OXFORD PRIVATE INTERNATIONAL
LAW SERIES

Series Editors
ANDREW DICKINSON

Solicitor
Fellow and Tutor, St Catherine's College
and Professor of Law, University of Oxford

JONATHAN HARRIS QC

Barrister, Serle Court
Professor of International Commercial Law,
Kings College, London

The Anti-Suit Injunction

Second Edition

THOMAS RAPHAEL QC

OXFORD PRIVATE INTERNATIONAL LAW SERIES

Series Editors: Andrew Dickinson & Jonathan Harris QC

The aim of this series is to publish works of quality and originality in a number of important areas of private international law. The series is intended for both scholarly and practitioner readers.

The Anti-Suit Injunction

Second Edition

THOMAS RAPHAEL QC

OXFORD
UNIVERSITY PRESS

OXFORD

UNIVERSITY PRESS

Great Clarendon Street, Oxford, OX2 6DP,
United Kingdom

Oxford University Press is a department of the University of Oxford.
It furthers the University's objective of excellence in research, scholarship,
and education by publishing worldwide. Oxford is a registered trade mark of
Oxford University Press in the UK and in certain other countries

First Edition published in 2010

Second Edition published in 2019

Published in the United States of America by Oxford University Press
198 Madison Avenue, New York, NY 10016, United States of America

British Library Cataloguing in Publication Data
Data available

Library of Congress Control Number: 2019936268

ISBN 978-0-19-877893-6

General Editors' Preface

The *Anti-Suit Injunction* is a remarkable legal creature. Its innocuous title belies its character as a heavy fetter on the exercise of the constitutional right of access to justice that is so prized and jealously defended by English judges within their own realm.

The first edition of Thomas Raphael's work, published in this series in 2008, cast much needed light on the nature, history, structures, and detailed regulation and operation of the anti-suit injunction. His commentary has provided valuable assistance to judges, practitioners, and scholars seeking to understand the potency and limitations of anti-suit relief, as well the jurisdictional and procedural technicalities that surround it.

Inevitably, the law has moved on in the intervening decade. The European Court of Justice has twice examined the place of anti-suit relief within the Brussels I regime. The first of those decisions (*Allianz SpA v West Tankers Inc* (2009)) was strongly influential in prompting reform of the arbitration exception in the recast Brussels I Regulation (Regulation (EU) No 1215/2012). The second (*'Gazprom' OAO v Lietuvos Respublika* (2015)), following that reform, examined the effects within the EU regime of anti-suit orders now frequently granted by arbitral tribunals. Notable decisions of the Supreme Court and Privy Council (*AES Ust-Kamenogorsk Hydropower Plant LLP v Ust-Kamenogorsk Hydropower Plant JSC* (2013); *Stichting Shell Pensioenfonds v Krys* (2014)) have interspliced a steady flow of decisions of the Court of Appeal and High Court. Other opportunities for much needed clarification of the doctrine at the highest level have passed by, with the withdrawal of appeals to the Supreme Court in *Petter v EMC Europe Ltd* (Court of Appeal, 2015) and The Yusuf Cepnioglu (Court of Appeal, 2016). The Supreme Court has also encouraged, and the English courts have embraced, the award of damages as a fully functioning part of the remedial armoury available to foreign defendants who allege that the proceedings against them have been brought in breach of a dispute resolution agreement (see *Starlight Shipping Co v Allianz Marine & Aviation Versicherungs AG* (Court of Appeal, 2014)). Finally, the UK's proposed—if increasingly obstacle strewn—exit from the European Union threatens to release the anti-suit injunction from the chains that have shackled it since the European Court's landmark decision in *Turner v Grovit* (2004). Should that event occur, proceedings before Member State courts will once again be within the range of this inter-systemic judicial missile.

As editors of the Oxford Private International Law Series, we are delighted to welcome the new edition of this work. Congratulating Mr Raphael on his achievement, we look forward to using this compendious work of reference in our own work and practice. Political and legal uncertainty notwithstanding, there is, perhaps, still hope for the anti-suit injunction to be tamed.

Professor Andrew Dickinson,
Oxford

Professor Jonathan Harris QC,
London
30 May 2019

Foreword to Second Edition

Despite the author's iconoclastic inclinations, *The Anti-Suit Injunction* is not a rallying call for further modernization in the commercial court. Robes fell by the wayside many years ago with no apparent loss of authority or prestige, but that might be a step too far.

On the contrary, it is a deadly serious subject.

With Dr Johnson we may wonder what it is that endows the English court with its extensive view, surveying mankind from China to Peru and remarking each anxious toil, each eager strife. (Was there ever, by the way, a better description of international commercial litigation?) How is it that this unique common law remedy, liberated from the diffidence which once constrained it, is so commonly and powerfully deployed to restrain the pursuit of legal proceedings all over the world?

All over the world, that is, except in those jurisdictions which are still at the time of writing our European partners. Lord Hoffmann in *West Tankers* regarded the ability to grant such an injunction as an important and valuable weapon promoting legal certainty and providing a competitive advantage over jurisdictions which choose to handicap themselves by disdaining such remedies. All that was some years ago now and the sky has not fallen in, but even so there was undoubted force in his remarks and the popularity of such injunctions shows no sign of abating. They are a vital weapon in the armoury of every international litigator.

So, a new edition of Thomas Raphael's book, written with his usual angelic grace, is more than welcome. It is everything that a legal textbook should be: a sound and succinct statement of the current law, already garlanded with the repeated *imprimatur* of the senior courts; a work of practical wisdom which never loses sight of the theoretical underpinnings of its subject; a polite but probing questioning of some of the more questionable judicial flights of fancy of which we are all sometimes found guilty; and a signpost pointing to the questions, and even better the answers, lurking and cleared for action just over the forensic horizon.

When the first edition of this book appeared (it seems only yesterday), I predicted that the most important question when a tricky point about these injunctions arose in future would be, 'What does *Raphael* say?' Ten years on, I see no reason to revise my prediction.

Sir Stephen Males
Royal Courts of Justice
1 November 2018

Preface

In 1665, the Earl of Clarendon, then Lord Chancellor, suggested in *Love v Baker* that an anti-suit injunction to restrain proceedings in Leghorn would be a '*dangerous case*'.[1] Perhaps Clarendon's long political and diplomatic experience led him to perceive that the extension of the common injunction into foreign countries could create awkward and troubling conflicts between states and courts.

This book was motivated by the perception that Clarendon was right—the anti-suit injunction is indeed a '*dangerous case*', which deserves a dedicated work in which the justification, structure, and development of the remedy can be thoroughly explored.

It is now almost eleven years since the first edition. Contrary to the fears of some, the anti-suit injunction is in robust health, and there has been a great deal of case law. It remains 'an antidote to jurisdictional shenanigans second to none'.[2] The anti-suit injunction now even benefits from real acceptance from a significant number of civil law thinkers and courts, whose growing understanding replaces a previous lack of sympathy.

To my great encouragement, this work has contributed to the debate and has been cited and followed by the judiciary on a heartening number of occasions, not only in England but also elsewhere in the common law world. This second edition has sought to take that discussion further. In a number of respects, the law is now clearer but the anti-suit injunction remains inescapably controversial. There are central issues of policy and principle on which more work needs to be done.

For this second edition I have also had the benefit of working with Belinda McRae, who is the co-author of the new chapters on Singapore and New Zealand, and who has brought a new perspective from the other side of the world. On this subject as others, the close common law countries[3] will continue to benefit from each other's thinking.

I have endeavoured to state the law of England and Wales as of 31 July 2018; Belinda and I have sought to state the law of Singapore and New Zealand to the same date. Subsequent developments have been taken into account where time, energy, and the publication process have permitted. In particular, the implications of Brexit have, where possible, been addressed up to 1 May 2019.

There are many people to whom I should express my thanks. Sir Peter Gross wrote a perceptive foreword to the first edition. Sir Stephen Males has gone out of his way to write a generous foreword to this edition which continues that tradition—among others. Belinda's

---

[1] *Love v Baker* (1664–65) Nels 103, 21 ER 801; (1665) 1 Chan Cas 67, 22 ER 698; see also *sub nom Lowe v Baker* (1665) 2 Freem Chy 125, 22 ER 1101. Leghorn is the old English name for Livorno.

[2] A Briggs, 'Anti-Suit Injunctions and Utopian Ideals' (2004) 120 LQR 529, 530.

[3] The 'close' common law countries are those whose law continues to have the closest resemblance, to English law and each other; such as England and Wales, Australia, New Zealand, and Singapore; the term therefore excludes countries such as the USA and India.

work and assistance has been invaluable for the commonwealth chapters, and also for dealing with the complications of Brexit.

Acknowledgments and gratitude, with the usual disclaimers, go to everyone who read chapters of the first edition or of this second edition and commented. For this second edition, thanks go in particular to Susannah Jones, Tom Corby, Andy Feld, Oliver Caplin, and Alexander Layton QC. A special mention should go to Sir Andrew Baker, who as Andrew Baker QC introduced me to the realities of anti-suit injunctions during *The Ivan Zagubanski*.[4] Scholars abroad who have helped over the years include in particular Gilles Cuniberti, Horatia Muir-Watt, Arnaud Nuyts, and Martin Illmer. Danny Ong gave some very valuable advice on Singapore law. Last but not least, the patience of the team at Oxford University Press in the face of continually extended deadlines, and late revisions, was again remarkable.

The first edition was dedicated to Sybille. This second edition is dedicated to Charlotte, as promised. Felix, Cléophée, and Jacques are celebrated in other ways, and every day.

Thomas Raphael QC
20 Essex Street, London
1 May 2019

---

[4] *Navigation Maritime Bulgare v Rustal Trading Ltd (The Ivan Zagubanski)* [2002] 1 Lloyds Rep 106.

Table of Contents

---

* Chapters 19 and 20 are co-authored with Belinda McRae.

Table of Cases

EUROPEAN UNION

EUROPEAN COURT OF HUMAN RIGHTS

INTERNATIONAL

Australia

Belgium

Brazil

British Virgin Islands

Canada

Vanuatu

Table of Legislation

TABLE OF CIVIL PROCEDURE
RULES AND RULES OF THE
SUPREME COURT

TABLE OF EUROPEAN LEGISLATION

Treaties and Conventions

Regulations

Decisions

TABLE OF INTERNATIONAL INSTRUMENTS

Abbreviations and Glossary

Bell	A Bell, *Forum Shopping and Venue in Transnational Litigation* (OUP 2003)
Briggs	A Briggs, *Civil Jurisdiction and Judgments* (6th edn, Routledge 2015)
Brownlie	J Crawford, *Brownlie's Principles of Public International Law* (8th edn, OUP 2012)
Brussels Convention	The Convention on Jurisdiction and Enforcement of Judgments in Civil and Commercial Matters, done at Brussels on 23 September 1968, as later amended by the accession conventions of 1978, 1982, 1989, and 1996
Brussels I Regulation	EC Regulation 44/2001
Brussels I Recast	EC Regulation 1215/2012
Brussels–Lugano Regime	The jurisdictional rules contained, collectively, in the Brussels I Regulation, the Brussels I Recast, the Brussels Convention, the New Lugano Convention, and the agreements with Denmark by which Denmark has brought itself within the Regulation and Recast
Brussels–Lugano zone	The territories of all the states that are party to the Brussels–Lugano regime
Cheshire & North	P North and J Fawcett, *Cheshire and North's Private International Law* (13th edn, OUP 1999)
Commission Proposal for Rome II	Proposal for a Regulation of the European Parliament and the Council on the law applicable to non-contractual obligations ('Rome II') Com (2003) 427.
CPR	Civil Procedure Rules
DAC Report	Departmental Advisory Committee on Arbitration Law Report on the Arbitration Bill, February 1996
Dicey	Lord Collins et al (eds), *Dicey, Morris & Collins on the Conflict of Laws* (15th edn, Sweet & Maxwell 2012)
Dickinson on Rome II	A Dickinson, *The Rome II Regulation: The Law Applicable to Non-Contractual Obligations* (OUP 2008)
ECHR	European Convention on Human Rights
ECJ	European Court of Justice
EEO	European Enforcement Order
Evrigenis and Kerameus Report	Report on the Accession of the Hellenic Republic to the Community Convention on Jurisdiction and the Enforcement of Judgments in Civil and Commercial Matters [1986] OJ C 298, 24 November 1986
GAFTA	Grain and Feed Trade Association
Gaillard (2005)	E Gaillard (ed), *Anti-Suit Injunctions in International Arbitration* (Juris 2005)
ILPr	International Litigation Procedure (Law reports)

Jenard Report	Report on the Convention on Jurisdiction and the Enforcement of Judgments in Civil and Commercial Matters, rapporteur P Jenard [1979] OJ C 59/1, 5 March 1979
Joseph	D Joseph QC, *Jurisdiction and Arbitration Agreements and their Enforcement* (3rd edn, Sweet & Maxwell 2015)
Layton & Mercer	A Layton and H Mercer, *European Civil Procedure* (2nd edn, Sweet & Maxwell 2004)
Lex fori	Law of the forum (ie the law of the court before which a case is heard applies its own law)
Meagher, Gummow and Lehane	RP Meagher, WMC Gummow, and JRF Lehane, *Equity Doctrines and Remedies* (4th edn, Butterworths LexisNexis 2002)
Model Law	UNCITRAL Model Law on International Commercial Arbitration
Mustill & Boyd	Sir MJ Mustill and Stewart C Boyd, *Commercial Arbitration* (2nd edn, LexisNexis 1989)
Mustill & Boyd Companion	Sir MJ Mustill and Stewart C Boyd, *Commercial Arbitration* (2nd edn, LexisNexis 2001 Companion Volume)
New Lugano Convention	The Convention on Jurisdiction and the Enforcement of Judgments in Civil and Commercial Matters, Containing a Set of Rules as between the Member States of the EC on the One Hand, and Norway, Iceland and Switzerland on the Other Hand, as revised, dated 30 October 2007
New York Convention	Convention on the Enforcement and Recognition of Foreign Arbitral Awards, 1958
Oppenheim	Sir R Jennings and Sir A Watts (eds), *Oppenheim's International Law* (9th edn, OUP 2008) Vol I
Plender & Wilderspin	R Plender and M Wilderspin, *The European Private International Law of Obligations* (3rd edn, Sweet & Maxwell 2009)
Rome Convention	Convention on the Law Applicable to Contractual Obligations, 1980
Rome I Regulation	EC Regulation 593/2008, on the Law Applicable to Contractual Obligations
Rome II Regulation	EC Regulation 864/2007, on the Law Applicable to Non-Contractual Obligations
RSC	Rules of the Supreme Court (the ancestors of the CPR)
Schlosser Report	Report on the Convention on the Association of the Kingdom of Denmark, Ireland and the United Kingdom of Great Britain and Northern Ireland to the Convention and to the Protocol on its interpretation by the Court of Justice, rapporteur Professor P Schlosser, [1979] OJ C 59/71, 5 March 1979
Yeo	TM Yeo, *Choice of Law for Equitable Doctrines* (OUP 2004)

1

Introduction

An anti-suit injunction, in its most typical form, orders a party to cease to pursue, or not **1.01** to commence, court proceedings abroad. It is backed by the threat of punishment for contempt of court if it is not obeyed. It is little surprise that it is one of the most controversial and contested remedies in the court's armoury.

Anti-suit injunctions have been criticized, especially by authors and judges from civil law **1.02** systems, where anti-suit injunctions are largely, although not entirely unfamiliar. It has been argued that they are irreconcilable with international comity and public international law, and amount to an unjustifiable interference with the sovereignty of the foreign state and the jurisdiction of the foreign court. Yet there should be little doubt about the power of the remedy as a practical tool.[1] In the game of 'multi-dimensional chess' that international litigation can become,[2] the anti-suit injunction can be a dramatic way of reducing the number of pieces on the board, and shaping the moves that can be taken. Experience also shows that it can, on occasion, be the only effective tool for achieving practical justice.

This book is intended to provide a detailed analysis of the principles and case law governing **1.03** the grant of anti-suit injunctions by the courts of England and Wales.[3]

The remainder of this Introduction will deal with the following topics: **1.04**

- Terminology and characterization (section A).
- The landscape of the remedy (section B).

---

[1] A Briggs, 'Anti-Suit Injunctions and Utopian Ideals' (2004) 120 LQR 529, 530, observes that 'as an antidote to jurisdictional shenanigans its usefulness is second to none'.

[2] The Hon Judge MR Wilkey, 'Transnational Adjudication: A View from the Bench' (1984) 18 Intl Lawyer 541, 543.

[3] In this work, 'England' will be used as a convenient abbreviation for England and Wales, and 'English law' likewise. Readers on the other side of Offa's Dyke are asked to forgive this.

- Anti-suit injunctions in other legal systems (section C)
- Anti-suit injunctions and comity (section D).
- Human rights law (section E).
- Anti-suit injunctions and public international law (section F).
- The Hague Convention on the Choice of Court (section G)
- The New York Convention (section H)
- Brexit (section I)

A. TERMINOLOGY AND CHARACTERIZATION

1.05   An anti-suit injunction is an order of the court requiring the injunction defendant not to commence, or to cease to pursue, or not to advance particular claims within, or to take steps to terminate or suspend, court or arbitration proceedings in a foreign country, or court proceedings[4] elsewhere in the court's own territorial jurisdiction. The order is addressed to, and binds, the actual or potential litigant in the other proceedings, and is not addressed to, and has no effect on, the other court.

1.06   Although a remedy of this type has formed part of English law for centuries, until recently it used to possess no convenient abbreviation. The label 'anti-suit injunction' is a late twentieth-century import from the USA,[5] but has become the usual name in modern English law.[6]

1.07   In *Turner v Grovit*, Lord Hobhouse suggested that the phrase 'anti-suit injunction' was misleading, 'since it fosters the impression that the order is addressed to and intended to bind the foreign court', and proposed the alternative terminology of 're-straining orders'.[7] It is true there is an ambiguity in the term 'anti-suit', which might suggest that the injunction affected the other court directly, when it only affects the party litigating there. So, referring to the 'anti-pursuit of suit' injunction would be more accurate, if unacceptably clumsy. Yet the phrase 'restraining order' is a little more than a tautology for any prohibitory injunction; it does not identify the particular type of restraint in which we are interested. Lord Hobhouse's recharacterization[8] has found no

---

[4]   Injunctions to restrain arbitrations in England are traditionally viewed as part of the court's supervisory jurisdiction over arbitration, rather than as anti-suit injunctions: Ch 11.

[5]   *Bank of Tokyo v Karoon* [1987] AC 45 (Note) (CA) 59F.

[6]   See eg *AES Ust-Kamenogorsk Hydropower Plant LLP v Ust-Kamenogorsk Hydropower Plant JSC* [2013] 1 WLR 1889 (HL) [25], [58].

[7]   *Turner v Grovit* [2002] 1 WLR 107 (HL) [16], [23]. In *Australian Broadcasting v Lenah Game Meats* (2001–02) 208 CLR 199 (Aus HC) 243, Gummow and Hayne JJ referred to 'what are somewhat loosely called anti-suit injunctions'.

[8]   Lord Hobhouse's relabelling should be seen as a one-off rhetorical device aimed, without success, at making the anti-suit injunction appear respectable to the European Court of Justice. His use of 'restraining order' formed part of his opinion on the question of whether the anti-suit injunction was compatible with the Brussels–Lugano regime, which the House of Lords was referring to the European Court. The linchpin of his argument that the injunction was unobjectionable was the contention that it was a merely personal remedy. So, language which shifted the jurisprudential focus onto the litigant abroad and away from the foreign proceedings was helpful. But the European Court was unmoved, viewing any such 'prohibition', however labelled, as incompatible with the Brussels–Lugano regime: Case C-159/02, *Turner v Grovit* [2004] ECR I-3565 [27]. In *Donohue v Armco* [2002] 1 Lloyds Rep 425 (HL) [43], [45], decided by the House of Lords on the same day that it ordered the reference in *Turner*, Lord Hobhouse was content to refer to the 'anti-suit injunction' (albeit on one occasion in inverted commas).

supporters, and the term 'anti-suit injunction' has become the uncontested and standard terminology.[9]

B. THE LANDSCAPE OF THE REMEDY

The English courts' willingness to grant anti-suit injunctions has waxed and waned, and there have been divergences of opinion and development of principle.[10]   **1.08**

However, the broad landscape of the law of the remedy is now settled for most purposes short of a root-and-branch challenge in the Supreme Court. Injunctions will be predominantly granted in two main situations: first, 'contractual' injunctions, where foreign proceedings are in breach of a contractual forum clause; and second, 'alternative forum' cases, where foreign proceedings overlap with matters that are being or can be litigated in England, and should be injuncted, in particular where they are considered to be vexatious and oppressive. There are also other less common categories where injunctions can be granted. These include injunctions to protect the insolvency jurisdiction of the English courts; 'single forum' cases, where injunctions are granted to restrain the pursuit of foreign proceedings abroad which can only be pursued abroad, and anti-anti-suit injunctions. Injunctions to restrain the pursuit of proceedings in England are possible, but rare in practice (outside the context of insolvency, where they are routine). Injunctions can in principle be granted to restrain the pursuit of foreign arbitration proceedings as well as the pursuit of court proceedings, but the supervisory role of the court of the seat of the arbitration, and the growing recognition of the principle of Competence-Competence,[11] make this rare.   **1.09**

The Brussels–Lugano regime, and the other instruments of European jurisdictional law, so long as they remain the law in England, impose restrictions on the grant of anti-suit injunctions where they seek to restrain proceedings in other Brussels–Lugano member states, following the decision of the European Court of Justice in *Turner v Grovit*.[12] The effect of Brexit is discussed in section I.   **1.10**

C. ANTI-SUIT INJUNCTIONS IN OTHER LEGAL SYSTEMS

Anti-suit injunctions have deep roots in English law common law and equity, and are part of the legal heritage which English law shares with the other common law legal systems to which it gave birth.[13]   **1.11**

---

[9] The language of 'anti-suit injunction' was also used in the International Law Association, Bruges Session (2003) Second Commission, Resolution: 'The Principles for Determining When the Use of the Doctrine of Forum non Conveniens and Anti-Suit Injunctions is Appropriate' (Rapporteurs L Collins, G Droz).

[10] *Donohue v Armco* [2002] 1 Lloyds Rep 425 (HL) [19]–[20].

[11] See Departmental Advisory Committee on Arbitration Law Report on the Arbitration Bill, February 1996 (hereafter 'DAC Report') paras 137–139.

[12] Case C-159/02, *Turner v Grovit* [2004] ECR I-3565. The restrictive effect of European jurisdictional law (so long as it applies) is discussed in Ch 12.

[13] See C McLachlan, *Lis Pendens in International Litigation* (Martinus Nijhoff 2009).

1.12   The common law legal systems all approach the anti-suit injunction with similar principles in mind. Outside the USA, the English case law is often applied,[14] and the jurisprudence of the Privy Council has been important in maintaining a common body of principle.[15]

1.13   We give, here, a brief *tour d'horizon* of the position in a number of the Commonwealth systems (and Hong Kong):

- Australian and Canadian law have pursued somewhat different paths to England, largely because of the different jurisdictional background. Yet the nature of the remedy is the same, and the principles to be applied have a strong family resemblance to English law.[16]
- In the British Virgin Islands and Brunei, the Privy Council has stated the law on anti-suit injunctions in terms drawing no distinction to English law.[17]
- Hong Kong law on anti-suit injunctions in substance follows English law.[18]
- Indian law recognizes anti-suit injunctions. The principles applied are similar to English law and draw on English and Commonwealth authorities.[19] But their application is sometimes unfamiliar. In recent years the international arbitration community has criticized the Indian courts for what has been perceived as excessive readiness to intervene in international arbitrations.[20]
- New Zealand and Singapore law essentially follow English law on anti-suit injunctions and the decisions of the Privy Council, although the jurisprudence of other commonwealth systems is also influential.[21]

1.14   This work addresses Singapore and New Zealand law on anti-suit injunctions in more detail in separate chapters (Chs 19 and 20, respectively).

1.15   In US law, the anti-suit injunction is an established remedy. Since the modern English anti-suit injunction developed after US independence, it is unsurprising that the US

---

[14] However, Australia is something of a *cavalier seul* on jurisdictional questions because of its rejection of the doctrine of *forum non conveniens* in *Voth v Manildra Flour Mills* (1990) 171 CLR 538 (HCA).

[15] *Société Nationale Industrielle Aérospatiale v Lee Kui Jak* [1987] AC 871 (PC) (Brunei); *Stichting Shell Pensionenfonds v Krys* [2015] AC 616 (PC) (British Virgin Islands, on appeal from the Eastern Caribbean Court of Appeal).

[16] The leading case in Australia is *CSR v Cigna Insurance Australia* (1997) 189 CLR 345 (HCA).

The leading case in Canada is *Amchem Products v British Columbia (Workers' Compensation Board)* [1993] 1 SCR 897 (Can SC). For the differences between the Canadian approach and the English approach see D McLean, 'A Common Inheritance? An Examination of the Private International Law Tradition of the Commonwealth' (1997) 260 Recueil des Cours 9, 67–69.

[17] *Société Nationale Industrielle Aérospatiale v Lee Kui Jak* [1987] AC 871 (PC) (Brunei); *Stichting Shell Pensionenfonds v Krys* [2015] AC 616 (PC) (British Virgin Islands, on appeal from the Eastern Caribbean Court of Appeal).

[18] In Hong Kong see *China Reit v Su Ping* [2007] HKEC 576; *Lucky Sun Development v Gainsmate International* [2007] HKCFA 1011; *Lioyang Shunfeng Iron and Steel v Yeung Tsz Wang* [2012] HKCA 246; *Compania Sub Americana de Vapores v Hin Pro International Logistics* [2015] HKCA 107, [2016] HKCFA 79 [57]–[58]; *Ever Judger Holding v Kroman Celik Sanayii Anonim Sirketi* [2015] 3 HKC 246; *Sea Powerful II Special Maritime Enterprises v Bank of China* [2016] 2 HKC 566, [2017] 1 HKC 153; *Arjowiggins HKK2 v Shandong Chenming* [2018] HKCFI 93. Some of the decisions have also drawn on Commonwealth authority, such as the decision of the Canadian Supreme Court in *Amchem*: see eg *China Light & Power v Wong To Sau Heung* [1993] HKCA 230.

[19] See eg *Oil and Natural Gas Commission v Western Company of North America* [1987] 1 SCC 496; *Modi Entertainment Network v WSG Cricket* (2003) 4 SCC 341; *Horlicks India v Heinz* (2010) (42) PTC 156 (Del) (DB).

[20] See eg WM Tupman, 'Staying Enforcement of Arbitral Awards under the New York Convention' 3 Arb Int 209 (1987); B Giaretta and A Kishore, 'Anti-Arbitration Injunctions: Mixed Signals from India' (Ashurst, January 2015).

[21] Singapore law is discussed in Ch 19. New Zealand law is discussed in Ch 20.

jurisprudence has a rather different cast.[22] But US judges have needed to confront many of the same problems as their English counterparts, and the solutions reached, though expressed differently, are often similar. English and US law on anti-suit injunctions have interacted, sometimes in conflict,[23] but also with mutual respect and influence.[24]

Scots law stands between the common law and the civil law systems, but in certain fields is strongly influenced by English law. The Scottish courts have a common law power to interdict (injunct) a foreign action, and have so far applied the same basic principles as English law.[25] In contrast, in South Africa, which also has a mixed civil and common law system, anti-suit injunctions have not yet been granted, and it is unclear whether they would be acceptable in principle.   **1.16**

The civil law countries have a different legal heritage, and the anti-suit injunction was an alien and often unwelcome idea to many civil lawyers.[26] Between 1980 to the early 2000s, when the anti-suit injunction became a focus of attention in Europe, there were hostile reactions from civil law writers and judges to English anti-suit injunctions.[27] Arbitrators from civil law backgrounds were also, initially, reluctant to grant anti-suit injunctions to protect arbitral references.   **1.17**

But it would be wrong now to view the civil law attitude to anti-suit injunctions as universal rejection. Remedies akin to anti-suits have occasionally been granted by some civil law systems. The former tendency for civil lawyers to react to anti-suit injunctions with incomprehension and hostility has become more nuanced, and anti-suit injunctions are sometimes met with a degree of acceptance and even occasionally sympathy,[28] which previously would have been surprising.   **1.18**

---

[22] See E Roberson, 'Comity be Damned: The Use of Anti-Suit Injunctions against the Courts of a Foreign Nation' (1998) U Penn Law Rev 409; C Lamm, E Hellbeck, and J Brubaker, 'Anti-Suit Injunctions in Aid of International Arbitration: The American Approach' (2009) 12 Intl ALR 115; G Bermann, 'Parallel Litigation: Is Convergence Possible?' in A Bonomi and GP Romano (eds) 13 Yearbook of Private International Law (De Gruyter 2011) 21 .

[23] The most infamous conflict was the *Laker Airways* litigation, discussed in L Collins, 'The Anti-Suit Injunction: Laker Airways and the Airlines' in *Essays in International Litigation and the Conflicts of Laws* (OUP 1994) 107–17. A recent example of conflict is *Petter v EMC* [2016] ILPr 3, and [2015] EWCA Civ 828 (judgment of 31 July 2015).

[24] *Bank of Tokyo v Karoon* [1987] AC 45 (CA) (Note) 57–58.

[25] *Young v Barclay* (1846) 8 D 774 (Ct of Sess); *Dawson's Trustees v Macleans* (1860) 22 D 685 (Ct of Sess); *Pan American Airways v Andrews* [1991] ILPr 41 (Ct of Sess); *Shell UK Exploration and Production v Innes* (1995) SLT 807 (Ct of Sess); *FMC v Russell* (1999) SLT 99 (Ct of Sess); P Beaumont and P McElheavy, *Anton's Private International Law* (3rd edn, Sweet & Maxwell 2011) paras 8.425–8.438. The modern Scottish cases have all treated *Aérospatiale* as stating Scots law and have identified no material difference to English law.

[26] See H Gaudemet-Tallon, 'Les régimes relatifs au refus d'exercer la compétence juridictionnelle en matiere civile et commercial: Forum non conveniens, lis pendens' (1994) 46 Rev Intl Dr Comp 423, 434 ('une intrusion intolérable dans le fonctionnement de la justice étrangère'). A general discussion is found in AT von Mehren, 'Theory and Practice of Adjudicatory Authority' (2002) 295 Recueil des Cours 327–28. J Fernandez Rozas, 'Anti-Suit Injunctions Issued by National Courts' in E Gaillard (ed), *Anti-Suit Injunctions in International Arbitration* (Juris 2005) (hereafter 'Gaillard (2005)') 75, 79–80, describes anti-suit injunctions as 'unknown in civil countries'; see also N Sifakis, 'Anti-Suit Injunctions in the European Union: A Necessary Mechanism in Resolving Jurisdictional Conflicts?' (2007) 13 JIML 100, 102–05. See in particular at nn 73 and 82 of this chapter.

[27] In 1989 the Brussels Civil Court held that an American anti-suit injunction could not be recognized in Belgium because it was repugnant to Belgian public policy and Article 6 of the European Convention on Human Rights (ECHR): *Civ Bruxelles* (18 December 1989) RW 1990–91, 676. In 1996, the Dusseldorf Regional Court of Appeal similarly declined to enforce an English anti-suit injunction saying that it interfered with the jurisdiction of the German court: *Re the Enforcement of an English Anti-Suit Injunction* [1997] IL PR 73. For civil law academic writers who have expressed opposition to anti-suit injunctions, see nn 26 and 82.

[28] See eg ML Niboyet, 'Le Principe de Confiance Mutuelle et Les Injonctions Anti-Suit' in P de Vareilles-Sommières, *Forum Shopping in the European Judicial Area* (Hart 2007) 77; and A Nuyts, *L'Exception de Forum non Conveniens* (Bruylant 2003) para 370.

1.19   In France, in *Banque Worms c Brachot*, the Cour de Cassation appears to have accepted the legitimacy of an order equivalent to an anti-suit injunction, enforceable by astreinte (a daily fine for non-compliance), to protect French insolvency proceedings.[29] Subsequently, at the crest of the wave of European hostility, in *Stolzenberg*,[30] the Cour de Cassation took the approach that anti-suit injunctions were inappropriate in principle. But in its more recent decision, *In Zone Brands*,[31] the Cour de Cassation concluded that a US anti-suit injunction to enforce an exclusive jurisdiction clause was not contrary to international public policy, nor the right of access to the court, and should be recognized and enforced by the French courts. Arguments that the injunction was an interference with French sovereignty and a breach of Article 6 of the European Convention on Human Rights (ECHR) were not accepted.[32]

1.20   Subsequently, in *Vivendi c Gerard*,[33] the Paris Court of Appeal rejected an appeal against the refusal by the Tribunal de Grande Instance ('TGI') to grant an anti-suit injunction restraining proceedings in the USA. But although it had been argued that French courts did not have power to grant such injunctions, the Court of Appeal of Paris (like the TGI) did not adopt that reasoning, rejecting the injunction on the grounds that the USA was a natural forum for the substantive litigation, there was no illegitimate 'forum shopping', and that the necessary 'fraude' (which can perhaps be best translated as wrongfulness, or even vexation) was not made out on the facts. The Court of Appeal abstained from commenting on the question of power.[34]

1.21   This work will leave it to French scholars to assess whether anti-suit injunctions will indeed become part of French legal practice.[35] But in Quebec, where the legal system is essentially French in heritage but influenced by the common law, anti-suit injunctions have been granted, and are accepted by many legal writers.[36]

1.22   Elsewhere in continental Europe, there have been decisions from the Netherlands and Belgium which are akin to anti-suit relief, although it is difficult for this writer to judge the extent to which they are anomalies.[37] In contrast, other continental courts and writers have

---

[29]   *Banque Worms c Brachot*, Cass Civ 1 (19 November 2002), noted H Muir Watt, 'Injunctive Relief in the French Courts: A Case of Legal Borrowing' [2003] CLJ 573.

[30]   *Stolzenberg v Daimler Chrysler Canada* [2005] ILPr 24 (Cour de Cassation) [4].

[31]   *In Zone Brands*, Cass Civ 1 (14 October 2009) No 08-16.369 and No 08-16.549 [2010] (Note H Muir-Watt).

[32]   L Perreau-Saussine, 'Forum Conveniens and Anti-Suit Injunctions before French Courts: Recent Developments' (2010) 59 ICLQ 519 and Cass Civ 1 (14 October 2009) Journal du Droit International (2010) 146 (Note S Clavel). The Juge-Rapporteur diverged from the comments in *Stolzenberg*: see H Muir-Watt, 'Surprise? Yes and No' (22 October 2009), at <http://conflictoflaws.net>.

[33]   *Vivendi c Gerard*, Cour d'Appel de Paris (28 April 2010) No 10/01643.

[34]   See for comment G Cuniberti, 'Abusive Forum Shopping', at <http://conflictoflaws.net/2010/abusive>.

[35]   Different views have been expressed: H Gaudemet Tallon, 'France' in J Fawcett, *Declining Jurisdiction in Private International Law* (Oxford, 1995) 175, 186, regarded anti-suit injunctions as an impossibility. But more recently, D Devot and A Pericard, 'France' in N Beale, B Lautenschlager, G Scotti, and L van den Hole, *Arbitration: Dispute Resolution Clauses in International Contracts* (Schultess 2013) 219–20, 228, envisage that French law might permit the grant of anti-suit injunctions to enforce forum clauses; and see G Cuniberti, 'Injonctions Provisoires et insolvabilité européene' (2017) 2 RC DIP 191.

[36]   *Lac d'amiante du Quebec c Lac d'amiante du Canada* 1999 CanLII 13500 (Quebec CA); *Opron v Aero System Engineering* [1999] RJQ 757, 777, 794; E Gaillard, 'Il est interdit d'interdire: Réflexions sur l'utilisation des Anti-Suit Injunctions dans l'arbitrage commercial international' (2004) Rev Arb 47, 53; P Desbiens, 'Les Anti-Suit Injunctions ont-ils leur place dans notre droit' (2005) 37(13) Journal du Barreau de Quebec.

[37]   See generally AT von Mehren, 'Theory and Practice of Adjudicatory Authority' (2002) 295 Recueil des Cours 327–28.

reaffirmed the view that anti-suit injunctions should not be granted as a matter of principle, or cannot operate within their own legal system.[38]

At the international level, a compromise was hammered out in the International Law **1.23** Institute's Bruges Resolution of 2003, which did not reject anti-suit injunctions, and comes close to giving them a grudging endorsement, if closely confined.[39]

The Dutch courts have issued orders restraining a party from commencing any further litigation in the Netherlands, on grounds of abuse of process: *Medinol v Cordis* (2004, President of the District Court of the Hague), noted in S Dack, 'Dutch Courage Ends Wasteful Litigation' (2004) 43 Euro Law 15; N Sifakis, 'Anti-Suit Injunctions in the European Union: A Necessary Mechanism in Resolving Jurisdictional Conflicts?' (2007) 13 JIML 100, 103. However, it is understood that in three previous cases the Dutch courts had refused anti-suit injunctions: cf Sifakis.

Similarly the Belgian courts have granted a form of anti-anti-suit injunction: Civ Bruxelles (18 December 1989) RW 1990–91, 676; noted in JT (1992) 438 (Note H Born and M Fallon); and commented on by A Nuyts, 'Les principes directeurs de l'Institut de Droit International sur le recours à la doctrine du forum non conveniens et aux anti-suit injunctions' (2003) 2 Revue Belge de Droit Intl, 536, 552–53. But this may be an isolated instance: R Asariotis, 'Anti-Suit Injunctions for Breach of a Choice of Forum Agreement: A Critical Review of the English Approach' (2000) Yearbook of European Law 447, 464.

Finally, an anti-arbitration injunction has apparently been granted by the Brazilian courts: Curitiba Court of First Instance (23 June 2003) *Compania Paranaense de Energia (COPEL) v UEG Arancaria*, discussed in A Lakatos and M Hilgard, 'Anti-Suit Injunctions in Defence of Arbitration: Protecting the Right to Arbitrate in Common and Civil Law Jurisdictions' Part II (2008) 2 Bloomberg Eur LJ 41 . However, Lakatos and Hilgard doubt that the anti-suit injunction is really part of Brazilian law.

---

[38] The Luxembourg Court of Appeal held that as a matter of principle there can be no such thing as an anti-suit injunction: 24 February 1998, Numéro 10047 (commented on in PB Carter, 'Anti-Suit Injunctions in Private International Law' (1997) 368 Vortrage, Reden und Berichte aus dem Europa Institut 22. Greek law also seems to regard anti-suit injunctions as unconstitutional: N Sifakis, 'Anti-Suit Injunctions in the European Union: A Necessary Mechanism in Resolving Jurisdictional Conflicts?' (2007) 13 JIML 100, 104–05.

A non-contractual anti-suit injunction has, it seems, been granted by the Supreme Court of Germany long ago in an international divorce case, Reinhard RG 03/03/1938, RGZ 157 (referred to in P Schlosser, 'Anti Suit Injunctions in International Arbitration' (2006) RIW 486 and M Lenenbach, 'Anti-Suit Injunctions in England, Germany and the United States: Their Treatment under European Civil Procedure and the Hague Convention' (1997–98) 20 Loy LA Intl & Comp LJ 257, 273–74). However, the decision has been described as dubious and not generalizable: H Schack, 'Germany' in J Fawcett (ed), *Declining Jurisdiction in Private International Law* (OUP 1995), 189 at 204; see also A Dutta and C Heinze, 'Anti-Suit Injunctions to Protect Arbitration Agreements' (2007) RIW 411, stating that anti-suit injunctions are not available in German law and A Lakatos and M Hilgard, 'Anti-Suit Injunctions in Defence of Arbitration: Protecting the Right to Arbitrate in Common and Civil Law Jurisdictions' Part II (2008) 2 Bloomberg Eur LJ 41 , stating that anti-suit injunctions are not available in German law. N Sifakis, 'Anti-Suit Injunctions in the European Union: A Necessary Mechanism in Resolving Jurisdictional Conflicts?' (2007) 13 JIML 100, 104, suggests that anti-suit injunctions may be available in Germany, but this seems to be out of line. The Oberlandesgericht (Dusseldorf), when rejecting an application for an anti-suit injunction to restrain the pursuit of proceedings before the German Cartel Office, accepted that such a power existed in principle, but rejected the injunction because the necessary 'special need for legal relief' by way of a preventative measure had not been made out. See I Klass, 'Case Comment: Oberlandesgericht (Dusseldorf) (DFL) (VI-Kart 1/09 (V)' [2010] ECLR N42–N43. But this domestic situation sheds little light on what would happen in relation to anti-suit injunctions to restrain proceedings before foreign courts.

In Switzerland, the Court of First Instance of Geneva, in Case C/10432005-15SP, *Air (Pty) Ltd v International Air Transport* (2 May 2005), trans (2005) 23 ASA Bull 739, 747, concluded that anti-suit injunctions were contrary to Swiss law, and this appears to be the general view: A Lakatos and M Hilgard, 'Anti-Suit Injunctions in Defence of Arbitration: Protecting the Right to Arbitrate in Common and Civil Law Jurisdictions' Part II (2008) 2 Bloomberg Eur LJ 41; M Scherer and W Jahnel, 'Anti-Suit and Anti-Arbitration Injunctions in International Arbitration: A Swiss Perspective' (2009) 12 Intl ALR 66; A Markus and S Giroud, 'A Swiss Perspective on *West Tankers* and its Aftermath' (2010) 28(2) ASA Bull 230, 243–44. In contrast, anti-suit awards are granted by Swiss arbitrators: Markus and Giroud; Scherer and Jahnel; M Scherer, 'Court Proceedings in Violation of an Arbitration Agreement: Arbitral Jurisdiction to Issue Anti-Suit Injunction and Award Damages for Breach of the Arbitration Agreement' (2011) 14(2) Intl ALR 43.

It has been said that the Italian legal system does provide for instruments similar to the anti-suit injunction: M Giorgetti, 'Anti-Suit, Cross-Border Injunction e Il Processo Cautelare Italiano' (2003) 53(2) Rivista di Diritto Processuale, 483 and G Carbone, 'Interference of the Court of the Seat with International Arbitration' (2012) 1 J Disp Res 217, 229.

[39] International Law Association, Bruges Session (2003) Second Commission, Resolution: 'The Principles for Determining When the Use of the Doctrine of Forum non Conveniens and Anti-Suit Injunctions is Appropriate' (Rapporteurs L Collins, G Droz).

1.24 Even within the framework of European Union (EU) law, the initial flat hostility reflected in the decision of the European Court of Justice (ECJ) in *Turner v Grovit* has since become more modified. The consequences of the decision in *The Front Comor*, which concluded that anti-suit injunctions could not be granted within Europe to enforce an arbitration clause, were regretted by many, even outside the world of the common law.[40] The high point of sympathy so far has been Advocate General Wautelet's bold opinion in the *Gazprom* case, where he went so far as to argue that in the light of Recital 12 of the Brussel I Recast, the Brussels–Lugano regime should not preclude the grant of anti-suit injunctions to restrain proceedings brought in breach of an arbitration clause.[41]

1.25 It would be going too far to suggest that the anti-suit injunction has conquered civil lawyers' affections. It seems unlikely that the remedy will be adopted by civil law systems in any general fashion. Nevertheless, civil law hostility to the injunction is no longer monolithic nor universal, and while disapproval persists, it is now tempered with greater understanding.

D. ANTI-SUIT INJUNCTIONS AND COMITY

1. Principles of Comity

1.26 In ordinary language, the word 'comity' refers to mutual courtesy or civility. In common law thinking on public and private international law, the phrase the 'comity of nations' refers to several different concepts that bear a family relationship. The linking idea is the underlying notion that different nations, and in particular their courts and legal systems, owe each other mutual and reciprocal respect, sympathy, and deference, where appropriate.[42] Comity is a principle *d'ordre public*, and not a question of private rights and duties; it reflects mutual respect between different states, legal systems, and courts.[43]

1.27 This underlying notion finds its expression variably in different contexts. Comity can refer to the mutual obligations imposed on states by public international law.[44] However, comity goes beyond the principles of public international law and includes more general imperatives of international public policy which do not amount to rules of law.[45] Reasoning based

---

[40] See eg C Kessedjian, 'Kessedjian on West Tankers' (12 February 2009), at <www.conflictoflaws.net>; A Markus and S Giroud, 'A Swiss Perspective on *West Tankers* and its Aftermath' (2010) 28(2) ASA Bull 230; M Moses, 'Arbitration/Litigation Interface: the European Debate' (2014) 35 NWJILB 1, 12–13, M Discours, 'L'Anti-Suit Injunction en Action: Étude Comparée des Modalités d'Attribution', (2014) Revue Libre de Droit, 89–97.

[41] Case C-536/61, *Gazprom*, EU:C:2015:316; AG [134], [188]. The ECJ did not feel the need to follow him on these points. See also European Parliament resolution of 7 September 2010 on the implementation and review of Council Regulation (EC) No 44/2001 on jurisdiction and the recognition and enforcement of judgments in civil and commercial matters (2009/2140(INI)), which at Recital M and para 10 recommended the reinstatement of anti-suit injunctions to enforce an arbitration clause. However, this was not picked up by the European Commission's drafting. The argument that Recital 12 of the Brussels I Recast removes the European preclusion of anti-suit injunctions to enforce arbitration clauses is not convincing: see Ch 12, paras 12.19–12.27.

[42] 'Judicial Comity is shorthand for good neighbourliness, common courtesy, and mutual respect between those who labour in adjoining judicial vineyards', per Sir John Donaldson MR in *British Airways Board v Laker Airways* [1984] QB 142 (CA) 186H (although cf S Males QC, 'Comity and Anti-Suit Injunctions' [1998] LMCLQ 543 at n 3); *Settebello Ltd v Banco Totta and Acores* [1985] 1 WLR 1050 (CA) 1057; *Agbaje v Agbaje* [2010] 1 AC 628 (SC) [52]–[53]. For an American perspective see R Raushenbush, 'Anti-Suit Injunctions and International Comity' (1985) 71 Va Law Rev 1039, 1064–66.

[43] *British Airways Board v Laker Airways* [1984] QB 142 (CA) 186H.

[44] *Buck v Attorney General* [1965] Ch 745 (CA) 770D, per Diplock LJ; *Treacy v Director of Public Prosecutions* [1971] AC 537 (HL) 561F–562C.

[45] M Akehurst, 'Jurisdiction in International Law' (1972–73) 66 BYBIL 145, 214–16.

on comity is deployed to justify particular rules of international and domestic law. Thus, comity is used to justify the principles of sovereign immunity,[46] and non-justiciability;[47] and to explain the cooperation that the English courts give to requests for international judicial assistance in evidence gathering.[48]

As relevant to anti-suit injunctions, the notion of comity underpins, or is deployed in, five main concepts in English jurisprudence: **1.28**

- the principle that jurisdiction should not be exercised in an exorbitant way;[49]
- the perception that one state's courts should not, without good reasons to do so, grant remedies that interfere even indirectly with the territorial and adjudicatory sovereignty of a foreign legal system;[50]
- the acceptance that the decisions and judgments, and decision-making independence, of foreign courts and states are entitled to a degree of deference, over and above the rules of *res judicata* and the recognition of foreign judgments;[51]
- the idea that each state's legal system has its own natural sphere of influence, within which the presumption against interference by another state's courts is of particular force, but outside which a state is entitled to a lesser degree of deference;[52]
- the converse concept that a court has a greater standing to intervene if a matter does fall within its own natural sphere of influence.[53]

Comity in this context is a set of principles or values, rather than a hard-edged rule, and is weighed against other principles or values.[54] The principles of comity have shaped the   **1.29**

---

[46] *The Parlement Belge* (1879–80) LR 5 PD 197 (CA) 214–15, 217; see also *Al-Fayed v Al-Tajir* [1988] QB 712 (CA) 730–31.

[47] *Luther v Sagor* [1921] 3 KB 532 (CA) 554–56; *Buck v Attorney General* [1965] Ch 745 (CA) 768E, 770G; *Yukos Capital v Rosneft Oil* [2014] QB 458 (CA) [66]; although this is subject to qualifications: *Belhaj v Straw* [2015] 2 WLR 1105 (CA) [53]–[55], [65]–[67], [2017] AC 964 (SC) [12], [56], [89], [222], [225].

[48] *State of Minnesota v Philip Morris* [1998] ILPr 170 (CA) 176.

[49] *JSC Bank of Moscow v Kekhman* [2015] 1 WLR 3737, [59].

[50] *Barclays Bank v Homan* [1993] BCLC 680, 690; *Credit Suisse Fides Trust v Cuoghi* [1998] QB 818 (CA) 827; *Airbus Industrie v Patel* [1999] 1 AC 119 (HL) 133H, 138G, 140A–B, F (requiring that the English court have a 'sufficient interest').

[51] *Barclays Bank v Homan* [1993] BCLC 680, 690, 692; *Yukos Capital v Rosneft Oil* [2014] QB 458 (CA) [87], [125]: 'comity … cautions that the judicial acts of a foreign state acting within its territory should not be challenged without cogent evidence'; *Stichting Shell Pensioenfonds v Krys* [2015] AC 616 (PC) [42].

[52] Thus, comity imposes fewer restraints on English courts where the foreign court seeks to exercise exorbitant jurisdiction over matters which do not fall within its own natural sphere of influence: *British Nylon Spinners v Imperial Chemical Industries* [1953] Ch 19 (CA) 27, 28; *Yukos Capital v Rosneft Oil* [2014] QB 458 (CA) [128]; or in a way contrary to international law: see, by analogy, *Kuwait Airways v Iraqi Airways* [2002] 2 AC 883 (HL) [24]–[29]. See *Société Nationale Industrielle Aérospatiale v Lee Kui Jak* [1987] AC 871 (PC) 894D–E and *Stichting Shell Pensioenfonds v Krys* [2015] AC 616 (PC) [42].

[53] *Airbus Industrie v Patel* [1999] 1 AC 119 (HL) 140D; *Deutsche Bank v Highland Crusader Offshore Partners* [2010] 1 WLR 1023 (CA) [50].

[54] *Deutsche Bank v Highland Crusader Offshore Partners* [2010] 1 WLR 1023 (CA) [50]. In the USA, see *Hilton v Guyot* 159 US 113 (1895) (US Sup Ct) 163–65; *Somportex v Philadelphia Chewing Gum*, 453 F 2nd 435 (3rd Cir 1971) 440; cert denied 405 US 1017 (1972).
In *Ecobank Transnational v Tanoh* [2016] 1 WLR 2231 (CA), the Court of Appeal discussed comity in terms that suggested it was principally relevant as a matter of transnational case management. These comments should be seen as focused on the contractual case before the court; and should not be interpreted as creating any new principle in non-contractual situations. The law in a line of cases from *Société Nationale Industrielle Aérospatiale v Lee Kui Jak* [1987] AC 871 (PC), to *Airbus Industrie v Patel* [1999] 1 AC 119 (HL), to *Deutsche Bank v Highland Crusader Offshore Partners LP* [2010] 1 WLR 1023 (CA) and *Stichting Shell Pensioenfonds v Krys* [2015] AC 616 (PC), firmly establishes that, at least outside the contractual case, comity does operate to discourage interference as a question of principle and judicial sovereignty, and not merely transnational case management.

existing rules for the grant or refusal of anti-suit injunctions; and comity also remains an independent consideration in the exercise of the court's discretion whether to grant an injunction.[55]

2. The English Courts' Commitment to the Anti-Suit Injunction

1.30   The principles of comity are in potential tension with the grant of anti-suit injunctions to restrain foreign proceedings,[56] although what comity actually demands in any particular case is debatable. Thus, in *Midland Bank v Laker*, Leggatt J at first instance took the view that 'comity with the courts of a friendly state required that any action which was properly commenced in the US courts in accordance with US procedure ought not to be restrained by the English court'; but the Court of Appeal begged to differ: 'comity in such a context as this is a matter on which different views can be held'.[57]

1.31   Indeed, it has been obvious from the very beginnings of the anti-suit injunction that it is a remedy with the potential to cause conflict with other legal systems. The first reported application for an anti-suit injunction to restrain foreign proceedings where the question of principle was discussed was rejected on the grounds that it was a 'dangerous case'.[58] Even the anti-suit injunction's domestic parent, the 'common injunction', by which the Court of Chancery restrained proceedings before the common law courts of England, gave rise to acute conflicts between the courts of common law and the Court of Chancery which lasted until after the Glorious Revolution.[59]

1.32   However, the legitimacy of the remedy has not faced a serious[60] root-and-branch challenge in England since *Bushby v Munday* in 1821, where it was contended that 'it would be a violation of the principles of international law to stay [the proceedings in the Scottish court] by

---

[55]   See Ch 4, section L, 'Comity'.

[56]   *Amchem Products v British Columbia (Workers Compensation Board)* [1993] 1 SCR 897 (SC Can) 913–14.

[57]   *Midland Bank v Laker Airways* [1986] QB 689 (CA) 705D. See also *R Griggs Group v Evans* [2005] 1 Ch 153, 159H–160B:

> In general, however, when our courts say that they intend to refrain from making a particular order because it would be a breach of international comity, they mean that, in their judgment, a foreign court would reasonably construe it as an invasion of the sovereignty of its country, and resent it accordingly. We do not mean to offend foreign courts, as by seeming to undermine their jurisdiction and authority, and expect a similar degree of self-imposed judicial restraint on their side. But how do we know where to draw the line? At times the line is tolerably clear, because it has been drawn in our own case law, or because it is demarcated by established concepts of international law. At other times the line is less clear.

[58]   *Love v Baker* (1665) 1 Chan Cas 67, 22 ER 698, (1664–65) Nels 103, 21 ER 801; also *sub nom Lowe v Baker* (1665) 2 Freem Chy 125, 22 ER 1101 (a claim for an injunction to restrain proceedings in the courts of Leghorn, that is to say Livorno).

[59]   See WS Holdsworth, 'A History of English Law', Vol 1 (Methuen 1903–38) 459–64; D Raack, 'A History of Injunctions in England before 1700' (1985–86) 61 Ind L J 539. It has been suggested that, 'as between the Courts of Chancery and common law, no questions of comity were involved': *Barclays Bank v Homan* [1993] BCLC 680 (Hoffmann J) 687. That, however, is the statement of a Chancery lawyer. The objections of the common law courts were, in substance, that the common injunction was a disregard of the 'comity' owed to them by the Court of Chancery.

[60]   In *Beazley v Horizon Offshore Contractors* [2005] Lloyds Rep IR 231, it was argued that the European Court of Justice's decision in Case C-159/02, *Turner v Grovit* [2004] ECR I-3565 should lead the English courts to review their view that anti-suit injunctions were compatible with comity, but this was rejected: 'The idea that the European Court of Justice has revealed "the emperor's new clothes" of the common law is fanciful. In recent times the common law has had a punctilious regard for the position of affected jurisdictions' (at [39]). Similar arguments were dismissed in *Midgulf International v Group Chimique Tunisien* [2010] 2 Lloyds Rep 543 (CA) [66]–[69].

the injunction of this court'. Sir John Leach VC dismissed the argument. He accepted that 'over the Court of Session this court has not, nor can pretend to have, any authority whatsoever' but thought this did not matter. He reasoned that:

> where parties Defendants are resident in England, and brought by subpoena here, this Court has full authority to act upon them personally with respect to the subject of the suit, as the ends of justice require; and with that view, to order them to take, or to omit to take, any steps or proceedings in any other Court of Justice, whether in this country, or a foreign country.[61]

The personal logic which lies at the heart of Sir John Leach's decision remains the starting point of the common law's response to the argument that the anti-suit injunction is irreconcilable with comity.[62] Although it has been criticized,[63] the personal logic of the anti-suit injunction is real, as the injunction does not seek to compel the foreign court.[64] Nevertheless, there has been a growing acceptance that the anti-suit injunction does *indirectly* interfere with the foreign court.[65] In recent case law, the anti-suit injunction has been tested against comity at the margins of the remedy.[66] But the question of whether the anti-suit injunction is *inherently* irreconcilable with comity has not been given a fresh examination in modern times.[67]   **1.33**

There is little prospect of any radical challenge to the anti-suit injunction succeeding before the English courts. The House of Lords, Supreme Court, and Privy Council have considered   **1.34**

---

[61] *Bushby v Munday* (1821) 5 Madd 297, 56 ER 908, 913, followed in *Stichting Shell Pensionenfonds v Krys* [2015] AC 616 (PC) [17]; see also *Ecobank Transnational v Tanoh* [2016] 1 WLR 2231 (CA). In *Amchem Products v British Colombia (Workers Compensation Board)* [1993] 1 SCR 897 (Can SC) 912, the approach taken in *Bushby v Munday* was viewed as 'parochial'.

[62] *Société Nationale Industrielle Aérospatiale v Lee Kui Jak* [1987] AC 871 (PC) 892C; and see the doubts expressed in *Philip Alexander Securities and Futures v Bamberger* [1997] ILPr 73 (CA) [48].

[63] See A Briggs, 'No Interference with Foreign Court' (1982) 31 ICLQ 189; T Hartley, 'Comity and the Use of Anti-Suit Injunctions in International Litigation' (1987) 35 AJCL 487, 506 (calling the personal logic 'sophistry'); C Ambrose, 'Can Anti-Suit Injunctions Survive European Community Law' (2003) 52 ICLQ 401, 408 (calling it 'superficially attractive'). See also Case C-159/02, *Turner v Grovit* [2004] ECR I-3565, AG [32], [34].

[64] See *Lord Portarlington v Soulby* (1834) 3 My & Ky 104, 40 ER 40, 41–42; *Beazley v Horizon Offshore Contractors* [2005] Lloyds Rep IR 231 [39]; *Stichting Shell Pensionenfonds v Krys* [2015] AC 616 (PC) [17]; *Ecobank Transnational v Tanoh* [2016] 1 WLR 2231 (CA). For defences of the personal logic, see *Kennedy v Cassillis* (1818) 2 Swans 313, 36 ER 635, 638 (where the injunction was dissolved on the ground that it was sought against the Scottish court itself); D Tan, 'Enforcing International Arbitration Agreements in Federal Courts: Rethinking the Federal Court's Remedial Powers' (2006) 47 Virg J Intl Law 545, 591–93 and M Lenenbach, 'Anti-Suit Injunctions in England, Germany and the United States: Their Treatment under European Civil Procedure and the Hague Convention' (1997–98)20 Loy LA Intl & Comp LJ 257, 293–94. The personal logic of the injunction is discussed in more detail at Ch 3, section D, 'Against Whom May an Anti-Suit Injunction be Granted?'.

[65] *British Airways Board v Laker Airways* [1985] AC 58 (HL) 95E; *Philip Alexander Securities and Futures v Bamberger* [1997] ILPr 73 (CA) [48]; *Airbus Industrie v Patel* [1999] 1 AC 119 (HL) 138G–H; *Deutsche Bank v Highland Crusader Offshore Partners* [2010] 1 WLR 1023 (CA) [50]; and see *Barclays Bank v Homan* [1993] BCLC 680, 686; *Beazley v Horizon Offshore Contractors* [2005] Lloyds Rep IR 231 [39]. The US courts have recognized this from the beginning: *Peck v Jeness* 48 US (7 How) 612 (US Sup Ct) 625; *China Trade v MV Choong* 837 F 2nd 33 (2nd Cir 1987) 35–36.

[66] See eg in *Airbus Industrie v Patel* [1999] 1 AC 119 (HL); *Star Reefers v JFC Group* [2012] 1 Lloyds Rep 376 (CA); *Stichting Shell Pensionenfonds v Krys* [2015] AC 616 (PC).

[67] Arguments based on comity were advanced by the injunction defendant in *West Tankers v Ras Riunione Adriatica di Sicurta (The Front Comor)* [2007] 1 Lloyds Rep 391 (HL) but Lord Hoffmann dismissed them by a curt reference to the first instance judge's reasoning: at [6]. However, Colman J had regarded the point as a matter of precedent, not principle, and had alluded to it only briefly: *West Tankers v Ras Riunione Adriatica di Sicurta (The Front Comor)* [2005] 2 Lloyds Rep 257 [51], [55]. Comity challenges based on the European Law approach were mounted in *Beazley v Horizon Offshore Contractors* [2005] Lloyds Rep IR 231 and in *Midgulf International v Group Chimique Tunisien* [2010] 2 Lloyds Rep 543 (CA) [66]–[69], but did not get far.

the anti-suit injunction on numerous occasions in recent years[68] and have given no hint that they were concerned about the nature of the remedy.[69]

3. Practical Justice

1.35   The English courts' commitment to the anti-suit injunction reflects a perception that it can be a vital tool for achieving practical justice. The court may be faced with a situation where it has concluded that the injunction defendant's pursuit of foreign litigation is clearly wrongful by English standards, and it has to hand an immediate and effective remedy to deal with the situation in the anti-suit injunction. Even if the foreign court will eventually reach the same conclusion, a similarly useful remedy may well not be available in the foreign court; for example if its procedure is notoriously slow, or if its procedure provides no means for a quick dismissal on jurisdictional grounds.[70] Letting the injunction defendant continue with his litigation will not only cause the innocent party to incur unnecessary costs abroad, but it can also change the result of the dispute between the parties.[71] The experienced litigator will know that it can be extremely difficult to conduct litigation in unfamiliar jurisdictions, and that even parties with strong claims, when faced with harassment on other fronts, can lose the will to fight.

1.36   Further, the anti-suit injunction is the only remedy capable of dealing with the situation where a well-funded party, convinced of the weakness of his prospects in the natural forum for the dispute, commences litigation in a multiplicity of other courts or arbitration tribunals. Requiring the injunction claimant to contest those claims in every single other court will be disproportionately burdensome.

1.37   These advantages must be weighed against the difficulties to which anti-suit injunctions can give rise when the foreign court objects.[72] Very real offence has been taken by foreign courts to the perceived interference with their sovereignty,[73] and anti-suit injunctions will often be refused enforcement abroad.[74] Between two countries that grant anti-suit injunctions, an escalating 'arms race' could result,[75] with anti-suit injunctions being met or pre-empted by

---

[68]   *Airbus Industrie v Patel* [1999] 1 AC 119 (HL); *Donohue v Armco* [2002] 1 Lloyds Rep 425 (HL); *Turner v Grovit* [2002] 1 WLR 107 (HL); *West Tankers v Ras Riunione Adriatica di Sicurta (The Front Comor)* [2007] 1 Lloyds Rep 391 (HL); *AES Ust-Kamenogorsk Hydropower Plant LLC v Ust-Kamenogorsk Hydropower Plant JSC* [2013] 1 WLR 1889 (SC); *Stichting Shell Pensionenfonds v Krys* [2015] AC 616 (PC).

[69]   In *The Front Comor*, the House of Lords made clear that they viewed the anti-suit injunction as a valuable and legitimate part of the court's armoury—*West Tankers v RAS Riunione Adriatica di Sicurta (The Front Comor)* [2007] 1 Lloyds Rep 391 (HL) [21], [28]–[30]—and gave short shrift to arguments that comity should preclude the grant of anti-suit injunctions: see n 67. The Privy Council has recently reasserted the equitable basis of the remedy: *Stichting Shell Pensionenfonds v Krys* [2015] AC 616 (PC).

[70]   In *Continental Bank v Aeakos* [1994] 1 Lloyds Rep 505 (CA) 511–12, the evidence of Greek procedure was that it was impossible to make a jurisdictional challenge without filing an expensive defence to the action at the same time.

[71]   See Sir P Gross, 'Anti-Suit Injunctions and Arbitration' [2005] LMCLQ 10, 24–25.

[72]   R Raushenbush, 'Anti-Suit Injunctions and International Comity' (1985) 71 Va Law Rev 1039, 1048–49.

[73]   *Re the Enforcement of an English Anti-Suit Injunction* [1997] ILPr 320 (Oberlandesgericht Düsseldorf); Case C-24/02, *Marseilles Fret v Seatrano Shipping* [2002] ECR I-3383 (Tribunal de Commerce de Marseille); *Shifco Somali High Seas International Fishing v Davies* (Tribunale di Latina, Italy, 29 May 2003) (an anti-suit injunction was an 'evident and fraudulent violation of the convention rules').

[74]   H van Houtte, 'May Court Judgments that Disregard Arbitration Clauses and Awards be Enforced under the Brussels and Lugano Conventions?' (1997) 13 Arb Intl 85, 91.

[75]   There would also, in theory, be a danger that in a dispute between A and B, the courts of state X might restrain party A from litigating on the merits before the courts of state Y, while the courts of state Y might restrain party

anti-anti-suit injunctions, which might in turn be met or pre-empted by anti-anti-anti-suit injunctions.[76] Clashes of this nature have occurred, most famously in the *Laker Airways* litigation,[77] but also on other occasions.[78] The perceived need to avoid such conflicts has led some writers to suggest that 'offensive' anti-suit injunctions should not be granted, and that courts should confine themselves to the grant of 'defensive' anti-anti-suit injunctions, where this is necessary.[79]

However, conflicts of this kind are likely to be rare provided that both legal systems pay   **1.38** sufficient regard to comity when considering whether to grant anti-suit injunctions, and in particular anti-anti-suit injunctions. [80] Where conflicts do arise, they can be resolved by the exercise of common sense. The grant of anti-suit injunctions as between common law courts has not disrupted the generally harmonious relations between them.[81] To abstain from *all* 'offensive' uses of the anti-suit injunction because of the risk of conflicts would be an overreaction.

Nevertheless, even if sufficient caution is deployed in the grant of anti-suit injunctions to   **1.39** render their use acceptable in practice, it is worth examining whether the anti-suit injunction can be reconciled with the principles of comity.

B from litigating in the courts of state X. If this were to happen, the parties would find themselves stymied—no one would be able to commence or continue substantive proceedings on pain of punishment. This was one of the objections raised by AG Kokott in Case C-185/07, *Allianz v West Tankers (The Front Comor)* [2009] ECR I-663, AG [72]. It is an uncommon scenario. There appear to be two examples in the reported English cases: *Amoco (UK) Exploration v British American Offshore* [1999] 1 Lloyds Rep 772, 776; and the situation resulting from the decision in *Petter v EMC* [2016] ILPr 3 (CA) (see Ch 4, paras 4.44–4.46). It can be avoided so long as the courts do not take an unjustifiably expansive approach to the anti-suit injunctions. The fact that this problem has apparently occurred in *Petter* is an illustration of the dangerously expansive nature of that decision: see T Raphael, 'Do as You Would be Done By? System-Transcendent Justification and Anti-Suit Injunctions' (2016) LMCLQ 256.

---

[76] For an example of an anti-anti-anti-suit injunction, see *GE Francona Reinsurance v CMM Trust No 1400* [2004] EWHC 2003 [10]. In theory the iteration could continue; but in reality, one does not tend to go further down the chain. Sufficiently broad drafting will ensure that an anti-anti-suit injunction is also in effect an 'anti-anti-anti-suit injunction'.

[77] Laker Airways Ltd, a British airline flying transatlantic, went into insolvency. Its liquidator commenced US anti-trust proceedings alleging a conspiracy by various British and European airlines to drive Laker out of business. 'Single forum' anti-suit injunctions were granted to restrain the US proceedings at first instance and by the Court of Appeal at the application of two British airlines: *British Airways Board v Laker Airways* [1984] QB 142 (applying the since discredited approach based on *forum non conveniens* derived from *Castanho v Brown & Root (UK)* [1981] AC 557 (HL)). These injunctions were subsequently discharged by the House of Lords because Laker and the other airlines, by operating on both sides of the Atlantic, had voluntarily brought themselves within the scope of US domestic law, including US anti-trust law, and therefore it was not unjust for US anti-trust law to be applied to them: *British Airways Board v Laker Airways* [1985] AC 58 (HL) 84. In the meantime, the US courts had reacted strongly to what was perceived as an unjustified interference with their jurisdiction. Anti-anti-suit injunctions were granted against other European airlines, including Sabena, which had not obtained anti-suit injunctions from the English courts but seemed likely to; and the English approach to anti-suit injunctions was criticized: *Laker Airways v Pan Am World Airways* 559 F Supp 1124, 1138 (DDC 1983), aff'd *Laker Airways v Sabena, Belgian World Airlines* 731 F 2nd 909 (DC Cir 1984). The *Laker Airways* imbroglio is discussed by R Raushenbush, 'Anti-Suit Injunctions and International Comity' (1985) 71 Va Law Rev 1039; T Hartley, 'Comity and the Use of Anti-Suit Injunctions in International Litigation' 35 AJCL 487 (1987); L Collins, 'The Anti-Suit Injunction: Laker Airways and the Airlines' in *Essays in International Litigation and the Conflicts of Laws* (OUP 1994) 107–17.

[78] See the conflict between the USA and the Indonesian courts in the *Pertamina* litigation: *Karaha Bodas v Perusahaan Pertambangan Minyak Dan Gas Bumi Negara* 335 F 3rd 357 (5th Cir 2003); discussed in E Gaillard, 'Il est interdit d'interdire: Réflexions sur l'utilisation des Anti-Suit Injunctions dans l'arbitrage commercial international' (2004) 1 Rev Arb 47, 56–57.

[79] R Raushenbush, 'Anti-Suit Injunctions and International Comity' (1985) 71 Va Law Rev 1039; see also G Bermann, 'The Use of Anti-Suit Injunctions in International Litigation' (1990) 28 Col J Transnl Law 589, 630–31.

[80] See AT von Mehren, 'Theory and Practice of Adjudicatory Authority' (2002) 295 Recueil des Cours 340–41.

[81] T Hartley, 'Anti-Suit Injunctions and the Brussels Convention' (2000) 49 ICLQ 166, 169.

4. The Absolute Challenge Based on Sovereignty and Jurisdiction

1.40   A fundamental challenge to the anti-suit injunction's legitimacy has been advanced by scholars and judges from civil law legal systems.[82] The challenge is made up of two main arguments. First, as a matter of sovereignty it must always be the court before which proceedings are brought, applying its own national law and policy, that should decide on whether those proceedings are or are not properly brought before it.[83] Second, it must always amount to an illegitimate interference with the adjudicatory jurisdiction of a court for another court to decide whether or not that adjudicatory jurisdiction can or cannot be invoked.[84]

1.41   From the perspective of these arguments, the common law analysis that there is no direct interference with the foreign court because the injunction operates *in personam* only is dismissed as irrelevant, since the production of the same result by indirect means is viewed as equally objectionable.[85]

1.42   The conflict between this absolute challenge and the common law approach to the anti-suit injunction derives from irreconcilably different assumptions as to the role of a legal system, and the values to which it should give primacy.

---

[82]   A Briggs, 'Anti-Suit Injunctions and European Ideals' (2004) 120 LQR 529, observes that 'it is well known that many continental lawyers have a peculiar hostility to the anti-suit injunction'.

For court decisions, see *Re the Enforcement of an English Anti-Suit Injunction* [1997] ILPr 320 (Oberlandesgericht Düsseldorf) [14]–[19] (criticized in J Harris, 'Restraint of Foreign Proceedings—The View from the Other Side of the Fence' [1997] CJQ 283, and reacted to in *Philip Alexander Securities & Futures Ltd v Bamberger* [1997] ILPr 73); *Ref Bruxelles* (18 December 1989) RW 1990–91, 676; noted in JT (1992) 438 (Note H Born and M Fallon); *Stolzenberg v Daimler Chrysler Canada* [2005] ILPr 24 (French Cour de Cassation) [4]. But as discussed at paras 1.18–1.25, some continental courts have now moved to an acceptance that at least contractual anti-suit injunctions are not inherently illegitimate.

For academic writing see H Gaudemet-Tallon, 'France' in J Fawcett (ed), Declining Jurisdiction in Private International Law (1995) 175 at 186–87; S Clavel, 'Anti-Suit Injunctions et Arbitrage' (2001) Rev Arb 669, 676–77, 701–06; A Nuyts, *L'Exception de Forum non Conveniens* (Bruylant 2003), esp paras 364–365; E Gaillard, 'Il est interdit d'interdire: Réflexions sur l'utilisation des Anti-Suit Injunctions dans l'arbitrage commercial international' (2004) Rev Arb 47; F Bachard, 'The Uncitral Model Law's Take on Anti-Suit Injunctions' in Gaillard (2005) 87ff; P Bonassies, 'L'entrée en vigueur du règlement communautaire no 44-2001 du 22 décembre 2000 concernant la competence judiciaire, la reconnaissance et l'exécution des décisions en matière civile et commerciale' (2002) 2 Revue Scapel 48–52, describing an anti-suit injunction to restrain proceedings in breach of an arbitration clause before the Tribunal de Commerce de Marseille as 'une méfiance insupportable à l'égard de cette jurisdiction non-britannique'; L Radicati di Brozolo, 'Arbitration and the Revised Brussels I Regulation: Seeds of Home Country Control and of Harmonisation' (2011) 7 J Priv Intl L 423, 430–32 (calling the anti-suit injunction 'imperialistic and condescending').

See also the discussion of the evidence of Belgian, French, and Italian lawyers in *OT Africa Line v Hijazy (The Kribi) (No 1)* [2001] 1 Lloyds Rep 76 [76]–[86], [95(5)]; *Navigation Maritime Bulgare v Rustal Trading (The Ivan Zagubanski)* [2002] 1 Lloyds Rep 106 [115]–[119], [121(5)] (where the evidence of Professor Bonassies was that the French courts would regard an anti-suit injunction as 'a grossly offensive intrusion to their own functioning'); *Evialis v SIAT* [2003] 2 Lloyds Rep 377 [52]–[58]; *West Tankers v Ras Riunione Adriatica di Sicurta (The Front Comor)* [2005] 2 Lloyds Rep 257 [43]–[46].

However, it is not the case that all 'civilian' lawyers are adamantly opposed to anti-suit injunctions. For examples of those who think the remedy has its place, see ML Niboyet, 'Le Principe de Confiance Mutuelle et Les Injonctions Anti-Suit' in P de Vareilles-Sommières, Forum Shopping in the European Judicial Area (2007) 77; A Nuyts, *L'Exception de forum non conveniens* (Bruylant 2003) para 370; and see the developing position discussed at paras 1.18–1.25 of this chapter.

[83]   *Re the Enforcement of an English Anti-Suit Injunction* [1997] ILPr 320 [14], [16]; F Bachard, 'The Uncitral Model Law's Take on Anti-Suit Injunctions' in Gaillard (2005) 102–03.

[84]   *Re the Enforcement of an English Anti-Suit Injunction* [1997] ILPr 320 [14], [17]; F Bachard, 'The Uncitral Model Law's Take on Anti-Suit Injunctions' in Gaillard (2005) 87ff, 102–03; for a summary of this 'continental perspective', see H Muir Watt, 'Injunctive Relief in the French Courts: A Case of Legal Borrowing' [2003] CLJ 573.

[85]   *Re the Enforcement of an English Anti-Suit Injunction* [1997] ILPr 320 [15]–[16]; Case C-159/02, *Turner v Grovit* [2004] ECR I-3565, AG [32], [34].

The 'civil law' arguments based on sovereignty and jurisdiction sketched out give priority to public judicial authority rather than private justice. The dominant consideration is not where a dispute should justly be resolved, but the doctrinal principle that the receiving court's authority to determine what litigation may be brought before it should be unquestioned by foreign courts. Compared to this principle of sovereignty, the private rights and obligations of the parties, and the practical consequences of upholding the principle, are of relatively little importance.[86]

In contrast, at the heart of the common law concept of civil justice is the imperative that a just resolution must be achieved for a private dispute. In relation to conflicts of jurisdiction, the question of principal importance, as a matter of justice, is where a dispute should be resolved in order to do practical justice between the parties, and in accordance with their private law rights.[87] Public law considerations of the sovereignty of foreign courts, and relations between courts, encapsulated in the concept of comity, are second-order constraints, to be deployed sparingly where they conflict with private justice. This conception of the function of courts and of justice naturally leads to a personal logic being applied to anti-suit injunctions, not merely as a matter of formality, but as a substantive reflection of the court's underlying concept of justice.[88]   **1.43**

There is a sense in which conflicts as deeply rooted as this[89] are not susceptible to resolution by argument.[90] It is no part of the purpose of this chapter to contend that all cases in which the English courts have granted anti-suit injunctions can be justified from an international perspective. Yet there are cases where a rigid application of a dogmatic conception of sovereignty would be unjustified, and would clash with principles as valid as those it seeks to uphold. Indeed, by giving overwhelming importance to the judicial sovereignty of the courts of the 'receiving' state Y, the sovereignty of the courts of the 'originating' state X to regulate their own proceedings could be undermined.   **1.44**

To take one example, it is standard in common law systems for one party to be required to disclose private documents to the other party, subject to controls, including obligations of confidentiality not to use the documents obtaining on disclosure or discovery in   **1.45**

---

[86] For an illustration of this mindset, see the ECJ's decision in Case C-281/02, *Owusu v Jackson* [2005] ECR I-1383; and see T Hartley, 'Anti-Suit Injunctions and the Brussels Jurisdiction and Judgments Convention' (2000) 49 ICLQ 166, 169–70.

[87] See A Briggs, 'The Impact of Recent Judgments of the European Court on English Procedural Law and Practice' Part II (2005) 124 Zeitschrift für Schweizerisches Recht Revue de droit Suisse 231 and A Clarke, 'The Differing Approach to Commercial Litigation in the European Court of Justice and the Courts of England and Wales II' (2006) 66 Amicus Curiae 2.

[88] At the risk of oversimplification, this 'civil law' approach, based on sovereignty, can be viewed as flowing from the inquisitorial concept of justice, under which it is the proper role and function of the court to seek out truth, and impose justice on the parties. In contrast, under the 'common law' approach, based on private justice, the court is more akin to a 'referee', whose function is to resolve justly a dispute between the parties which may properly be brought before it. From this perspective, the judicial sovereignty of the court to resolve cases before it is less important.

[89] See *Airbus Industrie v Patel* [1999] 1 AC 119 (HL) 131H for commentary on the fundamental differences between the civil and common law approaches to jurisdiction.

[90] See L Wittgenstein, *Philosophical Investigations* (2nd edn, Blackwell 1958), Remark 217: 'If I have exhausted the justifications I have reached bedrock, and my spade is turned. Then I am inclined to say: "This is simply what I do".' Briggs has referred to the clash between civil law and common law perspectives as like 'chickens talking to a duck; and if it is, it is pointless to say that one approach is right and the other is wrong': A Briggs, 'The Impact of Recent Judgments of the European Court on English Procedural Law and Practice' Part II (2005) 124 Zeitschrift für Schweizerisches Recht Revue de droit Suisse 231.

any other context or for any other purpose. Breaches of these obligations—for example by leaking protected information to the press—can be restrained by injunction, or even directly punished by contempt of court.[91] If a party who threatened to breach these obligations by deploying that material in foreign proceedings could not be prevented from doing so by injunction, the ability of the original court to control the proceedings before it would be seriously undermined.

1.46   Similarly, if an absolute rule based on sovereignty or jurisdiction were adopted, it would be impossible even to grant anti-anti-suit injunctions. Even those writers within the common law world who doubt the legitimacy of anti-suit injunctions tend to make an exception for anti-anti-suit injunctions to protect the jurisdiction of the originating state from inappropriate foreign anti-suit injunctions.[92]

1.47   To dismiss the personal logic of anti-suit injunctions as an irrelevant formalism is particularly inaccurate in cases where the injunction defendant owes a concrete personal jurisdictional obligation not to litigate abroad.[93] A contractual anti-suit injunction does, in a very real sense, enforce personal obligations of the injunction defendant. But once this is recognized, one of the foundations of the absolute 'civil law' challenge is weakened. Even if the injunction does indirectly affect the sovereignty or jurisdiction of the foreign court, this is a direct consequence of the personal obligations which the injunction defendant has assumed.[94] It appears to be a recognition of the force of this point that has driven the French courts to accept the legitimacy of foreign contractual anti-suit injunctions.[95]

---

[91] *Medway v Doublelock* [1978] 1 WLR 710; *Bourns v Raychem (No 3)* [1999] FSR 641 [11], [15]–[20], [55] (Laddie J) 679–82 (CA); *Bourns v Raychem (No 4)* [2000] FSR 841, 845–46 (referring to earlier unreported judgments).

[92] R Raushenbush, 'Anti-Suit Injunctions and International Comity' (1985) 71 Va Law Rev 1039, 1067–70. In contrast, civil law opponents of anti-suit injunctions tend to conclude that anti-anti-suit injunctions are equally objectionable: T Rauscher, *Europäisches Zivilprozessrecht Kommentar* (2nd edn, Beck 2006) 122, para 20ff; E Gaillard, 'Il est interdit d'interdire: Réflexions sur l'utilisation des Anti-Suit Injunctions dans l'arbitrage commercial international' (2004) 1 Rev Arb 47, 58–62.

[93] *Apple Corps v Apple Computer* [1992] RPC 70, 79; see also G Bermann, 'The Use of Anti-Suit Injunctions in International Litigation' (1990) 28 Col J Transnatl Law 589, 620–23.
In contrast, it is more doubtful whether injunctions granted on the basis of vexation or oppression (or unconscionability) enforce any real underlying substantive right, or correlative personal obligation: see Ch 3, section B, 'A Legal or Equitable Right?'. Even if as a matter of English law an underlying equitable obligation not to litigate abroad were identified, a foreign court could be forgiven if it were to view this 'obligation' as the expression of a conclusion that injunctive relief should be granted, rather than a genuine concrete personal obligation. In the absence of such a concrete personal obligation, the personal logic of the anti-suit injunction is more contestable. In *Barclays Bank v Homan* [1993] BCLC 680, 686, Hoffmann J explained:

> in theory the injunction merely operates in personam upon a person subject to the jurisdiction of the English court. There are cases, such as the enforcement by injunction of a contractual submission to the exclusive jurisdiction of the English court, in which this is a fair description of the proceedings. There are others where it is less realistic, as for example when the English court considers that the foreign proceedings would be unjust because the foreign court is asserting an excessive jurisdiction.

[94] The distinction between contractual and non-contractual anti-suit injunctions is taken seriously by a number of civilian writers. See Rev Crit DIP (2004) 93(2) 655 para 4 (Note H Muir-Watt), noting *Turner v Grovit*; P Schlosser, 'Anti-Suit Injunctions zur Unterstützung von internationalen Scheidsverfahren' (2006) RIW 486, 490–92. S Clavel, 'Anti-Suit Injunctions et arbitrage' (2001) Rev Arb 669, 674–75, 678–79 accepts that where an anti-suit injunction enforces a contractual obligation 'l'irrégularité est moins flagrante', and it may therefore be permissible. See also M Lenenbach, 'Anti-Suit Injunctions in England, Germany and the United States: Their Treatment under European Civil Procedure and the Hague Convention' (1997–98) 20 Loy LA Intl & Comp LJ 257, 290–92.

[95] See *In Zone Brands International v In Beverage International*, Cass Civ 1 (14 October 2009) Nos 08-16.369 and 08-16.549, discussed at para 1.19.

The English courts do not consider that a foreign anti-suit injunction is necessarily an il- **1.48**
legitimate interference with their own process.[96] Further, although the reaction from
foreign courts to English anti-suit injunctions has occasionally been hostile, this has not
always been the case. Unsurprisingly, the courts of common law legal systems that grant
anti-suit injunctions have accepted that injunctions restraining the pursuit of proceedings
before them may be legitimate;[97] and the French Cour de Cassation has accepted that a foreign contractual anti-suit injunction can be enforced in France.[98]

Consequently, at least in those cases where the jurisdictional relationships between the **1.49**
states in question are not regulated by a controlled 'closed system' of jurisdiction,[99] an absolute principle that comity must always preclude the grant of anti-suit injunctions to restrain
the pursuit of proceedings before the courts of a foreign state has little attraction other than
its simplicity.

5. Comity and the Right to Decide

There is a more subtle line of challenge, derived from considerations of comity, which has **1.50**
been articulated by some writers from both civil law and common law systems.

In many cases, the arguments that can be put before the originating court in support of an **1.51**
injunction, or parallels to them, can be put before the receiving court, on an application
to stay proceedings before it. If an argument can only be advanced with force before the
originating court, that will usually be because of a difference of national law and policy between the two states. Consequently, two questions must be asked: where the same points
or parallels to them *can* be made abroad, what is the *need*, or what gives the *right*, for the
originating court to intervene? And where the same points *cannot* be made abroad, what
gives the originating court the *right* to intervene (the need being obvious)?[100] It could be

---

[96] *Western Electric v Racal-Milgo* [1979] RPC 501, 511 (Whitford J), 518–19 (CA); *Through Transport Mutual Insurance Association (Eurasia) v New India Assurance* [2005] 1 Lloyds Rep 67 (CA) [91]; *Walanpatrias Stiftung v Lehman Brothers International (Europe)* [2006] EWHC 3034 [52]–[56]; *Winnetka Trading v Julius Baer International* [2009] Bus LR 1006.
 There are, however, examples where the English courts have objected to applications for foreign anti-suit injunctions which were perceived as illegitimate: *General Star International Indemnity v Stirling Cooke Brown Reinsurance Brokers* [2003] Lloyds Rep IR 719; *Tonicstar v American Home Insurance Co* [2005] Lloyds Rep IR 32.
[97] See eg *OT Africa Line v Magic Sportswear* [2007] 1 Lloyds Rep 85 (Can Fed Ct of Appeal) [55], [75], [81]–[82] (responding to the anti-suit injunction granted in *OT Africa Line v Magic Sportswear* [2005] 2 Lloyds Rep 170 (CA)).
[98] *In Zone Brands*, Civ Cass 1 (14 October 2009) Rev Crit DIP [2010] (Note H Muir-Watt).
[99] The Brussels–Lugano regime is the paradigm case of such a 'closed system' of jurisdiction (*OT Africa Lines v Magic Sportswear* [2005] 2 Lloyds Rep 170 (CA) [37]), and we now know from Case C-159/02, *Turner v Grovit* [2004] ECR I-3565 that it does preclude the grant of anti-suit injunctions within its territorial and material scope (so long as it remains the law). Resolution 1/2000 of the International Law Association, otherwise known as the Leuven/London principles, suggests that anti-suit injunctions should not be granted within closed systems of jur-isdiction which define the original jurisdiction of the courts of the parties: para 7.1.
 The Hague Convention on the Choice of Court (2005) establishes a partly controlled jurisdictional and mu-tual enforcement system. However, this does not preclude the power to grant anti-suit injunctions to enforce juris-diction clauses: see section G, 'The Hague Convention on the Choice of Court'.
[100] E Gaillard, 'Il est interdit d'interdire: Réflexions sur l'utilisation des Anti-Suit Injunctions dans l'arbitrage commercial international' (2004) Rev Arb 47, 51–52, observes with disapproval that:
 the core of the technique of the anti-suit injunction is to be found in the ambition to cause one's own view of which jurisdiction is competent, and where appropriate of whether an arbitration agreement is valid or invalid, to prevail, over the views of any other jurisdiction, whether state court or arbitral tribunal, which could be seised or has been seised with the question [author's translation].

argued that, if those questions are treated with sufficient seriousness, then it will be apparent that anti-suit injunctions should not be granted as a matter of comity, save perhaps in very limited circumstances, because the indirect interference with the foreign court is not justified by any need or right that can be identified. This argument has the attraction of flexibility, because it admits of the *possibility* that the originating court might have the need and right to intervene.

1.52   The English courts, and the Privy Council, have not been deaf to these questions. In *Aérospatiale*, a radical change in the case law was introduced by Lord Goff's conclusion that it would be inconsistent with comity for an injunction to be granted merely because there was a difference of view between the injuncting court and the foreign court as to which is the natural forum, and that something more was required to justify intervention.[101] Further, in *Airbus v Patel*, Lord Goff articulated the principle that, as a matter of comity, the English court must have a 'sufficient interest' in the matter to justify intervention.[102] Nevertheless, there are many cases where the English courts have answered, and continue to answer, the question of whether they have a need and right to intervene with a resounding affirmative.

1.53   Thus, in contractual cases, the English court has derived its *right* to intervene from the parties' contractual choice of England as the forum.[103] There are strong arguments to support this. It is possible to hypothesize a clear and clearly valid contractual clause which gives exclusive jurisdiction over any underlying dispute arising out of the contract to the courts of X, also gives exclusive jurisdiction over any dispute as to forum to the courts of X, and finally provides that the courts of X may award damages in respect of, and restrain by injunction, any breach of the clause committed by litigating elsewhere than in the courts of X. If such a clause has been agreed, then to prohibit the grant of the injunction for which it provides would interfere with freely assumed contractual obligations.[104] But this is the established interpretation given by the English courts to any standard English exclusive jurisdiction clause, an interpretation of which many well-advised contracting parties are well aware.[105] The same reasoning answers the objection raised by some scholars from civil law systems, that arbitration clauses and exclusive forum clauses create procedural rights only, capable of being effective only within a legal system by the grant of a stay of litigation before the court in question.[106] This, with respect, is a parochial perspective: arbitration clauses and exclusive forum clauses are viewed as substantive contractual obligations in a number of major legal systems, in particular systems with a common law heritage.[107] Parties who have agreed to an arbitration or exclusive jurisdiction clause governed by those laws have

---

[101]   *Société Nationale Industrielle Aérospatiale v Lee Kui Jak* [1987] AC 871 (PC) 895G–H.

[102]   *Airbus Industrie v Patel* [1999] 1 AC 119 (HL) 138G–H.

[103]   *Aggeliki Charis Compania Maritima v Pagnan (The Angelic Grace)* [1995] 1 Lloyds Rep 87 (CA) 96; *OT Africa Lines v Magic Sportswear* [2005] 2 Lloyds Rep 170 (CA) [27], [32], [58]–[61], [73].

[104]   See Rev Crit DIP (2004) 93(2) 655, para 4 (Note H Muir-Watt),.

[105]   *West Tankers v Ras Riunione Adriatica di Sicurta (The Front Comor)* [2007] 1 Lloyds Rep 391 (HL) [19]–[20]. See S Males QC, 'Comity and Anti-Suit Injunctions' [1998] LMCLQ 543, 552.

[106]   See P Ortolani, 'Anti-Suit Injunctions in Support of Arbitration under the Recast Brussels I Regulation' (2015) Max Planck Institute Working Paper 6, 11–12.

[107]   In English law there is no doubt that arbitration clauses and exclusive forum clauses create substantive contractual obligations not to sue abroad. See eg *Pena Copper Mines v Rio Tinto Co* (1911) 105 LT 846; *AES Ust-Kamenogorsk Hydropower Plant LLC v Ust-Kamenogorsk Hydropower Plant JSC* [2013] 1 WLR 1889 (SC) [1], [21]–[23], [24].

agreed to that analysis, and to its remedial consequences. A different civil law analysis is no warrant for overturning the parties' choice of law.

In turn, the *need* for the injunction follows from the fact that if the injunction is not granted, the injunction claimant will have to defend himself, or make an appearance to challenge jurisdiction, in the foreign court, which is exactly what he contracted to avoid,[108] as well as from the unjustified costs and expense that the continuation of the foreign proceedings (in breach of contract) will produce, and the risk that the defendant abroad may involuntarily submit to the jurisdiction of the foreign court.[109]   **1.54**

Nevertheless, these arguments do not get to the heart of the problem. The situations where the greatest controversy is likely to arise are those where the foreign jurisdiction applies different conflicts of laws rules, or mandatory rules of public policy, that invalidate an exclusive forum clause which English conflicts of laws rules and contract law would treat as valid.[110] In such a case, what gives the English court the *right* to impose its view of the validity of the clause over the injunction defendant's ability to invoke the possibly contrary view that might be taken by the foreign court?[111]   **1.55**

The primary response given by the English courts has been simply that they must apply their own conflicts of laws rules, and give effect to the contractual obligation that those rules dictate.[112] But from an international perspective, this may not be enough. It is arguable that, in order for an injunction in such a case to be reconcilable with comity, and to avoid parochialism, there would at least have to be some system-transcendent reason why it was appropriate for English conflicts of laws rules to be given overriding effect, and for the English court to intervene.[113] One possible candidate for a system-transcendent rationale is the principle of freedom of contract itself:[114] if the parties have elected to contract under a particular system of law, including that system's conflicts of laws rules, and for the exclusive jurisdiction of that system's courts, then their personal choices should be respected, and their personal obligations enforced; and it is legitimate for the chosen court to enforce those obligations.[115]   **1.56**

However, the opponent of anti-suit injunctions might respond that even this tribute to comity is insufficient, there being no such thing as a system-transcendent rationale, since no legal system can escape its own prejudices;[116] and that in any event, no such rationale   **1.57**

---

[108] *Aggeliki Charis Compania Maritima v Pagnan (The Angelic Grace)* [1995] 1 Lloyds Rep 87 (CA) 96; *West Tankers v Ras Riunione Adriatica di Sicurta (The Front Comor)* [2007] 1 Lloyds Rep 391 (HL) [19]–[20], [32]. See Sir P Gross, 'Anti-Suit Injunctions and Arbitration' [2005] LMCLQ 10, 24–25.

[109] Sir P Gross, 'Anti-Suit Injunctions and Arbitration' [2005] LMCLQ 10, 24–25.

[110] This problem can be called the 'conflict of conflicts'. See Ch 8, paras 8.31–8.44.

[111] A Nuyts, 'Les principes directeurs de l'Institute de Droit International sur le recours à la doctrine du *forum non conveniens* et aux anti-suit injunctions' (2003) 2 Revue Belge de Droit Intl 536, 556.

[112] See eg *West Tankers v Ras Riunione Adriatica di Sicurta (The Front Comor)* [2005] 2 Lloyds Rep 257, 262–63.

[113] For system-transcendence and the importance of symmetry, see T Raphael, 'Do as You Would be Done By? System-Transcendent Justification and Anti-Suit Injunctions' [2016] LMCLQ 256, which refers to the 'Golden Rule'—that you should do as you would be done by. On the same theme see *TS Production v Drew Pictures* (2008) 172 FCR 433 (FCA) [60].

[114] In *Apple Corps v Apple Computer* [1992] RPC 70, 79, Hoffmann J referred to the 'universal principle that until some good contrary reason has been shown, men should be held to their bargains'.

[115] *OT Africa Lines v Magic Sportswear* [2005] 2 Lloyds Rep 170 (CA) [27], [32], [58]–[61], [73].

[116] A Briggs, 'Anti-Suit Injunctions in a Complex World' in F Rose (ed), *Lex Mercatoria* (LLP 2000) 219, 237, suggests that the mere fact that an exclusive forum clause is governed by English law is insufficient to mean that the English court should 'claim the role as the exclusive enforcer of such a contractual term', as the court whose jurisdiction is allegedly excluded is at least as legitimate an enforcer of the clause.

would justify overriding the injunction defendant's right to rely on the foreign court's law and policy choices.

1.58   At this point of the analysis, we are therefore brought hard up against a fundamental choice between values: does the importance that comity places on the sovereignty of other legal systems, and their right to impose their own law and policy choices, require non-intervention, irrespective of any system-transcendent rationale? Or can the importance of doing practical justice, and enforcing a party's personal obligations, according to the originating system's own perception of what is right (especially on as system-transcendent a basis as is achievable), be sufficient to warrant an order against the party concerned, even at the price of tensions with comity? The common law chooses the latter result.[117] This is, again, a choice between fundamental values, which is as much a political as a legal issue.

1.59   Yet in defence of the common law answer, it can be noted that insisting on non-intervention is not a neutral solution. Although intervention by anti-suit injunction enforces the injuncting legal system's perception of what is right, insisting on non-intervention would conversely ensure that a party could, without interference, procure that his freely agreed obligations be overridden by finding a legal system that was willing to override them.[118] To give a practical example, the question in issue in *The Front Comor*[119] was not, from one perspective, whether the English court 'trusted' the Italian court: it was whether Italian or English conflicts of laws rules and contract law should be applied to determine whether an English law arbitration clause providing for arbitration in England is binding.[120]

1.60   A parallel and perhaps even more problematic debate arises where injunctions are sought on the basis that the foreign litigation is vexatious and oppressive. In these non-contractual cases, the interference to comity is not warranted by any concrete personal obligation, nor by any express or implied agreement that the originating court is the appropriate court to determine questions of forum. So, the argument that the originating court has a right to intervene necessarily starts from a weaker foundation.

1.61   The common law has recognized this, in particular by Lord Goff's imposition of the requirement that the court must have 'sufficient interest' in determining the question of forum before an injunction can be granted.[121] Yet the difficulty, and the debate, arises in identifying the level of connection or interest that *should* be required to give the originating court the right to intervene, notwithstanding the indirect interference with the foreign court that the

---

[117]   See, in Canada, *Amchem Products v British Columbia (Workers' Compensation Board)* [1993] 1 SCR 897, 934.

[118]   See Sir P Gross, 'Anti-Suit Injunctions and Arbitration' [2005] LMCLQ 10, 24.

[119]   *West Tankers v Ras Riunione Adriatica di Sicurta (The Front Comor)* [2007] 1 Lloyds Rep 391 (HL); see Ch 12.

[120]   The root of the problem, in arbitration cases within the European Community, is that arbitration is excluded from the Rome Convention and the Rome I Regulation, and thus arbitration clauses are not subject to the 'putative proper law' rule for choice of law provided for in Article 8 of the Rome Convention and Article 10 of the Rome I Regulation. See by analogy *XL Insurance v Owens Corning* [2000] 2 Lloyds Rep 500 (where the US court would apply the Federal Arbitration Act as the *lex fori* to override the agreed proper law of the contract). See also *OT Africa Line Ltd v Hijazy (The Kribi) (No 1)* [2001] 1 Lloyds Rep 76, where it seems that if no injunction had been granted, the consequence would have been that Belgian contract law rather than English contract law would have applied to determine the validity of an express English exclusive jurisdiction clause expressly governed by English law: see at [23], [73(3)].

[121]   *Airbus Industrie v Patel* [1999] 1 AC 119 (HL) 138G; the requirement of a sufficient interest is discussed further at Ch 4, paras 4.80–4.83. In *Masri v Consolidated Contractors (No 3)* [2009] QB 503 [81], Lawrence Collins LJ suggested that to grant an anti-suit injunction in a case which has no relevant connection with England 'may be a breach of international law'.

injection involves.[122] For example, under current English law, the English courts will have a sufficient interest if they view themselves as the natural forum for the dispute (and an injunction can then in broad terms be granted if the foreign litigation is vexatious and oppressive).[123] In contrast, some American circuits have taken a generally more restrictive approach, and require that anti-suit injunctions can only be granted to protect the forum's jurisdiction, to prevent evasion of the forum's important public policies, or where the foreign suit was brought in bad faith or to vex or harass the party seeking the injunction.[124] Some US scholarship has gone further and suggested that it is only where the originating legal system needs to protect its own judicial sovereignty by granting anti-anti-suit injunctions that it will have a legitimate ground to intervene.[125]

It is suggested that to preclude all non-contractual anti-suit injunctions, or to adopt restrictive and rigid rules in respect of them, would be inappropriate. For example, the English court has restrained applications to the US courts for the purpose of evidence gathering, where the actual substantive proceedings were in England, and the evidence-gathering methods in the USA would clash with the good management of an English trial.[126] These injunctions are clearly consistent with comity. The English courts were entitled to control the proceedings before them, and the evidence to be adduced therein, and it appears that the US courts may have welcomed the grant of appropriate injunctive relief by the court with jurisdiction over the merits.[127]   **1.62**

In principle, in order to pay due regard to comity, something more should be required, over and above a conclusion that the originating court is the natural forum for the litigation. To use the language of Hoffmann J (as he then was), there has to be some good reason why the decision to stop the litigation should be taken 'here rather than there'.[128]   **1.63**

However, it is unlikely, at least for the foreseeable future, that the English courts will accept that the barriers imposed by comity, even in non-contractual cases, should be raised high enough sharply to limit their powers to grant anti-suit injunctions. One of the fundamental assumptions of many of the writers who seek to restrict anti-suit injunctions is that one cannot criticize or suspect the quality of justice done in foreign courts, or the approach they   **1.64**

---

[122] R Fentiman, 'Anti-Suit Injunctions and the Brussels Convention' [2000] CLR 45, 45–46, argues that the grant of anti-suit injunctions to restrain duplicative litigation that harasses a party to litigation here is reconcilable with comity, because the interference with the English litigation is 'an issue uniquely within an English court's province'.

[123] *Airbus Industrie v Patel* [1999] 1 AC 119 (HL) 138H–139A.

[124] J Phillips, 'A Proposed Solution to the Puzzle of Anti-Suit Injunctions' (2002) 69 U Chic L Rev 2007.

[125] R Raushenbush, 'Anti-Suit Injunctions and International Comity' (1985) 71 Va Law Rev 1039. A Lowenfeld, 'Forum Shopping, Anti-Suit Injunctions, Negative Declarations, and Related Tools of International Litigation' (1997) 91 AJIL 314, who is in general an opponent of anti-suit injunctions, accepts their necessity in cases of 'fraud'.

[126] *Armstrong v Armstrong* [1892] P 98; *South Carolina Insurance v Assurantie Maatschappij 'De Seven Provincien'* [1987] 1 AC 24 (HL); *Bankers Trust International v PT Dharmala Sakti Sejahtera (No 1)* [1996] CLC 252; *Omega Group Holdings v Kozeny* [2002] CLC 132; *Nokia v Interdigital Technology* [2004] EWHC 2920 (Pat); *Benfield Holdings v Richardson* [2007] EWHC 171; and more recently *Royal Bank of Scotland v Hicks* [2011] EWHC 287, 94–96 (injunction refused on facts). In Australia, see *Allstate Life Insurance v Australian New Zealand Banking Group (No 4)* (1996) 64 FCR 61 (Aus Fed Ct).

[127] *Bankers Trust International v PT Dharmala Sakti Sejahtera (No 1)* [1996] CLC 252, 263B–F. Similarly, in *Allstate Life Insurance v Australian New Zealand Banking Group (No 4)* (1996) 64 FCR 61 (Aus Fed Ct) it appeared that the US court, far from objecting to the injunction, would welcome the exercise of control by the court with jurisdiction over the merits.

[128] *Barclays Bank v Homan* [1993] BCLC 680, 687 per Hoffmann J; followed in *Deutsche Bank v Highland Crusader Offshore Partners* [2010] 1 WLR 1023 (CA) [56]; and see *Stichting Shell Pensioenfonds v Krys* [2015] AC 616 (PC) [42].

take to their own jurisdiction. The English courts are hesitant to criticize foreign courts, and will usually refrain from doing so explicitly. But outside closed jurisdictional systems, such as the Brussels–Lugano regime, there is no reason to assume that foreign courts will exercise restraint in the exercise of jurisdiction.[129] By declining to intervene by injunction, the English court would be without an effective remedy in the face of exorbitant assumptions of jurisdiction by foreign courts.[130] Confronted with the 'jungle'[131] of independent jurisdictions that make up the world, the English courts are not likely unilaterally to disarm themselves, nor to adopt a degree of deference to comity which would preclude them from doing practical justice in the face of vexatious litigation abroad.

E. HUMAN RIGHTS LAW

1. The Right of Access to a Court

1.65 It has been argued[132] that the grant of an anti-suit injunction to restrain a party from litigating in the court of his choice is an infringement of his human rights, and in particular an unwarranted restriction on his right of effective 'access to a court', as guaranteed by Article 6 of the ECHR,[133] which the English courts are obliged to enforce.[134] However, it is suggested that such a sweeping view is unlikely to be right. We analyse the principles applicable under Article 6, and they do not support any absolute preclusion. The English courts, unsurprisingly, have rejected any suggestion that their anti-suit injunctions are contrary to Article 6.[135] In addition, the more recent case law of continental courts, and the ECJ, suggest that they too will accept that the anti-suit injunction is consistent with Article 6, at least in

---

[129] *Société Nationale Industrielle Aérospatiale v Lee Kui Jak* [1987] AC 871 (PC) 894E–F:

Their Lordships refer, in particular, to the fact that litigants may now be encouraged to proceed in foreign jurisdictions, having no connection with the subject matter of the dispute, which exercise an exceptionally broad jurisdiction and which offer such great inducements, in particular greatly enhanced, even punitive, damages, that they may tempt litigants to pursue their remedies there.

[130] For the necessity of the anti-suit injunction in a world outside controlled closed systems of jurisdiction, see *Airbus Industrie v Patel* [1999] 1 AC 199 (HL) 132G–133H; and see also *Amchem Products v British Columbia (Workers Compensation Board)* [1993] 1 SCR 897 (SC Can) 914–15.

[131] *Airbus Industrie GIE v Patel* [1999] 1 AC 119, 132C.

[132] This conclusion was reached by the Oberlandesgericht Düsseldorf in *Re the Enforcement of an English Anti-Suit Injunction* [1997] ILPr 320 [17]–[18]; and according to to JT (1992) 438 (Note H Born and M Fallon), was also deployed by the Belgian court in *Ref Bruxelles* (18 December 1989) RW 1990–91, 676. It was also the view of AG Kokott in Case C-185/07, *Allianz v West Tankers (The Front Comor)* [2009] ECR I-663, AG [58], but her analysis is brief and not well reasoned (eg she made no reference to the principle of waiver) and was not picked up by the ECJ in that case.

[133] Article 6 provides 'In the determination of his civil rights and obligations or of any criminal charge against him, everyone is entitled to a fair and public hearing within a reasonable time by an independent and impartial tribunal established by law.' The European Court of Human Rights (ECtHR) has held that a right of access to 'a' court is 'inherent' in Article 6: *Golder v UK* (1975) 1 EHRR 524 [28], [35]–[36]; and further that the individual has a right of *effective* access to 'a' court: *Airey v Ireland* (1979) 2 EHRR 305 [24], [28]. Sometimes the phase used is a 'right of access to court': see eg *TP and KM v UK* (2002) 34 EHRR 23 [96], [99]. The Convention protects foreigners as well as citizens (or subjects), including foreigners from non-Convention states: Article 1; while Article 6 protects companies as well as natural persons: see eg *Marpa Zeeland BV and Metal Welding BV v The Netherlands* (2005) 40 EHRR 407. The right is not absolute and may be subject to limitations which pursue a legitimate aim and are proportionate: *Radunovic v Montenegro* (2018) 66 EHRR 19 [62]–[63].

[134] The ECHR has been incorporated into English domestic law by the Human Rights Act 1998. The combined effect of ss 3 and 6 of the 1998 Act is that the power to grant anti-suit injunctions contained in s 37(1) of the Senior Courts Act 1981 must be exercised compatibly with the Convention rights.

[135] *OT Africa Line v Hijazy (The Kribi)* [2001] 1 Lloyds Rep 76 [28(9)], [41]–[44]; *Mauritius Commercial Bank v Hestia Holdings* [2013] 2 Lloyds Rep 121 [43].

many cases.[136] If Article 6 does impose any pertinent constraints, it is likely to be at the margins of the remedy.

2. Does the Right of Access to a Court Apply Extraterritorially?

Any restrictions imposed on rights of access to a court by anti-suit injunctions will limit the **1.66** injunction defendant's freedom to act in the state of the court of the proceedings restrained, not in the state of the court granting the injunction. Consequently, two threshold questions must be answered: first, does the injunction defendant fall within the originating state's jurisdiction for the purposes of the ECHR; and second, does the right of access to a court apply extraterritorially?

As to the first question, a defendant to an extraterritorial injunction granted by the courts **1.67** of a contracting state will probably fall within the 'jurisdiction' of that state for the purposes of the ECHR, and therefore be within the scope of the Human Rights Act 1998,[137] if the Convention right in question applies extraterritorially.

The question of whether the right of access to a court under Article 6 applies extraterritorially, **1.68** and can potentially be affected by the effect of anti-suit injunctions in the foreign state, is more difficult.

The general principle of the Strasbourg case law is that Article 1 only requires the con- **1.69** tracting states to ensure compliance with the Convention rights within their jurisdiction, which is principally their territorial jurisdiction.[138] Acts of the contracting states performed, or producing effects, outside their territories can constitute an exercise of jurisdiction within the meaning of Article 1 only in exceptional cases.[139] Exceptional cases may include where the state exercises effective control over an area in the foreign state; or even where state agents exercise physical power and control over the applicant in the foreign country, although the scope of the rights that apply to him will be tailored to the nature of the control.[140] In some cases, the Convention has been applied to the exercise of extraterritorial jurisdiction by national judges, albeit in cases where this has occurred with the consent of the 'receiving' state.[141]

---

[136] The Cour de Cassation has expressly concluded that a contractual anti-suit injunction is consistent with Article 6: *In Zone Brands International v In Beverage International*, Cass Civ 1 (14 October 2009) Nos 08-16.369 and 08-16.549. Similarly, Case C-536/61, *Gazprom*, EU:C:2015:316, accepted the legitimacy of anti-suit injunctions granted by arbitrators.

[137] The territorial scope of the protection given to the Convention rights by the Human Rights Act is congruent with the territorial scope of the protection offered by the Convention itself: *Al Skeini v Secretary of State for Defence* [2008] 1 AC 153 (HL) [56]–[59] (Lord Rodger); [133]–[151] (Lord Brown) (Baroness Hale and Lord Carswell agreed with Lords Rodger and Brown; Lord Bingham dissented).

[138] Article 1: 'The High Contracting Parties shall secure to everyone within their jurisdiction the rights and freedoms defined in Section I of this Convention.' The scope of the state's jurisdiction is primarily territorial: *Bankovic v Belgium* (2001) 11 BHRC 435 [59]–[61].

[139] *Catan v The Republic of Moldova and Russia*, No 43370/04, ECHR (2012) [103]–[106].

[140] *Al-Skeini v UK* (2011) 53 EHRR 18 [136]–[137]; *Hassan v UK* 38 BHRC 358; *Alseran v Ministry of Defence* [2018] 3 WLR 95 [79]–[80]; although see the doubts expressed in *Mohammed v Ministry of Defence* [2017] AC 821 (SC) [46]–[49].

[141] App Nos 7289/75 and 7349/76, *X and Y v Switzerland* (1977) 9 DR 57 (ECmHR) (the Swiss courts by agreement with Liechtenstein exercised jurisdiction over immigration into Liechtenstein; Switzerland was responsible under the Convention for their acts in doing so); *Al-Skeini v UK* (2011) 53 EHRR 18 [135]; *Jaloud v The Netherlands*, No 47708, ECHR (2014) [139]. See also App No 48205/99, *Gentilhomme v France* (14 May

1.70   Understanding whether this would apply in respect of the right of access to a court is not self-evident. The existing Strasbourg case law on the right of access to the court under Article 6 concerns only the obligations of states to protect, and not impede, the right of access to *their own* courts.[142] If this approach is extrapolated, the originating state will not have any general responsibility to ensure that individuals can access the courts of the foreign state, nor any obligations in respect of the fairness of proceedings in that state, which may not be party to the Convention.

1.71   However, the ECtHR has held that in extradition and deportation cases, Article 6 has a limited extraterritorial effect. A contracting state will breach Article 6 if the extradition or deportation creates a real risk that the individual will suffer a 'flagrant denial of justice' in the receiving state,[143] a phrase which is intended to set a higher threshold than a mere breach of Article 6.[144] These decisions do not expressly concern the extraterritorial application of the right of access to the court. Nevertheless, it is suggested that the Strasbourg Court might well conclude that the right of access to a court *does* have extraterritorial effect,[145] at least in respect of rights of access to the courts of other contracting states.[146]

2002) (Art 6(1) applied without query to the excessive length of French administrative court procedures relating to Algerian residents and facts in Algeria).

---

[142] See eg *Golder v UK* (1975) 1 EHRR 524 [35]–[36]; and *Wos v Poland* (2007) 45 EHRR 28 [98]; ECHR, Guide on Article 6: Right to a Fair Trial (civil limb) (2013). An argument that Article 6 relates only to access to a state's own courts gains some support from *Vasilescu v Romania* (1999) 28 EHRR 241 [43] (where it was said that in civil cases, Art 6(1) is merely a '*lex specialis*' of Art 13, the right to an effective remedy), since it is difficult to conceive of Article 13 having any effect in respect of other states' legal systems.

[143] *Soering v UK* (1989) 11 EHRR 439 [112]–[113]; *Mamatkulov and Askarov v Turkey* (2005) 41 EHRR 494 [84]–[91]; App No 7155/01, *Einhorn v France* (16 October 2001) [32] (where the extraterritorial operation of Art 6 was regarded as exceptional); App No 64599/01, *Razaghi v Sweden* (11 March 2003) 9; App No 17837/03, *Tomic v UK* (14 October 2003) 12; App No 24668/03, *Olaechea Cahuas v Spain* (10 August 2006) [59]–[62]; *Othman (Abu Qatada) v UK*, No 8139/09, ECHR (2012) [258]–[261]. Similarly, a court of a contracting state must refuse enforcement of a foreign judgment if the judgment is the result of a flagrant denial of justice in the foreign state: *Drozd and Janousek v France and Spain* (1992) EHRR 745 [101].

[144] *Othman (Abu Qatada) v UK*, No 8139/09, ECHR (2012) [260]:

> 'flagrant denial of justice' is a stringent test of unfairness. A flagrant denial of justice goes beyond mere irregularities or lack of safeguards in the trial procedures such as might result in a breach of Article 6 if occurring within the Contracting State itself. What is required is a breach of the principles of fair trial guaranteed by Article 6 which is so fundamental as to amount to a nullification, or destruction of the very essence, of the right guaranteed by that Article.

[145] The main justification for the extension of extraterritorial effect articulated in *Soering* (in relation to Art 3, which was the main issue in the case) was that extradition in circumstances that would lead to a breach of Article 3 'would be contrary to the spirit and intendment of the Art': at *Soering v UK* (1989) 11 EHRR 439 [88]. It would be arguable that an extraterritorial order that unjustifiably restricted rights of access to a foreign court (or rights of access globally) would be contrary to the spirit and purpose of Article 6. This conclusion also makes sense when tested in hypothetical situations. Imagine that Poland passed a law banning any person from commencing proceedings in the *German* courts for restitution of property seised at the end of the Second World War, on pain of criminal punishment in Poland; this could severely restrict individuals' rights of access to the courts. However, there would be no grounds for an application to be made against Germany, even though the restriction would bite in respect of rights of access to the German courts; the only state whose responsibility could be relevantly engaged would be Poland, and so concluding that the right of access to a court had no extraterritorial application would mean that there was no effective Convention remedy, and thus a potential 'gap or vacuum in human rights protection'. Any gap or vacuum of that kind should not be permitted, at least within the combined territories of the contracting states: see *Bankovic v Belgium* (2001) 11 BHRC 435 [80] (and n 146).

[146] In *Bankovic v Belgium* (2001) 11 BHRC 435 [80], the court noted that, when considering whether to extend the 'jurisdiction' of a state for the purposes of assessing its Convention responsibilities beyond its narrow territorial jurisdiction, it had only done so in cases where that extension was within the territory of the contracting states as a whole, because the Convention was designed to create a regional space of human rights protection and was not intended to be applied beyond the territories of the contracting states. See also *Al Skeini v Secretary of State for Defence* [2008] 1 AC 153 (HL) [77]–[79]. The concepts of 'jurisdiction', and the extraterritorial effects of the Convention rights, are not cleanly separable: see *Bankovic v Belgium* (2001) 11 BHRC 435 [68]. It could therefore

The injunction's effects on rights of access to courts in other countries are immediate and direct, and certainly 'proximate'.[147] Further, the exercise of control by injunction could be viewed as analogous to the case where a state agent exercises physical power and control over the applicant in the foreign state. Consequently, the grant of anti-suit injunctions may well be treated as one of those exceptional situations where the Convention rights can have extra-territorial effect.

In *McElhinney v Ireland*, the ECtHR was apparently prepared to accept, when considering whether Ireland had unjustifiably restricted access to its own courts, that the ability of the applicant to access the courts of the United Kingdom for the determination of the same matters was a material factor against a finding that Article 6 had been infringed,[148] illustrating that the right of access to a court can legitimately be assessed on a transnational basis.   **1.72**

However, even if the right of access to a court does apply extraterritorially, it remains to be seen whether it will only apply to prevent 'flagrant denials of justice',[149] or whether it will apply according to its ordinary logic without requiring a higher threshold. The reasons for the limited scope of the extraterritorial obligation in the extradition cases include the uncertainty of predictions as to an individual's future treatment, and the point that the extraditing state will not itself be directly involved in any violation of the applicant's rights. In contrast, where an anti-suit injunction is granted, any potential interference with the injunction defendant's rights of access to a court will follow directly from the orders of the courts of the state whose responsibility is said to be engaged. It is arguable that the right of access to the courts will apply to anti-suit injunctions extraterritorially without qualification. The discussion will proceed on that assumption; but it must be borne in mind that some higher threshold might be required.   **1.73**

3. The Right of Access to a Court and Contractual Anti-Suit Injunctions

Even if no higher threshold for the application of the right of access is required, the argument that anti-suit injunctions infringe the right of access to a court has little force in the standard 'contractual' case where an anti-suit injunction is sought to enforce an exclusive forum clause. The Strasbourg Court accepts that a party may 'waive' his Article 6 rights by a freely chosen exclusive arbitration clause.[150] There is no good reason why the same should   **1.74**

be argued that the responsibility of a state for the extraterritorial effect of the right of access to the court should not be interpreted to apply beyond the territories of the contracting states, within which, but not outside which, the right of access to the court should be protected. But this point seems unlikely to stand, as in the more recent case law of the European Court of Human Rights, the extraterritorial effects of the Convention Rights have extended beyond the territories of the contracting states: see eg *Al-Skeini v UK* (2011) 53 EHRR 18.

---

[147] In *Ilascu v Moldova and Russia* (2004) 40 EHRR 1030 [317], the European Court of Human Rights explained the *Soering* line of case law by saying: 'A State's responsibility may also be engaged on account of acts which have sufficiently proximate repercussions on rights guaranteed by the Convention, even if those repercussions occur outside its jurisdiction.'

[148] *McElhinney v Ireland* (2002) 34 EHRR 13 [39]; however, see the dissenting judgment of Judge Loicades (at 341), suggesting that, in assessing whether the right of access to the court was infringed, it was relevant to consider only the possibilities of access to the courts of the contracting state whose responsibility was allegedly engaged.

[149] Deploying the threshold test concepts used in the extradition cases: see para 1.71.

[150] See generally App No 1197/61, *X v Germany*, (1962) Yearbook of the ECHR 88, 94–96 (ECmHR); *Deweer v Belgium* (1980) 2 EHRR 439 [49]; App No 10881/84, *R v Switzerland* (1987) 51 DR 83 (ECmHR) 100–01; *Bramelid and Malmstrom v Sweden* (1986) 8 EHRR 116, 177 (ECmHR); App No 28101/95, *Nordström-Janzon v Netherlands* (27 November 1996); App No 31737/36, *Suovaniemi v Finland* (unreported) (23 February 1999); App No 46483/99,

not apply to exclusive court jurisdiction clauses. In turn, if a party has *waived* his Article 6 rights to access a particular court, there is no right which the anti-suit injunction could infringe. This is consistent with the reasoning of Popplewell J in *Mauritius Bank v Hestia*, where without reference to the waiver case law he concluded that a unilateral jurisdiction clause was not inconsistent with Article 6, because: 'Article 6 is directed to access to justice within the forum chosen by the parties, not to choice of forum.'[151] There might, however, be more credible Article 6 issues in cases where the consent of a party to the forum clause is deemed rather than real, since the waiver 'must be made in an unequivocal manner', and be 'knowing' and 'voluntary'.[152]

1.75   In addition, in *The Kribi*, Aikens J rejected an argument that Article 6 should preclude him from granting a contractual anti-suit injunction, without referring to the argument that the exclusive jurisdiction clause had waived the injunction defendant's rights of access to a court, on the simple and neat ground that the right of access to 'a' court does not entail a right of access to the court of your choice.[153]

Pastore v Italy, 25 May 1999; *Simeonovi v Bulgaria* (2018) 66 EHRR 2 [115]. In England, see *Fiona Trust v Privalov* [2007] 1 Lloyds Rep 391 (HL) [20]; *Di Placito v Slater* [2004] 1 WLR 1605 (CA) [51]; *Stretford v Football Association* [2007] Bus LR 1052 (CA) [43]–[66]; *Sumukan v Commonwealth Secretariat* [2007] 2 Lloyds Rep 87 [53]–[61]; *Warren v The Random House Group* [2009] QB 600 (CA) [32]. But the national arbitration law must permit appropriate court control of the arbitration process: *Nordstrom-Janzon v The Netherlands*, No 28101/95 (EComHR).

It would appear from the case law that the waiver must 'not run counter to any important public interest': App No 11960/86, *Axelsson v Sweden* (13 July 1990); *Stretford v Football Association* at [54]; *Warren v The Random House Group* at [32]; *Simeonovi v Bulgaria* (2018) 66 EHRR 2 [115]; but there is no case where an arbitration agreement has been held to run counter to any such interest; and in *Stretford v Football Association* it was held that arbitration under the FA rules and Arbitration Act 1996 was not contrary to any important public interest.

The Oberlandesgericht Düsseldorf did not refer to any of this jurisprudence in *Re the Enforcement of an English Anti-Suit Injunction* [1997] ILPr 320.

[151]   *Mauritius Commercial Bank v Hestia Holdings* [2013] 2 Lloyds Rep 121 [43]. See also the Cour de Cassation's reasoning in *In Zone Brands International v In Beverage International*, Cass Civ 1 (14 October 2009) Nos 08-16.369 and 08-16.549: 'there cannot have been deprivation of the right of access to the judge, since the decision taken by the Georgian judge had precisely the purpose of ruling on his own competence and, in the interests of finality, to ensure respect of the jurisdiction clause agreed by the parties'.

[152]   App No 11960/86, *Axelsson v Sweden* (13 July 1990); *Hakansson and Sturesson v Sweden* (1991) 13 EHRR 1, 16 [66]; *Transado-Transportes Fluviais do Sado v Portugal*, 35943/02, ECHR (2003); *Simeonovi v Bulgaria* (2018) 66 EHRR 2 [115], [128]; and in England *Stretford v Football Association* [2007] Bus LR 1052 (CA) [48], [60]. If arbitration is imposed by law, then the compulsory arbitration must respect the normal guarantees of the court which Article 6(1) envisages. This includes the requirement of publicity of debates which is inconsistent with most arbitration systems. See *Suda v Czech Republic*, No 1643/07, ECHR (2010), where provisions of Czech law requiring minority shareholder disputes to be brought before private arbitrators were held to be an infringement of Article 6(1). But this should be interpreted in a practical way. In *Stretford v Football Association* [2007] Bus LR 1052 (CA) [43]–[66] it was held that there was a valid waiver and no breach of Article 6 where a football agent was required, as condition of holding a license, to comply with the Football Association Rules, which included an arbitration provision, and where as a result as a matter of English law an arbitration clause was incorporated into his contract, even though there was no express voluntary agreement to arbitration.

[153]   *OT Africa Line v Hijazy (The Kribi)* [2001] 1 Lloyds Rep 76 [28(9)], [41]–[44]; discussed in J Fawcett, 'The Impact of Article 6(1) on the ECHR on Private International Law' (2007) 56 ICLQ 1, 11–12. This approach gains some support from the fact that the ECtHR has never yet considered that a requirement to use a particular court rather than any other within a national legal system could amount to a breach of the right of access to a court; in order to satisfy the right, all that has been necessary is that there is *a* court within the state in which the applicant's legal claims can be fully and fairly heard: *Alatulkkila v Finland* (2006) 43 EHRR 34 [41]–[43], [47]–[54] (applicants confined to review by the Finnish Supreme Administrative Court; the question was whether the hearing in that court was sufficient). Aikens J's analysis is also supported by JT (1992) 438 (Note H Born and M Fallon), criticizing *Ref Bruxelles* (18 December 1989) RW 1990–91, 676. See, however, *McElhinney v Ireland* (2002) 34 EHRR 13, discussed at para 1.72 .

It is therefore submitted that where there is a clear contractual agreement to the exclusive **1.76** forum clause any case for breach of Article 6 is unpromising.

4. The Right of Access to a Court and Alternative Forum Cases

The reasoning used by Aikens J in *The Kribi*, if correct, would also apply to all non-contrac- **1.77** tual alternative forum cases. However, it is not clear that Aikens J is right. A restriction on access to a particular court can in practice amount to a material hindrance on your rights of access to courts generally, especially where the restriction on your choice requires you to use one legal system rather than another. In another legal system, different procedural rules will operate, and if the choice of law rules are different, a different substantive law might also apply. Instead, the relevance of the availability of another court may well be that it reduces the seriousness of the restriction on access, and renders it more easily justifiable.[154] So it may well be necessary to consider whether the restrictions imposed by non-contractual alternative forum injunctions are permissible.

The Strasbourg case law makes clear that the right of access to a court does not entail un- **1.78** restricted access to any court at all, still less to the court of your choice. It is not an absolute right, but may be subject to limitations, provided those limitations do not impair the very essence of the right, pursue a legitimate aim, and comply with proportionality.[155] Thus, the various mechanisms by which legal systems terminate or stay unmeritorious litigation before them, or deny their own jurisdiction over litigation, can in principle be compatible with the right of access to a court enshrined in Article 6.[156] In particular, the English provisions restricting the commencement of actions by vexatious litigants before the English courts themselves are compatible with Article 6.[157]

However, from the point of view of the right of access to a court, the principal and per- **1.79** haps only difference between the courts of state X granting an injunction to restrain vexatious litigation (or litigation in breach of contract) in state Y, and state Y itself staying or dismissing such litigation, is the identity of the decision-maker. Consequently, in an alternative forum case, the only restriction which an anti-suit injunction inherently involves is a restriction of the right to select the court that will make the decision. There is no obvious reason why the right of access to a court should carry within it a right to insist that the question as to whether a party can proceed with his litigation in state X must be decided

---

[154] See eg *McElhinney v Ireland* (2002) 34 EHRR 13 [39], discussed.

[155] App No 727/60 (1960) Yearbook of the ECHR, 302, 309 (ECmHR) (restrictions on access to the court are permissible if they 'do not deviate from their exclusive purpose of assuring justice according to law'); *Golder v UK* (1975) 1 EHRR 524 [38]; *Ashingdane v UK* (1985) 7 EHRR 528 [55]–[57]; *Stubbings v UK* (1996) 23 EHRR 213 [52] at 226–27, [48] at 233. The state has a 'certain margin of appreciation' in deciding what limitations can be imposed: *Stubbings v UK* (1996) 23 EHRR 213 [48] at 233; *Wos v Poland* (2007) 45 EHRR 28 [98]; *Radunovic v Montenegro* (2018) 66 EHRR 19 [62]–[63].

[156] See *Tolstoy Miloslavsky v UK* (1995) 20 EHRR 442 [59]–[67] (security for costs order); *TP and KM v UK* (2002) 34 EHRR 23 [102] (striking out); *Z v UK* (2001) 34 EHRR 97 [95]–[100] (striking out); *Reid v UK* (21 June 2001); *Clunis v UK* (11 September 2001); *Al Adsani v UK* (2002) 34 EHRR 11 [52]–[56] (state immunity); *Carnduff v UK* (10 February 2004); *Luordo v Italy* (2005) 41 EHRR 26 [83]–[88] (restrictions on bankrupt's right to commence actions found disproportionate on the facts); *Banovic v Croatia*, No 44284/10, ECHR (2015) [43]–[44] (foreseeable limitation periods);

[157] *Golder v UK*, Series B, No 16 (ECmHR) 52 [95]; *H v UK* 45 DR 281 (1985) (ECmHR) 283–85; *Stone Court Shipping v Spain* (2005) 40 EHRR 31 [33]–[42].

in state X rather than state Y, as the substantive effect on the party's actual access to a court is broadly the same. This illustrates that many arguments against the anti-suit injunction which purport to be based on human rights are in reality driven by a hidden assumption as to what comity requires, and do not in truth derive from the right of access to a court.[158] So the degree of restriction on the right of access to a court imposed by a normal alternative forum anti-suit injunction is limited, even in a non-contractual case.

1.80   In many alternative forum cases, the injunction is granted to prevent a party from proceeding with duplicative litigation in a second court when the substance of his dispute is already being litigated in the injuncting court. The desire to proceed with duplicative litigation, which *ex hypothesi* will have been found to be vexatious and oppressive, does not deserve, and is unlikely to attract, extensive protection from the Strasbourg Court. It can be argued with force that the limitations imposed by normal alternative forum injunctions pursue a legitimate aim[159] and will be proportionate. Indeed, the injunction claimant's right not to be vexed and oppressed by duplicative litigation could also be viewed as an element of his own right to a fair trial.

1.81   However, even if the restrictions imposed by an anti-suit injunction were viewed as pursuing a legitimate aim (such as preventing vexatious litigation), it is by no means certain that the ECtHR would always accept that it was a proportionate method of pursuing that aim.

1.82   In particular, in alternative forum cases there could be situations where the inability of a party to obtain a determination of whether he can proceed before the courts of state X from those very courts could be viewed as a material restriction on the effectiveness of his rights of access to a court, for example where the party in question was a consumer resident in state X, and it would be burdensome for him to be involved in proceedings in state Y.[160]

1.83   Consequently, it is arguable that the English court should, in appropriate cases, take account of the possibility of restrictions on the right of access to a court in the exercise of its discretion whether or not to grant the injunction. However, it is to be hoped that the requirements of English law—such as that the injunction should only be granted when 'the ends of justice' require it, and that it should not be granted if it would 'deprive the [injunction defendant] of advantages in the foreign forum of which it would be unjust to deprive him'[161]—will already have created an adequate level of protection. If so, then save in marginal cases it may not be necessary to perform a second analysis specifically directed to Article 6.[162]

---

[158] ML Niboyet, 'Le Principe de Confiance Mutuelle et Les Injonctions Anti-Suit' in P de Vareilles-Sommières, *Forum Shopping in the European Judicial Area* (Hart 2007) 77, 85, rejects the argument that anti-suit injunctions to restrain vexatious conduct are contrary to Article 6.

[159] The good management of litigation is a legitimate aim. Thus, in particular, the aim of avoiding an appellate court's list being overloaded is legitimate: *García Mandibaro v Spain* (2002) 34 EHRR 6 [38].

[160] In *Re the Enforcement of an English Anti-Suit Injunction* [1997] ILPr 320, the German injunction defendants were consumers, which was one of the main reasons which led the English court to conclude that there was no arbitration clause binding on them, and to discharge the injunctions: see *Philip Alexander Securities & Futures Ltd v Bamberger* [1997] ILPr 73.

[161] See *Société Nationale Industrielle Aérospatiale v Lee Kui Jak* [1987] AC 871 (PC) 892A, 894G, 896G–H. The tests for anti-suit injunctions in general are explored in Ch 4.

[162] See by analogy *Lubbe v Cape* [2000] 1 WLR 1545 (HL), 1561.

5. Article 6 and Single Forum Cases

Article 6 is most likely to be relevant in 'single forum' cases (discussed in Chapter 5, section   **1.84**
D), where the grant of an injunction will not merely deprive the litigant of his choice of
court but will also prevent him from bringing a particular claim, which can only be brought
in one forum, in the only forum where it can be brought. The Strasbourg Court has held
that while procedural restrictions on the exercise of a right are permissible, 'the limitations
applied must not restrict or reduce the individual's access in such a way or to such an extent
as to impair the very essence of the right'.[163] It is submitted that this does not mean that a
single forum injunction is inherently irreconcilable with the right of access to a court.[164]
Single forum injunctions will only be granted if there is something inappropriate about the
targeted forum. If a party can effectively exercise such rights as he has under the appropriate law, as determined by an appropriate set of choice of law rules in the appropriate
forum, the fact that the injunction will prevent him from exercising a right which only
arises in an inappropriate forum should not be regarded as a necessarily disproportionate
restriction on his exercise of his rights. By analogy, Article 6 would not prohibit the striking
out of claims by the court before which the proceedings were brought on the grounds that
they are vexatious or oppressive, or an abuse of process, or brought in the wrong forum.
Nevertheless, the possibility of tension with Article 6 is real. This suggests, first, that greater
caution should be exercised before concluding that the grant of a single forum injunction is
indeed in 'the interests of justice' (a requirement which is in any event part of English law),
and second, that tampering with the high thresholds required for the grant of a single forum
injunction could well lead to Article 6 problems.

F. ANTI-SUIT INJUNCTIONS AND PUBLIC INTERNATIONAL LAW

It is a long-established principle of public international law that the territorial sovereignty of   **1.85**
independent states, including their adjudicatory sovereignty, should in general not be interfered with by other states, although this principle is not absolute.[165] However, the implications of the principle of territoriality for the exercise of extraterritorial civil jurisdiction by
states remain uncertain. A rigid application of the concept of territorial sovereignty to the
exercise of civil jurisdiction internationally would be unworkable,[166] and would not represent state practice. Indeed, it has been suggested that customary international law imposes

---

[163] *Zvolsky and Zvolska v Czech Republic*, No 46129/99, ECHR (2002) [47].

[164] But cf J Fawcett, 'The Impact of Article 6(1) on the ECHR on Private International Law' (2007) 56 ICLQ 1, 12.

[165] R Jennings and A Watts (eds), *Oppenheim's International Law* (9th edn, OUP 2008) Vol I (hereafter 'Oppenheim') 385–86; FA Mann, 'The Doctrine of Jurisdiction in International Law' Part I (1964) 111 Hague Recueil des Cours, 1, 26–28. *Lotus Case* PCIJ, Series A, No 10, 18; see also J Crawford, *Brownlie's Principles of Public International Law* (8th edn, OUP 2012) (hereafter 'Brownlie') 297–98. The principle of territoriality is not, however, an absolute principle: *Lotus Case* PCIJ, Series A, No 10, 20. The unquestioned doctrine that no anti-suit injunction can be granted against the foreign court itself is consistent with, and an implication of, the principle of territoriality. Similarly, the English court's powers to punish for contempt of court cannot be exercised within the foreign state: see FA Mann, 'The Doctrine of Jurisdiction in International Law' (1964) 111 Hague Recueil des Cours 1, 129.

[166] FA Mann, 'The Doctrine of Jurisdiction in International Law' (1964) 111 Hague Recueil des Cours 1, 43–51, describing a rigid approach based on territoriality as 'procrustean', and propounding a doctrine based on 'closeness of connection'.

no material limitations on the exercise of civil jurisdiction by municipal courts, other than established restrictions such as diplomatic and sovereign immunity.[167] Even if, as is likely, public international law does place certain substantive limitations on the exercise of municipal civil jurisdiction internationally, the restrictions imposed are neither numerous nor constricting.[168] A possible summary of the boundary drawn by the modern law is that the courts of a state can exercise jurisdiction over acts of a foreigner in a foreign state so long as there is a 'sufficiently close connection to justify the first state in regulating the matter.'[169] Brownlie suggests that 'there should be a real and not colourable connection between the subject-matter and the source of the jurisdiction ... the principle of non-intervention in the territorial jurisdiction of other states should be observed, notably in an enforcement context. Elements of accommodation, mutuality and proportionality should be taken into account.'[170]

1.86   This language is similar to the tests of comity applied to the grant of anti-suit injunctions by the English courts since *Airbus v Patel*.[171] However, the coincidence of phrasing by no means guarantees the international legitimacy of the English court's practice of granting relief, as public international law might not accept the English view that there can be a sufficiently

---

[167] M Akehurst, 'Jurisdiction in International Law' (1972–73) 66 BYBIL 145, 176–77.

[168] 'International law does not impose hard and fast rules on States delimiting spheres of international jurisdiction ... it does, however, postulate the existence of limits ...': Sir G Fitzmaurice, in *Case Concerning Barcelona Traction, Light and Power Ltd*, ICJ Reports (1970) 105 [70] (see also *The Lotus Case* PCIJ, Series A, No 10, 20). In *The Lotus Case* at 20, the PCIJ suggested that international law did not contain 'a general prohibition to States to extend the application of their laws and the jurisdiction of their courts to persons, property and acts outside their territory' and that:

> far from laying down a general prohibition to the effect that States may not extend the application of their own laws and the jurisdiction of their courts to persons, property and acts outside their territory, it leaves them in this respect a wide margin of discretion which is only limited in certain cases by prohibitive rules.

This decision is heterodox, in so far as it suggests that states have a discretion (see FA Mann, 'The Doctrine of Jurisdiction in International Law' (1964) 111 Hague Recueil des Cours 1, 34–36; and G Triggs, *International Law: Contemporary Practice and Principles* (LexisNexis 2006) para 7.10) but it does reflect the point that states have considerable freedom in the exercise of extraterritorial jurisdiction at the current stage of development of public international law. M Akehurst, 'Jurisdiction in International Law' (1972–73) 66 BYBIL 145, 170 observes that 'when one examines the practice of states ... one finds that states claim jurisdiction over all sorts of claim and parties having no real connection with them and that this practice has seldom if ever given rise to diplomatic problems'.

[169] Oppenheim, 457–58, 462, 467–68. Another phrasing is a 'direct and substantial connection between the state exercising jurisdiction and the matter in relation to which jurisdiction is exercised'. See also FA Mann, 'The Doctrine of Jurisdiction in International Law' Part I (1964) 111 Hague Recueil des Cours 1, 43–51, 78–81, and 'The Doctrine of International Jurisdiction' Part III (1984) 186 Hague Recueil des Cours, 29, 31, 67. However, for an even more liberal approach, see M Akehurst, 'Jurisdiction in International Law' (1972–73) 66 BYBIL 145, 176–77. Public international law draws a distinction between the exercise of jurisdiction over citizens abroad and over non-citizens abroad. The nationality of the injunction defendant was treated as a key factor in the earlier English case law: see *Carron Iron v Maclaren* (1855) 5 HLC 439, 442; *Re Distin* (1871) 24 LT 197; *Re Chapman* (1873) LR 15 Eq 75; *Ellerman Lines v Read* [1928] 2 KB 144 (CA) 152–53, 154–55. The modern English law of anti-suit injunctions does not cleave to such a bright line, and there is no hesitation in granting anti-suit injunctions against foreigners (see *Stichting Shell Pensioenfonds v Krys* [2015] AC 616 (PC) [33]–[40] and Ch 2, paras 2.12–2.13). However, the citizenship, residence, and domicile of the injunction defendant and the injunction claimant may remain relevant factors in the assessment, within the modern criterion of comity, of whether the English court has a sufficient connection with the matter in question for an injunction to be granted (see eg *General Star International Indemnity v Stirling Cooke Brown Reinsurance Brokers* [2003] Lloyds Rep IR 719, 722). This approach is consistent with public international law: see FA Mann, 'The Doctrine of Jurisdiction in International Law' Part I (1964) 111 Hague Recueil des Cours 1, 149–50, accepting the legitimacy of the grant of anti-suit injunctions in certain cases against non-residents or non-nationals.

[170] Brownlie, 486.

[171] *Airbus Industrie v Patel* [1999] 1 AC 119 (HL).

close connection between the originating court and the pursuit of litigation abroad by the injunction defendant, either at all or in any particular case.

Nevertheless, it seems, on the basis of the available materials, that customary international law does not materially conflict with the exercise of the current English principles that govern the power to grant anti-suit relief.   **1.87**

First, the principle of territorial sovereignty is a rule of customary international law derived from state practice. Anti-suit injunctions have been granted by common law courts for centuries without any apparent diplomatic protest by foreign states,[172] and with only limited occasions of significant judicial objection. In the circumstances, there is a forceful argument that state practice cannot support the conclusion that the principle of territorial sovereignty contains within it a prohibition of anti-suit injunctions.[173] Indeed, so far as there is state practice it would appear to establish rather than refute the legitimacy of anti-suit injunctions.   **1.88**

Second, the English courts have concluded that anti-suit injunctions can be reconciled with public international law, although the analysis has been relatively shallow. As discussed,[174] the argument that there was a conflict between the principle of territorial sovereignty and the grant of anti-suit injunctions was rejected by the English courts in *Bushby v Munday*,[175] on the basis that the injunction was granted against the defendant only, and did not interfere with the courts of the foreign state. Similarly, arguments that anti-suit injunctions to enforce arbitration clauses are inconsistent with the New York Convention have met with curt rejections by the English courts.[176]   **1.89**

Third, there is some support in international law writings for the conclusion that anti-suit injunctions can, in principle, be reconciled with international law. The International Law Association has recognized the legitimacy of anti-suit injunctions in limited circumstances which are seemingly modelled on the conditions imposed by English law;[177] and   **1.90**

---

[172] Although there have been protests by foreign courts and writers (see paras 1.17, 1.40), there appear not to have been any *diplomatic* protests by foreign states at the international level.

[173] M Lenenbach, 'Anti-Suit Injunctions in England, Germany and the United States: Their Treatment under European Civil Procedure and the Hague Convention' (1997–98) 20 Loy LA Intl & Comp LJ 257, 294. For state practice and international civil jurisdiction in general, see M Akehurst, 'Jurisdiction in International Law' (1972–73) 66 BYBIL 145, 177; *The Lotus Case*, PCIJ, Series A, No 10, 23, 29.

[174] See paras 1.32–1.33.

[175] *Bushby v Munday* (1821) 5 Madd 297, 56 ER 908.

[176] *West Tankers v Ras Riunione Adriatica di Sicurta (The Front Comor)* [2007] 1 Lloyds Rep 391 (HL) [8], referring to *West Tankers v Ras Riunione Adriatica di Sicurta (The Front Comor)* [2005] 2 Lloyds Rep 257 [53]–[58]; *Shashoua v Sharma* [2009] 2 Lloyds Rep 376 [35]–[39]; *Midgulf International v Group Chimique Tunisien* [2010] 2 Lloyds Rep 543 (CA) [66]–[69]. See further section H, 'The New York Convention', below.

[177] International Law Association, Bruges Session (2003), Second Commission, Resolution: 'The Principles of Determining When the Use of the Doctrine of Forum non Conveniens and Anti-Suit Injunctions are Appropriate' (Rapporteurs: Sir L Collins and G Droz), para 5:

> Courts which grant anti-suit injunctions should be sensitive to the demands of comity, and in particular should refrain from granting such injunctions in cases other than (a) a breach of a choice of court agreement or arbitration agreement; (b) unreasonable or oppressive conduct by a plaintiff in a foreign jurisdiction; or (c) the protection of their own jurisdiction in matters such as the administration of estates and insolvency.

For discussion see A Nuyts, 'Les principes directeurs de l'Institut de Droit International sur le recours à la doctrine du *forum non conveniens* et aux anti-suit injunctions' (2003) 2 Revue Belge de Droit International 536. However, Resolution 1/2000 of the International Law Association, (otherwise known as the 'Leuven/London principles') had been in slightly more restricted terms, less influenced by the common law: at para 7 it suggested that contractual anti-suit injunctions were permissible if a jurisdiction clause had been 'manifestly' breached, but otherwise that anti-suit injunctions should only be granted if the foreign court had not itself respected the jurisdictional principles outlined in the Leuven/London principles.

anti-suit injunctions have also received the approval of some 'highly qualified publicists'[178] on international law.[179] There are civil law writers who have adopted the contrary view, but thus far their arguments have consisted largely of assertion, and are not grounded in state practice.[180]

G. THE HAGUE CONVENTION ON THE CHOICE OF COURT

1.91   The Hague Convention on the Choice of Court agrees a common regime for the protection of exclusive jurisdiction clauses and the enforcement of judgments. It came into force with effect from 1 October 2015, but at the time of writing this section (1 May 2019), has been acceded to only by Mexico, the EU, Denmark, Montenegro, Singapore, and the United Kingdom.[181] Within its scope, the Convention confers a mandatory exclusive jurisdiction on the court designated by an exclusive jurisdiction clause, which is similar to, and overlaps with, the jurisdiction created by Article 25 of the Brussels I Recast,[182] and creates a mutual regime for the enforcement of judgments given by the courts designated by such a clause.

1.92   Since the Convention creates a coordinated regime for jurisdiction and the mutual recognition of judgments between the contracting states, in cases where there is a relevant exclusive jurisdiction clause selecting one of the contracting states, the question arises whether, like the Brussels–Lugano regime, it will preclude anti-suit injunctions between its contracting states. But the Convention does not purport expressly to abolish the anti-suit injunction within its domain, and it is implausible that common law members of the Hague Conference, like the USA, should be read as having consented tacitly to abolition by omission. Indeed, it is clear from the *Travaux Préparatoires* that the Convention on Choice of Court was not intended to preclude anti-suit injunctions to protect proceedings in the chosen court.[183] Whether and to what extent the Hague Convention may affect the

---

[178]   See Article 38(1) of the Statute of the International Court of Justice.

[179]   See eg FA Mann, 'The Doctrine of Jurisdiction in International Law' Part I (1964) 111 Hague Recueil des Cours 1, 149–50, accepting the legitimacy of the English approach in 'alternative forum' cases, and specifically approving of the decision in *Royal Exchange Assurance v Compania Naviera Santi (The Tropaioforos)* [1962] 1 Lloyds Rep 410: 'the principle upon which these English cases rest is sound and also highly significant from the point of view of the doctrine of international jurisdiction and … the cases which illustrate it are valuable examples of the test of closeness of connection and its advantages over the test of territory'; and FA Mann 'The Doctrine of International Jurisdiction' Part III (1984) 186 Hague Recueil des Cours 19, 47–48. P Schlosser, 'Anti Suit Injunctions in International Arbitration' (2006) RIW 486, 490–91 concludes that there is no basis in public international law for assertions that anti-suit injunctions are prohibited.

Judge Stephen Schwebel has argued that injunctions to restrain arbitrations abroad can amount to a 'denial of justice', because it prevents a party from proceeding before the forum where he is entitled to obtain justice: S Schwebel, 'Anti-Suit Injunctions in International Arbitration: An Overview' in Gaillard (2005) 5, 12–13. However, this contention is somewhat circular: it only has force if an injunction is granted to restrain a party from proceeding with valid arbitration proceedings; it does not follow that there is any denial of justice if a court has concluded, for example, that there is no valid arbitration agreement and grants an injunction on that basis.

[180]   See eg S Clavel, 'Anti-Suit Injunctions et Arbitrage' (2001) Rev Arb 669, 677.

[181]   There are complications related to the UK's accession and the transitional consequences of Brexit for the Hague Convention which we do not address here, but which are touched on in Ch 16, para 16.04.

[182]   The relationship between Article 25 of the Brussels I Recast and the Hague Convention is addressed in Ch 17, para 17.46.

[183]   Hague Conference on Private International Law, Report of the Second Meeting of the Informal Working Group on the Judgments Project (Prel Doc No 21) (6–9 January 2003) paras 15–16, and Minutes No 9 of the Second Commission Meeting of Monday 20 June 2005 (morning) in Proceedings of the Twentieth Session of the Hague Conference on Private International Law (Permanent Bureau of the Conference, Intersentia 2010), 622, 623–24. The point was not touched on in the Explanatory Report on the Convention, as it surely would have been, had any preclusion of anti-suit injunctions been the agreed intention of the contracting parties. See also M Ahmed

principles for, or exercise of discretion in relation to, the grant of anti-suit injunctions re-mains to be seen.[184]

H. THE NEW YORK CONVENTION

It has been argued that the New York Convention 1958 precludes the grant of anti-suit in-junctions to enforce arbitration clauses as between contracting states. Article II.3 requires the courts of the contracting states, when seised of an action covered by an arbitration clause, to 'refer' the matter to arbitration. The simplest and most direct argument is that this gives exclusive 'negative' competence to the courts seised with the substantive litigation, and thereby precludes the involvement of the court of the seat.[185] However, this is not con-vincing, save to those with a preconceived idea that anti-suit injunctions are inconsistent with international comity, and who are casting around for a weapon. Article II(3) simply does not address the question of whether or how arbitration clauses may be enforced by courts other than the court seised with the litigation; it does not confer exclusive jurisdic-tion on the court seised.[186] The imposition by Article II(3) of a duty to 'refer' on the court seised is not inconsistent with other courts enforcing the same policy by injunction.[187] The *Travaux Préparatoires* show that the subject was never addressed;[188] it is most unlikely that the common lawyers that participated in the formulation of the Convention[189] envisaged that it was abolishing anti-suit injunctions to enforce an arbitration clause; and the civil lawyer participants were probably not aware of the issue at all, given its lesser prominence at that time. The Convention is not a closed system analogous to the Brussels–Lugano regime because it does not control the jurisdiction of the courts of contracting states.[190] Were the

1.93

and P Beaumont, 'Exclusive Choice of Court Agreements: Some Issues on the Hague Convention on Choice of Court Agreements and its Relationship with the Brussels I Recast especially Anti-Suit Injunctions, Concurrent Proceedings and the Implications of BREXIT' (2001) Rev Arb 669, 677.

[184] See further Ch 7, para 7.09.

[185] In favour of exclusivity, see S Clavel, 'Anti-Suit Injunctions et Arbitrage' (2001) Rev Arb 669, 680–81; L Fumagalli, 'Antisuit injunction e arbitrato: una tutela troppo invasiva' (2005) Rivista dell' Arbitrato 583; F Bachand, 'The Uncitral Model's Take on Anti-Suit Injunctions' in Gaillard (2005) 87, 105–06; M Stacher, 'You Don't Want to Go There—Anti-Suit Injunctions in International Commercial Arbitration' (2005) 23 ASA Bull 640. Against ex-clusivity see J Rozas, 'Anti-Suit Injunctions Issued by National Courts: Measures Addressed to the Parties or to the Arbitrators' in Gaillard (2005) 73, 81–82; J Astigarraga, 'Control of Jurisdiction by Injunctions issued by National Courts' (2006) 13 Intl Arb 221; S Clavel, 'Anti-Suit Injunctions et Arbitrage' (2001) Rev Arb 669, 676; J Barcelo, 'Anti-Foreign-Suit Injunctions to Enforce Arbitration Agreements' (2007) Cornell Law Faculty Publications, Paper 87, 5; G Kim, 'After the ECJ's West Tankers: The Clash of Civilisations on the Issue of An Anti-Suit Injunction' (2011) 12 Cardozo J Conflict Res 573, 578–83. Bachand also argues that the presumption of non-intervention in Article 5 of the Uncitral Model law, and thus s 1(c) of the Arbitration Act 1996 which implements it, precludes anti-suit injunctions: see at 101–11.

[186] C Kessedjian, 'Arbitrage et droit européen: une désunion irrémédiable?' (2009) Recueil Dalloz 981, 983.

[187] Indeed, if Article II(3) were to apply at all, it might be said that its terms positively justify the grant of anti-suit injunctions to enforce the arbitration clause so as to 'refer' the parties to arbitration: J Fernandez Rozas, 'Anti-Suit Injunctions Issued by National Courts' in Gaillard (2005) 75, 81. See also G Kim, 'After the ECJ's West Tankers: The Clash of Civilisations on the Issue of An Anti-Suit Injunction' (2011) 12 Cardozo J Conflict Res 573, 578–83.

[188] And instead a proposal (ECOSOC, E Conf 26.2, 6 March 1958, paras 16–24) that control of the validity of arbitration awards should be exercised only in the state of enforcement was not accepted.

[189] The ad hoc committee of ECOSOC that drafted the initial version of the Convention was made up of the representatives of eight states including Australia, India, and the UK; and the UK representative was part of the drafting sub-committee. The UK submitted extensive comments to ECOSOC.

[190] *Shashoua v Sharma* [2009] 2 Lloyds Rep 376 [38].

argument for preclusion to be correct, it would also shut out the grant of anti-suit awards by arbitrators, which is now a growth industry.

1.94   In *The Front Comor*, the ECJ briefly addressed the relationship between the New York Convention and anti-suit injunctions in somewhat ambiguous terms, which could be read as supporting the proposition that the court seised should have exclusive jurisdiction. [191] But this is by no means clear; it may well be that the ECJ, like its Advocate General, was only observing, correctly, that the court seised had a jurisdiction of its own to enforce the arbitration clause, in support of its other conclusions of European Law,[192] and the ECJ has no power to interpret the New York Convention; if it was trying to do so, it was wrong. It is also commonly thought that the reasoning in *The Front Comor* was not the ECJ's finest hour;[193] and when the ECJ returned to anti-suit injunctions and arbitration in *Gazprom*, there was no suggestion of any inconsistency between the anti-suit injunction and the New York Convention.[194]

1.95   The English courts have firmly rejected all arguments that the New York Convention precludes the grant of anti-suit injunctions to enforce arbitration clauses.[195] It seems that a similar approach prevails in the USA.[196]

1.96   A more subtle argument would avoid absolutism, and focus on the demands of comity in the context of the New York Convention. It could be suggested, in particular, that since the

---

[191] Case C-185/07, *Allianz v West Tankers (The Front Comor)* [2009] ECR I-663, AG [55]–[56]; ECJ [33].
[192] This is how the ECJ's judgment was read in *Shashoua v Sharma* [2009] 2 Lloyds Rep 376 [35]–[39] and in *Midgulf International Ltd v Group Chimique Tunisien* [2010] 2 Lloyds Rep 543 (CA) [66]–[69] the Court of Appeal could not see that it made any difference.
[193] Cf C Kessedjian, 'Arbitrage et droit européen: une désunion irrémédiable?' (2009) Recueil Dalloz 981, 983, and more generally see Ch 12, paras 12.13–12.18.
[194] Case C-536/61, *Gazprom*, EU:C:2015:316. Advocate General Wautelet expressly concluded that the fact that an arbitration award contained an anti-suit injunction is not a ground to refuse to enforce it under the New York Convention (AG [180]–[188]), although strictly this was none of his business.
[195] The combined reasoning of the English courts on this point is terse, but is unlikely to change. This conclusion was arguably held to be the law in *Aggeliki Charis Compania Maritima v Pagnan (The Angelic Grace)* [1995] 1 Lloyds Rep 87 (CA) 94 (per Leggatt LJ; Millett LJ did not comment expressly on the point, although it is implicit in his conclusion that he agreed); see also *Toepfer International v Société Cargill France* [1998] 1 Lloyds Rep 379 (CA) 386. In *West Tankers v Ras Riunione Adriatica di Sicurta (The Front Comor)* [2005] 2 Lloyds Rep 257 [56]–[58], Colman J concluded that Article II(3) did not confer any exclusive jurisdiction on the court seised; and in the House of Lords [2007] 1 Lloyds Rep 391 (HL) [8], Lord Hoffmann, in a brief passage, which is nevertheless apparently *ratio decidendi*, and with which a majority of the House agreed, simply concluded that Colman J was right and that it is 'unnecessary to enlarge on the reasons that he gave'. Following the comments of the ECJ in *The Front Comor*, an attempt was made to re-argue the New York Convention point, but this was rejected by Cooke J in *Shashoua v Sharma* [2009] 2 Lloyds Rep 376 [35]–[39] and by the Court of Appeal in *Midgulf International v Group Chimique Tunisien* [2010] 2 Lloyds Rep 543 (CA) [66]–[69].
    It must, however, be mentioned that in *Toepfer International v Société Cargill France* [1998] 1 Lloyds Rep 379 (CA) 386, Phillips LJ raised the question of whether as a matter of practice, in light of the New York Convention, it might not usually be better to leave the matter to the court seised with the litigation. However, this hesitation has been overtrodden by the subsequent case law, following the more sweeping precedent of *Aggeliki Charis Compania Maritima v Pagnan (The Angelic Grace)* [1995] 1 Lloyds Rep 87 (CA).
[196] In *Karaha Bodas Co v Perusahaan Pertambangan Minyak Dan Gas Bumi Negara* 335 F 3rd 357 (5th Cir, 2003), the US Court of Appeals (5th Cir) held that 'there is nothing in the Convention which expressly limits the inherent authority of a federal court to grant injunctive relief'. However, the US Court of Appeals suggested that, where the arbitration award was made in state X, the structure of the Convention did discourage (although it did not preclude) the grant of anti-suit injunctions by the courts of state Y, where the award had been enforced, to restrain proceedings in respect of the validity of state Z, as the courts of state Y are only courts of 'secondary jurisdiction'. This is similar to the hesitations expressed by Phillips J in *Toepfer International v Société Cargill France* [1998] 1 Lloyds Rep 379 (CA) 386. For further discussion of the US approach to the interplay between the New York Convention and anti-suit injunctions, see C Lamm, E Hellbeck and J Brubaker, 'Anti-Suit Injunctions in Aid of International Arbitration: The American Approach' (2009) 12 Int ALR 115.

New York Convention envisages that the court seised will assess whether the arbitration clause is void, inoperable, or incapable of being performed, and implicitly accepts that it will do so applying its own conflicts of rules, so respect for the application of the other court's conflicts rules is consistent with the spirit of the Convention.[197] In turn, this could support the proposition that the grant of an injunction to impose the substantive law selected by English conflicts of laws rules, even where the foreign conflict rules would select a different substantive law, may be in tension with the spirit of, and implicit allocation of jurisdiction under, the Convention. If accepted, arguments along these lines could support a greater regard for the 'conflict of conflicts' than has so far been shown by the English courts.[198]

Arguments based on the New York Convention have more force in respect of anti-arbitration injunctions which restrain the pursuit of arbitration proceedings with a seat abroad—where, in any event, the English courts only grant injunctions in very limited circumstances.[199] However, it is important to distinguish two situations.   **1.97**

First, if a national court concludes that there is no binding foreign arbitration clause, the grant of an injunction to restrain the pursuit of the arbitration cannot be inconsistent with the New York Convention obligation to refer matters to arbitration, as *ex hypothesi* in the absence of a valid arbitration clause, the New York Convention obligation is not engaged. The argument that it should be for the court of the seat, not the injuncting court, to assess whether or not the arbitration clause is binding may have force as a matter of comity, but it is not an obligation that follows from the terms of the New York Convention itself: the Convention does not allocate any exclusive jurisdiction to the court of the seat, although Article V(e) does indicate the importance of the court of the seat.   **1.98**

The argument that anti-arbitration injunctions may be in tension with the New York Convention is at its strongest where it is accepted that there is a binding arbitration clause, and an anti-arbitration injunction is nevertheless sought to restrain the pursuit of the arbitration. In such a case there is a real prima facie sense in which interfering with the foreign arbitration could be in tension with the obligation to 'refer' to arbitration.[200] The English courts have, rightly, adopted a restrictive approach to the grant of injunctions in these situations.[201] Nevertheless, it is submitted that the New York Convention does not justify an absolute prohibition.[202] Such injunctions can be justified on the basis that they enforce separate obligations which are not inconsistent with the arbitration clause: if, for example, the pursuit of the arbitration would be duplicative and would amount to a vexatious and oppressive interference with existing national proceedings, then an injunction would be enforcing the separate obligation not to act vexatiously. There will also be cases where, as a matter of practical justice, a national court which is not the court of the seat is the appropriate forum to assess the question of whether proceedings should be permitted to proceed in arbitration; for example where a party has already litigated and lost in that court, and a   **1.99**

---

[197] J Barcelo, 'Anti-Foreign-Suit Injunctions to Enforce Arbitration Agreements' (2007) Cornell Law Faculty Publications, Paper 87, 5.

[198] For the 'conflict of conflicts' see Ch 8, paras 8.31–8.44 and T Raphael, 'Do as You Would be Done By? System-Transcendent Justification and Anti-Suit Injunctions' (2016) LMCLQ 256.

[199] See Ch 11, section B, 'Injunctions to Restrain Arbitrations in England'.

[200] S Schwebel, 'Anti-Suit Injunctions in International Arbitration: An Overview' in Gaillard (2005) 5, 10.

[201] See Ch 11, paras 11.17–11.19, 11.30–11.37.

[202] See further, see Ch 11, paras 11.22–11.24.

party seeks to pursue a duplicative arbitration on the same facts.[203] In principle, the position is not so very different to where an English court is asked to restrain proceedings before another court selected by an exclusive jurisdiction clause: there must be some very good reason why the English court would be an appropriate court to interfere, and in general strong factors of comity tending against an injunction, but no absolute bar to the grant of an injunction.[204]

I. BREXIT

1.100   On 23 June 2016 the majority of voters in the referendum on the United Kingdom's membership of the EU voted to leave the Union. That referendum was advisory and not self-executing, and at the date of writing this section (1 May 2019) its consequences remain uncertain in a number of dimensions. The Article 50 deadline has been extended to 31 October 2019, and it is still uncertain whether Brexit will happen, and if so when and on what terms; and it is also uncertain what will happen if there is no deal. This matters because English jurisdictional and choice of law rules are at present in large part contained in the European jurisdictional and choice of law instruments, in particular the Brussels I Recast and New Lugano Convention and the Rome I and Rome II Regulations. While it seems likely that the choice of law regime will at least initially remain the same whatever happens,[205] there is uncertainty as to the future for civil jurisdiction and the enforcement of judgments. There is a range of different possibilities, including continuation of or reversion to something very similar to the existing arrangements, during an initial transition period and perhaps even thereafter as part of the final status arrangements, but also including a breakdown of civil justice cooperation and a reversion to the common law, subject to the continued effect of the Hague Convention on the Choice of Court.[206]

1.101   So there are very different paths that English private international law may take. Which path we go down will affect a range of issues discussed in this work. Most directly it will affect the jurisdictional rules discussed in Chapters 16–18, and the constraints imposed on anti-suit injunctions by the Brussels–Lugano regime, discussed in Chapter 12. For the most part, this work proceeds on the assumption that something rather similar to the existing regimes will be preserved, but the position will need to be reviewed.

---

[203] S Schwebel, 'Anti-Suit Injunctions in International Arbitration: An Overview' in Gaillard (2005) 5, 15, accepts the potential legitimacy of such an injunction.

[204] See T Raphael 'Do as You Would be Done By? System-Transcendent Justification and Anti-Suit Injunctions' [2016] LMCLQ 256.

[205] If there is a deal, the draft Withdrawal Agreement of November 2018 would continue the Rome I and Rome II Regulations during the transition period. Further, it is the UK Government's intention that the Rome Regulations would continue after the end of any transition period subject to some limited modifications: see HM Government, 'Providing a Cross-Border Civil Judicial Cooperation Framework' (22 August 2017). For the Rome Regulations this can be done unilaterally without the EU's consent, in contrast to the jurisdictional instruments. Similarly, if there is no deal, the UK Government's no-deal legislation would continue the essential effect of the Rome I and Rome II regulations subject to limited modifications: see the relevant no-deal statutory instrument The Law Applicable to Contractual Obligations and Non-Contractual Obligations (Amendment etc) (EU Exit) Regulations 2019, SI 2019 No 834, and the guidance contained in HM Government, 'Cross-border civil and commercial legal cases after Brexit: Guidance for legal professionals', 29 March 2019.

[206] These issues are discussed in more detail in Ch 16, paras 16.04–16.05, 18.01, 18.40–18.41.

2

The History of an Unusual Remedy

A. INTRODUCTION

The history of the anti-suit injunction is marked by confusion and dissent over the central **2.01** tests to be satisfied in order for an injunction to be granted; and over the underlying basis of the injunction. This history remains important, as the conflicts have not always been neatly resolved, and the older decisions can be a treacherous guide to the modern law, unless their historical context is understood.

The exploration of the remedy's history that follows charts the rises and falls of the anti-suit in- **2.02** junction, and, in particular, seeks to trace the roots of the various tests that have been deployed.

B. THE COURT OF CHANCERY

The anti-suit injunction originally evolved from the 'common injunction', by which the **2.03** English Court of Chancery had restrained litigants before the English common law courts[1] from obtaining judgments which were contrary to the principles of equity.[2] A common injunction could be granted in two situations: where the common law would fail to protect an equitable right; and where the ends of justice required interference, for example to put an end to vexatious and oppressive litigation or a multiplicity of suits.[3] Equity did not accept any principle of initial deference to the common law courts, since as between the Courts of Chancery and common law, no considerations of the comity of nations were involved.[4]

---

[1] Until the fusion of the courts of law and equity by the Supreme Court of Judicature Acts 1873 and 1875, the English legal system was divided, with the common law courts and the Courts of Chancery forming separate and partly competing jurisdictions.

[2] For a discussion of the history of the common injunction, see WS Holdsworth, *A History of English Law* Vol 1 (1903–38) 459–64; D Raack, 'A History of Injunctions in England before 1700' (1985–86) 61 Ind L J 539. For a short but perceptive analysis of aspects of the history of the anti-suit injunction, see D Altaras, 'The Anti-Suit Injunction: Historical Overview' (2009) 75 Arbitration 327.

[3] See Lord Redesdale's Treatise on Equity, quoted in *Pennell v Roy* (1853) 3 De GM & G 126, 43 ER 50, 55.

[4] *Barclays Bank v Homan* [1993] BCLC 680, 685–86 (per Hoffmann J).

2.04   Foreign courts might also grant judgments which contravened English principles of equity, and so it was inescapable that the Court of Chancery would eventually have to consider whether an injunction could be granted to restrain litigants from pursuing foreign proceedings. The point appears to have been tested for the first time in the seventeenth-century case of *Love v Baker*, where Lord Clarendon LC feared that such a remedy might be 'a dangerous Case', and on the advice of the judges, dissolved the injunction.[5] But the reporter remarked '*sed quaere*, for all the bar was of another opinion'.[6]

2.05   By the late eighteenth century, it seems that the Bar's opinion had prevailed, and the personal logic of equity had overcome Lord Clarendon's concerns.[7] In the unreported case of *Grey v The Duke of Hamilton* it seems an injunction to restrain foreign proceedings may have been granted.[8] In *Lord Portland's Case*,[9] the Lord Keeper appears to have agreed that the court did have jurisdiction to restrain the pursuit of proceedings in Holland, on the basis of an argument that 'the partys living here, 'twas proper to bind their consciences by an injunction', although the injunction sought was refused on procedural grounds. Similarly, in *Foster v Vassall* in 1747, the court appears to have assumed in an *obiter* comment that it had the same powers to restrain inequitable proceedings abroad (or at least elsewhere in the Empire) as it did in respect of proceedings in England, on the basis that it acted in person on the litigant's conscience.[10]

2.06   In 1799, in *Wharton v May*,[11] an injunction was granted to restrain proceedings in Ireland, without discussion of the point of principle. During the early nineteenth century, the grant

---

[5] *Love v Baker* (1665) 1 Chan Cas 67, 22 ER 698 (a claim for an injunction to restrain proceedings in the courts of Leghorn, now Livorno), (1664–65) Nels 103, 21 ER 801; see also *sub nom Lowe v Baker* (1665) 2 Freem Chy 125, 22 ER 1101.

[6] *Love v Baker* (1665) 1 Chan Cas 67, 22 ER 698. In the report at (1664–65) Nels 103, 21 ER 801, the reporter wrote 'Barons' instead of 'Bar'; the third report *sub nom Lowe v Baker* (1665) 2 Freem Chy 125, 22 ER 1101, does not descend to this detail. R Eden, *A Treatise on the Law of Injunctions* (Butterworth & Cooke 1821) 141, considered that either reading was plausible, but concurred with the conclusion of the Bar (or the Barons): 'the doctrine [in *Love v Baker*] is certainly at variance with one of the first principles of a court of equity, which ... considers only the equities arising from the acts of the parties'.

[7] See the discussion of the history of the remedy in *Lord Portarlington v Soulby* (1834) 3 My & K 104, 40 ER 40, 41–42.

[8] The Lord Keeper in *Lord Portland's Case* referred to 'the case of Sir John Gray' as a previous authority for the grant of an injunction to restrain proceedings abroad. According to R Eden, *A Treatise on the Law of Injunctions* (Butterworth & Cooke 1821) 142, this was a reference to the unreported case of *Grey v Duke of Hamilton*. The reporter in *Kennedy v Cassillis* (1818) 2 Swans 313, 36 ER 635, 639 n 2 suggests that *Grey v Duke of Hamilton* was a case in which an anti-suit injunction to restrain proceedings abroad was granted. See also the discussion of the 'two instances' in the Hargrave MSS in *Lord Portarlington v Soulby* (1834) 3 My & K 104, 40 ER 40, 41, which also appears to include reference to *Grey* to the same effect. But it is not clear whether an injunction was granted in *Grey's* case, nor do we know what it concerned.

[9] *Lord Portland's Case*, 114 Harg MSS 166. As the Hargrave Manuscript is not easily accessible, Hargrave's report is set out in full, as best as I can transcribe it:

> Lord Portland's Case. Motion was for an injunction to stay the younger children's proceedings in Holland for part of their father's personal estates which they claimed under the marriage settlement by the Laws of Holland upon a surmise that he had given them one thousand pounds by his will which was intended in satisfaction of that Claim and not as an additional provision. Sir Joseph Jekill filed the case of ... where 'twas ruled that this court may take cognizance of contracts made in Holland and of the Laws there. Lord Keeper, put him in mind of the case of Sir John Grey and in the House of Lords to the same purpose which point seemed to be agreed. Sir Jos. Jekille said that the partys living here 'twas proper to bind their consciences by an injunction. I think it was denied in this case the Defendant not being in contempt nor having prayed time to answer, & therefore the motion was too early tho the whole matter had arisen within the jurisdiction of the Court.

[10] *Foster v Vassall* (1747) 3 Atkyns 587, 26 ER 1138, 1139.

[11] *Wharton v May* (1799) 5 Ves Jun 27, 31 ER 454, 476; (1789–1817) 1 Ves Jun Supp 489, 34 ER 887.

of injunctions to restrain proceedings in the other countries of the United Kingdom and the British Empire became well established;[12] and by the end of the century, injunctions had been granted to restrain proceedings in foreign countries that owed no allegiance to the Crown.[13]

In many of the earliest cases, the injunction was granted as if both categories of the common injunction could be legitimately applied in the international situation; and the pursuit of foreign litigation could be restrained on the simple ground that there was an equitable defence on the merits.[14]   **2.07**

However, beginning with *Bushby v Munday* in 1821,[15] where the legitimacy of the power was seriously tested for the first time since *Love v Baker*,[16] the courts began to approach injunctions to restrain foreign proceedings primarily within the framework of the second category, and the grant of an extraterritorial 'common' injunction solely on the grounds of a substantive equity fell into disuse.[17] One way of expressing the court's approach, and the formulation used in *Bushby* itself, was that the injunction claimant had to show that 'the ends of justice' required the injunction to be granted;[18] if he could, then he had a 'clear   **2.08**

---

[12] Between 1800 and 1840 we find *Kennedy v Cassillis* (1818) 2 Swans 313, 36 ER 635, 638 (Scotland, injunction dissolved on the ground that it was sought against the Scottish court itself); *Bushby v Munday* (1821) 5 Madd 297, 56 ER 908 (Scotland, the lead early case); *Harrison v Gurney* (1821) 2 Jac & W 563, 37 ER 743 (Ireland); *Beauchamp v The Marquis of Huntley* (1822) Jac 546, 37 ER 956 (Ireland); *Beckford v Kemble* (1822) 1 Sim & St 7, 57 ER 3 (Jamaica); *Lord Portarlington v Soulby* (1834) 3 My & K 104, 40 ER 40 (Ireland); *Marquess of Breadalbane v Marquess of Chandos* (1837) 2 My & Cr 711, 40 ER 811 (Scotland); *Booth v Leycester* (1837) 1 Keen 579, 48 ER 430 (Ireland); *Bunbury v Bunbury* (1839) 1 Beav 318, 48 ER 963 (Demerara, now part of Guyana, a British colony); *Wedderburn v Wedderburn* (1840) 2 Beav 208, 48 ER 1159, (1840) 4 My & Cr 585, 41 ER 225 (Scotland).

[13] With the possible exception of the unreported early case of *Grey v Duke of Hamilton* (see n 8) the first anti-suit injunction to restrain proceedings outside the British Empire appears to have been granted in *Hope v Carnegie* (1866) LR 1 Ch App 320 (Netherlands). *Pieters v Thompson* (1815) G Coop 294, 35 ER 563, as explained in *Peruvian Guano Co v Bockwoldt* (1882) 23 Ch D 225, 226–27, also concerned the courts of the Netherlands, but is (at most) a stay case.

[14] *Wharton v May* (1799) 5 Ves Jun 27, 31 ER 454, 476; (1789–1817) 1 Ves Jun Supp 489, 34 ER 887; *Harrison v Gurney* (1821) 2 Jac & W 563, 37 ER 743; *Beauchamp v The Marquis of Huntley* (1822) Jac 546, 37 ER 956; *Marquess of Breadalbane v Marquess of Chandos* (1837) 2 My & Cr 711, 40 ER 811 (although see the *obiter* comments to the effect that interference after judgment would be rare: at 820). The most explicit example of the extrapolation of the first category of common injunction was *Lord Portarlington v Soulby* (1834) 3 My & K 104, 40 ER 40, in which Lord Brougham justified an injunction to restrain proceedings before the courts of Ireland, where there was a potential equitable defence, on the ground that 'it suffices to say that the Court in which the action is brought is a court of common law, and has no ground to stop the proceeding on the ground now set forth': at 42.

[15] *Bushby v Munday* (1821) 5 Madd 297, 56 ER 908.

[16] *Love v Baker* (1665) 1 Chan Cas 67, 22 ER 698; (1664–65) Nels 103, 21 ER 801; see also *sub nom Lowe v Baker* (1665) 2 Freem Chy 125, 22 ER 1101.

[17] See *Jones v Geddes* (1846) 1 Ph 724, 41 ER 808, 809, where the injunction was rejected, although there would have been a potential substantive equity. There seems to be no case after *Lord Portarlington v Soulby* (1834) 3 My & K 104 40 ER 40, where an injunction to restrain the pursuit of foreign proceedings had been granted on the grounds of a substantive equity alone. In *Carron Iron v Maclaren* (1855) 10 ER 961, 5 HLC 416, 439, the House of Lords continued to assert that an injunction to restrain foreign proceedings could be granted in any situation where a common injunction could be granted to restrain English proceedings, but only if the foreign proceedings would be 'contrary to equity and good conscience', and they stressed that this did not mean the court had a duty so to act, 'if from any cause it appears likely to be more conducive to substantial justice that the foreign proceedings should be left to take their course'. In *Hyman v Helm* (1882) 24 Ch D 531, 541–43, the Court of Appeal held that there was no relevant substantive equity, but assumed that if such a substantive equity did exist, it could in principle have justified restraining the foreign proceedings.

[18] *Bushby v Munday* (1821) 5 Madd 297, 56 ER 908, 913; *Bunbury v Bunbury* (1839) 1 Beav 318, 48 ER 963, 967–68; *Carron Iron Co v Maclaren* (1855) 10 ER 961, 5 HLC 416, 437–38; 453; *Ainslie v Sims* (1854) 32 LJ (NS) Ch 161. See the historical discussions in *Masri v Consolidated Contractors (No 3)* [2009] QB 503 (CA) [39]; *Stichting Shell Pensioenfonds v Krys* [2015] AC 616 (PC) [17]–[18].

equity to be protected', which would affect the defendant's conscience.[19] Another way of phrasing the thresholds was that the injunction defendant's proceedings had to be 'contrary to equity and good conscience',[20] or inequitable.[21] But on either approach, the logic was not that an underlying substantive equity determined the court's decision as to whether proceedings should continue; instead, the court's assessment that the pursuit of the targeted proceedings should be restrained was the foundation for the equity.[22]

2.09   It was in *Bushby v Munday* that the tension with comity, posed by the indirect interference with foreign courts that the injunction creates, was first addressed. Leach V-C's justification of the injunction, which holds good today, depended on the 'personal logic' of the anti-suit injunction: the injunction does not bind the foreign court, applies only to the injunction defendant, and is justified by reference to his conscience.[23] *Bushby v Munday*, therefore, can be seen as the starting point of the modern jurisprudence on anti-suit injunctions.[24] The next leading case was *Portarlington v Soulby* in 1834, where Lord Brougham, again in reliance on the personal logic of the injunction, declined to follow the hesitations in *Love v Baker*.[25]

2.10   The run of the anti-suit injunction cases at this time concerned parallel litigation, or cases where the foreign litigation interfered with English insolvency or probate proceedings.[26]

---

[19] *Beckford v Kemble* (1822) 1 Sim & St 7, 57 ER 3, 7. The equity identified was not linked to any substantive equitable defence. However, it was clear that there must be something that would 'affect the consciences of the parties': *Pennell v Roy* (1853) 3 De GM & G 126, 43 ER 50, 55–56. In *Liverpool Marine Credit Co v Hunter* (1867) LR 4 Eq 62; (1868) LR 3 Ch App 479, 484, the criterion was that the conduct of the injunction defendant had to be inequitable.

[20] *Pennell v Roy* (1853) 3 De GM & G 126, 43 ER 50, 55–56; *Carron Iron v Maclaren* (1855) 10 ER 961, 5 HLC 416, 439; *Stichting Shell Pensionenfonds v Krys* [2015] AC 616 (PC) [17]–[18].

[21] *Liverpool Marine Credit Co v Hunter* (1867) LR 4 Eq 62; (1868) LR 3 Ch App 479, 484.

[22] The modern position may be that a substantive equity is not required at all, at least in alternative forum cases: see Ch 3, section B, 'A Legal or Equitable Right?', and *Masri v Consolidated Contractors (No 3)* [2009] QB 503 (CA) [39]–[59], [99]. However, in some cases a specific legal or equitable right will exist, such as the equitable right to an appropriate distribution of assets on insolvency identified in *Stichting Shell Pensionenfonds v Krys* [2015] AC 616 (PC) [19], [22].

[23] *Bushby v Munday* (1821) 5 Madd 297, 56 ER 908, 913; and see also previously *Foster v Vassall* (1747) 3 Atkyns 587, 26 ER 1138, 1139. For the personal logic more generally, see Ch 1, paras 1.32–1.33; Ch 3, section D, 'Against Whom May an Anti-Suit Injunction be Granted?'.

[24] *Stichting Shell Pensionenfonds v Krys* [2015] AC 616 (PC) [17].

[25] *Lord Portarlington v Soulby* (1834) 3 My & K 104, 40 ER 40; oddly, *Busby v Munday* was not cited. Lord Brougham LC instead relied on the otherwise unreported case of *Campbell v Houlditch* (1820).

[26] *Pieters v Thompson* (1815) G Coop 294, 35 ER 563 (plaintiff apparently put to his election as to where to sue when duplicate litigation brought); *Bushby v Munday* (1821) 5 Madd 297, 56 ER 908, 913 (England the more appropriate forum because crucial witness evidence could only be compelled there; Scottish litigation restrained); *Beckford v Kemble* (1822) 1 Sim & St 7, 57 ER 3, 7 (duplicate parallel litigation in Jamaica restrained); *Booth v Leycester* (1837) 1 Keen 579, 48 ER 430 (injunction claimed by the successful defendant in English proceedings to restrain new proceedings on the same claim in Ireland); *Bunbury v Bunbury* (1839) 1 Beav 318, 48 ER 963, 968–69 (substantive disputes ought to be decided primarily in England, injunction granted on terms that undertakings would be given); *Wedderburn v Wedderburn* (1840) 2 Beav 208, 48 ER 1159, (1840) 4 My & Cr 585, 41 ER 225 (security proceedings in Scotland could be restrained, but could proceed with the permission of the court if confined to seeking security only); *Jones v Geddes* (1846) 1 Ph 724, 41 ER 808, 809 ('the question for consideration in these cases is by what course of proceeding would justice, under all the circumstances, be most conveniently administered'; injunction dissolved on appeal as 'after weighing all the conveniences and inconveniences of the different course to be adopted, I think it is not advisable to interfere with the proceedings in the Court of Session'; the key factual consideration was that the proceedings in Scotland would proceed between other parties in any event, to the potential prejudice of the injunction defendant); *Parnell v Parnell* (1858) I Ch R 322 (administration suits in England and Ireland); *Venning v Loyd* (1859) 1 De G F & J 193, 45 ER 332, 337 (the Court of Chancery will injunct a suit 'improperly prosecuted in another country to determine questions which ought to be adjudicated upon here'); *Marquess of Bute v Stuart* (1861) 2 Giff 582, 66 ER 244 (injunction to restrain proceedings in Scotland which interfered with the process of the English court); *Hope v Carnegie* (1866) LR 1 Ch App 320 (injunction to restrain Dutch proceedings interfering with English probate); *Baillie v Baillie* (1867) LR 5 Eq 175 (Scottish proceedings interfering with the administration of English probate restrained); *Re South Eastern Portugal Railway* (1869) 17 WR

The vexatiousness of duplicate foreign proceedings was recognized as a ground for interference.[27] But the equitable jurisdiction was not confined to vexatiousness; there were other cases where the ends of justice could require an injunction, including where the foreign forum was inappropriate, or where the foreign proceedings would unjustifiably interfere with the fair distribution of assets in an English insolvency.[28]

The development of the injunction was, however, checked and limited by a growing realization of the inherent sensitivity of interfering with the pursuit of litigation abroad, and the courts began to develop limiting principles which can now be viewed as precursors of the modern deployment of comity.[29] In *Pennell v Roy*, where there were no parallel English proceedings, the Court of Chancery refused to grant an injunction which was sought on the ground that the Scottish proceedings were allegedly frivolous and vexatious, in the sense of wholly without merit, as this was a question for the Scottish courts to decide.[30]   **2.11**

In *Carron Iron v Maclaren*, Lord Cranworth LC's judgment contained language that might   **2.12**
have imposed a more serious check, stating:

> the first question is, whether there is any rule or principle of the Court of Chancery which, after a decree for administering a Testator's assets, would induce it to interfere with a foreign creditor resident abroad, suing for his debt in the courts of his own country? Certainly not. Over such a creditor the courts here can exercise no jurisdiction whatever. He is altogether beyond their reach, and must be left to deal as he may with his own forum, and to obtain such relief as the courts of his own country may afford.[31]

However, this statement did not form part of the judgments of the other Lords, and may not be part of the *ratio*.[32] It would be wrong to interpret it as establishing an absolute rule that anti-suit injunctions should not be granted to restrain a foreign party from claiming before

---

982 (proceedings in Portugal would evade the distribution of an English insolvency); *Re London and Colonial, ex parte Clark* (1869) LR 7 Eq 550 (Australian attachment proceedings interfering with English liquidation); *Re Distin* (1871) 24 LT 197 (where an English liquidation was underway, an injunction was granted to restrain creditors from claiming in foreign courts); *Re Oriental Inland Steam* (1874) LR 9 Eq 557 (injunction to restrain attachment proceedings in India which interfered with winding-up proceedings in England in which the injunction defendant had participated).

[27] *Carron Iron Co v Maclaren* (1855) 10 ER 961, 5 HLC 416, 437–38; see also *Jones v Geddes* (1846) 1 Ph 724, 41 ER 808, 809.

[28] *Carron Iron v Maclaren* (1855) 10 ER 961, 5 HLC 416, 437–39; *Stichting Shell Pensionenfonds v Krys* [2015] AC 616 (PC) [18]–[23]. In *Atlantic Star (Owners) v Bona Spes (Owners) (The Atlantic Star)* [1974] AC 436 (HL) 465A–B, Lord Cranworth LC's language was viewed by Lord Wilberforce as suggesting that the test applied in *Carron Iron* depended on vexation. But that appears to be wrong, as explained in *Shell v Krys*.

[29] *Carron Iron v Maclaren* (1855) 10 ER 961, 5 HLC 416, 437–38; and also *Maclaren v Stainton* (1855) 26 LJ (Ch) 332, 333. In *Hope v Carnegie* (1866) LR 1 Ch App 320, an injunction was granted to protect English probate proceedings by restraining probate proceedings in relation to the testator's assets in the Netherlands; however, it is clear that it would not have been granted, had the Dutch proceedings related only to real property situated in the Netherlands, as opposed to real and personal property. See also the historical discussion in *Barclays Bank v Homan* [1993] BCLC 680, 687.

[30] *Pennell v Roy* (1853) 3 De GM & G 126, 43 ER 50, 53–56. The modern law also adopts a reticent approach to grounding injunctions on the alleged weakness of the foreign claim; see Ch 5, paras 5.26–5.28.
It was also decided that an injunction would not be granted to restrain proceedings in a foreign country merely because the law that would be applied by the foreign court would be different: *Liverpool Marine Credit Co v Hunter* (1867) LR 4 Eq 62, 72; upheld (1868) LR 3 Ch App 479, 484–87.

[31] *Carron Iron v Maclaren* (1855) 10 ER 961, 5 HLC 416, 437, 441 (later applied in *Stainton v The Carron Co* (1855) 21 Beav 152, 52 ER 817).

[32] See Megaw J in *Royal Exchange Assurance v Compania Naviera Santi (The Tropaioforos) (No 2)* [1962] 1 Lloyds Rep 410, 417–18.

his own courts, and the courts have not done so.[33] In *Maclaren v Stainton*, very shortly afterwards, Lord Cranworth LC (sitting in Chancery) summarized his own previous judgment as meaning instead that a 'very strong case' would be required to restrain a foreigner from suing before his own courts.[34]

2.13   For a while *Carron Iron* induced hesitation in some cases;[35] but its effect diminished over time.[36] Recently, in *Shell v Krys* Lord Cranworth's comments were interpreted as referring only to an absence of personal territorial jurisdiction.[37] Similarly, occasional nineteenth-century concerns about granting an injunction in respect of foreign defendants resident in, and proceedings before, courts in 'purely foreign countries' outside Crown's dominions, on the basis that the injunction would be unenforceable against them,[38] have also faded away: the English courts now presume that parties will respect their extraterritorial injunctions, whether subject to the authority of the Crown or not.[39] The modern law certainly contains no prohibition on granting an injunction to restrain a foreigner from suing before his own courts, nor does it require a distinct higher threshold in such situations, as compared to non-contractual anti-suit injunctions generally. An anachronistic attempt to rely on the older case law to impose restrictions of this kind was rejected by the Privy Council in *Shell v Krys*. Instead, the modern law regards the foreign nationality of the injunction defendant as one factor, among others, that may be relevant to the assessment of comity; but it may not be a factor of particular significance.[40]

---

[33] In *Royal Exchange Assurance v Compania Naviera Santi (The Tropaioforos) (No 2)* [1962] 1 Lloyds Rep 410, Megaw J declined to follow Lord Cranworth LC's comment as representing the law; and even in *Re Vocalion (Foreign) Ltd* [1932] 2 Ch 196, 208, where the general approach in this regard in *Carron Iron* was given weight, this passage of *Carron Iron* was not quoted as representing the test. However, such an absolute interpretation of *Carron Iron* was adopted in the very brief judgment in *Re Boyse, Crofton v Crofton* (1880) 15 Ch D 591, 592–93.

[34] *Maclaren v Stainton* (1855) 26 LJ (Ch) 332, 333, in which there are hints that Lord Cranworth LC recognized that his earlier judgment was too sweeping in this regard, and in any event difficult to reconcile with the previous cases—in particular, Lord Brougham's decision in *Portarlington v Soulby* (1834) 3 My & K 104, 40 ER 40 had not been cited in *Carron Iron*. Similarly, Turner LJ in *Maclaren v Stainton* also regarded the rule as being that an 'exceedingly strong case' was required to restrain the defendant from proceeding before his own courts.

[35] See *Re Vocalion (Foreign)* [1932] 2 Ch 196, 208—although even there, however, *Carron Iron* was not cited as establishing a *rule* to that effect, and the injunction was refused on the grounds that it would not be 'conducive to the ends of justice'. But the decision in *Re Vocalion* was held not to represent modern law in *Stichting Shell Pensionenfonds v Krys* [2015] AC 616 (PC) [38].

[36] By the 1960s this aspect of Lord Cranworth's speech in *Carron Iron* was treated as of no binding force: *Royal Exchange Assurance v Compania Naviera Santi (The Tropaioforos) (No 2)* [1962] 1 Lloyds Rep 410.

[37] As explained in the joint opinion of Lords Sumption and Toulson in *Stichting Shell Pensionenfonds v Krys* [2015] AC 616 (PC) [33]–[35]. This appears to be inaccurate historically. It appears from Lord Cranworth's subsequent judgment in *Maclaren v Stainton* (1855) 26 LJ (Ch) 332, 333, where personal jurisdiction had been established, that the principle articulated in *Carron Iron* was one of substantive equity. Lords Sumption and Toulson justified their conclusion by referring to the fact that in *Carron Iron*, Lord Cranworth said that the result might have been different had the company sought relief in England (see *Carron Iron* at 443). But in fact, what Lord Cranworth said is equally, and perhaps more, consistent with reasoning based on substantive principles of equity, under which participation in the English proceedings would make it more substantively appropriate to exercise the equitable jurisdiction. Certainly, the case of *Beauchamp v Marquis of Huntley* (1822) Jac 546, 37 ER 956, to which he referred, appears to be a case about substantive equity.
Nevertheless, it would be fair to say that, at that early stage in the development of the English private international law, concepts of personal jurisdiction and the substantive equitable jurisdiction to grant extraterritorial relief were rather jumbled up. The Privy Council was right to treat this specific aspect of *Carron Iron* as providing no useful guidance as to modern substantive law. In contrast, *Carron Iron*'s establishment of 'the ends of justice' as the overall test, and its focus on the need for comity, remains good law.

[38] See *In re Chapman* (1872) 15 Eq 75, 77 and *In re International Pulp and Paper* (1876) 3 Ch D 594. But there were other cases where no hesitation was displayed on this ground (although other factors induced hesitation) and injunctions were granted even in respect of countries outside the Empire: see eg *Hope v Carnegie* (1866) LR 1 Ch App 320 (Netherlands); *Re South Eastern Portugal Railway* (1869) 17 WR 982 (Portugal); *In re North Carolina Estate* (1889) 5 TLR 328 (USA); *Heilmann v Falkenstein* (1917) 33 TLR 383 (USA).

[39] See *Stichting Shell Pensionenfonds v Krys* [2015] AC 616 (PC) [36]–[37].

[40] See generally Ch 4, para 4.23, n 42, para 4.86 and also para 4.95, n 249; *Stichting Shell Pensionenfonds v Krys* [2015] AC 616 (PC) [33]–[40]; *Star Reefers v JFC Group* [2012] 1 Lloyds Rep 376 (CA) [38].

Considerable hesitation about the grant of anti-suit injunctions persisted until the 1980s,[41] **2.14**
but as we shall see, this was derived from other sources and expressed in terms of different
concepts.

C. THE FUSION OF LAW AND EQUITY

After the fusion of the courts of law and equity in the Judicature Acts 1873 and 1875, **2.15**
the Court of Chancery became merely one division of the High Court, and equity
could be administered in any division of the High Court. In return, injunctions to
restrain extant proceedings before the High Court or Court of Appeal were prohibited.[42] It remained possible for extant proceedings before other courts of inferior or
concurrent jurisdiction to be restrained,[43] and it was also possible to restrain the commencement of proceedings even in the High Court,[44] but it was no longer necessary
to exercise these powers to ensure that the principles of equity were enforced over the
common law.

At the same time, and perhaps as an indirect consequence of the reforms, the principles **2.16**
relating to the grant of an anti-suit injunction were reformulated in terms less redolent of
the history of equity.

The impetus for change appears to have come from developments in the jurisprudence **2.17**
on the related subject of when the court would grant a stay of English proceedings.
During the 1880s, it became established in the series of cases starting with *McHenry
v Lewis* that the court would stay proceedings before it which were 'vexatious or oppressive' or 'an abuse of its process',[45] although the power was to be exercised with
'extreme caution'.[46] This test could be satisfied by English proceedings that were 'frivolous and vexatious', in the sense of without merit and bound to fail;[47] or by an action
brought in bad faith with the motive of vexatiously harassing the defendant.[48] It was
clear that neither the existence of duplicated proceedings nor the inconvenience of the

---

[41] See *Ecobank Transnational v Tanoh* [2016] 1 WLR 2231 (CA) [82].

[42] Supreme Court of Judicature Act 1873, s 24(5), replaced by Supreme Court of Judicature Act 1925, s 41. This restriction is no longer the law within England. For further discussion, see Ch 6, paras 6.02 and 6.05.

[43] *Besant v Wood* (1879) 12 Ch D 605; *Re Connolly Brothers* [1911] 1 Ch 731 (CA) (proceedings before Court of the County Palatine of Lancaster restrained).

[44] As they had not been commenced, they were therefore not 'pending' and thus not strictly within the terms of s 24(5) of the Supreme Court of Judicature Act 1873: see Ch 6, para 6.02.

[45] *McHenry v Lewis* (1881) 21 Ch D 202, (1882) 22 Ch D 397 (CA) 399–400, 405, 407–08 (this concept was drawn in part from the approach in *Carron Iron Co v Maclaren* (1855) 10 ER 961, 5 HLC 416, 437); *Peruvian Guano v Bockwoldt* (1882) 23 Ch D 225 (CA) 230–33. The main cases in the previous case law on stays of proceedings were *Lord Dillon v Alvares* (1798) 4 Ves Jun 357, 31 ER 182, (1779–1817) 1 Ves Jun Supp 445, 34 ER 867; *Pieters v Thompson* (1815) G Coop 294, 35 ER 563, as explained in *Peruvian Guano Co v Bockwoldt* (1882) 23 Ch D 225, 226–27; *The Bold Buccleugh* (1850) 3 W Rob 220, 166 ER 944, appealed as *Harmer v Bell* (1850–51) 7 Moo PC 267, 13 ER 884; *The Lanarkshire* (1855) 2 Sp Ecc & Ad 189, 164 ER 380; *The John and Mary* (1859) Swab 471, 166 ER 1221, appealed on other grounds (1862) 15 Moo PC 374, 15 ER 536; *Cox v Mitchell* (1859) 7 CB (NS) 55, 144 ER 734; *The Mali Ivo* (1869) LR 2 A&E 356; *Walsh v The Bishop of Lincoln* (1874) LR 4 A&E 242; and *The Catterina Chiazzare* (1876) 1 PD 368.

[46] *McHenry v Lewis* (1881) 21 Ch D 202, (1882) 22 Ch D 397 (CA) 406; see later *Logan v Bank of Scotland (No 2)* [1906] 1 KB 141 (CA) 149.

[47] *Castro v Murray* (1875) LR 10 Ex 213, 218 (a decision of the Court of Exchequer); *Dawkins v Prince Edward of Saxe Weimar* [1876] 1 QB 499, 502–03; *Peruvian Guano v Bockwoldt* (1882) 23 Ch D 225 (CA) 230.

[48] *McHenry v Lewis* (1882) 22 Ch D 397 (CA) 399, 407; *Peruvian Guano v Bockwoldt* (1882) 23 Ch D 225 (CA) 230, 233; *The Christiansborg* (1885) 10 PD 141 (CA) 157 (per Fry LJ); see also *Cohen v Rothfield* [1919] 1 KB 410 (CA) 414.

target forum was sufficient to establish vexation or oppression,[49] but duplicated proceedings could be vexatious if they did not give the double claimant some substantial advantage.[50]

2.18   Next, in *Hyman v Helm*, the Court of Appeal held that, at least where there was no independent substantive equity, the requirement of vexation or oppression developed in the stay cases was a necessary condition for the grant of an injunction to restrain foreign proceedings.[51]

2.19   The transference of the jurisprudence relating to stays was not fully explained in *Hyman v Helm*, and most of the previous authorities on anti-suit injunctions were not cited to the Court of Appeal.[52] Nevertheless, the criteria of vexation or oppression became established as the primary applicable test for the grant of anti-suit injunctions for almost the next hundred years,[53] although some cases held that injunctions could also be granted where the foreign proceedings would interfere with the process of the English court,[54] and a minority of decisions applied the older equitable concepts.[55]

---

[49]   *Hyman v Helm* (1883) 24 Ch D 531 (CA) 537, 540; *Guaranty Trust Co of New York v Hannay* [1915] 2 KB 536 (CA) 564, 574–75.

[50]   At this point in the development of the case law, duplicated proceedings were seen as vexatious if they were only of 'fanciful advantage' to the claimant, but not if there were 'substantial reasons of benefit' to him: *Peruvian Guano Co v Bockwoldt* (1882) 23 Ch D 225 (CA) 230, 232. The concept of proceedings that might be vexatious precisely because the foreign claimant might benefit from them in an *illegitimate* way was not articulated by the majority in *Peruvian Guano*, although Bowen LJ did allow that an injunction might be granted where the plaintiff's claim, although not frivolous, was claimed 'in a way which necessarily involves injustice': at 233. It was, however, clear that the mere fact of double proceedings on similar or related issues was not necessarily vexatious in itself. *McHenry v Lewis* (1882) 22 Ch D 397 (CA) 399, 409; *Peruvian Guano v Bockwoldt* (1882) 23 Ch D 225 (CA) 230, 233–34; *Cohen v Rothfield* [1919] 1 KB 410 (CA).

[51]   *Hyman v Helm* (1883) 24 Ch D 531 (CA) 537–38, 539–40, 540, 543. The Court of Appeal deliberately avoided deciding whether injunctions could ever be granted against a claimant in foreign proceedings who was only the defendant in England. However, this point was later resolved in the affirmative: *Re Connolly Brothers* [1911] 1 Ch 731 (CA) 745, relying on *Bushby v Munday* (1821) 5 Madd 297, 56 ER 908; *Cohen v Rothfield* [1919] 1 KB 410 (CA) 414–15 ('while, therefore there is a jurisdiction to restrain a defendant from suing abroad, it is a jurisdiction very rarely exercised'); cf, however, *Vardopulo v Vardopulo* (1909) 25 Times LR 518 (CA). It remained the case, at this stage of the development of the law, that where the defendant was domiciled abroad he would rarely be restrained from suing before the courts of his country: *Re Vocalion (Foreign)* [1932] 2 Ch 196, 209–10, and see also *Vardopulo v Vardopulo* (1909) 25 Times LR 518 (CA).

[52]   The Court of Appeal appear to have had only *Bushby v Munday* (1821) 5 Madd 297, 56 ER 908 cited to them, which they viewed as based on an independent equity. They were not taken to the other equitable cases where injunctions were granted on the basis of convenience and the interests of justice, without any independent equity being identified. The Court of Appeal also referred to the remedy sought, which was an application to restrain the pursuit proceedings before the courts of San Francisco, as a 'stay', rather than an injunction—a distinction which Baggallay LJ identified, but saw as a matter of 'form' only, in *The Christiansborg* (1885) 10 PD 141 (CA) 152.

[53]   This is how the history was correctly summarized in *Masri v Consolidated Contractors (No 3)* [2009] QB 503 (CA) [39]. See *Christian v Christian* (1897) 78 LT 86, 87–88; *Re Connolly Brothers* [1911] 1 Ch 731 (CA) 744, 746, 747–48; *Pena Copper Mines Ltd v Rio Tinto Co Ltd* (1912) 105 LT 846 (CA) 851 (*obiter*, a contract case); *Guaranty Trust Company of New York v Hannay* [1915] 2 KB 536 (CA) 564, 574–75 (*obiter*, a claim for a negative declaration); *Cohen v Rothfield* [1919] 1 KB 410 (CA) 414, 417; *Orr-Lewis v Orr-Lewis* [1949] P 347, 349; *Settlement Corp v Hochschild* [1966] 1 Ch 10. Although the words vexation or oppression were not used in *Armstrong v Armstrong* [1892] P 98, the reasoning recognizably descends from and develops the *McHenry v Lewis* line of cases. Change did not come until *Castanho v Brown & Root* [1981] AC 557 (HL).

[54]   A criterion which can be seen as the inverted equivalent of the concept, in stay cases, of an abuse of process of the English court: see *Armstrong v Armstrong* [1892] P 98, 100–02, where it was also a ground for the injunction that the foreign proceedings were 'injurious to the proper course of proceedings in this court'. See also *Royal Exchange Assurance v Compania Naviera Santi SA (The Tropaioforos) (No 2)* [1962] 1 Lloyds Rep 410, 416, where it was conceded that foreign proceedings could be restrained if they were an 'abuse of process of the English court'. However, the appropriateness of this type of language, which suggests that the *English* court's process is being abused, has been questioned in cases where all that is happening is litigation abroad: see Ch 4, para 4.68.

[55]   In *Ellerman Lines v Read* [1928] 2 KB 144 (CA) 152, 155, the injunction was granted to restrain foreign proceedings that were 'inequitable'; and in *Re Vocalion (Foreign) Ltd* [1932] 2 Ch 196, 210, the test applied, drawing

The new tests were accompanied by a hesitant approach to the grant of anti-suit injunctions, **2.20** exemplified by repeated warnings that, as the effect of the injunction was to interfere with proceedings in another jurisdiction, the power was to be exercised only with 'great caution', and 'very rarely'.[56]

Self-restraint was also imposed by the limited concept of pure vexation inherited from **2.21** *McHenry v Lewis*, under which proceedings were only vexatious if they were useless, and not if they gave real advantages to the claimant, whether or not those advantages were legitimate. A line of case law began to suggest that the notion of vexation could be developed to include proceedings which obtained only illegitimate advantages for the claimant,[57] and there was also authority to suggest that if the inconvenience of the targeted proceedings was sufficient to give rise to injustice, this could amount to vexation.[58] However, these ameliorations were not universally accepted, and in *Cohen v Rothfield*, the Court of Appeal approached a claim for an injunction on the basis that only the limited concept of pure vexation represented the law.[59]

As a result, the authorities in the hundred years that follow *Hyman v Helm* contain few decisions where anti-suit injunctions were granted to restrain foreign proceedings, and even **2.22** fewer where the injunction was granted in the absence of a contractual right.[60]

Further, at this stage in the development of the jurisprudence, no clear distinction had as **2.23** yet been drawn between injunctions to restrain foreign proceedings brought in breach of contract, and anti-suit injunctions in general.[61] Consequently, although contractual injunctions were in practice granted with fewer inhibitions,[62] they were often discussed in similarly cautious terms.[63]

---

on the older equitable authorities, was whether 'it will be more conducive to substantial justice that the foreign proceedings should be allowed to proceed'. The reasoning in *Re Derwent Rolling Mills Co, York City and County Banking Co v Derwent Rolling Mills* (1904) 21 Times LR 81 and *Re Low, Bland v Low* [1894] 1 Ch 147, is also redolent of the pre-Judicature Act cases, although no test was actually articulated.

[56] *Cohen v Rothfield* [1919] 1 KB 410 (CA) 413; *Ellerman Lines Ltd v Read* [1928] 2 KB 144 (CA) 158; *Settlement Corp v Hochschild* [1966] 1 Ch 10, 15G. In *Jopson v James* (1908) 77 LJ (Ch) 824, the tests of vexation and oppression were not referred to, but a similarly restrictive approach to the grant of an injunction was taken: at 828.

[57] *Armstrong v Armstrong* [1892] P 98, 100–02; *Re Connolly Brothers Ltd* [1911] 1 Ch 731 (CA) 744, 748.

[58] *Logan v Bank of Scotland (No 2)* [1906] 1 KB 141 (CA) 151–52; *St Pierre v South American Stores (Garth and Chaves) Ltd* [1936] 1 KB 382 (CA) 398.

[59] *Cohen v Rothfield* [1919] 1 KB 410 (CA) 414–15; followed in this respect in *Settlement Corp v Hochschild* [1966] 1 Ch 10, 15G; and regarded as the lead case in this period by *Masri v Consolidated Contractors (No 3)* [2009] QB 503 (CA) [39].

[60] As far as the reported cases tell, and leaving aside contractual injunctions and insolvency decisions, it seems that between 1883 (the date of the decision in *Hyman v Helm* (1883) 24 Ch D 531 (CA)) and 1979 (when *Castanho v Brown & Root* [1980] 1 WLR 833 was decided at first instance) non-contractual injunctions to restrain foreign proceedings were granted (and upheld where appealed) only in *Armstrong v Armstrong* [1892] P 98; *Moore v Moore* (1896) 12 TLR 221; *Christian v Christian* (1897) 67 LJP 18; *Heilmann v Falkenstein* (1917) 33 TLR 383; and *Ellerman Lines v Read* [1928] 2 KB 144 (CA). For an illustration of the hesitant approach taken by the courts at this time, see *Orr-Lewis v Orr-Lewis* [1949] P 347, 349 (divorce, injunction refused), where it was stated that no order to restrain proceedings brought in a foreign country by a defendant in England had been granted for thirty years.

[61] As observed in *Masri v Consolidated Contractors (No 3)* [2009] QB 503 (CA) [39].

[62] See eg *Pena Copper Mines v Rio Tinto* (1912) 105 LT 846 (CA); *Royal Exchange Assurance v Compania Naviera Santi (The Tropaioforos) (No 2)* [1962] 1 Lloyds Rep 410.

[63] *Settlement Corp v Hochschild* [1966] 1 Ch 10. The approach in contractual cases has now changed: see Ch 7.

D. 'FORUM NON CONVENIENS' AND
THE CASTANHO HERESY

2.24   The onerous requirement that a stay of English proceedings would not be granted unless they were vexatious or oppressive, or an abuse of process of the English court, meant that many actions which would most appropriately be determined elsewhere could proceed in England. This was a 'rather insular' doctrine, and in series of case beginning in the 1970s with *The Atlantic Star* and *MacShannon v Rockware Glass*,[64] and concluding in 1986 with *Spiliada v Cansulex*,[65] the House of Lords first diluted the requirements of vexation and oppression in stay cases, and then replaced them with the Scottish concept of *forum non conveniens*, under which proceedings in England would be stayed if the defendant could show that the foreign jurisdiction was clearly the more appropriate forum for the litigation.

2.25   The lowering of the threshold for the grant of a stay reflected greater deference to foreign legal systems, and meant that 'judicial chauvinism has been replaced by judicial comity'. But a parallel dilution of the conditions required for an anti-suit injunction would *decrease* deference and *increase* interference. To conclude that the adoption of *forum non conveniens* in relation to stays should produce a corresponding relaxation of the tests for an injunction was a *non sequitur*.[66]

2.26   Nevertheless, in *Castanho v Brown & Root*, Lord Scarman held that the principles applying to injunctions and stays should be the same, and that an anti-suit injunction could be granted on the sole ground that England was the most appropriate forum for the litigation, so long as the injunction would not deprive the injunction defendant of a legitimate juridical advantage in the foreign jurisdiction.[67] This was a heresy, and if it had been applied for any length of time, would have led to excessive levels of interference with litigation before foreign courts.[68]

2.27   However, Lord Scarman's approach was subsequently undermined by the criticisms of Lord Goff,[69] whose views triumphed in *Aérospatiale*, where the Privy Council held that to grant an injunction solely on the basis that the foreign court was an inconvenient forum would be inconsistent with comity, and that it would be wrong for the tests for stays, and injunctions were the same.[70]

---

[64]   *Atlantic Star (Owners) v Bona Spes (Owners) (The Atlantic Star)* [1974] AC 436 (HL) 453E–H; *MacShannon v Rockware Glass* [1978] AC 795 (HL).

[65]   *Spiliada Maritime Corp v Cansulex Ltd (The Spiliada)* [1987] AC 460 (HL) 474–78.

[66]   *The Abidin Daver* [1984] AC 398 (HL) 411G; see also *Bank of Tokyo v Karoon* [1987] AC 45 (CA) (Note) 62E, 63A–F; *Société Nationale Industrielle Aérospatiale v Lee Kui Jak* [1987] AC 871 (PC) 896D–E. P Carter, 'Decisions of British Courts during 1988: Private International Law' (1988) 59 BYBIL 267, 342, described the doctrinal connection between stays and injunctions as having 'an obvious but meretricious attraction'.

[67]   *Castanho v Brown & Root* [1981] AC 557 (HL) 574–77, per Lord Scarman; applied in *Smith Kline & French Laboratories Ltd v Bloch* [1983] 1 WLR 730 (CA) 737H–738G, 739H, 743B–G; 746F–747G; and also by the Court of Appeal in *British Airways Board v Laker Airways Ltd* [1984] QB 142 (CA) 187, although on appeal the House of Lords distinguished *Castanho* as not applying to 'single forum' situations [1985] AC 58 (HL) 80, 95. Lord Scarman's approach was also restated *obiter* as being the law by the majority in *South Carolina Insurance v Assurantie Maatschappij 'De Seven Provincien'* [1987] AC 24 (HL) 40F–G.

[68]   *Castanho* was immediately criticized for these reasons: A Briggs, 'No Interference with Foreign Court' (1982) 31 ICLQ 189.

[69]   Whose criticisms were first expressed (as Goff LJ) in *Bank of Tokyo v Karoon* [1987] AC 45 (CA) (Note) 61–63, and repeated in *South Carolina Insurance v Assurantie Maatschappij 'De Seven Provincien'* [1987] AC 24 (HL) 44F–45C.

[70]   *Société Nationale Industrielle Aérospatiale v Lee Kui Jak* [1987] AC 871 (PC) 894–96.

As a matter of strict precedent, the judgment in *Aérospatiale* was only a decision of Brunei   **2.28**
law, but a laudable flexibility was displayed in the application of the doctrine of precedent,
and the *Castanho* heresy was consigned to oblivion.[71]

E. UNCONSCIONABILITY AND THE RETURN TO EQUITY

A more durable difficulty has been created by the House of Lords' decision in *British*   **2.29**
Airways Board v Laker Airways, decided in the period of doctrinal confusion that followed
the decision in *Castanho v Brown & Root*. The case before the House was a 'single forum'
situation, in which there was no prospect of the foreign litigation being pursued in England
if its pursuit abroad was restrained. It was therefore apparent that an inverted application of
forum non conveniens was unworkable, and that some other criterion would be required to
control intervention.[72]

Without referring to authority, but in apparent reliance on the pre-Judicature Act deci-   **2.30**
sions,[73] Lord Diplock held that an injunction could be granted not only where there was a
legal or equitable right not to be sued in the foreign court, but also where equity would give
anticipatory effect to a substantive equitable defence by restraining the foreign proceedings.
To refer to the types of situations where such a substantive equitable defence might exist,
such as promissory estoppel or laches, he used the collective description of 'unconscionable conduct'.[74] Lord Scarman also relied on the concept of unconscionability, but in a more
flexible manner, holding that the court had power to grant the injunction 'if the bringing of
the suit in the foreign court is in the circumstances so unconscionable that in accordance
with our principles of a "wide and flexible" equity it can be seen to be an infringement of an
equitable right of the applicant'.[75]

---

[71] The subsequent case law generally treated the *Castanho* doctrine as having been 'developed' into non-
existence by *Aérospatiale*: see *Du Pont de Nemours v Agnew* [1988] 2 Lloyds Rep 240 (CA) 243–44, 249; *Barclays
Bank v Homan* [1993] BCLC 680 (CA) 697–99, 702, or simply applied *Aérospatiale*: see eg *Bouygues Offshore v
Caspian Shipping* [1997] 2 Lloyds Rep 485, 489–92.
    There was a limited number of cases where questions of precedent did occasionally cause difficulties, although
these were outliers and have been forgotten: see *Pathe Screen Entertainment Ltd v Handmade Films (Distributors) Ltd*
(11 July 1989), where Hobhouse J took the view that he was still bound by *Castanho* and *British Airways Board v Laker
Airways Ltd* [1985] AC 58 (HL), but attempted to reconcile *Aérospatiale* with them; and *Commercial Union Assurance
v Simat Helliesen & Eichner* [2001] Lloyds Rep IR 172, 175 (which must be viewed as erroneous in this respect).
    In recent times, the House of Lords has put the matter beyond doubt, albeit without ever expressly departing
from *Castanho* under the 1966 Practice Statement: *Airbus Industrie v Patel* [1998] 1 AC 119 (HL) 133C–F
(adopting *Aérospatiale*); *Turner v Grovit* [2002] 1 WLR 107 (HL) [24]–[25]; *Donohue v Armco* [2002] 1 Lloyds
Rep 425 (HL) [19] (adopting *Aérospatiale*, and wrily observing the 'development of principle'); see also [45],
[53], adopting *Aérospatiale*). It is now uncontested that *Castanho* does not represent the law in this regard: see
Masri v Consolidated Contractors (No 3) [2009] QB 503 (CA) [41], [47]; and *Deutsche Bank v Highland Crusader
Partners* [2010] 1 WLR 1023 (CA) [50]–[62] and *Stichting Shell Pensionenfonds v Krys* [2015] AC 616 (PC) [23]
treat *Aérospatiale* as stating the law.
[72] *British Airways Board v Laker Airways* [1985] AC 58 (HL) 80B–H.
[73] Some of the pre-Judicature Act authorities from the Court of Chancery were cited to the House: at 69H–70,
74C–F (including *Lord Portarlington v Soulby* (1834) 3 My & K 104, 40 ER 40, the last of the cases where an anti-
suit injunction was granted on the basis of a substantive equitable defence); however, the post-Judicature Act authorities establishing the test of vexation and oppression were not.
[74] *British Airways Board v Laker Airways* [1985] AC 58 (HL) 82C–F.
[75] *British Airways Board v Laker Airways* [1985] AC 58 (HL) 95F–H; drawing on his own speech in *Castanho
v Brown & Root* [1981] AC 557 (HL) 573, where he had held that 'the width and flexibility of equity are not to be
undermined by categorization …' and 'that the injunction can be granted against a party properly before the court,
where it is appropriate to avoid injustice', a passage which Lord Diplock also cited with approval in *British Airways
Board v Laker Airways*, at 81F–G.

2.31   Lord Diplock's anachronistic reliance on substantive equitable defences, which had not war-ranted an anti-suit injunction for well over a century, was not followed,[76] but the concept of 'unconscionable conduct' has become part of the court's tests for the grant of an anti-suit in-junction.[77] This does have the advantage of connecting the injunction back to the equitable history of the remedy, but as a guide to the exercise of the court's power the phrase is rather hollow. It is not specifically adapted to the remedy in question and gives little guidance as to the level of misconduct required. It would, therefore, have been unfortunate if 'unconscion-able conduct' were to have displaced concepts of vexation and oppression.

F. *AÉROSPATIALE* AND THE MODERN LAW

2.32   The law was returned to a sounder channel by *Aérospatiale*, where in a magisterial summary of the authorities, blending the equitable principles from the pre-Judicature Act case law with the line of cases descending from *McHenry v Lewis* and *Hyman v Helm*, Lord Goff held that an anti-suit injunction would be granted if the ends of justice required it, but that in general, an injunction would not be granted unless the foreign proceedings were vexatious or oppressive.[78] But as Lord Goff made clear, the ends of justice is a broader concept than vexation and oppression and injunctions can be granted, for example to protect the juris-diction of the court, even where the foreign proceedings are not vexatious.[79]

2.33   The use of the concept of 'the ends of justice' reiterated the breadth of the equitable power, and thus occupied much the same conceptual space as the concept of unconscionable con-duct deployed in *British Airways Board v Laker Airways*. The breadth of the power was controlled by the redeployment of the concepts of vexation and oppression, but these were refurbished to clean away some of the artificial limitations of the earlier case law. Lord Goff explained that the concept of vexation and oppression to be employed should be flexible, and that foreign proceedings could be 'oppressive' even where the claimant abroad could gain some substantial advantage, if the foreign forum was sufficiently inappropriate. The re-quirement that (non-contractual) anti-suit injunctions should only be granted with caution was reiterated, as a key device to ensure consistency with comity.[80]

---

[76]   In *Midland Bank v Laker Airways* [1986] QB 689 (CA), the concept of unconscionability was deployed as the test without reference to substantive equitable defences by Lawton LJ (at 699–700), while Dillon LJ based himself on Lord Scarman and not Lord Diplock's approach (at 701C–F). Neill LJ alone referred to Lord Diplock's categories of anticipatory defences, but described them as 'merely examples', and viewed the test as turning on the general question of whether the foreign proceedings were so inequitable that the English court had to intervene (at 712). In *South Carolina Insurance v Assurantie Maatschappij 'De Seven Provincien'* [1987] AC 24 (HL) 40D, the House of Lords employed the language of unconscionability without reference to Lord Diplock's categories of substantive defences. In the case law following *Société Nationale Industrielle Aérospatiale v Lee Kui Jak* [1987] AC 871 (PC), the concept of the pre-emptive recognition of an independent equitable defence has not surfaced. A more searching historical examination was undertaken in *Barclays Bank v Homan* [1993] BCLC 680, 686–87, where Hoffmann J suggested that application of the old tests for common injunctions in the modern context was no longer appro-priate. In *Masri v Consolidated Contractors (No 3)* [2009] QB 503 (CA), the comprehensive examination of the basis of the remedy by Lawrence Collins LJ (as he then was) did not reiterate this aspect of *Laker*, and confirmed that an equitable right was not a condition of the injunction at least in alternative forum cases: [39]–[59], [99].
[77]   *Midland Bank v Laker Airways* [1986] QB 689 (CA); *South Carolina Insurance v Assurantie Maatschappij 'De Seven Provincien'* [1987] AC 24 (HL) 40D; and see para 2.35.
[78]   *Société Nationale Industrielle Aérospatiale v Lee Kui Jak* [1987] AC 871 (PC) 896–97.
[79]   *Société Nationale Industrielle Aérospatiale v Lee Kui Jak* [1987] AC 871 (PC) 892–93; and *Stichting Shell Pensionenfonds v Krys* [2015] AC 616 (PC) [23].
[80]   *Société Nationale Industrielle Aérospatiale v Lee Kui Jak* [1987] AC 871 (PC) 892, 894, 902.

Despite *Aérospatiale*'s formal status as a decision of Brunei law only, it became accepted as **2.34** stating English law.[81] By the end of the 1990s, it was routine for Lord Goff's modernized concept of vexation and oppression to be applied as the relevant test without challenge.[82] In *Airbus v Patel*, and then *Donohue v Armco*, Lord Goff's tests were held to be the law by the House of Lords;[83] and the Privy Council has recently reiterated that *Aérospatiale* states the law.[84]

But the concept of unconscionable conduct did not go away, and it was re-used as the pri-   **2.35** mary test in Lord Hobhouse's *obiter* speech in *Turner v Grovit*, although that speech is, with respect, not a good guide to the law.[85] It has, therefore, been felt necessary to reconcile the language of unconscionable conduct, and the older equitable concepts, with the *Aerospatiale* tests. This has been achieved in different ways. Some courts use the *Aérospatiale* language as it is, on the basis that it expresses the necessary equitable considerations.[86] Others have created a blended test, in which the notion of unconscionable conduct is an umbrella concept which includes vexatious and oppressive conduct as its main example.[87] On this approach

---

[81] See *Du Pont de Nemours v Agnew* [1988] 2 Lloyds Rep 240 (CA) 243–44, 249; *Barclays Bank v Homan* [1993] BCLC 680 (CA) 697–99, 702; *Bouygues Offshore v Caspian Shipping* [1997] 2 Lloyds Rep 485, 489–549.

[82] *The Eras Eil Actions* [1995] 1 Lloyds Rep 64, 73, 79; *Simon Engineering v Butte Mining (No 1)* [1996] 1 Lloyds Rep 104, 106; *Simon Engineering v Butte Mining (No 2)* [1996] 1 Lloyds Rep 91, 95; *Deaville v Aeroflot Russian International Airlines* [1997] 2 Lloyds Rep 67, 73; *Bouygues Offshore v Caspian Shipping* [1997] 2 Lloyds Rep 485, 489–92; *Fort Dodge Animal Health v Akzo Nobel* [1998] FSR 222 (CA) 246; *Amoco (UK) Exploration v British American Offshore* [1999] 2 Lloyds Rep 772, 778; *National Westminster Bank v Utrecht-America Finance* [2001] 3 All ER 733 (CA) 744.

[83] *Airbus Industrie v Patel* [1998] 1 AC 119 (HL) 133C–F and *Donohue v Armco Inc* [2002] 1 Lloyds Rep 425 (HL) [19], [45], [53], where Lord Bingham observed with gentle irony 'some development of principle', and seemed to wish to consign *Castanho, Laker*, and *South Australia* to history. These more recent decisions of the House of Lords should be treated as the law. In *Donohue*, the conclusions on this point are part of the *ratio*.

[84] *Stichting Shell Pensionenfonds v Krys* [2015] AC 616 (PC) [17]–[18]. See also *Masri v Consolidated Contractors (No 3)* [2009] QB 503 (CA) [13], [39], [41] and *Deutsche Bank v Highland Crusader Partners* [2010] 1 WLR 1023 (CA) [50]–[62].

[85] *Turner v Grovit* [2002] 1 WLR 107 (HL) 117–18, per Lord Hobhouse at [24]–[25], relying on the contestable authority of Lord Diplock's speech in *British Airways Board v Laker* [1985] AC 58 (HL), and also *Lord Portarlington v Soulby* (1834) 3 My & K 104, 40 ER 40. Lord Hobhouse had always been a dissenter from the view that *Aérospatiale* reflected English law: *Pathe Screen Entertainment v Handmade Films (Distributors)* (Hobhouse J, 11 July 1989); *Airbus Industrie v Patel* [1997] 2 Lloyds Rep 8 (CA) 14–15 (per Hobhouse LJ), reversed [1998] 1 AC 119 (HL) (per Lord Goff); and see *Compagnie Européene de Céréals v Tradax Export* [1986] 2 Lloyds Rep 301, 304 (Hobhouse J). However, Lord Hobhouse's speech in *Turner v Grovit* was *obiter* on this point as the actual decision was to refer the questions of European law to the ECJ. Lord Hobhouse's discussion in this regard was merely a summary of English law as context for the European law issues; and in *Donohue v Armco* [2002] 1 Lloyds Rep 425 (HL), decided on the very same day, the House of Lords adopted *Aérospatiale* as being the law without dissent from him, although he was also one of the panel. It is submitted that his *obiter* summary in *Turner v Grovit* of the English law in relation to anti-suits was wrong on various points: see Ch 4, para 4.58, and nn 45, 164, 166, 183, 192, 200.

[86] See eg *Airbus Industrie v Patel* [1998] 1 AC 119 (HL) 133C–F; *Donohue v Armco* [2002] 1 Lloyds Rep 425 (HL) [19], [45], [53]; *Elektrim v Vivendi Holdings I Corporation* [2009] 1 Lloyds Rep 59 (CA) [82]; *Deutsche Bank v Highland Crusader Offshore Partners* [2010] 1 WLR 1023 (CA) [50]–[62]; *Stichting Shell Pensionenfonds v Krys* [2015] AC 616 (PC) [23]; *Ecobank Transnational v Tanoh* [2016] 1 WLR 2231 (CA) [97].

[87] See *Glencore International v Metro Trading International (No 3)* [2002] CLC 1090 (CA) [41]–[42]; *Sabah Shipyard (Pakistan) Ltd v Islamic Republic of Pakistan* [2003] 2 Lloyds Rep 571 (CA) 580–81; *Royal Bank of Canada v Cooperatieve Centrale Raiffeisen-Boerenleenbank* [2003] EWHC 2913 [29]; [2004] 1 Lloyds Rep 471 (CA), per Evans-Lombe J [8]–[10] (uncontested in argument), although Mance LJ probably should be read as preferring Lord Goff's approach: at [36–39]; *OT Africa Line v Magic Sportswear* [2005] 2 Lloyds Rep 170 (CA) [63]–[64], where the blended approach was supported by Rix LJ, although Longmore LJ preferred Lord Goff's approach, at [31]; *Seismic Shipping Inc v Total E&P UK* [2005] 2 Lloyds Rep 359 (CA) 368–70, where Evans-Lombe J's summary in *Raiffeisen* was applied, on the (over-simple) assumption that it had reflected the findings of the Court of Appeal as a whole in *Raiffeisen; Masri v Consolidated Contractors (No 3) (Anti-Suit Injunction)* [2009] QB 503 (CA) [48]; *Star Reefers v JFC Group* [2012] 1 Lloyds Rep 376 (CA) [25]–[27]; *Ahmed v Mustafa* 1 FLR 139 (CA). In many of these cases, the principles to be applied appear not to have been contested and so their authority is less decisive than it might be. See Ch 4, paras 4.60–4.61.

'unconscionable conduct' sits underneath 'the ends of justice' but above 'vexation or oppression'. In principle, there is room to doubt whether the interpolation of unconscionability in this way is a helpful additional concept. But such a blended test is now incorporated in a number of the modern statements of the principle. As a matter of precedent and authority the position is unnecessarily complicated and confused, and it would be helpful if the Supreme Court were to simplify matters. The position of this work, discussed in greater detail in Ch 4, section G, is that Lord Goff's approach in *Aérospatiale* is to be preferred as a matter of both precedent and principle, although there is no difficulty with including 'unconscionable conduct' alongside 'vexation and oppression' as another primary example of when it is in the interests of justice to grant an injunction. But the issue is essentially academic: either way the practical result is much the same.[88]

G. THE MODERN CONCEPT OF COMITY

2.36   The decision in *Airbus v Patel*[89] also contained Lord Goff's other great contribution to the jurisprudence on anti-suit injunctions, his subtle exploration of the requirements of the comity of nations. Drawing on authorities from other common law jurisdictions, he held that, in order to justify the grant of an injunction, comity required that the English court should have a sufficient interest in, or connection with, the matter in question to justify the indirect interference with the foreign court which an anti-suit injunction entails. This framework has enabled the rationalization of considerations which previously had not been adequately articulated; for example, the reluctance of the House of Lords in *Carron Iron v Maclaren*[90] to grant an injunction to restrain a foreign claimant from claiming before his own courts can now be conceptualized in terms of the possible absence of a sufficient connection between the matter and the English courts.

H. THE *ANGELIC GRACE* AND CONTRACTUAL CASES

2.37   The most important development in modern times has been the clarification and loosening, from the 1990s, of the tests to be applied to anti-suit injunctions sought in contractual cases. It had come to be thought that the requirement of caution should apply to contractual anti-suit injunctions just as much as non-contractual situations;[91] and that even where the foreign litigation was in breach of contract it was also necessary to show that it was vexatious and oppressive.[92] But in a line of cases commencing with *Continental Bank v Aeakos* and *The Angelic Grace*, and ratified by the House of Lords in *Donohue v Armco*,[93] it was

---

[88] Rix LJ regarded the two types of formulation as meaning much the same thing in *Star Reefers v JFC Group* [2012] 1 Lloyds Rep 376 (CA) [25]–[27].

[89] *Airbus Industrie v Patel* [1998] 1 AC 119 (HL).

[90] *Carron Iron v Maclaren* (1855) 10 ER 961, 5 HLC 416.

[91] As discussed in *AES Ust-Kamenogorsk Hydropower Plant LLP v Usk-Kamenogorsk Hydropower Plant JSC* [2013] 1 WLR 1889 (HL) [25].

[92] See eg *Settlement Corporation v Hochschild* [1966] Ch 10, discussed in *Masri v Consolidated Contractors (No 3)* [2009] QB 503 (CA) [39].

[93] *Continental Bank v Aeakos Compania Naviera* [1994] 1 Lloyds Rep 505 (CA); *Aggeliki Charis Compania Maritima v Pagnan (The Angelic Grace)* [1994] 1 Lloyds Rep 168 (Rix J), [1995] 1 Lloyds Rep 87 (CA); *Navigation Maritime Bulgare v Rustal Trading (The Ivan Zagubanski)* [2002] 1 Lloyds Rep 106; *Donohue v Armco* [2002] 1 Lloyds Rep 424 (HL).

established that where the injunction defendant's foreign proceedings were in breach of an exclusive jurisdiction or arbitration clause, an anti-suit injunction would be granted unless there were strong reasons not to do so. The existence of a contractual obligation justified applying a different set of tests to the general concepts of vexation or oppression. This has led to a great increase in the grant of anti-suit injunctions.[94] The subsequent case law has had to grapple with whether these new tests should also apply in more marginal situations, such as where there is no direct contractual relationship but the injunction defendant asserts contractual rights derived from the rights of the original parties to the jurisdiction clause.[95]

I. THE GROWTH OF THE ANTI-SUIT INJUNCTION

These modern tests have also been accompanied by a sea change in the English court's   **2.38**
attitudes to the grant of anti-suit injunctions. The hesitations of the past have greatly diminished and there has been what Lawrence Collins LJ (as he then was) referred to as an 'explosion' in the use of the anti-suit injunction since the 1980s.[96] The most marked change of approach has been in contractual anti-suit injunctions, following *The Angelic Grace*; but there have also been many more non-contractual anti-suit injunctions. In some cases, there is room to doubt whether the English courts are really applying a 'cautious' approach.[97] Why this is so is uncertain: the *Aérospatiale* tests themselves are not notably looser than what went before. It may be that the expansion of the contractual tests has led to a greater comfort with the grant of the remedy, which has transferred itself into a greater willingness to grant non-contractual injunctions.

This expansion has also brought the English anti-suit injunction to the attention of lawyers   **2.39**
from other legal systems, and in particular to scholars and courts from the civil law, who previously had not known about, or reflected on, this common law peculiarity. The initial civil law reaction was, in many cases, hostile, although greater familiarity has since led to greater understanding.[98]

J. *TURNER V GROVIT* AND EUROPEAN JURISDICTIONAL LAW

The growth of the anti-suit injunction occurred just as the United Kingdom was accus-   **2.40**
toming itself to the jurisdictional regime created by the Brussels Convention. It was inescapable that the anti-suit injunction's flexibility would find itself tested against the rigid rules of the Brussels–Lugano regime. This occurred in *Turner v Grovit*,[99] where the Court of Appeal asked the ECJ whether a non-contractual injunction to restrain abusive proceedings in Spain was permissible. When the reference reached the European Court of Justice (ECJ), to the surprise of few, but the disappointment of many English lawyers, the ECJ held, in

---

[94] As noted in *Ecobank Transnational v Tanoh* [2016] 1 WLR 2231 (CA) [84].
[95] See *Shipowners' Mutual Protection and Indemnity Association (Luxembourg) v Containerships Denizcilik Nakliyat ve Ticaret (The Yusuf Cepnioglu)* [2016] 1 Lloyds Rep 641 (CA).
[96] *Masri v Consolidated Contractors (No 3)* [2009] QB 503 (CA) [39].
[97] See eg *Samengo-Turner v Marsh & McLennan (Services)* [2008] ICR 18 and *Petter v EMC* [2016] ILPr 3 (CA) (criticized at Ch 4, paras 4.41–4.46).
[98] See Ch 1, paras 1.18–1.25.
[99] Case C-159/02, *Turner v Grovit* [2004] ECR I-3565.

trenchant terms, that the grant of an anti-suit injunction to restrain proceedings before the courts of other Brussels–Lugano member states was inconsistent with the principle of mutual trust established by the Brussels–Lugano regime. Five years later, in *The Front Comor*, the ECJ controversially extended this approach to anti-suit injunctions to enforce an arbitration clause.[100] Since then, European hostility to anti-suit injunctions has diminished, and in *Gazprom*[101] the ECJ held that anti-suit injunctions granted by arbitrators were not precluded by the Brussels–Lugano regime.

2.41   The English courts have refused any attempt to extend *Turner v Grovit* outside the Brussels–Lugano zone.[102] Far from diminishing, the anti-suit injunction has flourished, in respect of territories outside Europe. Within Europe, the prohibition on the grant of anti-suit injunctions has led to jurisprudential creativity, as the English courts develop other remedies, such as claims for damages, to respond to wrongful forum shopping.[103]

2.42   The effect of Brexit is currently unclear. If it happens, and if its consequence is that the United Kingdom is no longer constrained by European jurisdictional law or a similar regime, then these shackles on the anti-suit injunction will be removed.[104]

K. CONCLUSION

2.43   The anti-suit injunction can be viewed as an accident of English medieval history. If equity and common law had formed a single system, the common injunction would not have made it seem natural to English lawyers that proceedings before foreign courts could be restrained by injunction, in the same way as proceedings before the English courts of common law. But once established, the anti-suit injunction has given English courts a powerful tool to protect their own jurisdiction, and to enforce their own perceptions of justice on transnational litigation. There are no signs that they intend to give it up.

---

[100] Case C-185/07, *Allianz v West Tankers (The Front Comor)* [2009] ECR I-663.
[101] Case C-536/61, *Gazprom*, EU:C:2015:316.
[102] *Beazley v Horizon Offshore Contractors* [2005] Lloyds Rep IR 231; *Shashoua v Sharma* [2009] 2 Lloyds Rep 376 [35]–[39]; *Midgulf International v Group Chimique Tunisien* [2010] 2 Lloyds Rep 543 (CA) [66]–[69]. See Ch 12, section C, 'Both Sets of Proceedings within the Brussels–Lugano Regime and Zone'.
[103] See eg *West Tankers v Allianz (The Front Comor)* [2012] 2 Lloyds Rep 103 and *Starlight Shipping v Allianz Marine & Aviation Versicherungs (The Alexandros T)* [2012] 1 Lloyds Rep 162, [2014] 1 Lloyds Rep 544 (CA).
[104] See in particular Ch 1, section I, 'Brexit' and Ch 12, para 12.03.

3

Power, Nature, and Form

A. THE POWER TO GRANT INJUNCTIONS

The terms 'power' and 'jurisdiction' are difficult, and are abused interchangeably. In this work, *power* will be used to describe the scope of things a court can do, and in particular the extent of the remedies a court may grant, in claims which it is able to hear, assuming there are no relevant limits on the court's *jurisdiction*. In contrast, *jurisdiction* will be used to describe *territorial jurisdiction*, namely the limits on the court's ability to hear claims which are defined by reference to the degree of connection which those claims have with England and Wales. This section addresses power, not jurisdiction.[1]   **3.01**

In the High Court,[2] final injunctions in ordinary private law litigation are granted (in general) under section 37(1) of the Senior Courts Act 1981,[3] which restates and confirms the   **3.02**

---

[1] Jurisdiction, in the sense of territorial jurisdiction, is addressed in Chs 16–18.

[2] The other main civil courts have parallel statutory powers. First, the County Courts can grant injunctions under County Courts Act 1984, s 38(1) which, subject to exceptions 'prescribed' in the County Court Remedies Regulations 2014, SI 2014/982 (as amended), gives to the County Courts the same powers as the High Court. An anti-suit injunction is not prescribed, and so is available in the County Court. In practice it seems that parties use the High Court. In any case, the power granted by s 38(1) County Courts Act 1984 is subject to the same restrictions as s 37(1) Senior Courts Act 1981: *Khorasandjian v Bush* [1993] QB 727 (CA) 732B–D, 740H–741B; *Ali v Westminster City Council* [1999] 1 WLR 384 (CA) 388–89. Second, the Court of Appeal, which is also a creature of statute, has the same jurisdiction as the court from which appeal is made: Senior Courts Act 1981, s 15(3). Third, the Supreme Court is yet another statutory creation (in contrast to its predecessor the House of Lords). Section 40 of the Constitutional Reform Act 2005 provides that 'The Court has power to determine any question necessary to be determined for the purposes if doing justice in an appeal to it under any enactment.' This would be interpreted as including a power to grant anti-suit injunctions if required. In *Grobbelaar v News Group Newspapers* [2002] 1 WLR 3024 (HL) [25], [37], [62], it was held that on the hearing of an appeal the House of Lords had inherent power to exercise any power vested in the Court of Appeal.

[3] For the authorities showing that (subject to certain defined exceptional cases where the inherent jurisdiction, or other specific statutes, may used) injunctions should be granted under statute and generally under s 37(1) of the Senior Courts Act 1981: see *South Carolina v Assurantie Maatschappij 'De Seven Provincien'* [1987] AC 24 (HL) 39H; *AJ Bekhor v Bilton* [1981] 1 QB 923 (CA) 942G–943E; *Fourie v Le Roux* [2007] 1 WLR 320 (HL), and the further authorities at n 24.

powers of the pre-Judicature Act courts to grant injunctions,[4] and provides 'The High Court may by order (whether interlocutory or final) grant an injunction ... in all cases in which it appears to the court to be just and convenient to do so.'

Although recourse sometimes has been made to the inherent jurisdiction of the court as a basis for injunctions,[5] this is unnecessary in ordinary private law litigation, and would be a needless complication, since any inherent jurisdiction is unlikely to be wider than section 37(1).[6] There are some other specific statutory powers under which injunctions can be granted,[7] but they are not of general importance, and with the exception of powers relating to arbitration,[8] have been of little relevance to anti-suit injunctions. We come, therefore, to the thorny subject of what, if any, limitations are imposed on the general power in section 37(1).

---

[4] Section 37(1) is often viewed as *conferring* the court's powers to grant injunctions, but as Lord Scott pointed out in *Fourie v Le Roux* [2007] 1 WLR 320 (HL) [25], in fact s 37(1) of the Senior Courts Act 1981 (like its predecessors, s 25(8) of the Supreme Court of Judicature Act 1873, and s 45(1) of the Supreme Court of Judicature (Consolidation) Act 1925) actually only restates and confirms those powers, since the High Court would in any event have had all the powers of the pre-Judicature Act courts to grant injunctions under the continuation provisions of s 19 of the 1981 Act, and its predecessors, s 16 of the 1873 Act and s 18 of the 1925 Act. The Court of Chancery had a general power to grant injunctions where equity demanded this (see I Spry, *Equitable Remedies* (9th edn, Sweet & Maxwell 2014) 342); and the Common Law courts had also been given broad statutory powers to grant injunctions under s 82 of the Common Law Procedure Act 1854: see *L v K* [2014] Fam 35 [10]. This aspect of the analysis in *Fourie* was relied on in *L v K* [2014] Fam 35 [14]; *Cartier International v British Sky Broadcasting* [2015] RPC 7 [99], [2017] RPC 3 (CA) [40]–[41] (not addressed in the Supreme Court: [2018] 1 WLR 3259 [5]); and *Mezhdunarodniy Promyshlenniy Bank v Pugachev* [2016] 1 WLR 160 (CA) [45]–[47]. There is, however, no reason to suggest that the antecedent powers preserved by s 19 of the 1981 Act are any broader than the power restated in s 37(1). In the circumstances, it most convenient to analyse matters in terms of s 37(1) alone. This was how Lord Scott approached the issue in *Fourie v Le Roux* [2007] 1 WLR 320 (HL) [26]; see also *Richards v Richards* [1984] AC 174 (HL), 199G; *L v K* [2014] Fam 35 [14].

[5] For an example outside ordinary private law litigation, see the restraint of advertisement of abusive winding-up petitions by injunction, which it has been said is done under the inherent jurisdiction: *Mann v Goldstein* [1968] 1 WLR 1091, 1093H–1094A.

  The High Court also has an inherent jurisdiction, derived from the 'doctrine of necessity', exercised today by the Family Division, to grant injunctions to protect children, and adults who lack capacity to make their own decisions or are 'vulnerable', in the sense that their ability to take decisions for themselves has been compromised: see *In re Z (A Minor) (Identification: Restrictions on Publication)* [1997] Fam 1 (CA) 13–18; *In re F (Adult: Court's Jurisdiction)* [2001] Fam 38 (CA) 45–47 (in respect of declarations); *In re a Local Authority* [2004] Fam 96 [86]–[104]; *Sheffield City Council v E* [2005] Fam 326 [108]; *In re L (Vulnerable Adults with Capacity: Court's Jurisdiction) (No 2)* [2013] Fam 1 (CA) [22], [52]–[55]; *Re KL (a child) (abduction: habitual residence: inherent jurisdiction)* [2014] 1 All ER 999 [28].

  There were cases where the Family Division, and the Court of Appeal on appeal from the Family Division, had gone further and suggested that the High Court has an inherent jurisdiction to grant injunctive relief in other situations arising in family law, such as freezing injunctions in support of proceedings for ancillary relief on divorce: see *Khreino v Khreino* [2000] FCR 80 (CA); *ND v KP* [2011] EWHC 457 (Fam) [4] (Mostyn J). But the use of the term 'inherent jurisdiction' in those decisions may well have been no more than loose phrasing referring to the undoubted existence of power to grant injunctions outside the specific powers in the Matrimonial Causes Act 1973 (in particular under s 37(1) of the Senior Courts Act), and does not represent the law. In the more recent case law the Family Division has disavowed the possibility of any general power to grant injunctions in the inherent jurisdiction which is broader than s 37(1) and has confirmed that the Family Division has no wider powers than the other divisions of the High Court: *L v K* [2014] 2 WLR 914 [14] (Mostyn J); *C v C* [2016] Fam Law 20 [97]–[106].

  The anti-suit cases which refer to the inherent jurisdiction are discussed at para 3.06 and n 25; as explained there, the anti-suit injunction can be more neatly justified under s 37(1) of the Senior Courts Act 1981.

[6] See *Richards v Richards* [1984] AC 174 (HL) 199G; *L v K* [2014] Fam 35 [14]; *C v C* [2016] Fam Law 20 [97]–[106].

[7] See eg the insolvency powers discussed in n 26.

[8] See para 3.06 and n 27.

It used to be the law, in a line of authority starting with *North London Railway*,[9] and restored **3.03**
to prominence by *The Siskina*,[10] that in ordinary private law litigation,[11] a final injunction
could only be granted under section 37(1) Senior Courts Act 1981 to protect or enforce a
legal or equitable right or duty for the enforcement of which the defendant is amenable to
the jurisdiction of the court, except in certain exceptional cases.

This doctrine posed questions for non-contractual anti-suit injunctions, for which iden- **3.04**
tification of the relevant right is problematic. Relying, as was sometimes done in respect
of freezing injunctions,[12] on the rights being claimed in the underlying dispute would not
always work for anti-suit injunctions since a defendant might not have any claim based on
any underlying legal or equitable rights, but could still need protection against vexatious
litigation elsewhere, and in some cases single forum injunctions are sought independent of
any underlying claims. The case law upheld the legitimacy of such anti-suit injunctions; but
was ambivalent as to whether they were enforcing an equitable right or were one of the exceptional categories where a right was not required.[13]

However, the *North London Railway* doctrine (we may also call it the substantive doc- **3.05**
trine in *The Siskina*) was subject to extensive criticism,[14] and in *Fourie v Le Roux*, the

---

[9] *North London Railway v Great Northern Railway* (1883) 11 QBD 30 (CA), differing from *Beddow v Beddow*
(1878) 9 Ch D 89, but reaching the same result as *Day v Brownrigg* (1878) 10 Ch D 294 (CA). The decision in *North
London Railway* was followed grudgingly in *Kitts v Moore* [1895] 1 QB 253 (CA) 261, 262–63; and then followed
in *Montgomery v Montgomery* [1965] P 46, 50; *Thorne v BBC* [1967] 1 WLR 1104 (CA) 1109; *Duchess of Argyll v
Duke of Argyll* [1967] Ch 302, 344; *Gouriet v Union of Postal Workers* [1978] AC 435 (HL) 516A–G, 501D–E; *Paton
v BPAS Trustees* [1979] QB 276, 278–79; *Siskina v Distos Compania Naviera (The Siskina)* [1979] AC 210 (HL)
256F–H, 257A; *Bremer Vulkan Schiffbau Maschinenfabrik v South India Shipping Corp* [1981] AC 909, 959, 961
(CA) and 979–980, 992, 994–95 (HL); *Chief Constable of Kent v V* [1983] QB 34 (CA) 45E, 49D–50B; *Richards v
Richards* [1984] 1 AC 174 (HL) 200B–D; *Associated Newspapers v Insert Media* [1988] 1 Ch D 509, 514F–515B;
Khorasandjian v Bush [1993] QB 727 (CA) 732B–D; *Mercedes Benz AG v Leiduck* [1996] AC 284 (PC) 301A–D; *Ali
v Westminster City Council* [1999] 1 WLR 384 (CA) 388–89; *In re A Local Authority* [2004] Fam 96 [66]. See contra
Maclaine Watson v ITC (No 2) [1989] 1 Ch 286 (CA) 302G–H to 303A; *Worcestershire County Council v Tongue*
[2004] Ch 236 (CA) 249 [39]–[40]; *Department of Social Security v Butler* [1995] 1 WLR 1528 (CA) 1532H–1533C.

[10] *Siskina v Distos Compania Naviera (The Siskina)* [1979] AC 210 (HL) 249F, 256F–H, 257A (although the point
was assumed and not decided, and had been conceded).

[11] The position was different in public law cases, where no legal or equitable right was required (see *Broadmoor
Special Hospital Authority v Robinson* [2000] QB 775 (CA) [19]–[25], [49]–[50], [55]–[56]); and also possibly in
insolvency: see *In re Oriental Credit Ltd* [1988] Ch 204; *Morris v Murjani* [1996] 1 WLR 848 (CA) 852D–853 (CA).

[12] See the discussion in *Mercedes Benz v Leiduck* [1996] AC 284 (PC) 300F–301D.

[13] Contractual anti-suit injunctions do enforce a legal right, but there has long been debate as to whether this is
so for non-contractual anti-suit injunctions in general. In a trilogy of cases decided in the 1980s, the House of Lords
decided that final anti-suit injunctions could be reconciled with *North London Railway* and justified within s 37(1).
But there was a difference of approach. In *Castanho v Brown & Root* [1981] AC 557 (HL) 573 per Lord Scarman,
and *British Airways Board v Laker Airways* [1985] AC 58 (HL) per Lord Diplock at 80H–81G and per Lord Scarman
at 95–96, the House of Lords appeared to consider that there was an equitable right not to be subjected to unconscionable litigation abroad which could support a final anti-suit injunction. However, in *South Carolina v Assurantie
Maatschappij 'De Seven Provincien'* [1987] AC 24 (HL) 39–41, Lord Brandon's view for the majority was that no coherent legal or equitable right could be identified, but that anti-suit injunctions could nevertheless be granted under
s 37(1), as an exception to the *North London Railway* principle. In *Masri v Consolidated Contractors (No 3)* [2009]
QB 503 (CA) [31], [39]–[59], [99], Lawrence Collins LJ sought to reconcile these cases by concluding that in 'alternative forum' cases, no legal or equitable right is required, but in 'single forum' cases, such a right may well need to
exist. This issue is further discussed in section B, 'A Legal or Equitable Right?'.

[14] *South Carolina Insurance v Assurantie Maatschappij 'De Zeven Provincien'* [1987] AC 24 (HL) 44G–H (per
Lord Goff); *Channel Tunnel Group v Balfour Beatty Construction Ltd* [1993] AC 334 (HL) 343D–E (per Lord
Browne-Wilkinson, with whom Lords Goff and Keith agreed at 340G–341A); and see per Lord Mustill, at 362B–C.
In *Mercedes Benz v Leiduck* [1996] AC 284 (PC), the majority of the Judicial Committee of the Privy Council up-
held the *jurisdictional* doctrine in *The Siskina* (see n 47 of this chapter; and Ch 18, para 18.16, n 30 and n 32) but
expressly avoided expressing any opinion on the 'substantive' aspects of *The Siskina*: at 298A–C, 304F–G; and Lord
Nicholls, in his dissenting opinion on the question of jurisdiction, stated that in his opinion the power to grant injunctions should not be confined to rigid categories: at 208C–E.

House of Lords concluded that, provided that the court has *in personam* jurisdiction over the injunction defendant, section 37(1) gives the court the power to grant any final or interlocutory injunction, without any precondition that it must protect or enforce a legal or equitable right.[15] The House of Lords maintained that the court will not 'normally' grant an injunction save to protect or enforce a legal or equitable right,[16] but this is a limitation of principle and practice, which can be departed from, not a constraint on the court's powers.[17] For a time, this aspect of *Fourie v Le Roux* seemed to have escaped general notice, and some decisions persisted in following *North London Railway*;[18] but others did follow the *Fourie* approach.[19] In the recent case law, such as *Cartier v BskyB*, the *Fourie* analysis has become embedded.[20] Nevertheless, it remains the case under *Fourie* that as a matter of a practice and principle a legal or equitable right is generally required, and in its absence there are considerable barriers in the way of the grant of an injunction.[21]

3.06   Yet for our purposes, the practical result of these historically complicated developments is now for the most part simple, so far as concerns the power to grant anti-suit injunctions. Irrespective of whether anti-suit injunctions are justified by a correlative underlying legal or equitable right (a question that remains subject to debate[22]), and whether or not any requirement for a legal and equitable right is a question of power, or principle or practice, anti-suit injunctions are one of the established exceptions to any such requirements in the light of the House of Lords' decision in *South Carolina*,[23] and can be and are granted under section 37(1) of the Senior Courts Act 1981.[24] Further, it appears that anti-suit injunctions

---

[15]   *Fourie v Le Roux* [2007] 1 WLR 320 (HL) [30]. Lord Scott used the language 'jurisdiction in the strict sense' rather than 'power', but he was referring to the court's power: at [25].

[16]   *Fourie v Le Roux* [2007] 1 WLR 320 (HL) [32].

[17]   *Cartier International v British Sky Broadcasting* [2015] RPC 7 [104] (Arnold J).

[18]   The substantive doctrine in *The Siskina* was treated as still stating the law in this respect in *Elektrim v Vivendi (No 2)* [2007] 2 Lloyds Rep 8 [55] (*Fourie* not cited); *Masri v Consolidated Contractors (No 3)* [2009] QB 503 (CA) [34]–[38] (*Fourie* not referred to in the judgment); *AES Ust-Kamenogorsk Hydropower Plant LLP v Ust-Kamenogorsk Hydropower Plant JSC* [2010] 2 Lloyds Rep 493 (CA) [18]–[20] (*Fourie* not cited); *Law Society v Shah* [2015] 1 WLR 2094 [69] (*Fourie* not cited). See also the acceptance that the injunctive power in s 37(1) is 'not unfettered', referring to *The Siskina* but not *Fourie*, in the *obiter* comments in *Tasarruf Mevduati Sigorna Fonu v Merrill Lynch Bank & Trust* [2012] 1 WLR 720 (SC) [57].

[19]   The approach in *Fourie* was followed in *Secretary of State for the Environment, Food and Rural Affairs v Meier* [2009] 1 WLR 2780, (SC) [97]; *Royal Westminster Investments v Varma* [2012] EWHC 3439 [41]; *Revenue and Customs Commissioners v Ali* [2012] STC 42 [35]–[38]; *Cartier International v British Sky Broadcasting* [2015] RPC 7 [94]–[104] (Arnold J); and [2017] RPC 3 (CA) (point not addressed in SC: [2018] 1 WLR 3259 [5]). See also *Samsung Electronics (UK) v Apple* [2013] FSR 9 (CA) [73]–[74].

[20]   *Cartier International v British Sky Broadcasting* [2017] RPC 3 (CA) [42]–[50] (point not addressed in SC [2018] 1 WLR 3259 [5]); *Fujifilm Kyowa Kirin Biologics v Abbvie Biotechnology (No 2)* [2017] RPC 7 [45]; *UTB v Sheffield United* [2018] EWHC 1663 [30]–[34].

[21]   See eg *C v C* [2016] Fam Law 20 [167], [172]; *Coates v Octagon Overseas* [2017] 4 WLR 91 [21]–[22].

[22]   See section B, 'A Legal or Equitable Right?'.

[23]   *South Carolina Insurance v Assurantie Maatschappij 'De Zeven Provincien'* [1987] AC 24 (HL) 44G–H (per Lord Goff), applied in *Masri v Consolidated Contractors (No 3)* [2009] QB 503 (CA) [47]–[48].

[24]   For statements that contractual anti-suit injunctions are granted under s 37(1) (even in respect of arbitration clauses), see *West Tankers v Ras Riunione Adriatica di Sicurta (The Front Comor)* [2007] 1 Lloyds Rep 391 (HL) [10] and *AES Ust-Kamenogorsk Hydropower Plant LLP v Ust-Kamenogorsk Hydropower Plant JSC* [2013] 1 WLR 1889 (SC) [48], [55]–[59], among many others. For statements that non-contractual anti-suit injunctions are granted under s 37(1), see *South Carolina Insurance v Assurantie Maatschappij 'De Zeven Provincien'* [1987] AC 24 (HL) 44G–H (per Lord Goff); *Masri v Consolidated Contractors (No 3)* [2009] QB 503 (CA) [47]; and generally *AES Ust-Kamenogorsk Hydropower Plant LLP v Ust-Kamenogorsk Hydropower Plant JSC* [2013] 1 WLR 1889 (SC) [20], [23], [48], [55]–[59].

are granted under the court's statutory powers, and thus in general practice under section 37(1), and there is no need to deploy the inherent jurisdiction of the court.[25]

In principle, other statutory powers could also support an anti-suit injunction, but section 37(1) is the only power that is used by the High Court in the modern case law to restrain foreign proceedings.[26] It was previously thought that anti-suit injunctions to protect arbitration clauses could be granted under section 44 of the Arbitration Act 1996, but the Supreme Court has recently confirmed that both final and interim injunctions to protect arbitration proceedings are granted under section 37(1), and that interim injunctions to protect arbitration cannot be granted under section 44 of the Arbitration Act 1996.[27]

---

[25] It has occasionally been suggested that the court's inherent jurisdiction includes the power to grant anti-suit injunctions: IH Jacob, 'The Inherent Jurisdiction of the Court' (1970) 23 Current Legal Problems 23, 43–44; *The Eras Eil Actions* [1995] 1 Lloyds Rep 64, 73–74 (Potter J); *Glencore International v Metro Trading International (No 3)* [2002] CLC 1090 (Moore Bick J) [23]. But none of the cases cited by Jacob actually support the proposition that anti-suit injunctions are justified under the inherent jurisdiction (as opposed to the separate topic of orders to restrain vexatious litigants: see Ch 6, section G, 'Orders to Restrain Vexatious Litigants'). All the authorities to which he refers ground the anti-suit injunction in the principles of equity, or s 37(1). Further, with respect, Potter J's judgment in *The Eras Eil Actions* may be conflating questions of jurisdiction and power. The problem there was whether the Court could procedurally grant interim anti-suit injunctions, unlimited in time, in the context of the existing action without an independent basis of territorial jurisdiction. This can more conveniently be regarded as a question of the existence and scope of the 'ancillary jurisdiction' to grant ancillary relief, which the court has when it has territorial jurisdiction over the merits (see Ch 16, paras 16.18–16.20; Ch 17, section D, 'Interim Anti-Suit Injunctions'; Ch 18, paras 18.88–18.90), rather than a question of substantive power. Similarly, Moore Bick J's reasoning in *Glencore* was understood on appeal by Rix LJ as really concerned with questions of procedure and ancillary territorial jurisdiction. Any substantive inherent jurisdiction was unnecessary: 'there is no need to find in the inherent jurisdiction of the court the power to grant anti-suit injunctions, which is in any event provided by s 37(1) of the Act': see *Glencore International v Metro Trading International (No 3)* [2002] CLC 1090 (CA) [60]–[61]. Finally, the *obiter* comments in *Hospira UK v Eli Lilly* [2008] EWHC 1862 (Pat) [9], on close reading do not in fact support the proposition that anti-suit injunctions are granted under the inherent jurisdiction.
  If it were to turn out in the future that s 37(1) were to impose an unnecessary and artificial constraint on the grant of anti-suit injunctions, then the inherent jurisdiction could be deployed; but as matters stand it is not necessary, and simplicity suggests that anti-suit injunctions should be based on s 37(1).
  In Australia, the anti-suit injunction is derived in part from the inherent jurisdiction of the court: *CSR v Cigna Insurance Australia* (1997) 189 CLR 345 (HC Aus) 391–94; *Australian Broadcasting v Lenah Game Meats* (2001) 208 CLR 199 (HC Aus) [96]. But the Australian context is different, as there is no general equivalent to s 37(1).
[26] Once a winding-up petition has been presented, there is a power under s 126 of the Insolvency Act 1986 (the successor of the Companies Act 1862, s 85; Companies Act 1908, s 140; Companies Act 1948, s 226; and Companies Act 1948, s 521) to restrain proceedings before the English courts, and courts in other parts of the UK: *In re International Pulp and Paper* (1876) 3 Ch D 594 (rather confused); *Re Dynamics Corp of America* [1973] 1 WLR 63. However, this power does not apply to proceedings in foreign courts outside the UK: *Re Oriental Inland Steam* (1874) 9 Ch App 557 (CA); *In re Belfast Shipowners* [1894] 1 IR 321, 332 (note contra at first instance on this point: 327–28); *Re Vocalion (Foreign)* [1932] 2 Ch 196. In *Bloom v Harms Offshore AHT 'Taurus'* [2010] Ch 187 (CA) [16]–[21], this line of authority was extended to the analogous statutory provisions in respect of administration of companies, which were also held not to grant powers to restrain proceedings outside the UK. A similar approach applies in New Zealand: *Commissioner of Inland Revenue v Compudigm International* [2010] NZHC 1832 [13]–[14], discussed in Ch 20. It also appears that such powers are to be exercised by interim application rather than final claim: see Ch 13, para 13.23.
  Section 25 Civil Jurisdiction and Judgments Act 1982 has not been used to support anti-suit injunctions. This is probably because the English court is unlikely to have sufficient interest to grant an injunction in support of foreign proceedings. See Ch 4, para 4.83; Ch 7, section G, 'Injunctions in Support of a Foreign Forum'.
[27] *Ust-Kamenogorsk Hydropower Plant JSC (Appellant) v AES Ust-Kamenogorsk Hydropower Plant LLP* [2013] 1 WLR 1889 (SC), followed in *Southport Success SA v Tsingshan Holding Group Co Ltd* [2015] 2 Lloyds Rep 578 [19]–[25]. It was already clear that final injunctions to enforce an arbitration clause were granted under s 37(1) (*Welex v Rosa Maritime Ltd (The Epsilon Rosa)* [2003] 2 Lloyds Rep 509 (CA) [34]–[40]; *Starlight Shipping Co v Tai Ping Insurance Co (The Alexandros T)* [2008] 1 Lloyds Rep 230 [16]–[19]); but in *Ust-Kamenogorsk* the Supreme Court went further and confirmed that s 37(1) was also the basis of interim injunctions to enforce an arbitration clause. See Ch 13, section B, 'Power and Nature'.
  Injunctions to restrain English arbitrations can be granted under s 72 of the Arbitration Act 1996; but these are not anti-suit injunctions properly so called, but rather part of the court's supervisory jurisdiction over English arbitrations, and obey different principles: see Ch 11, section A, 'Introduction'.

3.07   No limit has been identified to the types of the foreign proceedings which may be affected by anti-suit injunctions. Injunctions have been granted to restrain the pursuit of ordinary civil proceedings, insolvency proceedings,[28] arbitrations, freezing injunctions and attachment proceedings,[29] and ship arrest proceedings.[30] There are, however, no cases where foreign criminal or public law proceedings have been restrained by the English courts, and any attempt to do so would raise serious concerns as to whether the grant of an injunction would be consistent with comity.[31]

3.08   The power to grant anti-suit injunctions under section 37(1) has not been removed by Article 6 of the European Convention on Human Rights, as the right of access to a court does not necessitate an unfettered choice of court, and any limitations on access to a court imposed by anti-suit injunctions are arguably justifiable. However, it is arguable that Article 6 should affect the exercise of the court's discretion to grant anti-suit injunctions and it is possible that it may exercise a material constraint on the grant of injunctions in certain situations, in particular in single forum cases.[32]

B. A LEGAL OR EQUITABLE RIGHT?

3.09   There has been considerable debate as to whether anti-suit injunctions are in all cases granted to enforce a legal or equitable right, and the issue is not yet settled. A detailed analysis is found in the Court of Appeal's decision in *Masri*, where it was concluded that 'alternative forum' injunctions did not need to enforce a legal or equitable right, but that, as a matter of precedent, free-standing 'single forum' injunctions were based on an equitable right.[33]

3.10   There is no doubt that in some cases, anti-suit injunctions do enforce specific legal or equitable rights. There is a legal right to enforce a valid contractual forum clause governed by

---

[28] See *Re the North Carolina Estate* (1889) 5 TLR 328; *Re Vocalion (Foreign) Ltd* [1932] 2 Ch 196, 210; *Stichting Shell Pensionenfonds v Krys* [2015] AC 616 (PC). This topic is discussed further at Ch 5, section E, 'Insolvency and Justice Between Creditors'.

[29] See eg *Bloom v Harms Offshore AHT 'Taurus'* [2010] Ch 187 (CA), where a mandatory injunction was granted requiring the injunction defendant to discharge in part a Rule B attachment obtained in New York.

[30] In respect of ship arrest proceedings, see *Petromin v Secnav Marine* [1995] 1 Lloyds Rep 603, 613–14; *OT Africa Line v Hijazy (The Kribi) (No 1)* [2001] 1 Lloyds Rep 76 [92]; *Kallang Shipping v Axa Assurances Senegal (The Kallang)* [2007] 1 Lloyds Rep 160; *Kallang Shipping Panama v Axa Assurances Senegal (The Kallang) (No 2)* [2009] 1 Lloyds Rep 124; *Sotrade Denizcilik Sanayi Ve Ticaret v Amadou Lo (The Duden)* [2009] 1 Lloyds Rep 145. In *Mike Trading and Transport v R Pagnan & Fratelli (The Lisboa)* [1980] 2 Lloyds Rep 546 (CA) 549, 552, the Court of Appeal would have prepared to grant a mandatory injunction to procure the vessel's release from arrest had the arrest proceedings been in breach of contract (which they were not). In *BSNC Leasing v Sabah Shipyard* [2000] 2 MLJ 70 (Malaysia CA) 96–97, a mandatory injunction was granted to require a foreign ship arrest to be lifted.

[31] In *Singh v Singh* [2010] FMCafam 949, the Federal Magistrates Court of Australia granted an injunction to restrain a potential complainant from instituting or participating in criminal proceedings in India. This decision has been criticized in S Harder, 'Recent Judicial Aberrations in Australian Private International Law' (2012) 19 Aust Intl Law J 161, 162–65.

[32] See Ch 1, section E, 'Human Rights Law'. The English courts have unhesitatingly rejected arguments that Article 6 should limit the grant of anti-suit injunctions: *OT Africa Line v Hijazy (The Kribi)* [2001] 1 Lloyds Rep 76 [28(9)], [41]–[44]; *Mauritius Commercial Bank v Hestia Holdings* [2013] 2 Lloyds Rep 121 [43]. The French Courts have agreed that contractual anti-suit injunctions do not, in themselves, unjustifiably restrict access to the court: *In Zone Brands*, Cass Civ 1 (14 October 2009) No 08-16.369 and No 08-16.549 [2010] Rev Crit DIP (Note H Muir-Watt).

[33] *Masri v Consolidated Contractors (No 3)* [2009] QB 503 (CA) [31], [39]–[59], [99].

English law, and this contractual right underpins contractual anti-suit injunctions;[34] and similarly quasi-contractual injunctions which prevent evasion of contractual forum clauses by third parties claiming derived rights are often viewed as based on equitable rights to enforce the clause.[35] But when one turns to non-contractual injunctions, it is difficult to identify relevant underlying legal rights. The possibility of relying on tortious legal rights to justify non-contractual anti-suit injunctions has not been pursued with enthusiasm,[36] and it is likely that any attempt to do so would be futile in most cases, because of the limited scope of the relevant torts.[37] Choice of law considerations could pose serious problems for any attempts to use a tortious basis, since it is arguable that the applicable law would be the law of the country of the litigation.[38] Consequently, if there is a substantive right which underpins the full breadth of the power to grant non-contractual anti-suit injunctions, it must be an equitable right.

There are some specific equitable rights which can support anti-suit injunctions in par-   **3.11**
ticular cases, such as the equitable right to require an assignee of a contract to comply with an exclusive jurisdiction clause in that contract when enforcing his assigned rights,[39] and the case law so far has taken the approach that there is generally an equitable right to enforce the forum clause against the third party in 'quasi-contractual' cases.[40] The Privy Council has also concluded that there is an equitable right to a fair distribution of assets in insolvency which can justify an anti-suit injunction to restrain litigation that would interfere with that distribution.[41] But again these specific rights are not sufficiently broad to support the vast bulk of the cases where non-contractual anti-suit injunctions are granted. In particular they will not apply in many of the situations where the foreign proceedings are restrained on the grounds that they are vexatious or oppressive or unconscionable; or where the injunction protects the jurisdiction of the English court.

---

[34] *Ust-Kamenogorsk Hydropower Plant JSC (Appellant) v AES Ust-Kamenogorsk Hydropower Plant LLP* [2013] 1 WLR 1889 (SC) [1], [21]–[24].

[35] See eg *Shipowners' Mutual Protection and Indemnity Association (Luxembourg) v Containerships Denizcilik Nakliyat ve Ticaret (The Yusuf Cepnioglu)* [2016] 1 Lloyds Rep 641 (CA) [16]–[33]. The issue is discussed in Ch 10, section C, 'An Obligation Not to Sue Elsewhere?'.

[36] A claim for an anti-suit injunction based on tort was originally advanced in *Schiffahrtgesellschaft Detlev von Appen v Voest Alpine Intertrading (The Jay Bola)* [1997] 1 Lloyds Rep 179, 183–84, but had been abandoned by the time of the hearing. Such an argument was advanced only indirectly, and not given weight, in *Amoco (UK) Exploration v British American Offshore* [1999] 2 Lloyds Rep 772, 780. A determined attempt to rely on tort was made in *OT Africa Line v Magic Sportswear* [2005] 1 Lloyds Rep 252 [19–25], but failed, for choice of law reasons: see Ch 4, paras 4.16, 4.38–4.39. In *Kallang Shipping v Axa Assurances Senegal (The Kallang)* [2007] 1 Lloyds Rep 160 [41], Gloster J held that a claim in tort against a third-party insurer for inducing its insured to breach an exclusive jurisdiction clause was arguable; but choice of law issues seem not to have been raised.

In the subsequent decisions in *Kallang Shipping Panama v Axa Assurances Senegal (The Kallang) (No 2)* [2009] 1 Lloyds Rep 124 [90]–[94] and *Sotrade Denizcilik Sanayi Ve Ticaret v Amadou Lo (The Duden)* [2009] 1 Lloyds Rep 145 [65]–[68], [90], insurers had manipulated insured cargo interests to bring proceedings in Senegal with the aim of pressuring shipowners to give up their right to arbitrate in London. Cargo interests were awarded damages against insurers on the basis they had wrongfully induced cargo interests' breach of the arbitration clause. Such a tortious claim would, in principle, be capable of supporting a claim for an anti-suit injunction. However, the judge made a point of observing, in both cases, that it was common ground that English law applied and that no case on Senegalese law was pleaded.

[37] See the discussion of possible relevant torts at Ch 4, section E, 'A Legal or Equitable Right'.

[38] Choice of law issues are discussed further at Ch 4, paras 4.38–4.39.

[39] See *Schiffahrtsgesellschaft Detlev von Appen v Voest Alpine Intertrading (The Jay Bola)* [1997] 2 Lloyds Rep 279 (CA) 286. See further Ch 4, paras 4.27–4.31 and Ch 10, section C, 'An Obligation Not to Sue Elsewhere?'.

[40] Ch 10, paras 10.14–10.19.

[41] *Stichting Shell Pensionenfonds v Krys* [2015] AC 616 (PC) [22].

3.12   The question is whether the courts should hold that there is a general substantive underlying equitable right not to be subjected to vexatious, oppressive, or unconscionable litigation elsewhere which can justify the full breadth of exercise of the power to grant non-contractual, and quasi-contractual, anti-suit injunctions.

3.13   On the one hand, anti-suit injunctions remain equitable remedies even though now granted under statutory powers.[42] Before the Judicature Acts 1873–75 they were granted in equity. The presumption that you cannot have a substantive remedy without an underlying right has intuitive attractions;[43] and is a comfortable corollary to the general principle that where you have a right you should have a remedy ('Ubi ius, ibi remedium').[44] It is arguable, therefore, that in order for equity to grant a non-contractual anti-suit injunction outside the cases of a defined specific equity it must be responding to a substantive equitable right not to be subjected to vexatious and oppressive or unconscionable litigation. This analysis has considerable support in precedent, both in the old Chancery authorities[45] and in more modern decisions, not least the House of Lords' decision in *Laker*.[46]

---

[42]   *Castanho v Brown & Root (UK)* [1981] AC 557 (HL) 573C; *British Airways Board v Laker Airways* [1985] 1 AC 58 (HL) 80H–81G, 95F–H; *Midland Bank v Laker Airways* [1986] 1 QB 689 (CA) 711B; *Barclays Bank v Homan* [1993] BCLC 680, 686–88 (Hoffmann J); *Turner v Grovit* [2002] 1 WLR 107 (HL) [22]; *Stichting Shell Pensioenfonds v Krys* [2015] AC 616 (PC) [18], [22]. Even a contractual anti-suit injunction is an equitable remedy to enforce a contractual right: *National Westminster Bank v Utrecht-America Finance* [2001] 3 All ER 733 (CA) [73]. Thus, anti-suit injunctions can be refused if the applicant does not have 'clean hands': *Royal Bank of Scotland v Highland Financial Partners* [2012] 2 CLC 109 [174]–[195], [2013] 1 CLC 596 (CA) [158].
(Cases such as *South Carolina v Assurantie Maatschappij 'De Seven Provincien'* [1987] AC 24 (HL) 39H–41C; *Donohue v Armco* [2002] 1 Lloyds Rep 425 (HL) [23]; *West Tankers v Ras Riunione Adriatica di Sicurta ('The Front Comor)* [2007] 1 Lloyds Rep 391 (HL) [8]; and *Deutsche Bank v Highland Crusader Offshore Partners* [2010] 1 WLR 1023 (CA) [50], use language that is less steeped in equity.)
[43]   See *Gouriet v Union of Post Office Workers* [1978] AC 435 (HL) per Lord Diplock at 499G–H, 500C, 501D–G, and also at 508G; *Kingdom of Spain v Christie, Manson and Woods* [1986] 1 WLR 1120, 1128–1129. However, for a refusal to follow the 'brocard', 'ubi remedium ibi ius', see *Harding v Wealands* [2007] 2 AC 1 [76].
   Amongst academic writers, Adrian Briggs thinks that such a general equitable right exists: A Briggs, *Agreements on Jurisdiction and Choice of Law* (OUP 2008) para 6.26; A Briggs, 'The Unrestrained Reach of an Anti-Suit Injunction: A Pause for Thought' [1997] LMCLQ 90, 92–93; and A Briggs, *Civil Jurisdiction and Judgments* (6th edn, Routledge 2015) para 5.99 (hereafter Briggs) (where, however the approach is more cautious). J Harris, 'Anti-Suit Injunctions—a Home Comfort?' [1997] LMCLQ 413, 415–16 also thinks that such a substantive equitable right exists, and observes 'if there is no recognized right, it is hard to see how the applicant should ever be entitled to a remedy'. See TM Yeo, *Choice of Law for Equitable Doctrines* (OUP 2004) para 4.30 (hereafter 'Yeo').
[44]   *Ashby v White* (1703) 92 ER 126, per Holt CJ: 'it is a vain thing to imagine a right without a remedy, for want of right and want of remedy are reciprocal'.
[45]   In *Beckford v Kemble* (1822) 1 Sim & St 7, 57 ER 3, 7, it was held that an anti-suit injunction would be granted as the applicant had a 'clear equity to be protected' (where the equity in question was not linked to any specific equitable defence); see also *Liverpool Marine Credit Co v Hunter* (1867) LR 4 Eq 62, 70 (where in considering whether to grant an injunction the question was if 'this species of equity exists'); (1868) LR 3 Ch App 479, 484–87. Care should be taken about some of the older cases, however, as in a number of them the injunction was granted to protect a specific substantive equitable defence which the foreign court might not give effect to (such as an estoppel), which is a different sort of equitable right to that in question here: see eg *Lord Portarlington v Soulby* (1834) 3 My & Ky 104, 40 ER 40.
[46]   In *British Airways Board v Laker Airways* [1985] AC 58 (HL) 81B–D, 95D–H, Lords Diplock and Scarman held that there was a legal or equitable right not to be sued in the foreign court if the action of the injunction defendant in suing there was unconscionable (Lord Diplock's discussion of the extent to which an anti-suit injunction should be viewed as an exception to *The Siskina*, at 81A–C, is not pellucid; but the best reading of his speech is probably that he was suggesting that the anti-suit injunction should be seen as an exception to the *procedural* doctrine of *The Siskina* (see para 3.14 below) and not to the existence of a legal or equitable right). See also *Castanho v Brown & Root (UK)* [1981] AC 557 (HL) 573. The approach taken in *British Airways Board v Laker Airways* was followed in *Midland Bank v Laker Airways* [1986] QB 689 (CA) 712B–G, 715F, and in *Compagnie Européene de Céréals v Tradax Export* [1986] 2 Lloyds Rep 301, 304–05 an injunction to restrain arbitration proceedings, where (it was said) the arbitrators had no jurisdiction to proceed because the matter was *res judicata*, was considered to be based on an equitable right. See also *Barclays Bank v Homan* [1993] BCLC 780, 787, adopting the language of an equitable right not to be sued from *Laker*.

This result has been given particular impetus in respect of final injunctions claimed as inde- **3.14**
pendent free-standing claims for final relief, because of the procedural doctrine[47] reflected
in *The Siskina*, according to which (a) a claim form seeking a final injunction must claim for
a substantive cause of action[48] over which the court has territorial jurisdiction; but (b) such
a cause of action for a final injunction can only exist if it enforces an underlying legal or
equitable right over which the court has jurisdiction; and (c) a 'right to an injunction' is insufficient without more, and cannot stand on its own.[49] But while limb (a) is a sound proposition (leaving aside some exceptional cases), because a cause of action is by definition
what must be pleaded in order to make out a valid claim for relief,[50] limbs (b) and (c) are
contestable (as will be discussed at paras 3.15, 3.24–3.26, and 3.30–3.31 below).

On the other hand, there is a forceful argument, supported by the House of Lords in *South* **3.15**
Carolina, that although the court may be exercising an equitable *power* when granting an
anti-suit injunction to restrain vexatious or oppressive litigation, it is not necessarily doing
so to protect any substantive equitable *right*, but is merely using its powers to respond to
vexatious or oppressive conduct, or conduct that interferes with the court's jurisdiction,
processes, and judgments, or is otherwise conduct that it is in the interests of justice to restrain. Since independent of the court's practice of granting anti-suit injunctions there is

The firmest modern statements that a substantive general equitable right does exist are contained in the decisions of Aikens J in *Donohue v Armco* [1999] 2 Lloyds Rep 649 [21] and *Youell v Kara Mara Shipping* [2000] 2 Lloyds
Rep 102 [41]–[45]. On appeal in *Donohue v Armco* [2000] 1 Lloyds Rep 579 (CA), the majority of the Court of Appeal
did not adopt Aikens J's analysis, but nor did they reject it, although Brooke LJ in the minority did take a different view
(at [90]). However, in the House of Lords [2002] 1 Lloyds Rep 425 (HL) 431 [18]–[21], Lord Bingham's analysis appeared to proceed on the basis that, if there was a good case for a general anti-suit injunction to be granted, then there
would be a 'substantial cause of action' underpinning the injunction (although on the facts of the case, the foreign
proceedings were not vexatious and oppressive). Lord Hobhouse's speech in *Turner v Grovit* [2002] 1 WLR 107 (HL)
does not directly confront this issue, but there are passages that suggest that he considered that in order for an injunction to be granted, an equitable right would be required: see at 118C–D (although cf also 117C–D). Following those
decisions there have been other authorities positively supporting the existence of an underlying substantive equitable
right. In *Glencore International v Metro Trading International (No 3)* [2002] CLC 1090 (CA) [42], Rix LJ referred to
'the right, legal or equitable but here equitable, for the protection of which an injunction should be granted'; and see
OT Africa Line v Magic Sportswear [2005] 2 Lloyds Rep 170 (CA) [63] and *Kallang Shipping v Axa Assurances Senegal
(The Kallang)* [2007] 1 Lloyds Rep 160 [20]. In *Nomihold Securities v Mobile Telesystems Finance* [2012] 1 Lloyds Rep
442 [27], Andrew Smith J stated that it was 'possible to regard' the right not to be subjected to vexatious proceedings
itself as an equitable right, but did not need to decide the point. Finally, in *Joint Stock Asset Management Company
Ingostrakkh Investments v BNP Paribas* [2012] 1 Lloyds Rep (CA) [46], the jurisdictional analysis proceeded on the
basis that the claim for injunction, if valid, reflected a right not to be sued. But the abstract question of whether or not
an injunction need reflect such a substantive right was not debated.

---

[47] This procedural doctrine is different to the substantive doctrine of *The Siskina*, namely that s 37(1) of the Senior
Courts Act only gives and confirms a power to grant injunctions in support of a legal and equitable right. That substantive doctrine is no longer the law, following *Fourie v Le Roux* [2007] 1 WLR 320: see paras 3.03–3.05. We distinguish also the *jurisdictional* doctrine of *The Siskina* (discussed Ch 18, para 18.16, n 30 and n 32), namely that only
claims for a cause of action for final substantive relief can be served out of the jurisdiction under CPR PD 6B para 3.1.
[48] *Mercedes-Benz v Leiduck* [1996] 1 AC 284 (PC) 310E.
[49] *Siskina v Distos Compania Naviera (The Siskina)* [1979] AC 210 (HL) 256C–E, 256G–H. This procedural
doctrine in *The Siskina*, which relates to the preconditions of an independent action, must be distinguished from
the substantive *North London Railway* doctrine, which concerned the powers of the court under s 37(1) Senior
Courts Act 1981.
[50] *Mercedes-Benz v Leiduck* [1996] 1 AC 284 (PC) 310D–F. A claim form can be struck out for failing to disclose
a cause of action: see among many others *Gouriet v Union of Post Office Workers* [1978] AC 435 (HL) 512F.
However, there are procedurally special cases where a claim form can validly be used to claim for free-standing
relief without a cause of action. Examples include *Norwich Pharmacal* orders; and interim injunctions in support
of foreign proceedings under s 25 of the Civil Jurisdiction and Judgments Act 1982, which are generally brought by
claim form: see Ch 13, paras 13.33–13.35. Arbitration claim forms are also used to make claims for interim relief,
including applications to subpoena witnesses or protect evidence.

no identifiable basis for a general substantive equitable right, it is circular to invent retrospectively a notional equitable right to fit the situations where the remedy will be granted.[51] It is arguable that provided that a fact pattern is accepted as justifying a cause of action for an injunction, it is not necessary to identify any distinct underlying right.[52] There are other cases where substantive relief will be granted without an underlying private law right, such as the court's power to enforce public rights, including the criminal law, at the suit of the Attorney General.[53] Any such 'right' would also become artificial and polymorphous: since the conditions in the case law are more complicated than simply allowing that vexation or oppression or unconscionability are necessary and sufficient, it would be difficult to articulate the equitable 'right' which underlies an injunction granted to protect the jurisdiction of the English court.[54] As Lawrence Collins LJ (as he then was) explained in *Masri*,

---

[51] In *South Carolina v Assurantie Maatschappij 'De Seven Provincien'* [1987] AC 24 (HL) 40H–41D, Lord Brandon concluded that an anti-suit injunction to restrain unconscionable (or vexatious and oppressive) conduct, as well as an anti-suit injunction to restrain proceedings in an inconvenient forum (mere inconvenience of the foreign forum is now no longer a sufficient justification for anti-suit injunctions without more: see *Masri v Consolidated Contractors (No 3)* [2009] QB 503 (CA) [48] and Ch 4, section J, 'Forum non Conveniens'), was not founded upon a legal or equitable right, as no such general right could be coherently formulated. Properly read, *Castanho v Brown & Root* [1981] AC 557, 573C–E, does not clearly support any general equitable right. *South Carolina* was followed in this regard in *ED&F Man (Sugar) v Yani Haryanto (No 2)* [1991] 1 Lloyds Rep 161, 167; and on appeal [1991] 1 Lloyds Rep 429 (CA), 438–39 (per Mann LJ); see also Neill LJ at 437. See in addition *The Eras Eil Actions* [1995] 1 Lloyds Rep 64, 70–71, 76, 79; and *Associated Newspapers Group v Insert Media* [1988] 1 WLR 509, 514H. However, for criticism of Lord Brandon's approach see A Briggs, 'The Unrestrained Reach of an Anti-Suit Injunction: A Pause for Thought' [1997] LMCLQ 90, 92, n 15; J Harris, 'Anti-Suit Injunctions—a Home Comfort?' [1997] LMCLQ 413, 415–16.

In *Mercedes-Benz v Leiduck* [1996] 1 AC 284 (PC) 301D–E, anti-suit injunctions were referred to as 'sui generis', and compared to freezing injunctions (which have no underlying cause of action) by Lord Mustill; and Lord Nicholls *dissentiens* at 310G–H analysed the underlying right as being essentially circular, to the extent it existed at all. In *Amoco (UK) Exploration v British American Offshore* [1999] 2 Lloyds Rep 772, 780–81, Langley J adopted Lord Mustill's comment and concluded that a claim for an injunction to restrain vexatious and oppressive conduct 'is not one which is designed to ascertain substantive rights but designed only to determine in which courts such rights should properly be determined'; he considered that an attempt to formulate an equitable right which underpinned the grant of an injunction did not amount to 'more than expressing in other terms the fact that an injunction should be granted'. (The knock-on effect according to Langley J was that the court had no jurisdiction under RSC Order 11, r 1(1) to permit service out of the jurisdiction of proceedings for a general anti-suit injunction (but this is a contestable conclusion, for many reasons, which it is submitted does not follow from the absence of an underling right: see n 62 of this chapter, para 3.27, and Ch 18, 'Can the Common Law Jurisdictional Gateways Apply?', paras 18.17–18.18. Langley J's approach to the jurisdictional question was adopted by Brooke LJ (in the minority) in *Donohue v Armco* [2000] 1 Lloyds Rep 579 (CA) [90], and was referred to without disapproval by Stuart-Smith LJ (see at [52]); but it was not adopted in the House of Lords: *Donohue v Armco* [2002] 1 Lloyds Rep 425 (HL) 431 [18]–[21]).

In *Turner v Grovit* [1999] 1 All ER (Comm) 445 [22], at first instance, David Donaldson QC concluded that in an extra-contractual case there was no obligation not to sue in a foreign country (overturned, on other grounds, *Turner v Grovit* [2000] QB 345 (CA)). Further, there are passages in Lord Hobhouse's speech in the House of Lords in *Turner v Grovit* [2002] 1 WLR 107 (HL) which suggest that he required only a 'legitimate interest' and not a substantive equitable right (at [24], [27]). In *Trafigura Beheer v Kookmin Bank (No 2)* [2007] 1 Lloyds Rep 669 [44(iii)], Field J interpreted Lord Hobhouse's analysis in *Turner v Grovit* as meaning that 'Absent an agreement to the exclusive jurisdiction of the court, or some other special factor, a person has no right to be sued in a particular forum'; and the reasoning in *Royal Bank of Scotland v Hicks* [2011] EWHC 2579 [62] is overall inconsistent with an underlying right.

Finally, in *Stichting Shell Pensioenfonds v Krys* [2015] AC 616 (PC) [22]–[23], it was held that an anti-suit injunction to protect equal distribution of assets on insolvency was justified by an equitable right; but the language used suggests that the Privy Council was distinguishing that situation to injunctions granted to restrain vexatious or oppressive conduct generally, in respect of which it was not suggested that there was any specific equitable right.

[52] See para 3.25.

[53] *Gouriet v Union of Post Office Workers* [1978] AC 435 (HL) 477–82.

[54] Take a case where the foreign litigation is vexatious but an injunction should not be granted as a matter of comity. Is there an equitable right which has been infringed, but one in respect of which there should be no injunction? Or is there no right at all?

there can be no objection to the expression 'right not to be sued' if the word 'right' is used in the same sense as it is in, for example, 'right to obtain disclosure'. The right not to be sued may involve a correlative duty, but it does not necessarily require a separate claim or cause of action any more than the right to obtain disclosure inter partes. In my judgment, on analysis those judges who have spoken, in alternative forum cases, of a right not to be sued, have not been indicating that there need be a separate cause of action, legal or equitable, but have simply been using the word 'right' in the sense of the thing which gives rise to a remedy.[55]

Applying this reasoning, Lawrence Collins LJ held in *Masri* that in 'alternative forum' cases, **3.16** in the light of *South Carolina*, it was not necessary to establish a substantive equitable right to underpin an anti-suit injunction. Such injunctions could be claimed as mere ancillary remedies in existing litigation. However, in 'single forum' cases, he appeared to accept that, in the light of *The Siskina* and *Laker*, as a matter of precedent (although not necessarily principle), the anti-suit injunction would still require, and be based upon, a substantive equitable right not to be sued abroad, founding a separate cause of action.[56] It was by this distinction between 'alternative forum' and 'single forum' cases that he managed to achieve a partial reconciliation of the clashing authorities.

However, there are difficulties with Lawrence Collins LJ's analysis, and it cannot be regarded **3.17** as the last word. The issue before him was the unusual question of whether it was necessary to make a separate claim, and establish separate territorial jurisdiction, for a post-judgment anti-suit injunction. This could have been resolved in a narrower way, on the basis that an interim anti-suit injunction, ancillary to existing proceedings, did not *procedurally* or *jurisdictionally* require a separate claim, whether or not there was an underlying equitable right not to be sued abroad.

As matter of legal history, the distinction between 'alternative forum' and 'single forum' **3.18** cases does not really reflect the previous authorities: in *Laker* the requirement of a right was conceived as being general and applying in alternative forum cases as well as single forum cases;[57] and the history of the remedy includes numerous cases where an equitable right was thought to exist in alternative forum situations.[58] Conversely, when in *South Carolina* the House of Lords held there was no underlying equitable right, their reasoning was not confined to 'alternative forum' cases.

Further, the distinction between 'alternative forum' and 'single forum' cases does not **3.19** work as a neat dividing line. An alternative forum injunction is granted where litigation could proceed in two different fora; a single forum injunction is sought where the claim in question could only proceed in the forum where the targeted litigation is brought.[59]

---

[55] At [52]. This was much the same analysis as Lord Nicholls' in *Mercedes Benz v Leiduck* [1996] AC 284 (PC) 310–11. See also *Associated Newspapers Group v Insert Media Ltd* [1988] 1 WLR 509, 514H, where Hoffmann J *obiter* suggested that anti-suit injunctions were founded on 'a right not to be sued in the foreign court' but not any 'independent cause of action'.

[56] *Masri v Consolidated Contractors (No 3)* [2009] QB 503 (CA) [31]–[59], [99].

[57] *British Airways Board v Laker Airways* [1985] AC 58 (HL) 81A–E, 95D–F. Although in the latter discussion Lord Scarman was, as it happens, addressing the single forum situation, the logic of his analysis of the equity would not be confined to single forum cases (*pace* Lawrence Collins LJ's reasoning in *Masri* at [43]).

[58] See nn 13, 45, 46.

[59] See Ch 5, section D, 'Single Forum Cases'.

But the difference is not always clear cut, for example where the claim that can be pursued in the other forum is similar but not quite the same. More importantly, an equity, if it exists, cannot coherently be confined to single forum situations. If vexatious conduct can contravene a substantive equitable right in a single forum case, it is difficult to see why conduct that is just as vexatious in alternative forum cases would not also contravene an equitable right.

3.20   In distinguishing 'single forum' cases, Lawrence Collins LJ appears to have been motivated by the difficulties of precedent, in the light of the procedural doctrine in *The Siskina*, of having an injunction without underlying English litigation to claim for a substantive cause of action to enforce a legal or equitable right.[60] But that problem does not neatly match up the distinction between 'alternative forum' and 'single forum' cases: it is possible to have an alternative forum situation where no litigation has been brought in England at all, but it could be. Conversely, it is also possible to claim for a 'single forum' injunction in the context of existing English proceedings if it is said that a related claim abroad should be restrained. So, to the extent that the procedural doctrine in *The Siskina* does continue to present a problem (we will return to this) it may be that *Masri* should be reframed as saying that an equitable right is required, and exists, only in relation to free-standing final claims for injunctions, as opposed to ancillary interim injunctions brought in the context of extant substantive proceedings. Yet it is difficult, again, to see why the underlying equitable rights should be different in the two situations, which may be identical so far as the conduct abroad is concerned.

3.21   If the question of principle was neutral in its consequences, and untrammelled by precedent, there would be much to be said for applying Occam's Razor,[61] and not inventing an artificial substantive right. Or it could be said that there should be a right only in the limited sense mentioned in *Masri*, that is a right to an injunction in the conditions identified by the case law, and not any more concrete underlying right. Seeking to create a more concrete right would be particularly problematic when set alongside the discretion not to grant the injunction.

3.22   But the existence or not of a substantive equitable right is interlinked with other issues of high importance, and cannot be decided in abstract. It interconnects, in particular, with four important questions of precedent and principle: first, whether a claim form for final relief can be issued if it does not claim in respect of any substantive underlying equitable right (the procedural doctrine of *The Siskina*); second, whether final anti-suit injunctions can be served out of the jurisdiction under the common law rules of territorial jurisdiction; third, whether choice of law rules should apply to anti-suit injunctions, and if so, how; fourth, what if any damages should be available for vexatious or oppressive conduct abroad.

3.23   We now turn to consider how the competing imperatives under each of these topics may be balanced and to sketch a possible solution.

---

[60] In oral argument Lawrence Collins LJ had said that the case law on these issues was 'bedeviled' by *The Siskina*.

[61] 'Essentia non sunt multiplicanda praeter necessitatem', or don't multiply things if you don't have to.

1. A Free-Standing Claim without a Legal or Equitable Right?

It is established that, whatever the theoretical analysis, there can be separate, free-standing, **3.24** claims for final non-contractual anti-suit injunctions to restrain vexatious and oppressive conduct abroad, brought by separate claim form, which enforce a valid cause of action.[62] But if the procedural doctrine reflected in *The Siskina*[63] remains good law, then this implies that such injunctions must be founded on an underlying equitable right and that a circular right to an injunction is not enough. However, there is a real argument that *The Siskina* should not be treated as gospel in this regard either.

It is accepted that a substantial cause of action is (normally) required for a valid claim for **3.25** final relief by claim form. But it should be possible to have a sufficient substantial cause of action to justify a final anti-suit injunction, and a valid free-standing claim form, even if there is no such separate equitable right. In *Mercedes-Benz v Leiduck*, the majority of the Privy Council doubted that there could be a valid free-standing claim form for a freezing injunction, and pointed to the conceptual incoherence of obtaining default judgment, or final judgment, on such a claim.[64] But such problems do not arise in relation to anti-suit injunctions which have no difficulties operating as final relief. In Lord Nicholls' minority opinion, while affirming that there was a cause of action for an anti-suit injunction which could validly be claimed by claim form for final relief, he pointed out that any underlying right would be 'elusive' and 'circular'. He did not endorse the conclusion that any such right needed to be identified, and observed that if needed it would at most a 'right not to be sued when that would be unconscionable'.[65] Similarly, *South Carolina's* approach that anti-suit injunctions are an exception to any need for an underlying right under section 37(1) could be regarded as having as a corollary that anti-suit injunctions are also an exception to any parallel procedural requirement.[66] Indeed, more generally it is arguable that the demise of the

---

[62] *British Airways Board v Laker Airways* [1984] QB 142 (CA) 148F, where the claims for the injunctions were commenced by writ; see also *Midland Bank v Laker Airways* [1986] QB 689 (CA) 691; *Mercedes Benz v Leiduck* [1996] AC 284 (PC) 310G; *Youell v Kara Mara Shipping* [2000] 2 Lloyds Rep 102 [44]; *Masri v Consolidated Contractors (No 3)* [2009] QB 503 (CA) [57]; *Steamship Mutual Underwriting Association (Bermuda) v Sulpicio* [2008] 2 Lloyds Rep 269 [10, 28]; *Joint Stock Asset Management Company Ingostrakkh Investments v BNP Paribas* [2012] 1 Lloyds Rep 649 (CA) [46]; *Golden Endurance Shipping v RMA Watanya* [2015] 1 Lloyds Rep 266 [8], [10(i)]. Further, the cause of action for the injunction is distinct to the cause of action on the underlying merits: *Toepfer International v Molino Boschi* [1996] 1 Lloyds Rep 510 [8]; *Masri v Consolidated Contractors (No 3)* [2009] QB 503 (CA) [55].

In *Amoco (UK) Exploration v British American Offshore* [1999] 2 Lloyds Rep 772, 780, Langley J held in relation to a non-contractual anti-suit injunction that 'the claim is not one designed to ascertain substantive rights but only to determine in which Court such rights should properly be ascertained', so that it could not fit within the powers to serve out under CPR 6.36 and PD 6B. This appears to suggest that he did not think that there was a real cause of action for a non-contractual injunction. However, it is suggested that Langley J was wrong. First, it may well be that a non-contractual anti-suit injunction does ascertain substantive rights, even if relatively circular and thin rights, such as a right to an injunction (per Lawrence Collins J in *Masri* at [52]) or a right not to be sued when that would be unconscionable (per Lord Nicholls in *Mercedes-Benz* at 310G). Second, even if there is no underlying right, it is submitted that there can be a cause of action, as the established legitimacy of such final relief shows. Third, the injunction plainly goes beyond merely determining where litigation should occur, even without any underlying right, as it will involve an assessment of whether the injunction defendant's conduct is vexatious and should be restrained in equity. Indeed, the end result of Langley J's reasoning was the conclusion that it was impossible to serve vexation-based non-contractual anti-suit injunctions out of the jurisdiction under CPR Part 6. It is submitted that this is an unnecessary and unhelpful result: see para 3.27 and Ch 18, paras 18.17–18.18.

[63] See para 3.14.

[64] *Mercedes Benz v Leiduck* [1996] AC 284 (PC) 298G–299A, 302H–303A.

[65] *Mercedes Benz v Leiduck* [1996] AC 284 (PC) 310E–311B.

[66] *South Carolina v Assurantie Maatschappij 'De Seven Provincien'* [1987] AC 24 (HL) 40D–E ('forms of injunction').

substantive doctrine of *The Siskina*, and of the limits it purported to impose on the power to grant injunctions under section 37(1),[67] should bring with it a corresponding liberalization of any matching procedural constraints—although given the *sui generis* nature of anti-suit injunctions, it is not necessary to take that step generally for our present purposes. Consequently, it is submitted that neither procedural principle, nor the need for a cause of action, compel the conclusion that free-standing (or single forum) anti-suit injunctions must be based upon a legal or equitable right. And if any underlying right is required, it may be enough to rely on a right to the injunction itself, as Lawrence Collins LJ envisaged in *Masri*. The near-circularity involved is benign.

3.26   It must be acknowledged, however, that unravelling the tangled cat's cradle of precedent which has built up around this issue would not be easy. Lord Diplock's speech in *Laker*, although not clear, appears to have qualified this aspect of *The Siskina* with regard to anti-suit injunctions in terms that preserved the need for a legal or equitable right;[68] so it would be necessary to regard this aspect of *Laker* as overtaken by *South Carolina*, and *Fourie v Le Roux*, with the help of the minority opinion in *Mercedes Benz*. But this might not fully work, as *South Carolina* could be interpreted in a more limited way, as dealing only with the situation of injunctions ancillary to existing proceedings and not free-standing claims, which is how Lawrence Collins LJ appears to have approached it in *Masri*. Further, the majority opinion in *Mercedes-Benz* requires, for proceedings to be served out of the jurisdiction under CPR 6.36 and PD 6B, that they be proceedings to ascertain or claim rights; and its logic suggests that proceedings which were not brought to ascertain rights in such a sense would not normally be valid claims for final relief, even if service out was not required. While the majority accepted that anti-suit injunctions were a *sui generis* exception to the general law for many purposes,[69] it is not quite as clear that they would have accepted that anti-suit injunctions should be an exception to this principle (the jurisdictional doctrine of *The Siskina*). In turn, the consequences of the demise of the substantive doctrine of *The Siskina* for the matching procedural doctrine have not yet been fully worked through in the case law. Consequently, Lawrence Collins LJ's pragmatic compromise in *Masri* might be treated for now, as a matter of *stare decisis* at Court of Appeal level, as requiring a legal or equitable right for a free-standing claim for a final anti-suit injunction, although not for an alternative forum injunction sought in existing English proceedings.[70]

2. The Problem of Territorial Jurisdiction

3.27   The problem in relation to territorial jurisdiction arises because of the opinion of the majority of the Privy Council in *Mercedes Benz* that in order for proceedings to be served out of the jurisdiction under CPR 6.36 and PD 6B, they must be designed to claim or ascertain substantive rights.[71] Although there is room to doubt that this is really correct under the CPR,[72] it has been treated as (in general) the law for the present.[73] In *Amoco*,

---

[67]   See paras 3.03–3.05.
[68]   *British Airways Board v Laker Airways* [1985] AC 58 (HL) 81A–E.
[69]   *Mercedes Benz v Leiduck* [1996] AC 284 (PC) 301F–302A, 301D.
[70]   *Masri v Consolidated Contractors (No 3)* [2009] QB 503 (CA) [44], [55]–[56].
[71]   *Mercedes Benz v Leiduck* [1996] AC 284 (PC) 301F–302D; see contra the minority opinion of Lord Nicholls at 310A–B, 313B–F.
[72]   See Ch 18, paras 18.16–18.18.
[73]   *Cruz City 1 Mauritius Holdings v Unitech* [2015] 1 Lloyds Rep 191 [79]–[80].

Langley J combined that principle with his conclusion that anti-suit injunctions based on vexation and oppression did not enforce any right, to arrive at the result that such vexation or oppression based injunctions could not be served out of the jurisdiction under CPR 6.36 and PD 6B. But it is suggested that this would be an unwelcome conclusion, and is wrong; it has not generally been followed.[74] It may be that anti-suit injunctions could be viewed as an exception to the *Mercedes-Benz* requirement (and the Privy Council were willing to treat anti-suits as a *sui generis* exception generally). But unless this or some other way is found to escape the result in *Amoco*, the courts could be driven to accept that there is an underlying equitable right of some sort, to avoid such jurisdictional difficulties.

3. Choice of Law

Conversely, a significant consideration against concluding that there is an underlying equit-   **3.28**
able right, or a right that is any more concrete than a 'right to an injunction', is that it might open a Pandora's box of choice of law difficulties. Choice of law for non-contractual obligations is now governed by the Rome II Regulation, and this is likely to apply to certain equitable obligations. The more concrete the underlying right, the more appropriate it would be to apply Rome II, which in contrast does not apply to questions of procedure. But if foreign law were to be applied, however, the practical result would almost certainly be to eliminate or drastically hamper the anti-suit injunction, since the law of the place of the litigation is unlikely to conclude that the action before it is wrongful in a relevant sense.[75] There are possible readings of Rome II under which English law would still be applied to govern anti-suit injunctions. But as discussed in Chapter 4, it is not guaranteed that the European Court of Justice would agree. In order to avoid losing tutelage over their prodigal child, the English courts may prefer to keep the anti-suit injunction as far as possible from the embrace of European law. One way to achieve this would be eliminate, or minimize, any concrete underlying right.

4. Damages

The existence of an underlying equitable right is also inextricably bound up with the ques-   **3.29**
tion of whether there should be a general right to damages for vexatious, or oppressive (or unconscionable) litigation abroad. We submit, later, that this would be a controversial new development.[76] But the more substantive the underlying right, the more conducive it is to a claim in damages, and *vice versa*.

---

[74] See Ch 18, paras 18.17–18.18. For example, in *BNP Paribas v Russian Machines* [2012] 1 Lloyds Rep 61, and (on appeal) *Joint Stock Asset Management Company Ingostrakkh Investments v BNP Paribas* [2012] 1 Lloyds Rep 649 (CA) [2], [69]–[78], Blair J and the Court of Appeal had no hesitation in permitting a non-contractual anti-suit injunction, based on unconscionability and vexation or oppression, to be served out of the jurisdiction under CPR 6. The *Amoco* point was, it seems, not even argued.
[75] *OT Africa Line v Magic Sportswear* [2005] 1 Lloyds Rep 252 [24].
[76] Ch 14, section B, 'Non-Contractual Damages'.

5. Conclusion: A Right or Not?

3.30 The existence of an underlying legal or equitable right is, therefore, not an innocent question. Its resolution will depend on what the courts wish to achieve, how they choose to steer their course between the competing imperatives, and how they resolve the interconnected issues of principle and precedent.

3.31 But it is submitted that an effective resolution as a matter of principle and policy, which steers between many of the reefs of precedent, would be as follows:

(1) It can be said that there is a general right to an anti-suit injunction in the circumstances defined by the case law, which is capable of supporting a cause of action for an injunction, but the right exists to that extent and no more, and there is no general concrete underlying equitable right.

(2) Such a 'right' and cause of action can support a claim form for final relief and such a claim form can be served out of the jurisdiction under CPR Part 6 PD 6B.

(3) Given the minimal and near-circular nature of this right, however, it is not *necessary* to use a classification in terms of rights, where this would be procedurally inappropriate, and so interim injunctions need not be analysed in terms of rights.

(4) Interim anti-suit injunctions can be claimed by application notice, as ancillary relief in existing proceedings, independent of whether a parallel final anti-suit injunction is claimed and irrespective of whether jurisdiction could be obtained over a free-standing claim for an anti-suit injunction.

(5) Any such general 'right' is insufficient to support a claim for damages, and whether there is a sufficient equity to support damages claims needs to be addressed separately.

(6) The minimal nature of any such 'right' means it is to be classified as procedural for the purposes of choice of law and so it is not necessary to analyse questions of choice of law under the Rome Regulations. (In any event, English law applies.[77])

C. THE FORM AND NATURE OF FINAL ANTI-SUIT INJUNCTIONS

1. Claims for Final Relief Brought by Claim Form

3.32 Final anti-suit injunctions can be and are claimed by claim form, and particulars of claim.[78] Such claims for final anti-suit injunctions are made in respect of, and to enforce, a cause of action for an injunction, which can be regarded as a substantive cause of action to the extent necessary[79] (whether or not that cause of action is based on an underlying legal or equitable right). Anti-suit injunctions can also be claimed by application notice in existing proceedings, in particular in 'alternative forum' situations.[80] However, this procedure is generally appropriate for interim injunctions only. It remains the case that even in alternative forum cases, a claim for a *final* anti-suit injunction can and it seems (at least generally) should[81]

---

[77] For the choice of law analysis, see Ch 4, section B, 'Applicable Law'.
[78] See *Masri v Consolidated Contractors (No 3)* [2009] QB 503 (CA) [57].
[79] See paras 3.04, 3.06, 3.15–3.16, 3.24–3.25.
[80] *Masri v Consolidated Contractors (No 3)* [2009] QB 503 (CA) [57].
[81] However, cf *Nomihold Securities v Mobile Telesystems Finance* [2012] 1 Lloyds Rep 442 [36], although the reasoning may not be very clear.

be claimed by claim form and particulars of claim, either in a free-standing action or by way of initial claim or amendment in the underlying action on the merits. Further, it seems likely that it must be shown that the court has a distinct jurisdictional basis for such a claim for a final injunction.[82]

In *Masri*, Lawrence Collins LJ gave as examples of claims for final anti-suit injunctions only   **3.33** injunctions to enforce an exclusive forum clause, or single forum injunctions, and suggested *obiter* that alternative forum injunctions would 'normally' be brought by application notice only. However, this is somewhat too narrow (not least as the boundary between single and alternative forum injunctions is not clear cut). It is true that interim alternative forum injunctions will often be brought only by application notice; and it is not necessary for there to be a corresponding claim for a final anti-suit injunction, as the interim anti-suit injunction can be brought ancillary to the underlying proceedings on the merits.[83] Nevertheless, final alternative forum injunctions can and have been brought by claim form in a number of cases.[84] The anti-suit injunction's ambivalence between interim and final form is one of the distinctive features of the remedy.

Either a Part 7 or a Part 8 claim form may be used, depending on whether or not the issues   **3.34** are likely to involve substantial contested issues of fact.[85]

Final injunctions to enforce arbitration clauses must be brought by way of arbitration claim   **3.35** form.[86]

2. Converting an Interim Hearing into a Trial

A hearing to determine an application for an interim anti-suit injunction can be converted   **3.36** into a trial of a claim for a final injunction, if there are no important disputes of fact, nor any interrelation with other final determinations which would make this course inappropriate,[87] and provided that the grant of final rather than interim relief is appropriate in the

---

[82] See Ch 16, paras 16.21–16.24; Ch 17, paras 17.06–17.09, and *Donohue v Armco* [2002] 1 Lloyds Rep 425 (HL) [17]–[21].

[83] *Glencore International v Metro Trading International (No 3)* [2002] CLC 1090 (CA) [59]–[61]; *Masri v Consolidated Contractors (No 3)* [2009] QB 503 (CA) [59]. See Ch 13, paras 13.08, 13.27.

[84] See eg *Simon Engineering v Butte Mining (No 2)* [1996] 1 Lloyds Rep 91, 93; *REC Wafer Norway v Moser Baer Photo Voltaic* [2010] 1 Lloyds Rep 410. See also *Joint Stock Asset Management Company Ingostrakkh Investments v BNP Paribas SA* [2012] 1 Lloyds Rep 649 (CA) [46], [80]–[82], where a final vexation-based anti-suit injunction was claimed to prevent evasion of an arbitration clause: this is also a form of alternative forum injunction.

[85] CPR 8.1(2)(a).

[86] Final (and interim) anti-suit injunctions to enforce an arbitration clause are sought under s 37(1) of the Supreme Court Act 1981, and not under the Arbitration Act 1996: see para 3.06. Nevertheless, such final injunctions must be brought by arbitration claim form, as they are regarded as 'affecting' the arbitration agreement, and so fall within CPR 62.2(1)(d), which engages the obligation to use an arbitration claim form in CPR 62.3. This was held in *AES Ust-Kamenogorsk Hydropower Plant LLP v Ust-Kamenogorsk Hydropower Plant JSC* [2013] 1 WLR 1889 (SC) [49], where *Sokana Industries v Freyre* [1994] 2 Lloyds Rep 57, 64–65 was regarded as only applicable to the narrower terms of the previous rules. For examples of this procedure, see *Steamship Mutual Underwriting Association (Bermuda) v Sulpicio* [2008] 2 Lloyds Rep 269 [10], [28] and *Mobile Telecommunications v Prince Hussam bin Saud bin Abdulaziz bin Saud* [2018] EWHC 1469. It also follows that the court has power to serve claims for such final injunctions out of the jurisdiction under CPR 62.5: see Ch 18, paras 18.78–18.79. So far as concerns the requirement in CPR 62.4 that the claimant must specify under which section of the 1996 Act the claim is made, it appears that this should be read with the addition of the words 'if any'.

[87] *Donohue v Armco* [1999] 2 Lloyds Rep 649, 664–65; *Navigation Maritime Bulgare v Rustal Trading (The Ivan Zagubanski)* [2002] 1 Lloyds Rep 106, 127 (injunction granted on an interim basis only).

circumstances.[88] The court will obviously be more willing to abbreviate the normal trial process in this way if both parties consent,[89] but even if one party objects, the court can and will in its discretion decide matters on a final basis in an appropriate case.[90] A similar procedural result can be produced through accelerating the hearing of the final claim by appropriate case management.[91]

3. Undertakings

3.37   The courts may accept undertakings from the injunction defendant in lieu of an injunction.[92]

4. Prohibitory and Mandatory Injunctions

3.38   The standard form of anti-suit injunction is prohibitory, restraining the injunction defendant from taking any further steps to pursue the foreign proceedings. However, this may not be enough to ensure that the injunction is practically effective. The foreign action may have a life of its own.[93] Consequently, in appropriate cases the court will also grant a mandatory anti-suit injunction requiring the injunction defendant to obtain the equivalent of a stay of the foreign proceedings or even to discontinue them.[94] Mandatory injunctions have also been granted requiring the injunction defendant to lift an arrest of a ship,[95] and to release monies attached by order of a foreign court.[96]

3.39   A mandatory anti-suit injunction can be seen as a more invasive form of relief, and there are a number of cases suggesting that a stronger case, and particular reasons, is required

---

[88]   Cf *Mobile Telecommunications v Prince Hussam bin Saud bin Abdulaziz bin Saud* [2018] EWHC 1469. The grant of final relief may be inappropriate where the anti-suit injunction is sought in the context of independent substantive proceedings for other relief, due to the possibility of changes in the relationship between the English substantive action and the foreign action, 'whereby the oppression originally complained of were relieved': see *The Eras Eil Actions* [1995] 1 Lloyds Rep 64 at 74. In *Skype Technologies v Joltid* [2011] ILPr 8 [41], the possibility of problems arising from a broad form of final injunction was dealt with by the inclusion of an express liberty to apply.

[89]   As occurred in *Pena Copper Mines v Rio Tinto Co* (1912) 105 LT 846 (CA) 849; *Samengo-Turner v J&H Marsh & McLennan (Services)* [2007] ILPr 52 (CA) [21]; *Golden Endurance Shipping v RMA Watanya* [2015] 1 Lloyds Rep 266 [10(i)].

[90]   *Donohue v Armco* [1999] 2 Lloyds Rep 649, 664–65; *West Tankers v Ras Riunione Adriatica di Sicurta (The Front Comor)* [2005] 2 Lloyds Rep 257, 273 [75]–[76].

[91]   As in *Mobile Telecommunications v Prince Hussam bin Saud bin Abdulaziz bin Saud* [2018] EWHC 1469.

[92]   See eg *Cadre v Astra Asigurari* [2006] 1 Lloyds Rep 560 [19]; *Société Nationale Industrielle Aerospatiale v Lee Kui Jak* [1987] AC 871 (PC) (Brunei) 896.

[93]   See eg the events in *Petter v EMC* [2016] ILPr 3 (CA), discussed in T Raphael, 'Do as You Would be Done By? System-Transcendent Justification and Anti-Suit Injunctions' [2016] LMCQ 256.

[94]   See eg *Mobile Telecommunications Company v Prince Hussam bin Saud bin Abdulaziz bin Saud* [2018] 2 Lloyds Rep 192.

  Mandatory anti-suit injunctions were granted, without specific discussion of their nature or any mention of a higher threshold, in a number of cases such as *British Airways Board v Laker Airways* [1984] QB 142 (CA) 203 (overturned on appeal on other grounds [1985] AC 58 (HL)); *Hemain v Hemain* [1988] 2 FLR 388 (CA) 389C; *Toepfer International v Société Cargill France* [1997] 2 Lloyds Rep 98, 102, 111 (this point was not raised on appeal, [1998] 1 Lloyds Rep 379 (CA) 386); *Turner v Grovit* [2000] QB 345 (CA) 350B, 364F, [2002] 1 WLR 107 (HL) 113–14 [16]; *Masri v Consolidated Contractors (No 3)* [2009] QB 503 (CA) [6]–[7]; *Compania Sud Americana de Vapores v Hin-Pro International Logistics* [2015] 1 Lloyds Rep 301 [36]; *Impala Warehousing and Logistics (Shanghai) v Wanxiang Resources (Singapore)* [2015] 2 All ER (Comm) 234 [143]. In *Petter v EMC* [2015] EWCA Civ 828 (31 July 2015), the Court of Appeal was moved to grant a mandatory anti-anti-suit injunction.

[95]   *Kallang Shipping v Axa Assurances Senegal (The Kallang)* [2007] 1 Lloyds Rep 160 [14].

[96]   *Bloom v Harms Offshore AHT 'Taurus'* [2010] Ch 187 (CA).

to justify it.[97] There are signs, however, that the courts are moving to a more sophisticated view. It can be artificial to treat the dividing line between mandatory and prohibitory relief in any rigid fashion. A so-called mandatory injunction requiring discontinuance may in truth be no more than the spelling out of the inevitable consequence of a prohibitory injunction preventing continuance of the foreign action. Further, stopping the foreign action may be a cleaner and clearer result than prohibiting it from being pursued and may require less policing. So, it may be that the mere fact that an injunction could be regarded as mandatory should not automatically trigger any different and more demanding regime: the focus should be on whether, in truth, the mandatory relief is more invasive in a way that should demand higher scrutiny.[98]

However, at least in general, mandatory injunctions should not be granted to force a party to take positive steps to arbitrate or litigate in the chosen forum, as parties are free to elect whether or not to advance a claim at all.[99]   **3.40**

There may be greater reluctance to grant an interim mandatory anti-suit injunction, unless the hearing is effectively a final hearing, especially if the effect of a mandatory injunction will be irreversible.[100] Nevertheless, interim mandatory injunctions have been granted in appropriate cases.   **3.41**

---

[97] In *Mamidoil-Jetoil Greek Petroleum v Okta Crude Oil Refinery* [2003] 1 Lloyds Rep 1, 36–37, Aikens J refused to grant a mandatory injunction. This was in part because the injunction was actually, in the unusual circumstances of that case, sought against a *defendant* in the foreign proceedings. But Aikens J observed that the facts in *Turner v Grovit* [2000] 1 QB 345 (CA), where a mandatory order had been granted, had been 'extreme'; and his other ground for declining to grant a mandatory injunction on the ground that it would be a 'direct interference with the procedure of a foreign court', which he thought raised serious problems of comity. There are a number of cases where the court has accepted that a higher threshold is required but gone on to grant the mandatory anti-suit injunction: see eg *Ecom Agroindustrial v Mosharaf Composite Textile Mill* [2013] 2 Lloyds Rep 196 [37]–[39]; *Evergreen Marine (Singapore) v Fast Shipping & Transportation C* [2014] EWHC 4893 (QB) [19]. Similarly, in *Credit Suisse First Boston (Europe) v Seagate Trading* [1999] 1 Lloyds Rep 784, 792–94, Rix J appeared to have considered that something additional would be required to justify mandatory relief. On the other hand, the authorities cited in n 94 do appear to show many cases of mandatory injunctions being granted without any additional hesitation.

[98] Cf *National Commercial Bank Jamaica v Olint* [2009] 1 WLR 1405 [20]; *Mobile Telecommunications v Prince Hussam bin Saud bin Abdulaziz bin Saud* [2018] 2 Lloyds Rep 192. See also the substance of the reasoning in *Evergreen Marine (Singapore) v Fast Shipping & Transportation* [2014] EWHC 4893 (QB) [19].

[99] As Cooke J has observed, failing to sue in England is not a breach of an exclusive forum clause, it is only the act of suing in the wrong forum which is a breach: *Compania Sud-Americana v Hin-Pro International Logistics* [2015] 1 Lloyds Rep 301 [38]. See also *Pena Copper Mines v Rio Tinto Co* (1911) 105 LT 846 (CA) 852:

> The parties could not be compelled to go to arbitration. They cannot now; but an appeal to the courts can be stopped, and that indirectly enforces the arbitration clause. Therefore the status of an arbitration clause in England is that it will not be specifically enforced, but by proper proceedings you can prevent the other party from appealing to the English courts in respect of any matter which by contract ought to be decided by arbitration.

There is also a line of authority that specific performance cannot be granted of arbitration agreements: *Street v Rigby* (1802) 6 Ves Jun 815, 31 ER 1323, 1324–25; *Gourlay v Duke of Somerset* (1815) 19 Ves Jun 429, 34 ER 576; *In Re Smith and Service* (1890) 25 QB 545 (CA).

The old case of *Penn v Lord Baltimore* (1750) 1 Ves Sen 444, 27 ER 1132, where specific performance was granted of a form of arbitration clause, under which commissioners were appointed to resolve a boundary dispute, arises out of exceptional facts, as the parties had expressly agreed that a particular set of disputes would be resolved by the commissioners. In the Canadian case of *Axio Supernet v Bell West* 2003 ABQB 195 (Alberta), a mandatory injunction requiring a recalcitrant party to arbitrate was granted. But again, the facts were unusual. The mandatory injunction appears to have been justified by the particular terms of the dispute resolution agreement, which provided that 'the parties have agreed to implement a dispute resolution mechanism to resolve issues in dispute in a timely and effective manner', and contained detailed positive obligations to negotiate, and then mediate, disputes before arbitration.

[100] For an example of an interim mandatory injunction being refused, see *Impala Warehousing and Logistics (Shanghai) v Wanxiang Resources (Singapore)* [2015] EWHC Comm 25 [24]. For an example of mandatory injunctions being granted at the interim stage, see *Evergreen Marine (Singapore) v Fast Shipping & Transportation* [2014]

D. AGAINST WHOM MAY AN ANTI-SUIT INJUNCTION BE GRANTED?

3.42   It is an essential feature of the anti-suit injunction that it is sought and granted against the injunction defendant personally, and does not purport to restrain the foreign court, nor directly to affect the foreign proceedings in themselves.[101]

3.43   The personal logic of the anti-suit injunction is a necessary condition of the enterprise of reconciling the remedy with the demands of comity. The grant of an injunction against the foreign court itself, even as a secondary defendant, would be obviously unacceptable.[102] The personal logic is not a mere artifice and has important consequences, not least the fact that, in contrast to a stay by the English court of English proceedings, the injunction does not have intrinsic and automatic effect on the proceedings in question.[103] But notwithstanding its personal logic, there has been growing acceptance that an anti-suit injunction is in effect 'however disguised and indirect, an interference with the process of justice in the foreign court',[104] and this recognition has driven the tightening

---

EWHC 4893 (QB) [19]. For a more detailed discussion of interim mandatory anti-suit injunctions, see Ch 13, section F, 'Mandatory Interim Injunctions'.

------

[101] This has been apparent since the very beginnings of the remedy. In *Love v Baker* (1664–65) Nels 103, 21 ER 801, (1665) 1 Chan Cas 67, 22 ER 698; see also *sub nom Lowe v Baker* 2 Freem Chy 125, 22 ER 1101, where the first reported claim for an anti-suit injunction was refused, the report observes that 'all the Bar was of another opinion. It was said, The Injunction did not lie for Foreign Jurisdictions, nor out of the King's Dominions. But to that it was answered, The Injunction was not to the Court, but to the Party.' This type of 'personal logic' was the principal argument advanced when the legitimacy of the remedy was accepted in principle in *Lord Portland's Case* 114 Harg MSS 166 (see Ch 2, para 2.05); and it formed the basis of the decision in the leading early case of *Bushby v Munday* (1821) 5 Madd 297, 56 ER 908, 913. In *Kennedy v Cassillis* (1818) 2 Swans 313, 36 ER 635, 638, Lord Eldon dissolved an injunction in part because 'the injunction is sought, not against the persons in whose name this bank stock stands, but against the Court of Session, which never can be made effectual' (although it can be noted that the summary in the report of the actual injunction sought, at 635–36, does not seem to bear out the surprising idea that the remedy was actually sought against the foreign court). See also *Lord Portarlington v Soulby* (1834) 3 My & Ky 104, 40 ER 40, 41–42 (describing the Bar's riposte in *Love v Baker* as 'a very sound answer'); *In re Artistic Colour Printing* (1880) 14 Ch D 502, 505.

In more recent authority the essential personal logic of the anti-suit injunction has been repeatedly confirmed. See *Castanho v Brown & Root* [1981] AC 557 (HL) 572F–573A; *Société Nationale Industrielle Aérospatiale v Lee Kui Jak* [1987] AC 871 (PC) 892C–D; *Donohue v Armco* [2002] 1 Lloyds Rep 425 (HL) [19]; *Turner v Grovit* [2002] 1 WLR 107 (HL) 117 [23]; *Glencore International v Metro Trading International (No 3)* [2002] CLC 1090 (CA) [42]; *Through Transport Mutual Insurance Association (Eurasia) v New India Assurance Co* [2004] 1 Lloyds Rep 206 [34] (overturned on appeal but not on this point, [2005] 1 Lloyds Rep 67 (CA)); *OT Africa Line v Magic Sportswear* [2005] 1 Lloyds Rep 252 [40(1)], [2005] 2 Lloyds Rep 170 (CA) [63]; *Beazley v Horizon Offshore Contractors* [2005] Lloyds Rep IR 231 [39]; *Stichting Shell Pensionenfonds v Krys* [2015] AC 616 (PC) [17]; *Ecobank Transnational v Tanoh* [2016] 1 WLR 2231 (CA).

[102] *Bushby v Munday* (1821) 5 Madd 297, 56 ER 908, 913: 'Over the Court of Session in Scotland this Court has not, nor can it pretend to have, any authority whatsoever … this Court does not pretend to any interference with the other Court.' Unsurprisingly, there has never been any attempt to seek contempt-of-court remedies against a foreign court or its staff where an injunction defendant has proceeded with his foreign proceedings in breach of an anti-suit injunction, as this would be regarded as wholly inappropriate: see *Castanho v Brown & Root (UK) Ltd* [1980] 1 WLR 833, 866B–D (dealing with the case of contempt proceedings against the foreign lawyers prosecuting the injunction claim; the case of the foreign court is *a fortiori*); *Smith Kline & French Laboratories Ltd v Bloch (No 4)* [1984] ECC 352 [66].

[103] For criticism that the personal logic is an 'artifice', see C Ambrose, 'Can Anti-Suit Injunctions Survive European Community Law?' (2003) 52 ICLQ 401, 407–10, and see generally Ch 1, para 1.33.

[104] Per Lord Scarman in *British Airways Board v Laker Airways* [1985] AC 58 (HL) 95. See also *South Carolina v Assurantie Maatschappij 'De Seven Provincien'* [1987] AC 24 (HL) 40D–E; *OT Africa Line v Magic Sportswear* [2005] 1 Lloyds Rep 252 [40(1)], [2005] 2 Lloyds Rep 170 (CA) [63]; *Masri v Consolidated Contractors (No 3)* [2009] QB 503 (CA) [81]. In *Barclays Bank v Homan* [1993] BCLC 680, 687, Hoffmann J suggested that the personal logic was less 'realistic' in a case based on vexation or oppression than in a case based on a contractual right to restrain an individual litigating abroad.

of the constraints imposed on the grant of the injunction by the modern doctrine of comity.[105]

Anti-suit injunctions can be sought against third parties in certain situations. The court has power to grant an injunction to protect an English action even against persons who are not parties to the underlying English action, but are parties to the foreign action.[106] Further, in appropriate situations, it is possible for an anti-suit injunction to be granted to restrain persons who are not formally parties to litigation at all, but who will otherwise assist or procure the formal parties to pursue wrongful proceedings.[107] Thus, in a case where foreign proceedings were brought in the name of a claimant but in reality by subrogated insurers, and the court restrained the nominal claimant from pursuing his action, the court was also willing to grant an anti-suit injunction against the insurers.[108]   **3.44**

However, it would, at least in most conceivable circumstances, be inappropriate to seek to restrain the lawyers acting for the injunction defendant in a foreign jurisdiction, or to seek contempt remedies against them for assisting in breaches of an anti-suit injunction against their client. First, to move from the client to the lawyer appears to be a transgression of the personal logic of the injunction. The foreign lawyers will not themselves be bound by any exclusive forum clause; nor does it follow from the fact their client is acting vexatiously that they are doing so. They will be acting on instructions from their client, and may be bound by their professional duties to their client to pursue the litigation, often as part of their duties to their own home state court. So the injunction would in effect purport to set the English court up as judge of the foreign lawyers' duties, and their relationship to their home court. Arguably, this would come close to interfering with the foreign court itself. Second, such an injunction would be in tension with comity more generally. The foreign lawyers will not owe any allegiance to the English court, and in general comity suggests   **3.45**

---

[105] It justified the requirement of 'caution' (outside the case of contractual and perhaps quasi-contractual anti-suit injunctions) in *South Carolina v Assurantie Maatschappij 'De Seven Provincien'* [1987] AC 24 (HL) 40D–E; and in *Airbus Industrie v Patel* [1999] 1 AC 119 (HL) 138G–H, it was held that the indirect interference with the foreign court was a matter which required justification, and in particular required that the English court had a 'sufficient interest' in the matter in question.

[106] In *Arab Monetary Fund v Hashim (No 6)*, (Hoffmann J, 14 July 1992), this was not seen as a problem, although the injunction was refused on other grounds. In *Murcutt v Murcutt* [1952] P 266, 269–70, which concerned other proceedings within England, the grant of an injunction against persons not party to the suit in which the injunction was sought was viewed as 'unusual and indeed extreme'. But this is from a different era.

[107] In *OT Africa Line v Magic Sportswear* [2005] 1 Lloyds Rep 252 [37], this was justified on the basis that if there is a power to grant an injunction to restrain a wrong committed by a primary wrongdoer then it follows that there will be power to restrain a third party from procuring or assisting the primary wrongdoer so to act: *Hubbard v Woodfield* (1913) 57 SJ 729; *Acrow (Automation) v Rex Chainbelt* [1971] 1 WLR 1676 (CA). However, a simpler analysis may be that the conduct of the third party is itself vexatious and oppressive. Once the injunction has been granted against the primary injunction defendant, a similar result could be produced by contempt proceedings against a third party who aids and abets, or procures, the injunction defendant to break the injunction: *Acrow (Automation) v Rex Chainbelt* [1971] 1 WLR 1676 (CA) 1682C–E.

In *Kallang Shipping v Axa Assurances Senegal (The Kallang)* [2007] 1 Lloyds Rep 160 [41], it was held that the insurers who were 'calling the shots' and causing their insured to breach the exclusive jurisdiction clause were arguably liable to be injuncted because their conduct was tortious, and amounted to inducement of a breach of contract, or interference with business relations, or conspiracy; and see to the same effect *Kallang Shipping SA Panama v Axa Assurances Senegal (The Kallang) (No 2)* [2009] 1 Lloyds Rep 124 [90–94]; *Sotrade Denizcilik Sanayi Ve Ticaret v Amadou Lo (The Duden)* [2009] 1 Lloyds Rep 145 [65–68]. But this analysis has its difficulties, not least because it could lead to serious problems in relation to the applicable law of the tort: see *OT Africa Line v Magic Sportswear* [2005] 1 Lloyds Rep 252 [19]–[24]. In *The Kallang (No 2)* at [90] and *The Duden* at [65] the court made the pointed observation that choice of law points had not been raised. See further Ch 4, paras 4.38–4.39.

[108] *OT Africa Line v Magic Sportswear* [2005] 1 Lloyds Rep 252 [29], [37], [2005] 2 Lloyds Rep 170 (CA) [14], [41], [82].

that the court should not seek to impose its sovereign authority in respect of the conduct of persons outside the scope of its territorial jurisdiction where they owe no substantive obligation over which the English court has jurisdiction.[109] Third, injunctions against lawyers personally would trample over the veil that normally covers lawyer–client relations in most legal systems.

3.46   The sound instinctive reaction of modern English judges faced with the idea of claims of this nature has with one partial and insubstantial exception, been to reject them out of hand.[110] In the US case of *SEC v Wang and Lee*, where the US first instance court had granted anti-suit injunctions that included injunctions against the primary injunction defendant's foreign lawyers, the British Government filed a diplomatic note protesting that this was a breach of customary international law and jurisdictional principles of international comity.[111]

3.47   The one partial exception is *The Duden*, where a previous *ex tempore* decision of Morison J is recorded in the report of the judgment of Jonathan Hirst QC. It appears the injunction defendants had previously been in breach of a without notice anti-suit injunction, restraining proceedings before the courts of Senegal. Applications were made for contempt and to join the injunction defendants' French avocats (who had offices in London) as defendants. In *obiter* oral comments during the course of the earlier *ex tempore* hearing, Morison J had suggested that there were 'good grounds for joining the French solicitors who also appear to be in contempt'. But it seems that Morison J's attention was not drawn to the previous authorities. One specific feature of *The Duden* was that the French avocats had misrepresented the nature of the anti-suit injunction to the Senegalese judge by apparently suggesting in oral argument before him that 'the English court holds him in contempt'.[112] Irritating though this must have been, it is submitted that as matter of principle, foreign lawyers should be left off the playing field.

E. CONTEMPT

3.48   Breach of an anti-suit injunction is a serious matter and the courts have been willing to commit contemnors to significant sentences of imprisonment.[113]

---

[109] *MacKinnon v Donaldson Lufkin & Jenrette* [1986] Ch 482, 493-94.

[110] In *Castanho v Brown & Root* [1980] 1 WLR 833 (CA), an injunction was granted to restrain the plaintiff 'by his servants or agents' from continuing proceedings in the Texan courts; and it seems that no relief was specifically granted against the plaintiff's Texan lawyers: see 865E. Nevertheless, contempt proceedings were brought against the Texan lawyers. This was regarded as an 'absurd episode' by Shaw LJ: see 866B–D (although see the different reasoning of Lord Denning MR, based on considerations of territorial jurisdiction, at 856G–H). For a similar unwillingness to target an injunction defendant's foreign lawyers, see *Smith Kline & French Laboratories v Bloch (No 4)* [1984] ECC 352 [66].

   There is very old precedent supporting the extension of common injunctions to the lawyers of the injunction defendant, where those lawyers were within the jurisdiction: *Cotes v Freston* (1558) Choyce Cases 108, 21 ER 67, but this does not appear to have been followed. It is submitted that it is no longer of any real persuasive value, in particular in respect of foreign lawyers.

[111] See L Collins, 'Public International Law and Extraterritorial Orders' in *Essays in International Litigation and the Conflicts of Laws* (Clarendon 1994) 102–07. The US Appellate Court never had an opportunity to rule on these issues, as the case settled.

[112] *Sotrade Denizcilik Sanayi Ve Ticaret v Amadou Lo (The Duden)* [2009] 1 Lloyds Rep 145 [26]–[28].

[113] *Trafigura v Emirates General Petroleum* [2010] EWHC 3007 (3 months); *Compania Sud Americana de Vapores v Hin-Pro International Logistics* [2013] EWHC 987 (12 months, concurrent); *Mobile Telecommunications v HRH Prince Hussam Bin Saud Bin Abdulaziz Al Saud* [2018] EWHC 3749 (Comm) (12 months). On specific facts, where contempt had been purged, see *Gulf Azov Shipping v Chief Idisi (No 1)* [2001] EWCA Civ 21 (3 months).

F. DEBARRED FROM DEFENDING

In certain cases, breach of an anti-suit injunction has led the English courts to order that   **3.49**
the injunction defendant be debarred from defending the substantive litigation. This can
be done by way of the law of contempt, under which the English courts can decline to hear
a contemnor, or more usually by an unless order, debarring a defence unless the anti-suit
injunction is complied with.[114] Debarring the right to defend the merits is a drastic remedy,
but the European Court of Justice has accepted that it can, in principle, be a legitimate sanction for breach of court orders, provided it is not disproportionate.[115] But its use in relation
to anti-suit injunctions is particularly sensitive: it may be that the injunction defendant did
not comply with the anti-suit injunction because from the perspective of his own conflicts
of law rules, he was not obliged to litigate before the court granting the injunction.

---

[114] *Access Bank v Rofos Navigation* [2013] EWHC 230, [2013] EWHC 748, [2013] EWHC 3861. See in Australia, *Cocoon Data Holdings v K2M3* [2011] VSC 355.
[115] Case C-394/07, *Gambazzi v DaimlerChrysler Canada* [2009] ECR I-02563; the Milan Court of Appeal even-tually concluded that the debarring order was not disproportionate.

4

Anti-Suit Injunctions: General Principles

A. THE GENERAL PRINCIPLES

The lead judgment on the general principles applicable to anti-suit injunctions is Lord **4.01**
Goff's magisterial judgment in *Aérospatiale*,[1] which is and remains English law.

In *Deutsche v Highland*, Toulson LJ summarized the modern principles governing the grant **4.02**
of anti-suit injunctions:[2]

1. Under English law the court may restrain a defendant over whom it has personal jurisdiction from instituting or continuing proceedings in a foreign court when it is necessary in the interests of justice to do.
2. It is too narrow to say that such an injunction may be granted only on grounds of vexation or oppression, but, where a matter is justiciable in an English and a foreign court,
   the party seeking an anti-suit injunction must generally show that proceeding before the
   foreign court is or would be vexatious or oppressive.
3. The courts have refrained from attempting a comprehensive definition of vexation or
   oppression, but in order to establish that proceeding in a foreign court is or would be

---

[1] *Société Nationale Industrielle Aérospatiale v Lee Kui Jak* [1987] AC 871 (PC). However, Lord Goff's requirement that the injunction defendant must be 'amenable to the jurisdiction' (892E) has turned out to be constraint
that is at best mild, and arguably empty. The modern position is that if personal jurisdiction is obtained, the injunction defendant is *ipso facto* 'amenable'. There is no additional requirement that the injunction defendant be
'amenable' in the sense of being exposed to the court's territorially confined powers to punish: *Stichting Shell
Pensionenfonds v Krys* [2015] AC 616 (PC) [27]–[39], and paras 4.84–4.85 below.
[2] *Deutsche Bank v Highland Crusader Partners* [2010] 1 WLR 1023 (CA) [50].

vexatious or oppressive <u>on grounds of forum non conveniens, it is generally necessary to show that (a) England is clearly the more appropriate forum ('the natural forum'),</u> and (b) justice requires that the claimant in the foreign court should be restrained from proceeding there.

4. If the English court considers England to be the natural forum and can see no legitimate personal or juridical advantage in the claimant in the foreign proceedings being allowed to pursue them, it does not automatically follow that an anti-suit injunction should be granted. For that would be to overlook the important restraining influence of considerations of comity.

5. An anti-suit injunction always requires caution because by definition it involves interference with the process or potential process of a foreign court. <u>An injunction to enforce an exclusive jurisdiction clause governed by English law is not regarded as a breach of comity, because it merely requires a party to honour his contract.</u> In other cases, the principle of comity requires the court to recognise that, in deciding questions of weight to be attached to different factors, different judges operating under different legal systems with different legal polices may legitimately arrive at different answers, without occasioning a breach of customary international law or manifest injustice, and that in such circumstances it is not for an English court to arrogate to itself the decision how a foreign court should determine the matter. The stronger the connection of the foreign court with the parties and the subject matter of the dispute, the stronger the argument against intervention.

6. The prosecution of parallel proceedings in different jurisdictions is undesirable but not necessarily vexatious or oppressive.

…

8. The decision whether or not to grant an anti-suit injunction involves an exercise of discretion and the principles governing it contain an element of flexibility.

4.03 Subject to three specific points, underlined above, Toulson LJ's summary is a good exegesis of most of the general principles in non-contractual alternative forum situations. (A specific set of principles applies in contractual situations, as discussed in Chapter 7.)

But it is an inevitable by-product of the common law method, and not a matter of reproach, that summaries formulated for one case may be slanted towards the questions there in issue. So, the summary in *Deutsche* does not cover: (a) injunctions to enforce a specific legal or equitable right; (b) injunctions to protect the processes, jurisdiction, or judgments of the court; (c) single forum injunctions; and (d) 'sufficient interest'. In particular points 4–6 are focused on alternative forum situations and require adaptation in other contexts.

4.04 As to the three underlined passages:

(1) It is a misstatement, in an *obiter* passing comment, to suggest that foreign proceedings can be vexatious 'on grounds of forum non conveniens': the doctrinal breakthrough in *Aérospatiale* was to separate vexation from *forum non conveniens*. The proof of vexation is analytically different and sets a higher threshold.[3] We discuss this in section J, *Forum non Conveniens*, below.

---

[3] *Société Nationale Industrielle Aérospatiale v Lee Kui Jak* [1987] AC 871 (PC) 895–96.

(2) It has often been accepted, following Lord Goff's speech in *Aérospatiale*, that for injunctions on grounds of vexation and oppression (although not in all other contexts), it is 'generally' (but <u>not</u> always) required that England is the natural forum for the litigation. But a closer reading of *Airbus v Patel* shows that, even in that context, Lord Goff wished to move away from any requirement in general of natural forum, and replace it with the more fluid concept of 'sufficient interest'.

(3) The second underlined passage, which is also *obiter*, opens up the controversy of whether respect for comity is dispensed with in relation to contractual anti-suit injunctions. There are authorities that support such a conclusion, but as addressed in Chapter 7, it is submitted it is not right. The presence of an exclusive jurisdiction clause can reduce comity concerns, but cannot eliminate them. [4]

With some temerity, therefore, this work ventures to propose its own summary. The general principles governing the grant of an anti-suit injunction to restrain the pursuit of foreign court[5] proceedings, can be summarized as follows.[6]   **4.05**

(1) The principles for the grant or refusal of an anti-suit injunction will be determined by English law.

(2) An anti-suit injunction, like any injunction, is a discretionary remedy and will only be granted if the court considers it is appropriate to do so in all the circumstances of the case.

(3) The injunction will be granted when 'the ends of justice' require it, or in other language, when it is in 'the interests of justice' to do so.

(4) Within that general principle, an anti-suit injunction may be granted to protect a substantive legal or equitable right not to be sued abroad.[7] Where foreign proceedings are in breach of a contractual forum clause not to be sued abroad, and in analogous situations, a special set of principles applies.[8]

(5) Where no such substantive legal or equitable right exists, an anti-suit injunction will generally only be granted to restrain foreign proceedings that are or will be vexatious or oppressive, or, in language that is sometimes used, unconscionable.[9]

(6) However, injunctions may also be granted where foreign proceedings are or will be an illegitimate interference with, or where the injunction is necessary for the protection of, the processes, judgments, and/or jurisdiction of the English court. In limited circumstances injunctions may also be granted where this is necessary to protect the important public policies of the forum.

---

[4] Ch 7, para 7.19; *Ecobank Transnational v Tanoh* [2016] 1 WLR 2231 (CA).

[5] Injunctions to restrain arbitration proceedings are addressed in Ch 11.

[6] The main authorities on which this summary is based are: *Société Nationale Industrielle Aérospatiale v Lee Kui Jak* [1987] AC 871 (PC); *Barclays Bank v Homan* [1993] BCLC 680 (Hoffmann J and CA); *Airbus Industrie v Patel* [1999] 1 AC 119 (HL); *Deutsche Bank v Highland Crusader Partners* [2010] 1 WLR 1023 (CA); *Stichting Shell Pensionenfonds v Krys* [2015] AC 616 (PC); and to a lesser extent (where it has been necessary to choose) *Glencore International v Metro Trading International (No 3)* [2002] CLC 1090 (CA) [41]–[42]. Aspects of the *Glencore* summary are, however, inaccurate: see paras 4.64, 4.80 n 192, 4.81 n 200.

[7] It has been held that an anti-suit injunction may be granted to protect a 'right' to be sued only according to the system of jurisdiction contained in the Brussels–Lugano regime: *Samengo-Turner v J&H Marsh & McLennan (Services)* [2007] ILPr 52 (CA); but this is wrong: see paras 4.41–4.46 below.

[8] See Ch 7.

[9] The question of whether (5) is logically an example of (4) is discussed at paras 4.26–4.28 below and in Ch 3, section B, 'A Legal or Equitable Right?'.

(7) Since the court is concerned with the ends of justice, account must be taken not only of the injustice to the injunction claimant if the injunction defendant is allowed to pursue his proceedings, but also of the injustice to the injunction defendant if he is not allowed to do so. The legitimate interests of the injunction defendant in pursuing the proceedings abroad, or the absence of such, are relevant considerations.

(8) In exercising the power to grant an anti-suit injunction, regard must be had to the principle of comity. As a result, save where the foreign proceedings are in breach of contract, the power must be exercised with caution.

(9) It is a consequence of comity that the court must have a sufficient interest in, or connection with, the matter in question to justify the indirect interference with the foreign court that an injunction involves. In an alternative forum case, where the injunction is based on vexation or oppression, the assessment of sufficient interest will involve consideration of whether the court is the natural forum for the resolution of the substantive disputes between the parties; or (perhaps) the natural forum for the resolution of disputes as to forum. But the concept of natural forum is only ever expressed as being 'generally' a requirement, and is too narrowly framed to serve as a limiting requirement in all cases. In particular, there is no need separately to identify the natural forum in relation to injunctions sought to protect the processes, jurisdiction, and judgments of the English court, or English public policy, as the court is always the appropriate court for that purpose.

(10) The principle of comity requires the court to recognize that, in assessing what is the appropriate forum for where litigation should proceed, different judges operating under different legal systems with different legal polices may legitimately arrive at different answers, and that it may not be appropriate for an English court to arrogate to itself the decision how a foreign court should determine the matter. In order for an injunction to be legitimate, there must be good reason why the decision to stop the litigation will be made by the English judge rather than the foreign judge. The stronger the connection of the foreign court with the parties and the subject matter of the dispute, the stronger the argument against intervention.

4.06 This summary is controversial in certain respects. Notably, there have been differences, which can be personified as a debate between Lord Goff and Lord Hobhouse,[10] as to whether the root concepts of the anti-suit injunction are Lord Goff's tests of 'the ends of justice' and 'vexation or oppression' on the one hand, or 'unconscionable conduct' on the other hand.[11] In the modern case law, Lord Goff's language is the most commonly used,[12] although sometimes there is a blending of the two phrasings.

4.07 Finally, these principles are (currently, and depending on the effect of Brexit[13]) subject to the limiting effect of the Brussels–Lugano regime. This is discussed in Chapter 12, but in

---

[10] For the history of this debate, see Ch 2, paras 2.29–2.35.
[11] The summary in para 4.05 is based principally on Lord Goff's thinking, but with the addition of the concept of unconscionable conduct, as an alternative phraseology, to reflect its use as one strand of the case law. The reasons why Lord Goff's tests are preferred are set out at paras 4.56–4.64 below.
[12] *Deutsche Bank v Highland Crusader Partners* [2010] 1 WLR 1023 (CA) [50]. For recent examples see *Kemsley v Barclays Bank* [2013] EWHC 1274; *Re Tadros* [2014] EWHC 2860 [45], [71]–[84]; *Stichting Shell Pensionenfonds v Krys* [2015] AC 616 (PC).
[13] The effect of Brexit is addressed in Ch 1, section I; Ch 12, section A; and also Ch 16, section B.

broad summary, where the underlying litigation concerns matters within the scope of the Brussels–Lugano regime, an anti-suit injunction cannot be sought to restrain proceedings before the courts of another Brussels–Lugano state.

B. APPLICABLE LAW

Under the law as it stands, the court will determine whether a non-contractual anti-suit injunction should be granted according to its own concepts of equity.[14] '[T]he injustice which can justify an anti-suit injunction must inevitably be judged according to English concepts of justice.'[15] Similarly, where the proper law of a forum clause is English law, the grant or refusal of an anti-suit injunction to enforce it will be governed by English principles.[16]   **4.08**

The current position on applicable law is clear. But it has been reached with little exploration of the principles of private international law. It has also not been tested in the context of the European choice of law rules put in place by the Rome II Regulation. The effect of that Regulation needs to be considered, since it seems likely that the Rome I and Rome II Regulations will, at least in substance, continue to occupy the field of most of English choice of law rules irrespective of how Brexit falls out (see Ch 1, section I, 'Brexit').   **4.09**

The assumption that non-contractual anti-suit injunctions should always be governed by English law appears to derive in large part from the traditional English conflicts analysis of equity, under which the existence and enforcement of equitable rights and powers was a matter for the *lex fori*.[17] But even before the Rome II Regulation, this had begun to be overtaken by the application of choice of law principles to the existence of substantive equitable rights and wrongs.[18]   **4.10**

The analysis of applicable law is dependent on the juridical foundations of the injunction: if the anti-suit injunction is viewed, in non-contractual cases, as founded upon a substantive equitable right, it becomes more difficult to avoid a choice of law analysis, and less easy to apply the *lex fori*.   **4.11**

Yet a choice of law analysis poses a potentially existential threat to English law on non-contractual anti-suit injunctions. It is by no means guaranteed that the European Court   **4.12**

---

[14] *Carron Iron v Maclaren* (1855) 10 ER 961, 5 HLC 416, 437; *British Airways Board v Laker Airways* [1985] AC 58 (HL) 81D; *Midland Bank v Laker Airways* [1986] QB 689 (CA) 701H–702A; *Barclays Bank v Homan* [1993] BCLC 680 (Hoffmann J) 687–88; quoted with approval in *Simon Engineering v Butte Mining (No 1)* [1996] 1 Lloyds Rep 104, 107. In general, English principles of equity have been assumed to apply without discussion. It has never been suggested in the case law that foreign law should apply. For the equitable nature of the anti-suit injunction, see Ch 3, section A, 'The Power to Grant Injunctions'.

[15] *Barclays Bank v Homan* [1993] BCLC 680 (Hoffmann J) 687–88.

[16] See Ch 7, section D, 'Choice of Law'.

[17] *Lord Cranstown v Johnston* (1796) 3 Ves Jun 170, 30 ER 952, 958–59; *In re Courtney, Ex parte Pollard* (1838–40) Mont & C 239, 250–51; *Carron Iron v Maclaren* (1855) 10 ER 961, 5 HLC 416, 437; *Re Anchor Line (Henderson Bros)* [1937] Ch 483, 488; RH Graveson, 'Choice of Jurisdiction and Choice of Law in the English Conflict of Laws' (1951) 28 BYBIL 273, 277; see also *El Ajou v Dollar Land Holdings* [1993] 3 All ER 717, 736, reversed on other grounds [1994] 2 All ER 685 (CA). This is the approach still taken today in Australia: *Paramasivam v Flynn* (1998-99) 160 ALR 203, 214–18 (Aus Fed Ct) [2001] NSWSC 29 [100]–[104] ('arguable' that this is the position).

[18] See *Macmillan v Bishopsgate Investment Trust (No 3)* [1995] 1 WLR 978, 989D, [1996] 1 WLR 387 (CA) 402D–E (disapproving of the *lex fori* approach taken in Australia and Canada) 407C, 408A; *Base Metal Trading v Shamurin* [2004] ILPr 5 [43]–[44] (reversed, but not on this point, [2005] 1 WLR 1157 (CA)); *Oil Company Yugraneft v Abramovich* [2008] EWHC 2613 [170]–[223].

of Justice (ECJ) would interpret (or would have interpreted) the Rome II Regulation so that English law could apply to anti-suit injunctions. But application of the law of the place where the targeted proceedings are brought could neuter anti-suit injunctions. The foreign legal system would be likely to treat the proceedings before its own courts as not contrary to any legal obligation in many cases where the English courts would regard foreign proceedings as vexatious and oppressive,[19] and perhaps in most cases where it really mattered.

1. The Rome II Regulation

4.13   The Rome II Regulation is part of English conflicts law for now. It applies to choice of law for 'non-contractual obligations in civil and commercial matters' (Art 1(1)). The concept of 'non-contractual obligations' will not be confined to tortious obligations: it will probably cover equitable obligations analogous to tort claims, such as claims for dishonest assistance in a breach of trust.[20] However, under Article 1(3) there is an exception for 'evidence and procedure'. The concept of 'procedure' is an autonomous European concept,[21] although its application may be influenced by the national law landscape. If a non-contractual matter falls outside Rome II, it will be governed by the English rules of the conflicts of laws.

4.14   For obligations within the scope of the Regulation, the primary[22] default choice of rule in Article 4 for a 'non-contractual obligation arising out of a tort/delict' is 'the law of the country where the damage occurs', which refers to where the *direct* and not the *indirect* damage occurs.[23] But the default rules can be displaced if 'the tort/delict is manifestly more closely connected' to another country. Further, under Article 15, 'the scope of the law applicable to non-contractual obligations under this Regulation shall govern … (d) within the limits of powers conferred on the court by its procedural law, the measures which a court may take to prevent or terminate injury or damage . . .', which is generally understood to cover injunctions.[24]

4.15   Given the potential awkwardness of applying Article 4, the English courts are likely to strive to avoid the conclusion that the choice of law rules in Rome II apply.[25] There are various ways in which this could be achieved. One is to analyse the anti-suit as not derived from an underlying non-contractual obligation, and as a procedural remedy granted under statute to enforce the court's perception of what procedurally is in the interests of justice, or to protect its own jurisdiction.[26] Another is to view any such equitable obligation as outside the scope of 'non-contractual obligation' in Rome II, not being the sort of conventional civil right or obligation *inter partes* to which that Regulation is directed: it is not an obvious

---

[19]   *OT Africa Line v Magic Sportswear* [2005] 1 Lloyds Rep 252 [19]–[25] and para 4.38 below.
[20]   L Collins et al (eds), *Dicey, Morris and Collins on the Conflict of Laws* (15th edn, Sweet & Maxwell 2012), paras 34-083–34-090 (hereafter 'Dicey').
[21]   *Actavis UK v Eli Lilly* [2016] RPC 2 (CA) [133]. See also the Commission Proposal for Rome II, 24.
[22]   Article 4(2) creates a default rule where both parties are resident in the same country.
[23]   Rome II, Recital 17; Commission Proposal on Rome II, 11; Dicey, para 35-024.
[24]   *Actavis UK v Eli Lilly* [2016] RPC 2 (CA) [143]. So far as concerns Article 15(c), which covers: 'the existence, the nature and the assessment of damage or the remedy claimed', this applies only to financial remedies, as explained in *Actavis* at [142].
[25]   Arguments for the application of foreign law are presented by C Sim, 'Choice of Law and Anti-Suit Injunctions: Relocating' (2013) 63 ICLQ 703.
[26]   See A Dickinson, 'The Rome II Regulation' (2008), para 4.111.

'tort/delict' within Article 4, but none of the other specific heads of Rome II apply.[27] However, if an anti-suit is viewed as based on an underlying equitable obligation, then the more concrete substance that is accorded to such an obligation, the more delicate these analyses become. From a European perspective, a substantive equitable obligation, which makes it a civil wrong to litigate vexatiously, might look rather like an obligation in tort/delict that should fall within 'non-contractual obligation'. If so, Article 15(d) suggests the law applicable to the substance of injunctive 'measures' to prevent damage arising from breach of such an obligation should be governed by the law applicable to such obligation.

If Rome II applies, the current English case law on the Brussels–Lugano regime suggests **4.16** that Article 4(1) may point to the law of the country of the targeted court, on the basis that the direct damage will occur where the 'wrongful' litigation will go ahead.[28] It might be argued that the damage would occur in England, where the injunction interferes with the jurisdiction of the English court, or with English litigation, but the contrary argument would be that these are indirect consequences, not the direct damage; and such logic would be more difficult to apply to some single forum injunctions.[29] If Article 4(1) were to point to the country of the targeted litigation, then for English law to apply, it would be necessary to show that the 'tort/delict' was 'manifestly more closely connected' to England.[30] The English court would be tempted to conclude that an anti-suit injunction to enforce its own ideas of justice would be manifestly most closely connected to England. When viewing the injunction as a remedy granted to enforce the English court's ideas of procedural justice, or to protect its own jurisdiction, or to prevent English litigation being vexatiously duplicated, the connections to England are strong. Yet the connections to the state where the targeted litigation would otherwise go ahead are real; so, it is not guaranteed that the ECJ would agree they are manifestly outweighed by the connections to England—although an English court is likely to regard this as *acte clair*. We return, also, to the question of whether there is an underlying right, as the connections to England will be more intimate if the injunction is viewed as essentially procedural or protective of the English jurisdiction.[31]

2. The Application of Residual English Principles

If anti-suit injunctions fall outside the scope of the Rome II Regulation (or if the Regulation **4.17** ceases to be part of English conflicts law), it is very likely that the English courts will continue to treat English law as applicable to the grant of anti-suit injunctions. In particular, if the anti-suit were to regarded as procedural for the purposes of Rome II, it would inevitably

---

[27] In *Committeri v Club Méditerranée* [2018] EWCA Civ 1889 [30]–[32], the Court of Appeal said, *obiter*, that anything that was not contractual would be non-contractual and within Rome II. It is submitted that this is wrong as a general statement; and the Court of Appeal was not considering the point now in issue. The European Court's judgment in *Ergo Insurance v IF P&C Insurance* [2016] ILPr 20 [44]–[46] indicates that Rome II applies only to certain non-contractual obligations, namely 'obligations ensuing from damage, that is to say, any consequence arising out of tort/delict, unjust enrichment, '*negotiorum gestio*' or '*culpa in contrahendo*'.

[28] See *OT Africa Line v Magic Sportswear* [2005] 1 Lloyds Rep 252 [19]–[21]; *AMT Futures v Marzillier* [2015] QB 699 (CA) [50]–[54].

[29] See A Dickinson, *The Rome II Regulation* (OUP 2008) para 4.109.

[30] See by analogy C-133/08, *Intercontainer Interfrigo v Balkenende Oosthuizen* [2010] QB 411 [63]–[64]; C-305/13, *Haeger Schmidt v MMA IARD* [2015] QB 319 [49].

[31] This shows that the choice of law analysis is more difficult for single forum injunctions than alternative forum injunctions. See Ch 3, para 3.28.

also be regarded as procedural under English common law conflicts of laws rules, and so governed by the *lex fori*.[32] If it fell outside the Rome II Regulation for other reasons, the same result would be likely to apply, although there are various ways in which this could be justified, the choice of which will interconnect with the question of whether there is an underlying substantive right. It may be, for example, that the anti-suit injunction would be regarded as a *sui generis* emanation of the English court's perception of procedural justice, which can only be governed by the *lex fori*, and to which the tendency to approach equitable obligations by means of choice of law rules should not apply.[33]

4.18   The English courts will wish to apply English law but it remains to be seen whether the European Court would accept this, if the point were ever referred. Yet the debate will be shaped by the extent to which the anti-suit injunction is based upon an underlying right; and this may in turn drive the English court's analysis of the juridical underpinnings of the injunction towards a more procedural analysis.[34]

C. A DISCRETIONARY REMEDY GOVERNED BY PRINCIPLE

4.19   The court's powers to grant a final anti-suit injunction will in most cases derive from section 37(1) of the Senior Courts Act 1981,[35] under which the court may grant an injunction if it is 'just and convenient' to do so.

4.20   Although the statutory wording of section 37(1) is in broad terms, the court will not exercise its power to grant an anti-suit injunction merely because it considers it 'just and convenient' to do so in abstract. The exercise of the court's discretion is governed by a set of principles and tests developed in the case law by the courts, which can preclude the grant of an injunction which might otherwise be thought intuitively to be just or convenient.[36]

---

[32] Under English conflicts of laws rules, matters of procedure are questions for the *lex fori*. The English law concept of 'procedure' includes all matters of 'remedy', and is broader than the European concept. See Private International Law (Miscellaneous Provisions) Act 1995, s 14(3); *Huber v Steiner* (1835) 2 Bing NC 202, 135 ER 80, 83 ('so much of the law as affects the remedy only, all that relates to the "ad litis decisionem", is taken from the "lex fori" of the country where that action is brought'); *Don v Lippmann* (1837) 5 Cl & Fin 1, 7 ER 303, 307; *Baschet v London Illustrated Standard* [1900] 1 Ch 73, 78; *Boys v Chaplin* [1971] AC 356 (HL) 378G–379A, 394C–F; *Olex Focas v Skodexport* [1998] 3 VR 380, 395; *Konamaneni v Rolls Royce* [2002] 1 WLR 1269 [45]–[50]; *Harding v Wealands* [2007] 2 AC 1 (HL) [24]–[31], [55], [66]–[67].

[33] *Midland Bank v Laker Airways* [1986] QB 689 (CA) 701H–702A: 'Since the jurisdiction to grant such injunctions is an English jurisdiction, the question whether it is unconscionable that Laker Airways should be allowed to pursue the plaintiff banks in a United States antitrust suit must be decided by the criteria of English law ...'.

[34] The question of whether from a purely domestic perspective it is possible to dispense with an underlying equitable right, is discussed in Ch 3, section B, 'A Legal or Equitable Right?'. It is submitted that it is.
The question of applicable law for anti-suit injunctions also connects to the contentious issue of claims for damages in equity for vexatious litigation abroad (independent of any specific concrete equity). Such a damages claim would appear to require the sort of substantive equity, in respect of which the case for applying Rome II, and the law of the targeted country, is stronger: which may illustrate why it is not clear that such a general damages right is sound. See Ch 14, section B, 'Non-Contractual Damages'.

[35] See Ch 3, section A, 'The Power to Grant Injunctions'.

[36] *Société Nationale Industrielle Aérospatiale v Lee Kui Jak* [1987] AC 871 (PC) 892A–F; *Donohue v Armco* [2002] 1 Lloyds Rep 425 (HL) [19], [23], [53]; see also *Turner v Grovit* [2002] 1 WLR 107 (HL) 116G–H; *Deutsche Bank v Highland Crusader Partners* [2010] 1 WLR 1023 (CA) [50], [65]. Although *Fourie v Le Roux* [2007] 1 WLR 320 (HL) has removed the rigid restrictions on the court's *powers* to grant injunctions under s 37(1), it has not abolished the principles, based on the case law, which guide the exercise of the court's discretion: see [3], [6], [45], [48]. Thus, the question whether the foreign proceedings are vexatious and oppressive is not a mere aspect of discretion but a question of evaluative judgment with a right answer, and so is readily open to examination on appeal: *Star Reefers Pool v JFC Group* [2012] 1 Lloyds Rep 376 (CA) [2].

Nevertheless, the injunction always remains a discretionary remedy. Even if the normal prin- **4.21**
ciples and tests for the grant of an anti-suit injunction are satisfied, relief can be always refused
as a matter of discretion.[37] In exercising its discretion, the court will take account of all relevant
facts which can affect whether or not it would be just or convenient, or unjust or inconvenient
to grant the remedy. Types of factual circumstances which can be of particular relevance to
discretion are discussed in section N, 'Other Discretionary Considerations' below.

D. THE ENDS OF JUSTICE

The power to grant an anti-suit injunction is to be exercised when the 'ends of justice' require **4.22**
it. The phrase 'in the interests of justice to do so' is sometimes used instead.[38] It makes no
difference. What justice requires must be judged according to English notions of justice.[39]

This test, propounded in modern times by Lord Goff, connects the modern law to the equit- **4.23**
able history of the remedy. The Court of Chancery would grant an injunction to restrain
foreign proceedings when 'the ends of justice' required it.[40] However, the flexibility of the
concept permits some liberties to be taken with history. It would not now be appropriate
to restrain foreign proceedings simply on the ground that under English principles of equity there would be a substantive equitable defence to which the foreign court might not
give effect.[41] Consequently, the use of the equitable notion of 'the ends of justice' does not
mean that an injunction will be granted in the same situations where the Court of Chancery
would have granted an injunction before the Judicature Act.[42] Instead, the phrase directs

---

[37] *Donohue v Armco* [2002] 1 Lloyds Rep 425 (HL) [24]; *Stichting Shell Pensionenfonds v Krys* [2015] AC 616
(PC) [41].
[38] *Bushby v Munday* (1821) 5 Madd 297, 56 ER 908, at 913; *Carron Iron v Maclaren* (1855) 5 HLC 416 (HL)
10 ER 961, 970; *Bank of Tokyo Ltd v Karoon* [1987] AC 45 (CA) 59, per Goff LJ ('whenever justice demands');
South Carolina Insurance v Assurantie Maatschappij 'De Seven Provincien' NV [1987] AC 24 (HL) 44H, per Lord
Goff, in the minority ('in the interests of justice'); *Société Nationale Industrielle Aérospatiale v Lee Kui Jak* [1987]
1 AC 871 (PC) 892A–B, per Lord Goff; *Airbus Industrie v Patel* [1999] 1 AC 119 (HL) 133C–D, 140B, per Lord
Goff; *Credit Suisse First Boston (Europe) v MLC Bermuda* [1999] 1 Lloyds Rep 767, 780–81 ('in the interests of
justice'); *Youell v Kara Mara Shipping* [2000] 2 Lloyds Rep 102, 113 [43] (although the analysis is controversial
on other points); *Donohue v Armco* [2002] 1 Lloyds Rep 425 (HL) [19], [45], [53]; *Glencore International v Metro
Trading International (No 3)* [2002] CLC 1090 (CA) [42]–[43]; *Cadre v Astra Asigurari* [2006] 1 Lloyds Rep 560
[6]; *Deutsche Bank v Highland Crusader Partners* [2010] 1 WLR 1023 (CA) [50], [60], [101] (both phrases used);
Star Reefers Pool v JFC Group [2012] 1 Lloyds Rep 376 (CA) [26]; *Petter v EMC* [2016] ILPr 3 (CA) [33], [48] (both
phrases used); *Stichting Shell Pensionenfonds v Krys* [2015] AC 616 (PC) [50] (a recent use of 'the ends of justice');
Ardila Investments v ENRC [2015] EWHC 1667 [56]–[57].
[39] *Barclays Bank v Homan* [1993] BCLC 680 (Hoffmann J), 687; quoted with approval in *Simon Engineering v
Butte Mining (No 2)* [1996] 1 Lloyds Rep 104, 107. Similarly, the concept of oppression must be judged by English
standards: *Omega Group Holdings v Kozeny* [2002] CLC 132. This approach is inextricable from the conclusion
that English law is the applicable law (discussed in section B, 'Applicable Law'; and see in particular para 4.08).
[40] Ch 2, para 2.03.
[41] *Barclays Bank v Homan* [1993] BCLC 680 (Hoffmann J), 686–87, contrary to the comments of Lord
Diplock in *British Airways Board v Laker Airways* [1985] AC 58 (HL) 81, which are not consistent with the
modern statements of the tests derived from *Aérospatiale* and have not been followed in modern case law. See
further para 4.30 below.
[42] The modern power is exercised in circumstances both broader and narrower than it was historically. The
Court of Chancery would, at least in the early years of the nineteenth century, restrain foreign proceedings merely
on the ground that England was a more convenient forum, but this is not the modern law, as it would 'disregard
the fundamental requirement that an injunction will only be granted where the ends of justice so require': *Société
Nationale Industrielle Aérospatiale v Lee Kui Jak* [1987] AC 871 (PC) 895G–H (see Ch 2, paras 2.03, 2.10, 2.26–
2.27). On the other hand, under the old law there was a reluctance to grant an injunction to restrain proceedings
brought by a foreigner before his own courts, if he had not voluntarily participated in the English process: *Carron
Iron v Maclaren* (1855) 5 HLC 416, 10 ER 961 (HL); *Maclaren v Stainton* (1855) 26 LJ (NS) 332, 333; *Re Distin*

the attention of the court to what justice demands in terms of the appropriate shape and location of future litigation.[43]

4.24   In principle, if 'the ends of justice' require it, an injunction may be granted without the need to satisfy any other criterion.[44] However, in the modern case law, the ends of justice are generally given concrete form through intermediate concepts, such as vexation or oppression, or illegitimate interference with the processes, jurisdiction, or judgments of the English court.[45]

4.25   The requirements of the 'ends of justice' also shape and direct, and in many cases subsume, the court's exercise of its discretion.[46] Thus, injunctions will be refused if the grant of relief would cause injustice to the injunction defendant that would outweigh the injustice to the injunction claimant if the remedy were refused.[47]

E. A LEGAL OR EQUITABLE RIGHT

4.26   An anti-suit injunction may be granted where the foreign proceedings infringe a relevant substantive legal or equitable right.[48]

4.27   The question of whether there is a general substantive equitable right not to be affected by litigation contrary to the interests of justice has been explored in Chapter 3, where it was concluded that the question is uncertain, but that in principle such a right could be dispensed with.[49] If a general substantive equitable right does exist, then all anti-suit injunctions are granted to enforce an equitable or legal right.

(1871) 24 LT 197; *Re Chapman* (1873) LR 15 Eq 75; *Ellerman Lines v Read* [1928] 2 KB 144 (CA) 152–53, 154–55 (see Ch 2, paras 2.11–2.12). But there is no such rigidity today, provided that the English court has a sufficient interest in the matter. However, the foreign domicile of the injunction defendant, and any lack of submission to the jurisdiction of the English courts, will be matters to be taken into account in the assessment of what comity requires: see *Cadre v Astra Asigurari* [2006] 1 Lloyds Rep 560; *Star Reefers Pool v JFC Group* [2012] 1 Lloyds Rep 376 (CA) [30]; *Stichting Shell Pensionenfonds v Krys* [2015] AC 616 (PC).

[43]   *Société Nationale Industrielle Aérospatiale v Lee Kui Jak* [1987] AC 871 (PC) 894F–G, 896F–H; *Donohue v Armco* [2002] 1 Lloyds Rep 425 (HL) 431. See eg *Du Pont de Nemours v Agnew* [1988] 2 Lloyds Rep 240 (CA) 245.

[44]   *Société Nationale Industrielle Aérospatiale v Lee Kui Jak* [1987] AC 871 (PC) 892A–C, 893E; *Stichting Shell Pensionenfonds v Krys* [2015] AC 616 (PC). In the Canadian case of *Amchem Products v British Colombia (Workers Compensation Board)* [1993] 1 SCR 897 (Can SC) 910, 932–33, Sopinka J held that a formulation based on the broad concept of injustice was to be preferred, without reference to vexation and oppression, which he considered to be vague and undefined terms. This does not reflect English law: *Bouygues Offshore v Caspian Shipping (No 2)* [1997] 2 Lloyds Rep 485, 490.

[45]   *Société Nationale Industrielle Aérospatiale v Lee Kui Jak* [1987] AC 871 (PC) 892A–894G, 902F–G. In *Turner v Grovit* [2002] 1 WLR 107 (HL) 117E–F, Lord Hobhouse thought that 'the basic principle of justice' could *only* be a background justificatory concept, but it is submitted that this is not the law.

[46]   *The Eras Eil Actions* [1995] 1 Lloyds Rep 64, 86; *Bouygues Offshore v Caspian Shipping (No 2)* [1997] 2 Lloyds Rep 485, 491–92; *Bouygues Offshore v Caspian Shipping (No 3)* [1997] 2 Lloyds Rep 493, 502–06; *Stichting Shell Pensionenfonds v Krys* [2015] AC 616 (PC) [41].

[47]   *Société Nationale Industrielle Aérospatiale v Lee Kui Jak* [1987] AC 871 (PC) 896G–H. See eg *The Eras Eil Actions* [1995] 1 Lloyds Rep 64, 84; *Bouygues Offshore v Caspian Shipping (No 2)* [1997] 2 Lloyds Rep 485, 491–92; *Bouygues Offshore v Caspian Shipping (No 3)* [1997] 2 Lloyds Rep 493, 502–06; *Bloch v Bloch* [2003] 1 FLR 1 [95]. See section K, 'Legitimate and Illegitimate Advantages' below.

[48]   *British Airways Board v Laker Airways* [1985] AC 58 (HL) 81C; *South Carolina Insurance Co v Assurantie Maatschappij 'De Seven Provincien'* [1987] AC 24 (HL) 40D; *Glencore International v Metro Trading International (No 3)* [2002] CLC 1090 (CA) [42]; *AES Ust-Kamenogorsk Hydropower Plant LLP v Ust-Kamenogorsk Hydropower Plant JSC* [2013] 1 WLR 1889 (SC) [20]; *Stichting Shell Pensionenfonds v Krys* [2015] AC 616 (PC) [22], [23], [25].

[49]   See Ch 3, section B, 'A Legal or Equitable Right?'.

There is a limited set of specific substantive rights not to be subjected to litigation elsewhere **4.28** in particular circumstances, which have an independent juridical basis. They include contractual rights, some tortious rights, and some substantive equitable rights.

1. Substantive Contractual Rights

Contractual rights not to be sued in particular locations, or at all, can be created by exclusive **4.29** forum clauses, arbitration clauses, and similar clauses.[50] Where these exist, the shape of the discretion to grant an injunction is transformed. The courts will, in general, restrain foreign proceedings in breach of contract unless there are strong reasons not to do so, and it is not necessary to show that the targeted proceedings are vexatious, or oppressive, or an interference with the process of the English courts.

2. Specific Equitable Rights

Before the Judicature Acts, the Court of Chancery would restrain proceedings before **4.30** the common law courts by means of the 'common injunction', where there was a risk that equitable defences would not be given effect by the common law courts. In the early development of the anti-suit injunction, the same principles were initially applied to foreign proceedings.[51] However, in modern times there has been no case where an injunction has been granted to restrain foreign proceedings merely on the grounds that the foreign court might reach a different decision to English principles of equity, and despite some comments to the contrary by Lord Diplock,[52] it is clear this is not a sufficient ground on which to interfere with foreign proceedings,[53] as it would be inconsistent with comity.

In order to be capable of supporting an anti-suit injunction, the substantive equitable right **4.31** in question must create obligations that apply to the conduct and location of litigation. In *Shell v Krys* the Privy Council made clear that the fair distribution of assets in insolvency was protected by an equitable right which would be breached by foreign proceedings aimed at producing an unbalanced distribution.[54] Another important example of such an equity is the third-party 'quasi-contractual' situation, where the injunction claimant has an equitable right to enforce a contractual exclusive forum clause against a party who is not bound by that obligation at common law.[55] Other forms of relevant substantive equity are also possible.[56] For example, if the grounds of complaint in the foreign action were based on information relied on in breach of a confidence owed in England, an injunction might lie

---

[50] Discussed in Chs 7 and 8.
[51] See generally Ch 2, paras 2.03–2.08, 2.29–2.31.
[52] *British Airways Board v Laker Airways* [1985] AC 58 (HL) 81C–F, discussed at 2.29–2.31.
[53] See the comments of Hoffmann J in *Barclays Bank v Homan* [1993] BCLC 680, 686–87.
[54] *Stichting Shell Pensionenfonds v Krys* [2015] AC 616 (PC) [18]–[25].
[55] *Shipowners' Mutual Protection and Indemnity Association (Luxembourg) v Containerships Denizcilik Nakliyat Ve Ticaret (The Yusuf Cepnioglu)* [2016] 1 Lloyds Rep 641 (CA) [33]. See Ch 10, section C, 'An Obligation Not to Sue Elsewhere?'.
[56] See the discussion of US law in G Bermann, 'The Use of Anti-Suit Injunctions in International Litigation' (1990) 28 Columbia J Transnl Law 589, 620–22.

to restrain the use of the confidential information, which would be similar in effect to an anti-suit injunction.[57]

3. Rights and Wrongs in Tort

4.32   It seems unlikely, with the possible but limited exception of claims for procurement of a breach of a jurisdiction clause, that tort obligations will provide a useful general basis for general, non-contractual anti-suit injunctions in respect of foreign proceedings. This is for three reasons. First, the existing torts under English law are confined, and not natural foundations for this purpose. Second, it is uncertain whether these torts should apply to litigation abroad. Third, there may be of choice of law difficulties.

4.33   With respect to tortious causes of action, two English law torts need to be considered: malicious prosecution, and the alleged tort of abuse of civil process.

4.34   The Supreme Court has recently decided in its controversial 5–4 decision in *Willers v Joyce* that there is a general tort of the malicious prosecution of civil proceedings, which is not confined to limited categories of proceedings.[58] However, to complete this cause of action, the criticized proceedings must have been brought maliciously, that is without a *bona fide* reason to bring the proceedings, and without reasonable and probable cause.[59] In respect of proceedings on the merits, they must have failed,[60] although this requirement does not generally apply to *ex parte* applications, arrests, or attachments.[61] The limited and old authorities that suggest this tort can apply to foreign litigation impose the same restrictions.[62]

4.35   There is authority to support the existence of a tort of abuse of civil process, under which it would be wrongful to use legal proceedings towards an improper end.[63] In *Land Securities v Fladgate Fielder* the Court of Appeal concluded that this tort did not extend to civil proceedings generally and was confined only to limited situations, which would not extend beyond the scope of the tort of malicious prosecution.[64] But in the light of *Willers v Joyce* it seems likely that this tort will be expanded to cover civil proceedings generally.[65]

---

[57]   Similarly, if a party were to seek to use, in foreign proceedings, documents which he had obtained in disclosure in English proceedings, in breach of the implied undertaking to the English court, it is likely that the court would restrain him from doing so by injunction: see *Bourns v Raychem (No 3)* [1999] FSR 641 [11], [15]–[20], [55] (Laddie J), 679–82 (CA); *Bourns v Raychem (No 4)* [2000] FSR 841, 845–46 (referring to earlier unreported judgments). In the USA, see *Omnium Lyonnais D'Etanchéité et Revêtement Asphalte v Dow Chemical*, 441 F Sup 1385 (CD Cal 1977) (where a French judgment was obtained by the use of discovery documents in breach of a US court order; and the claimants in France were restrained from enforcing the French judgment).

[58]   *Willers v Joyce* [2018] AC 779 (SC); following *Crawford Adjusters (Cayman) v Sagicor General Insurance (Cayman)* [2014] AC 366 (PC); and departing from *Gregory v Portsmouth City Council* [2000] 1 AC 419 (HL).

[59]   *Martin v Watson* [1996] AC 74 (HL) 80; *Willers v Joyce* [2018] AC 779 (SC) [56], [85]–[86].

[60]   *Castrique v Behrens* (1861) 3 El & El 709, 121 ER 608, 613; *Parton v Hill* (1864) 10 LT 414; *Basebé v Matthews* (1867) LR 2 CP 684; *Bynoe v Governor and Company of the Bank of England* [1902] 1 KB 467; *Everett v Ribbands* [1952] 2 QB 198 (CA).

[61]   *Congentra v Sixteen Thirteen Marine (The Nicholas M)* [2008] 2 Lloyds Rep 602 [38]–[44].

[62]   *Castrique v Behrens* (1861) 3 El & El 707, 121 ER 608, 613; *Taylor v Ford* (1873) 29 LT 392. See para 4.37 below.

[63]   *Grainger v Hill* (1838) 4 Bing (NC) 212, 132 ER 769, 773–74; *Parton v Hill* (1864) 10 LT 414; *Goldsmith v Sperrings* [1977] 1 WLR 478 (CA) 489H, 498; *Speed Seal Products Ltd v Paddington* [1985] 1 WLR 1327 (CA); *Metall und Rohstoff v Donaldson, Lufkin & Jenrette* [1990] 1 QB 391 (CA) 469–70; *Crawford Adjusters (Cayman) v Sagicor General Insurance (Cayman)* [2014] AC 366 (PC) [62]–[66] [79], [149]–[158].

[64]   *Land Securities v Fladgate Fielder* [2010] Ch 467 (CA); See also *De Medina v Grove* (1847) 10 QB 172, 116 ER 67; *Powell v Hoyland* (1851) 6 Exch 67, 155 ER 456, 459; *Digital Equipment Ltd v Darkcrest* [1984] Ch 512, 522–24.

[65]   In *Willers v Joyce* [2018] AC 779 (SC), the two torts were seen as difficult to distinguish: see at [25], although the scope of the tort of abuse of civil process was not decided. In *Crawford Adjusters (Cayman) v Sagicor General*

The scope of these rights in tort is far narrower than the scope of the general case law on   **4.36**
anti-suit injunction. Anti-suit injunctions can, and generally are granted where foreign proceedings are neither malicious nor motivated by a collateral purpose. It follows that such
tortious rights are not likely to be generally capable of supporting non-contractual anti-suit
injunctions; and they would be an awkward and unsatisfactory basis for the injunction even
within their scope.

It is also questionable whether such English tort law principles make sense as a basis to sup-   **4.37**
port anti-suit injunctions in respect of litigation abroad. It may well be that as a matter of
English law, torts of this kind should naturally be confined to litigation in England. There
are two old authorities which appear to proceed on the assumption that such English law
causes of action apply in relation to foreign proceedings, but in both cases the claim in tort
was rejected on the ground that the foreign proceedings had succeeded not failed, and that
just as in respect of English proceedings, it was necessary to prove the failure of the criticized proceedings. [66] But it does not appear to have been argued that the tort could not
in principle apply to foreign proceedings.[67] The point has not been considered in modern
times, and the torts of malicious prosecution and abuse of civil proceedings have never been
applied to anti-suit injunctions against foreign proceedings.[68] Instead, anti-suit injunctions
to restrain foreign proceedings have been granted on equitable bases and subject to their
own principles without regard to such torts.

There would be significant choice of law barriers to applying English law to such alleged   **4.38**
torts abroad. In contrast to the position in relation to equitable anti-suit injunctions, tort
claims of this kind would fall within the scope of the Rome II Regulation (so long as it remains the law). Applying Article 4(1) of Rome II Regulation, the current case law on the
application of the correlate concept 'the place where the damage occurred' would suggest
that the place where the direct damage occurred was the state where the allegedly malicious
or abusive litigation occurred.[69] It is also uncertain whether such torts could be viewed as
'manifestly more closely connected' to English law under Article 4(3). They concern malicious or abusive acts in the foreign jurisdiction causing damage there.[70] As discussed,
there are tenable arguments that the equitable jurisdiction to grant anti-suit injunctions is
most closely connected to England, because it is concerned (in general) with protection of
English litigation or policies. But, in contrast, these torts are not concerned with whether

---

Insurance (Cayman) [2014] AC 366 (PC) [62], [75], Lord Wilson JSC saw the two torts as marching together; and
they were conflated in *Gregory v Portsmouth City Council* [2000] 1 AC 419 (HL). See also *Congentra v Sixteen
Thirteen Marine (The Nicholas M)* [2008] 2 Lloyds Rep 602 [21]–[23], holding before *Willers v Joyce* that the limited
circumstances so far identified on the case law were capable of incremental expansion. However, it may be necessary for a further appeal to proceed up the judicial tree before all the precedents are rationalized.

[66] *Castrique v Behrens* (1861) 3 El & El 707, 121 ER 608, 613; *Taylor v Ford* (1873) 29 LT 392.
[67] This was argued in *British Airways Board v Laker Airways* [1985] AC 58 (HL) 65E–F. There was no express
decision on the point, but the House of Lords ignored tort as a basis for the anti-suit injunction.
[68] In some domestic cases, the tort of abuse of civil process has been considered as an additional possible basis
for the injunction: *Jacey (Printers) v Norton & Wright Group* [1977] FSR 475, 479; *Essex Electric v IPC Computers
(UK)* [1991] FSR 690, 699–701. See further Ch 6, paras 6.09–6.10.
[69] *OT Africa Line v Magic Sportswear* [2005] 1 Lloyds Rep 252 [19]–[21]; *AMT Futures v Marzillier* [2015] QB
699 (CA) [50]–[54].
[70] *Congentra v Sixteen Thirteen Marine (The Nicholas M)* [2008] 2 Lloyds Rep 602 [18] (applicable law of attachment proceedings is the law of the country of attachment).

the foreign litigation was intrinsically wrongful. It will only be in rare cases that litigation before foreign courts will be tortious under the foreign law.[71]

4.39   The only situation where the courts have, so far, given credence to the grant of anti-suit injunctions based on tort (leaving aside domestic injunctions) are the limited cases where the tort of inducing a breach of contract, and other economic torts, have been deployed against a third party who controls a party to a contractual forum clause and has directed the contracting party to breach its contractual obligations.[72] It is possible that such claims will be stymied by the application of choice of law principles.[73] However, there is a stronger case for the application of English law than in the case of the torts of malicious prosecution and abuse of civil process. In particular, it would be arguable that a claim for inducing a breach of a contractual forum clause would, under Article 4(3) of the Rome II Regulation, be 'manifestly more closely connected' to the contractual forum than the place of the wrongful litigation because the centre of gravity of the issue would be dominated by the contract.[74]

4.40   But in any event, it is not necessary to deploy tortious claims in order to achieve the objective of preventing third parties from procuring breaches of contractual forum clauses, as this can be achieved by other methods.[75] Anti-suit injunctions based on conventional equitable principles are capable of achieving this without difficulty, and it seems an unnecessary complication to impose an additional layer of tortious jurisprudence onto the question of whether an injunction should be granted.[76] The true relevance of the tort of procuring a breach of contract may be to whether damages claims should also be available.[77]

4. Injunctions to Enforce the Brussels–Lugano Regime?

4.41   The Brussels–Lugano regime (so long as it continues to apply) creates a closed system of jurisdiction, limiting the circumstances in which a defendant can be sued outside the state of his domicile. This system has been described as giving 'rights' to defendants not to be sued

---

[71]   *OT Africa Line v Magic Sportswear* [2005] 1 Lloyds Rep 252 [19]–[24].

[72]   *Kallang Shipping v Axa Assurances Senegal (The Kallang)* [2007] 1 Lloyds Rep 160 [41]; *Kallang Shipping Panama v Axa Assurances Senegal (The Kallang) (No 2)* [2009] 1 Lloyds Rep 124, [90]–[94]; *Sotrade Denizcilik Sanayi Ve Ticaret v Amadou Lo (The Duden)* [2009] 1 Lloyds Rep 145 [65]–[68]. A tort claim was also advanced in *Schiffahrtgesellschaft Detlev von Appen v Voest Alpine Intertrading (The Jay Bola)* [1997] 1 Lloyds Rep 179, 183; and Morison J thought a tort claim for damages would be a preferable way to resolve the problem in *Horn Linie v Panamericana Formas e Impresos (The Hornbay)* [2006] 2 Lloyds Rep 44 [26]. However, cf *OT Africa Line v Magic Sportswear* [2005] 1 Lloyds Rep 252 [19]–[24].

[73]   *OT Africa Line v Magic Sportswear* [2005] 1 Lloyds Rep 252 [19]–[24]. Choice of law problems were not addressed in *The Jay Bola, The Hornbay* or *The Kallang (No 1)* (see n 72). In *The Kallang (No 2)* and *The Duden,* English law was applied but the judge observed neither party had argued that Senegalese law should apply.

[74]   Article 4(3) makes clear that 'A manifestly closer connection with another country might be based in particular on a pre-existing relationship between the parties, such as a contract, that is closely connected with the tort/delict in question.'

[75]   The third party's conduct in procuring the contracting party's proceedings could be viewed as vexatious and oppressive. In addition, it has been held that if there is a power to grant an injunction to restrain a wrong committed by a primary wrongdoer, then it follows that there will be power to restrain a third party from procuring or assisting the primary wrongdoer so to act: *Hubbard v Woodfield* (1913) 57 SJ 729; *Acrow (Automation) v Rex Chainbelt* [1971] 1 WLR 1676 (CA); *OT Africa Line v Magic Sportswear* [2005] 1 Lloyds Rep 252 [37].

[76]   So, in *Kallang Shipping v Axa Assurances Senegal (The Kallang)* [2007] 1 Lloyds Rep 160 [36]–[37], the injunction was assessed by reference to principles of vexation, even though the underlying claims for damages included tortious claims for inducement.

[77]   As in *Kallang Shipping Panama v Axa Assurances Senegal (The Kallang) (No 2)* [2009] 1 Lloyds Rep 124 [90]–[94]; *Sotrade Denizcilik Sanayi Ve Ticaret v Amadou Lo (The Duden)* [2009] 1 Lloyds Rep 145 [65]–[68].

outside the defined jurisdictions.[78] Yet this is a misleading turn of phrase. The Brussels–Lugano regime allocates jurisdiction between courts as a matter of what may be called 'public' law; it does not create private rights.[79] Until recently, it was also clear that any such 'rights' were not sufficient to support an anti-suit injunction. In *The Eras Eil Actions*, Potter J rejected the conclusion that an anti-suit injunction to restrain proceedings in the USA could be founded on a 'right' to be sued only according to the rules of the Brussels–Lugano regime.[80]

However, in *Samengo-Turner v Marsh & Maclennan* the Court of Appeal concluded that where a freely agreed exclusive jurisdiction clause in favour of the courts of the USA conflicted with the mandatory jurisdiction regime for employees contained in section 5 of the Brussels I Regulation, the employee had a 'right' only to be sued according to the terms of section 5, and an anti-suit injunction would be granted to enforce that right and to restrain proceedings in the contractually agreed forum.[81]   **4.42**

This was a surprising decision, [82] and David Steel J had refused an injunction at first instance. The Court of Appeal appears to have been misled by its mistaken view that the Brussels–Lugano regime granted *rights* to the employee.[83] Further, even if the Brussels–Lugano regime creates 'rights' of some sort, it does not regulate the appropriateness of the commencement of proceedings in the USA in any way; and the 'rights' it might create are not the sort of rights that can support an anti-suit injunction.[84] The Court of Appeal reasoned that, once they had concluded that the US exclusive jurisdiction clause would not be given effect in England, it followed that an injunction should be granted, in order to   **4.43**

---

[78] *Samengo-Turner v J&H Marsh & McLennan (Services)* [2008] ICR 18 (CA) [23], [35], [43]. This language of rights was not adopted in *Petter v EMC* [2016] ILPr 3 (CA), discussed in paras 4.44-4.45 below. An argument that Article 2 of the Brussels–Lugano regime gave a defendant a 'statutory right' to be sued in the state of his domicile was not decided in *General Motors v Royal & Sun Alliance Insurance* [2007] 2 CLC 507 [46].

[79] In *The Eras Eil Actions* [1995] 1 Lloyds Rep 64, 74–76, Potter J observed:

> I incline to the view, as submitted for the foreign plaintiffs, that it is not helpful to categorize commencement of suit in a jurisdiction other than that laid down by the Convention as the invasion of a 'right' of the defendant in the traditional sense accorded to that term as a foundation for the grant of injunctive relief.

This is consistent with the analysis adopted by the ECJ. In C-281/02, *Owusu v Jackson* [2005] ECR I-1383 [40]–[42], the language of rights was not used. See T Raphael, 'Do as You Would be Done By? System-Transcendent Justification and Anti-Suit Injunctions' [2016] LMCLQ 256.

[80] *The Eras Eil Actions* [1995] 1 Lloyds Rep 64, 74–76. The decision was in part based on the conclusion, derived from *Re Harrods (Buenos Aires)* [1992] Ch 72 (CA), that the Brussels–Lugano regime did not affect the jurisdictional relationships of the contracting states outside the Brussels–Lugano zone, which is no longer good law since Case C-281/02, *Owusu v Jackson* [2005] ECR I-1383; but the remainder of the reasoning is sound. See also *Evialis v SIAT* [2003] 2 Lloyds Rep 377 [139(ii)]. In *Ultisol Transport Contractors v Bouygues Offshore* [1996] 2 Lloyds Rep 140, 146–48, Clarke J also concluded that Article 17 of the Brussels Convention (now Art 25 of the Recast) did not support an anti-suit injunction to restrain proceedings in South Africa, although the reasoning there was largely based on the now discredited approach in *Re Harrods*.

[81] *Samengo-Turner v J&H Marsh & McLennan (Services)* [2008] ICR 18 (CA) [38]–[44].

[82] The decision is criticized by academic writers. Professor Adrian Briggs, in 'Who is Bound by the Brussels Regulation?' [2007] LMCLQ 433, describes it as a 'calamity' and argues that it was decided *per incuriam*; see also A Briggs, *Agreements on Jurisdiction and Choice of Law* (OUP 2008), paras 3.46–3.47. Forceful criticism is found in A. Dickinson, 'Resurgence of the Anti-Suit Injunction: The Brussels I Regulation as a Source of Civil Obligations?' (2008) 57 ICLQ 465. L Merrett, *Employment Contracts in Private International Law* (OUP 2011), paras 9.36–9.39, is uncommitted.

[83] *The Eras Eil Actions* [1995] 1 Lloyds Rep 64 appears not to have been cited.

[84] *Evialis v SIAT* [2003] 2 Lloyds Rep 377 [139(ii)] (also not cited to the Court of Appeal in *Samengo-Turner*). In *Turner v Grovit* [2000] QB 345 (CA) 364E, the Court of Appeal optimistically concluded that the grant of an anti-suit injunction would 'underpin and support the proper application of the Brussels Convention'; but the ECJ most definitely did not agree: Case C-159/02, *Turner v Grovit* [2004] ECR I-3565.

protect the 'right' of the employee to be sued at his domicile: 'doing nothing is not an option'. This is a *non sequitur*. It has been clear since the rejection of the *Castanho* heresy[85] in *Aérospatiale* that it is not sufficient to justify an anti-suit injunction to conclude that a parallel English action should not be stayed.[86] The proceedings in the USA were not said to be vexatious or oppressive, and the injunction defendants had a contractual right to proceed there. Consequently, there was no sufficient basis for the grant of an anti-suit injunction; and by intervening by injunction merely to protect a mandatory rule of domestic jurisdictional law, the Court of Appeal paid insufficient respect to comity.

4.44   Such a dramatic arrogation of jurisdiction was not going to go away quietly. In *Petter v EMC* a similar injunction was sought. Yet again, at first instance the commercial judge, Cooke J, distinguished *Samengo-Turner* and refused an injunction as a matter of comity and discretion.[87] The Court of Appeal held that they were bound by *Samengo-Turner* to grant an injunction.[88] But their reasoning differed. Of the two commercial judges, Moore-Bick LJ simply applied precedent, while Vos LJ held that he was bound by precedent, but doubted the soundness of the injunction. In contrast, Sales LJ (a public and employment lawyer in a previous life) advanced a sophisticated argument in favour of the solution in *Samengo-Turner*. He relied on the previous case law under which injunctions could be granted to prevent the litigant's evasion of the important public policies of the forum (discussed in section I, 'Protection of English Public Policy', below), and concluded that the Brussels–Lugano regime's protections for employees reflected a public policy which the English court was bound to protect. Since that policy could only be given effect by an anti-suit injunction, there was 'considerable force' in the proposition that one should be granted. Party autonomy, and freedom of contract, was not the only value worthy of respect, and could be overridden. However, Sales LJ did not seek to defend the reasoning in *Samengo-Turner*, which relied on a supposed legal right derived from the Brussels–Lugano regime.[89] Permission to appeal was granted but the case settled before the hearing in the Supreme Court.

4.45   It is submitted that Sales LJ's reasoning based on public policy is unsound,[90] and that he gave insufficient attention to comity. As a matter of comity, the public policy behind the European mandatory rules, whose force is questionable, may well not justify the interference with the foreign court which the anti-suit injunction creates, and to suggest that it warrants interfering by injunction with the contractually agreed jurisdiction of another country is surprising. Further, relying on public policy on its own as sufficient to justify an anti-suit injunction is a bold step which could pose serious questions of comity, and the case law so far has only envisaged this in cases where the foreign court is being asked to exercise an exorbitantly wide jurisdiction.[91] But there was no attempt in *Petter* to consider the

---

[85] For the *Castanho* heresy, see Ch 2, section D, '*Forum non Conveniens* and the *Castanho* Heresy'; para 4.72 and n 165.

[86] See section J, '*Forum non Conveniens*' below.

[87] *Petter v EMC* [2015] EWHC 1498.

[88] *Petter v EMC* [2016] ILPr 3 (CA) (27 July 2015).

[89] Moore-Bick LJ did refer to the idea of such a right, but applied it as a matter of precedent, not principle. It appears not to have been argued that the Brussels–Lugano regime did not create relevant rights: see [29], [31].

[90] For a fuller exploration, see T Raphael, 'Do as You Would be Done By? System-Transcendent Justification and Anti-Suit Injunctions' [2016] LMCLQ 256.

[91] In *Barclays Bank v Homan* [1993] BCLC 680, 687–88, Hoffmann J said:

    a theme common to certain recent decisions is that the foreign court is, judged by its own jurisprudence, likely to assert a jurisdiction so wide either as to persons or subject-matter that to English notions it

proper scope of the use of public policy in itself as a ground for an anti-suit injunction, and it is not obvious why the jurisdiction asserted by the US court, pursuant to a freely agreed jurisdiction clause, was in any way exorbitant.

The adamant protection of English, or European, mandatory rules in *Samengo-Turner* and **4.46** *Petter*, and their use to override contractually agreed jurisdictional clauses, is difficult to reconcile with the converse line of decisions in which the English courts have justified the grant of anti-suit injunctions to enforce exclusive forum clauses in order to override comparable foreign mandatory laws,[92] on the basis that it was consistent with comity, or indeed demanded by comity, for the courts to enforce the parties' agreement. Indeed, from an international perspective, it may well be the English courts that have acted exorbitantly in *Petter*, not the US courts. It is no accident that the English anti-suit injunction led to the unhappy position of clashing anti-suit injunctions issued by both legal systems.[93]

F. VEXATIOUS OR OPPRESSIVE CONDUCT

Where no substantive legal or equitable right is infringed, an anti-suit injunction will gen- **4.47** erally only be granted where the foreign proceedings are vexatious or oppressive,[94] or in alternative language that is sometimes used, unconscionable.[95] But the concept of 'the ends of

> appears contrary to accepted principles of international law. In such cases the English court has sometimes felt it necessary to intervene by injunction to protect a party from the injustice of having to litigate in a jurisdiction with which he had little, if any, connection, or in relation to subject-matter which had insufficient contact with that jurisdiction, or both. Since the foreign court is *per hypothesi* likely to accept jurisdiction, this is a decision which has to be made here if it is to be made at all. These are cases in which the judicial or legislative policies of England and the foreign court are so at variance that comity is overridden by the need to protect British national interests <u>or</u> prevent what it regards as a violation of the principles of customary international law [Emphasis added to 'or'—these ideas are alternative].

This was adopted in *Stichting Shell Pensioenfonds v Krys* [2015] AC 616 (PC) [2015] 1 AC 616 [42]. See also *Airbus Industrie v Patel* [1999] 1 AC 119 (HL) 137–138; *Deutsche Bank v Highland Crusader Partners* [2010] 1 WLR 1023 (CA) [56]. The circumstances in which it may be legitimate to rely on public policy as a freestanding ground to support anti-suit injunctions are discussed in more detail in section I, 'Protection of English Public Policy' below.

In the quotation, Hoffmann J used, as one of his parameters, the concept of whether the foreign court's assumption of jurisdiction was in violation of 'customary international law'. But on closer analysis this may be an inaccurate metaphor. Customary public international law on the exercise of prescriptive civil jurisdiction does not, at present, have any very clearly defined content, or at the least its content is contested. A conventional view is that it states a broad discretion within parameters of 'reasonableness', but this is not very helpful. (See *Barcelona Traction (Belgium v Spain)* [1970] ICJ Rep 3 [70–72], Individual Opinion of Sir Gerald Fitzmaurice; AW Lowenfeld, 'International Litigation and the Quest for Reasonableness' Part I (1994) 245 Recueil des Cours 83, 94, 120–22; J Crawford, *Brownlie's Principles of Public International Law* (8th edn, OUP 2012) (hereafter 'Brownlie') 471–76.) Yet a conflicts rule can be exorbitant, and capable of criticism from an international perspective, even if it is not something that could be a breach of a clearly defined rule of public international law. Further, requiring national courts to identify rules of customary international law in this context would be demanding. So as a controlling concept the notion of customary international law would be difficult to apply. It would be better to frame this parameter, when asking whether it is justified to grant an anti-suit injunction by reference to public policy, in terms of whether the foreign court's jurisdiction would be exorbitant, from a non-parochial private international law perspective, which is what the courts probably had in mind. The yardstick of 'exorbitant' is commonly used in such internationally minded assessments (eg Brownlie, 472). In *Midland Bank v Laker* [1986] 1 QB 689 (CA) and *Airbus v Patel* [1999] 1 AC 119 (HL) the Court of Appeal and House of Lords asked whether the foreign court's exercise of jurisdiction was in fact exorbitant or consistent with comity, without reference to specific rules of customary international law.

---

[92] *Akai v People's Insurance* [1998] 1 Lloyds Rep 90 (criticized by the Australian courts in *The Comandate* [2008] 1 Lloyds Rep 119 [252]); *OT Africa Line v Magic Sportswear* [2005] 2 Lloyds Rep 170 (CA).
[93] *Petter v EMC* [2015] EWCA Civ 828 (second judgment, of 31 July 2015).
[94] *Société Nationale Industrielle Aérospatiale v Lee Kui Jak* [1987] AC 871 (PC) 896F–G; *Airbus Industrie v Patel* [1999] 1 AC 119 (HL) 133C; *Donohue v Armco* [2002] 1 Lloyds Rep 25 (HL) 431 [19]; *Deutsche Bank v Highland Crusader Partners* [2010] 1 WLR 1023 (CA) [50].
[95] For the concept of unconscionable conduct, see section G, 'Unconscionable Conduct' below.

justice' is not rigidly confined, and there are other situations for the grant of an injunction:[96] the main examples being where it is necessary to grant the injunction to protect the jurisdiction, processes, or judgments of the English courts, or to protect English public policy.[97]

4.48   It is sufficient that the foreign proceedings are either vexatious *or* oppressive. It is not necessary to show that they are vexatious *and* oppressive.[98] The criteria of vexation or oppression are the most important grounds on which a non-contractual anti-suit injunction may be granted.[99]

4.49   However, a finding of vexation or oppression is not a sufficient condition for the grant of an injunction. The injunction must always serve 'the ends of justice', and is in any event a discretionary remedy. The requirements of comity, or the conduct of the injunction claimant, can mean that even vexatious or oppressive foreign proceedings should not be restrained.[100]

4.50   The concepts of vexation or oppression should not be restricted by definition.[101] However, certain typical forms of vexation can be identified. Fact patterns in which findings of vexation or oppression may be made are explored in Chapter 5. Vexation can be subjective, such as where proceedings are motivated by bad faith or collateral harassment; but it can also be objective, and arise from the nature or effects of the criticized proceedings, while oppression is objective.[102]

4.51   In case law at the end of the nineteenth century, and the beginning of the twentieth century, the concept of vexation was restricted to foreign proceedings which were frivolous or pointless,[103] or brought *mala fide* with the intention of harassing the defendant,[104] or bound to fail;[105] and in contrast, proceedings which could give substantial actual benefit to the

---

[96]   *Stichting Shell Pensionenfonds v Krys* [2015] AC 616 (PC) [18]. In *Royal Bank of Canada v Cooperatieve Centrale Raiffeisen-Boerenleenbank* [2004] 1 Lloyds Rep 471 (CA) 475, Evans-Lombe J accepted the unchallenged proposition that, outside breach of contract cases, the court could *only* intervene where the pursuit of foreign proceedings would be vexatious and oppressive, but this is not the law: *Deutsche Bank v Highland Crusader Partners* [2010] 1 WLR 1023 (CA) [50].

[97]   See sections H, 'Interference with the Jurisdiction of the English Court' and and I, 'Protection of English Public Policy' below.

[98]   *Société Nationale Industrielle Aérospatiale v Lee Kui Jak* [1987] AC 871 (PC) 893–94, 899F; see also in Scotland *FMC v Russell* (1999) SLT 99 (Ct of Sess) 102.

[99]   *Société Nationale Industrielle Aérospatiale v Lee Kui Jak* [1987] AC 871 (PC) 893E.

[100]   *Barclays Bank v Homan* [1993] BCLC 680, 685–86; *Vitol Bahrain v Nasdec Trading* [2013] EWHC 3359 [41].

[101]   *Société Nationale Industrielle Aérospatiale v Lee Kui Jak* [1987] AC 871 (PC) 893F–G; *Elektrim v Vivendi Holdings 1* [2009] 1 Lloyds Rep 59 (CA) [83].

[102]   See Ch 5, paras 5.06–5.07.

[103]   See *Carron Iron v Maclaren* (1855) 5 HLC 416 (HL) 10 ER 961, 970–71, where it was accepted that foreign proceedings that were 'unnecessary and therefore vexatious' could be restrained; *Cohen v Rothfield* [1919] 1 KB 410 (CA) 414–15. See also in the modern case law, *Midland Bank v Laker Airways* [1986] QB 689 (CA) 700E–F; *Shell International Petroleum v Coral Oil (No 2)* [1999] 2 Lloyds Rep 606, 609.

[104]   This remains an element of the modern case law: 'vexatious harassment' has been viewed as a ground for the injunction: *Glencore International v Metro Trading International (No 3)* [2002] CLC 1090 (CA) [69], where an injunction was granted to restrain 'a strategy of harassment and vexation, designed to wear down Glencore by making it as difficult and expensive as possible for it to bear the burden of litigation on several fronts'; *Cadre v Astra Asigurari* [2006] 1 Lloyds Rep 560 [18]; *Star Reefers Pool v JFC Group* [2012] 1 Lloyds Rep 376 (CA) [30].

[105]   The modern case law on when the alleged weakness of the foreign claims can be relevant to vexation is discussed in more detail at Ch 5, paras 5.26–5.27. The exact approach is still developing. For reasons of comity, the courts are reticent to grant injunctions on this ground alone, as the foreign court may be the appropriate court to assess weakness under its own law. But vexation has been found on this basis where it is 'plain' that the foreign proceedings are 'bound to fail': *British Airways Board v Laker Airways* [1985] AC 58 (HL) 65; *Midland Bank v Laker Airways* [1986] QB 689 (CA) 700; *Shell International Petroleum Ltd v Coral Oil (No 2)* [1999] 2 Lloyds Rep 606, 609, although such cases are 'likely to be rare': *Star Reefers Pool v JFC Group* [2012] 1 Lloyds Rep 376 (CA) [31].

claimant abroad, and were brought in good faith, were considered not to be vexatious, and would not be restrained by injunction.[106]

However, the modern concept of vexation has expanded to allow that foreign proceedings may be vexatious, even where they bring substantial benefit to the claimant abroad, if the purposes sought to be achieved by the foreign proceedings are illegitimate.[107]   **4.52**

Further, foreign proceedings of substantial benefit to the claimant abroad can be so oppressive as to justify an injunction, if they would involve injustice to the injunction claimant.[108] But in order to justify an injunction, alleged oppression must go beyond mere inconvenience to the injunction claimant, and must include some element of injustice.[109]   **4.53**

Perhaps the most common example of oppression is where the injunction defendant has initially participated in the English litigation and now seeks a second bite of the cherry elsewhere.[110] Another example of possible oppression is where related third-party proceedings should, in the interests of justice, be heard together with the main proceedings, and this is possible in the natural forum but impossible in the foreign forum.[111] Foreign proceedings can also be made oppressive if the jurisdiction asserted by the foreign court would be excessive.[112] But simply choosing to ignore the English forum, not to submit to the English action, and to litigate in another forum in which legal advantages are available, is not in itself oppressive.[113]   **4.54**

The modern purpose of the concepts of vexation and oppression is to set a high threshold for the grant of an anti-suit injunction,[114] and to discourage the court from granting the potentially exorbitant remedy of an injunction whenever it might seem at first sight 'just and convenient' to do so. From this perspective, the criteria of vexation or oppression are part of the defences of comity.   **4.55**

G. UNCONSCIONABLE CONDUCT

In *Turner v Grovit*, Lord Hobhouse contended that the primary test for the grant of an anti-suit injunction is whether the injunction defendant's conduct is 'unconscionable'.[115]   **4.56**

---

[106] *McHenry v Lewis* (1882) 22 Ch D 397 (CA) 402–03; *Peruvian Guano v Bockwoldt* (1883) 23 Ch D 225, 230 (both stay cases); *Hyman v Helm* (1883) 24 Ch D 531 (CA) 538, 544; *Cohen v Rothfield* [1919] 1 KB 410 (CA) 414 (per Scrutton LJ; it is to be noted, however, that Eve J appears to have taken a broader approach). See Ch 2, paras 2.17–2.21.
[107] *Société Nationale Industrielle Aérospatiale v Lee Kui Jak* [1987] AC 871 (PC) 893–94. In *Star Reefers Pool v JFC Group* [2012] 1 Lloyds Rep 376 (CA) [36–37] the court envisaged that invocation of a legal advantage available under the foreign legal system's rules would be vexatious if it was 'hopelessly and cynically invoked'.
[108] *Société Nationale Industrielle Aérospatiale v Lee Kui Jak* [1987] AC 871 (PC) 894G, 902F.
[109] See *Arab Monetary Fund v Hashim (No 6)* (Hoffmann J, 14 July 1992): 'the court must be satisfied that the foreign proceedings are vexatious or oppressive in a sense which is likely to result in injustice'; *Deutsche Bank v Highland Crusader Partners* [2010] 1 WLR 1023 (CA) [50(3)].
[110] *Star Reefers Pool Inc v JFC Group Ltd* [2012] 1 Lloyds Rep 376 (CA) [32], [37]–[38].
[111] *Société Nationale Industrielle Aérospatiale v Lee Kui Jak* [1987] AC 871 (PC) 896G. Other examples of duplicative foreign proceedings that can amount to vexation and oppression are explored in Ch 5, section B, 'Alternative Forum Cases'.
[112] *Barclays Bank v Homan* [1993] BCLC 680 (Hoffmann J), 686, 688, and per Leggatt LJ at 702.
[113] *Star Reefers Pool v JFC Group* [2012] 1 Lloyds Rep 376 (CA) [36]–[39].
[114] *Société Nationale Industrielle Aérospatiale v Lee Kui Jak* [1987] AC 871 (PC) 896F–G.
[115] *Turner v Grovit* [2002] 1 WLR 107 (HL) 117C–F.

The notion of unconscionable conduct is a synonym for conduct that is 'contrary to equity and good conscience'.[116]

4.57   The introduction of this alternative phraseology has caused difficulties in the statement of the test. The simplest approach would have been to stick with Lord Goff's concepts of 'the ends of justice' and 'vexation or oppression' as formulated in *Aérospatiale*. This has been the approach taken in the subsequent House of Lords, Supreme Court, and Privy Council cases that have considered the test.[117] The influential summary of the law by the Court of Appeal in *Deutsche v Highland* essentially restated Lord Goff's tests, without use of unconscionable conduct.[118] Lord Hobhouse's speech in *Turner v Grovit* was itself *obiter*, and although it did pick up the language used in the earlier decisions in *British Airways v Laker* and *South Carolina*,[119] those decisions were regarded as superseded by *Aérospatiale* by the House of Lords in *Donohue v Armco*.[120] The balance of the recent Court of Appeal decisions also tends in favour of Lord Goff's language,[121] which was used in the Privy Council's recent decision in *Shell v Krys*,[122] and this is the tendency in the recent first instance case law.[123] It is therefore arguable that Lord Goff's tests should be viewed as established as being the law as a matter of precedent.

4.58   It is suggested that the language of 'the ends of justice' is also to be preferred as a matter of principle. Using unconscionability as the primary test brings with it the danger of excessive closeness to the historical equitable legacy of the common injunction.[124] It is also arguably a legal fiction. In many cases where anti-suit injunctions are granted, there is no real sense in which the injunction defendant's *conscience* is or should be engaged. 'Unconscionable conduct' fits particularly poorly as a way to describe situations where the injunction is granted to protect the jurisdiction of the English court, or English public policy. Further, the language of 'the ends of justice', or 'vexation and oppression' is a more appropriate way to frame

---

[116] The phrase used by Lord Cranworth LC in *Carron Iron v Maclaren* (1855) 5 HLC 416, 10 ER 961 (HL) 971, although elsewhere he referred to 'the ends of justice': at 970.

[117] The history of the competing tests is discussed in Ch 2, sections E–F. It is submitted that Lord Goff's tests have been established as the law, without reference to unconscionable conduct, through the adoption of Lord Goff's speech in *Société Nationale Industrielle Aérospatiale v Lee Kui Jak* [1987] AC 871 (PC) 891–97 by the House of Lords in *Airbus Industrie GIE v Patel* [1998] 1 AC 119 (HL) 133C–F (*obiter*) and *Donohue v Armco* [2002] 1 Lloyds Rep 425 (HL) [19], [45], [53] (*ratio*). The Privy Council also adopted *Aérospatiale* in *Stichting Shell Pensionenfonds v Krys* [2015] AC 616 (PC) [17]–[25].

[118] *Deutsche Bank v Highland Crusader Partners* [2010] 1 WLR 1023 (CA) [50]–[53].

[119] *British Airways Board v Laker Airways* [1985] AC 58, 81D–F; *South Carolina Insurance v Assurantie Maatschappij 'De Seven Provincien'* [1987] AC 24 (HL) 40D.

[120] *Donohue v Armco* [2002] 1 Lloyds Rep 425 (HL) [19], referring to the 'development of principle'; and see Ch 2, sections E–F.

[121] In *Deutsche Bank v Highland Crusader Partners* [2010] 1 WLR 1023 (CA) [50], of course, the *Aérospatiale* tests were used, and the same occurred in *Elektrim v Vivendi Holdings 1* [2009] 1 Lloyds Rep 59 (CA) [82]–[85]. The recent decision in *Michael Wilson v Emmott* [2018] 1 Lloyds Rep 299 (CA) [37]–[40] followed *Aérospatiale*. In *Masri v Consolidated Contractors (No 3)* [2009] QB 503 (CA) [39], [41], [44], [48], [95], Lawrence Collins LJ referred to both ways of stating the law without deciding between them. Further, the 'synthetic' cases like *Glencore International v Metro Trading International (No 3)* [2002] CLC 1090 (CA) (discussed at paras 4.60–4.65 below) represent a shift to a middle position seeking to combine *Turner v Grovit* and *Aérospatiale*.

[122] *Stichting Shell Pensionenfonds v Krys* [2015] AC 616 (PC) [18]–[23].

[123] For recent first instance decisions using the *Aérospatiale* tests or the *Deutsche v Highland* summary, see *Morris v Davies* [2011] EWHC 1272 [16]; *Re Tadros (Deceased)* [2014] EWHC 2860 [73]; *Dawnus Sierra Leone v Timis Mining Corporation* [2016] EWHC 236 [61]; *Team Y&R Holdings Hong Kong Limited v Ghossoub* [2017] EWHC 2401 [41]; *The Owners of the Ship 'Al Khattiya' v The Owners and/or Demise Charterers of the Ship 'Jag Laadki'* [2018] EWHC 389 [107]–[111].

[124] As illustrated by Lord Diplock's speech in *British Airways Board v Laker Airways* [1985] AC 58 (HL) 81D–F; see the comments of Hoffmann J in *Barclays Bank v Homan* [1993] BCC 680, 686–87.

those cases where features of the foreign litigation warrant the imposition of an injunction. The greater suitability of Lord Goff's tests is illustrated by the fact that in a number of cases where the concept of unconscionable conduct has been formally applied, it has merely served as a redundant, higher-level conceptual shell for the application of the underlying test of vexatious or oppressive behaviour.[125]

In addition, although Lord Hobhouse articulated the notion of 'unconscionable conduct' to **4.59** focus attention on the 'wrongful conduct of the individual',[126] it is submitted that this risks oversimplification. Anti-suit injunctions are not merely a matter of private law, but also inescapably involve public interests, because of the tensions with comity that they produce. Locating the concept of the 'ends of justice' at the heart of the relevant test compels the court to address not merely the conduct of the injunction defendant, but also the ends of justice as a whole.[127]

However, following *Turner v Grovit*, the concept of unconscionable conduct found its way **4.60** into a number of summaries of the law advanced in the Court of Appeal, sometimes as a substitute test, or sometimes as a synthetic test blended together with Lord Goff's concepts, in which unconscionable conduct stands either in the place of 'the ends of justice' or more commonly as an intermediary concept underneath 'the ends of justice', but sitting above and including 'vexation or oppression' and protection of the jurisdiction of the court.[128] This synthesis appears to have been driven by a desire to meld the two strands of the case law, although it is submitted that they are not capable of full reconciliation, but differ, at least in abstract. Yet it appears to have occurred without argument to the contrary, and in particular without it being contended that the *Aérospatiale* language was to be preferred.

---

[125] See eg *Glencore International v Metro Trading International (No 3)* [2002] CLC 1090 (CA) [65]–[70]; *Tonicstar v American Home Insurance* [2005] Lloyds Rep IR 32, 36–38; *Masri v Consolidated Contractors (No 3)* [2009] QB 503 (CA) [95]; *Star Reefers Pool v JFC Group* [2012] 1 Lloyds Rep 376 (CA) [2], [24], [31], [32].

[126] *Turner v Grovit* [2002] 1 WLR 107 (HL), 117E [24]. It can be suggested that, at least in part, the heavy emphasis put on wrongful conduct by Lord Hobhouse should be understood as a rhetorical effort to persuade the ECJ that the injunction operated *in personam* only, and did not therefore interfere with the jurisdiction of the courts of other member states of the Brussels–Lugano zone (his attempt was unsuccessful: see Case C-159/02, *Turner v Grovit* [2004] ECR I-3565, discussed at Ch 12, section B, 'The Collision'). Lord Hobhouse's focus on the wrongful conduct of the injunction defendant also led to his speech misstating the law in a number of other respects: see nn 45, 164, 166, 183, 192, 200.

[127] The corresponding analysis in the first edition of this work, supporting Lord Goff's approach, was agreed with by Choo Han Teck J in the High Court of Singapore in *AQN v AQO* [2015] 2 SLR 523 [24]–[26]. The discrepancy between Lord Hobhouse's analysis and the previous case law was also observed by A Briggs, 'Decisions of British Courts during 2001: Private International Law' (2001) BYBIL 437, 438.

[128] *Glencore International v Metro Trading International (No 3)* [2002] CLC 1090 (CA) [41]–[42] (Rix LJ); *Sabah Shipyard (Pakistan) v Islamic Republic of Pakistan* [2003] 2 Lloyds Rep 571 (CA) [38]–[39]; *Royal Bank of Canada v Cooperative Centrale Raiffeisen-Boerenleenbank* [2003] EWHC 2913 [29], [2004] 1 Lloyds Rep 471 (CA) [8] (per Evans Lombe J, although Mance LJ's approach at [36]–[39] in substance followed Lord Goff's approach; Thorpe LJ agreed with both [51]); and *Seismic Shipping v Total E&P UK* [2005] 2 Lloyds Rep 359 (CA) [44]–[45], where Evans-Lombe J's summary in *Raiffeisen* was applied, on the (incorrect) assumption that it reflected the point of view of the whole Court of Appeal in *Raiffeisen*. In *OT Africa Line v Magic Sportswear* [2005] 2 Lloyds Rep 170 (CA) [63]–[64], the 'synthetic' approach was again put forward by Rix LJ, but Longmore LJ preferred Lord Goff's approach: at [31]–[32].

However, since around 2005 and in particular since *Deutsche v Highland* in 2010 the bulk of the case law shows a move back towards the *Aérospatiale* concepts and away from this 'synthetic' approach and *Turner v Grovit*. The cases on this are set out in nn 117, 121, and 123 above.

One partial exception to that movement is *Star Reefers Pool v JFC Group* [2012] 1 Lloyds Rep 376 (CA) [26]–[27], where both the *Deutsche* and the *Glencore* summaries were used (by Rix LJ). In addition, in *Ahmed v Mustafa* [2015] 1 FLR 139 (CA) [12]–[15] a version of the 'unconscionable conduct' test was applied, but without argument to the contrary.

4.61   The most commonly cited summary of this kind comes from the judgment of Rix LJ in *Glencore v Metro*, where he summarized the essential test as being:

> … jurisprudence has limited the conditions under which such an injunction may be regarded as 'just and convenient'. The following conditions are necessary. First, the threatened conduct must be 'unconscionable'. It is only such conduct which founds the right, legal or equitable but here equitable, for the protection of which an injunction can be granted. What is unconscionable cannot and should not be defined exhaustively, but it includes conduct which is 'oppressive or vexatious or which interferes with the due process of the court' [per Lord Brandon of Oakbrook, South Carolina at 41D]. The underlying principle is one of justice in support of the 'ends of justice' [per Lord Goff of Chieveley, Société Aérospatiale at 892A, 893F]. It is analogous to 'abuse of process'; it is related to matters which should affect a person's conscience [per Lord Hobhouse of Woodborough, *Turner v Grovit* at para 24].[129]

4.62   Separately, some of the case law, including a passing comment of the House of Lords in *Airbus v Patel,* has suggested that the concept of 'unconscionable conduct' may be the test in respect of 'single forum' injunctions, even if it is not appropriate elsewhere.[130] In part this is historical accident; the single forum cases just happened to be ones in which the concept of unconscionable conduct was used.[131] It also reflects the debate, discussed elsewhere,[132] about whether the anti-suit injunction is based on an underlying legal or equitable right. One possible solution to that debate, reflected currently in the Court of Appeal's decision in *Masri v Consolidated Contractors (No 3)*, is that while alternative forum injunctions need not enforce an underlying substantive equitable right, single forum injunctions may depend on such a right, and accordingly Lawrence Collins LJ concluded that single forum injunctions might need to be 'fitt[ed] … into the mould of The Siskina by a right based on unconscionable conduct'.[133] However, this work has suggested previously that in principle a substantive underlying equitable right may well not be necessary even for a single forum injunction.[134] Further, the language of vexation or oppression is entirely workable for single forum cases as well and has been used for that purpose in various authorities;[135] while Lawrence Collins LJ's comments about single forum injunctions were *obiter*, and may well not reflect his concluded opinion. And given the fluidity of the boundary between single and alternative forum injunctions, a differentiated test would not be helpful.

4.63   For the hard-pressed textbook writer these conflicting strands of case law create a rat's nest of precedent that is awkward to resolve. But, as already noted, the post-*Turner* statements

---

[129] *Glencore International v Metro Trading International (No 3)* [2002] CLC 1090 (CA) [42]. Note that the further aspects of Rix LJ's summary at [42] are not the law, as discussed at paras 4.64, 4.80 n 192, and 4.81 n 200.

[130] *Airbus Industrie v Patel* [1999] 1 AC 119 (HL) 134D–E and *Masri v Consolidated Contractors (No 3)* [2009] QB 503 [44]. See Ch 5, para 5.29 n 86.

[131] *British Airways Board v Laker Airways* [1985] AC 58 (HL) 81E–81H, 84G; *Midland Bank v Laker Airways* [1986] QB 689 (CA)—which happened to be decided between *Castanho* and *Aérospatiale*—and it is the linguistic consequences of this happenstance that were picked up *en passant* in *Airbus Industrie v Patel* [1999] 1 AC 119 (HL) 134D–E.

[132] Ch 3, section B, 'A Legal or Equitable Right?'.

[133] *Masri v Consolidated Contractors (No 3)* [2009] QB 503 [44], although cf [55]–[56] suggesting that [44] may not be a concluded opinion.

[134] Ch 3, paras 3.17–3.26.

[135] *Pennell v Roy* (1853) 3 De Gm & G 126, 43 ER 50, 53–56; *Simon Engineering v Butte Mining (No 2)* [1996] 1 Lloyds Rep 91, 96, 100; *Shell International Petroleum v Coral Oil (No 2)* [1999] 2 Lloyds Rep 606, 610.

of the House of Lords, Supreme Court, and Privy Council, what seems to be the balance of the recent Court of Appeal authorities, and also the bulk of the recent first instance decisions, use approaches essentially derived from *Aérospatiale, Deutsche v Highland*, and Lord Goff's thinking, and not *Turner v Grovit*; while the use of the 'synthetic' approach seems to be diminishing.[136]

These two different ways of phrasing the law, as summarized in *Deutsche v Highland* and **4.64** *Glencore v Metro*, are not very different in substance or result. Indeed, in some cases, including *Star Reefers*, the courts have simply cited both summaries and applied them indifferently.[137] But they are not the same conceptually, and for a coherent statement of the law it is better to choose, and desirable to simplify. It is hoped that the Supreme Court will do so in due course. For the reasons given, it is the suggestion of this work that the essence of Lord Goff's approach in *Aérospatiale* is to be preferred, both as a matter of principle and precedent, both to Lord Hobhouse's approach and to the 'synthetic' approach.

But there is no real objection to including 'unconscionable conduct' as one instance of a **4.65** situation where an anti-suit injunction may be granted.[138] So to reflect those decisions granting anti-suit injunctions on the basis of 'unconscionable conduct', a pragmatic course is to include that phrase alongside 'vexation or oppression', as one of the typical situations in which an anti-suit injunction can be granted, or as an alternative form of language to describe essentially the same notions.[139] However, it should neither replace the overarching notion of the ends of justice[140] nor be used as an intermediate overarching concept under which 'vexation or oppression' must be placed. It is this compromise that has been used in the summary at para 4.05.

H. INTERFERENCE WITH THE PROCESSES, JURISDICTION, OR JUDGMENTS OF THE ENGLISH COURT

An injunction may also be granted if the foreign proceedings are an illegitimate[141] inter-   **4.66** ference with the processes, jurisdiction, or judgments of the English court,[142] or if an

---

[136] See nn 121, 123.

[137] *Star Reefers Pool v JFC Group* [2012] 1 Lloyds Rep 376 (CA) [26]–[27]; *Golden Endurance Shipping v RMA Watanya (The Golden Endurance)* [2015] 1 Lloyds Rep 266 [39], [40], [45]; *Re Tadros* [2014] EWHC 2860 [44]–[46] (although the court went on to apply vexation or oppression: [73]–[78]).

[138] To do so also reflects the alternative tests allowed for in *Carron Iron Co v Maclaren* (1855) 5 HLC 416, 10 ER 961 (HL) 970–71.

[139] There are numerous examples of the courts taking a similar pragmatic approach. See eg *Albon v Naza Motor Trading (No 4)* [2008] 1 Lloyds Rep 1 (CA) [7], where Longmore LJ stated the test as being whether the foreign litigation was 'oppressive and vexatious or (as it is sometimes said) unconscionable'; *Royal Bank of Scotland v Hicks* [2011] EWHC 287 [62]; *Joint Stock Asset Management Co Ingosstrakh-Investments v BNP Paribas* [2012] 1 Lloyds Rep 649 (CA) [58]; *Axa Corporate Solutions Assurance v Weir Services Australia* [2016] EWHC 904 [45].

[140] On one reading of *Turner v Grovit* [2002] 1 WLR 107 (HL), the notion of unconscionability could be seen as a second-level concept, derived from 'the basic principle of justice': 117E–F; but is submitted that the best reading of the judgment is that Lord Hobhouse saw unconscionability as the primary concept; his reference to 'the basic principle of justice' was calculated to relegate notions of justice to a background justification.

[141] The word 'illegitimate' is not used in any of the main statements of these concepts in the case law but it is submitted that it deserves to be infiltrated into them; it can derive some support from the reference to the 'due process' of the court in *South Carolina Insurance v Assurantie Maatschappij 'De Seven Provincien'* [1987] AC 24 (HL) 41D.

[142] *Bank of Tokyo v Karoon* [1987] AC 45 (Note) (CA) 60G ('interfering with the proper course of the administration of justice here'); *South Carolina Insurance v Assurantie Maatschappij 'De Seven Provincien'* [1987] 1 AC 24 (HL) 41D; *Omega Group Holdings v Kozeny* [2002] CLC 132 [23]; *Glencore International v Metro Trading*

injunction is necessary for the protection of the processes, jurisdiction, and judgments of the English court,[143] provided, of course, that it is in the interests of justice to do so.[144] If an anti-suit injunction is justified on this basis it is not necessary independently to show vexation or oppression,[145] and although vexation and oppression will often overlap in practice with illegitimate interference, they are not the same conceptually. [146]

4.67   Further, when an injunction of this kind is being considered, it is not generally necessary separately to demonstrate that England is the natural forum. The logical basis of the injunction is that the English court's jurisdiction needs to be protected, and if that is necessary then an injunction is legitimate whether or not the English court is the natural forum for the underlying litigation. The English court is the only appropriate court to assess the question of whether its processes need protection, and clearly has a 'sufficient interest' in doing so.[147] This point is blurred over (*obiter*) in some of the summaries of the law that have been given,[148] but if one goes back to bedrock, the distinction is clearly visible in Lord Goff's analysis in *Aérospatiale*.[149]

International (No 3) [2002] CLC 1090 (CA) [42]; *Masri v Consolidated Contractors (No 3)* [2009] QB 503 [26], [80]–[88], [100].

---

[143] *Bank of Tokyo v Karoon* [1987] AC 45 (Note) (CA) 60G ('necessary and proper for the protection of the exercise of the jurisdiction of the English court'); *South Carolina Insurance v Assurantie Maatschappij 'De Seven Provincien'* [1987] 1 AC 24 (HL) 45A–B; *Société Nationale Industrielle Aérospatiale v Lee Kui Jak* [1987] AC 871 (PC) 892H–893A ('to protect the jurisdiction of the English court'); *Masri v Consolidated Contractors (No 3)* [2009] QB 503 (CA) [26], [83]–[88], [100]; *Elektrim v Vivendi Holdings 1* [2009] 1 Lloyds Rep 59 (CA) [159]–[160]; *Stichting Shell Pensioenfonds v Krys* [2015] AC 616 (PC) [23]–[24]. See also *Morris v Davies* [2011] EWHC 1272 [37]–[38]; *Ardila Investments v ENRC* [2015] EWHC 1667 [57]–[58]. A striking example is *Royal Bank of Scotland v Hicks* [2011] EWHC 287.
    In Burton J's judgment in *Golden Endurance Shipping v RMA Watanya (The Golden Endurance)* [2015] 1 Lloyds Rep 266 [42]–[45], he appears on one reading to be denying the separate existence of such a head of anti-suit injunctions to protect the jurisdiction of the court. If so, that is not the law and was not necessary for his decision. His judgment is better read as being concerned with whether injunctions can be justified to prevent evasion of English public policy: see para 4.71 below.
[144] Before *Société Nationale Industrielle Aérospatiale v Lee Kui Jak* [1987] AC 871 (PC), it was suggested by Lord Goff that the concept of protection of the jurisdiction of the English court was 'the golden thread running through the rare cases where an injunction has been granted': see *Bank of Tokyo v Karoon* [1987] AC 45 (CA) 60F–G and *South Carolina Insurance v Assurantie Maatschappij 'De Seven Provincien'* [1987] 1 AC 24 (HL) 45A–B. But in *Aérospatiale*, the Privy Council, whose judgment was delivered by Lord Goff, concluded that this was 'too narrow a view'. The injunction was to be granted where the 'ends of justice' required it, and injunctions to restrain vexatious or oppressive behaviour were of equal if not greater importance to injunctions to prevent interference with the process of the English court: at 892A–893E.
[145] *Stichting Shell Pensioenfonds v Krys* [2015] AC 616 (PC) [25].
[146] See *Stichting Shell Pensioenfonds v Krys* [2015] AC 616 (PC) [23]–[25] and also *Arab Monetary Fund v Hashim (No 6)* (Hoffmann J, 14 July 1992).
[147] *The Owners of the Ship 'Al Khattiya' v The Owners and/or Demise Charterers of the Ship 'Jag Laadki'* [2018] EWHC 389 [110]–[111]. So in the cases of *Masri v Consolidated Contractors (No 3)* [2009] QB 503 (CA) [83]–[96] and *Stichting Shell Pensioenfonds v Krys* [2015] AC 616 (PC), where injunctions were required to protect the jurisdiction of the courts, no showing of natural forum was required. See also *Shell International Petroleum v Coral Oil (No 2)* [1999] 2 Lloyds Rep 606, 610 (suggesting that in pure vexation cases the relevant concept was whether the English forum was the natural forum to decide the question of forum).
[148] See eg *Star Reefers Pool v JFC Group* [2012] 1 Lloyds Rep 376 (CA) [17], [25]–[26]; but at [28] Rix LJ also quoted *Deutsche v Highland*, where—it is submitted more correctly—natural forum was stated as generally a criterion for injunctions based on vexation and oppression only. This point is returned to in more detail in sections K, 'Legitimate and Illegitimate Advantages' and L, 'Comity' below.
[149] *Société Nationale Industrielle Aérospatiale v Lee Kui Jak* [1987] AC 871 (PC) 894F–G, 896F–G; and see also in *Deutsche Bank v Highland Crusader Partners* [2010] 1 WLR 1023 (CA) [50], at point 3.

Reasoning akin to this head of jurisdiction has sometimes been phrased in terms of whether **4.68** the foreign proceedings were an 'abuse of process' of the English court.[150] But language of this kind may cause confusion, if all that is happening is litigation abroad, and so there is no actual abuse of the English court's own process. In *Wilson v Emmott* the Court of Appeal therefore discouraged this phrasing as a way of framing the issues generally in play.[151] However, there may be situations where the inter-relation between foreign and English litigation creates an abuse of the process of the English courts.

Illegitimate interference with the processes and jurisdiction of the English court can in-   **4.69** clude seeking to relitigate the merits abroad where a matter has been decided in England, or where it could and should have been decided in the English litigation,[152] or an illegitimate collateral attack on the effectiveness of the judgment of the English court.[153] It can also include foreign proceedings which harmfully distort the normal evidence-gathering procedures of an English trial.[154] Foreign anti-suit injunctions to restrain proceedings in England, if contrary to comity, can also amount to an illegitimate interference.[155]

Injunctions to protect the jurisdiction of the English court have been granted to restrain creditors from interfering with the forum's insolvency jurisdiction, and its policy of orderly and fair distribution among creditors, by bringing proceedings abroad with the aim of upsetting such distribution.[156]

---

[150] *Turner v Grovit* [2000] QB 345 (CA) 357F–358F, criticized in A Briggs, 'Private International Law' (1999) 69 BYBIL 332–35; *Glencore International v Metro Trading International (No 3)* [2002] CLC 1090 (Moore Bick J) [35]–[38], [40], affd in different terms [2002] CLC 1090 (CA); *Emmott v Michael Wilson* [2017] 1 Lloyds Rep 21 [57]–[59], departed from on this point in *Michael Wilson v Emmott* [2018] 1 Lloyds Rep 299 (CA) [54].

[151] *Michael Wilson v Emmott* [2018] 1 Rep 299 (CA) [54]. See also *Glencore International v Metro Trading International Inc (No 3)* [2002] CLC 1090 (CA) [42].

[152] *Elektrim v Vivendi Holdings 1* [2009] 1 Lloyds Rep 59 (CA) [83], [85]; *Emmott v Michael Wilson* [2017] 1 Lloyds Rep 21 [57]–[59], [62], as in part upheld by *Michael Wilson v Emmott* [2018] 1 Lloyds Rep 299 (CA) [55]–[58]; although see the cautious approach taken in *Zeeland Navigation v Banque Worms* (Waller J, 13 December 1995).

[153] *Masri v Consolidated Contractors (No 3)* [2009] QB 503 (CA) [83]–[95], [100]; *Elektrim SA v Vivendi Holdings 1* [2009] 1 Lloyds Rep 59 (CA) [159]; *Zeeland Navigation Company v Banque Worms* (Waller J, 13 December 1995); and for a recent example see *Ardila Investments v ENRC* [2015] EWHC 1667 [57]. This can also be viewed as protecting one of the court's judgments. For an example of an analogous form of reasoning in a different context, see *Cukurova Finance International v Alfa Telecom Turkey* [2015] 2 WLR 875 (PC). However, it is important to bear in mind that it is presumptively legitimate to resist enforcement of English judgments abroad, under the foreign legal system's own rules as to enforcement of judgments, in the normal way: see *Masri v Consolidated Contractors (No 3)* at [93].

[154] *Armstrong v Armstrong* [1892] P 98; *South Carolina Insurance v Assurantie Maatschappij 'De Seven Provincien'* [1987] AC 24 (HL); *Arab Monetary Fund v Hashim (No 6)* (Hoffmann J, 14 July 1992); *Bankers Trust International v PT Dharmala Sakti Sejahtera* [1996] CLC 252; *Omega Group Holdings v Kozeny* [2002] CLC 132; *Royal Bank of Scotland v Hicks* [2011] EWHC 287 [94]–[96]. See Ch 5, section G, 'Ancillary and Collateral Proceedings'. Similarly, foreign proceedings which seek to hold officers of the English court liable for their actions in the context of English court proceedings are likely to be restrained: see, in the context of the common injunction, *Aston v Heron* (1834) 2 My & K 390, 39 ER 993.

[155] See generally Ch 5, section H, 'Anti-Anti-Suit Injunctions'. However, such cases are often in fact analysed in terms of vexation or oppression. For example, the issues in both *General Star International Indemnity v Stirling Cooke Brown Reinsurance Brokers* [2003] Lloyds Rep IR 719, and *Tonicstar v American Home Assurance Co* [2005] Lloyds Rep IR 32, could have been analysed in terms of interference with the process of the English court, but were instead framed in terms of vexation or oppression. The sub-text of both decisions, however, is that it was the interference with the English court's process that was viewed as the strongest justification for relief: see *General Star* at [16]; and *Tonicstar* at [14].

[156] A recent example is *Stichting Shell Pensionenfonds v Krys* [2015] AC 616 (PC) [23]–[24]. See Ch 5, section E, 'Insolvency and Justice between Creditors'.

4.70   This type of justification for an anti-suit injunction also enables the grant of injunctions to restrain illegitimate interference with an English arbitration, or to prevent an illegitimate collateral attack on, or vexatious relitigation of, an English arbitration award.[157]

I. PROTECTION OF ENGLISH PUBLIC POLICY

4.71   In *Shell v Krys* the Privy Council has recently given some endorsement to a limited strand of authority (for the most part *obiter*) which suggests that an injunction may be granted where it is necessary to protect important public policies of the forum.[158] But in a number of cases, the public policy relied upon has been held not to be sufficient to justify an injunction.[159] Whether and if so when a sufficiently important and germane public policy can be an independent ground for anti-suit injunctions (within the overall assessment of what the ends of justice require), or a major factor contributing to it being appropriate to grant an injunction when combined with other factors, is not as yet settled. Different formulations have been used. In some cases where the possibility has been addressed, the focus has been 'whether an injunction is required to protect the policies of the English forum' or to 'prevent the evasion of the important public policies of the forum'.[160] In others, narrower formulations have been articulated. So in *Stichting Shell v Krys* the Privy Council referred to situations where 'the judicial or legislative policies of England and the foreign court are so at variance that comity is overridden by the need to protect British national interests or prevent what it regards as a violation of the principles of customary international law'. However, those narrower yardsticks were not clearly stipulated as necessary conditions.[161] We are at a very

---

[157] *Michael Wilson v Emmott* [2018] 1 Lloyds Rep 299 (CA) [55]–[58], in part upholding [2017] 1 Lloyds Rep 21 [57]–[59], [62].

[158] *Stichting Shell Pensioenfonds v Krys* [2015] AC 616 (PC) [41]–[42] (part of the ratio; but the case could have been decided on other grounds without reference to public policy). This followed *Barclays Bank v Homan* [1993] BCLC 680, 689G, and 686B (per Hoffmann J; and this part of his judgment was not endorsed by the Court of Appeal); in which the point was *obiter* and the injunction was refused. See also *Arab Monetary Fund v Hashim (No 6)* (Hoffmann J, 14 July 1992) (concepts of policy envisaged as relevant, but injunction rejected); *Deutsche Bank v Highland Crusader Partners* [2010] 1 WLR 1023 (CA) [56] (*obiter* en passant reference to what Hoffmann J had decided in *Homan*); *Petter v EMC* [2016] ILPr 3 [51], [52], [55], [61] (*obiter*, and Sales LJ only). Other decisions like *Airbus Industrie v Patel* [1999] 1 AC 119 (HL) 138-140; *Masri v Consolidated Contractors (No 3)* [2009] QB 503 (CA) [86] touch with fairly evident approval on the possibility of such a ground for an injunction without directly endorsing it. Similarly, while *Bank of Tokyo v Karoon* [1987] AC 45 (Note) (CA) 57–63 envisages the possibility of an injunction on this basis the actual decision was to reject the injunction applying other grounds (using concepts of *forum non conveniens* as the law then stood). So, the actual authority for the proposition is confined to the decision of the Privy Council in *Krys*; all the other English decisions are *obiter*.
    With respect to *Petter v EMC*, the decision itself is controversial for the reasons discussed at paras 4.41–4.46 above.

[159] See *British Airways Board v Laker Airways* [1984] QB 142, where the policy of the Protection of Trading Interests Act 1980 did not justify an injunction to restrain US anti-trust litigation: 163G–164B, 165H, 166E. Parker J's decision was overturned by the Court of Appeal [1984] QB 142 (CA), but restored by the House of Lords [1985] AC 58 (HL), where Lord Diplock apparently agreed with Parker J's conclusions on this issue: at 85E; and see Lord Scarman at 96B. Similarly, in *Golden Endurance Shipping v RMA Watanya (The Golden Endurance)* [2015] 1 Lloyds Rep 266 [45], Burton J declined to grant an injunction to enforce the public policy of the Hague Rules or Hague-Visby Rules as incorporated into English law, regarding this as inconsistent with comity.

[160] *Airbus Industrie v Patel* [1999] 1 AC 119 (HL) 139G-H; *Petter v EMC* [2016] ILPr 3 (CA) [51]; also *Bank of Tokyo v Karoon* [1987] AC 45 (Note) (CA) 63C, 63F–H; *Masri v Consolidated Contractors (No 3)* [2009] QB 503 (CA) [86].

[161] *Stichting Shell Pensioenfonds v Krys* [2015] AC 616 (PC) [41], adopting Hoffmann J in *Barclays Bank v Homan* [1993] BCLC 680, 686B, 689G.
    In addition, with regard to the idea that 'a violation of customary international law' might be required as an alternative to a need to protect 'British national interests', it would seem to be unhelpful and unnecessary to read

early stage in the development of this area of the law, and the language of *Krys* should not be read as a statute. Indeed, the reasoning of *Krys* itself is not entirely clear on whether public policy is being treated as a free-standing ground to justify an injunction, or rather as a strong and indeed decisive supporting ground for an injunction justified on other equitable grounds, which contributes to the conclusion that the injunction is consistent with comity—and essentially the same reasoning could have been framed without reference to policy within the overlapping concept of the need to protect the jurisdiction of the court. So the correct approach to public policy remains to be settled. It is suggested that as a matter of principle, anti-suit injunctions justified solely on the ground that the claims abroad would contradict the public policies of the forum may pose real questions of tension with comity, and it may well be that they will only be appropriate in unusual cases. It is perhaps illustrative of how things will develop that the bulk of the case law indicates that injunctions on grounds of public policy have generally only been envisaged where what the foreign court is being asked to do would be exorbitant from an international perspective.[162] Thus, the mere fact that foreign choice of law rules or substantive law are different cannot justify an injunction.[163] However, where there is a genuine need to protect English policy and the matter is sufficiently within the legitimate sphere of intervention of the English court that the grant of an injunction would be consistent with comity, there is no reason in principle why a need to protect public policy could not be a powerful, and even decisive, factor in support of the conclusion that the grant of an injunction is in the interests of justice.

J. *FORUM NON CONVENIENS*

It was for a brief interlude considered to be the law that an anti-suit injunction could be granted on the ground that the English court was the most natural forum and the foreign court was not. It is now clear this is not the law.[164] Although the inappropriateness of the   **4.72**

this literally. For the reasons discussed in more detail at n 91 above, the more germane question is whether the foreign court is acting in an exorbitant fashion, broadly assessed, rather than whether there is a technical breach of customary international law.

---

[162] See *Stichting Shell Pensioenfonds v Krys* [2015] AC 616 (PC) [42]; *Barclays Bank v Homan* [1993] BCLC 680, 686–91; *Airbus Industrie v Patel* [1999] 1 AC 119 (HL) at 138–40; another example may be in substance be *Midland Bank v Laker Airways* [1986] QB 689 (CA) (although not reasoned directly in terms of public policy). The counter-example to this is *Petter v EMC* [2016] ILPr 3 (CA).

[163] In *Barclays Bank v Homan* [1993] BCLC 680, 690F–G Hoffmann J commented that 'the foreign court is entitled, without thereby necessarily occasioning a breach of international law or manifest injustice, to give effect to the policies of its own legislation'. See also *Société Nationale Industrielle Aérospatiale v Lee Kui Jak* [1987] AC 871, 895; *Deutsche v Highland* [2010] 1 WLR 1023 [50]; *Star Reefers Pool v JFC Group* [2012] 1 Lloyds Rep 376 [34], [36], [39], suggesting that the contrary would be 'egoistic paternalism'; *Jewel Owner v Sagaan Developments Trading (The MD Gemini)* [2012] 2 Lloyds Rep 672 [21]; *Golden Endurance Shipping v RMA Watanya (The Golden Endurance)* [2015] 1 Lloyds Rep 266 [45].

[164] Until 1973, the courts required proceedings to be 'vexatious and oppressive', or an abuse of the process of the English court, before they would stay an English action: *St Pierre v South American Stores (Garth & Chaves)* [1936] 1 KB 382 (CA) 398; or grant an injunction to restrain the pursuit of a foreign action: *Hyman v Helm* (1883) 24 Ch D 531 (CA). However, in a series of cases beginning with *The Atlantic Star* [1974] AC 436 (HL) and *MacShannon v Rockware Glass Ltd* [1978] AC 795 (HL), the House of Lords first diluted and then abandoned the requirement of vexation in stay cases, and replaced it with the concept of *forum non conveniens*, under which proceedings in England would be stayed if the defendant could show that the foreign jurisdiction was clearly the more appropriate forum for the litigation: *Spiliada Maritime v Cansulex* [1987] AC 460 (HL) 474–78.

The lowering of the threshold for the grant of a stay reflected greater deference to foreign legal systems, and meant that 'judicial chauvinism has been replaced by judicial comity'. But conversely, a parallel dilution of the conditions required for an anti-suit injunction would decrease deference and increase interference. To conclude that foreign forum can be a factor in support of a conclusion that the injunction defendant's litigation is vexatious or oppressive,[165] the mere fact that the English court perceives the foreign forum as less appropriate than England cannot be sufficient ground for an injunction in itself, unless the inappropriateness goes further, and contributes to vexation or oppression.[166]

K. LEGITIMATE AND ILLEGITIMATE ADVANTAGES

4.73   Since the court is concerned with the ends of justice, account must be taken not only of injustice to the injunction claimant if the injunction defendant is allowed to pursue the

the adoption of *forum non conveniens* in relation to stays should produce a corresponding relaxation of the tests for an injunction was a *non sequitur: The Abidin Daver* [1984] AC 398 (HL) 411G; see also *Bank of Tokyo v Karoon* [1987] AC 45 (CA) (Note) 62E, 63A–F; *Société Nationale Industrielle Aérospatiale v Lee Kui Jak* [1987] AC 871 (PC) 896D–E. Nevertheless, in *Castanho v Brown & Root*, Lord Scarman held that the principles applying to injunctions and stays should be the same, and that an anti-suit injunction could be granted on the ground that England was the most appropriate forum for the litigation, so long as the injunction would not deprive the injunction defendant of a legitimate juridical advantage: *Castanho v Brown & Root* [1981] AC 557 (HL) 574–77, per Lord Scarman; applied in *Smith Kline & French Laboratories v Bloch* [1983] 1 WLR 730 (CA) 737H–738G, 739H, 743B–G; 746F–747G; and in *British Airways Board v Laker Airways* [1984] QB 142 (CA) 187, where, however, on appeal the House of Lords distinguished *Castanho* as not applying to 'single forum' situations [1985] AC 58 (HL) 80, 95. The heresy of *Castanho* was restated *obiter* by the majority in *South Carolina Insurance v Assurantie Maatschappij 'De Seven Provincien'* [1987] AC 24 (HL) 40F–G, but was criticized by Goff LJ (later Lord Goff), in *Bank of Tokyo v Karoon* [1987] AC 45 (CA) (Note) 61–63 (where he drew heavily on the American decision in *Laker Airways v Sabena, Belgian World Airlines* 731 F 2nd 909 (DC Cir 1984) [13]–[14], [17], [19]). As Lord Goff, he repeated his criticisms in his minority speech in *South Carolina*, 44F–45C. His view triumphed in *Aérospatiale*, 895–97, where the Privy Council, whose judgment Lord Goff delivered, held that to permit an injunction to be granted solely on the basis that the foreign court was an inconvenient forum would be inconsistent with comity, and that it would be wrong to conclude that the tests for stays and injunctions were the same (as to this see later *Amchem Products v British Colombia (Workers' Compensation Board)* [1993] 1 SCR 897 (Can SC) 913 and *Donohue v Armco* [2002] 1 Lloyds Rep 425 (HL) 433 [24]; the opinions to the contrary of Lord Hobhouse in *Turner v Grovit* [2002] 1 WLR 107 (HL) 118 [25], do not represent the law).

As a matter of strict precedent, the judgment in *Aérospatiale* was only a decision of Brunei law, but a laudable flexibility was displayed in the application of the doctrine of precedent, and the *Castanho* heresy consigned to oblivion. The subsequent case law generally treated the *Castanho* doctrine as having been 'developed' into non-existence by *Aérospatiale*: see *Du Pont de Nemours v Agnew* [1988] 2 Lloyds Rep 240 (CA) 243–44, 249; *Barclays Bank v Homan* [1993] BCLC 680 (CA) 697–99, 702, or simply applied *Aérospatiale*: see eg *Advanced Portfolio Technologies v Ainsworth* [1996] FSR 217; *Bouygues Offshore v Caspian Shipping* [1997] 2 Lloyds Rep 485, 489–92; although questions of precedent did occasionally cause hesitation: see *Pathe Screen Entertainment v Handmade Films (Distributors)* (11 July 1989), where Hobhouse J took the view that he was still bound by *Castanho* and *Laker* but attempted to reconcile *Aérospatiale* with them; and *Commercial Union Assurance v Simat Helliesen & Eichner* [2001] Lloyds Rep IR 172, 175. In recent times, the House of Lords has put the matter beyond doubt, albeit without ever expressly departing from *Castanho* under the 1966 Practice Statement: *Airbus Industrie v Patel* [1998] 1 AC 119 (HL) 133C–F (adopting *Aérospatiale*); *Turner v Grovit* [2002] 1 WLR 107 (HL) [24]–[25] (adopting the principle of unconscionability, and reinterpreting *Castanho*); *Donohue v Armco* [19] (adopting *Aérospatiale*, and observing the 'development of principle'; see also [45], [53]). See also *Masri v Consolidated Contractors) (No 3)* [2009] QB 503 (CA) [47]–[48].

The modern law on the point is conveniently stated in *Deutsche Bank v Highland Crusader Partners* [2010] 1 WLR 1023 (CA) [50]–[65].

---

[165] *Société Nationale Industrielle Aérospatiale v Lee Kui Jak* [1987] AC 871 (PC) 894F–G; *Donohue v Armco Inc* [2002] 1 Lloyds Rep 425 (HL) [19]; *Deutsche Bank AG v Highland Crusader Partners LP* [2010] 1 WLR 1023 (CA) [50], [53]–[62].
[166] *Société Nationale Industrielle Aérospatiale v Lee Kui Jak* [1987] AC 871 (PC) 895–6; *Donohue v Armco* [2002] 1 Lloyds Rep 425 (HL) [19]; see also *Glencore International v Metro Trading International (No 3)* [2002] CLC 1090 (CA) [42]. In this respect, the statement of Lord Hobhouse in *Turner v Grovit* [2002] 1 WLR 107 (HL) 118F–G that *forum non conveniens* 'is a weak complaint and is easily overridden by other factors or considerations' is overgenerous. It is clear from *Aérospatiale* that *forum non conveniens* cannot suffice in itself. See now *Deutsche Bank v Highland Crusader Partners* [2010] 1 WLR 1023 (CA) [50]–[65], and in particular the interpretation of *Turner* at [62].

foreign proceedings, but also of injustice to the injunction defendant if he is not allowed to do so. So the court will not grant an injunction if, by doing so, it will deprive the injunction defendant of advantages in the foreign forum of which it would be unjust to deprive him.[167] But only credible legitimate advantages are to be given weight; it is not unjust to deprive an injunction defendant of illegitimate or theoretical advantages,[168] or of purported advantages which are 'hopelessly and cynically invoked'.[169] Some cases have assessed whether the balance of legitimate advantages, or the 'balance of injustice',[170] is in favour of the foreign proceedings continuing.[171] But the concept of legitimate advantages is best seen as a control to be weighed in the balance; it should not be a central analytical concept defining the basis of the injunction, and that would not be consistent with principle. So the mere absence of apparent legitimate advantages does not automatically justify an injunction on its own as that would overlook the important restraining influence of comity.[172]

If the foreign forum is not an inappropriate forum for the litigation, then significant dif-   **4.74**
ferences in the law or procedure to be applied there, such as the availability of higher damages, or a broader disclosure regime, or more favourable rules of substantive law,[173] can be legitimate advantages for the injunction defendant. If, however, the foreign forum is clearly inappropriate, then those same differences may well be illegitimate, and can contribute to a finding of vexation or oppression.[174] Further, not all peculiarities of the foreign forum will be legitimate advantages, even if it is not an inappropriate forum. For example, it has been held that where a matter raises complex questions of fact and law it is not a legitimate advantage that it will be tried by jury.[175]

Similarly, it is a legitimate advantage to have issues of foreign law determined in the courts   **4.75**
of the relevant state,[176] provided that the foreign law is an appropriate law to govern the substantive dispute. Accrued procedural advantages in the foreign jurisdiction can also be

---

[167] *Société Nationale Industrielle Aérospatiale v Lee Kui Jak* [1987] AC 871 (PC) 896F–H; *Donohue v Armco* [2002] 1 Lloyds Rep 425 (HL) [19].

[168] *Smith Kline & French Laboratories Ltd v Bloch* [1983] 1 WLR 730, 738H, 743G, 748A (although the underlying jurisprudential approach in that case has now been discredited); *Spiliada Maritime v Cansulex* [1987] 1 AC 460 (HL) 473G, 476A, 482B–484D. For a recent example, see *Re Tadros* [2014] EWHC 2860 [74]–[77].

[169] *Star Reefers Pool v JFC Group* [2012] 1 Lloyds Rep 376 (CA) [36].

[170] *Bouygues Offshore v Caspian Shipping (No 2)* [1997] 2 Lloyds Rep 485, 491–92; *Bouygues Offshore v Caspian Shipping (No 3)* [1997] 2 Lloyds Rep 493, 502–06.

[171] *Bloch v Bloch* [2003] 1 FLR 1 [95].

[172] *Deutsche Bank v Highland Crusader Offshore Partners* [2010] 1 WLR 1023 (CA) [50(4)].

[173] *Star Reefers Pool v JFC Group* [2012] 1 Lloyds Rep 376 (CA) [36]–[38].

[174] *Simon Engineering v Butte Mining (No 1)* [1996] 1 Lloyds Rep 104, 110–11, which sought to summarize the effect of *Castanho v Brown & Root (UK)* [1981] AC 557 (HL) 577C–G; *Smith Kline & French Laboratories v Bloch* [1983] 1 WLR 730, 738H; and *Société Nationale Industrielle Aérospatiale v Lee Kui Jak* [1987] AC 871 (PC) 894D–G, 899G–H. See also *Simon Engineering v Butte Mining (No 2)* [1996] 1 Lloyds Rep 91, 99; *Bank of Tokyo v Karoon* [1987] AC 45, 51; *Morris v Davies* [2011] EWHC 1272 [35], [38]; but cf *The Eras Eil Actions* [1995] 1 Lloyds Rep 64, 85. It has been held that the unavailability of security for costs in the foreign forum is not a legitimate advantage: *Simon Engineering v Butte Mining (No 2)* [1996] 1 Lloyds Rep 91, 95. The position is the same in Scotland: *Shell UK Exploration and Production v Innes* (1995) SLT 807 (Ct of Sess), 823–24. For recent applications of the concepts, see *Star Reefers Pool v JFC Group Ltd* [2012] 1 Lloyds Rep 376 (CA) [36]–[38]; *Re Tadros* [2014] EWHC 2860 [74]–[77].

[175] *Smith Kline & French Laboratories v Bloch* [1983] 1 WLR 730 (CA) 738H, 742C, 747D; see also *Metall und Rohstoff v ACLI Metals (London)* [1984] 1 Lloyds Rep 598 (CA) 607 (where jury trial was seen as a serious *disadvantage*). There is, however, room for doubt about whether this approach is consistent with comity.

[176] *Moor v Anglo-Italian Bank* (1879) 10 Ch D 681, 690–91; *Re Belfast Shipowners* [1894] 1 IR 321, 333; *Settlement Corp v Hochschild* [1966] 1 Ch 10, 18–19; *Owners of Cargo Lately Laden on Board the Ship or Vessel Eleftheria v The Eleftheria (Owners) (The Eleftheria)* [1970] P 94, 105 (a contractual stay case); *Royal Bank of Canada v Cooperatieve Centrale Raiffeisen-Boerenleenbank* [2003] EWHC 2913 [75]; *Re Tadros* [2014] EWHC 2860 [75].

legitimate advantages. Thus, it has been held to be a legitimate advantage to have arrested property in the foreign jurisdiction, if the cessation of the foreign action could endanger the security,[177] although any weight will depend on the circumstances. If the injunction defendant has rights which are not time-barred abroad but are time-barred in England, this may be relevant; but whether it is treated as a legitimate advantage, and any weight, has in some decisions depended on whether the injunction defendant has created his own difficulty, and taken the risk of being time-barred in England, by his conduct in proceeding abroad.[178] Further, it is a legitimate advantage to be able to bring contribution proceedings in the foreign jurisdiction which could not be brought in England.[179]

4.76   In appropriate cases, potential injustice to the injunction defendant may be circumvented by requiring undertakings from the injunction claimant, or granting the injunction on terms, so as to ensure that the injunction defendant is not unjustly prejudiced.[180]

L. COMITY

4.77   In exercising the power to grant an anti-suit injunction, regard must be had to the principles of comity, which impose limits on the grant of the injunction.[181] Anti-suit injunctions will, in general, not be granted where to do so would be inconsistent with due respect for comity.[182] As a result, the tests for anti-suit injunctions are not the obverse of the tests for stays of English proceedings: a higher level of justification is required to warrant interference.[183] The usual level of respect due to comity can be diminished or displaced in certain circumstances, discussed below, but (outside the contractual situation) these are rare.[184]

4.78   The underlying principles of comity, which find their centre in the mutual respect due between courts and legal systems,[185] are discussed in Chapter 1, section C, 'Anti-Suit

---

[177] *Ascot Commodities v Northern Pacific Shipping (The Irini A)* [1999] 1 Lloyds Rep 196, 200.
[178] *Simon Engineering v Butte Mining (No 2)* [1996] 1 Lloyds Rep 91, 99–100; see also, in the contractual context, *Verity Shipping v NV Norexa* [2008] 1 Lloyds Rep 652.
[179] *Bitmac v Creosote Producers Association* (CA, 1 January 1986); this is the converse situation to *Société Nationale Industrielle Aérospatiale v Lee Kui Jak* [1987] AC 871 (PC).
[180] *Société Nationale Industrielle Aérospatiale v Lee Kui Jak* [1987] AC 871 (PC) 896H–897A; *Donohue v Armco* [2002] 1 Lloyds Rep 425 (HL) [19].
[181] *Airbus Industrie v Patel* [1999] 1 AC 119 (HL) 133H, 140A–B; *Deutsche Bank v Highland Crusader Partners* [2010] 1 WLR 1023 (CA) [50]–[65]. See also *Jopson v James* (1908) 77 LJ (Ch) 824, 828–30.
[182] *Airbus Industrie v Patel* [1999] 1 AC 119 (HL) 133H, 134E.
[183] The indirect interference with the foreign court's processes created by the injunction requires reconciliation with the principle of mutual respect, whereas in contrast a stay in favour of the foreign court is inherently respectful: *Société Nationale Industrielle Aérospatiale v Lee Kui Jak* [1987] AC 871 (PC) 895E–G; *Donohue v Armco* [2002] 1 Lloyds Rep 425 (HL) 433 [24]; *Airbus Industrie v Patel* [1999] 1 AC 119 (HL) 141G–H; *Deutsche Bank v Highland Crusader Partners* [2010] 1 WLR 1023 (CA) [50]–[65]. Lord Hobhouse in *Turner v Grovit* [2002] 1 WLR 107 (HL) at [25] made some *obiter* comments that could be read in the contrary sense, but these are not the law; and in *Deutsche v Highland*, the Court of Appeal interpreted them into nothing, to produce an orthodox result, eg at [62].
[184] Paragraphs 4.89–4.92.
[185] In *Ecobank Transnational v Tanoh* [2016] 1 WLR 2231 (CA), the Court of Appeal discussed comity in terms that suggested it was principally relevant as a matter of transnational case management, and that the question of interference in principle was less relevant than it had previously been. It is suggested, however, that these comments should be seen as focused on the contractual situation within which the Court was operating, and the question of delay which was before it; and do not create any new principle in the non-contractual case. The law as laid down by the Supreme Court and House of Lords and Court of Appeal firmly establishes that, outside the contractual case, comity does operate to discourage interference in principle: see para 4.80. For recent decisions illustrating the true role of comity as a question of principle and judicial sovereignty, and not merely transnational case management, see *Masri v Consolidated Contractors) (No 3)* [2009] QB 503 (CA) at [16], [81]; *Deutsche Bank v*

Injunctions in Other Legal Systems'. They influence the whole of the law on anti-suit injunctions. There are, however, a set of distinct constraints on the grant of the injunction which can be seen as the most direct emanations of comity; they are discussed in this section.

1. Non-Intervention and Caution

The respect due to the foreign court means that the English court should not inter- **4.79** fere, even indirectly, with the foreign court's policies and processes unless necessary.[186] Consequently, as an anti-suit injunction indirectly affects the foreign court,[187] the power to grant such an injunction must be exercised with caution,[188] save where the foreign proceedings are in breach of contract.[189] However, there will be no interference, and thus no reason for caution, in the occasional cases where it is apparent that the foreign court is willing to defer to the English court's views as to whether the foreign proceedings should continue.[190] It has also been suggested that, where the foreign jurisdiction itself exercises the power to grant anti-suit injunctions, the English court should pay little regard to allegations that the foreign court would be offended by a proper use of the remedy.[191]

Highland Crusader Partners [2010] 1 WLR 1023 (CA) [50]–[65]; *Stichting Shell Pensionenfonds v Krys* [2015] AC 616 (PC) [42]; and *Dawnus Sierra Leone v Timis Mining Corporation* [2016] EWHC 236 [66].

[186] *Barclays Bank v Homan* [1993] BCLC 680, 691–92 (Hoffmann J), upheld on appeal [1993] BCLC 680 (CA); *ED&F Man (Sugar) v Yani Haryanto (No 2)* [1991] 1 Lloyds Rep 161, 168 (Steyn J); [1991] 1 Lloyds Rep 429 (CA) 438, 440; *Deutsche Bank v Highland Crusader Partners* [2010] 1 WLR 1023 (CA) [50], [56].

[187] *Airbus Industrie v Patel* [1999] 1 AC 119 (HL) 138G–H; *Fort Dodge Animal Health v Akzo Nobel* [1998] FSR 222 (CA) 247; *Masri v Consolidated Contractors (No 3)* [2009] QB 503 (CA) [81].

[188] *Société Nationale Industrielle Aérospatiale v Lee Kui Jak* [1987] AC 871 (PC) 892E–F; *ED&F Man (Sugar) v Yani Haryanto (No 2)* [1991] 1 Lloyds Rep 429 (CA) 440; *Airbus Industrie v Patel* [1999] 1 AC 119 (HL) 133E–F; *Turner v Grovit* [2002] 1 WLR 107 (HL) [25]–[28]; *Masri v Consolidated Contractors (No 3)* [2009] QB 503 (CA) [81]; *Deutsche Bank v Highland Crusader Partners* [2010] 1 WLR 1023 (CA) [50], [53]; *Ellerman Lines v Read* [1928] 2 KB 144 (CA) 158. In a number of the earlier cases, the phrase 'great caution' was used: *Cohen v Rothfield* [1919] 1 KB 410, 413; *Settlement Corp v Hochschild* [1966] 1 Ch 10, 15 ('it is only exercised very rarely, with great caution'); *Mike Trading and Transport v R Pagnan & Fratelli (The Lisboa)* [1980] 2 Lloyds Rep 546 (CA) 549, 551 ('the jurisdiction will be exercised with great caution, especially where the defendant to the English proceedings is plaintiff in the foreign proceedings'); *Tracomin v Sudan Oil Seeds (Nos 1 and 2)* [1983] 1 WLR 1026 (CA) 1035; *Marc Rich v Società Italiana Impianti (The Atlantic Emperor) (No 2)* (Hobhouse J, 11 November 1991); *Bank of Tokyo v Karoon* [1987] AC 45 (CA) 59G ('extreme caution'); and see also *Barclays Bank v Homan* [1993] BCLC 680, 686 (Hoffmann J) ('great circumspection'). In *Royal Bank of Canada v Cooperatieve Centrale Raiffeisen-Boerenleenbank* [2004] 1 Lloyds Rep 471 (CA) 475, Evans-Lombe J accepted that 'great caution' had to be exercised. However, Mance LJ, in the same case, observed that the addition of the adjective 'great' did not reflect the authoritative statements of the law in *Airbus, Aérospatiale*, and (sic) *Turner v Grovit*: at 480 [39]. It is suggested that Mance LJ's approach is to be preferred, not least because, even if English judges are sometimes cautious when granting anti-suit relief, describing them as 'greatly' cautious does not reflect reality. In the recent authorities, the language used has been 'caution' not 'great caution': see eg *Masri v Consolidated Contractors (No 3)* [2009] QB 503 (CA) at [16], [81]; *Deutsche v Highland*, at [50]; *Star Reefers Pool v JFC Group* [2012] 1 Lloyds Rep 376 (CA) at [41]; *Stichting Shell Pensionenfonds v Krys* [2015] AC 616 (PC) at [41]; *Ecobank Transnational v Tanoh* [2016] 1 WLR 2231 (CA).

[189] *Aggeliki Charis Compania Maritima v Pagnan (The Angelic Grace)* [1995] 1 Lloyds Rep 87 (CA) 95. See generally Ch 7, section E, 'The *Angelic Grace* Principles'.

[190] *Bankers Trust International v PT Dharmala Sakti Sejahtera* [1996] CLC 252, 263B–F.

[191] *Beazley v Horizon Offshore Contractors* [2005] Lloyds Rep IR 231 [40].

2. Sufficient Interest or Connection

4.80   The respect due to the foreign court also means that, in general, the English court must have a sufficient interest in, or connection with, the matter in question to justify the indirect interference with the foreign court that an injunction involves.[192] A contractual clause providing for the exclusive or inclusive jurisdiction of the English courts will, however, generally establish a sufficient interest over connected matters.[193] The concept of sufficient interest includes, and corresponds to, the point that for an injunction to be granted 'there must be a good reason why the decision to stop the foreign proceedings should be made here rather than there'.[194]

4.81   In alternative forum cases,[195] where an injunction is sought on the basis that the foreign litigation is vexatious or oppressive, the requirement of a sufficient interest means that consideration must be given to whether the English court is the natural forum for the litigation. Indeed, it has often been said that in such cases an injunction will not, in general, be granted unless the English court is the natural forum for the resolution of the substantive disputes between the parties[196]—or perhaps the natural forum to resolve the question of forum.[197]

---

[192] *Airbus Industrie v Patel* [1999] 1 AC 119 (HL) 138G–140E; *Elektrim v Vivendi Holdings 1* [2009] 1 Lloyds Rep 59 (CA) at [114]; *Deutsche Bank v Highland Crusader Partners* [2010] 1 WLR 1023 (CA) [59]; see also *Shell International Petroleum v Coral Oil (No 2)* [1999] 2 Lloyds Rep 606, 609; *Vitol Bahrain v Nasdec General Trading* [2013] EWHC 3359 [41]. In *Turner v Grovit* [2002] 1 WLR 107 (HL) 117D, 119C–H, Lord Hobhouse sought (*obiter*) to redefine the concept of comity in terms of whether the injunction claimant, rather than the English court, has a 'legitimate interest' in restraining the injunction defendant's conduct, or a 'sufficient interest' in asking the English court for a remedy. This wording was adopted, again *obiter*, in *Glencore International v Metro Trading International (No 3)* [2002] CLC 1090 (CA) [42]. But Lord Hobhouse's approach is contradictory, and not complementary, to the authority of *Airbus v Patel*, and is thus not the law. It is also submitted, with respect, that Lord Goff's approach is correct in principle. When the court is assessing the demands of comity, it must move beyond the sphere of private right into the realm of public policy, and must assess not merely the legitimate interests of the injunction claimant, but also the adequacy of its own connection with the matters in question. The requirement of a sufficient interest or connection finds support in public international law: see FA Mann, 'The Doctrine of Jurisdiction in International Law' Part I (1964) 111 Recueil des Cours 1 149–50. In *Masri v Consolidated Contractors (No 3)* [2009] QB 503 (CA) [81], Lawrence Collins LJ suggested that 'Comity may be decisive where the English court is asked to grant an anti-suit injunction when the case has no relevant connection with England, since to grant an injunction in such a case may be a breach of international law.'

[193] In *Airbus Industrie v Patel* [1999] 1 AC 119 (HL) 138F–G, Lord Goff expressly excluded contractual cases from consideration when imposing this requirement. But there is no reason why the requirement of a 'sufficient interest' should not apply to contractual cases (see Ch 7, section G, 'Injunctions in Support of a Foreign Forum'), although it will be easily satisfied where there is an English exclusive forum clause.

[194] *Barclays Bank v Homan* [1993] BCLC 680, 686 (per Hoffmann J, upheld by Court of Appeal at 699–702; *Shell International Petroleum v Coral Oil (No 2)* [1999] 2 Lloyds Rep 606, 610; this aspect of *Homan* was adopted in *Mitchell v Carter* [1997] 1 BCLC 673, 687; *Deutsche Bank v Highland Crusader Partners* [2010] 1 WLR 1023 (CA) [50], [56]; *Bloom v Harms Offshore AHT 'Taurus'* [2010] Ch 187 (CA) [26]; *Stichting Shell Pensioenfonds v Krys* [2015] AC 616 (PC) [42].

[195] Alternative forum cases are those where the litigation could proceed in either or both of England or the foreign jurisdiction: see Ch 5, section B, 'Alternative Forum Cases'.

[196] *Société Nationale Industrielle Aérospatiale v Lee Kui Jak* [1987] AC 871 (PC) 896F–G; *Airbus Industrie v Patel* [1999] 1 AC 119 (HL) 138H, 140C; *Deutsche Bank v Highland Crusader Partners* [2010] 1 WLR 1023 (CA), [2010] 1 WLR 1023 [50]. If the other court is more natural, that tells against the granting of the injunction: *Jopson v James* (1908) 77 LJ (Ch) 824, 830; *Re Tadros (Deceased)* [2014] EWHC 2860 [78].

In *Star Reefers Pool v JFC Group* [2012] 1 Lloyds Rep 376 (CA) [25], the Court of Appeal, giving a summary of law as undisputed before it, said *obiter* that it was a necessary condition of the grant of a non-contractual injunction that England had to be the natural forum for the resolution of the dispute. That is not correct. It is clear that exceptions are possible to any requirement of natural forum. One example among others is that injunctions can be granted in 'single forum' cases. See S Males QC, 'Comity and Anti-Suit Injunctions' [1998] LMCLQ 543, 544–45, A Bell, *Forum Shopping and Venue in Transnational Litigation* (OUP 2003) paras 4.94–4.95 (hereafter 'Bell'); and Ch 5, section D, 'Single Forum Cases'.

[197] Paragraph 4.93.

However, on a close reading of *Airbus v Patel* we can see that Lord Goff's more developed conclusion was that 'any limiting principle requiring respect for comity cannot simply be expressed by reference to the question whether the English court may be the natural forum for the dispute', and that the true concept was 'sufficient interest'. As a result, even in alternative forum cases he preferred to use 'natural forum' merely as a factor, not a requirement, saying that in an 'alternative forum' case, assessing whether the general requirement of 'sufficient interest' is satisfied 'will involve consideration of the question whether the English court is the natural forum for the resolution of the dispute'.[198] In any event, natural forum is relevant as a criterion or consideration only 'generally' and not rigidly. No criterion of natural forum applies to injunctions sought to protect the processes, jurisdiction, and judgments of the English court, as already explained.[199] Nor does it apply in single forum cases. Further, contrary to some erroneous suggestions to the contrary, it is not necessary for there to be actual litigation in England which the injunction is sought to protect: there are numerous cases where free-standing anti-suit injunctions have been granted, such as single forum injunctions, injunctions to protect prospective English proceedings, and injunctions to restrain winding-up proceedings.[200] The concept of natural forum is further explored in section M, 'Natural Forum'.

In single forum cases,[201] the concept of 'sufficient interest' has not yet been fully explored. **4.82** However, a sufficient interest may (for example) potentially be provided if the substantive disputes can be characterized as dominantly English in character, by reason of the nationality or residence of the parties, the place where their dealings occurred, or the law to which they subjected their dealings.[202] A sufficient connection may also exist if the injunction is necessary to protect the jurisdiction of the English court,[203] or English public policy.[204] In these situations, the English court will be the appropriate court to decide questions of

---

[198] *Airbus Industrie v Patel* [1999] 1 AC 119 (HL) 134F, 135B, 138F–H.

[199] Paragraph 4.67 above.

[200] In *Turner v Grovit* [2002] 1 WLR 107 (HL) [27], it was suggested, *obiter*, that the injunction claimant *must* be a party to existing litigation in England which needs to be protected. This was adopted, again *obiter*, in the summary of the law in *Glencore International v Metro Trading International (No 3)* [2002] CLC 1090 (CA) [42], per Rix LJ. However, those *obiter* comments are not the law. They are inconsistent with the authoritative statements of the tests in the line of cases from *Aérospatiale* to *Airbus v Patel* to *Deutsche v Highland* and *Stichting v Krys* (see n 6) which contain no such requirement. They are also contrary to many previous decisions upholding the possibility of free-standing injunctions which are not sought to protect existing English proceedings. One example is single forum injunctions such as *Midland Bank v Laker Airways* [1986] QB 689 (CA); discussed further in Ch 5, section D. Another example is injunctions in the alternative forum situation to protect potential but not yet actual English proceedings: see eg in the contractual situation *AES Ust-Kamenogorsk Hydropower Plant LLP v Ust-Kamenogorsk Hydropower Plant JSC* [2013] 1 WLR 1889 (SC) and in non-contractual cases *Royal Bank of Scotland v Hicks* [2011] EWHC 287 [65], where Floyd J considered but did not follow the *obiter* comment in *Turner*. Other examples include patent cases where injunctions have been granted to restrain vexatious harassment of customers: *Landi den Hartog v Sea Bird (Clean Air Fuel Systems)* [1976] FSR 489; *Jacey (Printers) v Norton & Wright Group* [1977] FSR 475; and injunctions to restrain winding-up proceedings: see *Mann v Goldstein* [1968] 1 WLR 1091, and Ch 6, section F, 'Injunctions to Protect Winding-Up Proceedings'. See also Ch 5, para 5.23.

[201] Single forum cases are those where the litigation will either proceed in the foreign jurisdiction or not at all: see Ch 5, section D, 'Single Forum Cases'.

[202] *Midland Bank v Laker Airways* [1986] QB 689 (CA) 714–15; *Airbus Industrie v Patel* [1999] 1 AC 119 (HL) 138E, 139G; although see the reservations expressed about this in *Airbus* at 138C.

[203] *Airbus Industrie v Patel* [1999] 1 AC 119 (HL) 139G; *Bloom v Harms Offshore AHT 'Taurus'* [2010] Ch 187 (CA) [26], [33].

[204] *Stichting Shell Pensionenfonds v Krys* [2015] AC 616 (PC) [42]. As to protection of the policies of the English forum, see section I, 'Protection of English Public Policy'.

forum, which is another way of expressing the criterion of sufficient interest in the single forum situation.[205]

4.83   The English court will, in general, not have a sufficient interest in restraining proceedings in a second country, in order to protect litigation in a third country, to justify the grant of an injunction,[206] even if the second country is the natural forum but is itself unable to grant effective injunctive relief.[207] If the courts of the second country have requested the intervention of the English court, this may give the English court some interest in intervention, but even so, the respect owed to the courts of the third country means that this interest is unlikely to suffice.[208] Further, the same result cannot be achieved by the back door by obtaining an anti-suit injunction in the preferred foreign court and then seeking to enforce it in England, as the foreign anti-suit injunction will not be enforceable in England.[209]

3. Amenable to the Jurisdiction

4.84   It has frequently been said that it is a consequence of comity that an injunction will only be granted to restrain a person who is regarded as properly amenable to the jurisdiction of the English courts, against whom an injunction will be an effective remedy.[210] However, it was not entirely clear what this meant. The case law has now made clear that it means only that the court must have personal jurisdiction over the defendant to hear the claim for an injunction. It therefore adds little or nothing.[211]

---

[205] See eg *Arab Monetary Fund v Hashim (No 6)* (Hoffmann J, 14 July 1992); *General Star International Indemnity v Stirling Cooke Brown Reinsurance Brokers* [2003] Lloyds Rep IR 719, 721–22. The factors that determine which court is the appropriate one to determine questions of forum overlap with conventional *forum non conveniens* considerations, but they are not identical. The criterion of sufficient connection gives greater significance to jurisdictional factors, and less to difficulties of trial management.

[206] *Airbus Industrie v Patel* [1999] 1 AC 119 (HL) 138G–H, 140F–141C; *Evialis SA v SIAT* [2003] 2 Lloyds Rep 377, 403; *Dreymoor Fertilisers Overseas v Eurochem Trading* [2018] EWHC 2267 [71], [73]. See also the earlier case of *Hughes v Hannover* [1997] 1 BCLC 497 (CA), where the point was put in terms of the need for a 'relevant link' to England: at 504 (per Knox J). E Peel, 'Anti-Suit Injunctions: The House of Lords Declines to Act as an International Policeman' (1998) 114 LQR 543 considers that *Airbus* is a decision 'which should be viewed with some regret' and argues that 'it is difficult to see that the affront which may be caused is significantly greater where the court which grants the injunction is not itself the natural forum'. But for interesting commentary from a US perspective, see K Anderson, 'What can the United States Learn from English Anti-Suit Injunctions? An American Perspective on Airbus Industrie GIE v Patel', (2000) 25 YJIL 195.

[207] *Airbus Industrie v Patel* [1999] 1 AC 119 (HL) 140F–141C.

[208] In *Hughes v Hannover* [1997] 1 BCLC 497 (CA), the Bermudan court, before which insolvency proceedings were under way, asked the English court, by way of a letter of request, to grant an anti-suit injunction restraining proceedings in third countries. It was held that the English court would have power to grant such an order under s 426 of the Insolvency Act 1986: at 503–04 (per Knox J); 516–18. However, the injunction was refused on the facts. As the decision was reached before *Airbus v Patel*, the issue of comity was not sharply formulated. But it is submitted that the result can be viewed as confirmation of the proposition in the text.

[209] Foreign injunctions, including foreign anti-suit injunctions, are not enforceable in England at common law, or under the Administration of Justice Act 1920 or the Foreign Judgments (Reciprocal Enforcement) Act 1933: *Airbus Industrie v Patel* [1996] ILPr 465 (Colman J) [13]–[29]; Dicey, paras 14R-020 and 14-185. In theory, this barrier to enforceability may not exist under the Brussels–Lugano regime (so long as it applies); but the likelihood of the English court being asked to enforce an anti-suit injunction granted by a fellow Brussels–Lugano court is slim.

[210] See eg *In re North Carolina Estate* (1889) 5 TLR 328; *Bank of Tokyo v Karoon* [1987] AC 45 (CA) 59G; *Société Nationale Industrielle Aérospatiale v Lee Kui Jak* [1987] AC 871 (PC) 892E; *Donohue v Armco* [2002] 1 Lloyds Rep 425 (HL) [19].

[211] *Stichting Shell Pensionenfonds v Krys* [2015] AC 616 (PC) [27]; and see previously *ED&F Man (Sugar) v Yani Haryanto (No 2)* [1991] 1 Lloyds Rep 429 (CA) 438 (Mann LJ). *Donohue v Armco* [2002] 1 Lloyds Rep 425 (HL) [21]; *Masri v Consolidated Contractors (No 3)* [2009] QB 503 (CA) [27]–[29].

The injunction defendant's 'amenability' to the jurisdiction can also be understood as a label   **4.85**
for the idea that the injunction must be an effective remedy with respect to the particular
defendant in question. However, again, this appears to have disappeared as a separate requirement. It had previously been suggested that it is a necessary condition of granting the
anti-suit injunction that it can be enforced against the injunction defendant, either because
that defendant is or will be present within the jurisdiction, or because he, she or it has or
will have assets here.[212] But the recent decisions have not required this to be shown separately. The bold position adopted in the lead modern cases is that, in general, the court
does not contemplate the possibility that its order will not be obeyed,[213] and injunctions
have frequently been granted to restrain defendants who are not resident in England and
have no assets in the jurisdiction, even where there was no specific basis to assume that the
English injunction order could be enforced abroad.[214] It remains the case that the potential
unenforceability of an order, because the defendant and all his assets are out of the jurisdiction, is a matter of which the court can take account when considering whether it should
grant the remedy in its discretion.[215] But there would appear to be no meaningful separate
requirement of amenability in this regard either, for anti-suit injunctions. The cases reflect
little more than the weak general proposition, true of injunctions generally, that the court
will, in the exercise of its discretion, be disinclined to make orders which are futile.[216]

4. Comity and Discretion in General

The requirements of comity will also shape and influence the court's exercise of its dis-   **4.86**
cretion whether or not to grant an injunction, in ways that are not always captured by the
threshold tests which have so far been explored.

Thus, the closer the connection of the litigation with England and the English court, and
the more tenuous the link to the foreign jurisdiction, the weaker will be the inhibitions imposed by comity on the grant of the injunction,[217] while conversely, the more distant the

---

[212] *Turner v Grovit* [2002] 1 WLR 107 (HL) 117C.
[213] *Stichting Shell Pensionenfonds v Krys* [2015] AC 616 (PC) [36]–[37]; and see earlier *In re Liddell's Settlement Trusts* [1936] Ch 365 (CA) 373–74 (not an anti-suit case); *Royal Exchange Assurance v Compania Naviera Santi (The Tropaioforos) (No 2)* [1962] 1 Lloyds Rep 410, 420; *Castanho v Brown & Root* [1981] AC 557 (HL) 574B; *ED&F Man (Sugar) v Yani Haryanto (No 2)* [1991] 1 Lloyds Rep 429 (CA) 439 (Mann LJ).
[214] *Castanho v Brown & Root* [1981] AC 557 (HL) 574B–D; see also *Calenders and Diaries v Nuovo Instituto Italiano D'Arti Grafiche* (Wood J, 14 February 1986).
[215] *Royal Exchange Assurance v Compania Naviera Santi (The Tropaioforos) (No 2)* [1962] 1 Lloyds Rep 410, 420; *Board of Governors of the Hospital for Sick Children v Walt Disney Productions Inc* [1968] Ch 52 (CA) 68G–69B, 71C–71F, 77F; *Locabail International Finance v Agroexport* [1986] 1 WLR 657 (CA) 664H, 665F; *ED&F Man (Sugar) v Yani Haryanto (No 2)* [1991] 1 Lloyds Rep 429 (CA) 439; *Impala Warehousing and Logistics (Shanghai) v Wanxiang Resources (Singapore)* [2015] EWHC 811 [138]. This conclusion is not entirely easy to reconcile with the authorities, such as *Castanho v Brown & Root* and *Shell v Krys*, that articulate the sweeping proposition that the court, in making an order, does not contemplate the possibility that it will not be obeyed. But it is suggested that those cases need only be interpreted as rejecting any general rule that unenforceability should be treated as a decisive factor against the grant of an injunction. It is unnecessary to treat them as laying down a converse absolute rule that unenforceability can never be a relevant consideration to the exercise of the court's discretion, although the cases suggest that it will usually be a factor to which little weight should be accorded: see *Royal Exchange Assurance v Compania Naviera Santi (The Tropaioforos) (No 2)* [1962] 1 Lloyds Rep 410, 420; *Board of Governors of the Hospital for Sick Children v Walt Disney Productions* [1968] Ch 52 (CA) 68G–69B, 71C–71F, 77F.
[216] *Barclays Bank v Homan* [1993] BCLC 680, 691 (Hoffmann J). See also in the contractual context *Impala Warehousing and Logistics (Shanghai) v Wanxiang Resources (Singapore)* [2015] EWHC 811 [138].
[217] See eg *Moore v Moore* (1896) 12 TLR 221 (neither party domiciled in Austria).

connection to England, or the closer the connection to the foreign state, the greater the restraint to be exercised.[218] For example, where the underlying dispute concerns real property in the foreign jurisdiction, an anti-suit injunction is unlikely to be granted.[219] The US courts have concluded that injunctions should not generally be granted to restrain foreign proceedings concerning patents of the foreign state in question.[220] Similarly, if the injunction claimant has voluntarily brought its relations with the injunction defendant within the legitimate sphere of interest of the foreign law and legal system, then that will militate against the grant of an injunction.[221]

4.87   If there is evidence that the foreign court is likely, and with some system-independent justification, to regard the grant of an anti-suit injunction as an illegitimate interference, this may support an argument that comity requires that the injunction should not be granted.[222] However, the Court of Appeal has recently suggested that the force of such arguments has diminished;[223] and in any event it is doubtful that this reasoning applies in contractual cases.[224]

4.88   Delay in seeking an injunction can have important consequences for comity, and can be a powerful factor against the grant of an injunction, because the interference with the foreign court's jurisdiction is the greater if the foreign proceedings have been underway and the judicial resources of the foreign court have been used. Consequently, delay can defeat an injunction independent of prejudice to the injunction defendant.[225]

5. Bypassing or Overriding Comity

4.89   Comity is a mutual obligation. Consequently, the conduct of the foreign state can deprive it of the respect normally required by comity, and if so, the limits imposed by comity will be diminished or displaced.[226] Notably, an excessive assertion of jurisdiction by the foreign court may reduce the respect due to its processes.[227]

---

[218]   *Barclays Bank v Homan* [1993] BCLC 680, 691 (Hoffmann J), 701 (CA).

[219]   *Moor v Anglo-Italian Bank* (1879) 10 Ch D 681, 690–91; *Jopson v James* (1908) 77 LJ (Ch) 824, 830; and see *Impala Warehousing and Logistics (Shanghai) v Wanxiang Resources (Singapore)* [2015] EWHC 811 [138].

[220]   *Western Electric v Milgo Electronic Corp* 450 F Supp 835 (SD Fla 1978); D Tan, 'Anti-Suit Injunctions and the Vexing Problem of Comity' (2005) 45 Virg J Intl Law 283, 337–38.

[221]   *British Airways Board v Laker Airways* [1985] AC 58 (HL) 84E–G; *Midland Bank v Laker Airways* [1986] QB 689 (CA) 700D, 704H–705C, 715C–D; see also *Bitmac v Creosote Producers Association* (CA, 1 January 1986).

[222]   *Evialis v SIAT* [2003] 2 Lloyds Rep 377, 403; *Ecobank Transnational v Tanoh* [2016] 1 WLR 2231 (CA).

[223]   *Ecobank Transnational v Tanoh* [2016] 1 WLR 2231 (CA), saying that the question was not one of 'offence to individual judges', 'who are made of sterner stuff'.

[224]   See Ch 8, section E, 'Comity', paras 8.25–8.30.

[225]   *Ecobank Transnational v Tanoh* [2016] 1 WLR 2231 (CA).

[226]   *Airbus Industrie v Patel* [1999] 1 AC 119 (HL) 140D.

[227]   In *Barclays Bank v Homan* [1993] BCLC 680, 688, 691, upheld on appeal [1993] BCLC 680 (CA), Hoffmann J suggested that comity was no longer a restraint where 'the foreign court is, judged by its own jurisprudence, likely to assert a jurisdiction so wide either as to persons or subject matter that to English notions it appears contrary to accepted principles of international law'. However, he concluded on the facts before him that the assertion of US bankruptcy jurisdiction by the US court would not be 'so egregious a claim of extra-territoriality that justice requires that it should be prevented by injunction' (as to his specific language, see n 91). See also *Société Nationale Industrielle Aérospatiale v Lee Kui Jak* [1987] AC 871 (PC) 894E; *Deutsche Bank v Highland Crusader Partners* [2010] 1 WLR 1023 (CA) [50]–[65] and *Stichting Shell Pensioenfonds v Krys* [2015] AC 616 (PC) [42], where the injunction was justified in significant part because the Dutch court's jurisdiction was 'exorbitant'.

Further, a breach of comity by the foreign court can amount to a positive factor in sup-   **4.90**
port of an injunction. If the foreign court's assumption of jurisdiction is excessive, this can
amount to, or support a finding of, vexation or oppression.[228]

However, it will be difficult to view an assertion of jurisdiction by the foreign court as exces-   **4.91**
sive if the English courts would assert jurisdiction extraterritorially in an analogous case.[229]
It is also clear that the mere fact that the foreign court does not apply a doctrine analogous
to *forum non conveniens* is insufficient in itself to permit the inhibitions imposed by comity
to be displaced.[230]

Conversely, it has been suggested that, even where the foreign state's conduct has not dis-   **4.92**
placed comity, the inhibitions that comity would otherwise impose can be overcome if the
legislative policies of the English legal system and the foreign legal system are so at variance
that comity is overridden by the need to protect the national interest.[231] However, this will
only be relevant in rare cases.[232] The principle of mutual respect enshrined in the concept of
comity means that the foreign court must presumptively be entitled to give effect to the policies of its own national legislation, even if they conflict with the solution reached by English
law,[233] provided that there has been no excessive assertion of jurisdiction by the foreign
court, or the foreign proceedings are not otherwise vexatious or oppressive. The English
court will be reluctant to criticize the quality of justice available in the foreign forum, and
arguments of this kind will require cogent evidence.[234]

M. NATURAL FORUM

In alternative forum cases, the requirement of a sufficient interest means that an injunction   **4.93**
on grounds of vexation and oppression will not normally be granted unless the English
court is the natural forum for the resolution of the substantive disputes between the parties.[235] The concept of 'natural forum' has often been expressed as a general *requirement*
of such vexation and oppression-based alternative forum injunctions. But even viewed in
that way, it was only a general and not absolute requirement;[236] and it can be departed from
when appropriate.[237] Further, as discussed at para 4.81 above, the better view on a close
reading of *Airbus v Patel* is that 'natural forum' is only an important factor, and not a requirement. Lord Goff rephrased the point as merely being that in alternative forum cases

---

[228] Paragraph 4.54 and n 112.
[229] *Barclays Bank v Homan* [1993] BCLC 680, 688 (Hoffmann J).
[230] *Airbus Industrie v Patel* [1999] 1 AC 119 (HL) 140D–E.
[231] *Barclays Bank v Homan* [1993] BCLC 680, 688 (Hoffmann J); followed in *Stichting Shell Pensioenfonds v Krys* [2015] AC 616 (PC) [42].
[232] Further, reliance on English public policy on its own to justify the grant of an injunction is itself controversial: see section I, 'Protection of English Public Policy'. The proposition entertained here is more limited, namely
that public policy imperatives could justify a loosening of the constraints of comity.
[233] *Barclays Bank v Homan* [1993] BCLC 680, 690 (Hoffmann J); *Seismic Shipping v Total E&P UK (The Western
Regent)* [2005] 2 Lloyds Rep 359 (CA) [50], [59]; *Star Reefers Pool v JFC Group* [2012] 1 Lloyds Rep 376 (CA) [36]–
[40]; *Jewel Owner v Sagaan (The MD Gemini)* [2012] 1 Lloyds Rep 672 [21].
[234] *Dawnus Sierra Leone v Timis Mining Corporation* [2016] EWHC 236 [66].
[235] For the language of normally, see *Airbus Industrie v Patel* [1999] 1 AC 119 (HL) 134F.
[236] See among many others, *Société Nationale Industrielle Aérospatiale v Lee Kui Jak* [1987] AC 871 (PC) 894,
896; *Deutsche Bank v Highland Crusader Partners* [2010] 1 WLR 1023 (CA) [50], [53]–[56].
[237] For an example of departure, see *Shell International Petroleum v Coral Oil (No 2)* [1999] 2 Lloyds Rep
606, 610.

the assessment of 'sufficient interest' will involve 'consideration' of the question of whether the English court is the natural forum for the resolution of the dispute.[238] The general requirement of sufficient interest can be satisfied in other ways.[239] Further, in the recent case law there are signs that the concept of natural forum is expanding, so that in appropriate cases it will also suffice for this purpose if the English court is the natural forum to decide the question of forum,[240] and not merely the natural forum for the litigation. So, for example, the English court is the natural forum to grant injunctions to protect English arbitrations,[241] and it should not matter that it would not be able itself to hear the matter submitted to arbitration. However, in classic alternative forum situations, where an injunction is sought on the basis of vexation and oppression, the question of natural forum will be a central consideration, and failure to satisfy it will generally be determinative.[242]

4.94   Any criterion or consideration of natural forum does not, it seems, apply to injunctions granted to protect the processes, jurisdiction, and judgments of the English court,[243] nor to injunctions grounded on public policy, or to single forum injunctions.

4.95   The concept of natural forum for the trial of the action is derived from the case law on permission to serve claims out of the jurisdiction, and applications to stay English proceedings on the grounds of *forum non conveniens*.[244] The natural forum in this sense is 'that with which the action had the most real and substantial connection',[245] or, otherwise phrased, is the appropriate forum for the trial of the action.[246] In assessing which forum is natural in this sense, the court will evaluate the factors connecting the litigation with a particular forum, including factors affecting convenience or expense, but also other factors such as the law governing the relevant transaction,[247] the location of relevant property,[248] and the places where the parties respectively reside or carry on business.[249] In the recent case of *Re Tadros*, for example, it was unsurprisingly concluded that the Netherlands was the natural forum for deciding matters relating to a Dutch will.[250]

---

[238]   *Airbus Industrie v Patel* [1999] 1 AC 119 (HL) 134F, 135B, 138F–H.

[239]   *The Owners of the Ship 'Al Khattiya' v The Owners and/or Demise Charterers of the Ship 'Jag Laadki'* [2018] EWHC 389 [109].

[240]   *The Owners of the Ship 'Al Khattiya' v The Owners and/or Demise Charterers of the Ship 'Jag Laadki'* [2018] EWHC 389 [110] and *Shell International Petroleum v Coral Oil (No 2)* [1999] 2 Lloyds Rep 606, 610. This is perhaps also implicit in *Deutsche Bank v Highland Crusader Partners* [2010] 1 WLR 1023 (CA) [56].

[241]   *Michael Wilson v Emmott* [2018] 1 Lloyds Rep 299 (CA) [55].

[242]   See eg *Morris v Davies* [2011] EWHC 1272 [20], [32], [33]; *Re Tadros (Deceased)* [2014] EWHC 2860 [71]–[72]; *Vitol Bahrain v Nasdec General Trading* [2013] EWHC 3359.

[243]   Paragraph 4.67 above.

[244]   *The Abidin Daver* [1984] AC 398 (HL); *Spiliada Maritime v Cansulex* [1987] AC 460 (HL).

[245]   *The Abidin Daver* [1984] AC 398 (HL) 415F; approved in *Spiliada Maritime v Cansulex* [1987] AC 460 (HL) 478A; *Amchem Products v British Colombia (Workers Compensation Board)* [1993] 1 SCR 897 (Can SC) 916.

[246]   *Spiliada Maritime v Cansulex* [1987] AC 460 (HL) 475C, 477G, 478C, 482E, 483A and H.

[247]   See eg *Heilmann v Falkenstein* (1917) 32 TLR 383; *Vitol Bahrain v Nasdec General Trading* [2013] EWHC 3359; *Re Tadros (Deceased)* [2014] EWHC 2860 [72].

[248]   *Vitol Bahrain v Nasdec General Trading* [2013] EWHC 3359 [41]; *Re Tadros (Deceased)* [2014] EWHC 2860 [72].

[249]   *Spiliada Maritime v Cansulex* [1987] AC 460 (HL) 478A–B. It is worth noting that, although it is a material consideration that the injunction defendant is resident or domiciled abroad, there is no rule or presumption that injunctions will not be granted to restrain foreigners from suing before their own courts. Some of the older cases suggest that such a principle might exist, notably *Carron Iron v Maclaren* (1855) 10 ER 961, 5 HLC 416, 437, 441–44 (see further, Ch 2, paras 2.11–2.13), but under the modern approach following *Aérospatiale* the residence of the injunction defendant is merely one factor in the assessment of what is the natural forum: para 4.23, n 42.

[250]   *Re Tadros (Deceased)* [2014] EWHC 2860 [72]. See in contrast *Morris v Davies* [2011] EWHC 1272 [20], [32], [33].

The natural forum for the purposes of *forum conveniens* will, if nothing has changed, gen-   **4.96**
erally be the natural forum when considering whether or not to grant an anti-suit injunction.[251] However, a court which was not originally the natural forum for a particular claim
can become the natural forum due to the progress of litigation before it on the claim in
question, or on related claims.[252]

There is often no one forum that is clearly more appropriate than others,[253] and in con-   **4.97**
sidering whether to grant an injunction, the court will take account of different shades of
appropriateness in assessing vexation and oppression. Thus, even where England is the natural forum, it will weigh against a finding of vexation that the foreign court is *an* appropriate
forum.[254]

N.   OTHER DISCRETIONARY CONSIDERATIONS

The flexibility of the concepts of 'the ends of justice' and 'vexation and oppression', and   **4.98**
the tests of comity mean that there is less conceptual room for the operation of distinct
discretionary factors. Most considerations which are relevant to whether an injunction
should or should not be granted can be articulated within an assessment of whether it is
'in the interests of justice' to grant an injunction,[255] although the distinction between a
finding of vexation and oppression and the assessment of discretion is more easily drawn.
Nevertheless, the injunction always remains a discretionary remedy which responds to all
the circumstances.[256]

The exercise of the court's discretion, which always depends on all the facts of the case,   **4.99**
cannot be sensibly summarized in a textbook. Nevertheless, there are certain recurrent
types of situation which have been treated as distinctly relevant to the exercise of the court's
discretion, and which do not fall naturally under one of the tests discussed, perhaps because
they are essentially practical problems, and less redolent of 'justice'.

Thus, injunctions have been refused because of undue and unjustified delay,[257] or con-   **4.100**
versely, because the injunction was sought prematurely.[258] The injunction claimant's conduct in the competing proceedings can also disentitle him to relief, in particular if he can
be said to be acting in a vexatious or oppressive way himself.[259] If the order sought is likely

---

[251] *CNA International (UK) v Office Depot International (UK)* [2005] Lloyds Rep IR 658 [28].
[252] *Société Nationale Industrielle Aérospatiale v Lee Kui Jak* [1987] AC 871 (PC) 897–99; *Shell International Petroleum v Coral Oil (No 2)* [1999] 2 Lloyds Rep 606, 610; *Morris v Davies* [2011] EWHC 1272 [20], [32], [33]; *Salgaocar v Jitendra* [2018] SGHC 90 [48].
[253] *Amchem Products v British Colombia (Workers Compensation Board)* [1993] 1 SCR 897 (Can SC) 935 (although this case does not represent English law in other respects).
[254] *Ascot Commodities v Northern Pacific Shipping (The Irini A)* [1999] 1 Lloyds Rep 196, 200; however, cf *Cadre v Astra Asigurari* [2006] 1 Lloyds Rep 560 [17].
[255] Paragraph 4.25.
[256] *Deutsche Bank v Highland Crusader Partners* [2010] 1 WLR 1023 (CA) [50], [65].
[257] There was held to be no criticizable delay in *Cadre v Astra Asigurari* [2006] 1 Lloyds Rep 560, 564 [18]. Delay was excusable in *The Eras Eil Actions* [1995] 1 Lloyds Rep 64, 86; and was thought justifiable in *Sabbagh v Khoury* [2018] EWHC 1330 [33]–[36]. On the other hand, delay was not excusable, and contributed to the refusal to grant the injunction, in *Bloch v Bloch* [2003] 1 FLR 1 [57], [59]–[62], [85]; *Noble Assurance v Gerling-Konzern General Insurance* [2008] Lloyds Rep IR 1 [100]; and *Ecobank Transnational v Tanoh* [2016] 1 WLR 2231 (CA). See also *Moor v Anglo-Italian Bank* (1879) 10 Ch D 681, 690–91.
[258] *Berliner Bank v C Czarnikow Sugar (The Rama)* [1996] 2 Lloyds Rep 281, 298.
[259] See eg *Bloch v Bloch* [2003] 1 FLR 1 [57], [59]–[62], [85].

to be futile,[260] or if the same result can be achieved by less intrusive means, such as a declaration,[261] the court will be less likely to grant an injunction. Anti-suit injunctions can also be refused on the grounds that the injunction claimant has 'unclean hands', although strictly this is a matter of equitable principle, not discretion.[262]

O. QUIA TIMET

4.101 Anti-suit injunctions may be granted on a *quia timet* basis even before the targeted proceedings have commenced, if there is sufficient threat that they will be commenced; and that if so, they will be of a nature which will justify the injunction.[263] In one case, a mere reservation of rights to bring proceedings was held not to be sufficient to justify a *quia timet* injunction.[264]

---

[260] *Barclays Bank v Homan* [1993] BCLC 680 (Hoffmann J), 691–92.
[261] *Noble Assurance v Gerling-Konzern General Insurance* [2008] Lloyds Rep IR 1 [99]–[109]. See also *Banque Cantonale Vaudoise v Waterlily Maritime* [1997] 2 Lloyds Rep 347, 357–58, where in place of a full anti-suit injunction the court granted an order restraining the injunction defendant from advancing certain contentions pending the trial of the English action, which would be expedited.
[262] *Royal Bank of Scotland v Highland Financial Partners* [2012] 2 CLC 109 [175]–[195], [2013] 1 CLC 596 (CA) [158]–[172].
[263] *Hospira UK v Eli Lilly* [2008] EWHC 1862 (Pat) [11]–[13].
[264] *Hospira UK v Eli Lilly* [2008] EWHC 1862 (Pat) [11]–[13].

5

Non-Contractual Anti-Suit Injunctions

A. INTRODUCTION

This chapter explores the landscape of the cases in which non-contractual anti-suit injunctions have been sought in respect of proceedings abroad. It is divided into the following sections: **5.01**

- Alternative forum cases.
- Injunctions to prevent relitigation.
- Single forum cases.
- Insolvency and justice between creditors.
- The relevance of stay applications before the foreign court.
- Injunctions to restrain ancillary and collateral proceedings.
- 'Anti-anti-suit' injunctions.
- Anti-enforcement injunctions.

B. ALTERNATIVE FORUM CASES

A distinction needs to be drawn between 'alternative forum' and 'single forum' cases, although it is never absolute. In an alternative forum case,[1] the claim which is being made in the foreign action could be heard either in England or abroad, or in both jurisdictions. The possible claims in the competing jurisdictions do not need to be identical, provided that they are substantially similar.[2] In contrast, in a single forum case the foreign claim could   **5.02**

---

[1] Using the language of Lord Goff in *Airbus Industrie v Patel* [1999] 1 AC 119 (HL) 134B–C.
[2] If a contention could be raised by way of defence in the English action instead of by claim in the foreign action, then the situation can be treated as an alternative forum case: *Heilmann v Falkenstein* (1917) 32 TLR 383.

only be brought in the foreign country, and no similar claim could be brought in England.[3] But if additional and different remedies could be claimed abroad in respect of the same or similar substantive rights, the situation will probably still be treated as an alternative forum case.[4]

1. General Principles in Alternative Forum Cases

5.03   The existence of concurrent[5] proceedings on the same or substantially similar subject matters in England and abroad, where the claimant abroad is the defendant in England,[6] does not in itself mean that the pursuit of the foreign action is vexatious or oppressive, and is not a sufficient condition to justify the grant of an injunction.[7] In addition, a submission by the injunction defendant to the jurisdiction of the English court should not be treated as sufficient to justify an injunction,[8] as submission will occur in any English action which is defended after the failure of a jurisdiction challenge. Nor, conversely, is submission to the jurisdiction of the English courts a necessary condition of a finding of vexation or oppression (or unconscionability).[9] However, in general, the greater the positive and voluntary involvement of the injunction defendant in the English proceedings, and the longer the English action has been allowed to proceed before the commencement of the parallel foreign proceedings, the stronger the case for an injunction.[10] Thus vexation may be found in the facts that the injunction defendant has first submitted to English jurisdiction and then

---

[3]   In *OceanConnect UK v Angara Maritime* [2011] 1 Lloyds Rep 399 (CA), it was suggested, *obiter*, that a case would only be a single forum situation if there was no cause of action available to the injunction defendant that would enable him to win in the English courts. That is overstated: the likelihood of victory is not the point. The injunction is a 'single forum' injunction if it restrains a form of litigation in the only forum where that particular *kind* of claim can be pursued.

[4]   *Simon Engineering v Butte Mining (No 2)* [1996] 1 Lloyds Rep 91, 95.

[5]   For the case where the foreign proceedings are overlapping but *subsequent*, and the question is about whether the pre-existing judgment of the English court should be protected, see section C, 'Injunctions to Prevent Relitigation'.

[6]   For the 'double claimant' case, where the claimant abroad is also the claimant in England, see paras 5.14–5.16.

[7]   *Société Nationale Industrielle Aérospatiale v Lee Kui Jak* [1987] AC 871 (PC) 894C, 895E–F; *Credit Suisse First Boston (Europe) v MLC Bermuda* [1999] 1 Lloyds Rep 767, 781; *Royal Bank of Canada v Cooperatieve Centrale Raiffeisen-Boerenleenbank* [2003] EWHC 2913 [29], [2004] 1 Lloyds Rep 471 (CA) 474–75 (where this was not disputed); *Deutsche Bank v Highland Crusader Partners* [2010] 1 WLR 1023 (CA) [50], [63].

[8]   *Calendars and Diaries v Nuovo Instituto Italiano D'Arti Grafiche* (Wood J, 14 February 1986), where it was submitted by the injunction claimant that the injunction defendant's submission was decisive, but the injunction was refused; *Royal Bank of Canada v Cooperatieve Centrale Raiffeisen-Boerenleenbank* [2003] EWHC 2913 [2004] 1 Lloyds Rep 471 (CA) (where it was not contended to be a strong reason in favour of the grant of an injunction that the injunction defendant had submitted). The same result is also implicit in *Deutsche Bank v Highland Crusader Partners* [2010] 1 WLR 1023 (CA) and many other cases. However, see *CNA Insurance v Office Depot* [2005] Lloyds Rep IR 658 [27], where weight was placed on submission, among other factors.

[9]   *Star Reefers Pool v JFC Group* [2012] 1 Lloyds Rep 376 (CA) [30].

[10]   *Moore v Moore* (1896) 12 TLR 221; *CNA Insurance v Office Depot* [2005] Lloyds Rep IR 658 [27]; *Morris v Davies* [2011] EWHC 1272. In Singapore, see *PT Sandipala Arthaputra v ST Microelectronics Asia Pacific* [2015] SGHC 245 [136]–[137].

The inverse reasoning applies: see *Royal Bank of Canada v Cooperatieve Centrale Raiffeisen-Boerenleenbank* [2004] 1 Lloyds Rep 471 (CA) [50], where submission and participation in the foreign proceedings were viewed as a significant factor against an injunction (and see also in the contractual case, *Akai v People's Insurance* [1998] 1 Lloyds Rep 90, 105). Similarly, where the foreign proceedings are prior in time this may militate against the grant of an injunction: *Jopson v James* (1908) 77 LJ (Ch) 824, 829; *Star Reefers Pool v JFC Group* [2012] 1 Lloyds Rep 376 (CA) [29], although mere accidents of timing are a weak factor: at [28].

sought vexatiously and oppressively to prolong or multiply the litigation by commencing further proceedings abroad.[11]

It is also now established that foreign proceedings will not be vexatious or oppressive, and **5.04** an injunction cannot be justified, solely on the grounds that England is the natural forum for the litigation in the eyes of the English court, or that the English court has dismissed a stay on the grounds of *forum non conveniens*. The foreign proceedings must be shown to be vexatious or oppressive by reference to the circumstances as a whole, including some other factors, or there must be some additional reason why the ends of justice require the grant of an injunction.[12]

Nevertheless, if, in the eyes of the English court, England is the natural forum and the for- **5.05** eign jurisdiction is inappropriate, this can be a significant factor in support of a finding that parallel foreign proceedings are vexatious or oppressive.[13] The court recognizes the undesirable consequences that may result if concurrent actions in respect of the same subject matter proceed in two different countries. There may be conflicting judgments from the two courts concerned, or an 'ugly', or 'unruly' rush to get one action decided first to attempt to create a *res judicata* in the other court.[14]

2. Subjectively Vexatious Proceedings

If the parallel foreign proceedings have been brought in bad faith, or with the intention and **5.06** effect of harassing the injunction claimant, rather than actually seeking justice in the foreign forum, this can constitute subjective vexation, which can justify an injunction.[15] There is nothing inherently improper in preferring a foreign jurisdiction for tactical purposes.[16] But where no adequate explanation is advanced for why competing foreign proceedings have been brought, the court may well be willing to infer that the foreign proceedings are motivated by a deliberate strategy of harassment and vexation.[17]

---

[11] *Star Reefers Pool v JFC Group* [2012] 1 Lloyds Rep 376 (CA) [30]. The facts were not quite enough in *The Insurance Company of the State of Pennsylvania v Equitas Insurance* [2014] Lloyds Rep IR 195 [29].

[12] *Société Nationale Industrielle Aérospatiale v Lee Kui Jak* [1987] AC 871 (PC) 894B–G, 895E–G, 896F–H; *Donohue v Armco* [2002] 1 Lloyds Rep 425 (HL) [19] (Lord Bingham, with whom Lords Mackay and Nicholls agreed: at 438); *Glencore International v Metro Trading International (No 3)* [2002] CLC 1090 (CA) [42]; *Deutsche Bank v Highland Crusader Partners* [2010] 1 WLR 1023 (CA) [50], [54], [56], [63], [110], [117]–[119]; *Vitol Bahrain v Nasdec Trading* [2013] EWHC 3359 [46]–[48]. The contrary proposition would be to endorse Lord Scarman's error in *Castanho*: see further Ch 2, section D, 'Forum non Conveniens and the Castanho Heresy' and Ch 4, section J, 'Forum non Conveniens'.

[13] *Société Nationale Industrielle Aérospatiale v Lee Kui Jak* [1987] AC 871 (PC) 894E–G; *Turner v Grovit* [2002] 1 WLR 107 (HL) [25] (reasoned in terms of unconscionability). See eg *Moore v Moore* (1896) 12 TLR 221; *Simon Engineering v Butte Mining (No 1)* [1996] 1 Lloyds Rep 104, 111; *Tonicstar v American Home Assurance* [2005] Lloyds Rep IR 32, 37; *CNA Insurance v Office Depot International (UK)* [2005] Lloyds Rep IR 658 [27].

[14] *The Abidin Daver* [1984] AC 398 (HL) 423H–424A (a stay case); *Royal Bank of Canada v Cooperatieve Centrale Raiffeisen-Boerenleenbank* [2003] EWHC 2913 [29] (upheld on appeal [2004] 1 Lloyds Rep 471 (CA)); *Tonicstar v American Home Assurance* [2005] Lloyds Rep IR 32, 37; *Star Reefers Pool v JFC Group* [2012] 1 Lloyds Rep 376 (CA) [36].

[15] *Midland Bank v Laker Airways* [1986] QB 689 (CA) 702D–E; *Turner v Grovit* [2000] QB 345 (CA) 357–62, [2002] 1 WLR 107 (HL) [17], [29]; *Glencore International v Metro Trading International (No 3)* [2002] CLC 1090 (CA) [69]; *Cadre v Astra Asigurari* [2006] 1 Lloyds Rep 560 [18]; *Star Reefers Pool v JFC Group* [2012] 1 Lloyds Rep 376 at [31]; *Vitol Bahrain v Nasdec Trading* [2013] EWHC 3359 [49]–[50].

[16] *Evialis v SIAT* [2003] 2 Lloyds Rep 377 [140].

[17] *Glencore International v Metro Trading International (No 3)* [2002] CLC 1090 (CA) [69]; see also *The Owners of the Ship 'Al Khattiya' v The Owners and/or Demise Charterers of the Ship 'Jag Laadki'* [2018] EWHC 389 [111].

3. Objectively Vexatious or Oppressive Proceedings

5.07   Foreign proceedings can be vexatious or oppressive due to their nature or consequences. Duplicative foreign proceedings have been restrained where the foreign forum was not a natural forum and its remedial law contained alien and onerous remedies compared to the natural forum;[18] where a weak appeal, which was likely to be expensive and protracted, was brought against the foreign first instance court's decision to stay the proceedings before it, and England was clearly the natural forum;[19] where the aim of the foreign proceedings was to pre-empt proceedings in the natural forum;[20] where the foreign proceedings were viewed as an illegitimate attempts to 'hijack' the English court's determination of questions going to its own jurisdiction, although the English court was the natural forum to decide questions of forum;[21] where while participating in English proceedings one party brought foreign attachment proceedings as a pre-emptive strike to prevent any English judgment being effective;[22] where arrest proceedings were hopeless and served no purpose;[23] and where the injunction defendant proclaimed that he would be able to manipulate the foreign judiciary illegitimately.[24] It has been suggested that it would be oppressive to commence arrest proceedings abroad where the underlying claim in question has been stayed in England due to a failure to provide security for costs.[25]

5.08   Further, if the dispute between the injunction claimant and injunction defendant could necessitate the bringing of related proceedings against connected parties, which should as a matter of justice and sensible case management be determined in third-party proceedings heard together with the original action, and such third-party proceedings could be effectively brought in England, but would not be feasible in the foreign action, this can support a conclusion that the foreign proceedings would be oppressive.[26]

5.09   It is possible to support an argument of oppression on the basis that the foreign legal system is unfair or incapable of doing justice, but the English courts will be reluctant to make any such finding, and will not do so without concrete evidence.[27] This does not, however,

---

[18]   *Simon Engineering v Butte Mining (No 1)* [1996] 1 Lloyds Rep 104, 110–11; see also *Simon Engineering v Butte Mining (No 2)* [1996] 1 Lloyds Rep 91, although cf *The Eras Eil Actions* [1995] 1 Lloyds Rep 64, 83, 85. See also *Airbus Industrie v Patel* [1997] 2 Lloyds Rep 8 (CA) 18 (reversed [1999] 1 AC 119 (HL), but not on this point). However, if the foreign jurisdiction can be viewed as an appropriate forum, then its remedial peculiarities may well be analysed as legitimate advantages rather than grounds for oppression: *Simon Engineering v Butte Mining (No 1)* [1996] 1 Lloyds Rep 104, 110; and see *AWB (Geneva) v North America Steamships* [2007] 1 CLC 749 [31] (not addressed on appeal, [2007] 2 Lloyds Rep 315 (CA) [21], [33]).

[19]   *Simon Engineering v Butte Mining (No 1)* [1996] 1 Lloyds Rep 104, 112; *Simon Engineering v Butte Mining (No 2)* [1996] 1 Lloyds Rep 91, 101.

[20]   *Cadre v Astra Asigurari* [2006] 1 Lloyds Rep 560 [18]. See also *Heilmann v Falkenstein* (1917) 32 TLR 383.

[21]   *General Star International Indemnity v Stirling Cooke Brown Reinsurance Brokers* [2003] Lloyds Rep IR 719, 721–23; *Tonicstar v American Home Assurance* [2005] 1 Lloyds Rep IR 32, 37.

[22]   *Ardila Investments v ENRC* [2015] EWHC 1667 [56]–[57].

[23]   *The Owners of the Ship 'Al Khattiya' v The Owners and/or Demise Charterers of the Ship 'Jag Laadki'* [2018] EWHC 389 [111].

[24]   *A/S D/S Svendborg v Wansa* [1996] 2 Lloyds Rep 559, 574 (a contractual case, but analysed in terms of oppression); upheld [1997] 2 Lloyds Rep 183 (CA) 189.

[25]   *Petromin v Secnav Marine* [1995] 1 Lloyds Rep 603, 613–14.

[26]   *Société Nationale Industrielle Aérospatiale v Lee Kui Jak* [1987] AC 871 (PC) 899H–902G; *Simon Engineering v Butte Mining (No 1)* [1996] 1 Lloyds Rep 104, 112.

[27]   Any assessment of the quality of justice in the foreign court poses thorny problems of inter-judicial diplomacy. It will usually be presumed that a similar quality of justice is available in the foreign court: *Barclays Bank v Homan* [1993] BCLC 680 (Hoffmann J), 687; *Aggeliki Charis Compania Maritima v Pagnan (The Angelic Grace)* [1995] 1 Lloyds Rep 87 (CA) 96, followed *OT Africa Line v Magic Sportswear* [2005] 2 Lloyds Rep 170 (CA) 184. Further, the courts should be very slow to express views about the relative competence or suitability of a foreign legal system and

prevent the case for an anti-suit injunction being supported by evidence about unattractive practical consequences of the foreign litigation, such as the likely cost and length of the foreign proceedings.[28] There has been a considerable debate about whether certain features of the US legal system, such as contingency fees, treble damages, and jury trials, can be factors that support a finding of oppression: the prevailing view appears to be that these can amount to illegitimate advantages, and thus contribute to oppression, if the USA is clearly an inappropriate forum for the litigation.[29]

It is not inherently vexatious or oppressive to bring a claim to which the foreign court will apply a different substantive law than would be applied in England, even where this would give a significant advantage to the claimant abroad, although the position can be different if the foreign jurisdiction is not a natural forum for the dispute or the application of the foreign law would be inappropriate.[30] There are some authorities which suggest that foreign

5.10

the English courts to deal with particular disputes: *Aratra Potato Co v Egyptian Navigation (The El Amria)* [1981] 2 Lloyds Rep 119 (CA) 126–27; *Amin Rasheed Shipping v Kuwait Insurance* [1984] AC 50 (HL) 67D–G; 72F–73C; *The Abidin Daver* [1984] AC 398 (HL) 424G–425C (all stay cases); *Ascot Commodities v Northern Pacific Shipping (The Irini A)* [1999] 1 Lloyds Rep 196, 200. If the quality of justice afforded by a foreign court is to be criticized, this must be done candidly on the basis of clear positive evidence, and the English court should not pass judgment on the foreign legal system unless there is clear evidence of some incontestable procedural problem or deficiency: *Aratra Potato v Egyptian Navigation (The El Amria)* [1981] 2 Lloyds Rep 119 (CA) 126–27; *The Abidin Daver* [1984] AC 398 (HL) 411B–E (both stay cases); *Bankers Trust v PT Mayora Indah* (Colman J, 20 January 1999); see also Clarke J's evasion of the question in *A/S D/S Svendborg v Wansa* [1996] 2 Lloyds Rep 559, 574; *Middle Eastern Oil v National Bank of Abu Dhabi* [2008] 2 CLC 1026 [22]–[27]; *Agbaje v Agbaje* [2010] 1 AC 628 (HL) [53].

For a recent example of the English court refusing to criticize the justice available in the foreign court without cogent evidence, and refusing to grant an anti-suit injunction, see *Dawnus Sierra Leone v Timis Mining Corporation* [2016] EWHC 236 [66]. In *Mobile Telecommunications Company v Prince Hussam bin Saud bin Abdulaziz bin Saud* [2018] 2 Lloyds Rep 192 the court was open to such an argument but did not find it necessary to rule on it. For an example of the grant of an anti-suit injunction being driven in large part by the injunction defendant's assertion that he was able to manipulate the process of the foreign court, see *A/S D/S Svendborg v Wansa* [1996] 2 Lloyds Rep 559, 566, 574, [1997] 2 Lloyds Rep 183 (CA) 188–89.

In *Al-Bassam v Al-Bassam* [2004] EWCA Civ 857 [46], the Court of Appeal stated *obiter* that 'it is not for the English court to restrain a party in proceedings before it from suing in another jurisdiction on the grounds of its own perception as to the fairness or unfairness of proceedings in that other jurisdiction'. While there is sense to this as an exhortation, treated literally as an absolute principle it would not be correct, and it should not be treated as laying down any such considered doctrine. The Court of Appeal's approach should be interpreted as turning on the weakness of the factual evidence in the particular case before it and the specific issues addressed.

[28] See eg *Continental Bank v Aeakos Compania Naviera* [1994] 1 Lloyds Rep 505 (CA) 512 (a contractual case); *Simon Engineering v Butte Mining (No 1)* [1996] 1 Lloyds Rep 104, 108, 112.

[29] For decisions suggesting that features of US litigation like contingency fees, treble and punitive damages, and wide-ranging discovery are not oppressive, see *Castanho v Brown & Root* [1981] AC 557 (HL) 577; and Neill LJ in *Midland Bank v Laker Airways* [1986] QB 689 (CA) 714E–G. For decisions suggesting that such matters can contribute to oppression, at least where the USA is clearly an inappropriate forum, see *Smith Kline & French Laboratories v Bloch* [1983] 1 WLR 730 (CA) 738H, 747H; *Midland Bank v Laker Airways* [1986] QB 689 (CA) per Lawton and Dillon LJJ at 700, 703; *Société Nationale Industrielle Aérospatiale v Lee Kui Jak* [1987] AC 871 (PC) 894D–G, 899F–G; *Simon Engineering v Butte Mining (No 1)* [1996] 1 Lloyds Rep 104, 110–11; *Simon Engineering v Butte Mining (No 2)* [1996] 1 Lloyds Rep 91, 95; *Airbus Industrie v Patel* [1997] 2 Lloyds Rep 8 (CA) 16–17 (reversed, but not on this point, [1999] 1 AC 199 (HL)).

[30] *Liverpool Marine Credit v Hunter* (1867) LR 4 Eq 62, 72; upheld (1868) LR 3 Ch App 479 (CA) 484–87; *Société Nationale Industrielle Aérospatiale v Lee Kui Jak* [1987] AC 871 (PC) 899F–H (obiter hints); *R v R (Divorce: Hemain Injunction)* [2005] 1 FLR 386 [37]–[38], [71]; *Seismic Shipping v Total E&P UK (The Western Regent)* [2005] 2 Lloyds Rep 359 (CA) [55]; *Airbus Industrie v Patel* [1997] 2 Lloyds Rep 8 (CA) 17–18 (reversed [1999] 1 AC 119 (HL), but not on this point); *Jewel Owner v Sagaan Developments Trading (The MD Gemini)* [2012] 2 Lloyds Rep 672 [21]; *Navig8 v Al-Riyadh Co for Vegetable Oil Industry (The Lucky Lady)* [2013] 2 Lloyds Rep 104 [22]; *Golden Endurance Shipping v RMA Watanya (The Golden Endurance)* [2015] 1 Lloyds Rep 266 [46].

However, cf *Re Belfast Shipowners Co* [1894] 1 IR 321, 333–34 (injunction granted where the application of the foreign law would produce the 'wrong' result; although it may be that the decision should be explained by the need to protect insolvency proceedings).

proceedings may be vexatious if they seek to apply a law which is different from the parties' express choice of law.[31] However in *The Lucky Lady*, the fact that foreign conflicts rules might mean the foreign court would reach a different result on whether English law was the agreed choice of law was not sufficient to justify an injunction.[32]

5.11   In contrast, the mere inconvenience arising from the pursuit of the parallel foreign proceedings will not suffice to justify a finding of vexation or oppression, even if the inconvenience is significant, unless there is some aspect of the inconvenience which would amount to an injustice. This is so even if both sets of proceedings are likely to be tried at around the same time, with hearings and judgments overlapping.[33]

5.12   Further, the courts have concluded that foreign proceedings were not vexatious or oppressive in all the circumstances, in cases where the foreign jurisdiction was the most appropriate forum for the litigation;[34] where England was not a significantly more appropriate forum for the litigation;[35] where there would be overlapping proceedings in the competing jurisdictions whether or not the injunction was granted;[36] and where security that had been obtained in the foreign jurisdiction was a legitimate advantage for the injunction defendant.[37] In one case, where third-party proceedings were commenced by a defendant

---

For examples, see *Liverpool Marine Credit v Hunter* (1867) LR 4 Eq 62, 69, 72, (1868) LR 3 Ch App 479 (CA) 484 (injunction refused, even though the foreign law in question disregarded the comity of nations); *Calendars and Diaries v Nuovo Instituto Italiano D'Arti Grafiche* (Wood J, 14 February 1986) (injunction refused, although the Italian court would apply Italian law while the English court would apply English law, and this difference would determine the case); *Through Transport Mutual Insurance Association (Eurasia) v New India Assurance* [2005] 1 Lloyds Rep 67 (CA) 89; *Trafigura Beheer v Kookmin Bank* [2005] EWHC 2350 [50]–[52]; *Jewel Owner v Sagaan Developments Trading (The MD Gemini)* [2012] 2 Lloyds Rep 672 [21]. The concept of an 'appropriate' law is not yet developed, but it is less likely to be vexatious or oppressive to seek to rely on foreign law where the foreign law implements a widely accepted international convention, even if English law implements a different convention: *Bouygues Offshore v Caspian Shipping (No 2)* [1997] 2 Lloyds Rep 485, 491, or if the foreign court might give that convention a different but legitimate interpretation: *Deaville v Aeroflot Russian International Airlines* [1997] 2 Lloyds Rep 67, 69–70, 75.

[31]   *Cadre v Astra Asigurari* [2006] 1 Lloyds Rep 560 [18]; *Trafigura Beheer v Kookmin Bank (No 3)* [2007] 1 Lloyds Rep 669 [51]–[55]. This approach is in tension with the Court of Appeal's decision in *Petter v EMC* [2016] ILPr 3 (CA) (criticized elsewhere in this work at Ch 4, paras 4.41–4.46).
It has been suggested that it would be vexatious to advance claims abroad which purport to be claims governed by and under English law, where in truth no such claim exists under English law: *Pathe Screen Entertainment v Handmade Films (Distributors)* (Hobhouse J, 11 July 1989).

[32]   *Navig8 v Al-Riyadh Co for Vegetable Oil Industry (The Lucky Lady)* [2013] 2 Lloyds Rep 104 [22].

[33]   *Royal Bank of Canada v Cooperatieve Centrale Raiffeisen-Boerenleenbank* [2003] EWHC 2913 [79]–[83] (decision upheld on appeal [2004] 1 Lloyds Rep 471 (CA)); *Deutsche Bank v Highland Crusader Partners* [2010] 1 WLR 1023 (CA) [50]–[65]; *The Insurance Company of the State of Pennsylvania v Equitas Insurance* [2014] Lloyds Rep IR 195 [29].

[34]   *Donohue v Armco* [1999] 2 Lloyds Rep 649, 663, reversed [2000] 1 Lloyds Rep 579 (CA), but decision affirmed [2002] 1 Lloyds Rep 425 (HL); *Bloch v Bloch* [2003] 1 FLR 1 [82]; *Re Tadros* [2014] EWHC 2860 [74]–[78]. See also *Bitmac v Creosote Producers Association, The Times* (CA, 12 June 1986).
In *AWB (Geneva) v North America Steamships* [2007] 1 CLC 749 [31] (not addressed on appeal, [2007] 2 Lloyds Rep 315 (CA) [21], [33]), Field J held that an application by an insolvent Canadian company to a Canadian insolvency court to override the provisions of an English law contract was not vexatious or oppressive. It was 'predictable' that any insolvency proceedings relating to a Canadian company would be determined in Canada and it was a 'common feature of insolvency regimes that contractual rights can be overridden'.

[35]   *Royal Bank of Canada v Cooperatieve Centrale Raiffeisen-Boerenleenbank* [2003] EWHC 2913 [71] (decision upheld on appeal [2004] 1 Lloyds Rep 471 (CA)).

[36]   *Bouygues Offshore v Caspian Shipping (No 2)* [1997] 2 Lloyds Rep 485, 491; *Donohue v Armco* [1999] 2 Lloyds Rep 649, 663, [2002] 1 Lloyds Rep 425 (HL) [27], [29], [33]–[36], [46]–[47], [72]–[75].

[37]   *Ascot Commodities v Northern Pacific Shipping (The Irini A)* [1999] 1 Lloyds Rep 196, 200.

abroad, the fact that the defendant had not had a free choice as to where he was initially sued was a factor against a finding that the third-party proceedings were vexatious or oppressive.[38] It has also been held in one case that oppression is diminished where a potentially effective application to stay the foreign proceedings on *forum non conveniens* grounds could be, but has not been, made to the foreign court.[39]

Potential oppression can be disarmed by the provision of appropriate undertakings by the injunction defendant not to rely on features of the foreign proceedings that would otherwise be oppressive.[40]   **5.13**

4. Double Claims

In the normal alternative forum case, each party will have commenced litigation in his preferred forum, so that the claimant in England is the defendant abroad. However, in certain cases, a claimant will commence actions on the same subject matter in two different jurisdictions,[41] and this 'double claim' situation deserves separate treatment.   **5.14**

The response of the English courts to a double claim situation will depend on whether the double claimant has a legitimate purpose for bringing two claims in relation to the same subject matter in two different jurisdictions.[42] In one case it was held that where a claimant had commenced his second set of claims solely for the purposes of preventing a time bar in the second jurisdiction, and did not intend to pursue them if his primary set of claims can proceed in the first jurisdiction, there was no vexation.[43] Similarly, it may well be legitimate to commence duplicate claims where the secondary claim is intended only to obtain security, and will not be pursued on the merits.[44]   **5.15**

If, however, there is no legitimate reason for pursuing two claims on the same subject matter, then the pursuit of both proceedings is likely to be viewed as vexatious, or an abuse of process, and if so the claimant, on application by the defendant in the English proceedings, will   **5.16**

---

[38] *Dornoch v The Mauritius Union Assurance* [2005] EWHC 1887 [129].
[39] *Amoco (UK) Exploration v British American Offshore* [1999] 2 Lloyds Rep 772, 780. As to whether this is a general doctrine, see section F, 'Stay Applications in the Foreign Court'.
[40] *Société Nationale Industrielle Aérospatiale v Lee Kui Jak* [1987] AC 871 (PC) 899F–H; *Metall und Rohstoff v ACLI Metals (London)* [1984] 1 Lloyds Rep 598 (CA) 607; *Simon Engineering v Butte Mining (No 2)* [1996] 1 Lloyds Rep 91, 95; *Kemsley v Barclays Bank* [2013] EWHC 1274 [41]; *Stichting Shell Pensionenfonds v Krys* [2015] AC 616 (PC) [40].
[41] To fall within this category the claims must be genuinely duplicative. For examples where they were not, see *Kyrgyz Mobil Tel Ltd v Fellowes International Holdings Ltd (No 3)* [2005] EWHC 1314 and *Citicorp International Ltd v Shiv-Vani Oil & Gas Exploration Services* [2014] EWHC 245.
[42] *Merrill Lynch, Pierce Fenner & Smith v Raffa* [2001] ILPr 31 [22]; *Carnoustie Universal v International Transport Workers' Federation* [2002] 2 All ER (Comm) 657 [138]; *Beirut-Racy v Hawila* [2003] EWHC 1611 [54]–[55]. See also *Re Bank of Credit and Commerce International (No 9)* [1994] 3 All ER 764 (CA) 796–99 (in the slightly different context of whether undertakings to limit duplicative foreign litigation should be required as conditions of a *Mareva* injunction).
      The best view is that there is no presumption that a double claim abroad and in England is vexatious: *McHenry v Lewis* (1882) 22 Ch D 397 (CA); *Bank of Tokyo v Karoon* [1987] AC 45 (CA) (Note), 59, where it was stated *obiter* that 'it is not prima facie vexatious for the same plaintiff to commence two actions relating to the same subject matter, one in England and one abroad'; *Carnoustie Universal v International Transport Workers' Federation* [2002] 2 All ER (Comm) 657 [128]. The more rigid comments made in *Australian Commercial Research and Development v ANZ McCaughan Merchant Bank* [1989] 3 All ER 65, 69–70 were not followed in *Beirut-Racy v Hawila* [2003] EWHC 1611 [51] (upheld on appeal, [2004] EWCA Civ 209).
[43] See *Kyrgyz Mobil Tel v Fellowes International Holdings (No 3)* [2005] EWHC 1314 (Comm) [24].
[44] See, by analogy, Ch 7, section I, 'Foreign Proceedings to Obtain Security'.

be put to his election by the court as to which set of proceedings he wishes to continue.[45] If in such a case the 'double claimant' elects to pursue the English proceedings, the court will require him, as a condition of permitting them to proceed, to undertake to procure an adjournment, or stay, or discontinuance, as appropriate, of the foreign proceedings.[46] If he elects to pursue the foreign proceedings, he will have to bring the English proceedings to an end in one way or another.[47] If the English proceedings are stayed or discontinued, then there will be no basis to restrain the foreign proceedings unless there are independent grounds to restrain them such as vexation.[48] However, the 'double claimant' may not have a free election: there may be circumstances in which his involvement in English proceedings has been such that he will not be permitted to discontinue or stay them, in particular if it would now be an abuse or vexatious for him to do so. If so, the duplication caused by the continuation of the foreign proceedings may justify an injunction to restrain them.[49]

C. INJUNCTIONS TO PREVENT RELITIGATION

5.17   The recognition to be awarded to an English judgment by a foreign court is a matter of the foreign court's own national law, or international treaty.[50] It could therefore be argued that an anti-suit injunction should not be granted to restrain claims in a foreign country solely on the ground that they ignore, or seek to obtain a result contrary to, a pre-existing English judgment.[51] In *The Western Regent*, it was held that it was not vexatious and oppressive in

---

[45] *Australian Commercial Research and Development v ANZ McCaughan Merchant Bank* [1989] 3 All ER 65, 69–70; *Beirut-Racy v Hawila* [2003] EWHC 1611 [54]–[68], upheld on appeal, [2004] EWCA Civ 209. For recent examples where there was no abuse on the facts, see *Novoship (UK) v Mikhayluk* [2012] EWHC 1352 (Comm); *Akyuz v Akyuz* [2017] EWHC 2726 (Ch).

   In *The 'Hartlepool'* (1950) 84 Ll L Rep 145 and *The Soya Margareta* [1961] 1 WLR 709, 716–17 the defendant applied only for a stay, and the court did not put the double claimant to his election, but instead simply granted injunctions to restrain the foreign proceedings (in *The Hartlepool*, rather unusually, the injunction was granted at the double claimant's request). The modern approach would probably be to put the claimant to his election, and require undertakings. In *Advanced Portfolio Technologies v Ainsworth* [1996] FSR 217, Harman J refused to allow the double claimant to *stay* his English proceedings and as a result granted an injunction to restrain the New York proceedings; but it seems it would have been different if the claimant had been willing to *discontinue* his English proceedings.

[46] See eg *Beirut-Racy v Hawila* [2003] EWHC 1611 [54]–[68], upheld on appeal, [2004] EWCA Civ 209.

[47] In *Australian Commercial Research and Development v ANZ McCaughan Merchant Bank* [1989] 3 All ER 65, 69–70 it was held that the only option open to the claimant in England was a discontinuance, not a stay. Similarly, in *Advanced Portfolio Technologies v Ainsworth* [1996] FSR 217 Harman J refused to allow the claimant to stay his own proceedings. However, the modern cases appear to take a more flexible approach: a stay was sought and allowed in *Merrill Lynch, Pierce Fenner & Smith v Raffa* [2001] ILPr 31 [19] and *Beirut-Racy v Hawila* [2003] EWHC 1611 [46] (upheld on appeal, [2004] EWCA Civ 209).

[48] *Australian Commercial Research and Development v ANZ McCaughan Merchant Bank* [1989] 3 All ER 65, 69–70; *Merrill Lynch, Pierce Fenner & Smith v Raffa* [2001] ILPr 31 [24]. In *General Motors v Royal & Sun Alliance Insurance* [2007] 2 CLC 507, the duplicate claimant was restrained from pursuing his US proceedings because a consent order to which he had agreed in the English proceedings was construed as amounting to an agreement to the exclusive jurisdiction of the English courts.

[49] *Ardila Investments v ENRC* [2015] EWHC 1667; and see also *Advanced Portfolio Technologies v Ainsworth* [1996] FSR 217; *General Motors v Royal & Sun Alliance Insurance* [2007] 2 CLC 507; *Dana Gas v Dana Gas Sukuk* [2018] EWHC 277 (Comm) [40]–[41]. In *Castanho v Brown & Root* [1981] AC 557 (HL) 571–77, it was concluded that, on the facts of that case, the double claimant should be entitled to discontinue his English proceedings. The prejudice caused could be dealt with in costs.

[50] *Seismic Shipping v Total E&P UK (The Western Regent)* [2005] 2 Lloyds Rep 54, 61; [2005] 2 Lloyds Rep 359 (CA) [50], [66].

[51] See eg *ED&F Man (Sugar) v Yani Haryanto (No 2)* [1991] 1 Lloyds Rep 429 (CA) 437–38 (Neill LJ); *Seismic Shipping v Total E&P UK (The Western Regent)* [2005] 2 Lloyds Rep 54, 61; [2005] 2 Lloyds Rep 359 (CA) 369, 372. Similarly, in *Zeeland Navigation Co v Banque Worms*, The Times (26 December 1995), Waller J thought it was right to exercise considerable caution before granting an injunction based on *res judicata* alone.

itself to bring claims in a foreign jurisdiction for amounts which exceed a limitation de-cree granted by the English court.[52] It could therefore be argued that some additional factor over and above relitigation should be required to render foreign proceedings vexatious and oppressive.[53]

However, in *Masri v Consolidated Contractors*, Lawrence Collins LJ rejected this argument,   **5.18**
and concluded that the fact that the respondent is seeking to relitigate in a foreign jurisdic-tion matters which were already *res judicata* between himself and the applicant by reason of an English judgment could be a sufficient ground for the grant of an anti-suit injunc-tion. He described a case 'in which the judgment debtors are seeking to relitigate abroad the merits of a case which, after a long trial, they have lost in England' as 'a classic case of vexation and oppression'.[54] He also justified the injunction before him on the grounds that it was necessary to protect the 'jurisdiction' of the English court, in the form of protecting its 'judgments'.[55] *The Western Regent* was distinguished, Lawrence Collins LJ concluding that it did not lay down any general principle outside the unusual context of limitation decrees.[56]

Where a matter was not decided in the original English proceedings, but could and should   **5.19**
have been raised in those proceedings, it has been held that in appropriate circumstances it can be an 'abuse of process' and thus vexatious and oppressive, to seek to raise those matters in subsequent foreign litigation.[57]

Where foreign proceedings relitigate matters decided in arbitration, or amount to a col-   **5.20**
lateral attack on an arbitration award, this can also amount to vexatious relitigation.[58]

---

[52] *Seismic Shipping v Total E&P UK (The Western Regent)* [2005] 2 Lloyds Rep 54, 61, [2005] 2 Lloyds Rep 559 (CA) 369–70. The English court's self-restraint may depend, at least in part, on it being likely that the foreign court will also display sufficient respect for comity when considering the effect of the English judgment: *The Western Regent* at [49]–[50].

[53] Foreign proceedings which relitigated matters decided in England, but also were additionally vexatious for other specific reasons, were restrained in *Bank of Tokyo v Karoon* [1987] AC 45 (Note) (CA) 50G, 52B–H (per Bingham J); *Arab Monetary Fund v Hashim (No 6)* (Hoffmann J, 14 July 1992); *National Westminster Bank v Utrecht-America Finance* [2001] CLC 442 [54] (where the relitigation would be in breach of contract); on appeal [2001] 3 All ER 733 (CA), the breach of contract, not the relitigation, was viewed as the determining factor; *Law Debenture Trust v Concord Trust* [2007] EWHC 2255 [47], where the foreign proceedings were not only relitigation but were also hopeless (upheld with somewhat different reasoning, *Elektrim v Vivendi Holdings 1* [2009] 1 Lloyds Rep 59 (CA) [85]).

[54] *Masri v Consolidated Contractors (No 3)* [2009] QB 503 (CA) [83]–[96], [100]; followed in *Elektrim v Vivendi Holdings 1* [2009] 1 Lloyds Rep 59 (CA) [85]; and see to similar effect in principle *Michael Wilson v Emmott* [2018] 1 Lloyds Rep 299 (CA) [55]–[58], in part upholding *Emmott v Michael Wilson* [2017] 1 Lloyds Rep 21 [57]–[59], [62]. See also *Noble Assurance v Gerling-Konzern General Insurance* [2008] Lloyds Rep IR 1 [85]; *Berliner Bank v C Czarnikow Sugar (The Rama)* [1996] 2 Lloyds Rep 281, 298. For a recent example see *Ahmed v Mustafa* [2015] 1 FLR 139 (CA) [21].

[55] *Masri v Consolidated Contractors (No 3)* [2009] QB 503 (CA) [86]–[94], [100].

[56] *Masri v Consolidated Contractors (No 3)* [2009] QB 503 (CA) [96].

[57] By analogy to the principle in *Henderson v Henderson* (1843) 3 Hare 100, 67 ER 313. See *Zeeland Navigation Co v Banque Worms, The Times* (26 December 1995); *Glencore International v Metro Trading International* [2002] CLC 1090 (Moore-Bick J) [33]–[43], upheld on appeal (CA) [67]–[68] (although this case can be viewed as an example of concurrent, not consecutive litigation); *Noble Assurance v Gerling-Konzern General Insurance* [2008] Lloyds Rep IR 1 [95]; *Elektrim v Vivendi Holdings 1* [2009] 1 Lloyds Rep 59 (CA) [85]; *Nomihold Securities v Mobile Telesystems Finance* [2012] 1 Lloyds Rep 442 [42]–[43], [63] (injunction rejected on the facts). In *Royal Bank of Scotland v Highland Financial Partners* [2012] EWHC 1278, it was held that RBS had a prima facie strong case for an injunction on this basis, but the injunction was refused for lack of clean hands: [172], [194].

[58] *Michael Wilson v Emmott* [2018] 1 Lloyds Rep 299 (CA) [55]–[58], in part upholding *Emmott v Michael Wilson* [2017] 1 Lloyds Rep 21 [57]–[59], [62]; see also *Noble Assurance v Gerling-Konzern General Insurance* [2008] Lloyds Rep IR 1 [95]; *Nomihold Securities v Mobile Telesystems Finance* [2012] 1 Lloyds Rep 442 [42]–[43], [63] (injunction rejected on the facts); *Crescendo Maritime v Bank of Communications Company* [2016] 1 Lloyds Rep 414 [50]–[51]; *Mobile Telecommunications v Prince Hussam bin Saud bin Abdulaziz bin Saud* [2018] 2 Lloyds Rep 192.

Such conduct may also amount to breaches of the arbitration agreement or implied terms thereof.[59]

D. SINGLE FORUM CASES

5.21 The awkward but workable label of 'single forum' cases[60] describes situations where the claims made abroad can only be brought in the foreign forum, and cannot be brought in England.[61] To fall within this category, the foreign claims must be materially different to possible claims in England. It is insufficient that the foreign court will apply a different law to the same set of disputes.[62] Further, a case will not necessarily be a single forum case even if the foreign law provides for additional remedies, unavailable in England, for the same wrong.[63] The assessment of whether a possible English claim is a sufficiently close comparator will be a question of fact and degree in every case.

5.22 In a single forum case, England will not be the natural forum for the claims, as the only possible forum will be the foreign forum. The decision the court has to make is therefore not in which forum the claims should proceed, but rather whether they should proceed at all.[64] Any criterion or consideration that England should in general be the natural forum for the trial of the claim (to the extent this applies), is therefore inapplicable to single forum injunctions.[65] The risk of injustice if a single forum injunction is granted is real,[66] which means that particular caution must be displayed before granting such a drastic form of relief.[67]

---

[59]   See Ch 7, paras 7.66–7.67.

[60]   *British Airways Board v Laker Airways* [1985] AC 58 (HL) 80B–D, 86F–G; *Airbus Industrie v Patel* [1999] 1 AC 119 (HL) 134C; *Oceanconnect UK v Angara Maritime Ltd (The Fesco Angara)* [2011] 1 Lloyds Rep 399 (CA) [43].

[61]   *British Airways Board v Laker Airways* [1985] AC 58 (HL) 80B–D, 86F–G; *Midland Bank v Laker Airways* [1986] QB 689 (CA) 700B, 701B, 712B. See also *Bitmac v Creosote Producers Association* (CA, 12 June 1986).

[62]   See eg *Cadre v Astra Asigurari* [2006] 1 Lloyds Rep 560 [18]. The fact that foreign statutory law may be the applicable law of the claim is irrelevant, as the English court is able to apply foreign statute law, inter alia through the cause of action for breach of a statutory duty: *Crystal Decisions (UK) v Vedatech* [2004] EWHC 1872. For discussion of the difficulties in identifying the borderline between single and alternative forum cases, see A Bell, *Forum Shopping and Venue in Transnational Litigation* (OUP 2003) paras 4.97–4.99 (hereafter 'Bell').

[63]   In *Société Nationale Industrielle Aérospatiale v Lee Kui Jak* [1987] AC 871 (PC) 896E, Lord Goff treated as an alternative forum case any situation where 'a remedy for a particular wrong is available both in the English (or here the Brunei) court and the foreign court'. See *Simon Engineering v Butte Mining (No 2)* [1996] 1 Lloyds Rep 91, 95, where (a) it was suggested *obiter* that the unavailability of claims for treble damages under the US Racketeer Influenced and Corrupt Organizations (RICO) statute would not have prevented the case from being an alternative forum situation, as 'RICO provides a remedy rather than a cause of action'; (b) it was held that English statutory causes of action for securities fraud were sufficiently close comparators to US statutory causes of action for securities fraud.

[64]   This passage in the first edition was approved in *Oceanconnect UK v Angara Maritime (The Fesco Angara)* [2011] 1 Lloyds Rep 399 (CA) [43].

[65]   See *Airbus Industrie v Patel* [1999] 1 AC 119 (HL) 139F–G; Ch 4, sections L, 'Comity' and M, 'Natural Forum'. It may be that in a single forum case the more relevant question in relation to comity is not whether England is the natural forum for the trial of the claim but rather whether England is the natural forum to decide whether the claim is vexatious or oppressive: *Shell International Petroleum v Coral Oil (No 2)* [1999] 2 Lloyds Rep 606, 610.

[66]   See eg *Bitmac v Creosote Producers Association* (CA, 12 June 1986).

[67]   This passage in the first edition was approved in *Oceanconnect UK v Angara Maritime (The Fesco Angara)* [2011] 1 Lloyds Rep 399 (CA) [43]. See also *Midland Bank v Laker Airways* [1986] QB 689 (CA) 712B. However, see contra A Briggs, 'Anti-Suit Injunctions in a Complex World' in F Rose (ed), *Lex Mercatoria* (Informa 2000) 219, 240–41. It has been suggested that the necessary caution will make a true single forum injunction 'exceptional': *Star Reefers Pool v JFC Group* [2012] 1 Lloyds Rep 376 (CA) [30]. But the authority there relied on, *Airbus Industrie v Patel* [1999] 1 AC 119 (HL) at 139G, did not say this.

It is possible that the right of access to the court inherent in Article 6 of the European Convention on Human Rights (ECHR) should accentuate the court's hesitation before granting single forum anti-suit injunctions: see Ch 1, para 1.84.

In some general summaries of the law, it has been suggested *obiter* that (if contractual   **5.23**
cases are left to one side) an anti-suit injunction can only be granted if the injunction
claimant is a party to litigation in England, with which the injunction defendant's foreign proceedings interfere.[68] If so, single forum injunctions would be illegitimate in
principle. However, these summaries are mis-statements and not the law.[69] Although
the principles of comity mean, in general, that in non-contractual cases anti-suit injunctions are relatively rare without corresponding English proceedings such proceedings
here are not a requirement. Lord Goff expressly recognized in *Airbus v Patel* that the
courts may in principle grant single forum injunctions where there is a sufficient connection with the English forum.[70]

What is unclear is the breadth of the power to grant single forum injunctions. In *Airbus v*   **5.24**
Patel, Lord Goff did not identify what would amount to a sufficient connection in the single
forum case, observing merely that assessment of this question might involve consideration
of whether the relevant transactions were connected with England, and of whether the injunction was required to protect the policies of the English forum.[71] It follows that the past
case law provides an uncertain guide to the modern law on single forum injunctions; and
the following discussion, which analyses the historical cases, must be read subject to that
caution.

1. Types of Single Forum Injunction

The case law on single forum injunctions is sparse and the disparate decisions have not   **5.25**
yet been crystallized into any coherent order. Three main types of situation can be identified: (a) cases of 'pure vexation', where the foreign litigation is without any merit; (b) situations where litigation in the foreign forum would wrongfully impose foreign law or
jurisdiction onto essentially English relationships; and (c) injunctions granted to protect
the process of the English courts or the jurisdiction of the English courts.[72] However, these
situations should not be treated as exhaustive.

2. Weak and Hopeless Claims

In some 'single forum' cases it is alleged that the foreign litigation is said to be vexatious   **5.26**
because the foreign claims have no merit, or are sure to fail in the foreign forum, or are
brought in bad faith. However, single forum injunctions justified by the weakness of the foreign claim alone pose problems of comity. Especially where the foreign court has adequate

---

[68] *Turner v Grovit* [2002] 1 WLR 107 (HL) 119D–H; *Glencore International v Metro Trading International (No 3)*
[2002] CLC 1090 (CA) [42], per Rix LJ (both *obiter* on this point).
[69] See further Ch 4, para 4.81, n 200. Indeed, in *Star Reefers Pool v JFC Group* [2012] 1 Lloyds Rep 376 (CA) [30],
Rix LJ later himself recognized the legitimacy of single forum injunctions.
[70] *Airbus Industrie v Patel* [1999] 1 AC 119 (HL) 134B–C, 137C–138F, 139G. See eg *Shell International Petroleum
v Coral Oil (No 2)* [1999] 2 Lloyds Rep 606.
[71] *Airbus Industrie v Patel* [1999] 1 AC 119 (HL) 139F–G: 'these single forum cases demonstrate that any limiting principle requiring respect for comity cannot be simply expressed by reference to the question whether the
English court may be the natural forum for the dispute'.
[72] Contractual anti-suit injunctions can, in their practical effect, be single forum injunctions, but their logic is
different to injunctions based on vexation and oppression, and so they are not analysed here.

remedies to dismiss unsatisfactory claims at an early stage,[73] it should, in general, be a matter for the foreign court to determine whether a case before it will or should succeed, under its own law and procedure.[74] The English court is not the normal forum to engage in summary determinations of the merits of foreign proceedings.[75] Consequently, save in the rare case where it is 'plain' that the foreign case is 'bound to fail', or 'hopeless',[76] allegations of the weakness of the foreign claim should not on their own be capable of amounting to vexation.[77] But the inherent apparent weaknesses of the foreign claim can, when taken together with other matters, be important factors in the overall assessment of vexation or oppression.[78] Different phrasing has been used as to when a finding of hopelessness might be made to justify an injunction: in *Vitol Bahrain* Males J concluded that it would only be in an 'exceptional' case that this would be appropriate, but in *Midland Bank v Laker* the phrasing was that such a case was 'likely to be rare'.[79]

5.27   In *Elektrim v Vivendi*, the Court of Appeal appeared to conclude that, in one of the rare cases where hopelessness was proven, such a finding could be sufficient, without more, to justify an injunction, although the reasoning is not entirely clear.[80] However, although Lawrence Collins LJ did not consider in *Elektrim* the principle that the English court must always have a sufficient interest in, or connection with, the matter in question to justify intervention[81] it is submitted that this must be satisfied even where the foreign claim is perceived as being hopeless. In *Vitol Bahrain v Nasdec* Males J concluded that the requirement of sufficient interest had to apply.[82]

---

[73] *Smith Kline & French Laboratories v Bloch (No 2)* (Skinner J, 13 June 1984); *Midland Bank v Laker Airways* [1986] QB 689, 696B–C, 700D–G).

[74] *Arab Monetary Fund v Hashim (No 6)* (Hoffmann J, 14 July 1992); *Star Reefers Pool v JFC Group* [2012] 1 Lloyds Rep 376 (CA) [31], [39], where Rix LJ warned against 'egoistic paternalism'; *Vitol Bahrain v Nasdec Trading* [2013] EWHC 3359 (Comm) [50].

[75] See eg *Elektrim v Vivendi Holdings 1* [2009] 1 Lloyds Rep 59 (CA) [120]; *Vitol Bahrain v Nasdec Trading* [2013] EWHC 3359 [50].

[76] A finding of hopelessness was made in *Law Debenture Trust Corp v Concord Trust* [2007] EWHC 2255 [47]; *Elektrim v Vivendi Holdings 1* [2009] 1 Lloyds Rep 59 (CA) [114]–[122]; and *The Owners of the Ship 'Al Khattiya' v The Owners and/or Demise Charterers of the Ship 'Jag Laadki'* [2018] EWHC 389 [111].

[77] *Pennell v Roy* (1853) 3 De GM & G 126, 43 ER 50, 53–56; *British Airways Board v Laker Airways* [1984] QB 142, 166–67 (Parker J), reversed on appeal [1984] QB 142 (CA); decision restored in House of Lords [1985] AC 58 (HL) 86D–E; *Midland Bank v Laker Airways* [1986] QB 689 (CA) 700D–E, 703E–H; *Star Reefers Pool v JFC Group* [2012] 1 Lloyds Rep 376 (CA) [31] (an alternative forum case); *Vitol Bahrain v Nasdec Trading* [2013] EWHC 3359 (Comm) [50]–[56]. For examples of the failure of a claim for an injunction on this basis, see *Smith Kline & French Laboratories v Bloch (No 3)* [1985] ECC 85, [1985] ECC 230 (CA); *Smith Kline & French Laboratories v Bloch (No 2)* [1985] ECC 75; *Trafigura Beheer v Kookmin Bank* [2005] EWHC 2350.

[78] *Elektrim v Vivendi Holdings 1* [2009] 1 Lloyds Rep 59 (CA) [121].

[79] *Vitol Bahrain v Nasdec Trading* [2013] EWHC 3359 (Comm) [58]; see also *Star Reefers Pool v JFC Group* [2012] 1 Lloyds Rep 376 (CA) [31]–[39]; *Midland Bank v Laker Airways* [1986] QB 689 (CA) 700D–E.

[80] *Elektrim v Vivendi Holdings 1* [2009] 1 Lloyds Rep 59 (CA) [121]. In *Vitol Bahrain v Nasdec Trading* [2013] EWHC 3359 (Comm) [55], Males J appears to have regarded the decision in *Elektrim* as relying on hopelessness as only one factor among others. In *The Owners of the Ship 'Al Khattiya' v The Owners and/or Demise Charterers of the Ship 'Jag Laadki'* [2018] EWHC 389 [111] it was sufficient that the foreign proceedings, which overlapped with English proceedings, were self-evidently hopeless and served no legitimate purpose.

[81] *Airbus Industrie v Patel* [1999] 1 AC 119 (HL) 138G–H, 139; *Deutsche Bank v Highland Crusader Partners* [2010] 1 WLR 1023 (CA) [50(6)], [56]. See also *Arab Monetary Fund v Hashim (No 6)* (Hoffmann J, 14 July 1992); *Barclays Bank v Homan* [1993] BCLC 680, 687: 'the fact that the proceedings would, if brought in England, be struck out as vexatious or oppressive in the domestic sense, will not ordinarily in itself justify the grant of an injunction to restrain their prosecution in a foreign court'; *Shell International Petroleum v Coral Oil (No 2)* [1999] 2 Lloyds Rep 606, 610, where it was suggested that it needed to be shown that the English court was the appropriate court to decide questions of forum or to decide whether the foreign proceedings were vexatious.

[82] *Vitol Bahrain v Nasdec Trading* [2013] EWHC 3359 [50]–[56]. This is also consistent with the analysis and result in *Shell International Petroleum v Coral Oil (No 2)* [1999] 2 Lloyds Rep 606, 610.

Overall the trend of the authorities show a growing appreciation of the tensions with comity   **5.28**
created by injunctions driven by the apparent weakness of the foreign claim.[83] Yet the judiciary do not yet appear to have settled on a single view of the right balance. Thus, a relatively
restrictive approach was taken in *Vitol Bahrain v Nasdec*.[84] But in contrast Bryan J's recent
decision in *The Al Khattiya* does not display the same reticence.[85]

3. Disputes and Relationships Centred in England and Subject to English Law

In *Midland Bank v Laker*, the English liquidators of an English company brought US anti-   **5.29**
trust claims in the USA, which arose out of the provision and withdrawal of banking fa-
cilities in England, against English banks with no relevant connection to the USA. The
Court of Appeal upheld the grant of interim injunctions restraining the liquidator from
continuing with his US proceedings. The principal ground for the injunction was that it was
'unconscionable' to attempt to apply the alien remedies of US anti-trust law to acts done in
England and 'intended to be governed by English law', and in respect of which there would
be no claim under English law, where the banks had not 'submitted themselves' to US anti-
trust law, having no relevant business in the USA.[86] In effect, the injunction was chiefly
granted on the basis that the USA was an unnatural forum for the litigation, and that US law
was an unnatural law to govern the legal relationships involved.[87]

The decision in *Midland Bank v Laker* was, however, decided before *Airbus v Patel*, where   **5.30**
Lord Goff elaborated the modern tests of comity. In arriving at his conclusion that comity
required that the English court should have a 'sufficient interest' in the matter, Lord Goff
considered the decision in *Midland Bank v Laker* closely, and observed that the primary
justification for the injunction granted in that case was that 'the relevant transaction was
overwhelmingly English in character'. He observed that 'it can be said that, on this basis,
the decision was consistent with comity', but expressly reserved his position as to whether

---

[83] See the warnings against 'egoistic paternalism' in such cases in *Star Reefers Pool v JFC Group Ltd* [2012] 1
Lloyds Rep 376 (CA) [31]–[39].
[84] *Vitol Bahrain v Nasdec Trading* [2013] EWHC 3359 [50]–[56].
[85] *The Owners of the Ship 'Al Khattiya' v The Owners and/or Demise Charterers of the Ship 'Jag Laadki'* [2018]
EWHC 389 [111].
[86] *Midland Bank v Laker Airways* [1986] QB 689 (CA) 700B, 705B–C, 707E–F, 714H–715G. It should be noted,
however, that as with all anti-suit injunctions, everything depends on the facts. It was an important additional
factor in favour of the grant of an injunction that there was little or no evidential basis for the claims brought
against the bank: 710B, 713E–F, although cf Lawton LJ at 700G and Neill LJ at 713B–C.
In relation to 'unconscionability', the Court of Appeal was applying the test of unconscionable conduct rather than
vexation and oppression, because *Midland Bank v Laker* was decided between the decisions in *British Airways
Board v Laker Airways* [1985] AC 58 (HL), which first advanced the concept of unconscionable conduct, and
Société Nationale Industrielle Aérospatiale v Lee Kui Jak [1987] AC 871 (PC), which reintroduced the historical, and
now modern, test of vexatious or oppressive behaviour: see Ch 2, sections E, 'Unconscionability and the Return
to Equity' and F, '*Aérospatiale* and the Modern Law'. In *Airbus Industrie v Patel* [1999] 1 AC 119 (HL) 134D, Lord
Goff said in passing that 'in single forum cases, it is said that an injunction may be granted to restrain the pursuit
of proceedings overseas which is unconscionable'. It is suggested, however, that Lord Goff should not be treated
as ratifying the use of 'unconscionable' as the sole test in single forum cases. Vexation or oppression is an equally
appropriate juridical framework, and perhaps better. In *Shell International Petroleum v Coral Oil (No 2)* [1999] 2
Lloyds Rep 606, 610, Thomas J analysed a single forum case in terms of vexation, not unconscionability.
[87] *Airbus Industrie v Patel* [1999] 1 AC 199 (HL) 138D. The English court's ability to criticize a foreign court's exercise of jurisdiction as exorbitant may be limited if it would itself exercise jurisdiction over a foreigner in a parallel
situation: *Barclays Bank v Homan* [1993] BCLC 680, 689.

the case was correctly decided.[88] The soundness of *Midland Bank v Laker* is therefore open to question. Nevertheless, unless the Supreme Court overrules it, the case is authority that, in appropriate circumstances, single forum injunctions can be granted to prevent disputes and relationships centred in England being litigated abroad, if the imposition of the foreign law and jurisdiction would be unnatural.[89] However, this power should be exercised with additional caution.[90] In contrast, where the injunction claimant's conduct has brought the subject matter of the claim within the legitimate sphere of influence of the legal system of the foreign state, this will militate against the grant of the injunction.[91]

5.31   Differences between the foreign law under which the claim is made and English law, or between the foreign procedures and English procedure, are not in themselves sufficient to support a single forum injunction, provided that the exercise of the foreign jurisdiction and law over the subject matter is not unnatural or exorbitant. In *Barclays Bank v Homan*, Hoffmann J and then the Court of Appeal refused to grant an injunction to restrain US insolvency proceedings that would produce a different result from English insolvency proceedings.[92]

4. Protection of the Jurisdiction of the English Court

5.32   The grant of an anti-suit injunction can be justified by the need to protect the process or jurisdiction of the English court.[93] This justification is most commonly relevant in alternative forum cases, but it could also apply in the single forum situation. Foreign proceedings can illegitimately interfere with the process or jurisdiction of the English courts, even if the actual claims in the foreign litigation can only be brought abroad.

Thus, for example, injunctions have been granted to restrain foreign claims, where insolvency proceedings are under way in England, and the proceedings abroad seek to gain an unfair advantage for one creditor by evading the *pari passu* distribution of assets in an English insolvency.[94] These cases could perhaps be viewed as 'alternative forum' situations, but in

---

[88]   *Airbus Industrie v Patel* [1999] 1 AC 199 (HL) 138B–H.
[89]   See, by analogy, *Bloom v Harms Offshore AHT 'Taurus'* [2010] Ch 187 (CA) [28].
[90]   *Masri v Consolidated Contractors (No 3)* [2009] QB 503 (CA) [56].
[91]   *British Airways Board v Laker Airways* [1985] AC 58 (HL) 84E–G, 96A–B; *Midland Bank v Laker Airways* [1986] QB 689 (CA) 702B–C, 704F–705A; *Bitmac v Creosote Producers Association* (CA, 12 June 1986). In *Oceanconnect UK v Angara Maritime (The Fesco Angara)* [2011] 1 Lloyds Rep 399 (CA), an anti-suit injunction to restrain proceedings in the USA for a maritime lien was rejected. The availability of a US law maritime lien was a matter that should be determined by the US courts: [51], [56].
[92]   *Barclays Bank v Homan* [1993] BCLC 680: 'The foreign court is entitled, without thereby occasioning a breach of international law or manifest injustice, to give effect to the policies of its own jurisdiction' (at 690). Arguments that a claim for triple damages based on the US RICO statute was 'per se oppressive' were rejected in *The Eras Eil Actions* [1995] 1 Lloyds Rep 64, 85. In *Bitmac v Creosote Producers Association* (CA, 12 June 1986), the US imposition of no-fault liability without proof of specific causation by the defendant was not viewed as sufficient to justify an injunction, where the injunction claimant had placed his business within the sphere of interest of US law. In *Simon Engineering v Butte Mining (No 2)* [1996] 1 Lloyds Rep 91, 100, the deputy judge observed that 'in a single forum case it would be wrong for this court to criticize American procedures'. See also *Star Reefers Pool v JFC Group* [2012] 1 Lloyds Rep 376 (CA) [34], [36] and *Kemsley v Barclays Bank* [2013] EWHC 1274 (Ch) [38]–[39].
[93]   *Société Nationale Industrielle Aérospatiale v Lee Kui Jak* [1987] AC 871 (PC) 892H–893A; *Masri v Consolidated Contractors (No 3)* [2009] QB 503 (CA) [83]–[88]; Ch 4, section H, 'Interference with the Processes, Jurisdiction, or Judgments of the English Court'.
[94]   *Re North Carolina Estate* (1889) 5 TLR 328; discussed in *Barclays Bank v Homan* [1993] BCLC 680, 686 (Hoffmann J); *Re Distin* (1871) 24 LT 197.

many the English insolvency process was not a genuinely alternative forum for the claims in question.[95] So a better analysis of these cases may well be that the English court is protecting the integrity of its insolvency jurisdiction, which includes protecting the performance by liquidators or administrators of their functions as officers of the court.[96] In *Shell v Krys* the Privy Council has also recently justified a similar injunction on the basis that it is protecting the policy of English insolvency law;[97] but it is also possible to view the decision as based on the protection of the jurisdiction of the court.[98]

The decision in *Shell v Coral (No 2)* can also be viewed as an example of a single forum injunction granted to protect the jurisdiction of the English courts, although the phraseology was not expressly used. The English court had restrained the pursuit of earlier proceedings in Lebanon which were in breach of an exclusive forum clause. Further proceedings were then commenced by a related party, which were apparently hopeless and vexatious, and which also appeared to be an abusive attempt to evade the exclusive forum clause and the existing anti-suit injunction. Thomas J concluded that the court's involvement in restraining the prior claim was an important factor in giving it a sufficient interest in the matter for the grant of an injunction to be consistent with comity.[99]   **5.33**

Anti-anti-suit injunctions can also be viewed as examples of the grant of single forum injunctions to prevent interference with the process of the English court,[100] although they have not expressly been justified in those terms in England.[101] They are discussed in section H.   **5.34**

E. INSOLVENCY AND JUSTICE BETWEEN CREDITORS

In the nineteenth-century case law, injunctions were frequently granted to restrain creditors from evading England's insolvency jurisdiction, and its policy of fair division among creditors, by bringing proceedings to execute against assets abroad.[102] Anti-suit injunctions   **5.35**

---

[95] In *Barclays Bank v Homan* [1993] BCLC 680, 690, Hoffmann J viewed US insolvency proceedings as sufficiently different to English insolvency that an injunction to restrain them was in effect a single forum situation. Similarly, in *Stichting Shell Pensionenfonds v Krys* [2015] AC 616 (PC) the claims in question could only have been brought in the foreign court.

[96] See *Arab Monetary Fund v Hashim (No 6)* (Hoffmann J, 14 July 1992) and *Bloom v Harms Offshore AHT 'Taurus'* [2010] Ch 187 (CA) [24], [27], [33]. The cases on insolvency are discussed in detail in section E, 'Insolvency and Justice between Creditors'.

[97] *Stichting Shell Pensionenfonds v Krys* [2015] AC 616 (PC) [42].

[98] See *Stichting Shell Pensionenfonds v Krys* [2015] AC 616 (PC) at [40]: 'inimical to the proper winding up process'.

[99] *Shell International Petroleum v Coral Oil (No 2)* [1999] 2 Lloyds Rep 606, 608–10.

[100] See eg *General Star International Indemnity v Stirling Cooke Brown Reinsurance Brokers* [2003] Lloyds Rep 719; *Tonicstar v American Home Assurance* [2005] Lloyds Rep IR 32.

[101] In *Laker Airways v Sabena Belgian World Airlines* 731 F 2nd 909 (DC Cir 1984) [20]–[21], Judge Wilkey viewed anti-anti-suit injunctions as 'necessary to conserve the court's ability to reach a judgment' in certain circumstances.

[102] See *Graham v Maxwell* (1849) 1 Mac & G 71, 41 ER 1189; *Carron Iron v Maclaren* (1855) 5 HLC 416; *Re South Eastern Portugal Railway* (1869) 17 WR 982; *Re London and Colonial, ex parte Clark* (1869) LR 7 Eq 550; *Re Distin* (1871) 24 LT 197; *Re Oriental Inland Steam* (1874) LR 9 Ch App 557 (CA); *Re International Pulp and Paper* (1876) 3 Ch D 594 (based on Companies Act 1962, s 85); *Re the North Carolina Estate* (1889) 5 TLR 328; *Re Central Sugar Factories of Brazil, Flack's Case* [1894] 1 Ch 369; *Re Belfast Shipowners Co* [1894] 1 IR 321; *Re Vocalion (Foreign) Ltd* [1932] 2 Ch 196. Similar issues also arose in probate proceedings, where questions of the priority of creditors have had to be regulated: see *Maclaren v Stainton* (1852) 16 Beav 279, 51 ER 786; *Maclaren v Stainton* (1855) 26 LJ Ch (NS) 332.

to protect English insolvency proceedings are still legitimate in principle, and can be viewed as injunctions granted to protect the integrity of the English jurisdiction, or preventing the evasion of its important public policies.[103] These situations are on the cusp of the division between alternative forum and single forum cases: it may be that the foreign claim will be unavailable in England, if the foreign law permits creditors to claim in some different way from English insolvency law.[104]

5.36   However, the modern cases have adopted a different philosophy of intervention. In the nineteenth-century cases it appeared to be sufficient to justify an injunction that the foreign proceedings would produce a different result to the distribution of assets in an English insolvency. Yet, in *Bank of Tokyo Ltd v Karoon*, Robert Goff LJ doubted whether this part of the anti-suit injunction's history would be a good guide to the modern exercise of the power to restrain, and this has proved to be well founded.[105] In the modern context, the choice is now rarely between the operation of disciplined collective insolvency in England and a free-for-all abroad, as seems to have not uncommonly been the case in the nineteenth century.[106] Most developed countries have sophisticated insolvency laws and procedures enabling cross-border cooperation. Where the foreign jurisdiction has such laws, including procedures under which the orderly distribution of assets in the English insolvency can be protected where the foreign court thinks appropriate,[107] the underlying question will not be whether collective insolvency should be protected in principle, but rather whether the English court should impose its perception of what orderly collective insolvency requires in place of the foreign legal system's approach.

5.37   With this in mind, a series of modern cases has adopted a restrained approach. Provided that the foreign legal system has a developed insolvency law, which pays due regard to the fair distribution of assets in the English insolvency, the normal assumption is that it should be for the foreign court to decide whether or not to stay or restrain the proceedings before it under its own law.[108] Although there will inevitably be differences between national insolvency laws governing how insolvencies and distributions should be managed, such a difference in itself will not usually be a legitimate ground for the grant of an injunction on its own.[109] Thus, in *Barclays Bank v Homan*, Hoffmann J concluded, in a case where there

---

[103] *Arab Monetary Fund v Hashim (No 6)* (Hoffmann J, 14 July 1992); *Bloom v Harms Offshore AHT 'Taurus'* [2010] Ch 187 (CA) [24], [27], [33]; *Morris v Davies* [2011] EWHC 1272 (Ch) [38]–[39]; *Kemsley v Barclays Bank* [2013] EWHC 1274 (Ch) [38]–[41]; *Stichting Shell Pensionenfonds v Krys* [2015] AC 616 (PC) [40], [42].

[104] *Barclays Bank v Homan* [1993] BCLC 680, 691.

[105] *Bank of Tokyo v Karoon* [1987] AC 45 (Note) (CA) 63B–G, although it can be noted that no such doubt was expressed in *Société Nationale Industrielle Aérospatiale v Lee Kui Jak* [1987] AC 871 (PC) 892G–893A; 896D. In *Hughes v Hannover* [1997] 1 BCLC 497 (CA) 519–20, it was held that the historical cases concerning the restraint of creditors acting inconsistently with the collective insolvency proceedings should now be seen merely as illustrations of the applicability of the *Aérospatiale* principles, and that the question was always what the 'ends of justice' would require. See also *Kemsley v Barclays Bank* [2013] EWHC 1274 (Ch) [29], where the older authorities were not treated as a good guide.

[106] See eg *In re Distin* (1871) 24 LT 197.

[107] Such as eg s 304 of the United States Bankruptcy Code: see *Mitchell v Carter, Re Buckingham International* [1997] 1 BCLC 673, 676.

[108] *Barclays Bank v Homan* [1993] BCLC 680 (CA) 690–91 (Hoffmann J), 700 (Glidewell LJ); *Mitchell v Carter, Re Buckingham International* [1997] 1 BCLC 673 (CA) 676; followed in *Stichting Shell Pensionenfonds v Krys* [2015] AC 616 (PC) at [42]; *AWB Geneva v North America Steamships* [2007] 2 Lloyds Rep 315 (CA); and *Kemsley v Barclays Bank* [2013] EWHC 1274 (Ch) [29], [41]. The even more restrictive approach in *Re Vocalion (Foreign)* [1932] 2 Ch 196, 211 was not followed in *Krys* at [38]. See also the restraint shown in *Team Y&R Holdings Hong Kong v Ghossoub* [2017] EWHC 2401 (Comm) [113].

[109] See *Barclays Bank v Homan* [1993] BCLC 680, 685–86 (Hoffmann J), 700–01 (Glidewell LJ); *AWB Geneva v North America Steamships* [2007] 1 CLC 749 [31] (not challenged on appeal [2007] 2 Lloyds Rep 315 (CA));

was a difference of detail between the insolvency laws of the UK and the USA, that so long as the assertion of the foreign state's insolvency jurisdiction did not involve 'egregious' extra-territoriality, the interests of justice did not require it to be prevented by injunction.[110] His reasoning was essentially upheld by the Court of Appeal, who also concluded that there was nothing vexatious or oppressive about the US proceedings.[111] Similarly, if a party gives appropriate undertakings to ensure that the fair distribution of assets in the English insolvency is respected, this may well render his foreign proceedings not liable to be injuncted.[112]

Further, the questions of whether the English court has a sufficient interest to intervene, or is the natural forum, should always be borne in mind.[113] There is no rigid rule that injunctions will not be granted to restrain creditors resident abroad from making claims abroad in their 'home' courts;[114] the residence of the creditor is merely one factor to consider in assessing whether the injunction is appropriate. But in the specific context of insolvency law, if the centre of main interest of the insolvent party is in the foreign country, it is unlikely that the English courts would have a sufficient interest to interfere with litigation there.[115]   **5.38**

However, this restrained approach does not prevent injunctions being granted in the insolvency context where this is appropriate. Thus, injunctions can be granted in the insolvency context if there is something vexatious or oppressive about the foreign proceedings. In *Bloom v Harms*, the creditor companies used US attachment proceedings to create a trap for post-administration payments by administrators in circumstances which were judged by the court to be vexatious, oppressive, and unconscionable.[116] But vexation or oppression is not a necessary condition.[117] Even independent of vexation or oppression, injunctions can be granted where the foreign action would amount to an illegitimate interference with English insolvency proceedings (which includes illegitimate interference with the performance of the duties of administrators or liquidators, who are officers of the court, and so does not require extant court proceedings). The injunction in *Bloom v Harms* was also justified on this basis because the injunction was required to protect the proper performance of their functions by the administrators.[118] And, as envisaged by Hoffmann J in *Barclays Bank v Homan*,[119] injunctions can be justified where the foreign proceedings do involve an exorbitant interference with the fundamental policies of English insolvency law (again, independent of vexation or oppression). In *Shell v Krys*, the Privy Council confronted a situation   **5.39**

Kemsley v Barclays Bank [2013] EWHC 1274 (Ch) [38]–[47]. Maugham J also pointed out in *Re Vocalion (Foreign) Ltd* [1932] 2 Ch 196, 205 that often only some of the creditors abroad would be amenable to the jurisdiction of the English court, and thus the grant of an injunction could well lead to an unjustifiable discrimination between creditors abroad.

---

[110]   *Barclays Bank v Homan* [1993] BCLC 680, 685–86, 689–90 (Hoffmann J).
[111]   *Barclays Bank v Homan* [1993] BCLC 680 (CA) 700–02; Leggatt LJ expressed this conclusion in terms of unconscionability: at 703.
[112]   *Re Newton*, The Times (24 January 1956) and *Kemsley v Barclays Bank* [2013] EWHC 1274 (Ch) [41], cited with approval in *Stichting Shell Pensioenfonds v Krys* [2015] AC 616 (PC) at [40].
[113]   See generally Ch 4, sections L, 'Comity' and M, 'Natural Forum'.
[114]   *Stichting Shell Pensioenfonds v Krys* [2015] AC 616 (PC) at [33]–[34], [42].
[115]   *Kemsley v Barclays Bank* [2013] EWHC 1274 (Ch) [45]–[49].
[116]   *Bloom v Harms Offshore AHT 'Taurus'* [2010] Ch 187 (CA) [27]–[28], [33]. See also *Re the North Carolina Estate* (1889) 5 TLR 328; *Re Vocalion (Foreign)* [1932] 2 Ch 196, 210.
[117]   *Stichting Shell Pensioenfonds v Krys* [2015] AC 616 (PC) at [24].
[118]   *Bloom v Harms Offshore AHT 'Taurus'* [2010] Ch 187 (CA) [27]–[28], [33]. See also the comments of Lord Goff in *Société Nationale Industrielle Aérospatiale v Lee Kui Jak* [1987] AC 871 (PC) 892–93.
[119]   *Barclays Bank v Homan* [1993] BCLC 680, 688.

where Dutch law paid no regard to the existence of the English insolvency, and would have permitted the creditor to circumvent the fair distribution of assets. These rules were sufficiently exorbitant to justify an injunction even though the Privy Council specifically declined to find vexation or oppression.[120] However, the same result could probably have been justified in terms of protection of the English insolvency jurisdiction.

5.40   There are passages in *Shell v Krys* which suggest a return to the older approach of granting an injunction merely because the foreign proceedings would produce a different result to the English insolvency rules.[121] But the better reading of the case is that what actually justified the injunction was the specific and 'egregious' nature of the particular situation, where the Dutch rules contained no protection of fair distribution, and allowed a creditor to steal a march, in a way which was 'in principle inimical to the proper winding up process'. It was this that meant that 'there is no room for deference to the Dutch court's decision'.[122] It is submitted the Privy Council did not intend to depart from the modern approach developed in cases like *Barclays Bank v Homan*.[123]

5.41   In the New Zealand case of *Compudigm*, it was suggested that given the cooperative approach between courts dealing with insolvency internationally required by the UNCITRAL Model law on Cross Border Insolvency (which is in force in the UK[124]), it would be inappropriate to grant anti-suit injunctions to halt proceedings in a foreign court bound by the Model Law.[125] No such rigid restriction has been, nor is likely to be, accepted in England. But it may be that the operation of the Model Law in the 'target' state will be another reason supporting the restrained approach discussed.

F. STAY APPLICATIONS IN THE FOREIGN COURT

5.42   English law has not yet provided a fully consistent answer to whether an injunction claimant should first seek a stay or dismissal of the foreign proceedings in the foreign court, before applying to the English court for an injunction.

5.43   In a number of older decisions, the courts had suggested that if it was possible to apply to the foreign court for a stay on the basis of principles analogous to *forum non conveniens*,[126] a failure to do so first could be a significant factor against the grant of an anti-suit injunction based on vexation and oppression,[127] because 'generally speaking, in deciding whether or

---

[120] *Stichting Shell Pensionenfonds v Krys* [2015] AC 616 (PC) at [42].
[121] *Stichting Shell Pensionenfonds v Krys* [2015] AC 616 (PC), at [38]–[39].
[122] *Stichting Shell Pensionenfonds v Krys* [2015] AC 616 (PC), at [38], [40]–[43].
[123] Both *Barclays Bank v Homan* [1993] BCLC 680 (Hoffmann J and CA) and *Mitchell v Carter, Re Buckingham International* [1997] 1 BCLC 673 (CA) 676, were expressly cited with approval in *Stichting Shell Pensionenfonds v Krys* [2015] AC 616 (PC), at [42].
[124] Cross-Border Insolvency Regulations 2006.
[125] *Commissioner of Inland Revenue v Compudigm International Ltd* [2010] NZHC 1832 [29]. See further the discussion in Ch 20, paras 20.23–20.25.
[126] The relevance of the foreign court being able to apply principles analogous to *forum non conveniens* was discussed in *Société Nationale Industrielle Aérospatiale v Lee Kui Jak* [1987] AC 871 (PC) 894E–G.
[127] *Bouygues Offshore v Caspian Shipping (No 2)* [1997] 2 Lloyds Rep 485, 491 (although oddly Morison J appears to have thought that the contrary had been decided by the CA in *Barclays Bank v Homan*, which is not right); *Ascot Commodities v Northern Pacific Shipping (The Irini A)* [1999] 1 Lloyds Rep 196, 200; *Amoco (UK) Exploration v British American Offshore* [1999] 2 Lloyds Rep 772, 780. In *Amchem Products v British Colombia (Workers' Compensation Board)* [1993] 1 SCR 897 (Can SC) 931, the Canadian Supreme Court suggested that 'it is preferable that the decision of the foreign court not be pre-empted until a proceeding has been launched in that

not to order that a party be restrained in the pursuit of foreign proceedings, the court will be reluctant to take upon itself the decision whether a foreign forum is an inappropriate one'.[128] In contrast, in contractual cases it has long been established that there is no need for a prior application for a stay.[129]

However, any tendency to require a prior stay application appears to have faded out of the   **5.44** more recent case law, and there are many cases where non-contractual anti-suit injunctions have been sought but no weight has been given to the injunction claimant's failure to apply first to the foreign court for a stay.[130] In recent summaries of the law of considerable authority there is no suggestion of such a requirement.[131] In principle, it is doubtful that any preconception favouring a prior stay application is correct. It would pose risks of submission and could create unjustified delay, and would be inconsistent with the tendency of the modern case law to require expedition and discourage delay in seeking anti-suit injunctions. In *Glencore v Metro*, Moore-Bick J observed, in response to a submission that he 'should await the outcome of an application by Glencore to the District Court to stay the proceedings on the grounds of forum non conveniens' that:

> in my view this is only likely to lead to further difficulty. The proceedings before the District Court are still at the earliest stage. If I am satisfied, as I am, that the continued prosecution of those proceedings by the shipowners would be vexatious and abusive, it is far better that I grant relief now rather than seek to act at a later stage. The parties will be spared the cost of preparing and presenting a motion to challenge the jurisdiction of the District Court and,

---

court and the applicant for an injunction in the domestic court has sought from the foreign court a stay or termination of the foreign proceedings and failed'. (Although parts of *Amchem* were referred to with tentative approval in *Airbus Industrie v Patel* [2009] 1 AC 119 (HL), this passage was not amongst those mentioned.)

    This analysis is also consistent, in reverse, with *General Star International Indemnity v Stirling Cooke Brown Reinsurance Brokers Ltd* [2003] Lloyds Rep IR 719 [16], where the court concluded that the New York anti-suit injunction proceedings were vexatious because the 'logical and normal course' would have been to apply to the English court to stay the English proceedings on grounds of *forum non conveniens*.

[128] *Royal Bank of Canada v Cooperatieve Centrale Raiffeisen-Boerenleenbank* [2003] EWHC 2913 [29] (decision upheld on appeal [2004] 1 Lloyds Rep 471 (CA)); see also *Barclays Bank v Homan* [1993] BCLC 680 (CA) 691–92, 700 ('the normal assumption is that the foreign judge is the best person to decide whether an action in his court should proceed'). In *Kemsley v Barclays Bank* [2013] EWHC 1274 (Ch) [45]–[46], the appropriate course was for the US court first to decide whether Mr Kemsley's centre of main interest was in the USA and then to rule on a stay of the proceedings before it.

    This approach was supported by the International Law Association:

> In principle, the court first seised should determine the issues (including the issue whether it has jurisdiction) except (a) when the parties have conferred exclusive jurisdiction on the courts of another country, or (b) when the first seised court is seised in proceedings which are designed (eg by an action for a negative declaration) to frustrate proceedings in a second forum which is clearly more appropriate [International Law Association, Bruges Session (September 2003) Second Commission, Resolution: 'The Principles for Determining When the Use of the Doctrine of Forum non Conveniens and Anti-Suit Injunctions is Appropriate' (Rapporteurs L Collins, G Droz), section 4].

    See also A Lowenfeld, 'Forum non conveniens and Anti-Suit Injunctions: An Update' (1998) 92 AJIL 41, 41.

[129] Ch 7, para 7.17; Ch 8, paras 8.45–8.48.

[130] See eg *Société Nationale Industrielle Aérospatiale v Lee Kui Jak* [1987] AC 871 (PC) (although in that case the doctrine of *forum non conveniens* was not available in the foreign court); *Turner v Grovit* [2002] 1 WLR 107 (HL) (although the decision may be explained by the findings that the Spanish proceedings had been commenced in bad faith in order to harass the defendant in Spain); *Shell International Petroleum v Coral Oil (No 2)* [1999] 2 Lloyds Rep 606; *Al-Bassam v Al-Bassam* [2004] EWCA Civ 857; *Cadre v Astra Asigurari* [2006] 1 Lloyds Rep 560; *Morris v Davies* [2011] EWHC 1272; *Re Tadros* [2014] EWHC 2860; *Ardila Investments v ENRC* [2015] EWHC 1667.

[131] *Société Nationale Industrielle Aérospatiale v Lee Kui Jak* [1987] AC 871 (PC) 892–93; *Deutsche Bank v Highland Crusader Partners* [2010] 1 WLR 1023 (CA) [50].

in what I think is the unlikely event of the District Court's allowing the action to continue, this court will be spared the risk of causing offence to the District Court by intervening in the proceedings after it has decided to assume jurisdiction.

Moore-Bick J went on to observe that he saw no reason why, once the court had decided that foreign proceedings were vexatious and oppressive, the same approach as adopted in contractual cases should not apply.[132]

5.45 Even to the extent that any weight is given to the desirability of a a prior stay application to the foreign court in some cases, any such approach is riddled with exceptions. There are many situations where the absence of an application for a stay made to the foreign court is either insignificant or irrelevant. Thus, it can be so plain and obvious that the foreign proceedings are vexatious and oppressive that even requiring a party to apply for a stay or dismissal in the foreign court would be unjust.[133] Further, where the foreign court will not apply principles analogous to *forum non conveniens* in assessing whether or not to grant a stay,[134] where the foreign court is likely to assume an exorbitant jurisdiction,[135] or where the purpose of the injunction is to protect the jurisdiction of the English court,[136] the absence of a prior application for a stay abroad will not, it seems, be given material weight, as requiring it would be pointless or illogical.[137]

5.46 Where the foreign court has already heard but refused an application to stop the proceedings before it, and has done so after applying principles of *forum non conveniens* similar to those used in England, or by reaching a conclusion which is substantively consistent with such principles, it may well not be in the interests of justice, nor consistent with comity, for the English court to seek, in effect, to override that decision by the grant of an injunction

---

[132] *Glencore International v Metro Trading International (No 3)* [2002] CLC 1090 (Moore-Bick J, [42]; a challenge to this conclusion was not pressed on appeal, and the CA appeared to sympathize with Moore-Bick J's approach: (CA) [71]. See also *Arab Monetary Fund v Hashim (No 6)* (Hoffmann J, 14 July 1992), where Hoffmann J defined the criteria for the grant of an injunction as being that 'the court must be satisfied that the foreign proceedings are vexatious or oppressive in a sense which is likely to result in injustice unless the court grants an injunction rather than leaving the matter to a foreign court', and *Barclays Bank v Homan* [1993] BCLC 680 (CA) 699. In *CSR v Cigna Insurance Australia* (1996–97) 189 CLR 345 (HC Aus) 396–97, the High Court of Australia did not accept the 'proposed rule' that a stay should first be applied for, which had been advanced in *Amchem Products v British Colombia (Workers' Compensation Board)* [1993] 1 SCR 897 (Can SC) 931, and suggested that:

> there may be cases—for example, cases based on contentious or novel claims of unconscionable conduct—in which it is appropriate or desirable that an anti-suit injunction not be granted until an application has been made for a stay or dismissal of the foreign proceedings. However, that course is neither appropriate nor desirable if the application can be determined without that step being taken.

A Briggs, 'Anti-Suit Injunctions in a Complex World' in F Rose (ed), *Lex Mercatoria* (2000) 219, 226–27, argues it is wrong to require a prior stay application to the foreign court.
[133] *Arab Monetary Fund v Hashim (No 6)* (Hoffmann J, 14 July 1992); this may also be part of the explanation of the decision in *Glencore International v Metro Trading International (No 3)* [2002] CLC 1090 (Moore-Bick J) [42].
[134] In TC Hartley, 'Comity and the Use of Anti-suit Injunctions in International Litigation' (1987) 35 AJCL 487, 509, 510, Hartley suggests that although in general an injunction applicant should be expected first to seek a stay, it is a condition that 'the relevant law and policy of the foreign court must be substantially similar to that of the forum'.
[135] See *Midland Bank v Laker Airways* [1986] QB 689 (CA); *Stichting Shell Pensionenfonds v Krys* [2015] AC 616 (PC); TC Hartley, 'Comity and the Use of Anti-Suit Injunctions in International Litigation' (1987) 35 AJCL 487, 509–10.
[136] See again TC Hartley, 'Comity and the Use of Anti-suit Injunctions in International Litigation' (1987) 35 AJCL 487, 510.
[137] *CSR v Cigna Insurance Australia* (1996–97) 189 CLR 345, 398 (HC Aus). See *Midland Bank v Laker Airways* [1986] QB 689 (CA), where an application for a stay to the US court had failed, but the ground of the injunction was that the exercise of US anti-trust jurisdiction was exorbitant. There is no reason to suppose that the court would have been any more likely to decline an injunction had it been applied for before the hearing of the US stay application.

(unless some other factor justifies an injunction).[138] In contrast, if the foreign court has obtained and retained jurisdiction on a basis which appears to be alien or exorbitant, then a refusal of a stay by the foreign court has been given little significance.[139]

G. ANCILLARY AND COLLATERAL PROCEEDINGS

This section considers the distinct[140] category of cases where the foreign proceedings do **5.47** not decide the same substantive dispute, but instead interfere collaterally with an English trial or an English arbitration, for example by seeking remedies abroad that relate to the evidence to be used in the English hearing.

If foreign applications to obtain evidence abroad are sought with the authorization of orders **5.48** of the English court, they will obviously be legitimate. However, there are jurisdictions, notably the USA, which allow their evidence-collecting procedures to be engaged for the purposes of an English action without any prompting from the English court, and differences of laws and procedures can mean that evidence may be obtainable abroad where it would not be obtainable in England.

In principle, it is not in itself an interference with the process of the English court, nor in- **5.49** deed inherently illegitimate, to obtain evidence for use in English court proceedings by applications to foreign courts which are apparently lawful under the foreign law, even if the means by which the evidence is to be gathered would not be available under English law, or the scope of evidence to be obtained would be broader than the English disclosure process would encompass.[141] The foreign evidence-collecting proceedings in such cases merely expand, and do not interfere with, the English forensic process.[142]

---

[138] *Royal Bank of Canada v Cooperatieve Centrale Raiffeisen-Boerenleenbank* [2004] 1 Lloyds Rep 471 (CA) [47]–[48]; *Deutsche Bank v Highland Crusader Offshore Partners* [2010] 1 WLR 1023 (CA) [119] and (where this was not shown on the facts) *Dawnus Sierra Leone Limited v Timis Mining Corporation Limited* [2016] EWHC 236 [66].

See *Amchem Products v British Colombia (Workers' Compensation Board)* [1993] 1 SCR 897 (Can SC) 931-934, referred to with appreciation if not formal approval in *Airbus Industrie v Patel* [1999] 1 AC 119 (HL) 139; followed in relation to contractual injunctions in *Akai v People's* [1998] 1 Lloyds Rep 90, 105 and treated as a relevant principle in relation to non-contractual injunctions in *National Westminster Bank v Utrecht-America Finance* [2001] 3 All ER 733 (CA) [29] and *Royal Bank of Canada v Cooperatieve Centrale Raiffeisen-Boerenleenbank* [2003] EWHC 2913 [47].

Conversely, where a foreign first instance court has *declined* jurisdiction over competing foreign proceedings, it can be oppressive for the injunction defendant to appeal that decision in certain limited circumstances: *Simon Engineering v Butte Mining (No 1)* [1996] 1 Lloyds Rep 104, 108, 112; *Simon Engineering v Butte Mining (No 2)* [1996] 1 Lloyds Rep 91, 98–99, 101.

[139] *Midland Bank v Laker Airways* [1986] QB 689 (CA) 704E, *Société Nationale Industrielle Aérospatiale v Lee Kui Jak* [1987] AC 871 (PC) 886G–887B, 894E–G; *Stichting Shell Pensioenfonds v Krys* [2015] AC 616 (PC) [42]; and see also *Deutsche Bank v Highland Crusader Offshore Partners* [2010] 1 WLR 1023 (CA) [54].

[140] See *Bankers Trust International v PT Dharmala Sakti Sejahtera (No 1)* [1996] CLC 252, 254D–E.

[141] *South Carolina Insurance v Assurantie Maatschappij 'De Seven Provincien'* [1987] AC 24 (HL) 41G–44A (held that a direct application in the USA to obtain disclosure, outside the letter of request procedure, was not an interference with the process of the English court, and injunction refused); *Arab Monetary Fund v Hashim (No 6)* (Hoffmann J, 14 July 1992) (not an interference with an English action to bring foreign proceedings in order to cross-examine a witness in an English action, who otherwise would not have given oral evidence but only a written statement in the English proceedings; this case is perhaps an example of uncharacteristic restraint); *Bankers Trust International v PT Dharmala Sakti Sejahtera (No 1)* [1996] CLC 252, 254; *Nokia v Interdigital Technology* [2004] EWHC 2920 [25]–[26]; *Royal Bank of Scotland v Hicks* [2011] EWHC 287 [94]–[97].

[142] *Nokia v Interdigital Technology* [2004] EWHC 2920 [32]–[35]. However, if under the foreign procedures the request will be granted automatically, without consideration of relevance or proportionality, then the English court may have reasons for intervention, if it doubts the relevance of the material sought: at [34].

5.50   However, the court will always retain the power to intervene if the ends of justice so require, and in particular if the foreign evidence-collecting procedures would upset the process of the English trial[143] or English arbitration,[144] or otherwise be vexatious or oppressive or unconscionable. If the foreign application would subvert orders of the English court in relation to disclosure,[145] or would be oppressive in the light of the way in which the English litigation has developed or will develop,[146] the court will not hesitate to intervene by injunction.

5.51   The occasion for much of the case law on this issue has been section 1782 of Title 28 of the United States Code, under which a litigant in proceedings outside the USA can apply to the US Federal Court to obtain disclosure, or depositions, from persons resident in the USA, for the purposes of the foreign proceedings.

5.52   An injunction was refused where, well before the trial of the English action, the section 1782 proceedings were seeking disclosure of relevant documents from third parties that would otherwise not have been disclosed in the English proceedings.[147] The court also declined to intervene where, although there were doubts about the relevance of the material sought, the appropriateness of granting the application sought could be addressed before the US District Court.[148] In *Royal Bank of Scotland v Hicks*, a general anti-suit injunction restraining proceedings in the USA was qualified to permit section 1782 applications, subject to a requirement that 7 days prior notice was given, to deal with any concerns about potentially abusive *ex parte* applications.[149]

5.53   In contrast, an injunction was granted where the section 1782 application sought the taking of depositions and the disclosure of documents after the conclusion of the English trial, but before judgment,[150] and where the foreign proceedings would lead to the cross-examination of witnesses in the English action before the English trial, thus doubling the occasions on which they would be cross-examined.[151] The court would also probably restrain an application under section 1782 to the US courts where it was clear that the evidence sought was irrelevant to, or inadmissible in, the English action.[152]

5.54   Similarly, in *Benfield Holdings Ltd v Richardson*, the claimant in English proceedings had also commenced parallel New York proceedings, which were timetabled to be determined

---

[143]   *Armstrong v Armstrong* [1892] P 98; *Omega Group Holdings v Kozeny* [2002] CLC 132; *Royal Bank of Scotland v Hicks* [2011] EWHC 287 [94]–[97].

[144]   *Dreymoor Fertilisers Overseas v Eurochem Trading* [2018] EWHC 2267.

[145]   *Bankers Trust International v PT Dharmala Sakti Sejahtera (No 1)* [1996] CLC 252, 255F–256A (injunction granted to restrain applications for further discovery in the USA after the conclusion of the English trial, where the English court had previously rejected applications for disclosure of comparable documents).

[146]   *Bankers Trust International v PT Dharmala Sakti Sejahtera (No 1)* [1996] CLC 252, 255E. See also *Allstate Life Insurance v Australian New Zealand Banking Group (No 4)* (1996) 64 FCR 61 (Aus Fed Ct).

[147]   *South Carolina Insurance v Assurantie Maatschappij 'De Seven Provincien'* [1987] AC 24 (HL).

[148]   *Nokia v Interdigital Technology* [2004] EWHC 2920 [34]–[35].

[149]   *Royal Bank of Scotland v Hicks* [2011] EWHC 287 [94]–[97]. An injunction was also refused on the particular facts in *Dreymoor Fertilisers Overseas v Eurochem Trading* [2018] EWHC 2267.

[150]   *Bankers Trust International v PT Dharmala Sakti Sejahtera (No 1)* [1996] CLC 252, 255E.

[151]   *Omega Group Holdings v Kozeny* [2002] CLC 132; see also *Armstrong v Armstrong* [1892] P 98; a similar result was reached in *Allstate Life Insurance v Australian New Zealand Banking Group Ltd (No 4)* (1996) 64 FCR 61 (Aus Fed Ct). However, see contrary *Arab Monetary Fund v Hashim (No 6)* (Hoffmann J, 14 July 1992), where a Californian action for damages, whose underlying purpose was found probably to be to cross-examine in California a witness to the English action, was not restrained.

[152]   *Nokia v Interdigital Technology* [2004] EWHC 2920 [34]; *Allstate Life Insurance Co v Australian New Zealand Banking Group Ltd (No 4)* (1996) 64 FCR 61 (Aus Fed Ct).

after the English trial, and had proposed to apply in those New York proceedings for orders for deposition of England-based witnesses who would be testifying for the defendant, before the hearing of the English trial. It was alleged by the claimant that the purpose of these depositions was to support claims for interim injunctions in the New York action, but there was no evidence of any genuine intention to claim injunctions, or genuine need for the depositions for that purpose. Langley J concluded that the New York application would unfairly disrupt the defendant's trial preparation and give the claimant the unfair advantage of being able, in effect, to cross-examine the defendant's witnesses before trial, and granted an injunction restraining any such deposition until after determination of the English trial.[153]

The converse situation is where the foreign proceedings are brought to punish, dissuade, or prevent the use of evidence in the English action. The case law here is undeveloped.   **5.55**

However, it appears that the English court may well grant an injunction to restrain foreign proceedings which are brought, in bad faith, with the intention of dissuading a witness from giving evidence in England.[154] Further, if after the determination of an English action, the losing party then seeks damages in a foreign court on the basis of the winning party's conduct in England, it is possible that this will be viewed as a 'collateral attack' on the court's jurisdiction, and therefore restrained.[155]   **5.56**

H. ANTI-ANTI-SUIT INJUNCTIONS

Anti-suit injunctions, or analogous remedies, are granted by courts in legal systems around the world, and especially, but not exclusively, by courts in common law legal systems.[156] There have been many occasions when foreign courts have restrained the pursuit of English proceedings.[157] The English courts have generally accepted this with equanimity,[158] although vigorous objections have been expressed where it is felt that the foreign court has gone too far.[159]   **5.57**

It would be logically indefensible for the English courts to object to foreign anti-suit injunctions granted to restrain English proceedings in all situations. The repeated statements   **5.58**

---

[153] *Benfield Holdings v Richardson* [2007] EWHC 171.
[154] See *Arab Monetary Fund v Hashim (No 6)* (Hoffmann J, 14 July 1992), where it was held on the facts that there was no intention of dissuading the witness from giving evidence, and the injunction was refused.
[155] *Bank of Tokyo v Karoon* [1987] AC 45 (Note) (CA) 51–52 (per Bingham J at first instance); and see also *Unwired Planet International v Huawei Technologies* [2017] EWHC 2831 [8]–[10].
[156] Ch 1, section C, 'Anti-Suit Injunctions in Other Legal Systems'.
[157] There are numerous examples discussed in English cases: see eg *Western Electric v Racal-Milgo* [1979] RPC 501 (CA) 518–19; *Airbus Industrie v Patel* [1999] 1 AC 119 (HL) 136C–E; *Sabah Shipyard (Pakistan) v Islamic Republic of Pakistan* [2003] 2 Lloyds Rep 571 [5]–[11]; *Travelers Casualty and Surety Co of Canada v Sun Life Assurance Co of Canada (UK)* [2006] EWHC 2885 (Comm) [29]–[38]; *Winnetka Trading v Julius Baer International* [2009] Bus LR 1006 [6]–[12]; *Deutsche Bank v Highland Crusader Partners* [2010] 1 WLR 1023 (CA) [38]; *Enercon v Enercon (India)* [2012] 1 Lloyds Rep 519 [4], [26]; *Talos Capital v JSC Investment Holding XIV* [2014] EWHC 3977 [16] (set aside *inter partes*). See also *Parnell v Parnell* (1858) 7 IR Ch 322; and *Cukurova Finance International v Alfa Telecom Turkey* [2015] 2 WLR 875 (PC) [11]. It appears that the grant of a foreign anti-suit injunction will not prevent the English court, as a matter of English law, from hearing either the claim on the merits or an application for an anti-anti-suit injunction: see *Sabah*, at [9]–[15] [40]; the same is implicit in *Enercon*, at [50]–[52]; and in most cases the contrary has not even been argued: see eg *Deutsche*, at [38]. There is no known case of a foreign court seeking directly to restrain the English court itself.
[158] *Winnetka Trading v Julius Baer International* [2009] Bus LR 1006 [6], [13]–[14].
[159] *Tonicstar v American Home Assurance* [2005] 1 Lloyds Rep IR 32.

by English courts that an English anti-suit injunction operates *in personam* only, and that it does not directly or illegitimately interfere with the jurisdiction of the foreign court, and can be consistent with the comity of nations, must mean that there will be situations where a foreign anti-suit injunction to restrain the pursuit of English proceedings should be accepted as legitimate. Further, there should be consistency between the English court's 'offensive' and 'defensive' attitudes: if an English court would grant an anti-suit injunction in parallel circumstances, then any complaint about a foreign anti-suit injunction would be difficult to defend without hypocrisy.[160]

5.59   Nevertheless, where foreign claims for an anti-suit injunction can be characterized as vexatious and oppressive, or in breach of contract, there is no absolute reason of principle why an 'anti-anti-suit injunction' should not be granted to restrain the foreign anti-suit injunction. However, the particular sensitivity of this type of claim, and the inherent risks of escalating conflicts between legal systems, should probably mean that anti-anti-suit injunctions should be granted with particular caution.[161]

5.60   The English case law on anti-anti-suit injunctions is sparse.[162] They have not been treated as a separate category and are analysed under the same principles as general anti-suit injunctions. In non-contractual cases, the basic tests for non-contractual anti-suit injunctions, and thus most centrally the concepts of vexation and oppression (or unconscionability) have been applied,[163] sometimes with the modification that particular caution needs to be exercised.[164]

5.61   In some of the authorities, the English courts appear to have proceeded on the basis that if England was the natural form for the determination of the underlying dispute, and also for the determination of the question of forum, then an attempt to 'hijack' the determination of the question of forum by a claim for an anti-suit injunction abroad would be likely to be

---

[160] The converse does not follow: it would be parochial if the English court were to object to a foreign anti-suit injunction merely on the grounds that an English court would not grant an anti-suit injunction on the same basis.

[161] This passage of the first edition was followed in *Carlyle Capital Corporation v Conway* [2013] 2 Lloyds Rep 179 (Guernsey CA) [68]. See eg *General Star International Indemnity v Stirling Cooke Brown Reinsurance Brokers* [2003] Lloyds Rep IR 719 [15]; *Ecom Agroindustrial v Mosharaf Composite Textile Mill* [2013] 2 Lloyds Rep 196 [21]. In *Deutz v General Electric* (Thomas J, 14 April 2000), an anti-anti-suit injunction was refused, where the US court to which the application for an anti-suit injunction had been made was an appropriate court for the determination of questions of forum, and where all the relevant arguments on forum could be fairly advanced before the US court.

[162] Anti-anti-suit injunctions have been granted (although not always under that label) in *XL Insurance v Owens Corning* [2000] 2 Lloyds Rep 500, 504; *Sabah Shipyard (Pakistan) v Islamic Republic of Pakistan* [2003] 2 Lloyds Rep 571 (CA); *General Star International Indemnity v Stirling Cooke Brown Reinsurance Brokers* [2003] Lloyds Rep IR 719; *Tonicstar v American Home Assurance* [2005] 1 Lloyds Rep IR 32; *Goshawk Dedicated v ROP* [2006] EWHC 1730 [27]; *Ecom Agroindustrial v Mosharaf Composite Textile Mill* [2013] 2 Lloyds Rep 196 [21], [39]; *Swissmarine Services v Gupta Coal India* [2015] EWHC 265 [31]; *Tidewater Marine International v Phoenixtide Offshore Nigeria* [2015] EWHC 2748 [14]. See also *Carlyle Capital Corporation v Conway* [2013] 2 Lloyds Rep 179 (Guernsey CA) [63]–[85].

For other pertinent discussions see *EI Du Pont de Nemours v IC Agnew (No 2)* [1988] 2 Lloyds Rep 240 (CA) 242; *Dornoch v The Mauritius Union Assurance* [2005] EWHC 1887 (Comm) [127]–[130]; *Travelers Casualty and Surety Co of Canada v Sun Life Assurance of Canada (UK)* [2006] EWHC 2885.

[163] *Sabah Shipyard (Pakistan) v Islamic Republic of Pakistan* [2003] 2 Lloyds Rep 571 (CA) [13], [40]–[45] (and see also *Deutsche Bank v Highland Crusader Partners* [2010] 1 WLR 1023 (CA) [81]); *General Star International Indemnity v Stirling Cooke Brown Reinsurance Brokers* [2003] Lloyds Rep IR 719 [16]; *Carlyle Capital Corporation Ltd v Conway* [2013] 2 Lloyds Rep 179 (Guernsey CA) [68]–[116].

[164] *Carlyle Capital Corporation v Conway* [2013] 2 Lloyds Rep 179 (Guernsey CA) [68].

vexatious and oppressive, at least once the English court had determined that it was the natural forum.[165]

It is suggested, however, that in order for an anti-anti-suit injunction to be reconcilable with comity, the domestic court must be manifestly the appropriate forum for the determination of the question of forum. It would be inappropriate for an anti-anti-suit injunction to be deployed, in a case where there was a legitimate dispute as to the relative appropriateness of the different jurisdictions, merely because the domestic court had concluded that on balance it was the more natural forum for the trial of the merits.   **5.62**

If the parties have agreed to an exclusive English forum clause, a foreign anti-suit injunction to restrain substantive proceedings in England will be viewed as a breach of the clause, and can be restrained by injunction, on the basis that it is a breach of contract,[166] under the principles outlined in *The Angelic Grace*.[167] In *Sabah Shipyard v Government of Pakistan*, the parties had agreed to the non-exclusive jurisdiction of the English courts. A claim in Pakistan for an anti-suit injunction to restrain proceedings in England was held to be in breach of implied terms of the jurisdiction clause, and also to be vexatious and oppressive, as the parties had implicitly agreed at least that English litigation could not be treated as inappropriate, and an anti-anti-suit injunction was required to protect Sabah's rights to non-exclusive jurisdiction against the Pakistani anti-suit injunction.[168] However, probably due to the particular risks of conflict with foreign courts raised by anti-anti-suit injunctions, there is case law suggesting that the English courts are relatively willing to accept that there may be 'strong reasons' not to grant an anti-anti-suit injunction.[169]   **5.63**

Anti-anti-anti-suit injunctions may also be granted to protect the English court's anti-suit injunction jurisdiction. In general, they are granted as an ancillary injunction as part of an order for a primary anti-suit injunction,[170] although a free-standing anti-anti-anti-suit injunction has been granted in one reported case.[171] The case law has not yet explored the relevant tests, if any specific tests exist.   **5.64**

---

[165] *General Star International Indemnity Ltd v Stirling Cooke Brown Reinsurance Brokers* [2003] Lloyds Rep IR 719 [16]; *Tonicstar v American Home Insurance Co* [2005] 1 Lloyds Rep IR 32.

[166] This follows *a fortiori* from *Sabah Shipyard (Pakistan) v Islamic Republic of Pakistan* [2003] 2 Lloyds Rep 571 (CA) [37], [52], where the parallel conclusion was reached in relation to a non-exclusive English jurisdiction clause; and see *Deutsche Bank v Highland Crusader Partners* [2010] 1 WLR 1023 (CA) [81]. In relation to an exclusive jurisdiction clause, see *Ecom Agroindustrial Corp v Mosharaf Composite Textile Mill* [2013] 2 Lloyds Rep 196 [21], [36] (albeit undefended). See also *Goshawk Dedicated v ROP* [2006] EWHC 1730 [27] (where the parties had agreed to English arbitration, and an injunction was granted to restrain the pursuit of an 'anti-arbitration' application to the US courts).

[167] *Aggeliki Charis Compania Maritima v Pagnan (The Angelic Grace)* [1995] 1 Lloyds Rep 87 (CA). See generally Ch 7. But cf *Carlyle Capital Corporation v Conway* [2013] 2 Lloyds Rep 179 (Guernsey CA), where an anti-anti-suit injunction was issued in order to protect the Guernsey's court's insolvency jurisdiction notwithstanding exclusive jurisdiction clauses in favour of the other court.

[168] *Sabah Shipyard (Pakistan) v Islamic Republic of Pakistan* [2003] 2 Lloyds Rep 571 (CA) [36]–[37], [40]–[45]; *Deutsche Bank v Highland Crusader Partners* [2010] 1 WLR 1023 (CA) [81]. In *Deutsche v Highland* [78]–[87], the anti-suit injunction aspects of the reasoning in *Sabah* were treated as the legitimate justification for the result in the earlier case; otherwise *Sabah* was restrictively interpreted and its wider reasoning criticized.

[169] *Deutz v General Electric* (Thomas J, 14 April 2000); and perhaps *Ecom Agroindustrial v Mosharaf Composite Textile Mill* [2013] 2 Lloyds Rep 196 [21].

[170] An example of this is *Dell Emerging Markets (EMEA) v IB Maroc.com* [2017] EWHC 2397 (Comm), where anti-anti-anti-suit injunctions were granted both at the without notice and with notice stages, although this is not discussed in the report.

[171] *GE Francona Reinsurance v CMM Trust No 1400* [2004] EWHC 2003 [10].

I. ANTI-ENFORCEMENT INJUNCTIONS

5.65 The power to grant anti-suit injunctions includes the power to grant an anti-enforcement injunction, which restrains a party from seeking to enforce a foreign judgment, even in respect of potential enforcement in other foreign countries.[172]

5.66 However, the modern approach to comity suggests that, at least in non-contractual cases, worldwide anti-enforcement injunctions will now be granted only in rare circumstances.[173] Where a judgment has been given in foreign state X, and the judgment creditor seeks to enforce that judgment within foreign states Y and Z, it is in general a matter for the courts of Y and Z, under their own law of enforcement, to conclude whether or not the judgment should be enforced there. The English court will often not have a sufficient interest in, or connection with, the enforcement of the judgment within Y or Z to justify imposing its views on whether the judgment should be enforced by courts in Y or Z, still less in the rest of the world.[174]

5.67 In *Ellerman v Read*, the court held that it would grant an injunction to restrain enforcement of a foreign judgment obtained by breach of contract or by fraud, while Scrutton LJ appeared to consider that the court had sufficient interest to intervene because the contract was governed by English law, was partly to be performed in England, and the injunction defendant was a British subject.[175] But the fact that substantive foreign proceedings had been in breach of a London arbitration clause has been insufficient to warrant the grant of an anti-enforcement injunction in recent cases.[176] Instead, in the recent cases *Ellerman v Read* has been interpreted as depending on the proposition that the foreign judgment in that case was obtained by fraud.[177]

5.68 Further, delay in seeking the injunction until after the foreign judgment is a significant factor in the assessment of comity. It means that the injunction to restrain enforcement may well, in effect, be seeking to undo what has already been done by the foreign court. The English courts have tended to regard this as a considerable interference with the foreign court's jurisdiction, which is difficult to justify as a matter of comity.[178]

---

[172] *Ellerman Lines v Read* [1928] 2 KB 144 (CA) 152–53, 154–55, 158; *Mamidoil-Jetoil Greek Petroleum v Okta Crude Oil Refinery* [2003] 1 Lloyds Rep 1 [205]; *Masri v Consolidated Contractors (No 3)* [2009] QB 503 (CA) [93]–[94].

[173] *Masri v Consolidated Contractors (No 3)* [2009] QB 503 (CA) [93]–[94]; *Ecobank Transnational v Tanoh* [2016] 1 WLR 2231 (CA).

[174] *D&F Man (Sugar) Ltd v Haryanto (No 2)* [1991] 1 Lloyds Rep 161, 167–68, [1991] 1 Lloyds Rep 429 (CA) 438, 440; *Industrial Maritime Carriers (Bahamas) v Sinoca International (The Eastern Trader)* [1996] 2 Lloyds Rep 585, 602–03; *Akai v People's Insurance* [1998] 1 Lloyds Rep 90, 108; *Mamidoil-Jetoil Greek Petroleum v Okta Crude Oil Refinery* [2003] 1 Lloyds Rep 1, 35; see generally the discussion in *Ecobank Transnational v Tanoh* [2016] 1 WLR 2231 (CA).

[175] *Ellerman Lines v Read* [1928] 2 KB 144 (CA) 151–52 (per Scrutton LJ). In contrast Atkin LJ and Eve J did not seem to consider that comity imposed any restrictions in itself, and that fraud and breach of contract would suffice.

[176] It did not suffice in *ED&F Man (Sugar) v Haryanto (No 2)* [1991] 1 Lloyds Rep 161, [1991] 1 Lloyds Rep 429 (CA); nor in *Industrial Maritime Carriers (Bahamas) v Sinoca International (The Eastern Trader)* [1996] 2 Lloyds Rep 585, 602–03; and it would not have sufficed in *Akai v People's Insurance* [1998] 1 Lloyds Rep 90, 108.

[177] *Masri v Consolidated Contractors (No 3)* [2009] QB 503 (CA) [94]; *Ecobank Transnational v Tanoh* [2016] 1 WLR 2231 (CA).

[178] *Industrial Maritime Carriers (Bahamas) v Sinoca International (The Eastern Trader)* [1996] 2 Lloyds Rep 585, 602–03; *Ecobank Transnational v Tanoh* [2016] 1 WLR 2231 (CA).

A similarly hesitant approach to anti-enforcement injunctions applies even where the **5.69** foreign proceedings were in breach of a jurisdiction or arbitration clause, in particular because the delay can be a good reason not to grant the injunction.[179] It appears that in such situations the standard *Angelic Grace* principles may not apply and that 'caution' is required.[180]

The net result is that anti-enforcement injunctions have only been granted in two **5.70** cases: *Ellerman v Read*, which has been recently interpreted as turning on the proposition that the foreign judgment was obtained by fraud;[181] and *Bank St Petersburg v Archangelsky*, where the injunction was justified by a specific agreement not to bring the enforcement proceedings, and there was no objection on grounds of delay.[182] But an important aspect of the landscape is that the cases so far have largely concerned attempts to restrain post-judgment enforcement through normal measures of enforcement abroad, on the basis of objections to the legitimacy of the foreign proceedings which existed pre-judgment. In cases where the gravamen of the injunction depends on post-judgment matters, such as the potentially exorbitant nature of the foreign enforcement measures sought, different considerations will apply.[183]

Where the intended forum of enforcement is England, comity is no reason to withhold the **5.71** injunction; but the grant of an injunction to restrain enforcement may well be procedurally inappropriate or unnecessary: the appropriate course will often be to resist enforcement in England if and when it is sought.[184]

The question of whether and when anti-enforcement injunctions to restrain enforcement **5.72** proceedings elsewhere in the Brussels–Lugano zone are precluded by the principle of mutual trust is discussed (subject to the effect of Brexit) in Ch 12, paras 12.69–12.72.

---

[179] *Ecobank Transnational v Tanoh* [2016] 1 WLR 2231 (CA). In *Whitworths v Synergy Food and Processing BV* [2014] EWHC 2439 (QB) [68]–[74], the English court had granted an injunction to restrain pursuit of a foreign arbitration which it concluded was being pursued in breach of an agreement instead to arbitrate in England. Popplewell J refused to grant a further injunction to restrain enforcement in England of any arbitration award that might be the result; he viewed such enforcement as doomed to fail, not least because it would require the foreign arbitration to have been pursued in continuing contempt of court. Nevertheless, he concluded that it was premature, at that particular stage, to shut out the injunction defendant by an additional injunction from making any application to enforce the award, however doomed that might be, at least pending further developments in the arbitration. The decision does not involve a conclusion that an anti-enforcement injunction at a later point would never be appropriate.

[180] *Akai v People's Insurance* [1998] 1 Lloyds Rep 90 [104] and *Ecobank Transnational v Tanoh* [2016] 1 WLR 2231 (CA).

[181] *Ecobank Transnational v Tanoh* [2016] [2016] 1 WLR 2231 (CA); *Masri v Consolidated Contractors (No 3)* [2009] QB 503 (CA) [94].

[182] *Bank St Petersburg v Archangelsky* [2014] 1 WLR 4360 (CA) [34]–[39]; see the discussion in *Ecobank Transnational v Tanoh* [2016] [2016] 1 WLR 2231 (CA).

[183] See *Ecobank Transnational v Tanoh* [2016] 1 WLR 2231 (CA). The *Bank St Petersburg* case can be seen as depending on a 'post-judgment' objection, namely the agreement not to enforce which the Court of Appeal held existed.

[184] *EI Du Pont de Nemours v IC Agnew* [1988] 2 Lloyds Rep 240 (CA) 245, 249; *Industrial Maritime Carriers (Bahamas) v Sinoca International (The Eastern Trader)* [1996] 2 Lloyds Rep 585, 602–03; *Mamidoil-Jetoil Greek Petroleum v Okta Crude Oil Refinery* [2003] 1 Lloyds Rep 1 [202]; *Bank St Petersburg v Archangelsky* [2014] 1 WLR 4360 (CA) [27].

6

Injunctions in Relation to Proceedings in England and Wales

A. INTRODUCTION

The anti-suit injunction started at home. It developed from the 'common injunction', which before the Judicature Acts was granted by the Court of Chancery to restrain a party from pursuing inequitable proceedings before the common law courts of England.[1] It was only after centuries of injunctions to restrain court proceedings in England that the Court of Chancery, tentatively at first, began to restrain parties from pursuing proceedings abroad.[2] The modern position is reversed. It is now rare for injunctions to be granted to restrain the pursuit of proceedings in England.[3]   **6.01**

The cause of the change was the Judicature Act 1873, which fused the administration of common law and equity in the newly created High Court,[4] and in return prohibited the grant of injunctions to restrain actions 'pending' before the High Court or Court of Appeal.[5] The   **6.02**

---

[1] Ch 2, para 2.03. See eg *Cotesworth v Stephens* (1845) 4 Hare 185, 67 ER 612 (proceedings in Lord Mayor's Court restrained).

[2] See Ch 2, paras 2.04–2.06.

[3] Scotland and Northern Ireland, of course, have separate legal systems, and in relation to anti-suit injunctions, are foreign countries in most respects (although not under the Insolvency Act 1986, s 126: see n 65).

[4] Supreme Court of Judicature Act 1873, ss 22–25.

[5] Supreme Court of Judicature Act 1873, s 24(5): 'No cause or proceeding at any time pending in the High Court of Justice, or before the Court of Appeal, shall be restrained by prohibition or injunction …'. This was later replaced in the same terms by Supreme Court of Judicature (Consolidation) Act 1925, s 41, but was not carried through into the Supreme Court Act 1981, now the Senior Courts Act 1981. This has abolished the prohibition on injunctions, which has not been carried through implicitly into the 1981 Act: see *South West Trains v Wightman* [1998] Pens LR 113 [96]–[97]; *Omega Engineering v Omega* [2010] FSR 26 [86]–[88].
The previous provisions were applied in *Garbutt v Fawcus* (1875) 1 Ch D 155 (CA); *Wright v Redgrave* (1879) 11 Ch D 24 (CA) (where it was said that 'it was an evil that Courts of Equity had to interfere with proceedings in another court on equitable grounds': at 32); *In re Artistic Colour Printing Company* (1880) 14 Ch D 502; *Hart v Hart* (1881) 18 Ch D 670, 679–81; *In re General Service Co-Operative Stores* [1891] 1 Ch 496 (CA). Garnishee proceedings in the High Court were held to be proceedings within s 41 of the 1925 Act: *Llewellyn v Carrickford* [1970] 1 WLR 1124, and thus their pursuit could not be restrained by injunction. It also followed from s 24(5), and Supreme Court of Judicature Act 1875, s 11, that one division of the High Court would not stay proceedings in another division: *Garbutt v Fawcus* (1875) 1 Ch D 155 (CA) 158; *In re General Service Cooperative Stores* [1891] 1 Ch 496 (CA).

statutory prohibition was not decisive in itself, as it was interpreted narrowly and did not prohibit the grant of injunctions to restrain the *commencement* of proceedings in the High Court,[6] nor did it prohibit injunctions to restrain the pursuit of proceedings before the County Courts, other inferior courts, or indeed courts of coordinate jurisdiction.[7] More important was the fusion of the administration of common law and equity, which meant that any equitable right could be given substantive effect in the court before which the original proceedings were brought,[8] so that the need for common injunctions to enforce the principles of equity disappeared.[9] The fusion of the previously separate court systems also produced a change of judicial attitudes, with the common injunction coming to be seen as generally an unnecessarily heavy-handed tool to coordinate proceedings within what was now a single legal system.

6.03   Injunctions to restrain the pursuit of court proceedings within the jurisdiction were granted with some frequency in the immediate aftermath of the Judicature Acts.[10] But in modern times, the practice has become rare, with the exception of the special case of injunctions in the context of insolvency.[11] Nevertheless, the power to grant anti-suit injunctions in respect of English proceedings continues to exist, and can be exercised in appropriate situations.

B. POWERS TO GRANT INJUNCTIONS IN RELATION
TO ENGLISH PROCEEDINGS

6.04   The modern power to restrain proceedings[12] before another court or an arbitration tribunal[13] in England by injunction appears, on the best analysis, to be exercised (in general)

In general terms these provisions restricted only the High Court's powers, but the same applied to the County Court by implication: *Cobbold v Pryke* (1879) 4 ExD 315.

---

[6] As they had not been commenced they were not 'pending': *Besant v Wood* (1879) 12 Ch D 605, 630; *Hedley v Bates* (1880) 13 Ch D 498; *Cercle Restaurant Castiglione v Lavery* (1881) 18 Ch D 555 (s 24(5) not referred to); *Re a Company* [1894] 2 Ch 349, 351; *Re Maidstone Palace of Varieties Ltd* [1909] 2 Ch 283. Nor, apparently, did s 24(5) of the 1873 Act and its successors prohibit injunctions to restrain the use of evidence in other proceedings in the High Court: see *Medway v Doublelock* [1978] 1 WLR 710 (however, s 41 of the 1925 Act was not cited).

[7] *Re Connolly Brothers* [1911] 1 Ch 731 (CA) 739–40, 744–48.

[8] Supreme Court of Judicature Act 1873, s 24.

[9] *TC Trustees v JS Darwen (Successors)* [1969] 2 QB 295 (CA) 302B–C.

[10] Even if the cases related to winding up are left to one side, examples include *Besant v Wood* (1879) 12 Ch D 605, 630; *Hedley v Bates* (1880) 13 Ch D 498; *The Teresa* (1894) 7 Asp MLC 505; for a more restrictive approach see *Stannard v Vestry of St Giles, Camberwell* (1882) 20 Ch D 190 (CA) 196–97.

[11] For injunctions in the context of insolvency, see sections E, 'Injunctions to Restrain Winding-Up Petitions' and F, 'Injunctions to Protect Winding-Up Petitions'. In contrast, the court's separate powers to restrain vexatious *litigants* are frequently exercised: see section G, 'Orders to Restrain Vexatious Litigants'.

[12] Historically this included a power to restrain a party from issuing execution on a judgment: *Ochsenbein v Papelier* (1872) 8 Ch App 695 (CA) (foreign judgment; injunction not granted); *In re Low* [1894] 1 Ch 147 (CA) 162. But the existence of such power to restrain enforcement of an English judgment by injunction was doubted *obiter* (without citation of authority) by Evans-Lombe J in *Hillcourt (Docklands) v Teliasonera* [2006] EWHC 508 [18], where the appropriate course was thought to be a stay of execution. It is indeed likely that a stay of execution is likely to be the right approach at least in most cases, but it is submitted that Evans-Lombe's J's doubts as to the existence of any *jurisdiction* were unfounded.
  In the context of worldwide anti-enforcement injunctions, the court has had to consider whether it would be appropriate to grant an injunction restraining enforcement of a foreign judgment in England (by the usual methods of recognition and enforcement). In general, this has been thought not to be necessary or appropriate, for the practical reason that the judgment debtor can raise such objections as he has to enforcement before the English courts at the enforcement stage. See *ED&F Man (Sugar) v Haryanto (No 2)* [1991] 1 Lloyds Rep 429 (CA) 437; *Industrial Marine Carriers (Bahamas) v Sinoca International (The Eastern Trader)* [1996] 2 Lloyds Rep 585, 606; *Mamidoil-Jetoil Greek Petroleum v Okta Crude Oil Refinery* [2003] 1 Lloyds Rep 1 [202]; *Ecobank Transnational v Tanoh* [2016] 1 Lloyd Rep 360 (CA) [122]–[142]; *Whitworths v Synergy Food and Processing BV* [2014] EWHC 2439 (QB) [68]–[74]; and also the discussion in *Ecobank Transnational v Tanoh* [2016] 1 Lloyd Rep 360 (CA) [109], [111]. This was also in substance the ground for refusing the injunction in *Ochsenbein v Papelier*.

[13] Injunctions to restrain arbitrations in England are dealt with further in Ch 11.

under section 37(1) of the Senior Courts Act 1981.[14] In certain cases the injunction has been viewed as granted under the court's 'inherent jurisdiction' to prevent an abuse of its process,[15] but it is suggested that this is an unnecessary complication. Important and specific statutory powers to protect insolvency proceedings by injunction are also granted by the Insolvency Act 1986.[16] It appears that the exercise of these powers as between parties to a civil action is not precluded by the availability of remedies by way of judicial review against the targeted court itself.[17]

It appears that section 37(1), or indeed the inherent jurisdiction, are no longer constrained by the limited prohibition on the grant of injunctions to restrain proceedings 'pending' in the High Court, originally imposed by section 24(5) of the Judicature Act 1873, and re-enacted in section 41 of the Judicature Act 1925, as this was not re-enacted in the Senior Courts Act 1981. The High Court has concluded that it has not continued by implication.[18] Even if that were wrong, such a restriction cannot preclude injunctions restraining the commencement of proceedings, to which sections 24(5) and 41 never applied.[19] Further, Article 6 of the European Convention on Human Rights (ECHR) has been held not to create any absolute bar to such an injunction, and has been treated as being unlikely to be relevant.[20]   **6.05**

In contrast, a court has no power directly to order a *stay* of proceedings before another court or tribunal in England.[21] That would be incoherent, as a stay is a remedy which a court grants of proceedings before itself.[22]   **6.06**

---

[14] It is clear that injunctions to restrain proceedings abroad are based, in general, on s 37(1): see Ch 3, section A, 'The Power to Grant Injunctions'. The same should logically apply for injunctions to restrain proceedings in England. For authority, see *Sears v Sears, Roebuck* [1993] RPC 385, 388 and *Fujifilm Kyowa Kirin Biologics v AbbVie Biotechnology* [2017] RPC 7 [45]; upheld on appeal [2017] RPC 9 (CA) [107]–[108]. See also *Nursing and Midwifery Council v Harrold* [2015] EWHC 2254 [27], although cf [26], [37].
The court's statutory and common law powers to restrain vexatious litigants are juridically distinct from anti-suit injunctions. See generally paras 6.31–6.32. However, they can be viewed loosely as a form of injunctive relief: see *Nursing and Midwifery Council v Harrold* [2015] EWHC 2254 [27].
[15] *Mann v Goldstein* [1968] 1 WLR 1091, 1093H–1094A.
[16] Section F, 'Injunctions to Protect Winding-Up Proceedings'.
[17] *Sears v Sears, Roebuck* [1993] RPC 385, 392–93, where the doctrine in *O'Reilly v Mackman* [1983] 2 AC 237 (HL), which has moreover been much diluted since, was held not to apply to preclude domestic anti-suit injunctions. See also *Nursing and Midwifery Council v Harrold* [2015] EWHC 2254 [29]; and for recent examples of the power to injunct being held to exist, see *Omega Engineering v Omega* [2010] FSR 26 [86]–[88] and *Fujifilm Kyowa Kirin Biologics v AbbVie Biotechnology* [2017] RPC 7 [45], upheld on appeal [2017] RPC 9 (CA) [107]–[108].
   Where an injunction is claimed against the other litigant on the grounds that the court before which he seeks to pursue proceedings does not have jurisdiction, the overlap with remedies by way of judicial review against the inferior court is close, but even there, there has not been held to be any bar: see eg *The Teresa* (1894) 7 Asp MLC 505 (proceedings were brought before an inferior court that had no jurisdiction to hear them; prohibition could have been granted against the inferior court, and an injunction was granted to restrain the litigant before it); see also *R v Judge of County Court of Lincolnshire* (1888) 20 QBD 167, 169. In *Johns v Chatalos* [1973] 1 WLR 1437, it was argued that the existence of remedies by way of judicial review precluded the grant of an injunction *inter partes* against the other litigant, where the ground of complaint was that the inferior court was acting outside its jurisdiction; but Brightman J did not decide the point, as it was appropriate to refuse the injunction for discretionary reasons in any event.
[18] *South West Trains v Wightman* [1998] Pens LR 113 [96]–[97]; *Omega Engineering v Omega* [2010] FSR 26 [86]–[88].
[19] Paragraph 6.02 and n 6.
[20] *Fujifilm Kyowa Kirin Biologics v AbbVie Biotechnology* [2017] RPC 9 (CA) [107]–[108].
[21] *Clyde & Co v Bates van Winkelhof* [2012] ICR 928 [47]–[48]. The remainder of the reasoning in the case is questionable, but this aspect is correct.
[22] *Garbutt v Fawcus* (1875) 1 Ch D 155 (CA) 158.

6.07   In *Chorion v Lane*, the court adopted the alternative route of requiring the claimant in the other proceedings to apply for a stay to the other court or to consent to stay if applied for by the defendant there. This is in substance a form of mandatory anti-suit injunction. Although it might seem less of an intervention than a prohibitory injunction, in reality the distinction is no more than a device. In addition, requiring a party to make a grudging application against his or her own interests can be problematic. Consequently, a *Chorion*-style order should only be granted in the kind of situation, and on the basis of the same kind of principles, that would justify a prohibitory anti-suit injunction. In *Chorion* itself, Laddie J proceeded on the basis that he should in substance follow the injunction cases.[23] So it is not clear that the *Chorion* technique really adds much.

6.08   Even to the extent and so long as the Brussels–Lugano regime and European Union (EU) law (or any similar regime), remains effective in the UK, the principle of mutual trust laid down by the European Court of Justice (ECJ) in *Turner v Grovit*,[24] does not preclude the grant of injunctions by the English court to restrain the pursuit of proceedings before other courts in England (or the UK), because this is an internal matter with which the Brussels–Lugano regime is not concerned.[25]

C. PRINCIPLES GOVERNING INJUNCTIONS WITHIN ENGLAND

6.09   The case law since 1873 is sparse, and there has been little development of principles to govern when injunctions should be granted to restrain court proceedings in England. However, the main decisions have applied the familiar concepts of the ends of justice, and vexation or oppression,[26] although others have used a test of abuse of process.[27]

---

[23] *Chorion v Lane* (24 February 1999) (Laddie J) [17], [32]–[35]. In *Clyde & Co v Bates van Winkelhof* [2012] ICR 928, a restrictive approach was taken to *Chorion*, whose correctness was doubted. It is submitted that it is *Bates* itself which is doubtful, as the many previous authorities on domestic anti-suit injunctions were not put before the court. *Chorion* was discussed with approval (although treated as unusual) in *Mindimaxnox v Gover* (EAT, 7 December 2010) [42], [47] (where *Bates* was not cited).

[24] *Turner v Grovit* [2004] ECR I-3565.

[25] See Ch 12, section E, 'Injunctions and Proceedings in the United Kingdom'. The contrary *obiter* suggestions in *Clyde & Co v Bates van Winkelhof* [2012] ICR 928 [47], [50] are unconvincing and based on incomplete argument. Notably, the court in that case was not taken to the range of the authorities upholding domestic anti-suit injunctions.

[26] *Re Connolly Brothers* [1911] 1 Ch 731 (CA) 744–48 (in contrast to the references to 'convenience' at first instance: see 738–40); *Landi den Hartog v Sea Bird (Clean Air Fuel Systems)* [1976] FSR 489, 493–94 (where the point of principle was conceded); *Jacey (Printers) v Norton & Wright Group* [1977] FSR 475, 479; *Thames Launches v Trinity House Corp (Deptford Strond)* [1961] Ch 197, 204, 209 (although at 208 the concept actually applied seems to have been broader); *Thames Hudson v Design and Artists Copyright Society* [1995] FSR 153, 157–58 (where the power and the nature of the test was conceded); *Fujifilm Kyowa Kirin Biologics v AbbVie Biotechnology* [2017] RPC 7 [45], upheld on appeal [2017] RPC 9 (CA).

See also *Imperial Tobacco v Attorney General* [1981] AC 718 (HL) 752C, although the decision to grant an injunction in *Thames Launches* was treated with some reserve: at 718, 741–42, 746, 750–52 and *Ebert v Venvil* [2000] Ch 484 (CA) 492G–H, 497B–D, in the related context of orders to restrain vexatious litigants.

There are cases where the tests applied are looser: *Hedley v Bates* (1880) 13 Ch D 498, 503 ('just and convenient'); *Sears v Sears, Roebuck* [1993] RPC 385, 388–90; *Chorion v Lane* (24 February 1999) (Laddie J) [34] (inappropriate duplication was 'wrong', justifying an order that the defendant in the other proceedings should consent to a stay; but many of the lead authorities were not cited). However, to the extent that they are intended to lay down a different principle, it is suggested that they do not represent the law.

In *Medway v Doublelock* [1978] 1 WLR 710, no proof of vexation or oppression was expressly required. But it may be that the grant of an injunction in that case could be justified on the basis that use of the affidavits in the family proceedings, which was restrained by injunction, was a breach of the legal right created by the implied undertaking in respect of disclosed documents (see at 713H).

[27] *Stonegate Securities v Gregory* [1980] 1 Ch 576 (CA) 579H–580C; *Essex Electric v IPC Computers (UK)* [1991] FSR 690, 699–701.

It is submitted that the principles developed in relation to foreign proceedings can   **6.10**
be cross-applied, at least at a high level of generality, and with some modification.[28]
Consequently, the law can probably be summarized as follows. Within the scope of
the court's powers,[29] an injunction to restrain pending or future English proceedings
may be granted if—but only if—it is in the interests of justice to do so, and in general an injunction will not be granted unless the pursuit of other proceedings are or
will be vexatious or oppressive (or, to use other language, unconscionable),[30] or an
abuse of the process of the court, or inconsistent with a substantive legal or equitable right, such as a contractual right not to be sued in a particular forum or at a particular time, or a right not to be sued at all,[31] or an obligation of confidentiality.[32] One
example of a situation where an injunction may be granted is to restrain vexatious
relitigation.[33]

Some cases suggest that there is a wider power to grant an injunction (or to order   **6.11**
the respondent to consent to a stay) where otherwise there will be parallel duplicative proceedings, in a way that would be inefficient and wasteful, and contrary to
the overriding objective, but without any showing of vexation or oppression.[34] This
sort of 'case management' approach has been expressly rejected as an insufficient
ground for intervention internationally,[35] but a more flexible approach is possible
domestically, where considerations of comity are lessened. Yet this may be too low
a threshold for interference by injunction even within England, and if the justification is one of mere convenience, it may be that the most appropriate course should
usually be to apply for a stay to the court before which the targeted litigation is
proceeding.

The same principles apply to the restraint of the prosecution of criminal proceedings in   **6.12**
England, although it may be that the court will apply particular caution in the exercise
of its discretion in such a case.[36]

---

[28] In *Re Connolly Brothers* [1911] 1 Ch 731 (CA), the Court of Appeal did not perceive any distinction in principle between restraint of foreign proceedings and restraint of English proceedings: see at 744–46.

[29] The court's powers are, it seems, no longer restricted by the principle established in the Judicature Act
1873 that an injunction may not lie to restrain proceedings 'pending' in the High Court: see paras 6.02
and 6.05.

[30] In *Fujifilm Kyowa Kirin Biologics v AbbVie Biotechnology* [2017] RPC 7 [46(ii)], Arnold J suggested that in
relation to domestic anti-suit injunctions, proof of vexation or oppression would be a 'high threshold' to cross.
However, there is no direct support for this in the previous authorities, and the point was not picked up in the
Court of Appeal [2017] RPC 9 (CA) [107]–[108].

[31] *Omega Engineering v Omega* [2010] FSR 26 [61], [66], [85]–[94]; see also *Besant v Wood* (1879) 12 Ch D 605,
630; *Re Connolly Brothers* [1911] 1 Ch 731 (CA) 744, 748.

[32] This is a possible explanation of *Medway v Doublelock* [1978] 1 WLR 710.

[33] *Masri v Consolidated Contractors (No 3)* [2009] QB 503 (CA).

[34] *Chorion v Lane* (24 February 1999) (Laddie J) [34]; also *Hedley v Bates* (1880) 13 Ch D 498, 503 ('just and convenient'); *Sears v Sears, Roebuck* [1993] RPC 385, 388–90.

[35] Ch 4, section J, 'Forum non Conveniens'.

[36] *Thames Launches v Trinity House Corp (Deptford Strond)* [1961] Ch 197, 204–05; *Thames Hudson v Design
and Artists Copyright Society* [1995] FSR 153, 157–58; *Grand Junction Waterworks Co v Hampton Urban District
Council* [1898] 2 Ch 331, 342. Some of the authorities immediately after the Judicature Acts reflect a more re-
strictive approach in relation to criminal proceedings: *Saull v Browne* (1874–75) LR 10 Ch App 64; *Kerr v
Corporation of Preston* (1876) 6 Ch D 463. See, in the context of insolvency, *In re Briton Medical and General Life
Assurance Association* (1886) 32 Ch D 503; *Re Burrows (Leeds)* [1982] 1 WLR 1177, 1185.

6.13   The domestic context shapes the implementation of the general principles applicable to anti-suit injunctions to restrain the pursuit of foreign proceedings, and in some cases renders them inapplicable. For example, the doctrine of comity of nations is not directly transferable to injunctions within England and Wales. But a parallel logic to comity has led to the development of some analogous principles in the domestic case. Thus, in general, an injunction will not be granted, absent special circumstances, where the other English court is the jurisdiction to which Parliament has specifically assigned the determination of a particular matter, or is usually the appropriate court to decide a particular question,[37] provided the other court is acting within its jurisdiction.

6.14   In addition, some of the discretionary reasons in favour of restraint in granting injunctions may be reinforced within the United Kingdom.[38] If mutual trust between international courts is an aspiration,[39] between English courts it is a reality. Since the same arguments that might support an injunction can, in general, be deployed on an application to stay or transfer the other proceedings made in the court in which they were brought, and since there will be little reason for assuming that any different conclusion will be reached (in contrast to where the targeted litigation is in a foreign court), there will often be no practical reason for another English court to intervene in advance by injunction.[40] Indeed, a stay by the targeted court may be a preferable remedy to an injunction, as while an injunction has personal effect only, a stay directly affects the proceedings stayed.[41]

6.15   There is an obvious temptation for court A itself to intervene, once it has heard the matter and formed the view that, as a matter of case management, proceedings before court B should be stayed, even though normally court B would have heard any application to stay.[42] This is a temptation which should be resisted, as otherwise an injunction claimant could produce a *fait accompli*. There should be some good reason why it is legitimate for court

---

[37]   *Barnsley Canal Co v Twibell* (1843) 7 Beav 19, 49 ER 969; *Stannard v Vestry of St Giles, Camberwell* (1882) 20 Ch D 190 (CA) 196–97; *Grand Junction Waterworks Co v Hampton Urban District Council* [1898] 2 Ch 331, 345; *Merrick v Liverpool Corp* [1910] 2 Ch 449, 460–61 (the 'greatest possible caution' would be required before granting an injunction to restrain proceedings before magistrates); *Williams v Deptford Urban District Council* (1924) 41 TLR 47; *Murcutt v Murcutt* [1952] P 266, 269. In *Lord Auckland v Westminster Local Board of Works* (1872) 7 Ch App 597 (CA), a case before the Judicature Acts, the threatened proceedings before magistrates would have been outside their jurisdiction; see also *Hedley v Bates* (1880) 13 Ch D 498.
   For an example of the existence of the necessary special circumstances required to justify intervention (because there would otherwise have been a vexatious duplication of civil and criminal proceedings), see *Thames Launches v Trinity House Corp (Deptford Strond)* [1961] Ch 197. See also *St James Hall v London County Council* (1900) 53 LT 98.
[38]   See, in this regard, the comments of Arnold J in *Fujifilm Kyowa Kirin Biologics v AbbVie Biotechnology* [2017] RPC 7 [46(ii)]. The point was not picked up on appeal in the Court of Appeal's brief judgment [2017] RPC 9 (CA) [107]–[108] but their overall approach is redolent of restraint.
[39]   See A Dickinson 'A Charter for Tactical Litigation in Europe' [2004] LMCLQ 273; Sir P Gross 'Anti-Suit Injunctions and Arbitration' [2005] LMCLQ 10, 24.
[40]   There is old authority that an allegation that proceedings elsewhere in England have no real prospect of success is not a good ground to restrain them by injunction, as the appropriate step is to seek to strike them out in the court in which they are brought, at least 'until the experiment is repeated once or twice': *Pennell v Roy* (1853) 3 De GM & G 126, 43 ER 50, 53.
[41]   *Garbutt v Fawcus* (1875) 1 Ch D 155 (CA) 158.
[42]   This may be what happened in *Chorion v Lane* (24 February 1999) (Laddie J) [33].

A to intervene in advance. For example, there might be good reason where without the injunction there could be multiple future actions, or where the threat of future litigation may have a chilling effect on the injunction claimant's customers.

Given these practical considerations, injunctions to restrain the commencement or pursuit **6.16** of proceedings elsewhere in the United Kingdom will remain rare.[43] There are, however, three categories of case where intervention by injunction has become reasonably familiar.

First, injunctions to restrain the commencement of winding-up petitions are routine.   **6.17**

Second, injunctions have been granted with some frequency to restrain the commencement **6.18** or pursuit[44] of other proceedings within the United Kingdom, if there will otherwise be a vexatious duplication of proceedings,[45] and the problem will not appropriately be controlled by normal measures of stay, transfer, and consolidation. Some of the cases adopt a lower threshold and seem to regard it as sufficient to show that duplication would be wrong as a matter of case management, without a showing of vexation;[46] this may be too low a standard.

This type of case includes the restraint of criminal proceedings. In *Thames Launches Ltd v Trinity House*, an injunction was granted to restrain criminal proceedings that raised the same point of principle as a prior action for a declaration of right before the civil courts.[47] However, Buckley J noted that 'this court would be very slow to intervene with the course of criminal proceedings unless it was clear that the issues in the civil proceedings and the criminal proceedings really raised the same issue.'[48] It appears that the prior refusal of a stay

---

[43] The only reported cases in modern times of which the author is aware where, outside the context of insolvency, anti-suit injunctions to restrain civil proceedings in an inferior court in England have been granted are *Thames Launches v Trinity House (Deptford Strond)* [1961] Ch 197 (applied, in the context of an application for a stay, in *Royal Bank of Scotland v Citrusdal Investments* [1977] 1 WLR 1469); *Sears v Sears, Roebuck* [1993] RPC 385; and the patent cases of *Landi den Hartog v Sea Bird (Clean Air Fuel Systems)* [1976] FSR 489; *Jacey (Printers) v Norton & Wright Group* [1977] FSR 475; *Essex Electric v IPC Computers (UK)* [1991] FSR 690; and (in an alternative manner) *Chorion v Lane* (24 February 1999) (Laddie J), although injunctions have been granted to restrain the deployment of evidence in another court in breach of confidence: see section D, 'Injunctions to Restrain the Use of Confidential Information'. A general reluctance to intervene was apparent in *Johns v Chatalos* [1973] 1 WLR 1437, where the injunction was refused. In *Fujifilm Kyowa Kirin Biologics v AbbVie Biotechnology* [2017] RPC 7, upheld [2017] RPC 9 (CA), another patent case, it was held there was a real prospect of obtaining an injunction.

[44] It seems there is no longer any formal barrier to injunctions restraining the *pursuit* of other proceedings in the High Court: see para 6.05.

[45] *Re Connolly Brothers* [1911] 1 Ch 731 (CA) 744–48; *Chorion v Lane* (24 February 1999) (Laddie J) [34]. This category has a superficial similarity to the grant of orders to restrain a vexatious litigant, but they are not the same: see paras 6.31–6.32. Some of the cases seem to suggest that it is sufficient merely to show that duplicate proceedings would be inappropriate as a matter of case management: see *Chorion v Lane* (24 February 1999) (Laddie J) [34]. It is suggested that this may be insufficient to justify interference by injunction and that something more should, in general, be required.

[46] See eg *Chorion v Lane* (24 February 1999) (Laddie J) [34].

[47] The decision in *Thames Launches* was treated with some reserve by the House of Lords in *Imperial Tobacco Ltd v Attorney General* [1981] AC 718 (HL) 741–42, 746, 750–52, where it was held that it was not a proper exercise of the court's discretion to grant declaratory relief as to whether the elements of a criminal charge were made out, where the criminal proceedings had been commenced first, and were not vexatious.

[48] *Thames Launches v Trinity House Corp (Deptford Strond)* [1961] 1 Ch 197 (followed, in the context of an application for a stay, in *Royal Bank of Scotland v Citrusdal Investments Ltd* [1977] 1 WLR 1469). In that case, a prior attempt had been made to stay the criminal proceedings, but had failed, for no obvious reason. Buckley J treated as persuasive the older case of *Mayor and Corporation of York v Sir Lionel Pilkington* (1742) 2 Atk 302, 26 ER 584 (while a civil suit was pending, criminal proceedings were brought on the same topic before a magistrate's court

by the other court or tribunal is not an absolute reason to decline an injunction.[49] Nor is it always necessary to apply for a stay to the other court first.[50]

6.19   Third, injunctions have also been granted with some frequency to restrain the commencement or pursuit of other actions in England if the true purpose of the other proceedings is not legitimately to pursue legal rights, but rather unjustifiably to cause or threaten irrevocable collateral commercial damage to the injunction claimant, or otherwise vexatiously to harass the injunction claimant. Thus, in *Essex Electric v IPC*, Ferris J granted an interim injunction restraining the injunction defendant from commencing any actions alleging patent infringement against the injunction claimant's customers without the leave of the court, where the injunction defendant's claims of patent infringement were weak and appeared to be intended to put commercial pressure on the injunction claimant.[51]

6.20   The seriousness of the restrictions that orders preventing future litigation impose has meant that, in the recent case law, the orders granted have commonly not imposed absolute prohibitions on the commencement of actions, but have permitted the commencement of actions with the leave of the court.[52]

in which the prosecutors, who were parties in the civil proceedings, would be themselves the magistrates; and an injunction was granted).
    For another example of such an injunction being granted, see *Sears v Sears, Roebuck* [1993] RPC 385. For an example of a case where an injunction was refused, see *Thames & Hudson v Design and Artists Copyright Society* [1995] FSR 153, 159–61, where an injunction was refused on the grounds that the criminal proceedings were not vexatious, even though they overlapped with the civil proceedings, and even though the Chancery judge thought matters would be most efficiently resolved in the Chancery action.

---

[49] *Sears v Sears, Roebuck* [1993] RPC 385, 395–96; and a stay had also been refused in *Thames Launches v Trinity House (Deptford Strond)* [1961] Ch 197.
[50] *Chorion v Lane* (24 February 1999) (Laddie J) [33].
[51] *Essex Electric v IPC Computers (UK)* [1991] FSR 690, 700–01, 704–05, 707–09 (Ferris J concluded only that the targeted proceedings would 'arguably' amount to an abuse of process: at 704–05; this low threshold was used because the court applied *American Cyanamid* proceedings to the grant of an interim injunction (as to which, see Ch 13, section D, 'The Principles to be Applied to the Grant of Anti-Suit Injunctions'); see also *Landi den Hartog v Sea Bird (Clean Air Fuel Systems)* [1976] FSR 489, 493–94 (where the court granted an injunction having found that the injunction defendants 'have really been concerned not genuinely to assert their rights under the patents, but to harass [the injunction claimant] and … the present distributors of [the injunction claimant]'); and *Jacey (Printers) v Norton & Wright Group* [1977] FSR 475, 480–82 (where the basis for the injunction was weak; but the order sought was also limited).
[52] This has happened in a string of patent cases: *Landi den Hartog v Sea Bird (Clean Air Fuel Systems)* [1976] FSR 489; *Essex Electric v IPC Computers (UK)* [1991] FSR 690. In *Austria Tabakwerke v Port* (unreported, CA, 8 September 1989), this was held to be implicit in the injunctive order. In *Jacey (Printers) v Norton & Wright Group* [1977] FSR 475, 482, the order was even more limited, and only restrained the injunction defendant from commencing proceedings against the injunction claimant's customers without leave of the court unless the injunction claimant was also joined as a defendant. In *Fujifilm Kyowa Kirin Biologics v AbbVie Biotechnology* [2017] RPC 7 [61], Arnold J therefore concluded that domestic anti-suit injunctions of this kind would 'rarely' be granted without a qualification that claims could be brought with the leave of the court; and the Court of Appeal similarly indicated that a domestic injunction without that qualification might well be too broad: [2017] RPC 9 [107]–[108].
    Orders of this type are usually in effect 'single forum' injunctions and will prohibit the commencement of certain litigation at all (subject to the leave of the court). They thus arguably restrict the injunction defendant's right of access to the court, which is protected by Article 6 ECHR, and if so will only be permissible if they 'pursue a legitimate aim' and are proportionate. It is submitted that the limited orders granted in these cases were consistent with Article 6. See further Ch 1, section E, 'Human Rights Law'.

Similarly, if there is a real risk that an injunction defendant would commence relitigation of **6.21** a type that inevitably would be stayed or struck out, or would be inconsistent with existing decisions, an injunction might well be granted.[53]

Further, by analogy to the decisions on winding-up petitions,[54] it may be that injunctions **6.22** will be granted, in appropriate cases, to restrain other types of without notice applications if the orders granted without notice may cause irrevocable harm before they can be set aside.[55]

Injunctions to restrain arbitration proceedings in England form a distinct subject, ad- **6.23** dressed in Chapter 11.

D. INJUNCTIONS TO RESTRAIN THE USE OF CONFIDENTIAL INFORMATION

In *Medway v Doublelock*, Mr Medway had served affidavits of means in earlier family pro- **6.24** ceedings in the Family Division. In breach of the implied undertaking of confidentiality covering those affidavits, his estranged spouse disclosed those affidavits to a defendant in separate commercial litigation in the Queen's Bench division in which Mr Medway was also engaged, who then sought to deploy them on a security for costs application. Instead of applying to the judge in the Queen's Bench division to prevent the use of the affidavits, Mr Medway brought a third action in the Chancery division to restrain the defendant in the Queen's Bench action from using the affidavits in that litigation. Goulding J held that there was no jurisdictional bar to such an action and granted the injunction.[56]

The actual decision is open to some doubt. It might be wiser to encourage persons in Mr **6.25** Medway's position to apply either to the court in which the material in question was origin- ally disclosed, or to the judge hearing the case in which the material is sought to be used; there was no factor which meant that the Chancery division was a more appropriate div- ision of the High Court to decide the point.[57]

However, insofar as the decision confirms the existence of a power to restrain by injunc- **6.26** tion the abuse of confidential information, or information disclosed in breach of contract or undertaking, even where the information is to be used in other court proceedings in England, it appears to be sound.[58]

---

[53] See as a (somewhat unusual) example *Fujifilm Kyowa Kirin Biologics v AbbVie Biotechnology* [2017] RPC 7 [63]–[66], [2017] RPC 9 (CA) [107]–[108].

[54] See section E, 'Injunctions to Restrain Winding-Up Petitions'.

[55] See *Essex Electric v IPC Computers (UK)* [1991] FSR 690, where the injunction was granted because the threatened patent actions might cause irrevocable damage.

[56] *Medway v Doublelock* [1978] 1 WLR 710.

[57] In essence, Goulding J decided he should decide the point because the matter had been argued before him (at 712G); but that had the effect of ratifying, arguably inappropriately, the unilateral and rather strange choice of forum of the plaintiff.

[58] *Medway v Doublelock* was cited with approval in *S v S (Judgment in Chambers: Disclosure)* [1997] 1 WLR 1621. It can be noted that s 41 of the Judicature Act 1925 (preventing injunctions to restrain pending actions in the High Court—see paras 6.02 and 6.05) was not cited to Goulding J in *Medway v Doublelock*. However, the prohibition imposed by that section was probably inapplicable, as while the injunction restrained the use of evidence in the Queen's Bench division proceedings, it did not restrain 'the cause or proceeding pending' itself. Since then, as al- ready discussed, the s 41 restriction has not been continued in the Senior Courts Act 1981: see para 6.05.

E. INJUNCTIONS TO RESTRAIN WINDING-UP PETITIONS

6.27   An injunction may be granted to restrain the presentation of a winding-up petition,[59] where the petition would be an abuse of process.[60] Examples of this include where the petition is bound to fail;[61] where the debt is genuinely disputed, but there is nevertheless a threat to present a petition for winding up;[62] and where the petition is not presented in good faith but instead for ulterior motives.[63] There are decisive practical advantages to granting relief by way of injunction, rather than allowing the petition to be brought and then dismissed, because the mere presentation and publication of a winding-up petition can do irreparable economic harm.[64]

F. INJUNCTIONS TO PROTECT WINDING-UP PROCEEDINGS

6.28   The court has a specific statutory power under section 126(1) of the Insolvency Act 1986 to restrain by injunction the pursuit of proceedings against a company in courts other than the High Court[65] after a winding-up petition has been presented but before the petition has been heard.[66]

---

[59]   *Niger Merchants v Capper*, reported as a note to *Cercle Restaurant Castiglione v Lavery* (1881) 18 Ch D 555.

[60]   *Bryanston Finance v de Vries (No 2)* [1976] Ch 63 (CA) 76G–78H, 79D–E; *Re a Company (No 006273 of 1992)* [1992] BCC 794; *Re a Company (No 012209 of 1991)* [1992] 1 WLR 351; *Orion Media Marketing v Media Brook* [2002] 1 BCLC 184, 185; *James Dolman v Pedley* [2004] BCC 504 (CA) [10]. The threshold appears to be different for injunctions to restrain advertisement of a petition for winding up, which are not based on abuse of process: *In re a Company (No 007923 of 1994)* [1995] 1 WLR 953 (CA).

Injunctions to restrain winding-up petitions must be made to the Judge by the issue of an originating application: Practice Direction: Insolvency Proceedings, para 8.1.

For a similar jurisdiction in respect of injunctions to restrain proceedings to enforce tax liabilities, see *Biffin v HMRC* [2016] EWHC 2926.

[61]   *Charles Forte Investments v Amanda* [1964] Ch 240 (CA) 252, 259.

[62]   *John Brown v Keeble* [1879] WN 173; *Cadiz Waterworks v Barnett* (1874) LR 19 Eq 182; *Cercle Restaurant Castiglione v Lavery* (1881) 18 Ch D 555 (following *Niger Merchants v Capper*, which was reported as a note thereto); *Mann v Goldstein* [1968] 1 WLR 1091, 1096–99; *Stonegate Securities v Gregory* [1980] Ch 576 (CA) 580, 586–87, 589; *Re a Company (No 012209 of 1991)* [1992] 1 WLR 351; *Orion Media Marketing v Media Brook* [2002] 1 BCLC 184, 185; *James Dolman v Pedley* [2004] BCC 504 (CA) [5], [10]; *Ebbvale v Hosking* [2013] UKPC 1 [25]. For recent examples, see *LDX International Group v Misra Ventures* [2018] EWHC 275 (Ch) [22]; *J Carney Cleaning v Manchett Construction* [2018] EWHC 1101.

[63]   *In re a Company* [1894] 2 Ch 349, 351; *Mann v Goldstein* [1968] 1 WLR 1091, 1094B; *Ebbvale v Hosking* [2013] UKPC 1 [26]; *LDX International Group LLP v Misra Ventures Limited* [2018] EWHC 275 (Ch) [22]–[25].

[64]   *Niger Merchants v Capper* (1877), reported as a note to *Cercle Restaurant Castiglione v Lavery* (1881) 18 Ch D 555, at 558–59; *Charles Forte Investments v Amanda* [1964] 1 Ch 240 (CA) 252, 258; *Re A Company* [1986] BCLC 127.

[65]   It appears that the statutory powers under s 126 (1) apply only in respect of courts of the UK (which includes the courts of Scotland and, it appears, Northern Ireland): *In re International Pulp and Paper* (1876) 3 Ch D 594 (rather confused); *In re Belfast Ship Owners* [1894] 1 IR 321, 330, 332; *Re Dynamics Corporation of America* [1973] 1 WLR 63; *Bloom v Harms Offshore AHT 'Taurus'* [2010] Ch 187 (CA) [16]–[21], but not in respect of the restraint of proceedings in foreign courts outside the UK. However, a power remains in equity and under s 37(1) of the Senior Courts Act 1981 to restrain foreign proceedings anywhere in the world which would wrongly interfere with an English winding up: see Ch 3, section A, 'The Power to Grant Injunctions'; Ch 5, section E, 'Insolvency and Justice between Creditors'.

[66]   Section 126(1) provides:

> At any time after the presentation of a winding up petition, and before a winding up order has been made, the company, or any creditor of contributor may—(a) where any action or proceeding against the company is pending in the High Court or Court of Appeal in England and Wales or Northern Ireland, apply to the court in which the action or proceeding is pending for a stay of proceedings therein, and (b) where any other action or proceeding is pending against the company, apply to the

The discretion of the court under this section is not constrained by the traditional require-   **6.29**
ments for anti-suit injunctions, such as vexation and oppression, but is instead exercised in
order to ensure that the balance of interests enforced by insolvency law is protected, and to
protect the proper functioning of the winding up.[67] In particular, enforcement measures
which have been commenced before the winding-up petition is presented will not usually
be restrained unless there are special reasons rendering it inequitable[68] for those measures
to continue;[69] but in contrast, enforcement measures which are commenced after presentation of the petition will usually be restrained unless there are special reasons not to restrain
them.[70]

The prosecution of criminal or quasi-criminal proceedings can be restrained under this   **6.30**
section[71] if, for example, they will interfere with the orderly management of the winding
up.[72] However, in modern times the courts have indicated that this power is to be exercised
with caution.[73] Similarly, where a receiver has been appointed by the court, an injunction
may be granted to prevent actions being brought, in another court, against the receiver in
respect of his actions as receiver.[74]

court having jurisdiction to wind up the company to restrain further proceedings in the action or
proceeding.

Section 227 of the Insolvency Act 1986 extends this power in respect of unregistered companies. Once a
winding-up order has been made there is an automatic stay of proceedings against the company under Insolvency
Act 1986, s 130(2), unless the leave of the court is obtained.

The ancestors of s 126(1) were Companies Act 1862, s 85 (see eg *In re Artistic Colour Printing Co* (1880) 14
Ch D 502), Companies (Consolidation) Act 1908, s 140; Companies Act 1948, s 226 (see eg *In re Burrows (Leeds)*
[1982] 1 WLR 1177), and Companies Act 1985, s 521. The existence of s 126(1), and its predecessors, appears not to
preclude the grant of injunctions under s 37(1) of the Supreme Court Act in the insolvency context, where appropriate. In particular, it does not preclude applications for injunctions to restrain petitions for winding up (which
are frequently granted, but which are not provided for under s 126(1)).

---

[67] *Re Great Ship* (1863) 4 De GJ & S 63, 46 ER 839 (under s 201 of the Companies Act 1862, which related to unregistered companies, and is the ancestor of the modern ss 227–228 of the Insolvency Act 1986); *Re Perkins Beach*
(1878) 7 Ch D 371 (although the decision was wrong as a matter of jurisdiction, as it restrained pending proceedings in the High Court, in disregard of Judicature Act 1873, s 24(5): see *In re Artistic Colour Printing* (1880) 14 Ch
D 502); *Re Roundwood Colliery* [1897] 1 Ch 373 (CA) 381–82 (Stirling J; reversed, but not on this point, in CA);
Westbury v Twigg [1892] 1 QB 77, 80; *Venner's Electrical Cooking and Heating Appliances v Thorpe* [1915] 2 Ch 404
(CA) 407; *Herbert Berry Associates v Inland Revenue Commissioners* [1977] 1 WLR 1437 (HL); *Re Aro* [1980] 1 Ch
196, (CA) 204; *Re Memco Engineering* [1986] Ch 86, 95–96.

[68] Whether 'inequitability' was indeed a threshold question was debated in the House of Lords in *Herbert Berry
Associates v Inland Revenue Commissioners* [1977] 1 WLR 1437 (HL). Lord Simon thought not (at 1444), but Lord
Russell applied concepts of inequitability.

[69] *Re Great Ship* (1863) 4 De GJ & S 63, 46 ER 839; *Re Roundwood Colliery* [1897] 1 Ch 373 (CA) 381–82 (Stirling
J; reversed, but not on this point, in CA); *Venner's Electrical Cooking and Heating Appliances v Thorpe* [1915] 2 Ch
404 (CA) 407–08; *Herbert Berry Associates v Inland Revenue Commissioners* [1977] 1 WLR 1437 (HL) 1444–45; *Re
Bellaglade* [1977] 1 All ER 319, 320–21.

[70] *Re Roundwood Colliery* [1897] 1 Ch 373 (CA) 381–82 (Stirling J; reversed, but not on this point, in CA);
Anglo-Baltic and Mediterranean Bank v Barber [1924] 2 KB 410 (CA) 419.

[71] This was the case under the predecessors of s 126(1): *In re Briton Medical and General Life Assurance
Association* (1886) 32 Ch D 503 (injunction to restrain quasi-criminal proceedings granted under Companies Act
1862, s 85); *Re Burrows (Leeds)* [1982] 1 WLR 1177, 1185 (injunction to restrain criminal proceedings sought
under Companies Act 1948, s 226 but refused as a matter of discretion).

[72] *In re Briton Medical and General Life Assurance Association* (1886) 32 Ch D 503.

[73] *Re Burrows (Leeds)* [1982] 1 WLR 1177, 1185.

[74] *Re Maidstone Palace of Varieties* [1909] 2 Ch 283.

G. ORDERS TO RESTRAIN VEXATIOUS LITIGANTS

6.31 The court has an inherent jurisdiction,[75] which has been largely, although not entirely, over-written by specific statutory powers and procedural rules,[76] to grant 'civil restraint orders' to restrain vexatious litigants from issuing applications or commencing actions without the leave of the court.

6.32 These powers are distinct from anti-suit injunctions, even though both remedies restrain 'vexation', in a broad sense. Civil restraint orders are aimed at a particular litigant, not necessarily specific litigation; they are justified principally by reference to past conduct,[77] and not by the objectionable features of a particular proposed action or application; and they operate not by restraining the litigation from being pursued, but rather by requiring the litigant to obtain the permission of the court before issuing proceedings.[78] In contrast, anti-suit injunctions are not dependent on the past conduct of the litigant, and they are aimed at restraining specific vexatious litigation; further, an anti-suit injunction, if granted, will usually absolutely restrain that other litigation from being commenced or continued.[79] The remedies granted also operate in different ways. The anti-suit injunction relies on the law of contempt for its enforcement. In contrast, civil restraint orders operate within the court structure itself, and if granted, will have the effect that proceedings commenced without the leave of the court will be automatically dismissed without the other party having to respond at all.[80]

6.33 Nevertheless, the existence of civil restraint orders does illustrate that the anti-suit injunction is not a unique conceptual anomaly within the English legal system, but that it is instead one way among others of restraining vexatious conduct.[81]

---

[75] *Grepe v Loam* (1887) 37 Ch D 168 (CA); *Ebert v Venvil* [2000] Ch 484 (CA); *Bhamjee v Forsdick* [2004] 1 WLR 88 (CA).

[76] Supreme Court Act 1981, s 42; CPR 3.11 and CPR Part 3, PD C (civil restraint orders). It was clear that the relatively limited powers in the Supreme Court Act 1981, s 42 did not preclude the operation of the inherent jurisdiction to grant civil restraint orders: *Ebert v Venvil* [2000] Ch 484 (CA). However, it seems that the general codification of the court's inherent jurisdiction which has been undertaken in CPR 3.11 and the Practice Direction thereto will have a preclusive effect in most circumstances which fall within the type of situation which CPR 3.11 is intended to address, so that it will usually be inappropriate to grant civil restraint orders outside the scope of the rules: see *R (Kumar) v Secretary of State for Constitutional Affairs* [2007] 1 WLR 536 (CA) 549.

[77] *Grepe v Loam* (1887) 37 Ch D 168 (CA) 169; *Ebert v Venvil* [2000] Ch 484 (CA) 488–89; *Bhamjee v Forsdick* [2004] 1 WLR 88 (CA) [20], [39], [43]–[44], [50], [53]. Under CPR 3.11, for a civil restraint order to be granted, the party in question must have already made two applications which are 'totally without merit'.

[78] *Bhamjee v Forsdick* [2004] 1 WLR 88 (CA) [44].

[79] For examples of cases where anti-suit injunctions were granted requiring a party not to commence litigation without the leave of the court, see *Landi den Hartog v Sea Bird (Clean Air Fuel Systems)* [1976] FSR 489; *Jacey (Printers) v Norton & Wright Group* [1977] FSR 475; *Essex Electric v IPC Computers (UK)* [1991] FSR 690, discussed at para 6.19; and see also *Fujifilm Kyowa Kirin Biologics v AbbVie Biotechnology* [2017] RPC 7 [45]; upheld on appeal [2017] RPC 9 (CA) [107]–[108]. These cases therefore stand between 'civil restraint orders' and anti-suit injunctions; but they are still more analogous to anti-suit injunctions, as they are principally motivated not by the previous conduct of the injunction defendant but by the nature of his intended proceedings.

[80] See eg the draft forms of order annexed to CPR Part 3, PD C (civil restraint orders).

[81] For the centrality of the concept of vexatiousness to Civil Restraint Orders, see *Bhamjee v Forsdick* [2004] 1 WLR 88 [7]–[9].

7

Anti-Suit Injunctions and Exclusive Forum Clauses

A. INTRODUCTION

The court's approach to anti-suit injunctions is transformed where the injunction defendant is obliged by a contractual exclusive forum clause to resolve his disputes with the injunction claimant in an agreed forum.[1] **7.01**

There are two principal types of exclusive forum clause. An exclusive jurisdiction clause obliges parties to resolve disputes covered by the clause before a chosen court. An arbitration clause obliges them to resolve disputes covered by the clause before an arbitration tribunal. In both cases, the clause imposes negative as well as positive obligations, and so in general prohibits the contracting parties from litigating other than in the chosen forum.[2] Exclusive forum clauses are to be contrasted with non-exclusive forum clauses, under which the parties agree *positively* that each will submit to a particular jurisdiction if the other commences proceedings covered by the clause there, but do not expressly agree *negatively* that such proceedings shall not be brought in any other forum.[3] **7.02**

In contrast, so far, choice of law clauses have not been interpreted to include any correlative negative obligation. In substance the courts have concluded that choice of law clauses are a **7.03**

---

[1] *National Westminster Bank v Utrecht-America Finance* [2001] 3 All ER 733 (CA) 744–45.
[2] *AES Ust-Kamenogorsk Hydropower Plant LLC v Ust-Kamenogorsk Hydropower Plant JSC* [2013] 1 WLR 1889 (SC) [1], [21]–[28] and *Pena Copper Mines v Rio Tinto* (1911) 105 LT 84 (CA) 850–51, 852.
[3] The question of whether negative implied terms can be implied into non-exclusive jurisdiction clauses is considered in Ch 9, section B, 'Implied Terms'.

direction to a court or tribunal to apply the chosen law, if its choice of law rules so permit. But if a party litigates in a forum whose choice of law rules would apply a different law to that chosen by the clause, that is not a breach of the choice of law clause.[4]

7.04   This chapter considers claims for anti-suit injunctions in cases where it is contended that an exclusive forum clause applies. It addresses the following topics:

- the effect of the Brussels–Lugano regime;
- other international conventions;
- choice of law;
- the *Angelic Grace* principles;
- the scope and limits of exclusive forum clauses;
- injunctions in support of a foreign forum;
- injunctions to enforce arbitration clauses;
- foreign proceedings to obtain security.

7.05   The related question of what can amount to 'strong reasons' not to enforce an exclusive forum clause by injunction is addressed in Chapter 8.

B. THE EFFECT OF THE BRUSSELS–LUGANO REGIME

7.06   The decisions of the European Court of Justice (ECJ) in *Turner v Grovit*[5] and *The Front Comor*[6] have imposed important substantive limitations on the power to grant anti-suit injunctions in cases connected to the Brussels–Lugano zone (at least until Brexit, which may, but may also not, bring an end to the operation of European jurisdictional law and the Lugano Convention in the UK[7]). The detailed consequences of this are considered in Chapter 12. In brief summary, the current law is as follows, so long as the Brussels–Lugano regime, or any materially similar regime, continues to apply.

7.07   Where proceedings before the courts of another member state of the Brussels–Lugano regime fall within the material scope of the Brussels–Lugano regime, no anti-suit injunction may be granted by the English court, even if those proceedings are in breach of an exclusive jurisdiction or arbitration clause. However, this preclusive doctrine does not apply where the proceedings in respect of which the injunction is claimed are before a court in a state outside the Brussels–Lugano zone, or do not fall within the material scope of the Brussels–Lugano regime, or are before an arbitration tribunal, even if the seat of the arbitration is within the Brussels–Lugano zone. Where the Brussels–Lugano regime does not prohibit an anti-suit injunction, it has no effect on the exercise of the court's discretion. Further, the preclusive effect of the Brussels–Lugano regime has no effect on arbitrators who are not governed by its provisions and are entitled to make orders and awards akin to anti-suit injunctions irrespective of the Brussels–Lugano regime.

---

[4] *Navig8 v Al-Riyadh Co for Vegetable Oil Industry* [2013] 2 Lloyds Rep 104 [22]; *Golden Endurance Shipping v RMA Watanya (The Golden Endurance)* [2015] 1 Lloyds Rep 266 [42]–[45].

[5] Case C-159/02, *Turner v Grovit* [2004] ECR I–3565, [2005] 1 AC 101.

[6] Case C-185/07, *Allianz (formerly Riunione Adriatica di Sicurta) v West Tankers (The Front Comor)* [2009] ECR I-663.

[7] The possibilities are addressed in more detail in Ch 16, section B, 'Brexit'.

The following analysis of the English case law does not repeat these points at each stage, but **7.08** should always be read as stating the position subject to the restrictions which (so long as it continues to bind) are imposed by the Brussels–Lugano regime. If and to the extent that the effect of Brexit is that European jurisdictional law or any similar regime ceases to apply, then these shackles will be removed.

C. OTHER INTERNATIONAL CONVENTIONS

It is submitted that the Hague Convention on the Choice of Court, where it applies, will **7.09** not preclude the grant of anti-suit injunctions to enforce exclusive jurisdiction clauses.[8] Whether it will affect the applicable principles for the grant of anti-suit injunctions, or the exercise of the court's discretion, where the English court is the chosen court under a jurisdiction clause but the other proceedings are in another contracting state, remains to be seen.[9]

It has been decided, correctly, that the New York Convention does not preclude the grant of **7.10** anti-suit injunctions to enforce arbitration clauses.[10]

D. CHOICE OF LAW

Where an exclusive forum clause selects English arbitration or English exclusive jurisdic- **7.11** tion, and its proper law is English law, then English law and equitable principles will apply to determine the grant or refusal of an anti-suit injunction.[11] This is so even if under the law of the country where the target proceedings are brought there are mandatory rules of law that purport to override the exclusive forum clause.[12]

Exclusive forum clauses that select an English forum but are themselves governed by a for- **7.12** eign law are rare. If a claim were made to enforce such a clause by injunction, the proper law of the clause would determine the scope and effect of the contractual obligations it

---

[8] Ch 1, section G, 'The Hague Convention on the Choice of Court'.

[9] However, in contrast, if the court before which the proceedings sought to be restrained is the chosen court in another Hague Convention contracting state, this could militate against the grant of an anti-suit injunction to interfere with the pursuit of proceedings in the chosen court. See Minutes No 9 of the Second Commission Meeting of Monday 20 June 2005 (morning) in Proceedings of the Twentieth Session of the Hague Conference on Private International Law (Permanent Bureau of the Conference, Intersentia 2010), 622, 623–24; and M Ahmed and P Beaumont, 'Exclusive Choice of Court Agreements: Some Issues on the Hague Convention on Choice of Court Agreements and its Relationship with the Brussels I Recast Especially Anti-Suit Injunctions, Concurrent Proceedings and the Implications of BREXIT' (2017) 13 JPIL 386, 398. It would take something unusual to justify an injunction to restrain proceedings in a court chosen under an exclusive jurisdiction clause in any event.

[10] Ch 1, section H, 'The New York Convention'.

[11] There is no authority considering this point expressly, but this result is obviously right. Although there is a debate as to whether the applicable law is determined by the *lex fori* or the law of the contract, this makes no difference where the proper law of the clause is English law and the injunction is sought from the English courts. The English courts have always applied English law without question to the direct enforcement of English jurisdiction and arbitration clauses by way of anti-suit injunction: see eg *OT Africa Line v Magic Sportswear* [2005] 1 Lloyds Rep 252 [38]–[41], [2005] 2 Lloyds Rep 170 (CA) [50], [73]; *West Tankers v Ras Riunione Adriatica di Sicurta (The Front Comor)* [2005] 2 Lloyds Rep 257 [31]–[52]. As to the position in quasi-contractual cases, see Ch 10, section D, 'Third-Party Rights under Foreign Law'.

[12] *Bankers Trust International v RCS Editori* [1996] CLC 899, 904–06; *Shell International Petroleum v Coral Oil (No 1)* [1999] 1 Lloyds Rep 72, 78. For the relevance of foreign mandatory laws to whether there are 'strong reasons' not to grant the injunction, see Ch 8, paras 8.31–8.44.

created. The grant or refusal of an injunction is at least arguably determined by the *lex fori* rather than the law of the contract,[13] but the nature of the contractual obligations under the law of the contract should provide the foundations for the consideration of injunctive relief. Consequently, it can be doubted whether an anti-suit injunction should be granted to enforce a contractual forum clause under whose proper law anti-suit injunctions are unknown. Arguably it would be inappropriate if application of the *lex fori* were to create such a powerful extension to the contractual obligations, in a way that the *lex contractus* would not envisage.[14]

E. THE *ANGELIC GRACE* PRINCIPLES

7.13 Even when foreign proceedings are in breach of an exclusive forum clause, the decision whether or not to grant an anti-suit injunction is always discretionary,[15] and it must always

---

[13] Under the traditional common law rules for choice of law, the grant or refusal of an injunction to enforce a contractual obligation is a matter of procedure and remedy, and is thus a question for the *lex fori* and not the law of the contract: *Huber v Steiner* (1835) 2 Bing NC 202, 135 ER 80, 83 ('so much of the law as affects the remedy only, all that relates to the "ad litis decisionem", is taken from the "lex fori" of the country where that action is brought'); *Don v Lippmann* (1837) 5 Cl & Fin 1, 7 ER 303, 307 ('the law on this point is well settled in this country, where this distinction is properly taken, that whatever relates to the remedy to be enforced, must be determined by the *lex fori*'); *Baschet v London Illustrated Standard* [1900] 1 Ch 73, 78; *Boys v Chaplin* [1971] AC 356 (HL) 378G–379A, 394C–F.

Under the Rome I Regulation the line between *lex fori* and the law of the contract is drawn differently, because under Article 12, 'the law applicable to the contract by virtue of this Regulation shall govern in particular' 'within the limits of the powers conferred on the court by its procedural law, the consequences of a total or partial breach of obligations, including the assessment of damages in so far as it is governed by rules of law', as to which see *Actavis UK Ltd v Eli Lilly & Co* [2016] RPC 2 (CA) [143]. But by Article 1(2)(e), arbitration agreements and 'agreements on the choice of court' are excluded from the scope of the Regulation. This exclusion means that the 'formation, validity, and effects' of the forum clause are also outside the scope of the Regulation: see Report on the Rome Convention by Professors Mario Giuliano and Paul Lagarde (OJ 1980 No C282/1) (the 'Giuliano-Lagarde Report'), 12. So, it seems strongly arguable that the question of the applicable law for injunctions to enforce an exclusive forum clause falls outside the scope of the Rome I Regulation, remains determined in the English courts by the common law choice of law rules, and is therefore a matter for the *lex fori*. (NB, it is likely that the Rome I and II Regulations will in substance remain English law after Brexit, irrespective of how Brexit is resolved: see Ch 1, section I, 'Brexit'.)

Consistently with the common law's application of the *lex fori*, even in those rare cases where anti-suit injunctions have been sought to enforce exclusive forum clauses with a foreign proper law, English law has so far governed the conditions for the grant of the contractual anti-suit injunction: *A/S D/S Svendborg v Wansa* [1996] 2 Lloyds Rep 559, 563, 569–71, 575, [1997] 2 Lloyds Rep 183 (CA) 186–88; *The Owners of the 'MSC Dymphna' v Agfa-Gevaert* (David Steel J, 19 December 2001); and the courts of the British Virgin Islands and Bermuda have applied their own law to the enforcement by anti-suit injunction of English arbitration clauses: *Finecroft v Lamane Trading* (Eastern Caribbean SC, 6 January 2006) [36]–[47]; *OAO 'CT-Mobile' v IPOC International Growth Fund* (Bermuda SC, 6 October 2006) [77]–[92], [175], upheld in *IPOC International Growth Fund v OAO 'CT-Mobile'* (Bermuda CA, 23 March 2007) (although the argument that the *lex causae*, not the *lex fori* should apply appears not to have been advanced in any of these cases). See also the rather unclear decision in *Atlas Power v National Power and Despatch* [2018] EWHC 1052 [34]–[41], although that may be explained on the basis that the court may have found that the applicable law of the arbitration clause was English, not Pakistani law (notwithstanding that Pakistani law was the law of the contract).

[14] See *Phrantzes v Argenti* [1960] 2 QB 19, 35–36, and see also *Talleyrand v Boulanger* (1797) 3 Ves Jun 448, 30 ER 1099, 1100. However, cf contra *OAO 'CT-Mobile' v IPOC International Growth Fund* (Bermuda SC 6 October 2006) [11], [21], [175], [190], upheld in *IPOC International Growth Fund v OAO 'CT-Mobile'* (Bermuda CA, 23 March 2007) [5], [38], [40], where an anti-suit injunction was granted in part in support of a Swedish arbitration clause, even though Swedish law did not provide for the grant of anti-suit injunctions. (However, the injunction was also in part granted in support of English law agreements for Swiss arbitration.)

[15] The injunction claimant is not entitled to an anti-suit injunction as of right, even where he seeks to enforce a contractual clause. The conventional rule of equity that the court has no discretion to refuse an injunction to enforce a clear negative covenant, laid down in *Doherty v Allman* (1878) 3 App Cas 708 (HL) 719–20, does not apply to injunctions to restrain foreign proceedings because of the tensions with comity which are inherent in the indirect interference with the foreign court which the anti-suit injunction involves: *Settlement Corp v Hochschild*

be in the interests of justice to grant the injunction.[16] However, where an anti-suit injunction is sought to enforce an English exclusive forum clause, the court's discretion is governed by a distinct set of principles.[17] These will, for convenience, be referred to as the *Angelic Grace* principles, after the decision of the Court of Appeal in which the English courts laid aside, in contractual cases, the caution which had historically determined their approach to anti-suit injunctions.[18]

[1966] 1 Ch 10, 17G–18A; *Mike Trading and Transport v R Pagnan & Fratelli (The Lisboa)* [1980] 2 Lloyds Rep 546 (CA) 549, 550–51, 551; *Aggeliki Charis Compania Maritima v Pagnan (The Angelic Grace)* [1994] 1 Lloyds Rep 168, 175 (Rix J), upheld on appeal, it appears, without argument to the contrary on this point [1995] 1 Lloyds Rep 87 (CA) 95–96; *Mediterranean Shipping v Atlantic Container Line* (CA, 3 December 1998); *Donohue v Armco* [2002] 1 Lloyds Rep 425 (HL) [16], [23]; *National Westminster Bank v Utrecht-America Finance* [2001] CLC 442 [51], [2001] 3 All ER 733 (CA) [73]; *Skype Technologies v Joltid* [2011] ILPr 8 [30]–[31]; *Ecobank Transnational v Tanoh* [2016] 1 Lloyds Rep 360 (CA) [137]; *ADM Asia-Pacific Trading v PT Budi Semesta Satria* [2016] EWHC 1427 [34]; *Hamilton-Smith v CMS Cameron McKenna* [2016] EWHC 1115 [71].

In *Elektrim v Vivendi Holdings No 1* [2009] 1 Lloyds Rep 59 (CA) [81], a case concerning a 'no action' clause, it was conceded by the injunction defendant that if the 'no action clause' was applicable, then an injunction to restrain foreign proceedings was the appropriate remedy 'because the court would ordinarily enforce a negative covenant by injunction'. The Court of Appeal noted that the question of whether a party can sue at all is different to the question of appropriate or chosen forum. It can be doubted, however, whether this concession was correct, and the Court of Appeal was not referred to *National Westminster Bank v Utrecht-America Finance* [2001] CLC 442, [2001] 3 All ER 733 (CA), which also concerned a 'no action' clause but applied *The Angelic Grace*: see [30]–[35], [73]–[74]). It is submitted that, in principle, the same comity concerns underlying the earlier authorities should apply where an injunction is sought to restrain foreign proceedings on the basis of a 'no action' clause as where the injunction is sought to enforce an exclusive jurisdiction clause.

Similarly, the discretion to decline to grant an injunction continues to exist, even though the court from which the injunction is sought has jurisdiction over the merits under Article 25 of the Brussels I Recast, or under Article 5(1) of the Hague Convention of the Choice of Court (so that no *forum non conveniens* stay of English proceedings would be available). Whether a court should stay proceedings before itself, and whether it should restrain foreign proceedings, are inherently different questions, because the considerations of comity arising from the indirect interference with the foreign court caused by the injunction deserve independent attention: *Ultisol Transport Contractors v Bouygues Offshore* [1996] 2 Lloyds Rep 140, 146–48; *Skype Technologies v Joltid* [2011] ILPr 8 [21]–[28]. In *Nori Holding v Bank Otkritie Financial Corporation* [2018] 2 Lloyds Rep 80 [105] Males J suggested that the tests for the grant of a stay or an injunction to enforce an exclusive forum clause should be essentially the same, subject to questions of delay (in the common law context, not considering Art 25). It is respectfully submitted that this is wrong, even under the common law (see para 7.14 and n 19), and it would clearly be wrong under Article 25 or under the Hague Convention (which Males J was not considering; and the authorities mentioned above were, it seems, not cited to him.). Stays are different, and injunctions should have their own tests, whether Article 25 or the Hague Convention apply or not, although the necessity for a specific test for injunctions is most obviously clear in the Article 25 or Hague Convention context.

Nor does the New York Convention *remove* the court's discretion not to grant the injunction where it is sought to enforce an arbitration clause: see *Toepfer International v Société Cargill France* [1997] 2 Lloyds Rep 98, 110, where, although Colman J suggested that the mandatory effect of the New York Convention should limit the criteria which could be relied on as reasons to refuse to grant an injunction (a suggestion which it is submitted is wrong—see at n 41), he accepted that the court retained a discretion.

It is suggested that it is a fallacy to infer from the fact that a jurisdiction clause or arbitration clause would be mandatory in the context of stays that there is any mandatory or near-mandatory need to grant an injunction. The two situations are different, and the assessment of whether or not to grant an anti-suit injunction must always be discretionary.

---

[16]   See *Donohue v Armco* [2002] 1 Lloyds Rep 425 (HL) [19], [24].

[17]   *Donohue v Armco* [2002] 1 Lloyds Rep 425 (HL) [23].

[18]   The key authorities are *Aggeliki Charis Compania Maritima v Pagnan (The Angelic Grace)* [1995] 1 Lloyds Rep 87 (CA) 96; *Donohue v Armco* [2002] 1 Lloyds Rep 424 (HL) [24] (Lord Bingham) [45] (Lord Hobhouse); and *AES Ust-Kamenogorsk Hydropower Plant LLP v Ust-Kamenogorsk Hydropower Plant JSC* [2013] 1 WLR 1889 (SC) [25], [58]. In *West Tankers v Ras Riunione Adriatica di Sicurta (The Front Comor)* [2007] 1 Lloyds Rep 391 (HL) [8], *The Angelic Grace* was viewed as stating the law. For recent examples of the application of the test, see *Dell Emerging Markets (EMEA) v IBMaroc.com* [2017] EWHC 2397 [21] and *Nori Holding v Bank Otkritie Financial Corporation* [2018] 2 Lloyds Rep 80 [28], [103]–[114].

In *Philip Alexander Securities & Futures v Bamberger* [1997] ILPr 73 [79], Waller J commented that, 'the Court of Appeal in The Angelic Grace would appear to have relaxed the historic caution urged upon the English courts ...'; although in *Toepfer International v Molino Boschi* [1996] 1 Lloyds Rep 510, 516, Mance J commented

7.14   These tests are specific to anti-suit injunctions. While there are considerable conceptual similarities to the common law tests to be applied to stays in favour of exclusive jurisdiction clauses (with the same language of 'strong reasons' being used), the issues are not the same, because of the indirect interference with the foreign court created by the anti-suit injunction, and because discretionary considerations can always lead to the refusal of the injunction.[19]

7.15   Under the *Angelic Grace* principles, where actual or likely[20] foreign proceedings are or will be in breach of an English exclusive jurisdiction clause, or an agreement to arbitrate in England, the court will ordinarily[21] exercise its discretion to grant an anti-suit injunction to restrain the party in breach from commencing or continuing with those proceedings, unless the injunction defendant can show that there are 'strong reasons'[22] why the anti-suit

that, '*The Angelic Grace* itself only eliminated some of the diffidence previously felt about granting injunctive relief'. For earlier examples of the trend, see *Sohio Supply v Gatoil (USA)* [1989] 1 Lloyds Rep 588 (CA) 592; *Continental Bank v Aeakos Compania Naviera* [1994] 1 Lloyds Rep 505 (CA) (the Lloyds report of this case is preferable to the Weekly Law Reports version at [1994] 1 WLR 588, which accidentally omits some text).

---

[19]   As held in *Skype Technologies v Joltid* [2011] ILPr 8 [28] and *American International Specialty Lines Insurance v Abbott Laboratories* [2003] 1 Lloyds Rep 267, 275; and as explained by Goff J (as he then was) in *Marazura Navegacion v Oceanus Mutual Underwriting Association (Bermuda)* [1977] 1 Lloyds Rep 283, 287–88. It is submitted that this is the best reading of *Donohue v Armco* [2002] 1 Lloyds Rep 425 (HL) [24]. Further, it is submitted that these authorities are to be preferred to the comments in *Ultisol Transport Contractors v Bouygues Offshore* [1996] 2 Lloyds Rep 140, 148–49; *Akai v People's Insurance* [1998] 1 Lloyds Rep 90, 105; *Donohue v Armco* [1999] 2 Lloyds Rep 649, 655–56, [2000] 1 Lloyds Rep 589 (CA) 595; and *Society of Lloyds v White* (Cresswell J, 3 March 2000), to the extent that those say the contrary.

Although it is tempting to assimilate the tests for stays and injunctions to each other, it is a temptation to be resisted. The interference with foreign proceedings created by the grant of an anti-suit injunction, and the consequences for comity between national courts, mean that additional factors need to be taken into account, and indeed that the nature of the discretion to be exercised is different. Indeed, it is one of the major themes of the anti-suit case law since *Aérospatiale* that an injunction requires greater justification than a stay: see Ch 4, section J, 'Forum non Conveniens' and para 4.77; Ch 2, section D, 'Forum non Conveniens and the *Castanho* Heresy'.

In *Nori Holding v Bank Otkritie Financial Corporation* [2018] 2 Lloyds Rep 80 [103]–[105], Males J suggested that the tests for stays and injunctions to enforce a jurisdiction clause should be applied in the same way, apart from the impact of 'general equitable considerations' such as delay. It is submitted that even this modified assimilation is not correct. While the same language of 'strong reasons' is used in both tests and can be applied in broadly similar fashion, there is no broader identity of test. The House of Lords' decision in *Donohue v Armco* [2002] 1 Lloyds Rep 425 (HL), cited by Males J, does not demand any identity of test, even under the common law; and it seems the authorities mentioned above were not cited to Males J.

In addition, Males J was considering only the tests for stays under the common law, and not the mandatory impact of Article 25 of the Brussels I Recast (or the Hague Convention on the Choice of Court). It is clear that the mandatory effect of Article 25 will not be applied, by reflection, to anti-suit injunctions in cases where Article 25 would apply to questions of jurisdiction (see n 13). But following the coming into force of the Brussels I Recast, and so long as the Brussels–Lugano regime remains English law, Article 25 rather than the common law will now apply to questions of jurisdiction in the vast majority of cases involving English exclusive jurisdiction clauses. (Previously, under the Brussels I Regulation, Art 23 would only apply if one of the parties was domiciled in an EU state, but that limitation has now been removed.) If Brexit occurs, and the Brussels–Lugano instruments cease to apply, the Hague Convention on the Choice of Court (discussed in more detail at Ch 17, para 17.46) will probably become the dominant instrument. It also creates a mandatory jurisdiction (see Art 5), but again this should not deform the tests for injunctions.

[20]   *Navigation Maritime Bulgare v Rustal Trading (The Ivan Zagubanski)* [2002] 1 Lloyds Rep 106, 124–25.

[21]   *Donohue v Armco* [2002] 1 Lloyds Rep 424 (HL) [23]; *Royal Bank of Canada v Centrale Raiffeisen-Boerenleenbank* [2004] 1 Lloyds Rep 471 (CA) 475; though cf contra *Mediterranean Shipping v Atlantic Container Line* (CA, 3 December 1998) (where the Court of Appeal propounded a liberal reinterpretation of *The Angelic Grace* which has not been followed).

[22]   There has been a rather arid debate as to the exact phrasing of this test. In *Continental Bank v Aeakos Compania Naviera* [1994] 1 Lloyds Rep 505 (CA) 512, Steyn LJ used the language of 'special countervailing factors'. In *Aggeliki Charis Compania Maritima v Pagnan (The Angelic Grace)* [1995] 1 Lloyds Rep 87 (CA) 96, per Millett LJ (with whom Neill LJ agreed: at 97), originally used the language of 'good reason', and this was the test applied in many cases. However, in *Donohue v Armco* [2000] 1 Lloyds Rep 579 (CA) 588–89, 592, 594, the Court of Appeal

injunction should not be granted. The concept of 'strong reasons' frames the analysis of many possible factors, in particular those that relate to the injunction defendant's reasons for suing in the foreign court. But (as discussed further in Chapter 8) it does not subsume all possible discretionary considerations. As the qualification 'ordinarily' allows, there can be discretionary considerations allowing exceptions to the robust general rule, in particular those relating to the conduct of the claimant.[23] Thus, if anti-suit injunctions are not applied for promptly, in such a way as to make it just that the injunction should be refused, or if the injunction claimant has acted unconscionably (eg if he has 'unclean hands'), the injunction can be refused on such grounds alone, independent of the concept of 'strong reasons'.[24]

The burden of proof is on the party in breach to show that there are 'strong reasons'.[25] Where an injunction would otherwise cause some injustice to the injunction defendant, the court may require appropriate undertakings from the injunction claimant before granting relief.[26]   **7.16**

In contrast to the position in non-contractual cases, the court is not obliged to exercise caution[27] before granting an anti-suit injunction to enforce a contractual forum clause,   **7.17**

---

held, drawing on the language used in older stay cases, that the test should be whether there was 'strong cause' or 'strong reason'. Confusion reigned for a while, with some judges, in catholic fashion, using a combination of some of these phrases, or all of them together: see *OT Africa Line v Hijazy (The Kribi) (No 1)* [2001] 1 Lloyds Rep 76, 91. When *Donohue* was decided by the House of Lords, the wording 'strong reasons' was used: *Donohue v Armco* [2002] 1 Lloyds Rep 425 (HL) [24], [53], and this is the test on which most, but not all, of the subsequent case law has settled: see eg *Bank of New York Mellon v GV Films* [2010] 1 Lloyds Rep 365 [16]; *Oceanconnect UK v Angara Maritime (The Fesco Angara)* [2011] 1 Lloyds Rep 399 [41]; *Star Reefers Pool v JFC Group* [2012] 1 Lloyds Rep 376 (CA) [25]; *AES Ust-Kamenogorsk Hydropower Plant LLP v Ust-Kamenogorsk Hydropower Plant JSC* [2013] 1 WLR 1889 (SC) [25]; *ADM Asia-Pacific Trading v PT Budi Semesta Satria* [2016] EWHC 1427 [34]; *Nori Holding v Bank Otkritie Financial Corporation* [2018] 2 Lloyds Rep 80 [28], [103]–[114]. But for a recent case using 'good reasons', see *Shipowners' Mutual Protection and Indemnity Association (Luxembourg) v Containerships Denizcilik Nakliyat ve Ticaret (The Yusuf Cepnioglu)* [2016] 1 Lloyds Rep 641 (CA) [22]. All the various formulations mean much the same thing, and it is suggested that one should be chosen. If so, the best candidate is probably the phrase 'strong reasons', used by the House of Lords in *Donohue v Armco*, and the Supreme Court in *AES Ust-Kamenogorsk*.

From time to time, additional glosses have been put on this test, but it is submitted that they are not helpful: *Bouygues Offshore v Caspian Shipping (No 3)* [1997] 2 Lloyds Rep 493, 501–03 ('near certainty' that an exclusive forum clause would be enforced); *Bouygues Offshore v Caspian Shipping (Nos 1, 3, 4 and 5)* [1998] 2 Lloyds Rep 461 (CA) 464, 467 (an English exclusive jurisdiction clause 'exerts a powerful and all but irresistible pressure on both Bouygues and Ultisol to bring their disputes to England' and had a 'near-conclusive' effect). In *Donohue v Armco* and *AES Ust-Kamenogorsk* (and most other cases) the test of strong reasons was stated without any such gloss.

---

[23] For the relationship between strong reasons and discretion, see further Ch 8, paras 8.01–8.04.

[24] *Donohue v Armco* [2002] 1 Lloyds Rep 424 (HL) [33]–[34]; *ADM Asia-Pacific Trading v PT Budi Semesta Satria* [2016] EWHC 1427 [34]; *Nori Holding v Bank Otkritie Financial Corporation* [2018] 2 Lloyds Rep 80 [103]–[118]. For unclean hands see *Royal Bank of Scotland v Highland Financial Partners* [2012] 2 CLC 109 [175], [2013] 1 CLC 596 (CA) [158].

[25] *Aggeliki Charis Compania Maritima v Pagnan (The Angelic Grace)* [1995] 1 Lloyds Rep 87 (CA) 96; *Shell International Petroleum v Coral Oil (No 1)* [1999] 1 Lloyds Rep 72, 78; *Ecom Agroindustrial v Mosharaf Composite Textile Mill* [2013] 2 Lloyds Rep 196 [19] (adopting this passage of the first edition).

[26] *Tracomin v Sudan Oil Seeds (Nos 1 and 2)* [1983] 1 WLR 1026 (CA) 1037; *Schiffahrtsgesellschaft Detlev von Appen v Voest Alpine Intertrading (The Jay Bola)* [1997] 1 Lloyds Rep 179, 189 (injunction claimant required to undertake to pay the injunction defendant's legal costs in the foreign jurisdiction where he had delayed before seeking the injunction; not challenged on appeal [1997] 2 Lloyds Rep 279 (CA)).

[27] In non-contractual cases, 'caution' is required: see Ch 4, paras 4.02 and 4.05, and para 4.79. Before *The Angelic Grace*, 'caution' or even 'great caution' had been required even in some contractual cases: *Settlement Corp v Hochschild* [1966] 1 Ch 10, 15; *Mike Trading and Transport v R Pagnan & Fratelli (The Lisboa)* [1980] 2 Lloyds Rep 546 (CA) 549, 551; *Tracomin v Sudan Oil Seeds* [1983] 1 WLR 1026 (CA) 1035; *Marc Rich v Societa Italiana Impianti (The Atlantic Emperor) (No 2)* (Hobhouse J, 11 November 1991); but there were cases where no such threshold was imposed: *Pena Copper Mines v Rio Tinto* (1912) 105 LT 846 (CA) 850–51; *Royal Exchange Assurance v Compania Naviera Santi (The Tropaioforos) (No 2)* [1962] 1 Lloyds Rep 410, 418.

However, the decision of the Court of Appeal in *The Angelic Grace* [1995] 1 Lloyds Rep 87 (CA) was and is binding authority that 'caution' is not required in contractual cases. This approach was implicitly adopted in

and indeed has 'no good reason for diffidence' in enforcing the injunction defendant's promise.[28] Further, there is no need to make a prior application for a stay to the foreign court.[29] However, the full rigour of this approach only applies where there has been a determination that the exclusive forum clause has been breached, or where at the interim stage there is sufficient confidence—probably, a 'high degree of probability'—that this is so.[30]

7.18   In a number of the cases, particularly the older ones, the more expansive approach to anti-suit injunctions in contractual cases was justified on the grounds that breach of a contractual exclusive forum clause was in itself vexatious and oppressive (or unconscionable).[31] On this interpretation, the law in contractual cases would merely be a specialized application of the general equitable principles governing anti-suit injunctions.[32] However, the preponderance of the authorities, in particular in more recent times, treat the injunction as justified by the force of the contractual obligation itself,[33] and it is submitted that this is the better view in principle. The tendency to square the circle by equating vexation or oppression (or unconscionability) with breach of contract is neat but unsound. There may well be nothing vexatious or oppressive or unconscionable about a breach of contract.[34] Nevertheless, since

---

Donohue v Armco [2002] 1 Lloyds Rep 425 (HL) and explicitly in *AES Ust-Kamenogorsk Hydropower Plant LLP v Ust-Kamenogorsk Hydropower Plant JSC* [2013] 1 WLR 1889 (SC) [25]. See eg recently *Essar Shipping v Bank of China (The Kishore)* [2016] 1 Lloyds Rep 427 [35].

   From time to time 'caution' has surfaced in the contractual context (see eg *Navigation Maritime Bulgare v Rustal Trading (The Ivan Zagubanski)* [2002] 1 Lloyds Rep 106, 124; *Markel International v Craft (The Norseman)* [2007] Lloyds Rep IR 403 [30]), but it is submitted that this is not the law.

---

   [28] *Aggeliki Charis Compania Maritima v Pagnan (The Angelic Grace)* [1995] 1 Lloyds Rep 87 (CA) 96 (per Millett LJ, with whom Neill LJ agreed: at 97); but cf Leggatt LJ at 91, although even he was careful in his approach to the word 'caution'.
   [29] *Aggeliki Charis Compania Maritima v Pagnan (The Angelic Grace)* [1995] 1 Lloyds Rep 87 (CA) 95, 96, 97, restrictively distinguishing *World Pride Shipping v Daiichi Chuo Kisen Kaisha (The Golden Anne)* [1984] 2 Lloyds Rep 489; see also *Credit Suisse First Boston (Europe) v MLC (Bermuda)* [1999] 1 Lloyds Rep 767, 780–81; *Horn Linie v Panamericana Formas e Impresos (The Hornbay)* [2006] 2 Lloyds Rep 44 [25]. This issue is discussed in more detail in Ch 8, paras 8.45–8.46. For the question of whether a prior application for a stay to the foreign court is required in non-contractual cases (it is submitted not), see Ch 5, section F, 'Stay Applications in the Foreign Court'.
   [30] See Ch 13, paras 13.51–13.56.
   [31] *Royal Exchange Assurance v Compania Naviera Santi (The Tropaioforos) (No 2)* [1962] 1 Lloyds Rep 410, 418; *Sohio Supply v Gatoil (USA)* [1989] 1 Lloyds Rep 588 (CA) 592: 'it seems to me that the continuance of foreign proceedings in breach of contract may well be vexatious and oppressive in any given case'; *Continental Bank v Aeakos Compania Naviera* [1994] 1 Lloyds Rep 505 (CA) 512; *Bouygues Offshore v Caspian Shipping (No 2)* [1997] 2 Lloyds Rep 485, 489–90; *National Westminster Bank v Utrecht-America Finance* [2001] 3 All ER 733 (CA) 745. In *Donohue v Armco* [1999] 2 Lloyds Rep 649, 655, 664, Aikens J viewed all anti–suit injunctions as deriving from the same sources of unconscionability, within which the existence or not of contractual obligations were merely factors in the exercise of the discretion. But his approach was not followed on this point in either the Court of Appeal ([2000] 1 Lloyds Rep 589 (CA)) or the House of Lords ([2002] 1 Lloyds Rep 425 (HL)).
   [32] *Trafigura Beheer v Kookmin Bank (No 1)* [2005] EWHC 2350 [42(ii)].
   [33] *Pena Copper Mines v Rio Tinto* (1912) 105 LT 846 (CA) 850–51; *Castanho v Brown & Root* [1980] 1 WLR 833 (CA) 865–66 (overturned on other grounds [1981] AC 557 (HL); *British Airways Board v Laker Airways* [1985] AC 58 (HL) 81C–E; *South Carolina Insurance v Assurantie Maatschippij 'de Seven Provincien'* [1987] 1 AC 24 (HL) 40C–G; *Airbus Industrie v Patel* [1999] 1 AC 119 (HL) 138F; *Toepfer International v Société Cargill France* [1998] 1 Lloyds Rep 379 (CA) 384; *Credit Suisse First Boston (Europe) v MLC (Bermuda)* [1999] 1 Lloyds Rep 767, 779–80; *Donohue v Armco* [2000] 1 Lloyds Rep 589 (CA) 594–95, [2002] 1 Lloyds Rep 425 [23], [45], [53]; *OT Africa Line v Magic Sportswear* [2005] 2 Lloyds Rep 170 (CA) [33]; *West Tankers v Ras Riunione Adriatica di Sicurta (The Front Comor)* [2007] 1 Lloyds Rep 391 (HL) [14]; *AES Ust-Kamenogorsk Hydropower Plant LLP v Ust-Kamenogorsk Hydropower Plant JSC* [2013] 1 WLR 1889 (SC) [21]–[28]; *Crescendo Maritime v Bank of Communications* [2016] 1 Lloyds Rep 414 [41]; *Shipowners' Mutual Protection and Indemnity Association (Luxembourg) v Containerships Denizcilik Nakliyat ve Ticaret (The Yusuf Cepnioglu)* [2016] 1 Lloyds Rep 641 (CA) [33].
   [34] In *Toepfer International v Société Cargill France* [1998] 1 Lloyds Rep 379 (CA) 384, the Court of Appeal drew a clear distinction between 'intrinsically unconscionable' conduct and conduct which can be injuncted because it is in breach of contract, relying on comments of Scott VC in *Schiffahrtsgesellschaft Detlev von Appen v Voest Alpine*

an anti-suit injunction to enforce an exclusive forum clause is necessarily a discretionary equitable remedy, it will only be granted if the ends of justice so require.[35] The *Angelic Grace* principles are merely a crystallization into a general rule of what the ends of justice will ordinarily require in contractual cases.[36]

There is a debate as to whether in more marginal cases, where special comity concerns arise, the *Angelic Grace* approach can be displaced, even if a contractual forum clause is found to apply, so that it may remain appropriate for the court to exercise 'caution'. This is supported by a number of authorities, including observations of the House of Lords and Supreme Court.[37] However, there is also a line of Court of Appeal authority, led by Longmore LJ, holding that once it is concluded that an exclusive forum clause applies, there is little or no room to take further account of comity, as comity in fact mandates enforcement of the exclusive forum clause.[38] It is submitted that the best approach is that of Rix J in *Credit Suisse*: 'in a straightforward [contractual] case there is little mileage in a "ritual incantation" ... of the doctrine of comity', but comity should always remain a relevant consideration.[39]   **7.19**

In any event, the case law suggests that if the contractual injunction is a foreign anti-enforcement injunction, after the foreign judgment, rather than a normal anti-suit injunction, then 'caution' is appropriate.[40]   **7.20**

Subject to one differentiation, these principles apply in essentially the same fashion whether the injunction is sought to enforce an arbitration clause or an exclusive jurisdiction clause.[41]   **7.21**

Intertrading (The Jay Bola) [1997] 2 Lloyds Rep 279 (CA) 292. However, see the contrary views of Rix LJ in *OT Africa Line v Magic Sportswear* [2005] 2 Lloyds Rep 170 (CA) 183–84. Further, if unconscionability is interpreted broadly, so as to refer to anything equity will restrain, it follows trivially that, as equity will restrain a breach of contract, the breach of contract is in that sense unconscionable (see *Lett v Lett* [1906] 1 IR 618).

---

[35] *Donohue v Armco* [2002] 1 Lloyds Rep 425 (HL) [19], [24].
[36] *Crédit Suisse First Boston (Europe) v MLC (Bermuda)* [1999] 1 Lloyds Rep 767, 780.
[37] *Credit Suisse First Boston (Europe) v MLC (Bermuda)* [1999] 1 Lloyds Rep 767, 780–81; *Deutz v General Electric* (Thomas J, 14 April 2000); *Donohue v Armco* [2002] 1 Lloyds Rep 425 [25]; *AES Ust-Kamenogorsk Hydropower Plant LLP v Ust-Kamenogorsk Hydropower Plant JSC* [2013] 1 WLR 1889 (SC) [61]; *Ecobank Transnational v Tanoh* [2016] 1 Lloyds Rep 360 (CA) [100], [106], [134], [135]; and see S Males QC, 'Comity and Anti-Suit Injunctions' [1998] LMCLQ 543, 550–51. A Briggs, 'Anti-Suit Injunctions in a Complex World' in F Rose (ed), *Lex Mercatoria* (2000) 219, 236–39, argues that caution should be exercised even in standard contractual cases.
[38] *OT Africa Line v Magic Sportswear* [2005] 2 Lloyds Rep 170 (CA) [31]–[33]; *Shipowners' Mutual Protection and Indemnity Association (Luxembourg) v Containerships Denizcilik Nakliyat ve Ticaret (The Yusuf Cepnioglu)* [2016] 1 Lloyds Rep 641 (CA) [25], [34]–[35]; and also *Royal Bank of Scotland v Highland Financial Partners* [2012] 2 CLC 109 [154–158].
[39] *Credit Suisse First Boston (Europe) v MLC (Bermuda)* [1999] 1 Lloyds Rep 767, 780–81. See further the discussion in T Raphael, 'Do as You Would be Done By: System-Transcendent Justification and Anti-Suit Injunctions' [2016] LMCLQ 256, 260–61.
[40] *Akai v People's Insurance* [1998] 1 Lloyds Rep 90 [104] and *Ecobank Transnational v Tanoh* [2016] 1 Lloyds Rep 360 (CA) [110], [136]. See also the general discussion of anti-enforcement injunctions in Ch 5, section I, 'Anti-Enforcement Injunctions'.
[41] *Aggeliki Charis Compania Maritima v Pagnan (The Angelic Grace)* [1995] 1 Lloyds Rep 87 (CA) 94, 96; *AES Ust-Kamenogorsk Hydropower Plant LLP v Ust-Kamenogorsk Hydropower Plant JSC* [2013] 1 WLR 1889 (SC) [23]; *Essar Shipping v Bank of China (The Kishore)* [2016] 1 Lloyds Rep 427 [33]; *Aline Tramp v Jordan International Insurance (The Flag Evi)* [2017] 1 Lloyds Rep 467 [33]. See also *American International Specialty Lines Insurance v Abbott Laboratories* [2003] 1 Lloyds Rep 267, 275; *Through Transport Mutual Insurance Association (Eurasia) v New India Assurance (No 1)* [2005] 1 Lloyds Rep 67 (CA) 84 ('almost identical'); *Mike Trading and Transport v R Pagnan & Fratelli (The Lisboa)* [1980] 2 Lloyds Rep 546 (CA) 549 ('similar').
    In *Toepfer International v Société Cargill France* [1997] 2 Lloyds Rep 98, 110, Colman J suggested that, since under the Convention the English court would have no discretion whether or not to stay English proceedings brought in breach of the arbitration clause, it followed that when assessing whether or not there were 'strong reasons' not to enforce the arbitration clause by the grant of an anti-suit injunction, considerations of *forum non*

The fact that an international arbitration clause will usually have mandatory effect under the New York Convention, and so should preclude any discretion not to grant a stay, is a practical consideration affecting what happens if no injunction is granted,[42] which may influence whether there are 'strong reasons' not to enforce the clause, but it does not change the test. There is, however, one material dimension of difference introduced by the position of the arbitrators. As discussed below, when an injunction is sought to support an arbitration, the power to grant anti-suit injunctions must be exercised with sensitivity to the role of the arbitrators, and whether or not they are better placed to intervene.[43]

7.22   The approach in *The Angelic Grace* has not met with universal enthusiasm. In *Toepfer v Cargill*, Phillips LJ, although accepting that he was bound by *The Angelic Grace*, went out of his way to indicate that he thought its correctness was open to doubt, because 'there was much to be said for the view that, as a matter of comity and in the interests of procedural simplicity, the appropriate course was to leave the injunction claimant to seek a stay of the foreign proceedings in reliance on Article II.3 of the New York Convention.'[44]

---

conveniens and the risk of inconsistent decisions should be given little or no weight. This suggestion has attracted some limited sympathy: the Court of Appeal left the point open in *Mediterranean Shipping C v Atlantic Container Line* (CA, 3 December 1998); and see also *Credit Suisse First Boston (Europe) v MLC (Bermuda)* [1999] 1 Lloyds Rep 767, 780; *Welex v Rosa Maritime (The Epsilon Rosa) (No 2)* [2002] 2 Lloyds Rep 701 (Steel J) 706 (but see [2003] 2 Lloyds Rep 509 (CA) [45], [51], where the Court of Appeal did not adopt this aspect of Steel J's reasoning); S Males QC, 'Comity and Anti-Suit Injunctions' [1998] LMCLQ 543, 548.

   However, any such approach is probably precluded by *The Angelic Grace*, which envisages no such restriction on strong reasons in the arbitration context, and in the bulk of the case law, the principles have been applied to arbitration clauses in the same way as jurisdiction clauses, with no rigid restriction on the discretionary considerations that can be borne in mind. While it is, of course, true that the relevance of factors like *forum conveniens* will be considerably restricted by the parties' contractual agreement on a chosen forum, which will often be taken to have borne in mind and catered for questions of convenient forum (see Ch 8, paras 8.09–8.11), this is no more nor less so than for injunctions to enforce jurisdiction clauses. Cases where *forum conveniens* factors were thought to be potentially legitimate in appropriate cases in considering whether to refuse injunctions to enforce arbitration clauses include *Donohue v Armco* [1999] 2 Lloyds Rep 649 [23]; and *Welex v Rosa Maritime (The Epsilon Rosa)* [2003] 2 Lloyds Rep 509 (CA) [45], [51]; and this appears to be the better reading of *Crescendo Maritime v Bank of Communications Co* [2016] 1 Lloyds Rep 414 at [46]–[48] (there seems to be a missing 'not' before 'apply' in [47]). In *Donohue v Armco* [2002] 1 Lloyds Rep 425 (HL) [25], [53] and *AES Ust-Kamenogorsk Hydropower Plant LLP v Ust-Kamenogorsk Hydropower Plant JSC* [2013] 1 WLR 1889 (SC) [23] there was no suggestion that the analysis to be applied to arbitration clauses and exclusive jurisdiction clauses should be different.

   In principle, extrapolating the rigid mandatory approach required by the New York Convention in stay cases so as positively to demand the imposition of an injunction seems inappropriate. Different considerations apply to stays as compared to injunctions (as explained by Goff J (as he then was) in *Marazura Navegacion v Oceanus Mutual Underwriting Association (Bermuda)* [1977] 1 Lloyds Rep 283, 287–88).

   Recently, in *Nori Holding v Bank Otkritie Financial Corporation* [2018] 2 Lloyds Rep 80 [106], Males J cited *Toepfer* and took the approach that while the tests were the same, they might be applied differently because of the mandatory nature of arbitration clauses, which brought other considerations into play. There is no objection to this as such. It is plainly correct that where there will be no stay of matters submitted to arbitration in forum X, then this may affect the pragmatic considerations involved in assessing whether or not there are 'strong reasons' not to grant an injunction to restrain proceedings in forum Y. But it is submitted it would be wrong, if the mandatory nature of the arbitration clause with regard to stays was thought to bring with it a different test when enforcing it by injunction, such that the grant of an injunction was viewed as mandatory or closer to mandatory. Indeed, most exclusive jurisdiction clauses in favour of the English courts will now be mandatory under Article 25 of the Brussels I Recast (so long as it remains effective in English law), and the Hague Convention on the Choice of Court similarly precludes a court chosen under an exclusive jurisdiction clause within its scope from staying proceedings on grounds of *forum non conveniens*: see Article 5.

---

   [42] It is submitted that this is the correct interpretation of *Nori Holding v Bank Otkritie Financial Corporation* [2018] 2 Lloyds Rep 80 [106].

   [43] See *AES Ust-Kamenogorsk Hydropower Plant LLC v Ust-Kamenogorsk Hydropower Plant JSC* [2013] 1 WLR 1889 (SC) [60] and para 7.51.

   [44] *Toepfer International v Société Cargill France* [1998] 1 Lloyds Rep 379 (CA) 386; see also *Sokana Industries v Freyre* [1994] 2 Lloyds Rep 57, 66.

However, it seems insufficient to rely on the prospect that the foreign court will enforce **7.23**
the arbitration clause under the New York Convention, and therefore will stay the proceedings before it. Article II.3 of the New York Convention permits foreign courts to hold
that arbitration clauses are invalid on the basis of their own domestic law, and there can
be real risks that the foreign court will not enforce the arbitration clause, even though the
English court would do so.[45] In practice, claimants in foreign proceedings who resist an
anti-suit injunction to enforce a contractual forum clause often do so precisely because
they hope the foreign court may adopt a different view on whether the forum clause is
binding.

Further, the injunction defendant has agreed not even to invoke the jurisdiction of the other **7.24**
court, so there is no injustice in restraining him from doing so, while conversely there would
be injustice in compelling the injunction claimant to defend himself in a court where it had
been agreed that he would not have to appear.[46] Many jurisdictions do not have simple procedures for enforcing a jurisdiction clause in favour of another forum, or do not separate
the procedures for determining jurisdictional and substantive defences. In such cases, requiring injunction claimants to wait until after the determination of foreign stay applications before bringing an injunction would impose an unfair burden, not least because of
the ever-present risk that one false step in the foreign court might be viewed as a voluntary
submission to its jurisdiction.[47] Indeed, in recognition of the seriousness of this problem,
the English courts have regarded the unavailability of an easy and cheap procedure for
enforcing an exclusive forum clause before the foreign court as a significant factor in favour
of the grant of an injunction.[48]

In truth, the force of Phillips LJ's point arises out of the deeper concern as to whether it is **7.25**
appropriate, in principle, for the English court to impose its conclusion that the arbitration
clause or exclusive jurisdiction clause should be enforced, irrespective of the views of the
foreign court.[49] If it is accepted that this is legitimate, as under current English law it clearly
is, then the mutually binding obligations under the New York Convention do not provide
a strong reason for awaiting a foreign stay decision. Either there is no reason to believe that
the foreign court will not enforce the arbitration clause and grant a stay, in which case there
is no good reason for the English court to permit the proceedings to proceed,[50] or there is
a real risk that the foreign court will override or ignore the clause, which to English eyes
should be respected under the New York Convention; and in the latter case, provided that

---

[45] If the foreign state is not party to the New York Convention, it has been stated that 'the primary remedy' must
be to apply for an injunction: *Schiffahrtsgesellschaft Detlev von Appen v Voest Alpine Intertrading (The Jay Bola)*
[1997] 2 Lloyds Rep 279 (CA) 285.

[46] *Aggeliki Charis Compania Maritima v Pagnan (The Angelic Grace)* [1995] 1 Lloyds Rep 87 (CA) 96; *West
Tankers v Ras Riunione Adriatica di Sicurta (The Front Comor)* [2007] 1 Lloyds Rep 391 (HL) [30] (per Lord
Mance).

[47] *Aggeliki Charis Compania Maritima v Pagnan (The Angelic Grace)* [1994] 1 Lloyds Rep 168, 180, upheld
without specific discussion of this point [1995] 1 Lloyds Rep 87 (CA).

[48] In *Continental Bank v Aeakos Compania Naviera* [1994] 1 Lloyds Rep 505 (CA) 511–12 the rules of Greek
procedure were such that it was impossible to make a jurisdictional challenge without filing an expensive defence
to the action at the same time. The Court of Appeal would have treated this as a factor in favour of an injunction if
necessary.

[49] See Ch 1, paras 1.50–1.59.

[50] *Aggeliki Charis Compania Maritima v Pagnan (The Angelic Grace)* [1994] 1 Lloyds Rep 168 (Rix J) 182–83,
upheld, albeit in different terms, at [1995] 1 Lloyds Rep 87 (CA).

the English court is willing to impose its own view of the force of the clause, the only way in which the contractual clause will be given full effect is if the injunction is granted.[51]

7.26   It is also clear that Phillips LJ's comments do not reflect the current law, which has enshrined the *Angelic Grace* principles. The courts have repeatedly concluded that, even where the competing proceedings are in a New York Convention state, the New York Convention does not create a bar to the enforcement of arbitration clauses by way of anti-suit injunction, and further does not provide even a significant factor against the exercise of the court's discretion to grant the injunction.[52]

F. THE SCOPE AND LIMITS OF EXCLUSIVE FORUM CLAUSES

7.27   The *Angelic Grace* approach only applies directly if the foreign proceedings are in breach of the exclusive jurisdiction clause or can be treated as such. So, for it to apply, the injunction claimant must be entitled to enforce the clause, the injunction defendant has to be party to or otherwise in substance bound by the clause, the clause must be binding and not invalid, and the claim in the foreign proceedings must fall within its terms.

1. Parties and Third Parties

7.28   In recent years a developing line of case law has tested the boundaries of the effect of exclusive forum clauses with respect to third parties. The key questions are, first, when a non-party can enforce the clause; second, when a non-party can be bound by the clause; and third, when the contractual effect of the clause covers litigation with respect to non-parties.[53] The first two questions are covered in detail in Chapter 10. In brief summary, third parties can claim to enforce an exclusive forum clause where they have legal or equitable rights to do so, in a number of defined situations, for example as subrogees, assignees, or as third parties under the Contracts (Rights of Third Parties) Act 1999.[54] There are also cases where an apparent third party on analysis is a primary party to the contract, such as contracts through agency. Conversely, third parties can (in substance) be bound by the clause in a range of situations, in particular in cases where they seek to claim contractual rights in the shoes of one of the original contracting parties, for example as assignee, or under third-party rights statutes.

---

[51]   *Continental Bank v Aeakos Compania Naviera* [1994] 1 Lloyds Rep 505 (CA) 512. For arguments of principle supporting the application of the *Angelic Grace* principles, see S Males QC, 'Comity and Anti-Suit Injunctions' [1998] LMCLQ 543, 549–50.

[52]   *Navigation Maritime Bulgare v Rustal Trading (The Ivan Zagubanski)* [2002] 1 Lloyds Rep 106, 124, holding that this is the effect of *The Angelic Grace*; *Donohue v Armco* [2002] 1 Lloyds Rep 425 (HL) [23]–[25], [53] (ratifying the *Angelic Grace* approach); *Welex v Rosa Maritime (The Epsilon Rosa) (No 2)* [2003] 2 Lloyds Rep 509 (CA) [52]; *West Tankers v Ras Riunione Adriatica di Sicurta (The Front Comor)* [2005] 2 Lloyds Rep 257, 268–69, upheld [2007] 1 Lloyds Rep 391 (HL) [8]. Following the comments of the ECJ in *The Front Comor*, an attempt was made to re-argue the New York Convention point but this was rejected by Cooke J in *Shashoua v Sharma* [2009] 2 Lloyds Rep 376 [35]–[39] and by the Court of Appeal in *Midgulf International v Group Chimique Tunisien* [2010] 2 Lloyds Rep 543 (CA) [66]–[69]. The principles involved are discussed at Ch 1, section H, 'The New York Convention'.

[53]   For discussion, see A Briggs, 'The Subtle Variety of Jurisdiction Agreements' [2012] LMCLQ 364.

[54]   In *Horn Linie v Panamericana Formas e Impresos (The Hornbay)* [2006] 2 Lloyds Rep 44, [29], [34(2)], Morison J held, *obiter*, that a third party could be entitled to claim a contractual anti-suit injunction under an exclusive forum clause where he was entitled to be treated as a party to the contract by virtue of a *Himalaya* clause, and where he was joined to the proceedings as an additional party.

This section addresses the linked but different question of when an exclusive forum clause   **7.29**
covers litigation with respect to non-parties. It is different, because even if the clause does
cover litigation against non-parties, that does not mean the third party necessarily has the
right to enforce it. It may be that, even if A and B's contract includes a clause protecting C as
well as B, only B can enforce it by injunction, which B can do if he has a sufficient interest in
doing so.[55] It is linked, because the considerations affecting whether a third party C can enforce a clause interrelate with those underlying whether the clause covers litigation against
or by him; and because if the clause does not cover C, then any rights to enforce are without
relevant content.

The true principle is, or should be, relatively simple: in a contract between A and B the   **7.30**
starting point should be that the exclusive forum clause only contractually requires litigation between A and B to be brought in the chosen forum,[56] but specific terms, or the express
and implied terms of the contract and exclusive forum clause properly construed to apply
to particular situations, may mean that on its true interpretation the contract also requires
certain litigation against a connected party C to be brought in the chosen forum, or at least
prohibits such litigation against C being brought in any other forum.[57] But there will be
many situations where the exclusive forum clause only covers the parties to it.[58] In particular, there is a potential difficulty with giving the negative effect of arbitration clauses a
broad reading with respect to litigation against third parties. Unless the third party is also
itself bound by, and entitled to enforce, the exclusive forum clause, interpreting the negative effect of the clause to prevent litigation against the third party in any forum other than
that chosen could create a gap in judicial protection.[59] There is generally no need to distort

---

[55] See eg *Royal Bank of Scotland v Highland Financial Partners* [2012] 2 CLC 109 [153]; *Dell Emerging Markets (EMEA) v IBMaroc.com* [2017] EWHC 2397 [21].

[56] *Credit Suisse First Boston (Europe) v MLC (Bermuda)* [1999] 1 Lloyds Rep 767, 777–78; *Team Y&R Holdings Hong Kong v Ghossoub* [2017] EWHC 2401 [82].

[57] For examples of claims against third parties being covered, see eg *Deutsche Bank v Highland Crusader Offshore Partners* [2009] 1 CLC 535 [34] (held arguable; this point was not addressed on appeal [2010] 1 WLR 1023 (CA) where, however, the first instance decision was generally overturned); *Vitol v Arcturus Merchant Trust* [2009] EWHC 800 [36]; *Bannai v Erez* [2013] EWHC 3689 [13], [31]; *ICBCL Financial Leasing v CG Commercial Finance* [2014] EWHC 3156; *Starlight Shipping Co v Allianz Marine and Aviation Versicherungs (The Alexandros T) (No 2)* [2015] Lloyds Rep IR 54 [39] and [41]–[51]; *Dell Emerging Markets (EMEA) v IBMaroc.com* [2017] EWHC 2397 [14]–[21]. In *Royal Bank of Scotland v Highland Financial Partners* [2012] 2 CLC 109 [147]–[153], Burton J considered the contractual arguments, and appeared to be attracted by them, but in the end granted the injunction without distinguishing between contractual and non-contractual justifications: see the 'and/or' at [153].
It is worth briefly commenting on *Himalaya* clauses, on which there is case law pointing in different directions. In *The Mahkutai* [1996] AC 650 (JCPC) 665–68, Lord Goff concluded that an exclusive jurisdiction clause would not fall within the protection which the *Himalaya* clause afforded to the servants and agents of the carrier; as an exclu-sive jurisdiction clause was not a relevant 'provision'. Notwithstanding this, in the *Hornbay*, Morison J made the *obiter* suggestion that an exclusive jurisdiction clause would arguably be protected by the slightly different words of the *Himalaya* clause there: *Horn Linie v Panamericana Formas e Impresos (The Hornbay)* [2006] 2 Lloyds Rep 44 [29]–[30]. Finally, in *Whitesea Shipping and Trading v El Paso Rio Clara (The Marielle Bolten)* [2010] 1 Lloyds Rep 648 [21], the court concluded that an obligation in a *Himalaya* clause not to sue the connected third party could be enforced by anti-suit injunction by the original party to the contract.

[58] For examples of a connected party C not being covered by the A–B contract, see *Credit Suisse First Boston (Europe) v MLC (Bermuda)* [1999] 1 Lloyds Rep 767; *Citigroup Global Markets v Amatra Leveraged Feeder Holdings* [2012] 2 CLC 279 [55]; *Morgan Stanley v China Haisheng Juice Holdings* [2010] 1 Lloyds Rep 65; *Rochester Resources v Lebedev* [2014] EWHC 2926 [48]; *Crescendo Maritime v Bank of Communications Company* [2016] 1 Lloyds Rep 414; *Team Y&R Holdings Hong Kong v Ghossoub* [2017] EWHC 2401 [69]–[84]; and possibly *Bannai v Erez* [2013] EWHC 3689 at [32] (contrast [31]).

[59] cf *Morgan Stanley v China Haisheng Juice Holdings* [2010] 1 Lloyds Rep 65 [21]; *Crescendo Maritime v Bank of Communications* [2016] 1 Lloyds Rep 414 [56]; and see also *Team Y&R Holdings Hong Kong v Ghossoub* [2017] EWHC 2401 [78]–[82].

contract law, so as to protect exclusive forum clauses from evasion,[60] since contrived claims against connected third parties, brought to evade an exclusive forum clause, may in appropriate cases be treated as vexatious or oppressive and liable to be injuncted for that reason.[61] It is apparent, however, that there is a tension in the case law, with different judges taking different approaches and a more expansive attitude to construction tending to be adopted in cases where the injunction defendant's conduct is viewed as an illegitimate attempt to evade the forum clause.[62]

7.31   A complication has been created by *obiter* comments of Lord Scott in *Donohue v Armco*, where on one reading he suggested that in general, a jurisdiction clause between A and B will cover litigation against any C arising out of the matters substantively covered by the forum clause.[63] But it is submitted that those comments do not drive us to such a rigid doctrine. They were *obiter*, and a minority view; the point was not even argued before the House of Lords, and the other Lords made it clear they were not deciding it;[64] and they were made in the context of very specific facts, where B would be jointly and severally liable for A's claim against C. They are also difficult to reconcile with the views of Lord Goff in *The Mahkutai*, which was not cited in *Donohue*.[65] Although some cases have picked up these comments—perhaps without fully appreciating their controversial nature and fragility as authority[66]—the more persuasive decisions have treated them sceptically,[67] and in most of the case law they have not even been cited. The correct approach is to treat the question of whether C is protected as a matter for construction of the contract in each case.[68]

---

[60]   We do, however, assume that there is personal jurisdiction under CPR Part 6 PD 6B para 3.1(6) in respect of injunctions to prevent vexatious evasion of exclusive forum clauses (cf Ch 18, paras 18.48–18.52). If such jurisdiction did not exist, there would be greater pressure to impose a contract in A–B–C cases.

[61]   A number of the 'A–B–C' cases justify the injunction directly on vexation or oppression, such as eg *Bannai v Erez* [2013] EWHC 3689 [32] and *ICBCL Financial Leasing v CG Commercial Finance* [2014] EWHC 3156; and some do not distinguish between a contractual and a non-contractual justification: see eg *Royal Bank of Scotland v Highland Financial Partners LP* [2012] 2 CLC 109 [147]–[153]. But the mere fact of B being connected to A and/or B does not necessarily mean that it is vexatious for A to sue B in a forum different to that chosen between A and B, and this will depend on all the facts. The point is sometimes expressed in terms of whether the proceedings against the third party are a 'collateral attack' on the clause. See *Crescendo Maritime v Bank of Communications* [2016] 1 Lloyds Rep 414 [56]–[59] and *Midgulf International v Groupe Chimiche Tunisien* [2010] 2 Lloyds Rep 543 (CA) [52] (regarding collateral attack as a non-contractual ground for an injunction).

[62]   For a recent example of the expansive approach, see *Dell Emerging Markets (EMEA) v IBMaroc.com* [2017] EWHC 2397. For a more doctrinally conservative approach to contractual interpretation, see *Team Y&R Holdings Hong Kong v Ghossoub* [2017] EWHC 2401 [69]–[83]. It is difficult to view the thoughtful analysis in *Ghossoub* as representative of much of the recent case law.

[63]   *Donohue v Armco* [2002] 1 Lloyds Rep 425 [60]–[62].

[64]   *Donohue v Armco* [2002] 1 Lloyds Rep 425 [14], [23], [30, [48].

[65]   *The Mahkutai* [1996] AC 650 (PC) 665–68.

[66]   *Winnetka Trading v Julius Baer International* [2009] Bus LR 1006 [28]–[29] (although the facts involved a very close connection between the A–B and the A–C claims and it is not clear that a contractual relationship was found); *Royal Bank of Scotland v Highland Financial Partners* [2012] 2 CLC 109 [147]–[153], at [151] (although in the end Burton J granted the injunction without distinguishing between contractual and non-contractual justifications: see 'and/or' at [153]); *Dell Emerging Markets (EMEA) v IBMaroc.com* [2017] EWHC 2397 [12].

[67]   *Morgan Stanley & International v China Haisheng Juice Holdings* [2010] 1 Lloyds Rep 65 [30]; *Crescendo Maritime v Bank of Communications* [2016] 1 Lloyds Rep 414 [56]; *Team Y&R Holdings Hong Kong v Ghossoub* [2017] EWHC 2401 [72]–[75].

[68]   As Teare J put it in *Morgan Stanley & Co International v China Haisheng Juice Holdings* [2010] 1 Lloyds Rep 65 [21]:

> The true construction of the jurisdiction clause in the Master Agreement must depend on its terms.... The key question is whether clause 13 would reasonably be understood to mean that MSIP and CH promised each other that claims arising out or in connection with the Master Agreement would be brought in England regardless of whether the claims were against the other or a nonparty to the Master Agreement.

See also *Dell Emerging Markets (EMEA) v IBMaroc.com* [2017] EWHC 2397 [14] and the recent analysis in *Team Y&R Holdings Hong Kong v Ghossoub* [2017] EWHC 2401 [69]–[83].

2. Exclusive and Non-Exclusive Clauses

In order directly to trigger the *Angelic Grace* principles, the foreign proceedings must be an **7.32** actionable breach of contract (although quasi-contractual situations may be treated in the same way, as discussed in Ch 10). This will usually require that the clause is construed as exclusive as opposed to non-exclusive, as by definition foreign proceedings are generally not a breach of the express or even implied terms of a non-exclusive jurisdiction clause.[69]

It is not necessary, under English principles of contractual construction, for an exclusive **7.33** jurisdiction clause expressly to state that it is exclusive. The question is one of construction of the words of the clause in the context of the contract as a whole, and against its factual background.[70]

3. The Scope of the Clause

Whether a particular claim in foreign proceedings is covered by the clause must be resolved **7.34** by analysis of the nature of the foreign proceedings in the light of the construction of the particular words used. As a starting point:

> the construction of an arbitration clause should start from the assumption that the parties, as rational businessmen, are likely to have intended any dispute arising out of the relationship into which they have entered or purported to enter to be decided by the same tribunal. The clause should be construed in accordance with this presumption unless the language makes it clear that certain questions were intended to be excluded from the arbitrator's jurisdiction.[71]

These principles apply just as much to the construction of jurisdiction clauses.[72]

However, 'the essential task is to construe the jurisdiction clause in the light of the transac- **7.35** tion as a whole', and the presumption is capable of being rebutted without excessive difficulty in appropriate cases,[73] and may well not apply at all in less conventional situations,[74] such as where different parts of the same commercial relationship are governed by conflicting dispute resolution provisions.[75]

---

[69] See Ch 9, section B, 'Implied Terms'. Article 25 of the Brussels I Recast (so long as it remains effective in English law) and Article 3(b) of the Hague Convention on the Choice of Court provide similar but slightly different wording which deem jurisdiction clauses to be exclusive for the purposes of jurisdiction unless the contrary has been provided. The effect of a clause which has acquired deemed exclusivity in this way has not yet been explored in the reported decisions on anti-suit injunctions.

[70] The cases are reviewed in *Companhia Sub-America de Vapores v Hin-Pro International Logistics* [2015] 2 Lloyds Rep 1 (CA) [43]–[78]. Good illustrations of the modern approach are found in *BNP Paribas v Anchorage Capital* [2013] EWHC 3073 [82]–[88] and *Global Maritime Investments Cyprus v OW Supply and Trading* [2015] EWHC 2690 [46]–[52].

[71] *Fiona Trust & Holding Corp v Privalov* [2008] 1 Lloyds Rep 254 (HL) [5], [6]–[8], [13].

[72] See eg *Skype Technologies v Joltid* [2009] EWHC 2783 [14]–[19]; *UBS v HSH Nordbank* [2009] 2 Lloyds Rep 272 (CA) [82]–[84]; *Trust Risk Group v AmTrust Europe* [2015] 2 Lloyds Rep 154 (CA) [15]–[16], [40]–[49].

[73] *UBS v HSH Nordbank* [2009] 2 Lloyds Rep 272 (CA) [82]–[83].

[74] *Ryanair v Esso Italiana* [2013] 2 CLC 950 (CA) [42]–[49] (tortious claims unconnected to any viable contractual claim falling within the forum clause); followed by *Microsoft Mobile Oy v Sony Mobile* [2017] 5 CMLR 5 [47]–[54].

[75] *Deutsche Bank v Sebastian Holdings* [2011] 1 Lloyds Rep 106 (CA) [39]–[49]; *Trust Risk Group v AmTrust Europe* [2015] 2 Lloyds Rep 154 (CA) [16]–[17], [44]–[49].

7.36   By way of example, proceedings to enforce a judgment in an 'unchosen' forum, or to resist enforcement there, are not a breach of an exclusive jurisdiction clause, provided that they are not attempts to determine or relitigate the merits.[76] Further, it has been held that an application in insolvency proceedings in Canada, seeking a declaration that certain provisions of a contract should be overridden in the context of an insolvency, was not in breach of an English exclusive jurisdiction clause, because the disputes between the parties were not disputes 'under' the contract, nor a 'contractual issue'.[77]

4. Evasion of Exclusive Forum Clauses

7.37   Where concocted non-contractual claims are brought abroad in an abusive attempt to evade an English exclusive forum clause, or to interfere with proceedings in the chosen forum, they may be restrained on the grounds that they are vexatious and oppressive.[78] One example of this which has already been discussed is abusive claims on the same subject matter against connected third parties.[79] Another example is the use of foreign proceedings to effect a collateral attack on an arbitration.[80]

5. Clauses Prohibiting any Litigation at All

7.38   It is rarer, but not unknown, for parties to provide that no litigation at all may take place in relation to a particular matter. The court is unlikely to conclude that this was what was agreed without unusually clear language.[81] Even if an immunity has been contracted for, it will generally mean only that any claim should fail if brought, not that it would be a breach of contract for a claim even to be made before any court or tribunal.

7.39   Nevertheless, where clear language is used, the courts can give effect to such a clause by an injunction restraining foreign proceedings.[82] The principles set out in *The Angelic Grace*, or

---

[76] *Shashoua v Sharma* [2009] 2 Lloyds Rep 376 [40]–[41]; *Vitol v Capri Marine (No 2)* [2010] EWHC 458 [29]–[35].

[77] *AWB (Geneva) v North America Steamships* [2007] 2 Lloyds Rep 315 (CA) [25]–[28]; see similarly the nuanced approach taken in *Team Y&R Holdings Hong Kong v Ghossoub* [2017] EWHC 2401 [69]–[85] in relation to foreign winding-up proceedings.

[78] *Shell International Petroleum v Coral Oil Co (No 2)* [1999] 2 Lloyds Rep 606, 609–610; *Horn Linie v Panamericana Formas e Impresos (The Hornbay)* [2006] 2 Lloyds Rep 44 [25], [28]–[32]; *Starlight Shipping v Tai Ping Insurance (The Alexandros T)* [2008] 1 Lloyds Rep 230 [42] (although the court held that it had no personal jurisdiction over such a claim); *BNP Paribas v Russian Machines* [2012] 1 Lloyds Rep 61 [79]–[92], [2012] 1 Lloyds Rep 649 (CA) [49]–[58]; *Mace (Russia) v Retansel Enterprises* [2016] EWHC 1209 [12]; for examples where such an argument failed, see *Malhotra v Malhotra* [2013] 1 Lloyds Rep 285 [177]–[179]; *Team Y&R Holdings Hong Kong v Ghossoub* [2017] EWHC 2401 [85]–[88].

[79] Paragraphs 7.29–7.30.

[80] *Michael Wilson v Emmott* [2018] 1 Lloyds Rep 299 [55]–[58] and paras 7.66–7.67.

[81] *Crédit Suisse First Boston (Europe) v MLC (Bermuda)*[1999] 1 Lloyds Rep 767, 778; *National Westminster Bank v Rabobank Nederland (No 1)* [2007] EWHC 1056 [425]–[440]; *National Westminster Bank v Rabobank Nederland (No 3)* [2008] 1 Lloyds Rep 16 (a damages case); *Elektrim v Vivendi Holdings No 1* [2009] 1 Lloyds Rep 59 (CA) [78]–[95]. In *Apple Corps v Apple Computer* [1992] RPC 70, 73, 77, the legality of a 'no challenge' clause in relation to trade marks was disputed.

[82] *Apple Corps v Apple Computer* [1992] RPC 70, 73, 77; *National Westminster Bank v Utrecht-America Finance* [2001] 3 All ER 733 (CA) 739; *Elektrim v Vivendi Holdings No 1 Corp* [2009] 1 Lloyds Rep 59 (CA) [78]–[95]; *Whitesea Shipping & Trading v El Paso Rio Clara (The Marielle Bolten)* [2010] 1 Lloyds Rep 648 [56]–[64]; and see also *Nippon Yusen Kaisha v International Import & Export (The Elbe Maru)* [1978] 1 Lloyds Rep 206.

closely analogous principles, appear to apply.[83] If the English court has finally determined that the foreign proceedings are in breach of an agreement not to sue anywhere in respect of a matter, an injunction will usually be granted to restrain the continuance of those proceedings.[84] Further, a clause by which it is agreed that the only litigation in relation to a matter shall be conducted within a particular action has the understandable purpose of ensuring finality, and will be enforced without hesitation.[85] Similarly, where proceedings have been settled by a settlement agreement under which it is agreed that there will be no further litigation in relation to a dispute, the courts have restrained the pursuit of foreign litigation in breach of the settlement agreement.[86]

6. Challenging the Exclusive Forum Clause

A possible strategy for an injunction defendant confronted with an alleged exclusive jurisdiction clause is to attempt to impeach the validity of the clause itself, or of the contract in which it sits. The issues created by such arguments are most pressing in the context of interim injunctions (to which end they are discussed in Ch 13[87]), but can also arise on the trial of a final injunction, in particular where the claim for a final injunction is heard before the trial of the substantive dispute.   **7.40**

If the exclusive forum clause is contained in a separate contract which can be shown not to be binding, then it will have no contractual force, and thus cannot provide a contractual basis for an anti-suit injunction.[88] But where an exclusive forum clause is part of a broader contract, its validity is 'separable'. A ground of challenge that renders the main contract invalid, void, avoided, or unenforceable does not in itself render the forum clause invalid, unless the challenge either necessarily involves an attack on both the main agreement and the severable forum clause (for example where it is alleged that no contract was ever agreed), or unless the challenge directly and specifically undermines the agreement to the forum clause itself.[89]   **7.41**

There is some authority to suggest that, if the exclusive forum clause is specifically affected by a ground of challenge which justifies voidability, then even if the injunction defendant has not rescinded the contract as a whole, the clause will not be enforced by injunction against him. Either the separable forum clause can be separately rescinded, or its force has   **7.42**

---

[83] *National Westminster Bank v Utrecht-America Finance* [2001] 3 All ER 733 (CA) 744–45 [26]–[35], differing in this respect from *National Westminster Bank v Utrecht-America Finance* [2001] 2 CLC 442 [52]. In *Settlement Corp v Hochschild* [1965] 1 Ch 10, a 'cautious' approach was applied; but this was before the later development of the modern doctrine in *Aggeliki Charis Compania Maritima v Pagnan (The Angelic Grace)* [1995] 1 Lloyds Rep 87 (CA).

[84] *National Westminster Bank v Utrecht-America Finance* [2001] 3 All ER 733 (CA) [31]–[38], [73]–[74]. *National Westminster Bank v Utrecht-America Finance Co* [2001] 2 CLC 442 [49]–[56].

[85] *Royal Exchange Assurance v Compania Naviera Santi (The Tropaioforos) (No 2)* [1962] 1 Lloyds Rep 410.

[86] *Lett v Lett* [1906] 1 IR 618. See also by analogy *Starlight Shipping v Allianz Marine & Aviation Versicherungs (The Alexandros T)* [2014] 2 Lloyds Rep 544 (CA) (a damages claim).

[87] See Ch 13, paras 13.57–13.58.

[88] *Settlement Corp v Hochschild* [1966] 1 Ch 10, 19D–F (although the actual decision on the facts in that case probably would not be followed today); *Harbour Assurance (UK) v Kansa General International Insurance* [1992] 1 Lloyds Rep 81, 86.

[89] *Fiona Trust & Holding v Privalov* [2008] 1 Lloyds Rep 254 (HL) [17]–[19], [33]–[35]; *Deutsche Bank v Asia Pacific Broadband Wireless Communications* [2009] 2 All ER 129 (CA) [24]–[25], [27], [29].

been sufficiently 'impeached' for it not to support a contractual anti-suit injunction on *Angelic Grace* principles.[90]

G. INJUNCTIONS IN SUPPORT OF A FOREIGN FORUM

7.43   The case law has not yet resolved whether, or if so when, the English courts should grant an anti-suit injunction to enforce an exclusive jurisdiction clause in favour of a foreign court or an arbitration clause in favour of an arbitration with a foreign seat.

7.44   The general principle, established in *Airbus v Patel*, is that the English court should have a sufficient interest in or connection with the matter in question to justify the indirect interference with the foreign court which an anti-suit injunction entails.[91] In *Airbus v Patel*, the House of Lords held that the third-party court will usually have no sufficient interest in deciding before which of two foreign courts a matter should be heard, even if the injunction defendant is resident within its territorial jurisdiction, and even if the foreign court which would be most appropriate to hear the substantive case will not be able to grant effective anti-suit relief.[92] Lord Goff expressly observed that he was not reaching any conclusions as to the contractual situation,[93] but this is not a positive conclusion that the principle of sufficient interest does not need to be satisfied where there is a foreign exclusive forum clause. In *CSAV v Hin-Pro* the Court of Appeal of Hong Kong concluded that the requirement of sufficient interest derived from *Airbus* was applicable to, and should discourage, the grant of anti-suit injunctions to enforce a foreign jurisdiction clause, as a matter of comity.[94]

7.45   There is little English case law relating to the problem. David Steel J's reasoning in *The MSC Dymphna* suggests that it was his view that where the English court is a third-party court, it would be inclined not to enforce the foreign exclusive forum clause by injunction.[95] But the point was not explored in any depth.

---

[90] *Donohue v Armco* [1999] 2 Lloyds Rep 649 [34] (Aikens J); the point was not considered on appeal [2000] 1 Lloyds Rep 579 (CA), [2002] 1 Lloyds Rep 425 (HL).

[91] *Airbus Industrie v Patel* [1999] 1 AC 119 (HL) 138–41.

[92] *Airbus Industrie v Patel* [1999] 1 AC 119 (HL) 141A–C. See also *Evialis v SIAT* [2003] 2 Lloyds Rep 377 [139(i)]: 'the English court has no sufficient interest in protecting any interest that Evialis might have to be sued in France rather than Italy to protect it with injunctive relief', where the 'right' in question was a supposed 'right' to be sued in a particular jurisdiction under the Brussels Convention. Where the English court is the chosen court under an exclusive jurisdiction clause, it will *ipso facto* have a sufficient interest.

[93] *Airbus Industrie v Patel* [1999] 1 AC 119 (HL) 138F–G.

[94] *Compania Sudamerica de Vapores v Hin-Pro International Logistics* [2015] HKCA 107 [35]–[64]. This specific point was not disputed on appeal in the Court of Final Appeal [2016] HKCFA 79, which, however, overturned the Court of Appeal on other points, in ways that affect its overall reasoning.

[95] *The Owners of the 'MSC Dymphna' v Agfa-Gevaert NV* (David Steel J, 19 December 2001), where David Steel J held (in an unreserved judgment) that the court had no 'jurisdiction' to grant an injunction restraining proceedings in Belgium once he had held, contrary to the injunction claimant's submissions, that the relevant exclusive jurisdiction clause was actually a clause for exclusive US jurisdiction. The Judge observed that the claimant could apply to the US courts for any injunction.

In *OT Africa Line v Magic Sportswear* [2005] 2 Lloyds Rep 170 (CA) [32], Longmore LJ made *obiter* comments which, at least on one reading, suggest that the English courts will not hesitate to grant injunctions to protect exclusive jurisdiction clauses in favour of third-party courts. But it is doubtful that Longmore LJ was considering the third-party court situation. The case before Longmore LJ involved an exclusive jurisdiction clause in favour of the English courts. The issues of comity involved in interfering on behalf of another court were not considered.

In the unusual case of *A/S D/S Svendborg v Wansa* [1996] 2 Lloyds Rep 559, 563, 575, [1997] 2 Lloyds Rep 183 (CA) 186–88, an injunction was granted to restrain proceedings in Sierra Leone which were in breach of an Estonian exclusive jurisdiction clause. However, the injunction was not granted to force the parties to litigate in *Estonia*, but rather to ensure that the substantive claims were heard in *England* together with other linked substantive claims which

The point has been explored more fully in other common law countries. In *IPOC v CT-*   **7.46**
Mobile the Court of Appeal of Bermuda held that an injunction could be granted to enforce
a Swedish arbitration clause, where the Bermudan courts had personal jurisdiction over
the injunction defendant,[96] and a similar decision was reached by the Eastern Caribbean
Supreme Court in another case.[97]

The Singapore courts have been more reticent. In *People's Insurance v Akai* Mr Judicial   **7.47**
Commissioner Choo Han Teck of the High Court of Singapore dismissed an application for
an anti-suit injunction to restrain proceedings in Australia in order to enforce an English
exclusive jurisdiction clause, saying that the application should be made to the English
court, as 'the Singapore Court should not assume the role of an international busybody',
and 'where there are two courts having jurisdiction a third court with tenuous connection
should not influence the course unless there are strong reasons to do so'.[98] More recently, in
R1 International v Lonstroff, Judith Prakash J, before whom the point was not argued fully
and who was not required to decide it, did not exclude altogether the grant of an injunction to enforce a foreign arbitration clause. Yet she considered that strong reasons would
be required to justify the Singapore courts granting such an injunction, with one possible
situation being where the courts of the arbitration lack the power to grant effective interim
measures in support of arbitration[99] Finally, as noted, in *CSAV v Hin Pro*[100] the Hong Kong
courts concluded that it was necessary for them to have a 'sufficient interest' to grant an
injunction in support of an English jurisdiction clause; but the fact that the injunction defendant was within the territorial grip of the Hong Kong courts and not the English courts,
so that an English injunction would be ineffective or less effective, was not enough.

It is suggested that Mr Judicial Commissioner Choo Han Teck's approach has much to com-   **7.48**
mend it, at least in relation to exclusive jurisdiction clauses in favour of a foreign court and
governed by foreign law. There is no obvious reason why the requirement of a 'sufficient
interest' established in *Airbus v Patel* should not apply in the contractual case. While the
existence of a jurisdiction clause in favour of the English courts or an English arbitration
clause may diminish or even eliminate comity concerns about interfering with litigation in

---

were governed by English exclusive jurisdiction clauses. It could thus be said that the English court did have 'sufficient
interest', because of the intended proceedings before it. Even so, *Svendborg v Wansa* must be viewed as a marginal
decision, arising out of very unusual facts; the injunction defendant had boasted of his ability to subvert the process
of the courts of Sierra Leone: [1996] 2 Lloyds Rep 559, 566, 574, [1997] 2 Lloyds Rep 183 (CA) 188–89. If the parties
have agreed to a jurisdiction other than England, that should be a factor against the grant of an injunction restraining
proceedings in a third country in favour of English proceedings. At the very least, it is unlikely to be right to apply the
Angelic Grace principles without qualification in such a situation (as Clarke J may have done: [1996] 2 Lloyds Rep 559,
568–70, 574–75, since no separate test was articulated for the Estonian situation).

---

[96] *IPOC International Growth Fund v OAO 'CT-Mobile'* (Bermuda CA, 23 March 2007) upholding *OAO 'CT-
Mobile' v IPOC International Growth Fund* (Bermuda SC, 6 October 2006) [105]–[108].
[97] *Finecroft v Lamane Trading* (Eastern Caribbean SC, 6 January 2006). However, *Airbus v Patel* was not referred to and may not have been cited to the court.
[98] *People's Insurance v Akai* [1998] 1 SLR 206 (Sing HC) [12]–[13], quoted with apparent approval in *Akai v
People's Insurance* [1998] 1 Lloyds Rep 90, 108. See the discussion in Ch 19, section G, 'Injunctions in support of
foreign courts and tribunals'.
[99] *R1 International v Lonstroff* [2014] SGHC 69 [53]–[55].
[100] *Compania Sub Americana de Vapores v Hin-Pro International Logistics* [2015] HKCA 107 [35]–[64]. At [64]
the Hong Kong Court of Appeal approved the corresponding passages in the first edition of this work. The point
was not disputed on appeal in the Court of Final Appeal: [2016] HKCFA 79, but that decision overturned the Court
of Appeal on other points, in ways which affect and potentially undermine its overall reasoning.

an 'unchosen' forum, it does not follow that comity becomes irrelevant where the English forum has not itself been chosen.[101]

7.49   For an injunction by a 'third' court to be consistent with comity, there would need to be some factor which gave the third-party court a legitimate interest in intervention. The primary rationale that has been so far articulated in the case law is the overriding importance of the principle of *pacta sunt servanda*. But this creates no specific connection between the third court and the dispute. Further, even if the injunction defendant were resident within the third court's jurisdiction, it is uncertain whether this will be sufficient to justify, as a matter of comity, the indirect interference with the assessment by the other court of whether or not the proceedings before it are in breach of contract or should be stayed. Finally, it is doubtful that it will be sufficient that the contractually chosen court cannot itself grant anti-suit injunctions as a matter of its own law, as arguably this lacuna is part of the 'package' to which the parties have agreed.[102]

7.50   The Commonwealth cases where injunctions in support of a foreign forum have been granted so far all involve foreign arbitration clauses, and it could be argued that concerns about being an 'international busybody' are mitigated where the English court is not intervening to protect another court, but instead in support of an arbitration tribunal that cannot protect itself. Yet it is submitted that the English court, in general, does not have a sufficient interest to intervene by injunction in favour of a foreign arbitration clause. As Judith Prakash J suggested, some other specific good reason should be required to justify intervention.

H. INJUNCTIONS TO ENFORCE ARBITRATION CLAUSES

7.51   The effect of the case law, in summary, is that the *Angelic Grace* principles apply in much the same fashion to injunctions brought to enforce arbitration clauses and to those brought to enforce exclusive jurisdiction clauses.[103] Foreign substantive proceedings which are brought in breach of an agreement to arbitrate in England will therefore be restrained by injunction, unless there are 'strong reasons' not to do so. The one significant difference is that, in the arbitration context, the court must exercise sensitivity to the role of the arbitrators, and whether or not they are better placed to intervene.[104] But in general the court is not dissuaded from the grant of anti-suit injunctions by the overlapping role of the arbitrators, and anti-suit injunctions are frequently granted to protect arbitration.

---

[101] Little consideration appears to have been given to the problem that claiming an injunction from a third-party court may be a breach of the exclusive jurisdiction or arbitration clause itself. In *Akai v People's Insurance* [1998] 1 Lloyds Rep 90, 107, Thomas J was prepared to envisage that a 'justifiable' anti-suit injunction brought before the courts of Singapore to enforce an English exclusive jurisdiction clause 'might not' have been a breach of the clause, but this is not the last word. The somewhat parallel issues arising in relation to arbitration clauses are discussed at paras 7.55–7.58.

[102] See *West Tankers v Ras Riunione Adriatica di Sicurta (The Front Comor)* [2007] 1 Lloyds Rep 391 (HL) [17]–[18] and, in a different context, *The Bergen (No 2)* [1997] 2 Lloyds Rep 710, 718. In addition, if under the proper law of the clause anti-suit injunctions cannot be granted, it can be argued that the *lex fori* should not depart from the law of the contract in this respect: see paras 7.11–7.12.

[103] Paragraph 7.21.

[104] Paragraphs 7.21 and 7.65.

The issues arising from the interplay between the role of the court, the role of the arbitrators, **7.52** and the arbitration clause, will be considered in the following sections, which address in particular the following linked questions: (1) Does arbitration law or the arbitration clause itself preclude the grant of anti-suit injunctions by the court?; (2) What powers do the arbitrators have to grant anti-suit injunctions and when should they be exercised?; and (3) How should the arbitrators' role shape the parameters of when the court should and should not intervene?

We also discuss two other issues specific to the arbitration context: (4) injunctions sought **7.53** to protect arbitrations from vexatious relitigation of, or collateral attacks on, the arbitration process; and (5) injunctions to protect the English court's supervisory jurisdiction over the arbitration.

1. Does Arbitration Law or the Arbitration Clause Preclude an Anti-Suit Injunction?

The power to grant final[105] anti-suit injunctions to enforce arbitration clauses by restraining **7.54** court proceedings or arbitrations abroad[106] is contained in section 37(1) of the Senior Courts Act 1981.[107]

This power is not excluded by section 1 of the Arbitration Act 1996, which provides that the **7.55** courts 'should not intervene' in arbitrations. Section 1 provides guidance, rather than a jurisdictional restriction, and an anti-suit injunction to restrain the pursuit of other proceedings does not 'intervene' in the arbitration it seeks to protect.[108]

The grant of anti-suit injunctions by the court to protect arbitration clauses is also consistent **7.56** with, and not precluded by, the contractual agreement to submit disputes to arbitration, even if that agreement is worded in broad terms.[109] Anti-suit injunctions have frequently been granted to enforce arbitration clauses.

---

[105] Interim injunctions to enforce arbitration clauses are also granted under s 37 Senior Courts Act 1981, and not under s 44 Arbitration Act 1996: Ch 13, paras 13.10–13.12.

[106] Injunctions to restrain arbitrations in England are discussed in Ch 11, section A, 'Introduction'. They will generally be granted, if at all, under s 72 of the Arbitration Act 1996.

[107] *Welex v Rosa Maritime (The Epsilon Rosa) (No 2)* [2003] 2 Lloyds Rep 509 (CA) [40]; *West Tankers v Ras Riunione Adriatica di Sicurta (The Front Comor)* [2007] 1 Lloyds Rep 391 (HL) [10]; *Starlight Shipping v Tai Ping Insurance (The Alexandros T)* [2008] 1 Lloyds Rep 230 [16]; *Nomihold Securities v Mobile Telesystems Finance* [2012] 1 Lloyds Rep 442 [25]; *AES Ust-Kamenogorsk Hydropower Plant LLP v Ust-Kamenogorsk Hydropower Plant JSC* [2013] 1 WLR 1889 (SC) [48], [55]–[59]; *Southport Success v Tsingshan Holding Group* [2015] 2 Lloyds Rep 578 [19]–[25]; *Nori Holding v Bank Otkritie Financial Corporation* [2018] 2 Lloyds Rep 80 [28].

[108] *Steamship Mutual Underwriting Association (Bermuda) v Sulpicio Lines* [2008] 2 Lloyds Rep 269 [28]; *Nomihold Securities v Mobile Telesystems Finance* [2012] 1 Lloyds Rep 442 [25]; *AES Ust-Kamenogorsk Hydropower Plant LLP v Ust-Kamenogorsk Hydropower Plant JSC* [2013] 1 WLR 1889 (SC) [31]–[41], [55]–[62]; recently *HC Trading Malta v Tradeland Commodities* [2016] 1 Lloyds Rep 3120 [18] and *Starlight Shipping v Tai Ping Insurance (The Alexandros T)* [2008] 1 Lloyds Rep 230 [43]. Consequently, applications under s 9 of the Arbitration Act 1996 to stay claims for such anti-suit injunctions will fail: *Sheffield United FC v West Ham United FC* [2009] 1 Lloyds Rep 167 [37]–[41]; *Nomihold*, at [33]–[49].

However, for arguments that Article 5 of the UNCITRAL Model Law (and thus, by inference, its partial implementation in s 1 of the 1996 Act) should be read to preclude anti-suit injunctions to enforce an arbitration clause, see F Bachand, 'The UNCITRAL Model Law's Take on Anti-Suit Injunctions' in E Gaillard (ed), *Anti-Suit Injunctions in International Arbitration* (Juris 2005) 87 (hereafter 'Gaillard (2005)').

[109] *BNP Paribas v Russian Machines* [2012] 1 Lloyds Rep 61 [39]–[40] and [2012] 1 Lloyds Rep 649 (CA) [46], where the Court of Appeal said that there was 'neither dispute nor doubt' on the question; *Sheffield United FC v West Ham United FC* [2009] 1 Lloyds Rep 167 [39]–[40]; *Nomihold Securities v Mobile Telesystems Finance* [2012] 1 Lloyds Rep 442 [46]–[47]; and *Toepfer International v Société Cargill France* [1997] 2 Lloyds Rep 98, 107,

7.57 However, although the result is clear, the exact juridical rationale has been more trouble-some. In *Toepfer v Cargill* the Court of Appeal had, in *obiter* comments, justified the grant of anti-suit injunctions by the court to enforce an arbitration clause by saying that, as a matter of construction, claims for an anti-suit injunction to enforce the arbitration clause itself do not *fall within* the scope of even a broadly worded arbitration clause.[110] However, if a claim that foreign proceedings are in breach of an arbitration clause did not fall within the scope of the agreement to arbitrate, there would be surprising and unfortunate side effects. It would preclude arbitrators from granting a declaration that a given claim brought in a foreign court fell within the scope of the arbitration clause, or from awarding damages for breach of the clause; and it would also prevent arbitrators issuing final anti-suit injunctions themselves under section 48(5) of the Arbitration Act 1996. This is not the law.[111]

7.58 Instead, it is submitted that the correct analysis is as follows. While claims that foreign pro-ceedings are in breach of the obligation to arbitrate do generally fall within the scope of ar-bitration clauses, nevertheless, when contracting for arbitration in England under English law on normally worded arbitration clauses, the parties will generally be taken to have ac-cepted that the usual ancillary proceedings may also be brought before the English court (as the natural supervisory court) to assist and protect the arbitration. The permitted an-cillary proceedings will include claims for an anti-suit injunction,[112] and also a claim for a

---

[1998] 1 Lloyds Rep 379 (CA) 384–85, where the argument that an anti-suit injunction was precluded by the arbitration clause itself was described as 'a submission not lacking in effrontery', given that it came from a party who was himself in breach of the clause. Any suggestion that the arbitration clause itself precludes the grant of an anti-suit injunction to enforce it would also be inconsistent with the result in *AES Ust-Kamenogorsk Hydropower Plant LLC v Ust-Kamenogorsk Hydropower Plant JSC* [2013] 1 WLR 1889 (SC), where (although this particular point does not seem to have been taken) the ability to grant anti-suit injunctions to enforce an arbitration clause was resoundingly affirmed.

The analogous submission that a freezing injunction was also precluded by an arbitration clause in normal wording was also unsurprisingly rejected: *In Re Q's Estate* [1999] 1 Lloyds Rep 931, 933–38.

---

[110] *Toepfer International v Société Cargill France* [1998] 1 Lloyds Rep 379 (CA) 384–85, where the clause referred to arbitration of 'all disputes arising out of or under this contract'. The Court of Appeal referred the question to the ECJ, but the case settled before the reference was determined.

The two main reasons given by the Court of Appeal in *Toepfer v Cargill* do not seem to be valid under the Arbitration Act 1996 (which was not yet in force when it was decided). First, Phillips LJ argued that the issues arising on an injunction would probably be issues as to the arbitrators' jurisdiction, which are not suitable issues for the arbitrators to determine (at 385). But under the Arbitration Act 1996, ss 30–31, it is the general position that arbitrators can determine their own jurisdiction. Second, Phillips LJ suggested that an anti-suit injunction does not fall within the relief which arbitrators are in a position to provide (at 385). But that is not the modern law under the Arbitration Act 1996: see paras 7.59–7.64.

There was also an earlier line of authority in which it was held, in a yet broader approach, that even broadly worded arbitration clauses only applied to substantive 'proceedings to establish liability': *Mike Trading and Transport v R Pagnan & Fratelli (The Lisboa)* [1980] 2 Lloyds Rep 546 (CA) 548, per Lord Denning MR; *Toepfer International v Société Cargill France* [1997] 2 Lloyds Rep 98, 107 (Colman J). However, these decisions are not binding precedent: in *The Lisboa* only Lord Denning MR actually held this (at 548); the other two Lords Justices concluded only that the point was arguable (at 550–51). It is respectfully submitted that this approach is too broad, as the Court of Appeal in *Toepfer v Cargill* suggested (at 385). It would mean, for example, that arbitrators could not themselves grant anti-suit injunctions.

[111] It is generally accepted that damages can be awarded, including by arbitrators, for breaches of arbitration clauses committed by bringing proceedings in a foreign jurisdiction: *Mantovani v Carapelli* [1980] 1 Lloyds Rep 375 (CA) 381–84; London Arbitration 8/04, LMLN 14 April 2004; London Arbitration 11/06 (2006) 697 LMLN 2; *CMA CGM v Hyundai Mipo Dockyard* [2009] 1 Lloyds Rep 213 [10], [39]–[40] (point unchallenged); *West Tankers v Allianz (The Front Comor)* [2012] 2 Lloyds Rep 103 (where the point may not have been contested under English law). See also the difficult authority of *Sokana Industries v Freyre* [1994] 2 Lloyds Rep 57, 64, 66. Further, arbitrators do have the power to grant anti-suit awards: see paras 7.59–7.64. For further discussion, see Ch 14, para 14.04.

[112] And also, declarations as to the meaning and effect of an award: see *Noble Assurance v Gerling-Konzern General Insurance* [2008] Lloyds Rep IR 1 [97].

declaration as to the binding force of the arbitration clause,[113] so that bringing such claims before the English court is therefore not a breach of normal broadly worded arbitration clauses choosing London arbitration. This construction, or implied term, operates as an exception to the general scope of the arbitration clause, and permits the court and the arbitrators to exercise a concurrent jurisdiction. This line of analysis, as advanced in the first edition of this work, has been approved by the courts on two occasions, in *Sheffield United v West Ham* and *Nomihold v Mobile Telesystems*.[114]

2. Can an Anti-Suit Injunction be Sought from the Arbitrators?

Despite earlier but now outdated hesitation, it is now clear that arbitrators who have been granted jurisdiction by an arbitration agreement subject to English law have the power to grant anti-suit awards to enforce the arbitration agreement.   **7.59**

First, it is now clear that the arbitration agreement contains a negative contractual obligation not to litigate elsewhere,[115] and there is no good reason why arbitrators cannot enforce that obligation. Second, under section 48(5) of the Arbitration Act 1996, 'the tribunal has the same powers as the court—(a) to order a party to do or refrain from doing anything', and so since the court has power to grant final anti-suit relief, the arbitrators have a parallel power.[116] Third, it is arguable that the power to grant anti-suit awards or similar   **7.60**

---

[113] See Ch 15, paras 15.21–15.33.

[114] *Sheffield United FC v West Ham United FC* [2009] 1 Lloyds Rep 167 [39]–[40]; *Nomihold Securities v Mobile Telesystems Finance* [2012] 1 Lloyds Rep 442 [46]–[47]. See also earlier *Comdel Commodities v Siporex* [1997] 1 Lloyds Rep 424 at 425–29 and *Re Q's Estate* [1999] 1 Lloyds Rep 931, 937. It is submitted that it is also supported by the *obiter* discussion in *Toepfer International v Société Cargill France* [1998] 1 Lloyds Rep 379 (CA) 381–85, despite the contrary views of Flaux J in *B v S* [2011] 2 Lloyds Rep 18 [51]–[57]. In *BNP Paribas v Russian Machines* [2012] 1 Lloyds Rep 61 [39]–[40], where an interim injunction was sought under s 44 of the Arbitration Act 1996, Blair J reached a similar result on the basis that the court's statutory powers to support an arbitration under s 44 were not removed by an agreement to arbitrate in normal wording; and also relied on the fact that the arbitrator had given permission for the application for an injunction to be made to the court. It is suggested that Blair J's reasoning is consistent with, and can be seen as a specific example of, the analysis here. (On appeal, [2012] 1 Lloyds Rep 649 (CA) [25], [79] the Court of Appeal recorded that it was not disputed that the arbitration clause did not remove the power to grant the injunction, but did not analyse the juridical basis of that position.) Further, this approach is consistent with the principle in *C v D* [2007] 2 Lloyds Rep 367, [2008] 1 Lloyds Rep 239 (CA) (discussed at paras 7.68–7.70), under which the supervisory court of the seat has a special role in granting ancillary relief.

The reasoning of Flaux J in *B v S* [2011] 2 Lloyds Rep 18 is not wholly consistent with this logic. He concluded that a *Scott v Avery* arbitration clause (which precludes 'any action or other legal proceedings' before the arbitration award) prevented not only substantive proceedings but also ancillary proceedings for security, and he did not accept that there was a distinction between ancillary proceedings before the English courts and foreign courts. However, he was not concerned with anti-suit injunctions; and to the extent necessary, it is submitted that the analysis herein is to be preferred, at least in respect of arbitration clauses in normal wording, and at least so far as regards anti-suit injunctions. Indeed, in *Toepfer v Cargill*, both Colman J and the Court of Appeal firmly concluded that a *Scott v Avery* clause should not preclude the grant of an anti-suit injunction to enforce and protect the arbitration clause: *Toepfer International v Société Cargill France* [1997] 2 Lloyds Rep 98, 107, [1998] 1 Lloyds Rep 379 (CA) 384–85.

It can also be noted that in *Akai v People's Insurance* [1998] 1 Lloyds Rep 90, 107, Thomas J was prepared to envisage that a 'justifiable' anti-suit injunction brought before the courts of Singapore to enforce an English exclusive jurisdiction clause 'might not' have been a breach of the clause.

[115] *AES Ust-Kamenogorsk Hydropower Plant LLC v Ust-Kamenogorsk Hydropower Plant JSC* [2013] 1 WLR 1889 (SC) [1], [21]–[23], [24].

[116] *Welex v Rosa Maritime (The Epsilon Rosa)* [2003] 2 Lloyds Rep 509 (CA) [35]; *AES Ust-Kamenogorsk Hydropower Plant LLC v Ust-Kamenogorsk Hydropower Plant JSC* [2013] 1 WLR 1889 (SC) [40].

For the (incorrect) argument that the wording of s 48(5), which derives the arbitrators' powers from the court's powers, might limit the power to grant anti-suit awards where the court is prevented from granting an injunction by the Brussels–Lugano regime, see Ch 12, paras 12.52–12.55.

protective orders is inherent in the arbitrators' powers to control their own proceedings.[117] Consequently, arbitrators have the power to make a final[118] anti-suit award as regards matters within their jurisdiction.[119]

7.61   This may not have been the position before the Arbitration Act 1996. At that time, it was unclear whether arbitrators could grant any injunctions,[120] a problem section 48(5) was included to correct. Further, in the pre-1996 Act case law the courts had suggested that arbitrators could not grant anti-suit injunctions, although the issue had not been fully thought through.[121] But in the case law under the 1996 Act, it has been held without question that arbitrators do have such a power.[122]

7.62   Some scholars from civil law systems have contended that arbitrators do not have the power to grant anti-suit injunctions, on the basis that in their domestic systems the arbitration

---

[117] See R Moloo, 'Arbitrators Granting Antisuit Orders: When Should They and on What Authority?' (2009) 26 J Intl Arb 676, 678–81 and Ch 12, para 12.56.

[118] It appears that the combined effect of ss 39 and 48(5) of the 1996 Act is that arbitrators do not have power to grant *interim* injunctions absent express provision in the arbitration agreement or institutional rules: *Starlight Shipping v Tai Ping Insurance Co (The Alexandros T)* [2008] 1 Lloyds Rep 230 [20], [26]. However, the issue may not matter that much as the flexibility of arbitration procedure means the difference between final and interim proceedings is fluid. Further, many of the major institutional arbitration rules will contain powers to grant interim measures which can be construed to cover powers to make interim anti-suit awards: see M Black and R Reece 'Anti-Suit Injunctions and Arbitration Proceedings' (2006) 72 Arbitration 207, 213. For example, there is scope to grant such orders under the ICC Rules, Article 23. However, an interim decision by arbitrators may well not be an enforceable award under the New York Convention: see *Starlight Shipping v Tai Ping Insurance (The Alexandros T)* [2008] 1 Lloyds Rep 230 [26].

[119] See paras 7.34–7.38.

[120] Departmental Advisory Committee on Arbitration Law Report on the Arbitration Bill, February 1996 (hereafter 'DAC Report'), para 234 and Ch 12, para 12.56 n 81.

[121] In *Tracomin v Sudan Oil Seeds Co (Nos 1 and 2)* [1983] 1 WLR 1026 (CA) 1036–37, the Court of Appeal considered that it was a strong factor in favour of the grant of an anti-suit injunction to restrain proceedings brought in breach of the arbitration clause before the Swiss courts, that if the injunction were not granted, and the Swiss courts gave judgment on the claim, the Federation of Oils, Seeds & Fats Associations (FOSFA) arbitrators would have to decide whether the Swiss courts' judgment was right or wrong. The Court of Appeal considered that this would be a 'rather unseemly spectacle', 'and one which neither these courts, nor the Swiss courts if they were in a position to consider the matter, could contemplate with any degree of equanimity whatsoever'. In *Toepfer International v Société Cargill France* 1997] 2 Lloyds Rep 98, 107 and [1998] 1 Lloyds Rep 379 (CA) 385 both Colman J and the Court of Appeal thought that an anti-suit injunction was not within the relief that arbitrators are in a position to provide. However, this case appears to have been decided under the pre-1996 Act law.

[122] *Steamship Mutual Underwriting Association (Bermuda) v Sulpicio Lines* [2008] 2 Lloyds Rep 269 [28] (an uncontested hearing); *Welex v Rosa Maritime (The Epsilon Rosa)* [2003] 2 Lloyds Rep 509 (CA) [35]; *AES Ust-Kamenogorsk Hydropower Plant LLC v Ust-Kamenogorsk Hydropower Plant JSC* [2013] 1 WLR 1889 (SC) [40]; *Nori Holding Limited v Bank Otkritie Financial Corporation* [2018] 2 Lloyds Rep 80 [35]. There are many cases where the existence of the arbitrators' power is assumed (see eg *Southport Success v Tsingshan Holding Group* [2015] 2 Lloyds Rep 578 [27]).

In support of the existence of the power, see S Dutson and M Howarth, 'After West Tankers—Rise of the "Foreign Torpedo"' (2009) 75 Arbitration 334, 345.

However, Professor Charles Debattista has suggested (relying on *Kastner v Jason* [2005] 1 Lloyds Rep 397 (CA) [16]) that, as the arbitrators' powers under s 48(5) of the 1996 Act are confined to 'substantive awards', the powers thereby conferred cannot extend to anti-suit injunctions: see C Debattista, 'Arbitrators' Powers to Order Interim Measures Including Anti-Suit Injunctions' (2010) 76 Arbitration 421, 425. It is respectfully submitted that this does not follow. *Kastner v Jason* held only that s 48(5) was confined to 'final awards and substantive remedies on the merits'—which it was held did not include a freezing injunction. It is indeed correct that s 48(5) does not give power for an *interim* anti-suit award to be made by arbitrators. But there is no doubt that (as discussed in Ch 3 of this work) anti-suit injunctions can be granted by the court by way of final relief. In the circumstances, there is no reason why they should not be awarded by way of final award by arbitrators under the powers conferred by s 48(5).

For the (incorrect) argument that the wording of s 48(5), which derives the arbitrators' powers from the court's powers, might limit the power to grant anti-suit awards where the court is prevented from granting an injunction by the Brussels–Lugano regime, see Ch 12, paras 12.52–12.56.

agreement is given a procedural classification.[123] However, this misses the point: an arbitrator whose powers are conferred by English arbitration law as the applicable law of an English arbitration agreement will have the powers that English contract law confers.

The grant of anti-suit injunctions or equivalent awards by arbitration tribunals was in the past relatively uncommon. There were perhaps three main reasons for this: first, the relative powerlessness of an 'anti-suit award', which in itself merely creates a contractual obligation and does not give rise to a contempt of court sanctions, in contrast to a court injunction; second, a lingering perception that it was somehow inappropriate for arbitrators, as opposed to courts, to interfere indirectly with foreign judicial systems in this way; third, to international arbitrators with a civilian education, an anti-suit injunction was a strange and foreign remedy. **7.63**

However, the situation has changed. There is a growing number of recent reported decisions where arbitrators have granted anti-suit or equivalent relief.[124] Arbitrators from non-common law jurisdictions have become more comfortable with the remedy. Such orders are now sought and granted with some frequency in practice.[125] **7.64**

3. Sensitivity to the Arbitrators' Role

In *AES Ust-Kamenogorsk*, the Supreme Court made clear that the power to grant final or interim anti-suit injunctions under section 37(1) of the Senior Courts Act 'must be exercised sensitively and, in particular, with due regard for the scheme and terms of the 1996 Act when any arbitration is on foot or proposed'. In appropriate cases, this could require consideration of whether the arbitrators are better placed to grant any necessary final anti-suit relief, or whether the relief granted by the court should only be interim pending further **7.65**

---

[123] L Levy, 'Anti-Suit Injunctions Issued by Arbitrators' in Gaillard (2005), 115; P Ortolani, 'Anti-Suit Injunctions in Support of Arbitration under the Recast Brussels I Regulation', Max Planck Institute Working Paper 6 (2015) 11–12.

[124] A striking recent example is the arbitral anti-suit award held to be consistent with EU law in the ECJ's decision in Case C-536/61, *Gazprom OAO*, EU:C:2015:316, AG [37], [63]–[67], ECJ [18], [38]–[40]. L Mistelis and J Lew, *Pervasive Problems in International Arbitration* (Kluwer 2006) paras 10.2–10.13, refer to the 'spectacular development' of such awards, and discuss various cases. For discussion of a number of ICC arbitration awards granting or refusing anti-suit injunctions, see M Scherer and W Jahnel, 'Anti-Suit and Anti-Arbitration Injunctions in International Arbitration: A Swiss Perspective' [2009] Int ALR 66, 70–73 and 'Procedural Decisions in ICC Arbitration: Anti-Suit/Anti-Arbitration Injunctions' [2014] ICC Court of Arbitration Bulletin Vol 24, Suppl. Numerous anti-suit awards have been granted by ICSID tribunals, and by the Iran–US claims tribunal: see D Joseph QC, *Jurisdiction and Arbitration Agreements and their Enforcement* (3rd edn, Sweet & Maxwell 2015) paras 12.149–12.169 (hereafter 'Joseph').

For general discussion, see E Gaillard, 'Anti-Suit Injunctions Issued by Arbitrators' in *International Arbitration 2006: Back to Basics*, ICCA series no 13, at 235ff; M Black and R Reece, 'Anti-Suit Injunctions and Arbitration Proceedings' (2006) 72 Arbitration 3, 207, 213–14 (supporting the grant of anti-suit injunctions by arbitrators); T Landau, ' "Arbitral Lifelines": The Protection of Jurisdiction by Arbitrators' in *International Arbitration 2006: Back to Basics*, ICCA series no 13, at 282ff (arguing that arbitrators should grant relief of this type but that it should be conceptualized and structured differently to court injunctions); L Levy, 'Anti-Suit Injunctions Issued by Arbitrators' in Gaillard (2005), at 115ff; R Moloo, 'Arbitrators Granting Antisuit Orders: When Should They and on What Authority' (2009) 26 J Intl Arb 676. In 2004, the Uncitral Working Group on arbitration proposed that the Model Law be amended to give some recognition to anti-suit awards: see UNCITRAL Working Group on Arbitration, 'Report of the Working Group on Arbitration 40th Session', A/CN.9/547 (23–February 2004) paras 76–83, www.uncitral.org.

[125] This is the lesson of experience. See also 'Procedural Decisions in ICC Arbitration: Anti-Suit/Anti-Arbitration Injunctions' [2014] ICC Court of Arbitration Bulletin Vol 24, Suppl, 5.

awards by the arbitrators.[126] However, the existence of the arbitrators' overlapping powers to grant anti-suit awards has not in general led the courts to refrain from granting final, or indeed interim, anti-suit injunctions.[127] The court's power to grant injunctions can achieve results an award by arbitrators will not, because it is directly backed by punishment for contempt of court if breached,[128] and because in cases where anti-suits are relevant, the injunction respondent will usually be contesting the jurisdiction of the tribunal. As the Court of Appeal put it in *Wilson v Emmott*, the English court is 'the judicial guardian of the integrity of an arbitral process in London'.[129] In *Nori v Otkritie*, Males J concluded that availability of anti-suit relief from the arbitration tribunal did not affect the basic principle that, absent strong reasons to the contrary, an anti-suit injunction would ordinarily be granted by the court to enforce the arbitration clause.[130]

4. Injunctions to Restrain Relitigation of, or Collateral Attacks on, Arbitration

7.66   The court will grant injunctions to restrain proceedings which are a vexatious relitigation of matters decided in arbitration or a vexatious collateral attack on the arbitration process or the arbitration awards.[131] Injunctions on this ground can be granted even if the foreign litigation does not itself breach the arbitration clause, in which case they will be non-contractual injunctions justified on general principles, such as vexation, independent of the contractual logic of *The Angelic Grace*.[132]

7.67   However, in many cases foreign litigation which does amount to vexatious relitigation will also fall within the arbitration clause. Further, it may also be possible to view vexatious relitigation of the arbitration or a collateral attack on the arbitration as conduct which breaches obligations emanating from the arbitration clause or implied terms thereof, although the law is undeveloped in this regard, and the boundaries of any such terms are not yet clear. Thus, in one undefended case, conduct which was vexatious relitigation was also

---

[126]   *AES Ust-Kamenogorsk Hydropower Plant LLC v Ust-Kamenogorsk Hydropower Plant JSC* [2013] 1 WLR 1889 (SC) [60].

[127]   See *Nori Holding v Bank Otkritie Financial Corporation* [2018] 2 Lloyds Rep 80 [32]–[42]. For another recent example of final anti-suit relief to support an arbitration, see *Mobile Telecommunications v Prince Hussam bin Saud bin Abdulaziz bin Saud* [2018] 2 Lloyds Rep 192 [18], [20].
Similarly, the arbitrators' coeval powers have not discouraged the court from granting interim anti-suit injunctions: see Ch 13, paras 13.13–13.15.

[128]   The availability of the circuitous route of requiring a party to get an anti-suit award from the arbitrators, then enforcing it as a judgment of the court under s 66 of the Arbitration Act 1966, and then using the court's contempt jurisdiction to enforce that subsequent judgment, was not regarded as appealing, or an answer, by the Supreme Court in *Ust-Kamenogorsk*. Instead, it was better for the court to grant any necessary injunction directly: *AES Ust-Kamenogorsk Hydropower Plant LLC v Ust-Kamenogorsk Hydropower Plant JSC* [2013] 1 WLR 1889 (SC) [40]–[41].

[129]   *Michael Wilson v Emmott* [2018] 1 Lloyds Rep 299 [55].

[130]   *Nori Holding Limited v Bank Otkritie Financial Corporation* [2018] 2 Lloyds Rep 80 [32]–[42].

[131]   *Michael Wilson v Emmott* [2018] 1 Lloyds Rep 299 [55]–[58], in part upholding *Emmott v Michael Wilson* [2017] 1 Lloyds Rep 21 [57]–[59], [62]. See also *Noble Assurance v Gerling-Konzern General Insurance* [2008] Lloyds Rep IR 1 [95]; *Nomihold Securities v Mobile Telesystems Finance* [2012] 1 Lloyds Rep 442 [42]–[43], [63] (injunction rejected on the facts; reasoning rather confused); *Midgulf International v Groupe Chimiche Tunisien* [2010] 2 Lloyds Rep 543 (CA) [52]–[53]; *Crescendo Maritime v Bank of Communications* [2016] 1 Lloyds Rep 414 [50]–[51]; *Mobile Telecommunications v Prince Hussam bin Saud bin Abdulaziz bin Saud* [2018] 2 Lloyds Rep 192 [13].

[132]   See eg *Michael Wilson v Emmott* [2018] 1 Lloyds Rep 299 [41]–[50], [55]–[58].

viewed as a breach of an implied term of the arbitration agreement that the award should be respected and performed, and of the parallel express obligation in the London Court of International Arbitration (LCIA) rules.[133] As these lines of argument develop, non-contractual and contractual justifications for such injunctions may overlap.

5. Injunctions to Protect the Court's Supervisory Jurisdiction

By agreeing to arbitrate in England, the parties have submitted their substantive disputes within the scope of the clause to an arbitration tribunal whose seat will be in England, and have positively accepted the limited supervisory powers of the English courts under the Arbitration Act 1996. In a line of case law made binding precedent by *C v D*, the courts have held that by doing so the parties have also implicitly agreed to accept the *exclusive* supervisory jurisdiction of the English courts, creating an obligation 'analogous to an exclusive jurisdiction clause' so that attempts to engage the supervisory jurisdiction of other national courts will be a breach of contract,[134] and can be restrained by a contractual anti-suit injunction.[135] In some cases, the argument can be reinforced by institutional rules or terms of the arbitration agreement which require the parties to respect the award or preclude court challenges to awards.[136] This contractual line of justification involves an adventurous use of implied terms, but is established by precedent at the Court of Appeal level. In the past, injunctions have been granted to protect English arbitrations from wrongful supervisory interference by foreign courts, on grounds of vexation and oppression, without reliance on an implied contractual agreement that the English courts would have exclusive supervisory powers.[137] Such cases might now be analysed differently in terms of this new implied contractual obligation.   **7.68**

The scope of such a principle, if it exists, is inherently limited, as implied terms can be stretched only so far. On the current case law it appears to cover at least attempts to ask a foreign court to exercise a supervisory or appellate jurisdiction in competition with the powers conferred on the English courts in sections 67–69 of the Arbitration Act 1996,[138] and applications for other supervisory relief such as applications to remove an arbitrator on grounds of bias.[139] But it should not prevent a party from resisting enforcement of an award   **7.69**

---

[133] *Mobile Telecommunications v Prince Hussam bin Saud bin Abdulaziz bin Saud* [2018] 2 Lloyds Rep 192 [12]–[13]. See also the rather confused discussion in *Nomihold Securities v Mobile Telesystems Finance* [2012] 1 Lloyds Rep 442 [16], [30]–[31], [50], [62], where arguments along these lines were viewed as strongly arguable; the undeveloped one-sentence comment in *Midgulf International v Groupe Chimiche Tunisien* [2010] 2 Lloyds Rep 543 (CA) [52]; and the analysis in *Dreymoor Fertilisers Overseas v Eurochem Trading* [2018] EWHC 2267 [50], [84]–[85].
[134] *A v B (No 1)* [2007] 1 Lloyds Rep 237 [111(ii)], [112]; *A v B (No 2)* [2007] 1 Lloyds Rep 358 [16]–[19]; *C v D* [2007] 2 Lloyds Rep 367 [27]–[41], [51]–[54], [2008] 1 Lloyds Rep 239 (CA) [16]–[17], [33], followed inter alia in *Shashoua v Sharma* [2009] 2 Lloyds Rep 376 [14], [23], 41], [44]; *Nomihold Securities v Mobile Telesystems Finance* [2012] 1 Lloyds Rep 442 [29]–[31]; *Terna Bahrain Holdings v Al Shamsi* [2013] 1 Lloyds Rep 161 [131]–[135]; *Atlas Power v National Transmission and Despatch* [2018] 2 Lloyds Rep 113.
[135] *C v D* [2007] 2 Lloyds Rep 367, [54]–[58], [2008] 1 Lloyds Rep 239 (CA) [30].
[136] See eg *Nomihold Securities v Mobile Telesystems Finance* [2012] 1 Lloyds Rep 442 [29]–[31], [62], although the reasoning is not clear.
[137] *Tonicstar v American Home Insurance* [2005] Lloyds Rep IR 32; *Noble Assurance v Gerling-Konzern General Insurance* [2008] Lloyds Rep IR 1 [87]–[88], [95], [108].
[138] *C v D* [2007] 2 Lloyds Rep 367 [27]–[41], [51]–[54], [2008] 1 Lloyds Rep 239 (CA) [16]–[17], [33].
[139] *Midgulf International v Groupe Chimiche Tunisien* [2009] 2 Lloyds Rep 984 [59], referring to *Weissfisch v Julius* [2006] 1 Lloyds Rep 716 (CA).

before a foreign court in the normal way, even if that involves a contention that the award is unenforceable.[140]

7.70   Further, it is submitted that the *C v D* principle probably does not mean that normally worded arbitration clauses will preclude applications for interim relief to foreign courts in support of the arbitration. They may give implied exclusive supervisory jurisdiction, but that is not the same as exclusive supportive jurisdiction. So the most persuasive recent first instance decisions suggest that applications for interim relief in support of the arbitration in foreign courts are not precluded by any implied term of the arbitration agreement,[141] save perhaps where they amount to a collateral attack on the arbitration clause,[142] and instead should be regulated where necessary by non-contractual principles for anti-suit injunctions such as vexation and oppression. Some first instance decisions so far have suggested that applications for interim relief to a court other than the court of the seat should not be permitted save in 'exceptional' circumstances.[143] It is submitted that this goes too far. In general, the court of the seat will have the primary supportive role, and will be the most appropriate forum for interim relief in support of the arbitration.[144] In turn, if another court is not an appropriate forum, this will be a factor in support of a finding that seeking interim relief there is vexatious and oppressive. But it is too rigid to suggest that, outside 'exceptional circumstances', seeking relief before another court is inappropriate; and formulation of a contractual implied term along these lines would be difficult to justify on standard contractual logic.

I. FOREIGN PROCEEDINGS TO OBTAIN SECURITY

7.71   If the sole purpose of the foreign proceedings is to obtain security for a substantive claim to be brought in the agreed forum, the court will not normally grant an injunction to restrain their pursuit.[145] The pragmatic reason for this is obvious. Where a defendant's assets are

---

[140]   See by reverse analogy *HJ Heinz v EFL* [2010] 2 Lloyds Rep 727 [22].

[141]   *U&M Mining Zambia v Konkola Copper Mines* [2013] 2 Lloyds Rep 281 [56]–[61]; and see also *Toepfer International v Société Cargill France* [1997] 2 Lloyds Rep 98, 107–08. In *Evergreen Marine (Singapore) v Fast Shipping & Transportation* [2014] EWHC 4893 (QB) [9]–[12], Leggatt J suggested that the *C v D* principle did apply to prevent applications for interim relief being made to foreign courts other than the court of the seat—save in a wide range of supposedly 'exceptional' cases where it would be appropriate—but the point was not contested. Further, the court's reasoning appears to be based on a misinterpretation of the previous case law, which was not reasoned in contractual terms: neither *U&M Mining v Konkola* nor *Orient Express Lines (Singapore) v Peninsular Shipping Services* [2013] EWHC 3855 [23] framed matters in contractual terms. With respect, it is submitted that *Evergreen* is an illegitimate extension of the *C v D* principle and not reconcilable with normal contractual logic.

[142]   *Nomihold Securities v Mobile Telesystems Finance* [2012] 1 Lloyds Rep 442 [29]–[31]; although it may be better to rationalize such cases in terms of vexation and oppression: see eg *Noble Assurance v Gerling-Konzern General Insurance* [2008] Lloyds Rep IR 1 [28].

[143]   *Orient Express Lines (Singapore) v Peninsular Shipping Services* [2013] EWHC 3855, [23], purporting to apply *U&M Mining Zambia v Konkola Copper Mines* [2013] 2 Lloyds Rep 281 [63]; and *Evergreen Marine (Singapore) v Fast Shipping & Transportation* [2014] EWHC 4893 (QB) [9]–[12], applying *Orient Express* in turn. However, it is submitted that the *U&M Mining* case is actually more nuanced and does not support any more definitive rule other than the proposition that the court of the seat has the primary supportive role: see at [64]. This is the better approach.

[144]   *Econet Wireless v Vee Networks* [2006] 2 Lloyds Rep 428, [19]; *U&M Mining Zambia v Konkola Copper Mines* [2013] 2 Lloyds Rep 281 [63]–[64].

[145]   *Marazura Navegacion v Oceanus Mutual Underwriting Association (Bermuda)*[1977] 1 Lloyds Rep 283; *Mike Trading and Transport v R Pagnan & Fratelli (The Lisboa)* [1980] 2 Lloyds Rep 546 (CA); *Petromin v Secnav Marine* [1995] 1 Lloyds Rep 603, 613; *Ispat Industries v Western Bulk* [2011] EWHC 93 [41]–[45]; *Sam Purpose v Transnav Purpose Navigation (The Sam Purpose)* [2017] 2 Lloyds Rep 50 [24]–[30].

located outside the jurisdiction, security can often only be obtained effectively by application to the foreign court. However, the jurisprudential rationale for the court's approach needs some tidying up.

The case law has historically been troubled by the effects of the decision in *Mantovani v*   **7.72**
Carapelli, where it was held that proceedings brought before the Italian courts for security had been in breach of the arbitration clause, and therefore gave rise to a liability in damages,[146] even though the clause made no specific reference to prohibiting ancillary proceedings such as claims for security. However, the Court of Appeal's approach to construction in *Mantovani v Carapelli* depended on the presence of a *Scott v Avery* clause,[147] which prohibited any 'action *or other legal proceedings*' before the giving of the arbitration award.[148] It is also possible that the Court of Appeal's decision should be read only to apply to extreme measures such as the burdensome order for the sequestration of assets which had been obtained from the Italian courts in that case.[149]

In most of the subsequent case law, *Mantovani v Carapelli* has been distinguished. It is con-   **7.73**
fined to the unusual, and very broad, wording of *Scott v Avery* clauses, which have been held to exclude even applications for security to the English courts as the courts of the seat.[150] But in contrast, the modern case law suggests that arbitration clauses on normal wordings will be read to permit foreign proceedings for security only, provided that they are truly ancillary to, and assist, and do not hamper, the substantive proceedings in the chosen forum.[151]

---

[146] *Mantovani v Carapelli* [1978] 2 Lloyds Rep 63, 72–73, [1980] 1 Lloyds Rep 375 (CA) 381–84. No injunction had been sought.
[147] The clause was clause 26 of Contract 119 of the Grain and Feed Trade Association ('GAFTA') and provided:

   (a) Any dispute arising out of or under this contract shall be settled by arbitration in London in accordance with the Arbitration Rules [of GAFTA] ... (b) neither party hereto, nor any persons claiming under either of them, shall bring any action or other legal proceedings against the other of them in respect of any such dispute shall first have been heard and determined by the arbitrators ... and it is expressly agreed and declared that the obtaining of an award from the arbitrators, umpire or Board of Appeal, as the case may be, shall be a condition precedent to the right of either party hereto or of any person claiming under either of them to bring any action or legal proceedings against the other of them in respect of any such dispute.

   The second limb of clause 26 (b) was a form of *Scott v Avery* clause, named after the case of *Scott v Avery* (1856) 5 HLC 811, 10 ER 1121, as it goes beyond providing for an exclusive forum and additionally specifically prohibits the bringing of 'legal proceedings' in any other forum until after a decision has been given by the chosen forum.
[148] *Mantovani v Carapelli* [1980] 1 Lloyds Rep 375 (CA) 381, 382, per Lawton and Browne LJJ (although see Megaw LJ at 383–84). This ground of distinction appealed to Dunn LJ in *Mike Trading and Transport v R Pagnan & Fratelli (The Lisboa)* [1980] 2 Lloyds Rep 546 (CA) 551 (Lord Denning MR and Waller LJ also did not follow *Mantovani v Carapelli*, but without expressly explaining how they distinguished it: at 549–50). This distinction was also adopted by Rix J in *Re Q's Estate* [1999] 1 Lloyds Rep 931, 933–38, after a detailed examination of the case law.
[149] *Mantovani v Carapelli* [1980] 1 Lloyds Rep 375 (CA) 381, per Lawton LJ: '... I can see no reason at all for making an exception ... in favour of the kind of sequestration proceedings which were taken by the sellers in the Italian courts'; adopted by Browne LJ at 382; although see the broader approach of Megaw LJ at 383–84, adopting the reasoning of Donaldson J at first instance: *Mantovani v Carapelli* [1978] 2 Lloyds Rep 63, 72–73.
[150] See the controversial decision in *B v S* [2011] 2 Lloyds Rep 18, where it was concluded that a *Scott v Avery* clause excluded the application of the court's supportive powers under s 44 of the Arbitration Act 1996, and that the previous case law permitting supportive applications to the English but not foreign courts was to be explained by the different wording of s 12(6) of the previous Arbitration Act 1950. The result was, however, in large part driven by the conclusion that this was the effect of the binding precedent of *Mantovani v Carapelli* [1978] 2 Lloyds Rep 63. *B v S* has since been followed by Cooke J in *A v B* (27 November 2015).
[151] *Marazura Navegacion v Oceanus Mutual Underwriting Association (Bermuda)* [1977] 1 Lloyds Rep 283, 288–89; *Mike Trading and Transport v R Pagnan & Fratelli (The Lisboa)* [1980] 2 Lloyds Rep 546 (CA) 548–49, 550–51; *Toepfer International v Société Cargill France* [1997] 2 Lloyds Rep 98, 107; *Re Q's Estate* [1999] 1 Lloyds Rep 931, 933–38; *Bankgesellschaft Berlin v First International Shipping* (Langley J, 21 September 2000); *Green Flower Navigation Malta v SC Santierul Naval Constanta* (7 June 2002); *Kallang Shipping v Axa Assurances Senegal (The Kallang)* [2007] 1 Lloyds Rep 160 [17]; *Kallang Shipping v Axa Assurances Senegal (The Kallang) (No 2)* [2009] 1

On this approach, it has been held that seeking security in an unreasonable amount will not for that reason alone be a breach of contract.[152] In contrast, foreign security proceedings which go beyond seeking security only, including attempts to determine the merits, and probably also other collateral attacks on the forum clause, will be a breach of normally drafted exclusive forum clauses.[153] In particular, where the foreign security proceedings are aimed at, or include, compelling the injunction claimant to provide security to the foreign court in terms which will waive the injunction claimant's contractual rights to arbitrate or litigate in England, they will go beyond the scope of legitimate security proceedings, and will be a breach of contract that may be restrained.[154]

7.74   If foreign proceedings to obtain security are not a breach of contract, then there will be no contractual right to an injunction, and thus anti-suit relief will only be granted if the foreign security proceedings are vexatious or oppressive.[155] If adequate alternative security has been offered in England, this can mean the foreign security proceedings are vexatious and oppressive.[156]

7.75   This modern approach to construction is sensible. In general, businessmen will not wish to conclude an exclusive forum clause that excludes legitimate proceedings to obtain security in foreign courts, although there can be specific reasons to do this. It is only a partial answer to say that, even if the foreign security proceedings are a breach of contract, the English court will not normally grant an injunction to restrain them as a matter of discretion, because this could still allow a claim for damages as of right.[157] Consequently, the

---

Lloyds Rep 124 [79], [86]; *Ispat Industries v Western Bulk* [2011] EWHC 93 [41]–[45]; *Sam Purpose v Transnav Purpose Navigation (The Sam Purpose)* [2017] 2 Lloyds Rep 50 [24]–[30], [32]. However, cf partially contra *Petromin v Secnav Marine* [1995] 1 Lloyds Rep 603, 612–14.

[152]   *Ispat Industries v Western Bulk* [2011] EWHC 93 [47].

[153]   *Kallang Shipping v Axa Assurances Senegal (The Kallang)* [2007] 1 Lloyds Rep 160 [21]–[24], [36], [39]; *Kallang Shipping v Axa Assurances Senegal (The Kallang) (No 2)* [2009] 1 Lloyds Rep 124 [78]–[79], [86]; *Sotrade Denizcilik Sanayi ve Ticaret v Amadou LO (The Duden)* [2009] 1 Lloyds Rep 124 [55], [62]; *Sam Purpose v Transnav Purpose Navigation (The Sam Purpose)* [2017] 2 Lloyds Rep 50 [24]–[25], [32]. In *Ispat Industries v Western Bulk* [2011] EWHC 93 [41]–[45], it was suggested that only proceedings that amounted to an attempt to determine the merits could be a breach of contract. But *The Kallang, The Kallang No 2, The Duden,* and *The Sam Purpose* support the proposition that the principle goes wider and includes forms of collateral attack on the arbitration clause other than seeking to determine the merits.
   Similarly, even where a clause expressly permits proceedings to obtain security, it is unlikely to be interpreted to permit the bringing of *in rem* proceedings which go beyond the obtaining of security and aim also at a determination of the merits: *Ultisol Transport Contractors v Bouygues Offshore* [1996] 2 Lloyds Rep 140, 145–46 (reversed in *Bouygues Offshore v Caspian Shipping (Nos 1, 3, 4 and 5)* [1998] 2 Lloyds Rep 461 (CA), but not on this point).

[154]   *Kallang Shipping v Axa Assurances Senegal (The Kallang)* [2007] 1 Lloyds Rep 160 [36], [39] (where this was viewed as a breach of implied terms of the arbitration agreement, and also as oppressive); contrast *Kallang Shipping v Axa Assurances Senegal (The Kallang) (No 2)* [2009] 1 Lloyds Rep 124 [78]–[79], [86] (where this was viewed as breach of the express terms of the arbitration agreement on their true construction); similarly, *Sotrade Denizcilik Sanayi ve Ticaret v Amadou LO (The Duden)* [2009] 1 Lloyds Rep 124 [55], [62].

[155]   *Petromin v Secnav Marine* [1995] 1 Lloyds Rep 603, 613–14.

[156]   *Kallang Shipping v Axa Assurances Senegal (The Kallang)* [2007] 1 Lloyds Rep 160 [6], [36], [39] (where the attempt to insist on security that responded to the judgment of a court other than that agreed was also viewed as a breach of contract). In *Aggeliki Charis Compania Maritima v Pagnan (The Angelic Grace)* [1994] 1 Lloyds Rep 168, 176, Rix J suggested that 'the decision [in *The Lisboa*] would probably have been different if there had been an offer of alternative security in England'.

[157]   In *Mike Trading and Transport v R Pagnan & Fratelli (The Lisboa)* [1980] 2 Lloyds Rep 546 (CA) 549, Lord Denning MR (but not the other two Lords Justices: see Dunn LJ at 550) suggested that there should be no right for damages in respect of the bringing of foreign security proceedings. But the justification for such a restriction on the ability to claim damages as of right for a breach of contract (if there is such) is unclear. An argument might be made that in such circumstances a damages claim would be contrary to public policy (cf *Union Discount Co v Zoller* [2002] 1 WLR 1517), but it would be novel and radical, and in some tension with *Mantovani v Carapelli* [1980] 1 Lloyds Rep 375 (CA).

parties to a normal exclusive forum clause, even one in broad form,[158] should be taken to have impliedly accepted that it would not be a breach of the clause to bring proceedings in foreign courts whose sole purpose is to obtain appropriate security[159] to secure payment of the judgment of the chosen court or tribunal.

Even if a particular form of wording precludes foreign security proceedings, there may well **7.76** be 'strong reasons' for bringing the foreign proceedings provided that they are intended only to obtain security pending the determination of the agreed forum.[160] Further, where it is appropriate to grant an injunction in respect of foreign security proceedings, for example if they are not confined to seeking security only, it may be a condition of any injunction that the injunction claimant is willing to provide alternative security.[161]

[158] It is possible for security proceedings in foreign courts to be expressly prohibited, as was the case in *Ellerman Lines v Read* [1928] 2 KB 144 (CA) 145, and also appears to be the case under *Scott v Avery* clauses (if *Mantovani v Carapelli* [1980] 1 Lloyds Rep 375 (CA) is right). However, if they address the point at all, it is more common for exclusive forum clauses to expressly provide that proceedings in other courts to obtain security are permissible: *Ultisol Transport Contractors v Bouygues Offshore* [1996] 2 Lloyds Rep 140, 144–45, reversed in *Bouygues Offshore v Caspian Shipping (Nos 1, 3, 4 and 5)* [1998] 2 Lloyds Rep 461 (CA), but not on this point. See also LCIA Arbitration Rules (Effective 1 January 1998), clause 25; ICC Rules, Article 23.

[159] In *Toepfer International v Société Cargill France* [1997] 2 Lloyds Rep 98, 107–08, Colman J suggested that *any* application to a foreign court for provisional or protective measures under Article 24 of the Brussels Convention (Art 35 of the Recast) would not be a breach of the GAFTA arbitration clause in that case (even though it contained a *Scott v Avery* clause; *Mantovani v Carapelli* was not cited). It is submitted that this decision may go too far and is to be treated with care. Provisional or protective measures in other jurisdictions may well interfere with litigation in the chosen forum, and be a collateral attack on the arbitration clause, and if so, there would be a cogent argument that they could be a breach of contract. It is also difficult to reconcile Colman J's decision in *Toepfer v Cargill* with *Mantovani v Carapelli*, as a *Scott v Avery* clause was present in both cases.

[160] *Mike Trading and Transport v R Pagnan & Fratelli (The Lisboa)* [1980] 2 Lloyds Rep 546 (CA) 548, 550, 551; for a case where this was not so, see *Kallang Shipping v Axa Assurances Senegal (The Kallang)* [2007] 1 Lloyds Rep 160 and *Kallang Shipping v Axa Assurances Senegal (The Kallang) (No 2)* [2009] 1 Lloyds Rep 124.

[161] *Petromin v Secnav Marine* [1995] 1 Lloyds Rep 603, 613–14; *Ultisol Transport Contractors v Bouygues Offshore* [1996] 2 Lloyds Rep 140, 146, 152 (reversed in *Bouygues Offshore v Caspian Shipping (Nos 1, 3, 4 and 5)* [1998] 2 Lloyds Rep 461 (CA), but not on this point).

8

Strong Reasons and Discretion

A. THE RELATIONSHIP OF 'STRONG REASONS' AND DISCRETION

This chapter addresses the application of two key aspects of the *Angelic Grace* principles: the **8.01** concept of 'strong reasons' not to enforce an exclusive forum clause, and the operation of the court's discretion.

These two concepts overlap. The binding force of an exclusive forum clause shapes and **8.02** changes the exercise of the court's discretion. The exclusive forum clause will 'ordinarily' be enforced by anti-suit injunction unless there are 'strong reasons' not to do so.[1] But the anti-suit injunction remains a discretionary remedy. How do these two principles relate? Is discretion subsumed within 'strong reasons'? The answer is that it is not, and the term 'ordinarily' allows some discretion to operate.

Further, as foreshadowed by a dictum of Lord Bingham in *Donohue v Armco*, it seems, ac- **8.03** cording to the current case law, that the requirement of 'strong reasons' does not govern all discretionary factors. But the boundaries of the qualification are unclear. In *ADM v Budi Semesta Satria*, the Commercial Court concluded that 'strong reasons' relates 'primarily for justifications for suing in the foreign court'. It is not clear that this is quite the right line to draw. Lord Bingham's comment in *Donohue* was that 'I use the word "ordinarily" to recognize that where an exercise of discretion is called for there can be no absolute or inflexible rule governing that exercise, and <u>also</u> that a party may lose his claim to equitable relief by dilatoriness or other unconscionable conduct' (underlining added). This suggests three points. First, the test is not absolute and there is always a discretion in reserve as to whether or not to grant an injunction. Second, 'strong reasons' may be inapplicable to factors focused on the injunction claimant, through which the injunction claimant's conduct causes

---

[1] See Ch 7, section E, 'The *Angelic Grace* Principles'.

him to lose the right to an injunction—such as delay and unclean hands. Third, there may be cases where the 'strong reasons' framework is inappropriate altogether.[2]

8.04   The third point returns us to an important and as yet unresolved debate: whether, and if so when, situations that pose unanticipated problems of comity can displace the *Angelic Grace* tests. This has been discussed in Chapter 7, where it was suggested that there are situations where specific problems of comity mean that the '*Angelic Grace*' framework is an inappropriate straitjacket. But there is a strand of case law which, if taken literally, would treat comity as altogether irrelevant where an exclusive forum clause applies.[3]

8.05   This chapter considers the operation of the standard framework. It explores the cases which, applying the *Angelic Grace* tests, have developed and applied principles governing 'strong reasons', and shaping the court's discretion more generally, in relation to anti-suit injunctions in contractual situations.

8.06   Whether there are 'strong reasons', and whether or not it is right to grant or refuse an injunction in the court's discretion, depends on all the circumstances of the case,[4] and the textbook writer must be careful not to elevate into a principle what is no more than an application of discretion to specific facts. But the problems posed by anti-suit injunctions are not infinitely various. The court's assessment has been guided by gradually coalescing principles illuminating whether particular kinds of factor are acceptable reasons against the grant of an injunction; more generally, the case law is instructive as to how particular fact patterns may be treated.

8.07   The main potential 'strong reasons' that have so far been considered can be divided into three groups: reasons relating to the nature of the clause; factors relating to the nature of the targeted litigation; and principles of comity. These are addressed in this chapter, together with claimant-focused factors relevant to discretion, such as delay and unclean hands.

B. THE NATURE OF THE CLAUSE

8.08   It is not, in itself, a strong reason against the grant of an injunction that the clause in question was not individually negotiated by the party bound by it, although that can be relevant to the exercise of the court's discretion.[5] However, conversely, where an exclusive forum

---

[2] *Donohue v Armco* [2002] 1 Lloyds Rep 425 (HL) [24]; *ADM Asia-Pacific Trading v PT Budi Semesta Satria* [2016] EWHC 1427 (Comm) [33]–[34].
In *Royal Bank of Scotland v Highland Financial Partners* [2012] 2 CLC 109 [195], Burton J appears to have proceeded on the basis that *if* there were 'unclean hands', then there were 'strong reasons' not to enforce the clause; but the Court of Appeal addressed 'unclean hands' without express reference to the 'strong reasons' framework: [2013] 1 CLC 596 (CA) [172]. In *Team Y&R Holdings Hong Kong v Ghossoub* [2017] EWHC 2401 (Comm) [98]–[111], delay was analysed under the rubric of 'strong reasons' but without the contrary approach being considered.

[3] See Ch 7, para 7.19.

[4] *Donohue v Armco* [2000] 1 Lloyds Rep 579 (CA) 595, [2002] 1 Lloyds Rep 425 (HL) [24]. See, in relation to stay cases, *Owners of Cargo Lately Laden on Board the Ship or Vessel Eleftheria v The Eleftheria (Owners) (The Eleftheria)* [1970] P 94, 99H.

[5] *Welex v Rosa Maritime (The Epsilon Rosa) (No 2)* [2002] 2 Lloyds Rep 701, 706, [2003] 2 Lloyds Rep 509 (CA) [46]–[48]; *Impala Warehousing and Logistics (Shanghai) v Wanxiang Resources (Singapore)* [2015] EWHC 25 [28], [2015] 2 All ER (Comm) 234 [118]–[119]. Indeed, in *Bankers Trust v PT Jakarta International Hotels and Development* [1999] 1 Lloyds Rep 910, 915–16, Cresswell J concluded that it was a factor in favour of an injunction that the exclusive forum clause was contained in a set of commonly used standard form terms commonly used in international commerce. However, see *Through Transport Mutual Insurance Association (Eurasia) v New India*

clause has been individually negotiated and specifically agreed by the party who is now litigating elsewhere in breach of it, this may be a factor in favour of enforcing the clause.[6]

C. THE NATURE OF THE LITIGATION

1. Considerations of *'Forum Conveniens'*

English lawyers have acquired the habit of referring, in mangled Latin, to the set of practical **8.09** and legal factors that can make one court or tribunal more appropriate than another for the determination of a case as *forum conveniens* factors. Relevant *forum conveniens* considerations can include the location of evidence and witnesses; the connections of the parties with the competing jurisdictions; the substantive law to be applied; the legal or procedural reasons that one party may have for proceeding in a particular forum; whether a party would be prejudiced by having to proceed in one forum rather than another; whether there are overlapping proceedings in another forum; and whether a fair trial will be granted in a foreign court.[7]

If no exclusive forum clause has been agreed, such factors will be important to the assess- **8.10** ment of vexation and oppression and the court's discretionary decision as to whether to grant an anti-suit injunction.[8] But where an exclusive jurisdiction clause has been agreed, *forum conveniens* factors will in general be given little weight. Arbitration and jurisdiction clauses are often agreed precisely because the chosen forum has nothing to do with the parties or their affairs, and to give overriding weight to *forum conveniens* would defeat the intention of the parties. So considerations of relative convenience or inconvenience which the parties can be taken objectively to have foreseen at the time of the conclusion of the clause are encompassed by the parties' agreement, and should generally be insufficient to amount to 'strong reasons' against the grant of an injunction.[9] The same principle appears to apply to both exclusive jurisdiction and arbitration clauses.[10]

Assurance [2004] 1 Lloyds Rep 206 [39] (reversed on other points, [2005] 1 Lloyds Rep 67 (CA)), where the judge's reasoning suggests that if the clause had not been separately bargained for, he might not have enforced it.

---

[6] *Royal Exchange Assurance v Compania Naviera Santi (The Tropaioforos) (No 2)* [1962] 1 Lloyds Rep 410, 413–14. This appears to have been a factor underlying the court's willingness to grant an injunction in *Akai v People's Insurance* [1998] 1 Lloyds Rep 90, 93; see also *Welex v Rosa Maritime (The Epsilon Rosa)* [2003] 2 Lloyds Rep 509 (CA) [48].

[7] For a classic discussion, see *Aratra Potato v Egyptian Navigation (The El Amria)* [1981] 2 Lloyds Rep 119 (CA) 123–24, 129, drawing on *Owners of Cargo Lately on Board the Ship or Vessel Eleftheria v The Eleftheria (Owners) (The Eleftheria)* [1970] P 94, 99–100.

[8] Chapter 4, sections J, '*Forum non Conveniens*', K, 'Legitimate and Illegitimate Advantages', and L, 'Comity'.

[9] *Akai v People's Insurance* [1998] 1 Lloyds Rep 90, 105; *Bouygues Offshore v Caspian Shipping (Nos 1, 3, 4 and 5)* [1998] 2 Lloyds Rep 461 (CA) 466; *Donohue v Armco* [2000] 1 Lloyds Rep 579 (CA) 589, reversed on other grounds [2002] 1 Lloyds Rep 425 (HL); *Beazley v Horizon Offshore Contractors* [2005] 1 Lloyds Rep 231, 235–36; *Deutsche Bank v Highland Crusader Partners* [2010] 1 WLR 1023 [50(7)]; *Bank of New York Mellon v GV Films* [2010] 1 Lloyds Rep 365 [18]; *Morgan Stanley & Co International v China Haisheng Juice Holdings* [2010] 1 Lloyds Rep 265 [37]; *Skype Technologies v Joltid* [2011] ILPr 8 [32]–[37] (where the corresponding passage in the first edition of this work was agreed with); *Standard Chartered Bank (Hong Kong) v Independent Power Tanzania* [2015] 2 Lloyds Rep 183 [83]–[109] (a stay case, summarizing prior authorities); *Crescendo Maritime v Bank of Communications* [2016] 1 Lloyds Rep 414 [45]–[46]. In the context of stays, see also *Celltech R&D v Medimmune* [2004] EWHC 1522 (Pat), [2005] FSR 21 (CA).

   Further, it has been said that where the claim which the injunction defendant wishes to bring in the foreign forum cannot be brought in the contractual forum, considerations of *forum conveniens* do not arise at all: *Shell International Petroleum v Coral Oil (No 1)* [1999] 1 Lloyds Rep 72, 78.

[10] In *Toepfer International v Société Cargill France* [1997] 2 Lloyds Rep 98, 110, Colman J suggested that considerations of *forum non conveniens* and overlapping judgments should be given little or *no* weight in relation

8.11   In contrast, *forum non conveniens* factors which cannot be treated as encompassed by the parties' agreement, will not be rendered irrelevant by an exclusive jurisdiction clause in standard wording.[11] However, contracting parties in some cases will include stipulations waiving any right to object to proceedings in the chosen forum on the grounds that is inconvenient. In such a case, especially strong grounds will be required before the exclusive jurisdiction clause can be departed from on grounds of convenience.[12]

2. Conflicting and Overlapping Proceedings

8.12   The exclusive forum clause may cover only parts of an interconnected set of issues, so that enforcing it by injunction risks creating new problems, with conflicting and overlapping proceedings continuing in different countries. Problems of this nature are capable of amounting to strong reasons against an injunction.[13] It may be reasonable to suppose that serious problems due to conflicting and overlapping proceedings as a result of enforcing an exclusive forum clause are not something the parties would have had in mind at the time of agreeing the clause.[14] Nevertheless, the exclusive forum clause will always have considerable force and may well be enforced even at the price of multiplicity of proceedings, and this is the tendency in the recent case law.[15] Further, if there would be inconsistent proceedings even if the injunction is refused, the risk of a multiplicity of proceedings if the injunction is granted is of less significance.[16]

---

to anti-suit injunctions to enforce an arbitration clause, by analogy to the mandatory stay under the New York Convention. However, as discussed at Ch 7, para 7.21, the better view is that the test to be applied to arbitration clauses and exclusive jurisdiction clauses is essentially the same, and so considerations of *forum conveniens* can, in principle, be taken into account in relation to injunctions to enforce an arbitration clause to the same (limited) extent that they are relevant with regard to exclusive jurisdiction clauses: *Crescendo Maritime v Bank of Communications* [2016] 1 Lloyds Rep 414 at [46]–[48] (there seems to be a missing 'not' before 'apply' in [47]).

---

[11]   *Deutsche Bank v Sebastian* [2009] 2 CLC 949 [18]–[24]; *Skype Technologies v Joltid* [2011] ILPr 8 [34]; *Standard Chartered Bank (Hong Kong) v Independent Power Tanzania* [2015] 2 Lloyds Rep 183 [83]–[109] (a stay case).

[12]   *Bank of New York Mellon v GV Films* [2010] 1 Lloyds Rep 365 [18]; *Standard Chartered Bank (Hong Kong) v Independent Power Tanzania* [2015] 2 Lloyds Rep 183 [83]–[109] (a stay case, summarizing previous authorities).

[13]   *Donohue v Armco* [2002] 1 Lloyds Rep 425 (HL) 434; *Aratra Potato v Egyptian Navigation (The El Amria)* [1981] 2 Lloyds Rep 119 (CA) 128; and recently *Team Y&R Holdings Hong Kong v Ghossoub* [2017] EWHC 2401 (Comm) [89]–[92], [112]–[113].
For an illustration of the problems caused by an anti-suit injunction which produces a multiplicity of proceedings, see the *Bouygues v Caspian* debacle: *Ultisol Transport Contractors v Bouygues Offshore* [1996] 2 Lloyds Rep 140; *Bouygues Offshore v Caspian Shipping (No 2)* [1997] 2 Lloyds Rep 485; *Bouygues Offshore v Caspian Shipping (No 3)* [1997] 2 Lloyds Rep 493, 497, 502–03, 506; *Bouygues Offshore v Caspian Shipping (No 5)* [1997] 2 Lloyds Rep 533; *Bouygues Offshore v Caspian Shipping (Nos 1, 3, 4 and 5)* [1998] 2 Lloyds Rep 461 (CA).

[14]   *Donohue v Armco* [2002] 1 Lloyds Rep 425 (HL) [74]; *Import Export Metro v Compania Sud Americana de Vapores* [2003] 1 Lloyds Rep 405, 408–16. But it depends on the contractual context. For contrary examples, see *Skype Technologies v Joltid* [2011] ILPr 8 [36]–[37] and *Celltech R&D v Medimmune* [2004] EWHC 1522 (Pat), [2005] FSR 21 (CA).

[15]   *Hamilton-Smith v CMS Cameron McKenna* [2016] EWHC 1115 [47]–[76]; *Nori Holding v Bank Otkritie Financial Corporation* [2018] 2 Lloyds Rep 80 [113].

[16]   *Bouygues Offshore v Caspian Shipping (Nos 1, 3, 4 and 5)* [1998] 2 Lloyds Rep 461 (CA) [27]; *Donohue v Armco* [2002] 1 Lloyds Rep 425 (HL) 433–35; *C v RHL* [2005] EWHC 873; *Hamilton-Smith v CMS Cameron McKenna* [2016] EWHC 1115 [47]–[76]; *Nori Holding v Bank Otkritie Financial Corporation* [2018] 2 Lloyds Rep 80 [107]–[113].

Where the problems arise from the voluntary acts of the contract breaker in pursuing the   **8.13**
foreign litigation, the courts have tended to give the risk of conflicting proceedings less
weight.[17] Conversely, the interests of third parties have been taken more seriously.[18]

3. Enforceability Abroad

In *Impala v Wanxiang*, Blair J considered whether potential problems with enforcing the   **8.14**
English judgment abroad could be 'strong reasons'. He concluded that in principle they
could be, in particular where the claim involves property in the foreign jurisdiction, and
the unenforceability of the judgment there could render it nugatory. But on the facts of the
case before him, it was not unreasonable to hold the parties to the agreed clause. A relevant
factor was that the injunction claimant had offered to agree to English arbitration as a way
round potential problems with the enforceability of the English court judgment.[19]

4. Material Injustice to the Injunction Defendant

If an anti-suit injunction will significantly prejudice the legal position of the injunction de-   **8.15**
fendant, in a respect which is not a foreseeable consequence of the parties' bargain,[20] this
can amount to 'strong reason' not to grant an injunction.

For example, if the injunction defendant's substantive claims would be time-barred before   **8.16**
the contractual forum, then this may amount to strong reasons not to grant the injunction, depending on the circumstances, such as whether the injunction defendant acted reasonably in not commencing in the contractual forum before the time-bar.[21] However, this
factor may be defused if the injunction claimant is willing to undertake not to enforce the
time-bar as a condition of obtaining the injunction.[22] Similarly, if the effect of an anti-suit
injunction would be to cause the injunction defendant to lose security for his claims which
he has obtained in the foreign proceedings, then the injunction claimant may be required
to provide comparable security in the contractual forum as a condition of the injunction. In
the case law so far, an important factor has been the overall blameworthiness of the injunction defendant's conduct.[23]

---

[17] *Hamilton-Smith v CMS Cameron McKenna* [2016] EWHC 1115 [59], [62], [71].

[18] *Bouygues Offshore v Caspian Shipping (Nos 1, 3, 4 and 5)* [1998] 2 Lloyds Rep 461 (CA) 466; *Donohue v Armco*
[2002] 1 Lloyds Rep 425 (HL) [16], [25], [27]; *Verity Shipping v NV Norexa (The Skier Star)* [2008] 1 Lloyds Rep 652
[31]–[35].

[19] *Impala Warehousing and Logistics (Shanghai) v Wanxiang Resources (Singapore)* [2015] EWHC 25 [29],
[2015] 2 All ER (Comm) 234 [126]–[145].

[20] In contrast, if the effect on the injunction defendant is simply a direct consequence of the contractual
agreement on the exclusive forum clause, there is no 'strong reason'. See eg recently, *Aqaba Container Terminal
v Soletanche Bacy France* [2019] EWHC 471 (Comm) [39]–[42], where the effect of preventing the injunction
defendant from bringing a contractual claim outside of arbitration was that it was prevented from bringing a dependent constitutional claim which could not be arbitrated. It was held that this was a consequence of the parties'
agreement to arbitrate and not strong reasons against an injunction.

[21] *Toepfer International v Molino Boschi* [1996] 1 Lloyds Rep 510, 512; *Verity Shipping v NV Norexa (The Skier
Star)* [2008] 1 Lloyds Rep 652 [51]; *Essar Shipping v Bank of China (The Kishore)* [2016] 1 Lloyds Rep 427 [68].
However, the issue inter-relates with delay: if the injunction claimant has delayed until after the relevant time limit
before seeking the injunction, this may be a reason not to grant the injunction: *The Kishore* at [61].

[22] See eg *Tracomin v Sudan Oil Seeds Co (Nos 1 and 2)* [1983] 1 WLR 1026 (CA) 1037.

[23] *Mike Trading and Transport v R Pagnan & Fratelli (The Lisboa)* [1980] 2 Lloyds Rep 546 (CA) 548; *Sea
Premium Shipping v Sea Consortium* (David Steel J, 11 April 2001); *OT Africa Line v Hijazy (The Kribi) (No 1)*

D. THE CONDUCT OF THE INJUNCTION CLAIMANT

8.17   It seems, on the current case law, that unconscionable behaviour by the injunction claimant, such as 'unclean hands', and related factors undermining the injunction claimant's right to an injunction, such as a delay, are to be analysed outside the 'strong reasons' framework. They are instead considered from the perspective of whether they amount to considerations justifying the refusal of an injunction in the court's discretion.[24]

8.18   But the frontier is unclear and it is doubtful if it is wise to draw it. All these factors could be satisfactorily analysed within the framework of 'strong reasons' and some often have been. And even when they are approached outside the framework of 'strong reasons' the need to respect the exclusive forum clause remains a powerful consideration, so the net result is, or should be, little different to assessing them against the yardstick of 'strong reasons'.

1. Unclean Hands

8.19   An injunction is an equitable remedy, and the injunction claimant must 'come to equity with clean hands'. Improper or immoral conduct by the claimant, if it has an 'immediate and necessary relation to the equity sued for', can therefore be a reason against the grant of an injunction, although it must be weighed against hardship to the injunction claimant if the injunction is refused.[25] Although this has in the past been analysed in terms of 'strong reasons', the authorities now suggest it operates independently, and outside the 'strong reasons' framework.[26]

2. Delay

8.20   Delay by the injunction claimant can justify refusing an injunction even where the foreign proceedings are in breach of an exclusive forum clause. Again, on the most recent case law, it seems that delay is a consideration to be taken account in the court's discretion independently of the 'strong reasons' framework.[27]

8.21   The significance of delay will depend on all the circumstances of a particular case. But some principles have been identified in the case law. First, even where there is a binding exclusive forum clause, the injunction should be sought promptly, and before the foreign proceedings are too far advanced.[28] Second, the questions of delay and comity are linked. The more

---

[2001] 1 Lloyds Rep 76 [90]; *Welex v Rosa Maritime (The Epsilon Rosa)* [2003] 2 Lloyds Rep 509 (CA) [49]; *Starlight Shipping v Tai Ping Insurance (The Alexandros T)* [2008] 1 Lloyds Rep 230 [32]–[33].

[24] Paragraphs 8.01–8.03.
[25] *Royal Bank of Scotland v Highland Financial Partners* [2012] 2 CLC 109 [173]–[175], [2013] 1 CLC 596 (CA) [159].
[26] See paras 8.01–8.03 and in particular n 2.
[27] *ADM Asia-Pacific Trading v PT Budi Semesta Satria* [2016] EWHC 1427 (Comm) [33]–[34].
[28] *Aggeliki Charis Cia Maritima v Pagnan (The Angelic Grace)* [1995] 1 Lloyds Rep 87 (CA) 96; *Toepfer International v Molino Boschi* [1996] 1 Lloyds Rep 510, 516; *Royal Bank of Canada v Cooperatieve Centrale Raiffeisen-Boerenleenbank* [2004] 1 Lloyds Rep 471 (CA) [50]; *REC Wafer Norway v Moser Baer Photo Voltaic* [2011] 1 Lloyds Rep 410 [46]–[48]; *Ecobank Transnational v Tanoh* [2016] 1 WLR 2231 (CA) [85]–[87]; *Essar Shipping v Bank of China (The Kishore)* [2016] 1 Lloyds Rep 427. There are a number of cases where injunctions sought shortly before the foreign trial have been rejected: see eg *Toepfer International v Molino Boschi* [1996] 1 Lloyds Rep 510, 516; *Transfield Shipping v Chiping Xinfa Huayu Alumina* [2009] EWHC 3629 (QB) [75]–[79].

closely that the foreign court has become involved with the matter due to the delay, the greater the interference with foreign court that an injunction is likely to produce, and so the stronger the factors against the grant of an injunction.[29] Third, prejudice to the injunction defendant due to delay is significant, and if delay is not prejudicial it may be given significantly less weight.[30] But delay is not necessarily immaterial in the absence of prejudice to the injunction defendant. The need to avoid delay arises from a variety of reasons including, in addition to prejudice to the injunction defendant, waste of judicial resources, the need for finality, and comity towards the foreign court.[31] Fourth, and perhaps most importantly, the courts will take into account the extent to which the delay was justifiable or excusable in the circumstances; and will weigh delay against the importance of enforcing the forum clause. Even delay that can be criticized will often not be sufficient to justify refusing an injunction and thus permitting a breach of contract to continue.[32] It seems that time taken in challenging the foreign court's jurisdiction does not in itself justify delay in applying for an anti-suit injunction.[33]

---

[29] *Joint Stock Asset Management Co Ingosstrakh-Investments v BNP Paribas* [2012] 1 Lloyds Rep 649 (CA) [66]–[68]; *Ecobank Transnational v Tanoh* [2016] 1 WLR 2231 (CA) [105], [120]–[123], [127], [132]–[137]; and see also *Shell International Petroleum v Coral Oil (No 1)* [1999] 1 Lloyds Rep 72, 79; *Niagara Maritime v Tianjin Oil & Steel Group Co* [2011] EWHC 3035 [22]; *Team Y&R Holdings Hong Kong v Ghossoub* [2017] EWHC 2401 (Comm) [109]–[110].

 While considerations of comity are of reduced importance where an exclusive forum clause has been agreed, a forum clause does not render comity of no importance, and specifically does not remove the significance of delay for comity: *Ecobank* at [106]. As to the controversial question of whether the exclusive forum clause prevents comity being of significance outside the context of delay, see Ch 7, para 7.19.

 In one case it was held, following the first edition of this work, that the absolute duration of the delay was less important than the extent to which the foreign proceedings had gone ahead in the meanwhile: see *Niagara Maritime v Tianjin Oil & Steel Group* [2011] EWHC 3035 [22]. See also *Toepfer International v Société Cargill France* [1997] 2 Lloyds Rep 98, 108; *Verity Shipping v NV Norexa (The Skier Star)* [2008] 1 Lloyds Rep 652 [36]–[46]; *Rimpacific Navigation v Daehan Shipbuilding Co (The Jin Man)* [2010] 2 Lloyds Rep 236 [70]. However, in *Essar Shipping v Bank of China (The Kishore)* [2016] 1 Lloyds Rep 427 [52]. Walker J rejected this proposition, suggesting that the cases then cited for it do not lay down general principles. It is submitted that the proposition follows logically from the approach to comity adopted by the Court of Appeal in *Ecobank*.

[30] See eg *Ecobank Transnational v Tanoh* [2016] 1 WLR 2231 (CA) [123]–[124]; *Rimpacific Navigation v Daehan Shipbuilding Co (The Jin Man)* [2010] 2 Lloyds Rep 236 [70]. If delay has caused expense, but it is nevertheless just to restrain the foreign proceedings, the court may require the injunction claimant to provide an indemnity against that expense as a condition of the injunction: *Akai v People's Insurance* [1998] 1 Lloyds Rep 90, 108.

[31] *Ecobank Transnational v Tanoh* [2016] 1 WLR 2231 (CA) [126]–[137]. For cases taking into account delay without proof of prejudice, see *Toepfer International v Molino Boschi Srl* [1996] 1 Lloyds Rep 510; *Toepfer International v Société Cargill France* [1997] 2 Lloyds Rep 98; *Akai v People's Insurance* [1998] 1 Lloyds Rep 90; *Verity Shipping v NV Norexa (The Skier Star)* [2008] 1 Lloyds Rep 652 [36]–[46]; *Essar Shipping v Bank of China (The Kishore)* [2016] 1 Lloyds Rep 427 [42]–[43]. In *Donohue v Armco* [1999] 2 Lloyds Rep 649 (Aikens J), 664 (reversed [2000] 1 Lloyds Rep 579 (CA), upheld [2002] 1 Lloyds Rep 425 (HL), Aikens J suggested that prejudice was necessary, but the point was mentioned neither in the Court of Appeal nor in the House of Lords).

[32] *Toepfer International v Société Cargill France* [1997] 2 Lloyds Rep 98, 107–108; *Akai v People's Insurance* [1998] 1 Lloyds Rep 90, 108; *Shell International Petroleum v Coral Oil (No 1)* [1999] 1 Lloyds Rep 72, 79; *Niagara Maritime v Tianjin Oil & Steel Group* [2011] EWHC 3035 [22]; *Ecobank Transnational v Tanoh* [2016] 1 WLR 2231 (CA) [137] ('Whilst recognising that delay is not necessarily a bar to relief, and the importance of upholding the rights of those who are the beneficiaries of exclusive jurisdiction agreements...'); *Team Y&R Holdings Hong Kong v Ghossoub* [2017] EWHC 2401 (Comm) [108]; *Nori Holding v Bank Otkritie Financial Corporation* [2018] 2 Lloyds Rep 80 [118]. In *Essar Shipping v Bank of China (The Kishore)* [2016] 1 Lloyds Rep 427 [52], Walker J doubted that the similar proposition in the first edition of this work was a principle of law. With respect, however, it is submitted that it is sound, and supported by authority. In Singapore, see also the broad merits-based approach taken in *Sun Travel & Tours Pvt Ltd v Hilton International Mange (Maldives) Pvt Ltd* [2019] SGCA 10 [108]–[110].

[33] *Ecobank Transnational v Tanoh* [2016] 1 WLR 2231 (CA) [125]; *Magellan Spirit APS v Vitol (The Magellan Spirit)* [2016] 2 Lloyds Rep 1 [62], [64]; *Essar Shipping v Bank of China (The Kishore)* [2016] 1 Lloyds Rep 427. But time taken pending a jurisdictional challenge in the foreign court may be given less weight than periods of time during which there has been engagement with the merits: see eg *Team Y&R Holdings Hong Kong Limited v Ghossoub* [2017] EWHC 2401 (Comm) [109]–[110].

3. Voluntary Submission and Inconsistent Behaviour

8.22   A voluntary submission to the jurisdiction of the foreign court may in appropriate circumstances amount to a strong reason why a contractual injunction should not be granted.[34] However, only a submission that would be truly voluntary from the perspective of English law will have a powerful effect,[35] and if the injunction claimant has been doing what he can to resist the foreign court's assumption of jurisdiction, then any submission is less likely to be held against him. The foreign procedural framework may sometimes make submission unavoidable. Further, if the foreign court considers that a submission to its jurisdiction has been made, due to some merely technical step in the foreign proceedings, which the English court would not regard as a voluntary submission, then this is likely to be given less weight.[36]

8.23   If the injunction claimant behaves in a way which is inconsistent with the contractual forum being the sole forum for dispute resolution, such as himself starting proceedings in the non-contractual foreign court, this can be a powerful factor against enforcing an exclusive forum clause.[37] However, foreign proceedings whose purpose was only to obtain security for the main proceedings, or which are commenced merely to obtain protection against potential limitation difficulties, are not inconsistent with treating the contractual forum as the primary forum for resolution of the parties' substantive disputes.

---

[34] *Schiffahrtsgesellschaft Detlev von Appen v Voest Alpine Intertrading (The Jay Bola)* [1997] 1 Lloyds Rep 179, 189; *A/S D/S Svendborg v Wansa* [1996] 2 Lloyds Rep 559, 570, where in the 'exceptional' circumstances of the case it was decided that the voluntary submission should not prevent the grant of an injunction (at 572–75). The judge's decision on this point was held to be within his discretion on appeal: *A/S D/S Svendborg v Wansa* [1997] 2 Lloyds Rep 183 (CA) 188–89. See also *Akai v People's Insurance* [1998] 1 Lloyds Rep 90, 105.

[35] *Marc Rich v Societa Italiana Impianti (The Atlantic Emperor) (No 2)* (Hobhouse J, 11 November 1991); approved *obiter* in the Court of Appeal [1992] 1 Lloyds Rep 624, 633–34; *Advent Capital v Ellinas Imports-Exports (No 2)* [2005] 2 Lloyds Rep 607, 618; *Shashoua v Sharma* [2009] 2 Lloyds Rep 376 [36]–[48], [53]–[54]; *Bank of New York Mellon v GV Films* [2010] 1 Lloyds Rep 365 [19], [22]; *Jewel Owner v Sagaan Developments Trading (The MD Gemini)* [2012] 2 Lloyds Rep 672 [25] (where the injunction claimant had 'positively promoted' the other forum).
      The issues here may interrelate with the application of *res judicata*, but the law on that question is presently uncertain. In *The Atlantic Emperor (No 2)* it was held that voluntary submission meant the decision of the foreign court that no binding exclusive forum clause would be treated as *res judicata*, removing the basis for an anti-suit injunction: see Hobhouse J (11 November 1991) and (CA) 631–33. However, in *AES Ust-Kamenogorsk Hydropower Plant LLC v Ust-Kamenogorsk Hydropower Plant JSC* [2012] 1 WLR 90 (CA) [189]–[190] Rix LJ doubted the correctness of *The Atlantic Emperor (No 2)*, suggesting that foreign decisions as to the effect of jurisdiction and arbitration clauses would not be recognized here, even if there had been a submission, given the effect of s 32(3) of the Civil Jurisdiction and Judgments Act 1982; although Rix LJ's comments have in turn been doubted in *Spliethoff's Bevrachtingskantoor BV v Bank of China* [2015] 2 Lloyds Rep 123 [125]–[127].

[36] *Advent Capital v GN Ellinas Importers-Exporters (No 1)* [2004] ILPr 23 [25], [42]; *Advent Capital v Ellinas Imports-Exports (No 2)* [2005] 2 Lloyds Rep 607, 611–12; *Shashoua v Sharma* [2009] 2 Lloyds Rep 376 [36]–[48], [53]–[54]. See also *AES Ust-Kamenogorsk Hydropower Plant LLC v Ust-Kamenogorsk Hydropower Plant JSC* [2012] 1 WLR 90 (CA) [189]–[190]. In *Continental Bank v Aeakos Compania Naviera* [1994] 1 Lloyds Rep 505 (CA) 512 there was apparently uncontested evidence that by applying for an adjournment in Greece the injunction claimants had submitted to the Greek jurisdiction in the eyes of the Greek courts. The Court of Appeal did not give this any weight as a factor against the grant of an anti-suit injunction.

[37] *Banque Cantonale Vaudoise v Waterlily Maritime* [1997] 2 Lloyds Rep 347, 357; *Jewel Owner v Sagaan Developments Trading (The MD Gemini)* [2012] 2 Lloyds Rep 672 [25].

E. COMITY

The balance struck in *The Angelic Grace*[38] incorporates considerations of comity.[39] The force   **8.24**
of the contractual obligation on which the injunction relies means that the standard comity
concerns arising from the indirect interference with a foreign court which an injunction
produces have been dealt with in the framing of the test.[40] There are cases suggesting, further, that if a contractual forum clause has been held to apply, the *Angelic Grace* tests take
sufficient account of comity from all perspectives, so that comity considerations cannot
amount to strong reasons to refuse an injunction. It is clear that comity has reduced importance in the context of contractual forum clauses. Nevertheless, it is submitted that comity
remains relevant to contractual anti-suit injunctions, and where the circumstances create
specific tensions with the demands of comity, beyond those inherent in the grant of any injunction to restrain proceedings before a foreign court, this should be capable of amounting
to 'strong reasons' not to grant an injunction.[41]

Further, as previously discussed in Chapter 7, it is possible that the demands of comity can
be of sufficient importance that, in appropriate cases, they should be capable of displacing
the *Angelic Grace* tests altogether.[42]

1. Offence to the Foreign Court

There has been debate as to whether it can be a 'strong reason' to refuse an anti-suit in-   **8.25**
junction that the foreign court would be 'offended' by the injunction, but the trend of the
case law suggests that this is irrelevant. In *The Angelic Grace*, Millett LJ concluded that a
foreign court 'would not' be offended by the grant of an injunction to restrain a party from
breaching his contractual obligations not to sue in the foreign country.[43] In a line of subsequent first instance authorities, this was treated as ruling out a priori submissions that
the foreign court would be offended by the grant of an anti-suit injunction,[44] but not as
precluding the relevance of evidence that the foreign court would in fact be offended. The
judges in these cases were apparently prepared to accept that, if offence was proven, it could

---

[38] See Ch 7, section E, 'The *Angelic Grace* Principles'.

[39] *OT Africa Line v Magic Sportswear* [2005] 2 Lloyds Rep 170 (CA) [31]–[33]; *Shipowners' Mutual Protection and Indemnity Association (Luxembourg) v Containerships Denizcilik Nakliyat ve Ticaret (The Yusuf Cepnioglu)* [2016] 1 Lloyds Rep 641 (CA) [25], [34]–[35].

[40] *Aggeliki Charis Compania Maritima v Pagnan (The Angelic Grace)* [1995] 1 Lloyds Rep 87 (CA) at 96; *Credit Suisse First Boston (Europe) v MLC (Bermuda)* [1999] 1 Lloyds Rep 767, 780.

[41] The cases denying relevance to comity are *OT Africa Line v Magic Sportswear Corp* [2005] 2 Lloyds Rep 170 (CA) [31]–[33]; *Royal Bank of Scotland v Highland Financial Partners* [2012] 2 CLC 109 [156]; *Shipowners' Mutual Protection and Indemnity Association (Luxembourg) v Containerships Denizcilik Nakliyat ve Ticaret AS (The Yusuf Cepnioglu)* [2016] 1 Lloyds Rep 641 (CA) [25], [34]–[35], [58]. But there is real authority to support giving weight to non-standard considerations of comity to refuse contractual anti-suit injunctions in appropriate situ-ations: *Philip Alexander Securities & Futures v Bamberger* [199] ILPr 73 [78]–[84] (per Waller J); *Credit Suisse First Boston (Europe) v MLC (Bermuda)* [1999] 1 Lloyds Rep 767, 780–81; *Deutz v General Electric* (Thomas J, 14 April 2000); *Donohue v Armco* [2002] 1 Lloyds Rep 425 (HL) [24]–[25]; *AES Ust-Kamenogorsk Hydropower Plant LLP v Ust-Kamenogorsk Hydropower Plant JSC* [2013] 1 WLR 1889 (SC) [61]; *Ecobank Transnational v Tanoh* [2016] 1 Lloyds Rep 360 (CA) [100], [106], [134], [135], [137]; and in Australia, see *Comandate Marine v Pan Australia Shipping (The Commandate)* [2008] 1 Lloyds Rep 119 [252].

[42] See Ch 7, para 7.19. However, it does not matter much whether this approach is adopted, or whether comity concerns are incorporated within the analysis of 'strong reasons'.

[43] *Aggeliki Charis Compania Maritima v Pagnan (The Angelic Grace)* [1995] 1 Lloyds Rep 87 (CA) 96.

[44] *OT Africa Line v Hijazy (The Kribi) (No 1)* [2001] 1 Lloyds Rep 76, 93.

be a strong reason not to grant an anti-suit injunction.[45] There was, however, a division in approach. Certain judges were obviously reluctant to accept evidence that the foreign court would be offended, and tended to explain away insufficiently clear evidence,[46] while others accepted evidence of offence more readily.[47]

8.26   In *Through Transport*, the Court of Appeal, who did not have before them any evidence of actual offence,[48] went further, saying that there is no reason why any court 'should be' offended by an injunction granted to restrain a party from breaching his promise.[49] Nevertheless, the Court of Appeal did not address the question of the approach to take if the foreign court was in fact offended, and the point was not central to the issues before them.[50]

8.27   Subsequently, in *The Front Comor*, Colman J concluded that he was bound by the precedent of *The Angelic Grace* and *Through Transport* to conclude:

> that whatever terminology is adopted—'offended', 'affronted', or 'contrary to comity'— evidence that the foreign court would treat the order as an impermissible exercise of jurisdiction by the English courts is, as a matter of English conflicts of laws rules, not in itself any reason to withhold such an order to procure compliance with an agreement to arbitrate.[51]

Similarly, in *RBS v Highland*, Burton J concluded that it was unnecessary to resolve the disputed factual question of whether the foreign court would be offended, as the comity owed to a friendly foreign court should be addressed in the same way, whether or not evidence of offence existed.[52]

8.28   Colman J's contention that there was binding precedent for this result, at the time of his decision, is open to doubt.[53] But it is respectfully suggested that it is sound in principle.

---

[45]   *Philip Alexander Securities & Futures v Bamberger* [1997] ILPr 73, 83–84. In *OT Africa Line v Hijazy (The Kribi) (No 1)* [2001] 1 Lloyds Rep 76 [93], [94(5)], Aikens J held that there was insufficient evidence of offence before him for him to conclude that the Belgian court would be offended by the grant of an anti-suit injunction; but he stated that had such evidence been produced, then it would have been an important consideration.

[46]   See *OT Africa Line v Hijazy (The Kribi) (No 1)* [2001] 1 Lloyds Rep 76 (Aikens J) [94(5)]; *Navigation Maritime Bulgare v Rustal Trading (The Ivan Zagubanski)* [2002] 1 Lloyds Rep 106 (Aikens J) 126–27; *Electronic Arts v CTO* [2003] EWHC 1020 (Ian Glick QC) [113]; *West Tankers v Ras Riunione Adriatica di Sicurta (The Front Comor)* [2005] 2 Lloyds Rep 257 (Colman J) [45].

[47]   *Philip Alexander Securities & Futures Bamberger* [1997] ILP, 73 (Waller J) [83]–[84]; *Evialis v SIAT* [2003] 2 Lloyds Rep 377 (Andrew Smith J) 388–89.

[48]   The only evidence available was that the Finnish courts would not recognize or enforce the injunction: *Through Transport Mutual Insurance Association (Eurasia) v New India Assurance* [2004] 1 Lloyds Rep 206 [40]–[41], [2005] 1 Lloyds Rep 67 (CA) [77].

[49]   *Through Transport Mutual Insurance Association (Eurasia) v New India Assurance* [2005] 1 Lloyds Rep 67 (CA) [91].

[50]   *Through Transport Mutual Insurance Association (Eurasia) v New India Assurance* [2005] 1 Lloyds Rep 67 (CA) 85–88.

[51]   *West Tankers v Ras Riunione Adriatica di Sicurta (The Front Comor)* [2005] 2 Lloyds Rep 257, 266–68.

[52]   *Royal Bank of Scotland v Highland Financial Partners* [2012] 2 CLC 109 [55]. In *OT Africa Line v Magic Sportswear Corp* [2005] 2 Lloyds Rep 170 (CA) 186, Rix LJ made a glancing reference to the fact that the Canadian court would not take offence at the grant of an injunction. But this *obiter* comment does not merit the status of a positive endorsement of the relevance of evidence of offence.

[53]   The decision in *Aggeliki Charis Compania Maritima v Pagnan (The Angelic Grace)* [1995] 1 Lloyds Rep 87 (CA) can be viewed as proceeding on the basis of an assumption of fact, capable of subsequent rebuttal. The use of the word 'should' rather than 'would' by the Court of Appeal in *Through Transport Mutual Insurance Association (Eurasia) v New India Assurance Co* [2005] 1 Lloyds Rep 67 (CA) [91] does, on one reading, take the matter further, but the issue was not central to the reasoning of the Court of Appeal, nor even apparently argued before it, while the Court of Appeal may well not have intended to extend the reasoning in *The Angelic Grace* in this respect, and so their comments should be viewed as *obiter dicta*.

Subsequently, the practice of adducing expert evidence on whether the foreign court would be 'offended' has fallen away, which is a welcome development.

The concept of 'offence' is slippery, and means little. If it refers to an emotional reaction by the foreign court, this is not a relevant consideration. If it means that the foreign court would take the view that the English court's injunction would be an unacceptable interference with its own jurisdiction, it would be unsound for English law merely to accept the foreign court's view of the injunction without making its own assessment of that view's legitimacy.[54] There is little reason why proceedings before relatively 'protectionist' foreign jurisdictions should be immune from anti-suit injunctions when proceedings in other more laissez-faire jurisdictions will not be.[55] Illegitimate objections by a foreign court do not deserve great deference. But if the question is rephrased to ask whether the foreign court would have a *legitimate* ground to object to the anti-suit injunction, the concept of 'offence' has in effect disappeared, and been replaced by an objective assessment of the demands of comity between jurisdictions.[56]   **8.29**

Essentially this approach has now been adopted by the Court of Appeal in *Ecobank v Tanoh*, where without citation of the previous authorities, they made clear that the concept of 'offence' was really a question of comity, and of whether the foreign court 'may *justifiably* take objection'. As they saw it, that question 'is not based on any need to avoid offence to individual judges (who are made of sterner stuff)' but because illegitimate interference 'is not a sound method of conducting curial business'.[57] This, it is submitted, buttresses the correctness of Colman J's approach.   **8.30**

2. The Conflict of Conflicts

If all legal systems had the same conflicts of laws rules, and so applied the same choice of law rules and the same substantive contract law to exclusive forum clauses, the need for anti-suit injunctions to enforce such clauses would be less.   **8.31**

However, when contrasted to English law, the conflict of laws rules of foreign legal systems may be very different; their choice of law rules may apply different substantive laws to the determination of the parties' contractual obligations; they may use different legal principles to determine whether choice of law clauses or exclusive forum clauses are incorporated into contracts,[58] or as to whether connected third parties are bound by contracts at all;[59] and

---

[54] D Tan, 'Enforcing International Arbitration Agreements in Federal Courts: Rethinking the Federal Court's Remedial Powers' (2007) 47 Virg J Intl L 545, 591–92.

[55] It has been held that concerns about whether a foreign court will be offended are, in general, out of place where the foreign proceedings are in a jurisdiction which itself recognizes and exercises the anti-suit injunction: *Beazley v Horizon Offshore Contractors* [2005] 1 Lloyds Rep 231 [40]; and see *OT Africa Line v Magic Sportswear* [2005] 2 Lloyds Rep 170 (CA) 173, 186. This distinction is largely irrelevant, if Colman J's conclusions in *The Front Comor* represent the law. But it can be noted that despite the best hopes of the English courts, even the courts in other common law countries can react vividly to interference with their proceedings by anti-suit injunction: see eg the conflicts with the courts of the United States that arose in *British Airways Board v Laker Airways* [1984] QB 142 (CA) 185 (discussed at Ch 1, para 1.37, n 77).

[56] In *Royal Bank of Scotland v Highland Financial Partners* [2012] 2 CLC 109 [155] Burton J considered this passage in the first edition, and relied on it as support for his conclusion that the right approach would be to address the question of comity 'just as I would if I knew that without such express (contested) evidence a friendly foreign court were ready, willing and able to deal with proceedings'.

[57] *Ecobank Transnational v Tanoh* [2016] 1 Lloyds Rep 360 (CA) [134].

[58] As in *Navigation Maritime Bulgare v Rustal Trading (The Ivan Zagubanski)* [2002] 1 Lloyds Rep 106 [53(1)].

[59] *OT Africa Line v Hijazy (The Kribi) (No 1)* [2001] 1 Lloyds Rep 76, 82.

they may take different approaches to the enforcement of exclusive forum clauses, which may be overridden by mandatory domestic laws irrespective of the parties' choice of law.[60]

8.32   In any situation such as this, we are confronted with a conflict between conflict of laws rules, which may pose an acute problem of comity, namely whether it is legitimate for the English court to impose English principles of the conflict of laws by injunction in relation to the foreign proceedings, even though the foreign state has made different choices of policy which are incorporated in its different conflict of laws rules or mandatory laws.

8.33   In general, the English courts have adopted an uncompromising approach to the conflict of conflicts in anti-suit injunction cases, if the injunction defendant is in actionable breach of contract[61] by breaching an exclusive forum clause under the substantive law applied by English choice of law principles.[62]

8.34   Thus, in a number of cases the courts have held that it was not a 'strong reason' to refuse to enforce an exclusive forum clause by injunction that the foreign court will not enforce the clause because the foreign court applies a mandatory domestic statute which overrides the parties' choice of law and forum,[63] or because the foreign court would hold that the clause was not incorporated into the contract applying a different substantive law to that which the English court would apply,[64] or because the foreign court will refuse to enforce the forum clause in its discretion, applying principles contrary to those which would be deployed by an English court.[65] Recently, in *The Yusuf Cepnioglu*, Longmore LJ's reasoning, although not entirely explicit, can be read to suggest that questions of comity just do not arise when an exclusive forum clause has been agreed in the eyes of an English court, and that as a matter of principle foreign mandatory laws can be ignored.[66]

---

[60]   As in *Akai v People's Insurance* [1998] 1 Lloyds Rep 90, 92–94; *Bankers Trust International v RCS Editori* [1996] CLC 899, 906; *Shell International Petroleum v Coral Oil (No 1)* [1999] 1 Lloyds Rep 72, 78; *OT Africa Line v Magic Sportswear* [2005] 1 Lloyds Rep 252 [6]–[8]; *Aline Tramp v Jordan International Insurance (The Flag Evi)* [2017] 1 Lloyds Rep 467 [42]–[56].

[61]   A similarly robust approach has been applied in 'quasi-contractual cases', discussed in Ch 10. In a non-contractual case, different considerations apply: see eg *Seismic Shipping v Total E&P UK (The Western Regent)* [2005] 2 Lloyds Rep 359 (CA) [55] and *BNP Paribas v Russian Machines* [2012] 1 Lloyds Rep 61 [78].

[62]   *OT Africa Line v Magic Sportswear* [2005] 2 Lloyds Rep 170 (CA) 173, 177.

[63]   *Akai Pty v People's Insurance* [1998] 1 Lloyds Rep 90, 98–100, 104–05; *Bankers Trust International v RCS Editori* [1996] CLC 899, 905–06; *XL Insurance v Owens Corning* [2000] 2 Lloyds Rep 500, 509; *Electronic Arts v CTO* [2003] EWHC 1020 (Comm) [86]–[91]; *OT Africa Line v Magic Sportswear* [2005] 1 Lloyds Rep 252, 258–59 (Langley J); [2005] 2 Lloyds Rep 170 (CA) 178–80, 183–86; *Horn Linie v Panamericana Formas e Impresos (The Hornbay)* [2006] 2 Lloyds Rep 44 [20]; *Vitol v Arcturus Merchant Trust* [2009] EWHC 800 (Comm) [33]–[35]; *Sul America Cia Nacional de Seguros v Enesa Engenharia* [2012] 1 Lloyds Rep 275 [53]–[57] (the point was not pressed on appeal [2013] 1 WLR 102 (CA)); *Shipowners' Mutual Protection and Indemnity Association (Luxembourg) v Containerships Denizcilik Nakliyat ve Ticaret (The Yusuf Cepnioglu)* [2016] 1 Lloyds Rep 641 (CA) [17], [34, [58]; *Dell Emerging Markets (EMEA) v Systems Equipment Telecommunication Services* [2018] EWHC 702 [39].
    For possible qualifications see: *Philip Alexander Securities & Futures v Bamberger* [1997] ILPr 73, [51] (Waller J) and *Aline Tramp v Jordan International Insurance (The Flag Evi)* [2017] 1 Lloyds Rep 27 [41]–[56].

[64]   *Navigation Maritime Bulgare v Rustal Trading (The Ivan Zagubanski)* [2002] 1 Lloyds Rep 106 [53(1)]; *Welex v Rosa Maritime (The Epsilon Rosa)* [2002] 2 Lloyds Rep 701, 704–06, [2003] 2 Lloyds Rep 509 (CA) 517, although the 'conflict of conflicts' point was not directly argued in that case. In *Midgulf International v Group Chimique Tunisien* [2010] 2 Lloyds Rep 543 (CA) [55]–[66] the point was argued, but on analysis the Court of Appeal concluded that both Tunisian and English conflicts of laws rules would point to English substantive law.

[65]   *Akai Pty v People's Insurance Co* [1998] 1 Lloyds Rep 90, 105.

[66]   *Shipowners' Mutual Protection and Indemnity Association (Luxembourg) v Containerships Denizcilik Nakliyat ve Ticaret (The Yusuf Cepnioglu)* [2016] 1 Lloyds Rep 641 (CA) [34]–[37]. Moore-Bick LJ said he agreed with Longmore LJ but his own reasoning on this specific question is more open-textured: at [57]–[58]. The point was raised in *Midgulf International v Group Chimique Tunisien* [2010] 2 Lloyds Rep 543 (CA) [55]–[66], but did not need to be decided because of the way the facts fell out.

Indeed, if the foreign forum will apply the 'wrong' substantive law, which is likely to pro-   **8.35**
duce a significantly different result, the English courts may well view this as a reason in
favour of the grant of a contractual anti-suit injunction, in particular if the substantive law
that would be applied by English choice of law rules has been expressly chosen by the parties.[67] If the substantive law which the foreign court would decline to apply implements the
protections of an important multilateral convention, this factor may have added force.[68] An
injunction defendant who, nevertheless, seeks to persuade the court that there are strong
reasons why he should be allowed to continue in the non-contractual forum may find that,
as a condition of a refusal of the injunction, he will be required to give undertakings that he
will not seek to rely on the variant aspects of the foreign law.[69]

In such cases, the English court has imposed its answer to the conflict of conflicts by injunc-   **8.36**
tion, and held the parties to their bargain, even if that has the consequence that a substantive claim which could be brought in the foreign jurisdiction cannot be brought at all, as it
is not available in England under English principles of the conflict of laws. This has been
viewed as a consequence of the parties' bargain, which therefore causes no injustice.[70]

But the jurisprudential rationale for this approach is undeveloped. The traditional answer   **8.37**
is that the English court should apply its own law and its own conflict of laws rules to determining whether a contract is binding, and thus there is no reason why it should pay regard
to the legal rules that would be applied by the foreign court.[71] But although a sound rule in
other contexts, it is suggested that it may, from an international perspective, be an insufficient justification for the indirect interference with foreign sovereignty that an anti-suit
injunction involves.[72]

The problem has not gone entirely unrecognized. The courts have begun to identify justifi-   **8.38**
cations of policy that can be viewed as convincing from a neutral international perspective,
and go beyond simply saying that our law should be imposed by injunction because it is

---

[67] *Ultisol Transport Contractors v Bouygues Offshore* [1996] 2 Lloyds Rep 140, 151–52 (overturned on appeal,
but not on this point [1998] 2 Lloyds Rep 461 (CA)); *Shell International Petroleum v Coral Oil (No 1)* [1999] 1
Lloyds Rep 72, 78.
A similar approach is adopted in the partly analogous situations of service out of the jurisdiction, *Coast Lines
v Hudig & Veder* [1971] 2 Lloyds Rep 390, 392, 395; [1972] 2 QB 34 (CA) 43B–F, 45B–F, 49D–H; and stay
cases: *Seashell Shipping v Mutualidad de Seguros Del Instituto Nacional de Industria (The Magnum ex Tarraco
Augusta)* [1989] 1 Lloyds Rep 47 (CA) 53.
[68] *Ultisol Transport Contractors v Bouygues Offshore* [1996] 2 Lloyds Rep 140, 151–52 (overturned on appeal,
but not on this point [1998] 2 Lloyds Rep 461 (CA)); see *Coast Lines v Hudig & Veder* [1972] 2 QB 34 (CA) 43B–F,
49F–H, where the Netherlands was viewed as 'out of step' with international maritime law, and this was a reason to
reject a challenge to service of proceedings out of the jurisdiction.
[69] *Donohue v Armco* [2002] 1 Lloyds Rep 425 (HL) [39]; although note that Lord Scott would not have required
the undertaking: at [75].
[70] *Beazley v Horizon Offshore Contractors* [2005] 1 Lloyds Rep 231, 237–38, and see also *Southport Success v
Tsingshan Holding Group* [2015] 2 Lloyds Rep 578 [34], and n 20.
[71] *Youell v Kara Mara Shipping* [2000] 2 Lloyds Rep 102 [60]; *OT Africa Line v Magic Sportswear* [2005] 2 Lloyds
Rep 170 (CA) 173, 177, per Longmore LJ, although Rix LJ took a more nuanced approach, at 182–86; *West Tankers
v Ras Riunione Adriatica di Sicurta (The Front Comor)* [2005] 2 Lloyds Rep 257, 262–63. This may also be the rationale underpinning *Shipowners' Mutual Protection and Indemnity Association (Luxembourg) v Containerships
Denizcilik Nakliyat ve Ticaret (The Yusuf Cepnioglu)* [2016] 1 Lloyds Rep 641 (CA), in particular the judgment of
Longmore LJ.
[72] A Briggs, 'Anti-Suit Injunctions in a Complex World' in F Rose (ed), *Lex Mercatoria* (Routledge 2000) 219,
238, argues that where it is controversial whether an exclusive forum clause is binding, there is much to be said
for the view that the foreign court is best placed to evaluate the question. See also T Raphael, 'Do as You Would be
Done By: Anti-Suit Injunctions and System-Transcendent Justification' [2016] LMCLQ 256.

our law—which can be called system-transcendent justifications. In particular, it has been suggested that the contract should be enforced by way of injunction, despite the conflict of conflicts, because English law is giving effect to the parties' freely chosen bargain, and the foreign law is not.[73] On this approach, the legitimacy of the anti-suit injunction comes from a system-transcendent value, namely the moral force of the parties' promise.[74]

8.39   One reading of Moore-Bick LJ's judgment in *The Yusuf Cepnioglu* is that he thought there was a system-transcendent rationale for granting an injunction in the case before him. The case concerned whether an injunction could be granted to restrain foreign proceedings brought under a foreign statute giving third-party rights against insurers, where the contractual rights which the statute would give the third-party access to were inherently subject to an English arbitration clause. Moore Bick LJ concluded that:

> If legislation confers on an injured party the right to recover directly against the wrongdoer's liability insurer by giving him in substance the right to enforce the contract, he must accept what the legislation gives him, including the obligation to pursue any claim in arbitration. To hold him to that agreement is to give effect to the legislation while preserving the substance of the obligation which he seeks to enforce.

As a result, he viewed the case as in effect identical to one where an exclusive forum clause was freely agreed, and so thought that considerations of comity arising out of the conflict of conflicts did not arise.

8.40   However, the courts' practice goes well beyond this, and has not depended on the identification of a system-transcendent justification that can positively be identified. Anti-suit injunctions will be granted on *Angelic Grace* principles outside cases where there has indisputably been a freely chosen bargain in fact, independent of the perspective of English law and the English conflicts of laws. To take just one example, anti-suit injunctions can be justified on *Angelic Grace* principles against the third-party holders of bills of lading which incorporate charterparty forum clauses, even though there is little meaningful sense in which the holder has 'freely chosen' to agree to be bound by the exclusive forum clause, and many foreign laws take a different approach to incorporation.[75]

8.41   Nevertheless, in recent years, some regard has begun to be paid to the conflict of conflicts. There is a developing line of authority which suggests that a system-transcendent reason of sufficient weight in favour of the foreign law may be capable, in some particular cases,

---

[73] *Akai v People's Insurance* [1998] 1 Lloyds Rep 90, 98, where the case was particularly strong as the parties had specifically negotiated on and agreed English jurisdiction, and had not simply agreed a standard form contract incorporating an exclusive forum clause; *XL Insurance v Owens Corning* [2000] 2 Lloyds Rep 500, 509; *OT Africa Line v Magic Sportswear* [2005] 2 Lloyds Rep 170 (CA) 173, 183–85 (per Rix LJ, whose approach was, however, different to the more traditional approach of Longmore LJ); *West Tankers v Ras Riunione Adriatica di Sicurta (The Front Comor)* [2007] 1 Lloyds Rep 391 (HL) [19]–[20]; *Horn Linie v Panamericana Formas e Impresos (The Hornbay)* [2006] 2 Lloyds Rep 44 [20]. See also *Through Transport Mutual Insurance Association (Eurasia) v New India Assurance Co* [2004] 1 Lloyds Rep 206 [38]–[39], overturned on other grounds [2005] 1 Lloyds Rep 67 (CA).

[74] This justification is, of course, only imperfectly system-transcendent; it is inescapably the case that the English court is still imposing its view of what is transcendent between legal systems on the policy choices of the foreign legal system, and prioritizing freedom of contract is not politically neutral. Nevertheless, it does avoid the greater parochialism of imposing by injunction the solution arrived at by English law, merely because it is English law. For further discussion of system-transcendence, see Ch 1, paras 1.55–1.59.

[75] See eg *OT Africa Line v Hijazy (The Kribi) (No 1)* [2001] 1 Lloyds Rep 76, 82, 91; *Navigation Maritime Bulgare v Rustal Trading (The Ivan Zagubanski)* [2002] 1 Lloyds Rep 106 [53(1)] (although there the point was only hinted at in a half-hearted manner by the defendant).

of being a 'strong reason' against the grant of an injunction.[76] To date this remains merely a possibility floated in *obiter dicta*. The scope of any exception, if one exists at all, is unclear, and there is little sign as yet that it will be applied broadly.[77]

Thus, it has been suggested *obiter* that it may be a strong reason against enforcing an exclusive forum clause that the foreign law overrides the exclusive forum clause in circumstances where English domestic law would also have done so were the relevant events to have taken place in England.[78] Similarly, if the foreign law which overrides the exclusive forum clause is the product of an international convention to which the United Kingdom is a party, rather than being merely the idiosyncratic policy of a particular foreign country, it has been suggested *obiter* that this may be treated as a forceful system-transcendent consideration against the grant of an injunction.[79]   **8.42**

Similarly, it is possible that where a dispute or a public policy consideration is of a 'strongly domestic nature', and from a system-transcendent point of view can be seen as legitimately within the sphere of influence of the foreign state, a foreign mandatory statute overriding the parties' choice of law should be given weight. This is a principle which the courts should only apply, if at all, with care; but one candidate that has been suggested is a foreign statute for the protection of the foreign country's domestic consumers.[80] In contrast, a foreign statute which seeks to impose domestic public policy choices on international commercial transactions in defiance of the parties' freely chosen choice of law is less likely to be given system-transcendent weight by the English courts.[81]   **8.43**

Yet it is not at present easy to reconcile all the authorities. There are differences in the reasoning both within and between the key cases. So in *OT Africa* a more rigid approach is adopted by Longmore LJ compared to the more nuanced reasoning of Rix LJ; and there are also differences between the approaches of Longmore LJ and Moore-Bick LJ in *The Yusuf Cepnioglu*.[82] There is also an arguable inconsistency between the reasoning in *OT Africa* and *The Yusuf Cepnioglu* and the approach adopted in a converse situation in *Petter*   **8.44**

---

[76] *Philip Alexander Securities & Futures v Bamberger* [1997] ILPr 73 [51] (Waller J); *Aline Tramp v Jordan International Insurance (The Flag Evi)* [2017] 1 Lloyds Rep 27 [41]–[56]. See generally the views of Rix LJ in *OT Africa Line v Magic Sportswear* [2005] 2 Lloyds Rep 170 (CA) 185–86 (although Longmore LJ's approach reflected the traditional approach more closely); Sales LJ's view in *Petter v EMC* [2016] ILPr 1 (CA) [52]; and the *obiter* comment in *Ecobank Transnational v Tanoh* [2016] 1 WLR 2231 (CA) [54].

[77] The point was deliberately not decided in *Magellan Spirit APS v Vitol (The Magellan Spirit)* [2016] 2 Lloyds Rep 1 [74].

[78] *Philip Alexander Securities & Futures v Bamberger* [1997] ILPr 73 [51] (Waller J), not addressed on appeal [1997] ILPr 73 (CA). However, the analogy must be close: it is not sufficient that the foreign law restricts freedom of choice in some domains and English law restricts freedom of choice in other domains: see *Akai v People's Insurance* [1998] 1 Lloyds Rep 90, 98–99, rejecting the injunction defendant's argument based on *Owners of Cargo on Board the Morviken v Owners of the Hollandia (The Hollandia)* [1983] 1 AC 565.

[79] *OT Africa Line v Magic Sportswear* [2005] 1 Lloyds Rep 252 [40(v)], [2005] 2 Lloyds Rep 170 (CA) [75]–[76].

[80] *Philip Alexander Securities & Futures v Bamberger* [1997] ILPr 73 [82]–[83] (Waller J), not addressed on appeal [1997] ILPr 73 (CA); *OT Africa Line v Magic Sportswear* [2005] 2 Lloyds Rep 170 (CA) [77]; *Beazley v Horizon Offshore Contractors* [2005] 1 Lloyds Rep 231 [42]–[44]; *Aline Tramp v Jordan International Insurance Co (The Flag Evi)* [2017] 1 Lloyds Rep 27 [41]–[56].

[81] *Akai v People's Insurance* [1998] 1 Lloyds Rep 90, 98–100; *OT Africa Line v Magic Sportswear* [2005] 2 Lloyds Rep 170 (CA) 185–86, in particular at [77]; *Aline Tramp v Jordan International Insurance (The Flag Evi)* [2017] 1 Lloyds Rep 27 [41]–[56].

[82] *OT Africa Line v Magic Sportswear* [2005] 2 Lloyds Rep 170 (CA); *Shipowners' Mutual Protection and Indemnity Association (Luxembourg) v Containerships Denizcilik Nakliyat ve Ticaret (The Yusuf Cepnioglu)* [2016] 1 Lloyds Rep 641 (CA).

v EMC.[83] Still further, it is arguable that cases like *The Flag Evi,*[84] which show openness to the problem of the conflict of conflicts, are in tension with the wider propositions implicit in Longmore LJ's judgment in *The Yusuf Cepnioglu,* which suggest the conflict of conflicts should at least in general be ignored.[85] Whether and how weight can be given to the conflict of conflicts in certain situations will depend on how the case law develops.

3. Stay Applications in the Foreign Court

8.45   In *The Angelic Grace,* the Court of Appeal held that it is not a strong reason to refuse a contractual anti-suit injunction that the injunction claimant could, but has not yet made a jurisdiction challenge in the foreign court, or an application to the foreign court to stay the proceedings before it,[86] even if it is expected that the foreign court would enforce the exclusive forum clause and decline jurisdiction. Indeed, if there is no reason to expect the foreign court to reach a different decision as to where the litigation should be heard, this merely illustrates the lack of justification for the injunction defendant's intention to continue with the foreign proceedings.[87] This approach was at one time controversial, [88] but remains the law. Indeed, the modern case law emphasizes that anti-suit injunctions should be brought without delay,[89] and does not necessarily pardon delay even while a jurisdiction challenge is made in the foreign court.[90] That approach is inherently inconsistent with any requirement that a stay should first be applied for in the foreign court.

8.46   Similarly, it is not in itself a 'strong reason' against an injunction that such a jurisdiction challenge or stay application has been made to the foreign court, but has not yet been determined.[91]

8.47   In contrast, if the foreign stay hearing or jurisdiction challenge has taken place before the injunction hearing, and the foreign court has refused to stay or dismiss the proceedings before it, this can be a significant factor against the grant of an injunction, if the foreign court has applied principles relating to jurisdiction similar to those applied by the English court.[92]

---

[83]   *Petter v EMC* [2016] ILPr 1 (CA) 52. For an exploration of the inconsistencies, see T Raphael, 'Do as You Would be Done By: Anti-Suit Injunctions and System-Transcendent Justification' [2016] LMCLQ 256.
[84]   *Aline Tramp v Jordan International Insurance (The Flag Evi)* [2017] 1 Lloyds Rep 27.
[85]   See *Dell Emerging Markets (EMEA) v Systems Equipment Telecommunication Services* [2018] EWHC 702 [39], suggesting that the conflict of conflicts will 'ordinarily' be ignored.
[86]   *Aggeliki Charis Compania Maritima v Pagnan (The Angelic Grace)* [1995] 1 Lloyds Rep 87 (CA) 96; see also *Credit Suisse First Boston (Europe) v MLC (Bermuda)* [1999] 1 Lloyds Rep 767, 780–81; *Horn Linie v Panamericana Formas e Impresos (The Hornbay)* [2006] 2 Lloyds Rep 44 [25].
[87]   *Aggeliki Charis Compania Maritima v Pagnan (The Angelic Grace)* [1994] 1 Lloyds Rep 168, 182–83, [1995] 1 Lloyds Rep 87 (CA) 92. In *Toepfer International v Société Cargill France* [1997] 2 Lloyds Rep 98, 110–11, Colman J considered it a significant factor in favour of an injunction that he could see no way in which the French court could legitimately allow proceedings to continue under the terms of the New York Convention.
[88]   In particular, Phillips LJ expressed doubts in *Toepfer International v Société Cargill France* [1998] 1 Lloyds Rep 379 (CA) 386, as to which see generally Ch 7, paras 7.22–7.26.
[89]   See paras 8.20–8.21.
[90]   See eg *Ecobank Transnational v Tanoh* [2016] 1 WLR 2231 (CA) [124]–[126]; *ADM Asia-Pacific Trading v PT Budi Semesta Satria* [2016] EWHC 1427 (Comm) [42], [54].
[91]   *Aggeliki Charis Compania Maritima v Pagnan (The Angelic Grace)* [1994] 1 Lloyds Rep 168 (Rix J), 182, [1995] 1 Lloyds Rep 87 (CA) 95; *Toepfer International v Société Cargill France* [1997] 2 Lloyds Rep 98, 109; *Horn Linie v Panamericana Formas e Impresos (The Hornbay)* [2006] 2 Lloyds Rep 44 [25].
[92]   *Akai v People's Insurance* [1998] 1 Lloyds Rep 90, 105; *Society of Lloyd's v White* [2000] CLC 961, 972; *Transfield Shipping v Chiping Xinfa Huayu Alumina* [2009] EWHC 3629 (QB) [48]; and see the Canadian case of *Amchem Products v British Columbia (Workers Compensation Board)* [1993] 1 SCR 897 (Can SC) 931–32, 934.

Conversely, where the foreign court has applied markedly different principles in refusing a   **8.48**
jurisdiction challenge or stay, its refusal has generally been treated as of little or no weight as
a reason to refuse a contractual injunction,[93] at least if the application of different principles
is not the injunction claimant's fault.[94] In such a situation, however, it will be important to
consider whether the injunction claimant has delayed excessively in seeking an injunction
before the foreign court's decisions on jurisdiction.[95]

4. The Enforceability of the Injunction

In *Philip Alexander v Bamberger*, problems had arisen because the German courts had   **8.49**
refused to serve interim anti-suit injunctions, which they viewed as an infringement of
German sovereignty.[96] In response, Leggatt LJ suggested *obiter* that the English courts'
practice of granting anti-suit injunctions might require reconsideration, at least where the
defendant had no presence or assets in England and enforcement might require the cooperation of the foreign court, which might not be forthcoming.[97]

However, giving great weight to such a factor would be contrary to *The Angelic Grace*, where   **8.50**
the court granted an injunction without hesitation in exactly such a situation; and Leggatt
LJ's concerns have found little echo in the subsequent case law.[98] Anti-suit injunctions have
been granted in many cases where the defendant has no presence or assets in England,

---

[93] *Schiffahrtsgesellschaft Detlev von Appen v Voest Alpine Intertrading (The Jay Bola)* [1997] 1 Lloyds Rep 179,
188–89; *Akai v People's Insurance* [1998] 1 Lloyds Rep 90, 105; *Donohue v Armco* [2000] 1 Lloyds Rep 579 (CA)
591–92, 600, where it was significant that the foreign decision had been reached in part of the basis of an erroneous
understanding of English law (the Court of Appeal's decision was overturned, but not on this specific point [2002]
1 Lloyds Rep 425 (HL)): *Ecobank Transnational v Tanoh* [2016] 1 WLR 2231 (CA) [11]–[12], [50]. In *Society of
Lloyd's v White* [2000] CLC 961, 972 and *Transfield Shipping v Chiping Xinfa Huayu Alumina* [2009] EWHC 3629
(QB) [48], the court concluded that a foreign decision taken on different principles was in general of no weight. In
a non-contractual context, see *Airbus Industrie v Patel* [1997] IPLR 230 (CA) [57] (overturned on other grounds
[1999] 1 AC 119 (AC)).
   There are a significant number of recent decisions where there has been no attempt to rely on the fact of the
foreign court's decision to refuse a jurisdiction challenge as an argument which in itself justifies refusing the injunction, otherwise than as an element of the historical context of an argument based on delay or submission: see
eg *OT Africa Line v Magic Sportswear* [2005] 2 Lloyds Rep 170 (CA); *AES Ust-Kamenogorsk Hydropower Plant LLP
v Ust-Kamenogorsk Hydropower Plant JSC* [2012] 1 WLR 90 (CA), [2013] 1 WLR 1889 (SC); *ADM Asia-Pacific
Trading v PT Budi Semesta Satria* [2016] EWHC 1427 (Comm); *Impala Warehousing and Logistics (Shanghai) v
Wanxiang Resources (Singapore)* [2015] 2 All ER (Comm) 234, [106].
[94] In *Tracomin v Sudan Oil Seeds*, the Swiss courts would have applied English law on the incorporation of arbitration clauses, and stayed the Swiss proceedings in favour of arbitration, had evidence of English law been put before them, but due to an error by the injunction claimant, no such evidence was advanced, and so the Swiss courts,
applying Swiss law, held that there was no arbitration clause, and permitted the Swiss proceedings to continue. At
first instance, Leggatt J had held that the injunction claimant's error disentitled him from obtaining an anti-suit
injunction: *Tracomin v Sudan Oil Seeds Co (No 2)* [1983] 2 All ER 129, 137–38. However, the Court of Appeal disagreed, holding that the injunction claimant's negligence did not cancel out the blameworthiness of the injunction
defendant's breach of contract in proceeding in Switzerland: *Tracomin v Sudan Oil Seeds Co (Nos 1 and 2)* [1983] 1
WLR 1026 (CA) 1035–36.
[95] *Through Transport Mutual Insurance Association (Eurasia) v New India Assurance* [2004] 1 Lloyds Rep 206,
[32], overturned on other points [2005] 1 Lloyds Rep 67 (CA). As to delay in general, see paras 8.20–8.21.
[96] *Re the Enforcement of an English Anti-Suit Injunction* [1997] ILPr 320 (Oberlandesgericht Düsseldorf); see
also *Philip Alexander Securities & Futures v Bamberger* [1997] ILPr 73 [5] (Waller J) [48] (CA). The German injunction defendants, who were individual consumers, had ignored the interim injunctions granted.
[97] *Philip Alexander Securities & Futures v Bamberger* [1997] ILPr 73 (CA) [48] per Leggatt LJ, who had been one
of the unanimous court that decided *Aggeliki Charis Compania Maritima (The Angelic Grace)* [1995] 1 Lloyds Rep
87 (CA). The problems that arose with the German courts in the *Philip Alexander v Bamberger* case appear to have
caused Leggatt LJ to revisit, at least in part, the wisdom of his previous decision.
[98] However, see Sir P Gross, 'Anti-Suit Injunctions and Arbitration' [2005] LMCLQ 10, 15, 26.

without potential unenforceability abroad being viewed as a strong factor against the grant of the injunction.

8.51   To give significant weight to Leggatt LJ's concerns would also violate the principle that the court is not in the habit of proceeding on the assumption that its orders will not be obeyed.[99] The question of whether an injunction is likely to assist a claimant can usually be left to the claimant; and if an injunction defendant troubles to resist an injunction it can be fairly assumed that it will constrain his behaviour in some useful way. Consequently, it is suggested that while the doubtful enforceability of an injunction may be a relevant discretionary factor, it should generally not be viewed as a strong reason to refuse to grant relief.

---

[99] *Re Liddell's Settlement Trust* [1936] Ch 365 (CA) 374, where the Court of Appeal held that: 'It is not the habit of this court in considering whether or not it will make an order to contemplate the possibility that it will not be obeyed'; see also *Castanho v Brown & Root (UK)* [1981] AC 557 (HL) 574; *South Buckinghamshire (No 1) v Porter* [2003] 2 AC 558 (HL) [32]; and *Stichting Shell Pensionenfonds v Krys* [2015] AC 616 (PC) [37]. But this principle is not unquestioned: see in the family context *Hamlin v Hamlin* [1986] Fam 11 (CA) 18; *Wookey v Wookey* [1991] Fam 121 (CA) 130; *B v B* [2016] 2 WLR 487 (CA) [56].

9

Non-Exclusive Jurisdiction Clauses

A. INTRODUCTION

An exclusive forum clause binds the parties to litigate or arbitrate certain disputes exclusively in the chosen forum. In contrast, a non-exclusive jurisdiction clause permits litigation to proceed in the selected forum, but does not expressly prohibit litigation elsewhere. The purpose of a non-exclusive jurisdiction clause is 'to confer jurisdiction and avoid disputes about jurisdiction'.[1] It follows that litigation elsewhere is not in breach of a non-exclusive clause, unless in particular cases it can be said to be prohibited by an implied term of the contract, derived from the non-exclusive clause.[2]   **9.01**

Consequently, if there is a non-exclusive jurisdiction clause in favour of a particular jurisdiction, the general tests for the grant of anti-suit injunctions to restrain proceedings abroad will have to be satisfied, save where there is a relevant implied term prohibiting parallel litigation.[3] The *Angelic Grace* principles[4] do not apply, as this is not an injunction to restrain a breach of contract. Thus, it must be in the interests of justice to grant the injunction, and, in general, anti-suit relief will only be granted if the foreign proceedings are vexatious or oppressive.[5] There are cases where the court has used tests of vexation and oppression even where a relevant implied term has been found to exist,[6] but the more logical approach is that in such a situation the injunction should be treated as a contractual injunction governed by *Angelic Grace* principles, and this was the approach taken by the Court of Appeal in *Deutsche v Highland*.[7]   **9.02**

However, even if it brings with it no implied term restraining foreign litigation, the presence of a non-exclusive jurisdiction clause will be a relevant factor in assessing whether to grant an anti-suit injunction, as will be discussed further.   **9.03**

---

[1] *Pathe Screen Entertainment Ltd v Handmade Films (Distributors) Ltd* (Hobhouse J, 11 July 1989).
[2] *Deutsche Bank v Highland Crusader Partners* [2010] 1 WLR 1023 (CA) [105].
[3] *Sabah Shipyard (Pakistan) v Islamic Republic of Pakistan* [2003] 2 Lloyds Rep 571 (CA) [40]; *Royal Bank of Canada v Cooperatieve Centrale Raiffeisen-Boerenleenbank* [2004] 1 Lloyds Rep 471 (CA) 474–75; *Deutsche Bank v Highland Crusader Partners* [2010] 1 WLR 1023 (CA) [47]–[65], [105]–[106]. The key modern case is *Deutsche v Highland*, recently applied in *Dawnus Sierra Leone v Timis Mining Corporation* [2016] EWHC 236.
[4] Ch 7, section E, 'The *Angelic Grace* Principles'.
[5] *Deutsche Bank v Highland Crusader Partners* [2010] 1 WLR 1023 (CA) [47]–[65], [105]–[106]; for a recent example, see *Dana Gas v Dana Gas Sukuk* [2018] EWHC 277 (Comm) [40]–[41].
[6] *Sabah Shipyard (Pakistan) v Islamic Republic of Pakistan* [2003] 2 Lloyds Rep 571 (CA) [36]–[37], [42], although cf [52].
[7] *Deutsche Bank v Highland Crusader Partners* [2010] 1 WLR 1023 (CA) [110].

B. IMPLIED TERMS

9.04   It would be illogical, where the parties have expressly agreed only a non-exclusive jurisdiction clause, to imply a general term prohibiting proceedings in any other forum. Any implied term must therefore be limited to a prohibition of a limited set of foreign proceedings.

9.05   In *Sabah v Republic of Pakistan*, it was held that a claim for an anti-suit injunction abroad to restrain English proceedings where England had been selected by a non-exclusive jurisdiction clause was in a breach of an implied term of the non-exclusive jurisdiction agreement. By agreeing to England as a forum, the parties had impliedly agreed that England should not be prevented from being the forum.[8] However, this is an unusual situation, and in *Deutsche v Highland* the Court of Appeal confirmed that *Sabah* should be confined to those specific facts.[9]

9.06   It is now clear that in general, and without some specific basis in the wording for an implied term, a non-exclusive jurisdiction clause will not ordinarily support an implied term prohibiting litigation abroad. Instead, the starting point is that by contracting for non-exclusive jurisdiction, the parties have anticipated and accepted the possibility of some parallel proceedings.[10]

C. RELEVANCE OF THE CLAUSE TO THE INTERESTS OF JUSTICE

9.07   Where a non-exclusive jurisdiction clause does not clearly indicate whether prior or subsequent parallel proceedings in a non-selected forum are permitted or prohibited, the best interpretation will usually be that, by contracting for non-exclusive jurisdiction, the parties have anticipated and accepted the possibility of some parallel proceedings. As a result, the non-exclusive forum clause in favour of England does not create any presumption that the foreign proceedings are vexatious and oppressive, and only foreign proceedings which are vexatious and oppressive for some reason independent of the mere presence of the non-exclusive clause will be restrained by injunction.[11] The more expansive approach derived from *Sabah v Pakistan* has been checked in *Deutsche v Highland*, which confined *Sabah* to its own specific facts.[12]

---

[8] *Sabah Shipyard (Pakistan) v Islamic Republic of Pakistan* [2003] 2 Lloyds Rep 571 (CA) [6], [36]–[37], [41]–[43].
[9] *Deutsche Bank v Highland Crusader Partners* [2010] 1 WLR 1023 (CA) [85], [87], [112], [125]; *Evialis v SIAT* [2003] 2 Lloyds Rep 377 [101]–[103]. For another case where no such term was implied, see *ED & F Man Ship v Kvaerner Gibraltar (The Rothnie)* [1996] 2 Lloyds Rep 209. In general, it has not been argued that an implied term exists.
[10] *Deutsche Bank v Highland Crusader Partners* [2010] 1 WLR 1023 (CA) [105], relying on the first edition of this work. The previous authorities such as *Royal Bank of Canada v Cooperatieve Centrale Raiffeisen-Boerenleenbank* [2004] 1 Lloyds Rep 471 (CA) and *Catlin Syndicate v Adams Land & Cattle* [2006] 2 CLC 425, are now of lesser relevance.
[11] *Deutsche Bank v Highland Crusader Partners* [2010] 1 WLR 1023 (CA) [64], [105]–[114], [120]; and see also *Pathe Screen Entertainment v Handmade Films (Distributors)* (Hobhouse J, 11 July 1989); *Evialis v SIAT* [2003] 2 Lloyds Rep 377, 394–97.
[12] *Sabah Shipyard (Pakistan) v Islamic Republic of Pakistan* [2003] 2 Lloyds Rep 571 (CA), as discussed and distinguished in *Deutsche Bank v Highland Crusader Partners* [2010] 1 WLR 1023 (CA) [85], [87], [105]–[112], [126] (relying on the first edition of this work).

Nevertheless, even if there is no implied term prohibiting foreign proceedings, the pres- **9.08**
ence of an exclusive jurisdiction clause is still a relevant factor, as it can shape and influence
whether it is in the interests of justice to grant an injunction and whether the foreign proceedings are vexatious and oppressive. The courts take into account 'the spirit' of the clause,
and what types of foreign proceedings the parties can be taken to have 'envisaged'.[13]

A non-exclusive clause may affect the court's assessment of the interests of justice in respect **9.09**
of anti-suit injunctions in various ways, of which we mention two. First, the presence of such
a clause means that it will not be open for the injunction defendant to argue that England is
an inconvenient forum for the litigation, without strong reasons justifying oversetting the
clause.[14] Second, the clause may give more or less strong indications that parallel litigation
is either envisaged or deprecated.[15] But it will, it seems, require specific wording to confer
on the non-exclusively chosen forum any form of dominance.[16] It would appear that in this
context no special weight is to be given to which action was filed first.[17]

It may be that the foreign court has refused a jurisdiction challenge, and disregarded the **9.10**
non-exclusive choice of England, in circumstances where the English court would have respected a corresponding choice of another jurisdiction. This is not sufficient to justify an
injunction.[18]

---

[13] *Royal Bank of Canada v Cooperatieve Centrale Raiffeisen-Boerenleenbank* [2003] EWHC 2913 [64], [2004] 1
Lloyds Rep 471 (CA) 478.
[14] *Royal Bank of Canada v Cooperatieve Centrale Raiffeisen-Boerenleenbank* [2003] EWHC 2913 [66], not addressed on appeal [2004] 1 Lloyds Rep 471 (CA); *Deutsche Bank v Highland Crusader Partners* [2010] 1 WLR 1023
(CA) [64]; also *Sabah Shipyard (Pakistan) v Islamic Republic of Pakistan* [2003] 2 Lloyds Rep 571 (CA) [36], *BP v
National Fire Insurance Co* [2004] EWHC 1132 (Comm) [51].
[15] *Deutsche Bank v Highland Crusader Partners* [2010] 1 WLR 1023 (CA) [64], [115]; *Pathe Screen Entertainment
v Handmade Films (Distributors)* (Hobhouse J, 11 July 1989); *Sabah Shipyard (Pakistan) v Islamic Republic of
Pakistan* [2003] 2 Lloyds Rep 571 [40]; *Royal Bank of Canada v Cooperatieve Centrale Raiffeisen-Boerenleenbank*
[2003] EWHC 2913 [46], [65]–[68], [2004] 1 Lloyds Rep 471 (CA) [41]–[42].
[16] *Deutsche Bank v Highland Crusader Partners* [2010] 1 WLR 1023 (CA) [108], [120].
[17] *Deutsche Bank v Highland Crusader Partners* [2010] 1 WLR 1023 (CA) [117]; this is a somewhat different approach to *Royal Bank of Canada v Cooperatieve Centrale Raiffeisen-Boerenleenbank* [2003] EWHC 2913, [2004] 1
Lloyds Rep 471 (CA).
[18] *Deutsche Bank v Highland Crusader Partners* [2010] 1 WLR 1023 (CA) [50], [63]; *Dawnus Sierra Leone v
Timis Mining Corporation* [2016] EWHC 236 [67].

10

Quasi-Contractual Anti-Suit Injunctions

A. INTRODUCTION

The use of the term 'quasi-contractual' in this chapter is not meant to revive the shadows of **10.01** the old fiction of quasi-contractual promises used to justify restitutionary claims. Instead, it refers to anti-suit injunctions which are granted where the injunction defendant may not fully be party to and bound by a contractual forum clause as a matter of contract law, but should nevertheless be required to comply with the effect of the clause, 'as if' the injunction was contractual.[1] Substantively we are concerned with the 'penumbral' effect of forum clauses on third parties who are not fully contractually bound by the clause.

There are two types of case where quasi-contractual injunctions may be granted: third- **10.02** party situations, and cases where the injunction claimant himself denies that the exclusive forum clause is binding.

1. Third-Party Situations

Assume a contract between A and B which contains a forum clause. Between each other, **10.03** A and B must respect the clause. A third party, C, may obtain rights against A which flow from B's contractual rights against A. Two different ways in which he may have acquired rights against A must be distinguished.

First, there is a variety of rules under which a third party can become, or be deemed **10.04** to become, an actual contracting party who acquires the burden together with the benefit of the contract, such as collateral contracts, novation, the doctrine of un-disclosed principal, statutory succession,[2] and the Carriage of Goods by Sea Act

---

[1] The language of 'quasi-contractual' was used in *Sea Premium Shipping v Sea Consortium* (David Steel J, 11 April 2001) and also, paying regard to the first edition of this work, in *Dell Emerging Markets (EMEA) v IB Maroc. com* [2017] EWHC 2397 (Comm) [10], [22].

[2] *Donohue v Armco* [2000] 1 Lloyds Rep 579 (CA) [27] (reversed on other points, [2002] 1 Lloyds Rep 425 (HL)).

1992.[3] In those cases, the analysis is usually uncomplicated: C has become contractually bound by the forum clause and normal contractual principles apply. In such a situation, an anti-suit injunction is not quasi-contractual, but contractual.

10.05   Second, a third party may obtain *derived rights* under or in respect of a contract without becoming party to the contract, under rules such as assignment, subrogation, the Third Parties (Rights Against Insurers) Act 2010, the Contracts (Rights of Third Parties) Act 1999, or similar rules of foreign law. Anti-suit injunctions against a third party C with derived rights, which seek to compel C to respect the forum clause, on the ground that C cannot take the benefit of the contract without its burden, are quasi-contractual injunctions in the sense used here.

2. Where the Injunction Claimant Denies the Force of the Forum Clause

10.06   In some cases, the injunction defendant asserts, and the injunction claimant denies, that a contract containing an exclusive forum clause exists; but the injunction defendant nevertheless seeks to sue the injunction claimant on the merits, in a forum inconsistent with that provided for by the contract whose validity he himself asserts. The injunction defendant's contractual claims are potentially inherently inconsistent. An injunction sought by the injunction claimant in such a case can also be called *quasi*-contractual, because the injunction claimant does not himself assert that a contractual right exists, although the situation is not quite the same as more conventional quasi-contractual injunctions granted in cases of derived rights.

10.07   This chapter will consider third-party derived rights and quasi-contractual anti-suit injunctions, in Sections B–E. It will consider 'inconsistent claims' situations where the injunction claimant denies the existence of the forum clause in Section F, 'Inconsistent Contractual Claims'.

B. DERIVED RIGHTS AND FORUM CLAUSES

10.08   The English courts have consistently held that, where a third party makes claims for derived rights 'in the shoes' of an original party to a contract (the creditor) against the other party to the contract (the debtor), then however the third party acquired derived rights, those rights are subject to and should not be exercised inconsistently with any arbitration or jurisdiction clause[4] contained in the original contract.[5] This approach is uncontroversial when both the

---

[3] *OT Africa Line v Hijazy (No 1) (The Kribi)* [2001] 1 Lloyds Rep 76 [27(1)], [54]–[72]; *Aline Tramp v Jordan International Insurance (The Flag Evi)* [2017] 1 Lloyds Rep 467 [23]–[40].

[4] The same approach was applied to 'no-action' clauses in *Whitesea Shipping and Trading v El Paso Rio Clara (The Marielle Bolten)* [2010] 1 Lloyds Rep 648.

[5] The recent leading case is *Shipowners' Mutual Protection and Indemnity Association (Luxembourg) v Containerships Denizcilik Nakliyat ve Ticaret (The Yusuf Cepnioglu)* [2016] 1 Lloyds Rep 641 (CA). The Supreme Court granted permission to appeal but the case settled before the appeal hearing. See also *Firma C-Trade v Newcastle Protection and Indemnity Association (The Fanti and the Padre Island)* [1991] 2 AC 1 (HL) and *Schiffahrtsgesellschaft Detlev von Appen v Voest Alpine Intertrading (The Jay Bola)* [1997] 2 Lloyds Rep 279 (CA).

forum clause, and the method by which the third party acquires derived rights, are governed by English law.

Thus, an assignee is entitled to benefit from, and is bound by, any relevant contractual **10.09** forum clause governing the contract under which the assignor's rights against the debtor arose, when enforcing the assigned right.[6] Where an insurer brings claims in the name and right of his insured under the English doctrine of subrogation those claims are subject to any arbitration or jurisdiction clause binding on the insured in respect of the relevant right.[7] Further, it has been held that if an insured has tortious claims, but is bound by a forum clause in a connected contract which covers such connected tortious claims, then a subrogated insurer claiming in the shoes of the insured must respect the forum clause just as the insured would have been obliged to do—because the duty to arbitrate is an 'inseparable component' of the tortious rights transferred by subrogation to the insurer.[8] The same approach has been applied to trustees in bankruptcy.[9]

Similarly, where a third party brings a direct claim against an insurer under the Third **10.10** Parties (Rights Against Insurers) Act 2010,[10] and the contract of insurance contains a forum clause, any claim brought by the third party against the insurer is subject to the 'incidents' of the insured's claim against the insurer, including the forum clause. The third party's rights are subject to the forum clause; can benefit from the forum clause; and can only be claimed in the agreed forum.[11] The courts have rejected any distinction between derived rights

---

[6] *Pena Copper Mines v Rio Tinto* (1912) 105 LT 846; *Aspell v Seymour* (1929) WN 152 (CA); *Rumput (Panama) v Islamic Republic of Iran Shipping Lines (The Leage)* [1984] 2 Lloyds Rep 259, 262; *Montedipe v JTP-RO Jugotanker (The Jordan Nicolov)* [1990] 2 Lloyds Rep 11, 17; *Schiffahrtsgesellschaft Detlev von Appen v Voest Alpine Intertrading (The Jay Bola)* [1997] 1 Lloyds Rep 179, 187–88, [1997] 2 Lloyds Rep 279 (CA), 283, 285–86; *Glencore International v Metro Trading International (No 1)* [1999] 2 Lloyds Rep 632, 644–46; *Bankers Trust v PT Mayora Indah* (Colman J, 20 January 1999); *Nisshin Shipping v Cleaves* [2004] 1 Lloyds Rep 38, 45; *STX v Woori* [2012] 2 Lloyds Rep 99 [9]–[11] (undefended); *BNP Paribas v Russian Machines* [2012] 1 Lloyds Rep 61 [76] (adopting the corresponding passage in the first edition of this work); *Royal Bank of Scotland v Highland Financial Partners* [2012] 2 CLC 109 [139]–[141].

[7] *Schiffahrtsgesellschaft Detlev von Appen v Voest Alpine Intertrading (The Jay Bola)* [1997] 1 Lloyds Rep 179, 186, 188; *OT Africa Line v Hijazy (The Kribi) (No 1)* [2001] 1 Lloyds Rep 76 [67]; *Navigation Maritime Bulgare v Rustal Trading (The Ivan Zagubanski)* [2002] 1 Lloyds Rep 106 [52(4)], [112]–[119]; *West Tankers v RAS Riunione Adriatica di Sicurta (The Front Comor)* [2005] 2 Lloyds Rep 257 [15]–[34], [67] (the point was not certified for appeal to the House of Lords, and Colman J's conclusion was recorded without disapproval by Lord Hoffmann: [2007] 1 Lloyds Rep 391 (HL) [7]); *BNP Paribas v Russian Machines* [2012] 1 Lloyds Rep 61 [76]; *London Steam Ship Owners Mutual Insurance Association v Kingdom of Spain (The Prestige) (No 2)* [2014] 1 Lloyds Rep 309 [136]; *Aline Tramp v Jordan International Insurance (The Flag Evi)* [2017] 1 Lloyds Rep 467 [23]–[40].

[8] *West Tankers v Ras Riunione Adriatica di Sicurta (The Front Comor)* [2005] 2 Lloyds Rep 257 [25], [26], [30]–[33], [67]–[68].

[9] *Bannai v Erez* [2013] EWHC 3689 [3].

[10] Which has been described as in effect a 'statutory assignment': *Charterers Mutual Assurance Association v British & Foreign* [1998] ILPr 838 [38]; *Youell v Kara Mara Shipping* [2000] 2 Lloyds Rep 102 [58] and n 54; *Nisshin Shipping v Cleaves &* [2004] 1 Lloyds Rep 38, 45.

[11] *Socony Mobil Oil v The West of England Ship Owners Mutual Insurance Association (London) (The Padre Island) (No 1)* [1984] 2 Lloyds Rep 408, 414; *Socony Mobil Oil v The West of England Ship Owners Mutual Insurance Association (London) (The Padre Island) (No 2)* [1987] 2 Lloyds Rep 529, 533–34; *London Steamship Owners Mutual Insurance Association v Bombay Trading (The Felicie)* [1990] 2 Lloyds Rep 21, 26 (although much of the rest of the reasoning in that case has not been followed); *Firma C-Trade v Newcastle Protection and Indemnity Association (The Fanti and the Padre Island)* [1991] 2 AC 1 (HL) 33B–D; *Charterers Mutual Assurance Association v British & Foreign* [1998] ILPr 838 [37]–[38], [44]–[46]; *Nisshin Shipping v Cleaves &* [2004] 1 Lloyds Rep 38, 45; *BNP Paribas v Russian Machines* [2012] 1 Lloyds Rep 61 [76]; *London Steam Ship Owners Mutual Insurance Association v Kingdom of Spain (The Prestige) (No 2)* [2015] 2 Lloyds Rep 33 (CA) [30]; *Shipowners' Mutual Protection and Indemnity Association (Luxembourg) v Containerships Denizcilik Nakliyat ve Ticaret AS (The Cepnioglu)* [2016] 1 Lloyds Rep 641 (CA) [2], [46]–[47].

acquired by some form of voluntary transfer like assignment and subrogation, and derived rights acquired under statutes like the Third Parties (Rights Against Insurers) Acts 2010.[12]

10.11   The Contracts (Rights of Third Parties) Act 1999 has its own specific provisions in this regard, in sections 1(4), 8(1), and 8(2). The effect of these is that a third party enforcing his substantive rights under the Act has the ability to enforce against the promisor a forum clause which was intended to give rights to him,[13] and unless the original contracting parties objectively appear to have intended otherwise, the third party's rights can only be enforced consistently with any relevant exclusive jurisdiction or arbitration clause in the original contract.[14]

10.12   If an arbitration clause is subject to the Arbitration Act 1996, section 8(1) of the Contracts (Rights of Third Parties) Act 1999 goes further and provides expressly that if the third party seeks to enforce his rights against the promisor, and the original contract contained an arbitration clause governing the substantive rights in question, the third party shall be treated as a party to the arbitration agreement for the purpose of the 1996 Act.[15] However,

---

[12]   *Shipowners' Mutual Protection and Indemnity Association (Luxembourg) v Containerships Denizcilik Nakliyat ve Ticaret (The Yusuf Cepnioglu)* [2016] 1 Lloyds Rep 641 (CA) [27], [47].

[13]   See *Millen v Karen Millen Fashions* [2017] FSR 7 [336]–[341]. In the Law Commission Report which led to the Act, the original intention was that this would not be possible: Law Commission Report No 242, *Privity of Contract: Contracts for the Benefit of Third Parties*, paras 14.14–14.19, and consequently in the draft Bill attached to the Report, arbitration clauses and jurisdiction clauses were excluded from the scope of the Act at cll 6.2(d)–(e). See also A Burrows, 'Reforming Privity of Contract: Law Commission Report No. 242' [1996] LMCLQ 467, 481–82. However, the Law Commission subsequently changed its mind, and the Bill as introduced into Parliament reversed this position, as it omitted these exclusions, with the apparent purpose of allowing a third party to benefit from arbitration or jurisdiction clauses when enforcing his third-party rights, if this is consistent with the original contracting parties' intentions: *Hansard*, HL Deb, Vol 596, cols 27–28, 32–34 (11 January 1999); HL Deb, Vol 601, col 1059 (27 May 1999). Further if (as discussed in n 14) the effect of s 1(4) is that the third party will be *bound* by arbitration and jurisdiction clauses, it must follow that the third party can also *benefit* from such clauses.

[14]   This follows from s 1(4) of the Contracts (Rights of Third Parties) Act 1999, which provides that the Act 'does not confer a right to a third party to enforce a term of a contract otherwise than subject to and in accordance with any other relevant terms of the contract'. The conclusion is reinforced for arbitration clauses governed by the Arbitration Act 1996 by s 8(1) of the 1999 Act, but follows from s 1(4) in any event, and thus also applies to exclusive jurisdiction clauses, and arbitration clauses outside the Arbitration Act. See *Nisshin Shipping v Cleaves* [2004] 1 Lloyds Rep 38 [42], [47]–[48]; *Millen v Karen Millen Fashions* [2017] FSR 7 [336]–[344], [352]. This is not, on the true reading of the case, undermined by *Hurley Palmer Flatt v Barclays Bank* [2014] EWHC 3042 (TCC) [26], [32]–[38]); discussed in *Millen* at [340]. Further, in general, original contracting parties should be taken, unless they agree otherwise, to have intended that exclusive jurisdiction clauses and arbitration clauses should be binding on third-party claims by a 'conditional benefit' analysis: see *Nisshin Shipping v Cleaves* [2004] 1 Lloyds Rep 38 [47]–[48]; *Millen v Karen Millen Fashions* [2017] FSR 7 [343]–[344].

This analysis is supported by the pre-legislative materials, although the point is not quite as absolutely clear as one might wish. The Explanatory Notes, [9], [32], [33]–[35], point in this direction but are unclear. The point is made clearer by *Hansard*, HL Deb, Vol 601, cols 1054–1060 (27 May 1999), HC Deb, Second Reading Committee, col 4 (29 June 1999), where the Lord Chancellor explained that the third party would have to make use of agreed dispute resolution procedures (he used the language of 'alternative' but appears to have had in mind agreed forum clauses) where this was consistent with the original contracting parties' intentions, but that such parties could provide for certain dispute resolution clauses to apply only to themselves or the third party. It would, furthermore, be perverse if the third party's rights were bound by arbitration clauses, pursuant to s 8 of the 1999 Act, but not by exclusive jurisdiction clauses. The Law Commission's original comments in Law Commission Report No 242, paras 14.14–14.17 could be read as suggesting the contrary (see R Merkin (ed), *Privity of Contract* (Routledge 2000) para 5.123). However, the Law Commissioner responsible, Professor Burrows, subsequently explained that the Law Commission had intended only to produce the result that the third party would not have the *right* to enforce the forum clause but that the forum clause could still be a condition on the third party's substantive rights: A Burrows, 'Reforming Privity of Contract: Law Commission Report No 242' [1996] LMCLQ 467, 481–82. By the time of the passage of the 1999 Act, the Law Commission's views had evolved further, and the exclusions of arbitration and jurisdiction clauses from the draft bill were removed, with the apparent intention of enabling them to be both enforceable and effectively binding under s 1(4).

[15]   For discussion of s 8(1), and the back-up provision in s 8(2), see *Nisshin Shipping v Cleaves* [2004] 1 Lloyds Rep 38, 44–46; *Fortress Value Recovery Fund v Blue Skye Special Opportunities Fund* [2013] 1 WLR 3466 (CA), and

it seems that this provision had the narrower purpose of ensuring that the Arbitration Act 1996 would have full statutory effect in relation to the third party's claims, and possibly also to ensure that the third party has a positive right to arbitrate if he sues on his third-party claims, if this was otherwise in any doubt. It is submitted that it should not be treated as creating by statute a positive contractual right to prohibit litigation elsewhere which could support a full contractual anti-suit injunction.[16]

C. AN OBLIGATION NOT TO SUE ELSEWHERE?

The principle that someone who sues in the shoes of another should be subject to the same **10.13** conditions as the person he replaces could be viewed as merely imposing inherent restrictions on the exercise of rights without adding additional positive obligations, through a 'conditional benefit' analysis. Yet the English courts have gone further, and have held that there is a form of positive obligation on a third party who claims under derived rights not to sue in any forum other than the forum specified in the original contract (at least where all the relevant relationships are governed by English law). This applies not only where the third party acquires his derived rights under doctrines of equity such as assignment or subrogation but also, it seems, where he acquires them under third-party rights statutes such as the Third Parties (Rights Against Insurers) Acts 1930 and 2010[17] or the Contracts (Rights of Third Parties) Act 1999.[18]

The third party is not a party to the exclusive forum clause 'in the full sense', and is not under **10.14** full contractual obligations, but he is 'bound' by the forum clause by a form of obligation, at least if he has made a substantive claim on the underlying contractual obligations, and is treated as bound by the clause for the purposes of the Arbitration Act 1996[19] and the State Immunity Act.[20] The obligation in question has been held to be sufficient to support an

---

Millen v Karen Millen Fashions [2017] FSR 7 [340]–[341]. See also Arbitration Act 1996, s 82(2), defining a party to an arbitration agreement as including anyone who claims 'under or through a party to the agreement'.

---

[16] See the Explanatory Notes to the Contract (Rights of Third Parties) Act 1999, paras 33–35; HL Deb, Vol 601, cols 1059–1060 (27 May 1999), HL Deb, Vol 606, cols 1363–1364 (10 November 1999); *Millen v Karen Millen Fashions* [2017] FSR 7 [340]–[341]. The comments in *Fortress Value Recovery Fund v Blue Skye Special Opportunities Fund* [2013] 1 WLR 3466 (CA) [42]–[43], [45], [53]–[54], do not clearly address this question, but may best be read as regarding s 8(1) as imposing a 'procedural condition' on the substantive rights, not a substantive contractual obligation.

[17] *Charterers Mutual Assurance Association v British & Foreign* [1998] ILPr 838 [37]–[38], [44]–[46] (foreign third-party rights statute); *Youell v Kara Mara Shipping* [2000] 2 Lloyds Rep 102 [51], [56], [65] (ditto); *West Tankers v RAS Riunione Adriatica di Sicurta (The Front Comor)* [2005] 2 Lloyds Rep 257 [69]–[70] (reasoned, *obiter*, that there should be no distinction between statutory and equitable transfers of rights); *London Steam Ship Owners Mutual Insurance Association v Kingdom of Spain (The Prestige) (No 2)* [2014] 1 Lloyds Rep 309 [136] (foreign third-party rights statute); and on appeal [2015] 2 Lloyds Rep 33 (CA) [30] (apparently conceded on appeal); *Shipowners' Mutual Protection and Indemnity Association (Luxembourg) v Containerships Denizcilik Nakliyat ve Ticaret (The Yusuf Cepnioglu)* [2016] 1 Lloyds Rep 641 (CA) [1]–[2], [14], [16], [21], [33], [46]–[51] (foreign third-party rights statute).

[18] See *Nisshin Shipping v Cleaves* [2004] 1 Lloyds Rep 38 [34].

[19] *Through Transport Mutual Insurance Association (Eurasia) v New India Assurance (No 2)* [2005] 2 Lloyds Rep 378 [25]–[28]; *West Tankers v Ras Riunione Adriatica di Sicurta (The Front Comor) (No 2)* [2007] EWHC 2184 (Comm) [10]; *Shipowners' Mutual Protection and Indemnity Association (Luxembourg) v Containerships Denizcilik Nakliyat ve Ticaret AS (The Yusuf Cepnioglu)* [2016] 1 Lloyds Rep 641 (CA) [1]–[2], [14], [16], [21], [33], [46]–[51]; *Dell Emerging Markets (EMEA) v IBMaroc.com* [2017] EWHC 2397 [34].

[20] *London Steam Ship Owners Mutual Insurance Association v Kingdom of Spain (The Prestige) (No 2)* [2014] 1 Lloyds Rep 309 [136] and on appeal [2015] 2 Lloyds Rep 33 (CA) [55]–[71].

application for the appointment of an arbitrator against the third party provided that the third party has asserted claims in respect of the substantive rights under the contract;[21] to allow arbitrators to have jurisdiction to make declarations on the merits against the third party even if he denies they have jurisdiction;[22] to permit a declaration that the third party must make any claims arising from the contract in the chosen forum (although not a declaration that he is in *breach* of contract if he does not),[23] and to justify an application to enforce an award of declaratory relief under section 66(1) of the Arbitration Act 1996.[24] Further, the courts have also consistently concluded that the obligation is sufficient to support a quasi-contractual anti-suit injunction against the third party in appropriate cases.[25]

10.15   However, it is not entirely easy to identify the juridical basis of the obligation or obligations by which the third party with derived rights is bound, and this may vary, dependent on the nature of the way in which the derived rights arise.

10.16   The obligation will not, it seems, be an actual contractual duty, as that would amount to imposing the burden of a transferred contract on an assignee or subrogor or third party under the third-party rights statutes, which would be contrary to conventional principle.[26]

---

[21]   *Through Transport Mutual Insurance Association (Eurasia) v New India Assurance (No 2)* [2005] 2 Lloyds Rep 378; *West Tankers v Ras Riunione Adriatica di Sicurta (No 2)* [2007] EWHC 2184 (Comm) [10] (undefended); *London Steam Ship Owners Mutual Insurance Association v Kingdom of Spain (The Prestige) (No 2)* [2014] 1 Lloyds Rep 309, [2015] 2 Lloyds Rep 33 (CA).

[22]   It follows from the court's willingness to appoint an arbitrator that it would also uphold the tribunal's jurisdiction. Arbitrators have also upheld their own jurisdiction in such cases, as is illustrated by the cases which deal with the consequences of arbitration awards, such as *London Steam Ship Owners Mutual Insurance Association v Kingdom of Spain (The Prestige) (No 2)* [2014] 1 Lloyds Rep 309, [2015] 2 Lloyds Rep 33 (CA) and *West Tankers v Ras Riunione Adriatica di Sicurta (The Front Comor)* [2012] 2 Lloyds Rep 103.

[23]   *Through Transport Mutual Insurance Association (Eurasia) v New India Assurance* [2005] 1 Lloyds Rep 67 (CA) [63]–[65]; *London Steam Ship Owners Mutual Insurance Association v Kingdom of Spain (The Prestige) (No 2)* [2014] 1 Lloyds Rep 309 [136]. Declarations were also granted in *Charterers Mutual Assurance Association v British & Foreign* [1998] ILPr 838 [65].

[24]   *West Tankers v Ras Riunione Adriatica di Sicurta* [2011] 2 Lloyds Rep 117; *London Steam Ship Owners Mutual Insurance Association v Kingdom of Spain (The Prestige) (No 2)* [2014] 1 Lloyds Rep 309, [2015] 2 Lloyds Rep 33 (CA).

[25]   *Schiffahrtsgesellschaft Detlev von Appen v Voest Alpine Intertrading (The Jay Bola)* [1997] 2 Lloyds Rep 279 (CA); *Charterers Mutual Assurance Association v British & Foreign* [1998] ILPr 838 [44]–[46]; *Youell v Kara Mara Shipping* [2000] 2 Lloyds Rep 102 [51], [56], [65]; *OT Africa Line v Hijazy (The Kribi) (No 1)* [2001] 1 Lloyds Rep 76, [67]; *West Tankers v Ras Riunione Adriatica di Sicurta (The Front Comor)* [2005] 2 Lloyds Rep 257; *Through Transport Mutual Insurance Association (Eurasia) v New India Assurance* [2005] 1 Lloyds Rep 67 (CA) [63]–[65]; *Steamship Mutual Underwriting Association (Bermuda) v Sulpicio Lines* [2008] 2 Lloyds Rep 269 (undefended); *Royal Bank of Scotland v Highland Financial Partners* [2012] 2 CLC 109 [139]–[141]; *STX v Woori* [2012] 2 Lloyds Rep 99 [9]–[11] (undefended); *BNP Paribas v Russian Machines* [2012] 1 Lloyds Rep 61, [76]; *Shipowners' Mutual Protection and Indemnity Association (Luxembourg) v Containerships Denizcilik Nakliyat ve Ticaret (The Yusuf Cepnioglu)* [2016] 1 Lloyds Rep 641 (CA); *Dell Emerging Markets (EMEA) v IBMaroc.com* [2017] EWHC 2397 [10], [22]–[24], [34]; *Aline Tramp v Jordan International Insurance (The Flag Evi)* [2017] 1 Lloyds Rep 467 [40]. See also the recent (undefended) decision in *Qingdao Huiquan Shipping v Shanghai Dong He Xin Industry Group* [2018] EWHC 3009 [31].

[26]   *Schiffahrtsgesellschaft Detlev von Appen v Voest Alpine Intertrading (The Jay Bola)* [1997] 2 Lloyds Rep 279 (CA) 286 (per Hobhouse LJ, agreed with by Morritt LJ); *Through Transport Mutual Insurance Association (Eurasia) v New India Assurance (No 1)* [2005] 1 Lloyds Rep 67 (CA) [52], [65] (since doubted on other aspects, but not on this); *Shipowners' Mutual Protection and Indemnity Association (Luxembourg) v Containerships Denizcilik Nakliyat ve Ticaret (The Yusuf Cepnioglu)* [2016] 1 Lloyds Rep 641 (CA) [24], [32], [50], [56]; *Dell Emerging Markets (EMEA) v IBMaroc.com* [2017] EWHC 2397 [22]. There are some suggestions in the case law that the quasi-contractual injunction should be viewed as contractual rather than equitable, but they are a minority view: *The Jay Bola*, at 291–92 (per Scott VC) (in contrast the majority view of Hobhouse LJ and Morritt LJ was along more conventional conditional benefit/equitable lines). See further Ch 14, paras 14.26–14.28.

In the line of cases relating to the imposition on assignees of contractual burdens correlated with the contractual benefits claimed by the assignee (stemming from *Halsall v Brizell* [1957] Ch 169), there is some controversial case law suggesting that the obligations assumed by the assignee are not merely conditional but include

In some specific cases, such as assignment and subrogation, the third party's attempt to **10.17** evade the contractual jurisdiction clause will be inconsistent with an established independent substantive equity, such as the equitable principle that an assignee is subject to the equities that bind an assignor. But other situations where the third party acquires derived rights, such as claims under third-party rights statutes, do not fall within such pre-existing equitable doctrines.

It would be possible to escape the need for a substantive positive obligation, and to justify **10.18** and support the case law on quasi-contractual injunctions, by basing such injunctions on general principles of vexation and oppression. Where the third party's rights are derived from a contract between a creditor and a debtor, it is well arguable that it will often be vexatious and oppressive, and thus something which the court will restrain in the exercise of its powers under section 37(1) of the Senior Courts Act 1981 and in equity, for the third party to seek to claim those derived rights against the debtor without accepting the limitations to which they were inherently subject.[27]

The authorities are not definitive in this regard, although the bulk of the current case law appears to be best explained on the basis that the positive obligation binding on the third party **10.19** is a substantive equitable obligation, binding a third party not to seek to take the benefit of a contract without the burden of the exclusive forum clause to which that contract is subjected, which arises because it would be unconscionable, or contrary to good conscience,

---

independent contractual obligations. If this turns out to be the law, and if it applies to forum clauses, it could potentially apply to the burden of forum clauses with respect to assignees. Even to the extent it becomes the law it is submitted that this approach is best to be interpreted as the imposition of equitable obligations to respect such independent contractual obligations. These issues are discussed more closely in Ch 14, para 14.28 and n 58.

[27] *Royal Bank of Scotland v Highland Financial Partners* [2012] 2 CLC 109 [139]–[141]; *BNP Paribas v Russian Machines* [2012] 1 Lloyds Rep 61 [79]–[92], where on the specific facts the court was unconvinced that a quasi-contractual analysis was appropriate; *Jewel Owner v Sagaan Developments Trading (The MD Gemini)* [2012] 2 Lloyds Rep 672 [15]; *Dell Emerging Markets (EMEA) v IBMaroc.com* [2017] EWHC 2397 [21], [24], [33], [34]. See also *Shipowners' Mutual Protection and Indemnity Association (Luxembourg) v Containerships Denizcilik Nakliyat ve Ticaret (The Yusuf Cepnioglu)* [2015] 1 Lloyds Rep 567 [43]–[44], where Teare J approached an anti-suit injunction to restrain a claim under a third-party rights statute, on the basis that it would be vexatious and oppressive to ignore the contractual clause to which the insured's rights were subject; on appeal the Court of Appeal appears to have adopted an equitable analysis, following *The Jay Bola*: see [2016] 1 Lloyds Rep 641 (CA) [23], [27], [33], [35], [36] (per Longmore LJ), although Moore-Bick LJ's analysis was less definite in this regard: see [46]–[51], but also [55]–[56].
However, if there were no concrete positive obligation of any sort on the third party to comply with the contractual forum clause, and the injunction was based on vexation and oppression alone, this could have jurisdictional consequences. The current case law accepts a claim for a quasi-contractual anti-suit injunction falls within the gateways for claims 'in respect of a contract' which is 'governed by English law' or which 'contains a term to the effect that the court shall have jurisdiction to determine any claim in respect of the contract' in Practice Direction 6B, para 3.1(6)(c) and (d). In some cases, this has been justified on the basis that the third party is positively bound by the contractual forum clause, in equity not contract: *Schiffahrtsgesellschaft Detlev von Appen v Voest Alpine Intertrading (The Jay Bola)* [1997] 2 Lloyds Rep 279 (CA) 287; *Youell v Kara Mara Shipping* [2000] 2 Lloyds Rep 102 [51]. In *Shipowners' Mutual Protection and Indemnity Association (Luxembourg) v Containerships Denizcilik Nakliyat ve Ticaret (The Yusuf Cepnioglu)* [2015] 1 Lloyds Rep 567 [43]–[44], Teare J accepted that a quasi-contractual injunction preventing a third party from circumventing the arbitration clause (but which Teare J viewed as justified by vexation and oppression), was sufficiently 'in relation to a contract' to come within Practice Direction 6B para 3.1(6)(c) (see Ch 18, para 18.48). If Teare J is right, then the need to use an equitable analysis to avoid unwelcome jurisdictional difficulties is lessened; but given the confused case law on Practice Direction 6B para 3.1(6) the position in this regard deserves further clarification (see Ch 18, para 18.48, in particular at n 77).
The third side of the triangle is that (as discussed in Section D, 'Third-Party Rights under Foreign Law') a substantive equitable analysis may make the choice of law questions confronting anti-suit injunctions more intractable. The courts will need to settle on a juridical analysis which enables them to make both jurisdiction and choice of law work in a satisfactory manner.

for the third party to seek to do so.[28] This specific equity differs from the debatable general equitable rights and obligations which may (but may not) underlie non-contractual anti-suit injunctions in general,[29] as it means the third party is 'bound' to respect the clause. It is distinct from any such general equitable obligations and it may exist even if they do not. It appears that such specific equities may arise not only where the third party's derived rights themselves arise in contract or equity, but also where they arise under third-party rights statutes, although the law in this regard is not yet fully developed.[30]

10.20   The third party will have the right to elect to choose not to rely on the derived rights at all. If it does not, then no obligation will arise binding it with respect to the exclusive forum clause. However, it may not be necessary for the third party to have actually commenced proceedings: the assertion of derived claims which, if commenced, would be bound by the exclusive forum clause may be sufficient.[31]

---

[28] *Schiffahrtsgesellschaft Detlev von Appen v Voest Alpine Intertrading (The Jay Bola)* [1997] 2 Lloyds Rep 279 (CA) 286 (where on its true reading, Hobhouse LJ's reasoning is not confined to the narrow case of assignment; note, however, the different analysis of Scott VC at 291); *Charterers Mutual Assurance Association v British & Foreign* [1998] ILPr 838 [44]–[46] (although Judge Diamond QC seems to have thought that not only equitable but also legal rights would be infringed); *Youell v Kara Mara Shipping* [2000] 2 Lloyds Rep 102 [51], [56], [65]; *Donohue v Armco* [2000] 1 Lloyds Rep 579 (CA) [27] (not appealed on this point); *Nisshin Shipping v Cleaves* [2004] 1 Lloyds Rep 38, 44 (more general); *West Tankers v Ras Riunione Adriatica di Sicurta (The Front Comor)* [2005] 2 Lloyds Rep 257 [70]; *Through Transport Mutual Insurance Association (Eurasia) v New India Assurance (No 2)* [2005] 2 Lloyds Rep 37 [15]–[25]; *Whitesea Shipping and Trading v El Paso Rio Clara (The Marielle Bolten)* [2010] 1 Lloyds Rep 648 [21]; *Royal Bank of Scotland v Highland Financial Partners* [2012] 2 CLC 109 [139]–[141]; *London Steam Ship Owners Mutual Insurance Association v Kingdom of Spain (The Prestige) (No 2)* [2014] 1 Lloyds Rep 309 [136] (but see the CA decision, [2015] 2 Lloyds Rep 33 (CA), discussed in this regard at n 30); *Shipowners' Mutual Protection and Indemnity Association (Luxembourg) v Containerships Denizcilik Nakliyat ve Ticaret (The Yusuf Cepnioglu)* [2016] 1 Lloyds Rep 641 (CA) [1]–[2], [14], [16], [21], [33], [46]–[51] (although cf [55]–[56]); *Aline Tramp v Jordan International Insurance (The Flag Evi)* [2017] 1 Lloyds Rep 467 [40] ('obligation').
This analysis is in tension with aspects of the reasoning of *Through Transport Mutual Insurance Association (Eurasia) v New India Assurance* [2005] 1 Lloyds Rep 67 (CA), where [52]–[60], [63], [93] are consistent with an equitable obligation, but [89]–[90], [93] are less so. However, in *The Yusuf Cepnioglu*, at [32]–[33], [43], [54], [56] the Court of Appeal concluded that so far as there was a discrepancy, *Through Transport* was itself inconsistent with *The Jay Bola*, and that the *Jay Bola* was to be preferred.
[29]   For the vexed debate on whether such concrete general equitable obligations not to act vexatiously, oppressively, or unconscionably, do underpin non-contractual anti-suit injunctions in general, see Ch 3, section B, 'A Legal or Equitable Right?'.
[30]   *Charterers Mutual Assurance Association v British & Foreign* [1998] ILPr 838 [44]–[46]; *Youell v Kara Mara Shipping* [2000] 2 Lloyds Rep 102 [51], [56], [65]; *Through Transport Mutual Insurance Association (Eurasia) v New India Assurance (No 2)* [2005] 2 Lloyds Rep 378 [20]–[25], where Moore-Bick LJ discussed *The Jay Bola* and explained that the equitable analysis adopted there was not confined to situations of assignment and applied to all transferees, including claimants under third-party rights statutes; *West Tankers v Ras Riunione Adriatica di Sicurta (The Front Comor)* [2005] 2 Lloyds Rep 257 [69]–[70], where the point was not decided, but Colman J interpreted the case law as suggesting that no distinction should be drawn between an equitable and a statutory transfer of rights; *London Steam Ship Owners Mutual Insurance Association v Kingdom of Spain (The Prestige) (No 2)* [2014] 1 Lloyds Rep 309 [136] (not identifying the nature of the obligation) (but see the Court of Appeal decision discussed below); *Shipowners' Mutual Protection and Indemnity Association (Luxembourg) v Containerships Denizcilik Nakliyat ve Ticaret (The Yusuf Cepnioglu)* [2016] 1 Lloyds Rep 641 (CA) [1]–[2], [14], [16], [21], [33], [46]–[51].
In *London Steam Ship Owners Mutual Insurance Association v Kingdom of Spain (The Prestige) (No 2)* [2015] 2 Lloyds Rep 33 (CA) [30], the Court of Appeal concluded that for the purposes of characterization in the conflicts of laws, the question of whether the third party's claim should respect the forum clause to which the transferred rights were subject should be characterized as 'issues relating to an obligation sounding in contract' and therefore governed by the law applicable to the contract. They did not mention a possible equitable analysis. We submit, however, that this classification under private international law does not prevent the English law analysis being equitable as a matter of substantive law (see para 10.43). We address the the tension between the equitable analysis and finding a workable approach to choice of law, more generally, in section D, 'Third Party Rights Airing Under Foreign Law'.
[31]   *Through Transport Mutual Insurance Association (Eurasia) v New India Assurance (No 2)* [2005] 2 Lloyds Rep 378 [28], but compare cf *Aspen Underwriting v Kairos Shipping* [2017] EWHC 1904 (Comm) [48]–[51].

The question of whether a specific equitable obligation exists, and if so, what that means, **10.21** has not yet been fully examined. It intertwines with the choice of law analysis, with questions of territorial jurisdiction,[32] and also with the nature of the threshold tests for the grant of anti-suit injunctions.[33] The correct juridical basis is therefore not a technical question, nor to be blindly determined by authority: it must be shaped with open eyes to make the law work sensibly in multiple dimensions.

D. THIRD-PARTY RIGHTS ARISING UNDER FOREIGN LAW

Difficult questions of the conflicts of laws can be posed where the contract out of which **10.22** underlying rights arise or to which underlying rights were subject is governed by English law, but the third party's acquisition of rights is governed by a foreign law. Examples include where an insured creditor's relationship with his insurer is governed by an insurance contract which is subject to a foreign law, but the insured's contract with the debtor is an English law contract, which contains an exclusive forum clause; or where a third party claims under a foreign third-party rights statute to, in effect, enforce an English law contract against the debtor.

If the third party's acquisition of derived rights occurs under a foreign law which provides, **10.23** similarly to English law, that the third party's rights are subject to any contractual forum clause that would have bound the creditor, then no difficulty is likely to arise, and the third party's rights will be held to be subject to the forum clause.[34] Obviously the law of the transferred right cannot transfer more to the third party than the law of the transfer purports to transfer.

However, where the foreign law under which derived rights are conferred analyses the **10.24** issues in a different fashion, in particular if under the foreign law the third party's rights would not be subject to the forum clause in the original contract, the court is faced with a problem of conflicts of laws. Should the question of whether the third party's rights to sue the debtor are subjected to the forum clause be determined by English law, the law of the contract in which the forum clause is found, or should it be determined by the foreign law applying to the transaction under which the transference of rights to the third party was effected, or by some other law?

1. The *Through Transport* Approach: Classifying the Underlying Claim as Contractual

The response of the English courts has so far been consistent, wherever the underlying con- **10.25** tract between the initial debtor and creditor is governed by English law. The approach developed in a line of cases such as *Through Transport* and *The Prestige* is that the court will

---

[32] See n 27 and Ch 18, para 18.48.

[33] Section E, 'Principles for Quasi-Contractual Injunctions Based on Denied Rights'. It is also relevant to whether a claim in damages can be made in quasi-contractual situations (cf *Royal Bank of Scotland v Highland Financial Partners* [2012] 2 CLC 109 [139]–[141]). This is discussed at Ch 14, paras 14.25–14.29.

[34] *OT Africa Line v Hijazy (The Kribi) (No 1)* [2001] 1 Lloyds Rep 76 [68]; *West Tankers v Ras Riunione Adriatica di Sicurta (The Front Comor)* [2005] 2 Lloyds Rep 257 [35]–[41]; *Bannai v Erez* [2013] EWHC 3689 [3].

ask itself, from the perspective of English law,[35] whether the substance of the right which the third party sought to enforce against the debtor was contractual, and arose under the English law contract in which the contractual forum clause was found. If so, then whether or not the foreign law under which the third party was given rights would itself treat the third party's rights as bound by the forum clause, English law will be treated as the applicable law to determine whether the third party is obliged to respect the forum clause. As a result, the English law principles we have identified mean that the forum clause will be treated as requiring the third party to sue in the chosen forum, in any situation of derived rights which are in substance contractual, irrespective of the approach taken by the foreign law governing the conferral of the derived right.[36] On the existing case law, this applies to cases of statutory transfer under foreign third-party statutes, just as much as to transfer by voluntary doctrines such as assignment and subrogation, provided that the right conferred is characterized as a contractual and not an independent statutory right.

10.26   In *The Front Comor*, Colman J confronted a related situation where owners and charterers agreed a charterparty subject to an arbitration clause, which was broad enough to capture connected tortious claims. So, if charterers had sued owners in tort, they would have been obliged to arbitrate. The charterers' subrogated Italian insurers sought to bring the charterers' tortious claims by way of subrogation, in their own name as Italian insurance law allowed, without respecting the arbitration clause. It was argued that Italian law would permit this, and it was common ground that Italian law was the law of the tortious claims. This situation is not capable of being resolved by asking whether the transferred tortious rights are in themselves contractual. Colman J nevertheless concluded it was the law of the arbitration agreement which should govern whether the tortious claims could be brought independently of the arbitration clause, not the law of the tort, because this was a question of the effect of the arbitration clause on the tortious claims.[37]

---

[35]   The case law so far says the question of characterization must be answered using English law concepts of characterization: *Through Transport Mutual Insurance Association (Eurasia) v New India Assurance* [2004] 1 Lloyds Rep 206 [11] (upheld on appeal on this point, [2005] 1 Lloyds Rep 67 (CA) [55]–[64]); *BNP Paribas v Russian Machines* [2012] 1 Lloyds Rep 61 [78] (not addressed on appeal, *Joint Stock Asset Management Company Ingosstrakh Investments v BNP Paribas* [2012] 1 Lloyds Rep 649 (CA)); *London Steam Ship Owners Mutual Insurance Association v Kingdom of Spain (The Prestige) (No 2)* [2014] 1 Lloyds Rep 309 [52], [2015] 2 Lloyds Rep 33 (CA) [11]; *Shipowners' Mutual Protection and Indemnity Association (Luxembourg) v Containerships Denizcilik Nakliyat ve Ticaret (The Yusuf Cepnioglu)* [2015] 1 Lloyds Rep 567 [33], [2016] 1 Lloyds Rep 641 (CA) [14]–[16], [44]. But as discussed in para 10.32, this begs the question of whether European jurisdictional law concepts of characterization should not be the first port of call.

[36]   *Youell v Kara Mara Shipping* [2000] 2 Lloyds Rep 102 [54]–[61], [70], [73]; *Sea Premium Shipping v Sea Consortium* (David Steel J, 11 April 2001); *Through Transport Mutual Insurance Association (Eurasia) v New India Assurance* [2004] 1 Lloyds Rep 206, 209–11 (upheld on appeal on this point, [2005] 1 Lloyds Rep 67 (CA) [52]–[60], [63]–[64]); see also *Through Transport Mutual Insurance Association (Eurasia) v New India Assurance (No 2)* [2005] 2 Lloyds Rep 378, [4], [20]–[28] (commented on in J Harris, 'Arbitration Clauses and the Restraint of Proceedings in Another Member State of the European Union' [2005] LMCLQ 159, 162–64); *West Tankers v Ras Riunione Adriatica di Sicurta (The Front Comor)* [2005] 2 Lloyds Rep 257 [26]–[33]; *Starlight Shipping v Tai Ping Insurance (The Alexandros T)* [2008] 1 Lloyds Rep 230 [14]; *BNP Paribas v Russian Machines* [2012] 1 Lloyds Rep 61 [76]–[78] (this point was not cross-appealed in *Joint Stock Asset Management Company Ingosstrakh Investments v BNP Paribas* [2012] 1 Lloyds Rep 649 (CA)); *London Steam Ship Owners Mutual Insurance Association v Kingdom of Spain (The Prestige) (No 2)* [2014] 1 Lloyds Rep 309 [47]–[53], [2015] 2 Lloyds Rep 33 (CA) [10]–[30]; *Shipowners' Mutual Protection and Indemnity Association (Luxembourg) v Containerships Denizcilik Nakliyat ve Ticaret (The Yusuf Cepnioglu)* [2016] 1 Lloyds Rep 641 (CA) [1]–[4], [14]–[16], [46].

The point was apparently not contested in *Schiffahrtsgesellschaft Detlev von Appen v Voest Alpine Intertrading (The Jay Bola)* [1997] 2 Lloyds Rep 279 (CA) 284–85, or *Navigation Maritime Bulgare v Rustal Trading (The Ivan Zagubanski)* [2002] 1 Lloyds Rep 106.

[37]   *West Tankers v Ras Riunione Adriatica di Sicurta (The Front Comor)* [2005] 2 Lloyds Rep 257 [33]. But the reasoning is terse and compressed.

In contrast, if the third party is given an independent statutory right by the foreign statute, **10.27** the logic of the *Through Transport/Prestige* derived-rights approach does not impose the binding force of the forum clause by virtue of the application of the law of the contract.[38] Not all claims by third parties in respect of contracts are claims for derived rights. For example, in *BNP Paribas v Russian Machines*, a Russian company had concluded an English law guarantee allegedly subject to an arbitration clause with the injunction claimant. One of the company's Russian shareholders brought a claim before the Russian courts, to which the Russian company and injunction claimant were both defendants, to annul the guarantee on the basis that it was inconsistent with Russian company law. Blair J found the question of whether the Russian claim should be characterized as contractual, and so treated as subject to the forum clause in the guarantee by reference to English law, as of 'very considerable difficulty', and although he did not need to decide the point, was not persuaded that the Russian claim was subject to the clause. Indeed, the shareholder was not asserting any contractual rights against the injunction claimant, and it did not stand 'in the shoes' of the Russian company. Its claims were ones which would not have been available to the Russian company itself in an action against the injunction claimant.[39]

In such cases, an injunction could in principle be granted applying more general non- **10.28** contractual principles for anti-suit injunctions, such as vexation or oppression. There will be cases where the evasion of a forum clause in an underlying contract is vexatious even if the claim made abroad is not in substance contractual.[40]

The justifications given for the *Through Transport* approach have been variable, although the **10.29** courts have tended to proclaim their consistency. In *The Prestige*, Moore Bick LJ regarded the relevant issue as being 'whether the Club's liability can be enforced only in arbitration' and reasoned that if the underlying right transferred to the third party was essentially contractual, 'it is necessary to look to the contract of insurance to determine the extent of that right ... since that contract is governed by English law, it is necessary to turn to English law to determine the scope of the insurers' liability and the terms on which it may be enforced'.[41] This was essentially the approach he took in *The Yusuf Cepnioglu*, although he also added that in the view of English law, where the claimant must sue:

---

[38] In *Through Transport Mutual Insurance Association (Eurasia) v New India Assurance* [2004] 1 Lloyds Rep 206 [16], Moore-Bick J suggested that if the third party's claim was independent and not contractual, the foreign law under which it was created would determine the force of the forum clause. Things may not be so simple.

[39] *BNP Paribas v Russian Machines* [2012] 1 Lloyds Rep 61 [77]–[78] (this point was not cross-appealed in *Joint Stock Asset Management Company Ingosstrakh Investments v BNP Paribas* [2012] 1 Lloyds Rep 649 (CA)). Similarly in *Markel International v Craft (The Norseman)* [2007] 1 Lloyds Rep IR 403 [31], Morison J was prepared to accept it was arguable on the facts before him that the foreign third-party rights claim was brought independently of the contract (although distinguishing those facts from *Youell v Kara Mara Shipping* [2000] 2 Lloyds Rep 102, which was not cited to him, would have been difficult).

[40] As in *BNP Paribas v Russian Machines* [2012] 1 Lloyds Rep 61 [92].

[41] *London Steam Ship Owners Mutual Insurance Association v Kingdom of Spain (The Prestige) (No 2)* [2015] 2 Lloyds Rep 33 (CA) [29]–[30]. See also to similar effect *West Tankers v RAS Riunione Adriatica di Sicurta (The Front Comor)* [2005] 2 Lloyds Rep 257 [26]–[33]; *Starlight Shipping v Tai Ping Insurance (The Alexandros T)* [2008] 1 Lloyds Rep 230 [14]; *Navigation Maritime Bulgare v Rustal Trading (The Ivan Zagubanski)* [2002] 1 Lloyds Rep 106 [52(1)], [54].

For a different logic, see his earlier reasoning as Moore Bick J in *Through Transport Mutual Insurance Association (Eurasia) v New India Assurance* [2004] 1 Lloyds Rep 206 [16], approved [2005] 1 Lloyds Rep 67 (CA) [57]. As he put it there, the issue for characterization was whether the third party was bound by the clause; if the right transferred to the third party was a contractual rather than an independent right, then the issue was 'contractual' and should be treated as one of 'obligation', and thus should be governed by the proper law of the underlying contract creating the obligation.

depends on the system of law which governs the right he seeks to enforce, as that is characterised by English conflicts of laws rules. If that right is governed by a system of law other than that which provides a direct right of action, the latter will not be regarded under English law as capable of modifying it. (Moore-Bick LJ at para [42])

But for his part in *The Yusuf Cepnioglu*, Longmore LJ approached the characterization question differently, saying: 'it would be too narrow to characterise the issue in the case as whether the Club has the right not to be vexed by foreign proceedings or even whether the Club has the right to rely on the London arbitration clause in its rules'. Instead, he regarded the question as simply being 'whether the charterers' right to sue the Club direct is essentially a contractual right (in which case it will be governed by English law as the proper law of the contract) or an independent right (in which case it will be governed by Turkish law).'[42] As we will explain, we submit that it is Moore-Bick LJ's additional comments in *The Yusuf Cepnioglu* that give us a path to the best answer, although the issues are not easy.

10.30   In recent years, the compatibility of the *Through Transport/Prestige* analysis with the logic of private international law has been questioned. Distinguished academic commentary has contended for a different approach.[43] The Supreme Court granted permission to appeal in *The Yusuf Cepnioglu*, although the case settled before the hearing. The *Through Transport/ Prestige* approach appears at first sight to make robust sense, but on closer examination has an elusive, lapidary quality. At least in its simpler formulations, it does not seem to be a methodologically orthodox application of choice of law principles whether English or European, and with respect, it begs the question. In such third-party situations, the law of the original right between creditor and debtor, the law of any transfer, and even the law of the third party's claim against the debtor, could all be relevant. Simply stating that the derived right is in itself contractual does not answer why the conditions of its exercise in the hands of the third party must be governed by the law of the original contract with the debtor, nor demonstrate that the issue for characterization when assessing an anti-suit injunction is itself a contractual issue. Nor does it give an answer to the situation in *The Front Comor*, where the derived tortious right is plainly not contractual, and the question is whether the forum clause which would bind such right against the original victim should also affect it when claimed for by a transferee. And generally, the approach was initially formulated before the Rome I and Rome II Regulations and assumes without examination, even in the cases post-dating those Regulations, that the European instruments have no role to play. (In the following discussion we assume that the Rome I and II Regulations will continue to be the law; but as matters stand this is likely to be the case, in substance and so far as relevant, irrespective of how Brexit is resolved: see Ch 1, Section I, 'Brexit'.)

10.31   The following analysis therefore re-examines matters from first principle and concludes:

(1) The issue of whether there is a quasi-contractual obligation to enforce against the third party, or whether a quasi-contractual injunction should be granted, is a

---

[42] *Shipowners' Mutual Protection and Indemnity Association (Luxembourg) v Containerships Denizcilik Nakliyat ve Ticaret (The Yusuf Cepnioglu)* [2016] 1 Lloyds Rep 641 (CA) [16] (Longmore LJ), and [42] (Moore-Bick LJ).

[43] A Briggs, 'Direct Actions and Arbitration: All at Sea' [2016] LMCLQ 238; A Dickinson, 'The Right to Rome? The Law Applicable to Direct Claims against Insurers and Anti-Suit Injunctions' (2016) 132 LQR 536.

question which falls outside both Rome I and Rome II. The applicable law is therefore governed by English choice of law rules.

(2) The applicable law for that question is probably unaffected by Article 18 of Rome II, even in the limited cases of direct claims against insurers where Article 18 has potential relevance.

(3) As a matter of principle under English choice of law rules, the law to be applied to the quasi-contractual obligation and quasi-contractual injunction is the law of the underlying contract (or the law of the forum) and not the law of the transfer. The *Through Transport* result is thus right, although reached by different reasoning.

a) The Rome I and II Regulations

The initial problem is whether either, and if so which, of the European instruments apply   **10.32** (assuming that they remain the law, or are in substance continued). This poses a question of characterization that probably should be determined, not by English common law conflicts of laws principles, but by the autonomous interpretation of the Regulations or whatever continues their substantive effect.[44]

The Rome I Regulation applies to 'contractual obligations', although by Article 1.2(e) it does   **10.33** not apply to arbitration agreements and agreements on the choice of court; and both the Rome Regulations exclude 'evidence and procedure'. Further, Article 14(2) of Rome I states in terms that, in relation to voluntary assignment or contractual subrogation, the law governing the assigned or subrogated claim shall govern 'the relationship between the assignee or subrogee and the debtor' and 'the conditions under which the assignment or subrogation can be invoked against the debtor'. In contrast, the Rome II Regulation applies to 'non-contractual' obligations, and contains no exclusion for forum clauses. In relation to third-party claims against insurers, it contains a specific rule in Article 18, that the third party may bring his claim directly against the insurer 'if the law applicable to the non-contractual obligation or the law applicable to the insurance contract so permits'.

There is a range of different possible situations against which these issues need to be tested,   **10.34** including: (a) claims by third parties under general laws providing for third-party rights in contract (such as the Contract (Rights of Third Parties) Act 1999); (b) underlying contractual claims brought against debtors by assignees or subrogees; (c) underlying tortious claims against debtors brought by assignees or subrogees of a creditor who also has contractual claims subject to a forum clause (the *Front Comor* situation); (d) claims under statutes granting third-party rights against insurers, or similar, where the underlying claim against the debtor by the insured is contractual; (e) the same, where the underlying claim against the insured is tortious.

In this context, there are different ways of approaching the characterization question.   **10.35**

One threshold point is whether we should be focusing on underlying obligations at all, or   **10.36** whether the issue is instead merely whether the third party can be compelled to respect the forum clause—potentially, we are just characterizing the claim for an injunction itself, not any underlying obligation. If so, this may simplify the analysis.

---

[44] Case C-359/14, *Ergo Insurance v If P&C Insurance* [2016] ILPr 20, ECJ [43].

10.37   If, however, the analysis is focused on substantive underlying obligations, we can, like Moore Bick LJ, identify the relevant issue as being whether the third party's claim against the creditor is bound by the forum clause in the contract between creditor and debtor—or in other language the 'penumbral' effect of the forum clause—and seek to characterize that issue. But this may require further refinement: is the issue of whether the third party is 'bound' a question of conditional benefit, or positive obligation, or both; and are those separate issues or just parts of the overall question of whether the third party is 'bound'? The alternative approach, looking at the possible underlying obligations from the perspective of the third party, is to identify the relevant issue as being what are the incidents or conditions of the third party's claims against the creditor, or possibly against both debtor and creditor, and whether those incidents include the 'penumbral' effect of the clause.

10.38   Yet whichever way the issue is identified, it does seem incomplete to ask solely whether the third party's claim against the creditor is contractual or independent. That appears to be an element of the characterization and choice of law reasoning, rather than actually the issue to be characterized.

10.39   It is suggested that, if forced to confront the application of the Rome instruments, the English courts will be strongly tempted to regard these questions, however they are diced up, as outside both Rome I and Rome II, and in particular as outside Rome II. There are three principal ways this might be achieved.

10.40   First, a quasi-contractual anti-suit injunction, together with any non-contractual anti-suit injunction, could be regarded as a procedural matter, outside both Rome I and Rome II.[45]

10.41   Second, even if the question is viewed as one of substantive obligation, the relevant obligations could be regarded as non-contractual, but nevertheless outside Rome II, on the basis that Rome II applies to tort/delict obligations flowing from damage; while the obligation which the anti-suit injunction enforces, if equitable, should be regarded as of a different kind (and perhaps quasi-procedural).[46]

10.42   In Chapter 4, this work has suggested that something along the lines of these first and/or second solutions may be the right analysis for non-contractual anti-suit injunctions in general.[47]

10.43   Third, and in particular if the issue for characterization is identified as being whether the third party is bound by the clause or can be compelled to obey it, quasi-contractual

---

[45]   By virtue of Articles 1(3) of Rome I and Rome II. See *Turner v Grovit* [2002] 1 WLR 107 (HL) [30]–[40]. This is consistent with Case C–159/02, *Turner v Grovit* [2004] ECR I–3565, AG [26]–[27], [37], ECJ [22], [29], and Case C-195/07, *Allianz v West Tankers (The Front Comor)* [2009] ECR I-663, AG [33], [36]. The ECJ's case law proceeds on the basis that anti-suit injunctions to restrain proceedings in other Brussels–Lugano courts within the material scope of the Brussels–Lugano regime are inconsistent with the principle of mutual trust *even if* regarded as merely procedural.

   There is a potential tension between this analysis and the reasoning in *Hoteles Pinero Canarias v Keefe* [2016] 1 WLR 905 (CA), where it was held that the question of whether a direct action exists was substantive, not procedural: at [36(vii)], [77]. But that case was decided in a very specific context; and it is possible to distinguish between the (substantive) issue of whether a direct action exists and the (potentially procedural) issues of whether an injunction should lie to protect a forum clause.

[46]   Case C-359/14, *Ergo Insurance v If P&C Insurance* [2016] ILPr 20, ECJ [44]–[45], interpreting the Rome II Regulation as applying only to 'obligations ensuing from damage, that is to say, any consequentce arising out of tort/delict' (leaving aside other matters not relevant here).

[47]   Ch 4, section B, 'Applicable Law'.

injunctions or any substantive obligations they enforce could be characterized as contractual matters for the purposes of the conflict of laws (to the extent they are substantive and not procedural). This would be on the basis that any quasi-contractual equitable obligation, or quasi-contractual injunction based on vexation or oppression, is essentially concerned with whether the contractual obligation in the forum clause should be respected. It is a 'penumbral' obligation which exists around and in relation to that contractual obligation.[48] In all the situations where the original right is contractual, it would be difficult to characterize the issue of conditional benefit as anything other than contractual; and that conditional benefit must be very closely linked to any matching positive obligation.

In turn, the issue of whether the third party is bound by the forum clause, if viewed as contractual, would seem to be a matter relating to the arbitration clause, or the choice of court agreement (as the case may be), and so outside Rome I under Article 1(2)(e), with the result that the applicable law will be determined by English choice of law rules. But even if that were not so, and Rome I applied, it would seem unlikely that the law of the transfer would be applied. Where the underlying claim of the creditor against the debtor is contractual, Article 14(2) would suggest that in situations of transfer, all aspects of the relationship between **10.44**

---

[48] In *Youell v Kara Mara Shipping* [2000] 2 Lloyds Rep 102, the quasi-contractual claim for an injunction was considered to be 'in respect of a contract' for the purposes of the common law rules of jurisdiction because, in essence, it was seeking to enforce a contract against the injunction defendant: at [62]–[65].

In addition, the English courts have held that claims for derived contractual rights are themselves claims 'in matters relating to a contract' for the purposes of Article 7(1) of the Recast: *Atlas Shipping v Suisse Atlantique* [1995] 2 Lloyds Rep 188 [17]–[18]; *WPP Holdings Italy v Benatti* [2007] 1 WLR 2316 [54]–[55].

Otherwise, there is no decision directly on point, but assistance can be drawn from the following:

(1) In Case C-359/14, *Ergo Insurance v If P&C Insurance* [2016] ILPr 20, ECJ [54], [58], [62]; an insurer's liability to compensate a third party victim of his insured was viewed as a contractual matter for the purposes of Rome I, and not within Rome II, with the result that the law of the insurance contract applied; in turn, questions of subrogation between insurers (who were not in contractual relations) were also contractual.

Further, in *Verein für Konsumenteninformation v Amazon EU*, Case C-191/15 [2017] QB 252, AG [44]–[50], and see ECJ [49], the Advocate General (with whom the court agreed as to the result) reasoned that to be contractual within Rome I it was not necessary for the contractual commitment to be between the parties to the dispute; it was sufficient if the obligation in question had a contractual origin between A and B, who had agreed it even if it was being enforced against C.

(2) In Case C-27/02, *Engler v Janus Versand* [2005] ILPr 8, ECJ [33], it was said that to be contractual the obligation in question must be 'freely consented', and see Case C-51/97, *Reunion Europeene v Spliethoff's Bevrachtingskantoor* [2000] QB 690, AG [24], ECJ [20]. But in the recent case law this has been interpreted flexibly. Thus, it is sufficient if a contractual obligation has been freely consented between A and B, and the claim by A against C or by C against A derives from the contractual obligation between A and B, such that what is being enforced against by C is contractual even if he did not himself consent to it: Case C-419/11, *Ceska Sporitelna v Feichter* [2013] ILPr 22, ECJ [46]–[51]; Case C-548/12, *Brogsitter v Fabrication de Montres Normandes* [2014] QB 753, esp at ECJ [25]–[27]; Case C-274/16, *flightright v Air Nostrum Lineas Aereas del Mediterraneo* [2018] 1 Lloyds Rep 626, AG [53]–[54], ECJ [59]–[64]. (However, note the restrictive approach in Case C-375/13, *Kolassa v Barclays Bank* [2015] ILPr 14 ECJ [36]–[41], although cf AG [47].)

(3) The English authorities interpreting the ECJ cases, and applying them to the question of whether a matter is 'contractual' for the purposes of Rome I and Rome II, have concluded that it is not necessary for the third-party defendant C to be party to the contract, and that claims against C arising out of or penumbral to an underlying contract between A and B may be contractual, but the contract must be 'indispensable' for the claim against the third party, and the 'basis' of the claim against him: see *Committeri v Club Mediterranee* [2016] EWHC 1510 (QB) [48], [2018] EWCA Civ 1889 [42]–[56].

(4) An analogy can be derived from the European Court's case law under Article 25: see Ch 17, section B, 'Jurisdiction over Final Anti-Suit Injunctions under the Brussels–Lugano Regime', para 17.45.

(5) Finally, see the Dogauchi/Hartley Explanatory Memorandum to the 2005 Hague Convention on the Choice of Court (2013) at para 97.

debtor and third party, presumably including the binding effect of the forum clause, should be governed by the law of the debtor–creditor contract.

10.45   The contractual analysis will be all the stronger if surrounding aspects of the three-cornered relationship are also contractual in the particular case. Thus, where there is an assignment or subrogation to a third party of an underlying contractual claim against the debtor governed by a forum clause, it would be surprising if the question of conditional benefit, and any connected positive obligation, could be regarded as anything other than contractual matters. Similarly, if the third party has acquired rights from an English law contract under the Contracts (Rights of Third Parties) Act 1999, the question of conditional benefit (under ss 1(4) and/or 8(1)) will inevitably be contractual questions governed by English law[49] (and probably outside Rome I) and in turn it would be very difficult to give the scope of any positive obligation (equitable or otherwise) any different analysis. Even if a third party acquires rights against an insurer under a third-party rights statute, but the third party's original claim against the debtor was contractual, two sides of the triangle will push towards a contractual analysis.

10.46   Andrew Dickinson has advanced a contrary analysis in relation to the problem of third-party rights against insurers which arose in *The Yusuf Cepnioglu*. He regards the issue to be characterized as the existence or otherwise of the positive obligation, which he regards as substantive, and suggests that there is a 'strong, if not irresistible' argument that the correct characterization of that issue is tortious and so within Rome II. Applying the European Court's decision in *Engler* on Article 7 of the Brussels I Recast, he argues that the matter could only be contractual, and Rome I could only apply, if the third party had 'freely consented' to any actual contract with the insurer to respect the forum clause, but that this will not be the case for third parties claiming under such third party statutes.[50]

10.47   However, the European Court's case law on when an obligation has been 'freely consented' to, developed in the context of the Brussels–Lugano regime, is relatively flexible. It allows a contractual classification to be applied to a range of situations arising between A and C, where A and B have freely agreed a contract, there is no direct agreement between A and C, but C's claims against A derive from B's freely consented contractual rights.[51] Further, when characterizing matters for the Rome I and Rome II Regulation, in *Ergo v If* the European Court concluded that an insurer's liability to compensate a third-party victim of his insured was a contractual matter (to which the law of the insurance contract applied).[52] Dickinson's logic would risk applying different laws to the closely linked questions of on the one hand, conditional benefit—which is inescapably contractual—and on the other hand, of positive obligation on the third party.

10.48   It is suggested, therefore, that if we focus on the question of whether the third party is bound by the forum clause, the contractual analysis is the more persuasive.

---

[49]   *Committeri v Club Mediterranee* [2016] EWHC 1510 (QB) [48]; *Atlas Shipping v Suisse Atlantique* [1995] 2 Lloyds Rep 188 [17]–[18]; *WPP Holdings Italy v Bennatti* [2007] 1 WLR 2316 [54]–[55].

[50]   A Dickinson, 'The Right to Rome? The Law Applicable to Direct Claims against Insurers and Anti-Suit Injunctions' (2016) 132 LQR 536, applying Case C-27/02, *Engler v Janus Versand* [2005] ILPr 8.

[51]   See n 48.

[52]   Case C-359/14, *Ergo Insurance v If P&C Insurance* [2016] ILPr 20, ECJ [58], also AG [58], [71].

The arguments for a tortious characterization become more substantial where the third **10.49** party's claim against the creditor (or insured) is tortious, and where, additionally, the third party acquires his claim against the debtor (or insurer) by statutory transfer. It then becomes more credible to characterize the issue as being what are the incidents of the third party's separate tortious claim, and who is a legitimate defendant to that claim and on what conditions, and thus subject to the law applicable to the tort.[53] In another context, prior to Rome II, and with less at stake, Moore-Bick LJ was prepared *obiter* to characterize the question of whether a victim of injury had a direct claim against the wrongdoer's insurer as a question of substantive tort law.[54] Yet, even in such a tortious situation, the English courts are more likely to regard the issue in play for the purposes of anti-suit injunctions as being the penumbral effect of the forum clause—whether or not the third party is bound by the forum clause when claiming against the insurer—and so as a contractual question.

Finally, even if the question of the existence of such a penumbral equitable obligation **10.50** binding on the third party were tortious, there would be arguments that the obligation was 'manifestly more closely connected' to the contract under which the third party has acquired a conditional benefit (under Article 4(3) of Rome II).

b) Article 18 of Rome II

If the third party has acquired rights by way of a foreign statute creating third-party rights **10.51** against insurers, Article 18 of Rome II introduces an additional complication. It provides: 'The person having suffered damage may bring his or her claim directly against the insurer of the person liable to provide compensation if the law applicable to the non-contractual obligation or the law applicable to the insurance contract so provides.' This provision is difficult to grasp.

Two points should be made. First, it seems it will only apply to third-party rights based on **10.52** underlying tortious claims against the insured, not those based on underlying contractual claims—because if the underlying claim is contractual, there is no basis to apply Rome II to its incidents, and there is no equivalent in Rome I (where the closest analogy is the different provision of Article 14(2) of Rome I, albeit directly dealing with voluntary assignment only). Second, even for underlying tortious claims, Dickinson has suggested that Article 18 does not apply to direct actions against insurers brought outside the EU,[55] in which case it will be of little relevance to anti-suit injunctions (given *Turner v Grovit* and *Front Comor*).

In relation to those direct actions to which it applies, Article 18 supports an argument that **10.53** since it gives the third-party victim the option of suing the insurer under either the law applicable to the tort, or the law applicable to the non-contractual obligation, then the law applicable to the tort, if selected, will govern all incidents of the direct action, including

[53] Cf A Briggs, 'Direct Actions and Arbitration: All at Sea' [2016] 120 LMCLQ 328, 329.

[54] *Hoteles Pinero Canarias v Keefe* [2016] 1 WLR 905 (CA) [79]–[80] (Moore-Bick LJ). However, in that case, both the contractual analysis and the tortious analysis pointed to the same law and there was no question of whether or not the third party should comply with a forum clause. Gloster LJ, at [36(viii)], 40–41], and Black LJ at [60], did not find it necessary to decide the point. Further, Moore-Bick LJ's analysis depended on a characterization of the nature of the third-party right: that it equated to treating the insurer as vicariously liable for the tort of the insured. But in the *Through Transport/Prestige* line of cases, the third-party right in issue was viewed differently, as a right to acquire a claim under the contractual right of the insured against the insurer.

[55] Cf A Dickinson, 'The Right to Rome? The Law Applicable to Direct Claims against Insurers and Anti-Suit Injunctions' (2016) 132 LQR 536, 540.

whether the third party is bound by jurisdiction or arbitration clauses. This can be viewed as reinforced by *Pruller-Frey*, where the European Court of Justice concluded that:

> a person who has suffered damage is entitled to bring a direct action against the insurer of the person liable to provide compensation, where such an action is provided for by the law applicable to the non-contractual obligation, regardless of the provision made by the law that the parties have chosen as the law applicable to the insurance contract.[56]

10.54   However, *Pruller-Frey* should be treated with care. The European Court also made clear that Article 18 was not a true choice of law provision: 'it does not constitute a conflict-of-laws rule with regard to the substantive law applicable to the determination of the liability of the insurer or the person insured under an insurance contract', and 'merely makes it possible to bring a direct action where one of the laws to which it refers provides for such a possibility'. The European Court was not focusing on whether the exercise of the victim's option should be subject to jurisdiction or arbitration clauses, and the question in *Pruller-Frey* was the narrow point whether the choice of law provision in the insurer–insured contract would in itself override the power granted by Article 18 to use the law of the non-contractual obligation, which obviously should not be the case. The judgment of the European Court in *Ergo v If* also reiterates a narrow view of Article 18, stressing that it merely creates an option and that it cannot affect the scope of the insurer's obligations.[57]

10.55   It is possible to argue that Article 18 is concerned only with the limited question of whether the right of direct action exists, but does not affect the contractual question of whether the insurer's obligations under the insurance contract are inherently subject to a forum clause by conditional benefit, which must be determined by the law of the contract. In turn, it is arguable that Article 18 does not regulate the law applicable to whether the third party, when exercising any option to bring a direct action which the law of the non-contractual obligation gives him, must be 'bound' by the forum clause. In general, the effect of forum clauses is left out of the Rome instruments, and although there is no specific exclusion in those respects in Rome II, it is arguable that this is because such questions are contractual.

10.56   If the justification of the quasi-contractual injunction is emancipated from any underlying substantive obligation, and viewed instead as intended to prevent the vexatious conduct constituted by evasion of the forum clause to which the rights are conditionally benefit, then the issue is still further removed from Article 18.

10.57   The Article 18 issues are not simple. But it is suggested that the English court is likely to continue to regard the law of the underlying contract between debtor and creditor as the most attractive answer, and to be unwilling to accept that Article 18 produces a different rule for quasi-contractual anti-suit injunctions, even with regard to direct actions against insurers based on underlying tort claims—in particular when occurring outside the

---

[56] Case C-240/14, *Pruller-Frey v Brodnig* [2015] 1 WLR 2031, ECJ [40]–[45].
Similarly, although concerned with Brussels I and so not directly on point, Case C-368/16, *Assens Havn v Navigators Management (UK)* [2017] ILPr 30 can be viewed as evidencing a hostility, in the context of insurance, to treating third parties as bound by forum clauses to which they have not expressly consented.
[57] Case C-359/14, *Ergo Insurance v If P&C Insurance* [2016] ILPr 20, AG [79]; ECJ [54], [58]; and the Commission Proposal on Rome II, 37.

Brussels–Lugano zone. Choice of law rules are not mechanical, and should be used to identify the most appropriate law to govern the issue in question.[58]

c) The correct analysis under English choice of law principles

If, following such reasoning, the question of whether the third party is 'bound' is outside **10.58** Rome I and Rome II, or within the Article 1(2)(d) exception, applicable law will fall to be resolved by the common law rules. We could simply accept that the *Through Transport/ Prestige* analysis states the current law as a matter of precedent. However, given its incomplete logic, we propose to reconsider the issues in principle. It is submitted that the result achieved is sound, and can be justified by reference to wider precedent and underlying principle.

First, although the common law's development on this point has been confused, it may well **10.59** have evolved a rule that 'the conditions of assignability' are subject to the law of the underlying right. This rule is very similar to Article 14(2) of Rome I, and is likely to be interpreted parallel to Article 14(2).[59]

Second, such a rule is capable of extension, without much difficulty, to mean that the law of **10.60** the underlying right should govern conditional benefit with respect to derived rights. If so, then there is good reason to think it can be applied, outside the assignment situation, in all cases of derived rights. There is no meaningful distinction between assignment and contractual subrogation, and the courts have consistently regarded third parties with statutory rights against insurers as in effect statutory assignees.[60]

Third, this is sound in principle. The key principle which motivates the case law on choice **10.61** of law for the conditions of assignability is that an assignment should not be capable of expanding the underlying right, no matter what the content of the law of the transaction effecting the assignment.[61] By parity of reasoning, in any case of conditional benefit, the law of the transfer should not be capable of enabling the underlying right to be claimed independent of the conditions which, under the law applicable to the underlying right, are inherent limitations of that right. Logically, the same should be true for any transfer where the third party obtains a derived right, in which he stands in the shoes of the original creditor.

Although justified by policy, this is a valid principle of the conflicts of laws: it tells us why **10.62** the relevant law should not be the law of the transfer, still less the law of any claim by the third party against the debtor which leads to the transfer. This builds on the reasoning

---

[58] *Raiffeisen Zentralbank Osterreich v Five Star General Trading (The Mount I)* [2001] QB 825 (CA) 840–41.

[59] *Campbell Connolly & v Noble* [1963] 1 WLR 252, 255; *Compania Columbiana v Seguros v Pacific Steam Navigation (The Columbiana* [1965] 1 QB 101, 128; *Macmillan v Bishopsgate Investment Trust (No 3)* [1996] 1 WLR 387 (CA) 400–02, 410, 419; *Raiffeisen Zentralbank Osterreich v Five Star General Trading (The Mount I)* [2001] QB 825 (CA) 842, 844–45; *Wight v Eckhardt Marine* [2004] 1 AC 147 (PC) [12]–[15]. Sir L Collins et al (eds), *Dicey, Morris & Collins on the Conflict of Laws* (15th edn, Sweet & Maxwell 2012), paras 24R-050–24-055 (hereafter 'Dicey'), states the common law in the same terms as Article 14 of Rome I; but acknowledges that the basis in authority is thin. Some of the older cases turn on concepts which now seem antique, such as application of the *lex situs*.

[60] Paragraphs 10.09–10.10 and n 10.

[61] *Compania Columbiana v Seguros v Pacific Steam Navigation (The Columbiana)* [1965] 1 QB 101, 128; *Raiffeisen Zentralbank Osterreich v Five Star General Trading (The Mount I)* [2001] QB 825 (CA) 842, 844–45. See M Moshinsky, 'The Assignment of Debts in the Conflict of Laws' (1992) 108 LQR 591, 618–21. The same principle is also reflected in *National Bank of Greece and Athens v Metliss* [1958] AC 509 (HL) 525, 529, 531 and *Adams v National Bank of Greece and Athens* [1961] AC 255 (HL) 274–75, 280–81.

of Moore-Bick LJ in *The Yusuf Cepnioglu*,[62] but also connects it to wider authority and principle. Yet further, it illustrates why the focus of the *Through Transport/Prestige* line of authority, on whether the third party's claim is contractual, has resonance. If the third party's claim is in substance contractual, then it is a right derived from the underlying creditor–debtor contract, and if so, the law of the transfer should not be able to deform the original right.

10.63   Finally, if the law of the right transferred governs the question of conditional benefit, then it is submitted it should also govern the question of any penumbral positive obligation to comply with such conditions, at least for the purposes of anti-suit injunctions. It would be difficult sensibly to separate the two. We can add that if a third party chooses voluntarily to claim a benefit under a transferred right, then it is appropriate that it is the law which governs the conditions of the right assumed which should govern whether those conditions have a positive binding force, imposed by reason of his choice to assume the benefit.

10.64   The conclusion (if we use an analysis in terms of substantive obligations) is that as a matter of both authority and principle, the issue of conditional benefit and any parallel penumbral positive obligation is a question of the conditionality of the benefits of the underlying contract from which the third-party rights derive, and in turn, of the penumbral positive effect of the conditionality of those benefits on persons who seek to claim those benefits. It is therefore naturally governed by the law of that underlying contract, and inherently a contractual question.

10.65   Alternatively, if the quasi-contractual anti-suit injunction is viewed as a procedural matter, based on concepts of remedial equity, without requiring any positive obligation under which the third party is 'bound' by the forum clause, then English law as the *lex fori* will govern the conditions of the injunction.[63] On this approach, English law concepts of vexation will be applied to whether it is vexatious for the third party to claim the derived right abroad while not respecting the forum clause. However, the analysis will not in the end be very different, because whether or not there is vexation will be shaped by whether, as a matter of substantive contractual law, the benefit under the original contract is conditional on the forum clause.

E. PRINCIPLES FOR QUASI-CONTRACTUAL INJUNCTIONS BASED ON DERIVED RIGHTS

10.66   A third party who seeks to rely on a derived substantive contractual right in a forum other than that agreed will not, in quasi-contractual cases, generally be in actual actionable breach of contract, although he may be in breach of an equitable obligation to respect the forum clause. When we turn to consider the criteria for the grant of anti-suit injunctions, this raises a question: should the approach in *The Angelic Grace*[64] apply by analogy, as if the third party were fully bound by a contractual right, so that an injunction will be granted

---

[62] *Shipowners' Mutual Protection and Indemnity Association (Luxembourg) v Containerships Denizcilik Nakliyat ve Ticaret (The Yusuf Cepnioglu)* [2016] 1 Lloyds Rep 641 (CA) [42] and also Colman J's reasoning in *West Tankers v RAS Riunione Adriatica di Sicurta (The Front Comor)* [2005] 2 Lloyds Rep 257 [26], [31].

[63] Applying the analysis at Ch 4, section B, 'Applicable Law'.

[64] Ch 7, section E, 'The *Angelic Grace* Principles'.

unless there is 'strong reason' not to do so? Or should the lack of an actual contractual obligation weaken the force of the presence of the forum clause?

Until *Through Transport*,[65] the courts had uniformly concluded that the case of derived **10.67** rights was closely analogous to the direct contractual situation, so that an anti-suit injunction should in general be granted against a third party seeking to take the benefit without the burden of the contract unless there was strong reason not to do so, even where the third party's acquisition of rights occurred under a foreign law, and even if that foreign law might not require him to respect the forum clause.[66]

However, in *Through Transport*, where there was a claim under a Finnish third-party rights **10.68** statute, which under Finnish law could apparently ignore the arbitration clause in the original contract with insurers, the Court of Appeal did not use an *Angelic Grace* test. The third party's rights against insurers were characterized as contractual, and thus subject to the contractual right to arbitrate, and the Court of Appeal accepted that a declaration could be granted that the third party was 'bound' to arbitrate in England. Nevertheless, the Court of Appeal concluded that, in a situation where insurers had no contractual right to enforce the clause against the third party, and where the only reason why the third party could be treated as 'bound' by the clause was due to the imposition of English principles of characterization, the contractual principles in *The Angelic Grace* did not apply directly or by parity of reasoning. The relevant criterion was vexation and oppression, and the Court of Appeal held that relying on the Finnish statute in Finland was not in itself vexatious or oppressive. In all the circumstances, the injunction should not be granted.[67]

However, the decision was reached in the interregnum between *Turner v Grovit* and *The* **10.69** *Front Comor*.[68] Reading between the lines, there was a desire not to make a reference to the European Court on whether anti-suit injunctions to protect arbitration were precluded within the Brussels–Lugano zone. While the Court of Appeal held that the Brussels–Lugano regime did not preclude the grant of such injunctions, they nevertheless took the European context into account as a factor against granting the injunction.[69]

---

[65] *Through Transport Mutual Insurance Association (Eurasia) v New India Assurance* [2005] 1 Lloyds Rep 67 (CA).

[66] *Schiffahrtsgesellschaft Detlev von Appen v Voest Alpine Intertrading (The Jay Bola)* [1997] 1 Lloyds Rep 179, 188–90, [1997] 2 Lloyds Rep 279 (CA) 286 (Hobhouse LJ), 291 (Scott VC); *Charterers Mutual Assurance Association v British & Foreign* [1998] ILPr 838 [44]–[47], [52]–[54] (credible foreign law that forum clause not binding on third-party rights); *Youell v Kara Mara Shipping* [2000] 2 Lloyds Rep 102 [58]–[60], [70] (ditto); *Navigation Maritime Bulgare v Rustal Trading (The Ivan Zagubanski)* [2002] 1 Lloyds Rep 106 [52(4)], [112]–[119] (where *The Angelic Grace* was applied to all the defendants, including the third-party insurer defendants, although the derived rights point was not contested by the defendants); *Through Transport Mutual Insurance Association (Eurasia) v New India Assurance* [2004] 1 Lloyds Rep 206 [39]:

> There is a strong presumption that in commercial contracts of this kind parties should be free to make their own bargains and having done so should be held to them. By parity of reasoning those who by agreement or operation of law become entitled to enforce the bargain should equally be bound by all the terms of the contract.

[67] *Through Transport Mutual Insurance Association (Eurasia) v New India Assurance* [2005] 1 Lloyds Rep 67 (CA) [93]–[97].

[68] Case C-159/02, *Turner v Grovit* [2004] ECR I-3565; Case C-195/07, *Allianz v West Tankers (The Front Comor)* [2009] ECR I-663.

[69] *Through Transport Mutual Insurance Association (Eurasia) v New India Assurance* [2005] 1 Lloyds Rep 67 (CA) [82]–[97]. The conclusion that there was no preclusion in the Brussels–Lugano context was overturned in Case C-195/07, *Allianz v West Tankers (The Front Comor)* [2009] ECR I-663 (see further Ch 12).

10.70   This decision was not welcomed,[70] and outside the Brussels–Lugano context, it was not possible to reconcile its reasoning with the previous authorities on quasi-contractual injunctions. In particular, the conclusion that where there was no actionable breach of contract,
the *Angelic Grace* approach should not apply was (if generalizable outside the context of
third-party rights statutes) not consistent with the logic of Hobhouse LJ's approach in *The
Jay Bola*, where the Court of Appeal reasoned that a party claiming derived rights inherently subject to a forum clause should be treated as if contractually bound.[71] But *The Jay
Bola* had not been cited to the Court of Appeal in *Through Transport*.[72] There was also a
striking internal disconnection in the Court of Appeal's reasoning, which on the one hand
held that the third party was 'bound' by the forum clause, yet on the other hand gave no
apparent weight, when assessing vexation and oppression, to the vital factor that the third
party was claiming rights derived from a contract which were inherently conditional on the
forum clause.

10.71   In the subsequent first instance case law *Through Transport* was for the most part distinguished and confined to its specific facts, and either not followed as matter of wider principle, or simply ignored.[73]

10.72   The tension between *The Jay Bola* and *Through Transport* came to a head in *The Yusuf
Cepnioglu*, where the third-party victim sought to claim against a London insurer, under
a Turkish third-party rights statute which, it seemed, enabled it to disregard the London
arbitration clause in the insurance contract. The underlying issue of policy was whether
the third party would be able to ignore the 'pay to be paid' clause in the policy, which
would be enforced in London arbitration but which it seemed Turkish law might override. It was argued that the absence of any actual contractual obligation to abide by the
forum clause meant it was inappropriate to apply *The Angelic Grace*; the injunction should
be refused because the third party's conduct was not vexatious or oppressive, and because as a matter of comity he should be able to exercise the rights available to him under
Turkish law.

---

[70] J Harris, 'Arbitration Clauses and the Restraint of Proceedings in Another Member State of the European
Union' [2005] LMCLQ 159, 165–67, suggested it was incoherent, having concluded that New India was contractually bound to arbitrate in England, not to grant the injunction. Dicey, para 16–092, n 37, said the reasoning was
'hard to follow'. A Briggs, 'The Impact of Recent Judgments of the European Court on English Procedural Law and
Practice' (2005) 124-II Zeitschrift für Schweizerisches Recht/Revue de droit Suisse 231, described the reasoning as
'curiously unconvincing'. It was also criticized in the first edition of this work.

[71] *Schiffahrtsgesellschaft Detlev von Appen v Voest Alpine Intertrading (The Jay Bola)* [1997] 2 Lloyds Rep 279
(CA), per Hobhouse J at 286 (agreed to at 291) and 292.

[72] As a result, there were suggestions that *Through Transport* had been decided per incuriam: see *West Tankers
v Ras Riunione Adriatica di Sicurta (The Front Comor)* [2005] 2 Lloyds Rep 257 [59]–[72]; *Royal Bank of Scotland v
Highland Financial Partners* [2012] EWHC 1278 [139]–[141].
    Sir Anthony Clarke, speaking extrajudicially, later referred ruefully to the fact that *The Jay Bola* had not been
cited to the Court of Appeal in *Through Transport*: Sir A Clarke, 'The Differing Approach to Commercial Litigation
in the European Court of Justice and the Courts of England and Wales', Speech of 23 February 2006.

[73] See eg *West Tankers v Ras Riunione Adriatica di Sicurta (The Front Comor)* [2005] 2 Lloyds Rep 257 [59]–[72]
(subrogation; but the reasoning goes wider); *Starlight Shipping v Tai Ping Insurance (The Alexandros T)* [2008] 1
Lloyds Rep 230 [35] (subrogation under Chinese law; *Through Transport* not referred to); *STX v Woori* [2012] 2
Lloyds Rep 99 [10]–[13] (subrogation case; undefended); *Royal Bank of Scotland v Highland Financial Partners*
[2012] 2 CLC 109 [139]–[141] (assignment; conceded the injunction defendant could not rely on *Through
Transport*). However, in none of those cases does there seem to have been a credible case that the foreign law would
produce any different result.
    Some reliance was, however, placed on *Through Transport* in two cases: *Markel International v Craft (The
Norseman)* [2007] Lloyds Rep IR 403 [31] and *BNP Paribas v Russian Machines* [2012] 1 Lloyds Rep 61 [78].

In a robust judgment, the Court of Appeal adopted *The Jay Bola* and rejected *Through*   **10.73**
Transport.[74] In Longmore LJ's view, the third party claiming derived rights was bound in
equity to respect the contractual obligation in the forum clause to which the rights were
originally subject. It was right to apply the principles in *The Angelic Grace*. So, an injunction
would be granted unless there were strong reasons not to do so, and it was unnecessary to
show vexation and oppression.

Moore Bick LJ said he agreed with Longmore LJ (and Macfarlane LJ agreed with both), but   **10.74**
went on to advance a slightly more qualified analysis. He observed that while there was
no direct breach of contract, the case was much closer to a breach-of-contract situation
than one of alleged general non-contractual misconduct, because 'the right which equity
is called upon to protect by injunction is the same in the case of the [third party] as in the
case of an original party' and so 'there is no distinction of principle' to the contractual situation. So, the:

> commencement of proceedings contrary to the arbitration clause is … sufficiently vexatious
> and oppressive, or at any rate sufficiently unconscionable and unjust, to provide sufficient
> grounds for the court's intervention by way of the equitable remedy of an injunction … the
> rationale of the decision in *The Angelic Grace* applies equally to both cases.

Consequently, 'the existence of the arbitration clause … provided sufficient grounds for
the court to grant an anti-suit injunction'. But he did not directly use the framework of
'strong reasons'.

The difference, to the extent that there is one, is that Longmore LJ is saying that *The Angelic*   **10.75**
Grace applies;[75] Moore Bick LJ is saying that in the quasi-contractual situation, vexation
and oppression should be treated as applying in parallel to *The Angelic Grace*. The result is
almost the same.

The next stage of the analysis was then the same for both. Having concluded that *The Angelic*   **10.76**
Grace, or parallel principles, should apply, the Court of Appeal concluded that no considerations of comity could apply. The arguments that (a) the third party was merely claiming
Turkish statutory rights, which under Turkish law could be enforced in Turkey irrespective
of any agreed forum clause; and that (b) the imposition of the injunction would interfere
with Turkish public with regard to 'pay to be paid' clauses, were thought by Longmore LJ
simply not to be capable of amounting to strong reasons not to grant an injunction. Nor
were they even a relevant consideration of comity; comity did not apply where the question was whether to give effect to the arbitration clause by which the third party was treated
as bound.

For Moore-Bick LJ, who was not directly using the 'strong reasons' framework, any such
considerations of comity were incapable of meaning that the Turkish litigation was not
vexatious and oppressive or preventing the injunction from being granted. To him, also,
'comity in the established sense' did not apply, since the third party should be held to the

---

[74] *Shipowners' Mutual Protection and Indemnity Association (Luxembourg) v Containerships Denizcilik Nakliyat ve Ticaret (The Yusuf Cepnioglu)* [2016] 1 Lloyds Rep 641 (CA) [32]–[35], [50]–[56]. For a recent example, in an undefended case, of the courts applying *The Angelic Grace* in a quasi-contractual situation, see *Qingdao Huiquan Shipping v Shanghai Dong He Xin Industry Group* [2018] EWHC 3009 [31]–[36].
[75] Like *Youell v Kara Mara Shipping* [2000] 2 Lloyds Rep 102 [58]–[60], [70].

contract which was a condition of the rights he sought to exercise. He explained this by logic which purports to be universal:

> If legislation confers on an injured party the right to recover directly against the wrongdoer's liability insurer by giving him in substance the right to enforce the contract, he must accept what the legislation gives him, including the obligation to pursue any claim in arbitration. To hold him to that agreement is to give effect to the legislation while preserving the substance of the obligation which he seeks to enforce.[76]

10.77   The Supreme Court granted permission to appeal (and asked specifically for additional submissions on characterization), but the case settled before the hearing.

10.78   We are left with the Court of Appeal's decision in *The Yusuf Cepnioglu*. If we stand back, the combined result of its reasoning would, if generalized, be capable of producing a stark and adamant doctrine, because of its apparent rejection of any deference to the perspective of another legal system. In the case of actual contracts which a foreign law purports to override by mandatory provisions, the English court has sometimes justified the imposition by injunction of its own law, as the law indicated by its own conflict of law rules, by reference to the system-transcendent importance of freedom of contract.[77] The questions of the 'conflict of conflicts' this gives rise to have been discussed elsewhere, and it is the suggestion of this work that in appropriate cases the perspectives and policies of other legal systems should be capable of amounting to strong reasons not to grant an injunction.[78]

10.79   But in the quasi-contractual case, there is no actual contract, and the idea that a party claiming in another's shoes should always be bound by the forum clause in the original contract is not universally shared. It is true there is real moral force in the notion that a third party claiming in the shoes of an original party should be bound by the conditions of the original party's rights. Indeed, that notion is capable of being regarded as system-transcendent, and in *The Yusuf Cepnioglu*, Moore Bick LJ seems to have so viewed it. The error of *Through Transport* included giving no weight to it at all. Yet we can ask whether this concept's moral force is so self-evident that, in *all* cases, it should be right to impose it by injunction, irrespective of how the foreign legal system characterizes such claims, and irrespective of the policy reasons which lead the foreign system to take a different approach. It is submitted, therefore, that in appropriate cases, in quasi-contractual situations, the conflict of conflicts may be capable of amounting to 'strong reasons' not to grant an injunction; or potentially may even displace the rigid *Angelic Grace* framework.

10.80   In justifying his more rigid framework, Longmore LJ explained that 'invocation of comity in cases of this kind is not particularly apposite because it is never clear which country should give way to which' (see at [34]). Certainly, the English court will not wish to accept that it should defer automatically to any foreign characterization or mandatory rule. There will be many cases where it is right in principle and policy[79] to hold the third party to the

---

[76] *Shipowners' Mutual Protection and Indemnity Association (Luxembourg) v Containerships Denizcilik Nakliyat ve Ticaret (The Yusuf Cepnioglu)* [2016] 1 Lloyds Rep 641 (CA) [35]–[36] (Longmore LJ) [57]–[58] (Moore-Bick LJ).

[77] Ch 8, para 8.38, n 73.

[78] Ch 8, paras 8.31–8.44.

[79] The Club in *Shipowners' Mutual Protection and Indemnity Association (Luxembourg) v Containerships Denizcilik Nakliyat ve Ticaret (The Yusuf Cepnioglu)* [2016] 1 Lloyds Rep 641 (CA) argued that there were reasons

conditions of derived rights. It is true, also, that the evaluative judgments which any middle position requires may be awkward. But as a matter of comity, they may be preferable to imposing our law by injunction simply because it is our law.[80]

F. INCONSISTENT CONTRACTUAL CLAIMS

This section addresses the situation where the injunction claimant denies the very existence   **10.81**
of the contract under which he is sued, or otherwise denies the validity of the contract in a way which would also impeach the exclusive forum clause, or denies that he owes any contractual duties to or has any contractual rights against the injunction defendant (including derived duties or rights), but the injunction defendant in effect makes a claim under the contract, while seeking not to respect the forum clause which forms part of it. An anti-suit injunction sought in that context cannot be a contractual injunction, since the injunction claimant himself denies the existence or binding force of any relevant contractual right to enforce the forum clause. Nor can it be a conventional quasi-contractual injunction, of the kind discussed so far, because the injunction claimant cannot himself assert that the injunction defendant is bound by any derived contractual obligation.

The case law so far suggests that a form of quasi-contractual injunction may be granted   **10.82**
in such cases to restrain the injunction defendant from bringing contractual proceedings abroad, which are inconsistent with the exclusive forum clause to which his claims would be inherently subject if any contractual relationship exists, even if the injunction claimant denies there is any relevant contractual relationship.[81]

Injunctions may fall within this principle if the injunction defendant asserts there is a con-   **10.83**
tract with the injunction claimant (which the injunction claimant denies), under which he has a contractual claim, but seeks not to be bound by the exclusive forum clause to which any such contractual claims are inherently subject under the applicable law of the contract, if it exists.[82]

Perhaps more controversially, the case law shows that injunctions may also fall within this   **10.84**
principle even where the injunction defendant's substantive claims are said by the injunction defendant not to be contractual under the local law, and in turn are said not to fall within the exclusive forum clause, but would be viewed as contractual, and subject to the exclusive forum clause, under English law principles of characterization, if and to the extent

---

of policy for English law not to permit foreign legal systems to impose liabilities on insurers towards third parties which are inconsistent with what insurers have agreed under English law insurance contracts.

[80] Cf T Raphael, 'Do as You Would Be Done By: Anti-Suit Injunctions and System-Transcendent Justification' [2016] LMCLQ 256, 262–64.

[81] *Sea Premium Shipping Limited v Sea Consortium* (David Steel J, 11 April 2001); *Jewel Owner v Sagaan Developments Trading (The MD Gemini)* [2012] 2 Lloyds Rep 672 [15]; *Ace Seguradora v Fair Wind Navigation* [2017] EWHC 3352 (Comm) [7]–[8]; *Dell Emerging Markets (EMEA) v IB Maroc.com* [2017] EWHC 2397 (Comm) [34].
See also *Horn Linie v Panamericana Formas e Impresos (The Hornbay)* [2006] 2 Lloyds Rep 44 [28], [32], [34(2)]. (Contrary to the view of Teare J in *Dell*, the decision in *The Hornbay* appears to have included a quasi-contractual injunction, as the injunction was not merely granted to the injunction claimant who was a contractual party, the owner; Morison J also gave permission for the non-contractual injunction claimant, the agent, to be added to the claim for injunction by amendment: see at [34(2)].)

[82] *Jewel Owner v Sagaan Developments Trading (The MD Gemini)* [2012] 2 Lloyds Rep 672 [15].

they are coherent claims (even though the injunction claimant denies that there is, in fact, any such contractual relationship). In this context, the English court has characterized as contractual, and regarded as inherently bound by the exclusive forum clause, claims which are in substance an attempt to enforce the contract.[83] The approach is similar to that taken in cases of derived rights and can overlap with it.

10.85   However, the juridical underpinnings of this jurisprudence are at present underdeveloped. There would appear to be three possibilities. First, it may be arguable in some cases that, for the purposes of assessing whether an injunction should be granted, the injunction defendant should be estopped from denying the existence of the contract under which his substantive claims are made, even though the injunction claimant denies the existence of the contract.[84] Second, it would be possible to postulate an equitable obligation on the injunction defendant not to bring a claim in a forum inconsistent with that agreed under the contract which he alleges exists, or which is the necessary condition of his claims.[85] Third, it could be said that it is vexatious and oppressive to bring an internally inconsistent claim which does not respect the exclusive forum clause which would be the condition of any coherent claim.[86] In a recent decision, *Dell v IBMaroc*, Teare J used the language of both 'inequitable' and 'vexatious or oppressive' without needing to decide between the two, and made reference to the injunction defendant being 'bound', but did not make any clear finding that there was any independent concrete equitable right, and saw differences to the derived rights situation.[87]

10.86   In turn, the case law does not clearly resolve the issue, grappled with in *The Yusuf Cepnioglu*, as to whether the fact that the injunction defendant is seeking to advance a contractual claim (from the point of view of English law), inconsistently with the forum clause, means the appropriate test to apply is the logic of *The Angelic Grace*, applied quasi-contractually by analogy; or whether the situation is to be assessed by reference to the less adamant concepts of vexation and oppression, in which the fact of inconsistent claims is regarded as a (strong) factor in favour of a finding of vexation, or perhaps as in general inherently vexatious. The importance of the difference is that in the vexation-based analysis there would be more flexibility for other factors to defuse vexation.

10.87   In *Sea Premium v Sea Consortium*, David Steel J regarded the situation before him as sufficiently analogous to *The Jay Bola* and so subject to a test 'to similar effect' as *The Angelic Grace*.[88] But in *The MD Gemini*, Popplewell J's *obiter* reasoning was that it would generally

---

[83] *Sea Premium Shipping Limited v Sea Consortium Pte Limited* (David Steel J, 11 April 2001) and *Dell Emerging Markets (EMEA) v IB Maroc.com* [2017] EWHC 2397 (Comm) [34], and see *Horn Linie v Panamericana Formas e Impresos (The Hornbay)* [2006] 2 Lloyds Rep 44 [28], [32], [34(2)]. However, cf contra *Starlight Shipping v Tai Ping Insurance (The Alexandros T)* [2008] 1 Lloyds Rep 230 [36]–[41].

[84] *Sea Premium Shipping Limited v Sea Consortium* (David Steel J, 11 April 2001) 9, and by analogy *Boss Group v Boss France* [1997] 1 WLR 351 (CA) 356–57. But cf contra *Starlight Shipping v Tai Ping Insurance (The Alexandros T)* [2008] 1 Lloyds Rep 230 [36]–[41]; P Delebecque, 'Anti-Suit Injunctions and Arbitration: What Remedies?' (2007) Il Diritto Marittimo 979.

[85] In *Sea Premium Shipping Limited v Sea Consortium* (David Steel J, 11 April 2001), David Steel J regarded the injunction defendant as 'bound' by the clause.

[86] The language of vexation and oppression was used in *Starlight Shipping v Tai Ping Insurance (The Alexandros T)* [2008] 1 Lloyds Rep 230 [42]; *Jewel Owner v Sagaan Developments Trading (The MD Gemini)* [2012] 2 Lloyds Rep 672 [15]; and *Dell Emerging Markets (EMEA) v IB Maroc.com* [2017] EWHC 2397 [34].

[87] *Dell Emerging Markets (EMEA) v IB Maroc.com* [2017] EWHC 2397 (Comm) [32]–[34].

[88] *Sea Premium Shipping Limited v Sea Consortium* (David Steel J, 11 April 2001) 22–23; see also *Horn Linie v Panamericana Formas e Impresos (The Hornbay)* [2006] 2 Lloyds Rep 44 [28], [32], [34(2)].

be oppressive and vexatious for a party asserting a contractual right to seek to enforce the rights without respecting the forum clause.[89] In *Dell v IBMaroc*, Teare J's reasoning is somewhat ambivalent; there were references to the injunction defendant being 'bound' or being 'bound to accept' the contractual forum obligation, but his most concrete conclusion was that it would be 'inequitable or vexatious or oppressive for a party to a contract … to seek to enforce a contractual claim arising out of that contract without respecting the jurisdiction clause within that contract'. He was prepared to envisage that the approach in *The Yusuf Cepnioglu* might apply, but did not need to decide this, and observed that it might be distinguishable because in that case the injunction claimant was a party to the contract and was asserting a right that was quasi-contractual.[90]

The choice of law and characterization questions have not yet been explored in any detail.   **10.88**
But the English court has so far applied English law without hesitation, and in *Sea Premium v Sea Consortium* David Steel J held that the question of whether the injunction defendant should be treated as 'bound' by a forum clause governed by English law, for the purpose of assessing whether to grant a quasi-contractual injunction of this kind, was to be determined by English law.[91]

---

[89]   *Jewel Owner v Sagaan Developments Trading (The MD Gemini)* [2012] 2 Lloyds Rep 672 [15] and *Starlight Shipping v Tai Ping Insurance (The Alexandros T)* [2008] 1 Lloyds Rep 230 [42].
[90]   *Dell Emerging Markets (EMEA) v IB Maroc.com* [2017] EWHC 2397 (Comm) [34].
[91]   *Sea Premium Shipping v Sea Consortium* (David Steel J, 11 April 2001) 22–23.

11

Injunctions to Restrain Arbitration Proceedings

A. INTRODUCTION

11.01 It is legitimate, from an international perspective, for the courts of the seat of the arbitration to intervene to stop or suspend the arbitration in certain circumstances. Nevertheless, the modern tendency is for national arbitration laws to move towards a presumption of non-intervention. The acceptance of the principle of 'Competence-Competence'[1] means that the national court's control should in most cases be exercised after any award has been granted, by way of appeal or challenge before the court of the seat, or at the moment of enforcement. This tendency is reflected by the English Arbitration Act 1996, which to a considerable extent respects 'Competence-Competence', although it also confers a defined but limited power under section 72 of the 1996 Act by which the courts may intervene to restrain the pursuit of arbitrations with a domestic seat.

11.02 Three questions arise: first, whether section 72 of the 1996 Act exhausts the courts' powers to grant anti-suit injunctions to restrain domestic arbitration proceedings; second, if the court has wider powers to grant domestic anti-arbitration injunctions, in what conditions they may be granted; and third, whether anti-arbitration injunctions can be granted in respect of arbitrations with a foreign seat.

11.03 It appears that the modern law can be summarized as follows:

(1) The court has a general power under section 37(1) of the Senior Courts Act 1981 to grant an anti-arbitration injunction to restrain the commencement or pursuit of arbitration proceedings if (a) the arbitral proceedings are an infringement of a legal or equitable right of the injunction claimant; or (b) if the arbitration proceedings are vexatious or oppressive or unconscionable.

---

[1] The principle of 'Competence–Competence' is the internationally accepted principle, reflected in the UNCITRAL Model Law, that the arbitrators have competence to determine their own jurisdiction (or 'competence'). See *Dallah Real Estate and Tourism Holding v Ministry of Religious Affairs of the Government of Pakistan* [2011] 1 AC 763 [79]–[98]. See also Departmental Advisory Committee on Arbitration Law Report on the Arbitration Bill, February 1996, paras 137–139 (hereafter the 'DAC Report').

It is probably also the case that the scope of this power is co-extensive with the power to grant anti-suit injunctions in general, and so the anti-arbitration injunction can also be granted if it is in the 'interests of justice to do so'; although the primary situations where this will be satisfied is where (a) or (b) apply.

(2) The old pre-1986 case law, which imposed arbitrary distinctions between arbitration proceedings within the scope of an arbitration clause said to be void or invalid, and arbitration proceedings that are outwith the scope of an arbitration clause together, appears no longer to be the law. The court's powers to restrain arbitration proceedings exist in either case.

(3) Injunctions to restrain the pursuit of arbitrations whose seat is in England are also possible in defined circumstances under section 72 of the Arbitration Act 1996.

(4) The court's general power to grant anti-arbitration injunctions under section 37(1) of the Senior Courts Act 1981 is not removed by the Arbitration Act 1996, nor exhausted by section 72, in respect of domestic arbitrations, nor is the exercise of the court's power precluded by the existence of the arbitration agreement.

(5) The general power to grant anti-arbitration injunctions applies also to arbitrations with a foreign seat.

(6) However, the context of the Arbitration Act 1996, and the principle of Competence-Competence together exercise a significant constraint limiting when it will be *appropriate* to grant an injunction to restrain a domestic arbitration (outside the defined powers in the 1996 Act), and such power will therefore be exercised only 'very sparingly', or to use other language, in 'unusual circumstances'.

(7) Similarly, the effect of Competence-Competence and international comity is that anti-arbitration injunctions to restrain foreign arbitration proceedings may face a higher threshold before an injunction can be justified. Although the case law is not uniform, the burden of the authorities is that an injunction will in general be *appropriate* only in exceptional circumstances, provided the foreign court has appropriate supervisory jurisdiction, and unless it has been held, or can be shown to a high standard,[2] that the arbitrators have no jurisdiction or the pursuit of the arbitration proceedings would be in breach of contract.

B. INJUNCTIONS TO RESTRAIN ARBITRATIONS IN ENGLAND

1. The Law before *Compagnie Européene v Tradax*

11.04 Until the decision of Hobhouse J in *Compagnie Européene v Tradax*,[3] the rules of the common law and equity on the restraint by injunction of arbitrations in England had developed in an unsatisfactory and unclear manner.

11.05 The bulk of authority, deriving from the controversial decision in *North London Railway*, suggested that where a claim made in arbitration fell outside an existing arbitration agreement, and was therefore futile and vexatious, it nevertheless infringed no legal or equitable right of the unwilling respondent's, and was merely a nullity, with the result that the court

---

[2] The inconsistent case law on how high the standard should be is addressed in section C, 'Injunctions to Restrain Arbitrations with a Foreign Seat'.

[3] *Compagnie Européene de Céréals v Tradax Export* [1986] 2 Lloyds Rep 301.

had no power to restrain it.[4] If, on the other hand, the unwilling respondent could impeach the arbitration agreement by contending that it did not exist, was void or voidable, or had been discharged by frustration or by breach, then a legal right to restrain the arbitration proceedings by injunction existed;[5] and the courts also had power to grant an injunction where it was alleged that the terms of the arbitration agreement were being infringed, for example where there was said to be misconduct by the arbitrator.[6] There was also authority, of uncertain effect, to suggest that an injunction could be granted where the arbitration proceedings were dealing with a claim that was *res judicata*.[7]

These distinctions are unappealing. There is no good reason to distinguish between an arbitration claim that falls outside the terms of an existing arbitration agreement and an arbitration claim that is made under an alleged arbitration agreement that does not in fact exist. In   **11.06**

---

[4] *North London Railway v Great Northern Railway* (1883) 11 QBD 30 (CA) (distinguishing *Malmesbury Railway v Budd* (1876) 2 Ch D 113 and *Beddow v Beddow* (1878) 9 Ch D 89); *Wood v Lillies* (1892) 61 LJ Ch 158; *Steamship Den of Airlie v Mitsui* (1912) 17 Com Cas 116 (CA) 127, 130–31; *Bremer Vulkan Schiffbau und Maschinenfabrik v South India Shipping Corp* [1981] AC 909 (HL) 979–81 (per Lord Diplock, whose speech was supported by the majority); *Workplace Technologies v E Squared* (Judge David Wilcox, 16 February 2000) (a decision which appears to have been made under the common law, and not the Arbitration Act 1996, as it concerned an adjudication, not an arbitration). In contrast, a declaration could be made as to the scope of the matters covered by an arbitration agreement: *Government of Gibraltar v Kenney* [1956] 2 QB 410, 421.

   There was, however, contrary authority. *London and Blackwall Railway v Cross* (1885) 31 Ch D 354 (CA) per Chitty J (at 361) and Lindley LJ (at 368), but see contra Lopes LJ (at 373); Fry LJ reasoned in terms of discretion only (at 372). See also *Sissons v Oates* (1894) 10 TLR 392 (unclearly reported but difficult to reconcile with *North London Railway*); *Glasgow and South-Western Railway v Boyd & Forrest (No 3)* [1918] SC (HL) 14.

   It would be possible, although contestable, to describe Lord Diplock's speech in *Bremer-Vulkan* as *obiter* on this point, since Lord Diplock was only concerned directly with the question of whether the arbitration clause could be repudiated by delay. He did not need to conclude whether *North London Railway* was correct that injunctions could not be granted to restrain arbitrations which exceeded the scope of the arbitration clause. His reasoning did give a firm endorsement of *North London Railway* as authority; but as we shall see, things have moved on (see paras 11.07–11.09).

[5] See *Kitts v Moore* [1895] 1 QB 253 (CA); *Mylne v Dickinson* (1815) G Coop 195, 35 ER 528 (although the basis for the injunction is rather unclear); *Maunsell v Midland Great Western (Ireland) Railway* (1863) 1 H&M 130, 71 ER 58; perhaps *Edward Grey v Tolme and Runge* (1915) 31 TLR 137 (CA) (a decision that seems difficult to reconcile with the modern principle of the separability of arbitration clauses); *Compagnie Nouvelle France Navigation v Compagnie Navale Afrique du Nord (The Oranie and the Tunisie)* [1966] 1 Lloyds Rep 477 (CA) 486–87, 488–89; *Industrie Chimiche Italia Centrale v Alexander G Tsavliris and Sons Maritime (The Choko Star)* [1987] 1 Lloyds Rep 508 (CA); *Bremer Vulkan Schiffbau und Maschinenfabrik v South India Shipping* [1981] AC 909, 924–25, 932–33 (Donaldson J), 938–40, 954–56, 959–60 (CA) (later overturned on the question of whether a repudiatory breach had in fact occurred due to delay, but upheld on this point: 979–81 (HL)); *André v Marine Transocean (The Splendid Sun)* [1980] 1 Lloyds Rep 333 [1981] QB 694 (CA). If the validity of the arbitration clause was upheld, the injunction would be refused: see eg *Smith, Coney & Barrett v Becker, Gray* [1916] 2 Ch 86 (CA).

   There were contradictory decisions on whether there was jurisdiction to restrain an arbitration where the arbitration agreement was challenged on the grounds of alleged lack of authority of the agent concluding it. In *London and Blackwall Railway v Cross* (1885) 31 Ch D 354 (CA), such an injunction was refused (although only Lopes LJ clearly held the court had no jurisdiction), but in *Ben & v Pakistan Edible Oils, The Times*, 13 July 1998 (CA), such an injunction was granted, since a want of authority was viewed as a form of 'impeachment' of the arbitration clause.

[6] *Malmesbury Railway v Budd* (1876) 2 Ch D 113 ('corruption' of the arbitrator); *Beddow v Beddow* (1878) 9 Ch D 89 (personal unfitness or misconduct of the arbitrator); *Jackson v Barry Railway* [1893] 1 Ch 238.

[7] *Glasgow and South-Western Railway v Boyd & Forrest (No 3)* [1918] SC (HL) 14, a Scottish case of interdict; see also later *Compagnie Européene de Céréals v Tradax Export* [1986] 2 Lloyds Rep 301, 305–06. But the principle underlying these cases—that a claim which is *res judicata* is outside the arbitrators' jurisdiction and therefore can be restrained—is difficult to reconcile with *North London Railway*. The *Boyd & Forrest* case is arguably authority for Scottish law only; the English cases were not discussed.

   In the past, injunctions were also apparently granted on the ground that there was no actual dispute for the arbitrator to decide: *Sissons v Oates* (1894) 10 TLR 392 (although cf contra *Farrar v Cooper* (1890) 44 Ch D 323; and see the doubts of Mustill J in *Allied Marine Transport v Vale Do Rio Doce Navegação (The Leonidas D)* [1984] 1 WLR 1, 6H–7B, overturned on other points, [1985] 1 WLR 925 (CA)); but it is now clearly the law that arbitrators have jurisdiction to determine that there is no arguable dispute: *Halki Shipping Corp v Sopex Oils* [1998] 1 Lloyds Rep 465 (CA).

both cases, no arbitration agreement covers the claim made.[8] The analysis in *North London Railway* was also dubious in principle. If an arbitration claim exceeds the boundaries of the terms of an arbitration agreement, there is little logical difficulty in viewing its pursuit as a breach of the agreement to arbitrate.

11.07   Accordingly, in *Compagnie Européene v Tradax*, Hobhouse J concluded, without express reference to *North London Railway*,[9] that the contract created by an arbitration reference was a tripartite contract between the parties and the arbitrators, and that for the claimant to pursue, and the arbitrators to hear, a claim over which the arbitrators did not have jurisdiction, was a breach of contract which the court could restrain.[10] Hobhouse J also held that the court also had power in equity to restrain the arbitration claimant from pursuing 'unconscionable', or in other words, 'vexatious or oppressive', arbitration proceedings.[11]

11.08   Hobhouse J's contractual route to justify injunctions to restrain arbitrations where the arbitrators had no jurisdiction was, at the time, adventurous as a matter of precedent,[12] although sound in principle. Similarly, Hobhouse J's conclusion that he had a power to intervene as a matter of equity to restrain vexatious arbitration proceedings was also in

---

[8]   See the criticisms of Chitty J and Lindley LJ (not followed in this respect by Fry LJ and Lopes LJ) in *London and Blackwall Railway v Cross* (1885) 31 Ch D 354 (CA). In *Bremer Vulkan Schiffbau und Maschinenfabrik v South India Shipping* [1981] AC 909 (HL) 922–24, Donaldson J described the law as 'very strange'. In the Court of Appeal, Roskill and Cumming Bruce LJJ suggested that *North London Railway* decided no more than that the court would not intervene unless to protect some legal or equitable right, and they held that a legal or equitable right did exist 'to be protected against wasted costs in an arbitration in which such costs would be irrecoverable if the arbitrator had no power to determine the dispute': 959, 961; Lord Denning MR also thought that *North London Railway* was of little guidance today: 939. But in the House of Lords, Lord Diplock, who gave the lead decision for the majority, apparently viewed *North London Railway*, and the cases following it, as representing the law: at 979–88, although *North London Railway* was cogently criticized by Lords Fraser and Scarman, in the minority, at 992B–G, 993, 995. Nevertheless, as already mentioned, Lord Diplock's speech can be viewed as *obiter* on this point, as discussed in n 4.

[9]   It appears that the omission was deliberate, and that *North London Railway* had been cited: see [1986] 2 Lloyds Rep 301, 307, where the reference to '1883', the year of *North London Railway*, was a way for Hobhouse J to signal, without saying so expressly, that he thought that *North London Railway* had become outdated.

[10]   *Compagnie Européene de Céréals v Tradax Export* [1986] 2 Lloyds Rep 301, 305–06; *Siporex Trade v Comdel Commodities* [1986] 2 Lloyds Rep 428, 435. In *Compagnie Européene*, Hobhouse J concluded specifically that it would be outside the arbitrators' jurisdiction to rehear a claim that was *res judicata*. This can be doubted: the correct analysis is probably that it would be a matter for the arbitrators, and within their jurisdiction to de-cide whether to dismiss the claim on grounds of *res judicata*; *Nomihold Securities v Mobile Telesystems Finance* [2012] 1 Lloyds Rep 442 [42]–[44], [63]; *AmTrust Europe v Trust Risk Group* [2015] 2 Lloyds Rep 231 [20]. But in support of Hobhouse J's approach, see *Glasgow and South-Western Railway v Boyd & Forrest (No 3)* [1918] SC (HL) 14 (where, however, the conclusion that a claim that was precluded by a *res judicata* was outside the arbitrators' jurisdiction was apparently assumed without discussion, and perhaps without argument to the contrary).

[11]   *Compagnie Européene de Céréals v Tradax Export* [1986] 2 Lloyds Rep 301, 304–05, followed in *China Petroleum Technology and Development v LG Caltex Gas* (Andrew Smith J, 5 December 2000); and *Nomihold Securities v Mobile Telesystems Finance* [2012] 1 Lloyds Rep 442 [27] (where the point was unchallenged); *Sabbagh v Khoury* [2018] EWHC 1330 [19]–[20]. In *Compagnie Européene*, the relevant 'unconscionable' conduct was seeking to relitigate before the arbitrators a matter that was *res judicata*.

The Scottish courts had also held, following old authority, that they have power to intervene to restrain any reference to arbitration over which the arbitrator has no jurisdiction including references outside the arbitra-tion clause, and had not followed the older English authorities: see *Naylor v Greenacres Curling* [2001] SLT 1092 [9]–[10].

[12]   See the authorities at nn 4–5. For Hobhouse J's 'contractual' conclusion to be accepted, it was necessary to reject both *North London Railway* and *Steamship Den of Airlie*, and to distinguish or depart from Lord Diplock's speech, with which the majority agreed, in *Bremer Vulkan*. This amounts to accepting the arguments of the mi-nority in *Bremer Vulkan*, although it is possible to regard *Bremer Vulkan* as *obiter* on the point.

tension with much of the older case law, which was inconsistent on the point.[13] But again, it was sound in principle.

Both of Hobhouse J's conclusions can now be seen as justified in precedent as well as prin-   **11.09** ciple. Even in 1986, the development of the anti-suit injunction had reached the point where it was clear that there was a power,[14] derived from equity and exercisable by injunction, to restrain court litigation if it was contrary to the interests of justice, and in particular if it was vexatious or oppressive or unconscionable. Since then it has become still clearer that the juridical underpinnings of the older restrictions were unsound. *North London Railway* was driven by the doctrine that a legal or equitable right is a condition of the grant of an injunction in general. That doctrine, which was later given renewed life by Lord Diplock in *The Siskina*,[15] is now much qualified and may well no longer exist, in the light of decisions like *Fourie v Le Roux*.[16] Further, even if the *North London Railway/Siskina* doctrine still exists at all, it has been clear at least since 1987 that anti-suit injunctions are an exception to it. In a line of case law starting with the House of Lords' decision in *South Carolina* and recently reaffirmed by the Supreme Court in *Ust-Kamenogorsk* it has been held that anti-suit injunctions can be granted not only where the targeted proceedings infringe a separate legal or equitable right, but also where they are vexatious or oppressive (or unconscionable).[17]

Indeed, there may be no requirement of an underlying substantive legal basis at all.[18] There   **11.10** is no reason of principle why such a power should not also cover the restraint of unconscionable or vexatious arbitration proceedings, including where the reason why the arbitration was vexatious was that it simply fell outside the arbitration clause. Finally, the Arbitration Act 1996 entitles the courts to look at such matters afresh.[19]

---

[13] *North London Railway v Great Northern Railway* (1883) 11 QBD 30 (CA) 33–34 (per Cotton LJ intervening); *Farrar v Cooper* (1890) 44 Ch D 323, 328–29; and the cases cited at n 4. See also the doubts of Mustill J in *Allied Marine Transport v Vale Do Rio Doce Navegaçao (The Leonidas D)* [1984] 1 WLR 1, 6H–7B (overturned on other points, [1985] 1 WLR 925 (CA)).
      However, the existence of an equitable power to intervene to restrain inequitable arbitration proceedings, had been accepted before *North London Railway* in *Pickering v Cape Town Railway* (1865) 1 LR Eq 84. The existence of a power to restrain vexatious or oppressive arbitration proceedings was assumed in *The Ithaka* (1939) 64 Ll L Rep 259 (CA) 262–63. In *Compagnie Nouvelle France Navigation v Compagnie Navale Afrique du Nord (The Oranie and the Tunisie)* [1966] 1 Lloyds Rep 477 (CA) 486–87, 488–89, Sellers LJ accepted the existence of such a power (at 486–87); but Salmon LJ appeared to require that there should be prima facie evidence that the arbitration agreements be 'impeachable' (at 488–89). Lord Denning MR in *Bremer Vulkan Schiffbau und Maschinenfabrik v South India Shipping* [1981] AC 909 (HL) 939 also argued for existence of a power in similar terms; and although such a power was not supported by the other members of the Court of Appeal in *Bremer Vulkan*, nor any of the members of the House of Lords, it was not expressly rejected either. The Scottish case of *Glasgow and South-Western Railway v Boyd & Forrest (No 3)* [1918] SC (HL) 14 could also be viewed as an example of the exercise of such a power.
      The Court of Appeal in *North London Railway* may have rejected the existence of such an equity because of the authority of *Pennell v Roy* (1853) 3 De GM & G 126, where it had been held that the courts would have no power to restrain a claim before foreign courts merely because it was vexatious. However, the modern scope of the equitable power now clearly includes the power to restrain vexatious or oppressive or unconscionable litigation abroad, as discussed in Ch 3, , para 3.06 and Ch 4, paras 4.02 and 4.05.
[14] As to whether the equitable power comports a correlative equitable right, see Ch 3, section B, 'A Legal or Equitable Right?'.
[15] *Siskina v Distos Compania Naviera (The Siskina)* [1979] AC 210 (HL) 256F–H, 257A. See the discussion in Ch 3, para 3.03.
[16] *Fourie v Le Roux* [2007] 1 WLR 320 (HL) [25], [30], [32] (see Ch 3, section A, 'The Power to Grant Injunctions').
[17] *South Carolina Insurance v Assurantie Maatschappij 'De Zeven Provincien'* [1987] AC 24 (HL) 40; *Société Nationale Industrielle Aérospatiale v Lee Kui Jak* [1987] AC 871 (PC); *AES Ust-Kamenogorsk Hydropower Plant LLP v Ust-Kamenogorsk Hydropower Plant JSC* [2013] 1 WLR 1889 (SC) [19]–[20] (see Ch 3, section B, 'A Legal or Equitable Right?').
[18] See Ch 3, section B, 'A Legal or Equitable Right?'.
[19] *Elektrim v Vivendi Universal* [2007] 2 Lloyds Rep 8 [83].

11.11   In the subsequent case law on anti-arbitration injunctions, the approach adopted in *Compagnie Européene* has been either followed, or adopted without challenge, and the courts have accepted that they have a general power to restrain arbitrations if they infringe a legal or equitable right, or if the pursuit of the arbitration is vexatious and oppressive or unconscionable.[20] The old distinctions have not been persisted with, and it has not been considered to be a barrier to the grant of an injunction that the arbitration proceedings would fall outside the scope of the arbitration clause.[21] It is submitted, therefore, that the older restrictive case law has been overtaken by time and events, and the modern development of the anti-suit injunction and with it the anti-arbitration injunction.

11.12   Although the power to grant anti-suit and anti-arbitration injunctions grew out of common law and equity, in modern conditions anti-arbitration injunctions should be treated as being granted under section 37(1) of the Senior Courts Act 1981.[22] This is consistent with anti-suit injunctions to restrain court litigation,[23] and has the benefit of simplicity. There is no need to have recourse to independent powers under the common law or equity, as section 37(1) has sufficient breadth.

2. Injunctions under Section 37(1) in Respect of English Arbitrations

11.13   Section 1 of the Arbitration Act 1996 provides that the court 'should not intervene' in arbitrations with an English seat, governed by Part I of the Act, save as provided by Part I. The aim and effect of this section, and the scheme of the 1996 Act as a whole, is generally, but not absolutely,[24] to preclude the court from intervening in arbitrations, save through one of the

---

[20] *University of Reading v Miller Construction* (1994) 75 BLR 91, 111 (power accepted to exist on the basis of a concession); *Weissfisch v Julius* [2006] 1 Lloyds Rep 716 [33(v)] (brief statement permitting the restraint of foreign arbitrations in exceptional circumstances); *Intermet FZCO v Ansol* [2007] EWHC 226 [20]–[21] (common ground that power existed); *Elektrim v Vivendi Universal* [2007] 2 Lloyds Rep 8 [47]–[48], [51]–[52], [55] (power assumed to exist but not challenged); *J Jarvis & Sons v Blue Circle Dartford Estates* [2007] BLR 439 [39]–[40] (power held to exist, albeit in slightly different language; it is unclear whether the point of principle was challenged); *Albon v Naza Motor Trading* [2008] 1 Lloyds Rep 1 (CA) [6]–[7] (standard principles for anti-suit injunctions assumed to apply to anti-arbitration injunctions without any suggestion that effectively the same powers should not apply), *Republic of Kazakhstan v Istil Group (No 2)* [2008] 1 Lloyds Rep 382 [48] (power to restrain vexatious and unconscionable arbitration proceedings held to exist); *Claxton Engineering Services v TXM Olaj-és Gázjutató Kft* [2011] 1 Lloyds Rep 252 [27]–[34] (it is unclear whether the point was disputed as a matter of English law); *Nomihold Securities v Mobile Telesystems Finance (No 2)* [2012] 1 Lloyds Rep 442 [25]–[27], [32] (power not disputed); *Injazat Technology Capital v Najafi* [2012] EWHC 4171 [16]–[17] (power exercised but defendant not represented); *AmTrust Europe v Trust Risk Group* [2015] 2 Lloyds Rep 231 [25]; *Sabbagh v Khoury* [2018] EWHC 1330 [17]–[20]. Reference can also be made generally to the authorities on injunctions to restrain foreign arbitrations, which are based on the same power, and are equally unconfined by the old restrictions: see section C, 'Injunctions to Restrain Arbitrations with a Foreign Seat'. The same approach applies to adjudications: *Dorchester Hotel v Vivid Interiors* [2009] Bus LR 1026 [15], [17].

[21] See *Republic of Kazakhstan v Istil Group (No 2)* [2008] 1 Lloyds Rep 382 [48]; *Nomihold Securities v Mobile Telesystems Finance* [2012] 1 Lloyds Rep 442 [59]; *Sabbagh v Khoury* [2018] EWHC 1330 [17]–[20], [29], [42].

[22] See *Elektrim v Vivendi Universal* [2007] 2 Lloyds Rep 8, paras 47–48, 51–57 (on the basis of a concession); *Claxton Engineering Services v TXM Olaj-és Gázjutató Kft* [2011] 1 Lloyds Rep 252 [26]; *Excalibur Ventures v Texas Keystone* [2011] 2 Lloyds Rep 289 [54]; *AmTrust Europe v Trust Risk Group* [2015] 2 Lloyds Rep 231 [23], [25]; *Sabbagh v Khoury* [2018] EWHC 1330 [17]–[20].

[23] See Ch 3, section A, 'The Power to Grant Injunctions'.

[24] Section 1 of the 1996 Act provides only that the court 'should' not intervene, not that it 'shall' or 'must' not intervene: *Vale do Rio Doce Navegaçao v Shanghai Bao Steel Ocean Shipping* [2000] 2 Lloyds Rep 1, 11 [52]; *China Petroleum Technology and Development Corp v LG Caltex Gas* (Andrew Smith J, 5 December 2000); *AES Ust-Kamenogorsk Hydropower Plant LLP v Ust-Kamenogorsk Hydropower Plant JSC* [2012] 1 WLR 920 (CA) [47], [85], [100]–[105], [2013] 1 WLR 1889 (SC) [39]–[40]. Further, of course, certain arbitrations fall outside the scope of Part I of the 1996 Act.

restricted routes for intervention which the Act itself lays down. However, if the grant of a particular remedy is not an intervention in the arbitration, then section 1 does not apply.[25]

Part I of the 1996 Act applies (with exception of certain ancillary powers) only to arbitrations with an English seat, but it does not apply to all arbitrations in England. Arbitrations under an oral arbitration agreement fall outside it,[26] and it does not cover other kinds of alternative dispute resolution processes, such as adjudication[27] and mediation.   **11.14**

The grant of an injunction under section 37(1) of the Senior Courts Act 1981 by the English court to restrain arbitration proceedings in England clearly is an intervention in the arbitral process.   **11.15**

However, the modern case law has accepted that section 1(c) does not mean that grant of injunctions to restrain arbitration proceedings in England is precluded outside section 72 of the 1996 Act. Such injunctions can be granted under section 37(1) of the Senior Courts Act 1981 if the pursuit of the arbitration would infringe a legal or equitable right, or would be vexatious or oppressive or unconscionable, and probably also (to bring anti-arbitration injunctions in line with anti-suit injunctions generally[28]), if, more broadly, it would be in the interests of justice to do so.[29] There is no clear, binding precedent ratifying this interpretation of section 1(c), which has been adopted on the basis of accumulating concessions,[30] but it seems unlikely that the courts will reverse their course. Further, the fact that the arbitrators themselves might have the ability to decide on whether the arbitration proceedings   **11.16**

---

[25] Thus, a final or interim anti-suit injunction to restrain court proceedings in order to enforce an arbitration clause is unaffected by s 1, as it does not 'intervene' in the arbitration: see *AES Ust-Kamenogorsk Hydropower Plant LLP v Ust-Kamenogorsk Hydropower Plant JSC* [2013] 1 WLR 1889 (SC) [39]–[40] and Ch 7, para 7.55.

[26] Arbitration Act 1996, ss 2, 5.

[27] *Workplace Technologies v E Squared* (Judge David Wilcox, 16 February 2000).

[28] See Ch 4, paras 4.02 and 4.05.

[29] Most of the case law confines itself to reciting that for an anti-arbitration injunction to be granted it is necessary that there is to be an infringement of a legal or equitable right or for the arbitration to be vexatious or oppressive, or (in some cases) an abuse of process (see eg *Compagnie Nouvelle France Navigation v Compagnie Navale Afrique du Nord (The Oranie and the Tunisie)* [1966] 1 Lloyds Rep 477 (CA) 487); *Siporex Trade v Comdel Commodities* [1986] 2 Lloyds Rep 428; *J Jarvis & Sons v Blue Circle Dartford Estates* [2007] BLR 439 [39]–[40]; *Claxton Engineering Services v TXM Olaj-és Gázjutató Kft* [2011] 1 Lloyds Rep 252 [34]. However, anti-suit injunctions in general can be granted if it is in the interests of justice to do so, of which infringement of a legal or equitable right, or vexation or oppression or unconscionability, are merely the primary examples: see *Société Nationale Industrielle Aérospatiale v Lee Kui Jak* [1987] AC 871 (PC). In *Intermet FZCO v Ansol* [2007] EWHC 226 [20]–[21] it was common ground that such injunctions could be granted to serve 'the ends of justice' applying *Aerospatiale*; and in *Sabbagh v Khoury* [2018] EWHC 1330 [18], [20], the power was stated on the basis that an injunction could be granted if just and convenient, with vexation or oppression being an example. There is no particular reason why anti-arbitration injunctions should be more confined, in this regard, than anti-suit injunctions generally.

Consequently, it is suggested that the references to infringement of a legal or equitable right, or vexation or oppression or unconscionability should be read as condensations of the basic tests for anti-suit injunctions in general; and anti-arbitration injunctions should be regarded as granted on the same bases as other anti-suit injunctions, subject to the constraints dictated by the arbitration context, which as discussed in para 11.17, require such injunctions only to be granted 'very sparingly'. The broader approach is consistent with the language used in the recent case of *AmTrust Europe v Trust Risk Group* [2015] 2 Lloyds Rep 231 [23]–[25].

[30] See eg *Elektrim v Vivendi Universal* [2007] 2 Lloyds Rep 8 [47]–[48], [51]–[52], [55] (power assumed to exist but not challenged); *J Jarvis & Sons v Blue Dartford Estates* [2007] EWHC 1262 (TCC) [32]–[47]; *Republic of Kazakhstan v Istil Group (No 2)* [2008] 1 Lloyds Rep 382, [1]–[2]; and see also the other authorities granting injunctions to restrain domestic arbitrations, collected at nn 20, 22.

In *Fiona Trust & Holding Corp v Privalov* [2007] 2 Lloyds Rep 267 (CA) [34], Longmore LJ observed that if there was a valid arbitration agreement, an injunction could not be sought under s 72 of the Arbitration Act 1996 at all, and did not appear to contemplate the possibility of attack under s 37(1) of the Supreme Court Act 1981. But he was not asked to decide the latter point. (This issue appears not to have been argued in the House of Lords [2008] 1 Lloyds Rep 254 (HL)).

should, for example, be stayed as an abuse of process, on grounds that overlap with the basis for the injunction sought from the court does not mean that the claim for an injunction is a matter submitted to arbitration which the court has no jurisdiction to hear. The court's supervisory jurisdiction, which includes section 37(1), is part of what parties have agreed to when agreeing to arbitrate in England and is therefore not inconsistent with the arbitration clause.[31]

11.17   Nevertheless, the discretion to grant such anti-arbitration injunctions will be exercised 'very sparingly' or only in 'unusual circumstances'[32] and with due regard for the starting point of non-intervention, save where the 1996 Act provides for intervention.[33] Any broader power would permit an excessive degree of intervention inconsistent with the policy underlying the 1996 Act.[34]

11.18   In particular, section 72(1) of the 1996 Act provides a restricted route (as discussed in paras 11.25–11.29 under which an injunction to prevent an arbitration reference from proceeding can be claimed on the grounds that the tribunal has no jurisdiction.[35] Consequently, it should be difficult to justify an injunction to restrain an arbitration under section 37(1) of the 1981 Act on jurisdictional grounds if the conditions of section 72(1) of the 1996 Act are not satisfied.[36] The threshold condition of section 72(1) is that the injunction claimant

---

[31]   *Nomihold Securities v Mobile Telesystems Finance* [2012] 1 Lloyds Rep 442, [33]–[52]. It can be noted that this natural supervisory jurisdiction does not exist in relation to arbitrations with a foreign seat (see paras 11.32 and 11.37).

[32]   *China Petroleum Technology and Development v LG Caltex Gas* (Andrew Smith J, 5 December 2000); *Elektrim v Vivendi Universal (No 2)* [2007] 2 Lloyds Rep 8 [67]–[79]; *J Jarvis & Sons v Blue Dartford Estates* [2007] EWHC 1262 (TCC) [32]–[47] (from where 'very sparingly' is taken); *Claxton Engineering Services v TXM Olaj-és Gázjutató Kft* [2011] 1 Lloyds Rep 252 [27]–[34] ('exceptional' circumstances); *Nomihold Securities v Mobile Telesystems Finance* [2012] 1 Lloyds Rep 442 [55]–[66] ('unusual circumstances'); *Injazat Technology Capital v Najafi* [2012] EWHC 4171 [16]–[23] ('sparingly'); *Golden Ocean Group v Humpuss Intermoda Transportasi* [2013] 2 Lloyds Rep 421 [71]–[72]. The more relaxed earlier approach in *University of Reading v Miller Construction* (1994) 75 BLR 91 and *Intermet FZCO v Ansol* [2007] EWHC 226 does not represent the law.
   An attempt was made to challenge this approach, in a case concerning a foreign arbitration, *AmTrust Europe v Trust Risk Group* [2015] 2 Lloyds Rep 231 [21]–[26]. Andrew Smith was prepared to consider that a different approach might apply where 'there was no room for argument' that a jurisdiction clause, and so not the arbitration clause, covers the relevant claims. But he viewed the question of whether this was an exception to the test, or merely an application of 'exceptional circumstances', as an 'arid debate'. Further, in substance his decision displays the same caution and hesitancy.
   The same test should probably apply to injunctions to restrain the pursuit of adjudications: *Dorchester Hotel v Vivid Interiors* [2009] Bus LR 1026 [15], [17] ('very sparingly'). In *Mentmore Towers v Packman Lucas* [2010] BLR 393, standard principles of vexation and oppression were applied, but it was apparently not argued that any higher standard should be applied.

[33]   *J Jarvis & Sons v Blue Dartford Estates* [2007] EWHC 1262 (TCC) [37]–[47].

[34]   *Elektrim v Vivendi Universal (No 2)* [2007] 2 Lloyds Rep 8 [67]–[79]; *J Jarvis & Sons v Blue Dartford Estates* [2007] EWHC 1262 (TCC) [37]–[47]; *Nomihold Securities v Mobile Telesystems Finance* [2012] 1 Lloyds Rep 442 [55]–[59].

[35]   Section 72(1) is the only provision of the 1996 Act under which an injunction to restrain English arbitration proceedings can be justified. No injunction can be granted under s 32 or 45 of the Act in aid of decisions under those sections: *Welex v Rosa Maritime (The Epsilon Rosa)* [2003] 2 Lloyds Rep 509 (CA) [39]. A possible example of the relevant abnormal circumstances which might justify an injunction outside s 72 is *Republic of Kazakhstan v Istil Group (No 2)* [2008] 1 Lloyds Rep 382 [1]–[2], [48], where an arbitration claimant tried to continue arbitration proceedings under an arbitration clause which the English court had already held to be a nullity, on an appeal under Arbitration Act 1996, s 67. It was not contended in that case that s 72 could have applied, perhaps because the arbitration respondent had previously participated in the arbitration proceedings before the determination of the s 67 appeal.

[36]   *China Petroleum Technology and Development Corp v LG Caltex Gas* (Andrew Smith J, 5 December 2000). In *JT Mackley & v Gosport Marina* [2002] EWHC 1315 (TCC) (Judge Seymour QC), an unwilling arbitration respondent obtained a declaration that an arbitration reference was invalid, apparently outside of the terms of s 72: see [30]–[31]. Yet it appears that the judgment may have proceeded on a confused basis, and s 72 is not referred

must 'take no part' in the arbitration; so it will follow that taking part in a reference will, in the normal case, preclude any claim for an injunction to restrain arbitration proceedings in England on jurisdictional grounds. Further, since the principle of Competence-Competence indicates that it will in general be appropriate for arbitrators to determine their own jurisdiction in the first instance, the grant of an injunction to pre-empt this by imposing the court's own view of jurisdiction will in general not be appropriate.[37]

Similarly, a broad approach to intervention in cases where the arbitrators do have juris-   **11.19** diction would also be in tension with the parties' agreement to arbitrate. Such agreement brings with it a prima facie acceptance that the powers available to the arbitrators to regulate the proceedings before them are, in general, the most appropriate tools to control vexatious proceedings.[38] The court has no general supervisory power over arbitration proceedings[39] and in general should only intervene in them in the defined ways permitted by the 1996 Act. Consequently, although there is no absolute barrier to the grant of an anti-arbitration injunction where the jurisdiction of the arbitrators is not disputed,[40] in most cases the appropriate course will be to refuse the injunction and to permit the arbitrators to stay or adjourn or dismiss the proceedings before them if they think it appropriate.[41]

Cases where anti-arbitration injunctions may be appropriate under section 37(1) to restrain   **11.20** arbitrations with an English seat may include where the party commencing arbitration has agreed separately not to arbitrate;[42] or where the vexation or oppression arises from duplication between the arbitration and other proceedings,[43] in a way which cannot satisfactorily be controlled by the arbitrators' use of their own powers to control proceedings;[44] and one case that has been suggested is where there is 'no room for argument' that the relevant disputes are instead covered by an exclusive jurisdiction clause.[45]

Subject to these constraints, all the other principles which govern the grant of anti-suit in-   **11.21** junctions in general should apply, so far as applicable, and modified by the arbitration context as necessary. Thus, for example, since the injunction will only be granted if the interests

---

to at all. It is submitted that it is wrong, as illustrated by the convincing judgment of HHJ Waksman in *HC Trading Malta v Tradeland Commodities* [2016] 1 WLR 3120.

[37] *Elektrim v Vivendi Universal* [2007] 2 Lloyds Rep 8 [67]–[78]; see also *Fiona Trust & Holding Corp v Privalov* [2007] 2 Lloyds Rep 267 (CA) [34] (in relation to s 72; but the same policy should apply to s 37(1)).

[38] *Elektrim v Vivendi Universal* [2007] 2 Lloyds Rep 8 [67]–[78].

[39] *Elektrim v Vivendi Universal* [2007] 2 Lloyds Rep 8 [63] and *Bremer Vulkan v South India Shipping* [1981] AC 909 (HL) 979.

[40] *Nomihold Securities v Mobile Telesystems Finance* [2012] 1 Lloyds Rep 442 [55]–[66]; *Injazat Technology Capital v Najafi* [2012] EWHC 4171 [16]–[19] (defendant not represented).

[41] *Nomihold Securities v Mobile Telesystems Finance* [2012] 1 Lloyds Rep 442 [55]–[66]; and see by analogy *HC Trading Malta v Tradeland Commodities* [2016] 1 WLR 3120 [41].

[42] *Huyton v Peter Cremer* [1999] 1 Lloyds Rep 620 (in relation to a pre-1996 Act arbitration); *AmTrust Europe v Trust Risk Group* [2015] 2 Lloyds Rep 231 [23]–[26].

[43] See *Republic of Kazakhstan v Istil Group (No 2)* [2008] 1 Lloyds Rep 382 [48]; *Injazat Technology Capital v Najafi* [2012] EWHC 4171 [16]–[23] (foreign arbitration, defendant not represented).
    For older cases see: *Doleman v Ossett* [1912] 3 KB 257 (CA) 273; *Northern Regional Health Authority v Derek Crouch Construction* [1984] QB 644 (CA) 673G–H; *University of Reading v Miller Construction* (1994) 75 BLR 91, 108–11, 119. However, all these are pre-1996 Act cases and so of uncertain guidance.

[44] In *Elektrim v Vivendi Universal* [2007] 2 Lloyds Rep 8 [75], Aikens J refused the injunction as he thought that applications to the arbitrators for stays or an adjournment were the appropriate course. See also *Nomihold Securities v Mobile Telesystems Finance* [2012] 1 Lloyds Rep 442 [63].

[45] *AmTrust Europe v Trust Risk Group* [2015] 2 Lloyds Rep 231 [23]–[25] (in relation to a foreign arbitration).

of justice so require, it will not be granted if to do so would be unjust to the other party to the arbitration.[46] Similarly, anti-arbitration injunctions may be refused if there has been excessive delay.[47]

3. The New York Convention

11.22 There remains a question of whether the English courts' current approach is consistent with the New York Convention 1958, Article II(3) of which requires the courts of contracting states 'when seised of an action in a matter in respect of which the parties have made an agreement within the meaning of this article' to 'refer the parties to arbitration, unless it finds that the said agreement is null and void, inoperative, or incapable of being performed'. There is no difficulty if the basis of the injunction is that the arbitrators have no jurisdiction. But it has been argued that in cases where it is accepted that the arbitrators do have jurisdiction, the New York Convention obliges the UK to ensure that its courts 'refer' the matter to arbitration, as none of the Article II(3) exceptions of nullity, voidness, inoperability, or incapability of performance apply; and that by restraining the pursuit of the arbitration the court is doing the opposite of 'referring' the matter to arbitration.[48] This argument, if correct, would impose an absolute bar on the grant of injunctions to restrain the pursuit of arbitrations over which the arbitrators have jurisdiction. It is, therefore, inconsistent with the approach taken in the English case law so far.

11.23 The point has been directly addressed on three occasions. It was argued before Aikens J, who did not need to decide it, and reached no conclusion on it, in *Elektrim v Vivendi*.[49] Subsequently, in *Claxton Engineering Services*,[50] Hamblen J held, in brief terms, that the approach of the English courts was consistent with the New York Convention and Competence-Competence. Hamblen J did not explain his conclusion, but there are reasonable arguments to suggest that the grant of injunctions to restrain arbitrations over which the arbitrators have jurisdiction is consistent with the New York Convention, at least in cases concerning arbitrations with an English seat. First, in respect of injunctions to restrain arbitrations subject to English curial law, it has been held that arbitration agreement grants the court an implied supervisory jurisdiction, including the power to grant anti-arbitration injunctions.[51] The Arbitration Act 1996 undoubtedly does permit the English court as the court of the seat to intervene in ongoing arbitrations over which the arbitrators have jurisdiction, in certain cases, such as the courts' power to remove arbitrators and to overturn initial partial awards on grounds of serious irregularity. Second, it is arguable that the question of whether or not an arbitration is vexatious and oppressive, so that it can be restrained by the court, may not always be itself a matter submitted to arbitration by the agreement,

---

[46] *University of Reading v Miller Construction* (1994) 75 BLR 91, 111, adopting *Compagnie Nouvelle France Navigation v Compagnie Navale Afrique du Nord (The Oranie and the Tunisie)* [1966] 1 Lloyds Rep 477 (CA) 487.

[47] *Intermet FZCO v Ansol* [2007] EWHC 226 [25]–[26] (in respect of an arbitration with a foreign seat).

[48] See S Schwebel, 'Anti-Suit Injunctions in International Arbitration: An Overview' in E Gaillard (ed), *Anti-Suit Injunctions in International Arbitration* (Juris 2005) 1, 10–11 (hereafter 'Gaillard (2005)'); J Lew, 'Anti-Suit Injunctions Issued by National Courts to Prevent Arbitration Proceedings', in Gaillard (2005) 25, 31; and ICCA, 'Control of Jurisdiction by Injunctions Issued by National Courts', International Arbitration (2006), ICCA series no 13, 185, 215–18.

[49] *Elektrim v Vivendi Universal* [2007] 2 Lloyds Rep 8 [67]–[78].

[50] *Claxton Engineering Services v TXM Olaj-és Gázjutató Kft* [2011] 1 Lloyds Rep 252 [30].

[51] *Nomihold Securities v Mobile Telesystems Finance* [2012] 1 Lloyds Rep 442 [33]–[54].

which means that the court is not 'seised of an action in a matter in respect of which the parties have made an agreement'. Third, it might even be arguable that if the pursuit of an arbitration would be vexatious, then the arbitration agreement would be 'inoperative' or 'incapable of being performed', within the terms of the New York Convention. Fourth, it is well arguable that by restraining a party from arbitrating in a vexatious or oppressive manner, or in breach of a separate agreement not to arbitrate, the court is not refusing to refer a matter to arbitration, but simply enforcing an independent, and legitimate, restraint on the inequitable or non-contractual conduct of the party in question. The first basis, however, only applies to arbitration with an English seat.

The best view may well be that the New York Convention does not impose a direct bar to **11.24** the grant of such injunctions, but that the principles and policies underlying the New York Convention regime support a restrictive approach to the grant of injunctions to restrain arbitrations over which the arbitrators have jurisdiction, in particular if the arbitration has a foreign seat. Thus, Judge Stephen Schwebel, who in general contends that such injunctions are inconsistent with the New York Convention, allows for the possibility that there might be 'exceptional' circumstances in which there might be a basis for such an injunction, for example where a party has already arbitrated or litigated and lost—although even there, he considers that it might well be preferable for the questions of double litigation to be addressed by the arbitrators in the duplicative proceedings.[52] On this approach, the New York Convention is consistent with, and indeed can be seen as underlying, the current approach of the English courts permitting such injunctions in limited circumstances. Nevertheless, the question of whether it imposes an absolute bar deserves further consideration, at least in respect of foreign arbitration proceedings.

4. Injunctions under Section 72

The court has the power to grant both final and interim injunctions under section 72 of the **11.25** Arbitration Act 1996.[53] The section applies only to arbitrations with a seat in England.[54]

In order for the court to have power to grant relief under section 72, the claimant must not **11.26** 'take part in' the reference. If the claimant has not 'taken part', then section 72(1) allows him to 'question' by proceedings in the court for a declaration or an injunction whether there is a valid arbitration agreement, whether the tribunal is properly constituted, or what matters have been submitted to arbitration in accordance with the arbitration agreement.[55] This provision clearly establishes the court's power to grant an injunction, even where the

---

[52] See S Schwebel, 'Anti-Suit Injunctions in International Arbitration: An Overview', in Gaillard (2005) 1, 10–11; relied on in *Republic of Kazakhstan v Istil Group (No 2)* [2008] 1 Lloyds Rep 382 [2], [48].

[53] In *Zaporozhye Production Aluminium Plan, Open Shareholders Society v Ashly Limited* (Tomlinson J, 25 June 2002), the argument proceeded on the assumption that the power to grant interim relief existed, but should only be exercised in limited circumstances.

[54] As is apparent from s 2(1) of the 1996 Act. See *Arab National Bank v El-Abdali* [2005] 1 Lloyds Rep 541 [14].

[55] Section 72 is, however, compatible with the New York Convention, as the conditions for its exercise fall within the cases where Article II(3) of the Convention does not apply.

Injunctions can apparently be granted under s 72 even after an 'award' has been given. Thus, an injunction was granted under s 72 to restrain enforcement, and even publication, of an award made without jurisdiction and obtained by fraud: *Arab National Bank v El Abdali* [2005] 1 Lloyds Rep 541; *London Steamship Owners Mutual Insurance Association v Kingdom of Spain (The Prestige)* [2014] 1 Lloyds Rep 137 [83]; but cf contra *Bernuth Lines v High Seas Shipping (The Eastern Navigator)* [2006] 1 Lloyds Rep 537 [58].

unwilling respondent's objection is only that the arbitration claim falls outside the scope of the arbitration agreement. The *North London Railway* line of case law has therefore been reversed by statute.

11.27   The wording of section 72 does not clarify when the court should grant the remedies of declaration or injunction.[56] However, in *Fiona Trust v Privalov*, the Court of Appeal held that the 1996 Act contemplated, in general that, arbitrators should determine their own jurisdiction; and that the principle of non-interference expressed in section 1(c) 1996 meant the court should be 'very cautious' before deploying section 72 to grant either an injunction or a declaration.[57] In addition, even if there was an appropriate case to grant a declaration that the arbitration agreement was not binding under section 72, an injunction would normally only be necessary if there was some indication that the other party was intending not to comply with any declaration that the court might make.[58]

11.28   The case for caution will be even greater if what is sought is merely an interim injunction, as it will interfere with the arbitration without finally determining the question of jurisdiction.[59] In any event, an interim injunction will be refused if the balance of convenience weighs against granting it, for example if the application is brought under section 72 at a very late stage before the hearing of the jurisdiction challenge by the arbitrators.[60] Further, interim relief is unlikely to be necessary, as if a section 72 claim is brought, it will usually be sensible for arbitrators to wait for the section 72 claim to be concluded, rather than pressing on with the arbitration.[61]

11.29   If the court finds that the tribunal does have jurisdiction, it will not grant a declaration to that effect, but will simply dismiss the section 72 claim.[62]

C. INJUNCTIONS TO RESTRAIN ARBITRATIONS WITH A FOREIGN SEAT

11.30   The English courts have held that they have power to grant anti-arbitration injunctions to restrain the pursuit of arbitrations whose seat is abroad, under section 37(1) of the Senior Courts Act 1981, if the foreign arbitration proceedings are in breach of a legal or equitable right or are vexatious or oppressive or unconscionable (and probably also more generally if the grant of the injunction is 'in the interests of justice'). However, the English courts

---

[56]   There is no help to be found in the DAC Report: see para 295.

[57]   *Fiona Trust & Holding v Privalov* [2007] 2 Lloyds Rep 267 (CA) [34] (these points were not considered on appeal: [2008] 2 Lloyds Rep 254 (HL)); *British Telecommunications v SAE Group* [2009] EWHC 252 (TCC) [53], [71]; see also *Caparo Group v Fagor Arrasate Sociedad Cooperative* (Clarke J, 7 August 1998). This is a different approach to that apparently adopted in *Law Debenture Trust Corporation v Elektrim Finance* [2005] 2 Lloyds Rep 755 [48].

[58]   *Fiona Trust & Holding v Privalov* [2007] 2 Lloyds Rep 267 (CA) [36].

[59]   Sir MJ Mustill and SC Boyd, *Commercial Arbitration* (2nd edn, LexisNexis 2001 Companion Volume) 362 (hereafter 'Mustill and Boyd, Companion'.

[60]   *Zaporozhye Production Aluminium Plan, Open Shareholders Society v Ashly* [2002] EWHC 1410. For an illustration of the considerations of convenience that can arise where security has been given in the arbitration, see the pre-1996 Act case of *Industrie Chimiche Italia Centrale v Alexander G Tsavliris and Sons Maritime (The Choko Star)* [1987] 1 Lloyds Rep 508 (CA).

[61]   In *Azov Shipping v Baltic Shipping* [1999] 1 Lloyds Rep 68, 69, Rix J thought it would be 'unlikely' that an arbitrator would continue with the reference, but made it clear that he could do so. It can be noted that in contrast to s 32(4) of the 1996 Act, s 72 does not expressly provide that the arbitrator has the right to continue the reference in the meanwhile, but the right presumably exists nevertheless.

[62]   *Axa Re v Ace Global Markets* [2006] Lloyds Rep IR 683.

have, in most of the recent case law, suggested that it will only be appropriate to exercise such a power in 'exceptional' circumstances and 'with caution',[63] provided at least that the foreign court does not have an appropriate supervisory jurisdiction.[64] But there are differences of approach within the judiciary, and some judges have not required 'exceptional circumstances' or have essentially treated them as satisfied if there is a good case for an injunction.[65] There is, in particular, a logical tension in those cases where the foreign arbitration would be in breach of an English arbitration clause, or English exclusive forum clause, at least to English eyes, or this could be shown to the same standard as would normally be required to satisfy *The Angelic Grace*. In such a case, it might be said that there is no need for additional caution. It can be asked why, if there is a breach of contract, a foreign arbitration should benefit from any greater deference than foreign court proceedings.[66] Nevertheless, the majority of the more closely reasoned modern decisions do, for now, adopt the 'exceptional circumstances' threshold.

However, even if 'exceptional circumstances' are required, there are strong strands in the **11.31** case law which suggest that this higher threshold will not apply: (a) where it is already *res judicata* that the arbitrators have no jurisdiction or where there is no real argument to the contrary;[67] (b) where the pursuit of the arbitration can be shown to be (to a sufficient standard

---

[63] *Black Clawson International v Papierwerke Waldhof-Aschaffenberg* [1981] 2 Lloyds Rep 446, 457–58; *Weissfisch v Julius* [2006] 1 Lloyds Rep 716 (CA) [25], [33]; *A v B* [2007] 1 Lloyds Rep 237 [112]–[113], [124]–[125]; *Excalibur Ventures v Texas Keystone* [2011] 2 Lloyds Rep 289 [54]–[56]; *Claxton Engineering Services v TXM Olaj-és Gázjutató Kft* [2011] 1 Lloyds Rep 252 [29]; *Nomihold Securities v Mobile Telesystems Finance* [2012] 1 Lloyds Rep 442 [55]–[66] ('unusual circumstances'); *T v T (Hemain Injunction)* [2014] 1 FLR 96 [21]–[22]; *Golden Ocean Group v Humpuss Intermoda Transportasi* [2013] 2 Lloyds Rep 421 [71]–[72] (conceded); *AmTrust Europe v Trust Risk Group* [2015] 2 Lloyd Rep 231 [23]–[26]; *Sabbagh v Khoury* [2018] EWHC 1330 [19]–[20]. Any wider scope for intervention would require reconciliation with the cautious approach of the House of Lords in *Channel Tunnel Group v Balfour Beatty Construction* [1993] AC 334 (HL) 358F, 368B–H and would also create tensions with the New York Convention (see paras 11.22– 11.24 and 11.37).

[64] *Sabbagh v Khoury* [2018] EWHC 1330 [20].

[65] In *Intermet FZCO v Ansol* [2007] EWHC 226, it was assumed without challenge that standard principles for anti-suit injunctions should apply; but this is not how most of the latter case law has developed. In *Injazat Technology Capital v Najafi* [2012] EWHC 4171 [16]–[17], an anti-arbitration injunction was granted with no higher criterion of 'exceptional circumstances' being used but the relevant case law does not seem to have all been before the court, and the injunction defendant was not represented.

A more important contrary case is *Albon v Naza Motor Trading (No 4)* [2007] 2 Lloyds Rep 420, [2008] 1 Lloyds Rep 1 (CA) [16]–[18], where Lightman J and the Court of Appeal proceeded on the basis that it was sufficient for standard principles of vexation or unconscionability to be satisfied but that 'the caution exercised by the court relating to ant-suit injunctions should be increased or even redoubled in the case of an anti-arbitration injunction', at least in an 'ordinary case'. The injunction was then granted on the basis that this was not an ordinary case. However, the facts were specific: they included findings that it was properly arguable that the arbitration clause had been forged to defeat the English proceedings, that it had been agreed the English court would determine that very question; and that the injunction was made only on an interim basis pending determination of the question of forgery by the English courts. Further, it seems that key decisions in the previous case law on anti-arbitration injunctions (such as *Weissfisch* and *A v B*) were not cited. In any event, the formulation used is not greatly different to that of 'exceptional' circumstances.

Recently, see *Sabbagh v Khoury*, where the test of exceptional circumstances was referred to but not actually adopted and the court seemed to think that a finding of vexation might be sufficient: *Sabbagh v Khoury* [2018] EWHC 1330 [19]–[20].

[66] *Whitworths v Synergy Food and Processing* [2014] EWHC 2439 (QB) [63]–[66].

[67] *Sheffield United v West Ham United* [2009] 1 Lloyds Rep 167; *Claxton Engineering Services v TXM Olaj-és Gázjutató Kft* [2011] 1 Lloyds Rep 252 [33]–[44]; *AmTrust Europe v Trust Risk Group* [2015] 2 Lloyd Rep 231 [23]–[28]; and see also *Albon v Naza Motor Trading (No 4)* [2007] 2 Lloyds Rep 420, [2008] 1 Lloyds Rep 1 (CA) [16]–[18]; *Sabbagh v Khoury* [2018] EWHC 1330 [19].

However, the approach in *Sabbagh v Khoury* was perhaps more liberal, allowing for any requirement of exceptional circumstances to be displaced if arbitration was not agreed (without any requirement of 'no argument to the contrary'): [19], [48]. But the case was one where the inapplicability of the arbitration clause had already been established.

of proof) in breach of an exclusive forum clause (or, possibly, only where this is *clearly* the case or it has already been held to be the case).[68] But the boundaries of any such exceptions are not yet settled. Further, it may be that such situations can be viewed simply as examples of exceptional circumstances.[69]

11.32   This restrained approach flows, first, from the English court's acceptance that, consistently with the concept of Competence-Competence, the arbitrators should in general be permitted to determine their own jurisdiction in the first instance;[70] and second, from the principle that, as a matter of international comity, and possibly also the implied terms of the arbitration agreement, the natural supervisory court for an arbitration is generally the court of the seat of the arbitration.[71]

11.33   Thus, in *Claxton Engineering Services*, Hamblen J concluded that the test of exceptional circumstances was satisfied where the English court had already concluded that there was no binding arbitration agreement while instead an English exclusive jurisdiction agreement was binding. He also held, citing the first edition of this work, that even if such circumstances were not viewed as 'exceptional', nevertheless they were sufficient to justify an anti-arbitration injunction as an exception to any such requirement.[72]

---

[68]   *Claxton Engineering Services v TXM Olaj-és Gázjutató Kft* [2011] 1 Lloyds Rep 252 [33]–[44]; *Whitworths v Synergy Food and Processing* [2014] EWHC 2439 (QB) [63]–[66] (a more liberal approach; but a judgment given at an undefended hearing); *AmTrust Europe v Trust Risk Group* [2015] 2 Lloyd Rep 231 [23]–[28]. The case law on this point betrays a tension between (a) the argument that, if it can be shown to the relevant standard that the foreign arbitration is in breach of contract, the *Angelic Grace* principles should apply in the same way as they normally do, and there is no more reason to defer to arbitrators than there would be to defer to a foreign court in this context (cf *Whitworths* at [64]); and (b) the argument that in general the English court should allow the arbitrators themselves to decide whether the proceedings before them are in breach of contract, unless perhaps it is clear, or has already been held by the court, that the foreign arbitration is in breach of contract (cf *AmTrust* at [25]; *Claxton* is less clear).
   See also *Huyton v Peter Cremer* [1999] 1 Lloyds Rep 620, 623, 642, where the court enforced a separate agreement not to arbitrate by an injunction (in respect of an attempted arbitration in England).

[69]   *Claxton Engineering Services v TXM Olaj-és Gázjutató Kft* [2011] 1 Lloyds Rep 252 [33]–[44] and see also *AmTrust Europe v Trust Risk Group* [2015] 2 Lloyd Rep 231 [25].

[70]   Although English law does not adopt a wide and absolute view of Competence-Competence in its supervision of English arbitrations, as demonstrated by the existence of s 72 of the 1996 Act, the principle is receiving growing deference: *Fiona Trust & Holding Corp v Privalov* [2007] 2 Lloyds Rep 267 (CA) [34]; *Dallah Real Estate and Tourism Holding v Ministry of Religious Affairs of the Government of Pakistan* [2011] 1 AC 763; *HC Trading Malta v Tradeland Commodities* [2016] 1 WLR 3120. See P Fouchard, 'Anti-Suit Injunctions in International Arbitration: What Remedies' in Gaillard (2005) 153, 155.
   Nevertheless, the breadth of the principle of Competence–Competence should not be exaggerated. In Pace S Schwebel 'Anti-Suit Injunctions in International Arbitration: An Overview' in Gaillard (2005) 5, 15, there is little basis to assume that a broad interpretation of the principle of Competence-Competence reflects customary international law (as opposed to being a polemical position held by many writers on international arbitration), since many jurisdictions, notably the UK, do not fully accept the principle of Competence-Competence. See J Rozas, 'Anti-Suit Injunctions Issued by National Courts: Measures Addressed to the Parties or to the Arbitrators' in Gaillard (2005) 73, 81–82.

[71]   See *Black Clawson International v Papierwerke Waldhof-Aschaffenberg* [1981] 2 Lloyds Rep 446, 458; *Weissfisch v Julius* [2006] 1 Lloyds Rep 716 (CA) [25], [33]; *A v B* [2007] 1 Lloyds Rep 237 [112]–[113]; *Excalibur Ventures v Texas Keystone* [2011] 2 Lloyds Rep 289, [55]; *AmTrust Europe v Trust Risk Group* [2015] 2 Lloyds Rep 231 [23]–[26]. See also, in the different context of injunctions to support arbitration proceedings, *Channel Tunnel Group v Balfour Beatty Construction* [1993] AC 334 (HL) 358F, 368B–H; *Bank Mellat v Helliniki Techniki* [1984] 1 QB 291 (CA) 302E–F; *Naviera Amazonica Peruana v Compania Internacional de Seguros del Peru* [1988] 1 Lloyds Rep 116 (CA) 120. The Arbitration Act 1996 grants the English court only very limited powers in respect of arbitrations with a foreign seat: s 2(4). The only powers expressly conferred on the English court in relation to foreign arbitrations are the powers to secure the attendance of witnesses and to exercise court powers in support of arbitral proceedings in s 43 and 44 of the Act. Section 72 of the Act does not apply to foreign arbitrations.

[72]   *Claxton Engineering Services v TXM Olaj-és Gázjutató Kft* [2011] 1 Lloyds Rep 252 [33]–[44].

Similarly, in *AmTrust v Trust Risk*, Andrew Smith was prepared to envisage that where 'there   **11.34**
is no room for argument' that an exclusive jurisdiction clause covered the relevant claims,
and so there was a contractual agreement not to arbitrate, an anti-arbitration injunction
could be appropriate. He regarded the question of whether this was an exception to the test
of 'exceptional circumstances', or rather an example of 'exceptional circumstances', as an
arid debate. But in the case before him, there was a real dispute, which the arbitrators were
going to decide (with the Italian courts having supervisory jurisdiction over their award) as
to whether the Italian arbitration clause or the English jurisdiction cause applied to the dispute. He did not mechanistically apply the *Angelic Grace* approach—of granting injunctions
to enforce English jurisdiction clauses unless there is a strong reason not to do so—and
declined to grant the injunction. The right approach was for the injunction claimant to challenge jurisdiction before the arbitrators and, if necessary, before the Italian courts.[73]

Conversely, the English courts have accepted that, where the parties have 'unquestionably   **11.35**
agreed' to the foreign arbitration agreement, this is another significant factor against the
grant of an injunction. Nevertheless, they have said that the power to intervene by injunction still exists in such situations, even though the jurisdiction of the arbitrators will not
be challenged.[74] However, this conclusion was *obiter* in the two cases where it has been
pronounced.

The only reported case where an injunction has actually been granted to restrain a foreign   **11.36**
arbitration where the jurisdiction of the arbitrators was *not* challenged is *Injazat*.[75] In that
case, the basis for the anti-arbitration injunction was that the matter being arbitrated had
already been decided. But the injunction was granted at an undefended hearing at which
some of the key cases were not cited; and the approach adopted was out of line with the general approach in the case law discussed here: no showing of exceptional circumstances, nor
particular caution, was required. In principle, while relitigation or duplication may be capable of amounting to sufficient vexation to justify an anti-arbitration injunction,[76] it will always be necessary to consider whether such arguments should not instead be raised before
the arbitration tribunal, provided at least it has sufficient powers to deal with the problem[77]
(which is not necessarily the case[78]).

There is room to doubt whether even the current restrictive approach of the English courts   **11.37**
gives full weight to the considerations which militate against the grant of an injunction

---

[73] *AmTrust Europe v Trust Risk Group* [2015] 2 Lloyd Rep 231 [23]–[28].
[74] *Excalibur Ventures v Texas Keystone* [2011] 2 Lloyds Rep 289, [55]–[58]; and *Weissfisch v Julius* [2006] 1 Lloyds Rep 716 (CA) 722. In both *Excalibur* and *Weissfisch* the jurisdiction of the arbitrators was challenged.
[75] *Injazat Technology Capital v Najafi* [2012] EWHC 4171 [16]–[17].
[76] *Excalibur Ventures v Texas Keystone* [2011] 2 Lloyds Rep 289 [67]–[71].
[77] *Nomihold Securities v Mobile Telesystems Finance* [2012] 1 Lloyds Rep 442 [63].
[78] English arbitration tribunals applying English law have, it seems, powers to reject claims before them on grounds of *res judicata*: *Associated Electric & Gas Services v European Reinsurance of Zurich* [2003] 1 WLR 1041 (PC) [14], and may well have powers to reject claims before them on grounds of *Henderson v Henderson* abuse of process: *Nomihold Securities v Mobile Telesystems Finance* [2012] 1 Lloyds Rep 442 [40]–[44], [63], citing *HE Daniels v Carmel Exporters* [1953] QB 242, 256 (see also n 11). But the latter point in relation to *Henderson v Henderson* is debatable (see *Associated Electric*, at [16]). It is yet more doubtful whether they have powers to strike out claims on grounds of abuse of process more generally (see *Nomihold*, at [43]). However, the law on this is as yet undeveloped. Further, there are questions as to whether English law on *res judicata*, as developed in English court proceedings, is necessarily the applicable law to be applied by arbitrators to such questions, even where the arbitration has an English seat: see S Schaffstein, *The Doctrine of Res Judicata in International Commercial Arbitration* (OUP 2016), at Chs 5 and 6. And the position may be different before tribunals whose curial law is not English law.

to restrain foreign arbitration proceedings.[79] There are real arguments that if the juris-diction of the arbitrators is not challenged, such injunctions would be inconsistent with the New York Convention, save perhaps in exceptional circumstances.[80] In addition, the English courts themselves have insisted on the importance of the principle that the super-visory jurisdiction of the courts of the seat should be exclusive, and have relied on this to justify anti-suit injunctions to restrain foreign litigation that interferes with English arbi-tration awards.[81] In the circumstances, it is submitted that sufficient exceptional circum-stances should include some strong reason why the English court, as opposed to the courts of the seat, should intervene in the arbitration, and that cases where this is appropriate, as a matter of international comity, will be rare.[82] Taking the situation of relitigation or dupli-cate litigation, the English court may be given 'sufficient interest' to intervene[83] if the matter being relitigated, or litigated duplicatively, in a vexatious and oppressive manner, was ini-tially litigated in England, and if it would be unjust or inappropriate on the facts to force the injunction claimant to raise his objections to double litigation abroad before the arbitrators or the supervisory court.[84]

D. INJUNCTIONS AGAINST ARBITRATORS PERSONALLY

11.38   At common law, in most cases where injunctions to restrain arbitration proceedings have been granted, they were sought, and made, against the arbitration claimant alone.[85] However, there have been instances where injunctions were sought, and even made, against the arbitrator as well as the claimant.[86] The foundation for relief was the 'tripartite analysis' of the arbitration agreement, under which it is viewed as a three-way agreement between

---

[79] For arguments in favour of an even more restrictive approach to anti-arbitration injunctions, see J Lew, 'Does National Court Involvement Undermine the International Arbitration Process' (2009) 24(3) AUILR 489. For ar-guments in favour of anti-arbitration injunctions in appropriate cases, see N Poon, 'The Use and Abuse of Anti Arbitration Injunctions' [2013] 25 SAcLJ 244.

[80] See paras 11.22–11.24, 11.37.

[81] *C v D* [2007] 2 Lloyds Rep 367, [2008] 1 Lloyds Rep 239 (CA) [29]–[34]; *A v B* [2007] 1 Lloyds Rep 237 [112]–[113], [124]–[125]; *Nomihold Securities v Mobile Telesystems Finance* [2012] 1 Lloyds Rep 442 [29]–[31]; *Terna Bahrain Holding Company v Al Shamsi* [131]–[132]. The analytical basis and extent of the *C v D* principle is addressed at Ch 7, paras 7.68–7.70.

[82] See *A v B* [2007] 1 Lloyds Rep 237 [112]–[113], [124]–[125] and tacitly *Excalibur Ventures LLC v Texas Keystone* [2011] 2 Lloyds Rep 289 [55], [68]–[70]. This proposition is consistent with the approach taken in *Black Clawson International v Papierwerke Waldhof-Aschaffenberg* [1981] 2 Lloyds Rep 446, 457–58 and *Weissfisch v Julius* [2006] 1 Lloyds Rep 716 (CA) 722 [35(v)], and can be derived from ordinary principles of comity. However, a weaker approach was taken in *Excalibur Ventures v Texas Keystone* [2011] 2 Lloyds Rep 289, [55], although cf [68].

[83] Using the language in *Airbus Industrie v Patel* [1998] 1 AC 119 (HL) 138G–H.

[84] See *Excalibur Ventures v Texas Keystone* [2011] 2 Lloyds Rep 289 [69]–[70]; and see also the result in *Sabbagh v Khoury* [2018] EWHC 1330 [47]; although cf contra *Nomihold Securities v Mobile Telesystems Finance* [2012] 1 Lloyds Rep 442 [63].

[85] See eg *Bremer Vulkan v South India Shipping* [1981] AC 909 (HL) 915; *Black Clawson International v Papierwerke Waldhof-Aschaffenberg* [1981] 2 Lloyds Rep 446, 448; *Siporex Trade v Comdel Commodities* [1986] 2 Lloyd Rep 428, 430.

[86] Such an injunction was granted in *Compagnie Européene de Céréals v Tradax Export* [1986] 2 Lloyds Rep 301, 305–06. In *Workplace Technologies v E Squared* (Judge David Wilcox, 16 February 2000), which concerned an adjudication under Housing Grants, Construction and Regeneration Act 1996, s 108, the adjudicator as well as the claimant had been made a defendant to a claim for an injunction, and no objection was raised to the fact that the adjudicator was a party (although the injunction was refused). In *Government of Gibraltar v Kenney* [1956] 2 QB 410, 419, the arbitrator was initially sued as an additional defendant but the proceedings against him were not pursued when he undertook to abide by the court's judgment.

the parties and the arbitrator.[87] As a result, it has been held that it would be a breach of the arbitration agreement by the arbitrator to hear a claim outside his jurisdiction, so that he could be personally restrained by injunction.[88]

However, absent some situation of personal misconduct by the arbitrator, it seems unlikely **11.39** that injunctions will be granted personally against arbitrators today, even in arbitrations with an English seat. The Arbitration Act 1996 does not provide for any route by which injunctions may be granted against arbitrators. The removal of arbitrators is dealt with by the specific power in section 24. Section 72 is drafted in broad terms, which could potentially cover injunctions against arbitrators acting outside their jurisdiction, but an applicant would find it difficult to persuade the court that there were special circumstances sufficient to justify restraining an arbitrator personally.[89] Indeed, the 1996 Act and the CPR specify the cases where arbitrators need to be defendants to arbitration claims,[90] and where they must be given notice,[91] and these do not include section 72.

Further, injunctions to restrain the pursuit of arbitrations under section 37(1) will often **11.40** be based on grounds which are inapplicable to support injunctions against arbitrators personally. For example, in a case where it is appropriate to restrain an arbitration which is vexatious or oppressive, it will not usually be the arbitrator that will be acting in a vexatious or oppressive manner. Similarly, there will rarely be good discretionary reasons to restrain an arbitrator personally, especially where the real dispute is between the parties, and not between a party and the arbitrator.

Where the seat of the arbitration is outside England, the principle of comity will weigh **11.41** heavily against the grant of injunctive relief against an arbitrator personally, as the arbitrator owes no allegiance to England. International arbitrators have often ignored anti-suit

---

[87] *Compagnie Européene de Céréals v Tradax Export* [1986] 2 Lloyds Rep 301, 306 (Hobhouse J); *Montedipe v JTP-Ro Jugotanker (The Jordan Nikolov)* [1990] 2 Lloyds Rep 11, 16 (Hobhouse J); *K/S Norjarl v Hyundai Heavy Industries* [1991] 1 Lloyds Rep 524 (CA) 536–37 (where the point appears not to have been disputed: see [1991] 1 Lloyds Rep 260, 266); *Jivraj v Hashwani* [2010] ICR 1435 [14], [21]–[23].

[88] *Compagnie Européene de Céréals v Tradax Export* [1986] 2 Lloyds Rep 301, 306. But it could be argued that an arbitrator's only actual duty is to undertake 'quasi-judicial functions' (see *K/S Norjarl A/S v Hyundai Heavy Industries* [1991] 1 Lloyds Rep 524 (CA) 536–37), and thus to fairly and impartially consider any jurisdiction challenge made to him. If so, there would be no basis for restraining the arbitrator personally.

[89] In *Caparo Group v Fagor Arrasate Sociedad Cooperative* (Clarke J, 7 August 1998), it appeared that Clarke J would have been disinclined to grant an injunction if it had been sought against the arbitrator or the ICC, which it was not.

The international arbitration community (unsurprisingly) regards any injunctive interference with arbitrations, even by the courts of the seat, with hostility. International tribunals have even ignored injunctive relief granted against the tribunal itself by the courts of the seat of the arbitration (albeit in cases of manifestly abusive action by the state in question): J Werner, 'When Arbitration Becomes War—Some Reflections on the Frailty of the Arbitral Process in Cases Involving Authoritarian States' (2000) 17 J Intl Arb 97; ICC, 'ICC Arbitration 10623' (2003) 1 ASA Bulletin 59;M de Boisséson, 'Anti-Suit Injunctions Issued by National Courts' in Gaillard (2005) 65; J Werner, 'When Arbitration Becomes War—Some Reflections on the Frailty of the Arbitral Process in Cases Involving Authoritarian States' (2000) 17 J Intl Arb 97; J Lew, 'Control of Jurisdiction by Injunctions Issued by National Courts' (2006) International Arbitration, ICCA series no 13, 185, 208–10, 216, 218; A Redfern, M Hunter, and N Blackaby, *Law and Practice of International Commercial Arbitration* (6th edn, OUP 2015) paras 7.51–7.61. Leaving aside the merits of this resistance in other situations, we can note that under English law, a Tribunal with an English seat is bound by the English court's decisions: see *Naviera Amazonica Peruana v Compania Internacional de Seguros del Peru* [1988] 1 Lloyds Rep 116 (CA) 119.

[90] Civil Procedure Rule 62.6(1) requires that arbitrators are defendants to arbitration claims under ss 24, 28, or 56 of the 1996 Act.

[91] Arbitrators must be given notice of arbitration claims under ss 24, 48, 56, and 67–69 of the 1996 Act.

injunctions which have sought to restrain them personally.[92] In addition, in most such cases, the real dispute will not be about the arbitrator's conduct, but will instead concern the nature of the arbitration or the conduct of the other party. If so, the position of the foreign arbitrator in such a case is analogous to the position of the foreign court, and it is a fundamental principle of the law of anti-suit injunctions that they do not lie against the foreign court itself, but only against the litigating party.[93]

11.42   Even if the claim for the injunction is based on circumstances that relate directly to the arbitrator himself, it is still unlikely that any injunction will be granted where the seat of the arbitration is abroad. In *Weissfisch v Julius*, the agreed seat of the arbitration was in Zurich, and the substantive claims included contentions that the arbitrator had acted in breach of fiduciary duty in acting as arbitrator. An interim injunction was sought to restrain pursuit of the arbitration. The Court of Appeal rejected the application. The parties had unquestionably agreed to arbitrate in Zurich, and as a result, the issues raised by the claim were naturally to be resolved in Switzerland according to Swiss law. It followed that, save in exceptional circumstances, the English court would not grant a final injunction to restrain the arbitrator from hearing proceedings under the foreign arbitration agreement. Further, special circumstances would be required to justify the grant of interim relief, and none existed.[94]

11.43   The question remains whether, even if an injunction is not made against the arbitrator personally, he is bound by the law of contempt, as with third parties in general, not to interfere with the effect of the injunction, and so would himself be in contempt if he were to proceed with the arbitration. In *BHPB v Cosco*,[95] Finkelstein J in the Federal Court of Australia was of the view that the third-party effect of an anti-suit injunction should affect an arbitrator like any other third party and observed that the fact that a foreign arbitrator was not within the territorial jurisdiction of the Australian court would not necessarily relieve him of contempt liability, stating, with some menace: 'If Mr Oakley in fact took any step to further the arbitration after he became aware of the injunction, he may be in for a rude shock were he to find himself subject to the personal jurisdiction of the Federal Court.' With respect, this is an extraordinary result to reach, and may be explained by the fact that there was no one there to argue for Mr Oakley. No common law court has ever dreamed of mechanistically applying its rules of contempt to the judges or staff of foreign courts so as to enforce compliance with anti-suit injunctions and any attempt to use contempt to attack foreign lawyers acting for the injunction defendant would also be unsound.[96] It would be strange if the foreign arbitrator were any more exposed. Indeed, he will be subject to the arbitration law of the seat of the arbitration and bound by the arbitration clause and the terms of the reference, and therefore in general

[92] See n 89.
[93] See Ch 3, paras 3.42–3.43.
[94] *Weissfisch v Julius* [2006] 1 Lloyds Rep 716 (CA) 722. See also *Channel Tunnel Group v Balfour Beatty* [1993] AC 334 (HL) 368. It can also be noted that any such claim will face considerable difficulties of personal territorial jurisdiction, even if the arbitrator is domiciled in England: see the jurisdictional application made (but not considered by the Court of Appeal) in *Weissfisch* at 719. The substantive claims against the arbitrator were subsequently stayed by Colman J, who awarded indemnity costs against the claimants: *A v B* [2007] 1 Lloyds Rep 237; *A v B (No 2)* [2007] 1 Lloyds Rep 358.
[95] *BHPB Freight v Cosco Oceania Chartering* [2008] FCA 551 [6].
[96] See Ch 3, paras 3.43, 3.45–3.47.

will be contractually obliged to hear the arbitration before him. In contrast, a judgment of a non-curial court that is foreign to him will usually not be binding on the arbitrator and would give him no defence to his obligation to hear the arbitration. Seeking to put the arbitrator in a personally difficult position, by application of extraterritorial contempt powers, is hard to reconcile with comity.

12

Anti-Suit Injunctions and European Jurisdictional Law

A. BREXIT

The UK remains, as matters stand at the time of writing this section (1 May 2019), committed to Brexit. However, it is still necessary to address the interrelationship between anti-suit injunctions and European jurisdictional law, for numerous reasons. First, it is possible that Brexit will not occur. Second, if Brexit happens, under the current proposed draft withdrawal agreement of November 2018 if agreed, the European jurisdictional regime will continue to operate between the UK and the EU during the transitional period (with transitional provisions in Article 67 extending its effect in certain cases thereafter). Third, the final status arrangements may well include continuation of key elements of the European jurisdictional arrangements, including in particular the Brussels–Lugano regime. Fourth, while the consequences of 'No deal' would be the end of the operation of the Brussels–Lugano regime between the UK and the Brussels–Lugano states,[1] it is possible that something similar to the Brussels–Lugano arrangements might subsequently be agreed.[2]

12.01

Consequently, the remainder of this chapter analyses the relationship between anti-suit injunctions and European law as matters stand pre-Brexit, and on the working assumption

12.02

---

[1] This term will be used to describe the set of rules made up of the Brussels Convention, the New Lugano Convention, EC Regulation 44/2001, generally known as the Brussels I Regulation ('the Regulation'), its replacement EC Regulation 1215/2012, generally known as the Brussels I Recast ('the Recast') and the agreements with Denmark by which Denmark has brought itself within the Regulation and the Recast.

[2] See further Ch 1, section I, 'Brexit' and Ch 16, section B, 'Brexit'.

that the European jurisdictional instruments will continue to operate in similar form between the UK and the EU and Lugano states.

12.03   But in contrast, if the Brussels–Lugano arrangements cease to apply and are not reinstated, the restrictions imposed by European jurisdictional law on the grant of anti-suit injunctions (and possibly other remedies) will disappear. Subject to any transitional arrangements, there will no longer be any principle of mutual trust (see paras 12.08 and 12.09 below) and this chapter will become of historical interest only in England[3] (although it may still be of interest in other Brussels–Lugano states, like Ireland, that grant anti-suit injunctions). It is true that, in that situation, the UK will, subject to some transitional difficulties, become party to the Hague Convention on Choice of Court in its own right (as opposed to through its EU membership as now), and this will replace aspects of the Brussels–Lugano arrangements.[4] However, although the Hague Convention does create a closed system for jurisdiction and the enforcement of judgments between its contracting states, it seems that it will not create any preclusion of anti-suit injunctions even where the other proceedings are in a contracting state.[5]

B. THE COLLISION

12.04   A collision between the common law approach to anti-suit injunctions and the rigid jurisdictional rules of the Brussels–Lugano regime was inevitable from the moment of the United Kingdom's accession to the Brussels Convention, and its implementation by the Civil Jurisdiction and Judgments Act 1982.

12.05   In a line of cases starting with *Continental Bank v Aeakos*, the English courts saw no incompatibility between the grant of an anti-suit injunction and the United Kingdom's obligations under the Brussels–Lugano regime, although there was a lack of reasoning as to why this was so.[6] This approach was always unlikely to survive a trip to

---

[3] The ending of the UK's EU membership would automatically bring to an end UK participation in the Brussels I Regulation and the New Lugano Convention, which is part of EU law. Further, while there is a theoretical argument that Brexit would not terminate the old Brussels Convention itself which would revive, this does not appear to be being taken seriously by the participants, and all concerned are proceeding on the basis that the no-deal scenario would bring the Brussels–Lugano regime to an end between the UK and EU. Consistently with that, the UK government's current proposed no-deal legislation would bring the Brussels–Lugano regime to an end as a matter of domestic law, subject to preservation of the effect of limited parts of the consumer and employment protections in new ss 15A–15E of the Civil Jurisdiction and Judgments Act 1982: see the Civil Jurisdiction and Judgments (Amendment) (EU Exit) Regulations 2019 (No 479/ 2019). However, those limited provisions preserve only a unilateral jurisdictional regime and do not (and could not) maintain the mutual effect of the Brussels–Lugano regime between the UK and the EU member states on the international plane, which lapses on Brexit. Consequently, the principle of mutual trust and the shackles on anti-suit injunctions which it imposes (see paras 12.05–12.13 below) will come to an end upon any no-deal Brexit, and/or any final status arrangement which does not continue the effect of the Brussels–Lugano regime or something similar between the UK and the EU.
[4] The details of this are addressed in Ch 16, section B, 'Brexit'.
[5] See Ch 1, section G, 'The Hague Convention on the Choice of Court', and Ch 7, para 7.09.
[6] *Continental Bank v Aeakos Compania Naviera* [1994] 1 Lloyds Rep 505 (CA) 511–12 (injunction granted to restrain proceedings in Greece, although the point that the Brussels Convention imposed a bar on anti-suit injunctions was apparently not taken); *Aggeliki Charis Compania Maritima v Pagnan (The Angelic Grace)* [1995] 1 Lloyds Rep 87 (CA) 96 (again the point was not taken, but injunction granted to restrain proceedings in Italy); *Bankers Trust International v RCS Editori* [1996] CLC 899, 907C–E (arguments of principle were addressed and rejected); *Banque Cantonale Vaudoise v Waterlily Maritime* [1997] 2 Lloyds Rep 347; *Charterers Mutual Assurance Association v British & Foreign* [1998] ILPr 838 [48]–[52] (treating *Continental Bank* and *The Angelic Grace* as binding); *OT Africa Line v Hijazy (The Kribi) (No 1)* [2001] 1 Lloyds Rep 76 [28], [45], [75], [95(4)] (treating *Continental Bank* as binding); *Navigation Maritime Bulgare v Rustal Trading (The Ivan Zagubanski)* [2002] 1 Lloyds

Luxembourg,[7] which finally occurred in *Turner v Grovit*.[8] Since then the European Court's opposition to anti-suit injunctions within the Brussels–Lugano zone has been extended to apply to preclude anti-suit injunctions to restrain arbitration proceedings, in *The Front Comor*.[9]

In *Turner v Grovit*, an anti-suit injunction was granted by the Court of Appeal in a non-   **12.06** contractual case to restrain proceedings in Spain, which the Court of Appeal found had been brought in bad faith, in an apparent attempt to harass the pursuit of parallel proceedings in England.[10] The question of whether this injunction was compatible with the Brussels–Lugano regime was referred to the European Court by the House of Lords. It seems, from the delay in giving judgment, that there was internal debate as to the wisdom of the reference. Lord Hobhouse gave a speech intended to steer the European Court, contending that an anti-suit injunction was a purely personal remedy, and did not interfere with the jurisdiction of other Convention courts. He suggested that preclusion of anti-suit injunctions would go beyond the proper role of the Brussels Convention, as this was not a jurisdictional issue, but a question of the procedural remedies available to a national court.[11]

The European Court of Justice (ECJ) held that the Brussels Convention, and thus the   **12.07** Brussels–Lugano regime,[12] precluded the grant of an injunction whereby a court of a

Rep 106 [102]–[109] (treating *Continental Bank* as binding); *ACI Worldwide (EMEA) v National Organisation Systems & Technical Trading* [2002] EWHC 2581. These were all contractual cases.

In the non-contractual context, the English courts eventually also took the view that there was no incompatibility in *Turner v Grovit* [2000] QB 345 (CA) 357–58, [2002] 1 WLR 107 (HL) [30]–[39]. Previously they had shown more circumspection. In *Deaville v Aeroflot Russian International Airlines* [1997] 2 Lloyds Rep 67, a non-contractual case, an injunction was refused in respect of proceedings in France on grounds of comity, but the Brussels–Lugano regime was apparently not viewed as an absolute bar to the grant of relief. In *First National Bank Association v Compagnie Nationale Air Gabon* [1999] ILPr 617, Stephen Tomlinson QC refused to grant an injunction to restrain parallel proceedings in France where the English court was first seised: 'it is, to my mind, quite axiomatic that the whole shape of the Convention is that, as between Convention courts, the courts of one jurisdiction leave it to the courts of another Convention jurisdiction loyally to apply the Convention' (at [22]). See to the same effect, the decision of David Donaldson QC in *Turner v Grovit* at first instance: [1999] 1 All ER (Comm) 445.

---

[7]   A Briggs, 'Anti-Suit Injunctions and Utopian Ideals' (2004) 120 LQR 529, subsequently described the eventual result as being 'as inevitable as it is unpalatable' (at 529). For previous English academic commentary which gazed into the crystal ball, see: A Briggs, 'Decisions of British Courts during 1999: Private International Law' (1999) BYBIL 319, 332–35 (suggesting that the Court of Appeal's decision in *Turner v Grovit* [2000] QB 345 (CA) was wrong); J Harris, 'Use and Abuse of the Brussels Convention' (1999) 115 LQR 576 (predicting disaster); R Fentiman, 'Antisuit Injunctions and the Brussels Convention' [2000] CLJ 45 (supporting the Court of Appeal's decision, although noting its 'insecure foundations'); T Hartley, 'Antisuit Injunctions and the Brussels Jurisdiction and Judgments Convention' (2000) 49 ICLQ 166 (hoping our European partners would 'understand').

[8]   *Turner v Grovit* [1999] 1 All ER (Comm) 445 (David Donaldson QC, refusing the injunction—his decision afterwards looked rather prophetic); reversed [2000] QB 345 (CA) 357–58; reference made [2002] 1 WLR 107 (HL); the ruling on the reference is at Case C–159/02, *Turner v Grovit* [2004] ECR I–3565 (in effect reversing the Court of Appeal).

The English Court of Appeal had previously made a reference to the European Court on whether an anti-suit injunction to enforce an arbitration clause fell within the arbitration exception: *Toepfer International v Société Cargill France* [1998] 1 Lloyds Rep 379 (CA) 388, but the case settled before the reference was heard. The Tribunal de Commerce de Marseille had tried to construct an artificial reference to the European Court on the compatibility of anti-suit injunctions with the Brussels–Lugano regime, but neglected to observe that it had no jurisdiction to do so, since the power to refer was confined to courts of final appeal: Case C–24/02, *Marseille Fret v Seatrano Shipping* [2002] ECR I–3383.

[9]   Case C-195/07, *Allianz v West Tankers (The Front Comor)* [2009] ECR I-663.

[10]   *Turner v Grovit* [2000] QB 345 (CA) 357–58, reversing David Donaldson QC [1999] 1 All ER (Comm) 445.

[11]   *Turner v Grovit* [2002] 1 WLR 107 (HL) [30]–[40].

[12]   Although *Turner v Grovit* was formally a decision under the Brussels Convention only, there is no doubt that it also reflects the law under the Brussels–Lugano regime generally. The continuity of interpretation of the Brussels–Lugano regime has been repeatedly re-affirmed: see eg Case C-533/07, *Falco Privatstiftung v Weller-Lindhorst* [2010] Bus LR 210, ECJ [52], [53], [56].

contracting state prohibits a party from commencing or continuing legal proceedings before a court of another contracting state.[13]

12.08   The European Court[14] reasoned that the Brussels–Lugano regime is based on the principle of mutual trust between the courts of the contracting states. Except in limited situations, the regime does not permit the jurisdiction of a court of a contracting state to be reviewed by a court in another contracting state. Any 'prohibition imposed by a court, backed by a penalty, restraining a party from commencing or continuing proceedings before a foreign court', like an injunction, interferes with the jurisdiction of the other court and is thus inconsistent with the Brussels–Lugano regime. Even an injunction on the basis of abuse of process requires an assessment of the appropriateness of bringing proceedings before a court of another member state, and such an assessment runs counter to the principle of mutual trust. The argument that an injunction is merely a procedural measure intended to safeguard the integrity of proceedings before it, and thus a matter of national law alone, was no answer, because national procedural laws have only a limited autonomy, and are not allowed to impair the effectiveness of the regime.[15]

12.09   Three aspects of the decision were especially significant. First, the European Court's decision limited the English courts' exercise of their *power* to grant anti-suit injunctions, not their *jurisdiction* to hear cases concerning such injunctions.[16] Second, the English analysis under which anti-suit injunctions have personal effect only, and thus do not directly interfere with the foreign court, was dismissed. From the European Court's perspective, what was important was the substantive, if indirect, interference with the jurisdiction of the other court.[17] Third, although *Turner* itself was a non-contractual case, the European Court's reasoning by extension inevitably precluded injunctions to enforce an exclusive jurisdiction clause that restrained the pursuit of Brussels–Lugano proceedings.

---

[13]   Case C–159/02, *Turner v Grovit* [2004] ECR I–3565.

[14]   There was no British or Irish judge in the panel (the Advocate General was Spanish). Judge David Edward was present for the oral hearing, but had retired between then and the handing down of the judgment, and it appears did not participate in its formulation.

[15]   For criticism of the ECJ's decision, see A Briggs, 'Anti-Suit Injunctions and Utopian Ideals' (2004) 120 LQR 529; T Hartley, 'The European Union and the Systematic Dismantling of the Common Law of Conflict of Laws' (2005) 54 ICLQ 813; (2004) Rev Crit DIP 93(3) 655 (note H Muir-Watt on *Turner v Grovit*); and A Briggs, 'The Impact of Recent Judgments of the European Court on English Procedural Law and Practice' Part II (2005) 124 Zeitschrift fur Schweizerisches Recht/Revue de droit Suisse 231.

  The principle of mutual trust has come in for particular criticism. See J Mance, 'Exclusive Jurisdiction Agreements and European Ideals' (2004) 120 LQR 357, observing that the ECJ's reasoning in *Turner v Grovit* 'itself postulates an absence of mutual trust in a national court's ability to identify and restrain abuse in respect of litigation within its jurisdiction' (at 363); P Gross, 'Anti-Suit Injunctions and Arbitration' [2005] LMCLQ 10, 24, observing that 'trust in the foreign court to stay its proceedings' 'is no solution at all where—theory and Regulation assumptions notwithstanding—trust breaks down. The presumption that trust cannot break down does not address the practical difficulties when it does.' A Dickinson, 'A Charter for Tactical Litigation in Europe?' [2004] LMCLQ 273, expresses doubt as to whether the principle of mutual trust can bear the weight of reality; and from a more European perspective, F Blöbel and P Späth, 'The Tale of Multilateral Trust and the European Law of Civil Procedure' (2005) 30 EL Rev 528, suggest that the principle of mutual trust should be interpreted as a 'soft' and flexible concept, and not applied dogmatically. Nevertheless, the principle has been treated as established by the UK Supreme Court: *AMT Futures v Marzillier* [2018] AC 439 (SC) [11].

  There was a sting in the tail for Grovit, who did not get his costs, despite having won: *Turner v Grovit* (House of Lords, unreported, 21 October 2004).

[16]   The question of whether the Brussels–Lugano regime also restricts personal jurisdiction over anti-suit injunctions to restrain the pursuit of proceedings before courts outside the Brussels–Lugano zone is discussed at section C, 'Both Sets of Proceedings within the Brussels–Lugano Regime and Zone'.

[17]   [28] of the Judgment; see also [34] of the opinion of the Advocate General.

However, *Turner v Grovit* left a wide range of points unsettled, in particular at the frontiers   **12.10**
of the Brussels–Lugano regime. The most important debate was whether an anti-suit injunction to enforce an arbitration clause by restraining the pursuit of proceedings in other
Brussels–Lugano states would fall within the 'arbitration' exception to the material scope of
the regime, or whether it would also be precluded by the principle of mutual trust.

The English Courts had, initially, concluded that such an injunction was outside the   **12.11**
Brussels–Lugano regime; and that notwithstanding *Turner,* it was not precluded by the
European jurisdictional rules.[18] But it was apparent this might not be the answer that the
European Court would give, and the question was, yet again, loyally referred by the House
of Lords in *The Front Comor*, where an injunction had been granted to restrain the pursuit
of proceedings before the Italian courts which were (from an English perspective) in breach
of a London arbitration clause. Again, the House of Lords gave their views on the answer
in an attempt to persuade the European Court. Lord Hoffmann argued that such injunctions were obviously arbitration matters and within the arbitration exception. In turn, it
would be contrary to principle if the Regulation would preclude such injunctions, as that
would extend the application of the Regulation to orders made in proceedings to which the
Regulation did not apply, and ignored the practical realities of commerce.[19]

The reference gave rise to a problem of perspective: should the analytical focus be on the   **12.12**
grant of the injunction and the arbitration proceedings which the injunction was sought to
protect, or on the Brussels–Lugano proceedings whose pursuit it sought to restrain?

The European Court's judgment[20] concluded that the anti-suit injunction was not itself   **12.13**
within the scope of the Brussels–Lugano regime because it was sought to protect the right
to arbitrate, which meant that its subject matter was arbitration, so that it fell within the arbitration exception.[21] However, by virtue of the principle of effectiveness of European law,
even remedies which are themselves outside the scope of the Brussels–Lugano regime can
be precluded by the regime if they undermine its effectiveness.[22] The European Court concluded, first, that the Italian courts' own consideration of whether their own jurisdiction
should be precluded by the arbitration clause was a matter within the scope of the Brussels–
Lugano regime, because it was an incidental question to the substantive litigation before
them, which was civil and commercial litigation and so within the scope of the regime.
Second, even though such an injunction was itself outside the Brussels–Lugano regime,
it prevented a Brussels–Lugano court from exercising its own Brussels–Lugano jurisdiction and assessing whether that jurisdiction existed; it was therefore inconsistent with the

---

[18] See *Through Transport Mutual Insurance Association (Eurasia) v New India Assurance* [2005] 1 Lloyds Rep 67
(CA) [38]–[48]. The question of whether the injunction fell within or outside the arbitration exception had earlier
been referred to the European Court by the Court of Appeal in *Toepfer International v Société Cargill France* [1998]
1 Lloyds Rep 379 (CA), but the case had settled before the determination of the reference.

[19] *West Tankers v Ras Riunione Adriatica di Sicurta (The Front Comor)* [2007] 1 Lloyds Rep 391 (HL).

[20] Case C-195/07, *Allianz v West Tankers (The Front Comor)* [2009] ECR I-663. In effect this decision overrules the English case law leading up to *Through Transport Mutual Insurance Association (Eurasia) v New India
Assurance* [2005] 1 Lloyds Rep 67 (CA) (discussed at para 12.46 and n 66 below).

[21] This has the significant consequence that if a claim is made for an anti-suit injunction to enforce an arbitration clause, it will fall outside the jurisdictional rules of the Brussels–Lugano regime so that questions of territorial
jurisdiction are to be assessed under English national jurisdictional rules. See further Ch 16, para 16.26; Ch 17,
para 17.18 n 23.

[22] This conclusion has been criticized as overreaching: see Briggs, para 2.28, n 2 and para 2.30, suggesting that it
is inconsistent with Case 145/86, *Hoffmann v Krieg* [1988] ECR 654.

principle that Brussels–Lugano courts should assess their own jurisdiction; and therefore undermined the effectiveness of the Brussels–Lugano regime, and was inconsistent with the principle of mutual trust.[23]

12.14   The specific line of reasoning adopted by the European Court was abstract, and artificial. An illustration of its strained nature is the conclusion that the objection raised in the Italian court was an objection to the jurisdiction of the Italian court, when it was not: it was an argument that Brussels–Lugano jurisdiction should not be exercised because of the New York Convention. But it had important consequences. First, it followed logically that if the other proceedings are outside the Brussels–Lugano zone, there is nothing to prevent an injunction being granted, as the principle of mutual trust does not apply. Second, if the other proceedings are outside the material scope of the Brussels–Lugano regime, an injunction to restrain them would not be caught by the principle of effectiveness.

12.15   The decision in *The Front Comor* has been subject to considerable criticism, and not merely from lawyers from common law systems.[24] Even the anti-suit injunction found some friends from within civil law systems. It was recognized that *The Front Comor* risked creating an asymmetric situation in which arbitration could be undermined by national courts, which were not the courts for the seat of the arbitration, overriding agreements to arbitrate, while the courts of the seat were deprived of a useful remedy.[25] The European Commission acknowledged that it could open the door to procedural manoeuvring by which parties could use unjustified court litigation to undermine arbitration proceedings. The European Parliament issued a resolution arguing that *The Front Comor* should be reversed.[26]

---

[23]   See the analysis of *Gazprom* by Males J in *Nori Holding v Bank Otkritie Financial Corporation* [2018] 2 Lloyds Rep 80 [69]–[80].

[24]   For English academic discussion critical of the European Court of Justice's decision, see A Briggs, 'Fear and Loathing in Syracuse and Luxembourg' [2009] LMCLQ 161; R Fentiman, 'Arbitration and Anti-Suit Injunctions in Europe' [2009] CLJ 278; S Dutson and M Howarth, 'After West Tankers—Rise of the "Foreign Torpedo"' (2009) 75 Arbitration 334; E Peel, 'Arbitration and Anti-Suit Injunctions in the European Union', (2009) 125 LQR 365; J Tumbridge, 'European Anti-Suit Injunctions in Favour of Arbitration—A Sea Change?' [2010] ICCLR 177; H Seriki, 'Anti-Suit Injunctions, Arbitration and the European Court of Justice [2010] JBL 24; J Lurie, 'Court Intervention in Arbitration: Support or Interference' (2010) 76 Arbitration 447, 449–50; Y Baatz, 'A Jurisdiction Race in the Dark' [2010] LMCLQ 364.

     For continental academic discussion supportive of the ECJ's approach, see in advance: M Illmer and I Naumann, 'Yet Another Blow: Anti-Suit Injunctions in Support of Arbitration Agreements within the European Union' (2007) Intl ALR 147; and subsequently: K Lenaerts, 'The Contribution of the European Court of Justice to the Area of Freedom, Security and Justice' (2010) 59 ICLQ 255, 285–88; T Pfeiffer, 'Pfeiffer on West Tankers' (www.conflictoflaws.net); L Radicati di Brozolo, 'Arbitration and the Draft Revised Brussels I Regulation: Seeds of Home Country Control and of Harmonisation?' (2011) 7(3) J Priv IntL 423; M Illmer, 'Brussels I and Arbitration Revisited' (2011) 75 RabelsZ Bd 645–70.

     However, for continental academic discussion critical of the court's decision, see C Kessedjian, 'Kessedjian on West Tankers' and R Arenas 'Arenas on West Tankers' (both on www.conflictoflaws.net); H Muir Watt, 'Cour de justice des Communautés européennes (grande chambre)—10 février 2009—Aff C-185/07' (2009) 98 Revue Critique de Droit International Privé 373; S Bollée, 'Allianz et autre c/West Tankers Inc' (2009) Revue de l'arbitrage 413; C Kessedjian, 'Arbitrage et droit européen: une désunion irrémédiable?' (2009) Recueil Dalloz 981 ('la cour statue praeter legem … la cour encourage des parties de mauvaise foi …'); GA Dal, 'L'arrêt "West Tankers" et l'effet négatif du principe de compétence-compétence' (2010) Revue Pratique des Sociétés 22; S Bollée, 'L'arbitre peut-il octroyer des dommages-intérêts pour violation de la convention d'arbitrage?' (2012) Revue de l'Arbitrage 838–43. For a nuanced approach, see B Audit, note concernant la decision de la CJUE du 10 fev 2009 *West Tankers*, JDI no 4 (2009) 1281.

[25]   See B Hess, 'Hess on West Tankers' (www.conflictoflaws.net).

[26]   European Parliament resolution of 7 September 2010 on the implementation and review of Council Regulation (EC) No 44/2001 on jurisdiction and the recognition and enforcement of judgments in civil and commercial matters (P7_TA(2010)0304), recital M.

The conclusion that the Italian court's own 'incidental' decision on the applicability of the arbitration was itself a matter within the Brussels–Lugano regime—and therefore, apparently, would itself constitute a Brussels–Lugano judgment which would be enforceable under the Brussels–Lugano rules[27]—was subject to particular criticism.[28] This was unnecessary collateral damage, as the European Court could have concluded that the injunction undermined effectiveness and mutual trust on the broader basis that, by preventing the Italian court from deciding on whether to exercise jurisdiction over the proceedings before them, it interfered with the Italian courts' overall exercise or assessment of Brussels–Lugano jurisdiction, whether or not their decision on the arbitration clause was itself within the scope of the regime. Indeed, it is arguably possible to read the European Court's actual reasoning as depending, in part, on such a broader approach and thus remaining valid independent of the narrower issue of the characterization of the Italian court's decision, although the judgment is not very clear.[29]   **12.16**

But this narrower aspect was capable of producing unacceptably asymmetric consequences: on the one hand, the court of the seat's own positive conclusions that an arbitration clause was binding would not fall within the scope of the Brussels–Lugano regime, and would not be enforceable under the Brussels–Lugano regime, but on the other hand, the incidental determination of another court on the same question would fall within the scope of the regime and therefore have to be recognized even in the court of the seat.[30]   **12.17**

It was widely held across Europe that the existing position was unsatisfactory, although there was less agreement as to the remedy. A vigorous debate therefore fed into the ongoing process of reform of the Brussels I Regulation which was already under way.[31] The result is Recital 12 of the Brussels I Recast, which reinforces the arbitration exception. Although its effect is not entirely explicit, and it bears the hallmark of drafting by committee, it appears at the least to have reversed the unattractive side effect of *The Front Comor* under which the foreign court's incidental conclusion that an arbitration clause was not binding would itself be enforceable under the Brussels–Lugano recognition and enforcement rules.[32] No specific reference was made to anti-suit injunctions.   **12.18**

---

[27] The English courts held that this was indeed the effect of *The Front Comor* in *National Navigation v Endesa Generacion (The Wadi Sudr)* [2010] 1 Lloyds Rep 193 (CA).

[28] See C Kessedjian, 'Kessedjian on West Tankers", and R Arenas 'Arenas on West Tankers' (both on www.conflictoflaws.net).

[29] See the discussion in *Nori Holding v Bank Otkritie Financial Corporation* [2018] 2 Lloyds Rep 80 [69]–[76].

[30] In *National Navigation v Endesa Generacion (The Wadi Sudr)* [2010] 1 Lloyds Rep 193 (CA) [41], [46], it was said that *The Front Comor*'s result produced an unappealing 'lack of reciprocity'. The European Commission implicitly accepted that *The Front Comor* had the result that arbitration clauses were not given sufficient protection and proposed reforms: see the Commission Proposal for a new Brussels Regulation (Com (2010) 748 Final) at para 3.14. Somewhat different reforms have materialized in the Brussels I Recast.

[31] See Heidelberg Report (Study JLS/C4/2005/03) and Commission Green Paper for reform of the Brussels I Regulation (Com (2009) 175 Final); Commission Proposal for a new Brussels Regulation (Com (2010) 748 Final), none of whose proposals were adopted in this regard.

[32] See Recital 12, and in particular the second paragraph:

> A ruling given by a court of a Member state as to whether or not an arbitration agreement is null and void, inoperative, or incapable of being performed should not be subject to the rules of recognition and enforcement laid down in this Regulation, regardless of whether the court decided on this as a principal issue or as an incidental question.

> cf *Toyota Tsusho Sugar Trading v Prolat SRL* [2015] 1 Lloyds Rep 344 [15]–[17].

12.19   The interplay of these changes with *The Front Comor* presented an interesting possibility: has Recital 12 reversed the ECJ's conclusion that the foreign court's assessment of the binding force of the arbitration clause was itself a part of the foreign court's exercise of its Brussels–Lugano jurisdiction? And if so, does that remove the basis on which it was said that the anti-suit injunction was an interference with such Brussels–Lugano jurisdiction, and so precluded by the principle of effectiveness?[33] If the anti-suit injunction has been restored in this way, it would be a remarkable back-door legislative triumph for the UK negotiators.

12.20   In his opinion in *Gazprom*, Advocate General Wathelet concluded this would, indeed, be the effect of Recital 12. His reasoning is surprising—and in some ways refreshing to English lawyers, who have come to fear a lack of sympathy when English private international law is handled by the European legal institutions.

12.21   He seems to have been influenced by the continental academic criticism of *The Front Comor*, and concluded that the second paragraph of Recital 12 had shifted the boundaries of the arbitration exception outwards, so that where proceedings were brought before a national court in alleged breach of an arbitration clause, the national court's consideration of whether the arbitration clause was binding would not be within the Brussels–Lugano regime. Indeed, the proceedings before it would not be within the scope of the regime *until* the national court had concluded the arbitration clause was invalid. So, an injunction to restrain such consideration was not itself contrary to European jurisdictional law. Further, he reasoned that para 4 of Recital 12,[34] making clear 'ancillary proceedings' in support of arbitration were outside the Recast, would cover anti-suit injunctions. Consequently, Recital 12 meant the result of *The Front Comor* would be different under the Brussels I Recast. Anti-suit injunctions to enforce arbitration clauses by restraining Brussels–Lugano proceedings would be permissible.[35] He went so far as to suggest, pointing to the inconsistencies between *The Front Comor* and previous ECJ judgments like *Marc Rich*, that Recital 12 indicated the correct interpretation of the Brussels I Regulation, so that *The Front Comor* should no longer be treated as the law even before the Recast.[36]

12.22   The Advocate General's sympathy for anti-suit injunctions, especially when granted by arbitrators, is evident. He thought that an anti-suit award is the only effective remedy an arbitration tribunal can give to prevent breach of the arbitration agreement by litigation elsewhere, and concluded that anti-suit injunctions granted by arbitrators would anyway be unaffected by the Brussels–Lugano regime because arbitrators were not bound by mutual trust. He also observed that it would be compatible with the Brussels I Regulation for either a national court or an arbitration tribunal to award damages for breach of the arbitration clause by litigation before national courts.[37]

---

[33] This was suggested as a possibility by some authors: A Nuyts, 'La refonte du Reglement Bruxelles I (2013) RCDIP 1, 14–17; D Ndolo and M Liu, 'Does the Will of the Parties Supersede the Sovereignty of the State: Anti-Suit Injunctions in the UK Post Brexit' (2017) 83(3) Arbitration 254. For discussion, see also S Camilleri, 'Recital 12 of the New Regulation: A New Hope?' (2013) 62(4) ICLQ 899.

[34] 'This Regulation should not apply to any action or ancillary proceedings relating to, in particular, the establishment of an arbitral tribunal, the powers of arbitrators, the conduct of an arbitration procedure or any other aspects of such a procedure, . . .'.

[35] Case C-536/15, *Gazprom* EU:C:2015:316, AG [130]–[140].

[36] This appears to be the meaning of the Advocate General's opinion at Case C-536/15, *Gazprom* EU:C:2015:316, AG [141]–[143], [149].

[37] Case C-536/15, *Gazprom* EU:C:2015:316, AG [153]–[157].

However, none of the Advocate General's reasoning on the effect of Recital 12 on anti-suit **12.23** injunctions granted by courts was necessary to the decision of the case before him. *Gazprom* concerned the grant of anti-suit injunctions by arbitrators, and whether a national court could refuse to enforce such an anti-suit award. That could be decided without reversing *The Front Comor*'s prohibition of anti-suit injunctions by courts. Indeed, it would have been possible to decide the case by simply saying that whether or not to enforce an anti-suit award was a matter for national law, and the interpretation of the New York Convention, to which European law had no relevance.[38]

The European Court did not adopt AG Wathelet's wider reasoning nor engage with the rele- **12.24** vance of Recital 12. It concluded in brief terms that an injunction to enforce an arbitration clause by restraining proceedings before other Brussels–Lugano courts was inconsistent both with the principle of mutual trust and with the principle that member state courts should themselves decide their own jurisdiction and cannot be in a better position to de-cide on the jurisdiction of another court.[39] Despite their brevity, these conclusions are a clear implicit rejection of the argument that *The Front Comor* has been reversed, so far as concerns injunctions granted by courts, and they appear to apply as much under the Recast as under the Regulation—at the least, they provide a clear clue as to how the European Court would rule under the Recast. The European Court avoided the problem created by *The Front Comor*'s specific reasoning by concluding that the anti-suit injunction would in broader terms be an interference with the other court's consideration of, and exercise of, its own Brussels–Lugano jurisdiction, in the sense sketched above. Its reasoning is thus inde-pendent of the narrower point, which is affected by Recital 12, of whether the decision on the validity of the arbitration clause is itself within the Brussels–Lugano regime.[40]

Indeed, contrary to the Advocate General's suggestion, the fourth sentence of Recital 12 **12.25** is more naturally read to cover other kinds of ancillary measures and not anti-suit injunc-tions. More generally, it seems difficult to read Recital 12, as AG Wathelet did, as intended to reverse the existing position in relation to anti-suit injunctions. The better reading is that Recital 12 was intended rather to reverse the specific problems of enforceability of foreign rulings on the force of arbitration clauses created by *The Front Comor*.[41]

It is suggested, therefore, that although in *Gazprom* the European Court did not directly **12.26** consider the effect of the Recast and Recital 12, it is unlikely, without a change of doctrine, that it will treat Recital 12 as having permitted anti-suit injunctions to enforce arbitration clauses within the Brussels–Lugano zone.[42] This was the result reached in the Commercial Court by Males J in *Nori v Otkritie*, where he held that there is nothing in the Recast

---

[38] See Case C-536/15, *Gazprom* EU:C:2015:316, AG [158]. Notwithstanding this, AG Wathelet also reached various conclusions as to why enforcement of an anti-suit award could not be refused on grounds of public policy (Case C-536/15, *Gazprom* EU:C:2015:316, AG [160]–[188]). These display evident sympathy for the grant of anti-suit injunctions, at least by arbitrators. But it is difficult to see how they can be justified as conclusions of interpret-ation of the Brussels Regulation, which has nothing to say on when arbitration awards can be enforced.

[39] Case C-536/15, *Gazprom* EU:C:2015:316, ECJ [33]–[34].

[40] *Nori Holding v Bank Otkritie Financial Corporation* [2018] 2 Lloyds Rep 80 [81]–[98].

[41] *Nori Holding v Bank Otkritie Financial Corporation* [2018] 2 Lloyds Rep 80 [86]–[98].

[42] cf A Briggs, 'Arbitration and the Brussels Regulation Again' [2015] LMCLQ 284; B Demirkol, 'Ordering Cessation of Court Proceedings to Protect the Integrity of Arbitration Agreements under the Brussels I Regime' (2016) ICLQ 379, 402.

Regulation to cast doubt on the continuing validity of the decision in *The Front Comor* on the impermissibility of anti-suit injunctions, and disagreed with AG Wathelet's reasoning.[43]

12.27 However, as regards anti-suit awards made by arbitrators, the European Court in *Gazprom* did follow AG Wathelet, and agreed they were not affected by European jurisdictional law. The European Court held that arbitrators were not bound by the principle of mutual trust, which applied only between courts. Further, the principle that courts should decide on their own jurisdiction was not infringed, because it would always be a question for national courts as to whether or not to enforce the anti-suit award when considering their own jurisdiction. Finally, remedies for breach of the arbitration award would not involve the imposition of 'penalties' by a court of another member state.[44] Consequently, the Brussels–Lugano regime did not prevent the grant of anti-suit awards; and the enforcement of the anti-suit award was itself a matter outside of, and unaffected by, the Brussels–Lugano regime.[45]

1. The Unpersuasiveness of *The Front Comor*

12.28 At the end of this story, the practical results of the European Court's judgments are fairly clear, if no change of heart occurs (and so long as the Brussels–Lugano regime remains the law). But the fragility of their justification is apparent. The implications of *Gazprom* require abandoning most of the reasoning in *The Front Comor*, which was unpersuasive to begin with.

12.29 An injunction which is itself outside the scope of the regime can only interact with the regime through its effects; but any interference with the other court's assessment or exercise of its own jurisdiction caused by the injunction is not functionally different to the effect of an anti-suit award. They differ only in that the latter is awarded by the court and with somewhat different remedies for breach.[46]

12.30 Nor was there ever any true sense in which an anti-suit injunction in support of arbitration interfered with the other court's assessment of its own Brussels–Lugano jurisdiction. At most it only pre-empted the other court's assessment of whether or not to stay under the New York Convention, a matter inherently within the arbitration exception and outside the Brussels–Lugano regime, and so indirectly interfered with the exercise of Brussels–Lugano jurisdiction. And it would do so no more than an arbitral anti-suit award, which *Gazprom* says is legitimate.

12.31 Further, the idea that an anti-suit injunction interfered with the effectiveness of the Brussels–Lugano regime, by this indirect interference with the exercise of Brussels–Lugano jurisdiction, equally lacked credibility. By preventing a party from seeking to exercise a

---

[43] *Nori Holding v Bank Otkritie Financial Corporation* [2018] 2 Lloyds Rep 80 [81]–[99].

[44] Case C-536/15, *Gazprom* EU:C:2015:316, ECJ [35]–[40]. As regards English law, this aspect of the reasoning is incomplete: an anti-suit award can be enforced as a judgment by the English court and will then, in effect, be an injunction enforceable by contempt.

[45] Case C-536/15, *Gazprom* EU:C:2015:316, ECJ [36]–[39], [41], [44].

[46] The European Court in *Gazprom* suggested (at [38]) that an anti-suit award would not create any interference as the other court would have a choice as to whether to enforce it; but this creates no distinction, as both anti-suit awards and injunctions operate principally by their personal grip on the injunction defendant, while the other court would equally have a choice whether or not to enforce a court anti-suit injunction to enforce an arbitration clause (since that injunction would not be within the Brussels–Lugano enforcement regime).

court's Brussels–Lugano jurisdiction, the injunction no more undermines the effectiveness of the Brussels–Lugano regime than would an uncontested arbitration clause, which produces the same effect—as would, of course, an arbitral anti-suit award.

We are left with assertions that for a court, but not arbitrators, to operate by injunction, is contrary to mutual trust between courts. The principle of mutual trust was only ever an assertion of the desired result, rather than a justification. But it is particularly difficult to see why any principle of mutual trust created by the relationship of courts within the Brussels–Lugano regime should affect a court which is acting outside the regime, and acting in a way that affects only the decisions of the other court on whether to stay in favour of arbitration, which is again a matter outside the regime. The deeper logic of mutual trust flows from the structure of a harmonized jurisdictional system, but in matters such as arbitration where the member state courts are not bound by the same principles of European law, it is difficult to see why dogma of mutual trust should apply between courts. **12.32**

So the remaining contention when boiled down becomes little more than that European courts should not indirectly affect the exercise of each other's Brussels–Lugano jurisdiction by decisions on questions outside the scope of the Brussels–Lugano regime merely because they are courts who in other contexts are bound by a common jurisdictional regime, and even though, as *Gazprom* tells us, there is nothing wrong with arbitrators doing the same thing, and where uncontested arbitration agreements produce the same result. **12.33**

It becomes clear that the real underlying 'European' objection is to the English court rather than the court of the other proceedings deciding on the effect of the arbitration clause. But whatever the force of that objection as a matter of comity and international arbitration law, it is a question of 'arbitration' and is not a question on which the Brussels–Lugano regime has any legitimate purchase. The ECJ has sought to cloak an independent objection to the anti-suit injunction in the trappings of European jurisdictional law, and has overreached.[47] **12.34**

The extent of the overreaching is starkly apparent, once it is recognized that the effect of *The Front Comor* is to extend the Brussels–Lugano regime to override substantive contractual law[48]—since the anti-suit injunction is a component of the English law of contractual remedies—in respect to which the regime necessarily does not apply, and in a field where it does not provide its own remedies.[49] **12.35**

The current resting place of the European Court's reasoning on anti-suit injunctions to enforce arbitration clauses is therefore unsatisfactory and unpersuasive. But that does not mean it will change. **12.36**

In the rest of this chapter, we therefore proceed on the basis that the essential distinctions drawn so far by the European Court will remain the law, and explore their implications for the various situations in which anti-suit injunctions and related remedies may be sought. **12.37**

---

[47] As observed by S Bollée, 'Allianz et autre c/ West Tankers Inc' (2009) Revue de l'Arbitrage, 413, 415–16.

[48] See S Bollée, 'Allianz et autre c/ West Tankers Inc' (2009) Revue de l'Arbitrage, 413, 424–25, observing that the decision in *The Front Comor* creates 'de serieuses menaces sur l'effet negative du principe de competence-competence'.

[49] The Brussels I Recast does provide some remedies to deal with disrespect of exclusive jurisdiction clauses, notably the new provisions in Article 31 which override the usual rules of *lis pendens* in favour of the court chosen by a forum clause.

We address, in particular, situations where the other proceedings are outside the Brussels–Lugano zone, or outside the material scope of the Brussels–Lugano regime; and whether anti-enforcement injunctions should be treated differently. We will also consider the effect of the principles of effectiveness and mutual trust on alternative remedies such as claims for damages and declarations, and remedies sought from arbitrators.

C. BOTH SETS OF PROCEEDINGS WITHIN THE BRUSSELS–LUGANO REGIME AND ZONE

12.38   The effect of *Turner v Grovit* and *The Front Comor* is that if an anti-suit injunction is sought in court proceedings which are themselves within the material scope of the Brussels–Lugano regime, to restrain a party from invoking the Brussels–Lugano jurisdiction of another member state court, the principles of effectiveness and mutual trust will preclude the grant of an injunction as a matter of power, irrespective of the ground on which the injunction is based, irrespective of how the foreign court has assumed or will assume Brussels–Lugano jurisdiction, and irrespective of whether the injunction defendant is domiciled within the Brussels–Lugano zone.[50] It does not matter, for example, that by precluding contractual injunctions, the European jurisdictional regime has had the effect of removing one of the substantive rights available under the English law of contract, to which willing parties to English law jurisdiction and arbitration clauses can be considered to have agreed.[51] The root of both decisions is that it is inconsistent with the fundamental structure of the Brussels–Lugano regime for the courts of one member state to interfere, even indirectly, with the exercise of the regime jurisdiction of another member state court.

12.39   It seems likely that claims for injunctions which do not entirely or directly restrain Brussels–Lugano proceedings from being commenced or continued, but do nevertheless seek to restrain aspects of the way they are conducted in a manner analogous to an anti-suit injunction, will also be precluded by mutual trust.[52] There will be difficulties at the margin: for example, if the English court is asked to restrain a breach of confidence, where the mis-use of confidential information is or will be taking place in foreign proceedings, does the principle of mutual trust impose a barrier?[53] The answers will need

---

[50] For a recent example of the boundaries in action, see *SwissMarine Corp v OW Supply and Trading* [2015] 1 CLC 1040 [43]–[44]. *Panagaki v Apostoloupos* [2015] EWHC 2700 [59]–[63] was a hopeless attempt to distinguish *Turner v Grovit*.

[51] See Rev Crit DIP (2004) 93(3), 655, para 4 (Note H Muir-Watt on *Turner v Grovit*); J Krause, 'Turner/Grovit—Der EuGH erklärt Prozessführungsverbote für unvereinbar mit dem EuGVÜ' [2004] RIW 533, 539, 2(a).
This is how history has worked itself out, but was not an inevitable result. There is a clear distinction in the civil law reaction to contractual and non-contractual anti-suit injunctions, with the former being seen as less obviously illegitimate because they enforce a concrete obligation. There is room to wonder whether if a contractual case had been the first referred to Europe, things might have been different. But once the decision in *Turner* had been given in broad terms, the course of European law was set, and would not change.

[52] See *Polegoshko v Ibragimov* [2014] EWHC 1535 [26]–[28], where if it had been necessary to decide the point, the court would have concluded that an order that the injunction defendant should not take any steps in Lithuanian proceedings save as directed by the court was in substance the same as an anti-suit injunction and precluded by mutual trust. In *Banque Cantonale Vaudoise v Waterlily Maritime* [1997] 2 Lloyds Rep 347, 357–58, a temporary injunction was granted to restrain the injunction defendant from advancing particular arguments in Greek proceedings pending determination of those points in England, but this was before *Turner v Grovit* and was based on the *pre-Turner* approach of the English courts that anti-suit injunctions were not inconsistent with the Brussels–Lugano regime.

[53] For another example of the difficulties of this boundary, see *AMT Futures v Marzillier* [2015] QB 699 (CA) [59]–[61], suggesting *obiter* that, if X is inducing Y to sue in another member state, in breach of an English

to be worked out, but the problem illustrates the radical and ill-considered nature of the interference with substantive legal rights which the ECJ's current case law imposes.

D. COMPETING PROCEEDINGS OUTSIDE THE BRUSSELS–LUGANO ZONE

In contrast, the Brussels–Lugano regime does not preclude anti-suit injunctions which re-   **12.40**
strain the pursuit of proceedings before courts or arbitral tribunals outside the Brussels–Lugano zone. In such a case there can be no interference with the exercise of, or assessment as to whether to exercise a Brussels–Lugano jurisdiction, and the principle of mutual trust is not engaged.

Following *Turner* it was argued on occasion that the evident hostility displayed by the   **12.41**
European Court towards anti-suit injunctions meant that the Brussels–Lugano regime should be interpreted as inherently antipathetic to anti-suit injunctions, and that the English courts' powers to grant such injunctions should be restricted generally, or restricted in cases where personal jurisdiction was assumed under the Brussels–Lugano jurisdictional rules.[54] But this finds no basis either in the principle of mutual trust or in the rationale of *The Front Comor* and *Gazprom*. The English courts have taken the approach that the Brussels–Lugano regime has no effect either on the power[55] or the discretion[56]

---

jurisdiction clause, an injunction to restrain inducement of breach of contract would not be inconsistent with mutual trust. The Court of Appeal concluded it was not a 'collateral attack' on the jurisdiction of another member state's courts, but simply the restraint of a separate tort. The strange result is that you cannot restrain the direct breach of contract by Y but can restrain the indirect tortious inducement of Y's breach by X. The point was not addressed by the Supreme Court: [2017] 2 WLR 853 [44].

---

[54] T Kruger, 'The Anti-Suit Injunction in the European Judicial Space' (2004) 53 ICLQ 1030, 1038–40, regarded this question as 'open'. See also the decision of the Scottish courts in *Clarke v Fennoscandia (No 3)* (2005) SLT 511 [26] (although the point was conceded, and was not addressed on appeal [2007] UKHL 56 [15]). In *Petter v EMC* [2015] EWHC 1498 [69], Cooke J did refer to the Brussels–Lugano regime as 'essentially inimical' to the grant of anti-suit injunctions, but in a different context, namely whether Brussels–Lugano rights could in themselves justify an anti-suit injunction.

[55] *OT Africa Line v Magic Sportswear* [2005] 2 Lloyds Rep 170 (CA) [37]–[38], [51]; *Seismic Shipping v Total E&P UK (The Western Regent)* [2005] 2 Lloyds Rep 359 (CA) [50]; *Beazley v Horizon Offshore Contractor* [2005] Lloyds Rep IR 231 [35]–[47]; *West Tankers v Ras Riunione Adriatica di Sicurta (The Front Comor)* [2007] 1 Lloyds Rep 391 (HL) [8]; *Shashoua v Sharma* [2009] 2 Lloyds Rep 376 [35]–[39]; *Masri v Consolidated Contractors (No 3)* [2009] QB 503 (CA) [67]; *Midgulf International v Groupe Chimiche Tunisien* [2009] 2 Lloyds Rep 411 [62], [2010] 2 Lloyds Rep 543 (CA) [67]–[68]; *Morris v Davies* [2011] EWHC 1272 [11]; *Re Tadros* [2014] EWHC 2860 [43]; *Petter v EMC* [2016] ILPr 3 (CA) [32]; *Essar Shipping v Bank of China (The Kishore)* [2016] 1 Lloyds Rep 417 [2]. There are now many cases where anti-suit injunctions have been granted in respect of proceedings outside the Brussels–Lugano zone without any suggestion that either the court's powers should be limited or its discretion affected.

[56] There were initially some suggestions that *Turner v Grovit* might affect the exercise of the court's discretion even where *Turner* did not directly apply: see *Seismic Shipping v Total E&P UK (The Western Regent)* [2005] 2 Lloyds Rep 54 [34]–[35], [2005] 2 Lloyds Rep 359 (CA) [50]; *Through Transport Mutual Insurance Association (Eurasia) v New India Assurance* [2005] 1 Lloyds Rep 67 (CA) [78]–[97] and *Through Transport Mutual Insurance Association (Eurasia) v New India Assurance (No 2)* [2005] 2 Lloyds Rep 378 [18]. However, the approach in *Through Transport* was heavily influenced by the desire to avoid a reference on the question of whether there was a power to grant an injunction to enforce an arbitration clause within the Brussels–Lugano zone—and that horse has now bolted. In *Shipowners' Mutual Protection and Indemnity Association (Luxembourg) v Containerships Denizcilik Nakliyat ve Ticaret (The Yusuf Cepnioglu)* [2016] 1 Lloyds Rep 641 (CA) [33], [56], the Court of Appeal made clear that the reasoning in *Through Transport* was no longer regarded as sound.

The clear message of the modern authorities is that the court's discretion is unaffected by *Turner* where the other proceedings are outside the scope of the Brussels–Lugano zone or regime: *OT Africa Line v Magic Sportswear* [2005] 2 Lloyds Rep 170 (CA) [37]–[38], [51]; *Beazley v Horizon Offshore Contractors* [2005] Lloyds Rep IR 231

to grant anti-suit injunctions outside the 'closed system'[57] of the Brussels–Lugano regime.

E. INJUNCTIONS AND PROCEEDINGS IN THE UNITED KINGDOM

12.42   The Brussels–Lugano regime itself will have no effect on injunctions to restrain competing proceedings within the United Kingdom[58] because the situation has no 'international element', and thus the regime has no application.[59] The injunction would merely be one way of organizing the internal jurisdictional relationships of a state. In a hypothetical legal system, the same result could be produced by listing and transfer decisions imposed on an inferior court by a superior judicial authority, which could not be affected by the Brussels–Lugano regime. It follows that *Turner v Grovit* has no direct application to injunctions sought from the English courts to restrain proceedings brought before other courts in England and Wales.

12.43   The point needs to be looked at afresh in relation to Scotland and Northern Ireland, which have separate legal systems to England and Wales. Jurisdiction between the component parts of the United Kingdom is allocated under the provisions of the 'Modified Regulation' set out in section 16 and Schedule 4 of the Civil Jurisdiction and Judgments Act 1982,[60] whose terms mimic the substantive provisions of the Brussels–Lugano regime. It might be argued that this imposes a principle of mutual trust as between the legal systems of the United Kingdom,[61] and if so it could follow by inference that *Turner v Grovit* should

---

[35]–[47]; *Markel International v Craft* [2007] Lloyds Rep IR 403 [29]–[30] (saying that the comments in *Through Transport* were difficult to understand); *West Tankers v Ras Riunione Adriatica di Sicurta (The Front Comor)* [2005] 2 Lloyds Rep 257 [55], [2007] 1 Lloyds Rep 391 (HL) [8]; *Masri v Consolidated Contractors (No 3)* [2009] QB 503 (CA) [67]; *Shashoua v Sharma* [2009] 2 Lloyds Rep 376 [35]–[39]; *Midgulf International v Groupe Chimiche Tunisien* [2009] 2 Lloyds Rep 411 [62]; *Royal Bank of Scotland v Highland Financial Partners* [2012] 2 CLC 109 [155]–[157] (reversed on other grounds, CA); *Re Tadros* [2014] EWHC 2860 [43]; *Petter v EMC* [2016] ILPr 3 (CA) [32]. Indeed, any earlier hesitations now appear to have been completely forgotten. The argument that the discretion should be limited by analogy to European law is no longer mentioned, and the modern practice is for anti-suit injunctions in respect of proceedings outside the Brussels–Lugano zone to be addressed on the basis of established English principles without any suggestion that they should be modified by reference to European law. For two recent examples, see *Shipowners' Mutual Protection and Indemnity Association (Luxembourg) v Containerships Denizcilik Nakliyat ve Ticaret (The Yusuf Cepnioglu)* [2016] 1 Lloyds Rep 641 (CA) and *Ecobank Transnational v Tanoh* [2016] 1 Lloyds Rep 360 (CA).

This is right. The principles of mutual trust and effectiveness of European law have no meaningful application outside the territory of the Brussels–Lugano zone. To the extent that principles of comity of more general application can be extracted from *Turner v Grovit*, they are adequately allowed for already in the existing case law.

---

[57] For the langue of 'closed system', see *OT Africa Line v Magic Sportswear* [2005] 2 Lloyds Rep 170 (CA) [48], [51].

[58] For proceedings in England, see Ch 6.

[59] Case C–281/02, *Owusu v Jackson* [2005] ECR I–1383 [24]–[34]; Case C–346/93, *Kleinwort Benson v City of Glasgow District Council* [1995] ECR I–615, AG [20].

[60] As substituted by Civil Jurisdiction and Judgments Order 2001, SI 2001/3929, Article 4, Sch 2.

[61] Section 16(3) of the Civil Jurisdiction and Judgments Act 1982 provides that 'In determining any question as to the meaning and effect of any provision contained in Schedule 4—regard shall be had to any relevant principles laid down by the European Court in connection with Title II of the 1968 Convention or Chapter II of the Regulation.' However, *Turner v Grovit* is not, in fact, a decision under Title II or Chapter II. It might be said that it is not a decision under any specific provision of the Regulation or Convention at all—except perhaps recitals 16 and 17 of the Regulation, which mainly deal with a different issue. Certainly, apart from a glancing reference to Article 28 of the Brussels Convention, no specific provision was referred to by the ECJ as a basis for the principle of mutual trust on which the Convention is said to be 'necessarily based': Case C–159/02, *Turner v Grovit* [2004] ECR I–3565 [24]–[28].

preclude the grant of injunctions by the English court to restrain the pursuit of proceedings in Scotland or Northern Ireland, if not elsewhere in England and Wales.

However, it is far more likely that the Modified Regulation will not be interpreted as importing *Turner v Grovit* within the United Kingdom. The Modified Regulation does not preclude the operation of the doctrine of *forum non conveniens* within the United Kingdom, in particular because of the preservation of the power to stay in s 49 of the 1982 Act,[62] and this suggests that the Modified Regulation does not import the European Court's teleological approach to the Brussels–Lugano regime's structure into the internal jurisdictional affairs of the United Kingdom.[63] Furthermore, the principle of mutual trust as applied by the European Court appears more likely to be viewed by the English courts as an example of European legal imperialism, to be accepted but not extended, than as a persuasive interpretation of the inherent structure of closed systems of jurisdiction such as the Modified Regulation. And transference of the principle of mutual trust into the Modified Regulation will be still more unlikely if and when the UK has left the Brussels–Lugano regime.

12.44

F. INJUNCTIONS TO ENFORCE AN ARBITRATION CLAUSE

The Brussels–Lugano regime excludes 'arbitration' from its material scope.[64] This poses two questions: whether an anti-suit injunction to enforce an arbitration clause can be regarded as outside the scope of the regime ('the arbitration exception question') and whether this means it is unaffected by the principle of mutual trust ('the incompatibility question'). These

12.45

---

[62] L Collins and B Davenport, 'Forum Conveniens within the United Kingdom' (1994) 110 LQR 325; L Collins, 'The Brussels Convention within the United Kingdom' (1995) 111 LQR 541; *Cumming v Scottish Daily Record and Sunday Mail* [1995] EMLR 538 (Drake J, not following his previous decision in *Foxen v Scotsman Publications* [1995] EMLR 145); *Lennon v Scottish Daily Record and Sunday Mail* [2004] EWHC 359; *Ivax Pharmaceuticals v Akzo Nobel* [2006] FSR 43; *Sunderland Marine Mutual Insurance v Wiseman* [2007] 2 Lloyds Rep 308 [38]; *Cook v Virgin Media* [2016] 1 WLR 1672 (CA); *Kennedy v National Trust for Scotland* [2017] EWHC 3368.

[63] See L Collins and B Davenport, 'Forum Conveniens within the United Kingdom' (1994) 110 LQR 325, 327, for the argument that 'the spirit' of the Brussels Convention should not be applied to intra-UK cases.

[64] Article 1(2)(d) of the Recast. The Report on the Convention on Jurisdiction and the Enforcement of Judgments in Civil and Commercial Matters, rapporteur P Jenard [1979] OJ C 59/1, 5 March 1979 (hereafter 'Jenard Report') explained that this exception had been included because arbitration was regulated by other international conventions, in particular the New York Convention, and it meant that the regime 'does not apply for the purpose of determining the jurisdiction of courts and tribunals in respect of litigation relating to arbitration—for example, proceedings to set aside an arbitral award': Jenard Report, 13, Chapter III(D). The Report on the Convention on the Association of the Kingdom of Denmark, Ireland and the United Kingdom of Great Britain and Northern Ireland to the Contention and to the Protocol on its Interpretation by the Court of Justice, rapporteur Professor P Schlosser [1979] OJ C 59/71, 5 March 1979 (hereafter the 'Schlosser Report') noted there was a difference of interpretation between the United Kingdom, which considered that the exception 'covers all disputes which the parties had effectively agreed should be settled by arbitration, including any secondary disputes connected with the agreed arbitration', and the original member states, whose approach 'only regards proceedings before national courts as part of "arbitration" if they refer to arbitration proceedings, whether concluded, in progress or to be started' (para 61). It went on to observe:

> The 1968 Convention does not cover court proceedings which are ancillary to arbitration proceedings, for example the appointment and dismissal of arbitrators … In the same way a judgment determining whether an arbitration agreement is valid or not, or because it is invalid, ordering the parties not to continue the arbitration proceedings, is not covered by the 1968 Convention [para 64(b)].

The variant opinions of the Report on the Accession of the Hellenic Republic to the Community Convention on Jurisdiction and the Enforcement of Judgments in Civil and Commercial Matters [1986] OJ C 298, 24 November 1986 (hereafter the 'Evrigenis and Kerameus report') (at para 35) are to be given less weight; and were doubted by Darmon AG in Case C-190/89, *Marc Rich v Società Italiana Impianti (The Atlantic Emperor)* [1991] ECR I–3855, AG [43]–[46].

issues are of great practical importance,[65] as injunctions to enforce arbitration clauses in favour of London arbitration are perhaps the most common type of anti-suit injunctions granted by the English courts.

12.46   The English courts had concluded that an anti-suit injunction to enforce an arbitration clause was both outside the Brussels–Lugano regime and not incompatible with it, in a line of cases capped by *Through Transport v New India*,[66] where the Court of Appeal avoided having to make a reference because it refused to grant an injunction on the basis of some contorted reasoning as to the exercise of its discretion which is now no longer the law.[67]

---

[65]   This was Lord Hoffmann's reason for granting a reference to the European Court: *West Tankers v Ras Riunione Adriatica di Sicurta (The Front Comor)* [2007] 1 Lloyds Rep 391 (HL) [22]; see also Lord Mance at [28]. Colman J had agreed to certify the 'leapfrog' appeal because, as he said:

> It seems to me that the sooner the issues which are raised by the four questions which are proposed have been dealt with and considered by the House of Lords, and perhaps, if the House of Lords so considers, by the European Court of Justice, the better. The incidence of jurisdictional disputes relating to anti-suit injunctions in the Commercial Court is now so prevalent that it is important that a final authoritative ruling should be obtained on the very matters which have been raised by the four questions which are proposed in the application.

(This ruling is not itself reported.)

[66]   *Through Transport Mutual Insurance Association (Eurasia) v New India Assurance* [2005] 1 Lloyds Rep 67 (CA) [38]–[48]. For the previous debate, see *Partenreederei M/S 'Heidberg' v Grosvenor Grain and Feed (The Heidberg)* [1994] 2 Lloyds Rep 287, 297–303 (French court's decision that an arbitration clause was not binding held not within the scope of the exception—a controversial decision, doubted since); *Qingdao Ocean Shipping v Grace Shipping Establishment Transatlantic Schiffahrstskontor (The Xing Su Hai)* [1995] 2 Lloyds Rep 15, 21 (claims in respect of a time charterparty containing an arbitration clause, against unnamed parties, held not to be within the scope of the exception); *Arab Business Consortium International Finance and Business v Banque Franco-Tunisienne* [1996] 1 Lloyds Rep 485, 487 (registration in England of a French judgment to enforce an arbitration award held within the exception); *Toepfer International v Molino Boschi* [1996] 1 Lloyds Rep 510, 512–13 ((i) a declaration as to the existence of an arbitration clause which is designed to establish a cause of action for damages, or an issue estoppel, is not within the exception—not the law, since *Through Transport* and then Recital 12; (ii) anti-suit injunctions to enforce arbitration clauses are probably outside the exception, as they are 'directed to stopping foreign proceedings rather than actually bringing any arbitration into existence'—correct as a conclusion about the scope of the exception, but since *The Front Comor* no answer to the preclusive effect of the Brussels–Lugano regime); *Lexmar Corp and Steamship Mutual Underwriting Association (Bermuda) v Nordisk Skibsrederforening* [1997] 1 Lloyds Rep 289, 291–93 (a claim under letter of undertaking given in respect of security for the cost of an arbitration held to be outside the exception); *Toepfer International v Société Cargill France* [1997] 2 Lloyds Rep 98, 102–06 (anti-suit injunction to enforce an arbitration clause within the exception, because proceedings to enforce an arbitration clause are within the scope of the New York Convention; *The Heidberg* not followed); appealed at [1998] 1 Lloyds Rep 379 (CA) (arbitration exception point referred to the ECJ; the reference lapsed when the case was settled); *Union de Remorquage et de Sauvetage v Lake Avery (The Lake Avery)* [1997] 1 Lloyds Rep 540, 541, 546–50 (a claim for declaration as to the existence of a contract containing the arbitration clause held to be within the arbitration exception, the issue was not clearly addressed in relation to the claim for an injunction, which was left over, at 551); *Charterers Mutual Assurance Association v British & Foreign* [1998] ILPr 838 (anti-suit injunction to enforce an arbitration clause held to be outside the arbitration exception—again, no answer to the preclusive effect of the Brussels–Lugano regime following *The Front Comor*); *Vale do Rio Doce Navegacao v Shanghai Bao Steel Ocean Shipping* [2000] 2 Lloyds Rep 1 [9]–[19] (application for a declaration against a broker that he had validly concluded a contract containing an arbitration clause on behalf of another party held not to be within the exception); *Navigation Maritime Bulgare v Rustal Trading (The Ivan Zagubanski)* [2002] 1 Lloyds Rep 106 [61]–[101], per Aikens J ((i) an anti-suit injunction to enforce an arbitration clause is within the arbitration exception because arbitration is 'the principal focus or "essential subject matter" of the claim', 'because the claim is for relief to enforce the arbitration agreement'; (ii) the principal focus of a claim for a declaration that an arbitration agreement exists is also arbitration, and so such a claim is within the exception as well). Aikens J's reasoning was then followed in *Electronic Arts CV v CTO* [2003] EWHC 1020 [68]–[75]; and approved in *Through Transport Mutual Insurance Association (Eurasia) v New India Assurance* [2004] 1 Lloyds Rep 206 [24], [2005] 1 Lloyds Rep 67 (CA) [38]–[48]. Lord Hoffmann's reasoning in *West Tankers v Ras Riunione Adriatica di Sicurta (The Front Comor)* [2007] 1 Lloyds Rep 391 (HL) [14]–[16] is along the same lines as Aikens J in *The Ivan Zagubanski*, and resolved the debate within the English legal system. Consistently with this, in *A v B* [2007] 1 Lloyds Rep 237 [87]–[97], Colman J held that an injunction to restrain arbitration proceedings abroad fell within the arbitration exception.

[67]   See Ch 10, paras 10.67–10.80, and para 12.41 n 56 above.

But it was inevitable that the point would recur. In *The Front Comor*,[68] Colman J concluded that the anti-suit injunction should lie, but granted a certificate for a 'leapfrog' appeal to the House of Lords. The House of Lords referred the question to the European Court, with Lord Hoffmann, like Lord Hobhouse before him, attempting to give a desired steer.[69]

The effect of the European Court's decisions in *The Front Comor* and *Gazprom*,[70]   **12.47**
as discussed above, is that anti-suit injunctions to enforce arbitration clauses by re-straining Brussels–Lugano proceedings are in themselves 'arbitration' and outside the Brussels–Lugano regime.[71] Nevertheless, such injunctions are incompatible with the effectiveness of the regime, the principle of mutual trust, and the principle that a Brussels–Lugano court should be able to examine its own jurisdiction, if the other pro-ceedings are within the material scope of the Brussels–Lugano regime. This is so even if one of the preliminary issues within those proceedings will be whether the other court should stay its proceedings in favour of arbitration. Under Regulation 1215/2012, Recital 12 will mean that the other court's decision on the binding force of the arbitra-tion clause will not be enforceable under the Brussels–Lugano regime. However, it is unlikely, without a change of heart by the European Court, that it will have the more radical effect of changing the position with regard to anti-suit injunctions to enforce arbitration clauses by restraining the pursuit of substantive Brussels–Lugano proceed-ings before the other court. The prohibition of the injunction will continue, with the justification for it shifting to the Brussels–Lugano nature of the wider proceedings, which will be prevented.[72]

However, the principle of mutual trust has no effect on injunctions to enforce arbitra-   **12.48**
tion clauses by restraining proceedings outside the Brussels–Lugano zone,[73] or inside the Brussels–Lugano zone but outside the scope of the European jurisdictional instruments.[74] It is true that aspects of the brief language used in *Gazprom* articulate a prohibition on re-viewing the jurisdiction of another member state court in language that is not dependent on the other jurisdiction being a Brussels–Lugano jurisdiction.[75] But the logic of the case, and of *The Front Comor*, is dependent on the other proceedings being within the Brussels–Lugano regime.

---

[68] *West Tankers v Ras Riunione Adriatica di Sicurta (The Front Comor)* [2005] 2 Lloyds Rep 257 [9]–[10], [42], [48]–[52].

[69] *West Tankers v Ras Riunione Adriatica di Sicurta (The Front Comor)* [2007] 1 Lloyds Rep 391 (HL).

[70] Case C-195/07, *Allianz v West Tankers (The Front Comor)* [2009] ECR I-663; Case C-536/15, *Gazprom* EU:C:2015:316.

[71] *Nori Holding v Bank Otkritie Financial Corporation* [2018] 2 Lloyds Rep 80 [71].

[72] See paras 12.19–12.26 above, and as confirmed by Males J in *Nori Holding v Bank Otkritie Financial Corporation* [2018] 2 Lloyds Rep 80 [69]–[99].

[73] *Shashoua v Sharma* [2009] 2 Lloyds Rep 376 [35]–[39]; *Midgulf International v Groupe Chimiche Tunisien* [2009] 2 Lloyds Rep 411 [62], [2010] 2 Lloyds Rep 543 (CA) [67]–[68], and the authorities cited more broadly at nn 55 and 56 of this chapter. For a recent example, see *Essar Shipping v Bank of China (The Kishore)* [2016] 1 Lloyds Rep 417 [2].

[74] See *Morris v Davies* [2011] EWHC 1272 [11]; *Claxton Engineering Services v TXM Olaj-és Gázjutató Kft* [2011] 1 Lloyds Rep 252 [17]–[24]; *Re Tadros* [2014] EWHC 2860 [43]; *SwissMarine v OW Supply and Trading* [2015] 1 CLC 1040 [43]–[46], and the cases cited more generally at nn 55 and 56 of this chapter.

[75] For the wider phrasing see Case C-536/15, *Gazprom* EU:C:2015:316 at [33], first sentence; but for the true logic see *Gazprom* at [34].

12.49   Similarly, injunctions to restrain arbitration proceedings with seats in Brussels–Lugano countries—or outside the Brussels–Lugano zone—are unaffected by mutual trust and not prohibited by the Brussels–Lugano regime.[76]

G. ANTI-SUIT INJUNCTIONS SOUGHT FROM ARBITRATORS

12.50   The European Court's decision in *The Front Comor* posed the question on whether arbitrators could grant remedies akin to anti-suit injunctions, sometimes called anti-suit awards, to restrain Brussels–Lugano proceedings. The anti-suit award would obviously itself be within the arbitration exception in Article 1(2)(d) of the Recast since it was granted in proceedings before arbitrators, and so was 'arbitration', but the argument was that its effect on Brussels–Lugano proceedings might, as with court anti-suits, lead to the arbitral anti-suit being precluded by the principle of effectiveness of the Brussels–Lugano regime.

12.51   English arbitrators had generally taken the approach that they could continue to grant anti-suit awards, even though the grant of such relief by the English courts were now prohibited. This was also consistent with the decisions of the English courts in relation to damages and declarations, in which the courts had concluded that arbitrators were not affected by the principle of mutual trust or the principle of effective judicial protection within the Brussels–Lugano regime.[77] The European Court has now confirmed in *Gazprom* that anti-suit awards sought from arbitrators are not prohibited by the Brussels–Lugano regime, even where the seat of the arbitration is within the Brussels–Lugano zone or the *lex arbitri* is subject to the Brussels–Lugano regime.[78]

12.52   Since the Brussels–Lugano regime imposes no barriers on arbitrators granting such relief, and since English arbitrators generally have the power to grant anti-suit awards,[79] it would be strange if English law somehow removed that power when the competing proceedings were in the Brussels–Lugano zone. Yet it has been suggested that this is the effect of section 48(5) of the Arbitration Act 1996, which is often understood to be the basis of arbitrators' powers to grant injunctions in English arbitration law (absent specific agreement in the arbitration agreement or institutional rules).

12.53   Section 48(5) provides that, absent contrary agreement, 'the Tribunal has the same powers as the court—to order a party to do or refrain from doing anything'. It has been argued that, if the effect of *Turner v Grovit* is to preclude the 'power' of the court to grant an anti-suit injunction within the Brussels–Lugano zone, arbitrators will have no greater power. It is submitted that this is a non-existent problem. The purpose of section 48(5) is not to require

---

[76]   See, before *The Front Comor*, Colman J's decision in *A v B* [2007] 1 Lloyds Rep 237 [87]–[97]. Subsequently see *Sheffield United v West Ham United* [2009] 1 Lloyds Rep 167 [30]; *Claxton Engineering Services v TXM Olaj-és Gázjutató Kft* [2011] 1 Lloyds Rep 252 [17]–[25]. For academic commentary in support of this conclusion, see R Carrier, 'Anti-suit injonction: La CJCE met fin à un anachronisme' (2004) DMF 403, 412; A Dutta and C Heinze, 'Prozessführungsverbote im englischen und europäischen Zivilverfahrensrecht' (2005) Zeitschrift für Europäisches Privatrecht 428, 458–61.

[77]   *West Tankers v Allianz (The Front Comor)* [2012] 2 Lloyds Rep 103 [54]–[75]; and see also *CMA CGM v Hyundai Mipo Dockyard* [2009] 1 Lloyds Rep 213 [46]–[47].

[78]   Case C-536/15, *Gazprom* EU:C:2015:316 and *Nori Holding v Bank Okritie Financial Corporation* [2018] 2 Lloyds Rep 80 [82]–[83]. See also Case C-190/89, *Marc Rich v Società Italiana Impianti (The Atlantic Emperor)* [1991] ECR I-3855, ECJ [18]: 'the Contracting Parties intended to exclude arbitration in its entirety'.

[79]   Ch 7, paras 7.59–7.62.

arbitrators in each case to consider whether the court would or could grant a particular injunction, but instead to allow arbitrators to grant the same *types* of injunctive remedies as the courts. The court continues to have a power to grant an anti-suit injunction, where appropriate, under section 37(1) of the Supreme Court Act 1981, and section 48(5) transfers the full extent of that power to the arbitrators. The effect of European law is that the court's power cannot be *exercised* in respect of (for example) proceedings before the courts of another member state, but the existence of the power under English law, and so its transference to the arbitrators, is unaffected; and the Brussels–Lugano regime's limitation on the *exercise* of the court's power is then not a limitation that applies to the exercise of the *same power* by arbitrators, who are unaffected by the principle of mutual trust.[80] Another way of putting the same point is that any restriction of the court's powers under section 37(1) which is not a restriction which would logically apply to arbitrators does not meaningfully affect the powers transferred by section 48(5); if the powers are transferred subject to limitations that only affect courts, then any such limitations disappear once the power is in the hands of arbitrators.

So far as the author of this work is aware, on each occasion any argument based on section 48(5) has been raised, to the effect that arbitrators have no power to grant arbitral anti-suit awards, it has been rejected by distinguished arbitration tribunals. **12.54**

Any such problem, even were it to exist, would be specific to section 48(5) and would not arise where arbitrators have powers to grant injunctions derived from different sources such as the terms of the arbitration agreement or rules. Institutional rules often contain powers of sufficient breadth to support anti-suit awards. **12.55**

In addition, it has been argued that the power to grant anti-suit awards or similar protective orders is inherent in the arbitrators' powers to control their own proceedings,[81] and as such could be viewed as implicitly granted to tribunals by standard form modern arbitration agreements, independent of section 48(5) and without specific provision. However, under English arbitration law, this line of argument faces the difficulty that before the 1996 Act it was uncertain whether arbitrators had power to grant any injunctions at all.[82] **12.56**

1. Enforcement by Court Judgment of Anti-Suit Awards Made by Arbitrators

In *Nori v Otkritie*, Males J said *Gazprom* was 'crystal clear' that any court judgment to enforce an arbitral anti-suit award is outside the Brussels–Lugano regime, and is not precluded by mutual trust or effectiveness. He appeared to include the entry of judgment by the English **12.57**

---

[80] In *Starlight Shipping v Allianz Marine & Aviation Versicherungs* [2014] 2 Lloyds Rep 579 [89], [94], Flaux J held that the fact that the court was precluded from exercising the power to grant an anti-suit injunction did not remove the power to grant damages in lieu.

[81] T Landau, 'Arbitral Lifelines: The Protection of Jurisdiction by Arbitrators' (2006) Intl Arb: Back to Basics, 282, 290–93; R Moloo, 'Arbitrators Granting Antisuit Orders: When Should They and on What Authority?' (2009) 26 J Intl Arb 676, 678–81.

[82] See Departmental Advisory Committee on Arbitration Law Report on the Arbitration Bill, February 1996, para 234 (hereafter the 'DAC Report'), para 234; *Chandris v Isbrandtsen Moller* [1951] 1 KB 240; Sir MJ Mustill and SC Boyd, *Commercial Arbitration* (2nd edn, LexisNexis 1989) 390 (hereafter 'Mustill & Boyd'); although cf *Birtley and District Co-operative Society v Windy Nook and District Industrial Co-operative Society (No 2)* [1960] 2 QB 1.

court in terms of an anti-suit award,[83] even where the award, and so the court judgment enforcing it, would restrain in another member state.[84] It is respectfully submitted, however, that this is not what the European Court said. *Gazprom* was about whether the Brussels–Lugano regime prevented the *Lithuanian* courts from enforcing an anti-suit award, issued by a foreign arbitration tribunal, which would prevent proceedings continuing before the Lithuanian courts themselves.[85] It was not concerned with the enforcement by the courts of state X of an anti-suit award to restrain proceedings in another member state Y. When such an award is enforced by entry of judgment in the terms of the award under English law, this in effect creates an injunction from the English court restraining proceedings in the foreign court, backed by contempt. That is a different situation to what the European Court had in mind in *Gazprom*.

12.58   The literal words of the European Court's conclusion (at [44]) do not produce the result envisaged by Males J:

> Regulation 44/2001 must be interpreted as not precluding a court of a member state from recognising and enforcing, or from refusing to recognise and enforce, an arbitral award prohibiting a party from bringing certain claims before a court of *that member state*, since that Regulation does not govern the recognition and enforcement, in a member state, of an arbitral award issued by an arbitral tribunal in another member state [emphasis added].

Further, the reasoning was focused, in key respects, on why a court enforcing an award to restrain proceedings before itself was unproblematic;[86] and the European Court observed (at [38]) that the failure to comply with the anti-suit award was 'not capable of resulting in penalties being imposed upon [the respondent] by a court of another member state' which would not be the situation where there was entry of judgment in England in the terms of an anti-suit award restraining proceedings in another member state.

12.59   Consequently, contrary to Males J's suggestion, the legitimacy of entry of judgment in the terms of an anti-suit award is not established by *Gazprom*, where the award and judgment restrain proceedings in another member state.

12.60   In general, it is clear that the enforcement of arbitration awards is within the arbitration exception and unaffected by the Brussels–Lugano regime.[87] It could be said that applying the Brussels–Lugano regime to prevent enforcement of such an anti-suit award would be an intimate interference with the arbitral machinery, and directly inconsistent with the New York Convention, which requires enforcement of awards (cf Art III) and which by Article 73 of the Recast should be unaffected by the Recast's rules. The matter is, in a real sense, deeper within the arbitration exception than a direct court anti-suit injunction. Further, if such an award in itself is unaffected by the Brussels–Lugano regime, it would be odd if there could be no judgment enforcing such an award.

---

[83]   See eg under s 66 of the Arbitration Act 1966.
[84]   *Nori Holding v Bank Otkritie Financial Corporation* [2018] 2 Lloyds Rep 80 [83].
[85]   Case C-536/15, *Gazprom* EU:C:2015:316 [39], [41], [44].
[86]   Case C-536/15, *Gazprom* EU:C:2015:316 [35], [39], [40], [42].
[87]   Jenard Report, C59/13; Schlosser Report, para 65(c); Case C–391/95, *Van Uden Maritime v Kommanditgesellschaft in Firma Deco-Line* [1998] ECR I–7091 [32]; *Arab Business Consortium Corp International Finance & Investment v Banque Franco-Tunisienne* [1996] 1 Lloyds Rep 485, 487–89.

But whether considerations such as this are sufficient to immunize the enforcement of **12.61** an anti-suit award from the principles of mutual trust and effectiveness as interpreted by the European Court remains to be seen. From the perspective of the relationship between courts, it could be said there was little difference between a direct anti-suit injunction and a court judgment in the terms of an anti-suit award, with regard the indirect interference caused.

Whichever result is reached will produce arbitrary distinctions—between an anti-suit **12.62** award and a judgment enforcing it, on one side, or between an anti-suit award and a direct anti-suit injunction, on the other—which, again serve to illustrate the unsatisfactory nature of the European Court's reasoning in *The Front Comor*.

H. PROCEEDINGS OUTSIDE THE MATERIAL SCOPE OF THE REGIME

The Brussels–Lugano regime only covers 'civil and commercial matters', and in addition to **12.63** 'arbitration', it excludes:

(a) the status or legal capacity of natural persons, rights in property arising out of a matrimonial relationship or out of a relationship deemed by the law applicable to such relationship to have comparable effects to marriage; (b) bankruptcy, proceedings relating to the winding up of insolvent companies or other legal persons, judicial arrangements, compositions and analogous proceedings; (c) social security; ... (e) maintenance obligations arising from a family relationship, parentage, marriage or affinity; (f) wills and succession, including maintenance obligations arising by reason of death.[88]

English courts have historically granted anti-suit injunctions to protect English proceedings within these categories, and in particular, have granted injunctions to protect the equal and fair distribution of assets in insolvency proceedings from being interfered with by creditors trying unfairly to 'steal a march' in other jurisdictions.[89] The French Cour de Cassation has exercised a similar power to protect French bankruptcy proceedings from interference by the threatened actions of a creditor before the Spanish courts.[90]

It seems that anti-suit injunctions sought in or in respect of, and in order to protect, such **12.64** proceedings outside the material scope of the Brussels–Lugano regime are themselves claims outside the Brussels-Lugano regime because they partake of the same characterization as the underlying proceedings they protect.[91] This would mean, inter alia, that they would not need to satisfy Brussels–Lugano heads of territorial jurisdiction.

Nevertheless, the effect of the *Front Comor* and *Gazprom* appears to be that even if such **12.65** injunctions are themselves outside the scope of the regime, the grant of such injunctions

---

[88] Brussels I Recast, Article 1(2).

[89] *Liverpool Marine Credit v Hunter* (1867) LR 4 Eq 62, (1868) LR 3 Ch App 479, 484; *Re North Carolina Estate* (1889) 5 TLR 328; *Barclays Bank v Homan* [1993] BCLC 680.

[90] *Banque Worms c Epoux Brachot* Cass Civ 1 (19 November 2002), noted H Muir-Watt, 'Injunctive Relief in the French Courts: A Case of Legal Borrowing' [2003] CLJ 573.

[91] This was the view of Lord Hoffmann in *West Tankers v Ras Riunione Adriatica di Sicurta (The Front Comor)* [2007] 1 Lloyds Rep 391 (HL) [13], [16], [18]. The point is discussed in more detail at Ch 16, para 16.20 n 31.

to restrain Brussels–Lugano proceedings in other Brussels–Lugano courts is incompatible with the principles of mutual trust and effectiveness. [92]

12.66   In contrast, it seems clear that, if the other proceedings are inside the Brussels–Lugano zone but outside the material scope of the Brussels–Lugano regime, for example where they themselves fall within one of the exceptions, or are not civil and commercial matters, then the injunction will be unaffected by principles of mutual trust and effective judicial protection derived from the Brussels–Lugano regime itself. It is true that parts of the literal wording of the ECJ's decision in *Turner v Grovit* could be read as applying to preclude *any* injunction to restrain *any* proceedings before the courts of another member state,[93] and there are also aspects of the wording in *Gazprom* that could be read in this sense.[94] But the overall logic of *The Front Comor* and *Gazprom* leads clearly to the conclusion that there is no relevant mutual trust, and nothing relevant to protect, where the other proceedings fall outside the Brussels–Lugano regime or European jurisdictional law.[95] To use the words of Lord Hoffmann in *West Tankers v Ras Riunione Adriatica di Sicurta (The Front Comor)* [2007] 1 Lloyds Rep 391 (HL) [14], in such a case 'there is no set of uniform Community rules which the Member states can or must trust each other to apply'. The English case law has proceeded on this basis.[96]

12.67   Further, anti-suit injunctions to restrain arbitration proceedings outside the United Kingdom are unaffected by mutual trust and the Brussels–Lugano regime even if the seat of the foreign arbitration is within the Brussels–Lugano zone.[97]

12.68   However, a number of the subjects that fall within the exceptions to the scope of the Brussels–Lugano regime still fall within the net of European jurisdictional law under other instruments. Thus, jurisdiction over certain family law matters is covered by the Brussels II bis Regulation,[98] and jurisdiction in relation to insolvency is in many cases regulated by the Insolvency Regulations.[99] It is plausible that the European Court will view those

---

[92]   See the discussion at paras 12.08–12.14 and 12.38 above. This is the approach taken by the English courts in *Morris v Davies* [2011] EWHC 1272 [11]; *Re Tadros* [2014] EWHC 2860 [43]; *SwissMarine v OW Supply and Trading* [2015] 1 CLC 1040 [43]–[46].
It would follow that Banque *Worms c Epoux Brachot* Cass Civ 1 (19 November 2002) (discussed at para 12.63 and n 90 above) was wrongly decided, unless the Spanish proceedings themselves fell outside the scope of the Regulation, eg if they were also within the insolvency exception (which is not clear from the judgment). However, in *The Front Comor*, Lord Hoffmann observed that he was 'not surprised that it did not occur to the Cour de Cassation that such an order, made in proceedings excluded from the Regulation, might nevertheless conflict with it': *West Tankers v Ras Riunione Adriatica di Sicurta (The Front Comor)* [2007] 1 Lloyds Rep 391 (HL) [18].
[93]   Case C–159/02, *Turner v Grovit* [2004] ECR I–3565 [31]; but see [25], [26].
[94]   Case C–536/15, *Gazprom* EU:C:2015:316 at [33], first sentence.
[95]   For academic commentary supporting the conclusion that the principle of mutual trust does not preclude anti-suit injunctions to restrain the pursuit of proceedings before the courts of non-Brussels–Lugano states, see C Ambrose, 'Can Anti-Suit Injunctions Survive European Community Law?' (2003) 52 ICLQ 401, 421; T Kruger, 'The Anti-Suit Injunction in the European Judicial Space' (2004) 53 ICLQ 1030, 1038–39; A Dutta and C Heinze, 'Prozessführungsverbote im englischen und europäischen Zivilverfahrensrecht' (2005) Zeitschrift für Europäisches Privatrecht 428, 458–61.
[96]   *Morris v Davies* [2011] EWHC 1272 [11]; *Re Tadros* [2014] EWHC 2860 [43]; *SwissMarine v OW Supply and Trading* [2015] 1 CLC 1040 [43]–[46]. See similarly *Fortress Value Recovery Fund v Blue Skye Special Opportunities Fund* [2012] EWHC 1486 [106]–[111], where the point was it seems assumed.
[97]   Paragraph 12.49 above.
[98]   Regulation 2201/2003, replacing Reg 1347/2000, which covers 'civil matters relating to (a) divorce, legal separation or marriage annulment; (b) the attribution, exercise, delegation, restriction or termination of parental responsibility': see Article 1.
[99]   Regulation 1346/2000, and the Recast Insolvency Regulation, Reg 2015/848.

instruments as also creating closed jurisdiction systems which give rise to comparable principles of mutual trust within their scope as those applying within the Brussels–Lugano regime,[100] although the details of this have yet to be worked out.[101]

I. ANTI-ENFORCEMENT INJUNCTIONS

If a judgment from Brussels–Lugano state A is sought to be enforced under the Brussels–Lugano regime in Brussels–Lugano state B it would seem to be clear that the courts of B are being asked to engage a Brussels–Lugano jurisdiction, over which they have an exclusive jurisdiction under Article 24(5) of the Recast. Consequently, the logic of *Turner v Grovit* and *The Front Comor* suggests strongly that an anti-enforcement injunction to restrain enforcement proceedings in B would be contrary to mutual trust and an interference with the Recast jurisdiction of B. The English courts have not yet directly grappled with the point.[102]   **12.69**

If a judgment from outside the Brussels–Lugano zone is sought to be enforced in another Brussels–Lugano state, the position appears to be different. In *Bank St Petersburg v Archangelsky*,[103] it was common ground that the enforcement in another Brussels–Lugano court of a judgment of a court outside the Brussels–Lugano zone was not itself a Brussels–Lugano matter and so was not protected by the Brussels–Lugano regime from anti-enforcement injunctions, and the Court of Appeal therefore granted an injunction to restrain the pursuit of enforcement proceedings in France and Bulgaria.   **12.70**

However, this logic is only correct if Article 24(5) of the Recast, which creates an exclusive jurisdiction for the enforcement of 'judgments' in the state of enforcement, applies only to the enforcement of Brussels–Lugano judgments. On the face of the Recast, that appears to be correct, because 'judgments' are defined by Article 2(a) to include only Brussels–Lugano judgments.[104]   **12.71**

Yet this creates a puzzle in turn because if so, it is not clear on what jurisdiction basis a court in state A could assume jurisdiction, in an action for enforcement against assets in A, over a judgment debtor situated in Brussels–Lugano state B. The answer may be that enforcement of a non-Brussels–Lugano judgment is outside the Brussels–Lugano regime altogether and so there is no difficulty in obtaining jurisdiction over judgment debtors domiciled in the EU; but it is notable that enforcement is not an exception to the scope of   **12.72**

---

[100] The European Court of Justice has held that the principle of mutual trust applies to the Brussels II bis regulation, reflecting Recital 21 thereof: Case C-403/09, *Deticek v Sgueglia* [2010] Fam 104 [45]; Case C-4/14, *Bohez v Wiertz* [2016] 1 FLR 1159 [43]–[44], [52]; Case C-256/09, *Purrucker v Vallés Pérez (No 1)* [2010] ECR I-735 [81]. It has also reached the same conclusion in relation to the Insolvency Regulation 1346/2000: Case C–341/04, *In Re Eurofood* [2006] ECR I–3813 [40]–[42]; Case C-649/13, *Comité d'entreprise de Nortel Networks v Rogeau* [2016] QB 109 [53]. See also *West Tankers v Ras Riunione Adriatica di Sicurta (The Front Comor)* [2007] 1 Lloyds Rep 391 (HL) [12].

[101] The point did not arise in *SwissMarine v OW Supply and Trading* [2015] 1 CLC 1040 [43]–[46], because Denmark is not party to the Insolvency Regulations. In *Re Apcoa Parking Holdings* [2015] BCC 142 [280]–[281], the question arose of whether a clause in a scheme of arrangement which prevented litigation abroad was inconsistent with *Turner v Grovit* (schemes of arrangement are outside the Insolvency Regulations), but was resolved by agreement and did not need to be decided.

[102] *Mamidoil-Jetoil Greek Petroleum v Okta Crude Oil Refinery* [2003] 1 Lloyds Rep 1 [203], does not directly engage with the issue.

[103] *Bank St Petersburg v Archangelsky* [2013] EWHC 3529 [45] and [2014] 1 WLR 4360 (CA) [35].

[104] See Briggs, para 2.81.

the Brussels–Lugano regime in Article 1 of the Recast. If, in contrast, 'judgments' in Article 24(5) did include non-Brussels judgments, there would be an easy enforcement jurisdiction over Brussels–Lugano judgment debtors. But the consequence would also be that there would be an argument that an anti-enforcement injunction to restrain such enforcement elsewhere within the Brussels–Lugano zone, even of a non-Brussels–Lugano judgment, did infringe the effectiveness of European law.[105]

J. INJUNCTIONS IN GENERAL TERMS

12.73 It has been common for contractual anti-suit injunctions to be granted in negative and general terms, restraining proceedings before any courts other than the contractually agreed court. After *Turner v Grovit*, this is no longer appropriate, and where it may matter, general injunctions should be drafted to contain an express qualification to make clear that they do not restrain the pursuit of proceedings before the courts of another Brussels–Lugano state.[106] But not everyone is punctilious on the point.

K. INJUNCTIONS GRANTED BEFORE ACCESSION

12.74 In *Advent Capital v GN Ellinas Imports-Exports Ltd*, the court had granted a final anti-suit injunction to enforce an exclusive jurisdiction clause, restraining the pursuit of proceedings in Cyprus, before the accession of Cyprus to the EU. On accession, Cyprus became a member state to which the Brussels I Regulation applied. The injunction defendant applied to set aside the anti-suit injunction, relying on *Turner v Grovit*. Colman J held that if the effect of Cyprus's accession was that the right to an anti-suit injunction ceased to exist, this would be a change of circumstances which could warrant setting aside a permanent injunction. However, he held that the consequences of accession did not destroy the continuing right to an anti-suit injunction, the entitlement to which had been established by judgment before accession. There was nothing in the transitional provisions to the Regulation which would justify setting aside a pre-accession judgment.[107]

L. MANDATORY INJUNCTIONS AND SPECIFIC PERFORMANCE

12.75 It seems unlikely that the prohibition on injunctions to restrain Brussels–Lugano proceedings can be circumvented either by mandatory injunctions or orders for specific

---

[105] In *Ecobank Transnational v Tanoh* [2016] 1 Lloyds Rep 360 (CA) [136] it was suggested that 'intrinsically' it was a matter for the courts of another Brussels–Lugano state to decide on enforcement before it, which was a reason for 'caution' before granting an anti-enforcement injunction. But this is reasoning based on comity in general, not the principle of mutual trust derived from the Brussels–Lugano regime, and applies with much the same force in relation to anti-enforcement injunctions relating to non-Brussels–Lugano countries. Nor is it an absolute rule: as discussed in more detail at Ch 5, section I, 'Anti-Enforcement Injunctions', there are situations where anti-enforcement injunctions are legitimate including with regard to Brussels–Lugano countries. The Court of Appeal in *Tanoh* had indeed accepted that it was right to grant the injunction in *Bank St Petersburg v Archangelsky* [2014] 1 WLR 4360 (CA) which related to enforcement in France and Bulgaria.

[106] *Masri v Consolidated Contractors (No 3)* [2009] QB 503 (CA) [25], [97]; *Essar Shipping v Bank of China (The Kishore)* [2016] 1 Lloyds Rep 417 [2].

[107] *Advent Capital v Ellinas Imports-Exports (No 2)* [2005] 2 Lloyds Rep 607 [74], [101]–[102], [113]–[118].

performance, requiring a party positively to perform an exclusive forum clause by litigating in the chosen forum. First, as a matter of substantive English law, it is doubtful that a contractual forum clause creates a positive obligation to litigate. A party can always choose not to litigate in the chosen forum.[108] What is really being enforced is the negative obligation not to litigate outside the chosen forum. Second, however the order was framed, the same reasons of policy and principle would be likely to apply if in effect it amounted to an order backed by a penalty prohibiting the party in question from litigating abroad.

However, in two unusual situations, orders for specific performance of collateral contractual obligations arising out of settlement agreements, which had the result of affecting foreign litigation elsewhere in the Brussels–Lugano zone, have been viewed as compatible with mutual trust.   **12.76**

First, in *The Alexandros T*, a settlement agreement with insurers prohibited further claims but also provided for indemnification against any further claims. Greek proceedings were brought in breach of the settlement, and insurers sought not only damages but specific performance of the indemnity. Burton J ordered specific performance of the monetary obligation to indemnify[109] and a mandatory injunction to constitute a fund. In itself, this could be viewed as going little further than a monetary award such as damages (discussed below), but it is backed by contempt, which could strengthen arguments that the relief is a 'penalty' within the language used in *Turner v Grovit*.[110] However, these remedies were viewed by Burton J and the Court of Appeal as if there was no distinction to a monetary award. *Turner v Grovit* was distinguished on the straightforward basis that there was no restraint of the Greek proceedings.[111]   **12.77**

Second, subsequently (at a hearing at which the defendants did not attend), Flaux J further ordered specific performance of the settlement agreement by ordering the defendants to enter into a release-and-recognition agreement effectively acknowledging settlement and satisfaction. This was, it seems, intended to prevent the Greek proceedings having any material basis. It goes further than a monetary claim. Flaux concluded that it posed no problems from the perspective of mutual trust because it did not interfere with the jurisdiction of the Greek court, being no more than a determination of rights under the settlement agreement; the Greek court could elect whether or not to enforce the English judgment.[112] The order made, of course, did not actually restrain litigation in Greece. The issue illustrates the problematic nature of the interference with substantive contractual rights which flows from the decisions in *Turner v Grovit* and *The Front Comor*.   **12.78**

---

[108] See Ch 3, para 3.40.

[109] Burton J's judgment does not directly mention that specific performance of the indemnity, as opposed simply to indemnification, was sought: *Starlight Shipping Company v Allianz Marine & Aviation Versicherungs* [2012] 1 Lloyds Rep 162 [35]. But it seems from the later decision of Flaux J that Burton J did order specific performance: *Starlight Shipping Company v Allianz Marine & Aviation Versicherungs* [2014] 2 Lloyds Rep 579 [13], [20], [21]. The mandatory injunction to constitute a fund was discussed at [2012] 1 Lloyds Rep 162 [37]–[38].

[110] Case C–159/02, *Turner v Grovit* [2004] ECR I–3565 [34]; Case C-536/15, *Gazprom* EU:C:2015:316 [40].

[111] *Starlight Shipping Company v Allianz Marine & Aviation Versicherungs* [2012] 1 Lloyds Rep 162 [35]–[36], [2014] 2 CLC 492 (CA) [16].

[112] *Starlight Shipping v Allianz Marine & Aviation Versicherungs* [2014] 2 Lloyds Rep 579 [75].

M. DECLARATIONS

12.79   English courts have often granted declarations that an exclusive jurisdiction clause is contractually binding, and that a party is contractually bound to litigate before a given forum. The English courts have held without hesitation that such declarations are not precluded by *Turner v Grovit*, even where they do materially fall within the scope of the Brussels–Lugano regime.[113] There is no direct assessment of the jurisdiction of another member state's courts. Further, the declaration involves no 'penalty', and the threat of a penalty by a court was an important part of the reasoning in both *Turner* and *Gazprom*.[114] In contrast, declarations which purported to directly address the jurisdiction of the court of another member state, rather than set out the parties' contractual rights, or declarations about whether the foreign proceedings were in fact in breach of contract, would be in greater danger of being viewed as contrary to the principle of mutual trust.[115]

12.80   A claim for a declaration by the English court or a declaratory award by an arbitration tribunal, to the effect that an arbitration clause is binding or that specified matters should be arbitrated, is 'arbitration', and thus falls outside the scope of the Brussels–Lugano regime.[116] The ECJ's decision in *Gazprom* necessarily means that such declarations are not incompatible with the Brussels–Lugano regime when granted by arbitrators.[117] Further, it seems clear that the grant of such declarations by courts will not be precluded by the principles of mutual trust or effective judicial protection, on the basis that the declaration does not interfere even indirectly with the foreign court's functions.[118] English courts and arbitrators

---

[113] *Starlight Shipping v Allianz Marine & Aviation Versicherungs* [2014] 2 Lloyds Rep 544 (CA) [15]–[17] (and see [2014] 1 Lloyds Rep 223 (SC) [39]); *Barclays Bank v Ente Nazionale di Previdenza ed Assistenza dei Medici e Degli Odontoiatri* [2015] 2 Lloyds Rep 527 [112]–[122], [2016] 2 CLC 859 (CA) [32]–[37]. Declarations have on a number of occasions been granted without any objection being taken: see *Underwriting Members of Lloyds Syndicate 980 v Sinco* [2008] ILPr 49.

[114] Case C–159/02, *Turner v Grovit* [2004] ECR I–3565 [26], [28]; Case C–536/15, *Gazprom* EU:C:2015:316 [34].

[115] A non-contractual claim for declaration about the jurisdiction of another Brussels–Lugano court was refused in *Deaville v Aeroflot Russian International Airlines* [1997] 2 Lloyds Rep 67.

[116] This conclusion follows inevitably from the conclusion in Case C-195/07, *Allianz v West Tankers (The Front Comor)* [2009] ECR I-663 [22]–[24], that an anti-suit injunction to enforce an arbitration clause is in itself within the arbitration exception (albeit inconsistent with the Brussels–Lugano regime by virtue of its effects); see the discussion in *Nori Holding v Bank Otkritie Financial Corporation* [2018] 2 Lloyds Rep 80 [71]–[78]. That conclusion must apply *a fortiori* to declarations as to the effect of an arbitration clause (and see also Case C-391/95, *Van Uden Maritime v Kommanditgesellschaft in Firma Deco-Line* [1998] ECR I-7091 [56]–[57], ECJ [31]–[32] (adopting the views of the Schlosser Report, paras 64(b) and 65(c)). It is now reinforced by Recital 12 of the Recast; and is consistent with the logic of the European Court's decision in Case C-536/15, *Gazprom* EU:C:2015:316.

The English courts have so concluded: *Navigation Maritime Bulgare v Rustal Trading (The Ivan Zagubanski)* [2002] 1 Lloyds Rep 106 [72], [100(1)]; *Through Transport Mutual Insurance Association (Eurasia) v New India Assurance* [2005] 1 Lloyds Rep 67 (CA) [44]–[51], [63]; *A v B* [2007] 1 Lloyds Rep 237 [87]–[97] and *London Steamship Owners' Mutual Insurance v Kingdom of Spain (The Prestige) (No 2)* [2014] 1 Lloyds Rep 309 [193]. In *West Tankers v Ras Riunione Adriatica di Sicurta (The Front Comor)* [2005] 2 Lloyds Rep 257, a declaration of this type was granted by Colman J (although this is not apparent from the report), but while this was appropriate was not one of the questions certified for the House of Lords and it was not referred to the European Court. However, Lord Hoffmann's reasoning in relation to anti-suit injunctions is only consistent with the conclusion that a declaration of this type would be within the arbitration exception: [2007] 1 Lloyds Rep 391 (HL) [12]–[14].

This resolves the debates in the previous English case law: see *Toepfer International v Société Cargill France* [1997] 2 Lloyds Rep 98, 103–05 (for); *Partenreederei M/S 'Heidberg' v Grosvenor Grain and Feed (The Heidberg)* [1994] 2 Lloyds Rep 287, 299 (against—now not the law); *Toepfer International v Molino Boschi* [1996] 1 Lloyds Rep 510, 512–13 (partially against—now not the law); *Philip Alexander Securities & Futures v Bamberger* [1997] ILPr 73 [92]–[115] (unsure); *Union de Remorquage et de Sauvetage v Lake Avery (The Lake Avery)* [1997] 1 Lloyds Rep 540, 548–49 (for, with some nuances).

[117] This follows *a fortiori* from the reasoning in relation to anti-suit awards in *Gazprom* EU:C:2015:316.

[118] *Toyota Tsusho Trading v Prolat* [2015] 1 Lloyds Rep 344 [15]; and see before *Front Comor* the decision in *National Navigation v Endesa Generacion (The Wadi Sudr)* [2009] 1 Lloyds Rep 666 [119]–[121] (overturned on

have frequently made declaratory awards to such effect. In addition, where arbitrators have made such declarations, the English court has been willing to enter judgment in the terms of the award, and enforce such awards, where the principal purpose of the declaratory relief was to preclude any potential enforcement of inconsistent Brussels–Lugano judgments in England.[119]

N. CLAIMS FOR DAMAGES

A claim for damages for breach of an exclusive jurisdiction clause necessarily involves a **12.81** finding that the pursuit of the foreign proceedings is or was in breach of contract. It could therefore be contended that, where the foreign proceedings are within the Brussels–Lugano zone and within the material scope of the Brussels–Lugano regime, such a claim involves an illegitimate 'assessment of the appropriateness of bringing proceedings before the court of another member state', which imposes a 'penalty' for doing so,[120] and is therefore precluded by the principle of mutual trust.[121]

Whether the European Court would view the matter this way is unclear. The situation is **12.82** a long way from *Turner v Grovit*. A damages claim is less obviously offensive than an injunction, as it does not prohibit the pursuit of the foreign proceedings, but merely means that a retrospective price must be paid. It arguably does not equate even to the indirect interference[122] with the other court's jurisdiction, created by an anti-suit injunction, which was viewed as unacceptable by the European Court. Further, it could be argued that a

---

other grounds [2010] 1 Lloyds Rep 193 (CA)); and the result is parallel to the same conclusion reached in relation to jurisdiction clauses (see para 12.79 above).

This conclusion is also supported by authority on related points: (a) it is congruent with the reasoning in *London Steamship Owners Mutual Assurance Association v Kingdom of Spain (The Prestige) (No 2)* [2014] 1 Lloyds Rep 309 [190]–[194], where the court enforced a declaration by arbitrators as to their jurisdiction; (b) such declarations would be difficult to distinguish from applications to appoint an arbitrator which are unquestionably legitimate: *Union de Remorquage et de Sauvetage v Lake Avery (The Lake Avery)* [1997] 1 Lloyds Rep 540, 546–48; Case C-190/89, *Marc Rich v Società Italiana Impianti (The Atlantic Emperor)* [1991] ECR I–3855; (c) it is given further strength under the Brussels I Recast by Recital 12, reinforcing the breadth of the arbitration exception: cf *Toyota v Prolat*, at [16]–[17].

For academic discussion in favour of the legitimacy of such declarations, see M-L Niboyet, 'Quelle sanction pour les accords de compétence après les arrêts *Turner* et *West Tankers*' (2009) 148–149 Gaz Pal 8–10; for doubts see CJS Knight, 'Arbitration and Litigation after West Tankers' [2009] LMCLQ 285, 289.

---

[119] *West Tankers v Allianz (The Front Comor)* [2011] 2 Lloyds Rep 117, [2012] 1 Lloyds Rep 398 (CA); *African Fertilizers and Chemicals NIG (Nigeria) v BD Shipsnavo & Reederei* [2011] 2 Lloyds Rep 531; *London Steamship Owners Mutual Assurance Association v Kingdom of Spain (The Prestige) (No 2)* [2014] 1 Lloyds Rep 309 [181]–[197] (upheld on appeal on other grounds [2015] 2 Lloyds Rep 33 (CA)). The effectiveness of such judgments in terms of the award is discussed further at Ch 15, paras 15.09–15.20.

[120] Case C-159/02, *Turner v Grovit* [2004] ECR I–3565 [26], [28].

[121] See *Research in Motion UK v Visto* [2008] ILPr 34 (CA) (the point was not considered on appeal [2008] EWCA Civ 153; although see the observations at [31]–[34], [40]). However, this was in the rather different context of a free-standing damages claim, where the basis of the damages claimed was the alleged inherent wrongfulness of the use of the foreign jurisdiction, rather than the enforcement of an independent contractual right.

For arguments that damages judgments are contrary to mutual trust, or doubts as to whether they are compatible, see F Blöbel and P Späth, 'The Tale of Multilateral Trust and the European Law of Civil Procedure' (2005) 30 EL Rev 528, 545–46; S Bollée, 'L'arbitre peut-il octroyer des dommages-intérêts pour violation de la convention d'arbitrage?' (2012) *Revue de l'Arbitrage* 838–43; A Dickinson, 'Once Bitten: Mutual Distrust in European Private International Law' (2015) 131 LQR 186; J Ruddell, 'Monetary Remedies for Wrongful Foreign Proceedings' [2015] LMCLQ 10.

[122] Case C-159/02, *Turner v Grovit* [2004] ECR I–3565 [28].

contractual damages claim is not a direct 'assessment' of the jurisdiction of the other court, but rather the enforcement of a concrete personal legal obligation.[123] In the circumstances, it may be that the primary limitations on damages claims for breach of exclusive jurisdiction clauses will come not from the principle of mutual trust, but rather from the rules of *res judicata*[124] or *lis pendens*.[125]

12.83   The English courts have so far shown no hesitation in awarding contractual damages for breach of exclusive jurisdiction and arbitration clauses in respect of the bringing of proceedings in other Brussels–Lugano states and within the Brussels–Lugano regime,[126] or in enforcing contractual indemnities in settlement agreements as to the costs of subsequent proceedings, even where the subsequent proceedings are within the Brussels–Lugano regime and zone.[127] The same approach applies to damages in lieu of an injunction in a quasi-contractual situation.[128] In *AMT v Marzillier*, the Court of Appeal regarded a claim for damages for inducing a breach of contract, by inducing litigation in a Brussels–Lugano forum in breach of what the English courts regarded as a valid English exclusive jurisdiction clause, as consistent with the Brussels–Lugano regime.[129]

1. Damages for Breach of Arbitration Clauses

12.84   Even if claims for damages for breach of an exclusive jurisdiction clause are precluded by the principle of mutual trust, it does not follow that the same conclusion must apply in respect of damages for breach of an arbitration clause.

12.85   First, if the claim for damages for breach of an arbitration clause is made to the arbitrators themselves, it will be within the arbitration exception, and will not be incompatible with the Brussels–Lugano regime, as arbitrators are not subject to the principle of mutual trust.[130]

---

[123] *AMT Futures v Marzillier* [2015] QB 699 (CA) [59]–[61].

[124] See Ch 14, para 14.16–14.22.

[125] For the effect of the rules on *lis pendens* in Articles 27 and 28 of the Regulation on claims for damages for breach of exclusive jurisdiction clauses, see Ch 17, section C, '*Lis Pendens*'.

[126] *Starlight Shipping Company v Allianz Marine & Aviation Versicherungs* [2012] 1 Lloyds Rep 162 [31]–[36] (where the point of principle was apparently not addressed, and the English court had in any event held that it was the court first seised of the dispute on the merits), [2014] 2 CLC 492 (CA) [15]–[17] (and see [2014] 1 Lloyds Rep 223 (SC) [39]), [2014] 2 Lloyds Rep 579 [89], [94]; *Barclays Bank v Ente Nazionale de Previdenza ed Assistenza dei Medici e Degli Odontoiatri* [2015] 2 Lloyds Rep 527 [112]–[122], [2016] 2 CLC 859 (CA) [32]–[37]; *AMT Futures v Marzillier* [2015] QB 699 (CA) [59]–[62]; *AMT v Boural* [2018] EWHC 750 (no objection taken). In *West Tankers v Allianz (The Front Comor)* [2012] 2 Lloyds Rep 103 [74], Flaux J could see no material distinction between a declaration and an equitable damages claim for breach of the 'quasi-contractual' obligation to arbitrate imposed on a subrogated insurer.
The reasoning in *Research in Motion UK v Visto* [2008] ILPr 34 (CA) could be interpreted as hostile to all damages claims within the Brussels–Lugano zone, but has not been applied with respect to contractual damages claims: cf *West Tankers* (Flaux J) at [38]. (The point was not considered on appeal in *Research in Motion UK v Visto* [2008] ILPr 34 (CA); although see the observations at [31]–[34], [40].)

[127] *Starlight Shipping Company v Allianz Marine & Aviation Versicherungs* [2012] 1 Lloyds Rep 162 [31]–[36], [2014] 2 CLC 492 (CA) [15]–[17].

[128] *Starlight Shipping v Allianz Marine & Aviation Versicherungs* [2014] 2 Lloyds Rep 579 [73], [89]; *AMT Futures v Marzillier* [2015] QB 699 (CA) [62].

[129] *AMT Futures v Marzillier* [2015] QB 699 (CA) [59]–[61].

[130] *West Tankers v Allianz (The Front Comor)* [2012] 2 Lloyds Rep 103; Case C-536/15, *Gazprom* EU:C:2015:316; *Nori Holding v Bank Otkritie Financial Corporation* [2018] 2 Lloyds Rep 80 [102]; see also *CMA CGM v Hyundai Mipo Dockyard* [2009] 1 Lloyds Rep 213 [35], [41]–[47].

Second, if the claim for damages for breach of the arbitration agreement is made to **12.86** the court, it will still be within the arbitration exception, by parity of reasoning to the conclusion in *The Front Comor* that a court injunction to enforce an arbitration clause was 'arbitration'. It could be argued that it would nevertheless be incompatible with the Brussels–Lugano regime by reason of its effects on the other Brussels–Lugano proceedings. But, compared to the case of damages to enforce an exclusive jurisdiction clause, this would be at a yet further remove to the situation in *Turner v Grovit*. It engages an obligation with which the Brussels–Lugano regime is not directly concerned, an assessment of which does not inherently involve an assessment of the Brussels–Lugano jurisdiction of the other court, since the other court's decision whether or not to stay the proceedings on grounds of arbitration is itself a matter governed by the New York Convention and outside the Brussels–Lugano regime.[131]

The case law of the English courts suggests strongly that the award of damages by the court **12.87** for breach of the arbitration clause by litigating elsewhere in the Brussels–Lugano zone would not be precluded by the Brussels–Lugano regime.[132] However, it is arguable that, under English arbitration law, damages for breach of the arbitration clause are at least principally a matter for the arbitrators rather than the court.[133]

2. Non-Contractual Damages Claims

A claim for non-contractual damages for the allegedly wrongful or abusive commencement **12.88** of proceedings elsewhere in the Brussels–Lugano zone is more likely to be precluded by the principle of mutual trust.[134] From a European perspective, such a claim could well be viewed as nothing more than a direct assessment of the foreign court's assumption of jurisdiction, even if, as a matter of English law, such a claim would involve the enforcement of an underlying substantive equitable right.[135] However, in *AMT v Marzillier*, the Court of Appeal regarded a claim for damages for inducing a breach of contract, by inducing litigation in a

---

[131] As now confirmed by Recital 12 of the Brussels I Recast.

[132] This follows in particular from the logic of decisions allowing damages for breach of exclusive jurisdiction clauses (addressed at paras 12.81–12.83 above), in particular *Starlight Shipping v Allianz Marine & Aviation Versicherungs* [2014] 2 CLC 492 (CA) [15]–[17]. See also *West Tankers v Allianz (The Front Comor)* [2012] 2 Lloyds Rep 103 (in relation to damages awarded by arbitrators).

In *Nori Holding v Bank Otkritie Financial Corporation* [2018] 2 Lloyds Rep 80 [101]–[102] Males J considered claims for a declaration that the defendant, who had litigated in Cyprus in breach of an arbitration clause, should indemnify the claimant against costs and liabilities. He decided to defer addressing this indemnity claim, noting that the availability of damages and similar indemnities from arbitrators was a distinction to the position in relation to exclusive jurisdiction clauses. But that hesitation may reflect a concern that under English arbitration law, such damages and indemnities for breach of an arbitration clause may (at least primarily) be a matter for the arbitrators, not the court (see Ch 14, para 14.04), rather than a worry about the principle of mutual trust.

[133] See Ch 14, para 14.04 and see *Nori Holding v Bank Otkritie Financial Corporation* [2018] 2 Lloyds Rep 80 [102].

[134] See *Research in Motion UK v Visto* [2008] ILPr 34 (CA) (the point was not considered on appeal [2008] EWCA Civ 153; although see the supportive observations at [31]–[34], [40]); see further *West Tankers v Allianz (The Front Comor)* [2012] 2 Lloyds Rep 103 [37]. However, A Briggs, 'Anti-Suit Injunctions and Utopian Ideals' (2004) 120 LQR 529, 532, considers that even non-contractual damages claims do not infringe the principle of mutual trust.

[135] As to whether such a substantive equitable right exists, see Ch 3, section B, 'A Legal or Equitable Right?'.

Brussels–Lugano forum in breach of what the English courts regarded as a valid English exclusive jurisdiction clause, as consistent with the Brussels–Lugano regime. The Court of Appeal concluded that all that was engaged was a consideration of the claimant's rights in contract and tort and there was no assessment of the assumption of jurisdiction by the other Brussels–Lugano court.[136]

---

[136] *AMT Futures v Marzillier* [2015] QB 699 (CA) [59]–[62]; point not addressed on appeal [2018] AC 439 (SC) [44].

13

Interim Anti-Suit Injunctions

A. INTRODUCTION

Most anti-suit injunctions are sought and granted on an interim basis. The need to antici- **13.01**
pate hearings in the other proceedings means that interim relief is frequently a practical
necessity;[1] in many cases, the grant of an interim injunction will be decisive.[2]

Indeed, anti-suit injunctions can be granted as interim relief only, without corresponding final **13.02**
anti-suit relief.[3] And while some interim anti-suit injunctions meaningfully protect matching
causes of action for final anti-suit relief, such as a claim for breach of a jurisdiction clause, this
is often not the case. Interim alternative forum injunctions based on non-contractual grounds
often in reality protect only the distinct underlying claim on the merits, and even if a claim for
a final injunction is brought, it may have little material difference to the claim for the interim
injunction itself; while a trial of a final injunction is often neither expected nor required. But
the anti-suit injunction is not an inherently interim remedy, like a freezing injunction. It can
be granted on a final basis[4] and the factual disputes which need to be determined may include matters which, in principle, need to be resolved at a trial.[5] This procedural ambiguity

---

[1] See eg *Metall und Rohstoff v ACLI Metals (London)* [1984] 1 Lloyds Rep 598 (CA) 600. A similar result can
sometimes be produced by giving directions for the expeditious hearing of a final injunction: see *Tracomin v Sudan
Oil Seeds (No 2)* [1983] 2 All ER 129, 131.
[2] *Trafigura Beheer v Kookmin Bank* [2005] EWHC 2350 [42]; *Apple Corps v Apple Computer* [1992] RPC 70, 76.
[3] See paras 13.08 and 13.27.
[4] See Ch 3, para 3.32.
[5] See eg *Tracomin v Sudan Oil Seeds (No 2)* [1983] 2 All ER 129, 131.

corresponds to the juridical uncertainty, discussed earlier in this work, as to whether there is a true underlying substantive cause of action for interim non-contractual anti-suit relief at all, or whether such injunctions are in essence procedural remedies.[6]

13.03   The result is an unusual hybrid[7] which does not fit neatly into the categories established for standard interim injunctions claimed in support of substantive causes of action, such as an interim injunction to restrain a potential tortious wrong, sought and granted to hold the ring pending trial of a final injunction on the same cause of action. As we shall see, the ambiguous status of the remedy, and its unique procedural role, has caused difficulties in the formulation of the appropriate tests for the grant of interim relief.

13.04   The substantive restrictions imposed by the Brussels–Lugano regime on the grant of anti-suit injunctions (subject to the possible consequences of Brexit) are discussed in Chapter 12. They apply to interim injunctions as much as final injunctions. The following discussion is subject to those restrictions, so long as the Brussels–Lugano regime remains the law.

13.05   The remainder of this chapter will consider, in turn:

- the powers to grant interim anti-suit injunctions;
- procedure and form;
- the principles to be applied to the grant of interim anti-suit injunctions;
- the court's discretion;
- mandatory interim anti-suit injunctions.

B. POWER AND NATURE

1. The Primary Power: Section 37(1) of the Senior Courts Act 1981

13.06   In ordinary civil litigation in the High Court,[8] the power under which interim anti-suit injunctions are granted is section 37(1) of the Senior Courts Act 1981,[9] which provides

---

   [6] See Ch 3, section B, 'A Legal or Equitable Right?'.
   [7] For recognition of the 'sui generis' nature of anti-suit injunctions, see *Mercedes-Benz v Leiduck* [1996] 1 AC 284 (PC) 301D–E.
   [8] In the County Court, interim injunctions can be granted under s 38(1) County Courts Act 1984—although in practice anti-suit injunctions are a game played in the High Court alone.
There are some other miscellaneous statutory powers under which interim injunctions can be granted which could in principle support an interim anti-suit injunction. Thus, in the High Court, once a winding-up petition has been presented, there is a power under s 126 of the Insolvency Act 1986 (the successor of Companies Act 1862, s 85; Companies Act 1908, s 140, Companies Act 1948, s 226, and Companies Act 1948, s 521) to restrain proceedings before the English courts, and courts in other parts of the UK: *In re International Pulp and Paper* (1876) 3 Ch D 594 (rather confused); *Re Dynamics Corp of America* [1973] 1 WLR 63. However, this power does not apply to proceedings in foreign courts outside the UK: *Re Oriental Inland Steam* (1874) 9 Ch App 557 (CA); *In re Belfast Shipowners* [1894] 1 IR 321, 332 (note contra at first instance on this point: 327–28); *Re Vocalion (Foreign)* [1932] 2 Ch 196. In *Bloom v Harms Offshore AHT 'Taurus'* [2010] Ch 187 (CA) [16]–[22], the Court of Appeal thought it was likely (without deciding) that this approach should extend to the analogous statutory provisions in respect of administration of companies. See also *Tchenguiz v Grant Thornton UK* [2017] 2 BCLC 299 (CA) [69].
   [9] For authority holding that interim anti-suit injunctions are granted under s 37(1), see *Glencore International v Metro Trading International (No 3)* [2002] CLC 1090 (CA) [2], [60]; *Turner v Grovit* [2002] 1 WLR 107 (HL) [22]; *AES Ust-Kamenogorsk Hydropower Plant LLP v Ust-Kamenogorsk Hydropower Plant JSC* [2012] 1 WLR 920 (CA) [55], [62], [64], [125], [204], [2013] 1 WLR 1889 (SC) [19]–[20], [41], [48], [57], [60]; and among many others, *Nursing & Midwifery Council v Harrold* [2015] EWHC 2254 (QB) [27].
      For complete historical accuracy, it can be noted that strictly the power in s 37(1) restates and confirms, but does not replace, the inherent powers to grant interim injunctions which the High Court inherits from its

that the court has the power to grant interim as well as final injunctions if it is 'just and convenient' to do so.

It appears to be unnecessary to view interim anti-suit injunctions as being granted under the 'inherent jurisdiction' of the court.[10] **13.07**

In the contentious decision of *The Siskina*, it was considered that the power to grant an interim injunction under section 37(1) was confined to the protection or assertion of some underlying legal or equitable right.[11] Since the existence of a distinct legal or equitable right underlying non-contractual anti-suit injunctions is contestable,[12] there was a theoretical tension between the interim relief aspect of *The Siskina* and the anti-suit injunction. However, the courts finessed this problem by treating interim and final anti-suit injunctions as permissible either under a *sui generis* exception to the requirement of a legal or equitable right, or on the basis that injunctions can additionally be granted under section 37(1) if the respondent's conduct is 'unconscionable',[13] which could be viewed as covering all cases where non-contractual anti-suit injunctions are granted. An alternative route round *The Siskina* would have been to view the interim anti-suit injunction as granted in support of the underlying cause of action in the litigation on the merits between the parties.[14] Further, **13.08**

---

pre-Judicature Act forebears. It has often been viewed simplistically as *conferring* the court's powers to grant interim injunctions, but as Lord Scott pointed out in *Fourie v Le Roux* [2007] 1 WLR 320 (HL) [25], s 37(1) of the Senior Courts Act 1981 (like its predecessors, s 24(8) of the Supreme Court of Judicature Act 1873 and s 45(1) of the Supreme Court of Judicature (Consolidation) Act 1925) actually only restates and confirms those powers, since the High Court has inherited all the powers of the courts to grant injunctions which existed before the Judicature Acts 1873–75, by virtue of, in turn, s 16 of the Supreme Court of Judicature Act 1873, s 18 of the Supreme Court of Judicature (Consolidation) Act 1925, and finally Senior Courts Act 1981, s 19. See also *Cartier International v British Sky Broadcasting* [2015] RPC 7 (Arnold J) [94]–[95], [2017] RPC 3 (CA) [40]–[41] (point not addressed in the Supreme Court, [2018] 1 WLR 3259 [5]).

The powers preserved by s 19 of the 1981 Act are no broader than the power contained in s 37(1): *Day v Brownrigg* (1878) 10 ChD 294, 307; *L v K (Freezing Orders: Principles and Safeguards)* [2014] Fam 35 [14]; *Cartier* (Arnold J) at [95] and (CA) at [41]. In the modern case law, it is in reality the power in s 37(1) that is exercised.

In the circumstances, it is most convenient to analyse matters in terms of s 37(1) alone. This was how Lord Scott himself approached the issue in *Fourie v Le Roux* [26].

---

[10] In *The Eras EIL Actions* [1995] 1 Lloyds Rep 64, 72, Potter J accepted that an anti-suit injunction could be granted in the 'inherent jurisdiction' of the court. However, this conclusion was reached in order to resolve a procedural and jurisdictional problem, namely whether an interim anti-suit injunction could be applied for by application in the context of an existing action in which no claim for a final anti-suit injunction had been brought, to which Potter J gave a positive answer. As matters stand, however, it seems that the procedural and jurisdictional issues can be resolved by treating the court as having both procedural power and territorial jurisdiction to grant interim anti-suit injunctions ancillary to its jurisdiction over the merits of the underlying substantive action, even if no final claim for an anti-suit injunction is brought: see *Masri v Consolidated Contractors (No 3)* [2009] QB 503 (CA) [57]–[59]; *Glencore International v Metro Trading International (No 3)* [2002] CLC 1090 (CA) [59]; and paras 13.08 and 13.25–13.27. If so, there appears to be no reason why as a matter of substantive law the interim injunction cannot simply be granted under s 37(1), without needing to have recourse to the 'inherent jurisdiction': see *Glencore* (CA) at [2], [12], [60], treating the comments of Moore Bick J at first instance (at [23]) as turning solely on questions of procedure. See also Ch 3, para 3.33.

[11] *Siskina v Distos Compania Naviera (The Siskina)* [1979] AC 210 (HL) 254E, 256C–F; followed in *Bremer Vulkan Schiffbau und Maschinenfabrik v South India Shipping* [1981] AC 909 (HL) 979G–H, 992D–E, 994H–995A.

[12] See Ch 3, section C, 'The Form and Nature of Final Anti-Suit Injunctions'; Ch 4, section E, 'A Legal or Equitable Right'.

[13] *Castanho v Brown & Root* [1981] AC 557 (HL) 573C–E; *British Airways Board v Laker Airways* [1985] AC 58 (HL) 81, 95; *South Carolina Insurance v Assurantie Maatschappij 'De Zeven Provincien'* [1987] 1 AC 24 (HL) 40C–E; *Masri v Consolidated Contractors (No 3)* [2009] QB 503 (CA) [32]–[54]. In *AES Ust-Kamenogorsk Hydropower Plant LLP v Ust-Kamenogorsk Hydropower Plant JSC* [2013] 1 WLR 1889 (SC) [20] narrower language was used, focusing on unconscionability only, but *obiter* and without citation of all the relevant case law.

[14] See eg *Revenue and Customs Commissioners v Ali* [2012] STC 42. This line of justification is, however, more appropriate to alternative forum injunctions than single forum injunctions.

in any event, the restrictive interim relief doctrine of *The Siskina* has been under persistent attack,[15] and may well now have disappeared as an absolute restriction in the light of *Fourie v Le Roux*.[16] In the circumstances, *The Siskina* is not a relevant constraint on the grant of interim anti-suit injunctions. Interim anti-suit injunctions can therefore be granted in alternative forum cases, in the context of existing proceedings on the merits, even without a final claim for an anti-suit injunction.[17] However, where free-standing single forum injunctions are sought, it will probably be procedurally appropriate for the interim anti-suit injunction to be brought in the context of a final claim form for a final anti-suit injunction, as otherwise there will be no originating process.[18]

13.09   The breadth of the power to grant an interim injunction where it is 'just and convenient' to do so does not create an untrammelled discretion. The power must be exercised in accordance with principle, and thus will be governed by the tests for the grant of anti-suit injunctions developed in the authorities.[19]

2. Powers to Grant Injunctions in Support of Arbitrations

13.10   Section 44 of the Arbitration Act 1996 gives power to grant 'an interim injunction' 'for the purposes of and in relation to arbitral proceedings'. Section 44(3) and 44(4) allow injunctions only to be granted either in cases of 'urgency' for the purpose of preserving 'evidence or assets' or with the consent of the tribunal or the agreement of the other side. Section 44(5) provides that the court shall only act if the arbitral tribunal has no power or is unable for the time being to act effectively.

---

[15] Lord Diplock's speech in *The Siskina* provoked considerable concern and criticism for many years: see *Castanho v Brown & Root* [1981] AC 557 (HL) 573C–E; *South Carolina Insurance Co v Assurantie Maatschappij 'De Zeven Provincien'* [1987] 1 AC 24 (HL) 44–45; *Channel Tunnel Group v Balfour Beatty Construction* [1993] AC 334 (HL) 342H, 343C, 362–63; and *Mercedes Benz v Leiduck* [1996] AC 284 (PC), where the majority advice given by Lord Mustill declined to decide the point (298B–G, 304F–G); but Lord Nicholls in the minority suggested that *The Siskina* was wrong, or no longer applicable, in relation to interim relief (as well as jurisdiction): at 309–12. Lord Nicholls' views on the interim relief point have now in effect been adopted in *Fourie v Le Roux* [2007] 1 WLR 320 (HL): see n 16.

[16] *Fourie v Le Roux* [2007] 1 WLR 320 (HL) [30], followed in *Secretary of State for the Environment, Food and Rural Affairs v Meier* [2009] 1 WLR 2780 (SC) [97]; *Royal Westminster Investments v Varma* [2012] EWHC 3439; *Revenue and Customs Commissioners v Ali* [2012] STC 42 [35]–[38]; and now *Cartier International v British Sky Broadcasting* [2015] RPC 7 (Arnold J) [94]–[95], [2017] RPC 3 (CA) [40]–[41] (not addressed in Supreme Court, [2018] 1 WLR 3259 [5]). It should however be noted that in some of the subsequent case law, *Fourie v Le Roux* has not always been cited or applied in this sense, and *The Siskina* has been treated as having continued significance: see eg *Masri v Consolidated Contractors (No 3)* [2009] QB 503 (CA) [67]; *Octagon Overseas v Coates* [2017] 4 WLR 91 [15]–[22]. See also the obiter comments in *AES Ust-Kamenogorsk Hydropower Plant LLP v Ust-Kamenogorsk Hydropower Plant JSC* [2013] 1 WLR 1889 [20], leaving the point open, but where *Fourie* appears not to have been cited.
For the effect of the decision in *Fourie v Le Roux* on the court's power to grant final injunctions, see Ch 3, paras 3.05–3.06.

[17] *Glencore International v Metro Trading International (No 3)* [2002] CLC 1090 (CA) [59]. See also CPR 25.1(4). This is discussed further at para 13.27.

[18] See *Fourie v Le Roux* [2007] 1 WLR 320 [32]; *Octagon Overseas v Coates* [2017] 4 WLR 91 [15]–[22] (in a rather different context). In *Masri v Consolidated Contractors (No 3)* [2009] QB 503 (CA) [44], [55], [57], Collins LJ suggested that there would be a need for an underlying right and cause of action, and a final claim by claim form, for a free-standing single forum injunction.

[19] *Donohue v Armco* [2002] 1 Lloyds Rep 425 (HL) [23]; *Glencore International v Metro Trading International (No 3)* [2002] CLC 1090 (CA) [42]; see also in related contexts, the comments in *Fourie v Le Roux* [2007] 1 WLR 420 (HL) [3], [6], [33], [45], [48] and *Tasarruf Mevduati Sigorta Fonu v Merrill Lynch Bank & Trust Co (Cayman)* [2012] 1 WLR 1721 (PC) [57].

It used to be thought that interim anti-suit injunctions in support of arbitrations could also **13.11** be granted under section 44, and it was even occasionally envisaged that section 44 might be the exclusive basis for the grant of anti-suit injunctions in support of arbitration. This would have created difficulties, as the conditions of section 44 if applied unsympathetically would create inappropriate procedural restrictions.[20]

But in *AES Ust-Kamenogorsk* the Supreme Court held that section 44 did not cover such **13.12** anti-suit injunctions at all, as they were not 'for the purposes of' or 'in relation to' arbitration proceedings but instead sought to enforce the negative obligation in the arbitration agreement not to litigate elsewhere.[21] Consequently, interim anti-suit injunctions in support of arbitration are granted in ordinary civil litigation in the High Court under section 37(1) of the Senior Courts Act 1981. It seems the Supreme Court's reasoning also means that section 44 has 'no bearing' on such injunctions, so the procedural constraints in section 44 should not apply, even by analogy, and do not limit the discretion of the court under section 37(1).[22] At the most, the issues which the conditions of section 44 highlight *may* be paid

---

[20] It would be impractical if anti-suit injunctions could not be granted to support arbitration without the consent of the tribunal, as often time does not permit this, or the tribunal will not have been appointed, or it might be *functus*; and the other side's agreement is not realistically to be expected.

Consequently, in order to circumvent the barriers posed by s 44(3)–(4), before *AES Ust-Kamenogorsk* there was authority that suggested that the right to arbitrate under an arbitration clause could be treated as an 'asset' for this purpose (*Cetelem v Roust Holdings* [2005] 1 WLR 3555 [70]; *Starlight Shipping v Tai Ping Insurance (The Alexandros T)* [2008] 1 Lloyds Rep 230 [21]; *Sheffield United FC v West Ham United FC* [2009] 1 Lloyds Rep 167 [32]). This would have allowed anti-suit injunctions to be granted under s 44 in cases of urgency without the tribunal's consent. But the interpretation of 'assets' that permitted it was a rather artificial conclusion; Rix LJ viewed the point as 'unsettled' in *AES Ust-Kamenogorsk Hydropower Plant LLP v Ust-Kamenogorsk Hydropower Plant JSC* [2012] 1 WLR 920 (CA) [28]; and Lord Mance appeared similarly to find its logic unappealing in *Ust-Kamenogorsk* [2013] 1 WLR 1889 (SC) [47], which is part of the reason he concluded that s 44 did not apply at all.

Indeed, even if the 'assets' problem is interpreted away, or ignored, the restrictions of s 44 would still be inappropriate for interim anti-suit injunctions, even by analogy. Accordingly, even where the s 44 conditions have been thought relevant, they have been interpreted liberally, and they have not in practice been a significant constraint, whether applied directly or by analogy: see para 13.15.

[21] *AES Ust-Kamenogorsk Hydropower Plant LLP v Ust-Kamenogorsk Hydropower Plant JSC* [2013] 1 WLR 1889 (SC) [43]–[48], adopting the same approach as had previously been taken in *Sokana Industries v Freyre* [1994] 2 Lloyds Rep 57, 65, followed in *Industrial Maritime Carriers (Bahamas) v Sinoca International* [1996] 2 Lloyds Rep 585, 592. *Ust-Kamenogorsk* has been applied in *Rochester Resources v Lebedev* [2014] EWHC 2926 [52]; *Southport Success v Tsingshan Holding Group (The Anna Bo)* [2015] 2 Lloyds Rep 578.

The decision in *Ust-Kamenogorsk* overrules a number of previous cases in which interim anti-suit injunctions had been granted under s 44 or where it was held that interim anti-suit injunctions could in principle be granted under s 44 (often as an additional route available alongside s 37 (1)): *Starlight Shipping v Tai Ping Insurance (The Alexandros T)* [2008] 1 Lloyds Rep 230 [16]–[28]; *Niagara Maritime v Tianjin Iron & Steel Group* [2011] EWHC 3035 [11]–[12]—an undefended case); *BNP Paribas v Russian Machines* [2012] 1 Lloyds Rep 61 [38], [45] (where the point was conceded but Blair J thought it had been rightly conceded; the point was not addressed on appeal, *Joint Stock Asset Management Co Ingosstrakh-Investments v BNP Paribas* [2012] 1 Lloyds Rep 649 (CA)); *U&M Mining Zambia v Konkola Copper Mines* [2013] 2 Lloyds Rep 218 [24]; and see *AES Ust-Kamenogorsk Hydropower Plant LLP v Ust-Kamenogorsk Hydropower Plant JSC* [2012] 1 WLR 920 (CA) [101]–[105]. Similarly, in *West Tankers v Ras Riunione Adriatica di Sicurta (The Front Comor)* [2007] 1 Lloyds Rep 391 (HL) [10], Lord Hoffmann thought interim anti-suit injunctions could be granted under both s 37(1) and s 44.

[22] *AES Ust-Kamenogorsk Hydropower Plant LLP v Ust-Kamenogorsk Hydropower Plant JSC* [2013] 1 WLR 1889 (SC) [43], [48], [58] (departing from [2012] 1 WLR 920 (CA) [42]–[96], per Rix LJ); *Southport Success v Tsingshan Holding Group Co Ltd (The Anna Bo)* [2015] 2 Lloyds Rep 578 [19]–[25]; *Nori Holding v Bank Otkritie Financial Corporation* [2018] 2 Lloyds Rep 80 [32]–[42].

However, although in *The Anna Bo* Phillips J had concluded that the limitations of s 44 did not apply by analogy to anti-suit injunctions under s 37, in his own later decision in *Mace (Russia) v Retansel Enterprises* [2016] EWHC 1209 [19] the same judge held that 'regard' should be had to the limitations of s 44, without referring to his previous decision. In *Dreymoor Fertilisers Overseas v Eurochem Trading* [2018] EWHC 2267 [54]–[56], [82] Males J thought that although the s 44 considerations were 'not necessarily decisive', they 'may be taken into account so as to inform the exercise of the court's discretion'. It is suggested that the neatest reading of the Supreme Court's decision is that it is not even necessary to pay 'regard' to the specific conditions of s 44, and that *Southport* is the better

regard, to the extent relevant, in a loose, flexible, and non-restrictive manner, and ignoring aspects that are inappropriate, such as the reference to 'assets' in section 44(3).

13.13   As Lord Mance made clear, the court's power to grant anti-suit injunctions in support of arbitration must be exercised 'sensitively and, in particular, with due regard for the scheme and terms of the 1996 Act when any arbitration is on foot or proposed', which means 'having due regard for the role of the arbitrators and the forum in which the parties have agreed to determine their dispute'.[23] But this does not mean including the literal restrictions of section 44 by the back door.[24]

13.14   The case law suggests that this sensitivity to the scheme of the 1996 Act and the role of the arbitrators will not discourage the grant of injunctions in appropriate cases. In *Nori*, Males J explained that the fact that anti-suit relief was available from the arbitrators was not a sufficient reason for the court not to grant it, nor a reason to limit any interim injunction in time so that it lasted only until the Tribunal could consider whether to grant equivalent relief.[25]

13.15   In practice the section 44 factors have not in general been significant factors against the grant of injunctions. In most cases they are not considered at all,[26] and even where considered they are approached liberally and flexibly. Thus:

(1) The absence of the Tribunal's consent is not ordinarily treated as a strong factor against an injunction, and there is no obligation to seek consent.[27]

---

authority; considerations such as urgency may be separately relevant in principle but can be applied independent of the rather awkward terminology of s 44.

   Indeed, in *AES Ust-Kamenogorsk Hydropower Plant LLP v Ust-Kamenogorsk Hydropower Plant JSC* [2012] 1 WLR 920 (CA) [96] Rix LJ took the view that if s 44 was to apply by analogy, only ss 44(5) and 44(6), and not 44(3) and 44(4), could impose relevant constraints. At most, paying regard to the 'scheme' of the 1996 Act (as Lord Mance envisaged in *Ust-Kamenogorsk* at [60]) could involve paying a loose and inspecific regard to s 44 among other aspects of the Act.

---

[23]   *AES Ust-Kamenogorsk Hydropower Plant LLP v Ust-Kamenogorsk Hydropower Plant JSC* [2013] 1 WLR 1889 (SC) [60]; *Southport Success v Tsingshan Holding Group (The Anna Bo)* [2015] 2 Lloyds Rep 578 [25]. This is broadly also the approach of Rix LJ in *AES Ust-Kamenogorsk Hydropower Plant LLP v Ust-Kamenogorsk Hydropower Plant JSC* [2012] 1 WLR 920 (CA) [94], [96], [105].

[24]   *Southport Success v Tsingshan Holding Group (The Anna Bo)* [2015] 2 Lloyds Rep 578 [25]. However, cf contra *Mace (Russia) v Retansel Enterprises* [2016] EWHC 1209 [19], suggesting that 'regard' should be paid to the restrictions of s 44. This is discussed in n 22.

[25]   *Nori Holding v Bank Otkritie Financial Corporation* [2018] 2 Lloyds Rep 80 [32]–[42].

[26]   See among many others, *XL Insurance v Owens Corning* [2000] 2 Lloyds Rep 500, 503–04; *Navigation Maritime Bulgare v Rustal Trading (The Ivan Zagubanski)* [2002] 1 Lloyds Rep 106; *Through Transport Mutual Insurance Association (Eurasia) v New India Assurance* [2004] 1 Lloyds Rep 206, [2005] 1 Lloyds Rep 67 (CA).

[27]   See *Mace (Russia) v Retansel Enterprises* [2016] EWHC 1209 [19] (consent not sought and this was not thought to be a factor against the injunction); *Dreymoor Fertilisers Overseas v Eurochem Trading* [2018] EWHC 2267 [82] (no obligation to seek consent); and *AES Ust-Kamenogorsk Hydropower Plant LLP v Ust-Kamenogorsk Hydropower Plant JSC* [2010] 2 Lloyds Rep 233 [19]–[20]. Indeed, in *Starlight Shipping v Tai Ping Insurance (The Alexandros T)* [2008] 1 Lloyds Rep 230 at [29]–[31], the injunction was granted even though the arbitrators had *refused* consent. There are many cases where the consent of the arbitrators was not sought and this has not been considered to be a factor against the injunction.

   In *Dreymoor Fertilisers Overseas v Eurochem Trading* [2018] EWHC 2267 [54]–[56], [82], Males J observed that although there was no obligation to seek the Tribunal's consent, an absence of urgency combined with a lack of consent from the Tribunal might be 'highly relevant', although he made clear that there was 'no obligation' to seek their consent. That, however, was a case on unusual facts where the issue was whether an injunction should be granted to restrain evidence-gathering proceedings in the US court, where such evidence was to be used in the arbitration. The Tribunal's views on this might have been particularly pertinent. Males J regarded it as surprising that the Tribunal had not been informed of the injunction.

(2) Urgency is interpreted flexibly; and often no specific urgency is required. Indeed, it has been viewed as sufficient for urgency (if applicable), that without an injunction foreign proceedings in breach of the arbitration clause will continue.[28]

(3) With respect to section 44(5), the courts have accepted that, in general, the arbitrators will not be able to act as effectively as the court in relation to anti-suit relief because of the lack of contempt remedies for breach of awards; and because the respondent will generally not even accept the Tribunal's jurisdiction to make any anti-suit award. [29]

13.16 The power in section 37(1) permits the grant of interim anti-suit injunctions in support of arbitrations against non-parties to the arbitration clause, in appropriate cases. One example is where a party who is not contractually bound to arbitrate brings proceedings calculated to undermine the agreement to arbitrate or interfere with the arbitration.[30]

13.17 Section 37(1) also in principle permits the grant of interim anti-suit injunctions to enforce a foreign arbitration clause.[31] However, as discussed earlier, there are objections of comity and discretion to the grant of anti-suit injunctions in support of foreign arbitrations. For any interim remedy, the natural court to grant protective relief is usually the court of the seat of the arbitration, and there will need to be some special reason why it is appropriate to ask the English court to intervene in support of a foreign arbitration.[32] Further, seeking the invasive remedy of an anti-suit injunction in support of a foreign arbitration may pose real problems of comity.[33]

3. Arbitrators' Lack of Power to Grant Interim Injunctions

13.18 It is often accepted that under the Arbitration Act 1996, arbitrators lack the power to grant interim injunctions, unless the parties expressly grant them that power, either by special agreement (which is unlikely) or under the applicable arbitration rules.[34]

---

[28] In *Southport Success v Tsingshan Holding Group (The Anna Bo)* [2015] 2 Lloyds Rep 578 [26], urgency was considered satisfied (if it needed to be considered), even where the injunction had not been sought with any great speed, simply on the basis that it was important to prevent the foreign proceedings continuing in the near future. In *Starlight Shipping v Tai Ping Insurance (The Alexandros T)* [2008] 1 Lloyds Rep 230 [29]–[30], urgency was not considered relevant and only s 44(5) was applied by analogy under s 37.

[29] See *Southport Success v Tsingshan Holding Group (The Anna Bo)* [2015] 2 Lloyds Rep 578 [27]; *Starlight Shipping v Tai Ping Insurance (The Alexandros T)* [2008] 1 Lloyds Rep 230 [29]–[31]; *AES Ust-Kamenogorsk Hydropower Plant LLP v Ust-Kamenogorsk Hydropower Plant JSC* [2013] 1 WLR 1889 (SC) [40]–[41], [47]. See also the robust approach taken in *Nori Holding v Bank Otkritie Financial Corporation* [2018] 2 Lloyds Rep 80 [32]–[42].

[30] See eg *Joint Stock Asset Management Co Ingosstrakh-Investments v BNP Paribas* [2012] 1 Lloyds Rep 649 (CA) [46]–[58] and *Mace (Russia) v Retansel Enterprises* [2016] EWHC 1209.

[31] *Channel Tunnel Group v Balfour Beatty Construction* [1993] AC 334 (HL) 360–66.

[32] See *Econet Wireless v Vee Networks* [2006] 2 Lloyds Rep 423 [19]. See also *U&M Mining Zambia v Konkola Copper Mines* [2013] 2 Lloyds Rep 218 [63], concluding that where the seat of the arbitration is abroad, the court will need very good reason to exercise a jurisdiction under s 44 of the 1996 Act.

[33] See Ch 7, section G, 'Injunctions in Support of a Foreign Forum'. However, the courts of Bermuda and the Eastern Caribbean have granted anti-suit injunctions to enforce foreign arbitration clauses. See *Finecroft v Lamane Trading* (Eastern Caribbean SC, 6 January 2006); *IPOC International Growth Fund v OAO 'CT-Mobile'* (Bermuda CA, 23 March 2007).

[34] *Starlight Shipping v Tai Ping Insurance (The Alexandros T)* [2008] 1 Lloyds Rep 230 [20], [26] (relying, in particular, on the terms of Arbitration Act 1996, s 39); *Nori Holding v Bank Otkritie Financial Corporation* [2018] 2 Lloyds Rep 80 [35].

13.19 However, it is possible for arbitrators to produce similar results to interim injunctions by speedy final partial awards[35] granting injunctions in the course of the arbitration, or procedural orders. Their powers, at least under English arbitration law, include the power to grant 'anti-suit awards',[36] which can be shaped to grant relief which is limited in time.[37]

4. Section 25(1) of the Civil Jurisdiction and Judgment Act 1982

13.20 Section 25(1) of the Civil Jurisdiction and Judgments Act 1982, as extended by statutory instrument,[38] gives power to grant free-standing interim relief in support of foreign proceedings where substantive proceedings[39] have been or are to be commenced in any foreign court.[40] Section 25(2) provides that 'the court may refuse to grant that relief if, in the opinion of the court, the fact that the court has no jurisdiction apart from this section in relation to the subject-matter of the proceedings in question makes it inexpedient for the court to grant it'.

13.21 One important feature of this provision is that it has its own tailor-made jurisdictional gateway in CPR Part 6 PD 6B para 3.1(5). In contrast, if the proceedings to be protected are abroad, it may well be difficult in many cases to establish the court's territorial jurisdiction to hear an application for an interim injunction under section 37(1) of the Senior Courts Act 1981, and the role of section 37(1) in supporting foreign proceedings is in any event less well established and also bedevilled by the legacy of *The Siskina*.[41]

13.22 However, although section 25(1) of the Civil Jurisdiction and Judgments Act could in theory provide a basis for the grant of anti-suit injunctions,[42] it is unlikely that it will do so frequently if at all in practice, given the concerns based on comity which inhibit the grant of anti-suit relief in support of foreign courts. In *Airbus v Patel*, the House of Lords held that anti-suit injunctions would only be granted where the English court had 'sufficient interest' in the matter; and that where the question was in which of two foreign courts a substantive dispute would be litigated, some special factors would be required to give the English court a sufficient interest.[43] The same reasoning may mean that, in the language of section 25(1), it is generally 'inexpedient' to grant an interim anti-suit injunction in support of proceedings before a foreign court.

---

[35] Under Arbitration Act 1996, s 47.

[36] See Ch 7, paras 7.51–7.55.

[37] See *Kastner v Jason* [2004] 2 Lloyds Rep 397 [27]: 'the criterion for jurisdiction is that the relief is granted by the final award, not the final or interim character of the relief'.

[38] By Civil Jurisdiction and Judgments Act 1982 (Interim Relief) Order 1997, SI 1997 No 302.

[39] Section 25(1) only applies to give the English power to grant interim relief in support of substantive final foreign proceedings, and not in support of interim proceedings before foreign courts: *ETI Euro Telecom International v Republic of Bolivia* [2009] 1 WLR 665 (CA) [70]–[78].

[40] The s 25(1) power does not apply to interim relief in support of a foreign arbitration: *ETI Euro Telecom International v Republic of Bolivia* [2009] 1 WLR 665 (CA) [79]–[82].

[41] See the discussion of *The Siskina* in Ch 3, paras 3.04 and 3.14.

[42] The court can grant remedies under s 25(1) which the supported court could not grant: *Credit Suisse Fides Trust v Cuoghi* [1999] QB 818 (CA), so the inability of the supported court to grant anti-suit injunctions (as may well be the case) should not in itself be an absolute barrier.

[43] *Airbus Industrie v Patel* [1999] 1 AC 119 (HL) 138G–H, 139G. However, for examples of anti-suit injunctions being granted in support of foreign arbitration proceedings, see *Finecroft v Lamane Trading* (Eastern Caribbean SC, 6 January 2006); *IPOC International Growth Fund Ltd v OAO 'CT-Mobile'* (Bermuda CA, 23 March 2007). See generally Ch 4, para 4.83 and Ch 7, section G, 'Injunctions in Support of a Foreign Forum'.

5. Powers under the Insolvency Act 1986

Further, injunctions may be granted to restrain proceedings in England under sections 126 **13.23** and 227 of the Insolvency Act 1986; these powers are exercised on application on an interim basis.[44] These provisions, however, do not apply to injunctions to restrain foreign proceedings which must be brought under section 37(1) of the Senior Courts Act 1981.[45] Interim anti-suit injunctions can also, in theory, be granted in support of foreign insolvency proceedings at the request of the foreign court,[46] but considerations of comity may well be a serious barrier to the making of such injunctions.[47]

6. Powers of the Appellate Courts

The appellate courts can on appeal grant any relief which the court appealed from could **13.24** have granted.[48] In addition, the Court of Appeal,[49] the Privy Council,[50] and the Supreme Court,[51] have power to grant an interim injunction to preserve the status quo pending an appeal, as has the High Court. These powers have not yet been exercised to grant anti-suit injunctions on direct application to the appellate court, although there is no obvious reason in principle why they could not be. But in many cases, it will be more appropriate to claim anti-suit relief from the High Court rather than troubling the appellate court directly.

C. PROCEDURE AND FORM

1. Interim Anti-Suit Injunctions in the Context of Substantive Proceedings

An interim anti-suit injunction claimed under section 37(1) of the Senior Courts Act 1981 **13.25** should in general be sought within the framework of pre-existing substantive proceedings

---

[44] Section 126(1) expressly grants a power to 'apply' rather than 'claim'. See further Ch 3, para 3.06, n 26.

[45] *Re Oriental Inland Steam* (1874) 9 Ch App 557 (CA); *In re Belfast Shipowners* [1894] 1 IR 321, 332 (note contra at first instance on this point: 327–28); *Re Vocalion (Foreign)* [1932] 2 Ch 196; *Bloom v Harms Offshore AHT 'Taurus'* [2010] Ch 187 (CA) [16]–[22] (in respect of the parallel provisions relating to the administration of companies); *Tchenguiz v Grant Thornton UK* [2018] 2 WLR 834 (CA) [69].

[46] See eg *Hughes v Hannover* [1997] 1 BCLC 497 (CA) 500.

[47] An injunction was refused in *Hughes v Hannover* [1997] 1 BCLC 497 (CA) 520, 522–24, on the basis of reasoning which implicitly reflected concerns about comity; further, since *Airbus Industrie v Patel* [1999] 1 AC 119 (HL), the court's hesitation would be accentuated. See Ch 4, para 4.83.

[48] Senior Courts Act 1981, s 15(1) (in relation to the Court of Appeal); and Constitutional Reform Act 2005, ss 40–41 (in relation to the Supreme Court); see further Ch 3, para 3.03, n 2.

[49] *Polini v Gray* (1879) 12 Ch D 438 (CA) (injunction granted pending appeal to the House of Lords); *Novartis v Hospira UK* [2014] 1 WLR 1264 (CA). It appears that the Court of Appeal's power to grant such injunctions arises under s 37(1) of the Senior Courts Act 1981, which applies to the Court of Appeal under s 15 of that Act: *Ketchum International v Group Public Relations Holdings* [1997] 1 WLR 4 (CA) 8, 11; *Belize Alliance of Conservation Non-Governmental Organisations v Department of the Environment of Belize* [2003] 1 WLR 2839 (PC) [32].

[50] The Privy Council's power is an inherent power, derived by implication from the Judicial Committee Acts of 1833 and 1843: *Belize Alliance of Conservation Non-Governmental Organisations v Department of the Environment of Belize* [2003] 1 WLR 2839 (PC) [33]–[34]; *Cukurova Finance International v Alfa Telecom Turkey* [2013] UKPC 25 [17].

[51] Under s 40 of the Constitutional Reform Act 2005; see also *Grobbelaar v News Group Newspapers* [2002] 1 WLR 3024 (HL) [25], [37], [62].

brought by claim form,[52] and should be applied for by application notice under CPR Parts 23 and 25.[53]

13.26 The underlying proceedings can, but need not be, a claim for a final anti-suit injunction,[54] which may be commenced in order to provide a springboard for the interim application. Alternatively, the interim anti-suit injunction can be applied for in the context of substantive proceedings on the underlying dispute. Where underlying substantive proceedings have been commenced, an interim anti-suit injunction can be applied for by any party in the substantive action, whether defendant or claimant.[55]

13.27 Where substantive proceedings have been commenced on the underlying dispute on the merits, it is not necessary, as a matter of procedure, for an applicant for interim anti-suit relief also to commence a claim or counterclaim for a final anti-suit injunction,[56] provided that the purpose of the interim anti-suit injunction sought is to protect the substantive litigation.[57] Indeed, where substantive proceedings on the merits are already under way in England, it is more common for an anti-suit injunction to be sought by way of application notice only. The case law permits that such an interim injunction can be unlimited in time, provided it is subject to appropriate rights to vary upon a change of circumstances,[58] and it can extend beyond the trial of the action. In *Masri v Consolidated Contractors*, the Court of Appeal concluded that an application for an interim injunction brought after the trial, sought to restrain proceedings abroad relitigating the merits as decided in the trial judgment, could be viewed as interim relief brought within the context of the original action.[59] An injunction of this kind will have many functional resemblances to a final anti-suit injunction, which is illustrative of the hybrid nature of the remedy.

13.28 This doctrine that an anti-suit injunction can be granted without corresponding final relief has, in part, been driven by ulterior motives, as it allows territorial jurisdiction for interim injunctions to protect English litigation to be founded on the court's ancillary jurisdiction[60] to grant interim relief in the context of proceedings before it (which has not yet been

---

[52] CPR 23.2. See *Masri v Consolidated Contractors (No 3)* [2009] QB 503 (CA) [58].
[53] CPR 25.1(1)(a), 25.3, 23.1, 23.3. This is what was done eg in *Donohue v Armco* [1999] 2 Lloyds Rep 649 [18]; and *Youell v Kara Mara Shipping* [2000] 2 Lloyds Rep 102 [28]–[31]. The possibility of free-standing interim anti-suit injunctions is discussed at paras 13.33–13.35.
[54] See eg *Midland Bank v Laker Airways* [1986] QB 689 (CA) 694H–695C; *Donohue v Armco* [1999] 2 Lloyds Rep 649 [18].
[55] However, without the permission of the court, a defendant may not apply for an interim injunction before he has filed an acknowledgment of service or a defence: CPR 25.2(2)(c). For an example of an anti-suit injunction applied for by a defendant, see *Castanho v Brown & Root (UK) Ltd* [1981] AC 557 (HL).
[56] This proposition is given general support by CPR 25.1(4), and it is clearly established in relation to anti-suit injunctions: *Glencore International v Metro Trading International (No 3)* [2002] CLC 1090 (CA) [59]; *Masri v Consolidated Contractors (No 3)* [2009] QB 503 (CA) [58]. There are many examples of this: see *The Eras EIL Actions* [1995] 1 Lloyds Rep 64, 73 (concerning third-party defendants); *CNA Insurance Co Ltd v Office Depot* [2005] Lloyds Rep IR 658. The contrary was suggested in *Sokana Industries v Freyre* [1994] 2 Lloyds Rep 57, 66, but that is wrong.
[57] In contrast, if the anti-suit injunction was unconnected to the substantive litigation between the claimant and the defendant, then the principle in *Carter v Fey* [1894] 2 Ch 541 (CA) 543, 545 would probably apply, and the applicant would have to bring a separate claim for anti-suit relief.
[58] *The Eras Eil Actions* [1995] 1 Lloyds Rep 65, 74.
[59] *Masri v Consolidated Contractors (No 3)* [2009] QB 503 (CA) [4]–[5], [58], [66]. The Court of Appeal held that such an injunction was, however, necessarily subject to an implied liberty to apply: at [66], [97]. See also *Zeeland Navigation v Banque Worms* (14 December 1995).
[60] See Ch 17, paras 17.57–17.63; Ch 18, paras 18.90–18.92.

extended to cover final anti-suit relief[61]), and seeks to avoid the need to establish any separate and independent basis of jurisdiction for a claim for a final anti-suit injunction, which could be problematic in non-contractual cases.[62]

One question that has not yet been addressed is what would happen if, on such an application for an interim injunction, it became apparent that there were factual issues that could not fairly be resolved at a normal interlocutory hearing. One potential answer would be for directions to be given for their resolution by an ad hoc factual hearing (with cross-examination, or even disclosure, if necessary), within the framework of the interim application, without necessarily requiring a trial of a final injunction. Alternatively, if that approach was viewed as too heterodox, the problem could provide a reason to extend the ancillary jurisdiction to non-contractual final injunctions to protect existing proceedings.[63]   **13.29**

In urgent cases,[64] the application for an interim injunction may be made in advance of the commencement of planned substantive proceedings, which should then be issued without delay.[65]   **13.30**

2. Procedure for Injunctions in Support of Arbitration

As discussed, interim anti-suit injunctions in support of an arbitration clause or an arbitration can be claimed under section 37(1) of the Senior Courts Act. Section 44 of the Arbitration Act 1996 is no longer available for interim anti-suit injunctions.[66]   **13.31**

In many cases the interim anti-suit injunction will be sought in the context of, and to match and anticipate, a claim for a final anti-suit injunction in support of the arbitration. If so, the appropriate procedure is to issue substantive proceedings by arbitration claim form[67] claiming a final anti-suit injunction, and then to claim for interim relief by application notice in the context of the final claim.[68] If only an interim injunction is sought (for example pending the decision of the arbitrators), it would seem to be necessary to put the interim injunction in the arbitration claim form, although for good measure an application notice seeking the same interim relief may also be deployed as a procedural precaution.   **13.32**

---

[61]   As to whether the ancillary jurisdiction could and should apply to final relief as well, see Ch 16, para 16.23; Ch 17, paras 17.08–17.09.

[62]   See Ch 17, section B, 'Jurisdiction over Final Anti-Suit Injunctions under the Brussels–Lugano Regime'; Ch 18, section E, 'Can the Common Law Jurisdictional Gateways Apply?'.

[63]   See Ch 16, para 16.23; Ch 17, paras 17.08–17.09.

[64]   CPR 25.2.

[65]   Where it grants an interim remedy before a claim has been commenced, the court should give directions requiring a claim to be commenced: see CPR 25.2(3), and CPR PD 25A, para 5.1. The interim injunction may be discharged if substantive proceedings are not commenced in good time (even if there is no express order to do so, and *a fortiori* if there is): see *Siporex Trade v Comdel Commodities* [1986] 2 Lloyds Rep 428, 436.

[66]   See para 13.12.

[67]   For the appropriateness of using an arbitration claim form, see Ch 3, para 3.35.

[68]   This is what was done in eg *Navigation Maritime Bulgare v Rustal Trading (The Ivan Zagubanski)* [2002] 1 Lloyds Rep 106 [2], [26]–[27], [49]; in *BNP Paribas v Russian Machines* [2012] 1 Lloyds Rep 61 [2], [11], [26]–[27]; and also in *Ust-Kamenogorsk Hydropower Plant JSC v AES Ust-Kamenogorsk Hydropower Plant LLP* [2010] 2 Lloyds Rep 493 [1], [11]–[12], [2012] 1 WLR 920 (CA) [29], [32].

3. Free-Standing Interim Injunctions

13.33   Applications under section 25(1) of the Civil Jurisdiction and Judgments Act 1982 in support of foreign proceedings are necessarily free-standing. The appropriate procedure is not entirely clear. It seems most likely that a Part 8 claim form should be issued, together with an application notice if necessary, rather than merely a Part 23 application notice. A claim form is required in the Commercial Court.[69]

13.34   It would also be possible, at least in theory, for an interim anti-suit injunction to be claimed under section 37(1) of the Supreme Court Act 1981 by a free-standing application, independent of existing or proposed substantive proceedings in England. An example of this would be if an interim anti-suit injunction were sought to restrain foreign proceedings in one foreign state, in support of proceedings in another foreign state, or in support of a foreign arbitration.[70]

13.35   However, an applicant would face significant barriers to the grant of free-standing interim anti-suit relief under section 37(1) in support of foreign proceedings, because of the general comity constraints which the law imposes on the grant of anti-suit injunctions in support of foreign courts.[71] If such a free-standing application were made, the correct procedure is not entirely clear, with the available options being an application notice under CPR Part 23 and 25.4 or alternatively a Part 8 Claim Form, although the likelihood is that a claim form would be required, as otherwise there would be no originating process.[72] In particular, where the relief was sought in support of a foreign arbitration it would seem to need to be brought by arbitration claim form pursuant to CPR 62.2.

4. The Undertaking in Damages

13.36   As in the case of any other interim injunction, the court has a discretion to require an applicant for an interim anti-suit injunction to give an undertaking to pay damages to the defendant in case it is subsequently held that the interim injunction should not have been granted.[73]

---

[69]   Before the implementation of the CPR, applications under s 25(1) of the Civil Jurisdiction and Judgments Act 1982 had to be made by originating summons: Rules of the Supreme Court (RSC) Order 29, r 8A. Initially, the CPR also required, by reference back to the RSC procedure, that such applications by brought by Part 8 Claim Form: see the old CPR Part 8 Practice Direction B, paras A.1(3), A.2(1), A.3. However, under the current CPR Part 8 Practice Direction A, the use of the Part 8 Claim Form is not specifically required. Further, the wording of CPR 25.4 is capable of being read to suggest that an application in support of foreign proceedings should be brought by application notice pursuant to CPR 23. But the Commercial Court Guide requires a claim form: F15.15. The White Book also suggests that a claim form is also required at least for injunctions: paras 6HJ.13 and 25.4.2. In *Ras Al-Khaimah Investment Authority v Bestfort Development* [2015] EWHC 1955 [7]–[8], the court concluded that a claim form was the appropriate procedural mechanism, bearing in mind the provisions of CPR 25.2(3).

[70]   *Channel Tunnel Group v Balfour Beatty Construction* [1993] AC 334 (HL) 365H; *Fourie v Le Roux* [2007] 1 WLR 420 (HL) [25]–[30]; see also *Department of Social Security v Butler* [1995] 1 WLR 1528 (CA) 1534H–1535A (somewhat ahead of its time). This power has most relevance in relation to the support of foreign arbitration proceedings, because although the Civil Jurisdiction and Judgments Act 1982 s 25(1) gives an express power to grant interim relief in support of foreign court proceedings, it does not create a parallel power to grant interim relief in support of foreign arbitration proceedings: *ETI Euro Telecom International v Republic of Bolivia* [2009] 1 WLR 665 (CA) [79]–[82].

[71]   See Ch 4, para 4.83; Ch 7, section G, 'Injunctions in Support of a Foreign Forum'. It is also unlikely that anti-suit injunctions to support foreign proceedings would be granted under s 25(1): see paras 13.20–13.22.

[72]   See by analogy the position in respect of s 25 of the Civil Jurisdiction and Judgments Act 1982: see para 13.33.

[73]   CPR PD 25 para 5.1, which applies to all interim injunctions.

D. THE PRINCIPLES TO BE APPLIED TO THE GRANT OF INTERIM ANTI-SUIT INJUNCTIONS

1. The General Position: *American Cyanamid* Does Not Apply

The grant of an interim anti-suit injunction will often be decisive. If it is granted until the **13.37** trial of the merits it may well in effect determine where the substantive dispute is adjudicated,[74] since after the English trial it may be too late for any foreign trial. Further, when interim anti-suit injunctions are sought in the context of and to protect existing English proceedings, there will often be no claim for or trial of a final anti-suit injunction at all, with the hearing of the interim injunction being the only anti-suit hearing envisaged.[75] In addition, the grant of even an interim anti-suit injunction raises comity concerns, and can cause hostile reactions from foreign courts.[76]

These features of anti-suit injunctions mean that, with the exception of anti-suit injunctions **13.38** sought on a temporary basis to hold the ring pending a further hearing of the injunction, it will generally be inappropriate for anti-suit injunctions to be governed by the standard principles for interim injunctions derived from *American Cyanamid v Ethicon*.[77] Those principles are aimed at preserving the status quo until trial so far as possible, are dominated by the 'balance of convenience', and only require the applicant to show that there is 'a serious issue to be tried' on the merits of his case for a final injunction.

There is a small number of anti-suit cases in which *Cyanamid* reasoning has been used for **13.39** non-temporary interim anti-suit injunctions[78] but the courts have in general not followed

---

[74] *Apple Corps v Apple Computer* [1992] RPC 70, 76; *Trafigura Beheer v Kookmin Bank Co* [2005] EWHC 2350 [42]; *CSR v Cigna Insurance Australia* (1997) 146 ALR 402 (HC Aus) 437:

> Where, however, the issue is whether a matter should be litigated in the courts of one country or another and application is made for an interlocutory anti-suit injunction by reference to considerations which may fall for determination in proceedings in that other country, the injunction, if granted, operates with the consequence that the matter in question is heard and determined in the court granting the injunction … Thus, an interlocutory anti-suit injunction is effectively a final determination as to where the matter or some particular aspect of it is litigated.

[75] See *Dreymoor Fertilisers Overseas v Eurochem Trading* [2018] EWHC 2267 [48]–[53].
[76] As happened in *British Airways Board v Laker Airways* [1984] QB 142 (CA) 185.
[77] *American Cyanamid v Ethicon* [1975] AC 396 (HL).
[78] There are cases where *Cyanamid* has been applied to anti-suits that would be effectively determinative of the question of forum, but where it does not appear to have been argued that any other test should be applied: *Marazura Navegacion v Oceanus Mutual Underwriting Association (Bermuda)* [1977] 1 Lloyds Rep 283, 286–88; *Deutz v General Electric* (Thomas J, 14 April 2000). Recently, in *Petter v EMC* [2015] EWHC 1498 (QB) [59]–[71], Cooke J assumed that *American Cyanamid* would be the test—it appears without argument to the contrary—but then went on to refuse the injunction on what are in effect non-Cyanamid grounds.

> In another strand of the case law, *Cyanamid* has been applied only where the judges concluded that the grant of the interim injunction would not be determinative of the question of forum: *Apple Corps v Apple Computer* [1992] RPC 70, 76–77 (although Hoffmann J required 'caution'); and see *Golden Ocean Group v Humpuss Intermoda Transportasi TBK (The Barito)* [2013] 2 Lloyds Rep 421 [73] (where Burton J thought the injunction would only cause delay to the foreign proceedings; it is not clear whether it was argued that any different test should be applied). See also the *obiter* statements in *Joint Stock Asset Management Co Ingosstrakh-Investments v BNP Paribas* [2012] 1 Lloyds Rep 649 (CA) [83]; and *Dreymoor Fertilisers Overseas v Eurochem Trading* [2018] EWHC 2267 [48].

> There were passing references to 'balance of convenience' reasoning in *South Carolina Insurance v Assurantie Maatschappij 'De Zeven Provincien'* [1986] 1 QB 348 (CA) 359; but there was no echo of this in the House of Lords: [1987] 1 AC 24 (HL). In *Marc Rich v Societa Italiana Impianti (The Atlantic Emperor) (No 2)* (Hobhouse J, 11 November 1991), Hobhouse J thought that *American Cyanamid* 'provides the starting point for any application such as the present', but noted that 'the Court must also, even on an application for an interim injunction, have regard to the character of the injunction sought'; this led him to reintroduce elements of the threshold conditions for granting anti-suit injunctions as criteria, which meant that, in the end, his reasoning process was far from a simple *Cyanamid* approach. On appeal, the Court of Appeal described Hobhouse J as having applied *American Cyanamid*,

this approach, where the grant of an interim injunction would be determinative of the question of forum: 'it is not enough for the claimants to show that they have an arguable case that the suit would be unconscionable, and for them then to claim, on the principles in *American Cyanamid* ... an interlocutory injunction until the English action can be tried'.[79] Even the higher threshold, supported by some cases,[80] that the applicant for an interim injunction must show a prima facie right to a final anti-suit injunction, is probably insufficient, and does not represent the overall practice of the courts.

13.40   Instead, the case law adopts a higher threshold, although there is some uncertainty as to the right way to formulate this. First, much of the case law on non-contractual interim anti-suit injunctions assesses the grant of an interim anti-suit injunction effectively by reference to the tests used for the grant of final anti-suit injunctions, without reliance on the notion of some level of probability of establishing a right to final anti-suit relief at some later trial of a final injunction, although allowing for the inherent evidential limitations of an interim hearing.[81] This makes particular sense where it is not envisaged that there will be any trial

---

and generally approved his reasoning, but without directly considering whether *American Cyanamid* was appropriate: [1992] 1 Lloyds Rep 624 (CA) 628, 633–34.
    See also, in a domestic case, *Essex Electric (Pte) v IPC Computers (UK)* [1991] FSR 690.

---

[79]   *Midland Bank v Laker Airways Ltd* [1986] QB 689 (CA) 707C–E.
See also *Donohue v Armco* [1999] 2 Lloyds Rep 649 [33]; *Bankers Trust v Pt Mayora Indah* (Colman J, 20 January 1999); *Bankers Trust v PT Jakarta International Hotels and Development* (Cresswell J, 12 March 1999); *Sheffield United FC v West Ham United FC* [2009] 1 Lloyds Rep 167 [10]; *Dreymoor Fertilisers Overseas v Eurochem Trading Gmbh* [2018] EWHC 2267 [48].
In a domestic context, see *Bryanston Finance v de Vries (No 2)* [1976] Ch 63 (CA) 76–77, 79–81.
[80]   *Midland Bank v Laker Airways* [1986] QB 689 (CA) 707C–E; *Sheffield United FC v West Ham United FC* [2009] 1 Lloyds Rep 167 [10]. Similarly, in *Metall und Rohstoff v ACLI Metals (London)* [1984] 1 Lloyds Rep 598 (CA) 613 and *Pathe Screen Entertainment v Handmade Films (Distributors)* (Hobhouse J, 11 July 1989), it was suggested that a 'higher standard of proof' might be required for an anti-suit injunction than on an application for a stay.
[81]   There are many examples of this in the case law, although in general the cases operate simply by requiring that the juridical conditions of anti-suit relief be satisfied, without referring to any lower probabilistic threshold, rather than expressly grappling with what should be the test and concluding that a probabilistic approach is not appropriate.
    See with particular clarity: *National Westminster Bank v Utrecht-America Finance* [2001] 3 All ER 733 (CA) [28]–[29] (not itself an interim injunction); *Bloch v Bloch* [2003] 1 FLR 1 [47], [54]; *Trafigura Beheer v Kookmin Bank* [2005] EWHC 2350 [42]. See the *obiter* discussion at *Sheffield United FC v West Ham United FC* [2009] 1 Lloyds Rep 167 [9]–[11], [21] (quoting the corresponding passage in the first edition of this work); as well as *Dreymoor Fertilisers Overseas v Eurochem Trading* [2018] EWHC 2267, [48]–[53].
    Turning to lead decisions on anti-suit injunctions, this approach is consistent with and arguably implicit in the reasoning in *Société Nationale Industrielle Aérospatiale v Lee Kui Jak* [1987] AC 871 (PC); *Barclays Bank v Homan* [1993] BCLC 680 (CA); *Turner v Grovit* [2000] QB 345 (CA) 357–62; *Donohue v Armco* [2002] 1 Lloyds Rep 425 (HL) [19]–[20] (no suggestion of any lower threshold for interim injunctions); *Glencore International v Metro Trading International* [2002] CLC 1090, Moore-Bick J [24]–[43] (upheld on appeal, (CA) [65]–[70]); *Royal Bank of Canada v Cooperatieve Centrale Raiffeisen-Boerenleenbank BA* [2003] EWHC 2913 (upheld, [2004] 1 Lloyds Rep 471 (CA)); *Seismic Shipping v Total E&P UK (The Western Regent)* [2005] 2 Lloyds Rep 54 [29], [2005] 2 Lloyds Rep 359 (CA) [43]–[45].
    See also, for other examples of cases where this sort of approach has been taken, *Castanho v Brown & Root* [1980] 1 WLR 833 (CA) 836, 856, [1981] AC 557 (HL) 572–77; *EI Du Pont de Nemours v IC Agnew (No 2)* [1988] 2 Lloyds Rep 240 (CA) 244–45; *Arab Monetary Fund v Hashim (No 6)* (Hoffmann J, 14 July 1992); *The Eras EIL Actions* [1995] 1 Lloyds Rep 64, 66–67, 79, 86 (where both interim and final injunctions were sought and no distinction was drawn between the tests); *Simon Engineering v Butte Mining (No 1)* [1996] 1 Lloyds Rep 104 (where, significantly, it appears that the interim injunction was not determinative, as the final injunction hearing proceeded in *Simon Engineering v Butte Mining (No 2)* [1996] 1 Lloyds Rep 91); *Ascot Commodities v Northern Pacific Shipping (The Irini A)* [1999] 1 Lloyds Rep 196; *Commercial Union Assurance v SIMAT Helliesen & Eichner* [2001] Lloyds Rep IR 172, 175, 177; *Al-Bassam v Al-Bassam* [2004] EWCA Civ 857, [32], [47]–[48].
    For recent examples, see *Dawnus Sierra Leone v Timis Mining Corporation* [2016] EWHC 236 (TCC); *Wilson v Michael Emmott* [2018] 1 Lloyds Rep 299 (CA) [36]–[37], [58] (contrasting to [38]–[39]).
    See further n 84.

of a final anti-suit injunction. The substantive equivalence of the tests to be applied is illustrated by the court's willingness to convert an interim application hearing into a final judgment hearing, where it is apparent that further evidence is unlikely to produce a different result.[82] Second, another approach, which has been adopted in some recent case law, is to require proof of a high probability of success, at some (possibly notional) trial of a final injunction, either of disputed central factual elements, or perhaps of the entitlement to the injunction itself. [83] This is fairly clearly the test to be applied in contractual cases to proof of the existence of a binding exclusive jurisdiction clause.[84] What is uncertain is whether it should be applied more broadly.

2. Showing an Entitlement to the Injunction at the Interim Hearing

Under the first 'actually entitled' approach, the applicant for an interim anti-suit injunction in a non-contractual case, where a final trial of the anti-suit injunction is not envisaged, and/or where the interim injunction is in substance final, and possibly where there is a sufficient risk that the injunction will in effect be determinative of forum, will need to show, to the extent consistent with the inherent evidential limitations of an interim hearing, that the conditions for anti-suit relief *are* satisfied. Thus, it must be shown, on the material available, that it *is* in the interests of justice to grant the injunction and, for example (applying the most generally applicable criterion), that the targeted proceedings *are* vexatious and oppressive, or unconscionable (with the evidential threshold for so doing perhaps being the balance of probabilities).[85] It should not be sufficient or necessary for the applicant to establish some level of probability of establishing those matters at a later trial of a final anti-suit injunction, because *ex hypothesi* there will not be any such trial, or not at a meaningful moment. A similar way of putting this is that the court should simply ask itself who has the 'better case' on the material available at the point of considering the interim injunction.[86] There is a significant body of case law in favour of this solution, but the case law is not uniform, and as we shall see, there are a number of recent cases adopting the alternative 'high probability' approach.

13.41

---

[82] See eg *Navigation Maritime Bulgare v Rustal Trading (The Ivan Zagubanski)* [2002] 1 Lloyds Rep 106, [122] (where Aikens J declined to make an order on a final basis as it was possible that further evidence might arise).

[83] See paras 13.44–13.47 below.

[84] See paras 13.51–13.54 below.

[85] The examples of this approach being used in the case law are addressed at n 80. For cases which grapple with the point more expressly, and support the analysis in the text, see *Trafigura Beheer v Kookmin Bank* [2005] EWHC 2350, [42]; and the *obiter* comments in *Sheffield United FC v West Ham United FC* [2009] 1 Lloyds Rep 167 [9]–[11], [21] (quoting the corresponding passage in the first edition of this work). In *Apple Corps v Apple Computer* [1992] RPC 70, 77, Hoffmann J appears to have accepted that this would be the right approach in a case where *Cyanamid* could not apply, because the grant of the injunction would be determinative. Further, this appears to be what Stephenson LJ had in mind, in relation to injunctions to restrain winding-up proceedings, in *Bryanston Finance Ltd v de Vries (No 2)* [1976] Ch 63, 79–80; and see also the judgment of Sir John Pennycuick at 80–81 (however, Buckley LJ appears to have adopted a lower *'prima facie'* test: at 76–77). See also *British Caribbean Bank v Belize* [2013] CCJ 4.

In *Dreymoor Fertilisers Overseas v Eurochem Trading* [2018] EWHC 2267 [48]–[53], Males J adopted a similar approach for an anti-suit injunction which although interim in form was 'essentially final', and where it was not anticipated that there would be any further hearing of a final injunction. However, he envisaged (*obiter*) that 'high probability' would be the appropriate test to employ where the order for interim relief was 'likely in practice to be determinative'.

[86] *Magellan Spirit APS v Vitol (The Magellan Spirit)* [2016] 2 Lloyds Rep 1 [9]–[10].

13.42   Applying this 'actually entitled' approach, where there is some central[87] dispute of fact[88] which needs to be resolved in order to assess the appropriateness of interim anti-suit relief, but which cannot satisfactorily be resolved on the face of the witness statements at an interlocutory hearing, a different framework will be necessary, and it may be necessary to consider whether to make a temporary injunction on a short run basis pending a further intervening factual hearing[89] or trial of a final injunction,[90] which may need to be accelerated. A lower threshold will be required for such temporary 'holding-the-ring' injunctions.

13.43   However, in relation to alternative forum non-contractual injunctions, it is relatively rare for factual disputes to be central to the appropriateness of anti-suit relief.[91] It is usually possible, for example, to assess vexation or oppression on the basis of the essential uncontroversial facts as to the claims made in the foreign proceedings; and the courts take a pragmatic approach to disputes of fact in this context, to make the interim jurisdiction operate sensibly. Contractual injunctions are different, because the question of whether the foreign proceedings are in breach of contract will be often be central and may well involve triable issues of fact.

3. A Test of 'High Probability', Outside the Contractual Case?

13.44   The test of 'high probability' has been developed in relation to contractual injunctions. As will be discussed further, where the court is asking itself at the interim stage whether it has been shown to a sufficient level that foreign proceedings are in breach of contract, so that the rigorous *Angelic Grace* principles should apply, there is now a body of case law suggesting that the binding force of the forum clause must be proven at the level of 'high probability' that this will be shown to be the case at trial.[92] There are also some cases where this has slipped into being the test for the grant of the contractual injunction as a whole, although it is uncertain whether this is right.[93]

13.45   In non-contractual situations, there is now a strand of case law which suggests that, in cases where the grant of the non-contractual interim injunction is likely to be determinative, and perhaps even where there will be no final trial of the injunction, the relevant test is also whether the applicant has shown a 'high probability' that a final anti-suit injunction would be granted at the trial thereof.[94] However, this sort of cross-pollination requires some

---

[87]   Where appropriate, non-central points of fact which cannot be resolved at the interim stage can be left hanging: see eg *Mamidoil-Jetoil Greek Petroleum v Okta Crude Oil Refinery* [2003] 1 Lloyds Rep 1 [201].

[88]   Or perhaps even a difficult or time-consuming collateral matter of law which cannot be sensibly resolved at the interim stage: see *Apple Corps v Apple Computer* [1992] RPC 70, 79.

[89]   See para 13.29.

[90]   See eg *Midgulf International v Group Chimique Tunisienne* [2009] 2 Lloyds Rep 411 [36]–[43], [63] (a temporary injunction pending a speedy trial of whether the contract was agreed); and *CNA Insurance v Office Depot International (UK)* [2005] Lloyds Rep IR 658 [20] (a temporary holding injunction pending a further interim hearing).

[91]   In a number of important cases, the courts have not been hesitant in making robust findings of fact at interlocutory hearings for interim anti-suit injunctions: eg *Turner v Grovit* [2000] QB 345 (CA) 362C–D.

[92]   See paras 13.51–13.54.

[93]   See para 13.55.

[94]   The most express conclusion to this effect is in *Sabbagh v Khoury* [2018] EWHC 1330 [21], where Knowles J concluded that 'high probability' was right in principle, although the injunction would in effect be final and no further hearing was envisaged. But in fact, he granted the injunction on the basis that he was convinced that the foreign proceedings were vexatious (at [44]).

care.[95] Any probabilistic analysis could be strange in principle in those non-contractual, alternative forum cases where it is not envisaged that any final injunction will ever be sought or determined at all, or at any meaningful moment. However, it must be acknowledged that the recent cases have shown a tendency to use 'high probability', although without close analysis, and in *Sabbagh v Khoury*, Knowles J (briefly) considered the point and took a different view to that here proposed, concluding that 'high probability' would be the right test in principle.[96]

Where there are real factual disputes affecting the appropriateness of the injunction, and a **13.46** meaningful final trial of the anti-suit injunction is envisaged—for example together with the trial of the merits—but there is a real risk or likelihood that the grant of an interim injunction may in practice nevertheless have determinative effects as to forum in the meanwhile, a 'high probability' test would be less problematic in principle.[97]

Nevertheless, it is telling that this is not, in general, how the courts have proceeded in non- **13.47** contractual cases where the interim injunction is likely to be determinative. Instead, the general approach in practice has been to require at the interim stage that the court actually be satisfied, on the material available, that anti-suit relief should be granted.

4. Temporary Injunctions to Hold the Ring

Where the interim anti-suit injunction is sought only to hold the ring for a shorter period of **13.48** time pending a further hearing[98] or trial of the injunction, or where there will be sufficiently early trial of a final anti-suit injunction, so that the grant of an interim injunction will not be practically determinative of the question of forum, reasoning akin to *Cyanamid* is more appropriate. It may then be appropriate to grant relief on the basis of there being a sufficient probability of success, pending that further hearing or trial. In such a case, a trial of the final injunction may be accelerated.[99]

The Court of Appeal proceeded on the basis of such a test in *Joint Stock Asset Management Company Ingosstrakh Investments v BNP Paribas* [2012] 1 Lloyds Rep 649 (CA) [83]–[84], but the only alternatives put to the Court appear to have been *Cyanamid* or 'high probability', and they did not need to decide the issue. The use of 'high probability' was also common ground in *Mace (Russia) v Retansel Enterprises* [2016] EWHC 1209, [11] and *Team Y&R Holdings Hong Kong Limited v Ghossoub* [2017] EWHC 2401 [41]; and was used by the court in the undefended contractual decision in *Qingdao Huiquan Shipping v Shanghai Dong He Xin Industry Group* [2018] EWHC 3009 [27].

In *Dreymoor Fertilisers Overseas v Eurochem Trading* [2018] EWHC 2267 [48]–[53], Males J held that the right approach where the injunction was 'essentially final' would be to apply the tests for final injunctions, but he envisaged *obiter* that 'high probability' would apply to interim injunctions that were 'likely to be determinative'.

[95] In *Wilson v Michael Emmott* [2018] 1 Lloyds Rep 299 (CA) [36]–[39], [58] the Court of Appeal appears to have regarded the 'high probability' concept as applicable *only* to the proof of an exclusive forum clause in contractual injunction cases; they did not apply 'high probability' to vexation and oppression. Similarly, in *Stonehouse v Jones* [2012] EWHC 1089 [30], Hamblen J did not necessarily accept that 'high probability' was relevant to proof of vexation or oppression.

[96] *Sabbagh v Khoury* [2018] EWHC 1330 [21]; the point is also touched on in the reasoning of the Court of Appeal in *Ecobank Transnational v Tanoh* [2016] 1 WLR 2231 (CA) [90], although it seems without considering the alternative 'actually entitled' approach.

[97] This may be what Males J had in mind in *Dreymoor Fertilisers Overseas v Eurochem Trading* [2018] EWHC 2267 [48]–[53].

[98] See eg where an interim anti-suit injunction is sought for a short period pending a fuller interim hearing *inter partes* at which the matters can be properly debated: see eg *CNA Insurance v Office Depot International (UK)* [2005] Lloyds Rep IR 658 [20].

[99] See eg *Youell v Kara Mara Shipping* [2000] 2 Lloyds Rep 102, 122, 126.

13.49   In such a situation, the appropriate level of sufficient probability has not yet been clearly re-solved. There are temporary holding-the-ring cases where all that was required is *Cyanamid* or something similar.[100] There are cases where it was apparent that the interim injunction would not finally resolve the question of forum, but the court proceeded on the basis that a full showing of vexation and oppression would be required.[101] It may be that there is no single test for the range of situations, and that the correct test may turn on the circumstances.

13.50   In the current state of the case law we make only some tentative comments. It would seem that always requiring a 'high probability' of success would be setting the bar too high. Thus, in a short run situation where a final factual hearing can be listed in short order, and where an injunction to hold the ring will not cause delay to the foreign proceedings that is in ef-fect determinative of forum, a 'high probability' of success has not been demanded.[102] Nevertheless, even if the interim anti-suit injunction is not going to be determinative, it will still inevitably pose potential problems of comity, as its interim status does not prevent it interfering indirectly with the foreign court's jurisdiction. Consequently, it is submitted that the *American Cyanamid* tests should always require modification, to reflect the special context of anti-suit injunctions, and in particular the importance of comity. Caution will always be appropriate; and *Cyanamid* mechanically applied as a rubber stamp should not be sufficient.[103]

5. Contractual Injunctions

13.51   Under the principles developed in *The Angelic Grace*,[104] where the injunction defendant is in breach of contract, an anti-suit injunction should be granted unless there are 'strong reasons' not to do so. At the interim stage, this poses the question of what level of proof of a breach of contract is required.

13.52   Where the question of whether the injunction respondent is in breach of contract can be satisfactorily resolved at the interim hearing—for example where there is a straightforward dispute about the construction of the exclusive forum clause—the courts will usually re-quire the injunction applicant actually to convince the court, for the purposes of the interim hearing, that the foreign proceedings were indeed in breach of contract, in order to justify

---

[100] *Apple Corps v Apple Computer* [1992] RPC 70, 76–77; *ICBCL Financial Leasing v CG Commercial Finance* [2014] EWHC 3156; *Golden Ocean Group v Humpuss Intermoda Transportasi TBK (The Barito)* [2013] 2 Lloyds Rep 421 [73]–[74]. This may also be the explanation of *Youell v Kara Mara Shipping* [2000] 2 Lloyds Rep 102, 122, 126.
[101] See eg *Simon Engineering v Butte Mining (No 1)* [1996] 1 Lloyds Rep 104 (interim injunction hearing) and *Simon Engineering v Butte Mining (No 2)* [1996] 1 Lloyds Rep 91 (final injunction hearing where the same tests were applied); *Bloch v Bloch* [2003] 1 FLR 1 [88]–[90].
[102] See recently *Golden Ocean Group v Humpuss Intermoda Transportasi TBK (The Barito)* [2013] 2 Lloyds Rep 421 [73]–[74], and also *Midgulf International v Group Chimique Tunisienne* [2009] 2 Lloyds Rep 411 [36]–[43], [63], where Teare J would have refused an anti-suit injunction on the grounds that a 'high degree of probability' that the clause was binding had not been made out, but granted a temporary interim injunction pending a speedy trial of the question of the effect of the clause.
[103] Thus in *Apple Corps v Apple Computer* [1992] RPC 70, 77, where the injunction would not be determinative, although the *Cyanamid* principles were applied, Hoffmann J accepted that they had to be subject to the need for 'caution' in granting injunctions to restrain foreign proceedings; see also *Marc Rich v Societa Italiana Impianti (The Atlantic Emperor) (No 2)* (Hobhouse J, 11 November 1991). Regard was paid to comity when granting a temporary injunction in *Midgulf International v Group Chimique Tunisienne* [2009] 2 Lloyds Rep 411 [62].
[104] See Ch 7, section E, 'The *Angelic Grace* Principles'.

the application of the *Angelic Grace* principles at the interim stage.[105] If this can be shown, then the interim injunction will be granted unless the injunction respondent can show at the interim hearing that there are 'strong reasons' not to do so.[106]

On the other hand, if the question of breach of contract cannot properly be resolved fi-   **13.53**
nally in advance of a further factual hearing or trial (for example where the injunction respondent contends that an alleged exclusive forum clause was not in fact agreed, or that it
can be 'impeached'), it will be insufficient for the applicant to show that there is a serious
issue to be tried as to the validity of the clause, or that his case is arguable or strongly arguable.[107] Instead, the current approach reflected in most, although not all, of the case law appears to be that to justify the application of the *Angelic Grace* framework, the applicant will
have to show to a 'high degree of probability' that there is a binding and applicable exclusive
forum clause.[108] If so, then the injunction should be granted unless there are 'strong reasons'
not to do so.

However, once the relevant threshold of probability is passed for the establishment of the   **13.54**
force of the clause, it is suggested that the court is not then engaged in an exercise of probabilistic prediction of whether at a final trial, 'strong reasons' would or would not be held
to exist, or whether a final anti-suit injunction would be granted or refused at the court's
discretion. Instead, it is simply engaged in determining whether 'strong reasons' exist, and

---

[105] This appears to have been the approach adopted in *XL Insurance v Owens Corning* [2000] 2 Lloyds Rep 500, 508. There are numerous cases where a contractual injunction was granted on the basis that the injunction appli-cant had in fact shown that the foreign proceedings were in breach of contract, without it being suggested that he only had to satisfy a lower burden of proof: see eg *Sohio Supply v Gatoil (USA)* [1989] 1 Lloyds Rep 588 (CA) 592; *Continental Bank v Aeakos Compania Naviera* [1994] 1 Lloyds Rep 505 (CA) 509; *Credit Suisse First Boston (Europe) v MLC (Bermuda)* [1999] 1 Lloyds Rep 767; *Nori Holding v Bank Otkritie Financial Corporation* [2018] 2 Lloyds Rep 80.

[106] See eg *A/S D/S Svendborg v Wansa* [1996] 2 Lloyds Rep 559, 570; *OT Africa Line v Hijazy (The Kribi) (No 1)* [2001] 1 Lloyds Rep 76; *National Westminster Bank v Utrecht-America Finance* [2001] 3 All ER 733 (CA) [29]–[35]; *Donohue v Armco* [2002] 1 Lloyds Rep 425 (HL) [24], [53]; *Navigation Maritime Bulgare v Rustal Trading (The Ivan Zagubanski)* [2002] 1 Lloyds Rep 106 [112]–[113], [121]–[122]; *American International Specialty Lines Insurance v Abbott Laboratories* [2003] 1 Lloyds Rep 267, 272; *OT Africa Line v Magic Sportswear* [2005] 2 Lloyds Rep 170 (CA); *CNA Insurance v Office Depot International (UK)* [2005] Lloyds Rep IR 658, [27].

[107] *Donohue v Armco* [1999] 2 Lloyds Rep 649, [29]–[33]; not appealed on this ground, [2000] 1 Lloyds Rep 579 (CA) [22]; *American International Specialty Lines Insurance v Abbott Laboratories* [2003] 1 Lloyds Rep 267, 275. If an *American Cyanamid* approach were appropriate, then a different approach would have been taken in *Credit Suisse First Boston (Europe) v Seagate Trading* [1999] 1 Lloyds Rep 784, 797–98.
  In *Bouygues Offshore v Caspian Shipping (No 2)* [1997] 2 Lloyds Rep 485, 490, Morison J did use the language of 'arguable case'; but there was no finding that this was the appropriate test, nor was the question of what was the appropriate test discussed. Similarly, in *Rimpacific Navigation v Daehan Shipbuilding (The Jin Man)* [2010] 2 Lloyds Rep 236 [67], David Steel J proceeded on the basis that it was sufficient that the injunction claimant could show there was a 'strongly arguable' case on the existence of the jurisdiction clause. However, no authority was cited.

[108] *Ecobank Transnational v Tanoh* [2016] 1 WLR 2231 (CA) [74]–[79], [89]–[91]; *Wilson v Michael Emmott* [2018] 1 Lloyds Rep 299 (CA) [38]–[39].
  See also *Bankers Trust Co v PT Mayora Indah* (Colman J, 20 January 1999); *Bankers Trust Co v PT Jakarta International Hotels & Development* [1999] 1 Lloyds Rep 910, 913; *American International Specialty Lines Insurance v Abbott Laboratories* [2003] 1 Lloyds Rep 267, 275 (although in that case, the point actually could have been determined at the interim stage); *Transfield Shipping v Chiping Xinfa Huayu Alumina* [2009] EWHC 3629 (QB) [51]–[58]; *Stonehouse v Jones* [2012] EWHC 1089, [10] (where this passage in the first edition of this work was approved); not contested in *Malhotra v Malhotra* [2013] 1 Lloyd Rep 285 [68]–[74], [153], [176]; common ground in *Rochester Resources v Lebedev* [2014] EWHC 2926 [31]–[32]; *SwissMarine Corp v OW Supply and Trading AS* [2015] 1 CLC 1040, [16]; common ground in *Hamilton-Smith v CMS Cameron McKenna* [2016] EWHC 1115 [18] (also using the language of whether the court 'can point with confidence' to such a clause); *Emmott v Michael Wilson* [2017] 1 Lloyds Rep 21, [30] (apparently uncontested on the point); *Dell Emerging Markets (EMEA) Limited v Systems Equipment Telecommunications Services* [2018] EWHC 702 [28], [61]; *Perkins Engines v Ghaddar* [2018] 2 Lloyds Rep 197 [23].

whether the interim injunction should be granted in the court's discretion, on the material before it at the interim hearing. [109] 'Strong reasons' is a matter for the injunction defendant to prove; and asking how discretion would be exercised at trial is less relevant than how discretion should be exercised now.

13.55   It should be acknowledged that in some cases the court appears to have moved from requiring 'high probability' of success at trial as a requirement for proof of the force of the forum clause to regarding it as the overall requirement for the contractual injunction.[110] But there appears to have been no focus on the difference between the exercises in those cases, and in *Ecobank v Tanoh* and *Wilson v Emmott* the Court of Appeal recently restated the test in terms of 'high probability' being the requirement for proof of the forum clause.[111]

13.56   Where there is a substantial dispute of fact which means it cannot be shown at the initial interim hearing that there is a 'high probability' that the forum clause would be held binding at trial, then the appropriate course may be to grant a temporary injunction to hold the ring pending determination of a speedy trial on the force of the forum clause. In that situation, it appears that it is not necessary to satisfy a test of 'high probability', but only a lower threshold. Where that threshold should be set is discussed above.[112]

6. 'Impeachment'—No Separate Test

13.57   Some of the cases, when exploring the correct approach where the injunction defendant seeks to 'impeach' an otherwise prima facie binding exclusive forum clause (for example on grounds of misrepresentation), have used the language that, in order to displace the *Angelic Grace* principles, the injunction respondent will have to produce 'credible' evidence to 'impeach' the clause.[113] If the respondent's attempt at impeachment fails, then the *Angelic Grace*

[109] The approach is common in the case law and is reflected not least in *Aggeliki Charis Compania Maritima v Pagnan (The Angelic Grace)* [1994] 1 Lloyds Rep 168, [1995] 1 Lloyds Rep 87 (CA). Thus, in *Transfield Shipping v Chiping Xinfa Huayu Alumina* [2009] EWHC 3629 (QB) [51]–[58], [70], Christopher Clarke LJ applied 'high probability' to the existence of the clause but then approached questions of discretion at large: at [70]–[79]. Similarly, in *Ecobank Transnational v Tanoh* [2016] 1 WLR 2231 (CA) [74]–[79], [89]–[91]; 'high probability' was applied to proof of the clause, but questions of delay and comity were then analysed independent of 'high probability': at [137]–[141]. See for another recent example *Essar Shipping v Bank of China (The Kishore)* [2016] 1 Lloyds Rep 417, eg at [65]. However, cf contra the cases discussed in para 13.55.

[110] *Midgulf International v Group Chimique Tunisienne* [2009] 2 Lloyds Rep 411 [36]; *Mace (Russia) v Retansel Enterprises* [2016] EWHC 1209, [11] (but the point was common ground); *Impala Warehousing and Logistics (Shanghai) v Wanxiang Resources (Singapore)* [2015] EWHC 811 [53] (but no apparent argument to the contrary). Both strands of logic are present in *Bankers Trust v PT Mayora Indah* (Colman J, 20 January 1999); *Bankers Trust v PT Jakarta International Hotels & Development* [1999] 1 Lloyds Rep 910, 913.

[111] *Ecobank Transnational v Tanoh* [2016] 1 WLR 2231 (CA) [74]–[79], [89]–[91]; *Wilson v Michael Emmott & Partners* [2018] 1 Lloyds Rep 299 (CA) [38]–[39]; followed in *Perkins Engines v Ghaddar* [2018] 2 Lloyds Rep 197 [23]; see also the summary given in *Hamilton-Smith v CMS Cameron McKenna* [2016] EWHC 1115 [18]; and the recent undefended decision in *Qingdao Huiquan Shipping v Shanghai Dong He Xin Industry Group* [2018] EWHC 3009 [27].

[112] See paras 13.48–13.50.

[113] *SwissMarine Corp Ltd v OW Supply and Trading AS* [2015] 1 CLC 1040 [16], adopting the analysis in the first edition of this work (which was based on the earlier case law). See earlier *Donohue v Armco* [1999] 2 Lloyds Rep 649 [29]–[33] (Aikens J regarded 'credible' evidence as at least what was required, leaving open the possibility that a higher standard would be necessary); and see at [2000] 1 Lloyds Rep 579 (CA) [22], [50]; followed in *Society of Lloyds v White* (Cresswell J, 3 March 2000).

In *Mike Trading and Transport Ltd v R Pagnan & Fratelli (The Lisboa)* [1980] 2 Lloyds Rep 546 (CA) 551, Waller LJ (but not the other members of the Court of Appeal) considered it was sufficient in order to refuse an injunction that the respondent had an 'arguable case' that the foreign proceedings were not in breach of the clause; it is suggested this is an over-cautious approach; and it does not reflect the modern law.

principles will be applied on the basis that the court is sufficiently satisfied that the clause is binding.[114] It is suggested that these cases should now be viewed as consistent with, and examples of, the application of the 'high probability' test. If there is no 'credible' evidence to impeach the clause, then there is a high probability it will be enforced at trial.

However, it should be borne in mind that the doctrine of severability of the exclusive forum   **13.58** clause means that there are many cases where a challenge to the validity of the substantive contract, even if upheld, does not impeach the validity of the exclusive forum clause, because the parties' agreement to dispute resolution can be taken to comprise an agreement to resolve such arguments in the contractually agreed forum.[115] So in order to displace the application of the *Angelic Grace* principles at the interim stage, the injunction respondent must produce sufficiently credible evidence to impeach the forum clause itself, and not merely the underlying contract,[116] such that the injunction applicant cannot show there is 'high probability' that the forum clause will be enforced.

7. *Hemain v Hemain*

In the context of family law, a distinct approach had developed from the decision in *Hemain*   **13.59** *v Hemain*,[117] dealing with the situation where a defendant in divorce proceedings in England has delayed the progress of English proceedings by applying for a stay on jurisdictional grounds, and has in the meanwhile sought to progress duplicative proceedings in relation to the same divorce in a foreign jurisdiction.[118] In this type of case, short-term anti-suit injunctions were granted, to 'hold the ring' pending the determination of the English stay application. Injunctions of this nature have been formally justified on the basis that the injunction defendant's conduct in these circumstances was vexatious and oppressive. However, it was apparently assumed that vexation and oppression would follow from the mere fact of duplicative proceedings and the application for a stay in England. This was heterodox: there is nothing inherently vexatious in using the normal procedures of the foreign court; and the mere fact that competing foreign proceedings are likely to be determined first does not make them vexatious or oppressive.[119]

In the more recent case law, however, the signs are that the *Hemain* line of authority is de-   **13.60** veloping in a more orthodox direction. Thus, in *T v T*,[120] the normal criteria for anti-suit injunctions were required to be satisfied, and the injunction was refused despite the presence of duplicative proceedings. To the extent that some of the earlier family cases impose

---

[114] *SwissMarine Corp v OW Supply and Trading* [2015] 1 CLC 1040 [16]; *Donohue v Armco* [1999] 2 Lloyds Rep 649, [29]–[33], [40], [2000] 1 Lloyds Rep 579 (CA) [51], [59]–[65].

[115] For the operation of the doctrine of severability, see *Fiona Trust & Holding Corp v Privalov* [2008] 1 Lloyds Rep 254 (HL) and Ch 7, paras 7.40–7.42.

[116] *Donohue v Armco* [1999] 2 Lloyds Rep 649, [29]–[33], [2000] 1 Lloyds Rep 579 (CA) 592 [50]; *Crystal Decisions (UK) v Vedatech* [2004] EWHC 1872 [32]–[33]. For an example where impeachment was successful, because part of the mistake alleged was a mistake as to the jurisdiction and law applicable, see *Credit Suisse First Boston (Europe) v Seagate Trading* [1999] 1 Lloyds Rep 784, 797–98.

[117] *Hemain v Hemain* [1988] 2 FLR 388 (CA).

[118] *Hemain v Hemain* [1988] 2 FLR 388 (CA); *Bloch v Bloch* [2003] 1 FLR 1; *R v R (Divorce: Hemain Injunction)* [2005] 1 FLR 386; *JKN v JCN* [2011] 1 FLR 826.

[119] *Royal Bank of Canada v Cooperatieve Centrale Raiffeisen-Boerenleenbank* [2003] EWHC 2913, [2004] 1 Lloyds Rep 471 (CA) 474.

[120] *T v T* [2014] 1 FLR 96.

lesser requirements, they may be better viewed as an example of a lower threshold being applied to an interim anti-suit injunction where it will have a merely temporary and non-determinative effect.[121] In any event, to the extent that *Hemain* represents any other principle, it has not been, and will not be, followed outside the Family Division.

13.61   In any event, as the root cause of the problem in these situations is the delay caused by the English stay application, the most appropriate response is probably to use appropriate case management techniques in England to advance the stay hearing, or possibly to dismiss the stay application unless the injunction defendant gives undertakings that he will not advance the foreign proceedings pending the determination of the stay.[122]

E. THE COURT'S DISCRETION

13.62   Any interim anti-suit injunction, like any final anti-suit injunction, will always be a discretionary remedy.[123] However, at the interim stage the kind of circumstances which will be of particular relevance to the exercise of the court's discretion may be different. The exercise of discretion is always fact dependent and we give only some examples here.

13.63   An applicant can usually exercise much greater control over the timing of interim applications compared to final hearings, and consequently, timing is important to the court's discretion. Thus, interim anti-suit relief may be dismissed if the applicant has delayed unjustifiably.[124] Conversely, interim anti-suit injunctions have been dismissed on the ground that they had been applied for prematurely, for example where the court has concluded that a stay application should have first been made to the foreign court,[125] or where the injunction respondent had not yet given a sufficient indication that he would proceed in the foreign court.[126] Further, since the applicant can always pursue matters to a final hearing, or if appropriate pursue a second subsequent interim application, the benefit of the doubt may be given to the respondent where it is uncertain whether it is yet appropriate to grant an injunction, for example where the facts are not yet sufficiently clear.[127]

13.64   Interim anti-suit injunctions have not been refused on the grounds that damages would be an adequate remedy. The case law has consistently taken the view that, at least in general and perhaps in principle, damages will not be an adequate remedy, because damages cannot compensate for being sued in the wrong place, and because the counterfactual consequences of this occurring are difficult or impossible to predict.[128] However, in *ADM*

---

[121] See *R v R (Divorce: Hemain Injunction)* [2005] 1 FLR 386 (where a permanent injunction was refused but a temporary injunction pending determination of the English jurisdiction challenge was granted). Munby J held at [54] that in relation to *Hemain* injunctions it was not generally necessary to show that England was the natural forum.

[122] As suggested by the Court of Appeal in *Hemain v Hemain* [1988] 2 FLR 388 (CA) 393B–C and E–F.

[123] For the exercise of discretion in respect of final injunctions, see Ch 4, and in particular section N, 'Other Discretionary Considerations'.

[124] See eg *Markel International v Craft (The Norseman)* [2007] Lloyds Rep IR 403, [32]; *Transfield Shipping v Chiping Xinfa Huayu Alumina* [2009] EWHC 3629 (QB) [71]–[79].

[125] See eg *Seismic Shipping v Total E&P UK (The Western Regent)* [2005] 2 Lloyds Rep 54 [36].

[126] See eg *Hospira UK v Eli Lilly* [2008] EWHC 1862 (Pat) [11]–[13].

[127] *Berliner Bank v C Czarnikow Sugar (The Rama)* [1996] 2 Lloyds Rep 281, 298; *Industrial Maritime Carriers (Bahamas) v Sinoca International (The Eastern Trader)* [1996] 2 Lloyds Rep 585, 602–03.

[128] *Aggeliki Charis Compania Maritima v Pagnan (The Angelic Grace)* [1995] 1 Lloyds Rep 87 (CA) 96; *Starlight Shipping v Tai Ping Insurance (The Alexandros T)* [2008] 1 Lloyds Rep 230, [12]; *STX Pan Ocean v Woori* [2012] 2 Lloyds Rep 99 [16]; *AES Ust-Kamenogorsk Hydropower Plant LLP v Ust-Kamenogorsk*

Asia-Pacific, Phillips J rejected an injunction on the grounds that the applicant had delayed in seeking it and had for some considerable time taken the approach of preferring to resist the foreign litigation and claim the costs in damages.[129]

F. MANDATORY INTERIM INJUNCTIONS

The traditional form of an interim anti-suit injunction is prohibitory, as the respondent **13.65** is required not to take any further steps to pursue the targeted proceedings until further order. However, interim anti-suit injunctions can also be granted in mandatory form, such as requiring the respondent or defendant to stay, or even discontinue or withdraw, the foreign proceedings.[130] This is sometimes necessary, not least as there are foreign legal systems in which unless the foreign proceedings are discontinued, they will continue of their own accord.[131]

There is authority to support the proposition that the courts should generally be more reluc- **13.66** tant to grant interim mandatory injunctions than interim prohibitory injunctions in other contexts;[132] since interim mandatory relief is more likely to be irreversible it must genuinely be necessary,[133] and it has been said that it generally will require a 'high degree of assurance'.[134] However, as Lord Hoffmann explained in *National Commercial Bank Jamaica v*

Hydropower Plant JSC [2013] 1 WLR 1889 (SC) [25]; *Southport Success v Tsingshan Holding Group (The Anna Bo)* [2015] 2 Lloyds Rep 578 [35].
    For further authority, see *Continental Bank v Aeakos Compania Naviera* [1994] 1 Lloyds Rep 505, 512 (doubted on this point, and others, in A Briggs, 'Anti-European Teeth for Choice of Court Clauses' [1994] LMCLQ 158, 162); *Schiffahrtsgesellschaft Detlev von Appen v Voest Alpine Intertrading* [1997] 2 Lloyds Rep 279 (CA) 285; *Bankers Trust v PT Jakarta International Hotels & Development* [1999] 1 Lloyds Rep 910, 915; *OT Africa Line v Hijazy (The Kribi) (No 1)* [2001] 1 Lloyds Rep 76 [87]; *Starlight Shipping v Tai Ping Insurance (The Alexandros T)* [2008] 1 Lloyds Rep 230, [12]; *Sheffield United FC v West Ham United FC* [2009] 1 Lloyds Rep 167 [22]–[23]; *Steamship Mutual Underwriting Association (Bermuda) Ltd v Sulpicio Lines* [2008] 2 Lloyds Rep 269 [32] (a decision reached at an uncontested hearing); *Nomihold Securities v Mobile Telesystems Finance* [2012] 1 Lloyds Rep 442 [61]–[62]; *Skype Technologies v Joltid* [2011] ILPr 8 [33]; *U&M Mining Zambia v Konkola Copper Mines* [2013] 2 Lloyds Rep 218 [22]–[23]. C Ambrose, 'Can Anti-Suit Injunctions Survive European Community Law' (2003) 52 ICLQ 401, suggests contra that damages can be an adequate remedy. E Peel, 'Exclusive Jurisdiction Agreements: Purity and Pragmatism in the Conflict of Laws' [1998] LMCLQ 182, 207–09, suggests that the courts should consider in each case whether damages may not be an adequate remedy before granting an injunction. In practice that is not what happens.

---

[129] *ADM Asia-Pacific Trading v PT Budi Semesta Satria* [2016] EWHC 1427, [55].
[130] See eg *Hemain v Hemain* [1988] 2 FLR 388 (CA) 390C, recording the grant of an interim mandatory injunction at first instance (its mandatory aspect was not challenged on appeal); *Turner v Grovit* [2002] 1 WLR 107 (HL) [16], recording the grant of such an interim mandatory order by the Court of Appeal (the issue of a mandatory order was only mentioned and not explored in the Court of Appeal's reported judgment [2000] QB 345, 350B, 364F); *Comet Group v Unika Computer* [2004] ILPr 1 [39]–[45]; *Masri v Consolidated Contractors (No 3)* [2009] QB 503 [6]–[7]. A mandatory interim injunction was granted in *British Airways Board v Laker Airways* [1984] QB 142 (CA) 203 (overturned on appeal on other grounds, [1985] AC 58 (HL)), but was stayed until determination of Laker's appeal to the House of Lords: see *British Airways Board v Laker Airways (No 2)* [1984] ECC 304 (CA) [1]–[2] (where the terms of the mandatory order are set out). Mandatory interim injunctions were granted requiring the injunction defendant to release vessels from ship arrests abroad in *Kallang Shipping Panama v Axa Assurances Senegal (The Kallang) (No 2)* [2009] 1 Lloyds Rep 124 [20]–[26] and *Sotrade Denizcilik Sanayi Ve Ticaret v Amadou Lo (The Duden)* [2009] 1 Lloyds Rep 145 [23]–[29]. For final mandatory anti-suit injunctions, see Ch 3, paras 3.38–3.41.
[131] See eg *Evergreen Marine (Singapore) v Fast Shipping & Transportation* [2014] EWHC 4893 (QB) [18]–[19].
[132] *Shepherd Homes v Sandham* [1971] Ch 340, 348D–352A; *Locabail International Finance Ltd v Agroexport* [1986] 1 WLR 657 (CA) 663–64; *Nottingham Building Society v Eurodynamic Systems* [1993] FSR 468.
[133] *Frank Industries UK v Nike Retail* [2018] FSR 24 (CA).
[134] *National Crime Agency v N* [2017] 1 WLR 3938 [89].

Olint, the real question is what the practical consequences of the injunction are likely to be. It is wrong simply to say that because an interim injunction is mandatory in form, a 'high degree of assurance' is required for it. A 'high degree of assurance' would be required if the mandatory injunction would indeed be likely to create irreversible prejudice if wrongly granted, but if this is not the case, it may well not be appropriate to require any markedly higher threshold.[135]

13.67   In a number of first instance cases concerned with anti-suit injunctions, the courts have applied particular caution with regard to mandatory interim anti-suit injunctions, sometimes requiring thresholds such as a 'high degree of assurance' or even higher thresholds such as 'exceptional'.[136] Interim mandatory anti-suit injunctions requiring discontinuance have been described as involving a 'direct interference with the procedure of the foreign court',[137] and the indirect interference with the foreign court created by a mandatory injunction requiring discontinuance of the foreign proceedings may be seen as particularly striking, while a discontinuance could in some cases be irrevocable. Thus, at the interim stage the appropriate course may be to grant prohibitory relief only.

13.68   Nevertheless, if interim mandatory relief is required to make an interim prohibitory anti-suit injunction work, the courts will grant mandatory relief in appropriate cases, and their approach appears to have become more liberal in practice.[138] The first instance anti-suit case law mentioning a need for particular caution for interim mandatory relief has not, it seems, yet fully integrated the teachings of *Olint*, and should not be applied rigidly. As Lord Hoffmann saw in *Olint*, the issue is not whether the anti-suit injunction is mandatory in form but the actual consequences of granting the specific relief sought.[139]

---

[135] *National Commercial Bank Jamaica v Olint Corp* [2009] 1 WLR 1405 [16]–[20].

[136] See eg *Credit Suisse First Boston (Europe) v Seagate Trading* [1999] 1 Lloyds Rep 784, 792–93 (mandatory injunction refused on grounds of comity); *Commercial Union Assurance v SIMAT Helliesen & Eichner* [2001] Lloyds Rep IR 172, 177 (prohibitory interim injunction granted and mandatory interim injunction stood over with liberty to restore); *Al-Bassam v Al-Bassam* [2004] EWCA Civ 857, [30]; *Ecom Agoindustrial Corp v Mosharaf Composite Textile Mill* [2013] 2 Lloyd Rep 196 (undefended), [20], [37]. In *Mamidoil-Jetoil Greek Petroleum v Okta Crude Oil Refinery* [2003] 1 Lloyds Rep 1, [209], Aikens J observed that although a mandatory injunction had been granted in *Turner v Grovit* by the Court of Appeal (see [2002] 1 WLR 107 (HL), 114 (citing the Court of Appeal's order)), that had been an 'extreme' case.

In *Impala Warehousing and Logistics (Shanghai) v Wanxiang Resources (Singapore)* [2015] EWHC Comm 25, [24], a 'high degree of assurance' was required for any mandatory injunction; and higher thresholds were also propounded in Comet *Group v Unika Computer* [2004] ILPr 1, [39]–[45] ('unusually strong and clear'), and *Evergreen Marine (Singapore) v Fast Shipping & Transportation* [2014] EWHC 4893 (QB) [19] ('exceptional').

[137] *Credit Suisse First Boston (Europe) v Seagate Trading* [1999] 1 Lloyds Rep 784, 792–93; *Mamidoil-Jetoil Greek Petroleum v Okta Crude Oil Refinery* [2003] 1 Lloyds Rep 1 [210]. The interference in fact remains indirect, because the order is against the party, not the foreign court. The language of 'direct' interference is a metaphor; but it expresses the reality that the indirect interference created by a mandatory injunction to discontinue may be viewed as particularly invasive.

[138] See *Comet Group v Unika Computer* [2004] ILPr 1, [39]–[45]; *Evergreen Marine (Singapore) v Fast Shipping & Transportation* [2014] EWHC 4893 (QB) [18]–[19]; and also *Mobile Telecommunications v Prince Hussam bin Saud bin Abdulaziz bin Saud* [2018] 2 Lloyds Rep 192, [19] (this was a final injunction but a mandatory interim injunction had been granted at an earlier stage). See also the discussion at Ch 3, para 3.39.

[139] This is the approach applied in *Mobile Telecommunications v Prince Hussam bin Saud bin Abdulaziz bin Saud* [2018] 2 Lloyds Rep 192 [19].

14

Claims for Damages

A. DAMAGES FOR BREACH OF CONTRACT

1. Principles

Damages are, in general, an inadequate remedy for breach of an exclusive forum clause, **14.01** 'since its very nature requires the parties to have their disputes determined in [the chosen forum]. A party to such an agreement should not be put to the trouble of having disputes determined elsewhere in a manner contrary to the express contract between the parties.'[1] In *STX v Woori*, Flaux J observed that 'in cases such as this it is almost impossible to ascertain what the impact might be upon a claimant if, in breach of the arbitration agreement or in breach of the obligation to arbitrate, the defendant persists in taking proceedings in a foreign jurisdiction.'[2] One problem among many is the danger that if the injunction claimant is forced to defend the proceedings abroad he may end up submitting to the jurisdiction of the foreign court either inadvertently or due to the pressures of litigation,[3] which may in turn affect the ability to claim damages for breach of the forum clause.[4]

Exclusive forum clauses are viewed by English law as creating independent contractual **14.02** obligations which have, in principle, the same contractual force as any other contractual

---

[1] *Starlight Shipping v Tai Ping Insurance (The Alexandros T)* [2008] 1 Lloyds Rep 230 [12]. See also *Aggeliki Charis Compania Maritima v Pagnan (The Angelic Grace)* [1995] 1 Lloyds Rep 87 (CA) 96; *STX Pan Ocean v Woori* [2012] 2 Lloyds Rep 99 [16]; *AES Ust-Kamenogorsk Hydropower Plant LLP v Ust-Kamenogorsk Hydropower Plant JSC* [2013] 1 WLR 1889 (SC) [25]; *Southport Success v Tsingshan Holding Group (The Anna Bo)* [2015] 2 Lloyds Rep 578 [35]; and see Ch 13, para 13.64.

[2] *STX Pan Ocean v Woori* [2012] 2 Lloyds Rep 99 [16]. See also *Skype Technologies v Joltid Ltd* [2011] ILPr 8 [33].

[3] A party participating in the foreign proceedings in an attempt to avoid a judgment against him, while nevertheless seeking to avoiding submission, has to tread 'a legal tightrope': as submitted *arguendo* by Peter Gross QC in *Aggeliki Charis Compania Maritima v Pagnan (The Angelic Grace)* [1994] 1 Lloyds Rep 168, 180; and see P Gross, 'Anti–Suit Injunctions and Arbitration' [2005] LMCLQ 10, 13.

[4] See paras 14.15, 14.17–14.21.

obligation.[5] The obligations created include a positive obligation to litigate in the chosen forum and also a correlative negative obligation not to litigate in a different forum.[6] Consequently, where proceedings have been brought in breach of an exclusive forum clause, the innocent party is entitled to recover damages for any sufficiently proximate losses caused by the breach,[7] except where this is precluded by public policy.[8] Damages are available even if the party in breach has not sued elsewhere but has refused to cooperate in an agreed dispute resolution procedure.[9]

14.03   However, there are uncertainties which have not yet been fully clarified in relation to what can amount to a breach, what kinds of losses are sufficiently proximate, and what the

---

[5] *Owners of Cargo Lately Laden on Board the Ship or Vessel Eleftheria v The Eleftheria (Owners) (The Eleftheria)* [1970] P 94 (CA) 99G (a stay case; referring to suing in England 'in breach of an agreement to refer disputes to a foreign court'); *Sohio Supply v Gatoil (USA)* [1989] 1 Lloyds Rep 588, 592 (CA) (an injunction case; referring to 'the continuance of foreign proceedings in breach of contract'); *Continental Bank v Aeakos Compania Naviera* [1994] 1 Lloyds Rep 505 (CA) 512 (an injunction case, referring to the injunction defendant's 'clear breach of contract'); *Aggeliki Charis Compania Maritima v Pagnan (The Angelic Grace)* [1995] 1 Lloyds Rep 87 (CA) 96 (an injunction case, stating that the injunction defendant had 'promised not to bring' the foreign proceeding); *National Westminster Bank v Rabobank Nederland (No 1)* [2007] EWHC 1056 [438]–[439]; *National Westminster Bank v Rabobank Nederland (No 3)* [2008] 1 Lloyds Rep 16 [20]–[27]; *Kallang Shipping Panama v Axa Assurances Senegal (The Kallang) (No 2)* [2009] 1 Lloyds Rep 124 [97]–[101]; *Sotrade Denizcilik Sanayi Ve Ticaret v Amadou Lo (The Duden)* [2009] 1 Lloyds Rep 145 [72]–[79]; *Starlight Shipping v Allianz Marine & Aviation Versicherungs (The Alexandros T)* [2014] 1 Lloyds Rep 223 (SC) [132], [156] and [2014] 1 Lloyds Rep 544 (CA) [19]–[20]; *AMT Futures v Boural* [2018] EWHC 750 [31]–[40].
  See also E Peel, 'Exclusive Jurisdiction Agreements: Purity and Pragmatism in the Conflict of Laws' [1998] LMCLQ 182, 207–09.
  Some continental thinking has treated exclusive forum clauses as procedural agreements only that do not give rise to claims for damages: Ch 1, para 1.53. For academic analyses doubting that breaches of exclusive jurisdiction clauses should sound in damages, see LC Ho, 'Anti-Suit Injunctions in Cross-Border Insolvency: A Restatement' (2003) 52 ICLQ 697, 707–09; CH Tham, 'Damages for Breaches of English Jurisdiction Clauses; More than Meets the Eye' [2004] LMCLQ 46, 60; J Harris, 'Agreements on Jurisdiction and Choice of Law: Where Next?' [2009] LMCLQ 537, 548.
[6] *AES Ust-Kamenogorsk Hydropower Plant LLP v Ust-Kamenogorsk Hydropower Plant JSC* [2013] 1 WLR 1889 (SC) [1], [20]–[21].
[7] *Doleman v Ossett* [1912] 3 KB 257 (CA) 267–68 (although the case is not generally a sound guide to the law any more); *Mantovani v Carapelli* [1978] 2 Lloyds Rep 63, 72–73, [1980] 1 Lloyds Rep 375 (CA) 381–82, 383, 384 (distinguishing *Heyman v Darwins* [1942] AC 356 (HL) 374); *Mike Trading and Transport v R Pagnan & Fratelli (The Lisboa)* [1980] 2 Lloyds Rep 546 (CA) 549, 552; *A/S D/S Svendborg v Wansa* [1996] 2 Lloyds Rep 559, 575; *Industrial Maritime Carriers (Bahamas) v Sinoca International (The Eastern Trader)* [1996] 2 Lloyds Rep 585, 600; *Donohue v Armco* [2002] 1 Lloyds Rep 425 (HL) [48], [75] (although the point was apparently conceded: [36]); *A/S D/S Svendborg v Akar* [2003] EWHC 797 [37]; *Sunrock Aircraft v Scandinavian Airlines System Denmark-Norway-Sweden* [2007] 2 Lloyds Rep 612 (CA) [37] (damages for breach of an expert determination clause); *National Westminster Bank v Rabobank Nederland (No 1)* [2007] EWHC 1056 [438]–[439]; *National Westminster Bank v Rabobank Nederland (No 3)* [2008] 1 Lloyds Rep 16 [20]–[27]; *CMA CGM v Hyundai Mipo Dockyard* [2009] 1 Lloyds Rep 213 [39]–[40]; *Starlight Shipping Co v Allianz Marine & Aviation Versicherungs* [2012] 1 Lloyds Rep 162 (Burton J) [35]; [2014] 1 CLC 492 (CA) [19] and [2014] CLC 503 (Flaux J) [83]–[94] (damages in lieu of an injunction), while the Supreme Court when considering the *lis pendens* issues appears to have considered the damages claims to be sound [2014] 1 Lloyds Rep 223 (SC), in particular at [132], [156]; *Compania Sud Americana de Vapores v Hin-Pro International Logistics* [2015] 1 Lloyds Rep 301 [38]–[40] (undefended); *AMT Futures v Marzillier* [2015] QB 699 (CA) [61]–[62] (tort damages for procuring a breach of contract); *Swissmarine Services v Gupta Oil India Private Ltd* [2015] 1 Lloyds Rep 456 [33]; *Essar Shipping v Bank of China* [2016] 1 Lloyds Rep 417 [31], [74]–[76]; *AMT Futures v Boural* [2018] EWHC 750.
  In *Ellerman Lines v Landi (The Falernian)* (1927) 29 Ll L Rep 15, 22–24, overturned in part but not on this point *Ellerman Lines v Read* [1928] 2 KB 144 (CA) 153–54, 156–57, the courts awarded damages in respect of foreign litigation which was both fraudulent and in breach of contract, but without distinguishing between fraud and breach of contract.
[8] *Union Discount Co v Zoller* [2002] 1 WLR 1517 (CA) [34]–[38].
[9] *Sunrock Aircraft Corp v Scandinavian Airlines System Denmark-Norway-Sweden* [2007] 2 Lloyds Rep 612 (CA) [4]–[5], [36]–[38].

relevant rules of public policy should be.[10] Two main categories of loss need to be considered, namely legal costs and legal liabilities.

The law appears to be substantially the same for exclusive jurisdiction and arbitration **14.04** clauses. Arbitrators can award damages for breach of an arbitration agreement.[11] The court would also be able to award such damages, although it may be that such claims are at least primarily a matter for the arbitrators, and if damages are sought from the court, the claim may be susceptible to a stay in favour of arbitration.[12]

The grant of damages by courts for breach of jurisdiction or arbitration agreements is not **14.05** (on the current English case law) inconsistent with the Brussels–Lugano regime (while it remains English law), even where the competing proceedings are in the Brussels–Lugano zone and within the scope of the Brussels–Lugano regime.[13] It is clear that the Brussels–Lugano regime does not prevent the award of damages by arbitrators.[14]

---

[10] The arguments of principle for and against the use of damages to enforce exclusive forum clauses are considered in D Tan, 'Damages for Breach of Forum Selection Clauses, Principled Remedies, and Control of International Civil Litigation' (2005) 40 Tex Intl L J 623 and J Harris, 'Agreements on Jurisdiction and Choice of Law: Where Next?' [2009] LMCLQ 537.

[11] This is now commonplace and examples include: *Mantovani v Carapelli* [1978] 2 Lloyds Rep 63, [1980] 1 Lloyds Rep 375 (CA); London Arbitration 8/04, LMLN 14 April 2004; London Arbitration 11/06 (2006) 697 LMLN 2; *CMA CGM v Hyundai Mipo Dockyard Co Ltd* [2009] 1 Lloyds Rep 213 [10], [39]–[40] and the *obiter* comments in *Whitworths v Synergy Food and Processing* [2014] EWHC 2439 (QB) [73]–[74] (undefended). It was assumed damages in lieu of an injunction could be granted in a quasi-contractual case in *West Tankers v Allianz* [2012] 2 Lloyds Rep 103.

[12] The damages legitimated in *West Tankers v Allianz* [2012] 2 Lloyds Rep 103 were claimed from the arbitrators, not the court.

In relation to anti-suit injunctions, the law appears to be that standard arbitration agreements governed by English law permit (as a matter of construction or if necessary implied terms) the usual ancillary measures to be claimed from the English court as supervisory court without breach of the arbitration clause, including anti-suit injunctions in support of arbitration—and even though anti-suit awards would also fall within the scope of the arbitration clause and the arbitrators' jurisdiction: see Ch 7, para 7.58. But only the court has powers to grant a full anti-suit injunction, which is an inherently different remedy to an anti-suit award. There is no case law which has yet addressed directly whether a claim before the court for damages for breach of an arbitration agreement could fall within any similar implied exception. Claims for damages might therefore be stayed in favour of arbitration. Further, it remains to be seen whether the grant of damages by the court would be consistent with the sensitivity to the role of the arbitrators demanded in *AES Ust-Kamenogorsk Hydropower Plant LLC v Ust-Kamenogorsk Hydropower Plant JSC* [2013] 1 WLR 1889 (SC) [60].

The case law has not yet taken a grip on this problem. In *Nori Holding v Bank Otkritie Financial Corporation* [2018] 2 Lloyds Rep 80, [101]–[102] Males J expressed tentative concerns as to whether the availability of damages from the arbitrators might make it inappropriate to seek damages from the court, at least within the context of the Brussels–Lugano regime, and deferred consideration of damages. But in *Whitworths v Synergy Food and Processing* [2014] EWHC 2439 (QB) [73]–[74] (an undefended case), Cooke J granted permission to amend to plead a case for equitable damages on the basis that it had been wrongful to arbitrate abroad inconsistently with an English arbitration agreement, although he considered this was a matter that would fall within the arbitration agreement (it is not clear why damages were claimed in equity). He considered that such damages should 'primarily' be a matter for the arbitrators, but envisaged that the court might award damages if the arbitrators were for any reason unable to do so. In *Aqaba Container Terminal v Soletanche Bacy France* [2019] EWHC 471 (Comm) [47], the question of whether damages for breach of the arbitration clause could be claimed from the court or should be claimed from the arbitrators was debated, but left over.

For court declarations as to the effect of the arbitration clause, see Ch 15, paras 15.21–15.33.

[13] See Ch 12, section N, 'Claims for Damages'.

[14] Case C-536/15, *Gazprom* EU:C:2015:316, discussed at Ch 12, section B, 'The Collision', Ch 12, section G 'Anti-Suit Injunctions Sought from Arbitrators', and Ch 12, para 12.67.

2. Legal Costs in Respect of Proceedings Abroad in Breach of a Forum Clause

14.06   If proceedings abroad have been commenced in breach of an exclusive forum clause, the English courts will award damages in respect of the costs and expenses of having to resist the foreign litigation, unless public policy precludes recovery.[15] Despite some initial caution,[16] the recent case law suggests that (leaving aside the effect of the Brussels–Lugano regime[17]) public policy will not create a barrier to recovery in most situations. The main possibilities will be considered in turn.

(a)   Foreign proceedings dismissed on jurisdictional grounds

14.07   If foreign proceedings, in breach of an English exclusive forum clause, have been dismissed by the foreign court for want of jurisdiction, the English court or arbitration tribunal can award damages for the costs of those proceedings in appropriate cases provided, at least, the foreign court does not award costs in such case,[18] or can only award very limited costs.[19] The same approach would presumably apply where the foreign proceedings have been discontinued.

14.08   Further, even if the foreign court has the power to award substantial sums in respect of costs upon such a dismissal, it appears that the claim in damages will still lie, provided at least that the award of costs by the foreign court is not compensatory in principle, although credit will be given for any costs recovery abroad. There is an argument that, by analogy to the traditional exclusionary rule in relation to proceedings in England,[20] a damages claim for the

---

[15]   *Union Discount v Zoller* [2002] 1 WLR 1517 (CA) [38].

[16]   See *Union Discount v Zoller* [2002] 1 WLR 1517 (CA).

[17]   See Ch 12, section N, 'Claims for Damages'.

[18]   *Union Discount v Zoller* [2002] 1 WLR 1517 (CA) [38], not following in this respect the doubts expressed in *Industrial Maritime Carriers (Bahamas) v Sinoca International (The Eastern Trader)* [1996] 2 Lloyds Rep 585, 600, 602.

[19]   *National Westminster Bank v Rabobank Nederland (No 1)* [2007] EWHC 1056 [436]–[440] and *National Westminster Bank v Rabobank Nederland (No 3)* [2008] 1 Lloyds Rep 16 [20]–[27]; see in particular at [24]: 'the Californian court had no power to award as costs more than very limited items of expenditure'. The case before Colman J actually concerned a promise not to sue at all rather than an exclusive forum clause; but he held that the same principles applied to both: [2007] EWHC 1056 at [436]–[440]. See also *Campbell v Campbell* [2017] EWHC 182 [179]–[181].

[20]   The traditional position in relation to prior proceedings in England, developing from the cases of *Cockburn v Edwards* (1881) 18 Ch D 449, 459, 462; *Quartz Hill Consolidated Gold Mining Co v Eyre* (1883) 11 QBD 674 (CA) was summarized in *Carroll v Kynaston* [2011] QB 959 (CA) [23]–[31], where it was held that (leaving aside the case of prior criminal proceedings) damages would not in general be recoverable in respect of the costs of prior proceedings in England between the same parties. The recovery of those costs should be addressed by applications for costs in the prior proceedings under the court's costs rules, and claiming damages in respect of those costs, or in respect of such costs that had not been awarded under the court's cost rules, would in general involve double adjudication. This proposition was not affected by the fact that costs recovery under the CPR (like the RSC before it) does not in reality produce full compensation. The correctness of the analysis had been doubted in a number of cases (see *Berry v British Transport Commission* [1962] 1 QB 306 (CA); *National Westminster Bank v Rabobank Nederland (No 3)* [2008] 1 Lloyds Rep 16 [20]–[27]) but appeared to have been re-affirmed as a matter of binding precedent in *Carroll v Kynaston*.

However, in the recent decision of the Supreme Court in *Willers v Joyce* [2016] 3 WLR 477 (SC) [58] (over the dissent of Lord Mance at [124], [145]), damages were awarded in tort in respect of the costs of prior English proceedings where costs had been awarded on the standard basis only following a discontinuance, and an award of indemnity costs was not a matter the first instance judge was in a position properly to assess. The point was collateral to the main issues in debate, key authorities (including *Carroll v Kynaston*) were not cited to the Supreme Court, and the reasoning was brief. It is unclear, therefore, whether *Willers* creates merely an additional limited, fact-specific exception to the basic exclusionary rule, or whether it involves a new departure of principle. It is arguable, however, that it does involve a new approach. The new rule may be focused on whether the claim for additional costs involves an attempt at re-determination which is abusive.

difference should be precluded by the public policy against double adjudication. But this has, so far, not been adopted in relation to prior foreign determinations.[21]

In *Natwest v Rabobank*, Colman J held that where foreign proceedings were in breach of   **14.09** contract, there was no reason of public policy why he should not award by way of damages all costs that were reasonably incurred abroad. He also concluded that, in the case before him, the foreign costs decision could not create an issue estoppel, as the logic of the costs assessment abroad was wholly different and not compensatory.[22] This result can also be supported by those cases on damages in respect of liabilities abroad which suggest that the relevant counterfactual is where the foreign proceedings have not been brought at all.[23]

The final permutation is where the foreign jurisdiction has costs rules which award costs on   **14.10** an essentially compensatory basis. The reasoning of Colman J in *Natwest v Rabobank* suggests that, even here, a claim for damages should still lie for any difference—for example if the foreign court has declined to award costs on discretionary grounds, or if it limited costs recovery on grounds of 'proportionality'. Colman J thought that if there was 'demonstrable disparity between what, if anything, has been or will be recoverable in respect of costs in the foreign jurisdiction and what would be recoverable in damages in here, there is no policy reason for preventing proceedings in the English courts to recover as damages any such shortfall.'[24] This result is arguably also supported by the cases, on damages for liabilities abroad, holding that the relevant counterfactual is the position where the foreign proceedings were not brought at all.[25]

However, Colman J's reasoning depends, to a considerable extent, on a basic disagreement   **14.11** with the logic of the older cases supporting the traditional exclusionary rule in respect of prior English proceedings.[26] When in *Carroll v Kynaston* the Court of Appeal upheld the rule in relation to prior English proceedings, they distinguished *Natwest v Rabobank* and the other decisions on prior foreign proceedings, commenting *obiter* that in those cases, 'the foreign costs arose in foreign proceedings where there was no possibility of having them awarded in the foreign proceedings if so ordered'.[27] This does not fit with Colman J's

---

[21] Although the point had been left open in *Union Discount v Zoller* [2002] 1 WLR 1517 (CA) [38], the first instance case law has gone on to hold that damages could be awarded in such a situation: see *A/S D/S Svendborg D/S Af 1912 A/S Bodies Corporate Trading in Partnership as 'Maersk Sealand' v Akar* [2003] EWHC 797; *Crystal Decisions (UK) v Vedatech (No 2)* [2007] EWHC 1062 [62] (where *Union Discount v Zoller* was not cited, and the damages defendant was not represented by counsel); *National Westminster Bank v Rabobank Nederland (No 1)* [2007] EWHC 1056 [436]–[440]; *National Westminster Bank v Rabobank Nederland (No 3)* [2008] 1 Lloyds Rep 16 [20]–[27]; *West Tankers v Allianz (The Front Comor)* [2012] 2 Lloyds Rep 103 [77].
In *Carroll v Kynaston* [2011] QB 959 (CA) [23]–[31], the Court of Appeal commented *obiter* that prior foreign proceedings was distinguishable from the case of prior English litigation where there was 'no possibility' of the costs being awarded in the prior foreign proceedings. But the potentially restrictive force of this has now been undermined by *Willers v Joyce* [2016] 3 WLR 477 (SC) [58] which casts doubt on any attempt to cross-apply the traditional rule for prior English proceedings to the situation of foreign proceedings; and see also the broader approach in *Campbell v Campbell* [2017] EWHC 182 [179]–[181].
D Tan and N Yeo, 'Breaking Promises to Litigate in a Particular Forum: Are Damages an Appropriate Remedy?' [2003] LMCLQ 435, 440, suggest that the ability to recover substantial costs in the foreign jurisdiction should not preclude recovery in damages, but should be relevant, at most, to quantification.
[22] *National Westminster Bank v Rabobank Nederland (No 1)* [2007] EWHC 1056 [436]–[440].
[23] See paras 14.17–14.22, where the issue is explored.
[24] See *National Westminster Bank v Rabobank Nederland (No 3)* [2008] 1 Lloyds Rep 16, at [24]. See also *West Tankers v Allianz (The Front Comor)* [2012] 2 Lloyds Rep 103 [77]; and *Swissmarine Services v Gupta Oil India* [2015] 1 Lloyds Rep 456 [33].
[25] See paras 14.17–14.20.
[26] See *National Westminster Bank v Rabobank Nederland (No 3)* [2008] 1 Lloyds Rep 16, at [25].
[27] *Carroll v Kynaston* [2011] QB 959 (CA) [30] and *Campbell v Campbell* [2017] EWHC 182 [179].

reasoning in *Natwest v Rabobank*, which had adopted a broader policy, and it leaves open the possibility of foreign costs decisions having a exclusionary effect provided that the foreign cost rules were capable in principle of allowing for the award of costs in full. Yet the authority of *Carroll v Kynaston* has now been undermined by *Willers v Joyce*, where the Supreme Court has, it seems, qualified and possibly reshaped the traditional English rule in unclear terms, without analysing the previous case law (and with important cases not having been cited).[28] What this means for costs of foreign proceedings is unclear. So, the case law is in a state of some confusion, and we do not know where things will end up. One possibility, in the light of Lord Toulson's reasoning in *Willers*, is that it may be that recovery in damages for additional costs not awarded by the foreign court will only be precluded if such recovery is prevented by issue estoppel, *Henderson v Henderson* abuse of process, and/or perhaps a more flexible case by case operation of the principle against double adjudication.

(b) Foreign proceedings have failed on the merits

14.12 If the foreign proceedings brought by the other party have failed on the merits, rather than being dismissed on jurisdictional grounds, it appears that damages in respect of costs are recoverable in principle,[29] although the same questions as to whether and when the foreign court's approach to costs should have a preclusionary effect will recur. But if the defendant abroad has submitted to the jurisdiction of the foreign court or voluntarily participated in the foreign litigation, this may, although will not necessarily, amount to a waiver of the exclusive forum clause, or a breach of the chain of causation, which may on appropriate facts defeat claims for damages in respect of costs of the foreign proceedings.[30]

(c) Foreign proceedings are ongoing

14.13 The English courts have thus far had no hesitation in awarding damages, and declarations as to prospective damages, in respect of the ongoing costs of foreign litigation which has been brought in breach of an exclusive forum clause.[31] Arguments that the award of damages would be an unacceptable challenge to the authority of the foreign court have not gained any traction, at least in cases outside the scope of the Brussels–Lugano regime. English arbitration tribunals have also awarded damages for the breach of an arbitration agreement in respect of the costs of ongoing foreign proceedings.[32]

---

[28] *Willers v Joyce* [2016] 3 WLR 477 (SC) [58]. See n 20.

[29] *Donohue v Armco* [2002] 1 Lloyds Rep 425 (HL) 443 [75] (per Lord Scott, *obiter*); see the rather more qualified views of Lord Hobhouse at [48]; and see *Starlight Shipping v Allianz Marine & Aviation Versicherungs* [2014] 1 Lloyds Rep 223 (SC) per Lord Mance at [156]. See also *Ellerman Lines v Landi (The Falernian)* (1927) 29 Ll L Rep 15, 22–23, where damages for legal expenses of an unsuccessful defence were awarded (not raised on appeal in *Ellerman Lines v Read* [1928] 2 KB 144 (CA)). However, in that case the foreign proceedings were not only in breach of contract, but also involved a fraud.

[30] See *Aggeliki Charis Compania Maritima v Pagnan (The Angelic Grace)* [1995] 1 Lloyds Rep 87 (CA) 94; *Industrial Maritime Carriers (Bahamas) v Sinoca International (The Eastern Trader)* [1996] 2 Lloyds Rep 585, 602; *Donohue v Armco* [2002] 1 Lloyds Rep 425 (HL) 439, [48] (per Lord Hobhouse); *Starlight Shipping v Allianz Marine & Aviation Versicherungs* [2014] 1 Lloyds Rep 223 (SC) per Lord Mance at [156].

[31] *National Westminster Bank v Rabobank Nederland (No 1)* [2007] EWHC 1056 [435]–[451]; *A/S D/S Svendborg D/S Af 1912 A/S Bodies Corporate Trading in Partnership as 'Maersk Sealand' v Akar* [2003] EWHC 797; *Starlight Shipping Company v Allianz Marine & Aviation Versicherungs* [2012] 1 Lloyds Rep 162 [35], [36], [48], and see [2014] 1 Lloyds Rep 223 (SC) at [156] and [2014] 2 CLC 492 (CA) [19]–[20] (although the appellant did not attend before the Court of Appeal); *West Tankers v Allianz (The Front Comor)* [2012] 2 Lloyds Rep 103 [77]–[78] (held that the tribunal had jurisdiction to award damages in respect of ongoing Italian proceedings); *Compania Sud Americana de Vapores v Hin-Pro International Logistics* [2015] 1 Lloyds Rep 301 [38]–[40] (undefended); *AMT Futures v Marzillier* [2015] QB 699 (CA) [59]–[63] (damages in tort). See also *AMT Futures v Boural* [2018] EWHC 750.

[32] There are many examples of this in practice. For reported arbitral decisions, see London Arbitration 8/04, LMLN 14 April 2004; London Arbitration 11/06 (2006) 697 LMLN 2.

(d) Foreign proceedings successful

What if the foreign proceedings have been successful? It could be argued that the award   **14.14**
of damages would be an unacceptable challenge to the authority of the foreign court, and
contrary to comity. But such arguments have not found favour, at least in respect of foreign
proceedings outside the Brussels–Lugano zone. Further, in *Natwest v Rabobank*, Colman J
did not consider that a temporary stay of Californian proceedings, where the Californian
courts might later consider costs, was reason not to award damages for breach of contract.[33]
Consequently, the current authorities appear to suggest that, even where the wrongful foreign proceedings have been successful, the unsuccessful defendant abroad is entitled to
damages in respect of costs and expenses,[34] at least in the absence of a submission to the jurisdiction of the foreign court, or an issue estoppel or abuse of process arising in some other
way. (The effect of a foreign judgment is addressed in paras 14.17–14.22.)

If a jurisdiction challenge has been made before the foreign court and has failed, it is pos-   **14.15**
sible that claims for damages from the English court or tribunal may be precluded by an
issue estoppel as to the binding force of the exclusive forum clause.[35] However, this will not
be automatic: it will depend on the scope and nature of the foreign jurisdictional decision
and on whether it is recognizable in England under the applicable rules for the recognition
of judgments.

3. Legal Liabilities

It could be argued that principles of comity and public policy should preclude the award   **14.16**
of damages in respect of any liability awarded by the foreign court in proceedings brought
in breach of an exclusive forum clause. But this is not how English law has developed. The
courts have accepted that, subject to the effect of *res judicata* or submission to the jurisdiction of the foreign court, and possibly questions of waiver or abuse of process arising from
a submission (and leaving aside the effect, if any, of the Brussels–Lugano regime), damages

---

[33] *National Westminster Bank v Rabobank Nederland (No 1)* [2007] EWHC 1056 [435]–[451]. See also *A/S D/S Svendborg D/S Af 1912 A/S Bodies Corporate Trading in Partnership as 'Maersk Sealand' v Akar* [2003] EWHC 797.
[34] See the principles articulated in *Union Discount v Zoller* [2002] 1 WLR 1517 (CA) [31]–[32]; *Ellerman Lines v Read* [1928] 2 KB 144; *Mantovani v Carapelli* [1980] 1 Lloyds Rep 375 (CA); *OT Africa Line v Magic Sportswear* [2005] 1 Lloyds Rep 252 [25]. Such damages were awarded in *Mantovani v Carapelli* [1980] 1 Lloyds Rep 375 (CA) 382–84, although that related to a foreign interlocutory decision only. Similarly, in *Donohue v Armco* [2002] 1 Lloyds Rep 425, 439 [48], Lord Hobhouse considered that such damages could be recovered in principle in a case where the foreign action had succeeded, subject potentially to questions of *res judicata*, submission, and waiver; see also Lord Scott at [75]. However, the point was apparently conceded: cf [36]. In *Tracomin v Sudan Oil Seeds (Nos 1 and 2)* [1983] 1 WLR 1026 (CA) 1036–37, the question of costs was not considered; but a defeat abroad was not considered to be a bar to the recovery of damages for the liabilities under the foreign judgment (in a case where the foreign judgment would not be recognized: at 1030–31). See also *A/S D/S Svendborg D/S Af 1912 A/ S Bodies Corporate Trading in Partnership as 'Maersk Sealand' v Akar* [2003] EWHC 797 [37] (where damages in respect of costs were awarded, although the damages claimant's jurisdiction challenge abroad had failed up to that point). Finally, such damages were assumed to be possible by the Supreme Court (subject potentially to ques-tions of waiver, submission, *res judicata* and abuse of process) in *Starlight Shipping v Allianz Marine & Aviation Versicherungs AG (The Alexandros T)* [2014] 1 Lloyds Rep 223 (SC) [39], [132], [156], and they are consistent with the reasoning of the Court of Appeal (at a hearing in the same litigation where the appellant did not attend) in [2014] 2 CLC 492 (CA) [19]–[20]. See also recently *Compania Sud Americana de Vapores v Hin-Pro International Logistics* [2015] 1 Lloyds Rep 301, [37] (undefended).
    However, in *AMT Futures v Marzillier* [2015] QB 699 (CA) [63], the damages claimant deliberately chose to claim damages in respect only of those of the German actions which had not yet proceeded to judgment.
[35] *Marc Rich v Societa Italiana Impianti (The Atlantic Emperor) (No.2)* [1992] 1 Lloyds Rep 624.

should be recoverable in respect of any liability awarded against the damages claimant in the foreign proceedings.[36]

14.17 There has been debate about the right measure of damages. If the contractual forum has been able to proceed to judgment on the merits notwithstanding the existence of competing proceedings in a non-contractual court, then the 'correct' answer is known. In such a case, damages can be given for the amount of any inconsistent liabilities which may arise under the foreign judgment which has been obtained in breach of the clause.[37] But if the contractual forum has not yet been able to reach a decision on the merits, the question arises of whether damages can be awarded in respect of the liabilities awarded abroad without proof, by some form of trial within a trial, that the foreign court has reached the 'wrong answer', which is different to that which would or should be reached in the contractual forum. This was the approach taken in some of the earlier decisions, and in particular by the Court of Appeal in *Tracomin*.[38] But in the recent cases, such as *CMA CGM v Hyundai*, and *CSAV v Hin-Pro*, the courts have mostly taken the approach that this is unnecessary: since the foreign litigation is in breach of contract it should never have happened and so damages can be awarded to neutralise any liabilities imposed without any finding as to what would have happened in litigation in the contractual forum.[39] But they have done so without

---

[36] *Tracomin v Sudan Oil Seeds (Nos 1 and 2)* [1983] 1 WLR 1026 (CA) 1036–37; *Aggeliki Charis Compania Maritima v Pagnan (The Angelic Grace)* [1995] 1 Lloyds Rep 87 (CA) 94; *A/S D/S Svendborg v Wansa* [1996] 2 Lloyds Rep 559, 575, [1997] 2 Lloyds Rep 183 (CA) 189 (the quantum covered by a freezing injunction included potential damages in respect of liabilities that might be ordered in the wrongful foreign proceedings). In *CMA CGM v Hyundai Mipo Dockyard* [2009] 1 Lloyds Rep 213 [9]–[10], [39]–[40], Burton J upheld an arbitral award granting such damages. In *West Tankers v Allianz (The Front Comor)* [2012] 2 Lloyds Rep 103, Flaux J accepted that arbitrators had power to award such damages (on a quasi-contractual basis). Burton J allowed for such damages for breach of a jurisdiction clause in *Starlight Shipping v Allianz Marine & Aviation Versicherungs (The Alexandros T)* [2012] 1 Lloyds Rep 162 [35]; upheld [2014] 1 Lloyds Rep 544 (CA) [19]–[20] (appellant not represented). See also the comments of the Supreme Court in [2014] 1 Lloyds Rep 223 (SC), where no doubt was expressed about the availability of such damages in principle (at [39]) or where they were positively supported ([132], [156]). For a recent award of such damages for breach of a jurisdiction clause, see *Compania Sud Americana de Vapores v Hin-Pro International Logistics* [2015] 1 Lloyds Rep 301 [37]–[40] (undefended).
It has been suggested that if the foreign judgment is in reality unenforceable, theoretical liabilities imposed under it may have caused no loss: *Industrial Maritime Carriers (Bahamas) v Sinoca International (The Eastern Trader)* [1996] 2 Lloyds Rep 585, 600, 602.

[37] *CMA CGM v Hyundai Mipo Dockyard* [2009] 1 Lloyds Rep 213 [9]–[10], [39]–[40].

[38] *Tracomin v Sudan Oil Seeds (Nos 1 and 2)* [1983] 1 WLR 1026 (CA) 1036G–1037C (in the context of an arbitration clause, and as a collateral point while considering the justification for an injunction). In *Marc Rich v Società Italiana Impianti (The Atlantic Emperor) (No 2)* (Hobhouse J, 11 November 1991) (quoted in *Aggeliki Charis Compania Maritima v Pagnan (The Angelic Grace)* [1994] 1 Lloyds Rep 168, 179–80), Hobhouse J considered that proving a wrong answer as to liability was a precondition for a damages claim, which was impossible in the case before him, due to the effect of the *res judicata* findings of the foreign court (the point was not considered on appeal [1992] 1 Lloyds Rep 624 (CA)). Lord Bingham proceeded *obiter* on the assumption that this might be the right analysis in his glancing comments in *Donohue v Armco* [2002] 1 Lloyds Rep 425 [48]. See also *Toepfer International v Molino Boschi* [1996] 1 Lloyds Rep 510, 518. More recently, see the reasoning in *Essar Shipping v Bank of China* [2016] 1 Lloyds Rep 417 [74].
In relation to breach of an expert determination clause, see *Sunrock Aircraft v Scandinavian Airlines System Denmark-Norway-Sweden* [2007] 2 Lloyds Rep 612 (CA) [36]–[42]. For academic discussion, see S Dutson, 'Breach of an Arbitration or Exclusive Jurisdiction Clause: The Legal Remedies if It Continues' (2000) 16 Arb Intl 89, 97–100; D Tan, 'Damages for Breach of Forum Selection Clauses, Principled Remedies, and Control of International Civil Litigation' (2005) 40 Tex Intl L J 623, 653–54.

[39] *CMA CGM v Hyundai Mipo Dockyard* [2009] 1 Lloyds Rep 213 [39]–[40]; *Starlight Shipping v Allianz Marine & Aviation Versicherungs (The Alexandros T)* [2014] 1 Lloyds Rep 544 (CA) [19]–[20] (appellant not represented); *Compania Sud Americana de Vapores v Hin-Pro International Logistics* [2015] 1 Lloyds Rep 301 [37]–[40] (undefended).
This is also consistent with the views of Lord Neuberger in *Starlight Shipping v Allianz Marine & Aviation Versicherungs (The Alexandros T)* [2014] 1 Lloyds Rep 223 [132], where he reasoned, while addressing *lis pendens*, that there was no inconsistency between a damages claim reversing a foreign liability judgment, and the foreign

considering the previous case law, and on two important occasions, at undefended hearings; and the two strands of authority have not been reconciled.

The correct approach to the measure of damages will influence, and perhaps determine, the   **14.18**
consequences of an enforceable foreign judgment on the merits. Working with the notion
that the measure of damages depended on proving the foreign court had reached the 'wrong
answer', the earlier cases suggested *obiter* that if the judgment of the foreign court on the
merits will be recognized in England, even though given in foreign proceedings in breach
of an exclusive forum clause,[40] it would not be possible to claim damages for the liabilities
awarded by the foreign court, as the party who lost abroad would be precluded by *res judicata* from showing that any different result is 'correct'.[41]

But the potential shift away from the 'wrong answer' approach, in the cases following *CMA*   **14.19**
CGM v Hyundai, might produce a different answer. In *CMA CGM*, the arbitrators had suggested that the potential *res judicata* effect of the foreign judgment might be irrelevant, because if the contractual arbitration clause had been complied with, the foreign judgment
would never have existed, and so damages could be awarded on the basis that any *res judicata* effect of the foreign judgment could be ignored. Burton J appeared *obiter* to adopt
the same reasoning, also relying on the principle that the party litigating abroad cannot be
allowed to rely on his own wrong.[42] However, neither the arbitrators nor Burton J were referred to the previous case law to the contrary effect, and this result is controversial, since
it might be said that it is incoherent both to enforce a foreign judgment on the merits and
also award damages to neutralize its result. Further, the specific situation that Burton J was
dealing with in *Hyundai*, where the arbitrators had actually decided the merits, can also be
dealt with a simpler fashion: it was a necessary condition of the arbitrators deciding the underlying merits in favour of the damages claimant, as they had, that they were not treating
the contrary foreign judgment as a *res judicata*, and once they had done so any problem
with respect to damages claims did not arise.

In *The Alexandros T*,[43] the Supreme Court touched on these issues without reaching a clear   **14.20**
answer. The question was whether claims for damages or an indemnity for breach of a

---

liability judgment. But this is not or not clearly part of the reasoning of the other judges, who approached matters
differently: see [42]–[46] and [156].
    However, the reasoning in *Essar Shipping v Bank of China* [2016] 1 Lloyds Rep 417 [74], is more redolent of
the 'wrong answer' approach (again without referring to previous authority).

   [40] As to when and whether this is the case, see Ch 15.
   [41] *Marc Rich v Società Italiana Impianti (No 2)* (Hobhouse J, 11 November 1991), stating (*obiter*) that if the foreign court's decision would be recognized in England, then 'damages would never be an adequate remedy since [the plaintiff] could not establish one of the essential steps to its success'. See also *Aggeliki Charis Compania Maritima v Pagnan (The Angelic Grace)* [1995] 1 Lloyds Rep 87 (CA) 94 (Rix J, who merely said that if there was a submission, then 'all rights to arbitrate *may* be rendered nugatory' (emphasis added); the point was not considered on appeal [1992] 1 Lloyds Rep 624 (CA)); *OT Africa Line v Hijazy (The Kribi) (No 1)* [2001] 1 Lloyds Rep 76 [87] ('might be unfavourable'); *Industrial Maritime Carriers (Bahamas) v Sinoca International (The Eastern Trader)* [1996] 2 Lloyds Rep 585, 600, 602 (*obiter*); *Donohue v Armco* [2002] 1 Lloyds Rep 425 [48] ('may', *obiter*). If correct, this would be a striking example of a case where damages would not be an adequate remedy if an injunction is not granted.
   [42] *CMA CGM SA v Hyundai Mipo Dockyard Co Ltd* [2009] 1 Lloyds Rep 213 [37], [39]–[41]. See to similar effect E Peel, 'Exclusive Jurisdiction Agreements: Purity and Pragmatism in the Conflict of Laws' [1998] LMCLQ 182, 207–09.
   [43] *Starlight Shipping Co v Allianz Marine & Aviation Versicherungs (The Alexandros T)* [2014] 1 Lloyds Rep 233 (SC) [44]–[46], [58]–[59] (Lord Clarke for the majority) [132] (Lord Neuberger), and [156] Lord Mance.

jurisdiction clause and a settlement agreement by litigating abroad were the same cause of action as the foreign claim on the merits and so should be stayed under what is now Article 29 of the Brussels I Recast. None of the judges thought Article 29 should apply. Lord Clarke for the majority concluded this was so without engaging with whether a foreign *res judicata* on the merits would preclude a damages claim. Lord Mance similarly concluded Article 29 did not apply, but floated without resolving the question of whether any damages claim was 'subject to issues arising from the potential recognition of any Greek judgment . . .' or, if the Greek proceedings were defended 'subject to additional questions arising from any potential issue estoppel or application of the rule in *Henderson v Henderson*'. Lord Clarke did say that he generally agreed with Lord Mance on the Article 29 issues but without specifically identifying this aspect. Lord Neuberger, in contrast, did conclude that there was no inconsistency at all between a foreign judgment on the merit, and a damages or indemnity award in effect neutralizing any such liability. But his view was not positively that of the majority. Subsequently, in the Court of Appeal, Longmore LJ awarded summary judgment on the claims for damages, at an undefended hearing, on the basis that the breach of contract lay in bringing the claims at all; it was not necessary to prove a 'wrong answer' and so 'whether they succeed in Greece or would have failed in England is irrelevant'.[44] But since the English court was ruling first, he was not engaging with the effect of a prior recognized foreign judgment and the words 'whether they succeed in Greece . . . is irrelevant' appear to deal with the 'wrong answer' proposition he was rejecting. He did not engage with the difference between Lord Neuberger and Lord Mance.

14.21   It seems, therefore, that the issue of whether a prior recognized foreign judgment would preclude a damages claim has been left open. The key competing arguments of principle are: (a) against damages, the contention that (even if it is unnecessary for a damages claim to prove the foreign court has reached a wrong answer), it is incoherent both to recognize a foreign *res judicata* on the merits, and also to award damages to reverse that result; (b) in favour of damages, Lord Neuberger's opinion in *The Alexandros T* (at [132]) that there is no inconsistency and that the damages claim can coherently acknowledge (and indeed depend upon) the *res judicata* but then neutralize its practical result by a matching but not formally inconsistent liability in damages.

14.22   There is also some case law which suggests that submission to the jurisdiction of the foreign court may preclude a damages claim independent of *res judicata*, if the submission amounts to a waiver of the exclusive forum clause, or a breach of the chain of causation,[45] or means that the damages claim is an abuse of process.[46] It is suggested, however, that no absolute barrier should be created. A party may have no real choice to respond to wrongful foreign proceedings otherwise than by engagement and submission, in which case the cause of his losses is the wrongful commencement of those proceedings, not his involuntary submission.

---

[44]   *Starlight Shipping v Allianz Marine & Aviation Versicherungs (The Alexandros T)* [2014] 1 Lloyds Rep 544 (CA) [19]–[20] (appellant not represented).

[45]   *Marc Rich v Società Italiana Impianti (No 2)* (Hobhouse J, 11 November 1991), ('it could be said' to amount to a waiver; quoted without being directly adopted in *Aggeliki Charis Compania Maritima v Pagnan (The Angelic Grace)* [1994] 1 Lloyds Rep 168, 179–80; *Industrial Maritime Carriers (Bahamas) v Sinoca International (The Eastern Trader)* [1996] 2 Lloyds Rep 585, 600, 602 (*obiter*).

[46]   As floated by Lord Mance in *Starlight Shipping v Allianz Marine & Aviation Versicherungs (The Alexandros T)* [2014] 1 Lloyds Rep 223 (SC) at [156].

4. Other Losses

Where the foreign legal proceedings, in breach of a contractual jurisdiction clause, pro-   **14.23**
duce losses other than legal costs or legal liabilities, there is no reason of principle why
such losses should not be recoverable, subject to the usual restrictions of causation, re-
moteness, and possibly scope of duty. In *Ellerman Lines v Read*, the damages recoverable
for foreign proceedings, which were both fraudulent and in breach of contract, and which
led to the loss of the damages claimant's vessel, included consequential damages arising
from the loss of the vessel.[47]

5. Strong Reasons Not to Enforce the Clause

An important but often ignored question is whether damages can be awarded in cases   **14.24**
where the court has concluded, or would have concluded, that there were strong reasons not
to enforce the clause by injunction. Awkward results could follow if damages were awarded
in such a case. Thus, if there were strong reasons to refuse an injunction because of other
linked foreign litigation that would proceed anyway, and so the targeted proceedings were
not restrained, it would arguably be inconsistent if damages were awarded in respect of the
pursuit of the targeted proceedings—in particular if those damages included any liabilities
awarded therein, independent of whether they were the 'wrong answer'.[48] But on the other
hand, while 'strong reasons' may defeat the discretionary grant of an injunction, it is more
difficult conceptually to treat them as a defence to a claim for damages, which is a common
law claim as of right. If arguments of this kind are to be capable of providing a defence
to damages, this would presumably have to be justified as a *sui generis* doctrine of public
policy. The case law is, at present, undeveloped and inconsistent. The Court of Appeal in *The
Lisboa* appeared to assume that contractual damages will not lie if there are strong reasons
not to grant the injunction.[49] This finds an echo in the case law holding that if the English
court refuses a stay of English proceedings notwithstanding the existence of a foreign exclusive forum clause, there can be no claim in damages in England for the continuation of
the English litigation.[50] However, the more recent cases appear rather to proceed on the un-
tested assumption that, where foreign litigation is pursued in breach of an English exclusive
forum clause, then even if an injunction is refused the damages remedy can lie.[51] There is no
clearly reasoned or binding decision on the point.

---

[47] *Ellerman Lines v Read* [1928] 2 KB 144 (CA). Lord Mance's reasoning in *Starlight Shipping v Allianz Marine &
Aviation Versicherungs (The Alexandros T)* [2014] 1 Lloyds Rep 223 (SC) at [156] is also consistent with consequential loss being awarded.

[48] See D Tan, 'Damages for Breach of Jurisdiction Clauses' [2002] SALJ 342, 360–61, arguing that damages in
this situation would not make sense.

[49] See the comments in *Mike Trading and Transport v R Pagnan & Fratelli (The Lisboa)* [1980] 2 Lloyds Rep 546
(CA) 549, 552; and see by analogy (in the context of refusals to stay English proceedings) *Banco de Honduras v East
West Insurance* [1996] LRLR 74, 85. The point is not clearly addressed in *Navig8 d v Al-Riyadh Co for Vegetable Oil
Industry (The Lucky Lady)* [2014] 2 Lloyds Rep 104 [20]–[23].

[50] *Mantovani v Carapelli* [1980] 1 Lloyds Rep 375 (CA) 384; *Banco de Honduras v East West Insurance* [1996]
LRLR 74, 85.

[51] *Donohue v Armco* [2002] 1 Lloyds Rep 425 [48] (per Lord Bingham: 'may'—but 'complex' and *obiter*) [75]
(per Lord Hobhouse: 'no reason in principle' why damages in respect of costs should not be awarded; but the issues
were it seems not fully explored); *Essar Shipping v Bank of China* [2016] 1 Lloyds Rep 417 [74]–[76] (injunction
refused for delay, and claimant left to his claim in damages).

6. Quasi-Contractual Situations

14.25   In quasi-contractual situations, a third party who was not the original contracting party to the original contract and its forum clause brings claims derived from the contract in a different forum to that chosen by the clause. Whether claims for damages for breach of the exclusive jurisdiction clause will be available against the third party will depend on the features of the particular quasi-contractual situation. In some cases, the issue is unproblematic, as the third party will be, or will deemed to be, subject to the burdens of the contract including the exclusive jurisdiction clause: for example where the third party is the holder of a bill of lading or a statutory successor. However, in many quasi-contractual cases, the third party is not directly subject to positive contractual obligations, and cannot be liable in damages for breach of contract: the Court of Appeal so held in the case of a third party rights against insurers statute in *Through Transport*.[52] In such situations, damages will only be available if they can be claimed on a non-contractual basis: the extent to which this is possible is discussed in section B, 'Non-Contractual Damages'.

14.26   Whether there is a direct contractual claim for damages in cases of assignment or subrogation or similar voluntary transfers is at present doubtful.[53] It is clear that the assignee takes the substantive rights assigned to him subject to the restrictions imposed on the chose of action by the original contract. Consequently, the assignee's right to claim in respect of the assigned rights is inherently subject to any exclusive forum clause contained in the original contract, by a principle of conditional benefit.[54]

14.27   What is less clear, however, is whether the assignee's claim under the assignment can also be treated as creating a positive *contractual* obligation which can be enforced against the assignee independently. The conventional view in the case law on exclusive forum clauses would appear to be that it cannot: the assignee is 'bound' by the exclusive forum clause, but only in the sense that the duty to refer the claim to arbitration is 'an inseparable component of the subject-matter transferred'[55]: no independent contractual burden is imposed, and instead an anti-suit injunction in such a situation is not strictly a contractual injunction, but rather an injunction to enforce the assignee's equitable obligation to respect the condition of his exercise of the assigned rights. This analysis does not support a contractual claim for damages if the exclusive forum clause is not respected. In *The Jay Bola*, Hobhouse LJ (with whom Morritt LJ agreed) was of the view that the remedy for breach of the relevant

---

[52] *Through Transport Mutual Insurance Association (Eurasia) v New India Assurance* [2005] 1 Lloyds Rep 67 (CA) [52], [65], where the non-party's claim was based on a third-party rights statute and it was held the third party was not contractually bound, and so could not be sued in damages (or at least not for contractual damages); *Charterers Mutual Assurance Association v British & Foreign* [1998] ILPr 838, [53]; and see *Through Transport Mutual Insurance Association (Eurasia) v New India Assurance (No 2)* [2005] 2 Lloyds Rep 378 [25]–[28]; *London Steam Ship Owners Mutual Insurance Association v Kingdom of Spain (The Prestige) (No 2)* [2014] 1 Lloyds Rep 309 [136], [2015] 2 Lloyds Rep 33 (CA) [83]. The decision in *Shipowners' Mutual Protection and Indemnity Association (Luxembourg) v Containerships Denizcilik Nakliyat ve Ticaret (The Yusuf Cepnioglu)* [2016] 1 Lloyds Rep 641 (CA) [32]–[33], [56] does not appear to have departed from *Through Transport* on this point, but rather on the tests for injunctions.

[53] In *Through Transport Mutual Insurance Association (Eurasia) v New India Assurance (No 2)* [2005] 2 Lloyds Rep 378 [22], [28], Moore Bick LJ recognized that third-party rights statutes on the one hand, and doctrines such as assignment on the other, might be different in relation to this issue.

[54] *Rhone v Stephens* [1994] 2 AC 310 (HL) 322–23.

[55] *Schiffahrtsgesellschaft Detlev von Appen v Voest Alpine Intertrading (The Jay Bola)* [1997] 1 Lloyds Rep 179, 186–88; *West Tankers v Ras Riunione Adriatica di Sicurta (The Front Comor)* [2005] 2 Lloyds Rep 257 [33].

equitable obligation was an injunction only, in terms that seem difficult to reconcile with a claim for *contractual* damages,[56] and although Scott VC addressed the third party's obligations in contractual terms, it is Hobhouse LJ's approach which has generally been followed in the subsequent case law.[57]

However, much of the exclusive forum clause case law has been developed in the rather **14.28** different context of third-party rights statutes. There are decisions in the general law of assignment which suggest that principles of conditional benefit—by which an assignee who claims contractual benefits can only do so on the basis that he respects sufficiently closely linked contractual burdens—may be extended to allow imposition of independent contractual obligations on the assignee to respect such linked contractual burdens, or at least the imposition of an equitable obligation to accept the contractual force of the burden.[58] If applicable to contractual forum clauses, consistently with the analysis of Scott VC in *The Jay*

---

[56] See *Schiffahrtsgesellschaft Detlev von Appen v Voest Alpine Intertrading (The Jay Bola)* [1997] 2 Lloyds Rep 279 (CA) 286.

[57] *West Tankers v Ras Riunione Adriatica di Sicurta (The Front Comor)* [2005] 2 Lloyds Rep 257 [33]; *STX v Woori* [2012] 2 Lloyds Rep 99 [9]–[11] (undefended); *Aline Tramp v Jordan International Insurance (The Flag Evi)* [2017] 1 Lloyds Rep 467 [40]; and third-party rights statutes cases like *Charterers Mutual Assurance Association v British & Foreign* [1998] ILPr 838 [38], [53]. See generally Ch 10, section C, 'An Obligation Not to Sue Elsewhere?'.

[58] This arises from the cases following *Halsall v Brizell* [1957] Ch 169 (discussed in N Gravells, 'Enforcement of Positive Covenants Affecting Freehold Land' (1994) 110 LQR 346; *Davies v Jones* 1 All ER (Comm) 755 (CA)).

The basic rule is that an assignee cannot be liable under the burdens of a contract unless he is a party to that contract: *Rhone v Stephens* [1994] 2 AC 310 (HL at 316H–317A. In *IDC Group v Clark* [1992] 1 EGLR 187, 190, it was said *obiter* that the only means of enforcement in linked burden and benefit cases is to prevent the successor in title from enjoying the correlated benefits, save upon conditions that they give effect to the correlated obligations. The same approach appears to underpin Lord Templeman's reasoning in *Rhone v Stephens*, at 317F–318C, 322E–G. On this approach, there is no independent contractual obligation, and the correlated burden is enforced indirectly.

The question that arises, however, is whether such conditions can be imposed retrospectively on someone who has chosen to exercise the correlated benefit, where there is no prior occasion for putting them to their election as to whether to renounce the benefit or accept the condition. In a number of subsequent cases it has apparently been assumed that an assignee would become liable to perform appropriately linked burdens as independent contractual obligations, if he had elected to claim the linked benefits: see *Baybut v Eccles Rigg Country Park* (*Times*, 13 November 2006) [58]–[59]; *Thamesmead v Allotey* (2000) 79 P & CR 557 (CA) 564–65 (*obiter*); *Elwood v Goodman* [2014] 2 WLR 967 (CA) [24]–[31]; *Budana v Leeds Teaching Hospitals NHS Trust* [2018] 1 WLR 1965, [53] (*obiter*); and previously see *Elliston v Reacher* [1908] 2 Ch 665 (CA) 669 (*obiter* only). But the difference between the two approaches was in general not directly confronted.

In *Davies v Jones* [2010] 1 All ER (Comm) 755 [32]–[33], the Court of Appeal left open the possibility that the court would impose independent obligations, enforceable by a separate action, to perform correlated burdens, and doubted the comments in *IDC v Clark*. One jurisprudential mechanism envisaged in *Davies v Jones* was the imposition of a restitutionary obligation to pay for the benefit of the services received. But a neater and more coherent solution may be that the person who takes the linked benefit is obliged in equity to recognize the contractual force of the linked burden: this may be the analysis adopted in *Elwood v Goodman* [2014] 2 WLR 967 (CA) [24]–[31]; and *Budana v Leeds Teaching Hospitals NHS Trust* [2018] 1 WLR 1965 [53] (*obiter*).

However, it is unclear whether any such independent obligation doctrine, going beyond a purer conditional benefit analysis as per *IDC v Clark*, can be reconciled with *Rhone v Stephens* and the traditional rule that contractual burdens may not be imposed on assignors. And even if such a doctrine of positive obligation is sound in general, it is unclear whether it can apply to exclusive forum clauses, in particular in a situation where the damages defendant has claimed his positive rights abroad. As already discussed, the existing case law on assignment and exclusive forum clauses has as yet not adopted such an independent obligation analysis (with the partial exception of Scott VC's minority analysis in *The Jay Bola*): see para 14.27.

Longmore LJ in *The Yusuf Cepnioglu* regarded the principle in *Halsall v Brizell* as applying to contractual forum clauses, and to a third party claiming under a third-party rights statute, such that that party was 'bound' by the exclusive forum clause in a way sufficient to justify an injunction: *Shipowners' Mutual Protection and Indemnity Association (Luxembourg) v Containerships Denizcilik Nakliyat ve Ticaret (The Yusuf Cepnioglu)* [2016] 1 Lloyds Rep 641 (CA) [24]. But he was not focusing on damages, nor on an analysis under which the contractual forum clause became treated as independently binding, and he treated *both* Hobhouse LJ and Scott VC's analyses in *The Jay Bola* as correct.

Bola,[59] this approach could allow claims for *contractual* damages for breach of the forum clause in the quasi-contractual situation, at least in cases of assignment and similar voluntary transfers governed by the same equities.

14.29   The alternative possibility is that the equitable obligations imposed on the third party to respect the clause might themselves found a claim for equitable compensation or damages if the clause is not respected. This idea is addressed under 'Non-Contractual Damages' in section B. In the thin strand of case law in which damages have so far been awarded in quasi-contractual situations, it is this approach, not a contractual damages approach, which has been adopted.

B. NON-CONTRACTUAL DAMAGES

14.30   The possibility of awarding damages in respect of losses suffered as a result of supposedly 'wrongful' foreign proceedings which are not in breach of contract is territory which has only recently begun to be explored. There are three possible routes: damages in tort; damages or compensation in equity; or damages in lieu of an injunction under section 50 of the Supreme Court Act 1981.

1. Damages in Tort

14.31   Claims for damages in tort in respect of allegedly wrongful proceedings abroad are unlikely to be relevant in most situations. First of all, there are difficulties in showing that English law is the applicable law for any such tort. Second, with certain limited exceptions, the available tortious causes of action under English law do not seem to be relevant to, or capable of supporting, claims for damages for wrongful foreign litigation.

14.32   The relevant choice of law rules are contained in the Rome II Regulation.[60] Article 4(1) stipulates that the primary choice of law rule applies to the place where the direct damage occurred, which is likely to be the place where the allegedly wrongful litigation was pursued. Under Article 4(3), this primary rule can be displaced if the tort is 'manifestly more closely connected' with another country, but the European Court of Justice (ECJ) might not accept that the place where the litigation 'should' have happened is manifestly more closely connected to the tort than the place where it did happen.[61] One case that may demand a different treatment is the tort of inducing a breach of contract: there is force in the suggestion that such a tortious claim is manifestly more connected to the law of the contract.

---

[59] *Schiffahrtsgesellschaft Detlev von Appen v Voest Alpine Intertrading (The Jay Bola)* [1997] 2 Lloyds Rep 279 (CA) 291.

[60] EC Regulation No 864/2007 on the law applicable to non-contractual obligations (Rome II). As matters stand, the Rome I and Rome II Regulations appear likely to remain part of English conflicts rules, at least in substance, irrespective of how Brexit is resolved. See Ch 1, Section I, 'Brexit'.

[61] See, by analogy, the reasoning of Langley J in *OT Africa Line v Magic Sportswear* [2005] 1 Lloyds Rep 252 [19]–[24]; and the similar reasoning in *Congentra v Sixteen Thirteen Marine (The Nicholas M)* [2008] 2 Lloyds Rep 602 [18]–[19]. This is also consistent with the reasoning of the Court of Appeal and Supreme Court on the similar question of the application of Article 7(3) of the Brussels I Recast in *AMT Futures v Marzillier* [2015] QB 699 (CA) [49]–[58], [2018] AC 439 (SC) [25]–[27].

If, however, the law of the place of litigation is applicable, then any claim in tort will generally be either self-defeating or pointless, because in the rare cases where a foreign court might accept that the bringing of litigation before it is actionably wrongful,[62] it will usually itself provide procedural remedies to resolve the problem.   **14.33**

Even where choice of law difficulties could be surmounted, there would remain the problem   **14.34** in many situations of identifying a workable tort under English law. The tort of malicious prosecution, which now applies to civil proceedings generally,[63] requires that the criticized proceedings must have been brought maliciously and without reasonable and probable cause,[64] and must have failed.[65] Under the existing authorities, the same conditions apply in relation to foreign proceedings, so that if the claimant abroad has succeeded in his foreign proceedings, no cause of action will lie under English law.[66] The tort of abuse of civil proceedings, if it exists as a separate tort and generally,[67] has traditionally required the criticized proceedings to have been for an improper collateral purpose, which must be a purpose other than success in the action, although it may now best be viewed as merely an example of malicious prosecution and so require malice.[68] These limitations mean that those torts, even if they can be extended to proceedings abroad, cannot support general tortious liability for objectively vexatious and oppressive litigation abroad: there are many situations

---

[62] See eg *OT Africa Line v Magic Sportswear* [2005] 1 Lloyds Rep 252, 256, where an argument that the tort of inducing a breach of contract could be made out under Canadian law in respect of litigation that the Canadian courts had refused to stay was thought to be 'fanciful'.

[63] It had previously been understood that the tort was confined to criminal proceedings, and certain limited categories of civil proceedings: *Martin v Watson* [1996] 1 AC 74 (HL) 78; *Gregory v Portsmouth City Council* [2000] 1 AC 419 (HL) 432–33; *Crawford v Jenkins* [2016] QB 231 [48]–[49]. However, this has now changed following *Crawford Adjusters (Cayman) Ltd v Sagicor General Insurance (Cayman) Ltd* [2014] AC 366 (PC) and *Willers v Joyce* [2016] 3 WLR 477 (SC).

[64] *Martin v Watson* [1996] 1 AC 74 (HL) 80; *Crawford Adjusters (Cayman) v Sagicor General Insurance (Cayman)* [2014] AC 366 (PC) [45], [55], [57]–[58], [105], [119], 129; *Willers v Joyce* [2016] 3 WLR 477 (SC) [54].

[65] *Castrique v Behrens* (1861) 3 El & El 709, 121 ER 608, 613; *Basebé v Matthews* (1867) LR 2 CP 684; *Bynoe v Governor and Company of the Bank of England* [1902] 1 KB 467 (CA); *Everett v Ribbands* [1952] 2 QB 198 (CA); *Crawford Adjusters (Cayman) v Sagicor General Insurance (Cayman)* [2014] AC 366 (PC) [129]. The restriction that the previous proceedings must have failed applies only to substantive foreign proceedings which determine the merits, not to *ex parte* applications or attachments: *Congentra v Sixteen Thirteen Marine (The Nicholas M)* [2008] 2 Lloyds Rep 602 [38]–[44].

[66] *Castrique v Behrens* (1861) 3 El & El 709, 121 ER 608, 613; *Taylor v Ford* (1872) 29 LT 390.

[67] The existence of this tort is open to question. Historically, there was only a thin basis of authority to support it: see *Grainger v Hill* (1838) 4 Bing (NC) 212, 132 ER 767, 773–74; *Parton v Hill* (1864) 10 LT 414; *Goldsmith v Sperrings* [1977] 1 WLR 478 (CA) 489H, 498; *Speed Seal Products v Paddington* [1985] 1 WLR 1327 (CA); *Metall und Rohstoff v Donaldson, Lufkin & Jenrette* [1990] 1 QB 391 (CA) 469–70; *British Airways Board v Laker Airways* [1985] AC 58 (HL) 65E (concession in argument); and there was also authority to the contrary: see *De Medina v Grove* (1847) 10 QB 172, 116 ER 66; *Powell v Hoyland* (1851) 6 Exch 67, 155 ER 456, 459; *Digital Equipment v Darkcrest* [1984] Ch 512, 522–24. In *Land Securities v Fladgate Fielder* [2010] Ch 467 (CA) [67]–[70], [73], [77]–[78], [95]–[101], [113], the Court of Appeal observed that the tort had never been extended beyond the cases of compulsion by arrest, imprisonment, or other forms of duress, and held that it did not apply to judicial review proceedings; leaving undecided whether it could have any broader application in other civil proceedings. They also confined the recoverable loss to injury to person, damage to property, and damage to reputation. However, in *Crawford Adjusters (Cayman) v Sagicor General Insurance (Cayman)* [2014] AC 366 (PC) [62]–[66], [149]–[158], the Privy Council concluded that the tort of abuse of process could allow recovery of economic loss; and apparently assumed, without engaging with the contrary decision in *Land Securities* in this respect, that such a tort could be of general application to civil proceedings. Most recently, the reasoning in *Willers v Joyce* would also suggest that any such tort is not confined to particular civil proceedings, by extension of the new position for malicious prosecution; but Lord Toulson's *obiter* comments equally imply that the tort of abuse of civil process is not distinct to, and is merely an example of, the tort of malicious prosecution: *Willers v Joyce* [2016] 3 WLR 477 (SC) [25]. However, again *Land Securities* was not engaged with.

[68] *Crawford Adjusters (Cayman) v Sagicor General Insurance (Cayman)* [2014] AC 366 (PC) [62]–[66], [79]; *Willers v Joyce* [2016] 3 WLR 477 (SC) [23]–[25].

which the courts have been willing to call vexatious or oppressive for the purposes of the grant of an anti-suit injunction which go beyond the possible boundaries of such torts. It will also be arguable that, as a matter of public policy, such torts should in modern circumstances only be applicable to litigation in England, as foreign legal systems should in general have their own appropriate remedies to prevent malicious or abusive proceedings.[69]

14.35 Other tortious causes of action, such as misrepresentation, which do not directly target vexatious or oppressive foreign litigation, could theoretically overlap in unusual factual situations.[70]

14.36 It is therefore unsurprising that general non-contractual anti-suit injunctions have not in practice been based upon tortious causes of action.

2. Inducing a Breach of Contract and the Economic Torts

14.37 The tort of inducing a breach of contract, and possibly some of the other economic torts, may form a limited exception. In particular, where an exclusive forum clause is binding between A and B and a third party, C, who is in practical control of B, has directed B to breach the exclusive forum clause, some judges have accepted that anti-suit injunctions, or claims for damages, could be founded on the tort of inducing breach of contract, or possibly other economic torts.[71]

14.38 However, for this line of reasoning to work, the choice of law problem would need to be surmounted. In *OT Africa Line v Magic Sportswear*, Langley J faced an application to serve an

---

[69] It was argued in *British Airways Board v Laker Airways* [1985] AC 58 (HL) 65E–F that the tort of abuse of civil proceedings was confined to proceedings within the jurisdiction, but the point appears not to have engaged their Lordships' interest. In *Research in Motion UK v Visto* [2008] ILPr 34 (CA), Lewison J considered a claim for a defence to infringement of a patent, and a counterclaim for damage, on the basis that prior parallel Italian proceedings were an abuse of process. The damages claim was stayed under Article 28 of the Brussels I Regulation, and in relation to the defence, Lewison J observed that 'It is no part of the function of an English court to investigate whether the process of a foreign court has been abused' [28]. This suggests that a claim for damages for an abuse of civil process in the foreign court would not have been well received. See also the brief *obiter* comments of the Court of Appeal at [2008] ILPr 34 [40].

CH Tham, 'Damages for Breaches of English Jurisdiction Clauses; More than Meets the Eye' [2004] LMCLQ 46, 62, suggests that it is possible the tort might be extended to cover civil proceedings maliciously brought in non-English courts in breach of an exclusive jurisdiction clause.

[70] Possible examples of this are the tort of malicious falsehood, the tort of deceit or fraudulent misrepresentation, and also the economic torts (as to which see paras 14.37–14.40). In *A/S D/S Svendborg v Wansa* [1996] 2 Lloyds Rep 559, 562, 575, [1997] 2 Lloyd Rep 183 (CA) 189, the claimants claimed damages for fraudulent misrepresentation (as well as breach of contract) arising out of alleged forgeries which gave rise to a fraudulent cargo claim that was pursued before the courts of Sierra Leone. Clarke J upheld the grant of a freezing injunction against the defendants, under which the amount secured included damages claimed in respect of the costs and liabilities arising out of the Sierra Leone proceedings. Clarke J appears to have thought that this 'potential liability' was not incoherent in principle; although he may only have been thinking of the contractual claims made. In *Kallang Shipping Panama v Axa Assurances Senegal (The Kallang) (No 2)* [2009] 1 Lloyds Rep 124 [90]–[94], an alternative claim for unlawful interference in business relations was dismissed on the grounds that it added nothing to a claim for inducement of breach of contract [94], and a claim for conspiracy was rejected on the facts [96]; see also the parallel decision in *Sotrade Denizcilik Sanayi Ve Ticaret v Amadou Lo (The Duden)* [2009] 1 Lloyds Rep 145 [65]–[70].

[71] *Kallang Shipping v Axa Assurances Senegal (The Kallang)* [2007] 1 Lloyds Rep 160 [41]; *Horn Linie v Panamericana Formas e Impresos (The Hornbay)* [2006] 2 Lloyds Rep 44, [26]; *Kallang Shipping Panama v Axa Assurances Senegal (The Kallang) (No 2)* [2009] 1 Lloyds Rep 124 [90]–[94]; and *Sotrade Denizcilik Sanayi Ve Ticaret v Amadou Lo (The Duden)* [2009] 1 Lloyds Rep 145 [65]–[70]. However, the choice of law problem was not raised in these cases.

anti-suit injunction out of the jurisdiction, on the contractual party to the exclusive forum clause, who had breached the clause by commencing proceedings in Canada, and also on its third-party insurers. One of the bases for the injunction against the third-party insurers was the tort of inducing a breach of contract.[72] The judge applied the Private International Law (Miscellaneous Provisions) Act and concluded that under section 11, the 'most significant elements' of the tort occurred in Canada, where the insurers caused their insured to issue the proceedings. The claimants did not argue it was more appropriate for English law to apply under section 12; the judge observed that in his view they were right not to do so.[73] As a result Canadian law applied; and Langley J refused to accept that Canadian law would treat the Canadian proceedings as tortious, in a case where Canadian law treated the exclusive jurisdiction clause as non-binding. Had Langley J been considering the Rome II Regulation, it seems likely that he would have concluded that Canadian law applied under it as well.

This result is debatable; and even if correct it may not apply in all cases. It could be said that steps by insurers to manipulate a breach of an English exclusive forum clause are 'manifestly more closely connected' to England than to the place where the litigation occurs because of the connection with the forum clause, and therefore that Article 4(3) of the Rome II Regulation should displace the general rule in Article 4(1). If the third party or the contractual party had connections to England, then that could provide further support for applying Article 4(3).[74] There might also be cases where the third party's conduct was wrongful under the foreign law. **14.39**

In a number of subsequent cases, it has been assumed or held that the tort of inducing a breach of contract can support a claim for damages against a third party who has induced a breach of an English jurisdiction clause, applying English law, but the issue of choice of law was seemingly not raised.[75] **14.40**

3. Compensation in Equity

Monetary compensation (and possibly damages in equity[76]) can be awarded in equity for infringements of equitable rights, independent of section 50 of the Supreme **14.41**

---

[72] There was an alternative basis for relief against the insurers, which succeeded, namely the doctrine that there is jurisdiction to injunct those who threaten or intend to assist others to breach an injunction: see at [37].

[73] In *OT Africa Line v Magic Sportswear Corp* [2005] 1 Lloyds Rep 252 [19]–[25]. See also by analogy *Congentra v Sixteen Thirteen Marine (The Nicholas M)* [2008] 2 Lloyds Rep 602 [18]–[19].

[74] If both damages claimant and damages defendant were resident in the same country, then the law of that country will apply under Article 4(2), unless displaced by Article 4(3).

[75] In *AMT Futures v Marzillier* [2015] QB 699 (CA), the Court of Appeal assumed but did not decide (at [61]–[62]) that a tortious damages claim for inducing a breach of a contractual jurisdiction clause was an available claim in principle but questions of choice of law were not considered. Similarly, in *Kallang Shipping Panama v Axa Assurances Senegal (The Kallang) (No 2)* [2009] 1 Lloyds Rep 124 [90]–[94] and *Sotrade Denizcilik Sanayi Ve Ticaret AS v Amadou Lo (The Duden)* [2009] 1 Lloyds Rep 145 [65]–[70] damages claims for tortious inducement of a breach of contract were upheld but, as the Judge noted, it was assumed that English law applied. See also similarly *Kallang Shipping v Axa Assurances Senegal (The Kallang)* [2007] 1 Lloyds Rep 160 [41]; *Horn Linie GmbH v Panamericana Formas e Impresos (The Hornbay)* [2006] 2 Lloyds Rep 44 [26].

[76] It is probably better to refer to the remedy as one for equitable compensation rather than equitable damages, outside s 50 of the Senior Courts Act 1981. See *Target Holding v Redferns* [1996] AC 421, 434, 438–39; *Vestergaard Frandsen v BestNet Europe* [2010] FSR 2 [33]–[35] (partly overturned on appeal, but not on this point); *Force India Formula One Team v 1 Malaysia Racing Team* [2012] RPC 29 [392]–[393] (not challenged in this regard on appeal).

Court Act 1981.[77] In principle, therefore, compensation could be awarded in re-spect of foreign litigation that breached an equitable obligation not to pursue such litigation abroad.

14.42   However, if there is a general substantive equitable obligation not to commence vexatious and oppressive or unconscionable litigation abroad which is capable of supporting such a claim for compensation, it is a shy creature. There is no reported case where compensa-tion or damages have even been sought in equity in respect of such wrongful foreign liti-gation independent of Lord Cairns' Act;[78] and there is no principle of the traditional rules of equity on which a general claim for compensation could be based. The historical devel-opment of the anti-suit injunction is difficult to reconcile with the existence of a general claim for compensation or damages.[79]

14.43   As discussed previously in this work, it is uncertain whether there is any substantive equitable right which underpins general non-contractual anti-suit injunctions.[80] But even if there is a substantive equity it does not follow that it is an equity which supports a cause of action for equitable compensation or damages. Not all equitable relationships can do this.[81] It may well be, therefore, that any general substantive equity that may exist amounts to an equitable right to an injunction, but no more.[82] Even the authorities which support a concrete equitable right that could support an injunction contain no hint of any broader equity that could support a claim in damages.[83]

14.44   Further, if a general equitable right to compensation were to exist, it would confront and create serious problems. First, the scope of the equitable right would presumably have to match, or at least be related to, the scope of the injunction. But formulating a substan-tive right to compensation in terms which could flexibly mutate in accordance with the shaping of the discretion to grant an injunction, and the application of the principles of comity, would be challenging; and conversely, it would seem to be undesirable if an equit-able right to damages were to exist in many cases where an injunction should be refused as a matter of comity or discretion.[84]

---

[77] *Nocton v Lord Ashburton* [1914] AC 932 (HL); *Swindle v Harrison* [1997] 4 All ER 705 (CA); *Vestergaard Frandsen v BestNet Europe* [2010] FSR 2 [33]–[35] (partly overturned on appeal, but not on this point); *Force India Formula One Team Limited v 1 Malaysia Racing Team* [2012] RPC 29 [392]–[424] (not challenged in this regard on appeal).

[78] In *Whitworths v Synergy Food and Processing* [2014] EWHC 2439 (QB) [73]–[74], permission to amend to plead a case in equitable compensation was granted but the claim was for direct breach of an arbitration agree-ment; it is not clear why it was claimed in equity at all, and Cooke J regarded it as in substance a contractual claim.

[79] The principle of granting an injunction where 'the ends of justice' demand it developed first in *Bushby v Munday* (1821) 5 Madd 297, 56 ER 908, 913, and entrenched into the modern law in *Société Nationale Industrielle Aérospatiale v Lee Kui Jak* [1987] AC 871 (PC) 892C–D, is difficult to construe as supported by a concrete right to damages in equity.

[80] Ch 3, section B, 'A Legal or Equitable Right?'.

[81] ICF Spry, Equitable Remedies (9th edn, Reuters 2014) 647; J McGhee QC, *Snell's Equity* (33rd edn, Sweet & Maxwell 2017) para 20-028ff.

[82] The dissenting advice of Lord Nicholls, in *Mercedes Benz v Leiduck* [1996] AC 284 (PC) 310G–H, suggests that there may be no more than a right to an injunction, despite the near-circularity of such a formulation.

[83] See the authorities discussed in Ch 3, section B, 'A Legal or Equitable Right?'.

[84] In *Research in Motion UK v Visto* [2008] ILPr 34 (CA), Lewison J's reasoning is hostile to the idea of a damages right based on a direct assessment of the internal abusiveness of the foreign litigation. See also the brief *obiter* com-ments of the Court of Appeal at [2008] ILPr 34 [40].

Second, if such a general equitable right to compensation or damages exists, it will confront **14.45**
potential problems of choice of law. The question of how choice of law rules apply to equitable claims is complex and uncertain. But the more substantive the supposed equitable right
becomes, the more akin to a tortious right it looks, and so the more likely that the question
of applicable law should be determined by the Rome II Regulation.[85] If so, it is arguable
that the law of the place of the 'wrongful' litigation will be the applicable law, and if that is
right, the foreign law will usually preclude any claim based on a substantive equity, or any
analogous claim.

One way of resolving the tension between choice of law and equitable principles that **14.46**
arises if a substantive right not to be vexed by litigation abroad is considered to exist, is to
attenuate the substantive content of the right. The more any right becomes a right to an
injunction and nothing else, the easier it becomes to view it as not analogous to a claim
in tort, but instead as akin to a matter of procedure, and thus legitimately a matter for
English law alone, as the *lex fori*.[86] But if such an analysis is adopted, then any equitable
right may well have been so hollowed out that it will be incapable of supporting a claim in
damages.

Third, any equitable right to damages would confront the same logical problems, such as **14.47**
double adjudication, which confront claims for damages in the contractual case.

The landscape may be different in relation to specific equitable relationships which have **14.48**
a concrete existence independent of anti-suit injunctions and claims for damages, such
as the equitable relationship which links an assignee of a contract to the debtor under
the contract, or the subrogated insurer's relationship to the defendant to the subrogated claim; and perhaps other quasi-contractual situations (in the sense discussed in
Chapter 10 of this work). Equities of this nature may be sufficient to support a claim for
damages.[87]

In particular, in the assignment situation, there would be a credible argument that the **14.49**
assignee's equitable obligation not to claim the substantive rights under the original contract without respecting the exclusive foreign clause to which those rights are inherently
subject should be capable of supporting a claim for equitable compensation. If damages
were not available in such a situation, it would be easier to weaken the force of an exclusive
forum clause by assigning a contract to another linked party. It seems quite likely, therefore,
that a remedy in damages or compensation will be held to exist through one analysis or another, and that failing a direct contractual claim, liability will be justified either on the basis
that there is a claim for compensation in equity, or on the basis that the assignee is precluded
by equity from denying his liability in contractual damages.[88]

---

[85]   See Ch 4, section B, 'Applicable Law'.
[86]   See generally Ch 4, section B, 'Applicable Law'.
[87]   In *Whitworths v Synergy Food and Processing* [2014] EWHC 2439 (QB) [73]–[74], permission to amend to
plead a case in equitable compensation was granted, although the claim seems really to have been a claim for
breach of an arbitration agreement and appears to have been so regarded by Cooke J.
[88]   A claim for damages against an assignee was left to one side and did not need to be resolved in *Royal Bank of
Scotland v Highland Financial Partners* [2012] 2 CLC 109 [141].

14.50   In *West Tankers*, Flaux J thought there was a 'strong case' there would be a claim for 'equit-able damages' against a subrogated insurer who claimed abroad in breach of an arbitra-tion clause binding the assured, although it is possible (but unclear) that the damages were sought only *in lieu* under section 50 of the Senior Courts Act 1981. However, the juridical basis of the claim was not examined and the debate was focused on the question of whether European jurisdictional law barred the claim.[89]

14.51   It may also be possible to justify claims for damages in other quasi-contractual situations, where the third-party litigant abroad is making substantive claims in the shoes of a party whose claims are contractually subject by an English exclusive forum clause, on the basis of other doctrines. As discussed in Chapter 10, the case law in quasi-contractual situations, al-though fluid and unsettled, appears to support the proposition that the third party is bound by a specific positive equitable obligation to comply with a forum clause which is an in-herent condition of the derived contractual rights he wishes to assert against the debtor.[90] It should be borne in mind, however, that the existence of such an obligation is debatable, in particular in the situation of third parties under statutes transferring claims, where the im-position of equitable obligations is more ambitious than situations like assignment. In some of the case law, the courts have preferred to analyse the quasi-contractual situation on the basis that for the third party to litigate inconsistently with the forum clause which binds the original creditor would be vexatious and oppressive, without imposing any concrete posi-tive obligation.[91]

14.52   Such a positive obligation, if and where it exists, is capable of supporting a declaration that the third party is 'bound' by the arbitration or jurisdiction clause.[92] In turn, it is possible, but again debatable, that a positive equitable obligation could also support a claim for equitable compensation or damages. That result would be consistent with Flaux J's decision in *West Tankers*, although at least if a foreign third-party rights statute was involved, would require consideration of the meaning of the Court of Appeal's *obiter* comments about damages in *Through Transport*.[93]

14.53   The current case law suggests that the applicable law of such questions should be the law of the right transferred.[94]

---

[89]   *West Tankers v Ras Riunione Adriatica di Sicurta (The Front Comor)* [2012] 2 Lloyds Rep 103 [3], [49], [63], [74], [76]–[78].
[90]   See Ch 10, section C, 'An Obligation Not to Sue Elsewhere?'.
[91]   See eg Teare J in *Shipowners' Mutual Protection and Indemnity Association (Luxembourg) v Containerships Denizcilik Nakliyat ve Ticaret (The Yusuf Cepnioglu)* [2015] 1 Lloyds Rep 567 [43]–[44], and the cases discussed in Ch 10, section C, 'An Obligation Not to Sue Elsewhere?', para 10.18 n 27.
[92]   *West Tankers v Ras Riunione Adriatica di Sicurta* [2011] 2 Lloyds Rep 117; *The London Steam Ship Owners Mutual Insurance Association v Kingdom of Spain (The Prestige) (No 2)* [2014] 1 Lloyds Rep 309, [2015] 2 Lloyds Rep 33 (CA).
[93]   In *Through Transport Mutual Insurance Association (Eurasia) v New India Assurance* [2005] 1 Lloyds Rep 67 (CA) [65], the Court of Appeal stated simply (and *obiter*) that there could be no claim for damages in a quasi-contractual situation where the third party's claims were under a foreign third-party rights statute. But they seem to have been focusing solely on contractual damages and did not directly address equitable compensation or equit-able damages independent of contract.
[94]   See Ch 10, sections D, 'Third-Party Rights under Foreign Law' and F, 'Inconsistent Contractual Claims'.

4. Damages in Lieu of an Injunction: Section 50 of the Senior Courts Act 1981—Personal Jurisdiction

Where the court has power to grant an injunction, it can in its discretion grant damages in **14.54** lieu of an injunction under section 50 of the Senior Courts 1981,[95] which restates the powers granted by Lord Cairns' Act.[96] It has been suggested that this power could justify the grant of damages in place of an anti-suit injunction.[97] It would have the advantage, in contrast to a substantive equitable right to damages, that the award of damages under section 50 is discretionary, and thus flexible.

However, in the current state of the case law it is uncertain whether section 50 is a legitimate **14.55** independent basis for a claim for damages for 'wrongful' litigation abroad. First of all, there are conflicting authorities on the question of whether it is a precondition for the award of damages in lieu of an injunction under section 50 that a claim for damages would exist at common law (or equity) in respect of the wrong in question once it has occurred.[98] Second,

---

[95] Section 50 provides: 'Where the Court of Appeal or the High Court has jurisdiction to entertain an application for an injunction or specific performance, it may award damages in addition to, or in substation for, an injunction or specific performance.'

[96] The power to grant damages in lieu of an injunction was originally granted to the Court of Chancery by the Chancery Amendment Act 1858, s 2, commonly known as Lord Cairns' Act. It is often said that the relevant powers are now contained in s 50 of the Senior Courts Act 1981 alone: see eg *Lunn Poly v Liverpool & Lancashire Properties* [2006] EWCA Civ 430 [11]; *Regan v Paul Properties DPF No 1* [2007] Ch 135 (CA) [24]; *Force India Formula One Team v 1 Malaysia Racing* [2012] RPC 29 [389]. This, however, is not quite right. The formal position is that the powers contained in Lord Cairns' Act were transferred to the High Court, along with all the powers of the Court of Chancery, by s 16 of the Supreme Court of Judicature Act 1873 (and its successors, s 18 of the Supreme Court of Judicature (Consolidation) Act 1925, and s 19 of the Supreme Court Act 1981). Lord Cairns' Act was then itself abolished by the Statute Law Revision and Civil Procedure Act 1883, but the power earlier transferred to the High Court remained: *Leeds Industrial Co-operative Society v Slack* [1924] AC 851 (HL) 861–63; *Johnson v Agnew* [1980] AC 367 (HL) 400B; *Jaggard v Sawyer* [1995] 1 WLR 269 (CA) 276–77; *Attorney General v Blake* [2001] 1 AC 268 (HL) 281A. Section 50 of the Supreme Court Act 1981 then re-granted the powers in Lord Cairns' Act in modern language in 1981. Formally, therefore, the court has *both* the powers under s 50 and the powers derived from Lord Cairns' Act via s 19; the position is analogous to the relationship between the powers to grant injunctions contained in s 37(1) of the Supreme Court Act and the powers to grant injunctions transferred to the High Court by the Judicature Acts. However, there is no basis for suggesting that the powers in s 50 are any narrower than the powers derived from Lord Cairns' Act, and so separate discussion of the powers derived from Lord Cairns' Act is otiose; consequently, the discussion will analyse the issues by reference to s 50 alone.

[97] C Ambrose, 'Can Anti-Suit Injunctions Survive European Community Law' (2003) 52 ICLQ 401, 416, sees no problems with the grant of damages under s 50. CH Tham, 'Damages for Breaches of English Jurisdiction Clauses; More than Meets the Eye' [2004] LMCLQ 46, 68, also considers that damages under these provisions should be available in an appropriate case. See also, in the context of the American case law, D Tan, 'Damages for Breach of Forum Selection Clauses, Principled Remedies, and Control of International Civil Litigation' (2005) 40 Tex Intl L J 623, 646–47.

[98] In favour of the proposition that damages may be available under s 50 even if no damages could be awarded at common law once the wrong has occurred, see: *Eastwood v Lever* (1863) 4 De GJ & Sm 114, 46 ER 859; *Price v Strange* [1978] Ch 337 (CA) 358E–H, 369B–D (damages could be awarded in lieu even if common law damages would be barred by the Statute of Frauds); *Wrotham Park Estate Co Ltd v Parkside Homes Ltd* [1974] 1 WLR 79; *Jaggard v Sawyer* [1995] 1 WLR 269 (CA) 278H–279A, 283G, 284D, 290H–291B (differing from *Surrey County Council v Bredero Homes Ltd* [1993] 1 WLR 1361, and explaining *Johnson v Agnew* [1980] AC 367 (HL) 400B–D). This is consistent with the words of Lord Cairns' Act itself, which contain no limitation to the situation where an independent claim for damages would exist at common law or in equity. In *Lawrence v Fen Tigers* [2014] AC 822, the reasoning in *Jaggard v Sawyer* was generally referred to with approval (see [111]–[112], [120], [173]) and in terms that may imply agreement with the proposition that damages should be available under s 50 even if no common law claim for damages would lie (see [129], [159], [170]–[173], [248]), although without specific consideration of this point. *One-Step (Support) v Morris-Garner* [2018] 2 WLR 1353 (SC) [41]–[47], [95] regards damages in lieu of an injunction as targeted at replacing the injunction, but is not clear on whether an underlying common law right can be dispensed with (compare [46] to [95]).

  However, other authorities support the proposition that damages cannot be awarded under s 50 unless a claim for damages would lie at common law or equity once the wrong has occurred: see *Leeds Industrial Co-operative Society v Slack* [1924] AC 851 (HL) 857 (Viscount Finlay for the majority); see also 868–69 (per Lord Sumner in the

while it seems that damages are available under section 50 for breaches of purely equitable obligations,[99] there is a real argument that it would be wrong to award damages in lieu of an injunction if not only is there no common law cause of action but there is not even a underlying substantive equitable right that could sound in damages.[100] Thus, it is uncertain that section 50 could create a damages claim out of nothing, in cases where there is no relevant concrete positive equitable obligation.

14.56   In the old case of *Acraman v Price*, the Court of Chancery held that damages in lieu of an injunction were not available in respect of the pursuit of an improper action in the common law courts, although on the basis of very limited reasoning.[101] On the other hand, in *West Tankers* Flaux J was of the view that there was a 'strong case' that an equitable damages claim for wrongful litigation abroad in a quasi-contractual case would in principle lie under section 50, but the point of principle was apparently not contested, and *Acraman* was not cited.[102]

14.57   Consequently, outside the contractual case, it is uncertain whether section 50 Senior Courts Act 1981 provides a useful route to claim damages in respect of supposedly wrongful foreign litigation.[103]

C. THE BRUSSELS–LUGANO REGIME—PERSONAL JURISDICTION

14.58   The effect of the Brussels–Lugano regime on damages claims (so long as the regime remains English law) is considered in Chapter 12.

---

minority); *Johnson v Agnew* [1980] AC 367 (HL) 400B–D; *Experience Hendrix v PPX Enterprises* [2003] 1 All ER (Comm) 830 (CA) [34], [56]; *WWF-World Wildlife Fund for Nature v World Wrestling Federation Entertainment* [2007] Bus LR 1252 (CA) [54] (interpreting *Wrotham Park Estate v Parkside Homes* [1974] 1 WLR 79 as a case where damages were available at common law).

[99] In support of the award of damages under s 50 in support of a purely equitable right, see J McGhee QC, *Snell's Equity* (33rd edn, Sweet & Maxwell 2017) para 20-062 and *Eastwood v Lever* (1863) 46 ER 859 (CA) 865; *Attorney General v Observer* [1990] 1 AC 109, 286; and *Force India Formula One Team v 1 Malaysia Racing Team* [2012] RPC 29, at [393]; the discussion in ICF Spry, *Equitable Remedies* (9th edn, Reuters 2014) 662, is open. But see contra *Force India* at [390], [393]; and JD Heydon, MJ Leeming, and PG Turner (eds), *Meagher, Gummow & Lehane's Equity Doctrines and Remedies* (5th edn, LexisNexis 2015) paras 24-090–24-100. The reasoning in *One-Step (Support) v Morris-Garner* [2018] 2 WLR 1353 (SC) [41]–[47], [95] is unclear on the issue.

[100] J McGhee QC, *Snell's Equity* (33rd edn, Sweet & Maxwell 2017) para 20-062. *One-Step (Support) v Morris-Garner* [2018] 2 WLR 1353 (SC) [41]–[47], [95] is unclear on the question.

[101] *Acraman v Price* (1870) 18 WR 540. The court's reasoning on the point is only one short, conclusory sentence.

[102] *West Tankers Inc v Allianz Spa (The Front Comor)* [2012] 2 Lloyds Rep 103 [3], [63], [74]–[78].

[103] Choice of law issues would also need to be resolved. However, it is arguable that claims for damages in lieu of an injunction are a purely procedural matter and thus governed by the *lex fori*: see, under the existing law, *Harding v Wealands* [2007] 2 AC 1 (HL) and the discussion at Ch 4, section B, 'Applicable Law'.

15

Alternative Remedies

A. INTRODUCTION

Anti-suit injunctions, and claims for damages, are not the only available tools for resolving **15.01** or shaping conflicts of jurisdiction. This chapter considers alternative remedies which may be granted by the English courts to shape, pre-empt, or respond to the pursuit of litigation elsewhere. The limitations imposed by the Brussels–Lugano regime on anti-suit injunctions mean that this topic has grown in importance. This chapter proceeds (for the most part) on the assumption that the Brussels–Lugano regime, or something like it, will remain English law irrespective of Brexit.[1]

We consider in particular the following procedural remedies or strategies: **15.02**

- claims for declarations;
- applications for the appointment of an arbitrator;
- procedural management;
- resistance to enforcement.

B. DECLARATIONS

1. The Contractual Situation

Where foreign proceedings are in breach of a contractual exclusive jurisdiction or arbitra- **15.03** tion clause, the courts will in appropriate cases grant declarations that a given set of claims is covered by an English contractual forum clause,[2] or that the defendant is obliged to bring

---

[1] It also assumes that pursuant to Article 26(6) of the Hague Convention on the Choice of Court, the Hague Convention does not affect the operation of the Brussels–Lugano regime, on the assumptions that the situations discussed do not fall within the exceptions identified in Article 26(6). The operation of the Hague Convention (in cases within Article 26(6), or where the Brussels–Lugano regime does not apply) is outside the scope of this chapter, although the Convention will be touched on briefly at points.

[2] See eg *Toepfer International v Société Cargill France* [1997] 2 Lloyds Rep 98, 101, and Declaration §1 at 111.

those claims before the chosen forum or cannot bring them elsewhere,[3] or that the foreign proceedings are in breach of contract.[4] This has been done in numerous cases.[5]

15.04   There are arguments to the effect that parallel declarations to recognize or enforce an arbitration clause should only be granted in the limited circumstances envisaged in section 32 of the Arbitration Act 1996, but as discussed further at paras 15.21–15.31, these arguments have so far not prevented the court from granting such declarations to protect English arbitrations against competing foreign proceedings more widely, independent of section 32.

15.05   Such declarations are a legitimate form of relief when a party to such a clause has commenced, or may well commence, litigation before a foreign court which is not the agreed forum according to the clause, even if no parallel litigation or arbitration has yet been commenced in England.[6]

15.06   Whether and in what form declaratory relief will be appropriate in quasi-contractual cases will depend on the nature of the quasi-contractual connection to the contractual forum clause. In *Through Transport* the injunction defendant wished to make a substantive claim before the Finnish courts under a Finnish third-party rights statute, in respect of contractual rights subject to an English arbitration clause. The court was willing to grant a declaration that the injunction defendant was obliged to bring any claim arising out of the contract in the contractual forum, but not a declaration that the Finnish litigation was actually in breach of contract, as the claimant in Finland was not a party to the contract, and could not break it.[7]

15.07   A declaration of this kind is always a discretionary remedy. In general, declarations will be granted if they serve a useful purpose.[8] However, the court may decline to grant such declarations if they are inconsistent with comity. Thus, in *Toepfer v Molino Boschi* the foreign proceedings had been allowed to continue in breach of the arbitration clause for many years, with the result that it was inappropriate for the English court to grant a declaration with the aim of pre-empting the decision of the foreign court, at such a late stage.[9] However,

---

[3]   See eg *Toepfer International v Société Cargill France* [1997] 2 Lloyds Rep 98, 101, and Declaration §2 at 111; *Through Transport Mutual Insurance Association (Eurasia) v New India Assurance* [2005] 1 Lloyds Rep 67 (CA) [63]–[64]; *West Tankers v Allianz* [2012] 2 Lloyds Rep 103 [7]; *National Navigation v Endesa Generacion (The Wadi Sudr)* [2009] 1 Lloyds Rep 666 [74], [127] (overturned on appeal, but on a distinct point [2010] 1 Lloyds Rep 193 (CA) [133]); *AES Ust-Kamenogorsk Hydropower Plant LLP v Ust-Kamenogorsk Hydropower Plant JSC* [2012] 1 WLR 920 (CA), [2013] 1 WLR 1889 (SC) [2], [14]–[18].

[4]   See eg *Toepfer International v Société Cargill France* [1997] 2 Lloyds Rep 98, 101, Declaration §3 at 111; *Ust-Kamenogorsk Hydropower Plant JSC (Appellant) v AES Ust-Kamenogorsk Hydropower Plant LLP* [2013] 1 WLR 1889 (SC) [14]–[18]; *Ecom Agroindustrial v Mosharaf Composite Textile Mill* [2013] 2 Lloyds Rep 196 [15], [40]–[43].

[5]   *Ecom Agroindustrial v Mosharaf Composite Textile Mill* [2013] 2 Lloyds Rep 196 [41].

[6]   The contention that a declaration to enforce an arbitration clause could not be granted unless an arbitration had already been commenced was rejected in *Ust-Kamenogorsk Hydropower Plant JSC (Appellant) v AES Ust-Kamenogorsk Hydropower Plant LLP* [2013] 1 WLR 1889 (SC), upholding [2010] 2 Lloyds Rep 493, [2012] 1 WLR 920 (CA).

[7]   *Through Transport Mutual Insurance Association (Eurasia) v New India Assurance* [2005] 1 Lloyds Rep 67 (CA) [63]–[65].

[8]   *Messier-Dowty v Sabena* [2000] 1 WLR 2040 (CA). For relevant examples, see *Through Transport Mutual Insurance Association (Eurasia) v New India Assurance* [2005] 1 Lloyds Rep 67 (CA) [65] (in respect of the second declaration); *Toepfer International v Molino Boschi* [1996] 1 Lloyds Rep 510, 518; *Ecom Agroindustrial v Mosharaf Composite Textile Mill* [2013] 2 Lloyds Rep 196 [15], [40]–[43]; *London Steamship Owners' Mutual Insurance v Kingdom of Spain (The Prestige) (No 2)* [2014] 1 Lloyd Rep 309 [181]–[199].

[9]   *Toepfer International v Molino Boschi* [1996] 1 Lloyds Rep 510, 518.

a declaration raises fewer comity concerns than an anti-suit injunction in similar circumstances, and may be granted where an injunction would not be.[10]

There are also many ways in which such declarations can serve a useful purpose. First, they **15.08** can be used to create *res judicata* effects abroad.[11] Second, as discussed further at paras 15.09–15.20, such declarations may be used defensively in resistance to attempts to enforce the foreign judgment in England. Third, declarations that an exclusive forum clause is contractually binding can also provide a springboard for claims for damages; and they may assist in enforcing arbitration awards obtained under the terms of an arbitration clause.[12] The courts have, in general, taken a relatively liberal approach to the utility of such declarations. Thus, it has been considered appropriate to grant declarations that might assist in resisting enforcement of a prospective Brussels–Lugano judgment on the basis only that there was a 'real prospect' that the declaration would have such an effect, without deciding that it actually would do so.[13]

2. The Defensive Use of Declarations to Resist Enforcement

Section 32(1)(a) of the Civil Jurisdiction and Judgments Act 1982 provides that, outside **15.09** the Brussels–Lugano context, a foreign judgment will not be enforced if it is in breach of an exclusive forum clause, subject to certain exceptions, of which the most important is a submission to the jurisdiction of the foreign court.

---

[10] Declarations have been granted where anti-suit injunctions have been refused: see *Through Transport Mutual Insurance Association (Eurasia) v New India Assurance* [2005] 1 Lloyds Rep 67 (CA) [63]–[64] and *World Pride Shipping v Daiichi Chuo Kisen Kaisha (The Golden Anne)* [1984] 2 Lloyds Rep 489, 493, 496, 498; *Essar Shipping v Bank of China* [2016] 1 Lloyds Rep 417 [76] (injunction refused on grounds of delay, but declaration granted). See also *Ecom Agroindustrial v Mosharaf Composite Textile* [2013] 2 Lloyds Rep 196 [15], [40]–[43].

[11] If the competing litigation is in a non-Brussels–Lugano state, then the positive external effect of English declarations that exclusive forum clauses are binding will depend on the laws of recognition and *res judicata* of the country in question, and potentially the Hague Convention on the Choice of Court in another contracting state to the Hague Convention.

If the competing litigation is in another EU state, a declaration by the English court that an English exclusive jurisdiction clause is binding will be a Regulation judgment which should be treated as binding in other Regulation states and should lead other Regulation courts to decline jurisdiction automatically pursuant to Article 31(3) of the Brussels I Recast (see Case C-469/11, *Gothaer Allgemeine Versicherung v Samskip* [2013] QB 548). Further, the effect of Article 31(2) of the Recast is that the English court, as the agreed court, can determine its own jurisdiction even if the other court was seised first on the merits. This reverses Case C-116/02, *Erich Gasser v Misat* [2003] ECR I-14693.

However, the position is different for declarations as to the effect of an arbitration clause. A free-standing claim for a declaration that an arbitration clause is binding will be treated as 'arbitration', within the arbitration exception, and outside the Brussels–Lugano regime, and therefore will only be enforceable in other European states if their domestic rules of recognition and *res judicata* so permit. It is true that, under the Brussels I Regulation before the Brussels I Recast, it was held, controversially, that a decision that an arbitration clause was not binding reached in the course of proceedings that were otherwise within the scope of the Regulation would itself fall within the scope of the Regulation: C-185/07, *Allianz v West Tankers (The Front Comor)* [2009] ECR I-663 [26]. However, this would not apply to court proceedings whose focus was to obtain a declaration in respect of the binding force of the arbitration agreement. Further, under the Brussels I Recast the exclusion of arbitration is reinforced by Recital 12 so that even decisions on the scope of an arbitration clause in the context of Regulation proceedings should not be enforceable under the Brussels–Lugano regime.

[12] *Ecom Agroindustrial Corp Ltd v Mosharaf Composite Textile Mill Ltd* [2013] 2 Lloyds Rep 196 [15], [40]–[43].

[13] *West Tankers v Allianz (The Front Comor)* [2011] 2 Lloyds Rep 117, [28]–[31]; *African Fertilizers and Chemicals NIG v BD Shipsnavo* [2011] 2 Lloyds Rep 531 [27]–[28]; *London Steamship Owners' Mutual Insurance v Kingdom of Spain (The Prestige) (No 2)* [2014] 1 Lloyds Rep 309 [181]–[199].

15.10   A declaration that an exclusive forum clause is binding will therefore often provide an effective anticipatory defence to recognition of a non-Brussels–Lugano judgment obtained in breach of the clause, since it would establish in advance that section 32(1)(a) would apply.

15.11   A declaration as to the binding effect of an exclusive jurisdiction clause should also provide the practical answer to proceedings in another EU court in breach of that clause. Following the coming into force of the Brussels I Recast, Recital 22 and Article 31 of the Brussels I Recast should have the effect that if the English court is the agreed court under an exclusive jurisdiction clause, then even if it is second seised, the bringing of a claim before it for a declaration as to its own jurisdiction should lead to the temporary stay of the competing foreign proceedings pending its determination (Art 31(2)); and if the declaration is granted, the foreign court will then be required to decline jurisdiction (Art 31(3)). In addition, a prior English court judgment on the merits would prevent enforcement of a subsequent Brussels–Lugano judgment, which would be 'irreconcilable' with the prior English judgment under Article 45(1)(c) of the Recast.

15.12   The position in relation to arbitration clauses is less clear. Although in the course of the pre-legislative process that led to the Brussels I Recast there were proposals to give the courts of the seat of the arbitration the same primary role in relation to arbitration clauses as Article 31 of the Recast gives the chosen court in respect of exclusive jurisdiction clauses,[14] these proposals were not adopted. Instead, the philosophy of the Brussels I Recast in its final form was to seek to reinforce the exclusion of arbitration from the scope of the Brussels–Lugano regime, partly reversing the effect of *The Front Comor* through Recital 12.

15.13   Although the point has not yet been definitively decided, the better view appears to be that if an arbitration award on the merits has been obtained, and has been enforced as a judgment by the English court, then recognition of an inconsistent Brussels–Lugano judgment on the merits should be refused on grounds of irreconcilability under Article 45(1)(c) of the Brussels I Recast.[15] The English courts have so far accepted that it is legitimate to apply to

---

[14]   See See Professors Burkhard Hess and Thomas Pfeiffer, Report on the Application of Regulation Brussels I in the Member States, 2007, 350–51 (hereafter the 'Heidelberg Report'). Such a proposal was included in the initial Commission Memorandum: see Commission Proposal for a Regulation of the European Parliament and Council on jurisdiction and the recognition and enforcement of judgments in civil and commercial matters, COM(2010) 748 Final, 3.1.4. However, following resistance the proposal was not pursued.

[15]   *National Navigation v Endesa Generacion (The Wadi Sudr)* [2010] 1 Lloyds Rep 193 (CA) [63] (*obiter*); *West Tankers v Allianz (The Front Comor)* [2011] 2 Lloyds Rep 117 [28]–[31] (not finally decided, but concluding that there was a 'real prospect' of recognition being refused); *African Fertilizers and Chemicals NIG (Nigeria) v BD Shipsnavo* [2011] 2 Lloyds Rep 531 [27]–[28] (relating to the yet more difficult case of a declaration as to the force of the exclusion forum clause); see also *London Steamship Owners' Mutual Insurance v Kingdom of Spain (The Prestige) (No 2)* [2014] 1 Lloyds Rep 309 [181]–[199] (not deciding the point but similarly holding that there was a 'real prospect' that recognition might be refused, [187]).

The principal counter-argument is that the judgment enforcing the award is 'arbitration' and thus outside the scope of the Brussels–Lugano regime: see the decision of the French Cour de Cassation in *Republic of Congo v Groupe Antoine Tabet* (4 July 2007) Rev Crit DIP (2007) 822 (Note Usunier). The Brussels I Recast makes clear that the Regulation does not apply to any judgment concerning the enforcement of an arbitration award: see Recital 12. However, it is submitted that 'judgment' within Article 45(1)(c) should be read more broadly than 'judgment' in the recognition and enforcement provisions of the Brussels I Regulation, so as to include domestic judgments enforcing arbitration awards (and probably also declarations as to the effect of arbitration clauses): see Briggs, para 7.22, whose reasoning was cited with approval in *West Tankers v Allianz (The Front Comor)* [2011] 2 Lloyds Rep 117 [26]–[28]. The exclusion of such judgments from the scope of the Brussels–Lugano regime generally means they do not benefit from its recognition provisions abroad, but should not prevent them having effect as 'irreconcilable' judgments, since otherwise domestic rules of *res judicata* would be undermined in an incoherent way.

enforce as a judgment a declaratory arbitration award on the merits of the dispute for such a purpose.[16]

Indeed, if the arbitration award on the merits has been obtained, but not yet enforced as a **15.14** judgment by the English court, enforcement of the inconsistent foreign judgment should also be refused. Even if the award cannot be treated as a 'judgment' within Article 45(1) (c),[17] the prior award on the merits should still justify refusal of enforcement as a matter of public policy under Article 45(1)(a). If the award is an English arbitration award, then it is *res judicata* (unless successfully challenged under sections 67–69 of the Arbitration Act 1996).[18] Further, if it is a foreign award or an English award which is not a domestic award, the English court is bound to enforce it under Article III of the New York Convention, which takes precedence, and displaces the recognition rules of the Regulation by virtue of Article 73 of the Recast. The additional step of obtaining prior enforcement of the award by a judgment of the English court is thus an optional extra, which on this analysis is not necessary to prevent enforcement of a subsequent inconsistent Brussels–Lugano judgment.[19]

However, it is less clear whether a prior English arbitration award or court declaration as to **15.15** the binding effect of an arbitration clause, and which does not decide the merits of the dispute, will itself preclude the enforcement of an inconsistent Brussels–Lugano judgment on the merits of the dispute.

It is arguable that an English court declaration holding that an exclusive jurisdiction clause **15.16** or arbitration clause is binding would preclude enforcement in England of a Brussels–Lugano judgment obtained in breach of that clause, on the basis that the English declaration is 'irreconcilable' with the Brussels–Lugano judgment under Article 45(1)(c) of the

In principle it should also be arguable that the arbitration award should be treated as a 'judgment' for the purpose of Article 45(1)(c) and (d) of the Recast. As matters stand, such arguments face the difficulty that in the odd decision of Case C-414/92, *Solo Kleinmotoren v Emilio Boch* [1994] ECR I-2237 the European Court held that only judgments given by a court fell within Article 45(1)(c); but in the *Shipsnavo* case, Beatson J interpreted *Solo Kleinmotoren* as really only concerned with consensual settlements, and not to the outcome of the arbitration (at [28]). The better point may be that, in any event, enforcement of a foreign judgment that is inconsistent with a New York Convention award, and in turn with a prior English judgment enforcing such an award, would be inconsistent with the New York Convention, which takes precedence over the Brussels regime in this regard, under Article 73 of the Recast.

Recital 12 to the Brussels I Recast contains some unclear wording that if a court of a member state has determined that an arbitration agreement is null and void, 'this should not preclude' that court's judgment being enforced under the Brussels regime. This probably means only that the mere fact of an arbitration clause having been raised and dismissed does not exclude subsequent recognition; and the Recital goes on to make clear that such an approach 'should be without prejudice to the competence of the courts of the member states to decide on the recognition and enforcement of arbitration awards in accordance with [The New York Convention] which takes precedence over this Regulation'.

[16] *West Tankers v Allianz (The Front Comor)* [2011] 2 Lloyds Rep 117 [28]–[31] (upheld on appeal [2012] 1 Lloyds Rep 398 (CA), although Field J's exercise of discretion was not challenged: see at [38]); *African Fertilizers and Chemicals NIG (Nigeria) v BD Shipsnavo* [2011] 2 Lloyds Rep 531 [27]–[28] (relating to the more difficult case of a declaration as to the force of the exclusive forum clause). In *London Steamship Owners' Mutual Insurance v Kingdom of Spain (The Prestige) (No 2)* [2014] 1 Lloyds Rep 309 [181]–[199], the argument that granting a declaration for this purpose would subvert the scheme of the Regulation was rejected.

[17] See n 15.

[18] *Emirates Trading v Sociedade de Fomento Industrial* [2015] EWHC 1452 (Comm) [22]–[25]; and see also *Doe d Davy v Haddon* (1783) 3 Doug KB 310, 99 ER 969; *Commings v Heard* (1869) LR 4 QB 669; *Imperial Gas Light v Broadbent* (1859) 7 HL Cas 600; *Caledonian Railway v Turcan* [1898] AC 256; *Fidelitas Shipping v V/O Exportschleb* [1966] 1 QB 630; *Associated Electric & Gas Insurance Services v European Reinsurance Co of Zurich* [2003] 1 WLR 1041 [9], [15].

[19] Nevertheless, the cases permitting enforcement of such awards as judgments (see para 15.13 n 16) are still justifiable as the prior judgment is useful as a supplementary precaution.

Recast.[20] However, the point is uncertain, in particular[21] as the inconsistency is not as direct as between judgments or awards on the merits;[22] and the English case law suggests that for the purposes of Article 29 of the Recast claims for breach of an exclusive jurisdiction clause are not the same cause of action as the underlying claims for substantive relief.[23]

15.17   In *The Wadi Sudr*, Waller LJ made a rather cryptic *obiter* comment, in respect of declarations as to the effect of arbitration clauses, that may suggest he did not perceive any irreconcilability with a later foreign judgment on the merits, but the better reading may be that he was simply not addressing this point.[24] Conversely, in *African Fertilizers*, Beatson J was of the view that there was a real prospect that a declaration as to the effect of an arbitration clause would prevent the enforcement of a subsequent judgment on the merits obtained in breach of the clause, and was willing to enforce as a judgment an arbitration award declaring the binding force of the arbitration clause.[25]

---

[20] See *Philip Alexander Securities & Futures v Bamberger* [1997] ILPr 73 [112]–[113], [121], where Waller J suggested that such a declaration would preclude recognition because the subsequent Brussels–Lugano judgment would be 'irreconcilable' with the English judgment, within Article 45(1)(c) (then Art 34(3)). However, he may have changed his mind by the time of *The Wadi Sudr*: see *National Navigation v Endesa Generacion (The Wadi Sudr)* [2010] 1 Lloyds Rep 193 (CA) [63] (*obiter*), discussed at n 24.

[21] It is also arguable that such declarations, when made in respect of arbitration clauses, are 'arbitration' and so not judgments within Article 45(1)(c) at all, and Recital 12 of the Recast makes clear that such declarations do not benefit from the recognition and enforcement rules of the Brussels regime. However, the more attractive view is that 'judgment' is being used in two senses in the Recast, and that such a declaration can fall within Article 45(1)(c) for the purposes of domestic irreconcilability, even though it is not a 'judgment' for the purposes of Articles 39–45 of the Recast generally, and therefore does not have to be recognized in other EU states: see Briggs, para 7.22. In *African Fertilizers and Chemicals NIG v BD Shipsnavo* [2011] 2 Lloyds Rep 531 [9], [27]–[28], Beatson J rejected the proposition that Article 45(1)(c) does not apply to such judgments, although he did not consider the 'arbitration' exception point.

[22] In Case C-145/86, *Hoffmann v Krieg* [1988] ECR 645 [22] the ECJ laid down the principle that for judgments to be irreconcilable within Article 45(1)(c), they must 'entail legal consequences that are mutually exclusive'. The case concerned a foreign judgment that spousal maintenance had to be paid and a prior domestic judgment that the marriage had been dissolved by divorce. The ECJ concluded that the foreign maintenance judgment presupposed the continuing validity of the marital relationship and was therefore irreconcilable with the domestic judgment: at [25]. Similarly, in Case C-80/00, *Italian Leather v Weco Polstermöbel* [2002] ECR I-4995 [44]–[48], the ECJ accepted that 'irreconcilability lies in the effects of judgments' and extended beyond the limited case where one judgment had positively concluded the inverse of another. So, it could be argued, by analogy to *Hoffmann v Krieg*, that the foreign judgment presupposes that the forum clause is not binding and therefore is irreconcilable with the domestic declaration as to the binding force of the clause.

[23] *Starlight Shipping v Allianz Marine & Aviation Versicherungs (The Alexandros T)* [2014] 1 Lloyds Rep 223 (SC) [38].

[24] *National Navigation v Endesa Generacion (The Wadi Sudr)* [2010] 1 Lloyds Rep 193 (CA) [63]. Waller LJ commented *obiter* that where a declaration as to the binding effect of an arbitration clause had been obtained it was unlikely that the public policy exception 'would need to be invoked or could be invoked', because the claimant could proceed with the arbitration in England and obtain an award (and possibly judgment) on the merits. However, this does not clearly answer the question of irreconcilability with the declaration on the effect of the clause if no award (or judgment) on the merits has been obtained before enforcement of the Brussels–Lugano judgment, for example for reasons of procedural timing. In this respect, it is unclear whether Waller LJ's views had changed from *Philip Alexander Securities & Futures v Bamberger* [1997] ILPr 73 [112]–[113], [121], where he had concluded that such irreconcilability could be relied on.

[25] *African Fertilizers and Chemicals NIG v BD Shipsnavo* [2011] 2 Lloyds Rep 531 [7], [12], [26], [28]. However, Beatson J may not have paid sufficient regard to the distinction between an arbitration award on the merits and an award on the binding effect of the arbitration clause, and may therefore have over-interpreted the (somewhat cryptic) comments of Waller LJ in *The Wadi Sudr*. See also *London Steamship Owners' Mutual Insurance v Kingdom of Spain (The Prestige) (No 2)* [2014] 1 Lloyds Rep 309 [9], [181]–[199], where the awards enforced related to both the merits and the binding force of the arbitration clause, and it was concluded that there was 'real prospect of establishing the primacy of the award over any inconsistent judgment which may be rendered in Spain' [187]. However, no clear distinction was drawn between the award on the effect of the arbitration clause, and the award on the merits.

The other, and possibly stronger, argument is that recognition should be refused because it **15.18** would be 'manifestly contrary to public policy' under Article 45(1)(a) of the Recast to en- force a judgment which had been obtained inconsistently with a jurisdiction clause, or an arbitration clause, which an English judgment, or arbitration award enforceable in England, had held binding. The 'manifestly contrary' threshold is a high one, requiring infringement of 'some fundamental principle' of the domestic legal order,[26] and it could be said that re- fusing recognition would involve applying public policy to the foreign court's assumption of jurisdiction, which is precluded by Article 45(3) of the Recast.[27] In the *Wadi Sudr*, Waller LJ doubted *obiter* that public policy would permit refusal of recognition of a foreign judg- ment obtained inconsistently with an English declaration as to the existence of an arbitra- tion clause.[28]

Nevertheless, it is suggested that the correct answer in principle is that recognition of a **15.19** Brussels–Lugano judgment should be refused if there has been a prior declaratory judg- ment holding that the foreign litigation is in breach of the exclusive forum clause. The con- trary result would be incoherent: the English legal system would simultaneously be holding that the foreign judgment had been unlawfully obtained, by its prior declaration, which is capable of supporting a claim in damages; and also treating the foreign judgment as a binding source of legal obligation, by recognizing it. Notwithstanding the *obiter* views of Waller LJ, it is suggested such a situation could fairly be described as infringing a funda- mental principle of the domestic legal order.[29]

Further, it is also suggested that the same answer should also follow if there has been a **15.20** valid prior arbitration award declaring that the arbitration clause is binding, even if that award has not yet been enforced as a judgment of the court. There is a strong case in principle that it would be contrary to public policy, or directly contrary to the New York Convention, which takes precedence over the recognition and enforcement rules of the Recast via Recital 12 and Article 73 of the Recast, for the English court to be obliged to en- force a Brussels–Lugano judgment, if the English court is also bound by the prior arbitra- tion award as to the effect of the clause, where that award is *res judicata*. The binding effect of the award will necessarily mean the foreign judgment had been obtained unlawfully.[30]

---

[26] Case C-7/98 *Bamberski v Krombach* [2000] ECR I-1935 [20].

[27] Formerly Article 35(3) of the Brussels I Regulation. See *National Navigation v Endesa Generacion (The Wadi Sudr)* [2010] 1 Lloyds Rep 193 (CA) [125].

[28] See Waller LJ in *National Navigation v Endesa Generacion (The Wadi Sudr)* [2010] 1 Lloyds Rep 193 [63], [65]. This was a change of mind from his earlier *obiter* comments in *Philip Alexander Securities & Futures Ltd v Bamberger* [1997] ILPr 73 [112]–[113], [121]. The actual fact situation in *The Wadi Sudr* is, however, specific, and will not recur. There was no prior English judgment as to the enforceability of the arbitration clause. Instead, there was a prior Spanish judgment that the clause was not binding. Applying the law as it then stood in the light of *The Front Comor*, before the Brussels I Recast, this Spanish judgment was to be recognized in England, and was there- fore *res judicata* unless defeated by a public policy objection. In that context, the public policy arguments were weaker: see Moore-Bick LJ at [125]. However, now that Recital 12 of the Brussels I Recast has made clear that for- eign judgments on the effect of arbitration clauses do not come within the Brussels enforcement rules, the premise of the judgment in *The Wadi Sudr* would no longer exist.

[29] See Report on the Convention on Jurisdiction and the Enforcement of Judgments in Civil and Commercial Matters, rapporteur P Jenard [1979] OJ C59/1, 45 (the 'Jenard Report'): 'there can be no doubt that the rule of law in a state would be disturbed if it were possible to take advantage of two conflicting judgments'.

[30] This argument may be inconsistent, in cases where there has been a submission to the jurisdiction of the foreign court, with parts of the reasoning in the perplexing and incorrect decision of Carr J in *Spliethoff's Bevrachtingskantoor v Bank of China* [2015] 2 Lloyds Rep 623 [109]–[137]. Carr J concluded that, where there had been submission to the jurisdiction of the foreign court, anti-suit orders by arbitrators were not a ground to refuse

However, whether the European Court would adopt these solutions remains to be seen.[31]

3. Section 32 of the Arbitration Act 1996

15.21   The policy of the Arbitration Act 1996 is that challenges to the jurisdiction of the tribunal are primarily to be made before the arbitrators themselves under section 30, and the arbitrators may also grant declarations as to their own jurisdiction. Appeals from both lie to the court under section 67 of the Act. The 1996 Act also provides, in section 32, a restricted procedure for the grant of a declaration by the court that a tribunal has jurisdiction under an arbitration agreement. The permission of the tribunal or the opposing party is required to trigger the procedure; and even then, the court should only hear the claim in appropriate circumstances.

15.22   There was previously a line of first instance decisions in other contexts, led by *Vale do Rio Doce v Shanghai Bao Steel*, which suggested that section 32 is an exclusive remedy and that, save perhaps in abnormal circumstances,[32] declarations as to the jurisdiction of an arbitration tribunal should not be granted by the court independently of section 32,[33] as otherwise they would be an 'intervention' in the arbitration which the court should not commit, by reason of section 1(c) of the Arbitration Act. However, it was not clear whether this line of case law reflected a conclusion of jurisdiction or merely an approach to discretion.[34]

enforcement of a foreign judgment. However, that decision is wrong on many levels, and to the extent its reasoning touches on this particular issue (which it does not do clearly), is not a good guide. Indeed, the question of prior *res judicata* arising out of the arbitrators' anti-suit orders does not appear to have been addressed (and the nature of the arbitrators' decisions that led to those orders is not clear from the report). It is submitted that any suggestion that submission to a foreign judgment trumps what would otherwise be a public policy defence to recognition based on a prior *res judicata* must be wrong. Indeed, in many of the key cases where foreign judgments were refused recognition on grounds of a prior English *res judicata*, there had been submission to the jurisdiction of the foreign court, where the matter was fought out on the merits. See *Vervaeke v Smith* [1983] 1 AC 145 (HL).

We shall discuss further below at para 15.57 why (on top of considerations of *res judicata*) Carr J's reasoning in *Splietthoff's* is also wrong, more generally, in not accepting that breach of anti-suit arbitral awards should be a ground to refuse recognition as matter of public policy. See also para 15.56 n 88 (in relation to injunctions).

(Further, although the issue is beyond the scope of this book, Carr J's reasoning is yet further contestable because she did not follow Rix LJ's conclusions in *AES Ust-Kamenogorsk Hydropower Plant LLP v Ust-Kamenogorsk Hydropower Plant JSC* [2012] 1 WLR 920 (CA) [149]–[151], that recognition in the case of breach of an exclusive forum clause, even where there was submission, would remain a question of 'evaluative judgment'. The other recent authorities follow Rix LJ: see *Ecobank Transnational v Tanoh* [2015] EWHC 1874 (Comm) [27], [2016] 1 WLR 2231 (CA) [43]; and see the comment in *Exmek Pharmaceuticals v Alkem Laboratories* [2016] 1 Lloyds Rep 239 [39].)

[31]   Y Baatz, 'Should Third Parties be Bound by Arbitration Clauses?' [2015] LMCLQ 85, 109–10, regards the question as uncertain.

[32]   The existence or scope of any possible proviso for abnormal circumstances was not entirely clear. In *ABB Lummus Global v Keppel Fels* [1999] 2 Lloyds Rep 24, Clarke J appears to have considered that the exclusivity of s 32 was absolute. But in *Vale do Rio Doce Navegaçao v Shanghai Bao Steel Ocean Shipping* [2000] 2 Lloyds Rep 1, although Thomas J held that in the case before him the court had no power to grant a declaration that the tribunal had jurisdiction, part of his reasoning was that the circumstances of that case cannot have been unanticipated: see [53]–[54]. So, it appears Thomas J might have made an exception in certain abnormal and therefore unanticipated circumstances. Yet this is not certain; and Thomas J did not expressly differ from *ABB Lummus*. See also *JT Mackley v Gosport Marina* [2002] EWHC 1315 (TCC) [24]–[31], which might be read to allow a broader scope to the exception.

[33]   See *ABB Lummus Global v Keppel Fels* [1999] 2 Lloyds Rep 24, 30, 37. This was so even where the application for a declaration was made before the appointment of an arbitrator by the unwilling party: *Vale do Rio Doce Navegaçao v Shanghai Bao Steel Ocean Shipping* [2000] 2 Lloyds Rep 1, 10–12 [52].

[34]   *AES Ust-Kamenogorsk Hydropower Plant LLP v Ust-Kamenogorsk Hydropower Plant JSC v* [2012] 1 WLR 920 (CA) [47], [99]–[100].

But this line of case law would have been inconvenient, and has not been followed, in cases **15.23** where foreign court proceedings are competing with English arbitration proceedings, and where the declaration would serve to ratify and protect the English arbitration clause.

In many cases, where the argument that sections 1(c) and 32 of the Arbitration Act 1996 **15.24** preclude the grant of such declarations outside the narrow confines of section 32 appears not even to have been raised, the English courts had shown no hesitation in granting declarations as to the validity of English arbitration clauses, without reference to section 32, even after the Arbitration Act 1996 came into force.[35] This usually occurred in cases where a declaration was claimed as a parallel remedy alongside an anti-suit injunction, and where the declaration formalized the conclusions the court had reached on the force of the arbitration clause as part of its reasoning for the injunction.[36]

In the days when European law was not viewed as imposing a material restriction on the **15.25** grant of anti-suit injunctions, the question of whether such a declaration could also be granted was of lesser significance. But following the removal of the anti-suit injunction within the Brussels–Lugano regime from the court's toolbox, by European Court's decision in *The Front Comor*, the availability of a free-standing declaration has become of more importance.

The question whether section 32 precluded the grant of an injunction or a declaration in **15.26** support of arbitration was argued in *Ust-Kamenogorsk*, where in the Court of Appeal, Rix LJ held that he did not agree with any interpretation of *Vale do Rio* to the effect that there was a rule of *jurisdiction* which prevented the court granting a declaration outside section 32 to protect an arbitration clause against competing foreign proceedings. Instead, whether section 32 should lead a court to decline to grant a declaration was a question of principle or discretion dependent on the facts: 'a court asked to protect an agreement to arbitrate by granting declarations or injunctions in respect of it has to steer a careful path between: on the one hand, adequate support for the parties' agreement, without which support that agreement may be effectively nullified by foreign proceedings taken in breach of it; and on the other hand a proper concern not to intervene in an arbitration or prospective arbitration, or to usurp the role of arbitrators.'[37] He observed that a declaration by the court that an arbitration clause was definitively binding would not unacceptably trespass on the possibility that the arbitrators might in due course address the question of their own jurisdiction.

In the Supreme Court, Lord Mance decided the case on the narrower basis that any **15.27** preclusionary effect of section 32 could not apply to preclude the grant of an anti-suit injunction in a case where no arbitration proceedings were on foot or proposed.[38] However, his reasoning is also inconsistent with any rigid preclusionary doctrine of jurisdiction which would prevent the court from granting a declaration outside section 32 to protect

---

[35] See eg *Toepfer International v Société Cargill France* [1997] 2 Lloyds Rep 98 (involving a pre-1996 Act arbitration); *Navigation Maritime Bulgare v Rustal Trading (The Ivan Zagubanski)* [2002] 1 Lloyds Rep 106; *Through Transport Mutual Insurance Association (Eurasia) v New India Assurance* [2005] 1 Lloyds Rep 67 (CA).

[36] For a case where a declaration was granted, but an injunction was not, see *Through Transport Mutual Insurance Association (Eurasia) v New India Assurance* [2005] 1 Lloyds Rep 67 (CA).

[37] *AES Ust-Kamenogorsk Hydropower Plant LLP v Ust-Kamenogorsk Hydropower Plant JSC* [2012] 1 WLR 920 (CA) [99]–[100].

[38] *Ust-Kamenogorsk Hydropower Plant JSC v AES Ust-Kamenogorsk Hydropower Plant LLP* [2013] 1 WLR 1889 (SC) [40]–[42].

the arbitration clause, even if an arbitration had been commenced. He did not view the case law stemming from *Vale do Rio* as laying down any absolute rule; and regarded any limiting doctrine as justified by the principle of 'Kompetenz-Kompetenz' (Competence-Competence) which 'makes sense where a tribunal is asked to exercise a substantive jurisdiction and hears submissions at the outset as to whether it has such a jurisdiction'.[39] He concluded that the correct approach in relation to injunctions was that the power in section 37 of the Supreme Court Act 1981 should be exercised 'sensitively and, in particular, with due regard for the scheme and terms of the 1996 Act when any arbitration is on foot or proposed',[40] and it is submitted that the same logic applies in principle to declarations sought outside section 32 of the 1996 Act.

15.28   The other argument historically for a restrictive approach is the contractual contention that the binding force of the arbitration clause falls within the scope of the agreement to arbitrate, and therefore a declaration on the question is a matter within the exclusive jurisdiction of arbitrators. However, this argument has never found any favour.[41] There are numerous situations where the court has to decide on the binding effect of arbitration clauses, such as applications to stay court proceedings under section 9 of the Arbitration Act 1996. The best contractual rationalization appears to be that the preclusive contractual effect of the agreement to arbitrate is to be construed as expressly or impliedly qualified to allow for the court's ability to grant supportive measures, including declarations as to the effect of the agreement to arbitrate, in appropriate cases.[42] In such situations, the court and the arbitrators have a concurrent jurisdiction.[43]

15.29   The effect of *Ust-Kamenogorsk* was considered in *HC Tradeland Malta v Tradeland Commodities*, in which a claim was made for a declaration as to the force of the arbitration clause where there was no problem of competing foreign proceedings, and the claimant

---

[39]   *Ust-Kamenogorsk Hydropower Plant JSC v AES Ust-Kamenogorsk Hydropower Plant LLP* [2013] 1 WLR 1889 (SC) [39]–[40]. In *HC Tradeland Malta v Tradeland Commodities* [2016] 1 WLR 3120 [12]–[15], [27]–[29], the court similarly concluded that s 32 did not create any absolute bar of jurisdiction.

[40]   *Ust-Kamenogorsk Hydropower Plant JSC v AES Ust-Kamenogorsk Hydropower Plant LLP* [2013] 1 WLR 1889 (SC) [60].

[41]   Any such conclusion for arbitration clauses in general would be inconsistent with the result in the *Ust-Kamenogorsk* case.

Further, in *Toepfer International GmbH v Société Cargill France* [1997] 2 Lloyds Rep 98, 107, 109, Colman J rejected the argument that even a *Scott v Avery* clause should preclude the grant of injunctive relief, and also rejected the parallel argument that it precluded the grant of declaratory relief, because (a) the *Scott v Avery* clause applied only to substantive disputes; and (b) the declarations sought merely to establish the factual basis for the injunctions, and the fact that declarations were sought to ratify the court's conclusions on this point did not engage the *Scott v Avery* clause. On appeal, the Court of Appeal upheld the Judge's conclusion in respect of injunctive relief (albeit on slightly different grounds, and in terms that no longer reflect the law), and implicitly approved his grant of declarations, but did not specifically consider the question of declaratory relief: [1998] 1 Lloyds Rep 379 (CA) 385. It is submitted, with respect, that although Colman J's conclusion is correct, his reasoning may bear further examination. In particular, the conclusion that the arbitration clause only applied to substantive disputes is also dubious, as it would preclude the arbitrators themselves from granting parallel declarations. The better answer may be that, as is suggested in the main text, the court's ability to grant remedial measures in support of an arbitration, including injunctions to enforce the arbitration and declarations as to its scope, is an exception, if necessary by the implication of an implied term, to the preclusive scope of the arbitration clause (see also Ch 7, para 7.58).

[42]   Rix LJ referred to the parallel reasoning in the first edition of this work with apparent approval in *AES Ust-Kamenogorsk Hydropower Plant LLP v Ust-Kamenogorsk Hydropower Plant JSC* [2012] 1 WLR 920 (CA) [104]. The same analysis was also approved by Teare J in *Sheffield United FC v West Ham United FC* [2009] 1 Lloyds Rep 167 [40]; and Andrew Smith J in *Nomihold Securities v Mobile Telesystems Finance (No 2)* [2012] 1 Lloyds Rep 442 at [46]–[47]. The issues are discussed further in Ch 7, para 7.58, which addresses the difficult authority of *B v S* [2011] 2 Lloyds Rep 18 (at Ch 7, 7.58, n 114).

[43]   See *Nomihold Securities v Mobile Telesystems Finance (No 2)* [2012] 1 Lloyds Rep 442 at [46]–[51].

could, and intended to, commence arbitral proceedings in which any necessary declaration could be granted. The court accepted that there was no bar of jurisdiction to the grant of declarations as to the effect of arbitration clauses but held that on those facts it would be wrong to grant a declaration as a matter of principle, or anyway that it should decline to grant a declaration in its discretion. Granting a declaration in such a situation would circumvent sections 30 and 32 of the Act and usurp the arbitrators' role. But the court made clear that it was distinguishing what it called the 'anti-suit' situation; and it also distinguished the situation in *Through Transport*, where a declaration but not an injunction had been granted in a case of competing proceedings elsewhere in the Brussels–Lugano zone.[44]

In the circumstances, the best view of the law is that neither section 1(c) nor section 32, nor the contractual effect of the arbitration clause, impose any absolute or jurisdictional constraint on the grant of declarations to enforce arbitration clauses.   **15.30**

Instead, whether or not a declaration should be granted, or whether it should be left to the arbitrators, or sought only through section 32, is a question of principle and discretion, and depends on the context. In general, it is necessary to use 'sensitivity' to the arbitrators' role and the scheme of the 1996 Act,[45] and to avoid 'usurpation'[46] of the arbitrators' jurisdiction as to their own jurisdiction—their 'Competence-Competence'.   **15.31**

Even if an arbitration is underway or on the point of commencement, there will be situations where a declaration by a court will be appropriate. One such situation is where the court will, in reality, be resolving the question of jurisdiction in the context of an anti-suit injunction, and there is little purpose in requiring a further hearing before arbitrators before a declaration is granted. A further situation may be where (within the Brussels–Lugano zone) an injunction is prohibited and only a declaration can be granted by the court to protect the arbitration process, but the grant of a declaration would be of real utility. In contrast, where there is no reason not to use the normal arbitral processes other than a desire to avoid the normal process of an arbitral award on jurisdiction and then a subsequent appeal, and no issue of competing foreign proceedings, it seems in the light of *HC Tradeland* that it would be wrong in principle, or at least discretion, to grant a declaration.   **15.32**

In the light of this, the practice of granting declarations alongside or in place of anti-suit injunctions, to protect an arbitration against competing foreign proceedings, does not need to be abandoned. Nevertheless, the readiness with which declarations have been granted in the past may now deserve some rethinking. Indeed, the principle of avoiding usurpation of the arbitrators' role means that there may be circumstances, even if the court is intervening to protect the arbitration from competing foreign proceedings, where the final determination of the binding scope of the arbitration clause should be left to the arbitrators. This might mean, for example, that the appropriate relief will be an interim anti-suit injunction, rather than any final declaration.[47] But the appropriate resolution will be context-dependent.   **15.33**

---

[44] *HC Tradeland Malta v Tradeland Commodities* [2016] 1 WLR 3120.

[45] *Ust-Kamenogorsk Hydropower Plant JSC v AES Ust-Kamenogorsk Hydropower Plant LLP* [2013] 1 WLR 1889 (SC) [60].

[46] *AES Ust-Kamenogorsk Hydropower Plant LLP v Ust-Kamenogorsk Hydropower Plant JSC* [2010] 2 Lloyds Rep 493 [21], [2012] 1 WLR 920 (CA) [108]–[110] and *HC Tradeland Malta v Tradeland Commodities* [2016] 1 WLR 3120.

[47] See *AES Ust-Kamenogorsk Hydropower Plant LLP v Ust-Kamenogorsk Hydropower Plant JSC* [2010] 2 Lloyds Rep 493 [21], [2012] 1 WLR 920 (CA) [108]–[110]. In that case Burton J fashioned an apparent middle solution, in which a declaration was granted that the injunction defendant could not bring his claim otherwise than

4. Jurisdiction to Hear Claims for Contractual Declarations

15.34   Where a claimant seeks a declaration that an English exclusive jurisdiction clause is binding, the English courts will generally have jurisdiction under Article 25 of the Recast or the Hague Convention on the Choice of Court, or in the rarer cases where neither of these apply,[48] under CPR Part 6 PD 6B para 3.1(6)(c) and (d).[49]

15.35   Before the Brussels I Recast, there were potential *lis pendens* problems where the foreign proceedings in another EU state had been commenced first.[50] However, in *The Alexandros T* the Supreme Court adopted a robust approach to *lis pendens* and concluded that claims for declarations as to the effect of exclusive jurisdiction clauses were not 'the same cause of action' as foreign claims on the merits, and so did not have to be stayed under Article 29.[51] The Supreme Court further held that, although the declarations were related to the foreign proceedings on the merits, they should not be stayed in the court's discretion under Article 30, in particular because the English court as the chosen court was best placed to determine questions of the scope of the contractual agreements in question.[52]

15.36   Furthermore, all such *lis pendens* problems have now been removed under the Recast by Article 31, and Recital 22, which make clear that in cases concerning exclusive jurisdiction clauses the purportedly chosen court is entitled to determine its jurisdiction first.[53]

15.37   If a declaration is sought to establish the binding force of an arbitration clause, the claim will fall within the arbitration exception to the Brussels–Lugano regime.[54] As a result, the English court will usually have jurisdiction to hear a claim for a declaration that an English arbitration clause is binding, under CPR 62.5(1)(c), because the claim 'affects' an arbitration agreement, and it seems also under CPR PD 6B para 3.1(6)(c), as an agreement for

---

in arbitration. The aim was to avoid prejudging the arbitrators' determination of their own jurisdiction. It may, however, be doubted whether this is a valid middle solution. Even a declaration that claims cannot be brought otherwise than in arbitration will involve a final determination of the scope of the arbitration clause. An interim anti-suit injunction, in contrast, has the advantage of avoiding any final determination of the contractual scope of the clause.

---

[48]   Article 23 of the Brussels I Regulation applied only where one of the parties to the jurisdiction clause was domiciled within the EU: *Ravennavi v New Century Shipbuilding* [2007] 2 Lloyds Rep 24 (CA) [3]. But Article 25 of the Recast gives jurisdiction to the court chosen by the jurisdiction clause irrespective of domicile.

[49]   See *Gulf T Bank v Mitsubishi Heavy Industries* [1994] 1 Lloyds Rep 323, 327–28, under the RSC. The same result will follow under the broader wording of the CPR: see *Albon v Naza Motor Trading* [2007] 1 WLR 2489 [25]–[26]. The correctness of this is implicit from the existence of CPR PD 6B para 3.1(8), which permits service out of the jurisdiction of declarations that a contract does not exist.

[50]   In contrast, claims for declarations from arbitrators are not directly affected by the *lis pendens* rules of the Brussels–Lugano regime: see para 15.37.

[51]   *Starlight Shipping v Allianz Marine & Aviation Versicherungs (The Alexandros T)* [2014] 1 Lloyds Rep 223 (SC) [38]. The position was potentially different for declarations as to the effect of settlement agreements, which were arguably characterized as declarations of non-liability, as to which a reference was made to the European Court of Justice. The decision has been followed in *Barclays Bank v Ente Nazionale di Previdenza ed Assistenza dei Medici e Degli Odontoiatri* [2015] 2 Lloyds Rep 527 [63]–[91], [2016] 2 CLC 859 (CA) [20]–[28].

[52]   *Starlight Shipping v Allianz Marine & Aviation Versicherungs (The Alexandros T)* [2014] 1 Lloyds Rep 223 (SC) [91]–[97]; followed by *Barclays Bank v Ente Nazionale di Previdenza ed Assistenza dei Medici e Degli Odontoiatri* [2015] 2 Lloyds Rep 527 [92]–[97], [2016] 2 CLC 859 (CA) [29]–[31]. This was a difference of approach to some of the earlier case law: see *Toepfer International v Molino Boschi* [1996] 1 Lloyds Rep 510, 513–15 and *Toepfer International v Société Cargill* [1998] 1 Lloyds Rep 379 (CA) 388.

[53]   Discussed in *Dexia Crediop v Provincia di Brescia* [2016] EWHC 3261 [139]–[141].

[54]   See Ch 12, para 12.80.

arbitration in England will normally be governed by English law.[55] In addition, since they fall outside the regime, claims for declarations as to the effect of arbitration clauses will not be affected by *lis pendens* under Articles 29 and 30 of the Recast.[56]

5. Declarations by Arbitrators

Under English arbitration law, arbitrators have jurisdiction under sections 30 and 31 of the **15.38** Arbitration Act 1996 to grant awards that an arbitration clause is binding, either on the application of the arbitration claimant who wishes to uphold the validity of the clause, or when dismissing a jurisdiction challenge by the arbitration respondent.[57] Obviously, claims before arbitrators do not face difficulties of service out of the jurisdiction, nor are they affected by the *lis pendens* effect of prior proceedings elsewhere in the Brussels–Lugano zone.

If an award that an arbitration clause is binding, or that certain claims fall within the scope **15.39** of the arbitration clause, has been obtained, the successful party can either ask the court to enter judgment in the terms of the award by the summary procedure under section 66 of the Arbitration Act,[58] or, if necessary,[59] bring a common law claim on the award to obtain a court declaration ratifying the Tribunal's finding that the arbitration agreement is binding. A judgment by the court enforcing the arbitrators' declaration that an arbitration clause is binding should have the same effect and consequences as a declaration made by the court in the first instance. The English courts have so far been willing to permit enforcement of awards in order to assist with resisting enforcement of inconsistent foreign judgments, on the basis that there is a 'real prospect' that such enforcement would provide an (additional) ground to refuse recognition.[60] Where the arbitration award is an English award, and is *res judicata*, a court judgment enforcing the award may in the final analysis add little; as enforcement of a foreign judgment which contradicted a prior binding award should be contrary to public policy and section 54 of the Arbitration Act 1996.[61] But it may be a useful additional pre-emptive precaution, in particular in the face of a potential competing Brussels–Lugano judgment, since the correct interpretation of the Brussels–Lugano instruments in this regard has not yet been resolved.

---

[55] *Gulf Bank v Mitsubishi Heavy Industries* [1994] 1 Lloyds Rep 323, 327–28; *AES Ust-Kamenogorsk Hydropower Plant LLP v Ust-Kamenogorsk Hydropower Plant JSC* [2010] 2 Lloyds Rep 493 [19]–[20] (62.5(1)(c), [25], [2012] 1 WLR 920 (CA) [112]–[121], [127]–[128], [141]; [2013] 1 WLR 1889 (SC) [51]; *Shipowners' Mutual Protection and Indemnity Association (Luxembourg) v Containerships Denizcilik Nakliyat ve Ticaret (The Yusuf Cepnioglu)* [2015] 1 Lloyds Rep 567 [41]–[45], 48]–[49].

[56] Case C-190/89, *Marc Rich v Società Italiana Impianti (The Atlantic Emperor)* [1991] ECR I-3855, AG [95], ECJ [30]; *Toepfer International v Société Cargill* [1997] 2 Lloyds Rep 98, 105 (Colman J); *Sovarex v Alvarez* [2011] 2 Lloyds Rep 320 [57]–[65]; *London Steamship Owners' Mutual Insurance v Kingdom of Spain (The Prestige) (No 2)* [2014] 1 Lloyds Rep 309 [190]–[193].

[57] For a recent example, see *African Fertilizers and Chemicals NIG v BD Shipsnavo* [2011] 2 Lloyds Rep 531 [5].

[58] See eg *African Fertilizers and Chemicals NIG v BD Shipsnavo* [2011] 2 Lloyds Rep 531; *West Tankers v Allianz (The Front Comor)* [2011] 2 Lloyds Rep 117; *London Steamship Owners' Mutual Insurance v Kingdom of Spain (The Prestige) (No 2)* [2014] 1 Lloyds Rep 309 [9], [187]–[198].

[59] Applications under s 66 are the usual course as they are quicker and cheaper. A common law action on the award will only be necessary if for some reason a full trial is required to determine whether the award should be enforced, in which case the summary procedure would be inappropriate.

[60] *National Navigation v Endesa Generacion (The Wadi Sudr)* [2010] 1 Lloyd Rep 193 (CA) [63]; *West Tankers v Allianz (The Front Comor)* [2011] 2 Lloyds Rep 117 (upheld on appeal [2012] 1 Lloyds Rep 398 (CA); *African Fertilizers and Chemicals NIG v BD Shipsnavo* [2011] 2 Lloyds Rep 531; *London Steamship Owners' Mutual Insurance v Kingdom of Spain (The Prestige) (No 2)* [2014] 1 Lloyds Rep 309 [9] and [187]–[198].

[61] See para 15.14.

15.40   The court will have power to serve such proceedings out of the jurisdiction.[62] Claims to enforce an arbitration award declaring that the arbitrators have jurisdiction, whether under the common law or under section 66, will fall outside the scope of the Brussels–Lugano regime and should not be precluded by the principle of mutual trust.[63] Similarly, arguments that such section 66 applications should be stayed in favour of prior competing court proceedings in another EU state as a matter of public policy or discretion have also been rejected.[64]

6. Non-Contractual Declarations

15.41   In contrast, there is no reported example of an attempt to claim a declaration that foreign proceedings are vexatious or oppressive in a non-contractual case. The intangible nature of a substantive finding that foreign proceedings were vexatious or oppressive, independent of any concrete remedy, may mean that this is a remedy the court would be unlikely to grant. Further, a declaration of this nature might well be meaningless, since if no injunction were sought, there would appear to be no obvious remedial consequence.[65]

15.42   In *Deaville v Aeroflot*, where there were competing proceedings in England and France, and the case fell within the scope of the Warsaw Convention, the Judge concluded that it would be contrary to comity for the court to grant a declaration that the jurisdiction of the French courts was precluded by the Warsaw Convention.[66]

7. Pre-Emptive Declarations as to Recognition and Enforcement

15.43   The courts have in the past generally refused to grant pre-emptive declarations as to whether they will enforce foreign judgments,[67] or as to whether they will admit evidence which is being sought in foreign evidence-gathering proceedings,[68] preferring to reserve their position until the moment when enforcement is sought, or the evidence is adduced. However,

---

[62] In respect of actions to enforce an award, the relevant power is provided by CPR PD 6B para 3.1(10). In respect of summary enforcement of an award under Arbitration Act 1996, s 66, the relevant power is provided by CPR 62.18.

[63] See *National Navigation v Endesa Generacion (The Wadi Sudr)* [2010] 1 Lloyds Rep 193 (CA) [38(i)]; *Sovarex v Alvarez* [2011] 2 Lloyds Rep 320 [52]–[65]; *London Steamship Owners' Mutual Insurance v Kingdom of Spain (The Prestige) (No 2)* [2014] 1 Lloyds Rep 309 [187]–[198]. See further Ch 12, para 12.80.

[64] *Sovarex v Alvarez* [2011] 2 Lloyds Rep 320 [52]–[65]; *London Steamship Owners' Mutual Insurance v Kingdom of Spain (The Prestige) (No 2)* [2014] 1 Lloyds Rep 309 [186]–[198].

[65] A Briggs, 'The Unrestrained Reach of an Anti-Suit Injunction: A Pause for Thought' [1997] LMCLQ 90, 101, suggests that a declaration that the foreign proceedings were vexatious and oppressive would be useful and appropriate, as it could be relied on subsequently to resist enforcement or recognition of the foreign judgment. But within the Brussels–Lugano regime, this would seem to involve an evaluative assessment of the basis of the other Brussels–Lugano court's assumption of jurisdiction.

[66] *Deaville v Aeroflot Russian International Airlines* [1997] 2 Lloyds Rep 67, 70, 72, 75.

[67] *EI Du Pont de Nemours v IC Agnew (No 2)* [1988] 2 Lloyds Rep 240 (CA) 245, 249, 250; *Toepfer International v Molino Boschi* [1996] 1 Lloyds Rep 510, 518 (*obiter*); *Philip Alexander Securities & Futures v Bamberger* [1997] ILPr 73 [123] (Waller J) (the Court of Appeal declined to interfere with his discretion at [45]–[46], although in terms that suggested that an alternative conclusion could legitimately have been reached). However, such a declaration was granted in *Ellerman Lines v Landi (The Falernian)* (1927) 29 Ll L Rep 15, 23 (where it was viewed as a question of convenience; the point was not challenged on appeal). A Briggs, 'The Unrestrained Reach of an Anti-Suit Injunction: A Pause for Thought' [1997] LMCLQ 90, 100–02, suggests that such declarations may be appropriate.

[68] cf *Bankers Trust International v PT Dharmala Sakti Sejahtera (No 1)* [1996] CLC 252, 253H.

there are signs of change. In recent cases, the courts have been willing to enforce arbitration awards under section 66 of the Arbitration Act 1996 on the basis that such enforcement would give (additional) 'good prospects' of resisting enforcement.[69] The restrictions imposed by European law on the use of anti-suit injunctions may also encourage a more liberal approach.[70]

C. APPLICATIONS FOR THE APPOINTMENT
OF AN ARBITRATOR

A party who is bringing court proceedings abroad in arguable breach of an arbitration agreement, and whose case abroad depends on a denial that the arbitration clause is valid and binding, will frequently refuse to cooperate in the appointment of an arbitrator in the English arbitration. If the contractual appointment procedure has failed, the court can appoint an arbitrator under section 18 of the Arbitration Act 1996.   **15.44**

Applications to appoint an arbitrator fall outside the scope of the Brussels–Lugano regime,[71] and they do not infringe the principle of mutual trust.[72] The court has power to serve applications for the appointment of an arbitrator out of the jurisdiction under CPR 62.5.[73]   **15.45**

Where the English courts have concluded that an arbitration clause is binding and applicable, they are willing to deploy their powers to appoint an arbitrator to enable arbitration proceedings in England to be pushed forwards, ahead of competing court proceedings elsewhere, whether within the Brussels–Lugano regime, or outside it.[74]   **15.46**

D. PROCEDURAL MANAGEMENT

There is a range of procedural techniques available to litigants before the English courts that can be deployed to influence the result of conflicts of jurisdictions, without obtaining an anti-suit injunction, or any other substantive remedy. In this context 'the Court will exercise its discretion ... to give effect to the parties' rights and obligations as it understands them to be'.[75] Consequently, a party who can show that a particular procedural step will assist in ensuring that the substantive dispute will in effect be resolved in the contractual forum, or   **15.47**

---

[69] See n 15.

[70] D Tan, 'Enforcing International Arbitration Agreements in Federal Courts: Rethinking the Court's Remedial Powers' (2007) 47 Virg J Intl L 545, 609, argues that anticipatory declarations of non-recognition in respect of foreign litigation in breach of contract should be available in principle, under US law.

[71] Case C-190/89, *Marc Rich v Società Italiana Impianti (The Atlantic Emperor)* [1991] ECR I-3855, ECJ [19], upholding Hirst J in [1989] 1 Lloyds Rep 548; and see *Union de Remorquage et de Sauvetage v Lake Avery Inc (The Lake Avery)* [1997] 1 Lloyds Rep 540; *Nori Holding v Bank Otkritie Financial Corporation* [2018] 2 Lloyds Rep 80 [89]. This is confirmed by Recital 12 of the Recast.

[72] See Ch 12, nn 64 and 118.

[73] See Hirst J in *Marc Rich v Società Italiana Impianti (The Atlantic Emperor) (No 1)* [1989] 1 Lloyds Rep 548 (a decision under RSC Ord 73, r 7, the ancestor of CPR 62.5).

[74] *Through Transport Mutual Insurance Association (Eurasia) v New India Assurance (No 2)* [2005] 2 Lloyds Rep 378 [36]–[39]; *West Tankers Inc v Ras Riunione Adriatica di Sicurta (The Front Comor) (No 2)* [2007] EWHC 2184; see also *Atlanska Providba v Consignaciones Asturianas (The Lapad)* [2004] 2 Lloyds Rep 109 [25]–[34].

[75] *Through Transport Mutual Insurance Association (Eurasia) Ltd v New India Assurance Co Ltd (No 2)* [2005] 2 Lloyds Rep 378, 388.

in the otherwise most appropriate forum, will have a strong case to persuade the court to exercise its discretion in his favour.[76]

15.48   Where the substantive dispute is within the scope of the Brussels–Lugano regime, the simplest and most effective technique is to issue proceedings first, if necessary by way of an action for negative declaratory relief, and thus to ensure that there is a *lis pendens* under Article 29 of the Brussels I Recast, which should preclude any competing proceedings elsewhere in the Brussels–Lugano zone. However, the important new provisions of Article 31 of the Recast, which give the chosen court under a jurisdiction clause priority in the determination of its jurisdiction even if it was second seised, mean that the race for first seisin is now of less importance.[77] The chosen court, even if second seised, has priority to hear a declaration as to its own jurisdiction, and if it determines its own jurisdiction, that should lead to the automatic rejection of the jurisdiction of the other EU court.

15.49   The commencement of arbitration proceedings has no *lis pendens* effect, but the grant of an arbitration award on the merits, and even more so, the subsequent entry of judgment in the terms of that arbitration award, should preclude the recognition or enforcement in England of a contrary subsequent Brussels–Lugano judgment,[78] or any other foreign judgment.

15.50   If the foreign proceedings have been brought outside the Brussels–Lugano zone, or if the English or the foreign proceedings fall outside the material scope of the Brussels–Lugano regime, then the *lis pendens* rules of the Brussels I Recast will not automatically resolve the question of priority (Articles 33 and 34 of the Recast are discretionary even where they apply), and unless an application for a stay of proceedings succeeds either in England or abroad, both actions will proceed to judgment. Which action 'wins the race' and gets to judgment first can be of great importance, as the first decision can create a *res judicata*, possibly in the other action, or failing that in the courts of a third country where an attempt is made to enforce the second decision.

15.51   English courts and arbitration tribunals have undoubted powers to control proceedings before them, and have many devices at their disposal to accelerate a final decision, including the setting of tight timetables, the omitting of unnecessary procedural steps, and if necessary, an order for an expedited trial.[79] It is suggested that, in a case where the winning of the litigation race matters, and where the English court or tribunal has concluded that the foreign proceedings are in breach of contract, it is legitimate for the English court or tribunal to take appropriate procedural measures to advance the English action, so long as the requirements of a fair trial are not infringed.

15.52   A more aggressive procedural device would be for the court to use the threat of adverse procedural decisions to pressure the claimant abroad to give undertakings that he will not progress his proceedings abroad pending determination of the English proceedings. At least as matters currently stand, it is suggested that there would need to be some connection

---

[76] See by analogy *Sovarex v Alvarez* [2011] 2 Lloyds Rep 320 [52]–[65]; *London Steamship Owners' Mutual Insurance v The Kingdom of Spain (The Prestige) (No 2)* [2014] 1 Lloyds Rep 309 [186]–[198].

[77] The race to first seisin remains just as important under the Lugano Convention, for now, as the Lugano Convention has not yet been brought in line with the Brussels I Recast.

[78] See paras 15.13–15.14.

[79] See eg *Banque Cantonale Vaudoise v Waterlily Maritime* [1997] 2 Lloyds Rep 347, 357–58.

between the procedural step in question and the inconveniences produced by the continuation of the foreign litigation for it to be legitimate to require an undertaking of this kind.[80] However, it may be that the courts will become increasingly creative, now that the remedy of an anti-suit injunction is prohibited in many cases.

In *Hemain v Hemain*, the claimant abroad was vexatiously using the delay introduced by an **15.53** application for a stay of English proceedings on grounds of *forum non conveniens* to steal a march by advancing his foreign proceedings in the meanwhile. The Court of Appeal suggested that it would be a legitimate course to dismiss the stay application out of hand unless the claimant abroad gave undertakings to postpone his competing foreign litigation until after the determination of the stay application.[81]

E. RESISTING ENFORCEMENT

A party who considers that proceedings abroad are illegitimate or inappropriate in some **15.54** way can choose not to participate in the foreign proceedings, allowing judgment to be entered in his absence, with the intention of resisting enforcement of the foreign judgment in England, or any other relevant jurisdiction where he may have assets.

This is an easier strategy where the foreign proceedings are outside the Brussels–Lugano **15.55** zone or outside the material scope of the Brussels–Lugano regime,[82] because unless the defendant is present within the jurisdiction of the foreign court, or submits to the jurisdiction of the foreign court, or there is a jurisdiction clause in favour of the foreign court, or one of the limited statutory regimes for the registration of foreign judgments apply,[83] the foreign court's judgment will not be recognized in England.[84] Further, provided that the defendant did not submit to the jurisdiction of the foreign court, section 32 of the Civil Jurisdiction and Judgments Act 1932 provides that any foreign judgment which has been obtained in breach of an exclusive forum clause will not be enforceable in England.[85] There are also

---

[80] In *Credit Suisse First Boston (Europe) v MLC (Bermuda)* [1999] 1 Lloyds Rep 767, 783, Rix J considered that it would be a misuse of the court's discretion to make an extension of time for a defence in England conditional on the giving of an undertaking to discontinue competing foreign proceedings.

[81] *Hemain v Hemain* [1988] 2 FLR 388, 393B–C (CA) 393F–394A. It should be noted, however, that the authority of *Hemain* is questionable (in particular as regards injunctions): see Ch 13, paras 13.59–13.61.

[82] We leave aside here the effect of the Hague Convention on the Choice of Court where it is applicable.

[83] Namely, the Administration of Justice Act 1920, and the Foreign Judgment (Reciprocal Enforcement) Act 1920.

[84] See generally Briggs, para 7.37ff. The fact that foreign proceedings were 'vexatious and oppressive' is not in itself a ground to resist enforcement under the current law. However, A Briggs, 'The Unrestrained Reach of an Anti-Suit Injunction: A Pause for Thought' [1997] LMCLQ 90, 100–02, suggests that a declaration that foreign litigation is vexatious and oppressive should be a ground for subsequently resisting enforcement. The case law has not yet explored the overlap and differences between the concepts of a foreign judgment being contrary to public policy and it being obtained in a vexatious and oppressive manner.

[85] Civil Jurisdiction and Judgments Act 1982, s 32.

There is controversy as to whether, if there has been submission, there should then be enforcement irrespective of the forum clause (subject to any other separate defence to enforcement), or whether the effect of submission is solely to remove the automatic barrier to enforcement created by s 32, leaving a remaining question of evaluative judgment as to whether the foreign judgment should be enforced, notwithstanding the breach of the forum clause. In favour of the 'evaluative judgment' approach, see *AES Ust-Kamenogorsk Hydropower Plant LLP v Ust-Kamenogorsk Hydropower Plant JSC* [2012] 1 WLR 920 (CA) [149]–[151] (Rix LJ); *Ecobank Transnational v Tanoh* [2015] EWHC 1874 (Comm) [27], [2016] 1 WLR 2231 (CA) [43]; and see the comment in *Exmek Pharmaceuticals v Alkem Laboratories* [2016] 1 Lloyds Rep 239 [39]. Against, see *Spliethoff's Bevrachtingskantoor BV v Bank of China Ltd* [2015] 2 Lloyds Rep 623 [109]–[137]. The issue is beyond the scope of this work.

other defences to recognition of a foreign judgment, namely breach of English public policy, fraud, and breach of natural justice.[86] The public policy ground of recognition includes inconsistency with a prior English judgment that is *res judicata*,[87] and this principle must also apply to inconsistency with a prior English arbitration award that is *res judicata*.

15.56   Further, in principle, breach of an anti-suit injunction restraining pursuit of the foreign proceedings should also lead to refusal of recognition or enforcement of the foreign judgment, on grounds of public policy.[88] In any event, the party in breach of the injunction would be in contempt, and it could be forcefully argued that he could not be heard to enforce his judgment unless his contempt was purged by reversing that very judgment.[89]

15.57   In contrast, Carr J's decision in *Spliethoff's* holds that a foreign judgment obtained in breach of an anti-suit award given by English arbitrators should still be enforced in England, if

---

[86]   See generally Briggs, Ch 7.

[87]   *Vervaeke v Smith* [1983] 1 AC 145 (HL).

[88]   *Toepfer v Molino Boschi* [2006] 1 Lloyds Rep 510, 514 (Brussels–Lugano, *obiter*); *Philip Alexander Securities & Futures v Bamberger* [1997] ILPr 73 [120] (Waller J), [43] (CA); followed *obiter* in *Through Transport Mutual Insurance Association (Eurasia) v New India Assurance* [2004] 1 Lloyds Rep 206 [42]; *AK Investment v Kyrgyz Mobil Tel* [2012] 1 WLR 1804 (JCPC) [121] (injunction from third state court); *Whitworths v Synergy Food and Processing* [2014] EWHC 2439 (QB) [71]; see also *Navigation v Endesa Generacion (The Wadi Sudr)* [2010] 1 Lloyds Rep 193 (CA) [125]. In Singapore, see *WSG Nimbus Pte v Board of Control for Cricket in Sri Lanka* [2002] 3 SLR 603 (Sing HC) [58]–[65].

This principle should apply, at least in general, even if the injunction claimant has subsequently submitted to the jurisdiction of the foreign court. Indeed, all of the mentioned cases were either cases where submission had, or would have, occurred. Although submission is one of the initial preconditions for recognition at common law, it is a confusion to regard it as in itself overriding defences against recognition, and it should not, it is submitted, without more defeat the strong public policy against recognition of the foreign judgment where an anti-suit injunction has been breached. Any other result would undervalue the importance of enforcement of the court's orders, undermine the coherence of the anti-suit jurisdiction, and be inconsistent with the application of the law of contempt. It would put injunction claimants, faced by injunction defendants who are willing to be in contempt, in impossible positions, as the injunction claimant may then have no real choice but to engage in the foreign litigation while still insisting on the importance of respect for his injunction; sanctions for contempt of court may then be ineffective because of their territorial limitations. It would be strange if in such a situation the foreign judgment were then enforced in England merely on the grounds of a submission to the foreign court.

We need to consider whether *Golubovich v Golubovich* [2011] Fam 88 (CA), is a counter-example, but on analysis it is not. That judgment was reached in the context of very special facts: in the family law context, a divorce granted in Russia, and which as a matter of personal status would have effect similar to an *in rem* judgment, had been obtained in breach of an anti-suit injunction requiring the Russian proceedings to be suspended. Nevertheless, the divorce was recognized in England. But the circumstances were confused and the injunction claimant seemed to have been much to blame for the breach of the injunction. Further, as a matter of public policy, since the dissolution of the marriage would be recognized internationally, and it is important for all courts to speak with consistent clarity as to whether two persons are married or not, there were strong policy reasons to recognize the validity of the divorce ([75], [78]); the presumptive statutory obligation under the Family Law Act 1986 to recognize the foreign divorce therefore prevailed. Yet further, the recognition of the divorce did not matter much, in itself, as notwithstanding the *in rem* effect of the divorce itself, the Court of Appeal made clear that the English courts would retain jurisdiction over ancillary financial relief, and that the consequences of breach of the injunction could be visited on the husband in the context of any ancillary relief applications ([76]–[77]). Finally, the Court of Appeal's attention was not drawn to any of the previous authorities in the commercial context other than *Wadi Sudr*. It is submitted that the case is specific to the divorce context, and does not undermine the force of the basic principle that breach of an anti-suit injunction should in general suffice to justify refusal of enforcement of the resulting foreign judgment on grounds of public policy.

In *Spliethoff's Bevrachtingskantoor v Bank of China Ltd* [2015] 2 Lloyds Rep 623 [109]–[137], Carr J declined to apply the statements in *Bamberger*, *AK v Kyrgz*, and *WSG Nimbus* (the other authorities were not cited to her) to the separate and distinct question of enforcement of foreign judgments obtained in breach of anti-suit awards given by arbitrators (which are different to court injunctions in key respects), where there had been a submission to the jurisdiction of the foreign court. Aspects of her reasoning might also be read as being in tension with the conclusions in relation to court injunctions, although this is not very clear. With respect, however, it is submitted that to the extent there is a tension, it is the reasoning in *Spliethoff's* which is incorrect, and inconsistent with authority and principle, for the reasons given. The decision can in any event easily be distinguished and treated as applicable only, at most, to anti-suit awards.

[89]   *Whitworths v Synergy Food and Processing* [2014] EWHC 2439 (QB) [71]; see also *Fakih Bros v AP Moller (Copenhagen)* [1994] 1 Lloyds Rep 103, 108.

there has been submission to the jurisdiction of the foreign court,[90] but with respect the reasoning is unsatisfactory, and the result unattractive. (It is also distinguishable from the situation of anti-suit injunctions granted by the court, which are different juridically, since anti-suit awards have only contractual force.) Carr J reasoned that an arbitral anti-suit should be no more protection than an arbitration clause itself, and seemed to regard submission as determinative of public policy at least as regards anti-suit awards. But an anti-suit award *prima facie* should be *res judicata* (a point on which Carr J may not have been addressed). Submission should not in itself, reverse a *res judicata*; and as a matter of policy an anti-suit award goes further than a contestable arbitration clause since it decides, with what should be binding effect, that there should be protection from the foreign litigation.[91]

However, if the foreign proceedings are unfolding in another member state of the Brussels–Lugano regime, the opportunities for resisting the recognition or enforcement of any resulting judgment are less safe.[92]   **15.58**

Under Articles 36–51 of the Brussels I Recast, a Brussels–Lugano judgment must, in general, be recognized and enforced in England irrespective of whether the defendant submitted to the jurisdiction of the foreign court,[93] unless it is irreconcilable with a prior decision that is *res judicata*,[94] or unless recognition is 'manifestly contrary to public policy'.[95] Article 45(3) expressly states that 'The test of public policy ... may not be applied to the rules relating to jurisdiction.'[96] However, by Article 73, the Recast 'shall not affect' the operation of the New York Convention on international arbitration.   **15.59**

It seems likely that the judgment of another Brussels–Lugano court, within the material scope of the Brussels–Lugano regime, must be recognized under the Recast by the English courts, even if to English eyes it has been obtained in breach of an exclusive jurisdiction clause, as to refuse recognition on this ground would be contrary to the structure of the Recast.[97]   **15.60**

---

[90] *Spliethoff's Bevrachtingskantoor v Bank of China* [2015] 2 Lloyds Rep 623 [109]–[137].

[91] Carr J's reasoning on submission more generally also appears to be wrong: see n 30.

[92] The ability to resist enforcement is even more limited under Regulation 805/2004, creating a European Enforcement Order ('EEO'). This can apply where a judgment was uncontested in the state of origin. The court of origin can issue an EEO certificate, and if so, then unless there is a prior *res judicata*, recognition in another member state is automatic: Article 5. It has been argued that Article 20, which provides for enforcement to take place according to national law, preserves national law defences to enforcement (see G Cuniberti, 'The Recognition of Foreign Judgments Lacking Reasons in Europe: Access to Justice, Foreign Court Avoidance, and Efficiency (2008) 57 ICLQ 25, 50–51) but this is controversial, and could be said to undermine the purpose of the EEO Regulation. So, an uncontested judgment reached in breach of an exclusive forum clause might be automatically enforceable under the EEO Regulation. However, 'arbitration' is excluded from the scope of the EEO Regulation: see Article 2(d), and so for parallel reasons to those ventilated at paras 15.62–15.63, it is arguable that judgments reached in breach of arbitration clauses fall outside the scope of the EEO Regulation.

[93] Section 32 of the Civil Jurisdiction and Judgments Act 1982 provides no protection, because s 32(4)(a) provides that it shall not affect judgments which are required to be recognized or enforced under the Brussels–Lugano regime.

[94] Articles 45(1)(c) and 45(1)(d) of the Recast.

[95] Article 45(1)(a). It is for national law to determine what is contrary to public policy. However, recourse to the public policy exception can only be made in exceptional cases, and European law circumscribes the limits within which national public policy is allowed to operate: Case C-7/98, *Bamberski v Krombach* [2000] ECR I-1935, [22]–[23]; Case C-38/98, *Régie Nationale des Usines Renault v Maxicar* [2000] ECR I-2973, [30].

[96] See Case C-7/98, *Bamberski v Krombach* [2000] ECR I-1935, [23]. Further, a judgment cannot be refused on grounds of public policy merely because the state of judgment applied a different legal rule to that which would have been applied in the recognizing state: Case C-38/98, *Régie Nationale des Usines Renault v Maxicar* [2000] ECR I-2973, ECJ [29].

[97] Article 45(1)(e) of the Recast lists those sections which, if breached, in the opinion of the receiving court, entitle the receiving court to refuse recognition; but Section 7 (and Article 25) on jurisdiction clauses, is not included in the list. Thus, an argument that a jurisdiction clause has been breached would appear to amount to an illegitimate attempt to re-assess the foreign court's assumption of jurisdiction inconsistently with Article 45(3) of the Recast. In *The Wadi Sudr* it was held that the mere fact that the foreign court's decision on the applicability of an arbitration clause

15.61   The defendant's arguments against recognition would be stronger if the English courts had granted a declaration that an exclusive jurisdiction clause obliged the claimant abroad to litigate in England, although even in that case there remains a risk that the foreign judgment would have to be enforced under the Brussels–Lugano regime.[98] The best mechanism for protecting a jurisdiction clause in such a case is therefore to commence proceedings in the chosen court on the merits. In cases where the Recast applies, the chosen court will have priority even if it was second seised, pursuant to Article 31. In Lugano Convention cases, it will, however, remain important to ensure that the English court is first seised.

15.62   There has been considerable controversy about whether a judgment on the merits given by another Brussels–Lugano court must be recognized under the Brussels–Lugano regime by the English courts if it has been obtained in breach of an arbitration agreement. The United Kingdom and the existing contracting parties did not agree how to resolve this question on the United Kingdom's accession, and the text of the Brussels Convention as revised left it open.[99]

15.63   The writers of the various reports on the earlier Brussels instruments before the Recast, and the European Court's advocates general, approached this question in differing ways, none of which were decisive.[100] The variation of opinion reflects different attitudes to arbitration in the member states.[101]

---

is inconsistent with how an English court would have decided the point is not sufficient to justify a refusal of recognition: see *National Navigation v Endesa Generacion (The Wadi Sudr)* [2010] 1 Lloyds Rep 193 (CA) [125].

---

[98] See para 15.16.

[99] See Report on the Convention on the Association of the Kingdom of Denmark, Ireland and the United Kingdom of Great Britain and Northern Ireland to the Convention and to the Protocol on its Interpretation by the Court of Justice, rapporteur Professor P Schlosser, para 62 (hereafter the 'Schlosser Report), suggesting that the point could be dealt with in national implementing legislation. This was an opportunity which the UK did not take up, although it could be done by a suitable amendment to s 32 of the Civil Jurisdiction and Judgments Act 1982. In *Partenreederei M/S Heidberg v Grosvenor Grain and Feed (The Heidberg)* [1994] 2 Lloyds Rep 287, 301, Judge Diamond QC concluded that Parliament's failure to provide expressly to the contrary meant that s 32 should be understood to accept that Brussels–Lugano judgments reached in breach of an arbitration clause should be enforced; but the better view is that s 32 leaves the point open: *Philip Alexander Securities & Futures v Bamberger* [1997] ILPr 73 (Waller J), [94]–[97].

[100] The Schlosser Report (paras 61–62) discusses the arguments for and against recognition of judgment of the courts of other member states reached in breach of an arbitration clause but leaves the point open. The Report on the Accession of the Hellenic Republic to the Community Convention on Jurisdiction and the enforcement of Judgments in Civil and Commercial Matters [1986] OJ C 298, 24 November 1986 (hereafter the 'Evrigenis and Kerameus Report') (which is less influential) supports recognition (para 35). In Case C-190/89, *Marc Rich v Società Italiana Impianti (The Atlantic Emperor)* [1991] ECR I-3855, Darmon AG viewed the point as open, and appeared to disapprove of the statements in the Evrigenis and Kerameus report (AG [45]).

The European Court itself has not expressed a view. Arguments can be made that Case-145/86, *Hoffmann v Krieg* [1988] ECR 645 suggests that a judgment reached in breach of an arbitration clause need not be treated as Brussels–Lugano judgment, and also that Case C-391/95, *Van Uden Maritime BV v Kommanditgesellschaft in Firma Deco-Line* [1998] ECR I-7091 suggests the contrary; but neither case is directly on point.

The decision of the French Cour de Cassation, in *Assurances Générales de France v Goettgens* (No 98-21627, 14 November 2000) appears not to decide the point of principle, as the ground of the conclusion that the German judgment should be recognized notwithstanding the arbitration clause appears to have been that the defendant had not relied on the arbitration clause before the German court.

For academic opinions in favour of recognition, see P Kaye, 'The Judgments Convention and Arbitration: Mutual Spheres of Influence' (1991) 7 Arb Intl, 289, 291–92; for academic opinions against recognition see Briggs, paras 2.30–2.31, 7.08, 7.11, 7.13; Sir L Collins et al (eds), *Dicey, Morris & Collins on the Conflict of Laws* (15th edn, Sweet & Maxwell 2012) para 14.197; B Audit, 'Arbitration and the Brussels Convention' (1993) 9 Arb Intl 1, 20–25; D Hascher, 'Recognition and Enforcement of Judgments on the Existence and Validity of an Arbitration Clause under the Brussels Convention' (1997) 13 Arb Intl 33 (suggesting that the answer lies in the New York Convention and Art 57 of the Brussels Convention, now Art 71 of the Regulation); S Dutson, 'Breach of an Arbitration or Exclusive Jurisdiction Clause: The Legal Remedies if it Continues' (2000) 16 Arb Intl 89, 99 n 48; H Gaudemet-Tallon, *Compétence et Exécution des Jugements en Europe* (3rd edn, LDGJ 2002) para 363; C Ambrose, 'Arbitration and the Free Movement of Judgments' (2003) 19 Arb Intl, 3, 14–20.

[101] See Schlosser Report, para 62.

The English decisions have also expressed different views on the question.[102] Most recently,   **15.64**
in *The Wadi Sudr*, the Spanish court had reached a prior decision that an arbitration clause
was not binding.[103] Applying the law as it stood under Brussels I Regulation, in the light of
the *Front Comor*, this decision fell within the scope of the Regulation (because it had been
reached in the context of Regulation proceedings and the merits) and so was a binding and
enforceable Regulation judgment. The English court therefore had to recognize it, and treat
it as *res judicata*, unless public policy was a ground to refuse recognition. It was held that the
mere fact that the English court would have reached a different decision as to the force of the
arbitration clause was not enough to justify a refusal of recognition of the judgment as to the
effect of the arbitration clause on grounds of public policy. The *res judicata* on the force of
the clause was decisive.

This does not, however, definitively resolve the question of what happens if there is no   **15.65**
foreign judgment with *res judicata* effect on the force of the arbitration clause, nor what
happens now under the Brussels I Recast. The effect of para 2 of Recital 12 of the Brussels
I Recast (reversing the effect of *The Front Comor*) is that a foreign judgment on the force of
an arbitration clause is now *not* enforceable under the Recast. The *res judicata* effect of the
Spanish judgment on that very point, which was the heart of the decision in *The Wadi Sudr,*
will therefore not recur automatically.

Of the two judges that gave reasoned judgments in *Wadi Sudr*, Waller LJ's reasoning is fo-   **15.66**
cused on the situation where the foreign judgment on the effect of the arbitration clause
has *res judicata* effect. Moore Bick LJ's reasoning potentially goes broader. In terms that
may be applicable independently of a foreign *res judicata*, he concluded that breach of an
arbitration clause (to English eyes) would in general be insufficient, in itself, to render
enforcement of the foreign judgment contrary to public policy (and the logic would seem
to be the same, whether it is a judgment on the force of the clause or a judgment on the
merits). However, on what may be the crucial question, whether enforcement would be
contrary to the New York Convention if to English eyes there was a binding arbitration
clause, Moore Bick LJ's reasoning is apparently dependent on the *res judicata* effect of the
Spanish judgment.[104]

---

[102] In *Partenreederei M/S Heidberg v Grosvenor Grain and Feed (The Heidberg)* [1994] 2 Lloyds Rep 287,
301–02, it was held that the foreign judgment on the substance of the dispute should be recognized, even if
reached in breach of an arbitration clause; and in *Marc Rich v Società Italiana Impianti (The Atlantic Emperor)
(No 2)* [1992] 1 Lloyds Rep 624 (CA) 629–33, the point was left open. Further, in *Toepfer International GmbH
v Société Cargill France* [1997] 2 Lloyds Rep 98 (CA) 111, Colman J accepted that in light of *The Heidberg*, a
Brussels–Lugano judgment reached in breach of an arbitration clause 'might well be enforceable in another
Convention country'.
    However, in *Philip Alexander Securities & Futures v Bamberger* [1997] ILPr 73 [88]–[115], Waller J concluded
that a judgment reached in breach of an arbitration clause fell within the scope of the Brussels–Lugano regime but
suggested that recognition might be refused on grounds of public policy (the Court of Appeal held that this point
was referable but did not need to make the reference, at [44]); and in *Navigation Maritime Bulgare v Rustal Trading
Ltd (The Ivan Zagubanski)* [2002] 1 Lloyds Rep 106 [104], Aikens J referred to Waller J's decision with no apparent
disapproval (and refused to follow *The Heidberg* on other points, at [100(1)]). In *Banco Nacional de Comercio
Exterior v Empresa de Telecommuniciones de Cuba* [2007] ILPr 59, [14], Tomlinson J described the question as 'difficult and unresolved'. The most recent decision on the point is *The Wadi Sudr*, discussed in the main text, in which
Waller LJ reached different conclusions to his earlier views in the *Bamberger* case.
[103] *National Navigation Co v Endesa Generacion SA (The Wadi Sudr)* [2010] 1 Lloyds Rep 193 (CA).
[104] *National Navigation v Endesa Generacion (The Wadi Sudr)* [2010] 1 Lloyds Rep 193 (CA) [125], [127], [131].
Further, he observed that 'different considerations would arise if the judgment was obtained through conscious
wrongdoing, for example by pursuing proceedings in defiance of an injunction'.

15.67   This particular hot potato was tossed around during the pre-legislative debates that led to the Brussels I Recast.[105] The final result again bears the hallmarks of a messy compromise. Recital 12 of the Recast again does not clearly resolve the question, stating that:

> where a court of a Member State, exercising jurisdiction under this Regulation or under national law, has determined that an arbitration agreement is null and void, inoperative or incapable of being performed, this should not preclude that court's judgment from being recognised, or as the case may be, enforced in accordance with this Regulation.

This could be read as leaving the point open, by simply preventing preclusion of recognition based on the mere fact that an arbitration agreement has been previously raised before the original court. But it may reflect an implicit assumption that recognition is the likely starting point.

15.68   It follows that sitting back and relying on the existence of an arbitration clause, enforceable in the eyes of English law, is not a safe strategy when faced with litigation elsewhere in the Brussels–Lugano zone. In contrast, if a prior declaration has been obtained from the English court, or the arbitrators, holding that the arbitration clause was applicable and binding, then there would be strong arguments that a Brussels–Lugano judgment reached inconsistently with that declaration should not be recognized in England under the Brussels–Lugano regime.[106] If a prior arbitration award on the merits has been obtained, and *a fortiori* if such award has been enforced by a judgment in England, the case against enforcement of an inconsistent Brussels–Lugano judgment is even stronger.[107]

---

[105] See the Heidelberg Report, paras 106–136, summarizing aspects of the debate, stating that the current case law across Europe did not indicate that breach of an arbitration clause was not being treated as a public policy ground to refuse recognition, and suggesting that non-compliance with an arbitration clause should not be incorporated as a new express ground of refusal of recognition (para 128). The Commission Green Paper (Com(2009) 175 final) suggested that it might be appropriate to include a ground of refusal on the basis of irreconcilability with an arbitral award (see 9). The Commission Proposal for the Brussels I Recast (Com(2010) 748 final) addressed the problem in a completely different and more radical way. Picking up on suggestions in the Heidelberg Report, it included a proposal to bring arbitration partially within the Brussels–Lugano regime, including a mechanism (akin to Art 31 of the Recast for exclusive jurisdiction agreements) by which if an application had been made to the court of the seat of the arbitration, or if an arbitration tribunal had been seised of the dispute, competing court proceedings in another member state would have to be stayed. However, this radical suggestion was rejected, and does not feature in the eventual Recast.

[106] See paras 15.19–15.20. It is suggested that such declarations do not infringe the principle of mutual trust: see Ch 12, section M, 'Injunctions Granted before Accession'.

[107] See paras 15.13 and 15.14.

16

The Framework of Jurisdictional Law

A. INTRODUCTION

This chapter and Chapters 17 and 18 consider the court's jurisdiction to hear claims for **16.01** anti-suit injunctions. The term 'jurisdiction' is here used to refer to the limits on the court's *territorial* jurisdiction, not its *powers*.[1]

This chapter summarizes the framework of English jurisdictional law and then considers **16.02** the material scope of the Brussels–Lugano regime, and the other European jurisdictional instruments. Chapters 17 and 18 then address the application of the provisions of the Brussels–Lugano regime, and the Hague Convention on Choice of Court, and the traditional common law rules of jurisdiction, to anti-suit injunctions. Only issues of specific interest for anti-suit injunctions will be analysed.

B. BREXIT

These three chapters are written before Brexit has come to pass, at a time when European **16.03** law and related arrangements such as the Lugano Convention are still in force. For the most part, they proceed on the assumption that, even after Brexit (if it happens), the Brussels–Lugano regime and the other instruments of European jurisdictional law, as well as the Hague Convention on Choice of Court, will remain English law, whether as part of the transitional arrangements or more permanently.

Whether and when Brexit will happen, and if so what will happen on Brexit day, remains **16.04** unsettled at the time of writing this section (updated to 1 May 2019). But the current transitional provisions under the November 2018 Withdrawal Agreement (if that or something like it is eventually agreed) would continue European jurisdictional law during the post-Brexit transition period pending a final status agreement,[2] and are intended to achieve

---

[1] See Ch 3, para 3.01.
[2] Draft Withdrawal Agreement (November 2018), Articles 127–129, and Articles 66–69. Further, the transitional provisions would in certain respects continue the effect of the Brussels–Lugano regime for proceedings commenced before the end of the transitional period: see Article 67.
These arrangements appear to bring with them the continued effect of the agreement with Denmark by which Denmark is made in effect party to the Brussels I Recast, as that would seem to form part of Union law for the purposes of Article 127 by virtue of Article 2.

the same for the Lugano Convention, and the Hague Convention on the Choice of Court.[3] Further, it is the UK Government's policy to negotiate a continuation of the Brussels–Lugano regime and the other main European jurisdictional arrangements, or something very similar, as part of the final status agreements,[4] although the European Union (EU) has not yet agreed.[5] If there is no deal, then the Brussels–Lugano regime and other European jurisdictional arrangements would cease to apply (subject to complicated and awkward transitional issues). But no deal might not be the end of the story, as negotiations would continue, and future cooperative arrangements might include the reinstatement of the Brussels–Lugano framework or a similar regime.

16.05   If and to the extent that the Brussels–Lugano overlay is removed, either on a no-deal Brexit or after the conclusion of any transition under an agreed withdrawal, then England and Wales, so far as can presently be envisaged, will revert back to the common law rules on jurisdiction,[6] discussed in Chapter 18, subject to the effect of the Hague Convention on the

---

[3] There remains a wrinkle in relation to the Lugano Convention and, possibly more seriously, in relation to the Hague Convention. The New Lugano Convention of 2007, and the 2005 Hague Convention on the Choice of Court, were agreed by the EU on behalf of its member states, with the Lugano Convention states (Iceland, Norway, and Switzerland) and the Hague Convention states respectively. On Brexit day they therefore cease to apply, as such, between the UK and non-EU contracting states. Under Articles 2(a)(iv), 127, and 129 of the draft Withdrawal Agreement, European Union law, which includes international conventions to which the EU is party and thus includes the Lugano and Hague Conventions, continue in and in respect of the UK during the transition period, and the UK is bound by such conventions. The EU has further committed (by a footnote to Art 129) to notify the other parties to those conventions that the UK is to be treated as a member state during the transition period for the purposes of those agreements. The UK legislation to implement the Withdrawal Agreement (if passed) will presumably carry this into effect, so that the Lugano and Hague Conventions will be binding in the UK during the transition period. However, what remains uncertain is how, precisely, the Lugano Convention and Hague Convention states will react to this assertion and so whether *they* will treat themselves as bound towards the UK under those conventions. The likelihood is that the Lugano Convention states will seek to maintain a smooth continuity, but at the time of writing there appears to have been no published confirmation of their position. The position of the other Hague Convention states is unknown.

In the meanwhile, while the UK acceded to the Hague convention in its own right by a notification of 28 December 2018, to take effect on 1 April 2019 (at a time when the Article 50 period was going to expire on 28 March 2019), this has now been put off. Following the EU's extensions of the Article 50 period to 31 October 2019, the UK has suspended its accession to the Hague Convention, with the agreement of the depositary (The Netherlands Ministry of Foreign Affairs), to 1 November 2019. It is likely that any further extensions of the Article 50 period would be matched by further suspensions (or possibly withdrawals) so that the UK will not become a member of the Hague Convention in its own right until just after Brexit day (if there is no deal) or the end of the transitional period (if there is a deal). As a result, there is no immediate difficulty so long as the Article 50 period continues to be extended, because the UK will remain a full EU member state and so party to the Hague Convention as such. However, if there is a deal on the terms of the draft Withdrawal Agreement, then as matters stand, during the transition period the UK will need to rely on the mechanism described above.

Further, there are complications relating to transitional provisions and what happens to jurisdictional agreements concluded after Brexit day but before full UK membership takes effect; although we do not go into the detail here. For the UK's own interests, the better course would have been for the UK to join the Hague Convention in its own right, as soon as possible, whether or not this overlapped with EU membership of the Convention. However, that approach would have been in tension with the EU's asserted exclusive external competence, which appears to be the explanation for the suspensions (and see Article 129(4) of the draft Withdrawal Agreement).

[4] UK Government, 'Providing a Cross-Border Civil Judicial Co-Operation Framework—A Future Partnership Paper', 22 August 2017, HM Government, 'Framework for the UK-EU partnership: Civil judicial cooperation', 13 June 2018; and 'The Future Relationship between the United Kingdom and the European Union', Cm 9593 (July 2018), para 128(g).

[5] The EU has been willing, so far, only to agree to continue the European jurisdictional arrangements during the transition period: see European Commission, 'Position Paper on Judicial Cooperation in Civil and Commercial Matters', 13 July 2017.

[6] Regulations 82–91 of the Civil Jurisdiction and Judgments (Amendment) (EU Exit) Regulations 2019, SI 2019 No 479, would bring the European jurisdictional arrangements and the Lugano Convention (as well as the Brussels Convention 1968) to an end on Brexit day in the event of no deal. This is subject to one exception, namely the transference into English law of much of the essential effect of the protective European jurisdiction regimes for consumer and employment cases by new sections 15A–15E of the Civil Jurisdiction and Judgments Act 1982,

Choice of Court, to which the United Kingdom will become party in its own right.[7] The UK Government would seek membership of the Lugano Convention in that situation,[8] but this would require the consent of the EU and Lugano states, and has not yet been agreed.

C. THE FRAMEWORK OF ENGLISH JURISDICTIONAL LAW

The rules governing the jurisdiction of the English courts are currently comprised of two main[9] overlapping systems: the traditional 'common law' rules of jurisdiction, based on service, and the European rules of jurisdiction imposed by the Brussels–Lugano regime, and the other European jurisdictional instruments.[10] A third component, which overlaps with the corresponding elements of the European rules while they remain in force, is the Hague Convention on Choice of Court.[11] Within their scope, the European jurisdictional instruments (so long as they apply) and the Hague Convention are dominant and override the common law rules.   **16.06**

The principal component of the Brussels–Lugano regime is Regulation 1215/2012, the 'Brussels I Recast', in this work generally abbreviated to 'the Recast'.[12] The Lugano Convention regulates jurisdiction as between the EU and the Lugano states, namely Switzerland, Norway, and Iceland. Its terms are parallel to those of the previous Brussels   **16.07**

---

which would be brought about by Regulation 26. It is also subject to complicated transitional arrangements contained in Regulations 92–95. The EU would take its own approach to transition, which, however, will not be quite the same: see EU Commission, 'Notice to Stakeholders, Withdrawal of the United kingdom and EU rules in the Field of Civil Justice and Private International Law' (Rev 1), 18 January 2019. In the event of a deal, Articles 67–69 of the draft Withdrawal Agreement also set up transitional arrangements to deal with the effect of the European jurisdictional arrangements after the end of the transition period.

[7] On 28 December 2018, the UK deposited a notification of accession to the Hague Convention which, provided there is no deal, was to take effect on 1 April 2019, three days after 28 March 2019, then the scheduled date for the UK's departure from the EU. However, when the Article 50 period was extended on 22 March 2019 and then on 11 April 2019 to 31 October 2019, the UK communicated to the Hague Convention depositary (the Netherlands Ministry of Foreign Affairs) that the UK's accession should be suspended, for now until 1 November 2019, and the depositary has accepted this.
   As a matter of UK law, this is implemented, with detailed transitional provisions, by Civil Jurisdiction and Judgments (Hague Convention on Choice of Court Agreements 2005) (EU Exit) Regulations 2018, SI 2018 No 1124.
[8] UK Government, 'The Future Relationship between the United Kingdom and the European Union', Cm 9593 (July 2018), para 128(g).
[9] In narrow fields, jurisdiction also exists under specific statutory rules, giving effect to certain international conventions, such as the Carriage of Goods by Road Act 1965, implementing the Convention on the Contract for the International Carriage of Goods by Road (CMR Convention). These are outside the scope of this work.
[10] In particular: (a) EC Regulation 848/2015, the 'Insolvency Regulation', whose scope is collective insolvency proceedings, subject to certain exceptions (see Art 1), and thus covers many of the matters excepted by Article 1(2)(b) of the Brussels I Recast; (b) EC Regulation 2201/2003, the 'Brussels II Bis Regulation', which covers 'civil matters relating to (i) divorce, legal separation, or marriage annulment; (ii) the attribution, exercise, delegation, restriction, or termination of parental responsibility' (see Art 1), and thus deals with some of the matters excepted by Article 1(2)(a) of the Brussels I Recast; and (c) EC Regulation 4/2009 on jurisdiction, applicable law, recognition and enforcement of decisions, and cooperation in matters relating to maintenance obligations (which poaches maintenance from the scope of the Brussels I Regulation: see Recital 44). The United Kingdom has not participated in EU Regulation 650/2012 on Succession and Wills.
[11] The relationship of the Hague Convention on Choice of Court to the Brussels-Lugano regime is addressed by Article 26(6) of the Convention. This is a complex subject which is touched on briefly at para 16.10 below.
[12] Denmark is not party to the Recast because of an opt-out from European legislation on Justice and Home Affairs but is in effect covered by the same arrangements under an agreement with the EU that means the effect of the Recast is paralleled.

I Regulation, EC Regulation 44/2001. However, for simplicity we will analyse matters by reference to the provisions of the Brussels I Recast alone.[13]

16.08   If the defendant is domiciled in the Brussels–Lugano zone,[14] and the matter falls within the material scope of the Brussels–Lugano regime, the court's jurisdiction over him is determined by the rigid substantive rules of jurisdiction laid down by the regime. The starting point is that a defendant must be sued in the state of his domicile, unless there is some head of special or exclusive jurisdiction allowing him to be sued in another state. However, where the defendant is domiciled outside the Brussels–Lugano zone, Article 6 of the Recast provides that jurisdiction is to be exercised according to national law, unless the exclusive jurisdiction provisions of the Recast apply, in which case the Recast's rules will govern jurisdiction.[15]

16.09   The Brussels–Lugano regime is generally only concerned with the allocation of jurisdiction between and not within member states.[16] However, in civil and commercial matters, jurisdiction as between the component parts of the United Kingdom is allocated by the 'Modified Regulation' contained at Schedule 4 of the Civil Jurisdiction and Judgments Act 1982, which broadly works in parallel to the European instruments (and which, on the current no-deal legislation, will remain in force within the UK even after a no-deal Brexit).

16.10   The Hague Convention on Choice of Court, to which the United Kingdom is at present party through the EU's accession thereto, confers jurisdiction on the English courts if they are the designated court under an exclusive jurisdiction agreement. This has important consequences in terms of the ability to enforce a judgment in the other contracting states (as of 1 May 2019, outside the EU member states, Mexico, Montenegro, and Singapore). However, so long as the Brussels–Lugano regime remains in force, the Hague Convention has little effect in terms of the English court's domestic rules of jurisdiction. Although jurisdiction under the Hague Convention appears to apply in international cases irrespective of where the parties are domiciled,[17] the reconciliation provisions in Article 26(6) of the Hague Convention provide that it does not 'affect' jurisdiction under the Brussels–Lugano regime, unless one of the parties is domiciled in a Hague Convention state which is not a Brussels–Lugano state. Where, accordingly, the Hague Convention's rules are consistent with Brussels–Lugano jurisdiction, it would seem that in principle, Hague Convention jurisdiction can and should still apply in addition to and alongside Brussels–Lugano jurisdiction, but this will be an essentially notional point, save where Hague Convention jurisdiction is broader. There will be few cases where that is so, because the scope and effect of Article 25 of the Brussels I Recast has deliberately been extended to cover most of the same terrain, so far as regards exclusive[18] jurisdiction clauses, as the scope of the Hague

---

[13]   Case C-533/07, *Falco Privatstiftung v Weller Lindhorst* ECJ [52], [53], [56].

[14]   The Brussels–Lugano zone is, collectively, the territory of the EU member states (and certain territories belonging to them), plus the territories of the Lugano Convention states, namely Switzerland, Norway, and Iceland.

[15]   See Article 6, excepting Articles 18(1), 21(2), 24, and 25.

[16]   There are some minor exceptions to this, as the Brussels–Lugano regime's allocation of jurisdiction in some cases identifies not only the member state in question but also the court within it, for example Article 7(1) of the Recast.

[17]   See Article 1 of the Convention.

[18]   There is a material difference with regard to non-exclusive jurisdiction clauses, which fall within Article 25 of the Recast, but do not fall within the Hague Convention unless states make an appropriate declaration under Article 22 of the Convention.

Convention.[19] The position is little different in those situations where one of the parties is domiciled in a non-EU Hague state, and the Hague Convention therefore can 'affect' Brussels–Lugano jurisdiction. Again, the similarity of Hague Convention jurisdiction with regard to exclusive jurisdiction clauses to the scope of Article 25 of the Brussels I Recast means that in most cases there will be little change in terms of the essential scope of jurisdiction.

On the other hand, if the Brussels–Lugano arrangements cease to apply following Brexit, then the Hague Convention will become more significant and will become the dominant jurisdictional regime for claims under exclusive jurisdiction clauses, since in terms of domestic jurisdiction, it applies in international cases irrespective of whether defendants are domiciled in other contracting states, provided only that the case has international elements. It should be borne in mind, however, that it has important subject matter carve outs defined in Article 2(2), such as employment, and the carriage of goods by sea.   **16.11**

Where neither the Brussels–Lugano regime nor the Hague Convention applies, jurisdiction will be governed by English national law on jurisdiction. This is, in general,[20] contained in the common law rules of jurisdiction, principally[21] framed by the rules on service in CPR Part 6.   **16.12**

Under the common law rules of jurisdiction, if the defendant is present within England and Wales even temporarily, and is served with proceedings while he is there, then the court possesses personal jurisdiction over him. However, if the defendant can show that another country's courts are a more appropriate forum for the litigation, the proceedings in England can be stayed under the doctrine of *forum non conveniens*.[22]   **16.13**

In contrast, if the defendant is outside the jurisdiction, he can only be served with proceedings out of the jurisdiction under the common law rules if the court gives permission. The principal rules governing permission to serve out of the jurisdiction are contained in CPR 6.36, and CPR PD 6B para 3.1, which give the court power to grant permission in a list of   **16.14**

---

[19] One example where the Hague Convention might have greater breadth is with respect to an exclusive jurisdiction agreement concluded in a case that is not 'civil and commercial' (and so excluded from Brussels–Lugano jurisdiction), but which does not fall within the exceptions to the scope of the Hague Convention in Article 2. Conversely, there are significant respects in which the Hague Convention is narrower than the Brussels I Recast due to the carve outs in Article 2(2) of the Convention, which exclude a range of important subject matters such as the carriage of goods by sea.

[20] There are also some specific statutory jurisdictional regimes which apply under English law in limited fields, usually implementing international conventions, eg the Carriage of Goods by Road Act 1965, implementing the CMR Convention, which contains its own jurisdictional regime at Article 31. These specific statutory regimes will not be considered further in this work.

In addition, the UK's no-deal legislation would retain the operation of the special European jurisdiction regimes for employment and consumer cases which would be transferred into UK law by new sections 15A–15E of the Civil Jurisdiction and Judgments Act 1982, as implemented by Civil Jurisdiction and Judgments (Amendment) (EU Exit) Regulations 2019, SI 2019 No 479, Regulation 26. However, we will not address those employment and consumer regimes (as transferred into English law) in this work and in the discussion that follows (and in Ch 18) we will assume we are dealing with cases where they would not apply.

[21] Parts of the common law rules on jurisdiction are also contained in specific service regimes elsewhere in the CPR, such as CPR 62.5 (for arbitration) and CPR 63.14 (for intellectual property).

[22] Where the defendant is domiciled in England, the Brussels–Lugano regime prohibits the application of the doctrine of *forum non conveniens*: Case C-281/08, *Owusu v Jackson* [2005] ECR I-1383.

situations defined primarily by reference to the nature of the claim and its connection to England.

16.15   So when assessing whether the English court has jurisdiction, it is necessary first to assess whether the claim falls within the material scope of the Brussels–Lugano regime, or the other European jurisdictional instruments,[23] so long as they remain in force, or where relevant the Hague Convention on the Choice of Court.[24]

D. THE MATERIAL SCOPE OF THE BRUSSELS–LUGANO REGIME

16.16   Article 1 of the Recast provides that it applies in civil and commercial matters (which are defined not to include, in particular, revenue, customs, or administrative matters), save that it shall not apply to (a) the status and capacity of natural persons, rights in property arising out of a matrimonial relationship, wills and succession; (b) bankruptcy, proceedings relating to the winding up of insolvent companies or other legal persons, judicial arrangements, compositions, and analogous proceedings; (c) social security; (d) arbitration; (e) maintenance obligations; or (f) wills and succession.

16.17   It seem clear that, where the underlying substantive litigation does not fall within one of the exceptions, a claim for an anti-suit injunction sought in ordinary civil litigation[25] will be a 'civil and commercial' matter.[26] Further, although it is possible that 'merely procedural' applications fall outside the scope of the Brussels–Lugano regime altogether, it is questionable that an anti-suit injunction would be viewed as 'merely procedural', as even an interim anti-suit injunction seeks substantive relief.[27]

16.18   In *Masri v Consolidated Contractors (No 3)*, Lawrence Collins LJ observed that the claim for an anti-suit injunction in the case before him did not involve the injunction defendant being 'sued' for the purposes of Articles 4 and 5 of the Recast. However, he reached that conclusion with regard to interim alternative forum anti-suit injunctions in the context of

---

[23] The scope of the other European jurisdictional instruments will not be analysed in any detail in this work.

[24] The scope of the Hague Convention on the Choice of Court is defined in Article 2.

[25] It is theoretically possible that an anti-suit injunction might not be a 'civil and commercial' matter if it was sought in a revenue, customs, or administrative case. But there is no example in the reported cases of an anti-suit injunction being sought in, or in order to protect, revenue, customs, or administrative litigation in England.

[26] This is implicit in Case C-185/07, *Allianz v West Tankers (The Front Comor)* [2009] ECR I-663. In Case C-292/08, *German Graphics Graphische Maschinen v Holland Binding* [2009] ECR I-8421, the European Court indicated that 'civil and commercial matters' should be interpreted broadly. The application of the concept of 'civil and commercial matters' to anti-suit injunctions was conceded in *The Eras Eil Actions* [1995] 1 Lloyds Rep 64, 77, and in *Toepfer International v Molino Boschi* [1996] 1 Lloyds Rep 510, 512–13; Mance J reasoned on the basis that the Brussels Convention would apply to an anti-suit injunction if the arbitration exception did not. As a matter of logic and language anti-suit injunction appears to be a 'civil and commercial' matter, at least in most situations.

[27] See Case C-159/02, *Turner v Grovit* [2004] ECR I-3565, AG [26], [27], [37], ECJ [29]. The argument of principle that merely procedural measures fell outside the scope of the regime was accepted by the Advocate General, but treated with reserve by the European Court. Although the United Kingdom's argument that anti-suit injunctions were 'merely procedural' was not expressly rejected, it was handled with some suspicion, and was not considered to be sufficient to protect the injunction from the preclusive effect of the principle of mutual trust (see Ch 12, para 12.08). The idea that anti-suit injunctions are 'merely procedural' was not picked up in the later European case law.

existing English substantive proceedings. He viewed the court as having jurisdiction over such anti-suits as an ancillary jurisdiction derived from its jurisdiction over the merits of the substantive claims, so that the anti-suit was not a fresh claim. This does not mean that freestanding single forum injunctions would not be regarded as 'suing' within Brussels–Lugano, and Lawrence Collins LJ treated those separately.[28]

It seems correct that interim anti-suit injunctions sought within, and ancillary to, sub-   **16.19**
stantive proceedings over which the English court otherwise has jurisdiction under the Brussels–Lugano regime, are within the scope of this 'ancillary' jurisdiction; this is discussed in Chapter 17.[29] In the circumstances, they will share the characterization of the underlying substantive proceedings, and will be 'civil and commercial', and there is no need for any fresh jurisdictional basis.[30]

What of interim anti-suit injunctions which are sought in the context of, and to protect,   **16.20**
substantive proceedings which are outside the material scope of the Brussels–Lugano regime? It seems likely that these, also, should be treated as sharing the characterization of the underlying substantive proceedings.[31] Consequently, whether the court has jurisdiction will be determined by the common law rules of jurisdiction. But similarly to the position under Brussels–Lugano, it seems that jurisdiction to grant such injunctions follows from jurisdiction over the substance and it is not necessary to make a fresh jurisdictional showing.[32]

In contrast, if in a single forum situation there are no existing English proceedings, and if a   **16.21**
final anti-suit injunction is sought by claim form in free-standing proceedings, or if a free-standing anti-suit injunction is sought by application notice, then it would seem that this

---

[28] *Masri v Consolidated Contractors (No 3)* [2009] QB 503 (CA) [31], [60]–[67], [99]; *The Eras Eil Actions* [1995] 1 Lloyds Rep 64, 72–74. For the ancillary jurisdiction, see Case C-391/95, *Van Uden Maritime v Kommanditgesellschaft in Firma Deco-Line* [1998] ECR I-7091 [19]; *National Justice Compania Naviera v Prudential Assurance (The Ikarian Reefer) (No 2)* [2000] 1 WLR 603 (CA) 616; and *Golden Endurance Shipping v RMA Watanya (The Golden Endurance)* [2015] 1 Lloyds Rep 266 [25]–[30]. For the contrasting position in relation to free-standing single forum injunctions, see paras 16.21–16.22; Ch 17, paras 17.06–07 and para 17.67 n 100.

[29] See Ch 17, section D, 'Interim Anti-Suit Injunctions'.

[30] The position in relation to final alternative forum injunctions, claimed in existing proceedings, is less clear: see paras 16.23–16.24. But in general, alternative forum injunctions are sought on an interim basis only.

[31] This was the view of Lord Hoffmann in *West Tankers v Ras Riunione Adriatica di Sicurta (The Front Comor)* [2007] 1 Lloyds Rep 391 (HL) [13], [16], [18]. See also *Babanaft International v Bassatne* [1990] Ch 13 (CA) 29–32 and *Masri v Consolidated Contractors (No 3)* [2009] QB 503 [30]–[31], [60]–[67], [99]. It is also consistent with the ECJ's reasoning, in the arbitration context, in Case C-195/07, *Allianz v West Tankers (The Front Comor)* [2009] ECR I-663 [22]–[23], and more generally in Case C-406/09, *Realchemie Nederland v Bayer Cropscience* [2011] ECR I-9773 [41]–[42]; Case C-4/14, *Bohez v Wiertz* [2015] ILPr 43; Case 143/78, *Cavel v Cavel* [1979] ECR 1055 [9]; *CHW v GJH* [1982] ECR 1189, ECJ [8] and AG [1].
However, it is worth noting that the arbitration context is not necessarily the same as the other exceptions, and see the difficult case of C-391/95, *Van Uden Maritime v Kommanditgesellschaft in Firma Deco-Line* [1998] ECR I-7091 [26]–[34], as well as *Re Hayward* [1997] Ch 45, 54–55 (claim by trustee in bankruptcy against third parties to recover property of the bankrupt not within bankruptcy exception, because the claim itself was not a matter of bankruptcy law); approved and followed in *Ashurst v Pollard* [2001] Ch 595 (CA) 601–02. The arguments are potentially affected by whether the injunction is interim or final and whether anti-suit injunctions are viewed as enforcing a substantive underlying right.

[32] *Golden Endurance Shipping v RMA Watanya (The Golden Endurance)* [2015] 1 Lloyds Rep 266 [25]–[30]; and see previously *The Eras Eil Actions* [1995] 1 Lloyds Rep 65, 72–74; see also *Glencore International v Metro Trading International (No 3)* [2002] CLC 1090 (CA) [59]–[60]. The point is discussed further at Ch 18, section J, 'Jurisdiction and Interim Anti-Suit Injunctions', paras 18.90–18.92.

is a free-standing 'civil and commercial' matter, which is also 'suing'.[33] Jurisdiction would need to be established independently under the Brussels–Lugano regime if the injunction defendant was domiciled in the Brussels–Lugano zone.

16.22   Further, a free-standing contractual claim to enforce an exclusive jurisdiction clause by final relief would probably also be treated as a separate 'civil and commercial' claim to enforce a contractual right, over which jurisdiction would need to be established.

16.23   It is possible that a different analysis is required for final anti-suit injunctions, sought in alternative forum cases to protect substantive English proceedings, as an additional final claim in those proceedings.[34] It may be debated whether these can be treated as ancillary to the underlying substantive claims, even if 'final' as a matter of English procedural law, or whether they are truly a fresh separate claim which requires an independent characterization and an independent basis of jurisdiction. In *The Eras Eil* actions Potter J was inclined to consider that the form of the injunction should not be determinative, provided at least that any injunction was not fully final, and was subject to a liberty to apply and a right to vary upon a change of circumstances.[35]

16.24   The current English case law suggests that any claim which is final in English procedural terms, that is, brought by claim form, requires a separate jurisdictional basis, and so a separate characterization.[36] On this basis only interim injunctions, brought by application notice, could fall within the ancillary jurisdiction. This would appear to create no major practical difficulty as matters stand, because alternative forum anti-suit injunctions can be, and in general are, sought by interim application within the underlying substantive final proceedings, without the need for final relief, and thus clearly fall within the ancillary jurisdiction.[37] The fact that they may be unlimited in time will not render them 'final' in any sense that could take them outside the ancillary jurisdiction, provided they are subject to appropriate rights to vary upon a change of circumstances.[38] However, this is a solution driven by the jurisdictional conundrum and there is some procedural awkwardness in treating such anti-suit injunctions, which are often effectively final, as purely interim.[39] So it may become necessary in the future to consider whether or not to extend the scope of the ancillary jurisdiction to such protective final relief.

16.25   If and to the extent a final anti-suit injunction within the scope of the regime is not within the ancillary jurisdiction, and a fresh jurisdictional determination is required, the heads of jurisdiction in the Brussels–Lugano regime are available and can apply, but must be satisfied according to their individual terms.[40]

---

[33]   This is the implication of *Masri v Consolidated Contractors (No 3)* [2009] QB 503 [30]–[31], [60]–[67], [99].

[34]   Lawrence Collins LJ noted, by way of distinction, that final relief was not sought in *Masri v Consolidated Contractors (No 3)* [2009] QB 503 (CA) [99].

[35]   *The Eras Eil Actions* [1995] 1 Lloyds Rep 65, 72–74; see also *Glencore International v Metro Trading International (No 3)* [2002] CLC 1090, Moore-Bick J at [22].

[36]   *Donohue v Armco* [2002] 1 Lloyds Rep 425 (HL) [17]–[21]; *Masri v Consolidated Contractors (No 3)* [2009] QB 503 (CA) [74]–[76].

[37]   Ch 13, paras 13.08 and 13.27; also paras 16.19–16.20 of this chapter; Ch 17, paras 17.57–17.62; Ch 18, paras 18.90–18.92.

[38]   *The Eras Eil Actions* [1995] 1 Lloyds Rep 65, 74.

[39]   See Ch 13, paras 13.27–13.29.

[40]   *The Eras Eil Actions* [1995] 1 Lloyds Rep 65, 77–79.

Where the underlying matter is subject to an arbitration clause, there may be no English   **16.26** court proceedings at all other than the anti-suit injunction, and so the ancillary jurisdiction will not exist. It is, however, clear that an anti-suit injunction to protect and enforce an arbitration clause is 'arbitration' and falls outside the scope of the Brussels–Lugano regime. The European Court so held in *The Front Comor*,[41] and that result is reinforced by Recital 12 of the Recast. This should apply whether the anti-suit injunction is sought on a final or interim basis or both.

---

[41] Case C-185/07, *Allianz v West Tankers (The Front Comor)* [2009] ECR I-663 [22]; and see recently *Nori Holdings v Bank Otkritie Financial Corp* [2018] 2 Lloyds Rep 80. See also Case C-190/89, *Marc Rich v Società Italiana Impianti* [1991] ECR I-3855 [19].

17

Jurisdiction under the Brussels–Lugano Regime

A. INTRODUCTION

This chapter considers the application of the jurisdictional rules of the Brussels–Lugano **17.01**
regime to anti-suit injunctions which fall within the material scope of the regime.[1] It is relevant so long as, and to the extent that, the Brussels–Lugano regime remains English law in
the light of Brexit, and proceeds on that assumption.[2]

The Brussels–Lugano regime imposes restrictions on the substantive *power* to grant anti- **17.02**
suit injunctions in relation to court proceedings elsewhere in the Brussels–Lugano zone,
which have been discussed in Chapter 12. In short, if the other proceedings are elsewhere
within the Brussels–Lugano zone, and are within the material scope of the Brussels–Lugano
regime, then so long as the regime remains the law, the English court will be precluded from
granting anti-suit injunctions.

---

[1] The material scope of the regime is discussed in Ch 16, section C, 'The Framework of English Jurisdictional Law'.
[2] It also proceeds on the assumption that the rules of the Brussels–Lugano regime are not displaced by the
Hague Convention on the Choice of Court, which will only occur (as matters stand) in limited cases, defined in
Article 26(6) of the Convention. The operation of Article 26(6) is touched on briefly below at para 17.46.

17.03 In contrast, the application of the *jurisdictional* rules of the Brussels–Lugano regime imposes no inherent barrier to anti-suit injunctions. The English case law accepts that (a) final anti-suit injunctions are capable of falling within the Brussels–Lugano heads of jurisdiction;[3] and that (b) interim anti-suit injunctions are capable of falling within the ancillary jurisdiction available under the Brussels–Lugano rules, where the court has jurisdiction over the merits.[4]

17.04 In *Masri v Consolidated Contractors (No 3)* it was argued that the Brussels–Lugano regime's jurisdictional rules carried with them a preclusion of the grant of anti-suit injunctions against persons domiciled within the Brussels–Lugano zone, and over whom jurisdiction was asserted under the Brussels–Lugano rules, even in respect of target litigation outside the Brussels–Lugano zone. The Court of Appeal unsurprisingly rejected this argument.[5] Their conclusion is consistent with the reasoning in *The Front Comor*,[6] where the prohibition on anti-suit injunctions in support of arbitration was justified on the grounds that this was an illegitimate interference with the Brussels–Lugano jurisdiction of the court where the other proceedings would otherwise proceed. There is no reason why the Brussels–Lugano regime's rules should in themselves preclude jurisdiction over anti-suit injunctions in respect of proceedings outside the Brussels–Lugano zone, simply because the injunction defendant is domiciled in the zone.[7]

17.05 This chapter considers the application of the jurisdictional heads of the Brussels–Lugano regime to anti-suit injunctions. Section B considers jurisdiction over final anti-suit injunctions under the primary jurisdictional heads of the Brussels I Recast. The only heads of jurisdiction which appear to be real, practical candidates to support an anti-suit injunction are Articles 4, 6, 7(1), 7(5), 8, 20, 25, and 26 of the Recast.[8] The chapter also touches briefly on the overlapping jurisdiction which may exist, where an exclusive jurisdiction clause applies, under the Hague Convention on the Choice of Court. For the most part this duplicates and does not change jurisdiction under Article 25 of the Recast. Section C considers *lis pendens*. The ancillary jurisdiction for applications for interim injunctions is addressed in Section D.

B. JURISDICTION OVER FINAL ANTI-SUIT INJUNCTIONS UNDER THE BRUSSELS–LUGANO REGIME

1. Is Final Relief to Protect Existing Proceedings a Fresh Claim?

17.06 The threshold question is whether a claim for a final anti-suit injunction would amount to 'suing' and so be a fresh claim over which jurisdiction needs to be established separately under the Brussels–Lugano regime—in contrast to an interim anti-suit injunction sought to protect existing proceedings, for which jurisdiction does not need to be separately

---

[3] *The Eras Eil Actions* [1995] 1 Lloyds Rep 64, 77–79 and *Glencore International v Metro Trading International (No 3)* [2002] 2 CLC 1090, Moore Bick J [22].

[4] *Masri v Consolidated Contractors (No 3)* [2009] QB 503 (CA) [31], [60]–[67], [99], building on *Masri v Consolidated Contractors (No 2)* [2009] QB 450 (CA) [92]–[107] and addendum; also *The Eras Eil Actions* [1995] 1 Lloyds Rep 64, 82–74. See further paras 17.07–17.11, 17.57–17.63.

[5] *Masri v Consolidated Contractors (No 3)* [2009] QB 503 (CA) [67]. See also, before Case C-159/02, *Turner v Grovit* [2004] ECR I-3565, *The Eras Eil Actions* [1995] 1 Lloyds Rep 64, 77.

[6] Case C-185/07, *Allianz v West Tankers (The Front Comor)* [2009] ECR I-663.

[7] See further, Ch 12, paras 12.40–12.41.

[8] References below will be to the Articles of the Brussels I Recast.

established, as (applying *Masri* and *Van Uden*) ancillary jurisdiction follows from jurisdiction over the merits.[9] The issues in this regard have been touched on in Chapter 16.

In summary, free-standing claims for final anti-suit injunctions, such as a claim for a single **17.07** forum injunction, or a free-standing claim for a final injunction to enforce an exclusive jurisdiction clause, do seem to be fresh claims which would be regarded as 'suing' and over which jurisdiction would need to be separately established. Jurisdiction over them therefore can, and needs to be, established under one or more of the individual Brussels–Lugano heads of jurisdiction.[10]

The position is more problematic if an alternative forum injunction is sought to protect ex-   **17.08** isting proceedings, but claimed on a final basis in the context of those proceedings, whether by amendment or in the initial claim form. It is clearly possible for jurisdiction over such final injunctions to be obtained under the primary jurisdictional heads of the regime, where the injunction can be fitted within those the terms of the relevant jurisdictional head,[11] but the question is whether one or more of those heads *needs* to be satisfied.

The current case law suggests, applying a conventional English procedural perspective, that   **17.09** a claim for such a final injunction would be a separate claim which would not fall within the ancillary jurisdiction and for which a separate jurisdictional basis must be established.[12] However, in principle, from the perspective of the Brussels–Lugano regime, it might be possible to view this as an inappropriate cross-application of English procedural categories, and to treat such protective relief, albeit final in form, as being something that could be brought within the ancillary jurisdiction addressed in *Masri*.[13]

This constraint does not matter much, as matters stand, since it is possible to seek the alter-   **17.10** native forum anti-suit injunction on an interim basis, within and ancillary to the substantive proceedings, without corresponding final relief, and without a fresh separate jurisdictional basis,[14] while the interim injunction can be unlimited in time provided it can be varied upon a change of circumstances.[15] This use of ancillary jurisdiction was the solution applied in *Masri* to the jurisdictional objections in that case.[16]

However, either way, as a matter of principle and policy, it should be possible to bring ap-   **17.11** propriate alternative forum injunctions within the ancillary jurisdiction. Otherwise there could be artificial restrictions on the court's territorial jurisdiction to grant injunctions to protect its own proceedings against parties domiciled in the Brussels–Lugano zone, since in

---

[9] See section D, 'Interim Anti-Suit Injunctions', paras 17.57–17.62; *Masri v Consolidated Contractors (No 3)* [2009] QB 503 (CA) [31], [60]–[67], [99], relying on *Van Uden Maritime v Kommanditgesellschaft in Firma Deco-Line* [1998] ECR I-7091 [19], and building on *Masri v Consolidated Contractors (No 2)* [2009] QB 450 (CA) [92]–[107] and addendum; and *The Eras Eil Actions* [1995] 1 Lloyds Rep 65, 77–79.

[10] Ch 16, paras 16.17, 16.23–16.24.

[11] See the authorities at n 3 above; and Ch 16, para 16.25, also para 16.22.

[12] *Donohue v Armco* [2002] 1 Lloyds Rep 425 (HL) [17]–[21] (in a non-Brussels–Lugano case) and *Masri v Consolidated Contractors (No 3)* [2009] QB 503 (CA) [74]–[76].

[13] *Masri v Consolidated Contractors (No 3)* [2009] QB 503 (CA) [61]–[62]; Ch 16, paras 16.23–16.25.

[14] This approach is driven by the jurisdictional constraints. On the potentially awkward consequences of treating effectively final relief as interim relief, see Ch 13, section C, 'Procedure and Form', paras 13.27–13.29.

[15] *Masri v Consolidated Contractors (No 3)* [2009] QB 503 (CA) [58]–[59], [66], [76], 96]–[97]; *Glencore International v Metro Trading International (No 3)* [2002] 2 CLC 1090 (CA) [59]–[60]; *The Eras Eil Actions* [1995] 1 Lloyds Rep 64, 73–74; Ch 3, paras 3.08, 3.27, 3.33; Ch 13, paras 13.08–13.27; Ch 16, paras 16.19–16.20.

[16] *Masri v Consolidated Contractors (No 3)* [2009] QB 503 (CA) [57].

non-contractual cases there will often be no available distinct head of special jurisdiction for anti-suit injunctions.

17.12 In what follows, we assess the primary jurisdictional heads of the Recast on the assumption that a claim for final anti-suit injunction is 'suing' and requires an independent jurisdictional basis.

2. Service of Proceedings Falling within the Brussels–Lugano Regime

17.13 Where the English court has jurisdiction under one of the heads of jurisdiction of the Brussels–Lugano regime, the claim form can be served on the defendant out of the jurisdiction without the permission of the court, under CPR 6.33.

3. Jurisdiction Based on Domicile: Article 4

17.14 If the injunction defendant is domiciled in England, the courts will have jurisdiction to hear a claim for a final anti-suit injunction under Article 4 of the Recast (which will attribute jurisdiction to the courts of the United Kingdom) and Article 2 of the Modified Regulation[17] (which sub-allocates jurisdiction to the English courts within the United Kingdom).

4. Domicile Outside the Brussels–Lugano Zone: Article 6

17.15 If the injunction defendant is domiciled outside the Brussels–Lugano zone, then Article 6 of the Recast means the jurisdiction of the English courts will be determined by English national law on jurisdiction, and thus in general the traditional common law rules of jurisdiction,[18] unless the exclusive jurisdiction provisions of Article 24 or the prorogated jurisdiction provisions of Article 25 of the Recast apply, and subject to the rules of *lis pendens*.

5. Domicile Elsewhere in the Brussels–Lugano Zone

17.16 If the injunction defendant is domiciled elsewhere in the Brussels–Lugano zone, and the anti-suit injunction falls within the material scope of the regime, the English court will only have jurisdiction over a final claim for an anti-suit injunction if the claimant can show that one of the Brussels heads of jurisdiction applies in favour of the English courts (unless, in alternative forum cases, jurisdiction can be derived from the substantive English proceedings, as discussed previously[19]). This may well be difficult in relation to non-contractual single forum injunctions.

---

[17] Civil Jurisdiction and Judgments Act 1982, s 16 and Sch 4.
[18] Discussed in Ch 18.
[19] See paras 17.07–17.12 of this chapter; see also Ch 16, paras 16.21–16.23.

6. Article 7(1) in General: Place of Performance of a Contract

Leaving aside contracts for the sale of goods or the provision of services, where a specific re-   **17.17**
gime applies,[20] Article 7(1) gives special jurisdiction 'in matters relating to a contract, to the
courts for the place of performance of the obligation in question'. Where a particular claim
relates to part of a contract or set of contractual obligations, it is only the obligation which
forms the actual basis of the claim which is relevant.[21] The place of performance of an obligation is to be determined by the applicable national law as determined by the conflicts of
laws rules of the court deciding the issue.[22] Consequently, the English courts will not have
independent jurisdiction over a claim for a final anti-suit injunction merely because a substantive provision of an underlying contract is to be performed in England. It is only if any
contractual obligation which founds the claim for an anti-suit injunction is to be performed
in England that the basic rules of Article 7(1) could apply.

As a result, Article 7(1) will be of little relevance as an independent basis for jurisdiction   **17.18**
over final anti-suit injunctions. The principal examples of contractual obligations which
themselves found claims for anti-suit injunctions are exclusive jurisdiction and arbitration
clauses. But if an exclusive jurisdiction clause agreeing to English exclusive jurisdiction satisfies the conditions of Article 25, the English courts will have exclusive jurisdiction over the
claim for an anti-suit injunction to enforce it, and Article 7(1) will be superfluous; while it is
now clear that claims to enforce an arbitration clause by anti-suit injunction fall within the
arbitration exception to the scope of the Brussels–Lugano regime and are governed by the
common law jurisdictional rules.[23]

Anti-suit injunctions are sometimes sought to enforce settlement agreements, or negative   **17.19**
contractual obligations not to bring any claim at all within a certain category, or settlement agreements.[24] These are not exclusive jurisdiction clauses in themselves. In general,
it will not be possible to obtain jurisdiction over such claims under Article 7(1), because
the obligation in question will not be an obligation to do something in England, but rather
a negative obligation not to act in a particular way anywhere in the world. So 'the' place of
performance will not be in England.[25] Similarly, the place of breach will not be England either, but where the foreign litigation occurs.[26]

---

[20] Paragraphs 17.20–17.21.
[21] Case 266/85, *Shenavai v Kreischer* [1987] ECR 239 [20]; Case C-420/97, *Leathertex Divisione Sintetici v
Bodetex* [1999] ECR I-6747 [32], [42]; *Union Transport v Continental Lines* [1992] 1 WLR 15 (HL); Case C-440/97,
Groupe Concorde v Master of the Vessel 'Suhadiwarno Panjan' [1999] ECR I-6307 (ECJ). The position is different for
contracts for the sale of goods or the provision of services: see paras 17.20–17.21.
[22] Case 12/76, *Industrie Tessili Italiana Como v Dunlop* [1976] ECR 1473.
[23] Case C-185/07, *Allianz v West Tankers (The Front Comor)* [2009] ECR I-663 [21]–[23]; applied in *National
Navigation v Endesa Generacion (The Wadi Sudr)* [2009] 1 Lloyds Rep 666, [67]–[71], [2010] 1 Lloyds Rep 193
(CA) [22]–[27], [134]–[137]; *Nori Holdings v Bank Otkritie Financial Corp* [2018] 2 Lloyds Rep 80. It is consequently now unnecessary to address the question, previously debated, of whether an English arbitration clause had
its place of performance in England: Case C-190/89, *Marc Rich v Società Italiana Impianti (The Atlantic Emperor)*
[1991] ECR I-3855, AG [79]–[85]; *Toepfer International v Molino Boschi* [1996] 1 Lloyds Rep 510, 512; *Navigation
Maritime Bulgare v Rustal Trading (The Ivan Zagubanski)* [2002] 1 Lloyds Rep 106 [120].
[24] See eg, respectively, *National Westminster Bank v Utrecht-America Finance* [2001] 3 All ER 733 (CA) and
Royal Exchange Assurance v Compania Naviera Santi (The Tropaioforos) [1962] 1 Lloyds Rep 410.
[25] Case C-256/00, *Besix v Wasserreinigungsbau Alfred Kretzschmar* [2002] ECR I-1699; *Canyon Offshore v GDF
Suez E&P Nederland* [2015] ILPr 8 [49]–[53].
[26] See, by analogy, *AMT Futures v Marzillier* [2018] AC 439 (SC) [25]–[26].

7. Article 7(1)(b): Goods and Services

17.20   Article 7(1)(b) provides, in the case of contracts for the sale of goods, that the place of perform-ance is autonomously defined as the place where the goods were delivered or should have been delivered, and in the case of contracts for the provision of services, that the place of perform-ance is autonomously defined as the place where the services were provided or should have been provided.

17.21   In *Color Drack v Lexx* the European Court of Justice has held that these defined places of performance govern the application of Article 7(1) for *all claims* founded on the relevant contract, even if the claim in question has nothing to do with delivery of goods or the per-formance of services.[27] This might apply to a contractual injunction brought to enforce a con-tractual obligation, other than an English exclusive jurisdiction clause or arbitration clause, contained in a contract for the sale of goods or provision of services. However, it would not apply to a claim for a non-contractual anti-suit injunction, brought to protect litigation in respect of such a contract, but itself based on vexation or oppression, as this would not be within Article 7(1) at all.

8. Tort (and Equitable Wrongs): Article 7(2)

17.22   Article 7(2) of the Recast provides that special jurisdiction will exist 'in matters relating to a tort, delict or quasi-delict, in the courts for the place where the harmful event oc-curred or may occur'. This should cover, in principle, anti-suit injunctions to enforce tor-tious rights, such as anti-suit injunctions to restrain interference with breach of contract.

17.23   However, in English law, anti-suit injunctions are not generally claimed to enforce tortious rights.[28] In non-contractual cases, anti-suit injunctions are usually analysed as equitable remedies which respond to conduct that is vexatious or oppressive, or unconscionable, and thus contrary to equity. However, it is at present unclear whether they enforce underlying substantive equitable rights or not.[29]

17.24   The concept of 'tort or delict' will be given an autonomous European meaning and will not be shackled by the English distinction between common law and equity.[30] The European Court has often said that Article 7(2) covers all claims which 'seek to estab-lish the liability of a defendant' but which are not contractual, and so are not within Article 7(1).[31] The exact scope of the concept of 'liability' is not entirely clear. It will

---

[27]   Case C-386/05, *Color Drack v Lexx International Vertriebs* [2007] ECR I-3699 [26]; Case C-19/09, *Wood Floor Solutions Andreas Domberger v Silva Trade* [2010] 1 WLR 1900 [43]; *Cube Lighting & Industrial Design v Afcon Electra Romania* [2011] EWHC 2565 [40].

[28]   Ch 3, para 3.10; Ch 4, paras 4.32–4.40.

[29]   Ch 3, section B, 'A Legal or Equitable Right?'.

[30]   Case 189/87, *Kalfelis v Bankhaus Schroeder Münchmeyer Hengst* [1988] ECR 5565 [15]–[16]; Case C-167/00, *Verein für Konsumenteninformation v Henkel* [2002] ECR I-8111 [33]; *Hewden Tower Cranes v Wolffkran* [2007] 2 Lloyds Rep 138 [30].

[31]   See eg Case 189/87, *Kalfelis v Bankhaus Schroeder Münchmeyer Hengst* [1988] ECR 5565 [17]. For an example of a claim that falls outside Article 7(2), see Case C-261/90, *Reichert and Kockler v Dresdner Bank (No 2)* [1992] ECR I-2149, where the European Court of Justice (ECJ) held that the French 'action paulienne' which is deployed to set aside certain transactions concluded by a person who has since become bankrupt, did not seek to establish liability.

probably cover normal claims in English law which seek to establish liability for equitable wrongs.[32]

But whether this concept of 'liability' could, in principle, apply to non-contractual anti-suit in-   **17.25**
junctions based on general notions of equity is uncertain. In *Henkel*, the European Court held
that a claim for an injunction brought under statutory powers by a consumer association to
restrain the threatened use of unlawful or unconscionable contractual terms and conditions
could be a tortious claim within Article 7(2), even though no actionable damage was alleged.[33]
This approach to 'liability' would arguably be broad enough to cover non-contractual anti-suit
injunctions, even if not viewed as enforcing a substantive equitable right. But from a European
perspective the anti-suit injunction is an anomalous form of remedy, and the European Court
might not accept that it was a form of liability that could fall within Article 7(2).[34]

In any event, even if Article 7(2) can apply to anti-suit injunctions, it is unlikely it would   **17.26**
give special jurisdiction to the English courts. Although the concept of the 'place where the
harmful event occurred' has been broadly interpreted and includes either 'the place where
the damage occurred or the place of the event giving rise to it',[35] the European Court has
made clear that the place where the damage occurred is the place where the initial damage
occurs, not where its financial consequences, or other indirect results, subsequently occur.[36]
For an anti-suit injunction, the place of the event giving rise to the damage will be the courts
before which the vexatious litigation is being brought, and at least in general, that will also
be the place where the immediate damage occurred (namely, the need to defend the litigation and expend legal costs). In *AMT v Marzillier*, the Court of Appeal and Supreme Court
concluded that, in relation to a claim for damages for tortiously inducing breach of a jurisdiction clause, the place where the damage occurred was where the wrongful foreign litigation was commenced.[37]

9. Connected Claims: Article 8(1)

Article 8(1) provides that: **17.27**

> a person domiciled in a Member State may also be sued: ... where he is one of a
> number of defendants, in the courts for the place where any one of them is domiciled,

---

[32] In *Casio Computer v Sayo* [2001] ILPr 43 (CA) [10]–[16], a claim for the equitable wrong of dishonest assistance was held to fall within Article 7(2); and in *Dexter v Harley* (Lloyd J, 8 March 2001) [13], *Casio* was applied
to constructive trusts and knowing receipt. However, see contra *Kitechnology v Unicor* [1994] ILPr 560 (CA) [43]
(viewing the applicability of Art 7(2) to dishonest assistance as unclear and referable).

[33] Case C-167/00, *Verein für Konsumenteninformation v Henkel* [2002] ECR I-8111 [22], [41], [50].

[34] Article 7(2), like the other heads of special jurisdiction, is to be interpreted narrowly: Case 189/87, *Kalfelis v
Bankhaus Schroeder Münchmeyer Hengst & Co* [1988] ECR 5565 [19].

[35] Case 21/76, *Handelswekerij GJ Bier v Mines de Potasse d'Alsace* [1976] ECR 1735 [19], [25].

[36] Case C-364//93, *Marinari v Lloyds Bank* [1995] ECR I-2719 [14]–[15], [21].

[37] *AMT Futures v Marzillier* [2015] QB 699 [51]–[57], [2018] AC 439 (SC) [25]–[35]. See also the unusual case
of *Sandisk v Koninklijke Philips Electronics* [2007] ILPr 22 [35]–[39], [41]. In *OT Africa Line v Magic Sportswear*
[2005] 1 Lloyds Rep 252 [20], the injunction claimant sought to support his claim for an injunction against third-
party insurers, who were inducing his contractual counterparty to litigate in Canada in breach of an exclusive
jurisdiction clause, by relying on the tort of inducing a breach of contract. However, Langley J concluded, in part
on the basis of concessions, that for the purposes of the tests for choice of law in tort contained in ss 11 and 12 of
the Private International Law (Miscellaneous) Provisions Act, which have some conceptual similarity to Article
7(2), the tort of inducing a breach of contract was governed by the law of the state where the targeted litigation was
taking place (Canada) and not by English law.

provided the claims are so closely connected that it is expedient to hear and determine them together to avoid the risk of irreconcilable judgments resulting from separate proceedings.

17.28   In *The Eras Eil Actions*, Potter J held that Article 8(1) could in principle apply to anti-suit injunctions, and that where parallel anti-suit injunctions based on the same arguments of unconscionability were claimed against numerous injunction defendants there was a sufficiently close connection between the claims to satisfy Article 8(1).[38] It would seem that a claim against the 'anchor' defendant must be a claim for substantive relief.[39] However, an anti-suit injunction would, it is suggested, be treated as a claim for substantive relief for these purposes, even if based solely on vexation and oppression.[40]

10. Third-Party Proceedings: Article 8(2)

17.29   Article 8(2) provides that a person domiciled in another member state may be sued 'as a third party in an action on a warranty or guarantee or in any other third party proceedings'. Anti-suit injunctions are not actions on warranties or guarantees. But an anti-suit injunction could in theory be 'third party proceedings'.

17.30   The conditions imposed under the Recast for Article 8(2) to apply to third-party proceedings are not restrictive. First, there must be a sufficient connection between the original proceedings and the third-party proceedings to show that the third-party proceedings do not amount to an abuse aimed at removing the third-party defendant from the jurisdiction of the court which would otherwise be competent to hear the case.[41] Second, it may also be required that the third-party proceedings are linked or closely linked to the original proceedings or that there is a 'close connection', although this means much the same thing as the basic no abuse requirement.[42] Third, it appears that Article 8(2) can only apply to

---

[38] *The Eras Eil Actions* [1995] 1 Lloyds Rep 64, 74–79.

[39] *Mölnlycke v Procter & Gamble* [1992] 1 WLR 1112 (CA) 1117A.

[40] This was conceded in *The Eras Eil Actions* [1995] 1 Lloyds Rep 64, 79. However, cf *Amoco (UK) Exploration v British American Offshore* [1999] 2 Lloyds Rep 772, 780 (in relation to service out of the jurisdiction under the common law rules).

[41] Case C-77/04, *Réunion Européene v Zurich España* [2005] ECR I-4509, ECJ [31]–[33], [36]; C-521/14, *SOVAG—Schwarzmeer und Ostsee Versicherungs-Aktiengesellschaft v If Vahinkovakuutusyhtio* [2016] QB 780 (ECJ) [47]. The wording of Article 8(2) is ambiguous: on one reading it is the *original proceedings* which should not have been instituted 'with the object of removing' the third party from the jurisdiction of the court, which would otherwise be competent. However, after *Réunion Européene v Zurich España*, it appears that it is the *third-party proceedings* which are subject to this control, which makes more sense: *Barton v Golden Sun Holidays* [2007] ILPr 57 [22]–[23] and *SOVAG* at [45]–[47].

[42] Case C-521/14, *SOVAG—Schwarzmeer und Ostsee Versicherungs-Aktiengesellschaft v If Vahinkovakuutusyhtio* [2016] QB 780 (ECJ) [45]–[47]; applied in this sense by *PHP Tobacco Carib v BAT Caribbean* [2016] EWHC 3377 [45]–[46], [51], [53]; and *Roberts v Soldiers, Sailors, Airmen and Families Association—Forces Help* [2017] PNLR 10 [27], where it was said that 'the connection must be such that it is rational, and that the harmonious and efficacious administration of justice requires the court to hear both claim and third party proceedings in the same action'. The requirement of a close connection has been the consistent approach in the English decisions: *Barton v Golden Sun Holidays* [2007] ILPr 57; and previously *Kinnear v Falconfilms* [1996] 1 WLR 920, 925–27 (requiring some 'nexus'); *Waterford Wedgwood v David Nagli* [1999] ILPr 9 [20] ('it must be shown to be expedient in the interests of justice and good administration that the two actions or claims be heard by the same court'); *Summers v Stubbs* [2002] EWHC 3213 [39]; *Shekhar Dooma Shetty v Al Rushaid* [2011] EWHC 1460 [31] (following *Barton*).

However, the language in *SOVAG* is not entirely clear, and the previous judgment of the European Court in Case C-77/04, *Réunion Européene v Zurich España* [2005] ECR I-4509 [33] appeared to have held that no such additional requirement of close connection should be required: 'Art 6(2) of the Convention does not require

proceedings which can be genuinely classified as third-party proceedings.[43] However, at present it is not clear what this comprises. It will, of course, include the classic case of third-party proceedings where liability is passed on by a defendant, but may well include a range of other situations where it is appropriate to bind in a third party.[44] In the circumstances there may be some room for bringing claims for anti-suit injunctions, in appropriate cases, under Article 8(2). This will be particularly so where there is a claim for anti-suit relief between the original parties and it is appropriate for the third party to be joined into that claim. Where there is no original claim for an anti-suit injunction, but the claim sought to be added is an anti-suit by or against the third party, it remains to be seen whether in principle such a new claim would be regarded as having a sufficiently close link to the underlying claims on the merits for the purposes of Article 8(2).[45]

The procedural restrictions on third-party proceedings imposed by English procedural law   **17.31**
would also have to be satisfied.[46] The anti-suit injunction claimant would have to persuade the English court that third-party proceedings were procedurally appropriate, in the light of the criteria set out in CPR 20.9. The current English law tests are not entirely clear.[47] But they do not restrict third-party claims to claims seeking to pass on liability and will cover a range of situations where it is useful to bind a third party into the litigation.[48] However, if

---

the existence of any connection other than that which is sufficient to establish that the choice of *forum* does not amount to an abuse'; while the degree of connection required for this purpose appeared to be a matter which should be determined by national law: [34]–[35]. While it seems likely that *SOVAG* has moved matters beyond *Zurich Espana*, this is not certain.

[43]   In Case C-77/04, *Réunion Européene v Zurich España* [2005] ECR I-4509, the ECJ appeared to consider that Article 8(2) would only apply to proceedings that could be 'regarded as' or had the 'classification' of third-party proceedings: at [26]–[32]. The Report on the Convention on Jurisdicton and the Enforcement of Judgments in Civil and Commercial Matters, rapporteur P Jenard [1979] OJ C 59/1, 5 March 1979 (hereafter the 'Jenard Report') stated at 28:

> the simplest definition of third party proceedings is to be found in Articles 15 or 16 of the Belgian Judicial Code, which provides that 'Third party proceedings are those in which a third party is joined as a party to the action. They are intended either to safeguard the interest of the third party or of one of the parties to the action, or to enable judgment to be entered against a party.

In *Shekhar Dooma Shetty v Al Rushaid* [2011] EWHC 1460 [34], the English court concluded (a) that third-party proceedings under Article 8(2) were not confined to claims over against a third party, reflecting or passing on any liability claims made by the original proceedings; (b) that Article 8(2) simply meant any proceedings involving a third party which can be brought as additional claims under national rules. The first point is probably right: and indeed the European Court has held in *SOVAG* that Article 8(2) can apply to claims by the third party against one of the parties to the original proceedings and is not confined to claims against the third party (Case C-521/14, *SOVAG—Schwarzmeer und Ostsee Versicherungs-Aktiengesellschaft v If Vahinkovakuutusyhtio* [2016] QB 780 (ECJ) [47]). But the second is probably not. The European Court is likely to interpret 'third-party proceedings' as a European law concept that excludes certain national law peculiarities.

[44]   See the Jenard Report, 28, quoted in n 43 and *National Justice Compania Naviera v Prudential Assurance (The Ikarian Reefer) (No 2)* [2000] 1 WLR 603 (CA) 616 (an alternative ground).

[45]   See *Glencore International v Metro Trading International (No 3)* [2002] 2 CLC 1090, Moore Bick J at [22] and (CA) at [59], where (under English procedural rules) an anti-suit was seen as sufficiently closely connected to the substantive claims to be treated as a counterclaim, even though, in the unusual procedural circumstances of that case, the injunction defendant may not formally have been a claimant on the merits.

[46]   National procedural restrictions as to when third-party proceedings are admissible can be imposed within the context of Article 8(2), provided that they do not impair the practical effectiveness of the jurisdictional rules of the regime: Case C-365/88, *Kongress Agentur Hagen v Zeehaghe* [1990] ECR I-1845, AG [33(2)], ECJ [21].

[47]   Annoyingly, CPR 20.9 sets out only criteria, but no test, in contrast to the more helpful provisions of the old RSC Ord 16 r 1(1), which required that the third-party proceedings must be 'relating to or connected with the original subject matter of the action'.

[48]   *Shekhar Dooma Shetty v Al Rushaid* [2011] EWHC 1460 [31]–[34].

there is no connection or 'nexus' between the third-party proceedings and the original proceedings, then permission to bring the third-party claim in the same proceedings should probably be refused,[49] as the bringing of the third-party claim together with the original claim would probably not be 'convenient and effective' for the purposes of CPR 20.1. In this respect, the English procedural requirements appear to march in step with the requirements of Article 8(2) as presently interpreted.

17.32   When and how an anti-suit injunction brought against a third party would be considered to have a sufficient 'nexus' to be a legitimate Part 20 claim within CPR 20.9 remains to be determined.

11. Other Available Heads of Special Jurisdiction

17.33   There are a number of heads of special jurisdiction in the Regulation, of lesser importance, which could support jurisdiction over claims for anti-suit injunctions in certain circumstances, but which require little discussion here, as they do not give rise to any obvious problems specific to anti-suit injunctions.

17.34   Thus, Article 7(5) gives jurisdiction 'as regards a dispute arising out of the operations of a branch, agency, or other establishment, in the courts for the place where the branch, agency or other establishment is situated'. The 'dispute' in relation to this article will probably be the conduct of the foreign litigation, rather than the substantive underlying dispute.

17.35   Article 7(6) permits a person to be sued 'in his capacity as a settlor, trustee or beneficiary of a trust' 'in the courts of the state where the trust is domiciled'; this will presumably apply where the claim for an anti-suit injunction seeks to restrain foreign proceedings concerning trust claims pursued by the settlor, trustee, or beneficiary.

17.36   Under Article 8(3), a person domiciled in another member state can be sued in England by a counterclaim 'arising out of the same contract or facts on which the original claim is based'. There is no reason why this should not apply to anti-suit injunctions, which can be brought by substantive counterclaim.[50] However, it remains to be seen when an anti-suit injunction will be treated as 'arising out of the same facts' as the substantive litigation it seeks to protect.

---

[49]   The general trend of the pre-CPR authorities was to require some form of legitimate 'nexus' or connection, in the light of the terms of RSC Ord 16 r 1(1): *Kinnear v Falconfilms* [1996] 1 WLR 920, 926; *Caltex Trading v Metro Trading International* [1999] 2 Lloyds Rep 724. The criterion of a sufficient 'nexus' appears also to have been applied under CPR 20.9: *Trustor v Barclays Bank* (Rimer J, 24 October 2000) [55]–[56]; *Summers v Stubbs* [2002] EWHC 3213 [38] (although these decisions are difficult to apply, because they are in part based on a mistaken approach to Art 8(2)). In *Barton v Golden Sun Holidays* [2007] ILPr 57, Wyn Williams J required a 'close connection'; but this was a result of his interpretation of Article 8(2), not an application of national law. In *Shekhar Dooma Shetty v Al Rushaid* [2011] EWHC 1460 [32], Christopher Pymont QC, sitting as a deputy, did not require a 'nexus', but applied analogous reasoning in concluding that there was a sufficient 'connection' between the original proceedings and the intended third-party claim for it to be a 'proper case' for the third-party claim to be allowed to be brought.

[50]   Ch 18, section G, 'Jurisdiction by Way of Counterclaim', para 18.73.

12. Heads of Special Jurisdiction which are Unlikely to Apply

The Recast also includes other heads of special jurisdiction, which are either conceptually **17.37** inapplicable to anti-suit injunctions, or are unlikely to be of practical relevance to anti-suit injunctions.

The heads of special jurisdiction which appear to be inapplicable include Article 7(3), which **17.38** relates to civil claims for damages or restitution in criminal proceedings; Article 7(4), relating to civil claims for the recovery of a cultural object; and Article 9, which covers claims for the limitation of liability for maritime claims. Article 8(4), which covers contractual claims in matters relating to rights in rem in immovable property, appears unlikely to apply to anti-suit injunctions.

Article 7(7) applies to 'disputes concerning the payment of remuneration claimed in respect **17.39** of the salvage of a cargo or freight'. It is submitted that, even where the underlying litigation concerned salvage, the dispute with which a claim for a final anti-suit injunction would be concerned would be the dispute over which forum was appropriate, not the 'payment of remuneration'.

13. The Special Protective Regimes: Insurance, Consumer Contracts, and Employment

Sections 3, 4, and 5 of Chapter II of the Recast set up special protective jurisdictional re- **17.40** gimes 'in matters relating to insurance',[51] in 'matters relating to a contract concluded by … a consumer … for a purposes which can be regarded as outside his trade or profession',[52] and 'in matters relating to individual contracts of employment'.[53] The special regimes limit a claimant's ability to sue the insured, the consumer, or the employee otherwise than in his or her state of domicile; and conversely grant rights to sue the insurer, the business, or the employer in the state of domicile of the insured, the consumer, or the employee, respectively. Their purpose is to protect the weaker party by rules of jurisdiction more favourable to him than the general rules.[54]

The question that arises is whether, if the underlying substantive litigation does or would **17.41** fall within these sections, a final anti-suit injunction to protect that litigation would be viewed as a 'matter relating to' insurance, consumer contracts, or individual employment contracts, or whether it would be seen as a separate civil and commercial matter, which did not itself fall within the special regime. This remains to be determined,[55] and the point must be viewed as unclear.[56]

---

[51] Article 10.
[52] Article 17.
[53] Article 20.
[54] In relation to insurance, see Case C-347/08, *Vorarlberger Gebietkrankenkasse v WGV-Schwäbische Allgemeine Versicherungs* [2009] ECR I-8661 [40]–[41].
[55] In *National Justice Compania Naviera v Prudential Assurance (The Ikarian Reefer) (No 2)* [1999] 2 Lloyds Rep 621 (Rix J), 630, [2000] 1 WLR 603 (CA) 616–17, the Court of Appeal concluded that if a claim for third-party costs in insurance litigation was viewed as a fresh matter (which they doubted), then it would be regarded as about costs, not insurance, and so not within the protective regime.
[56] See, for analogies, the decisions on the scope of Article 1 in Case 143/78, *De Cavel v De Cavel (No 1)* [1979] ECR 1055 and Case 25/81, *CHW v GJH* [1982] ECR 1189; Case C-406/09, *Realchemie Nederland v Bayer Cropscience* [40]–[44].

14. Exclusive Jurisdiction: Article 24

17.42   In relation to 'proceedings which have as their object' or are 'concerned with' a range of matters which have close and distinctive connections to particular states and their territories, such as rights *in rem* in immovable property, the dissolution of companies, entries in public registers, and patents, Article 24 gives exclusive jurisdiction to the state in question. In addition, in 'proceedings concerned with the enforcement of judgments, the courts of the member state in which the judgment has been or is to be enforced has exclusive jurisdiction'. It may be that 'concerned' has to be read as 'principally concerned', although the different language versions and the cases are not consistent; and one gloss on the Recast's wording, which also reflects some language versions, is that claims fall within Article 24 if their 'subject matter' and possibly 'principal subject matter' falls within its terms.[57] Article 24 applies irrespective of domicile.

17.43   It is suggested that the 'subject matter' of a claim for a final anti-suit injunction will usually be where the litigation should be decided, not the underlying substantive dispute; or in the words of the English text of Article 24, the proceedings will usually have as their object, or be concerned with, the right not to be vexed by the foreign litigation, rather than the underlying substantive issues.[58] If so, then if jurisdiction for final anti-suit injunctions needs to be separately established (as discussed in para 17.07 of this chapter), claims for final anti-suit injunctions would probably not fall within Article 24, even where the UK has exclusive jurisdiction over the substantive dispute. But the point is contestable; and anyway, does not limit the ancillary jurisdiction for interim relief (discussed in section D, 'Interim Anti-Suit Injunctions').

15. Jurisdiction Clauses: Article 25

17.44   Article 25 gives jurisdiction to the court of a member state which the parties have agreed shall have jurisdiction, although 'consensus' to that agreement must be sufficiently established.[59] It is clear that 'court' in this context means public courts of law and not arbitration tribunals.[60] If there is a jurisdiction clause in favour of the English courts, they will have

---

[57]   We do not seek to resolve those questions here. For the difference between the language versions, see *Fujifilm Kyowa Kirin Biologics v Abbvie Biotechnology* [2017] RPC 7 [73]–[78]; Case C-144/10, *Berliner Verkehrstriebe (BVG), Anstalt des offentlichen Rechts v JP Morgan Chase Bank* [2011] 1 WLR 2087 (ECJ), [26]; and *JP Morgan Chase v Berliner Verkehrsbetriebe (BVG) Anstalt des Offentlichen Rechts* [2012] QB 176 (CA) [54]. For discussion in relation to whether the test includes 'principally' or 'principal', and/or whether 'subject matter' is an appropriate phrasing, see Jenard Report, 34; *Webb v Webb* [1994] QB 689, AG [11]–[12], although cf ECJ [17]; and Case C-144/10, *Berliner v JP Morgan* (ECJ) [26], [38], [44] (supporting 'principal subject matter' at least for Article 24(2)). But many cases simply apply the language of the individual heads of Article 24, such as Cases C-343/04, *Land Oberösterreich v ČEZ* [2006] ECR I-4557 and C-605/14, *Komu v Komu* [2016] ILPr 8 (ECJ). It may be that 'principally concerned', and/or 'principal subject matter' have been held to be required only for Article 24(2), and not other sub-heads of Article 24. In the English cases, see eg *Ashurst v Pollard* [2001] Ch 595 (CA) 597C; *JP Morgan Chase v Berliner* (CA) [83]; *Re Zavarco* [2016] Ch 128 [27]; *Fujifilm* at [73]–[78]; *Eli Lilly v Genentech* [2018] 1 WLR 1755, [41]; *Koza v Akcil* [2018] EWHC 384 [23]–[25] . Recently, the discussion in *Magiera v Magiera* [2017] Fam 327 (CA) [52]–[54] leaves the point open.

[58]   In Case C-343/04, *Land Oberösterreich v ČEZ* [2006] ECR I-4557 [34], the ECJ adopted a restrictive approach to Article 24 and concluded that an action for cessation of a nuisance did not constitute a dispute having as its object rights *in rem* in immovable property.

[59]   For discussion of the requirement of consensus, see Briggs, paras 2.138 to 2.135.

[60]   Case 102/81, *Nordsee Deutsche Hochseefischerei v Reederei Mond Hochseefischerei Nordstern* [1982] ECR 1095 [12]–[14] (in the context of Art 234 EC).

jurisdiction over claims for an anti-suit injunction, as well as over the underlying substantive dispute, provided that the anti-suit injunction falls within the terms of the clause, as will usually be the case for jurisdiction clauses governed by English law.[61] It is to be noted that this head (and not the common law rules of jurisdiction via Article 6) applies to give jurisdiction even against a defendant domiciled outside the Brussels–Lugano zone provided that the court selected is within the Brussels–Lugano zone.

Article 25 can cover certain 'quasi-contractual' situations where a third party C has rights **17.45** derived from a contract between A and B containing a jurisdiction clause. The question that arises is whether a separate agreement by the third party to the clause is required or whether his claiming in the shoes of B will suffice. The European Court has held that, in cases outside the special protective regimes (for consumers, workers, and insurance), where a third party C has genuinely 'succeeded' to the contractual rights of B against A (or been 'substituted' for B), there is a sufficient 'consensus' between A and C for the purposes of Article 25, and no separate agreement to the clause is required.[62] The concept of 'succession' or 'substitution' has not been defined with any clarity but seems to be a broad concept of derived rights, and includes holders of bills of lading,[63] assignees,[64] subrogating insurers,[65] acquirers of bonds,[66] and claimants under third-party rights in contract,[67] where the third party would be entitled to benefit from and be bound by the clause under the applicable national law. The general approach is that the third party cannot, in principle, acquire more rights than the original contracting party, and by being vested in the original party's rights, also becomes subject to all the obligations to which the rights acquired are subject. The answer in any particular case would appear to be influenced by whether there is a European consensus as to how to analyse it.[68] The boundaries will not necessarily be the same as English law.[69] So a third party claiming under a third-party rights against insurers statute is not bound by the

---

[61] *OT Africa Line v Hijazy (The Kribi) (No 1)* [2001] 1 Lloyds Rep 76 [27], [29], [54]–[72].

[62] Case C-71/83, *Partenreederei Tilly Russ v Haven & Vervoebedrijf Nova* [1985] QB 931 [24]–[26]; Case C-159/97, *Trasporti Castelletti Spedizioni Internazionali v Hugo Trumpy* [1999] ILPr 492 (ECJ), AG [78]–[85], [139]–[140], ECJ [40]–[42]; *Coreck Maritime v Handelsveem* [2000] ECR I-9337 [23]–[27]; Case C-24/89, *Powell Duffryn v Petereit* [1992] ECR I-1745 [19]–[21] (shareholders' claims under articles of association); Case C-112/03, *Société Financière et Industrielle du Peloux v Axa Belgium* [2006] ECR I-3707, AG 93; Case C-543/10, *Refcomp v AXA Corporate Solutions Assurance* [2013] ILPr 17, AG 56 n 48, ECJ [36]–[38] (language of 'substitution' used); Case C-368/16, *Profit Investment Sim v Ossi* [2016] 1 WLR 3832 [31]–[37]. In England, see *Knorr-Bremse Systems v Haldex Brake Products* [2008] ILPr 26 [30]; *Goldman Sachs International v Novo Banco* [2015] 2 CLC 475 [75]–[92]. See also *Boss Group v Boss France* [1997] 1 WLR 351, 356–57 (in relation to inconsistent positions).
However, it seems that this approach does not apply to third parties who are protected by the special protective regimes; it may be necessary for them to have separately agreed to the jurisdiction clause in a way that specifically satisfies the requirements of those regimes. See Case C-201/82, *Gerling Konzern Speziale Kreditversicherung v Amminstrazione del Tesoro dello Stato* [1984] 3 CMLR 638, [20]; *Tilly Russ* at [23]; and Case C-368/16, *Assens Havn v Navigators Management (UK)* [2017] ILPr 30 [35]–[42].

[63] Case C-71/83, *Partenreederei Tilly Russ v Haven & Vervoebedrijf Nova* [1985] QB 931 [24]–[26]; Case C 159/97, *Trasporti Castelletti Spedizioni Internazionali v Hugo Trumpy* [1999] ILPr 492, AG [78]–[85], [139]–[140], ECJ [40]–[42]; Case C-387/98, *Coreck Maritime v Handelsveem* [2000] ECR I-9337 [23]–[27]. For an example of the uncontested operation of this in England, see *AP Moller-Maersk v Sonaec Villas Cen Sad Fadoul* [2011] 1 Lloyds Rep 1.

[64] Case C-159/97, *Trasporti Castelletti Spedizioni Internazionali v Hugo Trumpy* [1999] ILPr 492 (ECJ), AG [73]–[76]; *Firswood v Petra Bank* [1996] CLC 608, 617.

[65] Case C-453/10, *Refcomp v AXA Corporate Solutions Assurance* [2013] ILPr 17, AG [56] n 48.

[66] Case C-368/16, *Profit Investment Sim v Ossi* [2016] 1 WLR 3832 [31]–[37].

[67] Case C 159/97, *Trasporti Castelletti Spedizioni Internazionali v Hugo Trumpy* [1999] ILPr 492, AG [73]–[76].

[68] Case C-543/10, *Refcomp v AXA Corporate Solutions Assurance* [2013] ILPr 17 [38].

[69] In *Dresser v Falcongate Freight Management* [1992] QB 503 (CA) 508–11, 524, it was held that the doctrine of bailment on terms did not satisfy Article 25.

forum clause in the insurance contract under Article 25 without specific additional agreement to the clause, as the specific conditions of the protective regime for insurance would not be satisfied.[70]

17.46   If a matter falls within an exclusive jurisdiction clause which is within the temporal and material scope of the Hague Convention on the Choice of Court, then it seems that an overlapping jurisdiction will exist either alongside[71] Brussels–Lugano jurisdiction under Article 25, or outside Article 25 if Article 25 does not apply but the Convention does.[72] The Convention is directly effective in the United Kingdom (until Brexit) under EU law.[73] However, this will generally change little (so long as the Brussels–Lugano regime remains the law[74]). First of all, the jurisdictional rules of the Hague Convention are at least for most purposes, and for most jurisdiction clauses, the same as Article 25.[75] In most cases, therefore, it will be sufficient to rely on jurisdiction under Article 25 without needing to focus closely on the Hague Convention, and the existence of parallel jurisdiction under the Hague Convention will make little difference. Second, in any event, Article 26(6) of the Convention provides that the Convention shall not 'affect' the operation of Brussels–Lugano jurisdiction save in limited circumstances, namely where at least one of the parties is resident in a contracting state which is not a Brussels–Lugano state, which (at present) is a small number of cases.[76] Third, the rules of Article 25 and the Hague Convention are very similar in most cases. For most practical purposes, therefore, parallel jurisdiction under the Hague Convention is of little relevance unless and until the United Kingdom leaves the Brussels–Lugano regime. If Brexit brings an end to European jurisdictional co-operation, the Convention will assume much greater significance, and its role as part of the common law rules of jurisdiction in that situation is addressed in Chapter 18.

17.47   The application of the Hague Convention on the Choice of Court to quasi-contractual claims has not yet been explored.[77]

---

[70]   Case C-368/16, *Assens Havn v Navigators Management (UK)* [2017] ILPr 30, [35]–[42]; and see also Case C-112/03, *Société Financière et Industrielle du Peloux v Axa Belgium* [2006] ECR I-3707 [40]–[43].

[71]   For the question of whether Brussels–Lugano jurisdiction and Hague jurisdiction are parallel or mutually exclusive, see Ch 16, para 16.10.

[72]   The Hague Convention applies temporally to exclusive jurisdiction clauses concluded after 1 October 2015 (although some complicated transitional issues may arise post-Brexit). Its material scope is defined in Articles 2 and 16. A detailed comparison of the material scope of the Hague Convention and the Brussels–Lugano regime is outside the scope of this work. It is sufficient to say that in general Brussels–Lugano is broader, but there will be some cases of jurisdiction clauses which might be outside Brussels–Lugano but are within Hague, such as jurisdiction clauses agreed in public law matters.

[73]   Under Article 216 Treaty on the Functioning of the European Union (TFEU) and Council Decision 2014/887-EU. (After Brexit, if there is a deal, the Convention will remain directly effective under the Withdrawal Agreement and the EU Withdrawal Act 2018; if there is no deal, the Hague Convention will become law in the UK under the no-deal legislation and by virtue of the UK's independent accession thereto: see Ch 16, para 16.05). The power to serve proceedings under the Hague Convention out of the jurisdiction is given procedural form in England by CPR 6.33(2B).

[74]   There are complicated possible transitional consequences for the Hague Convention arising out of Brexit. We do not address these here.

[75]   To take one point, there is a slight difference in the wording relating to when clauses which do not expressly define themselves as either exclusive or should be deemed to be exclusive: compare Article 3(b) of the Convention to Article 25. Whether this makes a difference in practice remains to be seen. Another possible material difference is that the Convention's rules in Article 5 as to when a jurisdiction clause is binding, which refer to the chosen national law, may differ in abstract to the autonomous European law conditions of Article 25.

[76]   At the date of writing this footnote (1 May 2019), the contracting states outside the EU (and the UK) are only Mexico, Montenegro, and Singapore.

[77]   There is some relevant discussion at paras 94–97 of Trevor Hartley and Masato Dogauchi, *Explanatory Report on the Convention of 30 June 2005 on Choice of Court Agreements* (2013).

16. Entering an Appearance: Article 26(1)

Article 26(1) provides that a court before which a defendant enters an appearance shall **17.48** have jurisdiction. A defendant will be treated as entering an appearance before the English courts if, for example, he submits to the jurisdiction of the English court by filing an acknowledgment of service without indicating an intention to challenge jurisdiction,[78] and then filing a defence; or if he indicates an intention to challenge jurisdiction and then does not issue an application to challenge jurisdiction within the time for doing so.[79] The commission of other positive acts before the court, which are inconsistent with denying the court's jurisdiction, can also amount to a submission under English law and thus the 'entry of an appearance' under European law. This provision applies to claims for final anti-suit injunctions as it applies to any other claim for final relief.

C. *LIS PENDENS*

One of the distinctive characteristics of the Brussels–Lugano regime is its strict rules of *lis* **17.49** *pendens*.[80] Under Article 29, if 'proceedings involving the same cause of action and between the same parties' have been commenced first in another state, then the court second seised must stay or dismiss proceedings brought before it. Under Article 30, 'where related actions are pending in the courts of different Member States, any court other than the court first seised may stay its proceedings'. Actions are 'deemed to be related where they are so closely connected that it is expedient to hear and determine them together to avoid the risk of irreconcilable judgments resulting from separate proceedings'. However, even if actions are related, there is a discretion whether or not to stay.

There is an exception to the basic rule of *lis pendens* under Article 31, where the second **17.50** seised court has jurisdiction conferred on it by an exclusive clause compliant with Article 25. In that case, the non-chosen court must stay its proceedings pending determination of its own jurisdiction by the court chosen; and if the chosen court determines it has jurisdiction, then all other courts must decline jurisdiction. Consequently, even if the chosen court is seised second it does not need to stay the proceedings before it.

Article 33 and 34 create a parallel but more flexible regime where the prior proceedings are **17.51** outside the Brussels–Lugano zone, with Article 33 addressing the situation where the prior third country proceedings involve the same cause of action and Article 34 dealing with the case where they are related. In particular, a stay will only be required if it is required or necessary for 'the proper administration of justice', even if the prior proceedings involve the same cause of action. There is no direct equivalent to Article 31; but it is submitted that

---

[78] Not indicating an intention to challenge the jurisdiction on the acknowledgment of service form is not in itself sufficient to amount to a submission if an application to challenge the jurisdiction is then issued before a defence needs to be filed: *IBS Technologies v APM Technologies (No 1)* (Michael Briggs QC, 7 April 2003); *Global Multimedia International v Ara Media Services* [2006] EWHC 3107 [28]; *Maple Leaf Macro Volatility Master Fund v Rouvroy* [2009] EWHC 257 [186].

[79] CPR 11.5. However, the court has power to extend the time limit: *Sawyer v Atari Interactive* [2006] ILPr 129 [46]–[47]; *Texan Management v Pacific Electric Wire & Cable Company* [2009] UKPC 46 [73]–[77]; *Newland Shipping & Forwarding v Toba Trading* [2017] EWHC 1416 [52]–[96].

[80] Case C-116/02, *Gasser v MISAT* [2003] ECR I-14693.

there is no need, as the same priority for exclusive forum clauses can and should be taken into account in assessing what the proper administration of justice requires.

17.52 Only Articles 33 and 34 are likely to be of direct relevance to anti-suit injunctions because anti-suit injunctions cannot be sought to restrain the pursuit of Brussels–Lugano proceedings in any event. Further, where the English proceedings for anti-suit relief, or damages or declarations, are based on an English exclusive forum clause, Article 31 will mean that the English court can proceed irrespective of prior foreign proceedings. In the circumstances, questions of *lis pendens* are now of less importance than they were under the Brussels I Regulation.

17.53 In *The Alexandros T* the Supreme Court concluded that claims for declarations that foreign proceedings were in breach of exclusive jurisdiction clauses, and for damages for that breach, were not the same cause of action as the prior foreign claims on the merits.[81] This should mean, by parity of reasoning, that an anti-suit injunction is also not the same cause of action as the underlying claims on the merits.

17.54 A final claim for an anti-suit injunction might be 'related' in a broad factual sense to prior underlying claims on the merits, in particular if the basis of the injunction, such as a claim that the foreign proceedings are in breach of an exclusive forum clause, is part of what is being disputed in the prior foreign proceedings. This does not necessarily mean it would be related for the purposes of Article 30 or Article 34. In *Toepfer v Molino,* Mance J concluded that there was no risk of irreconcilable judgments between an anti-suit injunction and proceedings on the merits, and in any event that it would not be 'expedient' to stay the anti-suit to avoid irreconcilable judgments, nor to hear it together with the main proceedings.[82] This reasoning, however, is partly suspect: there are numerous ways in which an anti-suit injunction could involve conclusions that are irreconcilable with foreign proceedings on the merits. It is suggested, therefore, that subject to the question of expediency, which flows into the issue of whether a stay should be granted in the court's discretion, an anti-suit

---

[81]   *Starlight Shipping v Allianz Marine & Aviation Versicherungs (The Alexandros T)* [2014] 1 Lloyds Rep 223 (SC) [36]–[39], [135]. This was the overall effect of the previous English authorities, although they were not entirely consistent.

Previous decisions concluding that an anti-suit injunction was not the same cause of action as a previous foreign claim on the merits included: *Alfred C Toepfer International v Molino Boschi* [1996] 1 Lloyds Rep 510, 513; *Toepfer International v Société Cargill France* [1997] 2 Lloyds Rep 98, 106; and the same conclusion was reached in relation to claims for damages for breach of a jurisdiction clause in *Underwriting Members of Lloyd's Syndicate 980 v Sinco* [2009] 1 Lloyds Rep 365, [50], [54]. Similarly, in *Continental Bank v Aeakos Compania Naviera SA* [1994] 1 Lloyds Rep 505 (CA), the first instance judge concluded (at 510) that the anti-suit injunction was not the same cause of action as the prior claim on the merits. (The Court of Appeal approached matters differently, at 510–12).

In *Toepfer v Cargill* on appeal [1998] 1 Lloyds Rep 379 (CA), 387, 388, Phillips LJ considered that the question of whether a subsequent anti-suit was caught by Article 29 was open to doubt because of the overlap between the claim for breach of the forum clause which justified the anti-suit and the jurisdictional challenge based on the same clause in the prior foreign proceedings, and made a reference to the European Court, which was not decided, as the case was then settled. However, this doubt was not followed in the later cases and has now been overridden by *The Alexandros T*.

In *Advent Capital v GN Ellinas Imports-Exports (No 2)* [2005] 2 Lloyds Rep 607, [38], [49(ii)], [105]–[112], a claim for negative declarations on the merits was brought in circumstances where the English court was second seised, together with a claim in the alternative for damages for breach of the jurisdiction clause. Colman J concluded, correctly, that the claim for negative declarations on the merits must be stayed. He appears also to have concluded that the claim for damages must be stayed, although this is not entirely clear from the judgment. If so, it is unclear on what basis that decision was reached; and the question of 'same cause of action' does not seem to have been debated. In any event, again, this aspect of his decision has now been overtaken by *The Alexandros T*.

[82]   *Toepfer International v Molino Boschi* [1996] 1 Lloyds Rep 510, 513–15.

injunction might well be regarded as 'related' in abstract to prior foreign proceedings on the merits, for the purposes of Article 30 and 34, depending on the facts. In *The Alexandros T* it was conceded that the subsequent claims for damages for breach of the jurisdiction clause were 'related' to the prior foreign merits proceedings said to be in breach thereof, and this was regarded as correct by the Supreme Court.[83] The reasoning in *Toepfer v Molino* is capable of being reinterpreted as showing why the anti-suit injunction should not be stayed as a matter of expediency, and discretion.

However, this is only the first step. Even if English claims for damages, or declarations for **17.55** breach of an exclusive forum clause, or anti-suit injunctions, may be treated as 'related' in abstract to the prior foreign claim on the merits, subject to expediency, the English courts have consistently refused applications to stay such claims under Article 30 on grounds of discretion or expediency. Their reasoning has relied on the importance of protecting the exclusive jurisdiction clause, and the wrongfulness of the foreign proceedings. This was the approach taken in *The Alexandros T*.[84] As Mance J put the point, in relation to an anti-suit injunction, in *Toepfer v Molino Boschi*:

> Taking the injunctive claims first, their purpose is, as explained, to stop Molino Boschi pursuing the Italian proceedings (or any other proceedings, save arbitration). It would be quite contrary to that purpose, and inexpedient, to require the present claims to be heard and determined together with the Italian proceedings which it is their very object to stop.[85]

Accordingly, it is unlikely that any Article 34 stay would be granted in relation to any proper claim for a contractual anti-suit injunction to restrain prior substantive proceedings outside the Brussels–Lugano zone.

Different considerations may arise in relation to non-contractual anti-suit injunctions. In **17.56** *Research in Motion v Visto*, Lewison J held that a vague and ill-formulated claim for non-contractual damages arising from the allegedly abusive pursuit of foreign proceedings in another EC member state should be stayed under Article 30, because the foreign court would necessarily have to decide on the validity of its own process, and it was the most appropriate court to consider such questions.[86] The decision was, however, heavily influenced

---

[83] *Starlight Shipping v Allianz Marine & Aviation Versicherungs (The Alexandros T)* [2014] 1 Lloyds Rep 223 (SC) [74]. The point was also conceded in *Barclays Bank v Ente Nazionale de Previdenza ed Assistenza dei Medici e Degli Odontoiatri* [2015] 2 Lloyds Rep 527, [62]. On the unusual facts of *Research in Motion UK v Visto* [2007] EWHC 900, [25], it was held that English proceedings claiming damages for Italian proceedings that were said to be an abuse of process were 'related' to the Italian proceedings. However, the facts were unusual (see para 17.56); and the issues do not appear to have been closely analysed—for example, expediency was not addressed. (The stay was conceded on appeal [2008] ILPr 34, [23].)
  In *Advent Capital v GN Ellinas Imports-Exports* [2005] 2 Lloyds Rep 607 [109] relatedness was also assumed, but this conclusion may have been intended to apply only to the claim for negative declarations on the merits, and not the alternative claim for damages for breach of the jurisdiction clause; there was no distinct reasoning as to the damages claim.
[84] *Starlight Shipping Co v Allianz Marine & Aviation Versicherungs AG (The Alexandros T)* [2014] 1 Lloyds Rep 223 (SC) [95]–[97], upholding the decision of Burton J at [2012] 1 Lloyds Rep 544 [47]. This approach has been followed in *Barclays v Ente Nazionale de Previdenza ed Assistenza dei Medici e Degli Odontoiatri* [2015] 2 Lloyds Rep 527 [96]; *Commerzbank Aktiengesellschaft v Liquimar Tankers Management* [2017] 1 Lloyds Rep 273, [97]. Before *The Alexandros T*, see *JP Morgan v Primacom* [2005] 2 Lloyds Rep 665. An Article 30 stay of an anti-suit injunction was refused in *Toepfer International v Molino Boschi* [1996] 1 Lloyds Rep 510, 513–15.
[85] *Toepfer International v Molino Boschi* [1996] 1 Lloyds Rep 510, 514.
[86] *Research in Motion UK v Visto* [2007] EWHC 900, [25]–[26] (on appeal [2008] ILPr 34 [20]–[40], this point was no longer live).

by the unusual specific facts of the case, and Lewison J's perception that the damages claim in question was inherently ill-founded and would be caught by *Turner v Grovit*. It is likely to be of limited assistance in relation to whether stays should be granted under Article 34 in respect of well-formulated claims for non-contractual anti-suit injunctions in respect of prior substantive proceedings outside the Brussels–Lugano zone.

D. INTERIM ANTI-SUIT INJUNCTIONS

1. The Ancillary Jurisdiction

17.57 The European Court has held in *Van Uden* that a court having jurisdiction as to the substance of a case over a defendant in accordance with Articles 4 and 7–26 of the Recast[87] has ancillary jurisdiction against that defendant to order any 'provisional or protective' measure which may prove necessary.[88]

17.58 In *Masri (No 2)* and *Masri (No 3)*, Lawrence Collins LJ (as he then was) held that the ancillary jurisdiction also extends to any orders ancillary to the substantive dispute, even if they are not 'provisional or protective': 'the English court seised of the substantive dispute has the power to grant ancillary orders in that dispute, both prior to judgment and after judgment …'.[89] He concluded that an interim anti-suit injunction, sought on an alternative forum basis, to protect English proceedings, did not involve a new separate cause of action and was not 'suing'. Independent jurisdiction therefore did not need to be established under the Brussels–Lugano regime, even against a Brussels–Lugano defendant and instead the interim anti-suit injunction could be brought within the court's ancillary jurisdiction. However, alternatively and if necessary, he considered that such an interim anti-suit injunction was a 'provisional, or protective measure', because it was 'designed to protect the underlying rights of [the injunction claimant]', and so would fall within the ancillary jurisdiction

---

[87] See Case C-391/95, *Van Uden Maritime v Kommanditgesellschaft in Firma Deco-Line* [1998] ECR I-7091 [19]; Case C-99/96, *Mietz v Intership Yachting Sneek* [1999] ECR I-2277 [41]. In contrast, if the English court has jurisdiction over the substance under Article 6 of the Recast and the common law rules of jurisdiction applicable thereunder, this principle will not apply, as jurisdiction is to be determined 'by the law of that Member State'. The omission of any reference to Article 6 in *Van Uden*, [19], was presumably deliberate (in *Mietz*, [41], the European Court used the language of 'one of the heads of jurisdiction laid down in the Convention', but this was probably not meant to refer to Art 6). Consequently, if the defendant is domiciled outside the Brussels–Lugano zone, ancillary jurisdiction over interim relief will be determined by the common law rules of jurisdiction. However, they will create an ancillary jurisdiction with at least the same breadth. See Ch 18, section J, 'Jurisdiction and Interim Anti-Suit Injunctions', paras 18.90–18.92.

[88] See Case C-391/95, *Van Uden Maritime v Kommanditgesellschaft in Firma Deco-Line* [1998] ECR I-7091 [19]–[20]; Case C-99/96, *Mietz v Intership Yachting Sneek* [1999] ECR I-2277 [40]–[41]; applied in *JP Morgan Europe v Primacom* [2005] 2 Lloyds Rep 665 [70]; restated by the Advocate General in Case C-539/03, *Roche Nederland v Primus* [2006] ECR I-6535, AG [46] (suggestive of a broad approach) and in Case C-616/10, *Solvay v Honeywell* (2012), AG [45]. This principle of ancillary jurisdiction does not follow from Article 35, but rather as a necessary implication from the jurisdictional rules of the regime. The limitations imposed on measures granted under Article 35 (which will apply only where the court granting interim relief does not have jurisdiction over the substantive dispute), such as the requirement of a close territorial link, do not restrict the ancillary jurisdiction itself: *Van Uden* at [19], [22].

[89] *Masri v Consolidated Contractors (No 2)* [2009] QB 450 (CA) [92]–[107] and addendum; *Masri v Consolidated Contractors (No 3)* [2009] QB 503 (CA) [60]–[65], [99]. This is consistent with the decision, before *Van Uden*, in *The Eras Eil Actions* [1995] 1 Lloyds Rep 64, 72–74. See also in a non-Brussels–Lugano context, *Star Reefers Pool v JFC Group* [2012] 1 Lloyds Rep 376 (CA) [42]–[43]; *Golden Endurance v RMA Watanya* [2015] 1 Lloyds Rep 266 [26]–[29]; *Deutsche Bank v Sebastian Holdings (No 2)* [2017] 1 WLR 3056, [6].

even if being 'provisional, or protective' was a necessary condition.[90] As a result, he concluded that an English court with jurisdiction over the merits under the Brussels–Lugano regime will in turn have jurisdiction to grant interim anti-suit injunctions against the parties to that litigation.[91] This was so, even in relation to an interim anti-suit injunction that was sought without limit of time, and post-judgment.

Lawrence Collins LJ's approach to the ancillary jurisdiction has support in academic writing.[92]   **17.59**
The attribution of a general ancillary jurisdiction to the court with jurisdiction over the merits produces a practical and principled allocation of international jurisdiction. It is also consistent with other decisions in which the European Court of Justice (ECJ) has accepted that a range of ancillary measures, granted as part of, and to protect and pursue, underlying litigation, fell within, or were incidents of, jurisdiction over the merits of the substantive litigation. An example of this is *Realchemie v Bayer*, where a fine ordered by the German court for breach of a German court order was enforceable under the Brussels–Lugano regime.[93]

As a matter of English procedural law, interim anti-suit injunctions may be sought within   **17.60**
existing proceedings, even if they are indefinite in effect, and even if no corresponding final injunction has been claimed.[94] The effect of *Masri (No 3)* is therefore that where the court has substantive jurisdiction over the merits against a party, it will also have ancillary jurisdiction under the Brussels–Lugano regime to grant an interim anti-suit injunction to protect the proceedings by application against that party in the existing proceedings, even against a party domiciled elsewhere in the Brussels–Lugano zone, and even if there is no independent jurisdiction to hear a claim for a final anti-suit injunction against that party, or none is claimed.

Even if, contrary to *Masri (No 3)*, it were thought that interim alternative forum anti-suit   **17.61**
injunctions did not fall within the ancillary jurisdiction, it might be possible to view them as 'procedural' measures and so not as matters over which independent substantive jurisdiction needed to be established.[95]

---

[90] An interim anti-suit injunction is arguably not conservatory in the relevant sense, as it will usually be intended to create final and irreversible effects. Nevertheless, the English courts are unlikely to change course on this point, unless compelled.

[91] *Masri v Consolidated Contractors (No 3)* [2009] QB 503 (CA) [31], [60]–[66], [99].

[92] See Briggs, paras 6.08–6.09; see also Sir L Collins et al (eds), *Dicey, Morris & Collins on the Conflict of Laws* (15th edn, Sweet & Maxwell 2012) para 8.025.

[93] Case C-406/09, *Realchemie Nederland v Bayer CropSciences* [2011] ECR I-9773, [40], [44]. See also *CHW v GJH* [1982] ECR 1189, ECJ [8] and AG [1].

[94] *Glencore International v Metro Trading International (No 3)* [2002] 2 CLC 1090 (CA) [59]; *The Eras Eil Actions* [1995] 1 Lloyds Rep 64, 72–74; *Masri v Consolidated Contractors (No 3)* [2009] QB 503 (CA) [58]–[59], [66], [76], 96]–[97]. See Ch 3, para 3.33; Ch 13, paras 13.27–13.29.

[95] Lawrence Collins LJ concluded that such interim alternative forum anti-suit injunctions, sought in existing proceedings, were not 'suing' and did not involve a separate cause of action, in *Masri v Consolidated Contractors (No 3)* [2009] QB 503 (CA) [31]–[32], [59]–[66], [99]. There are suggestions in the case law of the European Court that measures of a purely procedural nature do not fall within the Brussels–Lugano regime, and thus do not need to comply with its rules on jurisdiction, although even if that is right, they must still not interfere with the effectiveness of the regime or cut across its general scheme (Case C-365/88, *Kongress Agentur Hagen v Zeehaghe* [1990] ECR I-1845, AG [33(2)], ECJ [19]–[20]; Case C-159/02, *Turner v Grovit* [2004] ECR I-3565, AG [37], ECJ [22], [29]). It is possible that at least non-contractual anti-suit injunctions may be viewed as procedural matters for the purposes of the Rome II Regulation: see Ch 4, section B, 'Applicable Law', para 4.15. However, it has not yet been accepted that an interim anti-suit injunction should be treated as a measure of a purely procedural nature for the purpose of the Brussels–Lugano regime. In *Turner v Grovit*, ECJ [29], the ECJ was apparently sceptical of such an argument: 'Even if it is assumed that, as has been contended, an injunction may be regarded as a measure of a

17.62   Further, where applicable, the *Van Uden* doctrine of ancillary jurisdiction (in contrast to Article 31 of the Brussels I Regulation) constitutes a positive grant of jurisdiction under the Brussels–Lugano regime.[96] As a result, applications for interim relief which fall within it can be served out of the jurisdiction on parties to the proceedings without the permission of the court. This will include interim alternative forum anti-suit injunctions.

17.63   As a matter of machinery, this can be effected under CPR 6.33, read together with CPR 6.2(c) if the application notice is issued before the claim form. If the substantive proceedings have already been brought, it might be possible to serve the ancillary application within the jurisdiction at the address for service which is required under CPR 6.23 or, where necessary, by alternative service; and in any event, an implied power to serve documents relating to the proceedings out of the jurisdiction, would appear to exist as an implied consequence of CPR 6.38(1).[97]

17.64   It is unclear at present to what extent and in what conditions the Brussels–Lugano ancillary jurisdiction can apply to give jurisdiction towards third parties not parties to the substantive litigation.[98]

---

procedural nature … it need merely be borne in mind that the application of national procedural rules may not impair the effectiveness of the Convention.'

[96] This appears to be the correct reading of Case C-391/95, *Van Uden Maritime v Kommanditgesellschaft in Firma Deco-Line* [1998] ECR I-7091, [18]–[22]; *Masri v Consolidated Contractors (No 2)* [2009] QB 450 (CA) [92]–[107] and addendum; *Masri v Consolidated Contractors (No 3)* [2009] QB 503 (CA) [60]–[67]. See also *Masri v Consolidated Contractors (No 4)* [2010] 1 AC 90, (CA) [30]–[35], [67]. (The Court of Appeal's decision in *Masri (No 4)* was overturned on appeal, but without discussion of the issues of European jurisdictional law, because at the stage of permission to appeal the House of Lords had indicate that a reference would be made on European law issues, and the European law points were hived off pending determination of the English law points: [2010] 1 AC 90, [39]. This does not necessarily mean that all the European jurisdictional law questions relating to the ancillary jurisdiction were considered to be referable. Other European law issues were in play and the scope of any reference was never in the event defined.) This is in contrast to Article 35, which merely allows national rules of jurisdiction to operate in respect of interim relief irrespective of the general jurisdictional limitations imposed by Article 2. However, note that the discussion in Case C-159/02, *Turner v Grovit* [2004] ECR I-3565, ECJ [22], [29] does not clearly support this conclusion.

[97] CPR 6.38(1) requires that if permission is required to serve the claim form out of the jurisdiction, permission is also required to serve any other document in those proceedings out of the jurisdiction. The power to grant permission for such other documents is found, as a matter of mechanics, in 6.37(5)(b)(ii), which includes a power to grant permission to serve application notices out of the jurisdiction. It is implicit in 6.38(1) that if permission is not required to serve the claim form out of the jurisdiction, permission is not required for such other documents, including application notices ancillary to and within the proceedings. See *Masri v Consolidated Contractors (No 4)* [2010] 1 AC 90 (HL) [28], discussing the previous 6.30(2), which was in materially identical terms to what is now 6.38(1); and *Star Reefers v JFC Group* [2010] EWHC 3003, [28], [2012] 1 Lloyds Rep 376 (CA) [42]; holding that 'documents' within CPR 6.37 and 6.38 includes applications for interim anti-suit injunctions.

[98] The Court of Appeal thought the Brussels–Lugano ancillary jurisdiction could apply to third parties in *Masri v Consolidated Contractors (No 4)* [2010] 1 AC 90 (CA) at [30]–[35], [66], [67], relying on *National Justice Compania Naviera SA v Prudential Assurance Co Ltd (The Ikarian Reefer) (No 2)* [2000] 1 WLR 603 (CA). In addition, Lawrence Collins LJ's approach to the ancillary jurisdiction in *Masri v Consolidated Contractors Ltd (No 3)* [2009] QB 503 (CA) [31], [60]–[67], is consistent with the ancillary jurisdiction being capable of applying to third parties.

But in *Masri (No 4)*, when appealed to the Supreme Court, the European law issues had been hived off and were not addressed (the Supreme Court had indicated a reference to the ECJ would be required). In respect of the issues arising under the *common law* jurisdictional rules, the House of Lords concluded that any ancillary jurisdiction did not apply automatically towards third parties, and doubted aspects of *The Ikarian Reefer*: at [2010] 1 AC 90 (HL) [26]–[34], [36]. The Court of Appeal's conclusions as to the ancillary jurisdiction and third parties therefore have a questionable status. The distinction between ancillary relief sought against the parties to litigation on the one hand, and against non-parties on the other hand, is also reflected in *Belletti v Moricci* [2009] 2 CLC 525 [16]–[43].

2. Jurisdiction over Interim Relief under the Heads of Jurisdiction in the Regulation

17.65 The court will also have jurisdiction over a claim for an interim injunction if the interim injunction sought can itself be made to fit within one of the primary heads of jurisdiction in Articles 4 and 7–26 of the Recast. If the court would have jurisdiction over a claim for a final anti-suit injunction against a defendant, then it will have jurisdiction over a parallel interim injunction, either under the ancillary jurisdiction derived from its jurisdiction over the merits if the final injunction is also claimed by claim form, or because the interim injunction if free-standing, is treated as a claim in its own right, which is 'suing' and over which independent jurisdiction can and should be obtained under the jurisdictional heads of the regime.

17.66 Where such jurisdiction exists, the application notice can be served out of the jurisdiction without the permission of the court, either under CPR 6.33 read together with CPR 6.2(c), if the application is brought before the claim form is brought, or by inference from CPR 6.38(1), if the substantive proceedings have already commenced.[99]

3. Interim Injunctions in Single Forum Cases

17.67 If an interim injunction is sought in a 'single forum' case, where there are and will be no underlying English proceedings, and the only possible substantive litigation is the targeted litigation, the applicant will have to bring the interim injunction within one of the substantive heads of jurisdiction of the regime.[100] There will be no ancillary jurisdiction, as there will be no underlying substantive jurisdiction.[101] However, if jurisdiction does exist under one of the heads of the regime, it will be possible to serve any application notice out of the jurisdiction either ancillary to any final claim for a single forum injunction, or if the application is brought before any such claim form, under CPR 6.33 read together with CPR 6.2(c).

However, if there is no ancillary Brussels–Lugano jurisdiction towards third parties, problems could arise in relation to a wide range of ancillary matters such as contempt, *Chabra* injunctions, and anti-suit injunctions. The difficulties are greater than under the common law rules because of the relative inflexibility of the Brussels–Lugano regime, and because problems cannot be fixed simply by the Rules Committee amending the procedural rules. Solutions might be found in Article 35, or by treating certain ancillary matters as purely procedural and outside the scope of the Brussels–Lugano regime (Art 8 of the Recast might also be a possibility, but *Belletti v Morici* at [41] suggests that it cannot be used for interim relief). But failing such alternative solutions, there may be a practical pressure for the Brussels–Lugano ancillary jurisdiction to cater for certain forms of relief against third parties. The Supreme Court did not need to consider these problems in *Masri No 4*.

---

[99] See para 17.63.

[100] Even an interim anti-suit injunction is a civil and commercial matter within the scope of the Brussels–Lugano regime (Ch 16, para 16.17) and if it is claimed by free-standing application and is not concerned with the protection of existing proceedings in England, it should probably be regarded as 'suing' for the purposes of the Brussels–Lugano regime. In *Masri v Consolidated Contractors (No 3)* [2009] QB 503 (CA) [31], Lawrence Collins LJ observed that 'the claim for an anti-suit injunction did not involve CCIC being "sued" for the purposes of the Brussels I Regulation'. However, on a true reading of his judgment this comment applies only to interim alternative forum injunctions, which he viewed as falling within the ancillary jurisdiction, and as not amounting to 'suing' for substantive relief for that reason: [52]. Indeed, Lawrence Collins LJ regarded single forum injunctions as juridically and jurisdictionally different to alternative forum injunctions (see at [34]–[59]), and observed that it would be a 'very rare case' where the court would have jurisdiction to hear a claim for a single forum injunction against a non-English party: at [56].

[101] See *Masri v Consolidated Contractors (No 3)* [2009] QB 503 (CA) [56], [59].

4. Interim Injunctions Sought in English Court Proceedings
Outside the Regime

17.68   If the substantive proceedings in an English court fall outside the scope of the regime, for example if they concern wills or succession,[102] it seems that interim anti-suit injunctions applied
for in those proceedings should be treated as 'borrowing' the characterization of the underlying claim, and thus fall within the relevant exception, and outside the scope of the Brussels–
Lugano regime.[103] If so, the relevant rules of jurisdiction will be the common law rules.[104]

5. Injunctions in Support of Proceedings Elsewhere

17.69   It is possible, in theory, that an interim anti-suit injunction could be sought to protect substantive proceedings in another country. If this were attempted, jurisdiction could in principle be obtained under Articles 2–24 if they applied, in the situations discussed above.

17.70   In addition, under Article 35 of the Recast, the English court has jurisdiction to grant such
'provisional, including protective' measures against a defendant domiciled in another
member state as may be available under English law, even if a court of another member state
has jurisdiction over the substantive dispute.[105] This does not cover the situation in which
the English court itself has jurisdiction over the substance, where jurisdiction for interim
relief is covered by the ancillary jurisdiction established in *Van Uden*.[106]

17.71   In principle, Article 35 of the Recast could also be used to give the English court jurisdiction
to hear claims for interim[107] anti-suit injunctions in support of proceedings in the court of
another member state. However, there would be barriers in the way.

---

[102] See the exceptions in Article 1(2) of the Regulation, set out in Ch 16, section C, 'The Framework of English
Jurisdictional Law', para 16.16.

[103] See Ch 16, section D, 'The Material Scope of the Brussels–Lugano Regime', para 16.20.

[104] Unless the Hague Convention or some other specific regime applies. For the common law rules of jurisdiction in respect of interim relief see Ch 18, section J, 'Jurisdiction and Interim Anti-Suit Injunctions'.

[105] Case C-391/95, *Van Uden Maritime v Kommanditgesellschaft in Firma Deco-Line* [1998] ECR I-7091
[18]–[21].

[106] Case C-391/95, *Van Uden Maritime BV v Kommanditgesellschaft in Firma Deco-Line* [1998] ECR I-7091,
[19]; and see more generally paras 17.57–17.62.

[107] It can be doubted whether a final anti-suit injunction (if regarded as an independent final claim over which
jurisdiction needs to be freshly established) would fall within the concept of 'provisional, including protective
measures', since it is irrevocable final relief. In Case C-391/95, *Van Uden Maritime v Kommanditschaft in Firma
Deco Line* [1998] ECR I-7091, [38]–[48] (following and expanding Case 125/79, *Denilauler v Couchet Frères* [1980]
ECR 1553 [16]), the ECJ held that, for a measure to fall within Article 35, the national court must be able to impose a time limit and to impose conditions to safeguard the provisional nature of the measure ordered (and thus,
orders for interim payment would not fall within Art 35 unless they included appropriate guarantees of repay-
ment). A final anti-suit injunction is not reversible in that sense, even though it can be set aside on a change of
circumstances. In *Masri v Consolidated Contractors (No 3)* [2009] QB 503 (CA) [66], [99], Lawrence Collins LJ
concluded *obiter* that an interim anti-suit injunction 'qualifies as a protective measure', but his reasoning expressly
distinguished final injunctions, in terms which clearly suggest he thought they would not fall within Article 35. In
Navigation Maritime Bulgare v Rustal Trading (The Ivan Zagubanski) [2002] 1 Lloyds Rep 106 [52]–[53], [120], it
was argued that a final anti-suit injunction could be justified under Article 35. Aikens J showed little enthusiasm
for the argument, and declined to decide the point.
    In addition, jurisdiction under Article 35 is permissive, not facultative: Article 35 permits national courts
to assume jurisdiction under their own rules. In England, the power to grant interim relief in support of foreign courts is contained in Civil Jurisdiction and Judgments Act, 1982, s 25 (extended by Civil Jurisdiction and
Judgments Act 1982 (Interim Relief) Order 1997), and proceedings under s 25 can be served out of the jurisdiction
with the permission of the court under CPR 6.36 and PD 6B para 3.1(5). But this applies to interim relief only.
A claim for a final anti-suit injunction in support of a foreign court could therefore not be brought under s 25 and

First, while Lawrence Collins LJ has concluded that an interim anti-suit injunction is a 'provisional, including protective measure',[108] the contrary could be arguable, since interim anti-suit injunctions are not necessarily reversible. **17.72**

Second, for interim measures to satisfy the conditions for the application of Article 35, there must **17.73** be a 'real connecting link between the subject matter of the measures sought and the territorial jurisdiction of the Contracting State before which those measures are sought'.[109] It remains to be seen whether the courts would accept that a claim for an anti-suit injunction to restrain proceedings before the courts of a country outside the Brussels–Lugano regime, where the competing substantive proceedings that are to be protected are abroad, will have a 'real connecting link' to England. Even if this is possible in principle, it might be necessary to show some specific connecting link to England and Wales, such as the injunction defendant or his assets being within the jurisdiction and therefore susceptible to the coercive jurisdiction of the English court.[110]

Third, Article 35 does not provide a positive grant of jurisdiction but instead refers back to the **17.74** applicable rules of national law. In England these have, in substance, been provided by section 25 of the Civil Jurisdiction and Judgments Act 1982 and CPR PD 6B para 3.1(5).[111] To fall within section 25, it must not be 'inexpedient' for the English court to grant interim relief in support of the foreign court. The English courts are generally reluctant, on grounds of comity, to grant anti-suit injunctions in support of proceedings in another country.[112]

6. Interim Injunctions to Protect Arbitration Proceedings in England (or Abroad)

An interim anti-suit injunction may be claimed to protect arbitration proceedings in England, **17.75** and in principle even in support of a foreign arbitration.[113]

It follows from the decision of the ECJ in *The Front Comor* that anti-suit injunctions, including interim anti-suit injunctions, to enforce an arbitration clause or protect an arbitration fall outside the scope of the Brussels–Lugano regime.[114] Consequently jurisdiction over them will be determined by the common law rules.[115] **17.76**

would have to be claimed under s 37(1) of the Senior Courts Act. Even if it were a legitimate form of substantive relief (as to which see Ch 4, section L, 'Comity', para 4.83; Ch 7, section G, 'Injunctions in Support of a Foreign Forum') it therefore would not be able to benefit from the jurisdictional head in PD 6B para 3.1(5).

---

[108] *Masri v Consolidated Contractors (No 3)* [2009] QB 503 (CA) [66], [99].
[109] Case C-391/95, *Van Uden Maritime BV v Kommanditgesellschaft in firma Deco–Line* [1998] ECR I-7091, [40].
[110] *Belletti v Morici* [2009] ILPr 525 [25]–[26], [54]–[55], [58]; and see Briggs, para 6.05.
[111] As extended by Civil Jurisdiction and Judgments Act 1982 (Interim Relief) Order 1997, SI 1997/302. (If and when Brexit occurs then, as matters stand, this will be amended by the current 'No Deal' legislation, but its material effect will not change.)
[112] See Ch 4, para 4.83; Ch 7, section G, 'Injunctions in Support of a Foreign Forum', and in particular *Airbus Industrie v Patel* [1999] 1 AC 119 (HL). While in principle relief could also be granted under s 37(1) of the Senior Courts Act 1981 (cf Ch 3, paras 3.06–3.07), it is unlikely that this could legitimately be used to evade the restrictions of principle imposed by s 25 of the Civil Jurisdiction and Judgments Act 1982: see *Anan Kasei v Molycorp Chemicals and Oxides (Europe)* [2017] ILPr 8, [39]–[41]. In any event, if an anti-suit was 'inexpedient' under s 25, it is difficult to see how it would be 'in the interests of justice' to grant it under s 37.
[113] Ch 13, paras 13.10–13.17 and paras 13.31–13.32.
[114] Case C-185/07, *Allianz v West Tankers (The Front Comor)* [2009] ECR I-663, [22]–[23]; see recently *Nori Holding v Bank Otkritie Financial Corp* [2018] EWHC 1343 [69]–[86].
[115] See Ch 18, sections I, 'Arbitration Claims', and J, 'Jurisdiction and Interim Anti-Suit Injunctions'.

18

Jurisdiction under the Common Law Rules

A. INTRODUCTION

18.01 The 'common law' rules of jurisdiction, which are principally contained in the rules on service in CPR Part 6,[1] are the main relevant rules for jurisdiction (subject to the effect of the Hague Convention on the Choice of Court[2]) where the subject matter of the proceedings is outside the material scope of the Brussels–Lugano regime, and also, through Article 6 of

---

[1] The common law rules can also be regarded as including the jurisdictional rules contained in other parts of the CPR, such as CPR 62.5 on arbitration and CPR 63.14 on intellectual property.

English law also contains some separate statutory regimes for jurisdiction for defined subject matters. See eg Carriage of Goods by Road Act 1965, Sch 1, incorporating the Convention on the Contract for the International Carriage of Goods by Road (CMR Convention), which has its own jurisdiction regime in Article 21. These separate regimes are not explored in this work.

[2] In matters concerning an exclusive jurisdiction clause which falls within the scope of the Hague Convention on Choice of Court, jurisdiction will exist under the Convention on top of and outside the 'common law' rules. Where jurisdiction exists under the Hague Convention, service can be effected without permission under 6.33(2B). So long as the Brussels–Lugano regime continues to apply, Hague Convention jurisdiction will in most cases apply in parallel to jurisdiction under Article 25 of the Brussels I Recast (see Ch 16, para 16.10) and will often be of little practical import. But if Brexit leads to the ending of European jurisdictional co-operation, and (as is anticipated) the UK's accession to the Hague Convention then takes effect (see Ch 16, para 16.05), the role of the Hague Convention will be much more significant. It will become the primary jurisdictional basis for claims under jurisdictional clauses (within its material scope). Its operation alongside the common law rules in that situation is discussed at paras 18.40–18.41 of this chapter.

the Recast, where the defendant is domiciled outside the Brussels–Lugano zone.[3] If the consequence of Brexit is that the Brussels–Lugano regime ceases to operate, then the common law rules of jurisdiction will become again the primary rules governing territorial jurisdiction, combined with the Hague Convention in cases concerning jurisdiction clauses.[4]

18.02   Jurisdiction under the common law rules is based on service of originating process on the defendant.[5] However, at common law proceedings can in general only be served within 'the jurisdiction', that is England and Wales, unless there is statutory authority permitting service out of the jurisdiction.[6] The common law rules of jurisdiction therefore consist, in essence, of the rules by which service may be effected within the jurisdiction; and the rules which give the court power to grant permission to serve proceedings out of the jurisdiction.

18.03   The analysis in this chapter considers jurisdiction over claims or applications for anti-suit injunctions under the common law rules, and also under the Hague Convention on the Choice of Court. It is not intended to be a general survey of the rules of jurisdiction. Only issues of particular relevance to anti-suit injunctions are analysed in detail.

B. SERVICE WITHIN THE JURISDICTION

18.04   The rules for service of claim forms within the jurisdiction have not, so far, given rise to any questions of specific interest in relation to anti-suit injunctions.

18.05   In ordinary civil litigation, claim forms can be served within the jurisdiction on any person or entity present within the jurisdiction under the rules set out in CPR Part 6 sections I and II, and also, in relation to companies, under the Companies Act 2006.[7] In brief, these rules permit claim forms to be served: by personal service on the defendant within the jurisdiction;[8] by sending them to defined addresses within the jurisdiction, including in particular the defendant's residence, principal or registered office, or place of business, within the jurisdiction (if such exists);[9] at an address for service given by the defendant;[10] on the defendant's solicitor with authority to receive service;[11] by a contractually agreed method;[12] or in certain cases on the defendant's agent in respect of a contract.[13]

---

[3]   Subject to Articles 18(1), 21(2), 24, and 25 of the Brussels I Recast, and the effect of the Hague Convention of the Choice of Court.

[4]   On the Hague Convention, see n 2 and paras 18.40 and 18.41 of this chapter, and Ch 16, paras 16.05, 16.10. In addition, in the event of a no-deal Brexit, as matters stand, the no-deal provisions contained in Civil Jurisdiction and Judgments (Amendment) (EU Exit) Regulations 2019, SI 2019 No 479 will transfer into English law the essential effect of the protective employment and consumer regimes contained in the Brussels Recast, by Regulation 26 adding new sections 15A–15E of the Civil Jurisdiction and Judgments Act 1982. We do not seek to address the effect of those possible provisions in this chapter.

[5]   *Dresser UK v Falcongate Freight Management* [1992] QB 502 (CA) 518H, 523A–D; *Masri v Consolidated Contractors (No 4)* [2010] 1 AC 90 (HL) [32]–[39].

[6]   The traditional position is that all service of originating process out of the jurisdiction requires statutory authority, because under the common law the monarch's writ only runs within England and Wales: *Siskina v Distos Compania Naviera (The Siskina)* [1979] AC 210 (HL) 254F–255C; *Masri v Consolidated Contractors (No 4)* [2010] 1 AC 90 (HL) [32]. The point is also expressly reconfirmed in CPR 6.6(1) in respect of claim forms.

[7]   Companies Act 2006, s 1139.

[8]   CPR 6.3(1)(a) and 6.5.

[9]   Under CPR 6.3(1)(b)–(d), and 6.9, or under Companies Act 2006, s 1139.

[10]   CPR 6.8.

[11]   CPR 6.7.

[12]   CPR 6.11.

[13]   CPR 6.12.

Even temporary presence in the jurisdiction is sufficient for personal service on a nat-   **18.06**
ural person.[14] However, personal service on a company, by service on one of its officers
within the jurisdiction, can only be effective if the company carries on business within the
jurisdiction.[15]

If difficulties with the normal rules of service arise, an application can be made to   **18.07**
the court to permit service by an *alternative* method,[16] or to dispense with service altogether,[17] although these rules cannot be used to circumvent the jurisdictional constraints imposed by the rules which govern when service out of the jurisdiction is
permissible.[18]

In addition, if a defendant has been purportedly but invalidly served with proceedings   **18.08**
within the jurisdiction, the court will nevertheless have jurisdiction over the case if the defendant submits to the jurisdiction of the court.

C. FORUM NON CONVENIENS

Proceedings that have been validly served within the jurisdiction can be stayed under CPR   **18.09**
Part 11 on the grounds of *forum non conveniens*, if the defendant can show that there is
some other available forum, having competent jurisdiction, in which the case may be tried
more suitably for the interests of all the parties and the ends of justice. The burden is on the
defendant to show that there is another forum which is clearly or distinctly more appropriate than the English forum.[19]

The power to stay on grounds of *forum non conveniens* cannot be exercised if the defendant   **18.10**
is domiciled within England and Wales and the matter falls within the scope of the Brussels–
Lugano regime.[20]

However, there is little room for the application of the doctrine of *forum non conveniens*   **18.11**
in relation to anti-suit injunctions. If there is a reasonable case on the merits for the
grant of an anti-suit injunction to protect proceedings in England, or for a 'single forum'
injunction,[21] or even an injunction to protect proceedings abroad, then it will usually
be obvious that England is the most convenient forum to hear the claim for an anti-suit
injunction.[22] The limitations on the grant of the remedy incorporate, via the principles of

---

[14] *Colt Industries v Sarlie* [1966] 1 WLR 440; *Maharanee of Baroda v Wildenstein* [1972] 2 QB 283 (CA) 291, 294,
298; *Adams v Cape Industries* [1990] Ch 433 (CA) 518–19.
[15] *SSL International v TTK LIG* [2012] 1 WLR 1842 (CA) [61].
[16] CPR 6.15.
[17] CPR 6.16.
[18] *Field v Bennett* (1886) 56 LJQB 89; *Kyrgyz Republic Ministry of Transport Department of Civil Aviation v Finrep*
[2006] 2 CLC 402 [43]; *Honda Motor v Neesam* [2007] EWHC 581 [29]–[37]; *Koza v Akcil* [2018] EWHC 384
[23]–[25].
[19] *Spiliada Maritime v Cansulex* [1987] AC 460 (HL).
[20] Case C-281/02, *Owusu v Jackson* [2005] ECR I–1383.
[21] For the distinction between 'single forum' and 'alternative forum' cases, see Ch 5, para 5.02.
[22] See eg *Joint Stock Asset Management Co Ingosstrakh-Investments v BNP Paribas* [2012] 1 Lloyds Rep 649 (CA)
[80]–[82]. See also *Donohue v Armco* [1999] 2 Lloyds Rep 649 [63]–[69]; *Youell v Kara Mara Shipping* [2000] 2
Lloyds Rep 102 [72]–[75]; *Navigation Maritime Bulgare v Rustal Trading (The Ivan Zagubanski)* [2002] 1 Lloyds
Rep 106 [52(11)], [101].

comity, essentially the same constraints as the doctrine of *forum non conveniens* imposes in terms of jurisdiction.

D. SERVICE OUT OF THE JURISDICTION

18.12   Under the common law rules, proceedings can only be served on defendants outside the jurisdiction if the court grants permission to do so.[23] In ordinary civil litigation, the court has power to grant permission, in its discretion, under statutory powers contained principally in CPR 6.36 and Practice Direction 6B ('PD 6B').[24] Other powers to permit service out in litigation on specific topics are concerned in other CPR rules such as CPR 6.33(2B) for the Hague Convention, CPR 62.5 for arbitration, certain other subject-specific rules, and certain statutes;[25] of those, this work will address only the Hague Convention and CPR 62.5.

18.13   In order to persuade the court to exercise its discretion to grant permission to serve proceedings out of the jurisdiction, the claimant must show in respect of each of his claims that (a) there is a serious issue to be tried (or a reasonable prospect of success, which has been held to be the same thing);[26] (b) there is a good arguable case that the claim falls within one of the gateways for jurisdiction (for example the heads in PD 6B para 3.1); and (c) that England is clearly the appropriate forum for the trial of the action.[27] Applications for permission to serve proceedings out of the jurisdiction are usually made and determined on paper, without notice to the defendant, who then has the right to apply to set aside service under CPR Part 11.

E. CAN THE COMMON LAW JURISDICTIONAL GATEWAYS APPLY?

18.14   Where an anti-suit injunction is granted to restrain vexatious or oppressive (or unconscionable) conduct, or because it is otherwise in the interests of justice to grant the injunction,

---

[23] Leaving aside the case where a defendant has given as an address for service the address of a lawyer in Scotland, Northern Ireland, or the European Economic Area (EEA): CPR 6.7(2) and (3), in which case he can be served as if he was within the jurisdiction. However, in the event of a no deal Brexit the ability to serve on an EEA lawyer will be removed by the current no-deal statutory instruments: Civil Procedure Rules 1998 (Amendment) (EU Exit) Regulations 2019.

[24] The 'common law' rules on service out of the jurisdiction, once considered of sufficient importance to require direct primary legislation in the Common Law Procedure Act 1852, have come down in the world. Having spent an intermediary century as Rules of Court (first Order XI and Order 11 of the Rules of the Supreme Court, and then CPR 6.20), they are now framed by CPR 6.36 and 6.37, but contained in PD 6B para 3.1. The constitutional implications of permitting the court's extraterritorial jurisdiction to be regulated by a mere practice direction appear not to have been taken seriously. Compared to this, it is a minor complaint that for the practising litigator, 'Practice Direction 6B, paragraph 3.1(3)' is distinctly unwieldy to pronounce. See also the hostility to this change expressed by A Dickinson, 'Restrained No More? Service out of the Jurisdiction in the 21st Century' [2010] LMCLQ 1, 12–13.

[25] See n 1.

[26] *Seaconsar Far East v Bank Markazi Jomhouri Islami Iran* [1994] 1 AC 438 (HL) 456G–H, 457B established the 'serious issue to be tried' test under the RSC. Under the CPR, the different wording of rule 6.37(1)(b) requires that the claimant's evidence confirms that each of his heads of claim has 'reasonable prospects of success'. The courts have held that the tests mean the same thing, and are in effect the same as the merits threshold for summary judgment: *BAS Capital Finding v Medfinco* [2004] 1 Lloyds Rep 652 [151]–[153]; *Altimo Holdings and Investment v Kyrgyz Mobil* [2012] 1 WLR 1804 (PC) [71]; *Al-Sanea v Saad Investments* [2012] EWCA Civ 313 [29]; *Fujifilm Kyowa Kirin Biologics v Abbvie Biotechnology* [2017] RPC 7 [86].

[27] *Spiliada Maritime Corporation v Cansulex* [1987] AC 460 (HL) 464H–465A, 480G–481A; *Altimo Holdings and Investment v Kyrgyz Mobil* [2012] 1 WLR 1804 (PC) [71]; CPR 6.37(3) (using the language of 'the proper place to bring the claim').

it is in general ordered under section 37(1) of the Senior Courts Act 1981 to give effect to principles of equity.[28]

There is an unresolved debate about whether a non-contractual anti-suit injunction of this **18.15** nature enforces a substantive underlying equitable right, or whether it is a claim for an injunction which responds as a matter of equitable principle to vexation and oppression or unconscionability independent of such an underlying right.[29] The answer is of more than merely academic interest, not least because it may affect whether it is possible to bring anti-suit injunctions based on such principles of equity within CPR 6.36 at all.

The Privy Council had concluded in *Mercedes Benz v Leiduck* that in order for a writ to be **18.16** served under RSC Order 11, the ancestor of CPR 6.36, the proceedings must be 'designed to ascertain substantive rights'.[30] It was held that at first instance in *Cool Carriers* this doctrine also governs the application of what was CPR 6.20, the immediate predecessor of the current CPR 6.36,[31] although there is reason to doubt whether this can be right.[32]

In *Amoco v British American Offshore*, Langley J considered the implications of *Mercedes* **18.17** *Benz v Leiduck*, and concluded *obiter* that as a claim for an anti-suit injunction based on vexation and oppression did not assert any legal or equitable right against the injunction

---

[28] Ch 3, section B, 'A Legal or Equitable Right?'. Tortious rights have only played a very limited role in relation to anti–suit injunctions: see Ch 3, para 3.10; Ch 4, paras 4.26–4.40.

[29] See Ch 3, section B, 'A Legal or Equitable Right?'; and see the following paragraphs in this chapter.

[30] *Mercedes Benz v Leiduck* [1996] AC 284 (PC), 302C–E, where it was held that it was not possible to serve a writ claiming a freezing injunction under the Hong Kong equivalent of RSC Ord 11, because such an injunction was not designed to ascertain substantive rights but was 'proceedings which are merely peripheral'. This was a development of the jurisdictional doctrine articulated in *Siskina v Distos Compania Naviera (The Siskina)* [1979] AC 210 (HL) 256G–H, where Lord Diplock had held that to come within the then RSC Ord 11 r 1 (i) (later RSC Ord 11 r 1(2), the predecessor of PD 6B para 3.1(2) as it now is):

> the injunction sought in the action must be part of the substantive relief to which the plaintiff's cause of action entitles him; and the thing that it is sought to restrain the foreign defendant from doing in England must amount to an invasion of some legal or equitable right belonging to the plaintiff in this country and enforceable here by a final judgment for an injunction.

[31] *Cool Carriers v HSBC Bank USA* [2001] 2 Lloyds Rep 22, 29–30 (interpleader summons not within CPR 6.20 (as it then was), the predecessor of what is now CPR 6.36). The correctness of *Cool Carriers* was accepted, *obiter,* apparently without argument to the contrary, and without consideration of the full implications, in *Eastern Trading Engineering v Vijay Construction (Proprietary)* [2018] EWHC 1539 [36].

[32] The rigidity of the jurisdictional doctrine of *The Siskina*, even as modernized in *Mercedes Benz v Leiduck*, has received considerable criticism: see, in particular, the dissenting speech of Lord Nicholls in *Mercedes Benz v Leiduck* [1996] AC 284 (PC) 312–14. The House of Lords abolished the equally criticized substantive doctrine of *The Siskina* in *Fourie v Le Roux* [2007] 1 WLR 320 (HL), and so the auguries for the jurisdictional doctrine of *The Siskina* are perhaps poor. See *Krohn v Varna Shipyard (No 2)* [1998] ILPr 614 (Royal Court of Jersey) [10]–[11], refusing to follow the jurisdictional doctrine of *The Siskina*.

Further, it is arguable that *Mercedes Benz v Leiduck* is inapplicable under the CPR, whose wording is different to the RSC. CPR 6.36 provides that the claim form may be served out of the jurisdiction 'in any proceedings' covered by the common law rules of jurisdiction if the grounds set out in para 3.1 of PD 6B apply, and there is no verbal reason why a claim for a final anti-suit injunction should not fall within this, even if it is not based on any underlying substantive right. In addition, CPR 6.2(c) makes clear that applications for interim injunctions, if sought before the commencement of substantive proceedings, can be fitted within CPR 6.36 and para 3.1 of PD 6B. In *Masri v Consolidated Contractors (No 3)* [2009] QB 503 (CA) [59], the Court of Appeal assumed that applications for interim anti-suit injunctions could if necessary be fitted within the heads of CPR 6.20, whose wording was in this respect similarly structured to the current rules (by virtue of the definitional effect of CPR 6.18, which had a similar effect to CPR 6.2(c)), and did so even though they were proceeding on the basis that there was no underlying cause of action for an interim alternative forum anti-suit injunction.

In *Cruz City 1 Mauritius Holdings v Unitech* [2015] 1 Lloyds Rep 191 [79]–[80] Males J proceeded *obiter* on the basis that the doctrine in *Mercedes-Benz v Leiduck* 'generally' represented the position, subject to any contrary indication in the terms of particular gateways. But the point was not central, and the contrary appears not to have been argued.

defendant, it was not 'designed to ascertain substantive rights', but designed only to determine in which court such rights should properly be determined. It followed that it could not be served out of the jurisdiction under RSC Order 11.[33]

18.18   If correct, and if it applied to the CPR, the *obiter* reasoning in *Amoco* would have far-reaching consequences; it would mean that the court would have jurisdiction over final anti-suit injunctions based on equitable principles of vexation, oppression, and unconscionability only in respect of defendants who could be served with proceedings within England and Wales.[34] But this would be a very impractical result, and it is submitted that Langley J's conclusion is not the law. To begin with, it is possible that anti-suit injunctions based on vexation or oppression can be viewed as enforcing a substantive equitable right, in both 'single forum' and 'alternative forum' cases.[35] In any event, even if that is not so, and even if *Mercedes Benz* remains the law under the CPR, which is doubtful, it is suggested that an anti-suit injunction is a form of *sui generis* substantive relief which can legitimately be brought within CPR 6.36, even if it enforces no underlying substantive equitable right: it does claim for a substantive cause of action irrespective of the existence of any such underlying right.[36] In contrast to freezing injunctions, anti-suit injunctions can undoubtedly form the sole claim in conventional proceedings for final relief.[37] *Amoco* has not been applied in practice in the subsequent case law and the courts have on a number of occasions upheld service out of the

---

[33]   *Amoco (UK) Exploration v British American Offshore* [1999] 2 Lloyds Rep 772, 780–81.

[34]   It appears that the scope for founding non-contractual anti-suit injunctions on tortious rights is limited: see Ch 3, para 3.10; Ch 4, paras 4.26–4.40.

[35]   The Court of Appeal has accepted that claims for final anti-suit injunctions do enforce substantive legal or equitable rights in 'single forum' cases, but not in 'alternative forum' cases: *Masri v Consolidated Contractors (No 3)* [2009] QB 503 (CA) [44], [46], [52]. However, that distinction is open to some doubt. It is possible that a legal or equitable right should be viewed as underpinning final claims for 'alternative forum' anti-suit injunctions as well (Ch 3, section B, 'A Legal or Equitable Right?') although that conclusion would bring with it problems in terms of choice of law (see Ch 4, section B, 'Applicable Law'). It is also arguable that non-contractual anti-suit injunctions should not be seen as enforcing underlying substantive rights at all, whether in single or alternative forum cases. If the price of overcoming the supposed jurisdictional lacuna identified in *Amoco* were the inference of a substantive legal or equitable right in alternative forum cases as well, it is a price that would probably be paid: see Ch 3, para 3.27. The appropriate solution is likely to be one that will reconcile the competing tensions to conclude that non-contractual anti-suit injunctions can be fitted within the heads of PD 6B para 3.1, while not posing unnecessary problems in terms of choice of law. In any event, it is possible that in certain circumstances particular types of non-contractual anti-suit injunction may be founded on specific equitable or tortious rights: see Ch 3, paras 3.10–3.11; Ch 4, paras 4.30–4.31, 4.39.

[36]   See Ch 3, paras 3.09–3.31. In *Mercedes Benz v Leiduck* [1996] AC 284 (PC) 302E, 302F–H, the contrast with which Lord Mustill was concerned was between proceedings for 'substantial relief', which could be begun by claim form, and 'incidental' or 'peripheral' claims, which could only be brought by application notice in the context of other substantive proceedings. Within that framework, it is submitted that final anti-suit injunctions based on vexation and oppression fall on the 'substantial' side of the line, even if there is no underlying equitable right, and thus can fall within CPR 6.36 and PD 6B, para 3.1 on any basis. It can be noted that in Lord Nicholls' dissent, he observed that a writ could be issued claiming a 'vexation' anti-suit injunction alone, and by implication that this could be served out of the jurisdiction (see 310G); and this was not a matter on which he viewed himself as dissenting. The only express comment that Lord Mustill, speaking for the majority, made on anti-suit injunctions was to note that they were 'sui generis': at 301C. In *Masri v Consolidated Contractors (No 3)* [2009] QB 503 (CA) [51], Lawrence Collins LJ treated Lord Nicholls' speech as stating the law in this respect, and it is consistent with his reasoning that even final anti-suit injunctions based on vexation and oppression are capable of fitting within CPR 6.36 and para 3.1 of PD 6B, provided that they can be brought within a relevant head of jurisdiction: see [55]–[56], [59].

[37]   See Ch 3, para 3.25. For example, a claim form claiming a final injunction for an anti-suit injunction to restrain vexation, in contrast to an application for a freezing injunction, can ground judgment in default. The inability of a freezing injunction to ground judgment in default was viewed as a telling reason why a writ claiming a freezing injunction alone was not sufficiently 'substantive' to be served out of the jurisdiction in *Mercedes Benz v Leiduck* [1996] AC 284 (PC) 301F–H, 302A–F.

jurisdiction of anti-suit injunctions based on vexation, oppression, and unconscionability under CPR 6.36 and para 3.1 of PD 6B, or assumed that this would be possible in principle.[38] Any contrary result would be strange. It would mean, for example, that where a valid, vexation-based, single forum injunction was claimed against an English-domiciled defendant and there was a necessary and proper party to that injunction claim who was domiciled abroad, service out of the jurisdiction on the co-defendant would be impossible.

The following analysis therefore assumes that it is possible in principle to serve a claim for   **18.19** final anti-suit injunction based on vexation, oppression, or unconscionability out of the jurisdiction under the CPR gateways for jurisdiction if they apply.

Quasi-contractual anti-suit injunctions, sought against a third party pursuing rights   **18.20** derived from a contract containing an exclusive forum clause, have been viewed as grounded, on the balance of the case law so far, on an equitable right of the original debtor's not to be sued by the third party in a forum which is not that agreed by the original creditor.[39] On that basis, no problems with *Mercedes-Benz v Leiduck* would arise. In any event, it is clear from the authorities that such injunctions can be served out of the jurisdiction under CPR 6.36 and PB 6B para 3.1(6), and also CPR 62.5 where they relate to an arbitration clause.[40]

---

[38] For examples of vexation- and oppression-based injunctions being served out of the jurisdiction under para 3.1 of PD 6B see *OT Africa Line v Magic Sportswear* [2005] 1 Lloyds Rep 252 [29] (not appealed on this point), where Langley J himself permitted service out of the jurisdiction under what is now para 3.1(3) of PD 6B, although the injunction claimant had no direct contractual claim against the insurers (without commenting on his prior decision in *Amoco*); *Albon v Naza Motor Trading* [2007] 2 Lloyds Rep 420 [19]–[20] (albeit that the finding that what is now para 3.1(6) of PD 6B applied is controversial for other reasons); *Joint Stock Asset Management Co Ingosstrakh-Investments v BNP Paribas* [2012] 1 Lloyds Rep 649 (CA) [2], [69]–[78] (again permitting service out of the jurisdiction of an anti-suit injunction based on vexation under PD 6B para 3.1(3)); *Shipowners' Mutual Protection & Indemnity Association (Luxembourg) v Containerships Denizcilik Nakliyat ve Tikaret (The Yusuf Cepnioglu)* [2015] 1 Lloyds Rep 567 [40]–[47] (applying PD 6B para 3.1(6) to an injunction viewed as based on vexation); *Talos Capital v JSC Investment Holdings XIV* [2014] EWHC 3977 [58]; *Fujifilm Kyowa Kirin Biologics v Abbvie Biotechnology* [2017] RPC 7.
    For examples of cases where it was considered, or assumed, that if a head of para 3.1 of PD 6B applied on its terms, a vexation- or oppression-based injunction could be served out of the jurisdiction under such a head, see *Donohue v Armco* [1999] 2 Lloyds Rep 649 (Aikens J) [62]–[65] (although NB the comments of the Court of Appeal in that case, addressed below); *Youell v Kara Mara Shipping* [2000] 2 Lloyds Rep 102 (Aikens J) [44]–[46]; *Navig8 Pte v Al-Riyadh Co for Vegetable Oil Industry (The Lucky Lady)* [2013] 2 Lloyds Rep 104 [14].
    On the other hand, in *Donohue v Armco* [2000] 1 Lloyds Rep 579 (CA) (reversed [2002] 1 Lloyds Rep 425 (HL) without comment on this issue), Brooke LJ, in the minority, treated Langley J's judgment in *Amoco* as being the law (at [90]), in an *obiter dictum* made apparently without argument to the contrary (Sedley LJ did not comment on the point; and Stuart-Smith LJ referred to *Amoco* neutrally without approving of the proposition in issue here: at [52]).
    In *Masri v Consolidated Contractors (No 3)* [2009] QB 503 (CA) [55], Lawrence Collins LJ referred *obiter* to Langley's decision in *Amoco* as suggesting that in the situation of a single forum injunction, a separate cause of action 'may have to be established' (emphasis added). But in *Masri* Lawrence Collins LJ was dealing with what he had held to be an interim, not a final injunction, over which he considered the court had jurisdiction independent of what was then CPR 6.20 (now CPR 6.36 and PD 6B para 3.1), and so he did not need to consider whether the restrictions imposed by *Amoco* on the jurisdiction to serve claims for final injunctions out of the jurisdiction were appropriate. He was also proceeding on the basis that there could be an underlying substantive cause of action for an anti-suit injunction in single forum cases: see at [57]. At [59] of the judgment he seemed to assume that anti-suit injunctions could be fitted within the heads of jurisdiction in what was then CPR 6.20. He should not, therefore, be taken as adopting the *Amoco* doctrine that non-contractual anti-suit injunctions cannot be fitted within PD 6B para 3.1. Consequently, it is submitted that the comments in *Donohue* and *Masri* do not solidify *Amoco* as the law.
[39] See Ch 10, section C, 'An Obligation Not to Sue Elsewhere?'.
[40] *Shipowners' Mutual Protection & Indemnity Association (Luxembourg) v Containerships Denizcilik Nakliyat ve Tikaret (The Yusuf Cepnioglu)* [2015] 1 Lloyds Rep 567 [40]–[61], following *Schiffahrtsgesellschaft Detlev von Appen v Voest Alpine Intertrading (The Jay Bola)* [1997] 2 Lloyds Rep 279 (CA) 286–288; *Youell v Kara Mara Shipping* [2000] 2 Lloyds Rep 102 [47]–[51], [57], [63]–[69]. The issues arising are discussed at paras 18.48–18.49.

18.21   A claim for a final injunction for an anti-suit injunction which is based on an exclusive juris-diction clause, or another contractual right not to be sued save in the chosen, forum, is clearly a claim 'designed to ascertain substantive rights' to the extent required. Such a claim may be served out of the jurisdiction under CPR 6.36 and PD 6B where a relevant head of PD 6B applies,[41] and where it enforces an arbitration clause, can be served out of the jurisdiction under CPR 62.5.[42]

F. THE HEADS OF JURISDICTION UNDER CPR PD 6B PARAGRAPH 3.1

18.22   PD 6B para 3.1 contains a list of specific jurisdictional gateways, defined generally by sub-ject matter, but sometimes by characteristics of the defendant and sometimes by the nature of the remedy sought. They will need to be considered in turn. As will be seen, the heads of jurisdiction which are of real practical use in relation to final anti-suit injunctions are prin-cipally PD 6B para 3.1(3) and (6), para 3.1(4A), and CPR 62.5.

18.23   This section considers only claims for final relief, and thus does not discuss PD 6B para 3.1(5). Jurisdiction over applications for interim relief are considered in section J, 'Jurisdiction and Interim Anti-Suit Injunctions'.

18.24   However, it should be noted that the effect of CPR 6.38(1) and 6.37(5)(b)(ii), as interpreted in *Star Reefers*[43] and read together with *Masri (No 3)*,[44] is that the court will generally have jurisdiction under the common law rules over interim anti-suit injunctions against the existing parties to litigation already before the courts.[45] Further, as a matter of English pro-cedural law, it is possible to obtain an interim anti-suit injunction in the context of existing proceedings without corresponding final relief.[46] In most cases, it will be sufficient to ob-tain alternative forum injunctions between the parties to litigation on an interim basis, and a final injunction is not necessary, nor required. Consequently, it is only where a free-standing single forum injunction is sought, or in situations posing analogous problems, that the constraints imposed by PD 6B are likely to be of decisive importance.[47]

1. Domicile: PD 6B Paragraph 3.1(1)

18.25   PD 6B para 3.1(1) allows service out of the jurisdiction where 'a claim is made for a remedy against a person domiciled within the jurisdiction'. This is an available head of jurisdiction

---

[41] Unless Article 25 of the Recast or the Hague Convention apply, in which case the proceedings can and should be served out of the jurisdiction without permission under CPR 6.33; see paras 18.40–18.41, 18.45–18.46.

[42] See section I, 'Arbitration Claims'.

[43] *Star Reefers v JFC Group* [2010] EWHC 3003 [28], [2012] 1 Lloyds Rep 376 (CA) [42].

[44] *Masri v Consolidated Contractors (No 3)* [2009] QB 503 (CA) [26].

[45] See eg *Golden Endurance Shipping v RMA Watanya (The Golden Endurance)* [2015] 1 Lloyds Rep 266 [24]–[29]. See further, section J, 'Jurisdiction and Interim Anti-Suit Injunctions'.

[46] *Masri v Consolidated Contractors (No 3)* [2009] QB 503 (CA) [58]–[59], [66], [76], 96]–[97]; *Glencore International v Metro Trading International (No 3)* [2002] 2 CLC 1090 (CA) [59]–[60]; *The Eras Eil Actions* [1995] 1 Lloyds Rep 64, 73–74; Ch 3, para 3.33; Ch 13, paras 13.08 and 13.27.

[47] See *Masri v Consolidated Contractors (No 3)* [2009] QB 503 (CA), where Lawrence Collins LJ also observed that it would only be in a very rare case where the English court would have jurisdiction to grant a single forum injunction against a non-English party (at [56]).

for anti-suit injunctions, although it will be of limited significance in practice, as it will only apply outside the subject matter scope of the Brussels–Lugano regime (as matters stand), and only as against persons temporarily abroad.

2. Injunctions: PD 6B Paragraph 3.1(2)

PD 6B para 3.1(2) allows service out of the jurisdiction where 'a claim is made for an injunc-   **18.26** tion ordering the defendant to do or refrain from doing an act within the jurisdiction'. This has a negative limb and a positive limb.

The negative limb of CPR 6.20(2), relating to claims for injunctions ordering the de-   **18.27** fendant to 'refrain from doing an act within the jurisdiction', will cover injunctions to restrain a defendant from pursuing proceedings in England.[48] However, the negative limb will not be applicable to claims for injunctions which are in substance intended to restrain foreign proceedings, even where in theory the injunction could also cover proceedings within the jurisdiction of the English courts, because in substance the act which the defendant is meant to be restrained from doing is the act of litigating before the foreign court.[49]

In *Amoco v British American Offshore*, an injunction was sought to restrain proceedings   **18.28** in Texas. It was argued that this could be brought within the predecessor of PB 6B para 3.1(2) because the order restraining the Texan proceedings would also restrain the service in England of documents produced in the Texan proceedings. This argument was curtly rejected; it would mean that 'the tail would indeed be wagging the dog'.[50]

The positive limb of PD 6B para 3.1(2) covers injunctions sought to order a party 'to   **18.29** do' an act within the jurisdiction. However, an anti-suit injunction in mandatory form, requiring a party to discontinue or stay proceedings abroad, would not fall within this. Similarly, the typical prohibitory form of anti-suit injunction, restraining a party from pursuing proceedings abroad, is not an order relating to the performance of acts in England. A party could not in general be positively required to sue in England, or in any particular court, even if it were appropriate to restrain him from suing elsewhere.[51] An order requiring a party to sue 'only' in England would in substance be a prohibitory order relating to the foreign proceedings, and would not fall within the spirit of PD 6B para 3.1(2), as the aim of the prohibition would be to prevent foreign proceedings, not compel English proceedings.[52]

---

[48] *Fujifilm Kyowa Kirin Biologics v Abbvie Biotechnology* [2017] RPC 7 [116]–[121].

[49] See *OT Africa Line v Magic Sportswear* [2005] 1 Lloyds Rep 252, [20] (in relation to choice of law). No attempt was made in that case to argue that an anti-suit injunction to restrain the pursuit of proceedings abroad fell within PD 6B para 3.1(2).

[50] *Amoco (UK) Exploration v British American Offshore* [1999] 2 Lloyds Rep 772, 778.

[51] See Ch 3, para 3.40.

[52] See in other contexts *GAF v Amchem Products* [1975] 1 Lloyds Rep 601, 606; *Innovia v Frito-Lay* [2012] RPC 24 [114]–[120]; *Conductive Inkjet Technology v Uni-Pixel Displays* [2014] FSR 22 [61]; *Unlockd v Google Ireland* [2018] EWHC 1363 [45].

18.30 Consequently, PD 6B para 3.1(2) will not provide a workable jurisdictional gateway for the service out of the jurisdiction of injunctions to restrain foreign proceedings.[53] It will be available for anti-suit injunctions to restrain proceedings in England.[54]

3. Additional Defendants: PD 6B Paragraph 3.1(3)

18.31 PD 6B para 3.1(3) permits service out of the jurisdiction on a secondary defendant who is a 'necessary and proper party' to a claim against a primary defendant, provided that (a) there was a 'serious issue to be tried' between the claimant and the primary defendant; (b) the court has jurisdiction over the primary defendant in some other way, and the claim has been or will be served on him;[55] and (c) the additional defendants would have been proper parties to the action had they all been present in England.[56] This gateway is available for anti-suit injunctions. For example, if the court has jurisdiction to hear a claim for an anti-suit injunction against injunction defendant A, it can also have jurisdiction under para 3.1(3) to hear a claim for a non-contractual injunction against connected defendant B where B's vexatious and oppressive conduct is bound up with A's conduct.[57] However, it is a head of jurisdiction to be used with 'care' and 'forbearance'.[58]

4. Additional Claims: PD 6B Paragraph 3.1(4)

18.32 PD 6B para 3.1(4) permits service out of the jurisdiction where the claim for which permission is sought is an 'Additional Claim' brought by a party to an existing action; and the intended defendant to the additional claim is a necessary and proper party to the 'claim or additional claim'.

---

[53] In *Golden Endurance Shipping v RMA Watanya (The Golden Endurance)* [2015] 1 Lloyds Rep 266 [25], it was the unchallenged position of the injunction defendant that PD 6B para 3.1(2) could not apply.

In *Ust-Kamenogorsk Hydropower Plant JSC v AES Ust-Kamenogorsk Hydropower Plant LLP* [2013] 1 WLR 1889 (SC) [51] Lord Mance observed in passing that 'leave was in fact obtained under CPR PD 6B, paragraph 3.1(2)', as well as under CPR 62.5(1)(b) and (c). However, this appears to be a typographical error. Leaving aside 62.5(1)(b) and (c), leave had in fact been granted without notice (and upheld by Burton J) under CPR PD 6B para *3.1(20)*, not *3.1(2)*: see [2010] 2 Lloyds Rep 493 [24].

(In any event, it seems that Burton J was wrong to uphold service under para 3.1(20), as the Court of Appeal had explained in [2012] 1 WLR 920 (CA) [192], [207], and [126]. Lord Mance's comment does not amount to authority to the contrary; see paras 18.64 – 18.71).

[54] As occurred without challenge to the applicability of the gateway in *Fujifilm Kyowa Kirin Biologics v Abbvie Biotechnology* [2017] RPC 7 [13], [116]–[121].

[55] However, this does not mean that, if D1 is abroad, permission to serve out of the jurisdiction on D1 must have already been obtained before permission is sought in respect of D2. It is sufficient if it is clear that permission to serve out on D1 will be obtained. See *Joint Stock Asset Management Company Ingosstrakh-Investments v BNP Paribas* Lloyds Rep 649 (CA) [69]–[78]. Thus, the law on this point is no longer as reflected in *Amoco (UK) Exploration v British American Offshore* [1999] 2 Lloyds Rep 772, 779.

[56] *Donohue v Armco* [1999] 2 Lloyds Rep 649, [62]; *Altimo Holdings and Investment Ltd v Kyrgyz Mobil* [2012] 1 WLR 1804 (PC) [87].

[57] See eg *OT Africa Line v Magic Sportswear Corp* [2005] 1 Lloyds Rep 252 [29]; *Joint Stock Asset Management Co Ingosstrakh-Investments v BNP Paribas* [2012] 1 Lloyds Rep 61 (Blair J) [50]–[55] ('Where the allegation is that parties are acting in concert, one party will usually be a necessary or a proper party to the claim against the other party'), upheld [2012] 1 Lloyds Rep 649 (CA) [69]–[78]; see also *Talos Capital v JSC Investment Holdings XIV Limited* [2014] EWHC 3977 [58].

[58] *Massey v Heynes* (1888) 21 QBD 330 (CA) 334; *Arab Monetary Fund v Hashim (No 4)* [1992] 1 WLR 553, 557, affirmed [1992] 1 WLR 1176 (CA); *Altimo Holdings and Investment Ltd v Kyrgyz Mobil* [2012] 1 WLR 1804 (PC) [73]; see also *Cruz City 1 Mauritius Holdings v Unitech* [2015] 1 Lloyds Rep 191 [68]–[81].

The 'additional claims' that fall within this provision include counterclaims against the ori-   **18.33**
ginal claimant, and counterclaims which have additional defendants,[59] as well as third-party
claims more broadly. This head of jurisdiction is available in principle for anti-suit injunctions. (Counterclaims are addressed in section G, 'Jurisdiction by Way of Counterclaim'.)

On its face, PD 6B para 3.1(4) could create a surprisingly broad jurisdiction for additional   **18.34**
claims, because the words 'claim or additional claim' include the additional claim itself as well as
the claim against the original defendant.[60] If applied without constraint, this would be too broad,
as it could permit the service out of proceedings against a new defendant who is a 'necessary and
proper party' to the additional claim for which jurisdiction is sought even though the additional
claim has no connection to the underlying claim. However, the court should and will control
and exclude jurisdiction over unconnected additional claims. This could be done procedurally,
by use of its procedural powers to require an inappropriate additional claim to be dealt with separately under CPR 20.9 and 3.1(2)(e) and (j). Or it could be achieved by implication into para
3.1(4) of an implied condition that there must be a sufficient connection between the additional
claim and the original claim, or a similar restriction which will produce the result that, in effect,
the new defendant must be a necessary and proper party to the existing litigation.[61] In *Goldstone
v Goldstone* the Court of Appeal interpreted 3.1(4) as intended to enable the English court to
exercise jurisdiction 'if it is just to do so because he is a necessary and proper party to litigation
which is already before the court'.[62] Excessively broad application of this gateway could also be
controlled by application of the principle that permission to serve proceedings out of the jurisdiction will not be given where England is not the proper place to bring the claim.[63]

This head of jurisdiction has so far been of limited practical relevance to anti-suit injunctions.   **18.35**
Anti-suit injunctions by defendants against the original claimants are usually brought by interim injunction rather than counterclaim, and on the court's current broad approach to the
ancillary jurisdiction, face few jurisdictional difficulties. Even when anti-suit injunctions are
brought by way of final counterclaim, it will usually be possible to serve them on the address for
service which claimants are required to give under CPR 6.23.[64] Thus far, anti-suit injunctions
have not been brought by way of 'third-party' claim, and the factual situations where this could
be done naturally may well be rare. However, there may be cases where this head will be of real
use, for example where a final anti-suit injunction is claimed by way of counterclaim against
not only the original claimant but also other parties involved in the foreign litigation. In such a
case, it may be possible to use PD 6B para 3.1(4) to obtain permission to serve the counterclaim
out of the jurisdiction on the other parties, as additional defendants to the counterclaim for an
injunction, provided that they are 'necessary and proper' parties and there are sufficient connections between the various parties and the respective facts to satisfy the criteria of CPR 20.9.

---

[59]   CPR Part 20 covers 'Counterclaims and other additional claims'.
[60]   Compare the wording of CPR 6.20(3A) in the immediately preceding version of the rules which permitted
service where 'The claim is an additional claim and the person to be served is a necessary and proper party to the
claim against the Part 20 claimant.'
[61]   In *CH Offshore Limited v PDV Marina SA* [2015] EWHC 595 [41]–[58], the application of 'necessary and
proper party' was assessed only by reference to the action as a whole (including existing inter-defendant third
party claims), and not by reference solely to whether the new defendant was a necessary and property party to the
additional claim against itself.
[62]   *Goldstone v Goldstone* [2011] EWCA Civ 39 [61]; applied in *CH Offshore Limited v PDV Marina SA* [2015]
EWHC 595 [36].
[63]   CPR 6.37(3).
[64]   Counterclaims are addressed further at section G, 'Jurisdiction by Way of Counterclaim'.

5. Connected Claims: PD 6B Paragraph 3.1(4A)

18.36   The revisions to the CPR that came into force on 1 October 2015 introduced new PD 6B para 3.1(4A), which provides that a claim may be served out of the jurisdiction where: 'A claim is made against the defendant in reliance on one or more of paras (2), (6) to (16), (19) or (21) and a further claim is made against the same defendant which arises out of the same or closely connected facts.' This is a radical change to the common law rules of jurisdiction. For the first time, it permits jurisdiction to be established towards a defendant over a claim which would not otherwise fall within the rules, merely because of the connection between that claim and one which does fall within the rules.[65] No parallel exists under the Brussels–Lugano regime. Many questions arise as to how far this 'connected claim' jurisdiction can extend, and the case law has so far given only partial answers. Overall, head 4A seems to be applied relatively broadly and flexibly.[66]

18.37   In *Eli Lilly v Genentech*, Birss J concluded as a matter of principle that while a 'close' connection was required, this would not preclude jurisdiction where the second claim has some facts unique to it and distinct to those in issue on the anchor claim; nor was it necessary for there to be a 'single investigation'. On whether the connection was sufficiently close:

> Given that the defendant is already properly subject to the court's jurisdiction, pragmatic factors are appropriate matters to take into account in deciding whether the connection between the facts is sufficiently close to justify service out having regard to the overall justice of the circumstances. The purpose of gateway (4A) is to allow the joinder of a further claim against the same defendant based on the same or closely connected facts so as to further the interests of justice, including taking into account practical considerations such as procedural economy and an avoidance of inconsistent results.[67]

18.38   However, the drafting of 3.1(4A) is strange and appears to create arbitrary distinctions, because on its face it does not apply in all cases where jurisdiction is obtained under the common law rules or otherwise, but only where jurisdiction is obtained under a limited set of defined heads of PD 6B 3.1, namely 3.1(2), (6)–(16), and (19)–(21). If applied literally, this would create odd results. Take, for example, the case where jurisdiction is obtained over the initial claim of a party by service within the jurisdiction, who then leaves the jurisdiction;

---

[65]   New PD 6B 3.1(4A) was introduced following the report of the Chancery Working Group dated 12 June 2015, which explained at para 13:

> Its purpose is to enable claims against the same defendant which have a close factual relationship to be tried together in this jurisdiction, even if the further claim would not by itself satisfy any of the relevant gateways. There is a risk that this extension might be considered exorbitant, but we think the risk is outweighed by the practical advantages of enabling closely related claims against the same defendant to be tried together.

In *Eurasia Sports v Aguad*, [2018] EWCA Civ 1742 [63]–[64], Longmore LJ commented that 'the intention of this new gateway must be that claims arising out of the same or closely connected facts should be tried together. That is eminently sensible and should be encouraged', and that any decision in relation to service out of the jurisdiction 'is generally a pragmatic one in the interests of the efficient conduct of litigation in an appropriate forum'. (The latter point relying on Lord Sumption's contentious comments in *Abela v Baadarani* [2013] 1 WLR 2043 (SC), as to which see *Cruz City 1 Mauritius Holdings v Unitech* [2015] 1 Lloyds Rep 191 [16].)

[66]   *Eli Lilly v Genentech* [2018] 1 WLR 1755 [30]–[36]; *Unlockd v Google Ireland* [2018] EWHC 1363 [48]; *Eurasia Sports v Aguad*, [2018] EWCA Civ 1742 [49]–[50]. The Chancery Working Group had said (at para 15) that the test of same or closely connected facts in proposed gateway 4A 'would probably be interpreted rather more stringently than one of close connection, and for that reason too would be preferable, given that the new gateway involves an extension of the present position which (as we have said) could be viewed as exorbitant'.

[67]   *Eli Lilly v Genentech* [2018] 1 WLR 1755 [30]–[36].

but the claim was one which could have been served out of the jurisdiction under one of the defined heads, had the defendant been out of the jurisdiction from the beginning. It is then desired to add a new claim which is sufficiently connected within 4A. But 4A does not apply on its literal words, because as it happens the initial claim was not served 'in reliance on paragraphs (2), (6) to (16) … etc'. It would be artificial if the connected claims jurisdiction could not apply in this case, but the courts have not yet confronted the problem. Separately, it seems to have been illogical to leave out PD 6B para 3.1(1), as there are cases where a person's domicile has changed.[68]

CPR 3.1(4A) will be relevant in various ways to claims for anti-suit injunctions, depending on the specific facts of particular cases. The most important question, however, will be how it works where the court has jurisdiction over the merits under one of the defined heads—for example in a basic contractual claim under an English law contract, where 3.1(6) applies to the main claim, or an action in tort where 3.1(9) applies—but it would not have been possible to fit a final claim for an anti-suit injunction within any of the other heads of PD 6B para 3.1. There are real difficulties in bringing final claims for non-contractual, vexation based, anti-suit injunctions brought to protect existing proceedings in England, within the other heads of PD 6B para 3.1. In such a case, is the claim for a final anti-suit injunction one that arises out of the 'same or closely connected facts' as the underlying claims on the merits it seeks to protect? The question is open on the face of the words. It could be said (in many cases) that the claim for an injunction arises not out of the facts disputed in the underlying contractual or tortious action, but out of the separate facts relating to the foreign litigation. But it is likely that the English court will conclude that the connection between the protective injunction and the English litigation is sufficient. Using the logic of Birss J in *Eli Lilly v Genentech*, this is consistent with pragmatic considerations and overall procedural justice. It will usefully fill what was otherwise a lacuna in the rules and also enable the jurisdiction for final injunctions to match the ancillary jurisdiction over interim injunctions to protect the existing proceedings (which is discussed in sub-sections 6–11 following). **18.39**

6. Contract: The Hague Convention on the Choice of Court

If European jurisdictional law remains law, the Hague Convention on the Choice of Court will have limited additional importance. Claims under exclusive jurisdiction clauses, or to enforce them by injunction, will principally be brought under Article 25 of the Brussels I Recast (cf Ch 17, paras 17.44–17.47). In most cases governed by Article 25, it appears there will be overlapping parallel Hague Convention jurisdiction, provided they fall within the scope of the Convention.[69] But Article 25 of the Recast will remain the primary jurisdictional basis, unless the case falls within the (currently) limited cases addressed by Article 26(6) of the Convention, where the Convention can override the Brussels–Lugano regime **18.40**

---

[68] If jurisdiction over X for claim A is obtained under PD 6B 3.1, and then jurisdiction over Y is obtained for claim A under 3.1(3) on the basis that Y is a connected party, it will not be possible to obtain connected claim jurisdiction over Y in respect of connected claim B, because 3.1(3) is not within the 3.1(4A) list. This is so even though there would potentially be jurisdiction over X for claim B if the facts were sufficiently closely connected. In *Eurasia Sports v Aguad* [2018] EWCA Civ 472 [47], the Court of Appeal thought that this might be a principled and intended result, because building gateway on gateway in this way could produce an exorbitant result against the connected party.

[69] See Ch 16, para 16.10.

(and then only if there is a material difference, which generally there will not be); or in cases where the defendant is domiciled outside the Brussels Lugano zone, and jurisdiction is broader under the Convention than Article 25 (for example where the definition of an agreement under Article 3 of the Convention is broader than the required 'consensus' under Article 25).

18.41   However, if the effect of Brexit is to take the United Kingdom out of the Brussels–Lugano regime, the Hague Convention will become much more significant. Although at present the contracting states are limited in number (the EU, potentially the UK, Mexico, Montenegro, and Singapore), the domestic jurisdiction that is conferred by the convention applies (in international cases) irrespective of the domicile of the defendant and whether or not defendants are domiciled in contracting states. Thus, the Hague Convention will become the principal (although not exhaustive) jurisdictional basis for all claims (in international cases), brought under jurisdiction clauses within its temporal and material scope.[70] Service out of the jurisdiction, for claims over which the court has jurisdiction under the Convention, can be effected without permission under CPR 6.33(2B).

7. Contract: PD 6B Paragraph 3.1(6)–(8)

18.42   PD 6B para 3.1(6) provides that proceedings may be served out of the jurisdiction if:

> a claim is made in respect of a contract where the contract—
>
> (a) was made within the jurisdiction;
> (b) was made by or through an agent trading or residing in the jurisdiction;
> (c) is governed by English law; or
> (d) contains a term to the effect that the court shall have jurisdiction to determine any claim in respect of the contract.

18.43   There have been significant disputes as to the scope of PD 6B para 3.1(6) in general, which have not yet been fully resolved, and have consequences for the scope of jurisdiction to hear claims for anti-suit injunctions. Debates have concerned the extent to which the words 'in respect of a contract' extend beyond contractual claims conservatively conceived, in two main dimensions: whether and when words can cover claims by or against persons not party to the contract, and how far they extend to cover claims that do not assert positive contractual rights.

18.44   We will turn first to direct contractual claims for injunctions, before addressing the more complicated issues which arise in relation to quasi-contractual injunctions, or injunctions based on vexation and oppression.

a) Direct contractual claims for anti-suit injunctions

18.45   The analysis in relation to direct contractual claims to enforce exclusive jurisdiction clauses is simple. If, in a civil and commercial matter which falls within the scope of the Brussels–Lugano regime, or where the Hague Convention on the Choice of Court applies,[71] an

---

[70] See Articles 1, 2, and 16(1) of the Convention.
[71] The application of the Hague Convention of the Choice of Court, and its relationship to Article 25, is discussed in Ch 16, para 16.10; Ch 17, para 17.46.

anti-suit injunction is sought to enforce an exclusive or non-exclusive jurisdiction clause in favour of the English courts against a party to such a clause, and the anti-suit injunction itself falls within the scope of the clause as properly interpreted, then the English courts will have jurisdiction under Article 25 of the Recast, or under the Convention, or both, and both of those statutory regimes will apply regardless of domicile. Consequently, service out of the jurisdiction can be effected without permission under CPR 6.33.[72]

This is a change compared to Article 23 of Regulation 44/2001, which applied only where one of the parties was domiciled within a Brussels–Lugano state. It follows that para 3.1(6)(d) will now often be unnecessary in contractual cases. However, para 3.1(6)(d) will still be relevant for claims to enforce jurisdiction clauses by injunction if the litigation is outside the scope of the Brussels–Lugano regime or the Hague Convention but is covered by a jurisdiction clause. In such a case, para 3.1(6)(d) will apply as the injunction is a claim 'in respect of' the jurisdiction clause.[73] In addition, Article 25 and the Convention do not preclude the application of para 3.1(6)(d) where it is broader. Thus, even within the material scope of the Brussels–Lugano regime, provided the injunction defendant is outside the Brussels–Lugano zone, para 3.1(6)(d) may also be used in respect of contractual claims which satisfy the common law criteria for a contract but not the potentially more restrictive thresholds for Article 25 (the Hague Convention may also be an available route in some such cases).   **18.46**

In addition, although PD 6B para 3.1(6)(d) does not apply to arbitration clauses, permission to serve out anti-suit injunctions to enforce arbitration clauses governed by English law can be obtained under para 3.1(6)(c), as they are claims 'in respect of a contract' 'governed by English law', in addition to under the specific arbitration power in CPR 62.5 (to which we will return). Arguments that CPR 62.5 should be the exclusive head in respect of injunctions to enforce an arbitration clause have been rejected, which is a sensible approach.[74]   **18.47**

b) Quasi-contractual claims

A third-party quasi-contractual anti-suit injunction is sought to enforce a contractual forum clause against a third party who brings claims derived from the original creditor's contractual rights against the original debtor, but seeks not to comply with a contractual   **18.48**

---

[72] *Ravennavi v New Century Shipbuilding* [2007] 2 Lloyds Rep 24 (CA) [3].
[73] This appears never to have been contested, when para 3.1(6)(d) was more generally relevant, before the coming into force of the Brussels I Recast. Permission to serve out of the jurisdiction has frequently been granted in such cases. See *Amoco (UK) Exploration British American Offshore* [1999] 2 Lloyds Rep 772, 775–77; *OT Africa Line v Hijazy (The Kribi) (No 1)* [2001] 1 Lloyds Rep 76, 80 (although possibly Art 23 of Regulation 44/2001 should have been used, as the claimants were domiciled in England).
In *OT Africa Line v Magic Sportswear* [2005] 1 Lloyds Rep 252 [11], permission to serve out was obtained against the cargo interests, who were party to the jurisdiction clause, as well their subrogating insurers. A jurisdiction challenge was filed by both groups of defendants; but the challenge advanced by the cargo interests was not pursued. See also *Beazley v Horizon Offshore Contractors* [2005] 1 Lloyds Rep 231 [47].
[74] This was held to be the case (in respect of the predecessor of the current arbitration provisions) in *Navigation Maritime Bulgare v Rustal Trading (The Ivan Zagubanski)* [2002] 1 Lloyds Rep 106 [52(5)], [53(2)], [101], [120]. In *BNP Paribas v Russian Machines* [2012] 1 Lloyds Rep 61 [56]–[58], it was conceded that PD 3.1(6)(c) could apply to claims for anti-suit injunctions to enforce arbitration clauses. In *Ust-Kamenogorsk Hydropower Plant JSC (Appellant) v AES Ust-Kamenogorsk Hydropower Plant LLP* [2013] 1 WLR 1889 (SC) [51], Lord Mance commented *obiter* that 3.1(6)(c) could apply to such claims. Finally, in *Shipowners' Mutual Protection & Indemnity Association (Luxembourg) v Containerships Denizcilik Nakliyat ve Tikaret (The Yusuf Cepnioglu)* [2015] 1 Lloyds Rep 567 [41]–[42], Teare J relied on Lord Mance's comments in *Ust-Kamenogorsk*, rejected the argument that CPR 62.5 was exhaustive, and upheld service out of an anti-suit injunction to enforce an arbitration clause under CPR Part 6 PD 6B para 3.1(6)(c). The arguments as to whether CPR 62.5 is exhaustive are examined in more detail at para 18.84.

forum clause that was binding on the creditor under the original contract.[75] It has been consistently held, most recently by Teare J in *The Yusuf Cepnioglu*, that this sort of quasi-contractual claim is made 'in respect of a contract' within PD 6B para 3.1(6), even though the third-party injunction defendant is not actually a party to the contract,[76] and it is submitted this is the correct analysis.[77]

---

[75] See Ch 10.

[76] *Schiffahrtsgesellschaft Detlev von Appen v Voest Alpine Intertrading (The Jay Bola)* [1997] 1 Lloyds Rep 179, 185–88, [1997] 2 Lloyds Rep 279 (CA) 286–88; *Youell v Kara Mara Shipping* [2000] 2 Lloyds Rep 102 [47]–[51], [57], [63]–[69], both decided under RSC Ord 11 r 1(1)(d); *Navigation Maritime Bulgare v Rustal Trading (The Ivan Zagubanski)* [2002] 1 Lloyds Rep 106 [101]; and under the CPR, *Shipowners' Mutual Protection & Indemnity Association (Luxembourg) v Containerships Denizcilik Nakliyat ve Tikaret (The Yusuf Cepnioglu)* [2015] 1 Lloyds Rep 567 [41]–[61]. See also *Ace Seguradora v Fair Wind Navigation* [2017] EWHC 3352, [7], [10].

[77] There is an unresolved dispute in the general case law on CPR PD 6B para 3.1(6) as to whether and when the claimant and/or the defendant need to be a party to the contract in question in order for a claim to fall within para 3.1(6). However, whichever way this is resolved, it seems likely that quasi-contractual injunctions will continue to fit within para 3.1(6).

In *Finnish Marine Insurance v Protective National Insurance* [1989] 2 Lloyds Rep 99, 101–02, Adrian Hamilton QC sitting as a deputy had held that RSC Ord 11 r 1(1)(d), the ancestor of CPR PD 6B para 3.1(6), which applied to claims 'brought to enforce … or otherwise affect' a contract, did not permit service out of proceedings relating to a contract which the plaintiff contended did not exist, in particular where the purpose of those proceedings was to obtain a declaration that the contract did not exist. However, the law developed to allow for a broader and more flexible position. The result of *Gulf Bank v Mitsubishi Heavy Industries* [1994] 1 Lloyds Rep 323, 327 (a declaration case); *DR Insurance v Central National Insurance* [1996] 1 Lloyds Rep 74, 77–78; *Schiffahrtsgesellschaft Detlev von Appen v Voest Alpine Intertrading (The Jay Bola)* [1997] 1 Lloyds Rep 179, 185–88, [1997] 2 Lloyds Rep 279 (CA) 286–88; and *Youell v Kara Mara Shipping* [2000] 2 Lloyds Rep 102 [47]–[51], [57], [63]–[69], was that Ord 11 r 1(1)(d) applied to a wide range of contractual claims and claims related to contracts. It was not in fact necessary for there to be a contract between the claimant and the defendant, and it was sufficient if the claim was sought to *enforce* the clause or its substantive effect against the third party. Consequently, a claim for an quasi-contractual anti-suit injunction against a third party would fall within RSC Ord 11 r 1(1)(d), as it did seek to enforce *a* contract containing an exclusive jurisdiction clause against the third party, even though he was not strictly party to such a contract, as held in *The Jay Bola* and *Kara Mara*.

Similarly, even under the CPR, where the wording 'in respect of a contract' is perhaps slightly narrower, the law has not adopted a rigid position that the claimant and the defendant need to be party to the contract in question. There is, however, an ongoing dispute as to the exact nature of the connection that is required. In *Albon v Naza Motor Trading* [2007] 1 WLR 2489 [20], [26]–[27], Lightman J held that a claim did not need actually to be made under a contract, and that it was sufficient if it was 'connected'. This led him, in *Albon v Naza Motor Trading (No 4)* [2007] 2 Lloyds Rep 420 [20], to conclude that an anti-suit injunction to prevent vexatious parallel litigation in respect of a contract governed by English law was within what was then CPR 6.20(5)—a decision which may well have gone too far, although the point was not addressed on appeal [2008] 1 Lloyds Rep 1 (CA): see further para 18.56. Next, in *Greene Wood & McClean v Templeton Insurance* [2009] 1 WLR 2013 (CA) [18]–[19] the Court of Appeal concluded *obiter* that it was sufficient for para 3.1(6) if the claim 'has a connection to a contract governed by English law' and it was not necessary that the contract be one to which the intended defendant and intended claimant were party.

The breadth of these decisions has been criticized: see A Dickinson, 'Restrained No More? Service out of the Jurisdiction in the 21st Century' [2010] LMCLQ 1, and subsequently, in *Cecil v Bayat* [2010] EWHC 641 [49], Hamblen J confined this approach, holding that a 'legal' and not merely a 'factual' connection must exist between the claim and the contract—which may put a question mark over *Albon v Naza (No 4)*. However, even if Hamblen J's slightly narrower approach is adopted, there will be no difficulty with quasi-contractual injunctions of this kind satisfying PD 6B para 3.1(6).

In contrast, a far narrower approach to PD 6B para 3.1(6) was adopted in *Global 5000 v Wadhawan* [2012] EWCA Civ 3, [64], where Rix LJ suggested, *obiter,* that the *defendant* had to be party to the relevant contract (an analysis supported by A Dickinson, 'Service Out of the Jurisdiction in Contract Cases: Straightening out the Deck Chairs?' [2012] LMCLQ 181). Further, in *Alliance Bank v Aquanta* [2013] 1 Lloyds Rep 175 (CA) [71], Tomlinson LJ stated *obiter* that (a) he was 'attracted' by the reading that para 3.1(6) would not apply 'where the contract in question is not one to which the defendant is party', but also gave tentative approval to the criterion (b) that it must be the case that 'the claimant is suing in order to establish a contractual right or a right which has arisen out of non-performance of a contract', which he said would ordinarily only apply in respect of contracts to which the intended defendant is party. However, Tomlinson LJ's actual decision was only that a 'clear connection' or connection with 'real content to the contract' was required and this would be more difficult to establish in situations where the intended defendant was not party to the contract.

Consequently, the court can have jurisdiction over such claims under PD 6B para 3.1(6)(d), **18.49** if the contract contains an exclusive jurisdiction clause in favour of the English courts,[78] or under PD 6B para 3.1(6)(c) if it contains an arbitration clause governed by English law.

Similarly, a claim for a declaration that an English exclusive jurisdiction clause is in effect **18.50** binding against the third party can also fall within PD 6B para 3.1(6).[79]

c) Inconsistent claims

A more difficult situation arises where, on the injunction claimant's own case, he is not party **18.51** to the underlying contract, but the injunction defendant's substantive claims against the injunction claimant are contractual, and inherently subject to an exclusive forum clause in the contract.

In *The Alexandros T*, claims were brought in the Chinese courts by cargo owners not only **18.52** against the ship's owners (in breach of an arbitration clause) but also against the ship's managers. The managers alleged that as a matter of Chinese law, the claims against them were contractual (or in bailment), if they had any substance at all, although the managers denied they owed any obligations to the cargo owners of any sort. In contrast, the cargo owners alleged that their Chinese claims were statutory and not contractual. Cooke J could not resolve this dispute of expert evidence but concluded that, however it was answered,

---

The case law has not yet reached any clear finding that Tomlinson LJ's narrower approaches (or one of them) are right. Strand (b) of his reasoning in *Aquanta* was adopted by Andrew Smith J in *Navig8 v Al-Riyadh Co for Vegetable Oil Industry (The Lucky Lady)* [2013] 2 Lloyds Rep 104 [14], who concluded that an anti-suit injunction based solely on vexation and oppression could not fall within CPR 3.1(6), even though it was protecting underlying litigation in respect of a contract; and the correctness of this result was conceded and followed in *Golden Endurance Shipping v RMA Watanya (The Golden Endurance)* [2015] 1 Lloyds Rep 266 [24]–[29]. This was a different result to *Albon v Naza Motor Trading (No 4)* [2007] 2 Lloyds Rep 420, although reached without reference to *Albon*. However, these cases were not concerned with quasi-contractual injunctions. See also *Erste Group Bank (London) v JSC (VMZ Red October)* [2013] EWHC 2926 [132]–[140] (tort claims against non-parties for interference with contractual relations not 'in respect of a contract', no clear conclusion as to the principles).

If the narrower approach articulated in the *obiter dicta* in *Wadhawan* and in strand (a) of *Aquanta* were to be applied literally, it could exclude jurisdiction over quasi contractual anti-suit injunctions of this kind—although it would be arguable that Tomlinson LJ's strand (b) could apply to quasi-contractual injunctions. But neither of these two distinguished judges was focusing on the current situation, where the essence of the claim for the injunction is that although the injunction defendant may not formally be bound by the contract, he should be treated as if he were, and therefore restrained by injunction. In substance, the injunction claimant in such a case *is* 'suing in order to establish a contractual right'. In such a case, it is appropriate for such a claim to be treated as if it were 'in respect' of a contract for the purposes of a jurisdiction, even if generally PD 6B para 3.1(6) would require the defendant to be a party to the contract in question.

Consequently, it is submitted that however 'in respect of' is interpreted, this kind of quasi-contractual injunction should fall within para 3.1(6). Teare J had no hesitation in reaching this conclusion in *Shipowners' Mutual Protection & Indemnity Association (Luxembourg) v Containerships Denizcilik Nakliyat ve Tikaret AS (The Yusuf Cepnioglu)* [2015] 1 Lloyds Rep 567 [41]–[61], in which he used a broad test of 'sufficient connection' to the contract, and his conclusion was not challenged on appeal. There is no inconsistency between this result and *The Lucky Lady* and *The Golden Endurance*, which are concerned with injunctions that have no quasi-contractual foundation.

---

[78] However, if a quasi-contractual claim to enforce an English exclusive jurisdiction clause can be brought within Article 25 of the Recast and/or the Hague Convention on the Choice of Court, then jurisdiction will exist under the Recast and CPR 6.33 and/or under the Hague Convention and CPR 6.33(2B) without permission to serve out being required, and so it will not be necessary to use CPR PD 6B para 3.1(6). For whether quasi-contractual claims can come within Article 25, see Ch 17, para 17.45. The applicability of the Hague Convention to quasi-contractual claims has not yet been explored, although there is some relevant discussion at paras 94–97 of Trevor Hartley and Masato Dohauchi, *Explanatory Report on the Convention of 30 June 2005 on Choice of Court Agreements* (2013).

[79] *Gulf Bank v Mitsubishi Heavy Industries* [1994] 1 Lloyds Rep 323, 327–38; *Youell v Kara Mara Shipping* [2000] 2 Lloyds Rep 102 [99]–[100] (although there the declaration was in respect of the substantive scope of the contract); see also *Navigation Maritime Bulgare v Rustal Trading (The Ivan Zagubanski)* [2002] 1 Lloyds Rep 106 [100]–[101] (although the point was little debated). This is consistent with PD 6B para 3.1(8), which permits service out of the jurisdiction of claims for a declaration that a contract does not exist.

in circumstances where no party alleged that the managers were party to the arbitration agreement, the claim for an anti-suit injunction by the managers could not be a contractual claim, and thus did not fall within what is now PD 6B para 3.1(6).[80]

18.53   It is doubtful whether this decision is correct. If the claim in China was in substance contractual from the perspective of English law, then the managers' claim for an anti-suit injunction could be viewed as a quasi-contractual injunction, which sought in effect to prevent a party whose substantive claims were contractual from not being able to claim the benefit of the contract without the burden of the contractual forum clause.[81] If so, it is well arguable that such a claim is 'in respect of a contract', as the essence of the juridical right asserted to justify the injunction is contractual.[82] This situation is close in practice to the quasi-contractual injunction over which jurisdiction was accepted in *Yusuf*, and using Teare J's approach in *The Yusuf Cepnioglu*, it can be said that there is a 'sufficient connection' to the contract.[83] The case for applying PD 6B para 3.1(6) will be *a fortiori* where, although the claimant denies there is a contract, the defendant itself alleges that its claims are contractual.[84]

18.54   The eventual answer, or at least the reasoning used, may depend in part on the resolution of the current debate in the authorities about whether PD 6B para 3.1(6) should be broadly interpreted as covering any claims sufficiently 'connected' to the contract (which can be called Longmore LJ's view), or whether in contrast it covers only claims under contracts to which the defendant is alleged to be a party, or only claims to assert a contractual right (which can be called Tomlinson LJ's view).[85]

d) Injunctions based on vexation and oppression in respect of contractual litigation

18.55   What if the underlying contract is governed by English law, but contains no exclusive forum clause, and an anti-suit injunction is sought to protect ongoing English proceedings on that contract and to restrain vexatious and oppressive litigation abroad, the subject matter of which relates to the underlying contract? In this case the anti-suit injunction is not enforcing a contractual right not to be sued abroad in any sense, whether directly or quasi-contractually.

18.56   In *Albon v Naza (No 4)*, Lightman J held that, in such a case, the claim for an anti-suit injunction was 'in respect of a contract', and fell within what is now para 3.1(6) because the

---

[80] *Starlight Shipping Co v Tai Ping Insurance Co Ltd (The Alexandros T)* [2008] 1 Lloyds Rep 230 [36]–[42].

[81] As discussed at Ch 10, section F, 'Inconsistent Contractual Claims', there are three main possible analyses of the managers' claim for an injunction against the cargo owners. First, if the cargo owners' claim was inherently contractual, then even if the managers did not accept the existence of the contract, the cargo owners could be estopped from denying its existence for the purposes of the claim for an injunction. Second, the claim for an anti-suit injunction could be viewed as enforcing the substantive equitable obligation on the cargo owners not to bring a claim in a forum inconsistent with that selected under the contract which was an inherent part of their claim. Third, the cargo owners' claim could be viewed as a vexatious and oppressive attempt to evade the purpose of the forum clause agreed between them and their primary counterparty. On the first two analyses, the managers' claim was clearly 'in respect of a contract' as a matter of natural language. But even on the third analysis it was very closely related to the contract.

[82] In contrast to the position in *Navig8 v Al-Riyadh Co for Vegetable Oil Industry (The Lucky Lady)* [2013] 2 Lloyds Rep 104 [14], where the injunction was brought in respect of a contract but to claim a non-contractual equitable anti-suit injunction.

[83] *Shipowners' Mutual Protection & Indemnity Association (Luxembourg) v Containerships Denizcilik Nakliyat ve Tikaret (The Yusuf Cepnioglu)* [2015] 1 Lloyds Rep 567 [41]–[61]. There are cases where jurisdiction asserted on this basis has not been challenged: see eg *Dell Emerging Markets (EMEA) v IB Maroc.com* [2017] EWHC 2397.

[84] See *Ace Seguradora v Fair Wind Navigation* [2017] EWHC 3352, [7], [10].

[85] See the discussion at n 78.

anti-suit injunction was 'in connection with' the contract.[86] This is debatable. The claim for an anti-suit injunction was based on equitable principles, and was not enforcing the forum clause. Even if a broad interpretation of PD 6B para 3.1(6) is adopted, and it covers claims 'connected' to the contract, it is uncertain whether such an injunction is sufficiently connected to the underlying contract.[87] And if Tomlinson LJ's narrower approach to para 3.1(6) is adopted,[88] and it covers only claims *under* the contract, then *Albon v Naza (No 4)* will not be followed.

In *The Lucky Lady*, the English arbitration clause in a charterparty was not incorporated   **18.57** into the bill of lading, but it was arguable that the agreement to English law was incorporated. Andrew Smith J, following Tomlinson LJ's approach, concluded that a claim for an anti-suit injunction against the bill of lading holder, based exclusively on 'vexation or oppression', did not fall within para 3.1(6) because no contractual right was asserted to justify the injunction (although *Albon* was not cited). This has been the approach in other recent authorities.[89]

However, such limitations may not matter much in practice. Provided there is English liti-   **18.58** gation on the merits, it is possible to obtain jurisdiction for an interim anti-suit injunction to protect the English litigation under the ancillary jurisdiction, even if there is no jurisdiction under PD 6B para 3.1 to serve a final anti-suit injunction out of the jurisdiction, and that is what happened in *The Golden Endurance*.[90] This is discussed in section D, 'Service Out of the Jurisdiction'. In addition, para 3.1(4A) may provide a relevant basis for a claim for a final injunction, on the basis that the injunction is sufficiently closely connected to the underlying claim on the merits, although this is yet to be determined.[91]

PD 6B para 3.1(7), which covers claims 'in respect of a breach of contract committed within   **18.59** the jurisdiction' will not normally apply to injunctions to restrain the pursuit of proceedings abroad. Where an injunction defendant breaches an English exclusive jurisdiction clause by litigating abroad, his breach of contract will take place abroad.[92]

PD 6B para 3.1(8), which covers claims for declarations that no contract exists, is not dir-   **18.60** ectly applicable to anti-suit injunctions.

---

[86] *Albon v Naza Motor Trading (No 4)* [2007] 2 Lloyds Rep 420 [20]; the judge also upheld jurisdiction on an alternative ground derived from the injunction defendant's submission to the jurisdiction of the court: at [21]–[22], and jurisdiction was not considered on appeal: [2008] 1 Lloyds Rep 1 (CA) [9].

[87] *Cecil v Bayat* [2010] EWHC 641 [49].

[88] See again n 78.

[89] *Navig8 v Al-Riyadh Co for Vegetable Oil Industry (The Lucky Lady)* [2013] EWHC 328 [14]; which would have been followed, if necessary, in *Talos Capital Ltd v JSC Investment Holdings XIV* [2014] EWHC 3977 [58]; also followed, albeit unchallenged, in *Golden Endurance Shipping v RMA Watanya (The Golden Endurance)* [2015] 1 Lloyds Rep 266 [24]–[25].

In *The Lucky Lady* an alternative argument was advanced that the injunction was 'in respect of a contract' because it was sought to defend the contractual choice of English law which would be overridden by Jordanian law in the competing Jordanian proceedings. Andrew Smith J did not decide whether this alternative claim was within para 3.1(6), instead holding that there was no good arguable case on the facts, and also because in principle a choice of English law did not on its own bring with it a promise not to sue in any jurisdiction where the local conflicts of law principles would not apply English law: see [21]–[22]; see to similar effect *The Golden Endurance* at [38]–[47]. The issue has been more fully explored, to similar effect, in the thoughtful Australian decision in *Ace Insurance Ltd v Moose Enterprises Pty Ltd* [2009] NSWSC 724, where it was held that a choice of law clause is usually 'declaratory of the parties' intention, not promissory'.

[90] *Golden Endurance Shipping v RMA Watanya (The Golden Endurance)* [2015] 1 Lloyds Rep 266 [26]–[29].

[91] Paragraphs 18.36–18.39 of this chapter.

[92] See *OT Africa Line v Magic Sportswear* [2005] 1 Lloyds Rep 252 [20] (in respect of choice of law).

8. Tort: PD 6B Paragraph 3.1(9)

18.61   PD 6B para 3.1(9) permits service out of the jurisdiction where 'a claim is made in tort' and either 'the damage was sustained within the jurisdiction' or the damage 'resulted from an act committed within the jurisdiction'.

18.62   Non-contractual anti-suit injunctions have historically been based on equity, not tort, and it is unlikely that tortious rights and duties will prove to be a productive basis for claims for anti-suit injunctions in most cases.[93] In addition, in *AMT v Marzillier* the Supreme Court concluded, in respect of a claim for damages for inducing a breach of a jurisdiction clause by inducing the party bound by the clause to sue in a foreign court, that the place where the harmful event occurred was in the foreign court, not England, for the purpose of Article 7(3) of the Recast. The same reasoning is likely to apply to para 3.1(9). Consequently, absent special facts, this gateway is unlikely to support jurisdiction in England for an anti-suit injunction based on tort.[94]

9. Claims in Relation to Administration: PD 6B Paragraph 3.1(13)

18.63   PD 6B para 3.1(13) permits service out of the jurisdiction where 'A claim is made for any remedy which might be obtained in proceedings for the administration of the estate of a person who died domiciled within the jurisdiction'. This is arguably broad enough to cover an anti-suit injunction to restrain foreign proceedings that might interfere with that administration, because of the words 'any remedy'. On the other hand, it might be said that the provision is focused only on the substantive remedies in the administration proceedings. If it does cover anti-suit injunctions, its breadth is merely an accident of language, as illustrated, for example, by the comparison to the trust heads of jurisdiction. In the circumstances, if it does cover anti-suit injunctions, it would probably only be used with some caution.

10. Claims under Enactments: PD 6B Paragraph 3.1(20)

18.64   PD 6B para 3.1(20)(a) allows permission to serve out of the jurisdiction if 'A claim is made–(a) under any enactment which allows proceedings to be brought and those proceedings are not covered by any of the other grounds referred to in this paragraph'. The reference to 'any enactment which allows proceedings to be brought' is more open than the corresponding wording in CPR 6.20(18), which like its predecessor in RSC Order 11(1)(o)–(s) and (u), permitted service out of the jurisdiction if a claim was made under one of a list of miscellaneous

---

[93]   See Ch 3, section B, 'A Legal or Equitable Right?'; Ch 4, paras 4.26–4.40. However, it is possible that the tort of inducing a breach of contract may be of assistance in some cases: *Kallang Shipping SA v Axa Assurances Senegal (The Kallang)* [2007] 1 Lloyds Rep 160 [41]; and see also *Kallang Shipping v Axa Assurances Senegal (The Kallang) (No 2)* [2007] 1 Lloyds Rep 160 [90]–[96]; *Sotrade Denizcilik Sanayi Ve Ticaret v Amadou Lo (The Duden)* [2009] 1 Lloyds Rep 145 [65]–[70].

[94]   *AMT Futures v Marzillier* [2017] 2 WLR 853 (SC) [25]–[26]. See also by analogy *OT Africa Line v Magic Sportswear* [2005] 1 Lloyds Rep 252 [19]–[24]. In *Kallang Shipping v Axa Assurances Senegal (The Kallang)* [2007] 1 Lloyds Rep 160 [41]–[43], Gloster J appears to have accepted that service out of the jurisdiction of an interim anti-suit injunction based on the torts of inducing breach of contract, interference with business relations, and conspiracy, could be upheld. However, the applicable heads of jurisdiction under CPR 6.20 (now PD 6B para 3.1) were not analysed.

specified statutes, such as the Nuclear Installations Act 1965, and the Financial Services and Markets Act 2000.

This new wording poses an important question. Was it intended to create a general juris-   **18.65**
dictional head for claims based on statute, extending beyond service of claims under the previous rag-bag of miscellaneous enactments—which were of relatively little importance in civil litigation? If so, what kinds of statutory claims are intended to be covered?

In *AES Ust-Kamenogorsk*, Burton J held that para 3.1(20)(a) was an 'obvious catch-all clause'   **18.66**
and there was 'no connection' between it and the previous provisions that had operated by way of list. Consequently, a claim for an anti-suit injunction under Senior Courts Act 1981 section 37(1) was a claim under 'an enactment' which could fall under para 3.1(20)(a).[95] Since anti-suit injunctions are always, or at least can always be, based on section 37(1),[96] this decision would have meant, if correct, that the court would always have a gateway to permit service of claims for anti-suit injunctions out of the jurisdiction. Either they would come within one of the other heads of PD para 3.1, or they would fall within para 3.1(20)(a). However, on appeal the Court of Appeal disagreed. The majority (Wilson LJ and Burnton LJ) concluded *obiter* that section 37 of the Senior Courts Act did not fall within para 3.1(20)(a); and although Rix LJ did not decide the point, he concluded that there was a 'serious argument' that this was the case.[97]

The reasoning was terse (on this point). Burnton LJ's logic was that section 37 was not 'an   **18.67**
enactment which allows proceedings to be brought'. But this was because section 37 'con-fers a power to grant injunctions in proceedings properly within the jurisdiction', which reads strangely, as section 37 covers final injunctions. Rix LJ's reasoning was that section 37 merely allows for a particular remedy within proceedings whose legal basis has to be found elsewhere; but this is in tension with the many cases that hold that anti-suit injunc-tions are granted under section 37, which is therefore not just about remedy: such as *Ust-Kamenogorsk* in the Supreme Court itself.[98] The para 3.1(20) point does not appear to have been debated on appeal to the Supreme Court, although Lord Mance commented in passing that 'leave was in fact obtained under CPR PD 6B, paragraph 3.1(2)' in what seems to have been a typographical error for para 3.1(20).[99]

The case law has since become more complex. In the recent decision of *Orexim v Mahavir*,[100]   **18.68**
the Court of Appeal considered whether applications under section 423 of the Insolvency Act 1986 could fall within para 3.1(2). They reviewed the law on para 3.1(20) and its pre-decessors, and contrasted it to the narrower power in CPR 6.33(3), and departing from the narrower previous test set down for the earlier wordings in *Re Harrods*,[101] concluded that

---

[95] *AES Ust-Kamenogorsk Hydropower Plant LLP v Ust-Kamenogorsk Hydropower Plant JSC* [2010] 2 Lloyds Rep 493 [24].

[96] Ch 3, section A, 'The Power to Grant Injunctions'.

[97] *AES Ust-Kamenogorsk Hydropower Plant LLP v Ust-Kamenogorsk Hydropower Plant JSC* [2012] 1 WLR 920 (CA) [192], [207], and [126]; interpreted in *ED&F Man Capital Markets v Obex Securities* [2018] 1 WLR 1708 [19].

[98] *Ust-Kamenogorsk Hydropower Plant JSC (Appellant) v AES Ust-Kamenogorsk Hydropower Plant LLP* [2013] 1 WLR 1889 (SC) [60]; *South Carolina v Assurantie Maatschappij 'De Seven Provincien'* [1987] AC 24 (HL) 39H; *Cartier International v British Sky Broadcasting* [2015] RPC 7 [99], [2016] EWCA Civ 658 [40]–[41] (not addressed on this point in the Supreme Court: [2018] 1 WLR 3259 [5]); and Ch 3, paras 3.02 and 3.06.

[99] *Ust-Kamenogorsk Hydropower Plant JSC v AES Ust-Kamenogorsk Hydropower Plant LLP* [2013] 1 WLR 1889 (SC) [51].

[100] *Orexim Trading v Mahavir Port and Terminal* [2018] EWCA Civ 1660 [35], [47].

[101] *Re Harrods (Buenos Aires)* [1992] Ch 72 (CA).

'if, as a matter of construction, the enactment in question allows proceedings to be brought against persons not within England and Wales, then the court has power to allow those proceedings to be served abroad'. They suggested that no restrictions should be implied into the literal wording of the gateway. Applied literally, this reasoning could apply to section 37(1), because there is no doubt that section 37(1) allows, substantively, the grant of injunctions against persons outside the jurisdiction in relation to facts outside the jurisdiction.

18.69   However, *Ust-Kamenogorsk* was not cited, and the Court of Appeal does not appear to have fully considered all the potential issues relating to the boundaries of para 3.1(20). A test which allowed para 3.1(20) to cater for service out of claims brought under statutes which implicitly envisaged a distinct and additional extraterritorial jurisdiction, but not otherwise, might well have covered section 423 without bringing in section 37(1) by side wind. However, although there are shades of this sort of concept in the Court of Appeal's reasoning in *Orexim* (see at [48]), it is not expressly articulated in the test used, at [35], although it might be said that this is what is really meant by 'allowed'. The true boundaries of *Orexim* and its effect on section 37(1) are therefore unclear.

18.70   An answer may, however, be found that in the fact that section 37(1) is a *sui generis* provision of entirely general application, whose historical role was merely to confirm the court's existing jurisdiction to grant injunctions and declarations, and not to confer a power which did not exist before.[102] The position is different to statutes which create specific powers in circumstances which bring with them specific extraterritorial jurisdiction. Thus, even if anti-suit injunctions are 'brought' under section 37(1), it may be correct to say that section 37(1) does not '*allow* them to be brought against persons not within England and Wales' in the sense which the Court of Appeal had in mind in *Orexim*; because 'allow' appears to convey some sense that the relevant statute not only confirms but also creates the substantive power, and also creates an extraterritorial jurisdiction for that power. A shorter answer (not explored in *Ust-Kamenogorsk*) might be that since injunctions are specifically catered for by para 3.1(2), they are not 'proceedings not covered by any of the other grounds referred to in this paragraph', so that para 3.1(20) is inapplicable. But this would leave outstanding the other oddity that the appointment of receivers, which is covered by section 37(1) but not by any of the specific heads of PD 6B para 3.1, would then remain within para 3.1(20).

18.71   As matters stand, the conclusion in *Ust-Kamenogorsk* that anti-suit injunctions do not follow within para 3.1(20)(a) has been put in doubt by the unclear ambit of the reasoning in *Orexim*. But it would be surprising if para 3.1(20) were to create a general head of jurisdiction emancipating anti-suit injunctions from the confines of the other heads of CPR 6.36 and PD 6B para 3.1.

11. Heads of Jurisdiction Irrelevant to Anti-Suit Injunctions

18.72   A number of the heads of jurisdiction in PD 6B para 3.1 clearly have no connection to anti-suit injunctions, because they apply only to claims with specific subject matters.

---

[102] *Cartier International v British Sky Broadcasting* [2017] RPC 7 (CA) [40]–[42].

- PD 6B para 3.1(10) applies to claims to 'enforce' a judgment or arbitral award; but an anti-suit injunction is not an enforcement process.
- PD 6B para 3.1(11) applies where 'the whole subject matter of a claim relates to property within the jurisdiction'; an anti-suit injunction primarily relates to litigation.
- PD 6B para 3.1(10) applies only to 'a probate claim' or 'a claim for a rectification of a will'. The latter clearly does not, and the former should similarly not, cover anti-suit injunctions.
- PD 6B para 3.1(15) applies to claims for a remedy against a defendant as constructive trustee; but the anti-suit injunction's foundations in equity are not based on trust.
- PD 6B para 3.1(16) applies only to claims 'for restitution'.
- PD 6B para 3.1(17) only covers claims by the Commissioners for HM Revenue and Customs relating to duties and taxes.
- PD 6B para 3.1(18) covers claims for third-party costs.
- PD 6B para 3.1(19) applies only to admiralty claims.

G. JURISDICTION BY WAY OF COUNTERCLAIM

The court will have jurisdiction to hear any counterclaim which may as a matter of procedure appropriately be heard together with the claimant's claim, provided it is sufficient connected with the subject matter of the proceedings.[103] By bringing his claim, the claimant has submitted to the court's jurisdiction to hear any appropriate counterclaim, even if jurisdiction could not have been obtained over the counterclaim if it brought in separate proceedings.[104] Final anti-suit injunctions can be claimed by counterclaim[105] and so this form of jurisdiction will apply to them. It will generally be unnecessary to obtain permission to serve such claims out of the jurisdiction, since a claimant should in any event have given an address for service within the jurisdiction under CPR 6.23.[106] Permission to serve out of the jurisdiction can also, if necessary, be obtained under the 'Additional Claims' head of jurisdiction in PD 6B para 3.1(4), for example if it is necessary to add an additional defendant to the counterclaim.   **18.73**

---

[103] The modern rules as to when a counterclaim can properly be brought in the same proceedings as the original claim are contained in CPR 20.9 and 3.1(2)(e) and (j), but they are hardly clear. See *Glencore International v Metro Trading International (No 3)* [2002] CLC 1090 (Moore-Bick J), [19]; *In re a Debtor (No 87 of 1999)* (Rimer J, 17 January 2000); *Jones v Longley* [2016] EWHC 1309 [39]–[47].

[104] *Derby v Larsson* [1976] 1 WLR 202 (HL) 205H; *Republic of Liberia v Gulf Oceanic* [1985] 1 Lloyds Rep 539 (CA) 542, 544–45, 547–48; *Metal Scrap Trade v Kate Shipping (The Gladys)* [1990] 1 WLR 115 (HL); *Balkanbank v Taher (No 2)* [1995] 1 WLR 1067 (CA) 1075–1076, 1081–82; *Altimo Holding and Investment v Krygz Mobil* [2012] 1 WLR 1804 (PC) [72]. This principle has been extended to Part 20 claims made in complicated multi-party litigation: see *Glencore International v Metro Trading International (No 3)* [2002] CLC 1090, (Moore Bick J) [17]–[22], (CA) [44]–[60].

There is some authority to the effect that if the consequences of ordering a counterclaimant to bring his counterclaim in a separate action would be that the counterclaim could never be brought in England, as the counterclaimant could not independently obtain jurisdiction for the counterclaim, then the court will not exercise its discretion to order separation: *Metal Scrap*, 130B; *Balkanbank v Taher*, 1076C. This is inconsistent with the older cases: *South African Republic v La Compagnie Franco-Belge du Chemin de Fer du Nord* [1897] 2 Ch 487 (CA) 493, and it seems doubtful in principle.

[105] *Glencore International v Metro Trading International (No 3)* [2002] CLC 1090, per Moore Bick J at [22]; upheld in terms which suggest this is correct at CA [57], [59].

[106] *Derby v Larsson* [1976] 1 WLR 202 (HL) 205H–206A.

18.74   However, in many cases a defendant in such a situation does not trouble with claiming a final anti-suit injunction against a claimant by claim form and instead chooses only to seek anti-suit relief by way of application notice.[107] Jurisdiction will usually be unproblematic in this situation under the court's ancillary jurisdiction to grant ancillary relief in substantive proceedings over which it already has jurisdiction (which is discussed further in section J, 'Jurisdiction and Interim Anti-Suit Injunctions').

H. DISCRETION UNDER CPR PARAGRAPHS 6.36 AND 6.37

18.75   Even if it has been shown that a claim for an anti-suit injunction falls within one of the heads of jurisdiction in PD 6B para 3.1, the injunction claimant must still show that it is proper case for the proceedings to be served out of the jurisdiction, in the discretion of the court, under CPR 6.36 and 6.37.

18.76   In relation to ordinary substantive claims, the central question for the court's exercise of its discretion is where it is most appropriate for the matter to be tried. But it is an inherent feature of anti-suit injunctions that they should only be granted if the English court has a close interest in the matter.[108] Logically, if there is a good case for an anti-suit injunction on the merits, it will in most circumstances follow that England is the most appropriate jurisdiction for the matter to be tried.[109]

18.77   Other separate discretionary factors, such as a failure by the claimant to discharge his duty of full and frank disclosure when applying without notice, or delay, can also affect the court's discretionary decision as to whether permission for service out of the jurisdiction should be granted or maintained.

I. ARBITRATION CLAIMS

18.78   Final injunctions to enforce an arbitration clause providing for arbitration in England can be claimed under Senior Courts Act 1981 section 37(1),[110] and can and must be brought by arbitration claim form.[111] They can be served out of the jurisdiction under CPR 62.5(1)(c),[112] which allows proceedings commenced by arbitration claim form to

---

[107]   It is not necessary in order for an interim anti-suit injunction to be applied for by a defendant, for a final anti-suit injunction to have been claimed by way of counterclaim, as the interim injunction can be simply sought by way of application in the context of the action before the court: *Glencore International v Metro Trading International (No 3)* [2002] CLC 1090 (CA) [59], distinguishing *Carter v Fey* [1894] 2 Ch 541 (CA); *Masri v Consolidated Contractors (No 3)* [2009] QB 503 (CA) [58].

[108]   Ch 4, section L, 'Comity'.

[109]   See *Joint Stock Asset Management Co Ingosstrakh-Investments v BNP Paribas SA* [2012] 1 Lloyds Rep 649 (CA) [80]–[82]. See also *Amoco (UK) Exploration v British American Offshore* [1999] 2 Lloyds Rep 772, 780; *Donohue v Armco* [1999] 2 Lloyds Rep 649 [63]–[69]; *Youell v Kara Mara Shipping* [2000] 2 Lloyds Rep 102 [72]–[75]; *Navigation Maritime Bulgare v Rustal Trading (The Ivan Zagubanski)* [2002] 1 Lloyds Rep 106 [52(11)], [101].

[110]   *Welex v Rosa Maritime (The Epsilon Rosa)* [2003] 2 Lloyds Rep 509 (CA) [34]–[40]; *AES Ust-Kamenogorsk Hydropower Plant LLP v Ust-Kamenogorsk Hydropower Plant JSC* [2012] 1 WLR 920 (CA) [29], [36]–[37], [42]–[104], [204], [2013] 1 WLR 1889 (SC) [48], [55]–[62]. See further Ch 3, section A, 'The Power to Grant Injunctions'.

[111]   Ch 3, para 3.35.

[112]   CPR 62.5(1)(b), which permits service out of the jurisdiction of claims for orders under s 44 of the Arbitration Act 1996, does not apply to final anti-suit injunctions, since s 44 is capable of supporting interim injunctions only.

be served out of the jurisdiction where the claimant seeks a remedy, or requires a question to be decided by the court, 'affecting an arbitration (whether started or not), [or] an arbitration agreement', and the seat of the arbitration is or will be within the jurisdiction.[113] CPR 62.5(1)(c) is not confined to claims under the Arbitration Act 1996 and so can support injunctions under section 37(1) of the Senior Courts Act.[114] It permits service out of the jurisdiction of injunctions to enforce an arbitration clause, because the anti-suit injunction 'affects' the arbitration or the arbitration agreement by enforcing the implied negative obligation in the arbitration agreement not to litigate relevant disputes outside arbitration or otherwise protecting the arbitration.[115] It has been held to apply in a case where the injunction was sought to prevent a vexatious collateral attack on the arbitration award.[116]

The wording of CPR 62.5(1)(c) makes clear that it will apply even where no arbitration has yet been commenced; and the Supreme Court has also held that it will be satisfied even if neither party intends to commence an arbitration, but the injunction claimant wishes to prevent the injunction defendant litigating otherwise than in the agreed arbitration, because the requirement in 62.5(c)(ii) that 'the seat of the arbitration is or will be within the jurisdiction' must be read as satisfied if the seat of any arbitration, if any were to be commenced, would be within the jurisdiction.[117] **18.79**

Teare J has held that CPR 62.5(1)(c) applies to give jurisdiction to quasi-contractual claims for an injunction to enforce an arbitration clause against a third party claiming derived rights in the shoes of a party bound by the arbitration clause, as such an injunction 'affects' an arbitration or an arbitration agreement. He concluded that insofar as CPR 62.5 requires that the defendant be a party to the arbitration clause, a third party in the **18.80**

---

[113] CPR 62.5 can also apply, even if the seat of the arbitration is not in England, if s 2(4) of the Arbitration Act 1996 applies. This provides:

> The court may exercise a power conferred by any provision of this Part not mentioned in subsection (2) or (3) for the purpose of supporting the arbitral process where—(a) no seat of the arbitration has been designated or determined, and (b) by reason of a connection with England and Wales or Northern Ireland the court is satisfied that it is appropriate to do so.

See *Western Bulk Shipowning III v Carbofer Maritime Trading (The Western Moscow)* [2012] 2 Lloyds Rep 163 [103]–[109].

[114] *AES Ust-Kamenogorsk Hydropower Plant LLP v Ust-Kamenogorsk Hydropower Plant JSC* [2012] 1 WLR 920 (CA) [114]–[120]; *Ust-Kamenogorsk Hydropower Plant JSC (Appellant) v AES Ust-Kamenogorsk Hydropower Plant LLP* [2013] 1 WLR 1889 (SC) [49]–[51], overruling comments to the contrary in *Vale do Rio Navegacao v Shanghai Bao Steel Ocean Shipping* [2000] 2 Lloyds Rep 1 [59].

[115] This has now been conclusively confirmed in *Ust-Kamenogorsk Hydropower Plant JSC (Appellant) v AES Ust-Kamenogorsk Hydropower Plant LLP* [2013] 1 WLR 1889 (SC) [49]–[51] and was conceded in respect of parties to the arbitration agreement in *Shipowners' Mutual Protection & Indemnity Association (Luxembourg) v Containerships Denizcilik Nakliyat ve Tikaret (The Yusuf Cepnioglu)* [2015] 1 Lloyds Rep 567 [48]–[50] (where the fight was about third parties); see also *Emmott v Michael Wilson* [2017] 1 Lloyds Rep 21 [66]–[67]; *AES Nigeria Barge v Federal Republic of Nigeria* [2013] EWHC 3860 [9].

For previous authority to the same effect, see *BNP Paribas v Russian Machines* [2012] 1 Lloyds Rep 61 [46]–[49] (not addressed on appeal in *Joint Stock Asset Management Company Ingosstrakh-Investments v BNP Paribas* [2012] 1 Lloyds Rep 649 (CA) [79]); *Navigation Maritime Bulgare v Rustal Trading (The Ivan Zagubanski)* [2002] 1 Lloyds Rep 106 [56], [101], where the question was effectively conceded (in relation to para 8.1 of the old Arbitration Practice Direction, the ancestor of CPR 62.5(1)(c)).

[116] *Emmott v Michael Wilson* [2017] 1 Lloyds Rep 21 [66]–[67].

[117] *Ust-Kamenogorsk Hydropower Plant JSC (Appellant) v AES Ust-Kamenogorsk Hydropower Plant LLP* [2013] 1 WLR 1889 (SC) [50], [2010] 2 Lloyds Rep 493 [19]–[23], and [2012] 1 WLR 920 (CA) [106]–[121].

quasi-contractual situation is to be treated as a party to the arbitration clause for that purpose.[118]

18.81   Outside the quasi-contractual situation, there is a broader debate as to whether CPR 62.5(1)(c) can apply to permit service out of the jurisdiction of claims against a third party who is not party to the arbitration clause. In a line of cases flowing from *Vale do Rio* to *The Alexandros T* (Cooke J) and capped by *Cruz City* (Males J), it has been held that CPR 62.5(1)(c) only applies to parties to the arbitration clause. The key rationale of principle is that it is only parties to the arbitration who have agreed to submit themselves to the English jurisdiction for the purposes of CPR 62.5.[119] But this is a controversial conclusion, and there are contrary decisions and suggestions in the case law.[120] Before *Cruz City*, in *BNP Paribas v Russian Machines*, Blair J had accepted that there was force in the submission that an anti-suit injunction, claimed against a person not party to the arbitration agreement to prevent them interfering vexatiously with the arbitration, would fall within CPR 62.5(1)(c).[121] Further, in *The Yusuf Cepnioglu* Teare J concluded, distinguishing *Cruz City*, that CPR 62.5(1)(c) would apply to third parties in quasi-contractual situations, on the basis that they would be treated as 'parties' to the arbitration agreement in a sufficient sense. As a result, he did not need to determine whether *Cruz City* was right; but his reasoning suggests he might well have doubted its correctness had it been necessary to do so.[122]

18.82   The debate encapsulated in *Cruz City* is of particular relevance in relation to the question (parallel to that arising in relation to 3.1(6)(c)) whether CPR 62.5(1)(c) can apply in the 'inconsistent claims' situation, where the injunction claimant himself denies that he is party to the contract containing the arbitration clause, but the injunction defendant's substantive claim, if coherent, is necessarily subject to the clause. In *The Alexandros T* (discussed at para 18.36) Cooke J held that CPR 62.5(1)(c) could not so apply, with the result that an injunction claimant who denied any contract with the injunction defendant, but who was seeking an injunction to restrain the injunction defendant from acting inconsistently with the arbitration clause in the contract, could not come within CPR 62.5(1)(c).[123]

---

[118] *Shipowners' Mutual Protection & Indemnity Association (Luxembourg) v Containerships Denizcilik Nakliyat ve Tikaret (The Yusuf Cepnioglu)* [2015] 1 Lloyds Rep 567 [48]–[61]; distinguishing *Cruz City 1 Mauritius Holdings v Unitech* [2015] 1 Lloyds Rep 191 [25]–[52]. This conclusion can be reinforced, in appropriate cases, by s 82(2) of the Arbitration Act 1996, which provides that 'references in this Part to a party to an arbitration agreement include any person claiming under or through a party to the agreement'.

[119] *Vale do Rio Navegacao v Shanghai Bao Steel Ocean Shipping* [2000] 2 Lloyds Rep 1 [20]–[42]; *Starlight Shipping v Tai Ping Insurance (The Alexandros T)* [2008] 1 Lloyds Rep 230 [36]–[42]; *Cruz City 1 Mauritius Holdings v Unitech* [2015] 1 Lloyds Rep 191 [25]–[52]. See also *DTEK Trading v Morozov* [2017] 1 Lloyds Rep 126 [11]–[57]. It is to be noted, however, that there is a flaw in the logic of *DTEK v Morozov* as it assumes incorrectly at [28] that interim anti-suit injunctions to protect arbitration are sought under s 44 of the Arbitration Act 1996, which is (now) not the case: see Ch 13, paras 13.10–13.12. It would seem that *Ust-Kamenogorsk Hydropower Plant JSC (Appellant) v AES Ust-Kamenogorsk Hydropower Plant LLP* [2013] 1 WLR 1889 (SC) was not cited.

[120] *Tedcom Finance v Vetabet Holdings* [2011] EWCA Civ 191; *BNP Paribas v Russian Machines* [2012] 1 Lloyds Rep 61 [49] (although cf on appeal [2012] 1 Lloyds Rep 649 (CA) [79], [88]); *Vseukrainskyi Aktsionernyi Bank v Maksimov* [2013] EWHC 3203 [72]–[83]; *Western Bulk Shipowning III A/S v Carbofer Maritime Trading (The Western Moscow)* [2012] 2 Lloyds Rep 163 [110]–[113].

[121] *BNP Paribas v Russian Machines* [2012] 1 Lloyds Rep 61 [49], relying on *AES Ust-Kamenogorsk Hydropower Plant LLP v Ust-Kamenogorsk Hydropower Plant JSC* [2012] 1 WLR 920 (CA), where the reasoning in *Vale do Rio* was not followed in various other respects. The point was considered to be 'not straightforward' on appeal from Blair J in *Joint Stock Asset Management Company Ingosstrakh-Investments v BNP Paribas* [2012] 1 Lloyds Rep 649 (CA) [79], [88].

[122] *Shipowners' Mutual Protection & Indemnity Association (Luxembourg) v Containerships Denizcilik Nakliyat ve Tikaret (The Yusuf Cepnioglu)* [2015] 1 Lloyds Rep 567 [48]–[61].

[123] *Starlight Shipping v Tai Ping Insurance (The Alexandros T)* [2008] 1 Lloyds Rep 230 [36]–[42].

There is room to doubt whether *The Alexandros T* is correct, even if *Cruz City* is right. First, **18.83** the law accepts that such 'inconsistent claims' injunctions are in principle legitimate injunctions akin to quasi-contractual injunctions,[124] and it would be strange not to have a jurisdictional basis for them. Second, the cases following *Vale do Rio* and *Cruz City* concern distinct situations, for example whether a third-party *Chabra* defendant with nothing to do with the arbitration can be brought within the jurisdiction, as in *Cruz City*. In none of them was there an argument that the defendant could not deny that he was bound by the clause. Third, in *The Yusuf Cepnioglu* Teare J was willing to extend the boundaries of CPR 62.5(1)(c), and to treat the third party in a quasi-contractual case as in effect party to the arbitration clause for jurisdictional purposes.[125] But that quasi-contractual argument is analogous to the logic of the 'inconsistent claims' situation, and it could be argued that 'inconsistent claims' should also be distinguished from *Cruz City*. Fourth, in *BNP Paribas* Blair J saw force in the contention that CPR 62.5(1)(c) could in principle apply broadly as against non-parties.[126] It is submitted the better view is that in a quasi-contractual 'inconsistent claims' situation the injunction defendant should be treated as party to the arbitration agreement for the purpose of CPR 62.5(1)(c), if necessary, or that in any event the injunction against him should be viewed as 'affecting' the arbitration agreement. This is, however, subject to how the central case law on CPR 62.5(1)(c) and PD 6B para 3.1(6)(c) continues to evolve. In any event, the case for applying CPR 62.5(1)(c) will be even stronger where, although the claimant denies there is a contract, the defendant itself alleges that its claims are contractual.[127]

Furthermore, on the current case law, CPR 62.5 is not the exclusive route for service out of **18.84** the jurisdiction of 'arbitration claims', and consequently final anti-suit injunctions to enforce arbitration clauses can also be served out of the jurisdiction under any heads of PD 6B para 3.1 that are available.[128] This has important consequences in respect of third parties. The available heads will include PD 6B para 3.1(6)(c), permitting service out in respect of a contract governed by English law, as an arbitration clause providing for arbitration in England will be such a contract, although the breadth of that head is subject to debate.[129] In addition, in *Joint Stock v BNP Paribas* it was held that PD 6B para 3.1(3) was capable of justifying service out of a vexation-based anti-suit injunction against a defendant who was not party to the arbitration clause, but who was said to be acting in concert with the party subject to the arbitration clause in order to procure determination of the matters submitted to arbitration before the Russian courts, in an allegedly vexatious manner.[130]

---

[124] *Dell Emerging Markets (EMEA) v IB Maroc.com SA* [2017] EWHC 2397 [22]–[35], relying on previous authority. The topic is discussed in the round at Ch 10, section F, 'Inconsistent Contractual Claims'.

[125] *Shipowners' Mutual Protection & Indemnity Association (Luxembourg) v Containerships Denizcilik Nakliyat ve Tikaret AS (The Yusuf Cepnioglu)* [2015] 1 Lloyds Rep 567 [48]–[61].

[126] *BNP Paribas v Russian Machines* [2012] 1 Lloyds Rep 61 [46]–[49], albeit that the Court of Appeal saw the point as difficult: [2012] 1 Lloyds Rep 649 (CA) [79], [88].

[127] See *Ace Seguradora v Fair Wind Navigation* [2017] EWHC 3352, [7], [10].

[128] *Shipowners' Mutual Protection & Indemnity Association (Luxembourg) v Containerships Denizcilik Nakliyat ve Tikaret S (The Yusuf Cepnioglu)* [2015] 1 Lloyds Rep 567 [41]–[42], following *Ust-Kamenogorsk Hydropower Plant JSC (Appellant) v AES Ust-Kamenogorsk Hydropower Plant LLP* [2013] 1 WLR 1889 (SC) [51]. See also the Court of Appeal in *Ust-Kamenogorsk* [2012] 1 WLR 920 (CA) [123]–[144], although cf Burton J at [2010] 2 Lloyds Rep 493 [25]. The same conclusion is assumed in *BNP Paribas v Russian Machines* [2012] 1 Lloyds Rep 61 [50]–[66] and *Joint Stock Asset Management Company Ingosstrakh-Investments v BNP Paribas* [2012] 1 Lloyds Rep 649 (CA) [78]–[79].

[129] The extent to which para 3.1(6)(c) can apply to non-contractual claims is discussed elsewhere in this chapter at paras 18.55–18.57.

[130] *BNP Paribas SA v Russian Machines* [2012] 1 Lloyds Rep 61 [50]–[66]; and *Joint Stock Asset Management Company Ingosstrakh-Investments v BNP Paribas* [2012] 1 Lloyds Rep 649 (CA) [69]–[78].

18.85   The use of para 3.1(6)(c) and (d) provides another way of dealing with quasi-contractual situations, including potentially the case of 'inconsistent claims'.[131] And para 3.1(3) creates a broad power to bring in third parties in other cases where the third party is not subject to the arbitration clause, where there is an 'anchor' claim for an injunction against the party subject to the arbitration clause.

18.86   The effect of the current case law is a patchwork, as the results produced by CPR para 3.1 go beyond the boundaries of CPR 62.5 as interpreted in *Cruz City* (at least so far as regards third parties who are not bound by any form of quasi-contractual reasoning), and the logic of *Cruz City*'s restrictive approach to CPR 62.5 has not been reconciled with the broad operation of CPR para 3.1. The whole area would benefit from a comprehensive reconsideration.

18.87   Finally, it appears that where the court has power to serve an arbitration claim form out of the jurisdiction under CPR 62.5, the exercise of its discretion will be governed by similar discretionary considerations as those that apply under CPR 6.36 and 6.37.[132]

J. JURISDICTION AND INTERIM ANTI-SUIT INJUNCTIONS

18.88   This section considers the court's scope of the court's jurisdiction over applications for interim anti-suit injunctions under the common law rules.

18.89   The rules relating to jurisdiction over interim applications and ancillary documents have not been the Rules Committee's finest hour; they have been through various iterations, whose incomplete drafting has caused the courts to engage in some contortions to make the rules work. But the end result appears to be fairly clear and workable.

1. The Ancillary Jurisdiction

18.90   If the court has jurisdiction over the substance under the Brussels–Lugano regime (so long as it remains the law), then ancillary documents, including applications for interim anti-suit injunctions, can be served out of the jurisdiction on parties to the substantive proceedings. This follows as an ancillary jurisdiction derived from the court's primary Brussels–Lugano jurisdiction over the substance.[133] The machinery of service will be provided by CPR 6.33, together with 6.2, and/or by implication from 6.38(1).[134]

18.91   The position is parallel under the common law rules. If the court has jurisdiction over the substance, it will in principle have jurisdiction over ancillary matters, including interim anti-suit injunctions to protect the substantive proceedings.[135]

---

[131] See paras 18.51–18.54.
[132] Sir L Collins et al (eds), *Dicey, Morris & Collins on the Conflict of Laws* (15th edn, Sweet & Maxwell 2012), para 16.046.
[133] Ch 17, paras 17.57–17.62.
[134] Ch 17, para 17.63.
[135] For the ancillary jurisdiction, see *Masri v Consolidated Contractors (No 3)* [2009] QB 503 (CA) [26], [30], [60]–[66], [99] and *Glencore International v Metro International Trading* [2002] CLC 1090 [59]. (See also *Masri v Consolidated Contractors (No 4)* [2010] 1 AC 90, (CA) [30]–[35], although that decision was overturned by the Supreme Court on the specific points in issue in that case). Those cases focus on Brussels–Lugano ancillary jurisdiction but their reasoning is cross-applicable to the common law rules. The same approach to ancillary

This common law ancillary jurisdiction is matched by the court's powers to permit   **18.92**
service out of the jurisdiction. First, if the court has given permission to serve the underlying claim form out of the jurisdiction, there is power to give permission to serve
ancillary documents out of the jurisdiction under CPR 6.37(5)(b)(ii) and CPR 6.38, and
this power includes applications for interim anti-suit injunctions.[136] Second, once proceedings are underway, it should in general be possible to serve applications on the address for service required under CPR 6.23. Third, if permission to serve the claim form
out of the jurisdiction has not yet been granted, it will be possible to serve an interim
anti-suit application out of the jurisdiction under the combination of CPR 6.2(c) and
CPR 6.36, provided the application can be fitted independently within the heads of jurisdiction in PD 6B para 3.1.[137] Fourth, if the injunction respondent is present in the
jurisdiction, he can be served under the domestic rules of service in Part 6. Finally, if
other service machinery is not available for any specific reason, but ancillary jurisdiction exists in principle, it should be possible to use alternative service under CPR 6.15 to
fill any lacuna.

The Hague Convention on the Choice of Court makes clear that it does not confer or   **18.93**
affect interim measures of protection (see Art 7). It is highly likely therefore, that if the
court has substantive jurisdiction under the Hague Convention (but Brussels–Lugano
jurisdiction does not apply), it will also have a parallel ancillary jurisdiction under the
common law, including jurisdiction to grant interim anti-suit injunctions. In any event,
it would not be difficult to fit such jurisdiction within other heads of jurisdiction, as the
interim relief would be protecting a contractual choice of English jurisdiction.

---

jurisdiction has been adopted under the common law rules in *Golden Endurance Shipping v RMA Watanya (The Golden Endurance)* [2015] 1 Lloyds Rep 266 [24]–[29].

[136] *Star Reefers v JFC Group* [2010] EWHC 3003, [28], [2012] 1 Lloyds Rep 376 (CA) [42]; and this is supported by implication by the conclusion in *Masri v Consolidated Contractors (No 4)* [2010] 1 AC 90, [28] with regard to service out of the jurisdiction without permission under 6.38(1) (then CPR 6.30(2)). This was the previous pos-ition under RSC Order 11 rule 9(4) which, it seems, the CPR in substance has been trying to emulate and is now approximating to.
　　Before CPR Part 6 was reformed on 1 October 2008 to introduce CPR 6.37(5)(b)(ii), it was possible that the service machinery was not general in this way and was restricted to applications that could independently be fitted within the heads of PD 6B para 3.1 (see *C v L* [2001] 1 Lloyds Rep 459 [95(1)], and *Vitol v Capri* [2009] Bus LR 271 [9]; although cf *Masri v Consolidated Contractors (No 3)* [2009] QB 503 (CA) [60]–[66], [99], which implies that this is not necessary; it is submitted that the reference to *Vitol v Capri* in *Masri (No 4)* [2010] 1 AC 90 (SC) [28] was not intended to be an adoption of this specific element of *Vitol v Capri*). However, following the introduction of CPR 6.37(5)(b)(ii) in 2008, any such restrictions are clearly no longer the law, and it is clear that the ancillary service power is general. It is no longer necessary to fit applications for interim anti-suit injunctions, applied for in existing proceedings, within particular heads of PD 6B: *Golden Endurance Shipping v RMA Watanya (The Golden Endurance)* [2015] 1 Lloyds Rep 266 [29].
　　There is also a possibility that a power to permit service out of the jurisdiction of ancillary documents can be derived directly from the ancillary jurisdiction when the court has jurisdiction over the substance, without any specific CPR rule. This is arguably the implication of the confirmation of the ancillary jurisdic-tion in *Masri (No 3)*; and in *Star Reefers* (CA), Rix LJ thought this was a possibility at [42]; while in *The Golden Endurance* there was no specific reference to CPR 6.37(5)(b)(ii). See also earlier *Glencore International v Metro International Trading* [2002] CLC 1090, Moore-Bick J at [23] and CA at [60] and *The Eras Eil Actions* [1995] 1 Lloyds Rep 64, 72–74. However, CPR 6.37(5)(b)(ii) would appear to have filled the gap for most practical pur-poses and in most cases.
[137] There is no reason why this would not additionally be possible. See *Glencore International v Metro International Trading* [2002] CLC 1090, Moore Bick J at [22] and CA at [58]; *C v L* [2001] 1 Lloyds Rep 459 [94(1)]; *Vitol v Capri* [2009] Bus LR 271 [9].

2. Jurisdiction under CPR Paragraph 6.36 and PD 6B Paragraph 3.1

18.94   In addition to the ancillary jurisdiction, it should be possible to obtain jurisdiction for interim relief, and serve application notices in existing proceedings out of the jurisdiction, provided that the application can be fitted independently within the heads of jurisdiction in PD 6B para 3.1. But the growing recognition of the ancillary jurisdiction in principle means that this should now generally merely form part of the machinery of service.

3. Jurisdiction by Presence

18.95   If the injunction respondent is present in England, then jurisdiction can be obtained by service on him here.

4. Free-Standing Interim Injunctions

18.96   If an attempt is made to seek a free-standing interim injunction, and assuming this is possible as a matter of basic substantive and procedural law,[138] it should be possible in principle to obtain jurisdiction under CPR 6.36, or 6.36 combined with 6.2(c), provided that the application (whether sought by claim form or application notice) can be fitted independently within the heads of jurisdiction in PD 6B para 3.1.

5. The Ancillary Jurisdiction and Third Parties

18.97   It seems that the common law ancillary jurisdiction, being derived from the court's jurisdiction over the parties to litigation before it, does not, or does not automatically, give jurisdiction over third parties. The logic of *Masri (No 4)* is that no such ancillary jurisdiction towards third parties can be derived from CPR 6.38(1) or CPR 6.37(5)(b)(ii).[139] Thus, jurisdiction over an interim injunction against a third party would seem to require an independent jurisdictional basis. For example, service out of the interim injunction against the third party could be justified if the injunction application against him could in itself be independently fitted within the heads of jurisdiction in CPR PD 6B para 3.1. The necessary and proper party head in PD 6B 3.1(3) may provide a solution in some cases.

6. Interim Relief in Support of Foreign Proceedings: PD 6B Paragraph 3.1(5)

18.98   CPR PD 6B para 3.1(5), provides a specific, and exclusive,[140] jurisdictional head for claims for interim relief in support of proceedings in a foreign court made under section 25(1) of the

---

[138] See Ch 13, paras 13.33–13.35.

[139] *Masri v Consolidated Contractors (No 4)* [2010] 1 AC 90 (SC) [28]–[29], adopting *Vitol v Capri* [2009] Bus LR 271 [9]. See also *Linsen International v Humpuss Sea Transport* [2012] 2 CLC 773 [9].

The new CPR since 1 October 2008 also contains a new CPR 6.39 dealing with service out of the jurisdiction on non-parties. However, this appears to be merely procedural and not intended to create any new general jurisdiction over non-parties.

[140] *Belletti v Morici* [2009] ILPr 57 [43].

Civil Jurisdiction and Judgments Act 1982. If an interim anti-suit injunction can be credibly applied for under section 25(1), then there is no reason why 6B para 3.1(5) should not apply to give jurisdiction. However, as a matter of substantive law, comity is likely to discourage the grant of anti-suit injunctions in support of foreign proceedings.[141] It may be that such applications have to be made by claim form rather than freestanding application notice.[142]

7. Jurisdiction over Interim Injunctions in Support of Arbitration

Interim anti-suit injunctions to enforce arbitration clauses can applied for under section 37(1) of the Senior Courts Act 1981. It used to be thought that interim anti-suit injunctions to enforce arbitration clauses could also be applied for under section 44 of the Arbitration Act 1996. However, the Supreme Court has now held that section 44 does not apply to anti-suit injunctions at all, as such anti-suit injunctions are not sought 'for the purposes of and in relation to arbitral proceedings'.[143] Where such an interim injunction is sought within proceedings for a final injunction, it can be sought by interim application notice in the context of an arbitration claim form seeking a final injunction. But if there is no claim for final relief, such interim applications must be sought within the arbitration claim form, or possibly by a combination of an arbitration claim form seeking the interim relief and a parallel interim application notice.[144]   **18.99**

CPR 62.5(1)(c) gives power to permit service out of the jurisdiction of such an arbitration claim form seeking an interim anti-suit injunction, provided that the seat of the arbitration is or will be in England, or there is a sufficiently close connection with England and Wales for the purposes of Arbitration Act 1996 section 2(4). In addition, in respect of an arbitration clause governed by English law, the arbitration claim form can be served out of the jurisdiction under CPR 6.36 and PD 3.1(6)(c). Other heads of PD 6B para 3.1 may also be appropriate in particular cases, such as PD para 3.1(3) for necessary and proper parties. The scope and limits of CPR 62.5 and PD 6B para 3.1 with regard to injunctions, for example with respect to third parties, are discussed earlier in this chapter.   **18.100**

If service out of the jurisdiction of the arbitration claim form has not yet been permitted, then by virtue of CPR 6.2(c) the same heads of jurisdiction under CPR 6.36 and PD 3B para 3.1 can apply to justify service of an application notice for an interim injunction in support of the arbitration, if and to the extent they are applicable to the relief sought, as discussed above.   **18.101**

Further, if permission to serve an arbitration clause form out of the jurisdiction seeking a final (or interim) anti-suit injunction in support of arbitration has been obtained, then it would seem that an application notice for an injunction seeking an interim anti-suit injunction paralleling the final injunction sought, or more generally in the context of the claim for a final injunction, can be served out of the jurisdiction as an application notice within the existing action, under CPR 6.37(5)(2)(b)(ii).   **18.102**

---

[141] See *Airbus Industrie GIE v Patel* [1999] 1 AC 119 (HL). This issue is analysed at Ch 4, para 4.83 and Ch 7, section G, 'Injunctions in Support of a Foreign Forum'.

[142] See Ch 13, para 13.33.

[143] *Ust-Kamenogorsk Hydropower Plant JSC (Appellant) v AES Ust-Kamenogorsk Hydropower Plant LLP* [2013] 1 WLR 1889 (SC) [48] and Ch 13, paras 13.10–13.16.

[144] See Ch 13, paras 13.31–13.32.

19

*Singapore Law**

A. INTRODUCTION

Singapore law has a close relationship with English law that persists today.[1] **19.01**

The Singapore law on anti-suit injunctions follows the broad contours of English law[2] **19.02** and the jurisprudence of the Privy Council, with both the Singapore High Court and the Singapore Court of Appeal contributing to its development. There has been a steady stream of claims and applications for such injunctions since the Singapore courts first had the occasion to consider the question in 1993.[3]

We consider the case law as it has developed in Singapore below. References to the High **19.03** Court and to the Court of Appeal are to the Singapore courts. We do not seek to capture every aspect of Singapore law on anti-suit injunctions, for which reference can be made to other works on Singapore law, but only to those issues specific to anti-suit injunctions.[4]

---

[*] Co-authored with Belinda McRae

[1] English law was generally understood to have been imported into Singapore (and the other Strait Settlements) by way of the Second Charter of Justice on 27 November 1826. After independence, the application of English law in Singapore was clarified and codified in the Application of English Law Act (Cap 7A, 1994 Rev Ed). This Act provided that the English common law would continue to be part of the law of Singapore, to the extent that it was already part of it before the date of enactment: see s 3(1). Decisions of the English courts are often cited and relied upon by their Singaporean counterparts. Chief Justice Sundaresh Menon has described the relationship between Singaporean and English law as 'umbilical': 'The Somewhat Uncommon Law of Commerce' (2014) 26 SAcLJ 23, [9].

[2] With the obvious exception of European jurisdictional law, so long as and to the extent that this remains part of English law in the light of Brexit.

[3] See *Bank of America National Trust and Savings Association v Djoni Widjaja* [1994] 2 SLR(R) 898, which was the first reported application for an anti-suit injunction. It was an appeal from an application heard on 23 June 1993 before Kan Ting Chiu JC. There has been a marked increase in reported cases concerning anti-suit injunctions in recent years.

[4] In addition, this work has not sought to analyse Singapore law on the Singapore court's supervision of arbitrations with a seat in Singapore.

B. SOURCES AND POWERS

19.04   Leaving aside the context of injunctions to protect arbitration, permanent and interim anti-suit injunctions are granted in Singapore under the broad powers conferred on the High Court by section 18(2) and para 14 of Schedule 1 of the Supreme Court of Judicature Act (Cap 322, 2007 Rev Ed) (the 'SCJA') to grant 'all reliefs and remedies at law and in equity', and section 4(10) of the Civil Law Act (Cap 43, 1999 Rev Ed) (the 'CLA').[5] The best view seems to be that permanent anti-suit injunctions are granted under para 14 of Schedule 1 SJCA; and interim anti-suit injunctions are granted under section 4(10) CLA. These powers are not qualified by the Hague Convention on the Choice of Court (see section H, 'The Hague Convention on the Choice of Court').

19.05   The powers in section 210(10) of the Singapore Companies Act (Cap 50, 2006 Rev Ed) to restrain court proceedings during consideration of schemes of arrangement are territorially confined and do not give a power to restrain foreign proceedings abroad.[6] However, in 2017, new powers were introduced in section 211B–C of the Act, enabling the Singapore courts to impose a 'moratorium' during considerations of schemes of arrangement or compromises with creditors. These powers in effect amount to a power to grant anti-suit injunctions, as the High Court recognized in *IM Skaugen*.[7] They are not territorially limited in the same way as section 210(10), and permit the restraint of specified court or arbitration

---

[5] *R1 International v Lonstroff AG* [2014] 3 SLR 166 [40]–[43]; *BC Andaman v Xie Ning Yun* [2017] SGHC 64 [53], making the comment that para 14 Sch 1 of the SCJA combined with s 4(10) CLA 'broadly mirror' s 37 of the English Senior Courts Act 1981; *Hilton International Manage (Maldives) v Sun Travels & Tours* [2018] SGHC 56 [38]–[43]; see also *Swift-Fortune v Magnifica Marine* [2007] 1 SLR(R) 629 [64].

Section 18(2) of the SCJA provides that the High Court shall have the powers set out in Sch 1 to the Act. Paragraph 14 of Sch 1 of the SCJA provides as follows: 'Power to grant all reliefs and remedies at law and in equity, including damages in addition to, or in substitution for, an injunction or specific performance.' At points in this chapter, we shall refer merely to para 14 of Sch 1 for brevity; and s 18(2) should be taken as read. Section 4(10) CLA reads as follows:

> A Mandatory Order or an injunction may be granted or a receiver appointed by an interlocutory order of the court, either unconditionally or upon such terms and conditions as the court thinks just, in all cases in which it appears to the court to be just or convenient that such order should be made.

The Singapore International Commercial Court is taken to have the same powers as the High Court, with certain exceptions that are not relevant here: see Supreme Court of Judicature Act, s 18I(1).

In *R1 International v Lonstroff* [2014] 3 SLR 166 [40]–[44], Judith Prakash J thought that s 4(10) CLA would suffice for permanent injunctions. Her decision was appealed, but the arguments in the appeal did not focus on the powers of the court: *R1 International v Lonstroff* [2015] SLR 521 [2]. This particular strand of reasoning in her decision is unsound, as s 4(10) CLA pertains only to interlocutory orders: see *Swift-Fortune v Magnifica Marine* [2007] 1 SLR(R) 629 [64]. This was subsequently made clear in *Hilton International Manage (Maldives) v Sun Travels & Tours* [2018] SGHC 56 [38]–[43], where Belinda Ang Saw Ean J disagreed with this aspect of *R1 International*, concluding that s 4(10) CLA was not the basis for the power to grant permanent anti-suit injunctions, which were instead granted under para 14 of Sch 1. Her decision was overturned on appeal in *Sun Travel & Tours v Hilton International Manage (Maldives)* [2019] SGCA 10, but on other grounds. On the question of statutory basis (which does not appear to have been debated on appeal), the Court of Appeal at [42] referred to Belinda Ang Saw Ean J's reasoning without disapproval, although without specific approval either.

The restricted effect of s 4(10) CLA creates no difficulty, as the broad words of para 14 of Sch 1, as incorporated by s 18(2) SJCA, can clearly support final injunctions.

[6] *Pacific Andes Resources Development* [2016] SGHC 210 [16]–[21]. This parallels the position under the corresponding English and New Zealand statutes: see Ch 3, para 3.06 n 26; Ch 20, paras 20.13–20.15.

[7] *Re IM Skaugen* [2018] SGHC 259 [39].

proceedings abroad, provided that the respondent is in Singapore or within the territorial jurisdiction of the Singapore courts.[8]

Although the power to grant anti-suit injunctions is exercised under statute, it is, like that of its English counterparts, based upon equity, both historically and in terms of the nature of the principles engaged.[9]   **19.06**

With one exception, it does not appear to have been suggested that the power derives from the High Court's inherent jurisdiction to protect its own processes.[10]   **19.07**

The one exception is *Pacific Andes*, where an injunction was sought to restrain proceedings abroad in order to protect a Singapore scheme of arrangement. Kannan Ramesh JC concluded that no such injunction should be granted. In the course of doing so he discussed the accepted category of injunctions to protect Singapore liquidation or administration proceedings by restraining foreign proceedings, which he described as based on the inherent jurisdiction. However, in the context of the issues he had to describe, the 'inherent jurisdiction' did not need to mean anything more than the High Court's basic general power in equity and under para 14 of Schedule 1 SCJA and section 4(10) CLA to grant such injunctions. He needed only to contrast the court's basic powers with the specific power in section 210(10) of the Companies Act, which he held could not apply. He was not considering, and it seems there had been no submissions made to him about, the difference between that basic jurisdiction and the 'inherent jurisdiction' properly so called. Indeed, his key reasoning was that such injunctions were grounded in equity. It is submitted, therefore, that *Pacific Andes* is not clear authority to ground anti-suit injunctions in the inherent jurisdiction properly so called. In any event, it is unnecessary, and simplest not to do so, as the powers in equity and under statute are sufficient.[11]   **19.08**

1. Injunctions in Existing Proceedings

An interim anti-suit injunction, sought on a non-contractual alternative forum basis to protect existing proceedings, may be sought by an application in existing proceedings without a fresh claim for final anti-suit relief.[12]   **19.09**

---

[8] *Re IM Skaugen* [2018] SGHC 259 [39], [85]–[87] explaining and relying on s 221(B)(5)(b). Sub-section 221(C)(5)(b) is to the same effect in relation to s 221(C).

[9] *Sun Travel & Tours v Hilton International Manage (Maldives)* [2019] SGCA 10 [64], [105]–[106], [113]. See previously *Regalindo Resources v Seatrek Trans* [2008] 3 SLR(R) 930 [30]; *Evergreen International v Volkswagen Group Singapore* [2004] 2 SLR(R) 457 [15], [41]; *BC Andaman v Xie Ning Yun* [2017] SGHC 64 [52]–[53]. Thus, equitable doctrines like 'unclean hands' apply: *Beckkett v Deutsche Bank* [2011] 1 SLR 524 [38]; *Lakshmi Anil Salgaocar v Jhaveri Darsan Jitendra* [2018] SGHC 90 [68]–[70].

[10] The Singapore courts have an inherent jurisdiction to prevent an abuse of their own processes: see *Lai Shit Har v Lau Yu Man* [2008] 4 SLR (R) 348 [22]; this is a jurisdiction that could be deployed to support anti-suit injunctions if necessary (as occurs in Australia: see *CSR v Cigna Insurance Australia* (1997) 189 CLR 345 (HCA). Thus, in *Beckkett v Deutsche Bank* [2011] 2 SLR 96 [19]–[20], the Singapore court referred to its power to restrain by injunction foreign proceedings which were an abuse of process due to their impact on local litigation. The application of the court's inherent jurisdiction has been engaged in the context of stays of proceedings (see eg *Roberto Building Material v Oversea-Chinese Banking* [2003] 2 SLR (R) 353 [15]–[17]; *Chan Chin Cheung v Chan Fatt Cheung* [2010] 1 SLR 1192 [47]).

[11] *Pacific Andes Resources Development* [2016] SGHC 210 [22]–[29]. Specific statutory provision has now been made in the field of insolvency in s 211B–211C of the Companies Act, discussed at para 19.05.

[12] *PT Sandipala Arthaputra v STMicroelectronics Asia Pacific* [2015] 5 SLR 873 [45]–[56], relying on the English approach. The court suggested that there might be a more compelling argument that if a contractual injunction was sought, originating process would be necessary: at [57].

2. Injunctions in Support of Arbitration

19.10   Permanent anti-suit injunctions in support of arbitrations with a seat in Singapore are granted under section 18(2) and para 14 of Schedule 1 of the SCJA, and not under section 12(A) of the International Arbitration Act (Cap 143A, 2002 Rev Ed) (the 'IAA').[13]

19.11   On the current case law, interim anti-suit injunctions in support of arbitrations with a seat in Singapore may be granted under section 12(A) IAA.[14]

19.12   There is as yet no clear decision on whether in cases of interim anti-suit injunctions to support arbitration, section 12(A) is exhaustive of the court's powers and can be used exclusively. But the wider case law, including that dealing with the previous provision, suggests that section 12(A) is exhaustive of the court's powers to grant interim injunctions in support of arbitration in general.[15] If so, and if this means that section 4(10) CLA cannot be used to ground interim anti-suit injunctions in support of arbitration independent of section 12(a), this creates a problem. Anti-suit injunctions are not well suited to the constraints of section 12(A), which imposes unnecessary restrictions, such as a need for urgency, or the consent of the Tribunal, or proof that the Tribunal is unable to act effectively.

19.13   In English law, this problem has been dealt with by the conclusion of the Supreme Court in *Ust-Kamenogorsk* that anti-suit injunctions in support of arbitration fall outside the corresponding section 44 of the English Arbitration Act 1996 altogether and so are instead governed by section 37(1) of the English Senior Courts Act 1981. The Supreme Court's logic was that an anti-suit injunction was not 'for the purposes of' or 'in relation to' arbitration proceedings, but instead sought to enforce the negative obligation in the arbitration agreement not to litigate.[16] This logic, if accepted in Singapore, would suggest that section 4(10) CLA should be the relevant statutory basis for interim injunctions in support of arbitration, and that section 12(A) IAA should not cover anti-suit injunctions at all. However, this approach has not yet been taken in the Singapore case law, which regards section 12(A) as applicable at least to interim anti-suit injunctions in support of arbitration[17] and so it seems, by implication, exhaustive in that regard.

---

[13] *Hilton International Manage (Maldives) v Sun Travels & Tours* [2018] SGHC 56 [39]–[43] (her decision was overturned on other grounds, but not on this point, in *Sun Travel & Tours v Hilton International Manage (Maldives)* [2019] SGCA 10, where this aspect of her decision was referred to without disapproval at [42]); *R1 International v Lonstroff* [2014] 3 SLR 166 [40]–[43]. In *R1 International*, Judith Prakash J had held, it is submitted incorrectly, that the court's power to issue permanent anti-suit injunctions in support of arbitration was found in s 4(10) of the CLA. Belinda Ang Saw Ean J disagreed with this view in *Hilton* (at [42]), holding correctly that s 4(10) applies only to interim injunctions and that the basis for permanent injunctions in support of arbitration was s 18(2) SJCA and para 14 of Sch 1: see para 19.04 above. However, Judith Prakash J's conclusion in *R1 International* that s 12(A) of the IAA was not a basis for permanent injunctions in support of arbitration is, with respect, clearly right and was adopted by Belinda Ang Saw Ean J in *Hilton International*.

[14] *Maldives Airports v GMR Male International Airport* [2013] 2 SLR 449 [33]–[43]; *R1 International v Lonstroff* [2014] 3 SLR 166 [43], [54]. In this respect, as matters stand, the position is different to English law following *AES Ust-Kamenogorsk Hydropower Plant LLP v Ust-Kamenogorsk Hydropower Plant JSC* [2013] 1 WLR 1889, where it was held that s 44 of the English Arbitration Act 1996 did not cover anti-suit injunctions to support arbitrations. See further paras 19.13–19.14 and Ch 13, paras 13.10–13.15.

[15] *Maldives Airports v GMR Male International Airport* [2013] 2 SLR 449 [33], and in relation to the previous provisions of s 12(7), deleted with effect from 1 October 2010 in favour of the new s 12A, *Swift-Fortune v Magnifica Marine* [2007] 1 SLR(R) 629 [37], [96].

[16] *AES Ust-Kamenogorsk Hydropower Plant LLP v Ust-Kamenogorsk Hydropower Plant JSC* [2013] 1 WLR 1889 (SC) [43]–[48], and Ch 13, paras 13.10–13.15.

[17] *Hilton International Manage (Maldives) v Sun Travels & Tours* [2018] SGHC 56 [39]–[43] (overturned, but not on this point, *Sun Travel & Tours v Hilton International Manage (Maldives)* [2019] SGCA 10); compare *Maldives*

If the Singapore case law continues to house anti-suit injunctions in support of arbi-   **19.14**
tration under section 12(A), then it seems likely that the Singapore courts will interpret
the conditions of section 12(A) flexibly for anti-suit injunctions.[18] Thus, the right to rely
on an arbitration clause has been interpreted as an 'asset', enabling an injunction to be
granted under section 12(A) in cases of urgency without the consent of the other party
(see s 12(A)(4)).[19] The English case law has, where necessary, interpreted the requirement
of 'urgency' in section 12(A)(4) flexibly to permit the grant of anti-suit injunctions where
required: urgency is constituted by the need to prevent the foreign proceedings going further. [20] Similarly, it seems likely that the Singapore courts will interpret the requirement
in section 12(A)(6) that the Tribunal must be unable to act effectively to permit anti-suit
inunctions in most cases, on the basis that the court's coercive powers of enforcement are
required.[21] Certainly, there is no sign in the case law of any hesitation in granting interim
anti-suit injunctions in support of arbitration, as we discuss under section E, 'Contractual
Injunctions' below.

The power under section 12(A) of the IAA also (on the current case law) confers a power   **19.15**
to grant an interim anti-suit injunction to protect an arbitration with a foreign seat,[22] and
the powers under para 14 of Sch 1 of the SCJA also probably include a power to grant a permanent anti-suit injunction to protect an arbitration with a foreign seat.[23] The question of
whether and if so when it is sound in principle to do so is a separate matter, and discussed at
section F, 'Arbitration' below.

The power to grant anti-suit injunctions in support of arbitration is not precluded by Article   **19.16**
5 of UNCITRAL Model Law on arbitration, which is in force in Singapore pursuant to
section 3 IAA. Article 5 is intended to prevent unnecessary court intervention in the arbitral process and does not apply to anti-suit injunctions.[24]

C. THE TESTS

The analytical framework for the High Court's determination of an anti-suit injunction   **19.17**
application has been derived principally from the English and Privy Council authorities.

Airports v GMR Male International Airport [2013] 2 SLR 449 [33]–[43]; *R1 International v Lonstroff* [2014] 3 SLR
166 [43], [54].

---

[18] See the flexible interpretation of the parallel conditions of s 44 of the English 1996 Act, discussed at Ch 13,
para 13.15.
[19] *Maldives Airports v GMR Male International Airport* [2013] 2 SLR 449 [33]–[43].
[20] See Ch 13, para 13.15.
[21] *NCC International v Alliance Concrete Singapore* [2008] 2 SLR(R) 565 [41]. For the English cases see Ch 13,
para 13.15 and inter alia recently *Southport Success v Tsingshan Holding Group (The Anna Bo)* [2015] 2 Lloyds Rep
578 [27]–[28].
[22] *R1 International v Lonstroff* [2014] 3 SLR 166 [52]–[53]. The new s 12(A) IAA, in force from 1 October 2010,
was deliberately expanded to cover arbitrations in this respect. The previous authorities on s 12 IAA, holding
that it does not apply to foreign arbitrations, are no longer the law: cf *Swift-Fortune v Magnifica Marine* [2007] 1
SLR(R) 629.
[23] *R1 International v Lonstroff* [2014] 3 SLR 166, [54], although Judith Prakash J did not reach a decision on the
point. Judith Prakash J referred only to s 4(10) CLA. However, as discussed at para 19.04 and n 5 above, para 14 of
Sch 1 SJCA is the better source for permanent injunctions, and this would apply to injunctions to support foreign
proceedings as well, by parity of reasoning.
[24] *Hilton International Manage (Maldives) v Sun Travels & Tours* [2018] SGHC 56 [54]–[57].

19.18   When the Court of Appeal came to consider the tests for anti-suit injunctions under Singapore law for the first time in *Widjaya* (an undefended appeal), it described the law governing anti-suit injunctions as 'well-settled' on the basis of those authorities.[25]

19.19   The Court of Appeal in *Widjaya* recited four enumerated principles set out in Lord Goff's speech in the Privy Council's decision in *Aérospatiale* (an appeal from Brunei), namely:[26]

  (i) an anti-suit injunction should be issued only when the 'ends of justice' require it;
  (ii) an anti-suit injunction is directed against the party bringing or threatening to bring foreign proceedings, not the foreign court;
  (iii) the defendant must be amenable to the court's jurisdiction; and
  (iv) the jurisdiction must be exercised with caution,[27] in the light of the indirect impact of an anti-suit injunction on the foreign court.

These propositions have been repeatedly restated in the subsequent Singapore case law. They were recently re-iterated by the Court of Appeal in *Sun Travel v Hilton International*,[28] together with the further propositions in *Kirkham v Trane*, to which we turn in para 19.21.

19.20   The Court of Appeal in *Widjaya* also adopted *Aérospatiale* generally, and in particular the key passages of *Aérospatiale* in which we see the following propositions (numbering added):

  (v) 'as a general rule the ... court must conclude that it provides the natural forum for the trial of the action' but
  (vi) an injunction would not be granted on the basis solely that the foreign court was viewed as not the natural forum;[29]
  (vii) in alternative forum cases, 'the court will, generally speaking, only restrain the plaintiff from pursuing proceedings in the foreign court if such pursuit would be vexatious and oppressive';
  (viii) 'since the court is concerned with the ends of justice, that account must be taken not only of injustice to the defendant if the plaintiff is allowed to pursue the foreign proceedings,

---

[25] *Bank of America National Trust and Savings Association v Djoni Widjaja* [1994] 2 SLR(R) 898 [10]; and see also recently *Sun Travel & Tours v Hilton International Manage (Maldives)* [2019] SGCA 10 [65].

[26] *Bank of America National Trust and Savings Association v Djoni Widjaja* [1994] 2 SLR(R) 898 [11]. See *Société Nationale Industrielle Aérospatiale v Lee Kui Jak* [1987] AC 871 (PC) 892. Those four enumerated principles have since been applied or approved by the Singaporean courts on numerous occasions: see *Kischinchand Tiloomal Bhojwani v Sunil Kishinchand Bhojwani* [1996] 1 SLR(R) 861 [9]; *Koh Kay Yew v Inno-Pacific Holdings* [1997] 2 SLR(R) 148 [13]; *Evergreen International v Volkswagen Group Singapore* [2004] 2 SLR(R) 457 [15]; *Regalindo Resources v Seatrek Trans* [2008] 3 SLR(R) 930 [12]; *VH v VI* [2008] 1 SLR(R) 742 [37]–[38]; *Kirkham v Trane US* [2009] 4 SLR(R) 428 [24]–[25]; *Relfo Ltd (in liquidation) v Bhimji Velji Jadva Varsani* [2009] 4 SLR(R) 351 [10]; *BC Andaman Co v Xie Ning Yun* [2017] SGHC 64 [54]; *Sun Travel & Tours v Hilton International Manage (Maldives)* [2019] SGCA 10 [65].

[27] See the discussion at para 19.47 below as to whether the Singapore courts have adopted a higher threshold than 'caution'.

[28] *Sun Travel & Tours v Hilton International Manage (Maldives)* [2019] SGCA 10 [65].

[29] A point also specifically picked up on in a number of other cases such as *Kirkham v Trane US* [2009] 4 SLR(R) 428 [45], [48]; *UBS v Telesto Investments* [2011] 4 SLR 503 [106], [119(b)], [134]–[135]; *Hong Hin Kay Albert v AAHG* [2014] SGHC 206 [48]–[49].

but also of injustice to the plaintiff if he is not allowed to do so. So the court will not grant an injunction if, by doing so, it will deprive the plaintiff of advantages in the foreign forum of which it would be unjust to deprive him.'[30]

For a conventional alternative forum case like that before it, and leaving to one side quali- **19.21** fications which are principally relevant in less typical cases, those propositions led the Court of Appeal in *Widjaya* to focus for the heart of its analysis on the logic that 'If it is the case that the court in Singapore is the natural forum for the determination of the dispute, an injunction should only be granted if the pursuit of [foreign] proceedings ... would be vexatious or oppressive and, in this connection, account must be taken of any injustice [to either party].'[31] But it would be wrong to regard this as a statement of rigid necessary conditions. Instead, as Andrew Ang J said in *Regalindo*, 'it is well settled that the court's jurisdiction to restrain foreign proceedings is exercised on the basis of the "ends of justice" and that there are several distinct and discrete grounds on which the court could grant an anti-suit injunction'.[32] This is also the approach since adopted by the Court of Appeal in *Kirkham v Trane*.[33]

The Singapore case law also makes repeatedly clear (just as Lord Goff did in *Aérospatiale* **19.22** and later in *Airbus v Patel*[34]) that (ix) international comity is a central consideration, and that if an injunction is in tension with comity, this may lead to be being refused.[35]

While the subsequent Singapore cases[36] have not always articulated propositions (v)–(ix) **19.23** above in a convenient list of standard principles, they represent Singapore law; the Singapore courts have not intended to do anything different than adopt the essence of Lord Goff's approach in *Aérospatiale*. In many subsequent cases the Singapore courts have referred directly to *Aérospatiale*,[37] or to English textbook summaries of English law.[38] Recently, they have also adopted the law as set out in the Privy Council's decision in *Shell v Krys* (an appeal from the British Virgin Islands), which itself applies English law principles as representative of the general common law in this internationally minded field.[39]

---

[30] *Bank of America National Trust and Savings Association v Djoni Widjaja* [1994] 2 SLR(R) 898 [14]–[15].

[31] *Bank of America National Trust and Savings Association v Djoni Widjaja* [1994] 2 SLR(R) 898 [15].

[32] *Regalindo Resources v Seatrek Trans* [2008] 3 SLR(R) 930 [11].

[33] *Kirkham v Trane US* [2009] 4 SLR(R) 428 [27]–[28]; and see also *VH v VI* [2008] 1 SLR(R) 742 [40]; *Evergreen International v Volkswagen Group Singapore* [2004] 2 SLR(R) 457 [16] (regarding vexation as merely one example of where an injunction may be granted); *Grover v SetClear* [2012] 2 SLR 625 [37]; and the other cases following *Kirkham*, collected at n 42 below. There is further discussion at paras 19.25–19.34 below.

[34] *Airbus Industrie v Patel* [1999] 1 AC 119, 133H, 140A–B.

[35] *Evergreen International SA v Volkswagen Group Singapore* [2004] 2 SLR(R) 457 [32]; *Kirkham v Trane US* [2009] 4 SLR(R) 428 [29], [45]; *Beckkett v Deutsche Bank* [2011] 1 SLR 524 [43]–[46]; *Beckkett v Deutsche Bank* [2011] 2 SLR 96 [24]; *Morgan Stanley Asia (Singapore) v Hong Leong Finance* [2013] 3 SLR 409 [33], [35]; *Grover v SetClear* [2012] 2 SLR 625 [37]; *BC Andaman v Xie Ning Yun* [2017] SGHC 64, [55]; *Sun Travel & Tours v Hilton International Manage (Maldives)* [2019] SGCA 10 [69], [74]–[75], [77]–[78], [80]–[81], [114(a)].

[36] Including those cited in nn 26 and 37.

[37] *Regalindo Resources v Seatrek Trans* [2008] 3 SLR(R) 930 [11]; *R1 International v Lonstroff* [2014] 3 SLR 166 [48]; *Evergreen International v Volkswagen Group Singapore* [2004] 2 SLR(R) 457 [26]; *VH v VI* [2008] 1 SLR(R) 742 [37]; *Sun Travel & Tours v Hilton International Manage (Maldives)* [2019] SGCA 10 [65].

[38] See eg *BC Andaman v Xie Ning Yun* [2017] SGHC 64 [55]; *Lakshmi Anil Salgaocar v Jhaveri Darsan Jitendra* [2018] SGHC 90 [15].

[39] *Pacific Andes Resources Development* [2016] SGHC 210, applying *Stichting Shell Pensionenfonds v Krys* [2015] AC 616 (PC).

19.24   Since, like any injunction, the anti-suit is a discretionary equitable remedy,[40] it can be re-fused in the court's discretion, which will be influenced by factors such as 'unclean hands' and delay. This discretion can, however, be viewed as encapsulated within the test of 'ends of justice'.[41]

19.25   In the more recent cases, the Singapore courts have also identified the following factors,[42] to be considered in the round,[43] as relevant in assessing whether it serves the ends of justice—or is in 'the interests of justice'[44]—to grant the injunction. These can be called the *Kirkham* list of factors, following the case of that name:

> (a) whether the defendant is amenable to the jurisdiction of the Singapore court;
>
> (b) whether Singapore is the natural forum for the resolution of the dispute between the parties;
>
> (c) whether the foreign proceedings are vexatious or oppressive to the plaintiff if they are allowed to continue;
>
> (d) whether an anti-suit injunction would cause any injustice to the defendant by depriving the defendant of legitimate juridical advantages sought in the foreign proceedings; and
>
> (e) whether the commencement of the foreign proceedings is in breach of any agreement between the parties.

19.26   In the recent Court of Appeal decision in *Sun Travel v Hilton International*, these *Kirkham* factors were recited after the *Widjaya* conditions.[45]

19.27   It will be seen that *Kirkham* factors (a)–(d) are consistent with, and indeed flow out of the principles already identified above from Lord Goff's judgment in *Aérospatiale*, while the relevance of factor (e), in contractual cases, is entirely consistent with *Aérospatiale*. The phrasing of them being *factors* as opposed to *conditions* has the advantage of making clear that Lord Goff's principles set out at (v)–(vii) in para 19.20 have not been calcified into supposed necessary conditions, when that is not how they were intended. They are factors that need to be considered 'in the round'.[46]

19.28   The above *Widjaya* and *Kirkham* sets of principles essentially follow the 'ends of justice/ vexation or oppression' approach adopted by Lord Goff in *Aérospatiale*, rather than the

---

[40] *Sun Travel & Tours v Hilton International Manage (Maldives)* [2019] SGCA 10 [106].

[41] *Lakshmi Anil Salgaocar v Jhaveri Darsan Jitendra* [2018] SGHC 90 [70].

[42] *Evergreen International v Volkswagen Group Singapore* [2004] 2 SLR(R) 457 [15]–[16]; *Kirkham v Trane US* [2009] 4 SLR(R) 428 [28]–[29] (adopting and expanding *Evergreen*); *UBS AG v Telesto Investments* [2011] 4 SLR 503, 541 [108]; *Grover v SetClear* [2012] 2 SLR 625 [37]; *Morgan Stanley Asia (Singapore) v Hong Leong Finance* [2013] 3 SLR 409 [26]–[27]; *Hong Hin Kay Albert v AAHG* [2014] SGHC 206 [29]; *AQN v AQO* [2015] 2 SLR 523 [16]; *PT Sandipala Arthaputra v STMicroelectronics Asia Pacific* [2015] 5 SLR 873 [72]; *BC Andaman v Xie Ning Yun* [2017] SGHC 64 [56]; *Lakshmi Anil Salgaocar v Jhaveri Darsan Jitendra* [2018] SGHC 90 [17].

[43] *Morgan Stanley Asia (Singapore) v Hong Leong Finance* [2013] 3 SLR 409 [26]; *PT Sandipala Arthaputra v STMicroelectronics Asia Pacific* [2015] 5 SLR 873 [115]; *BC Andaman v Xie Ning Yun* [2017] SGHC 64 [56].

[44] Both phraseologies are used in England: see Ch 4, sections A, 'The General Principles', F, 'Vexatious or Oppressive Conduct', and G, 'Unconscionable Conduct'; and 'the interests of justice' has also been used in Singapore: see *AQN v AQO* [2015] 2 SLR 523 [25]–[26], adopting the relevant passage in the first edition of this work.

[45] *Sun Travel & Tours v Hilton International Manage (Maldives)* [2019] SGCA 10.

[46] *Sun Travel & Tours v Hilton International Manage (Maldives)* [2019] SGCA 10 [66]–[67].

'unconscionability' phrasing sometimes used in the English case law, which is derived from Lord Hobhouse's language.[47] The language of unconscionability has also been used in the Singapore case law from time to time, [48] and could therefore, be used as an alternative touchstone, in place of vexation and oppression, within the overall framework of the ends of justice.

The Singapore Court of Appeal has not needed to resolve the difference between those two approaches; but in the one case where the conflict between the two ways of framing the test has been squarely confronted, Choo Han Teck J (adopting the analysis in the first edition of this work[49]) concluded that Lord Goff's approach is to be preferred.[50]   **19.29**

Importantly, the *Widjaya* and *Kirkham* summaries addressed above do not as yet distinctly address the established availability of non-contractual anti-suit injunctions on grounds independent of vexation and oppression, although within the overall requirement of 'the ends of justice' (or the 'interests of justice'). While vexation or oppression is the principal intermediate basis used within and under 'the ends of justice', and encapsulates most of the Singapore case law, there are other available bases at the same conceptual level that have been acknowledged in the Singapore case law,[51] which has followed the English case law in this regard.   **19.30**

Thus, (a) independent of vexation or oppression, an injunction can be granted where this is necessary to protect the processes, jurisdiction and judgments of the Singapore court;[52] (b) injunctions have been granted where the foreign litigation amounts to an abuse of process;[53] (c) injunctions may also be granted to protect the injunction claimant's legal or equitable rights, even outside the simple case of contractual jurisdiction clauses.[54] Further, (d) there is some limited support in the case law for the proposition that injunctions may be granted to give effect to Singapore public policy.[55]   **19.31**

---

[47] See Ch 4, sections F, 'Vexatious or Oppressive Conduct' and G, 'Unconscionable Conduct'.

[48] *BC Andaman v Xie Ning Yun* [2017] SGHC 64 [53]; *Beckkett v Deutsche Bank AG* [2011] 2 SLR 96 [19] (relying on *Turner v Grovit* [2002] 1 WLR 107 (HL) 117); *Evergreen International v Volkswagen Group Singapore* [2004] 2 SLR(R) 457 [41], [53], [64]; *Kirkham v Trane US* [2009] 4 SLR(R) 428 [47]; *Sun Travel & Tours v Hilton International Manage (Maldives)* [2019] SGCA 10 [68].

[49] Now set out at Ch 4, section G, 'Unconscionable Conduct'.

[50] *AQN v AQO* [2015] 2 SLR 523 [24]–[26].
This is not the first time this work and Choo Han Teck J have found themselves in agreement. Both the first and second editions of this work have supported and relied on his reasoning with regard to the difficulties of injunctions sought in support of a foreign forum expressed in *People's Insurance v Akai* [1998] 1 SLR 206 (Sing HC) [12]–[13]; see now Ch 7, paras 7.43–7.50.

[51] *Regalindo Resources Pt v Seatrek Trans* [2008] 3 SLR(R) 930 [11], quoted at para 19.19 above.

[52] *Evergreen International v Volkswagen Group Singapore* [2004] 2 SLR(R) 457 [51]–[55], [63]–[64]; *Beckkett v Deutsche Bank* [2011] 1 SLR 524 [34]–[35], [2011] 2 SLR 96 [19]–[20]; *PT Sandipala Arthaputra v STMicroelectronics Asia Pacific* [2015] 5 SLR 873 [79]. See also *Regalindo Resources v Seatrek Trans* [2008] 3 SLR(R) 930 [11]. In English law, see Ch 4, section H, 'Interference with the Jurisdiction of the English Court'.

[53] See *Beckkett v Deutsche Bank* [2011] 2 SLR 96 [19]–[20]. However, in principle, it seems unlikely that 'abuse of process' actually adds much to the bases of vexation/oppression/ unconscionability; or interference with the processes and jurisdiction of the Singapore courts. See Ch 4, para 4.68.

[54] *Evergreen International v Volkswagen Group Singapore Pt* [2004] 2 SLR(R) 457 [53], [55]. Compare Ch 4, section E, 'A Legal or Equitable Right'.

[55] *Evergreen International SA v Volkswagen Group Singapore* [2004] 2 SLR(R) 457 [51]–[55]. Compare Ch 4, section I, 'Protection of English Public Policy'.

(These propositions can be regarded as expansions, by way of alternative grounds to vexation and oppression, to proposition (vii) in para 19.20 above.)

19.32   A strong recent example of points (a) and (b) is the decision in *Pacific Andes*[56] where the High Court, following the Privy Council's decision in *Shell v Krys*, stated that where there were Singapore insolvency proceedings and competing foreign proceedings, an anti-suit injunction could be granted in order to protect the equitable right to a fair distribution in insolvency, and also in order to protect the insolvency jurisdiction of the Singapore courts.

19.33   Separately, a different and more rigorous test is appropriate in contractual situations, and we return to this at section E, 'Contractual Injunctions'.

19.34   Consequently, the *Widjaya* and *Kirkham* summaries identify the central features of Singapore law on anti-suit injunctions, and are, read together, a convenient starting point in most cases. Nevertheless, it is submitted that they are not comprehensive statements of Singapore law outside the central case of non-contractual injunctions to restrain vexatious or oppressive conduct. Singapore law on anti-suit injunctions goes wider. It includes the further propositions identified in para 19.31, and it is respectfully submitted that it can also be summarized, on a broader basis, by the synthesis of English law put forward in Ch 4, para 4.05.

19.35   Indeed, there is good reason to expect that Singapore law will develop along similar lines to the general English law on the tests for anti-suit injunctions, as and when it becomes necessary to explore less central situations in more detail, although the Singapore courts will no doubt add their own contributions to the jurisprudence. As yet, no significant difference of principle has been identified between English and Singapore law, with the possible exception of whether Singapore law will dispense with the inclusion of unconscionability in the test (see para 19.28 above).

---

[56] *Pacific Andes Resources Development* [2016] SGHC 210 [22]–[27]. The specific issue in that case was whether an injunction should be granted, under the general powers to the court, to restrain foreign proceedings in order to protect a situation where a scheme of arrangement was being negotiated, although such would be protected domestically by an application under s 210(10) of the Companies Act. It was held that no such injunction should be granted, as the case for protection was less strong than if administration or liquidation was under way. However, the court envisaged that the position might well be different if the scheme of arrangement had actually been sanctioned by the Singapore court—this would mean that there was a case that the integrity of the sanctioned scheme would justify protection.

But this decision is open to some criticism and has in large part been overtaken by subsequent events. First of all, Kannan Ramesh JC expressed himself in terms that there was no 'jurisdiction' to grant an injunction to restrain foreign proceedings in order to protect mere negotiations for a scheme of arrangement (at [27]–[28]). With respect, however, this may be an inaccuracy of phrasing. Even at the time of *Pacific Andes* the better way to describe the situation was that the jurisdiction—ie power—existed under the relevant statutory powers in s 4(10) CLA and para 14 Sch 1 of the SGCA, and the real question was whether it was right in principle to exercise it. Second, at the time of *Pacific Andes* the only specific statutory power in the area was the power in s 210 of the Companies Act, which did not permit the restraint of foreign proceedings (see para 19.05 above). But the statutory context has changed, as ss 211B and 211C of the Companies Act have since 2017 specifically introduced a power to restrain specific foreign proceedings in support of a moratorium where a compromise or scheme of arrangement is merely being considered. This expression of the legislature's will may indicate that the situations where anti-suit injunctions should be granted should be broader than envisaged in *Pacific Andes*. In *Re IM Skaugen* [2018] SGHC 259 [39], [85]–[87], little hesitation was shown in granting relief under s 211B to restrain specific foreign proceedings, and not just Singapore proceedings, in order to give breathing space to negotiate compromises and schemes of arrangement, although these had not yet been sanctioned by the Singaporean court; and this relief was regarded as substantively parallel to an anti-suit injunction.

The Singapore courts do, however, have the significant advantage that they are uncon-   **19.36**
strained by the Brussels–Lugano regime and therefore face no artificial restrictions on the
grant of injunctions to restrain proceedings in Europe.

We now turn to consider some key aspects of the main principles identified above, as devel-   **19.37**
oped in the Singapore case law.

1. Amenable to the Jurisdiction (*Widjaya* (i); *Kirkham* (a))

The injunction defendant must be amenable to the jurisdiction of the Singapore court.   **19.38**
However, this criterion will be satisfied if the court has *in personam* jurisdiction over
the defendant, either by way of valid service, or submission to the court's jurisdiction.[57]
While there are comments in the case law which have suggested that the criterion of
amenability means, additionally, that the injunction must be an effective remedy, [58] the
developing case law has made clear that amenability does not mean that the injunction
defendant must have a presence or assets in the jurisdiction which means that an injunction can be enforced against him in practice; the Singapore courts can, and in appropriate cases will, grant an injunction even where its order may be ineffective in practice
and will not contemplate that its order will be disobeyed.[59] In this regard, the development of Singapore law has matched and anticipated the Privy Council's recent decision
in *Shell v Krys*.[60]

2. Natural and Proper Forum (*Aérospatiale* (v); *Kirkham* (b))

In some Singapore cases, the criterion of Singapore being the natural forum for the litiga-   **19.39**
tion has been stated to be a necessary condition for the grant of an injunction.[61] However,
it is respectfully submitted that as an unqualified proposition this would be wrong. It is not
what *Aérospatiale* says—Lord Goff qualified his statements there on natural forum with the
words 'in general'; and watered down any requirement still further in *Airbus v Patel*. Nor
does it seem that an unqualified doctrine has been adopted by the Singapore courts. So,
for example, in *Evergreen*, Belinda Ang Saw Ean J applied *Aérospatiale* as requiring natural

---

[57]   *Koh Kay Yew v Inno-Pacific Holdings* [1997] 2 SLR(R) 148 [17], [29]; *PT Sandipala Arthaputra v STMicroelectronics Asia Pacific* [2015] 5 SLR 889 [75]–[76]; *Lakshmi Anil Salgaocar v Jhaveri Darsan Jitendra* [2018] SGHC 90 [18]. The Court of Appeal in *Koh Kay* understood 'amenable' as meaning that the defendant is 'liable or accountable to this jurisdiction' (at [17]). On amenability by submission, see *Bank of America National Trust and Savings Association v Djoni Widjaja* [1994] 2 SLR(R) 898 [15]–[16]; *Kischinchand Tiloomal Bhojwani v Sunil Kishinchand Bhojwani* [1996] 1 SLR(R) 861 [11].

[58]   *Koh Kay Yew v Inno-Pacific Holdings* [1997] 2 SLR(R) 148 [28]. This is no doubt derived from Lord Goff's reference to an 'effective remedy' in the context of the defendant's amenability to the jurisdiction: *Société Nationale Industrielle Aérospatiale v Lee Kui Jak* [1987] AC 871 (PC) 892 ('an injunction will only be issued restraining a party who is amenable to the jurisdiction of the court, against whom an injunction will be an ef-fective remedy').

[59]   *Evergreen International v Volkswagen Group Singapore* [2004] 2 SLR(R) 457, 465 [22]–[25]; however, cf *People's Insurance v Akai* [1997] 2 SLR(R) 291 [9], [12].

[60]   *Stichting Shell Pensioenfonds v Krys* [2015] AC 616 (PC) [36]–[37]; and see Ch 4, paras 4.84–4.85.

[61]   *Koh Kay Yew v Inno-Pacific Holdings* [1997] 2 SLR(R) 148 [18]–[19]; *Ram Parshotam Mittal v Portcullis Trustnet (Singapore)* [2014] 3 SLR 1337 [44]; *PT Sandipala Arthaputra v STMicroelectronics Asia Pacific* [2015] 5 SLR 873 [81].

forum only as a 'general rule', but not an 'invariable one'.[62] Numerous other cases adopting the *Kirkham* factors have regarded natural forum as an important factor, but not a necessary condition.[63] It is a factor among others to be considered 'in the round'.[64]

19.40   This more nuanced position is the right approach in principle. A showing of natural forum remains a central factor in conventional alternative forum cases; if Singapore is not the natural forum, then in such cases it is likely to be difficult to show that the other litigation is vexatious and oppressive or that the grant of an injunction would be consistent with comity. But in other types of situation, requiring that Singapore be the natural forum *for* the litigation would be either inappropriate, or something that can be deemed to be the case without any independent showing of natural forum by reference to the connections of the parties. In particular, where a single forum injunction is sought, Singapore will never be the natural forum for the issues in play in the foreign litigation.[65] Further, if the injunction is granted to protect a Singapore (or foreign) arbitration, the Singapore courts have a sufficient connection to grant the injunction, even though they may well not be otherwise the natural forum in terms of connections to the underlying facts. Similarly, where an injunction is necessary to protect the jurisdiction, processes, and judgments of the Singapore court, it should be granted irrespective of whether the Singapore court is the natural forum for the litigation; the Singapore court is self-evidently the right, or natural court to protect itself and its processes.[66]

19.41   When assessing the natural forum for the litigation in a conventional way, the court will seek to identify the forum with which the dispute has the most real and substantial connection. This is not a mechanical process; instead, the court will take into account a multitude of factors.[67] The fact that Singapore proceedings are well advanced is a factor which may mean that Singapore is, or has become, the natural forum.[68]

3. Vexation or Oppression (*Kirkham* (c))

19.42   The criterion of vexation or oppression, referred to in *Widjaja*, has sometimes been stated as being, or summarized as if it were, a necessary condition of the grant of an injunction.[69]

---

[62]   *Evergreen International v Volkswagen Group Singapore* [2004] 2 SLR(R) 457 [15], [26].
[63]   See paras 19.21 and 19.26.
[64]   *Sun Travel & Tours v Hilton International Manage (Maldives)* [2019] SGCA 10 [66]–[67].
[65]   For discussion of single forum injunctions, see Ch 4, paras 4.81–4.82; Ch 5, section D, 'Single Forum Cases'.
[66]   See Ch 4, para 4.67 and para 4.94.
[67]   See *Kirkham v Trane US* [2009] 4 SLR(R) 428 [34]; *AQN v AQO* [2015] 2 SLR 523 [18]; *PT Sandipala Arthaputra v STMicroelectronics Asia Pacific* [2015] 5 SLR 873 [82], [97]; *Hong Hin Kay Albert v AAHG* [2014] SGHC 206 [36]. For particular examples of relevant factors and their weighting, see *Evergreen International v Volkswagen Group Singapore* [2004] 2 SLR(R) 457 [31] (fact that tort occurred in Singapore conducive to Singapore being natural forum); *Kirkham v Trane US* [2009] 4 SLR(R) 428 [37]–[38] (not decisive against Singapore that no parties in Singapore; non-compellability of third-party witnesses outside Singapore may be relevant); *Grover v SetClear* [2012] 2 SLR 625 [38] (location of parties in Singapore and Singapore law applying conducive to natural forum); *Morgan Stanley Asia (Singapore) v Hong Leong Finance* [2013] 3 SLR 409 [56]–[58] (non-exclusive jurisdiction clause in favour of Singapore conducive factor).
[68]   *PT Sandipala Arthaputra v STMicroelectronics Asia Pacific* [2015] 5 SLR 885 [102]–[105], [127]. Alternatively, the advanced state of the Singapore proceedings has been treated as a factor supporting a finding of vexation: see eg *Kischinchand Tiloomal Bhojwani v Sunil Kishinchand Bhojwani* [1996] 1 SLR(R) 861 [14].
[69]   This is one possible reading of *Widjaja* itself: *Bank of America National Trust and Savings Association v Djoni Widjaja* [1994] 2 SLR(R) 898 [15]—although it is submitted that is not the right reading, as discussed at para 19.20 above; and see also *Koh Kay Yew v Inno-Pacific Holdings* [1997] 2 SLR(R) 148, 155 [19].

But that would not be a correct reading of *Aérospatiale*, under which vexation or oppression is only required 'in general'. Vexation or oppression is the most centrally relevant criterion to whether an injunction is in the interests of justice; but not the only possible springboard[70]—for example, as discussed above, under *Aérospatiale* injunctions can also be granted where necessary to protect the processes, jurisdiction, and judgments of the local courts.[71] Nor does any more rigid rule seem to be the right reading of Singapore law. In the subsequent Singapore cases, and in particular those applying *Kirkham*, there are numerous examples of the Singapore courts reflecting the more nuanced approach to vexation and oppression under which it is not a necessary condition,[72] but instead, again, is a factor to be considered with others 'in the round'.[73]

The circumstances in which vexation or oppression will arise cannot exhaustively de-   **19.43**
fined: every case will turn on its own facts.[74] Factual findings which have supported findings of vexation or oppression include where the foreign proceedings: (a) were instituted in bad faith or an improper purpose or for no good reason;[75] (b) are bound to fail;[76] (c) will cause extreme inconvenience;[77] or (d) amount to an attack on the plaintiff's legal rights.[78]

In addition, vexation or oppression can be made good, (e), where foreign proceedings   **19.44**
are duplicative of Singapore proceedings to a vexatious or oppressive extent.[79] But, importantly, there is no presumption that a multiplicity of proceedings is vexatious or oppressive per se. Something additional is required to make the duplication vexatious.[80] In this regard, the Singapore courts have adopted the remark in the first edition of this work that 'the greater the positive and voluntary involvement of the injunction respondent in the local proceedings, and the longer the local suit has been allowed to proceed before the commencement of the parallel foreign proceedings, the stronger the case for an injunction.'[81]

---

[70] See *Regalindo Resources v Seatrek Trans* [2008] 3 SLR(R) 930 [11]; *VH v VI* [2008] 1 SLR(R) 742 [40]; *Evergreen International SA v Volkswagen Group Singapore* [2004] 2 SLR(R) 457 [15]–[16]; *Kirkham v Trane US Inc* [2009] 4 SLR(R) 428 [27]–[28] (adopting and expanding *Evergreen*).

[71] See para 19.31 and Ch 4, section H, 'Interference with the Jurisdiction of the English Court'.

[72] See the authorities at nn 33, 37, and 43 above.

[73] *Sun Travel & Tours v Hilton International Manage (Maldives)* [2019] SGCA 10 [66]–[67].

[74] Belinda Ang Saw Ean J observed that whilst previous cases might 'provide useful guidance ... everything depends on the circumstances of the case and new circumstances will emerge': *Evergreen International v Volkswagen Group Singapore* [2004] 2 SLR(R) 457 [33]. See further *Hong Hin Kay Albert v AAHG* [2014] SGHC 206 [56] ('What amounts to vexation or oppression has never been exclusively defined.')

[75] *Kirkham v Trane US* [2009] 4 SLR(R) 428 [47]. See eg *Bank of America National Trust and Savings Association v Djoni Widjaja* [1994] 2 SLR(R) 898 [24]; *Regalindo Resources v Seatrek Trans* [2008] 3 SLR(R) 930 [22]; *PT Sandipala Arthaputra v STMicroelectronics Asia Pacific* [2015] 5 SLR 873 [130]–[137]; *Hong Hin Kay Albert v AAHG* [2014] SGHC 206 [56]–[57].

[76] *Kirkham v Trane US* [2009] 4 SLR(R) 428 [47].

[77] *Kirkham v Trane US* [2009] 4 SLR(R) 428 [47].

[78] *Evergreen International v Volkswagen Group Singapore hers* [2004] 2 SLR(R) 457 [46]–[64] (circumvention of rights to limit). The reasoning in this particular case may benefit from being tested against the contrasting English decision in *Seismic Shipping v Total E&P UK (The Western Regent)* [2005] 2 Lloyds Rep 359 (CA).

[79] See eg *PT Sandipala Arthaputra v STMicroelectronics Asia Pacific* [2015] 5 SLR 873 [118]–[137].

[80] *Kirkham v Trane US* [2009] 4 SLR(R) 455 [48]; *Relfo Ltd (in liquidation) v Bhimji Velji Jadva Varsani* [2009] 4 SLR(R) 351 [12]; *UBS v Telesto Investments* [2011] 4 SLR 503 [106], [119], [134]–[137]). Singapore law has therefore reached the same landing as English law: see Ch 4, paras 4.02, 4.05, 4.72; Ch 5, para 5.04.

[81] *PT Sandipala Arthaputra v STMicroelectronics Asia Pacific* [2015] 5 SLR 873 [137]. See also *Lakshmi Anil Salgaocar v Jhaveri Darsan Jitendra* [2018] SGHC 90 [48].

19.45   If a claimant pursues parallel proceedings in Singapore or abroad, he may be forced to elect to pursue one claim or the other.[82] If he elects to pursue the foreign action and to stay or discontinue the Singapore action, he may still be restrained from pursuing the foreign action if this would be vexatious or oppressive.[83]

4. The Balance of Legitimate Advantages and Injustice (*Kirkham* (d))

19.46   If there is a prima facie case of vexation or oppression, the court will then examine the alleged injustice that the defendant would suffer if he were deprived of the advantages sought in the foreign proceedings.[84] At this stage, any legitimate juridical advantages[85] will be identified and balanced against the vexation or oppression caused to the plaintiffs.[86]

5. Caution, Circumspection, and 'the Clearest of Circumstances' (*Widjaya* (iv))

19.47   In *Widjaya*, following *Aérospatiale*, the Singapore Court of Appeal made clear that caution would be required for the grant of a non-contractual anti-suit injunction, in order to ensure consistency with comity.[87] The language of 'caution' has been used in many subsequent cases.[88] However, there is a strand of the Singapore case law which has stated that vexation or oppression should only be found in 'the clearest of circumstances'.[89] Similarly, it has been said that (in non-contractual situations) the jurisdiction is to be

---

[82]   *Koh Kay Yew v Inno-Pacific Holdings* [1997] 2 SLR(R) 148 [22]; *Yusen Air & Sea Service v KLM Royal Dutch Airlines* [1999] 2 SLR(R) 955 [16]–[32]; *Belbana v APL* [2014] SGHC 17 [20]–[21]. If the claimant has elected to pursue the claim in Singapore, an anti-suit injunction may be granted to preclude it from pursuing any overseas proceedings: see *Yusen* at [34], [47]; *Virsagi Management v Welltech Construction* [2013] 4 SLR 1097 [35]; or the same may be achieved by undertakings.

[83]   *Yusen Air & Sea Service v KLM Royal Dutch Airlines* [1999] 2 SLR(R) 955 [36]; *Virsagi Management v Welltech Construction* [2013] 4 SLR 1097, 1108 [36]; see also *Rappo v Accent Delight International* [2017] SLR 265 [64].

[84]   The third and fourth elements are 'two sides of the same coin', as the focus shifts from the plaintiff's interests in obtaining the injunction to the defendant's interests in continuing the foreign proceedings: *Kirkham v Trane US* [2009] 4 SLR(R) 428 [29]. Note the emphasis on injustice in *BC Andaman v Xie Ning Yun* [2017] SGHC 64 [52] ('…the injunction can be granted against a party properly before the court where it is appropriate to avoid injustice').

[85]   For examples of the exploration of this concept in the case law, see *Bank of America National Trust and Savings Association v Djoni Widjaja* [1994] 2 SLR(R) 898 [19]–[22]; *Kischinchand Tiloomal Bhojwani v Sunil Kishinchand Bhojwani* [1996] 1 SLR(R) 861 [20]; *Regalindo Resources v Seatrek Trans* [2008] 3 SLR(R) 930 [21]–[31] (where the availability of security in the foreign proceedings was the key factor); *UBS v Telesto Investments* [2011] 4 SLR 503 [153]–[155]; *AQN v AQO* [2015] 2 SLR 523 [31] (where the interim nature of the injunction and the fact that it did not preclude the enforcement of a contractual claim at a later stage meant that no juridical advantage had been lost); *Rappo v Accent Delight International* [2017] SLR 265 [107]–[112] (where it was unsuccessfully alleged that the respondents would be deprived of certain remedies if the matter were to proceed in Singapore); *Lakshmi Anil Salgaocar v Jhaveri Darsan Jitendra* [2018] SGHC 90 [68] (where the defendant's argument that he would need to bring fresh proceedings in Singapore to vindicate his contractual rights if the anti-suit injunction was described as 'not very compelling').

[86]   *Evergreen International v Volkswagen Group Singapore* [2004] 2 SLR(R) 457 [32]. See also *Kischinchand Tiloomal Bhojwani v Sunil Kishinchand Bhojwani* [1996] 1 SLR(R) 861 [23]; *BC Andaman v Xie Ning Yun* [2017] SGHC 64 [104].

[87]   See para 19.19.

[88]   See the cases reciting the *Widjaya* tests at n 26 above; see also *VH v VI* [2008] 1 SLR(R) 742 [38], [50]; *Beckkett v Deutsche Bank* [2011] 2 SLR 96 [24] ('circumspection'); *Relfo Ltd (in liquidation) v Bhimji Velji Jadva Varsani* [2009] 4 SLR(R) 351 [11]–[12]; *Sun Travel & Tours v Hilton International Manage (Maldives)* [2019] SGCA 10 [69].

[89]   *Koh Kay Yew v Inno-Pacific Holdings* [1997] 2 SLR(R) 148 [25]; *Regalindo Resources v Seatrek Trans* [2008] 3 SLR(R) 930 [13]; *Kirkham v Trane US* [2009] 4 SLR(R) 428 [46]; *Relfo Ltd (in liquidation) v Bhimji Velji Jadva Varsani* [2009] 4 SLR(R) 351 [16]; *UBS v Telesto Investments* [2011] 4 SLR 503 [109].

exercised sparingly and in exceptional cases.[90] As a matter of language this might be seen as a higher test, which if so, is not reflected in the jurisprudence of other common law countries. However, the Singapore courts have not stated that they are intending to impose any higher threshold compared to the approach taken in the wider common law, and in *Kirkham* the Court of Appeal considered the 'clearest of circumstances' language alongside the previous English and Privy Council authorities and did not consider it adopted any different test. Most recently, the Court of Appeal in *Sun Travel v Hilton International* used the language of 'caution' for anti-suit injunctions in general, and reserved the language of 'exceptional' circumstances for the more specific situation of anti-enforcement injunctions.[91] It is suggested that 'caution', and no higher threshold, best represents Singapore law.

D. ANTI-ENFORCEMENT INJUNCTIONS

Anti-suit injunctions may be granted to restrain the enforcement of foreign judgments. But where the injunction is being sought after the foreign judgment, this will usually mean that there has been delay in seeking it. This factor, and the heightened significance of comity where the Singapore court is being asked to interfere with the pursuit of foreign proceedings where the foreign court has already given judgment, have led the Singapore court to say that 'anti-enforcement' injunctions will be granted only in 'exceptional' cases.[92]   **19.48**

E. CONTRACTUAL INJUNCTIONS

As discussed in Chapter 7, the English courts have adopted a distinct set of tests for contractual cases, where the foreign proceedings are in breach of an injunction. These are often known as *The Angelic Grace* principles,[93] following the 1995 English Court of Appeal decision of that name. Where the foreign litigation is in breach of an exclusive forum clause, an injunction to restrain it will ordinarily be granted unless there are 'good reasons' or 'strong reasons' not to do so; although there is always a discretion to refuse to grant an injunction. As Millett LJ explained, where there is a breach of a jurisdiction or arbitration clause, there is no need for 'diffidence', and the caution which is a requirement in non-contractual cases need not be applied.[94]   **19.49**

In the *Kirkham* summary, the relevance of an exclusive forum clause was mentioned merely as a factor relevant to the grant of an injunction.[95] But it is clear from *Kirkham* itself and the developed Singapore case law that has followed it, that the Singapore courts do not treat the presence of a binding exclusive forum clause merely as a factor within an overall assessment of vexation. Instead, the recent case law has therefore adopted a distinct rigorous test   **19.50**

---

[90] *PT Sandipala Arthaputra v STMicroelectronics Asia Pacific* [2015] 5 SLR 873 [71].
[91] *Sun Travel & Tours v Hilton International Manage (Maldives)* [2019] SGCA 10 [69].
[92] *Sun Travel & Tours v Hilton International Manage (Maldives)* [2019] SGCA 10 [99], [114], building on the English decision in *Ecobank Transnational v Tanoh* [2016] 1 Lloyds Rep 360 (CA).
[93] See Ch 7, section E, 'The *Angelic Grace* Principles'.
[94] *Aggeliki Charis Compania Maritima SA v Pagnan Spa (The Angelic Grace)* [1995] 1 Lloyds Rep 87 (CA) 95–96.
[95] *Kirkham v Trane US* [2009] 4 SLR(R) 428 [29].

in contractual cases, which is substantially the same as the English *Angelic Grace* test.[96] The breach of the exclusive forum clause is a sufficient and independent basis for the injunction and the injunction should, in general, be granted unless there are strong reasons not to do so.[97]

19.51   The adoption of the *Angelic Grace* approach in Singapore has been driven in part by Singapore public policy in favour of arbitration. As Lee Seiu Kin JC explained in *WSG Nimbus*, maintenance of Singapore's position as a centre for international legal services and international arbitrations requires a 'robust approach', and is consistent with the New York Convention.[98] The Singapore courts are confident that this is consistent with comity.

19.52   There have been some variations in manner of expression. In *WSG Nimbus* the court expressed itself in terms that if there is an arbitration agreement the court 'has a duty to uphold that agreement and prevent any breach of it', without reference to an exception for 'strong reasons'; but the court had earlier referred to, with approval, the passage in *The Angelic Grace* containing the 'good reasons' exception.[99] Further, although there was no express reference to discretion in *WSG Nimbus*, it is clear from the other case law that the court does retain a discretion to refuse to enforce an exclusive forum clause by injunction.[100] In *Grover v SetClear*, the first instance judge referred to the need for 'special or exceptional reason' to show why the injunction should not be granted.[101] In other cases, however, like *Maldives*, the decision in *The Angelic Grace* has simply been stated as being the law,[102] or the test that the injunction should generally be granted unless there are strong reasons not to do so has been expressly adopted.[103] It is submitted that these occasional variations of expression do not change the essence of the tests, and in *Hilton v Sun* the English tests were

---

[96]   This is clearly stated by the Court of Appeal in *Sun Travel & Tours v Hilton International Manage (Maldives)* [2019] SGCA 10 [67]–[68]; upholding Belinda Ang Saw Ean J at first instance in *Hilton International Manage (Maldives) v Sun Travels & Tours* [2018] SGHC 56 [47]–[54]. See previously *WSG Nimbus v Board of Control for Cricket in Sri Lanka* [2002] 1 SLR (R) 1088 [79]–[91]; *Maldives Airports v GMR Male International Airport* [2013] 2 SLR 449 [34], [42]–[43]; *UBS v Telesto Investments* [2011] 4 SLR 503 [109], [119](d); *Grover v SetClear* [2012] 2 SLR 625 [25], [35], [38(f)][42]; *Morgan Stanley Asia (Singapore) v Hong Leong Finance* [2013] 3 SLR 409 [29] (citing *Donohue v Armco* [2002] 1 Lloyds Rep 425 (HL), another of the key English contractual cases); *R1 International v Lonstroff* [2015] 1 SLR 521 (where it was assumed that if a contract existed, the injunction would follow); *BC Andaman v Xie Ning Yun* [2017] SGHC 64 [65].
       There are two cases where it has been suggested that *Aérospatiale* and not any distinct contractual test should be applied in contractual situations: *People's Insurance v Akai* and *R1 International v Lonstroff*. However, *People's Insurance Co Ltd v Akai Pty Ltd* [1997] 2 SLR(R) 291 [10] was about a very different question, namely injunctions to protect an agreed foreign forum (and it seems *Angelic Grace* may not have been cited). In *R1 International v Lonstroff* [2014] 3 SLR 166, 176 [39]–[40] the High Court suggested *obiter* that in contractual situations where Singapore was selected, the *Aérospatiale* tests should apply; and had been applied in Singapore law to contractual cases by *Maldives Airports v GMR Male* (this point was not addressed on appeal in *R1 International v Lonstroff* [2015] 1 SLR 521). However, the better view, as explained, is that Singapore law is actually applying a specific set of tests in contractual situations. Those contractual tests can most properly be regarded as independent of *Aérospatiale*, although they are, of course, consistent with it.
[97]   *Sun Travel & Tours v Hilton International Manage (Maldives)* [2019] SGCA 10 [67]–[68]. This is subject to considerations of delay and unconscionable conduct by the injunction claimant, discussed at paras 19.56–19.57.
[98]   *WSG Nimbus v Board of Control for Cricket in Sri Lanka* [2002] 1 SLR (R) 1088 [90]–[91].
[99]   *WSG Nimbus v Board of Control for Cricket in Sri Lanka* [2002] 1 SLR (R) 1088 [85] and [91].
[100]   *UBS v Telesto Investments* [2011] 4 SLR 503 [119](d).
[101]   *Grover v SetClear* [2012] 2 SLR 625 [25].
[102]   *Maldives Airports v GMR Male International Airport* [2013] 2 SLR 449 [42]–[43]; *BC Andaman v Xie Ning Yun* [2017] SGHC 64 [65].
[103]   As in *Morgan Stanley Asia (Singapore) v Hong Leong Finance* [2013] 3 SLR 409 [29]; *BC Andaman v Xie Ning Yun* [2017] SGHC 64 [65], [68]

adopted without modification,[104] subject potentially to one point about the role of comity (to which we will return).

As a result, in contractual cases it is not necessary to show that Singapore is the natural   **19.53** forum for the litigation, as the agreement to Singapore either as the exclusive jurisdiction or the seat of the arbitration gives the Singapore courts sufficient interest. In *BC Andaman* Quentin Loh J explained: 'the principle of comity is also not violated when a court grants an anti-suit injunction to protect interests arising from proceedings before an arbitral tribunal whose seat is in the forum, or to enforce an arbitration agreement conferring jurisdiction on such a tribunal'.[105]

Similarly, it is not necessary to show that the foreign proceedings are vexatious or oppres-   **19.54** sive or satisfy one of the other non-contractual thresholds: the breach of contract is sufficient basis. [106]

There is, however, one dimension in which the Singapore courts may be beginning to de-   **19.55** velop a difference of thinking to the English courts. There is some English case law that suggests that the importance of upholding the exclusive forum clause means that where foreign proceedings are in breach of an exclusive forum clause, comity has no further significance (at least outside the situation of delay).[107] The Singapore case law, however, suggests that although the presence of the exclusive forum clause will reduce the importance of comity, it may remain a relevant factor.[108]

Since the injunction is discretionary, the conduct of the injunction claimant can lead to it   **19.56** being refused, even where the foreign proceedings are in breach of contract. Factors that can lead to refusal are 'unclean hands',[109] or other conduct that amounts to unconscionability by the injunction claimant.[110]

As part of this, the case law requires that, even where the foreign proceedings are in   **19.57** breach of contract, anti-suit injunctions should be brought promptly and without delay.[111] Unjustified and unconscionable delay in seeking the injunction can warrant its refusal. Delay engages comity, and the longer the delay and the more advanced the foreign court proceedings become, the stronger the considerations of comity against the grant of the injunction will be.[112]

---

[104] *Sun Travel & Tours v Hilton International Manage (Maldives)* [2019] SGCA 10 [67]–[68].
[105] *BC Andaman v Xie Ning Yun* [2017] SGHC 64 [54]–[55].
[106] *Sun Travel & Tours v Hilton International Manage (Maldives)* [2019] SGCA 10 [67]–[68]; *Kirkham v Trane US* [2009] 4 SLR(R) 428 [29]; *UBS v Telesto Investments* [2011] 4 SLR 503, 541 [109]; *Grover v SetClear* [2012] 2 SLR 625 [38](f), and the authorities cited at n 96.
However, cf the application of *Aérospatiale* directly in *People's Insurance Co Ltd v Akai Pty Ltd* [1997] 2 SLR(R) 291 [10]; *R1 International v Lonstroff* [2014] 3 SLR 166, 176 [39]–[40], discussed at n 96, second paragraph.
[107] See Ch 7, para 7.19.
[108] *Sun Travel & Tours v Hilton International Manage (Maldives)* [2019] SGCA 10 [114(a)]; see also *Kirkham v Trane US* [2009] 4 SLR(R) 428 [29]; *BC Andaman v Xie Ning Yun* [2017] SGHC 64 [65].
[109] See eg (in a non-contractual case) *Beckkett v Deutsche Bank* [2011] 1 SLR 524 [38].
[110] *Sun Travel & Tours v Hilton International Manage (Maldives)* [2019] SGCA 10 [68], [106].
[111] *Hilton International Manage (Maldives) v Sun Travels & Tours* [2018] SGHC 56 [60]–[63]; *Sun Travel & Tours v Hilton International Manage (Maldives)* [2019] SGCA 10 [82]–[87]. For other cases illustrating the significance of delay, see *VH v VI* [2008] 1 SLR(R) 742 [34]–[35] (in a non contractual case); *PT Sandipala Arthaputra v STMicroelectronics Asia Pacific* [2015] 5 SLR 873, 906 [141] (again a non-contractual case).
[112] *Sun Travel & Tours v Hilton International Manage (Maldives)* [2019] SGCA 10 [82]–[87], [106], [113] (citing the first edition of this work with approval). As a result, the current Singapore case law has said that if the

19.58   Care must of course be taken as to whether the foreign proceedings are indeed in breach of contract. For example, in *Regalindo*, New York security proceedings were not regarded as a breach of an arbitration clause and so the question of whether the security should be injuncted was assessed by reference to non-contractual principles of vexation and oppression.[113] Further, a non-exclusive forum clause in favour of Singapore does not create any contractual obligation not to litigate abroad; and mere duplication is not enough to justify an injunction. Instead, where the clause is non-exclusive, some independent and additional wrongfulness, such as vexation and oppression independent of the clause, is required.[114]

F.   ARBITRATION

19.59   The Singaporean courts have recognized that an anti-suit injunction can be granted in support of and to protect arbitration proceedings. In *Hilton v Sun*, Belinda Ang Saw Ean J observed (applying Lord Hoffmann's comments in *The Front Comor*) that 'the exercise of the jurisdiction to restrain foreign court proceedings is generally regarded as an important and valuable weapon in the hands of a court exercising supervisory jurisdiction over the arbitration'.[115] As discussed in section B, 'Sources and Powers', the power to grant a permanent and interim injunction in support of arbitration exists under statute, and has not been removed by the UNCITRAL Model Law.[116]

19.60   Where the foreign proceedings are in breach of the arbitration agreement, the strong contractual principles discussed above, derived from *The Angelic Grace*, apply. The Singapore courts have adopted the reasoning in the English Supreme Court's decision in *Ust-Kamenogorsk* that an arbitration agreement contains an implied negative obligation not to litigate outside the contractual forum, which can be enforced by injunction even if no arbitration has yet been commenced.[117]

19.61   The High Court has emphasized that, consistent with the policy underlying the International Arbitration Act, the court must take a 'robust approach' and ensure that the parties' arbitration agreement is upheld.[118] However, recently in *Sun Travel v Hilton International*, an anti-enforcement injunction to restrain the enforcement of a foreign judgment obtained in breach of an arbitration clause was refused, because of the delay and the comity concerns involved in intervening after the foreign judgment.[119]

19.62   In addition, if the foreign proceedings are a collateral attack on the arbitration award (even if not a direct breach of the arbitration agreement), this will be a strong ground to support

injunction to enforce the exclusive forum clause is an anti-enforcement injunction, it will only be granted in exceptional cases: see Section D, 'Anti-Enforcement Injunctions'.

[113]   *Regalindo Resources v Seatrek Trans* [2008] 3 SLR(R) 930 [16]–[17].
[114]   *UBS v Telesto Investments* [2011] 4 SLR 503, 119–26, (following the analysis in Ch 9 of the first edition of this work, and *Deutsche Bank v Highland Crusader Partners* [2010] 1 WLR 1023); *Morgan Stanley Asia (Singapore) v Hong Leong Finance* [2013] 3 SLR 409 [30]–[35].
[115]   *Hilton International Manage (Maldives) v Sun Travels & Tours* [2018] SGHC 56 [28].
[116]   See para 19.16.
[117]   *Hilton International Manage (Maldives) v Sun Travels & Tours* [2018] SGHC 56 [50]–[51], applying *AES Ust-Kamenogorsk Hydropower Plant LLP v Ust-Kamenogorsk Hydropower Plant JSC* [2013] 1 WLR 1889 (SC); see also to similar effect *Sun Travel & Tours v Hilton International Manage (Maldives)* [2019] SGCA 10 [67].
[118]   *WSG Nimbus v Board of Control for Cricket in Sri Lanka* [2002] 1 SLR (R) 1088, 1130 [90]–[91].
[119]   *Sun Travel & Tours v Hilton International Manage (Maldives)* [2019] SGCA 10, discussed in relation to anti-enforcement injunctions at section D, 'Anti-Enforcement Injunctions'.

an injunction on the basis that the foreign proceedings are vexatious, or that it is necessary to protect the arbitral jurisdiction, or it is otherwise in the interests of justice to do so.[120] In this post-award situation, it has been held that greater caution is required than where the foreign proceedings are in breach of the arbitration agreement during the continuance of the arbitration, and so the *Angelic Grace* principles do not apply with the same rigidity.[121]

G. INJUNCTIONS IN SUPPORT OF FOREIGN COURTS AND TRIBUNALS

The statutory powers of the Singapore courts include powers that are broad enough to sustain anti-suit injunctions in support of foreign arbitrations or foreign court proceedings.[122] It is, however, a separate question whether it is appropriate for the Singapore courts to do so. As we have seen, comity is a central restraining factor under Singapore law on anti-suit injunctions.[123] In English law, comity requires that the English courts have a 'sufficient interest' in the matter to grant an injunction, and in *Airbus v Patel*, this led the House of Lords to refuse to grant a non-contractual anti-suit injunction in support of litigation in the courts of India.[124] While the Singapore case law has not yet had cause to adopt *Airbus*, it is likely that the Singapore courts would apply similar principles; although as we shall see they have currently used the language of requiring 'strong reasons' rather than a sufficient interest.   **19.63**

Indeed, before the modern English doctrine of comity had been laid down by the House of Lords in *Airbus*, the Singapore High Court had anticipated its reasoning. In *People's Insurance v Akai*, where there was a dispute between whether the English or Australian courts should have jurisdiction, and an English jurisdiction clause which Australian law purported to override, Choo Han Teck JC (as he then was) was asked to grant an anti-suit injunction to support English proceedings. He declined, saying: **19.64**

> the Singapore courts should not assume the role of international busybody and direct that the parties litigate in England … the courts of the two competing jurisdictions are entitled to come to different conclusions and that does not concern the Singapore courts unless the parties come to this jurisdiction for the purpose of enforcing their respective judgments …
>
> …
>
> where there are two courts both having jurisdiction a third court with tenuous connections should not influence the course unless there are strong reasons to do so.[125]

His judgment was given after the English Court of Appeal's decision in Airbus, which had upheld the injunction, but before the House of Lord's reversal of the Court of Appeal; and in   **19.65**

---

[120] Accepted in principle in *BC Andaman v Xie Ning Yun* [2017] SGHC 64 [80]–[81]; and now see *Hilton International Manage (Maldives) v Sun Travels & Tours* [2018] SGHC 56 [54]–[57] (overturned on other grounds on appeal, with this point not addressed, *Sun Travel & Tours v Hilton International Manage (Maldives)* [2019] SGCA 10). In English law, see Ch 7, paras 7.66–7.67.

[121] *Hilton International Manage (Maldives) v Sun Travels & Tours* [2018] SGHC 56 [54]–[57] (overturned, but not on this point, *Sun Travel & Tours v Hilton International Manage (Maldives)* [2019] SGCA 10) This development is a sophisticated extension that the English courts have not, so far, adopted.

[122] See para 19.15 above.

[123] See para 19.22 above.

[124] *Airbus Industrie v Patel* [1999] 1 AC 119 (HL).

[125] *People's Insurance v Akai* [1997] 2 SLR(R) 291 [12]–[13].

many respects his reasoning was prophetic of, and anticipated, Lord Goff's approach in the House of Lords.

19.66   Choo Han Teck JC's approach does not, however, amount to a blanket exclusion. In *R1 v Lonstroff*, Judith Prakash adopted his approach, and applied it to the case of foreign arbitrations. She concluded that it is only where 'strong reasons are present' that the Singapore courts would grant an anti-suit injunction to protect a foreign arbitration. She commented *obiter* that one possible situation where this might be so was where the forum in which the arbitration is to take place does not provide for effective interim measures in support of arbitration, but she did not need to decide the point.[126]

H. HAGUE CONVENTION ON THE CHOICE OF COURT

19.67   Singapore is one of the contracting states to the Hague Convention on the Choice of Court. However, for reasons already discussed in this work, the Hague Convention should not preclude the grant of anti-suit injunctions between its contracting states. Whether it will affect the discretion to grant anti-suit injunctions remains to be seen.[127]

---

[126]   *R1 International Pte Ltd v Lonstroff* [2014] 3 SLR 166 [55]. See the discussion in Ch 7, section G, 'Injunctions in Support of a Foreign Forum'.

[127]   See Ch 1, Section G, 'The Hague Convention on the Choice of Court'.

20

*New Zealand Law**

A. INTRODUCTION

New Zealand has a 'distinct national legal identity'.[1] Although New Zealand law has a close **20.01** relationship with English law,[2] the New Zealand courts depart from English case law where conditions in New Zealand are different or where case law in other common law countries is a better guide.[3]

However, New Zealand law on anti-suit injunctions, as it has so far developed, is much the **20.02** same as English law,[4] and has generally followed the English decisions, while also paying particular regard to the judgments of the Privy Council on the subject.

In contrast, Australian anti-suit decisions have not been influential in New Zealand. **20.03** Australian law on jurisdictional matters is in key respects marked off from other Commonwealth systems, due to the effect of the rejection of the doctrine of *forum non conveniens* in Australia.[5] In contrast, New Zealand, like most of the close common law countries[6] has followed the doctrine of *forum non conveniens* developed in *Spiliada*.[7]

---

* Co-authored with Belinda McRae

[1] R Cooke, 'The New Zealand National Identity' (1987) 3 Cant LR 171, 180.

[2] M Kirby, 'Robin Cooke, Human Rights and the Pacific Dimension' (2008) 39(1) VUWLR 119, 132: 'despite the evolution of a uniquely New Zealand law, English law remained (and probably still remains) the most important influence on the development of New Zealand law'.

[3] R Cooke, 'The New Zealand National Identity' (1987) 3 Cant LR 171, 180; *Invercargill City Council v Hamlin* [1996] 1 NZLR 513, 519–20.

[4] With the obvious exception of the effect of European jurisdictional law, if and so long as that continues to be part of English law after Brexit.

[5] See *Voth v Manildra Flour Mills* (1990) 171 CLR 538 (HCA), building on *Oceanic Sun Line Special Shipping v Fay* (1988) 165 CLR 197 (HCA).

[6] The 'close' common law countries are those whose law continues to have the closest resemblance to English law and each other; such as England and Wales, Australia, New Zealand and Singapore; the term therefore excludes countries such as the United States and India.

[7] The lead English decision is *Spiliada Maritime v Cansulex* [1987] AC 460 (HL), adopted in New Zealand by *Oilseed Products (NZ) v HE Burton* (1987) 1 PRNZ 313, 316–17 (NZ HC); *Club Mediterranée NZ v Wendell* [1989] 1 NZLR 216 (NZ CA). For discussion, see S Gallacher, 'After the *Spiliada*—Forum non Conveniens in New Zealand and Australia' (1996) 8 Otago LR 63; Report of the New Zealand Law Commission, 'Electronic Commerce Part One: A Guide for the Legal and Business Community' [1998] NZLCR 50 [281ff].

20.04   However, New Zealand jurisprudence on the subject is limited, as there have been few applications for anti-suit injunctions in New Zealand.[8] It appears that the New Zealand courts have granted only one anti-suit injunction and directly considered the possibility of an anti-suit injunction in one other case.[9]

20.05   The New Zealand judiciary appears to accept that anti-suit injunctions are a justifiable tool in principle. Hugh Williams J, writing extra-judicially, has said: 'although the anti-suit injunction must be contained within proper national limits informed by proper regard for international comity and notions of sovereignty, such injunctions may nonetheless have a valuable part to play and, perhaps, have an as yet unrealised potential in maritime law'.[10]

20.06   We address the case law as it has developed so far in New Zealand. References are to the courts of New Zealand, and references to statutes are to New Zealand statutes, unless specified.

B. SOURCES AND POWERS

20.07   The New Zealand courts have confirmed that they have the power to grant anti-suit injunctions without addressing the source of the power. In *Jonmer v Maltexo*, the court stated that there was '... no question that the [New Zealand] Court has the jurisdiction to make such an order'.[11] In addition, in *Compudigm*, the possible anti-suit injunction was discussed and rejected on the facts without any question that the power to grant it exists.[12]

20.08   This jurisprudence has not discussed the source of the power, but the answer appears to be clear. In New Zealand, injunctions are not granted under an express statutory power specifically conferring or confirming the power to grant injunctions, in contrast to section 37(1) of the English Senior Courts Act 1981. Instead, sections IV, V, and XVI of the Supreme Court Act 1860 conferred on the New Zealand High Court all the jurisdiction possessed by the superior courts of England in 1860. That jurisdiction included the power to grant injunctions, including anti-suit injunctions to restrain domestic or foreign proceedings.[13] All such powers were continued in section 16 of the Supreme Courts Act 1882, section 16 of the Judicature Act 1908, and now in section 12(a) of the Senior Courts Act 2016, which also provides in section 12(b)[14] that the High Court has 'the judicial jurisdiction that may

---

[8]   Sir H Williams, 'Anti-Suit Injunctions: Damp Squib or Another Shot in the Maritime Locker' (2006) ANZMLJ 3: 'Anti-suit injunctions have scarcely figured in New Zealand, by contrast with the wealth of litigation on the subject in Australia. It is almost impossible to find a case in this country on the topic.'

[9]   *Jonmer v Maltexo* (1996) 10 PRNZ 119 (NZ HC); and *Commissioner of Inland Revenue v Compudigm International* [2010] NZHC 1832 (see section C, 'Principles for Non-Contractual Anti-Suit Injunctions').

[10]   Sir H Williams, 'Anti-Suit Injunctions: Damp Squib or Another Shot in the Maritime Locker' (2006) ANZMLJ 3.

[11]   *Jonmer v Maltexo* (1996) 10 PRNZ 119, 120. In the New Zealand Law Commission's report, 'Electronic Commerce Part One: A Guide for the Legal and Business Community' [1998] NZLCR 50, the jurisdiction to issue an anti-suit injunction was described as 'undoubtedly available for exercise'.
The existence of the power was also recognized in *Perpetual Trustee Company v Downey* (2011) 21 PRNZ 28 [46]; *TTAH v Koninklijke Ten Cate* [2015] NZCA 348 [63]; see also *Flujo Holdings Pty v Merisant* [2017] NZHC 1656 [43].

[12]   *Commissioner of Inland Revenue v Compudigm International* [2010] NZHC 1832.

[13]   See Ch 3, para 3.02 n 4; Ch 2, section B, 'The Court of Chancery'; Ch 6, para 6.04.

[14]   The 1882 and 1908 Acts had similar provisions to s 12(b) of the 2016 Act.

be necessary to administer the laws of New Zealand.'[15] In *TV3 v Everready*, the Court of Appeal confirmed that 'the remedy of injunction should be available whenever required by justice'.[16]

As in English law, the power to grant injunctions, and specifically anti-suit injunctions, is an **20.09** 'equitable jurisdiction'.[17] New Zealand law has followed the general principles of injunctions under English law.[18]

It appears, therefore, that the power of the New Zealand courts to grant permanent and **20.10** interim anti-suit injunctions is derived from equity, and is based upon the donation to the New Zealand courts of the pre-1860 powers of the English courts by the chain of statutes leading to section 12 of the 2016 Act; if necessary, the power could also be based on section 12(b) of the 2016 Act.

It might also be suggested that the anti-suit injunction could also be founded in the inherent **20.11** jurisdiction of the court, as it is in part in Australia[19] although not in England.[20] In *Carter v Holt*,[21] the High Court was considering whether it could 'stay', that is restrain the pursuit of, an arbitration in New Zealand, and discussed the issues under the rubric of the court's 'inherent jurisdiction to order a stay of arbitration proceedings'.[22] However, *en passant* references like this to the 'inherent jurisdiction' are sometimes best understood as referring to the court's general jurisdiction or power to grant injunctions rather than the inherent jurisdiction properly so called. The court's supervisory jurisdiction over domestic arbitrations is generally viewed as a separate matter to its power to grant anti-suit injunctions.[23] There does not appear to have been argument directed to whether grounding the power in the 'inherent jurisdiction' was indeed appropriate; still less was there any consideration of the basis of the power to grant anti-suit injunctions in general; and the English authorities referred to by the court in *Carter v Holt* were themselves injunction authorities that made no reference to the inherent jurisdiction.[24] In the circumstances, it is submitted that this decision does not appear to be persuasive authority to treat anti-suit injunctions as founded in the High Court's inherent jurisdiction, at least not in general, and there is no apparent need to do so.

There is no reason to assume that understanding the High Court's power as derived from the **20.12** pre-1860 powers of the English courts will create any material difference to the modern approach to the grant of injunctions in England under the statutory power in section 37 of the English Senior Courts Act 1981. While English law on anti-suit injunctions has developed

---

[15] Section 12 of the 2016 Act is explained in *AG v Taylor* [2018] NZSC 104 [86]–[87]; and touched on in *Meder v Official Assignee* [2018] NZAR 632 [32]. See also Sir M Casey, 'Injunctions' in *The Laws of New Zealand* (LexisNexis, 14 March 2018) para 1 n 1.

[16] *TV3 Network v Eveready New Zealand* [1993] 3 NZLR 435 (CA) 438; see also at 447.

[17] *Commissioner of Inland Revenue v Compudigm International* [2010] NZHC 1832 [17].

[18] See generally Sir M Casey, 'Injunctions' in *The Laws of New Zealand* (LexisNexis, 14 March 2018).

[19] *CSR v Cigna Insurance Australia* (1997) 189 CLR 345 (HCA); *Herold v Seally (No 2)* [2017] FCA 543 [34(6)] (FCA).

[20] Ch 3, paras 3.02 and 3.06.

[21] *Carter Holt Harvey v Genesis Power* [2006] 3 NZLR 794 (HC) [12], [27], [32].

[22] For the inherent jurisdiction more generally, see *R v Moke* [1996] 1 NZLR 263; *Meder v Official Assignee* [2018] NZAR 632.

[23] See Ch 11, sections A, 'Introduction' and B, 'Injunctions to Restrain Arbitrations in England'; Ch 3, para 3.06 n 27.

[24] *University of Reading v Miller Construction* (1995) 75 BLR 91; *Doleman v Ossett* [1912] 3 KB 257 (CA).

since 1860 in terms of the principles as to when an injunction should be granted, the essence of the power has not changed.

1. Injunctions in Support of Insolvency Proceedings

20.13   The New Zealand court has held that section 248(1)(c)(i) of the Companies Act, preventing the commencement or continuance of legal proceedings against a company in liquidation does not apply to foreign legal proceedings.[25] In turn, the power to grant injunctions to restrain litigation against the company in liquidation in section 247 of the act will also only apply to proceedings in New Zealand.[26]

20.14   However, the general equitable power to grant anti-suit injunctions permits the grant of anti-suit injunctions to restrain foreign proceedings in order to protect the insolvency jurisdiction of the New Zealand court.[27]

20.15   But where both countries are party to the UNCITRAL Model Law on Cross-Border Insolvency, the exercise of this power may be limited by considerations of comity. This point is discussed at paras 20.25–20.26.

2. Injunctions in Support of Arbitration

20.16   It seems clear that the New Zealand courts will have power to grant permanent and interim anti-suit injunctions in support of arbitration, including the power to restrain competing court and arbitration proceedings abroad.[28] The statutory basis of the power has not yet been addressed.

20.17   It is submitted that permanent anti-suit injunctions in support of arbitration would be founded on the court's general powers to grant injunctions, discussed above.[29] Such a power would not be inconsistent with the presumption of non-intervention derived from Article 5[30] of the UNCITRAL Model Law on International Commercial Arbitration,[31] because the court would not be interfering in, but instead protecting, the arbitration.[32]

20.18   So far as concerns interim anti-suit injunctions in support of arbitration, the exact basis of the power is somewhat less clear, although it is clear that some basis will exist. Possibilities

---

[25] *Commissioner of Inland Revenue v Compudigm International* [2010] NZHC 1832 [13]–[14].

[26] Matching with the English position under the English Insolvency Act 1986, discussed in Ch 3, para 3.06 n 26.

[27] *Commissioner of Inland Revenue v Compudigm International* [2010] NZHC 1832 [17]–[23].

[28] This work does not address the question of the New Zealand courts' powers to supervise, or to restrain, arbitrations whose seat is in New Zealand.

[29] See by analogy the position in English law (Ch 3, para 3.06 and n 27) and Singapore law (Ch 19, paras 19.10–19.15); this was addressed in the UK Supreme Court's decision in *AES Ust-Kamenogorsk Hydropower Plant LLP v Ust-Kamenogorsk Hydropower Plant JSC* [2013] 1 WLR 1889 (SC).

[30] Article 5 provides: 'in matters governed by this law, no Court shall intervene except where so provided by this law'.

[31] Which forms part of New Zealand law by virtue of s 5 of Sch 1 of the Arbitration Act 1996.

[32] *Carter Holt Harvey v Genesis Power* [2006] 3 NZLR 794 (HC) [12], [27], [32]; discussed in Professor DAR Williams QC, 'Defining the Role of the Court in Modern International Commercial Arbitration' (2012), Herbert Smith Freehills–SMU Asian Arbitration Lecture, Singapore 10–13; see Ch 7, para 7.55. Indeed, the UNCITRAL Model law recognizes the arbitrators' powers to grant interim anti-suit relief: see Article 17A.

include the general powers inherited from the English courts,[33] as discussed above; or Article 9(2) of Schedule 1 of the New Zealand Arbitration Act 1996, combined together with Articles 17 and 17A of the Schedule, or perhaps with section 12 of the Act.

C. PRINCIPLES FOR NON-CONTRACTUAL ANTI-SUIT INJUNCTIONS

The New Zealand courts appear likely to continue to follow the basic principles in respect   **20.19** of the grant of non-contractual anti-suit injunctions derived from Lord Goff's judgment in *Aérospatiale*,[34] and the English cases that have developed *Aérospatiale*. Those principles are summarized in Chapter 4 of this work. In short and incomplete summary, their central features are that (a) an anti-suit injunction can be granted where the ends of justice so require; (b) generally the foreign proceedings must be vexatious and oppressive, and it is not sufficient merely that in the eyes of the New Zealand court it is the more appropriate forum; (c) the foreign proceedings must not give the injunction defendant a legitimate advantage of which it would be unjust to deprive him; (d) the New Zealand court must have a sufficient interest in the matter; (e) comity must be taken into consideration; and (f) the injunction will only be granted with caution. A fuller summary is found at Ch 4, para 4.05. It seems likely that New Zealand law, like English law, will also accept the legitimacy of anti-suit injunctions to protect the processes of the New Zealand court from interference.

Aérospatiale and the English case law developing it has been applied in the two New Zealand   **20.20** cases that have directly considered anti-suit injunctions, *Jonmer v Maltexo*,[35] and *Compudigm*,[36] which we discuss below. The logic of *Aérospatiale* has been applied by other Commonwealth courts in the Pacific.[37] Other leading English decisions on anti-suit injunctions have also been treated as representing New Zealand law in other cases on other topics.[38]

In *Jonmer v Maltexo*,[39] a claim was brought in Texas by Maltexo, a New Zealand company,   **20.21** against Jonmer, a Texas company, to recover a debt owed under the agreement concluded between them for the distribution of Maltexo's traditional New Zealand product. Jonmer, on the other hand, brought proceedings against Maltexo in New Zealand for breach of the distribution agreement. Following Maltexo's failed attempt to resist jurisdiction in New Zealand on grounds of *forum non conveniens*, Jonmer applied to the High Court in New Zealand to restrain Maltexo from its pursuit of its debt claim in Texas. In considering this application, Robertson J cited and applied the *Aérospatiale* test, as summarized above, and

---

[33] See in England *AES Ust-Kamenogorsk Hydropower Plant LLP v Ust-Kamenogorsk Hydropower Plant JSC* [2013] 1 WLR 1889 (SC) [48], holding that interim anti-suit injunctions in support of arbitration fall outside the English Arbitration Act 1996; discussed at Ch 13, paras 13.10–13.15.

[34] *Société Nationale Industrielle Aérospatiale v Lee Kui Jak* [1987] AC 871 (PC).

[35] *Jonmer v Maltexo* (1996) 10 PRNZ 119.

[36] *Commissioner of Inland Revenue v Compudigm International* [2010] NZHC 1832.

[37] See the decision of the Court of Appeal of Vanuatu in *Chang Wing (Vanuatu) v Motis Pacific Lawyers* [1998] VUCA 6. However, see by contrast the decision of the High Court of Fiji in *Mount Kasi v Range Resources* [1999] 45 FLR 16 (applied in *Lowing v Howell* [2015] FJHC 693). The first two decisions are commented on in R Mortensen, 'Duty Free Forum Shopping: Disputing Venue in the Pacific' (2001) 32(3) VUWLR 673. See also *AKR v SP* [2011] NZHC 1509 [30]–[31] (where an unsuccessful application in the Fiji High Court is discussed).

[38] See eg *TTAH v Koninklijke Ten Cate* [2015] NZCA 348 [63] (referring with approval to *Airbus v Patel* [1999] 1 AC 119; also *Marac Finance v Vero Liability Insurance* [2014] NZHC 1974 [48]).

[39] *Jonmer v Maltexo* (1996) 10 PRNZ 119, 120, 122–23.

the English cases developing it.[40] He found that New Zealand was the natural forum for the dispute, as it was where the parties' bargain was struck and where the most relevant witnesses were likely to reside. Robertson J also held that it was 'an exceptional case' that was likely to 'create oppression and abuse' if the smaller debt claim was allowed to be heard in Texas, in circumstances where there was 'no demonstrable benefit or advantage' to proceeding in that jurisdiction. Ultimately, the court granted an order restraining Maltexo from continuing the Texas proceedings, but on the condition that Jonmer consented to judgment in Texas if the debt was found to be due.

20.22   A significant feature of Robertson J's decision is that he correctly recognized that the mere existence of parallel proceedings does not constitute vexation and oppression (see 122). This reflects the key doctrinal developments in English law and the Privy Council in the 1980s, rejecting the *Castanho* heresy (under which it had been temporarily but wrongly accepted that an anti-suit injunction could be granted solely on the basis that the English court had concluded that it and not the forum court was the convenient forum).[41]

20.23   In *Commissioner of Inland Revenue v Compudigm*,[42] a claim was brought in Nevada against an insolvent New Zealand company. The Nevada court requested the consent of the New Zealand court before the Nevada proceedings continued. The liquidator did not oppose the application for consent, but the High Court concluded that its consent was not necessary. However, as part of its reasoning, the High Court considered the analogous question of whether it would have granted an anti-suit injunction had such been sought (it had not). In doing so, the High Court applied the basic principles derived from the English cases, following *Aérospatiale*, of *Barclays Bank v Homan* and *Bloom v Harms*.[43] The central tests deployed were whether the Nevada proceedings were vexatious or oppressive or unconscionable (see at [19]–[23]). The High Court also considered it was necessary to satisfy itself that 'there must be good reason why the decision to stop foreign proceedings should be made here rather than there' (cf [18]),[44] an element of the English requirement of a 'sufficient interest' that has been developed since *Barclays Bank v Homan*. On the facts, the High Court concluded that since the Nevada proceedings were not a 'blatant attempt' to undermine the New Zealand liquidation, no anti-suit injunction would have been granted (at [34]).

20.24   However, the High Court then went further and considered the implications of the UNCITRAL Model Law on Cross-Border Insolvency 1997, which has been implemented in both the United States and New Zealand, but which neither party had cited. The Model Law on Cross-Border Insolvency contains provisions as to the mutual recognition of insolvency decisions, and for stays pending determination of the foreign insolvency proceeding, in appropriate cases. In the light of this, although without reaching any decision, the court

---

[40] Namely, *Barclays Bank v Homan* [1993] BCLC 680 and *Société Commerciale de Reassurance v Eras International (No 2)* [1995] 2 All ER 278.
Robertson J also observed that an applicant for an anti-suit injunction faces 'a very high threshold'. This is understood to be a description of the *Aérospatiale* tests and their general requirement for vexation or oppression and caution, and not an attempt to set any different threshold.

[41] Ch 4, section J, '*Forum non Conveniens*'.

[42] *Commissioner of Inland Revenue v Compudigm International* [2010] NZHC 1832.

[43] *Barclays Bank v Homan* [1993] BCLC 680; *Bloom v Harms Offshore AHT 'Taurus'* [2010] 2 WLR 349.

[44] See Ch 4, para 4.80.

suggested that the grant of an anti-suit injunction to restrain foreign insolvency proceedings would in general be inappropriate where both countries implemented the Model Law,[45] absent unusual circumstances such as urgency.[46] This approach has some resemblance to the approach of the European Court of Justice (ECJ) to anti-suit injunctions within the closed jurisdictional system of the Brussels–Lugano regime.[47]

It is respectfully submitted that the approach in *Compudigm* is too absolute a policy, as contested argument might have revealed. The operation of the Model Law's regime between the two states in question may well affect and limit the grant of anti-suit injunctions in various ways. For example, its provisions on which state should have jurisdiction in insolvency may shape which court is the natural forum. Its provisions on mutual recognition and stays may shape whether the foreign proceedings are indeed vexatious, or whether an injunction is appropriate as a matter of discretion, or whether the appropriate course is in general to seek a stay in the foreign proceedings. All these points will need to be considered, taking into account the particular way in which the Model Law is implemented in any particular state. The framework of the Model Law may also be influential in assessing the restraining influence of comity. But it is submitted that it would be too rigid to suggest that the Model Law will mean, in general, that an anti-suit injunction will be inappropriate outside cases of urgency. Even within the framework of the Model Law, parties could seek to use the other countries' insolvency proceedings in a vexatious fashion, and its implementation may vary. Thus, in principle, there can be situations where even requiring recourse to be made to the foreign court would in itself be oppressive, or where the centre of gravity of the issues is located in the domestic court in a way that makes it consistent with comity for the domestic court itself first to assess the question of vexation. One example of this may be where the claimant abroad has already participated in, and submitted to, the domestic insolvency regime and then, disliking the results, seeks to have another spin of the wheel elsewhere.[48]   **20.25**

D. CONTRACTUAL ANTI-SUIT INJUNCTIONS

Where the foreign litigation is in breach of a contractual exclusive forum clause, the English case law adopts a stronger and distinct set of principles, derived from cases such as *The Angelic Grace* and *Donohue v Armco*. In short, where the foreign proceedings are in breach of contract, the anti-suit injunction will ordinarily be granted unless there are a strong reasons not to do so.[49]   **20.26**

The sole New Zealand case which has addressed this question, *Product Development Solutions v Parametric Technology Corporation*, indicates that the same basic principles will be adopted in New Zealand. The High Court was considering an application to stay proceedings before it, notwithstanding that there was an exclusive jurisdiction clause in favour of Auckland. It observed that the party arguing for New Zealand jurisdiction 'could also rely   **20.27**

---

[45] Citing LC Ho, 'Anti-Suit Injunctions in Cross-Border Insolvency: A Restatement (2003) 52(3) ICLQ 697, 733–34: see [2010] NZHC 1832 [29].
[46] The difference from the result in the English decision in *Bloom v Harms Offshore AHT 'Taurus'* [2010] 2 WLR 349 was explained by the Court in *Compudigm* on the basis that there was a need for urgency in *Bloom*.
[47] See Ch 12.
[48] See further Ch 5, section E, 'Insolvency and Justice between Creditors'.
[49] Ch 7, section E, 'The *Angelic Grace* Principles'.

on that same clause to seek an anti-suit injunction to prevent [the other party] bringing proceedings against it in Australia. The approach of the courts is to enforce exclusive jurisdiction clauses unless there are very strong reasons why they should not be.'[50] This is a strong indication that the essence of the approach in *The Angelic Grace* would be applied in New Zealand.[51] It does not seem that the use of 'very strong' as opposed to 'strong' is intended to create any departure from the English jurisprudence.

20.28   It will, however, be a matter for the New Zealand courts to consider whether they wish to apply the more controversial aspects of the rigorous English approach.[52]

E. INJUNCTIONS IN SUPPORT OF ARBITRATION

20.29   The existence of a power to grant anti-suit injunctions in support of arbitration and to protect an arbitration clause has already been discussed.[53] Where the foreign proceedings are in breach of the arbitration clause, it seems likely that the same or similar principles will be applied as in respect of foreign proceedings in breach of exclusive jurisdiction clauses.[54] The New Zealand courts are also likely to have power to grant anti-suit injunctions to prevent collateral attacks on arbitrations.

F. THE TRANS-TASMAN REGIME

20.30   The Agreement between Australia and New Zealand on Trans-Tasman proceedings (the 'Trans-Tasman Agreement') provides for the mutual enforcement of judgments and judicial cooperation between New Zealand and Australia.[55] It is implemented in New Zealand by the Trans-Tasman Proceedings Act 2010.[56] The regime contains provisions for the courts of each country to stay proceedings if the courts of the other country are the more

---

[50] *Product Development Solutions v Parametric Technology Corporation* [2013] NZHC 33 [46].

[51] The Australian courts have also adopted a strong approach to anti-suit injunctions to enforce exclusive forum clauses. They have in general concluded that such injunctions can be granted to enforce the contractual obligation without needing to satisfy the tests for non-contractual anti-suit injunctions; or to much the same effect, they have taken the approach that where the foreign proceedings are in breach of contract they are for that reason vexatious. See eg *CSR v Cigna Insurance Australia* (1997) 146 ALR 402, 434 (HCA) (where the High Court of Australia, at nn 61 and 62, expressly referred to the English case law); *Great Southern Loans Pty Ltd v Locator Group Pty Ltd* [2005] NSWSC 438 [34]–[39] (analysing matters contractually but concluding in the alternative that if vexation needed to be shown, the breach of contract would establish vexation) and [52] (in cases of contractual anti-suit injunctions, the court need not 'withhold its hand' for reasons of comity); *Alkimos Shipping Company v Hind Leer Chemicals* [2004] FCA 969, [25] (referring to English case law); *MRT Performance v Mastro Motors* [2005] NSWSC 316 [24]–[25]; *Rectron Australia v Lu* [2014] NSWSC 1367 [57]; *Insurance Commission of Western Australia v Woodings* [2017] WASC 122 [17].

[52] As discussed in Chs 7 and 8.

[53] See paras 20.16–20.18.

[54] Professor DAR Williams QC, 'Defining the Role of the Court in Modern International Commercial Arbitration' (2012), Herbert Smith Freehills–SMU Asian Arbitration Lecture, Singapore 10–13.

[55] Agreement between the Government of Australia and the Government of New Zealand on Trans-Tasman Court Proceedings and Regulatory Enforcement, signed at Christchurch on 24 July 2008, with entry into force on 11 October 2013 (henceforth 'the Trans-Tasman Agreement'). This is discussed generally in R Mortensen, 'The Hague and the Ditch: The Trans-Tasman Judicial Area and the Choice of Court Convention' (2009) JPIL 213 and R Mortensen, 'A Trans-Tasman Judicial Area: Civil Jurisdiction and Judgments in the Single Economic Market' (2010) 16 Canterbury Law Rev 61.

[56] It is implemented in Australia by the Trans-Tasman Proceedings Act 2010 (Cth).

appropriate forum.[57] So, *forum non conveniens* does operate by statute between Australian and New Zealand.

In turn, it was thought appropriate to restrict the scope of anti-suit injunctions between New **20.31** Zealand and Australia. Section 28 of the Trans-Tasman Proceedings Act 2010 provides that a New Zealand court must not restrain a person from commencing, or taking steps in, a civil proceeding in an Australian court 'on the grounds that the Australian court is not the appropriate forum for the proceeding'. The Australian implementing legislation has an identical provision.[58] Both implement Article 8(5) of the Trans-Tasman Agreement, which uses the same central language.

The scope of Article 8(5), section 28 of the New Zealand Act, and the corresponding provision **20.32** in the Australian implementing legislation, is consciously limited. They are not intended to preclude all anti-suit injunctions between New Zealand and Australia, but only those based on considerations of appropriate forum.

A significant part of their background was, it seems, the Australian experience of anti-suit **20.33** injunctions between the states and territories of Australia and within the Australian federal structure. The Australian courts had concluded that (within their respective scopes) neither the Service and Execution of Process Act 1992 (Cth) ('SEPA'),[59] nor the Australian cross-vesting legislation[60] which enables the transfer of litigation to the more appropriate Australian forum,[61] should preclude anti-suit injunctions within Australia. In particular, section 21 of SEPA provides, in terms similar to Article 8(5) of the Trans-Tasman Agreement, that anti-suit injunctions may not be granted to restrain proceedings served under SEPA on the ground that the place of issue is not the appropriate forum. But, in *Great Southern Loans*, the New South Wales court concluded that it did not preclude contractual injunctions, nor it seems injunctions based on vexation or oppression.[62]

Further, considerations of comity between Australian courts have not prevented intra- **20.34** Australia anti-suit injunctions from being a thriving and vigorous jurisdiction. While significant decisions in some Australian courts have taken the approach that on grounds of comity considerable caution should be exercised before an anti-suit injunction could be granted to restrain proceedings in another Australian court,[63] others have displayed

---

[57] Trans-Tasman Agreement, Art 8. In New Zealand, Trans-Tasman Proceedings Act 2010, Part 2(2). In Australia, see Trans-Tasman Proceedings Act 2010 (Cth), Part 3.

[58] Trans-Tasman Proceedings Act 2010 (Cth), s 22.

[59] SEPA, an Australian federal statute, facilitates service and enforcement between the states of Australia (as defined in s 5 to include certain territories). It creates a mechanism for staying proceedings served under SEPA on grounds of appropriate forum, and to complement this, s 21 SEPA provides, in terms similar to Article 8(5)(b) of the Trans-Tasman Agreement, that anti-suit injunctions may not be granted to restrain proceedings served under SEPA on the ground that the place of issue is not the appropriate forum.

[60] For discussion of the cross-vesting legislation (ie Jurisdiction of Courts (Cross-vesting) Act 1987 (Cth) and its state and territory counterparts), see *BHP Billiton v Schultz* (2004) 221 CLR 400.

[61] For the conclusion that the cross-vesting location should not preclude anti-suit injunctions, see *Santos Ltd v Helix Energy Services Pty Ltd* (2009) 28 VR 595, 602–03; see also *Pegasus Leasing Ltd v Cadoroll Pty Ltd* (1996) FCA 1245 and *Wigmans v AMP Ltd* [2018] NSWSC 1045 [50]–[55].

[62] *Great Southern Loans v Locator Group* [2005] NSWSC 438, [73]–[78]. The tentative *obiter* comments in *Beecham v Roque* (1987) 11 NSWLR 1, 3D–E (NSW CA) suggesting that particular hesitation might be appropriate in the context of SEPA were not picked up in *Great Southern Loans*. Note, however, the reasoning in *Greinert v Jarrett* [2004] NSWSC 209 [42]–[43], distinguished in *Great Southern Loans* at [54]–[55].

[63] cf eg *Beecham v Roque* (1987) 11 NSWLR 1, 3, and 6; *Construction, Forestry, Mining and Energy Union v Mirvac Constructions* [2000] FCA 341 [36]; *Greinert v Jarrett* [2004] NSWSC 209, [41]; *Reale v Reale* [2006] NSWSC 227, [26]; *Lederer v Hunt* [2007] FamCA 55 [33]–[37].

lesser[64] or no such hesitation,[65] and it has even been suggested by Brereton J in the New South Wales court that 'anti-suit injunctions are more readily granted within the confines of the federal system, than where proceedings have been issued in a foreign court and a local court'.[66] Further, in any event, such comity-induced self-restraint does not apply in contractual cases, where one Australian court is enforcing an exclusive forum clause prohibiting litigation in another Australian forum.[67] In the round, there are numerous cases of intra-Australian anti-suit injunctions.

20.35   During the preparatory work for the Trans-Tasman Agreement, in the initial Trans-Tasman Working Group Discussion Paper of 2005, there was express reference to the possibility of anti-suit injunctions on other grounds, such as vexation, or protection of the processes of the court, and 'not the appropriate forum' was treated as a more narrow concept (also described as an anti-suit injunction 'on forum grounds'). The Discussion Paper asked consultees whether anti-suit injunctions on grounds other than not being the appropriate forum should also be excluded,[68] but the Working Group Report of 2006 did not make any such recommendation. Instead, the Report explained the proposed restriction solely on the basis that it was necessary to prevent circumvention of the power to stay on grounds of *forum non conveniens*.[69] This discussion seems to have had in mind the prior Australian experience. Against this background, it seems clear that the narrow wording of Article 8(5) of the Treaty is a consciously limited preclusion, which does not preclude anti-suit injunctions generally.[70]

20.36   The linguistic result is somewhat inapposite in relation to New Zealand law, and indeed Australian law, under both of which non-contractual anti-suit injunctions are not based directly on the inappropriateness of the foreign forum.[71] Indeed, the essence of the principles in *Aérospatiale* is that mere inappropriateness of the foreign forum is not a sufficient

---

[64]   *Tsyzu v Fightvision* [2001] NSWCA 103 [44]–[47].

[65]   See eg *Total Development Supplies v GRD Building* [2007] FCA 2032; *Whirlpool (Australia) v Castel Electronics* [2015] FCA 906; *Pratten & McPherson* [2016] FamCA 775. See also the discussion of earlier anti-suit case law in R Mortensen, 'Autochthonous Essential: State Courts and a Cooperative National System of Civil Jurisdiction' (2003) 22 UTasLR 103, 120–21, 134, 138. R Mortensen, 'A Trans-Tasman Judicial Area: Civil Jurisdiction and Judgments in the Single Economic Market' (2010) 16 Canterbury Law Rev 61, 78, suggests that anti-suit injunctions within Australia are now granted without significant restraint.

[66]   See the *obiter* comments of Brereton J in *Valceski v Valceski* [2007] NSWSC 440, [76], relying on *Dibeek Holdings Pty Ltd v Notaras* (1997) 141 FLR 364, 373–74 (which, however, does not say the same thing). R Mortensen, 'A Trans-Tasman Judicial Area: Civil Jurisdiction and Judgments in the Single Economic Market' (2010) 16 Canterbury Law Rev 61, 78, suggests that the *Valceski* approach is the modern one, which has overtaken the earlier more restrained approach in *Beecham* and the cases following it (see n 63). It is unclear that this is right, and it is striking that *Beecham* was not referred to in *Valceski*. But the exact resolution is a question of Australian law and is beyond the scope of this work.

[67]   See *Great Southern Loans v Locator Group* [2005] NSWSC 438, [52]–[55]; distinguishing *Beecham v Roque* (1987) 11 NSWLR 1, 3 and 6 (NSW CA); see also *Greinert v Jarrett* [2004] NSWSC 209 [41]; *Insurance Commission of Western Australia v Woodings* [2017] WASC 122 [17].

[68]   Trans-Tasman Working Group Discussion Paper (2005) paras 5.15–5.16.

[69]   Trans-Tasman Working Group Report (December 2006) 20. See also the Explanatory Memorandum to the Australian Act and the Bill Note for the New Zealand Act.

[70]   For an academic suggestion that the effect of the Trans-Tasman Agreement is to create a general ban on anti-suit injunctions (save in contractual cases), see R Mortensen, 'A Trans-Tasman Judicial Area: Civil Jurisdiction and Judgments in the Single Economic Market' (2010) 16 Canterbury Law Rev 61, 79–80, 85.

[71]   For New Zealand law, see para 20.19 above and Ch 4. For Australian law, cf *Great Southern Loans v Locator Group* [2005] NSWSC 438 (NSW SC) [75]–[76], and the leading case of *CSR v Cigna Insurance Australia* (1997) 189 CLR 345 (HCA).

ground for an anti-suit injunction, and instead anti-suit injunctions are based on higher thresholds and wider considerations such as the interests of justice, vexation, or oppression. The Australian *Great Southern Loans* decision refers to this mismatch, and one possible reading of the New South Wales court's reasoning is that section 21 of SEPA—and by analogy Article 8(5) of the Agreement and section 28 of the New Zealand Act—may simply miss the point, and do not affect the actual bases on which anti-suit injunctions are granted. But this would appear to be an overreading of the case, whose reasoning was focused on the situation before it, namely, an injunction based on a contractual clause.[72]

It is suggested that this accidental linguistic dead end should not render section 28 meaningless. The better view is that where the underlying grounds of a non-contractual anti-suit injunction are in reality based on the alleged inappropriateness of the Australian forum, but formulated in different terms, such as vexation or oppression, then either an anti-suit injunction based on such concepts should be precluded by section 28; or the circumvention of section 28 should be a strong discretionary factor against an injunction. On the other hand, if the grounds of the injunction are independent of the posited inappropriateness of the Australian forum, section 28 should not directly preclude an anti-suit injunction. Thus, for example, the decision in *Great Southern Loans* suggests that injunctions based on the protection of the jurisdiction and judgments of the New Zealand courts would be outside the sphere of influence of section 28. The exact boundaries of the distinction will need to be worked out over time.   **20.37**

However, even where section 28 does not apply directly to preclude anti-suit injunctions, the question arises as whether, and if so how far, the context of the Trans-Tasman Agreement and considerations of comity between the Australian and New Zealand courts, will operate as a restraining factor in principle or as a matter of discretion to the grant of an anti-suit injunction, with an application for a stay to the other court being regarded as a preferred remedy. The Australian case law suggests that, at least where considerations of vexation and oppression overlap with questions of appropriate forum, then section 28 may well serve as a significant if flexible discouraging factor.[73] It is perhaps striking that there appear to have been no examples of Trans-Tasman anti-suit injunctions since the Trans-Tasman Agreement. But it seems that neither the New Zealand nor the Australian courts have yet had to rule on Article 8(5) of the Treaty and their respective implementing legislation.   **20.38**

Separately, it is clear that section 28 will not preclude anti-suit injunctions granted to enforce exclusive jurisdiction clauses or arbitration clauses. Such injunctions are not based on the inappropriateness of the Australian court as a forum, but instead on the contractual right not to be sued there.[74] In turn, the Australian case law suggests that where the injunction enforces a direct breach of an exclusive forum clause, the Trans-Tasman regime will not amount to a significant discretionary constraint.[75]   **20.39**

---

[72] *Great Southern Loans v Locator Group* [2005] NSWSC 438 (NSW SC) [74]–[78].
[73] See para 20.33–20.34, and 20.37 above.
[74] *Great Southern Loans v Locator Group* [2005] NSWSC 438 (NSW SC); see R Mortensen, 'A Trans-Tasman Judicial Area: Civil Jurisdiction and Judgments in the Single Economic Market' (2010) 16 Canterbury Law Rev 61, 85–86.
[75] See the authorities cited at nn 62 and 67 above.

Index

www.ingramcontent.com/pod-product-compliance
Ingram Content Group UK Ltd.
Pitfield, Milton Keynes, MK11 3LW, UK
UKHW051311031225
9359UKWH00006B/43